INTRODUCTION

Whether you're a three star chef or just enjoy making dinner for the family, you're bound to have built up a collection of favourite recipes. Some are probably begged and borrowed from friends, others clipped from magazines and cookery books, while a good few are probably your own creations, attributable to inspired luck.

The same is true both for the professional cocktail bartender and for the home mixologist. This tome is a comprehensive compilation of the 2,000 cocktails I've collected to date and published over the past year in our diffordsguide quarterly bookazines.

I'd like to thank the many amateur cocktail makers and professional bartenders who've emailed me their recipes and suggestions. Some of the drinks I've included may have originally been created using brands other than those stated, or with slightly differing proportions. Occasionally I've 'adapted' recipes in order to make them simpler or to avoid obscure ingredients. I have endeavoured to credit drink inventors while making it clear that my adaptation varies slightly from their original creation.

I'd be the first to admit that some of the recipes are better than others (most definitely including my own). Thus I've graded cocktails on a scale of one to five and discreetly indicated this score by dots above each drink's name.

Anyone looking to start a cocktail cabinet at home should begin with the fourteen 'Key Ingredients' featured in the opening pages. These are the most frequently used cocktail ingredients and by combining them with such easy-to-find ingredients as fruits and juices you will be able to make literally hundreds of drinks.

This guide is intended not only to encourage more people to make and enjoy cocktails at home but to help them appreciate them when drinking out. A great cocktail is as luxuriously satisfying as a fine wine, a vintage champagne or a family reserve cognac. However, while many have had the opportunity to taste a great wine, fairly few have ever experienced a truly great cocktail.

Cheers

Simon Difford
simon@diffordsguide.com

Bartending Basics	2
Glassware	12
Essential Ingredients	14
Cocktails A-Z	18
Ingredients Index	322
Great Bars Of The World	358

diffordsguide are:

Publisher & Editor Simon Difford, **Design & Art Direction** Dan Malpass, **Photography** Rob Lawson
Published by Sauce Guides Limited, Milngavie Business Centre, 17 Station Road, Milngavie, G62 8PG. **www.diffordsguide.com**

Don't blame us:

This guide is intended for adults of legal drinking age. • Please enjoy alcohol and cocktails in a responsible manner. • Consumption of alcohol in excess can be harmful to your health. • The high sugar levels in some cocktails may mask their alcohol content. • Please do not consume cocktails and drive or operate machinery. • Great care should be exercised when combining flames and alcohol. • Consumption of raw and unpasteurised eggs may be harmful to health. • Please follow the alcohol content guidelines included in this guide where a shot is equal to 25ml or 1 US fluid ounce (29.6ml) at most. A 25ml measure of spirit at 40% alc./vol. is equal to 1 unit of alcohol. Most men can drink up to three to four units of alcohol a day and most women can drink up to two to three units of alcohol a day without significant risks to their health. • Women who are trying to conceive or who are pregnant should avoid getting drunk and are advised to consume no more than one to two units of alcohol once or twice a week.

BARTENDING BASICS

PLEASE READ THE FOLLOWING INSTRUCTIONS BEFORE ATTEMPTING TO FOLLOW THE RECIPES IN THIS GUIDE.

By definition any drink which is described as a cocktail contains more than one ingredient. So if you are going to make cocktails you have to know how to combine these various liquids. Firstly, as in cooking, there is a correct order in which to prepare things and with few exceptions that runs as follows:

1. Select glass and chill or pre-heat (if required).
2. Prepare garnish (if required).
3. Pour ingredients.
4. Add ice (if required - add last to minimise melt).
5. Combine ingredients.
6. Add garnish (if required).
7. Consume or serve to guest.

Essentially, there are four different ways to mix a cocktail: shake, stir, blend and build. (Building a drink means combining the ingredients in the glass in which the cocktail will be served.)

A fifth construction method, 'layering', isn't strictly mixing. The idea here is to float each ingredient on its predecessor without the ingredients merging at all. At the heart of every cocktail lies at least one of these five methods. So understanding these terms is fundamental.

SHAKE

When you see the phrase 'shake with ice and strain', you should place all the necessary ingredients with cubed ice in a cocktail shaker and shake briskly for about twenty seconds. Then you should strain the liquid into the glass, leaving the ice behind in the shaker.

Shaking not only mixes a drink. It also chills and dilutes it. The dilution is as important to the resulting cocktail as using the right proportions of each ingredient. If you use too little ice it will quickly melt in the shaker, producing an over-diluted cocktail - so always fill your shaker at least two-thirds full of fresh ice.

Losing your grip while shaking is likely to make a mess and could result in injury, so always hold the shaker with two hands and never shake fizzy ingredients.

Although shakers come in many shapes and sizes there are two basic types.

STANDARD SHAKER

A standard shaker consists of three parts and hence is sometimes referred to as a three-piece shaker. The three pieces are **1.** a flat-bottomed, conical base or 'can', **2.** a top with a built-in strainer and **3.** a cap.

I strongly recommend this style of shaker for amateurs due to its ease of use. Be sure to purchase a shaker with a capacity of at least one pint as this will allow the ice room to travel and so mix more effectively.

TO USE:

1. Combine all ingredients in the base of the shaker and fill two-thirds full with ice.
2. Place the top and cap firmly on the base.
3. Pick up the closed shaker with one hand on the top and the other gripping the bottom and shake vigorously. The cap should always be on the top when shaking and should point away from guests.
4. After shaking briskly for a count of around 20 seconds, lift off the cap, hold the shaker by its base with one finger securing the top and pour the drink through the built-in strainer.

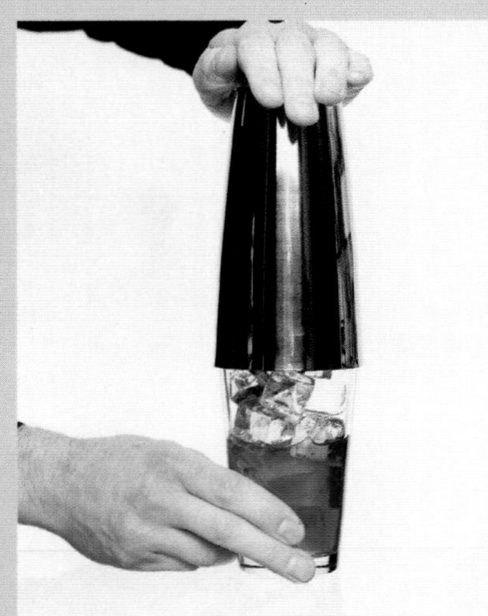

BOSTON SHAKER

A Boston shaker comprises two flat-bottomed cones, one larger than the other. The large cone, or 'can', is made of stainless steel while the smaller cone can be either glass or stainless steel. I prefer glass as this allows both mixer and guest to see the drink being made.

Avoid Boston shakers that rely on a rubber ring to seal. I use Alessi Boston tins as I find these seal without a thump and open with the lightest tap. However good your Boston shaker, these devices demand an element of skill and practice is usually required for a new user to become proficient.

TO USE:

1. Combine ingredients in the glass or smaller of the two cans.

2. Fill the large can with ice and briskly upend over the smaller can (or glass), quickly enough to avoid spilling any ice. Lightly tap the top with the heel of your hand to create a seal between the two parts.

3. Lift shaker with one hand on the top and the other gripping the base and shake vigorously. The smaller can (or glass) should always be on the top when shaking and should point away from guests.

4. After shaking for around 20 seconds, hold the larger (base) can in one hand and break the seal between the two halves of the shaker by tapping the base can with the heel of your other hand at the point where it meets the upper can (or glass).

5. Before pouring place a strainer with a coiled rim (also known as a Hawthorne strainer) over the top of the can and strain the mixture into the glass, leaving the ice cubes behind.

STIR

If a cocktail recipe calls for you to 'stir with ice and strain', stir in a mixing glass using a bar spoon with a long, spiralling stem. If a lipped mixing glass is not available, one half of a Boston shaker, or the base of a standard shaker, will suffice.

Combine the ingredients in the mixing glass, adding the ice last. Slide the back of the spoon down the inside of the mixing glass and stir the drink. Then strain into a glass using a strainer (or the top of a standard shaker if you are using a standard shaker base in place of a mixing glass).

Some bartenders (and I'm one) prefer to use the flat end of a bar spoon to stir a drink. Simply place the flat end on top of the ice in the mixing glass and start to stir, working the spoon down the drink as you go.

FINE STRAIN

Most cocktails that are served 'straight up' without ice benefit from an additional finer strain, over and above the standard strain which keeps ice cubes out of the drink. This 'fine strain' removes small fragments of fruit and fine flecks of ice which can spoil the appearance of a drink. All you need to do is strain a cocktail through the strainer you would normally use while holding a fine sieve, like a tea strainer, between the shaker and the glass. Another popular term for this method is 'double strain'.

BLEND

When a cocktail recipe calls for you to 'blend with ice', place ingredients and ice into a blender and blend until a smooth, even consistency is achieved. Ideally you should use crushed ice, as this lessens wear on the blender's blades. Place liquid ingredients in the blender first, adding the ice last, as always. If you have a variable speed blender, always start slowly and build up speed.

LAYER

As the name would suggest, layered drinks include layers of different ingredients, often with contrasting colours. This effect is achieved by carefully pouring each ingredient into the glass so that it floats on its predecessor.

The success of this technique is dependent on the density (specific gravity) of the liquids used. As a rule of thumb, the less alcohol and the more sugar an ingredient contains, the heavier it is. The heaviest ingredients should be poured first and the lightest last. Syrups are non-alcoholic and contain a lot of sugar so are usually the heaviest ingredient. Liqueurs, which are high in sugar and lower in alcohol than spirits, are generally the next heaviest ingredient. The exception to this rule is cream and cream liqueurs, which can float.

One brand of a particular liqueur may be heavier or lighter than another. The relative temperatures of ingredients may also affect their ability to float or sink. Hence a degree of experimentation is inevitable when creating layered drinks.

Layering can be achieved in one of two ways. The first involves pouring down the spiral handle of a bar spoon, keeping the flat, disc-shaped end of the spoon over the surface of the drink. Alternatively you can hold the bowl end of a bar spoon (or a soup spoon) in contact with the side of the glass and over the surface of the drink and pour over it.

The term 'float' refers to layering the final ingredient on top of a cocktail.

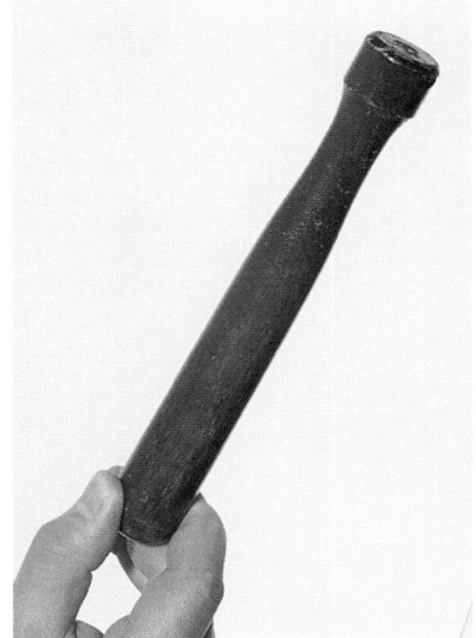

MUDDLE

Muddling means pummelling fruits, herbs and/or spices with a muddler (a blunt tool similar to a pestle) so as to crush them and release their flavour. (You can also use a rolling pin.) As when using a pestle and mortar, push down on the muddler with a twisting action.

Only attempt to muddle in the base of a shaker or a suitably sturdy glass. Never attempt to muddle hard, unripe fruits in a glass as the pressure required could break the glass. I've witnessed a bartender slash his hand open on a broken glass while muddling and can't over-emphasize how careful you should be.

FLAME

The term ignite, flame or flambé means that the drink should be set alight. Please exercise extreme care when setting fire to drinks. Be particularly careful not to knock over a lit drink and never attempt to carry a drink which is still alight. Before drinking, cover the glass so as to suffocate the flame and be aware that the rim of the glass may be hot.

ICE

A plentiful supply of fresh ice is essential to making good cocktails. When buying bagged ice avoid the hollow, tubular kind and the thin wafers. Instead look for large, solid cubes of ice. I have a Hoshizaki ice machine which produces large solid cubes, and thoroughly recommend it.

When filling ice cube trays, use bottled or filtered water to avoid the taste of chlorine often apparent in municipal water supplies. Your ice should be dry, almost sticky to the touch. Never use 'wet' ice that has started to thaw.

When serving a drink over ice, always fill the glass with ice, rather than just adding a few cubes. This makes the drink much colder, the ice lasts longer and so melting ice does not dilute the drink.

Never use ice in a cocktail shaker twice, even if it's to mix the same drink as last time. You should always throw away ice after straining the drink and use fresh ice to fill the glass if required.

Unless otherwise stated, all references to ice in this guide mean cubed ice. If crushed ice is required for a particular recipe, the recipe will state 'crushed ice'. This is available commercially. Alternatively you can crush cubed ice in an ice-crusher or simply bash a bag of it with a rolling pin.

If a glass is broken near your ice stocks, melt the ice with warm water, clean the container and re-stock with fresh ice. If this occurs in a busy bar and you are not immediately able to clean the ice well, mark it as being contaminated with a liberal coating of red grenadine syrup and draw ice from another station.

MEASURING

Balancing each ingredient within a cocktail is key to making a great drink. Therefore the accuracy with which ingredients are measured is critical to the finished cocktail.

In this guide I've expressed the measures of each ingredient in 'shots'. Ideally a shot is 25ml or one US fluid ounce (29.6ml), measured in a standard jigger. (You can also use a clean medicine measure or even a small shot glass.) Whatever measure you use should have straight sides to enable you to accurately judge fractions of a shot. Look out for measures which are graduated for quarter and half shots.

The measure 'spoon' refers to a bar spoon, which is slightly larger than a standard teaspoon.

Some bartenders attempt to measure shots by counting time and estimating the amount of liquid flowing through a bottle's spout. This is known as 'free-pouring' and can be terribly inaccurate. I strongly recommend the use of a physical measure.

GARNISHES

Garnishes are used to decorate cocktails and are often anchored to the rim of the glass. Strictly speaking, garnishes should be edible, so please forget about paper parasols. Anything from banana chunks, strawberries or redcurrants to coffee beans, confectionery, basil leaves and slices of fresh ginger can be used as a garnish. The correct garnish will often enhance the aroma and flavour as well as the look of a drink.

Fruit should be unblemished and washed prior to use. Olives, in particular, should be washed thoroughly to prevent oil from spoiling the appearance of a drink. Cut citrus fruits have a maximum shelf life of 24 hours when refrigerated. Cherries and olives should be stored refrigerated and left in their own juices.

Olives, cherries, pickled onions and fresh berries are sometimes served on cocktail sticks. A whole slice of citrus fruit served on a cocktail stick 'mast' is known as a 'sail': this is often accompanied by a cherry.

Celery sticks may be placed in drinks as stirring rods while cinnamon sticks are often placed in hot drinks and toddies.

To sprinkle chocolate on the surface of a drink you can either shave chocolate using a vegetable peeler or crumble a Cadbury's Flake bar. The instruction 'dust with chocolate' refers to a fine coating of cocoa powder on the surface of a drink. (When dusting with nutmeg it is always best to grate fresh nutmeg as the powdered kind lacks flavour.)

Citrus peels are often used as a garnish. Besides the variations listed under 'zest twist' overleaf, thin, narrow lengths of citrus peel may be tied in a 'knot'. A 'Horse's Neck' is the entire peel of either an orange, a lemon or a lime, cut in a continuous spiral and placed so as to overhang the rim of the glass.

Wedges of lemons and limes are often squeezed into drinks or fixed to the glass as a garnish. A wedge is an eighth segment of the fruit. Cut the 'knobs' from the top and bottom of the fruit, slice the fruit in half lengthwise, then cut each half into four equal wedges lengthwise.

Mint sprigs are often used to garnish cups and juleps.

ZEST TWIST

This term refers to flavouring a drink by releasing the aromatic oils from a strip of citrus zest. Using a knife or peeler, cut a half inch (12mm) wide length of zest from an unwaxed, cleaned fruit so as to leave just a little of the white pith. Hold it over the glass with the thumb and forefinger of each hand, coloured side down. Turn one end clockwise and the other anticlockwise so as to twist the peel and force some of its oils over the surface of the drink. Deposit any flavoursome oils left on the surface of the peel by wiping the coloured side around the rim of the glass. Finally, drop the peel onto the surface of the drink. (Some prefer to dispose of the spent twist.)

A flamed zest twist is a dramatic variation on this theme which involves burning the aromatic oils emitted from citrus fruit zest over the surface of a drink. Lemons and limes are sometimes treated in this way but oranges are most popular. Firm, thick-skinned navel oranges, like Washington Navels, are best.

You will need to cut as wide a strip of zest as you can, wider than you would for a standard twist. Hold the cut zest, peel side down, between the thumb and forefinger about four inches above the drink and gently warm it with a lighter flame. Then pinch the peel by its edges so that its oils squirt through the flame towards the surface of the drink - there should be a flash as the oils ignite. Finally, wipe the zest around the rim of the glass.

SALT/SUGAR RIM

Some recipes call for the rim of the glass to be coated with salt, sugar or other ingredients such as desiccated coconut or chocolate: you will need to moisten the rim first before the ingredient will hold. When using salt, whip a cut wedge of lime around the outside edge of the rim, then roll the outside edge through a saucer of salt. (Use sea salt rather than iodised salt as the flavour is less biting.) For sweet ingredients like sugar and chocolate, either use an orange slice as you would a lime wedge or moisten a sponge or paper towel with a suitable liqueur and run it around the outside edge of the glass.

Whatever you are using to rim the glass should cling to the outside edge only. Remember, garnishes are not a cocktail ingredient but an optional extra to be consumed by choice. They should not contaminate your cocktail. If some of your garnish should become stuck to the inside edge of the glass, remove it using a fresh fruit wedge or a paper towel.

It is good practice to salt or sugar only two-thirds of the rim of a glass. This allows the drinker the option of avoiding the salt or sugar. If you rim glasses some hours prior to use, the lime juice or liqueur will dry, leaving a crust of salt or sugar crystals around the rim. The glasses can then be placed in a refrigerator to chill ready for use.

A professional piece of equipment with the unfortunate title of a 'rimmer' has three sections, one with a sponge for water or lime juice, one containing sugar and another containing salt. Beware, as this encourages dipping the glass onto a moist sponge and then into the garnish, and so contaminating the inside of the glass.

GLASSWARE

Cocktails are something of a luxury. You don't just ping a cap and pour. These drinks take time and skill to mix so deserve a decent glass.

Before you start, check your glassware is clean and free from chips and marks such as lipstick. Always handle glasses by the base or the stem to avoid leaving finger marks and never put your fingers inside a glass.

Ideally glassware should be chilled in a freezer prior to use. This is particularly important for martini and flute glasses, in which drinks are usually served without ice. It takes about half an hour to sufficiently chill a glass in the freezer.

If time is short, you can chill a glass by filling it with ice (ideally crushed, not cubed) and topping it up with water. Leave the glass to cool while you prepare the drink, then discard the ice and water once you are ready to pour. This method is quicker than chilling in the freezer but not nearly so effective.

To warm a glass ready for a hot cocktail, place a bar spoon in the glass and fill it with hot water. Then discard the water and pour in the drink. Only then should you remove the spoon, which is there to help disperse the shock of the heat.

There are thousands of differently shaped glasses, but if you own those mentioned here you have a glass to suit practically every drink and occasion. Failing that, a set of Collins, Martini and Old-fashioned or Rocks glasses, and possibly flutes if you fancy champagne cocktails, will allow you to serve the majority of drinks in this guide. Use a Martini in place of a Coupette and a Collins as a substitute for Hurricane and Sling glasses.

1. Martini

Those in the old guard of bartending insist on calling this a 'cocktail glass'. It may once have been! But to most of us today a V-shaped glass is a Martini glass. Anything bigger than 7oz is ridiculous, as a true Martini warms up too much in the time it takes to drink such a large one. Chill before use.
Capacity to brim: 7oz / 20cl

2. Sling

This elegant glass has recently become fashionable again – partly due to the popularity of long drinks such as the Russian Spring Punch.
Capacity to brim: 11oz / 32cl

3. Shot

Shot glasses come in all shapes and sizes. You'll need small ones if you're sensible and big ones if you're not!
Capacity to brim (pictured glass): 2oz / 6cl

4. Flute

Flutes are perfect for serving champagne cocktails as their tall, slim design helps maintain the wine's fizz. Chill before use.
Capacity to brim: 6oz / 17cl

5. Collins

In this guide I refer to a tall glass as a 'Collins'. A hi-ball is slightly squatter than a Collins but has the same capacity. A 12oz Collins glass will suffice for cocktails and is ideal for a standard 330ml bottle of beer. However, I favour 14oz glasses with the occasional 8oz for drinks such as Fizzes which are served tall but not very long.
Capacity to brim: 14oz / 40cl or 8oz / 24cl

6. Coupette

This is commonly referred to as a 'Margarita glass' since it is used to serve the hugely popular cocktail of the same name. Its rim cries out for salt.

Capacity to brim: 8oz / 24cl

7. Goblet

Not often used for cocktails, but worth having, if for no other reason than to enjoy your wine. An 11oz glass is big enough to be luxurious.

Capacity to brim: 11oz / 32cl

8. Boston

A tall, heavy conical glass with a thick rim, designed to be combined with a Boston tin to form a shaker. It can also be used as a mixing glass for stirred drinks.

Capacity to brim: 17oz / 48cl

9. Hurricane

Sometimes referred to as a 'poco grande' or 'Piña Colada' glass, this big-bowled glass is commonly used for frozen drinks. It screams out for a pineapple wedge, a cherry and possibly a paper parasol as well. Very Del Boy.

Capacity to brim: 15oz / 43cl

10. Old-fashioned

Another glass whose name refers to the best-known drink served in it. It is also great for enjoying spirits such as whiskey. Choose a luxuriously large glass with a thick, heavy base. Alternatively, the similarly shaped 'Rocks' glass has a thick rim and is usually made from toughened glass so better suited to drinks that require muddling in the glass.

Capacity to brim: 11oz / 32cl

11. Snifter

Sometimes referred to as a 'brandy balloon'. The bigger the bowl, the more luxurious the glass appears. Use to enjoy cocktails and deluxe aged spirits such as Cognac.

Capacity to brim: 12oz / 35cl

12. Toddy

Frequently referred to as a 'liqueur coffee glass', which is indeed its main use, this glass was popularised by the Irish Coffee. Toddy glasses have a handle on the side, allowing you to comfortably hold hot drinks.

Capacity to brim: 8.5oz / 25cl

13. Sour

This small glass is narrow at the stem and tapers out to a wider lip. As the name would suggest, it is used for serving Sours straight-up. I favour serving Sours over ice in an Old-fashioned but any of the recipes in this guide can be strained and served 'up' in this glass.

Capacity to brim: 4oz / 12cl

14. Rocks

Like an Old-fashioned with a thick rim, this is usually made from toughened glass - perfect for drinks that require muddling in the glass. A hardy glass, if there is such a thing.

Capacity to brim: 9oz / 27cl

THE 14 KEY INGREDIENTS

MAKE MORE THAN 400 COCKTAILS IN THIS GUIDE WITH JUST 14 BASE INGREDIENTS.

You don't need a fully stocked bar to start mixing cocktails. After all, many of the greatest cocktails require few ingredients: a Martini is made with just two and a Margarita three ingredients.

With just the fourteen Key Ingredients opposite, a few mixers, some fresh fruit, copious amounts of ice and a handful of kitchen basics you will be able to make the over four hundred cocktails listed over the next page.

Add your favourite spirits and liqueurs to these fourteen and then refer to our full ingredients appendix on page 322 to find the additional drinks you will be able to make.

KETEL ONE VODKA

PLYMOUTH GIN

LIGHT WHITE RUM

SAUZA HORNITOS TEQUILA

BOURBON

BLENDED SCOTCH WHISKY

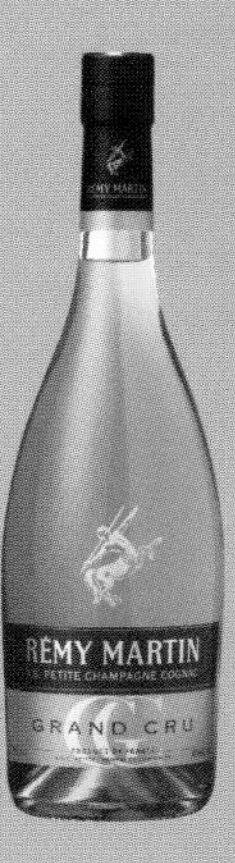

COGNAC

COINTREAU LIQUEUR

COFFEE LIQUEUR

GRAND MARNIER LIQUEUR

APRICOT BRANDY

RICH BERRY LIQUEUR

DRY VERMOUTH

CHAMPAGNE

ESSENTIAL JUICES & MIXERS

CRANBERRY JUICE

ORANGE JUICE

PRESSED APPLE JUICE

PINK GRAPEFRUIT JUICE

PINEAPPLE JUICE

SODA WATER

COLA

GINGER ALE & GINGER BEER

TONIC WATER

FRIDGE & LARDER ESSENTIALS

SUGAR (GOMME) SYRUP

GRENADINE SYRUP

LIME CORDIAL

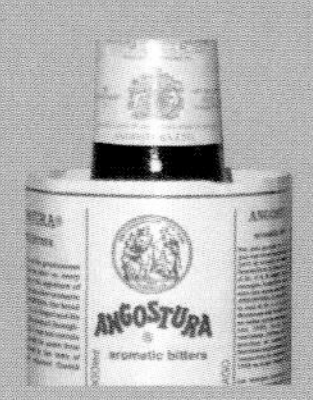

ANGOSTURA AROMATIC BITTERS

FRESH LEMONS

FRESH LIMES

FRESH MINT

STRAWBERRIES

RASPBERRIES

MARASCHINO CHERRIES

VANILLA PODS

DOUBLE CREAM

MILK

EGGS

SUGAR CUBES

RUNNY HONEY

FILTER & ESPRESSO COFFEE

EARL GREY TEA

NOT FORGETTING... ICE - THE MOST IMPORTANT COCKTAIL INGREDIENT

Ace
Agent Orange
Aggravation
A.J.
Alan's Apple Breeze
Alice In Wonderland
Anita's Attitude Adjuster
Apple Daiquiri
Apple Martini #1
Apple Of One's Eye
Apple Virgin Mojito
Apricot Lady Sour
Apricot Mango Martini
Apricot Martini
Apricot Sour
Arizona Breeze
Attitude Adjuster
Balalaika
Bald Eagle Martini
Barnum
Basil & Honey Daiquiri
Basil Grande
Bay Breeze
Beach Iced Tea
Bebbo
Bee's Knees #2
Between the Sheets
Beverly Hills Iced Tea
Biarritz
Bingo
Bitter Sweet Symphony
Black Russian
Bling! Bling!
Blinker
Blue Blazer
Blueberry Martini #2
Bora Bora Brew
Boston
Bourbon Smash
Bourbonella
Bradford
Brandy Buck
Brandy Fizz
Brandy Flip
Brandy Smash
Brandy Sour
The Buck
Bulldog
Bull's Blood
C C Kazi
Cactus Banger
Caipirissima
Caipirovska
Call Me Old-fashioned
Cape Codder
Cappercaille
Celtic Margarita
Cham Cham
Champagne Cup
Cinderella
Claret Cobbler
Claridge
Classic Daiquiri
Clipper Cocktail
Clockwork Orange
Clover Leaf Martini
Coffee & Vanilla Daiquiri
Colonel Collins
Colonel T
Colorado Bulldog
Cowboy Martini
Cuba Libra
Cuban Master
Cuban Special
Cucumber & Mint Martini
Daiquiri On The Rocks
Daisy Duke
Damn-The-Weather
Delmonico Special
Derby Daiquiri
Derby Fizz
Detroit Martini
Diamond Fizz
Dickens' Martini
DNA
Dorian Gray
Dowa
Dreamsicle
Dry Martini #1 (Traditional)
Dry Martini #2 (Naked)
Dyevitchka

Earl Grey Mar-tea-ni
East India #2
Easy Tiger
Egg Nog #1 (Cold)
Egg Nog #2 (Hot)
El Burro
El Presidente Daiquiri
El Torado
Elegante Margarita
Espresso Daiquiri
Espresso Martini
Esquire #1
Fantasia
Fine & Dandy
Fizz
Flip
The Flirt
Flirtini #1
Flirtini #2
Florida Cocktail
Florida Sling
Floridita Margarita
Flutter
Flying Tigre Coctel
Fog Horn
Forbidden Fruits
Frankenjack
Franklin Martini
French 75
French 76
French Daiquiri
French Martini
French Mojito
French Mule
Fresca Nova
Frozen Daiquiri
Frozen Margarita
Fruit Sour
Fruit Tree Daiquiri
Full Circle
Gentle Breeze
Gibson
Gimlet #1
Gimlet #2
Gin & Sin
Gin & Tonic
Gin Berry
Gin Fix
Gin Fixed
Gin Fizz
Gin Gin Mule
Gin Sour
Ginger & Lemongrass Martini
Gin-Ger & Tonic
Ginger Cosmos
Ginger Mojito
Gin-Ger Tom
Golden Fizz #1
Golden Fizz #2
Golden Screw
Golf Cocktail
Grand Margarita
Grand Mimosa
Grand Sidecar
Grande Champagne Cosmo
Grape Martini
Grapefruit Julep
Grapple Martini
Greyhound
Gypsy Martini
Hair Of The Dog
Hard Lemonade
Havanatheone
Hobson's Choice
Honey & Marmalade Dram'tini
Honey Bee
Honey Daiquiri
Honey Limeaid
Honeysuckle Daiquiri
Honolulu
Hoopla
Hop Toad #1
Hop Toad #2
Horse's Neck With a Kick
Hot Red Blooded Frenchman
Hot Tub
Ice 'T' Knee
Icy Pink Lemonade
Iguana
Incognito
Jack Dempsey

Jackie O's Rose
Jade Garden #2
Jalisco
Jalisco Espresso
Jambouree
Ja-Mora
John Collins
Jose Collins
Judy
Julep Martini
Jules Delight
Jungle Juice
Kamikaze
Katinka
Kee-Wee Martini
Kentucky Jewel
Kentucky Muffin
Kentucky Tea
Kiwi Collins
Kiwi Martini (simple)
Klondike
Lazarus
LCB Martini
Lemon Drop
Lemon Lime & Bitters
Lime Blush
Livingstone
Lolita Margarita
Lonely Bull
Long Island Iced Tea
Loved Up
Lucky Lily Margarita
Lucky Lindy
Lush
Lutkins Special Martini
Madras
Madroska
Maiden's Blush
Maiden's Prayer
Mainbrace
Major Bailey #1
Major Bailey #2
Magic Bus
Mango Collins
Mango Daiquiri
Mango Margarita #1
Mango Margarita #2
Manhattan Dry
Maple Old-Fashioned
Maple Leaf
Maple Pomme
Margarita #1
Margarita #2
Margarita #3
Marguerite Martini
Maria Theresa Margarita
Marmalade Martini
Marmarita
Marny Cocktail
Marquee
Martinez
Matador
Mayan
Mayan Whore
Mayfair Cocktail
Melon Martini #2
Mesa Fresca
Merry-Go-Round Martini
Mexican
Mexican 55
Mexican Coffee (Hot)
Mexican Mule
Mexican Surfer
Mexican Tea (Hot)
Mexico City
Mexicano (Hot)
Miami Beach
Miami Daiquiri
Milk & Honey
Millionaire
Millionaire's Daiquiri
Mimosa
Mint Collins
Mint Daiquiri
Mint Julep
Mint Limeade
Mississippi Punch
Mojito
Mojito de Casa
Momo Special
Moscow Mule

Nacional Daiquiri #1
Nacional Daiquiri #2
Nantucket
Naranja Daiquiri
Natural Daiquiri
Nautilus
New Orleans Mule
New Yorker
Niagara Falls
Nicky's Fizz
Not So Cosmo
November Seabreeze
Oh Gosh!
Old Fashioned #1
Old Fashioned #2
Olympic
Opal
Orange Bloom Martini
Orange Blossom
Paisley Martini
Palermo
Paradise #1
Paradise #2
Park Lane
Passion Fruit Daiquiri
Passion Fruit Martini #1
Pavlova Shot
Pedro Collins
Perfect Martini
Periodista Daiquiri
Pharmaceutical Stimulant
Pierre Collins
Piña Martini
Pineapple & Cardamom Martini
Pineapple & Ginger Martini
Pineapple Blossom
Pineapple Daiquiri #1
Pineapple Daiquiri #2
Pineapple Margarita
Pink Gin #1
Pink Gin #2
Pink Gin & Tonic
Pink Grapefruit Margarita
Pink Hound
Pink Lady
Pink Lemonade
Pink Palace
Pino Pepe
Planter's Punchless
Playa Del Mar
Playmate Martini
Plum Daiquiri
Plum Martini
Plum Sour
Pogo Stick
Poinsettia
Polly's Special
Pomegranate Margarita
Pomegranate Martini
Pompanski Martini
President
Presidente
Prince Of Wales
Princeton Martini
Purple Haze
Purple Hooter
Pussyfoot
Raspberry Margarita
Raspberry Martini #1
Raspberry Mule
Raspberry Watkins
Ray's Hard Lemonade
Real Lemonade [Mocktail]
Red Lion #1 (Modern)
Red Lion #2 (Embury's)
Red Marauder
Remsen Cooler
Resolute
Rosarita Margarita
Roselyn Martini
Roy Rogers
Royal Mojito
Rude Cosmopolitan
Rude Ginger Cosmopolitan
Sage Margarita
Sage Martini
Saigon Cooler
St Kitts
La Sang
Sangaree
Santiago Daiquiri

Satan's Whiskers (Straight)
Scotch Milk Punch
Screwdriver
Seabreeze #1 (Simple)
Seabreeze #2 (Layered)
Shady Grove Cooler
Shirley Temple
Showbiz
Sidecar #1
Sidecar #2 (Difford's)
Sidecar #3 (Embury's)
Silent Third
Silver Fizz
Sleepy Hollow
Sling
Sloppy Joe
Smoky Martini #1
Snood Murdekin
Snow White Daiquiri
Snyder Martini
South Of The Border
Southside Royal
Spencer Cocktail
Speyside Martini
Spiked Apple Cider (Hot)
Sputnik #2
Stanley Cocktail
Stork Club
Strawberry & Balsamic Mojito
Strawberry Daiquiri
Strawberry Frozen Daiquiri
Strawberry Margarita
Strawberry Martini
Summer Time Martini
Sundowner #1
Sunshine Cocktail #1
Sunstroke
Swizzle
Tango Martini #1
Tequila Fizz
Tequila Slammer
Tequila Sour
Tequila Sunrise
Tequila Sunset
Tequila'tini
Tex Collins
Texas Iced Tea
Texsun
Thai Lady
Three Miler
Thriller From Vanilla
Tipperary #2
Tom Collins
Tomahawk
Tre Martini
Tres Compadres Margarita
Turkish Coffee Martini
U.S. Martini
Valencia
Vanilla & Raspberry Martini
Vanilla Daiquiri
Vanilla Margarita
Vavavoom
Venus Martini
The Vesper Martini
Vodka Collins
Vodka Espresso
Vodka Gimlet
Vodka Sour
Vodkatini
Waltzing Matilda
Wanton Abandon
Ward Eight
Watermelon & Basil Martini
Watermelon Martini
Webster Martini
Wet Martini
What The Hell
Whiskey Cobbler
Whiskey Collins
Whiskey Daisy
Whiskey Sour #1
(Classic)
Whiskey Sour #2
(Difford's)
Whisky Fizz
White Lady
White Lion
White Russian
The Zamboanga 'Zeinie'
Zoom

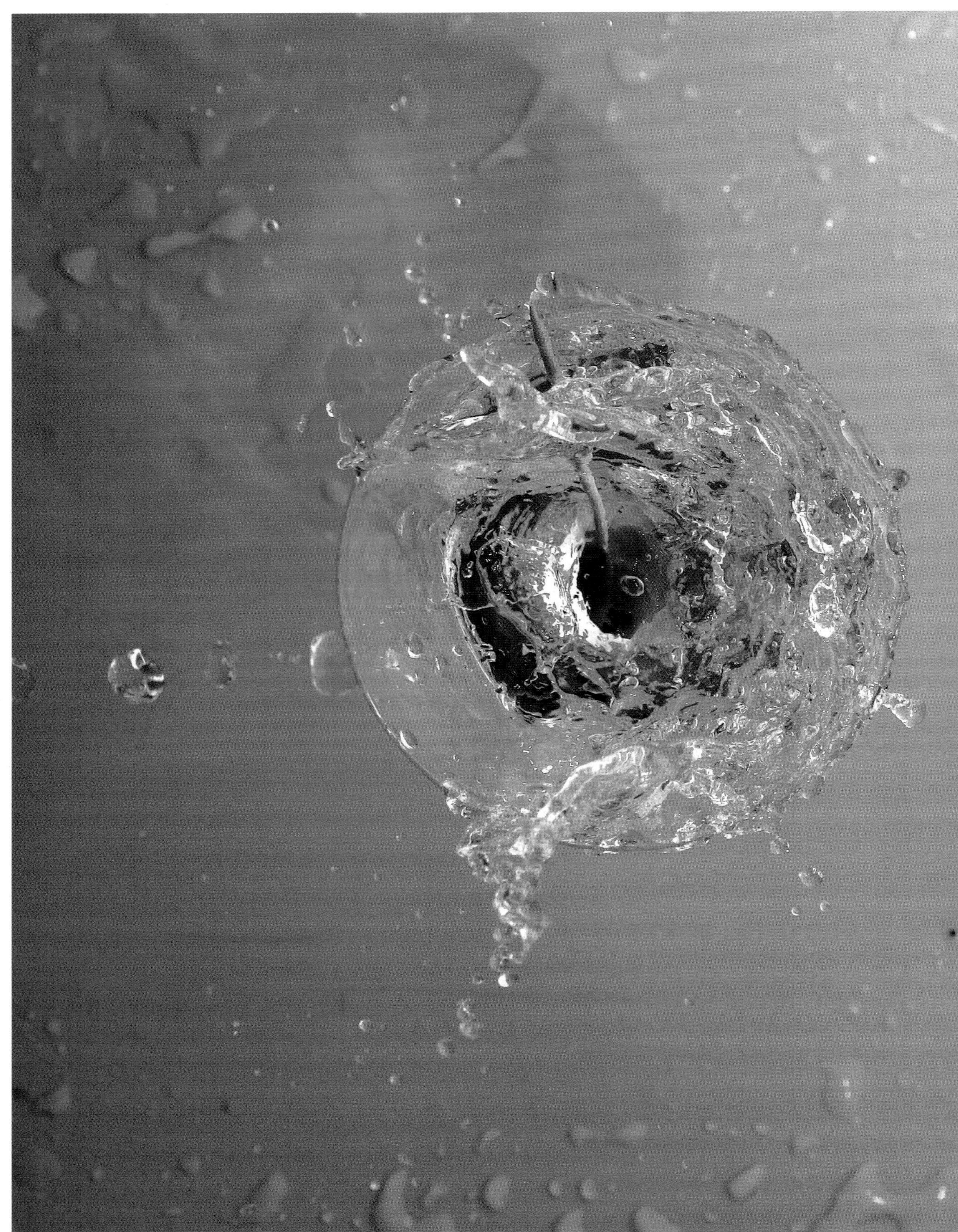

COCKTAILS A-Z

A

ABACAXI RICAÇO [NEW]

Glass: Pineapple shell
Garnish: The overly keen may like to cut a straw sized hole in the top of the pineapple and replace it as a lid.
Method: Cut the top off a small pineapple and carefully scoop out the flesh from the base to leave a shell with 12mm (1/2") thick walls. Place the shell in a freezer to chill. Remove the hard core from the pineapple flesh and place in blender. Add the rest of the ingredients and **BLEND** with one 12oz scoop of crushed ice. Pour into the pineapple shell and serve with straws. (The flesh of one pineapple blended with the following ingredients will fill at least two shells).

1 fresh **Pineapple**
3 shot(s) **Mount Gay golden rum**
3/4 shot(s) **Freshly squeezed lime juice**
1/2 shot(s) **Sugar (gomme) syrup**

Origin: Purloined from David Embury's classic book, The Fine Art Of Mixing Drinks. Pronounced 'Ah-bah-Kah-shee Rich-kah-SO', the Portuguese name of this Brazilian drink literally translates as 'Extra Delicious Pineapple'.
Comment: Looks good but a lot of hassle – personally I'd juice the pineapple and serve drink in a glass.

ABACI BATIDA

Glass: Collins
Garnish: Pineapple wedge on rim
Method: **SHAKE** all ingredients with ice and strain into glass filled with crushed ice.

2 1/2 shot(s) **Sagatiba cachaça**
3 shot(s) **Freshly extracted pineapple juice**
1/2 shot(s) **Sugar (gomme) syrup**
1/2 shot(s) **Freshly squeezed lemon juice**

Origin: The Batida is a traditional Brazilian drink and 'Abaci' means pineapple in Portuguese, the official language of Brazil.
Comment: Unfortunately, this excellent drink has not transferred as quickly from its homeland as the Caipirinha.

ABBEY MARTINI

Glass: Martini
Garnish: Orange zest twist
Method: **SHAKE** all ingredients with ice and fine strain into chilled glass.

2 shot(s) **Plymouth gin**
1 shot(s) **Rosso (sweet) vermouth**
1 shot(s) **Freshly squeezed orange juice**
3 dashes **Angostura aromatic bitters**

Origin: This 1930s classic cocktail is closely related to the better known Bronx.
Comment: A dry, orangey, herbal, gin laced concoction.

A.B.C.

Glass: Shot
Method: Refrigerate ingredients then **LAYER** in chilled glass by carefully pouring in the following order.

1/2 shot(s) **Luxardo Amaretto di Saschira**
1/2 shot(s) **Baileys Irish cream liqueur**
1/2 shot(s) **Rémy Martin cognac**

Comment: A stripy shooter with almond, whiskey, cream and cognac.

ABSINTHE COCKTAIL [NEW]

Glass: Martini
Garnish: Mint leaf
Method: **SHAKE** all ingredients with ice and fine strain into chilled glass.

1 shot(s) **La Fée Parisian 68% absinthe**
1 shot(s) **Chilled mineral water**
1/4 shot(s) **Sugar (gomme) syrup**

Variant: If grenadine (pomegranate syrup) is substituted for the sugar syrup this becomes a Tomate.
Origin: Dr. Ordinaire perfected his recipe for absinthe in 1792 and from day one it required the addition of water and sugar to make it palatable.
Comment: Absinthe tamed and served up.

ABSINTHE FRAPPÉ [NEW]

Glass: Old-fashioned
Garnish: Mint sprig
Method: **SHAKE** all ingredients with ice and fine strain into glass filled with crushed ice.

1 1/2 shot(s) **La Fée Parisian 68% absinthe**
1/2 shot(s) **Anisette liqueur**
1/8 shot(s) **Sugar (gomme) syrup**

Origin: Created in 1874 by Cayetano Ferrer at Aleix's Coffee House, New Orleans, which consequently became known as 'The Absinthe Room'. Today the establishment is fittingly known as the 'Old Absinthe House' but sadly US law prevents it from actually serving absinthe.
Comment: Aniseed and the fire of absinthe moderated by sugar and ice but still dangerous.

ABSINTHE SOUR

Glass: Old-fashioned
Garnish: Lemon zest twist
Method: **SHAKE** all ingredients with ice and strain into ice-filled glass.

1 shot(s) **La Fée Parisian 68% absinthe**
1 shot(s) **Sugar (gomme) syrup**
1 shot(s) **Freshly squeezed lemon juice**
1/2 fresh **Egg white**

Variant: Served 'up' in sour glass.
Comment: A touch of the sours for absinthe lovers.

ABSINTHE SUISESSE [NEW]

Glass: Old-fashioned
Garnish: Mint sprig
Method: SHAKE all ingredients with ice and strain into glass filled with crushed ice.

1½	shot(s)	La Fée Parisian (68%) absinthe
½	shot(s)	Orgeat (almond) sugar syrup
1	fresh	Egg white
½	shot(s)	Double (heavy) cream
½	shot(s)	Milk

Origin: New Orleans 1930s.
Variant: Also spelt 'Suissesse' and sometimes made with absinthe, vermouth, sugar, crème de menthe and egg white shaken and topped with sparkling water.
Comment: Absinthe smoothed with cream and sweet almond.

ABSINTHE WITHOUT LEAVE

Glass: Shot
Method: Refrigerate ingredients then LAYER in chilled glass by carefully pouring in the following order.

¾	shot(s)	Pisang Ambon liqueur
¾	shot(s)	Baileys Irish cream liqueur
½	shot(s)	La Fée Parisian (68%) absinthe

Origin: Discovered in 2003 at Hush, London, England.
Comment: This green and brown stripy shot is easy to layer but not so easy to drink.

ABSOLUTELY FABULOUS

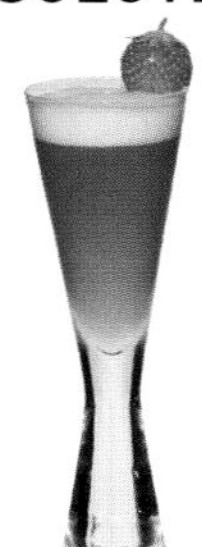

Glass: Flute
Garnish: Strawberry on rim
Method: SHAKE first two ingredients with ice and strain into glass. TOP with champagne.

1	shot(s)	Stolichnaya vodka
2	shot(s)	Cranberry juice
Top up with		Bollinger champagne

Origin: Created in 1999 at Monte's Club, London, England, and named after the Absolutely Fabulous television series where Patsy consumed copious quantities of Stoli and Bolly – darlings.
Comment: Easy to quaff – Patsy would love it.

ACAPULCO

Glass: Collins
Garnish: Pineapple wedge on rim
Method: SHAKE all ingredients with ice and strain into ice-filled glass.

1	shot(s)	Sauza Hornitos tequila
1	shot(s)	Mount Gay Eclipse golden rum
1	shot(s)	Freshly squeezed grapefruit juice
2½	shot(s)	Pressed pineapple juice
½	shot(s)	Sugar (gomme) syrup

Comment: An innocuous, fruity mixture laced with tequila and rum.

ACAPULCO DAIQUIRI

Glass: Martini
Garnish: Lime wedge on rim
Method: SHAKE all ingredients with ice and fine strain into chilled glass.

1½	shot(s)	Light white rum
½	shot(s)	Cointreau / triple sec
¾	shot(s)	Freshly squeezed lemon juice
¾	shot(s)	Rose's lime cordial
½	fresh	Egg white

Comment: A smooth, yet citrus-rich Daiquiri.

ACE [NEW]

Glass: Martini
Garnish: Maraschino cherry on rim
Method: SHAKE all ingredients with ice and fine strain into chilled glass.

2	shot(s)	Plymouth gin
½	shot(s)	Pomegranate (grenadine) syrup
½	shot(s)	Double (heavy) cream
½	shot(s)	Milk
½	fresh	Egg white

Comment: Pleasant, creamy, sweetened gin. Add more pomegranate syrup to taste.

ACE OF CLUBS DAIQUIRI [NEW]

Glass: Martini
Garnish: Dust with cocoa powder
Method: SHAKE all ingredients with ice and fine strain into chilled glass.

2	shot(s)	Mount Gay Eclipse golden rum
½	shot(s)	White crème de cacao liqueur
½	shot(s)	Freshly squeezed lime juice
⅛	shot(s)	Sugar (gomme) syrup

Origin: A long lost classic thought to have heralded from the Bermudian nightclub of the same name.
Comment: A Daiquiri with a hint of chocolate.

ACHILLES HEEL [NEW]

Glass: Collins
Garnish: Apple slice
Method: SHAKE all ingredients with ice and strain into ice-filled glass.

2	shot(s)	Zubrówka bison vodka
¼	shot(s)	Chambord black raspberry liqueur
¼	shot(s)	Peach schnapps liqueur
1	shot(s)	Pressed apple juice
½	shot(s)	Freshly squeezed lemon juice

Origin: Created in 2005 at Koba, Brighton, England.
Comment: If you like French Martinis you'll love this semi-sweet Tatanka with knobs on.

A B C D E F G H I J K L M N O P Q R S T U V W X Y Z

A

ADAM AND EVE

Glass: Old-fashioned
Garnish: Lemon zest twist
Method: **SHAKE** all ingredients with ice and strain into ice-filled glass.

2	shot(s)	**Bourbon whiskey**
½	shot(s)	**Galliano liqueur**
½	shot(s)	**Sugar (gomme) syrup**
4	dashes	**Angostura aromatic bitters**

Comment: Lovers of the Sazerac will appreciate this herbal, bourbon-laced concoction.

ADIOS

Glass: Shot
Method: Refrigerate ingredients then **LAYER** in chilled glass by carefully pouring in the following order.

¾	shot(s)	**Kahlúa coffee liqueur**
¾	shot(s)	**Sauza Hornitos tequila**

Comment: Surprisingly tasty with a potent agave reminder of what you've just knocked back.

ADONIS

Glass: Martini
Garnish: Orange zest twist
Method: **STIR** all ingredients with ice and strain into chilled glass.

3	shot(s)	**Tio Pepe fino sherry**
1½	shot(s)	**Rosso (sweet) vermouth**
3	dashes	**Fee Brothers orange bitters**

Origin: Thought to have been created in 1886 to celebrate the success of a Broadway musical.
Comment: Surprisingly delicate, dry, aromatic oldie.

AFFINITY

Glass: Martini
Garnish: Lemon zest twist
Method: **STIR** all ingredients with ice and strain into chilled glass.

2	shot(s)	**The Famous Grouse Scotch**
1	shot(s)	**Rosso (sweet) vermouth**
1	shot(s)	**Dry vermouth**
3	dashes	**Angostura aromatic bitters**

AKA: Scotch Manhattan
Variant: Rob Roy & Violet Affinity
Comment: This classic cocktail may be something of an acquired taste for many modern drinkers.

AFTER EIGHT

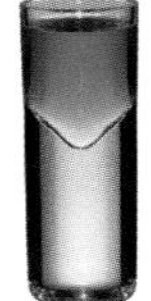

Glass: Shot
Method: **SHAKE** all ingredients with ice and fine strain into chilled glass.

½	shot(s)	**Ketel One vodka**
½	shot(s)	**White crème de cacao liqueur**
½	shot(s)	**Green crème de menthe**

Comment: Looks like mouthwash but tastes like liquid After Eight chocolates.

AFTER SIX SHOT

Glass: Shot
Method: Refrigerate ingredients then **LAYER** in chilled glass by carefully pouring in the following order.

½	shot(s)	**Kahlúa coffee liqueur**
½	shot(s)	**White crème de menthe liqueur**
½	shot(s)	**Baileys Irish cream liqueur**

Comment: A layered, creamy, coffee and mint shot.

AFTERBURNER

Glass: Snifter
Method: **POUR** all ingredients into glass, swirl to mix, flambé and then extinguish flame. Please take care and beware of hot glass rim.

1	shot(s)	**White crème de menthe liqueur**
1	shot(s)	**Kahlúa coffee liqueur**
½	shot(s)	**Wray & Nephew overproof rum**

Comment: A surprisingly smooth and moreish peppermint-laced drink.

AFTERNOON TEA-NI [NEW]

Glass: Martini
Garnish: Lemon zest twist
Method: **SHAKE** all ingredients with ice and fine strain into chilled glass.

1½	shot(s)	**Polstar Cucumber vodka**
1½	shot(s)	**Pimm's No.1 Cup**
1	shot(s)	**Krupnik honey liqueur**

Origin: Discovered in 2003 at Claridge's Bar, London, England.
Comment: Looks and even tastes remarkably like sweetened black tea.

DRINKS ARE GRADED AS FOLLOWS:

DISGUSTING · PRETTY AWFUL · BEST AVOIDED · DISAPPOINTING · ACCEPTABLE · GOOD · RECOMMENDED · HIGHLY RECOMMENDED · OUTSTANDING / EXCEPTIONAL

B C D E F G H I J K L M N O P Q R S T U V W X Y Z

AGED HONEY DAIQUIRI [NEW]

Glass: Martini
Garnish: Lime wedge on rim
Method: **STIR** honey with rum in base of shaker until honey dissolves. Add lime juice and water, **SHAKE** with ice and fine strain into chilled glass.

2	shot(s)	**Appleton Estate V/X aged rum**
1½	spoons	**Runny honey**
½	shot(s)	**Freshly squeezed lime juice**
½	shot(s)	**Chilled mineral water (omit if wet ice)**

Comment: Sweet honey replaces sugar syrup in this natural Daiquiri. Try experimenting with different honeys. I favour orange blossom honey.

AGENT ORANGE

Glass: Old-fashioned
Garnish: Orange zest twist
Method: **SHAKE** all ingredients with ice and strain into ice-filled glass.

1	shot(s)	**Ketel One vodka**
½	shot(s)	**Grand Marnier**
½	shot(s)	**Cointreau / triple sec**
2	shot(s)	**Freshly squeezed orange juice**

Comment: Fresh orange is good for you. This has all of the flavour but few of the health benefits.

AGGRAVATION

Glass: Old-fashioned
Garnish: Dust with freshly grated nutmeg
Method: **SHAKE** all ingredients with ice and strain into ice-filled glass.

2	shot(s)	**The Famous Grouse Scotch**
1	shot(s)	**Kahlúa coffee liqueur**
¾	shot(s)	**Double (heavy) cream**
¾	shot(s)	**Milk**
¼	shot(s)	**Sugar (gomme) syrup**

Comment: If you like Scotch and enjoy creamy drinks, you'll love this.

AIR MAIL

Glass: Martini
Garnish: Mint leaf
Method: **STIR** honey with rum in base of shaker until honey dissolves. Add lemon and orange juice, **SHAKE** with ice and fine strain into chilled glass. **TOP** with champagne.

1	shot(s)	**Mount Gay Eclipse golden rum**
2	spoons	**Runny honey**
½	shot(s)	**Freshly squeezed lime juice**
½	shot(s)	**Freshly squeezed orange juice**
Top up with		**Piper-Heidsieck brut champagne**

Origin: This old classic is basically a Honeysuckle topped up with champagne.
Comment: Rum, honey and a touch of citrus freshness make this one of the better champagne cocktails.

A.J.

Glass: Martini
Garnish: Dust with cinnamon powder
Method: **SHAKE** all ingredients with ice and fine strain into chilled glass.

2	shot(s)	**Calvados (or applejack brandy)**
2	shot(s)	**Freshly squeezed grapefruit juice**
½	shot(s)	**Sugar (gomme) syrup**

Comment: Amazingly simple and beautifully balanced. I hope you like apple brandy as much as I do.

ALABAMA SLAMMER #1

Glass: Martini
Garnish: Orange zest twist
Method: **SHAKE** all ingredients with ice and fine strain into chilled glass.

1	shot(s)	**Ketel One vodka**
1	shot(s)	**Southern Comfort**
2	shot(s)	**Freshly squeezed orange juice**
¼	shot(s)	**Pomegranate (grenadine) syrup**

Comment: Medium sweet, fruity and scarlet.

ALABAMA SLAMMER #2

Glass: Old-fashioned
Garnish: Peach wedge on rim
Method: **SHAKE** all ingredients with ice and strain into ice-filled glass.

1	shot(s)	**Southern Comfort**
½	shot(s)	**Plymouth sloe gin liqueur**
½	shot(s)	**Luxardo Amaretto di Saschira**
2¼	shot(s)	**Freshly squeezed orange juice**
1	shot(s)	**Freshly squeezed lemon juice**

Comment: Rich and quite sweet with a citrus bite.

THE ALAMAGOOZLUM COCKTAIL [NEW]

Glass: Martini
Garnish: Pineapple wedge on rim
Method: **SHAKE** all ingredients with ice and fine strain into chilled glass.

1	shot(s)	**Jonge jenever**
¾	shot(s)	**Yellow Chartreuse**
¾	shot(s)	**Wray & Nephew overproof white rum**
¼	shot(s)	**Grand Marnier**
¾	shot(s)	**Sugar (gomme) syrup**
1	shot(s)	**Chilled mineral water (reduce if wet ice)**
¼	shot(s)	**Angostura aromatic bitters**
¼	fresh	**Egg white**

Origin: My adaptation of a long lost classic from the 1930s. In his book 'The Fine Art Of Mixing Drinks', David Embury says, "This cocktail is supposed to have been a speciality of the elder Morgan of the House of Morgan, which goes to prove as a bartender he was an excellent banker."
Comment: Even Mr Embury would approve of this version. Overproof Jamaican rum and copious amounts of bitters make this drink.

ALAN'S APPLE BREEZE

Glass: Collins
Garnish: Apple wedge on rim
Method: **SHAKE** all ingredients with ice and strain into ice-filled glass.

- 2 shot(s) **Light white rum**
- $\frac{3}{4}$ shot(s) **Apricot brandy liqueur**
- 2 shot(s) **Pressed apple juice**
- 2 shot(s) **Cranberry juice**
- $\frac{1}{2}$ shot(s) **Freshly squeezed lime juice**
- $\frac{1}{2}$ shot(s) **Sugar (gomme) syrup**

Origin: Created in 2002 by Alan Johnston at Metropolitan, Glasgow, Scotland.
Comment: A sweet, tangy version of the Apple Breeze.

ALASKA MARTINI [UPDATED]

Glass: Martini
Garnish: Orange zest
Method: **SHAKE** all ingredients with ice and fine strain into chilled glass.

- $2\frac{1}{2}$ shot(s) **Plymouth gin**
- $\frac{3}{4}$ shot(s) **Yellow Chartreuse**
- 1 shot(s) **Tio Pepe fino sherry**
- 3 dashes **Fee Brothers orange bitters**

AKA: Nome
Origin: Adapted from the Alaska in The Savoy Cocktail Book. The addition of dry sherry is recommended in David Embury's The Fine Art Of Mixing Drinks.
Comment: If you like gin and Chartreuse, you'll also love this strong and complex Martini.

ALESSANDRO

Glass: Martini
Method: **SHAKE** all ingredients with ice and fine strain into chilled glass.

- 2 shot(s) **Opal Nera black sambuca**
- $\frac{3}{4}$ shot(s) **Plymouth gin**
- $\frac{3}{4}$ shot(s) **Double (heavy) cream**
- $\frac{3}{4}$ shot(s) **Milk**

Comment: Hints of aniseed, elderflower and gin emerge from this grey, creamy drink.

ALEXANDER

Glass: Martini
Garnish: Dust with freshly grated nutmeg
Method: **SHAKE** all ingredients with ice and fine strain into chilled glass.

- $1\frac{1}{2}$ shot(s) **Plymouth gin**
- $1\frac{1}{4}$ shot(s) **White crème de cacao liqueur**
- $\frac{3}{4}$ shot(s) **Double (heavy) cream**
- $\frac{3}{4}$ shot(s) **Milk**

AKA: Gin Alexander or Princess Mary
Comment: A Prohibition favourite – white, smooth and better than you'd imagine.

ALEXANDER THE GREAT [UPDATED]

Glass: Martini
Garnish: Dust with freshly grated nutmeg
Method: **SHAKE** all ingredients with ice and fine strain into chilled glass.

- $1\frac{3}{4}$ shot(s) **Ketel One vodka**
- $\frac{1}{2}$ shot(s) **Kahlúa coffee liqueur**
- $\frac{3}{4}$ shot(s) **White crème de cacao liqueur**
- $\frac{3}{4}$ shot(s) **Double (heavy) cream**
- $\frac{3}{4}$ shot(s) **Milk**

Comment: A tasty combination of coffee, chocolate and cream, laced with vodka.

ALEXANDER'S BIG BROTHER [UPDATED]

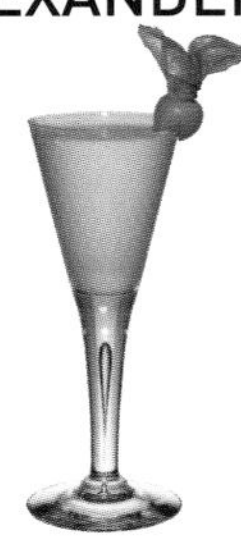

Glass: Martini
Garnish: Physalis (Cape gooseberry) on rim
Method: **SHAKE** all ingredients with ice and fine strain into chilled glass.

- $1\frac{1}{2}$ shot(s) **Plymouth gin**
- $\frac{1}{4}$ shot(s) **Cointreau / triple sec**
- $\frac{3}{4}$ shot(s) **Blue curaçao liqueur**
- $\frac{3}{4}$ shot(s) **Double (heavy) cream**
- $\frac{3}{4}$ shot(s) **Milk**

Comment: Orangey in taste and creamy blue in colour - mildly better than pink for the macho out there.

ALEXANDER'S SISTER

Glass: Martini
Garnish: Mint leaf
Method: **SHAKE** all ingredients with ice and fine strain into chilled glass.

- $1\frac{1}{2}$ shot(s) **Plymouth gin**
- $\frac{3}{4}$ shot(s) **White crème de menthe liqueur**
- $\frac{3}{4}$ shot(s) **Double (heavy) cream**
- $\frac{3}{4}$ shot(s) **Milk**

Comment: A green minty thing for dairy lovers.

ALEXANDRA

Glass: Martini
Garnish: Dust with freshly grated nutmeg
Method: **SHAKE** all ingredients with ice and fine strain into chilled glass.

- $1\frac{1}{2}$ shot(s) **Pusser's navy rum**
- 1 shot(s) **Kahlúa coffee liqueur**
- 1 shot(s) **Double (heavy) cream**
- 1 shot(s) **Milk**

Comment: Surprisingly potent and spicy, despite the ladylike name.

ALFONSO [UPDATED]

Glass: Flute
Garnish: Twist of lemon
Method: Coat sugar cube with bitters and drop into glass. **POUR** Dubonnet and then champagne into chilled glass.

1	cube	**Sugar**
4	dashes	**Angostura aromatic bitters**
1/2	shot(s)	**Dubonnet Red**
Top up with		**Piper-Heidsieck brut champagne**

Origin: Named after the deposed Spanish king Alfonso XIII, who first tasted this drink while exiled in France.
Comment: Herbal variation on the classic Champagne Cocktail.

ALGONQUIN [UPDATED]

Glass: Old-fashioned
Garnish: Cherry on stick
Method: **SHAKE** all ingredients with ice and strain into ice-filled glass.

2	shot(s)	**Rye whiskey**
1 1/4	shot(s)	**Dry vermouth**
1 1/4	shot(s)	**Pressed pineapple juice**
2	dashes	**Peychaud's aromatic bitters**

Origin: One of several classic cocktails accredited to New York City's Algonquin Hotel in the 1930s. Its true origins are lost in time.
Comment: Pineapple juice adds fruit and froth, while Peychaud's bitters combine subtly with the whiskey in this dry, aromatic drink.

ALICE FROM DALLAS

Glass: Shot
Method: Refrigerate ingredients then **LAYER** in chilled glass by carefully pouring in the following order.

1/2	shot(s)	**Kahlúa coffee liqueur**
1/2	shot(s)	**Grand Marnier**
1/2	shot(s)	**Sauza Hornitos tequila**

Comment: Coffee and orange spiked with tequila.

ALICE IN WONDERLAND

Glass: Shot
Garnish: Lime wedge
Method: Refrigerate ingredients then **LAYER** in chilled glass by carefully pouring in the following order.

1	shot(s)	**Sauza Hornitos tequila**
1/2	shot(s)	**Grand Marnier**

Comment: Brings a whole new dimension to tequila and orange.

ALEXANDER

The original Alexander, a mix of gin, crème de cacao and cream, came into existence early in the twentieth century, certainly before 1917. It became a Prohibition favourite as the cream and nutmeg garnish disguised the rough taste of homemade 'bathtub' gin. While the original, gin based Alexander has slipped from popularity, its successors, particularly the Brandy Alexander, have an enduring place on the world's cocktail lists.

Alexander variations include
Alessandro
Alexander the Great
Alexander's Big Brother
Alexander's Sister
Alexandra
Bird of Paradise
Brandy Alexander
Cherry Alexander
Irish Alexander

A B C D E F G H I J K L M N O P Q R S T U V W X Y Z

ALL FALL DOWN

Glass: Shot
Method: Refrigerate ingredients then **LAYER** in chilled glass by carefully pouring in the following order.

1/2	shot(s)	**Kahlúa coffee liqueur**
1/2	shot(s)	**Sauza Hornitos tequila**
1/2	shot(s)	**Pusser's Navy (54.5%) rum**

Comment: Too many of these and you will.

ALL WHITE FRAPPÉ

Glass: Old-fashioned
Garnish: Lemon zest
Method: **BLEND** ingredients with 6oz scoop of crushed ice. Pour into glass and serve with short straws.

1	shot(s)	**Luxardo Sambuca dei Cesari**
1	shot(s)	**White crème de cacao liqueur**
1	shot(s)	**Peppermint schnapps liqueur**
1	shot(s)	**Freshly squeezed lemon juice**

Comment: Aniseed, chocolate, peppermint and lemon juice are an unlikely but tasty combination for summer afternoons.

ALMOND & APRICOT MARTINI [NEW]

Glass: Martini
Garnish: Apricot on rim
Method: **SHAKE** all ingredients with ice and fine strain into chilled glass.

2	shot(s)	**Almond flavoured vodka**
3/4	shot(s)	**Apricot brandy liqueur**
1/4	shot(s)	**Dry vermouth**
3/4	shot(s)	**Chilled mineral water (omit if wet ice)**
3	dashes	**Angostura aromatic bitters**

Origin: Created in 2005 by yours truly.
Comment: Dilution is key to this drink. Cheat by adding water or shake for bloody ages.

ALMOND & COCONUT MARTINI [NEW]

Glass: Martini
Garnish: Dried coconut
Method: **SHAKE** all ingredients with ice and fine strain into chilled glass.

1 3/4	shot(s)	**Almond flavoured vodka**
1 1/2	shot(s)	**Fresh coconut water**
1/4	shot(s)	**Sugar (gomme) syrup**
1/4	shot(s)	**Dry vermouth**

Origin: Created in 2005 by yours truly.
Comment: Two nuts flavour this sweetened Martini.

ALMOND & SAKE MARTINI [NEW]

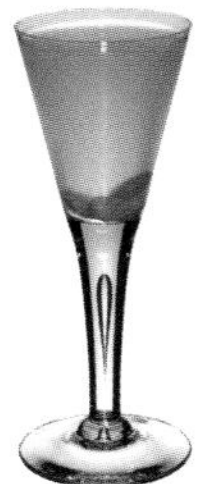

Glass: Martini
Garnish: Sink three chilled almonds
Method: **STIR** honey with vodka in base of shaker until honey dissolves. Add sake, **STIR** with ice and strain into chilled glass.

1	spoon	**Runny honey**
2	shot(s)	**Almond flavoured vodka**
2	shot(s)	**Sake**

Origin: Created in 2005 by yours truly.
Comment: Almond vodka and sake combine well, especially when sweetened with honey.

ALMOND COLLINS [NEW]

Glass: Collins
Garnish: Lemon slice
Method: **SHAKE** first three ingredients with ice and strain into ice-filled glass. **TOP** with soda.

2	shot(s)	**Almond flavoured vodka**
1	shot(s)	**Freshly squeezed lemon juice**
1/2	shot(s)	**Sugar (gomme) syrup**
Top up with		**Soda water**

Origin: Created in 2005 by yours truly.
Comment: Long and refreshing. Fortified almond with a clean lemon citrus finish.

ALMOND MARTINI #1

Glass: Martini
Garnish: Sink three roasted almonds
Method: **SHAKE** all ingredients with ice and fine strain into chilled glass.

2	shot(s)	**Ketel One vodka**
1/2	shot(s)	**Freshly squeezed lemon juice**
1/2	shot(s)	**Almond (orgeat) sugar syrup**
1	shot(s)	**Pressed apple juice**
2	dashes	**Fee Brothers peach bitters (optional)**

Origin: Created in 2004 by Matt Pomeroy at Baltic, London, England.
Comment: Almond inspired with hints of apple and lemon juice.

ALMOND MARTINI #2 [NEW]

Glass: Martini
Garnish: Sink three almonds
Method: **SHAKE** all ingredients with ice and fine strain into chilled glass.

2	shot(s)	**Almond flavoured vodka**
1/2	shot(s)	**Luxardo Amaretto di Saschira**
1/4	shot(s)	**Dry vermouth**
3/4	shot(s)	**Chilled mineral water (omit if wet ice)**

Origin: Created in 2005 by yours truly.
Comment: A delicate, almond flavoured Vodka Martini.

ALMOND OLD FASHIONED [NEW]

Glass: Old-fashioned
Garnish: Orange zest twist
Method: STIR one shot of tequila with two ice cubes in a glass. Add amaretto, agave syrup, bitters and two more ice cubes. Stir some more then add another two ice cubes and the remaining tequila. Stir lots more so as to melt ice then add more ice. The melting and stirring in of ice cubes is essential to the dilution and taste of the drink.

2	shot(s)	**Sauza Hornitos tequila**
1/4	shot(s)	**Luxardo Amaretto di Saschira**
1/4	shot(s)	**Agave syrup**
3	dashes	**Fee Brothers orange bitters**

Origin: Created in 2005 by Mark Pratt at Maze, London, England.
Comment: One to please fans of both tequila and the Old Fashioned drinks genre.

AMARETTO SOUR

Glass: Old-fashioned
Garnish: Cherry & lemon slice sail
Method: SHAKE all ingredients with ice and strain into ice-filled glass.

2	shot(s)	**Luxardo Amaretto di Saschira**
1 1/4	shot(s)	**Freshly squeezed lemon juice**
1/2	fresh	**Egg white**
2	dashes	**Angostura aromatic bitters**

Comment: Sweet 'n' sour – frothy with an almond buzz

AMARO DOLCE [UPDATED]

Glass: Old-fashioned
Method: MUDDLE lime in glass to release the juices and oils in its skin. **POUR** rest of ingredients into glass, add crushed ice and churn (stir) with bar spoon. Serve with a straw.

1	whole	**Lime cut into eighths**
1	shot(s)	**Raspberry flavoured vodka**
1	shot(s)	**Campari**
1/2	shot(s)	**Freshly squeezed lime juice**
1/2	shot(s)	**Sugar (gomme) syrup**

Origin: Created in 2002 by Alex Kammerling, London, England.
Comment: Not to everyone's taste, this Caipirinha-like drink features that distinctive bitter Campari edge.

AMBER

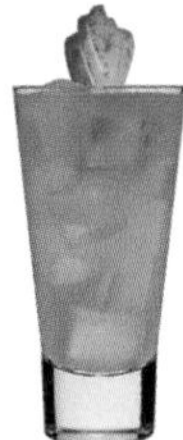

Glass: Collins
Garnish: Apple chevron & nutmeg dust
Method: MUDDLE ginger in base of shaker. Add other ingredients, **SHAKE** with ice and strain into glass filled with crushed ice.

2	slices	**Fresh root ginger (thumbnail sized)**
1 1/2	shot(s)	**Zubrówka bison vodka**
4	shot(s)	**Pressed apple juice**
1/2	shot(s)	**Ginger sugar syrup**
1/2	shot(s)	**Apple schnapps liqueur**

Origin: Created in 2001 by Douglas Ankrah for Akbar at the Red Fort, Soho, London, England.
Comment: A fantastic combination of adult flavours in a long, thirst-quenching drink. Also great served up.

AMBROSIA [UPDATED]

Glass: Flute
Method: SHAKE first four ingredients with ice and strain into glass. **TOP** with champagne.

1	shot(s)	**Rémy Martin cognac**
1	shot(s)	**Calvados (or applejack brandy)**
1/4	shot(s)	**Freshly squeezed lemon juice**
1/4	shot(s)	**Cointreau / triple sec**
Top up with		**Piper-Heidsieck brut champagne**

Comment: Dry, fortified champers with a hint of apple.

AMBROSIA'TINI

Glass: Martini
Garnish: Dust with freshly grated nutmeg
Method: SHAKE all ingredients with ice and fine strain into chilled glass.

3/4	shot(s)	**Rémy Martin cognac**
2	shot(s)	**Advocaat liqueur**
1	shot(s)	**Cuarenta Y Tres (Licor 43) liqueur**
1/2	shot(s)	**Yellow Chartreuse**

Origin: I created this drink and named it after the Greek for 'elixir of life, the food of the gods'. In Britain Ambrosia is a brand of custard, so advocaat seemed appropriate, while, if there is a God, he/she/it surely drinks Chartreuse.
Comment: Easy-drinking but complex with a herbal edge.

HOW TO MAKE SUGAR SYRUP

To make your own sugar syrup, gradually pour TWO cups of granulated sugar into a saucepan containing ONE cup of hot water. Stir as you pour and carry on stirring and simmering until the sugar is dissolved. Do not let the water even come close to boiling and only simmer for as long as it takes to dissolve the sugar. Allow syrup to cool and pour into an empty bottle. Ideally, you should finely strain your syrup into the bottle to remove any undissolved crystals which could otherwise encourage crystallisation. If kept in a refrigerator this mixture will last for a couple of months.

AMERICAN BEAUTY

Glass: Martini
Garnish: Float rose petal
Method: **SHAKE** first six ingredients with ice and fine strain into chilled glass. Use the back of a soup spoon to **FLOAT** red wine over drink.

2½	shot(s)	**Rémy Martin cognac**
½	shot(s)	**Dry vermouth**
½	shot(s)	**White crème de menthe liqueur**
½	shot(s)	**Freshly squeezed orange juice**
½	shot(s)	**Pomegranate (grenadine) syrup**
¾	shot(s)	**Chilled mineral water (omit if wet ice)**
¼	shot(s)	**Red wine**

Origin: Adapted from a recipe found in David A. Embury's The Fine Art Of Mixing Drinks.
Variant: When served in a tall glass with crushed ice this is called an American Beauty Punch.
Comment: Both fresh and refreshing - a subtle hint of peppermint gives zing to this cognac cocktail.

AMERICAN PIE MARTINI [NEW]

Glass: Martini
Garnish: Apple wedge on rim
Method: **SHAKE** all ingredients with ice and fine strain into chilled glass.

1½	shot(s)	**Bourbon whiskey**
½	shot(s)	**Apple schnapps liqueur**
½	shot(s)	**Crème de myrtille (bilberry) liqueur**
¾	shot(s)	**Cranberry juice**
½	shot(s)	**Pressed apple juice**
¼	shot(s)	**Freshly squeezed lime juice**

Origin: Adapted from a recipe discovered at Oxo Tower Restaurant & Bar, London, England.
Comment: This berry and apple pie has a tangy bite.

AMERICANA [UPDATED]

Glass: Flute
Garnish: Peach slice
Method: Coat sugar cube with bitters and drop into glass. **POUR** bourbon and then champagne into chilled glass.

1	cube	**Sugar**
4	dashes	**Angostura aromatic bitters**
¼	shot(s)	**Bourbon whiskey**
Top up with		**Piper-Heidsieck brut champagne**

Comment: The Wild West take on the classic Champagne Cocktail.

AMERICANO

Glass: Collins
Garnish: Orange slice
Method: **POUR** Campari and vermouth into ice-filled glass and **TOP** with soda. Stir and serve with straws.

2	shot(s)	**Campari**
2	shot(s)	**Cinzano Rosso sweet vermouth**
Top up with		**Soda water (club soda)**

Origin: First served in the 1860s in Gaspare Campari's bar in Milan, this was originally known as the 'Milano-Torino' as Campari came from Milano (Milan) and Cinzano from Torino (Turin). It was not until Prohibition that the Italians noticed an influx of Americans who enjoyed the drink and so dubbed it Americano.
Comment: A bitter, fizzy, long refreshing drink, which you'll love if you like Campari.

ANIS'TINI

Glass: Martini
Garnish: Star anise
Method: **MUDDLE** star anise in base of shaker. Add other ingredients, **SHAKE** with ice and fine strain into chilled glass.

2	dried	**Star anise**
1	shot(s)	**Ketel One vodka**
¾	shot(s)	**Luxardo Sambuca dei Cesari**
½	shot(s)	**Pernod anis**
1½	shot(s)	**Chilled mineral water**

Origin: Discovered in 2002 at Lot 61, New York City, USA.
Comment: Specks of star anise are evident in this aniseedy Martini.

ANITA'S ATTITUDE ADJUSTER

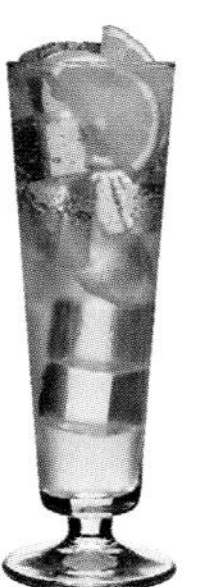

Glass: Sling
Garnish: Lemon slice
Method: **SHAKE** first seven ingredients with ice and strain into ice-filled glass. **TOP** with champagne and gently stir.

½	shot(s)	**Cointreau / triple sec**
½	shot(s)	**Sauza Hornitos tequila**
½	shot(s)	**Light white rum**
½	shot(s)	**Plymouth gin**
½	shot(s)	**Ketel One vodka**
½	shot(s)	**Freshly squeezed lime juice**
½	shot(s)	**Sugar (gomme) syrup**
Top up with		**Piper-Heidsieck brut champagne**

Comment: Anita has a problem – she's indecisive when it comes to choosing base spirits.

To make your own sugar syrup, gradually pour **TWO cups of granulated sugar into a saucepan containing ONE cup of hot water.** Stir as you pour and carry on stirring and simmering until the sugar is dissolved. Do not let the water even come close to boiling and only simmer for as long as it takes to dissolve the sugar. Allow syrup to cool and pour into an empty bottle. Ideally, you should finely strain your syrup into the bottle to remove any undissolved crystals which could otherwise encourage crystallisation. If kept in a refrigerator this mixture will last for a couple of months.

APACHE

Glass: Shot
Method: Refrigerate ingredients then **LAYER** in chilled glass by carefully pouring in the following order.

3/4	shot(s)	**Kahlúa coffee liqueur**
1/2	shot(s)	**Midori melon liqueur**
1/2	shot(s)	**Baileys Irish cream liqueur**

AKA: Quick F.U.
Comment: A coffee, melon and whiskey cream layered shot.

APHRODISIAC

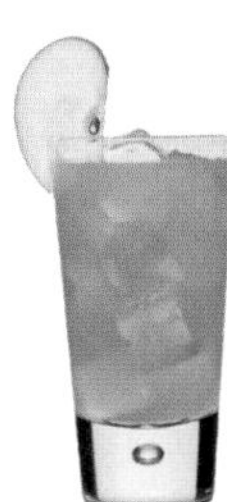

Glass: Collins
Garnish: Apple slice on rim
Method: **MUDDLE** ginger in base of shaker. Add other ingredients, **SHAKE** with ice and fine strain into ice-filled glass.

3	slices	**Fresh root ginger (thumbnail sized)**
2	shot(s)	**Vanilla-infused vodka**
1/2	shot(s)	**Green Chartreuse**
2 1/2	shot(s)	**Pressed apple juice**
2	shot(s)	**Sauvignon Blanc wine**

Origin: Created in 2002 by Yannick Miseriaux at The Fifth Floor Bar, London, England.
Comment: As strong in flavour as it is high in alcohol.

APPLE & BLACKBERRY PIE [NEW]

Glass: Martini
Garnish: Apple slice dusted with cinnamon
Method: **SHAKE** all ingredients with ice and fine strain into chilled glass.

7	fresh	**Blackberries**
2	shot(s)	**Apple flavoured vodka**
1	shot(s)	**Pressed apple juice**

Origin: Created in 2005 by yours truly.
Comment: A dessert in a glass, but not too sweet.

APPLE & CRANBERRY PIE

Glass: Martini
Garnish: Dust with cinnamon powder
Method: **SHAKE** first four ingredients with ice and fine strain into chilled glass. **FLOAT** cream on surface of drink by pouring over back of spoon.

1 1/2	shot(s)	**Cranberry flavoured vodka**
3/4	shot(s)	**Apple schnapps liqueur**
1	shot(s)	**Cranberry juice**
1/2	shot(s)	**Freshly squeezed lime juice**
3/4	shot(s)	**Double (heavy) cream**

Origin: I created this drink in 2003 for Finlandia.
Comment: Sip apple and cranberry through a creamy cinnamon layer

APPLE & CUSTARD MARTINI

Glass: Martini
Garnish: Apple wedge on rim
Method: **SHAKE** all ingredients with ice and fine strain into chilled glass.

2	shot(s)	**Advocaat liqueur**
1 1/2	shot(s)	**Calvados (or applejack brandy)**
1/2	shot(s)	**Apple schnapps liqueur**
1/4	shot(s)	**Vanilla sugar syrup**

Origin: I created this in 2002 after rediscovering advocaat on a trip to Amsterdam.
Comment: Smooth and creamy, this tastes like its name.

APPLE & ELDERFLOWER COLLINS

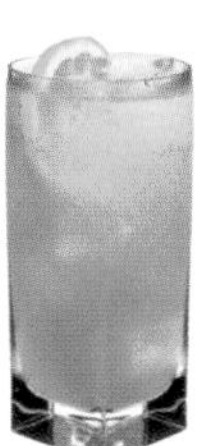

Glass: Collins
Garnish: Lemon slice
Method: **SHAKE** all ingredients with ice and strain into ice-filled glass. **TOP** with soda, stir and serve with straws.

2	shot(s)	**Plymouth gin**
1 1/2	shot(s)	**Freshly squeezed lemon juice**
2	shot(s)	**Pressed apple juice**
3/4	shot(s)	**Elderflower cordial**
Top up with		**Soda water (club soda)**

Origin: Formula by yours truly in 2004.
Comment: A John Collins laced with apple and elderflower.

APPLE & MELON MARTINI

Glass: Martini
Garnish: Apple wedge on rim
Method: **SHAKE** all ingredients with ice and fine strain into chilled glass.

2	shot(s)	**Ketel One vodka**
1	shot(s)	**Sour apple liqueur**
1/2	shot(s)	**Midori melon liqueur**
1/2	shot(s)	**Freshly squeezed lime juice**

Comment: The ubiquitous Green Apple Martini with extra colour and flavour thanks to a dash of melon liqueur.

APPLE & SPICE

Glass: Shot
Garnish: Dust with cinnamon powder
Method: Refrigerate ingredients then **LAYER** in chilled glass by carefully pouring in the following order.

3/4	shot(s)	**Calvados (or applejack brandy)**
3/4	shot(s)	**Double (heavy) cream**

Comment: Creamy apple shot.

A

APPLE BRANDY SOUR

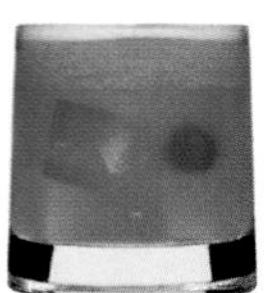

Glass: Old-fashioned
Garnish: Lemon sail (cherry & lemon slice)
Method: **SHAKE** all ingredients with ice and strain into ice-filled glass.

2	shot(s)	**Calvados (or applejack brandy)**
3/4	shot(s)	**Freshly squeezed lemon juice**
1	shot(s)	**Sugar (gomme) syrup**
4	dashes	**Angostura aromatic bitters**
1/2	fresh	**Egg white**

Comment: Sour by name - balanced sweet and sour apple by nature.

APPLE BREEZE

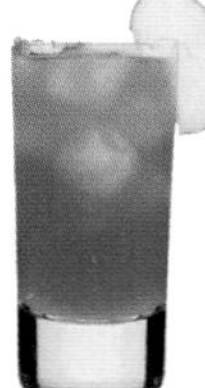

Glass: Collins
Garnish: Apple wedge on rim
Method: **SHAKE** all ingredients with ice and strain into ice-filled glass.

2 1/2	shot(s)	**Zubrówka bison vodka**
3	shot(s)	**Pressed apple juice**
2	shot(s)	**Cranberry juice**

Variant: Substitute vodka for Zubrówka bison vodka.
Comment: A lot more interesting than the better known Sea Breeze.

APPLE BUCK [NEW]

Glass: Collins
Garnish: Apple wedge
Method: **SHAKE** first four ingredients with ice and strain into ice-filled glass. **TOP** with ginger ale.

1 1/2	shot(s)	**Calvados (or applejack brandy)**
1/2	shot(s)	**Sour apple liqueur**
1	shot(s)	**Pressed apple juice**
1/2	shot(s)	**Freshly squeezed lime juice**
Top up with		**Ginger ale**

Origin: Adapted from a drink created in 2004 by Wayne Collins.
Comment: A refreshing long number with a taste reminiscent of cider.

APPLE CART

Glass: Martini
Garnish: Apple slice on rim
Method: **SHAKE** all ingredients with ice and fine strain into chilled glass.

2	shot(s)	**Calvados (or applejack brandy)**
3/4	shot(s)	**Cointreau / triple sec**
1/2	shot(s)	**Freshly squeezed lemon juice**
1/2	shot(s)	**Sugar (gomme) syrup**
1/2	shot(s)	**Chilled mineral water (omit if wet ice)**

AKA: Calvados Sidecar
Origin: This classic cocktail is an adaptation of the even older Sidecar.
Comment: A serious combination of apple with orange and sweet with sour.

APPLE CRUMBLE MARTINI #1

Glass: Martini
Garnish: Apple wedge on rim
Method: **SHAKE** all ingredients with ice and fine strain into chilled glass.

2	shot(s)	**The Famous Grouse Scotch**
1/4	shot(s)	**Butterscotch schnapps liqueur**
1	shot(s)	**Pressed apple juice**
1/2	shot(s)	**Freshly squeezed lemon juice**
1/2	shot(s)	**Sugar (gomme) syrup**

Comment: That's the way the apple crumbles - in this case enhancing the flavour of the Scotch.

APPLE CRUMBLE MARTINI #2

Glass: Martini
Garnish: Dust with cinnamon powder
Method: **SHAKE** all ingredients with ice and fine strain into chilled glass.

2	shot(s)	**Tuaca Italian liqueur**
1/2	shot(s)	**Freshly squeezed lemon juice**
2	shot(s)	**Pressed apple juice**

Origin: Created in 2002 by Eion Richards at Bond's Bar, London, England.
Comment: Easy to make and equally easy to drink.

APPLE DAIQUIRI

Glass: Martini
Garnish: Apple wedge on rim
Method: **SHAKE** all ingredients with ice and fine strain into chilled glass.

2	shot(s)	**Light white rum**
1 1/2	shot(s)	**Pressed apple juice**
1/2	shot(s)	**Freshly squeezed lime juice**
1/4	shot(s)	**Sugar (gomme) syrup**

Origin: Formula by yours truly in 2004.
Comment: A classic Daiquiri with a very subtle hint of apple.

APPLE MAC

Glass: Martini
Garnish: Float apple slice
Method: **SHAKE** all ingredients with ice and strain into ice-filled glass.

2	shot(s)	**The Famous Grouse Scotch**
2 1/2	shot(s)	**Pressed apple juice**
1/2	shot(s)	**Stone's Original green ginger wine**

Variant: Also suits being served over ice in an old-fashioned glass.
Origin: I created this twist on the classic Whisky Mac in 2004.
Comment: Scotch, ginger and apple are a threesome made in heaven.

APPLE MANHATTAN

Glass: Martini
Garnish: Apple slice on rim
Method: **SHAKE** all ingredients with ice and fine strain into chilled glass.

2 shot(s) **Bourbon whiskey**
1½ shot(s) **Apple schnapps liqueur**
½ shot(s) **Rosso (sweet) vermouth**

Origin: My take on a drink created by David Marsden at First on First in New York City and latterly popularised by Dale DeGroff. Traditionalists may want to stir it.
Comment: Rusty gold in colour, this is a flavoursome number for bourbon lovers.

APPLE MARTINI #1 (SIMPLE VERSION)

Glass: Martini
Garnish: Cherry in base of glass
Method: **SHAKE** all ingredients with ice and fine strain into chilled glass.

2½ shot(s) **Ketel One vodka**
2 shot(s) **Pressed apple juice**
¼ shot(s) **Sugar (gomme) syrup**

Variant: Sour Apple Martini, Caramelised Apple Martini
Origin: Formula by yours truly in 2004.
Comment: This is subtitled the simple version for good reason but, if freshly pressed juice is used, it's as good if not better than other Apple Martini recipes.

APPLE MARTINI #2

Glass: Martini
Garnish: Apple wedge on rim
Method: **SHAKE** all ingredients with ice and fine strain into chilled glass.

2 shot(s) **Ketel One vodka**
¾ shot(s) **Apple schnapps liqueur**
2 shot(s) **Pressed apple juice**

Comment: There are as many different recipes for this drink as there are varieties of apple and brands of apple liqueur: this is one of the more popular.

APPLE MARTINI #3 [NEW]

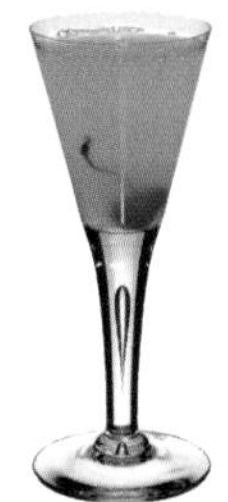

Glass: Martini
Garnish: Maraschino cherry in glass
Method: **SHAKE** all ingredients with ice and fine strain into chilled glass.

2 shot(s) **Apple flavoured vodka**
¼ shot(s) **Apple schnapps**
1¾ shot(s) **Pressed apple juice**

Origin: Created in 2005 by yours truly.
Comment: Another subtle twist on the Apple Martini theme, this one with apple flavoured vodka.

APPLE MOJITO [NEW]

Glass: Collins
Garnish: Mint sprig
Method: **MUDDLE** mint in base of glass. Add other ingredients, half fill glass with crushed ice and **CHURN** (stir) with bar spoon. Fill glass to brim with more crushed ice and churn some more. Serve with straws.

12 fresh **Mint leaves**
1¾ shot(s) **Apple flavoured vodka**
½ shot(s) **Light white rum**
1 shot(s) **Freshly squeezed lime juice**
½ shot(s) **Apple schnapps liqueur**
¼ shot(s) **Sugar (gomme) syrup**

Origin: Created in 2005 by yours truly.
Comment: An enduring classic given a touch of apple.

APPLE OF MY EIRE

Glass: Martini
Garnish: Clove
Method: **MUDDLE** cloves and cinnamon in base of shaker, add Drambuie and continue to muddle. Add the rest of the ingredients, **SHAKE** with ice and fine strain into chilled glass.

7 whole **Cloves**
¼ spoon **Ground cinnamon powder**
1 shot(s) **Drambuie liqueur**
1 shot(s) **Passoã passion fruit liqueur**
½ shot(s) **Grand Marnier**
¾ shot(s) **Pressed apple juice**
¾ shot(s) **Cranberry juice**

Origin: Adapted from a recipe created by Elaine in 2002 at The Living Room, Liverpool, England. The original uses a blend of apple purée with cloves and cinnamon.
Comment: Cinnamon and cloves combine with a veritable fruit basket to produce a drink reminiscent of cold mulled wine – very refreshing.

APPLE OF ONE'S EYE

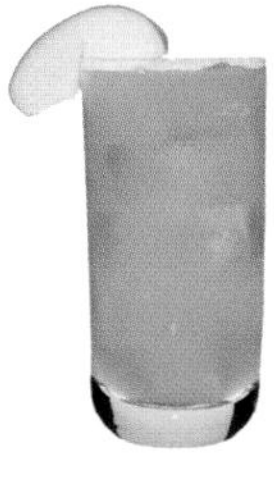

Glass: Collins
Garnish: Apple wedge on rim
Method: **SHAKE** first three ingredients with ice and strain into ice-filled glass. **TOP** with ginger beer.

2 shot(s) **Rémy Martin cognac**
½ shot(s) **Freshly squeezed lime juice**
3 shot(s) **Pressed apple juice**
Top up with **Jamaican ginger beer**

Comment: This spicy concoction is definitely something to cherish.

DRINKS ARE GRADED AS FOLLOWS:

● DISGUSTING ●◐ PRETTY AWFUL ●● BEST AVOIDED
●●◐ DISAPPOINTING ●●● ACCEPTABLE ●●●◐ GOOD
●●●● RECOMMENDED ●●●●◐ HIGHLY RECOMMENDED
●●●●● OUTSTANDING / EXCEPTIONAL

A B C D E F G H I J K L M N O P Q R S T U V W X Y Z

A

APPLE PIE MARTINI

Glass: Martini
Garnish: Apple wedge on rim
Method: **SHAKE** all ingredients with ice and fine strain into chilled glass.

1½	shot(s)	**Zubrówka bison vodka**
½	shot(s)	**Goldschläger cinnamon schnapps**
2	shot(s)	**Pressed apple juice**
1	shot(s)	**Cranberry juice**

Origin: Created in 2000 by Alexia Pau Barrera at Sand Bar, Clapham, England.
Comment: There's a good hit of cinnamon in this apple pie.

APPLE PIE SHOT [UPDATED]

Glass: Shot
Garnish: Dust with cinnamon powder
Method: **SHAKE** first two ingredients with ice and strain into chilled glass. Float cream on drink by carefully pouring over the back of a spoon.

1	shot(s)	**Apple schnapps liqueur**
½	shot(s)	**Hazelnut (crème de noisette) liqueur**
¼	shot(s)	**Double cream**

Comment: Nuts, apple, cinnamon and cream – pudding, anyone?

APPLEISSIMO [UPDATED]

Glass: Collins
Garnish: Apple slice on rim
Method: **SHAKE** first three ingredients with ice and strain into ice-filled glass. Top with anis and serve with straws.

1½	shot(s)	**Apple schnapps liqueur**
2	shot(s)	**Pressed apple juice**
1½	shot(s)	**Cranberry juice**
1½	shot(s)	**Pernod anis**

Comment: Stir the anis in with straws before drinking. Anis is best added last as it reacts on contact with ice.

APPLE SPRITZ

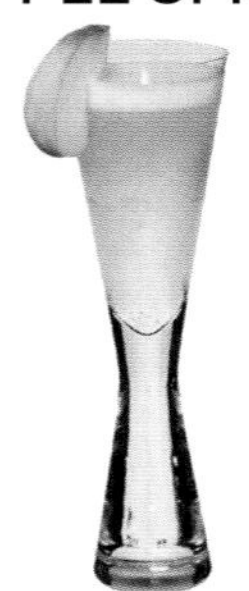

Glass: Flute
Garnish: Peach or apple slice on rim
Method: **POUR** first two ingredients into glass and top with champagne.

¾	shot(s)	**Apple schnapps liqueur**
¼	shot(s)	**Peach schnapps liqueur**
Top up with		**Piper-Heidsieck brut champagne**

Origin: Discovered in 2003 at Paramount Hotel, New York City, USA.
Comment: Sweet, fruity champagne – oh yeah, baby.

APPLE STRUDEL MARTINI

Glass: Martini
Garnish: Dust with cinnamon powder
Method: **SHAKE** first five ingredients with ice and fine strain into chilled glass. Carefully **FLOAT** cream by pouring over the back of a spoon.

1	shot(s)	**Apple schnapps liqueur**
½	shot(s)	**Goldschläger cinnamon schnapps**
½	shot(s)	**White crème de cacao liqueur**
½	shot(s)	**Dark crème de cacao liqueur**
1	shot(s)	**Pressed apple juice**
¾	shot(s)	**Double (heavy) cream**

Variant: May also be served as a shot.
Origin: Created in 1999 by Alex Kammerling, London, England.
Comment: This sweet dessert cocktail tastes just like mum's home-made apple pie with cream.

APPLE STRUDEL MARTINI #2

Glass: Martini
Garnish: Dust with cinnamon powder
Method: **SHAKE** all ingredients with ice and fine strain into chilled glass.

2	shot(s)	**Vanilla flavoured vodka**
2	shot(s)	**Pressed apple juice**
¼	shot(s)	**Apple schnapps liqueur**

Comment: The flavour of this drink is just what it says on the tin.

APPLE SUNRISE

Glass: Collins
Garnish: Apple slice
Method: **SHAKE** all ingredients with ice and strain into ice-filled glass.

2	shot(s)	**Calvados (or applejack brandy)**
½	shot(s)	**Sisca crème de cassis**
3½	shot(s)	**Freshly squeezed orange juice**

Origin: Created in 1980 by Charles Schumann, Munich, Germany.
Comment: A pleasing blend of fruits with the apple punch of Calvados.

FOR MORE INFORMATION SEE OUR INGREDIENTS APPENDIX ON PAGE 322

APPLE VIRGIN MOJITO (MOCKTAIL) [NEW]

Glass: Collins
Garnish: Mint sprig
Method: **MUDDLE** mint in base of glass. Add apple juice, sugar and lime juice. Half fill glass with crushed ice and **CHURN** (stir) with bar spoon. Fill glass to brim with more crushed ice and churn some more. Continue adding crushed ice and churning until glass is filled. Serve with straws.

12	fresh	**Mint leaves**
2	shot(s)	**Pressed apple juice**
1	shot(s)	**Freshly squeezed lime juice**
1/4	shot(s)	**Sugar (gomme) syrup**

Variant: Add three dashes of Angostura aromatic bitters.
Comment: As non-alcoholic cocktails go this is one of the best.

APPLESINTH

Glass: Old-fashioned
Garnish: Apple wedge on rim
Method: **SHAKE** all ingredients with ice and strain into glass filled with crushed ice.

1	shot(s)	**La Fée Parisian (68%) absinthe**
1	shot(s)	**Apple schnapps liqueur**
2	shot(s)	**Pressed apple juice**
3/4	shot(s)	**Freshly squeezed lime juice**
1/2	shot(s)	**Passion fruit sugar syrup**

Origin: Created in 1999 by Alex Kammerling, London, England.
Comment: Hints of apple and liquorice combine to make a very moreish cocktail.

APPLES 'N' PEARS [NEW]

Glass: Martini
Garnish: Apple or pear slice on rim
Method: **SHAKE** all ingredients with ice and fine strain into chilled glass.

1	shot(s)	**Pear flavoured vodka**
1	shot(s)	**Calvados (or applejack brandy)**
3/4	shot(s)	**Xanté pear brandy liqueur**
1 1/2	shot(s)	**Pressed apple juice**

Origin: Created in 2005 by yours truly.
Comment: 'Apples and pears' means stairs. Well worth climbing.

APPLILY MARRIED [NEW]

Glass: Martini
Garnish: Dust with cinnamon powder
Method: **STIR** honey with vodka in base of shaker until honey dissolves. Add other ingredients, **SHAKE** with ice and fine strain into chilled glass.

2	spoons	**Runny honey**
2 1/2	shot(s)	**Apple flavoured vodka**
1/2	shot(s)	**Pressed apple juice**

Origin: Created in 2005 by yours truly.
Comment: Apple and honey are indeed a marriage made in heaven.

APRICOT COSMO

Glass: Martini
Garnish: Apricot slice
Method: **STIR** apricot preserve with vodka until preserve dissolves. Add other ingredients, **SHAKE** with ice and fine strain into chilled glass.

2	shot(s)	**Ketel One vodka**
1	spoon	**Apricot preserve (St. Dalfour)**
1	shot(s)	**Cranberry juice**
1/4	shot(s)	**Passion fruit sugar syrup**
1/2	shot(s)	**Freshly squeezed lime juice**
2	dashes	**Fee Brothers orange bitters**

Origin: Created in 2004 at Aura Kitchen & Bar, London, England.
Comment: The apricot preserve adds a flavoursome tang to the contemporary classic.

APRICOT FIZZ

Glass: Collins
Garnish: Lemon wedge
Method: **SHAKE** first four ingredients with ice and strain into ice-filled glass. **TOP** with soda water.

2	shot(s)	**Apricot brandy liqueur**
1	shot(s)	**Freshly squeezed orange juice**
1 1/4	shot(s)	**Freshly squeezed lime juice**
1/4	shot(s)	**Sugar (gomme) syrup**
Top up with		**Soda water (club soda)**

Comment: This low-alcohol, refreshing cocktail is perfect for a summer afternoon.

APRICOT LADY SOUR

Glass: Old-fashioned
Garnish: Lemon sail (lemon slice & cherry)
Method: **SHAKE** all ingredients with ice and strain into ice-filled glass.

1 1/2	shot(s)	**Light white rum**
1	shot(s)	**Apricot brandy liqueur**
1	shot(s)	**Freshly squeezed lemon juice**
1/4	shot(s)	**Sugar (gomme) syrup**
1/2	fresh	**Egg white**

Comment: This seemingly soft and fluffy, apricot flavoured drink hides a most unladylike rum bite.

APRICOT MANGO MARTINI

Glass: Martini
Garnish: Mango slice
Method: **MUDDLE** mango in base of shaker. Add other ingredients, **SHAKE** with ice and fine strain into glass.

1	cupful	**Fresh diced mango**
2	shot(s)	**Plymouth gin**
1/2	shot(s)	**Apricot brandy liqueur**
3/4	shot(s)	**Freshly squeezed lemon juice**
1/2	shot(s)	**Sugar (gomme) syrup**

Variant: Use one-and-a-half shots of mango purée in place of fresh mango and halve amount of sugar syrup.
Comment: A simple, great tasting variation on the fresh fruit Martini.

A

APRICOT MARTINI

Glass: Martini
Garnish: Lemon zest twist
Method: **SHAKE** all ingredients with ice and fine strain into chilled glass.

$1^1/2$	shot(s)	**Plymouth gin**
1	shot(s)	**Apricot brandy liqueur**
$^1/4$	shot(s)	**Freshly squeezed lemon juice**
$^1/8$	shot(s)	**Pomegranate (grenadine) syrup**
3	dashes	**Angostura aromatic bitters**
$^3/4$	shot(s)	**Chilled mineral water (omit if wet ice)**

Comment: This scarlet cocktail combines gin, apricot and lemon juice.

APRIL SHOWER

Glass: Martini
Garnish: Orange zest twist
Method: **SHAKE** all ingredients with ice and fine strain into chilled glass.

2	shot(s)	**Rémy Martin cognac**
$^1/2$	shot(s)	**Bénédictine D.O.M. liqueur**
2	shot(s)	**Freshly squeezed orange juice**

Comment: This mustard coloured, medium dry, cognac-based drink harnesses the uniquely herbal edge of Bénédictine.

APRICOT SOUR [NEW]

Glass: Old-fashioned
Garnish: Lemon zest twist
Method: **STIR** apricot jam (preserve) with bourbon until it dissolves. Add other ingredients, **SHAKE** with ice and fine strain into ice-filled glass.

2	spoons	**Apricot jam (preserve)**
$1\ ^1/2$	shot(s)	**Bourbon whiskey**
$^1/2$	shot(s)	**Apricot brandy liqueur**
1	shot(s)	**Pressed apple juice**
$^1/2$	shot(s)	**Freshly squeezed lemon juice**

Origin: Created in 2005 by Wayne Collins for Maxxium UK.
Comment: Short and fruity.

AQUARIUS [UPDATED]

Glass: Old-fashioned
Method: **SHAKE** all ingredients with ice and strain into ice-filled glass.

2	shot(s)	**The Famous Grouse Scotch whisky**
1	shot(s)	**Cherry (brandy) liqueur**
$1^1/2$	shot(s)	**Cranberry juice**

Comment: A sweet cherry edge is balanced by the dryness of cranberry and Scotch.

ARIZONA BREEZE

Glass: Collins
Garnish: Grapefruit wedge on rim
Method: **SHAKE** all ingredients with ice and strain into ice-filled glass.

$2^1/2$	shot(s)	**Plymouth gin**
3	shot(s)	**Cranberry juice**
2	shot(s)	**Freshly squeezed grapefruit juice**

Comment: A tart variation on the Sea Breeze – as dry as Arizona.

ARNAUD MARTINI

Glass: Martini
Garnish: Blackberry on rim
Method: **STIR** all ingredients with ice and strain into chilled glass.

$1^1/2$	shot(s)	**Plymouth gin**
$1^1/2$	shot(s)	**Dry vermouth**
$1^1/2$	shot(s)	**Sisca crème de cassis**

Origin: A classic cocktail named after the pre-war stage actress Yvonne Arnaud.
Comment: An interesting balance of blackcurrant, vermouth and gin. Sweet palate and dry finish.

ARTLANTIC

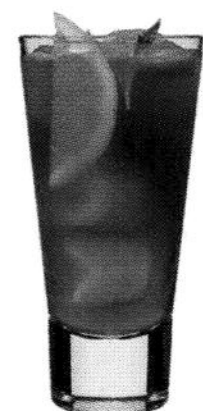

Glass: Collins
Garnish: Orange wedge
Method: **SHAKE** all ingredients with ice and strain into ice-filled glass.

1	shot(s)	**Spiced rum**
$^1/2$	shot(s)	**Luxardo Amaretto di Saschira**
$^1/2$	shot(s)	**Blue curaçao liqueur**
$^1/2$	shot(s)	**Freshly squeezed lime juice**
3	shot(s)	**Pressed apple juice**

Origin: Atlantic Bar & Grill, London, England.
Comment: This sea green cocktail tastes much better than it looks.

ASIAN GINGER MARTINI [NEW]

Glass: Martini
Garnish: Ginger slice on rim
Method: **MUDDLE** ginger in base of shaker. Add other ingredients, **SHAKE** with ice and fine strain into chilled glass.

2	slices	**Fresh root ginger (thumbnail sized)**
$1^1/2$	shot(s)	**Ketel One vodka**
$2^1/4$	shot(s)	**Sake**
$^1/4$	shot(s)	**Sugar (gomme) syrup**

Origin: Adapted from a recipe created in 2004 by Chris Langan of Barnomadics.
Comment: Lightly spiced with ginger, distinctly oriental in character.

ASIAN MARY [NEW]

Glass: Collins
Garnish: Lemongrass
Method: **MUDDLE** ginger in base of shaker and add vodka. Squeeze wasabi paste onto bar spoon and **STIR** with vodka and ginger until dissolved. Add other ingredients, **SHAKE** with ice and fine strain into ice-filled glass.

3	slices	**Fresh root ginger (thumbnail sized)**
3	peas	**Wasabi paste**
2	shot(s)	**Ketel One Citroen vodka**
1	spoon	**Soy sauce**
4	shot(s)	**Tomato sauce**
$\frac{1}{2}$	shot(s)	**Freshly squeezed lemon juice**

Comment: An aptly named Bloody Mary with plenty of Asian spice.

ASIAN PEAR MARTINI

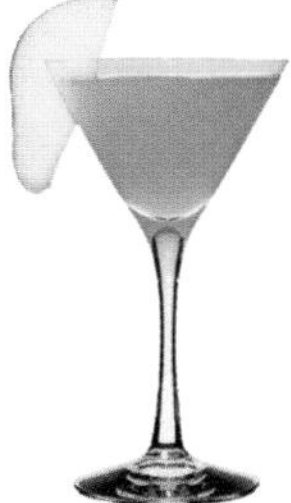

Glass: Martini
Garnish: Pear slice on rim
Method: **SHAKE** all ingredients with ice and fine strain into chilled glass.

2	shot(s)	**Sake**
$\frac{1}{4}$	shot(s)	**Xanté pear brandy liqueur**
$\frac{1}{2}$	shot(s)	**Poire William eau de vie**
$1\frac{1}{2}$	shot(s)	**Freshly extracted pear juice**
$\frac{1}{4}$	shot(s)	**Freshly squeezed lemon juice**

Origin: Created in 2002 by yours truly.
Comment: Sake and pear juice with a kick.

ASSISTED SUICIDE

Glass: Shot
Method: **SHAKE** first two ingredients with ice and strain into chilled glass. **TOP** with cola.

1	shot(s)	**Wray & Nephew overproof rum**
$\frac{1}{2}$	shot(s)	**Jägermeister**
Top up with		**Cola**

Comment: Not for the faint-hearted.

FOR MORE INFORMATION SEE OUR
INGREDIENTS APPENDIX ON PAGE 322

ATHOLL BROSE [NEW]

Glass: Martini
Garnish: Dust with freshly grated nutmeg
Method: Prepare oatmeal water by soaking three heaped tablespoons of oatmeal in half a mug of warm water. Stir and leave to stand for fifteen minutes. Then strain to extract the creamy liquid and discard what's left of the oatmeal.

To make the drink, **STIR** honey with Scotch until honey dissolves. Add other ingredients, **SHAKE** with ice and fine strain into chilled glass.

2	spoons	**Runny heather honey**
2	shot(s)	**The Famous Grouse Scotch**
$1\frac{1}{2}$	shot(s)	**Oatmeal water**
$\frac{1}{4}$	shot(s)	**Drambuie liqueur**
$\frac{1}{4}$	shot(s)	**Luxardo Amaretto di Saschira**
$\frac{1}{2}$	shot(s)	**Double (heavy) cream**

Origin: My adaptation of a Scottish classic. Legend has it that Atholl Brose was created by the Earl of Atholl in 1475 when he was trying to capture Iain MacDonald, Lord of the Isles and leader of a rebellion against the king. Hearing rumours that MacDonald was drawing his drinking water from a small well, the Earl ordered it to be filled with honey, whisky and oatmeal. MacDonald lingered at the well enjoying the concoction and was captured.
Comment: Forget the porridge and kick start your day with a Atholl Brose.

ATLANTIC BREEZE

Glass: Collins
Garnish: Orange slice
Method: **SHAKE** all ingredients with ice and strain into ice-filled glass.

$1\frac{1}{2}$	shot(s)	**Light white rum**
$\frac{1}{2}$	shot(s)	**Apricot brandy liqueur**
$\frac{1}{4}$	shot(s)	**Galliano liqueur**
$2\frac{1}{2}$	shot(s)	**Pressed pineapple juice**
$\frac{1}{2}$	shot(s)	**Freshly squeezed lemon juice**

Comment: A fruity, tropical cocktail finished with herbal and citrus notes.

ATOMIC COCKTAIL [NEW]

Glass: Martini
Garnish: Orange zest twist
Method: **SHAKE** first three ingredients with ice and fine strain into chilled glass. **TOP** with champagne.

$1\frac{1}{4}$	shot(s)	**Ketel One vodka**
$1\frac{1}{4}$	shot(s)	**Rémy Martin cognac**
$\frac{1}{2}$	shot(s)	**Amontillado sherry**
Top up with		**Piper-Heidsieck brut champagne**

Origin: Created in the early 50s in Las Vegas. A-bomb tests were being conducted in Nevada at the time.
Comment: Golden and flavoursome – handle with care.

A B C D E F G H I J K L M N O P Q R S T U V W X Y Z

ATOMIC DOG

Glass: Collins
Garnish: Pineapple wedge on rim
Method: **SHAKE** all ingredients with ice and strain into ice-filled glass.

1½	shot(s)	**Light white rum**
¾	shot(s)	**Midori melon liqueur**
¾	shot(s)	**Malibu coconut rum liqueur**
2½	shot(s)	**Pressed pineapple juice**
¾	shot(s)	**Freshly squeezed lemon juice**

Comment: A long, refreshing tropical drink with melon, coconut and pineapple juice.

ATTITUDE ADJUSTER

Glass: Hurricane
Garnish: Orange sail (orange slice & cherry)
Method: **SHAKE** first three ingredients with ice and strain into ice-filled glass. **TOP** with cola then **DRIZZLE** orange and coffee liqueurs.

2	shot(s)	**Plymouth gin**
1	shot(s)	**Cointreau / triple sec**
¾	shot(s)	**Freshly squeezed lime juice**
Top up with		**Cola**
¼	shot(s)	**Grand Marnier**
¼	shot(s)	**Kahlúa coffee liqueur**

Comment: I've simplified and tried to improve this somewhat dodgy but popular cocktail – sorry, I failed!

AULD ACQUAINTANCE

Glass: Martini
Garnish: Dust with freshly grated nutmeg
Method: **SHAKE** all ingredients with ice and fine strain into chilled glass.

1½	shot(s)	**The Famous Grouse Scotch**
1½	shot(s)	**Drambuie Cream liqueur**
1½	shot(s)	**Freshly squeezed orange juice**
¾	shot(s)	**Mandarine Napoléon liqueur**

Origin: Created in 2001 by Wayne Collins at High Holborn, London, England.
Comment: Creamy with a subtle hint of Scotch and orange zestiness.

AUNT AGATHA

Glass: Old-fashioned
Garnish: Orange zest twist
Method: **SHAKE** first three ingredients with ice and strain into glass filled with crushed ice. **SHAKE** bitters over surface.

1½	shot(s)	**Pusser's navy rum**
2	shot(s)	**Freshly squeezed orange juice**
1	shot(s)	**Pressed pineapple juice**
3	dashes	**Angostura aromatic bitters**

Origin: Aunt Hagatha was one of Samantha's aunts in the 1960s TV series 'Bewitched'; Aunt Agatha was Bertie Wooster's terrifying aunt in P.G. Wodehouse's books.
Comment: A most unusual looking, tropical tasting concoction.

AUNT EMILY [NEW]

Glass: Martini
Garnish: Apricot wedge on rim
Method: **SHAKE** all ingredients with ice and fine strain into chilled glass.

1½	shot(s)	**Plymouth gin**
1½	shot(s)	**Calvados (or applejack brandy)**
¾	shot(s)	**Apricot brandy liqueur**
¾	shot(s)	**Freshly squeezed orange juice**
⅛	shot(s)	**Pomegranate (grenadine) syrup**

Origin: A forgotten classic.
Comment: Aunt Emily is onto something as these ingredients combine to make a stylish fruity Martini.

AUNTIE'S HOT XMAS PUNCH

Glass: Toddy
Garnish: Cinnamon stick in glass
Method: **POUR** all ingredients into glass and stir. **MICROWAVE** for a minute (vary time depending on your microwave oven), stir again and serve.

¾	shot(s)	**Freshly squeezed lemon juice**
1½	shot(s)	**Pedro Ximénez sherry**
2¼	shot(s)	**Rémy Martin cognac**
3	shot(s)	**Pressed apple juice**
4	dashes	**Peychaud's aromatic bitters**

Origin: I created this drink to serve live on Christmas Eve 2002 during a broadcast on BBC radio. 'Auntie' is a nickname for the BBC and the drink uses the traditional punch proportions of 1 sour, 2 sweet, 3 strong and 4 weak.
Comment: A fruity seasonal warmer.

AUTUMN MARTINI

Glass: Martini
Garnish: Orange zest twist
Method: Cut passion fruit in half and scoop out flesh into shaker. Add other ingredients, **SHAKE** with ice and fine strain into chilled glass.

1	fresh	**Passion fruit**
2	shot(s)	**Zubrówka bison vodka**
1	shot(s)	**Pressed apple juice**
½	shot(s)	**Passion fruit sugar syrup**
½	fresh	**Egg white**

Origin: Created in 2004 by yours truly, inspired by Max Warner's excellent Autumn Punch.
Comment: An easy drinking, smooth, fruity cocktail with grassy hints courtesy of bison vodka.

DRINKS ARE GRADED AS FOLLOWS:

● DISGUSTING ●◐ PRETTY AWFUL ●● BEST AVOIDED
●●◐ DISAPPOINTING ●●● ACCEPTABLE ●●●◐ GOOD
●●●● RECOMMENDED ●●●●◐ HIGHLY RECOMMENDED
●●●●● OUTSTANDING / EXCEPTIONAL

AUTUMN PUNCH

Glass: Sling
Garnish: Physalis (Cape gooseberry) on rim
Method: Cut passion fruit in half and scoop out flesh into shaker. Add vodka, passion fruit sugar syrup, pear and lemon juice, **SHAKE** with ice and strain into ice-filled glass. **TOP** with champagne.

1	fresh	**Passion fruit**
2	shot(s)	**Zubrówka bison vodka**
1/4	shot(s)	**Passion fruit sugar syrup**
1	shot(s)	**Freshly extracted pear juice**
1/2	shot(s)	**Freshly squeezed lemon juice**
Top up with		**Piper-Heidsieck brut champagne**

Origin: Created in 2001 by Max Warner at Baltic Bar, London, England.
Comment: Autumnal in colour with a wonderful meld of complementary flavours.

AVALANCHE [UPDATED]

Glass: Collins
Garnish: Banana slice on rim
Method: BLEND ingredients with 12oz scoop of crushed ice. Pour into glass and serve with straws.

2	shot(s)	**Crème de bananes liqueur**
1	shot(s)	**White crème de cacao liqueur**
1/2	shot(s)	**Luxardo Amaretto di Saschira**
1	shot(s)	**Double (heavy) cream**
1	shot(s)	**Milk**
1/2	fresh	**Peeled banana**

Origin: Created in 1979 at Maudes Bar, New York City, USA.
Comment: Creamy, rich and smooth. Fluffy but lovely.

AVALANCHE SHOT

Glass: Shot
Method: Refrigerate ingredients then **LAYER** in chilled glass by carefully pouring in the following order.

1/2	shot(s)	**Kahlúa coffee liqueur**
1/2	shot(s)	**White crème de cacao liqueur**
1/2	shot(s)	**Southern Comfort**

Comment: Rich, smooth and sticky – peculiarly, this has an almost nutty taste.

AVENUE [NEW]

Glass: Martini
Garnish: Orange zest twist
Method: Cut passion fruit in half and scoop flesh into shaker. Add other ingredients, **SHAKE** with ice and fine strain into chilled glass.

1	fresh	**Passion fruit**
1	shot(s)	**Bourbon whiskey**
1	shot(s)	**Calvados (or applejack brandy)**
1/4	shot(s)	**Pomegranate (grenadine) syrup**
1/8	shot(s)	**Orange flower water**
3/4	shot(s)	**Chilled mineral water (omit if wet ice)**

Origin: A modern adaptation of a classic.
Comment: Fruity and floral.

AVIATION [UPDATED]

Glass: Martini
Garnish: Lemon zest twist
Method: SHAKE all ingredients with ice and fine strain into chilled glass.

2 1/2	shot(s)	**Plymouth gin**
1/2	shot(s)	**Luxardo maraschino liqueur**
1/2	shot(s)	**Freshly squeezed lemon juice**
1/2	shot(s)	**Chilled mineral water (omit if wet ice)**

Variant: Bee's Knees, Blue Moon
Origin: A classic cocktail thought to have originated in 1916.
Comment: This is a fantastic, tangy cocktail and dangerously easy to drink – too many of these and you really will be flying.

AVIATOR [NEW]

Glass: Martini
Garnish: Lemon zest twist
Method: STIR all ingredients with ice and strain into chilled glass.

1	shot(s)	**Plymouth gin**
1	shot(s)	**Dry vermouth**
1	shot(s)	**Rosso (sweet) vermouth**
1	shot(s)	**Dubonnet Red**

Origin: A classic cocktail of unknown origins. This recipe is from The Savoy Cocktail Book.
Comment: On the bitter side of bittersweet.

AWOL

Glass: Shot
Method: LAYER in chilled glass by carefully pouring ingredients in the following order. Then **FLAME** drink and allow to burn for no more than ten seconds before extinguishing flame and consuming. Take extreme care and beware of hot glass.

1/2	shot(s)	**Midori melon liqueur**
1/2	shot(s)	**Pressed pineapple juice**
1/2	shot(s)	**Ketel One vodka**
1/2	shot(s)	**Wray & Nephew overproof rum**

Origin: Created in 1993 by Lane Zellman at Louis XVI Restaurant, St. Louis Hotel, New Orleans, USA.
Comment: A strong but surprisingly palatable shot.

FOR MORE INFORMATION SEE OUR
INGREDIENTS APPENDIX ON PAGE 322

A B C D E F G H I J K L M N O P Q R S T U V W X Y Z

AZURE MARTINI

Glass: Martini
Garnish: Apple slice on rim
Method: **SHAKE** all ingredients with ice and fine strain into chilled glass.

2	shot(s)	**Sagatiba cachaça**
1/4	shot(s)	**Goldschläger cinnamon schnapps**
1	shot(s)	**Pressed apple juice**
1/2	shot(s)	**Freshly squeezed lime juice**
1/4	shot(s)	**Sugar (gomme) syrup**

Origin: Created in 1998 by Ben Reed at the Met Bar, London, England, and originally made with muddled fresh apple.
Comment: A tangy cocktail – reminiscent of a cinnamon laced apple pie. Shame it's not blue.

B2C2 [NEW]

Glass: Martini
Garnish: Orange zest twist
Method: **SHAKE** first three ingredients with ice and strain into ice-filled glass. **TOP** with champagne.

1	shot(s)	**Rémy Martin cognac**
1	shot(s)	**Bénédictine D.O.M. liqueur**
1	shot(s)	**Cointreau / triple sec**
Top up with		**Piper-Heidsieck brut champagne**

Origin: Named after the four ingredients and created in France during World War II by American soldiers using ingredients liberated from retreating Germans.
Comment: Strong and sweet. This wartime drink can still be deadly if not handled with care.

B5200

Glass: Shot
Method: Refrigerate ingredients then **LAYER** in chilled glass by carefully pouring in the following order.

1/2	shot(s)	**Kahlúa coffee liqueur**
1/2	shot(s)	**Baileys Irish cream liqueur**
1/2	shot(s)	**Wood's 100 rum**

Origin: Discovered in 2003 at Circus Bar, London, England.
Origin: Layering this drink is as easy as inflating a lifejacket – drink a few and you'll need one.

B-52 SHOT

Glass: Shot
Method: Refrigerate ingredients then **LAYER** in chilled glass by carefully pouring in the following order.

1/2	shot(s)	**Kahlúa coffee liqueur**
1/2	shot(s)	**Baileys Irish cream liqueur**
1/2	shot(s)	**Grand Marnier**

Origin: Named after B-52 bombers in Vietnam.
Comment: Probably the best-known and most popular shot.

B-53 SHOT

Glass: Shot
Method: Refrigerate ingredients then **LAYER** in chilled glass by carefully pouring in the following order.

1/2	shot(s)	**Kahlúa coffee liqueur**
1/2	shot(s)	**Baileys Irish cream liqueur**
1/2	shot(s)	**Ketel One vodka**

Comment: Why settle for a 52 when you can have a 53?

B-54 SHOT

Glass: Shot
Method: Refrigerate ingredients then **LAYER** in chilled glass by carefully pouring in the following order.

1/2	shot(s)	**Luxardo Amaretto di Saschira**
1/2	shot(s)	**Kahlúa coffee liqueur**
1/2	shot(s)	**Baileys Irish cream liqueur**

Comment: Layered and sticky – but nice.

B-55 SHOT

Glass: Shot
Method: Refrigerate ingredients then **LAYER** in chilled glass by carefully pouring in the following order.

1/2	shot(s)	**Kahlúa coffee liqueur**
1/2	shot(s)	**Baileys Irish cream liqueur**
1/2	shot(s)	**La Fée Parisian (68%) absinthe**

Comment: The latest and scariest of the B-something range of layered shots.

B-52 FROZEN

Glass: Old-fashioned
Garnish: Crumbled Cadbury's Flake bar
Method: **BLEND** ingredients with 6oz scoop of crushed ice. Pour into glass and serve with straws.

1	shot(s)	**Baileys Irish cream liqueur**
1	shot(s)	**Grand Marnier**
1	shot(s)	**Kahlúa coffee liqueur**

Comment: The classic shot blended with ice.

B & B

Glass: Old-fashioned
Garnish: Lemon zest twist
Method: **STIR** ingredients with ice and strain into ice-filled glass.

2	shot(s)	**Bénédictine D.O.M. liqueur**
2	shot(s)	**Rémy Martin cognac**

Origin: Created in 1937 by a bartender at New York's famous 21 Club.
Comment: Honeyed and spiced cognac.

B. J. SHOT

Glass: Shot
Garnish: Thin layer of single cream
Method: Refrigerate ingredients then **LAYER** in chilled glass by carefully pouring in the following order.

1/2	shot(s)	**Grand Marnier**
1/2	shot(s)	**Baileys Irish cream liqueur**

Comment: You know what the letters stand for – tastes better!

BABY BLUE MARTINI [UPDATED]

Glass: Martini
Garnish: Orange zest twist
Method: SHAKE all ingredients with ice and fine strain into chilled glass.

2	shot(s)	**Plymouth gin**
3/4	shot(s)	**Blue curaçao liqueur**
3/4	shot(s)	**Squeezed pink grapefruit juice**
3/4	shot(s)	**Pressed pineapple juice**

Comment: Turquoise blue, easy drinking, fruity gin.

BABY GUINNESS

Glass: Shot
Method: Refrigerate ingredients then **LAYER** in chilled glass by carefully pouring in the following order.

1	shot(s)	**Kahlúa coffee liqueur**
1/2	shot(s)	**Baileys Irish cream liqueur**

Comment: Looks like a miniature pint of Guinness stout.

BABY WOO WOO

Glass: Shot
Garnish: Lime wedge
Method: SHAKE all ingredients with ice and fine strain into chilled glass.

1/2	shot(s)	**Ketel One vodka**
1/2	shot(s)	**Peach schnapps liqueur**
1/2	shot(s)	**Cranberry juice**

Comment: Pink, sweet and all too easy to shoot.

BACARDI COCKTAIL

Glass: Martini
Garnish: Maraschino cherry
Method: SHAKE all ingredients with ice and fine strain into chilled glass.

2 1/2	shot(s)	**Bacardi light rum**
1	shot(s)	**Freshly squeezed lime juice**
1/2	shot(s)	**Pomegranate (grenadine) syrup**
3/4	shot(s)	**Chilled mineral water (omit if wet ice)**

Origin: In 1936, a bar in New York was found to be selling the Bacardi Cocktail – without including Bacardi rum. To protect their brand, Bacardi sued. A premise of their case was that Bacardi was a unique rum: although the president of the company refused to reveal any details of production, the court found that it was indeed unique. The judge ruled that a Bacardi Cocktail must be made with Bacardi.
Comment: This classic pink drink is a perfectly balanced combination of the flavour of rum, the sourness of lime juice and the sweetness of grenadine.

BAHAMA MAMA

Glass: Collins
Garnish: Pineapple wedge & cherry
Method: SHAKE all ingredients with ice and strain into ice-filled glass.

3/4	shot(s)	**Pusser's navy rum**
3/4	shot(s)	**Appleton Estate V/X aged rum**
1	shot(s)	**Malibu coconut rum liqueur**
1 3/4	shot(s)	**Freshly squeezed orange juice**
2 1/2	shot(s)	**Pressed pineapple juice**
3	dashes	**Angostura aromatic bitters**

Comment: A tropical, fruity number laced with flavoursome rum.

BAHAMAS DAIQUIRI

Glass: Martini
Garnish: Pineapple wedge on rim
Method: SHAKE all ingredients with ice and fine strain into chilled glass.

1 1/2	shot(s)	**Myers's Planter's Punch rum**
3/4	shot(s)	**Malibu coconut rum liqueur**
1/4	shot(s)	**Kahlúa coffee liqueur**
1 1/2	shot(s)	**Freshly extracted pineapple juice**
1/2	shot(s)	**Freshly squeezed lime juice**

Origin: Adapted from the Bahamas Martini created in 2002 by Yannick Miseriaux at the Fifth Floor Bar, London, England.
Comment: Totally tropical with a sweet tangy edge.

HOW TO MAKE SUGAR SYRUP

To make your own sugar syrup, gradually pour **TWO cups of granulated sugar into a saucepan containing ONE cup of hot water.** Stir as you pour and carry on stirring and simmering until the sugar is dissolved. Do not let the water even come close to boiling and only simmer for as long as it takes to dissolve the sugar. Allow syrup to cool and pour into an empty bottle. Ideally, you should finely strain your syrup into the bottle to remove any undissolved crystals which could otherwise encourage crystallisation. If kept in a refrigerator this mixture will last for a couple of months.

A **B** C D E F G H I J K L M N O P Q R S T U V W X Y Z

●●●◐○

BAJAN MOJITO [NEW]

Glass: Collins
Garnish: Passion fruit slice / mint sprig
Method: Cut passion fruit in half and scoop flesh into glass. Add mint and gently **MUDDLE** (just to bruise mint). Add Mount Gay, lime juice, sugar and crushed ice. **CHURN** drink in glass to mix. **DRIZZLE** passion fruit liqueur.

1	fresh	**Passion fruit**
8	fresh	**Mint leaves**
2	shot(s)	**Mount Gay Eclipse golden rum**
½	shot(s)	**Freshly squeezed lime juice**
½	shot(s)	**Sugar (gomme) syrup**
¼	shot(s)	**Passoã passion fruit liqueur**

Origin: Created by Wayne Collins for Maxxium UK
Comment: A laid-back fruity Mojito.

●●●●○

BAJAN PASSION [NEW]

Glass: Martini
Garnish: Float passion fruit slice
Method: Cut passion fruit in half and scoop flesh into shaker. Add other ingredients, **SHAKE** with ice and fine strain into chilled glass.

1	fresh	**Passion fruit**
1½	shot(s)	**Mount Gay Eclipse golden rum**
½	shot(s)	**Apricot brandy liqueur**
1	shot(s)	**Freshly squeezed lime juice**
¼	shot(s)	**Sugar (gomme) syrup**
¼	shot(s)	**Vanilla sugar syrup**

Origin: Created in 2004 by Wayne Collins for Maxxium UK.
Comment: A Daiquiri laced with fruit and spice.

●●●●◐

BAJITO [NEW]

Glass: Collins
Garnish: Mint sprig
Method: Lightly **MUDDLE** mint and basil in glass just enough to bruise. Add rum, sugar and lime juice. Half fill glass with crushed ice and **CHURN** (stir) with bar spoon. Add more crushed ice and churn some more. Continue adding crushed ice and churning until glass is full.

6	fresh	**Basil leaves**
6	fresh	**Mint leaves**
2	shot(s)	**Light white rum**
1	shot(s)	**Freshly squeezed lime juice**
¼	shot(s)	**Sugar (gomme) syrup**

Origin: Discovered in 2004 at Excelsior Bar, Boston, USA.
Comment: Basically a Mojito with basil as well as mint.

FOR MORE INFORMATION SEE OUR
INGREDIENTS APPENDIX ON PAGE 322

●●●●○

BALALAIKA

Glass: Martini
Garnish: Orange zest twist
Method: **SHAKE** all ingredients with ice and fine strain into chilled glass.

1½	shot(s)	**Ketel One vodka**
1½	shot(s)	**Cointreau / triple sec**
1½	shot(s)	**Freshly squeezed lemon juice**

Comment: Richly flavoured with orange and lemon.

●●◐○○

BALD EAGLE SHOT

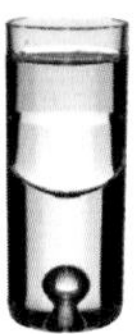

Glass: Shot
Method: Refrigerate ingredients then **LAYER** in chilled glass by carefully pouring in the following order.

½	shot(s)	**White crème de menthe liqueur**
¾	shot(s)	**Sauza Hornitos tequila**

Comment: Minty tequila – fresh breath tastic.

●●●●◐

BALD EAGLE MARTINI

Glass: Martini
Garnish: Salt rim
Method: **SHAKE** all ingredients with ice and fine strain into chilled glass.

2	shot(s)	**Sauza Hornitos tequila**
1	shot(s)	**Freshly squeezed pink grapefruit juice**
½	shot(s)	**Cranberry juice**
½	shot(s)	**Freshly squeezed lime juice**
½	shot(s)	**Freshly squeezed lemon juice**

Origin: Created for me in 2001 by Salvatore Calabrese at The Lanesborough Library Bar, London, England.
Comment: If you like Tequila and you like your drinks on the sour side, this is for you.

●●●◐○

BALI TRADER

Glass: Martini
Garnish: Banana chunk on rim
Method: **SHAKE** all ingredients with ice and fine strain into chilled glass.

2	shot(s)	**Ketel One vodka**
1	shot(s)	**Pisang Ambon green banana liqueur**
1	shot(s)	**Pressed pineapple juice**

Comment: A tasty Caribbean combination of banana and pineapple.

DRINKS ARE GRADED AS FOLLOWS:

● DISGUSTING ●◐ PRETTY AWFUL ●● BEST AVOIDED
●●◐ DISAPPOINTING ●●● ACCEPTABLE ●●●◐ GOOD
●●●● RECOMMENDED ●●●●◐ HIGHLY RECOMMENDED
●●●●● OUTSTANDING / EXCEPTIONAL

BALLET RUSSE

Glass: Martini
Garnish: Lime wedge on rim
Method: **SHAKE** all ingredients with ice and fine strain into chilled glass.

2	shot(s)	**Ketel One vodka**
3/4	shot(s)	**Sisca crème de cassis**
1	shot(s)	**Freshly squeezed lime juice**
1/4	shot(s)	**Sugar (gomme) syrup**

Comment: Intense sweet blackcurrant balanced by lime sourness.

BALTIC BREEZE [NEW]

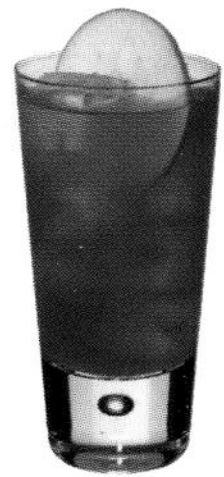

Glass: Collins
Garnish: Apple slice
Method: **SHAKE** all ingredients with ice and strain into ice-filled glass.

1 1/2	shot(s)	**Raspberry flavoured vodka**
1/2	shot(s)	**Apricot brandy liqueur**
2	shot(s)	**Pressed apple juice**
2	shot(s)	**Cranberry juice**
1/4	shot(s)	**Freshly squeezed lime juice**

Origin: Created in 2004 by Wayne Collins for Maxxium UK.
Comment: Long, pink and hardly challenging to drink.

BALTIC SPRING PUNCH [NEW]

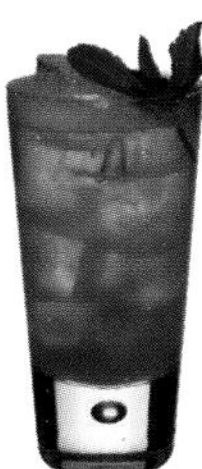

Glass: Collins
Garnish: Mint sprig
Method: **MUDDLE** peach in base of shaker. Add other ingredients, **SHAKE** with ice and fine strain into ice-filled glass.

1	ripe	**Peach skinned and diced**
1 1/2	shot(s)	**Rose petal liqueur**
1/2	shot(s)	**Freshly squeezed lemon juice**
1/4	shot(s)	**Sugar (gomme) syrup**
Top up with		**Piper-Heidsieck brut champagne**

Variant: If using peach purée omit the sugar.
Origin: Created in 2002 at Baltic, London, England.
Comment: Just peachy, baby.

BALTIMORE EGG NOG

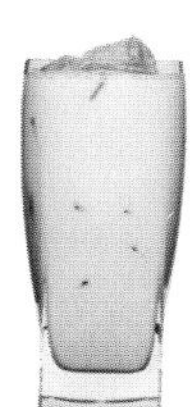

Glass: Collins
Garnish: Dust with freshly grated nutmeg
Method: **SHAKE** all ingredients with ice and fine strain into ice-filled glass.

1 1/2	shot(s)	**Rémy Martin cognac**
1 1/2	shot(s)	**Madeira**
1	shot(s)	**Pusser's Navy rum**
1	shot(s)	**Double (heavy) cream**
1	shot(s)	**Milk**
1	shot(s)	**Sugar (gomme) syrup**
1	fresh	**Beaten egg**

Comment: A flavoursome liquid meal.

BAMBOO

Glass: Martini
Garnish: Orange zest twist
Method: **STIR** all ingredients with ice and strain into chilled glass.

2	shot(s)	**Tio Pepe fino sherry**
2	shot(s)	**Dry vermouth**
1/4	shot(s)	**Cointreau / triple sec**
3	dashes	**Fee Brothers orange bitters**

Variant: East Indian
Origin: A classic and all but forgotten cocktail from the 1940s.
Comment: Dry, refined and subtle - for sophisticated palates only.

BANANA BATIDA [NEW]

Glass: Collins
Garnish: Banana chunk on rim
Method: **BLEND** ingredients with 12oz scoop of crushed ice. Pour into glass and serve with straws.

2 1/2	shot(s)	**Sagatiba cachaça**
1	shot(s)	**Crème de bananes liqueur**
3/4	shot(s)	**Freshly squeezed lemon juice**
1	fresh	**Peeled banana**

Origin: The Batida is a traditional Brazilian drink.
Comment: A wonderfully tangy drink for a summer's afternoon.

BANANA BLISS

Glass: Martini
Garnish: Banana chunk on rim
Method: **STIR** all ingredients with ice and strain into chilled glass.

2	shot(s)	**Crème de bananes liqueur**
2	shot(s)	**Rémy Martin cognac**
1	shot(s)	**Chilled mineral water (reduce if wet ice)**
2	dashes	**Fee Brothers orange bitters**

AKA: Golden Brown
Comment: Crème de bananes and cognac go shockingly well together.

BANANA BOOMER [UPDATED]

Glass: Martini
Garnish: Banana chunk on rim
Method: **SHAKE** all ingredients with ice and strain into chilled glass.

1	shot(s)	**Ketel One vodka**
1	shot(s)	**Crème de bananes liqueur**
1/2	shot(s)	**Apricot brandy liqueur**
1/2	shot(s)	**Cherry (brandy) liqueur**
3/4	shot(s)	**Freshly squeezed orange juice**
3/4	shot(s)	**Pressed pineapple juice**

Comment: Fortified bubble gum for the young at heart.

A B C D E F G H I J K L M N N P Q R S T U V W X Y Z

BANANA COLADA [UPDATED]

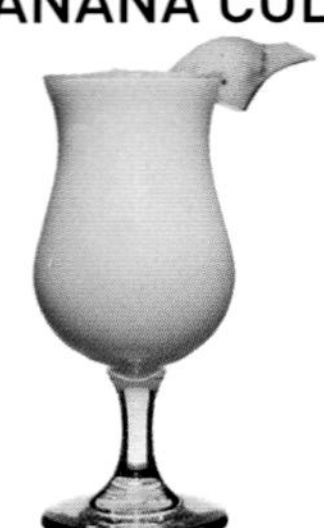

Glass: Hurricane
Garnish: Banana chunk on rim
Method: **BLEND** ingredients with 12oz scoop of crushed ice. Pour into glass and serve with straws.

2	shot(s)	**Mount Gay Eclipse golden rum**
1/2	shot(s)	**Crème de bananes liqueur**
4	shot(s)	**Pressed pineapple juice**
1	fresh	**Peeled banana**
1	shot(s)	**Coco López cream of coconut**

Comment: Don't skimp, use a whole banana per drink for real flavour.

BANANA DAIQUIRI [UPDATED]

Glass: Hurricane
Garnish: Banana chunk on rim
Method: **BLEND** ingredients with 12oz scoop of crushed ice. Pour into glass and serve with straws.

2	shot(s)	**Light white rum**
1	shot(s)	**Crème de bananes liqueur**
1/2	shot(s)	**Freshly squeezed lime juice**
1	fresh	**Peeled banana**

Comment: A tangy banana disco drink that's not too sweet.

BANANA SMOOTHIE (MOCKTAIL) [NEW]

Glass: Hurricane
Garnish: Banana chunk on rim
Method: **BLEND** ingredients with 12oz scoop of crushed ice. Pour into glass and serve immediately with straws.

3	shot(s)	**Pressed apple juice**
7	spoons	**Natural yoghurt**
3	spoons	**Runny honey**
1	fresh	**Banana**

Origin: Created in 2005 by Lisa Ball, London, England.
Comment: Serve with breakfast cereal and you'll be set up for the day. The high fresh banana content means this drink will quickly turn brown if left. This can be countered by adding fresh lemon juice and balancing with more honey but this detracts from the fresh banana flavour.

BANANAS & CREAM

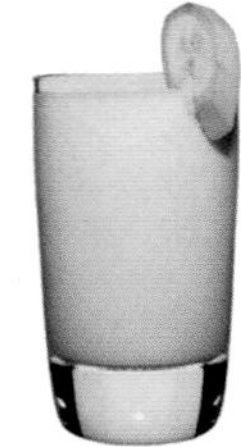

Glass: Collins
Garnish: Banana chunk on rim
Method: **BLEND** ingredients with 12oz scoop of crushed ice. Pour into glass and serve with straws.

2	shot(s)	**Crème de bananes liqueur**
1	shot(s)	**Luxardo Amaretto di Saschira**
1	shot(s)	**Baileys Irish cream liqueur**
1	shot(s)	**Double (heavy) cream**
2	shot(s)	**Milk**

Comment: Banana and cream frappé with hints of almond – one for a summer afternoon.

BANOFFEE MARTINI

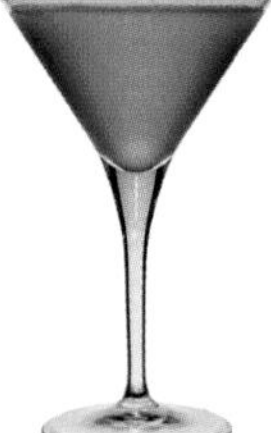

Glass: Martini
Garnish: Dust with cocoa powder
Method: **MUDDLE** banana in base of shaker. Add other ingredients, **SHAKE** with ice and fine strain into chilled glass.

1/4	fresh	**Banana**
1 1/2	shot(s)	**Vanilla flavoured vodka**
3/4	shot(s)	**Butterscotch schnapps liqueur**
3/4	shot(s)	**Crème de bananes liqueur**
1	spoon	**Maple syrup**
1/2	shot(s)	**Double (heavy) cream**
1/2	shot(s)	**Milk**

Origin: Adapted from a recipe created in 2002 by Barry Wilson, Zinc Bar & Grill, Edinburgh, Scotland.
Comment: Thick and rich, one for after the cheese course.

BANSHEE

Glass: Shot
Method: **SHAKE** all ingredients with ice and fine strain into chilled glass.

1/2	shot(s)	**Crème de bananes liqueur**
1/2	shot(s)	**White crème de cacao liqueur**
1/2	shot(s)	**Double (heavy) cream**

Comment: Creamy chocolate banana.

BARBARA

Glass: Martini
Garnish: Dust with freshly grated nutmeg
Method: **SHAKE** all ingredients with ice and fine strain into chilled glass.

2	shot(s)	**Ketel One vodka**
1	shot(s)	**White crème de cacao liqueur**
1	shot(s)	**Double (heavy) cream**
1	shot(s)	**Milk**

Comment: Quite neutral and subtle – the nutmeg garnish is as important to the flavour as cacao.

BARBARA WEST [NEW]

Glass: Martini
Garnish: Lemon twist
Method: **SHAKE** all ingredients with ice and fine strain into chilled glass.

2	shot(s)	**Plymouth gin**
1	shot(s)	**Amontillado sherry**
1/2	shot(s)	**Freshly squeezed lemon juice**
1/4	shot(s)	**Sugar (gomme) syrup**
2	dashes	**Angostura aromatic bitters**

Origin: A classic from the 1930s.
Comment: Well balanced but for serious gin and sherry drinkers only.

BARBARY COAST HIGHBALL

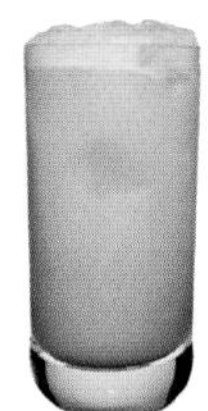

Glass: Collins
Method: SHAKE all but soda with ice and strain into ice-filled glass. **TOP** with soda and stir.

1	shot(s)	**Bourbon whiskey**
1	shot(s)	**Plymouth gin**
1	shot(s)	**Dark crème de cacao liqueur**
1/2	shot(s)	**Double (heavy) cream**
1/2	shot(s)	**Milk**
Top up with		**Soda water (club soda)**

Variant: Omit soda and serve straight-up in a Martini glass.
Comment: Looks like a glass of frothy weak tea - bourbon and chocolate predominate.

BARBARY COAST MARTINI

Glass: Martini
Garnish: Dust with cinnamon powder
Method: SHAKE all ingredients with ice and fine strain into chilled glass.

1 1/4	shot(s)	**The Famous Grouse Scotch**
1 1/4	shot(s)	**Plymouth gin**
1 1/4	shot(s)	**White crème de cacao liqueur**
1 1/4	shot(s)	**Double (heavy) cream**

Origin: Adapted from a 1947 edition of Trader Vic's Bartender's Guide.
Comment: It may be creamy, but this is a serious drink.

BARNACLE BILL [NEW]

Glass: Old-fashioned
Garnish: Mint sprig
Method: SHAKE all ingredients with ice and strain into glass filled with crushed ice.

1/2	shot(s)	**Yellow Chartreuse**
1/2	shot(s)	**Parfait Amour liqueur**
1/2	shot(s)	**Pernod anis**
1/2	shot(s)	**Chilled mineral water (omit if wet ice)**

Origin: Adapted from a recipe in the 1947 edition of Trader Vic's Bartender's Guide.
Comment: This sweetie is great after a meal on a warm night.

BARNAMINT

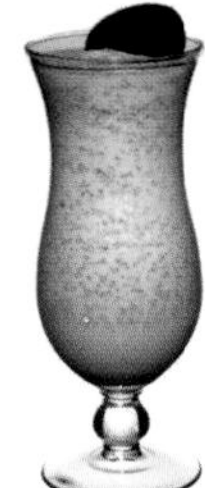

Glass: Hurricane
Garnish: Oreo cookie
Method: BLEND ingredients with 12oz scoop of crushed ice. Pour into glass and serve with straws.

2	shot(s)	**Baileys Irish cream liqueur**
1 1/2	shot(s)	**Green crème de menthe**
1	shot(s)	**Double (heavy) cream**
1	shot(s)	**Milk**
2	scoops	**Vanilla ice cream**
3	whole	**Oreo cookies**

Origin: This original TGI Friday's cocktail is named after the Barnum & Bailey Circus, which also inspired the red and white awnings outside Friday's restaurants.
Comment: If you're after a drinkable dessert, then this TGI classic may be the cocktail for you.

BARNUM [NEW]

Glass: Martini
Garnish: Lemon twist
Method: SHAKE all ingredients with ice and fine strain into chilled glass.

2	shot(s)	**Plymouth gin**
3/4	shot(s)	**Apricot brandy liqueur**
1/2	shot(s)	**Freshly squeezed lemon juice**
1/2	shot(s)	**Chilled mineral water (omit if wet ice)**
3	dashes	**Angostura aromatic bitters**

Origin: A classic from the 1930s.
Comment: A classic cocktail flavour combination that still pleases.

BARTENDER'S MARTINI

Glass: Martini
Garnish: Orange zest twist
Method: SHAKE all ingredients with ice and fine strain into chilled glass.

1	shot(s)	**Plymouth gin**
1	shot(s)	**Tio Pepe fino sherry**
1	shot(s)	**Dubonnet Red**
1	shot(s)	**Dry vermouth**
1/2	shot(s)	**Grand Marnier**

Comment: This classic cocktail resembles an aromatic Martini. Hints of sherry and orange are followed by a dry finish.

BARTENDER'S ROOT BEER

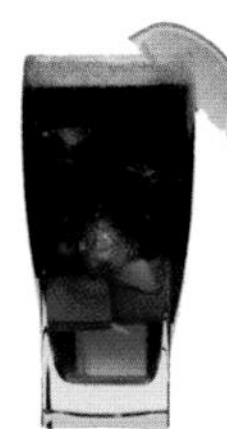

Glass: Collins
Garnish: Lime wedge on rim
Method: POUR first three ingredients into ice-filled glass and top up with cola.

1	shot(s)	**Galliano liqueur**
1	shot(s)	**Kahlúa coffee liqueur**
1/4	shot(s)	**Freshly squeezed lime juice**
Top up with		**Cola**

Comment: Not quite the root of all evil, but tasty all the same.

BASIL & HONEY DAIQUIRI [NEW]

Glass: Martini
Garnish: Float basil leaf
Method: STIR honey and rum in base of shaker until honey dissolves. Add basil leaves and lightly **MUDDLE** just enough to bruise. Add lime juice, **SHAKE** with ice and fine strain into chilled glass.

2	spoons	**Runny honey**
2	shot(s)	**Light white rum**
6	fresh	**Basil leaves**
1/2	shot(s)	**Freshly squeezed lime juice**

Origin: Formula by yours truly in 2005.
Comment: I love Daiquiris and this is one of the best variations I've tried.

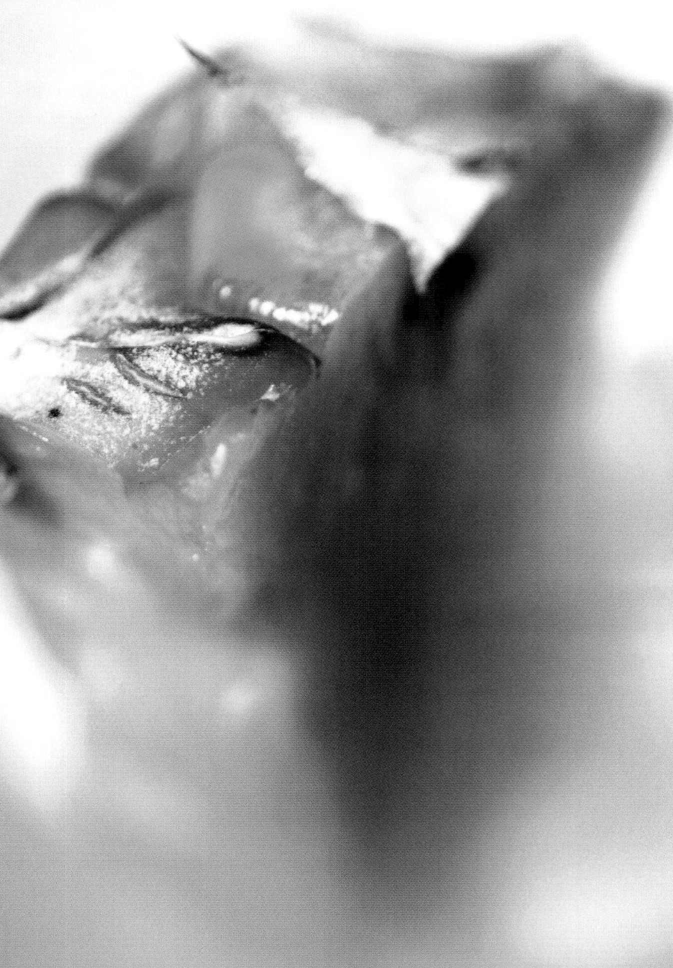

BATIDA

The Batida is a traditional Brazilian drink based on cachaça mixed with fresh fruit, sugar and/or sweetened condensed milk (leite condensado). They are usually blended with crushed ice or shaken and served over crushed ice.

In Brazil the most popular Batidas are made with passion fruit (batida de maracujá) and coconut milk (batida de coco). Unfortunately, this excellent drink has not transferred as quickly from its homeland as the Caipirinha.

Batida variations include
Abaci (pineapple) Batida
Banana Batida
Batida de Coco (with coconut milk)
Carneval (mango) Batida
Goiaba (guava) Batida
Mango Batida
Maracujá (passion fruit) Batida
Milho Verde (sweetcorn) Batida
Morango (strawberry) Batida

●●●●○

BASIL BEAUTY

Glass: Martini
Garnish: Pineapple wedge on rim
Method: Lightly **MUDDLE** basil in base of shaker just enough to bruise. Cut passion fruit in half and scoop flesh into shaker. Add other ingredients, **SHAKE** with ice and fine strain into chilled glass.

4	fresh	**Basil leaves**
1	whole	**Passion fruit**
2	shot(s)	**Ketel One Citroen vodka**
2	shot(s)	**Pressed pineapple juice**
1/4	shot(s)	**Freshly squeezed lime juice**
1/2	shot(s)	**Coconut syrup (or sugar syrup)**

Origin: Created in 2003 by Wayne Collins for Maxxium UK.
Comment: Pineapple, passion fruit, hints of lime, basil and coconut all laced with citrus vodka.

●●●●○

BASIL BRAMBLE SLING [NEW]

Glass: Sling
Garnish: Mint sprig
Method: **MUDDLE** basil in base of shaker. Add rest of ingredients, **SHAKE** with ice and strain into ice-filled glass. Serve with straws.

7	fresh	**Basil leaves**
2	shot(s)	**Plymouth gin**
1 1/2	shot(s)	**Freshly squeezed lemon juice**
1/2	shot(s)	**Sugar (gomme) syrup**
1/2	shot(s)	**Crème de mûre (blackberry) liqueur**

Origin: Created in 2003 by Alexandra Fiot at Lonsdale House, London, UK.
Comment: Wonderfully refreshing and balanced.

●●●●○

BASIL GRANDE [UPDATED]

Glass: Martini
Garnish: Strawberry and dust with black pepper.
Method: **MUDDLE** strawberries and basil in base of shaker. Add other ingredients, **SHAKE** with ice and fine strain into glass.

4	fresh	**Hulled strawberries**
5	fresh	**Basil leaves**
3/4	shot(s)	**Ketel One vodka**
3/4	shot(s)	**Chambord black raspberry liqueur**
3/4	shot(s)	**Grand Marnier**
2	shot(s)	**Cranberry juice**

Origin: Created in 2001 by Jamie Wilkinson at Living Room, Manchester, England.
Comment: Fruity, with interest courtesy of the basil and grind of pepper.

DRINKS ARE GRADED AS FOLLOWS:

● DISGUSTING ●◐ PRETTY AWFUL ●● BEST AVOIDED
●●◐ DISAPPOINTING ●●● ACCEPTABLE ●●●◐ GOOD
●●●● RECOMMENDED ●●●●◐ HIGHLY RECOMMENDED
●●●●● OUTSTANDING / EXCEPTIONAL

BASIL MARY [NEW]

Glass: Collins
Garnish: Basil leaf
Method: Lightly **MUDDLE** basil in base of shaker just enough to bruise. Add other ingredients, **SHAKE** with ice and fine strain into ice-filled glass.

7	fresh	**Basil leaves**
2	shot(s)	**Pepper flavoured vodka**
4	shot(s)	**Pressed tomato juice**
1/2	shot(s)	**Freshly squeezed lemon juice**
8	drops	**Tabasco pepper sauce**
4	dashes	**Lea & Perrins Worcestershire sauce**
1/2	spoon	**Horseradish sauce**
1/2	shot(s)	**Tawny port**
2	pinch	**Celery salt**
2	pinch	**Black pepper**

Origin: Discovered in 2004 at Indigo Yard, Edinburgh, Scotland.
Comment: A particularly spicy Mary with a herbal twist.

BASILICO [NEW]

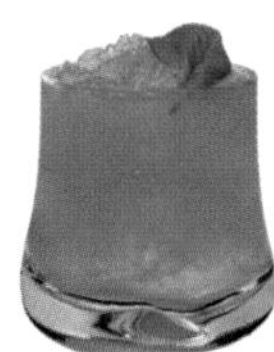

Glass: Old-fashioned
Garnish: Basil leaf
Method: **MUDDLE** basil in base of shaker. Add other ingredients, **SHAKE** with ice and strain into glass filled with crushed ice.

7	fresh	**Basil leaves**
2	shot(s)	**Ketel One vodka**
1/2	shot(s)	**Luxardo limoncello**
1/2	shot(s)	**Freshly squeezed lemon juice**
1/2	shot(s)	**Sugar (gomme) syrup**

Origin: Discovered in 2004 at Atlantic Bar & Grill, London, England.
Comment: A lemon Caipirovska with basil.

BATIDA DE COCO [NEW]

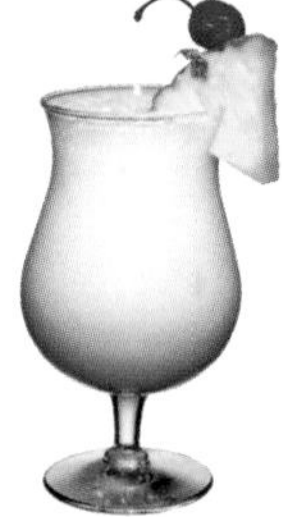

Glass: Collins
Method: **BLEND** ingredients with 12oz scoop of crushed ice. **POUR** into glass and serve with straws.

2 1/2	shot(s)	**Sagatiba cachaça**
1 1/2	shot(s)	**Coco López cream of coconut**
1	shot(s)	**Coconut milk**

Origin: Traditional Brazilian drink.
Comment: Sweet, almost creamy coconut with a hint of cachaça.

BAY BREEZE

Glass: Collins
Garnish: Pineapple wedge
Method: **SHAKE** all ingredients with ice and strain into ice-filled glass.

2 1/2	shot(s)	**Ketel One vodka**
4	shot(s)	**Cranberry juice**
2	shot(s)	**Pressed pineapple juice**

Comment: Pink, fluffy, sweet and easy to drink.

BAY OF PASSION

Glass: Collins
Garnish: Maraschino cherry
Method: **SHAKE** all ingredients with ice and strain into ice-filled glass.

1	shot(s)	**Passoã passion fruit liqueur**
1	shot(s)	**Ketel One vodka**
3 1/2	shot(s)	**Cranberry juice**
2	shot(s)	**Pressed pineapple juice**

Comment: Variation on a Bay Breeze - fruity with a tropical tinge.

BAZOOKA

Glass: Shot
Method: **SHAKE** all ingredients with ice and fine strain into chilled glass.

3/4	shot(s)	**Southern Comfort**
1/2	shot(s)	**Crème de bananes liqueur**
1/8	shot(s)	**Pomegranate (grenadine) syrup**
1/4	shot(s)	**Double (heavy) cream**

Comment: A sticky, pink shot.

BAZOOKA JOE

Glass: Shot
Method: Refrigerate ingredients then **LAYER** in chilled glass by carefully pouring in the following order.

1/2	shot(s)	**Blue curaçao liqueur**
1/2	shot(s)	**Crème de bananes liqueur**
1/2	shot(s)	**Baileys Irish cream liqueur**

Comment: Banana and orange topped with whiskey cream.

BBC

Glass: Martini
Garnish: Dust with freshly grated nutmeg
Method: **SHAKE** all ingredients with ice and fine strain into chilled glass.

1 1/4	shot(s)	**Rémy Martin cognac**
1	shot(s)	**Bénédictine D.O.M. liqueur**
3/4	shot(s)	**Double (heavy) cream**
3/4	shot(s)	**Milk**

Origin: Thought to have originated in the UK in the late 1970s and named, not after the British Broadcasting Company, but brandy, Bénédictine and cream.
Comment: Brandy and Bénédictine (a classic combo) smoothed with cream. Drier than you might expect.

A B C D E F G H I J K L M N N P Q R S T U V W X Y Z

A B C D E F G H I J K L M N N P Q R S T U V W X Y Z

BE-TON

Glass: Collins
Garnish: Squeezed lime wedge in glass
Method: **POUR** Becherovka into ice-filled glass, then top up with tonic water and stir.

2	shot(s)	**Becherovka (Carlsbad Becher)**
Top up with		**Tonic water**

Origin: Becherovka (or Carlsbad Becher as it's sometimes known) is the Czech national liqueur. Matured in oak, it contains cinnamon, cloves, nutmeg and other herbs.
Comment: This spicy drink is the Czech Republic's answer to the Gin 'n' Tonic.

BEACH BLONDE

Glass: Collins
Garnish: Banana slice on rim
Method: **BLEND** ingredients with 12oz scoop of crushed ice. Pour into glass and serve with straws.

1/2	fresh	**Peeled banana**
1	shot(s)	**Wray & Nephew overproof white rum**
3	shot(s)	**Advocaat liqueur**
3	shot(s)	**Freshly squeezed orange juice**

Origin: Created in 2002 by Alex Kammerling, London, England.
Comment: Fruity, creamy holiday drinking.

BEACH ICED TEA

Glass: Sling
Garnish: Lemon slice
Method: **SHAKE** all ingredients with ice and strain into ice-filled glass.

1/2	shot(s)	**Light white rum**
1/2	shot(s)	**Plymouth gin**
1/2	shot(s)	**Ketel One vodka**
1/2	shot(s)	**Sauza Hornitos tequila**
1/2	shot(s)	**Cointreau / triple sec**
1	shot(s)	**Freshly squeezed lemon juice**
1/2	shot(s)	**Sugar (gomme) syrup**
3	shot(s)	**Cranberry juice**

Comment: A Long Island Iced Tea with cranberry juice instead of cola.

BEACHCOMBER

Glass: Martini
Garnish: Lime wedge on rim
Method: **SHAKE** all ingredients with ice and fine strain into chilled glass.

2	shot(s)	**Light white rum**
1/2	shot(s)	**Cointreau / triple sec**
3/4	shot(s)	**Freshly squeezed lime juice**
1/4	shot(s)	**Luxardo maraschino liqueur**
3/4	shot(s)	**Chilled mineral water(less if wet ice)**

Comment: A Daiquiri with the addition of a dash of triple sec and maraschino.

BEAM-ME-UP SCOTTY

Glass: Shot
Method: Refrigerate ingredients then **LAYER** in chilled glass by carefully pouring in the following order.

1/2	shot(s)	**Kahlúa coffee liqueur**
1/2	shot(s)	**Crème de bananes liqueur**
1/2	shot(s)	**Baileys Irish cream liqueur**

Comment: A layered shot with a taste reminiscent of banana flambée.

BEBBO [NEW]

Glass: Martini
Garnish: Lemon twist
Method: **STIR** honey with gin in base of shaker until honey dissolves. Add other ingredients, **SHAKE** with ice and fine strain into chilled glass.

2	spoons	**Runny honey**
2	shot(s)	**Plymouth gin**
1/2	shot(s)	**Freshly squeezed orange juice**
1	shot(s)	**Freshly squeezed lemon juice**

Origin: A long lost relation of Bee's Knees below. This recipe is based on one from Ted Haigh's 'Vintage Spirits & Forgotten Cocktails'.
Comment: Fresh, clean and fruity. One for a summer's evening.

BEE STING [NEW]

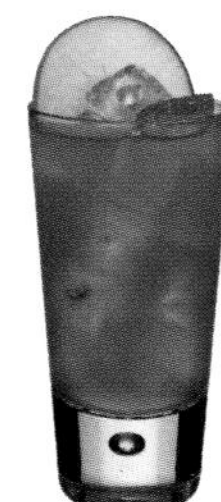

Glass: Collins
Garnish: Apple slice
Method: **STIR** honey with whiskey in base of shaker until honey dissolves. Add tequila and apple juice, **SHAKE** with ice and strain into ice-filled glass. **TOP** with a splash of ginger ale.

1	spoon	**Runny honey**
1	shot(s)	**Jack Daniel's Tennessee whiskey**
1	shot(s)	**Sauza Hornitos tequila**
2	shot(s)	**Pressed apple juice**
Top up with		**Ginger ale**

Origin: Discovered in 2005 at The Royal Exchange Grand Café & Bar, London, England.
Comment: A delicately spiced, long, refreshing drink.

BEE'S KNEES #1

Glass: Martini
Garnish: Orange zest twist
Method: **STIR** honey with rum until honey dissolves. Add other ingredients, **SHAKE** with ice and fine strain into chilled glass.

1 1/4	shot(s)	**Light white rum**
1 1/4	shot(s)	**Pusser's navy rum**
2	spoons	**Runny honey**
1	shot(s)	**Freshly squeezed orange juice**
1/2	shot(s)	**Double (heavy) cream**
1/2	shot(s)	**Milk**

Comment: Smooth and orangey to start, with a rum and honey finish.

BEE'S KNEES MARTINI # 2

Glass: Martini
Garnish: Orange wedge
Method: In base of shaker **STIR** honey with gin until honey dissolves. Add lemon and orange juice, **SHAKE** with ice and fine strain into chilled glass.

2	shot(s)	**Plymouth gin**
4	spoons	**Runny honey**
1	shot(s)	**Freshly squeezed lemon juice**
1	shot(s)	**Freshly squeezed orange juice**

Variant: Made with light rum in place of gin this drink becomes a Honeysuckle Martini.
Origin: Adapted from a recipe in David Embury's The Fine Art Of Mixing Drinks.
Comment: This honeyed citrus concoction really is the bee's knees.

BEETLE JEUSE [NEW]

Glass: Collins
Garnish: Mint sprig
Method: Lightly **MUDDLE** mint in base of shaker just enough to bruise. Add other ingredients, **SHAKE** with ice and strain into ice-filled glass.

7	fresh	**Mint leaves**
1	shot(s)	**Green Chartreuse**
1	shot(s)	**Zubrówka bison vodka**
3½	shot(s)	**Pressed apple juice**
¼	shot(s)	**Passion fruit sugar syrup**

Origin: Created in 2003 by Milo Rodriguez at Raoul's Bar, Oxford, and named after Beetlejuice, the Tim Burton black comedy about a young couple whose premature death leads them to a series of bizarre afterlife exploits.
Comment: Long and refreshing with a flavour reminiscent of caramelised apple.

BEHEMOTH

Glass: Martini
Garnish: Lemon zest twist
Method: **SHAKE** all ingredients with ice and fine strain into chilled glass.

1½	shot(s)	**Bourbon whiskey**
1	shot(s)	**Cinzano Rosso vermouth**
¾	shot(s)	**White crème de cacao liqueur**
¾	shot(s)	**Freshly squeezed lemon juice**
½	shot(s)	**Sugar (gomme) syrup**
½	fresh	**Egg white (optional)**
2	dashes	**Peychaud's aromatic bitters (optional)**

Origin: This monstrous beast was created in 2004 by yours truly.
Comment: Tangy, citrus bourbon with a hint of chocolate.

DRINKS ARE GRADED AS FOLLOWS:

● DISGUSTING ●◐ PRETTY AWFUL ●● BEST AVOIDED
●●◐ DISAPPOINTING ●●● ACCEPTABLE ●●●◐ GOOD
●●●● RECOMMENDED ●●●●◐ HIGHLY RECOMMENDED
●●●●● OUTSTANDING / EXCEPTIONAL

BEJA FLOR

Glass: Martini
Garnish: Banana chunk on rim
Method: **SHAKE** all ingredients with ice and fine strain into chilled glass.

2	shot(s)	**Sagatiba cachaça**
1	shot(s)	**Cointreau / triple sec**
1	shot(s)	**Crème de bananes liqueur**
½	shot(s)	**Freshly squeezed lemon juice**

Comment: Sharp and quite dry but with a sweet banana twang.

BELLA DONNA DAIQUIRI

Glass: Martini
Garnish: Wipe rim with lemon & dust with cinnamon powder
Method: **SHAKE** all ingredients with ice and fine strain into chilled glass.

1½	shot(s)	**Gosling's Black Seal rum**
1½	shot(s)	**Luxardo Amaretto di Saschira**
½	shot(s)	**Freshly squeezed lemon juice**
¼	shot(s)	**Sugar (gomme) syrup**
½	shot(s)	**Chilled mineral water**

Origin: Adapted from a drink discovered in 2003 at Bellagio, Las Vegas, USA.
Comment: This was the hit cocktail for diffordsguide staff at the Bellagio, Las Vegas, after working at the Nightclub & Bar Beverage Convention. Try one and see why.

BELLINI #1 (ORIGINAL)

Glass: Flute
Garnish: Peach slice on rim
Method: **STIR** all ingredients with ice and strain into chilled glass.

1	shot(s)	**Puréed white peaches (with added sugar and lemon juice)**
2	shot(s)	**Prosecco sparkling wine (chilled)**

Origin: Created in 1934 by Giuseppe Cipriani at Harry's Bar, Venice, Italy.
Comment: It's hard not to like this blend of peaches and sparkling wine.

BELLINI #2 (DIFFORD'S FORMULA)

Glass: Flute
Garnish: Peach slice on rim
Method: **SHAKE** first four ingredients with ice and fine strain into chilled glass. **TOP** with Prosecco and gently stir. (Alternatively, refrigerate all ingredients, blend quickly without ice and serve in chilled glass.)

2	shot(s)	**Puréed white peaches**
¼	shot(s)	**Peach schnapps liqueur**
¼	shot(s)	**Peach eau de vie (de pêche)**
⅛	shot(s)	**Freshly squeezed lemon juice**
Top up with		**Prosecco sparkling wine**

Origin: Created in 2003 by yours truly.
Comment: My version is more alcoholic and drier than the classic Bellini.

BELLINI

The original Bellini consists of puréed white peaches with added sugar and lemon juice mixed with Prosecco sparkling wine. It was created by Giuseppe Cipriani at Harry's Bar, Venice, in 1945, fourteen years after he opened his tiny bar on the edge of the Grand Canal, not far from St. Mark's Square. Cipriani named his cocktail after the 15th-century Venetian painter Giovanni Bellini due to the drink's pink hue and the painter's penchant for using rich pinks on his canvases.

Like many other legendary bars around the world, Harry's owes some of its notoriety to being patronised by probably the world's greatest drinker, Ernest Hemingway. It was also the haunt of Sinclair Lewis, Orson Welles, F. Scott Fitzgerald and Dorothy Parker, and continues to attract celebrities to this day. But you don't have to be a celebrity to go to Harry's Bar. Cocktail aficionados from around the world make pilgrimages to the birthplace of the Bellini to sample the original recipe.

Prosecco is a sparkling wine which must come from a specific region in Northern Italy. White peaches are in season in Italy from May to September, so in Venice the best bars only sell the drink between May and October. Bars which serve the drink year round use frozen purée.

BELLINI VARIATIONS INCLUDE

Bellini (original)
Bellini (Difford's formula)
Bellini-Tini
Kiwi Bellini
Puccini (tangerine/mandarin) Bellini
Raspberry Bellini
Rhubarb & Honey Bellini
Rossini (strawberry)
Tintoretto (pomegranate) Bellini
Tiziano (Fragola grape) Bellini

●●●●○

BELLINI-TINI [UPDATED]

Glass: Martini
Garnish: Peach wedge
Method: **SHAKE** all ingredients with ice and fine strain into chilled glass.

2	shot(s)	**Ketel One vodka**
1/2	shot(s)	**Peach schnapps liqueur**
2	shot(s)	**Fresh white peach purée**
3	dashes	**Peach bitters (optional)**

Comment: Peachy, peachy, peachy! Based on the Bellini, funnily enough.

●●●○○

BELLISSIMO [NEW]

Glass: Old-fashioned
Garnish: Orange slice
Method: **SHAKE** all ingredients with ice and fine strain into ice-filled glass.

1	shot(s)	**Hazelnut (crème de noisette) liqueur**
1	shot(s)	**Campari**
1	shot(s)	**Luxardo Limoncello liqueur**
1/2	shot(s)	**Freshly squeezed lemon juice**

Origin: Adapted from a drink created in 2003 by Ben Davidson at Posh Lounge, Sydney, Australia.
Comment: An unusual meld of flavours, but Campari lovers should give this a try.

●●●●○

BENTLEY [UPDATED]

Glass: Old-fashioned
Garnish: Orange zest twist
Method: **STIR** all ingredients with ice and strain into ice-filled glass.

1 1/2	shot(s)	**Calvados (or applejack brandy)**
1 1/2	shot(s)	**Dubonnet Red**

Variant: Served straight-up.
Comment: Dry spiced wine impregnated with apple – pretty good.

●●●●○

BERRY CAIPIRINHA

Glass: Old-fashioned
Method: **MUDDLE** lime and berries in base of glass. Add other ingredients and fill glass with crushed ice. **CHURN** drink with bar spoon and serve with short straws.

3/4	fresh	**Lime cut into wedges**
3	fresh	**Raspberries**
3	fresh	**Blackberries**
2	shot(s)	**Sagatiba cachaça**
3/4	shot(s)	**Sugar (gomme) syrup**

Variant: Black 'N' Blue Caipirovska
Comment: A fruity version of the popular Brazilian drink.

BERRY NICE

Glass: Collins
Garnish: Blackberries
Method: **MUDDLE** blackberries in base of shaker. Add next three ingredients, **SHAKE** with ice and strain into ice-filled glass. **TOP** with ginger beer.

9	fresh	**Blackberries**
2	shot(s)	**Raspberry flavoured vodka**
1/4	shot(s)	**Chambord black raspberry liqueur**
1/2	shot(s)	**Freshly squeezed lemon juice**
Top up with		**Jamaican ginger beer**

Origin: Adapted from a drink created in 2001 in the UK's The Living Room chain of bars.
Comment: Rich blackberry flavour with a strong ginger finish.

BESSIE & JESSIE

Glass: Collins
Garnish: Orange slice
Method: **SHAKE** all ingredients with ice and strain into ice-filled glass.

2	shot(s)	**The Famous Grouse Scotch**
2	shot(s)	**Advocaat liqueur**
3 1/2	shot(s)	**Milk**

Comment: Malty, creamy and eggy, but tasty.

BETWEEN THE SHEETS

Glass: Martini
Garnish: Flamed orange zest twist
Method: **SHAKE** all ingredients with ice and fine strain into chilled glass.

1	shot(s)	**Light white rum**
1	shot(s)	**Rémy Martin cognac**
1/2	shot(s)	**Cointreau / triple sec**
3/4	shot(s)	**Freshly squeezed lemon juice**
1/2	shot(s)	**Sugar (gomme) syrup**
1/2	shot(s)	**Chilled mineral water**

Origin: Created in the 1930s by Harry MacElhone, of Harry's New York Bar in Paris, and derived from the Sidecar.
Comment: When made correctly this is a beautifully balanced drink to rival even a Daiquiri.

BEVERLY HILLS ICED TEA [UPDATED]

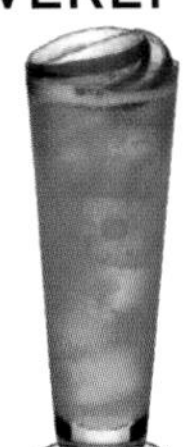

Glass: Sling
Garnish: Lime zest spiral
Method: **SHAKE** first five ingredients with ice and strain into ice-filled glass. **TOP** with champagne and gently stir.

3/4	shot(s)	**Plymouth gin**
3/4	shot(s)	**Ketel One vodka**
1	shot(s)	**Cointreau / triple sec**
1/2	shot(s)	**Freshly squeezed lime juice**
1/2	shot(s)	**Sugar (gomme) syrup**
Top up with		**Piper-Heidsieck brut champagne**

Comment: Very strong and refreshing.

BIARRITZ

Glass: Old-fashioned
Garnish: Orange slice & cherry (orange sail)
Method: **SHAKE** all ingredients with ice and strain into ice-filled glass.

2	shot(s)	**Rémy Martin cognac**
1	shot(s)	**Grand Marnier**
3/4	shot(s)	**Freshly squeezed lemon juice**
1/2	fresh	**Egg white**
3	dashes	**Angostura aromatic bitters**

Comment: Basically a brandy sour with a little something extra from the orange liqueur.

BIG APPLE MARTINI

Glass: Martini
Garnish: Apple wedge on rim
Method: **SHAKE** all ingredients with ice and fine strain into chilled glass.

2 1/2	shot(s)	**Ketel One vodka**
1	shot(s)	**Sour apple liqueur**
1	shot(s)	**Apple schnapps liqueur**

AKA: Apple Martini, Sour Apple Martini
Comment: There's no apple juice in this Martini, but it has an appealing light minty green hue.

THE BIG EASY

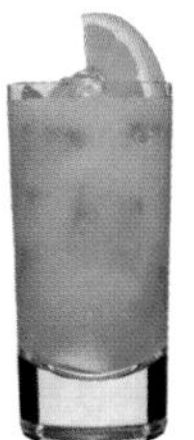

Glass: Collins
Garnish: Half orange slice
Method: **SHAKE** first three ingredients with ice and strain into ice-filled glass. **TOP** with ginger ale.

1 3/4	shot(s)	**Southern Comfort**
3/4	shot(s)	**Cointreau / triple sec**
2	shot(s)	**Freshly squeezed orange juice**
Top up with		**Ginger ale**

Comment: Fruity and refreshing with a hint of spice.

BIKINI MARTINI

Glass: Martini
Garnish: Orange zest twist
Method: **SHAKE** all ingredients with ice and fine strain into chilled glass.

2	shot(s)	**Plymouth gin**
3/4	shot(s)	**Blue curaçao liqueur**
1/4	shot(s)	**Peach schnapps liqueur**
1/4	shot(s)	**Freshly squeezed lemon juice**
3/4	shot(s)	**Chilled mineral water (omit if wet ice)**

Origin: Adapted from a cocktail created in 1999 by Dick Bradsell for an Agent Provocateur swimwear launch.
Comment: A vivid blue combination of lemon, orange and peach laced with gin.

A
B
C D E F G H I J K L M N O P Q R S T U V W X Y Z

BINGO

Glass: Collins
Garnish: Lemon wheel
Method: SHAKE first four ingredients with ice and strain into ice-filledglass. Top with soda water.

1	shot(s)	**Ketel One vodka**
1	shot(s)	**Grand Marnier**
1	shot(s)	**Apricot brandy liqueur**
1/2	shot(s)	**Freshly squeezed lemon juice**
Top up with		**Soda water (club soda)**

Comment: Refreshing, fruity long drink.

BIRD OF PARADISE

Glass: Martini
Garnish: Dust with freshly grated nutmeg
Method: SHAKE all ingredients with ice and fine strain into chilled glass.

1 1/4	shot(s)	**Sauza Hornitos tequila**
3/4	shot(s)	**White crème de cacao liqueur**
1/2	shot(s)	**Luxardo Amaretto di Saschira**
1	shot(s)	**Double (heavy) cream**
3/4	shot(s)	**Milk**

Comment: If you like tequila and creamy drinks, the two don't mix much better than this.

BISHOP

Glass: Toddy
Garnish: Dust with freshly grated nutmeg
Method: Place bar spoon in glass, **POUR** ingredients and stir.

2 1/2	shot(s)	**Warre's Otima Tawny port**
1	shot(s)	**Freshly squeezed orange juice**
1/2	shot(s)	**Sugar (gomme) syrup**
Top up with		**Boiling water**

Origin: A variation on the 18th century Negus - reputedly a favourite of the writer Dr. Johnson.
Comment: Mulled wine without the spice.

BIT-O-HONEY [NEW]

Glass: Shot
Method: Refrigerate ingredients then **LAYER** in chilled glass by carefully pouring in the following order.

3/4	shot(s)	**Butterscotch schnapps liqueur**
3/4	shot(s)	**Baileys Irish cream liqueur**

Variant: Layered with butterscotch, then honey liqueur and an Irish cream float.
Comment: A sweet but pleasant tasting shot.

BITTER ELDER [NEW]

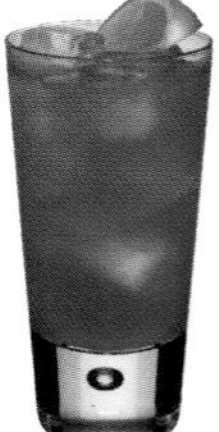

Glass: Collins
Garnish: Lemon wedge
Method: SHAKE all ingredients with ice and strain into ice-filled glass.

2	shot(s)	**Plymouth gin**
2	shot(s)	**Pressed apple juice**
3/4	shot(s)	**Freshly squeezed lemon juice**
1/2	shot(s)	**Elderflower cordial**
3	dashes	**Angostura aromatic bitters**

Origin: Adapted from a short drink created in 2005 by Tonin Kacaj at Maze, London, England.
Comment: The eponymous elderflower is well balanced with the other ingredients to make a dry refreshing long drink.

BITTER SWEET SYMPHONY

Glass: Martini
Garnish: Apricot slice
Method: SHAKE all ingredients with ice and fine strain into chilled glass.

1/2	shot(s)	**Ketel One vodka**
1	shot(s)	**Cointreau / triple sec**
1	shot(s)	**Apricot brandy liqueur**
1/2	shot(s)	**Freshly squeezed lime juice**
1 1/2	shot(s)	**Freshly squeezed grapefruit juice**

Origin: Adapted from a drink created in 2003 by Wayne Collins for Maxxium UK.
Comment: This roller coaster ride of bitter and sweet mainly features apricot and grapefruit.

BITTEREST PILL

Glass: Shot
Method: Refrigerate ingredients then **LAYER** in chilled glass by carefully pouring in the following order.

1/2	shot(s)	**Passion fruit sugar syrup**
1/2	shot(s)	**Campari**
1/2	shot(s)	**Ketel One vodka**

Created by: Alex Kammerling, London, England
Comment: The bitterness of Campari, toned down by passion fruit sugar syrup.

BLACK & TAN [NEW]

Glass: Boston
Method: POUR lager into chilled glass then float Guinness on top.

1/2	pint	**Lager**
1/2	pint	**Guinness stout**

Comment: Lager downstairs, Guinness upstairs.

BLACK & WHITE DAIQUIRI

Glass: Martini
Garnish: Blackberry in drink
Method: **MUDDLE** berries in base of shaker. Add other ingredients, **SHAKE** with ice and fine strain into chilled glass.

12	fresh	**Blackberries**
2	shot(s)	**Malibu coconut rum liqueur**
1	shot(s)	**Light white rum**
$^3/_4$	shot(s)	**Crème de mûre (blackberry) liqueur**
$^1/_2$	shot(s)	**Freshly squeezed lime juice**
$^1/_2$	shot(s)	**Chilled mineral water**

Origin: I named this drink after the black berries and the white Malibu bottle.
Comment: Blackberries and coconut add depth to the classic Daiquiri.

BLACK BEARD

Glass: Boston
Method: **POUR** ingredients into glass and serve.

2	shot(s)	**Spiced rum**
$^1/_2$	pint	**Guinness** (chilled)
Top up with		**Cola** (chilled)

Origin: Thought to have originated in Stirling, Scotland, during the late 1990s.
Comment: Something of a student drink, this tastes better than it sounds.

BLACK BISON MARTINI

Glass: Martini
Garnish: Apple wedge
Method: **SHAKE** all ingredients with ice and fine strain into chilled glass.

2	shot(s)	**Plymouth gin**
$^1/_2$	shot(s)	**Apple schnapps liqueur**
$1^1/_2$	shot(s)	**Pressed apple juice**
$^1/_4$	shot(s)	**Dry vermouth**

Origin: Adapted from a drink discovered in 2001 at Oxo Tower Bar, London, England.
Comment: A fragrant cocktail with a dry finish. As the name suggests, also works well with Zubrówka bison vodka in place of gin.

BLACK BISON MARTINI #2

Glass: Martini
Garnish: Apple wedge
Method: **SHAKE** all ingredients with ice and fine strain into chilled glass.

$1^1/_2$	shot(s)	**Plymouth gin**
$^1/_2$	shot(s)	**Apple schnapps liqueur**
2	shot(s)	**Pressed apple juice**
$^1/_4$	shot(s)	**Dry vermouth**

Origin: Adapted from a drink discovered in 2001 at Oxo Tower Bar, London, England.
Comment: A dry, fragrant cocktail, which, as the name suggests, also works well with Zubrówka bison vodka in place of gin.

BLACK DREAM

Glass: Shot
Method: Refrigerate ingredients then **LAYER** in chilled glass by carefully pouring in the following order.

$^1/_2$	shot(s)	**Opal Nera black sambuca**
$^1/_2$	shot(s)	**Baileys Irish cream liqueur**

Comment: Slippery Nipple with black sambuca.

BLACK FOREST GATEAU MARTINI

Glass: Martini
Garnish: Dust with cocoa powder
Method: **SHAKE** first four ingredients with ice and strain into chilled glass. **FLOAT** cream on drink.

2	shot(s)	**Ketel One vodka**
$^3/_4$	shot(s)	**Chambord black raspberry liqueur**
$^3/_4$	shot(s)	**Crème de fraise (strawberry) liqueur**
$^1/_4$	shot(s)	**Sisca crème de cassis**
1	shot(s)	**Double (heavy) cream**

Origin: Created in 2002 at Hush, London, England.
Comment: Dessert by name and dessert by nature. Wonderfully moreish, naughty but very nice.

BLACK IRISH

Glass: Hurricane
Garnish: Dust with cocoa powder
Method: **BLEND** ingredients with 12oz scoop of crushed ice. Pour into glass and serve with straws.

1	shot(s)	**Ketel One vodka**
1	shot(s)	**Baileys Irish cream liqueur**
1	shot(s)	**Kahlúa coffee liqueur**
2	scoops	**Vanilla ice cream**

AKA: Frozen Black Irish
Comment: Like a very sweet, alcoholic, frozen caffè latte.

BLACK JACK

Glass: Shot
Method: Refrigerate ingredients then **LAYER** in chilled glass by carefully pouring in the following order.

$^3/_4$	shot(s)	**Opal Nera black sambuca**
$^3/_4$	shot(s)	**Jack Daniel's Tennessee whiskey**

Comment: Whiskey sweetened with sambuca.

A B C D E F G H I J K L M N N P Q R S T U V W X Y Z

BLACK MAGIC

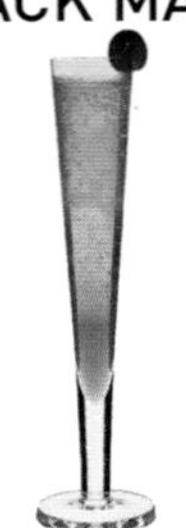

Glass: Flute
Garnish: Black grape on rim
Method: POUR first two ingredients into glass and top up with champagne.

2	shot(s)	**Red grape juice**
1/2	shot(s)	**Grand Marnier**
Top up with		**Piper-Heidsieck brut champagne**

Comment: Subtle and dry, though dependent on your red grape juice.

BLACK MARTINI

Glass: Martini
Garnish: Float grated white chocolate
Method: SHAKE all ingredients with ice and fine strain into chilled glass.

1 1/2	shot(s)	**Light white rum**
1 1/2	shot(s)	Dark crème de cacao liqueur
1 1/2	shot(s)	**Espresso coffee (cold)**

Origin: Created in March 2004 by yours truly.
Comment: This flavoursome mix of coffee and chocolate is further enhanced if vanilla-infused rum is used.

BLACK MUSSEL

Glass: Flute
Garnish: Orange zest twist discarded
Method: POUR first two ingredients into glass and top up with champagne.

1/2	shot(s)	**Blue curaçao liqueur**
1/4	shot(s)	**Sisca crème de cassis**
Top up with		**Piper-Heidsieck brut champagne**

Comment: Blue curaçao adds a hint of orange to a Kir Royale.

BLACK 'N' BLUE CAIPIROVSKA [UPDATED]

Glass: Old-fashioned
Method: MUDDLE berries in base of glass. Add other ingredients. Fill glass with crushed ice, **CHURN** (stir) with bar spoon and serve with straws.

6	fresh	**Blackberries**
10	fresh	**Blueberries**
2	shot(s)	**Ketel One vodka**
1/2	shot(s)	**Freshly squeezed lime juice**
3/4	shot(s)	**Sugar (gomme) syrup**

Comment: A great fruity twist on the regular Caipirovska.

BLACK NUTS

Glass: Shot
Method: LAYER in chilled glass by carefully pouring ingredients in the following order.

3/4	shot(s)	**Opal Nera black sambuca**
3/4	shot(s)	**Hazelnut (crème de noisette) liqueur**

Comment: It's something of a challenge to get the Hazelnut liqueur to float on the black sambuca. If you store the Opal Nera in a freezer and the Hazelnut liqueur at room temperature, this helps.

BLACK RUSSIAN

Glass: Old-fashioned
Garnish: Lemon slice
Method: STIR all ingredients with ice and strain into ice-filled glass.

2	shot(s)	**Ketel One vodka**
1/2	shot(s)	**Kahlúa coffee liqueur**

Variants: 1/ Served straight-up in a Martini glass. 2/ Topped with cola and served over ice in a Collins glass. 3/ Made into a White Russian.
Comment: Most popularly served with cola. With or without, this drink is not that interesting.

BLACK VELVET

Glass: Flute
Garnish: Shamrock or mint leaf
Method: POUR ingredients into chilled glass.

2 1/2	shot(s)	**Guinness stout**
Top up with		**Piper-Heidsieck brut champagne**

Origin: Thought to have originated in 1861 at Brook's Club, London, after the death of Prince Albert. Some credit it to the Shelbourne Hotel, Dublin, Ireland.
Comment: A fitting tipple for Saint Patrick's Day in honour of Ireland's patron saint, who's credited with banishing snakes from the island back in 441 AD.

BLACK WIDOW

Glass: Martini
Garnish: Liquorice
Method: SHAKE all ingredients with ice and fine strain into chilled glass.

1	shot(s)	**Opal Nera black sambuca**
1	shot(s)	**Crème de fraise (strawberry) liqueur**
1	shot(s)	**Malibu coconut rum liqueur**
1/2	shot(s)	**Double (heavy) cream**
1/2	shot(s)	**Milk**

Comment: This sticky, fruity, liquorice cocktail tastes a little like an Allsort sweet.

BLACKTHORN ENGLISH

Glass: Martini
Garnish: Flamed orange zest twist
Method: **SHAKE** all ingredients with ice and fine strain into chilled glass.

1½	shot(s)	**Plymouth sloe gin liqueur**
¾	shot(s)	**Plymouth gin**
¾	shot(s)	**Rosso (sweet) vermouth**
3	dashes	**Fee Brothers orange bitters**
1	shot(s)	**Chilled mineral water**

Origin: A classic cocktail whose origins are unknown.
Comment: A dry, subtle rust-coloured Martini.

BLACKTHORN IRISH

Glass: Martini
Garnish: Flamed lemon zest twist
Method: **SHAKE** all ingredients with ice and fine strain into chilled glass.

1½	shot(s)	**Irish whiskey**
1	shot(s)	**Dry vermouth**
¼	shot(s)	**Pernod anis**
4	dashes	**Angostura aromatic bitters**
1	shot(s)	**Chilled mineral water**

Origin: A classic cocktail whose origins are unknown.
Comment: A dry and aromatic Martini with hints of anis. Some may prefer to add a dash of sugar syrup.

BLIMEY

Glass: Old-fashioned
Garnish: Lime wedge
Method: **MUDDLE** blackberries in base of shaker. Add other ingredients, **SHAKE** with ice and fine strain into glass filled with crushed ice. Serve with straws.

8	fresh	**Blackberries**
2	shot(s)	**Lime flavoured vodka**
1	shot(s)	**Freshly squeezed lime juice**
¾	shot(s)	**Sisca crème de cassis**
⅛	shot(s)	**Sugar (gomme) syrup**

Origin: Created in 2002 by yours truly. Named by Tarja Tuunanen.
Comment: This blackberry and lime blend is both fruity and aptly named.

BLING! BLING!

Glass: Shot
Method: **MUDDLE** raspberries in base of shaker. Add vodka, lime and sugar, **SHAKE** with ice and fine strain into glass. **TOP** with champagne.

8	fresh	**Raspberries**
½	shot(s)	**Ketel One vodka**
½	shot(s)	**Freshly squeezed lime juice**
½	shot(s)	**Sugar (gomme) syrup**
Top up with		**Piper-Heidsieck brut champagne**

Origin: Created in 2001 by Phillip Jeffrey at the GE Club, London, England.
Comment: An ostentatious little number.

BLINKER [NEW]

Glass: Martini
Garnish: Lemon twist
Method: **SHAKE** all ingredients with ice and fine strain into chilled glass.

2	shot(s)	**Bourbon whiskey**
1½	shot(s)	**Freshly squeezed pink grapefruit juice**
¼	shot(s)	**Pomegranate (grenadine) syrup**

Origin: A 1930s classic revisited.
Comment: Back in the 1930s David Embury wrote of this drink, "One of a few cocktails using grapefruit juice. Not particularly good but not too bad." Times have changed and now there are many grapefruit juice cocktails.

BLOOD & SAND

Glass: Martini
Garnish: Orange zest twist
Method: **SHAKE** all ingredients with ice and fine strain into chilled glass.

1	shot(s)	**The Famous Grouse Scotch**
¾	shot(s)	**Cherry (brandy) liqueur**
¾	shot(s)	**Rosso (sweet) vermouth**
1	shot(s)	**Freshly squeezed orange juice**

Origin: Made for the premiere of the 1922 Rudolph Valentino movie, Blood and Sand.
Comment: One of the best Scotch whisky based cocktails.

BLOODHOUND

Glass: Collins
Garnish: Lime wedge
Method: **SHAKE** all ingredients with ice and strain into ice-filled glass.

2	shot(s)	**Campari**
1	shot(s)	**Ketel One vodka**
3½	shot(s)	**Freshly squeezed grapefruit juice**

Comment: A dry, tart, refreshing long drink.

BLOOD ORANGE [NEW]

Glass: Collins
Garnish: Raspberries
Method: **MUDDLE** raspberries in base of shaker. Add other ingredients, **SHAKE** with ice and fine strain into ice-filled glass.

7	fresh	**Raspberries**
2	shot(s)	**Orange flavoured vodka**
½	shot(s)	**Crème de framboise (raspberry) liqueur**
2	shot(s)	**Freshly squeezed orange juice**
1¼	shot(s)	**Cranberry juice**
½	shot(s)	**Freshly squeezed lime juice**

Origin: Created in 2005 by Mark Pratt at Maze, London, England.
Comment: A long refreshing fruity number.

BLOODY MARY

The Bloody Mary was originally created in 1920 by Fernand Petiot, at that time a young bartender at Harry's New York Bar in Paris. Contrary to popular belief the drink was not named after Queen Mary the First, whose nickname was 'Bloody Mary' for her persecution of Protestants in the 17th century, or even after the silent-movie actress Mary Pickford. The drink was actually named by one of Petiot's customers, entertainer Roy Barton, as a homage to the Bucket of Blood nightclub in Chicago, where he once performed. The first version contained just vodka and tomato juice.

Petiot left Paris for the US in 1933 and was hired as a bartender at the King Cole Bar in Manhattan's Hotel Saint Regis. Here he mixed his drink for Serge Obolansky, the hotel's President, who pronounced it "too flat". Petiot mixed him another with added salt, pepper, lemon juice and Worcestershire sauce and so gave birth to this classic drink.

Vincent Astor, who owned the hotel, found the name Bloody Mary a little crude for his clientele and so the drink was officially renamed the Red Snapper – although customers continued to order Bloody Marys. (Nowadays a Red Snapper is a Bloody Mary made with gin.)

Petiot's rich and famous clientele helped spread the popularity of the Bloody Mary which quickly gained a reputation as a restorative to be consumed the morning after.

The celery stick garnish dates back to 1960 when a bartender at the Ambassador Hotel in Chicago noticed a lady stirring her drink with a celery stick.

Bloody Mary recipes are as personal as Martinis. Purists will only use Tabasco, Worcestershire sauce, salt and lemon to spice up tomato and vodka but everything from oysters to V8 can be added.

The Bloody Mary's many variations include
Asian Mary (with wasabi, ginger & soy sauce)
Bloody Bull (with beef consommé)
Bloody Caesar (with clam juice)
Bloody Joseph (with Scotch whisky)
Bloody Maria (with tequila)
Bloody Maru (with sake)
Bloody Mary (original)
Bloody Mary (modern)
Bloody Shame (mocktail)
Bullshot (with beef bouillon)
Cubanita (with rum)
Peppered Mary (with pepper vodka)
Red Snapper (with gin)

BLOODY JOSEPH

Glass: Collins
Garnish: Stick of celery
Method: **SHAKE** all ingredients with ice and strain into ice-filled glass.

2	shot(s)	**The Famous Grouse Scotch**
4	shot(s)	**Pressed tomato juice**
1/2	shot(s)	**Freshly squeezed lemon juice**
8	drops	**Tabasco pepper sauce**
4	dashes	**Lea & Perrins Worcestershire sauce**
1/2	spoon	**Horseradish sauce**
1/2	shot(s)	**Tawny port**
2	pinch	**Celery salt**
2	pinch	**Black pepper**

Comment: A Bloody Mary with whisky.

BLOODY MARIA

Glass: Collins
Garnish: Salt & pepper rim plus celery stick
Method: **SHAKE** all ingredients with ice and strain into ice-filled glass.

2	shot(s)	**Sauza Hornitos tequila**
4	shot(s)	**Pressed tomato juice**
1/2	shot(s)	**Freshly squeezed lemon juice**
8	drops	**Tabasco pepper sauce**
4	dashes	**Lea & Perrins Worcestershire sauce**
1/2	spoon	**Horseradish sauce**
1/2	shot(s)	**Tawny port**
2	pinch	**Celery salt**
2	pinch	**Black pepper**

Comment: Tequila adds a very interesting kick to the classic Bloody Mary.

BLOODY MARU [NEW]

Glass: Collins
Garnish: Lemonglass stick
Method: **SHAKE** all ingredients with ice and strain into ice-filled glass.

3	shot(s)	**Sake**
3	shot(s)	**Pressed tomato juice**
1/2	shot(s)	**Freshly squeezed lemon juice**
8	drops	**Tabasco pepper sauce**
4	dashes	**Lea & Perrins Worcestershire sauce**
2	pinch	**Celery salt**
2	pinch	**Black pepper**

Origin: A Bloody Mary based on sake.

FOR MORE INFORMATION SEE OUR
INGREDIENTS APPENDIX ON PAGE 322

BLOODY MARY (1930S RECIPE)

●●◐○○

Glass: Old-fashioned
Garnish: Salt & pepper rim
Method: **SHAKE** all ingredients with ice and strain into empty glass.

2	shot(s)	**100-proof (50% alc./vol.) vodka**
2	shot(s)	**Thick pressed tomato juice**
1/4	shot(s)	**Freshly squeezed lemon juice**
5	dashes	**Lea & Perrins Worcestershire sauce**
4	pinch	**Salt**
2	pinch	**Black pepper**
2	pinch	**Cayenne pepper**

Variant: Red Snapper
Origin: A 1933 version of the classic created in 1920 by Fernand Petiot at Harry's New York Bar, Paris, France.
Comment: Fiery stuff. The modern version is more user friendly.

BLOODY MARY (MODERN RECIPE)

●●●●◐

Glass: Collins
Garnish: Salt & pepper rim plus celery stick
Method: **SHAKE** all ingredients with ice and strain into ice-filled glass.

2	shot(s)	**Ketel One vodka**
4	shot(s)	**Pressed tomato juice**
1/2	shot(s)	**Freshly squeezed lemon juice**
8	drops	**Tabasco pepper sauce**
4	dashes	**Lea & Perrins Worcestershire sauce**
1/2	spoon	**Horseradish sauce**
1/2	shot(s)	**Tawny port**
2	pinch	**Celery salt**
2	pinch	**Black pepper**

Comment: A fiery Mary with the heat fuelled by horseradish. If you like to fight a hangover with spice, this is for you.

BLOODY SHAME (MOCKTAIL)

●●●◐○

Glass: Collins
Garnish: Celery stick
Method: **SHAKE** all ingredients with ice and strain into ice-filled glass.

5	shot(s)	**Pressed tomato juice**
1/2	shot(s)	**Freshly squeezed lemon juice**
8	drops	**Tabasco pepper sauce**
4	dashes	**Lea & Perrins Worcestershire sauce**
1/2	spoon	**Horseradish sauce**
2	pinch	**Celery salt**
2	pinch	**Black pepper**

AKA: Virgin Mary
Comment: Somehow missing something.

DRINKS ARE GRADED AS FOLLOWS:

● DISGUSTING ●◐ PRETTY AWFUL ●● BEST AVOIDED
●●◐ DISAPPOINTING ●●● ACCEPTABLE ●●●◐ GOOD
●●●● RECOMMENDED ●●●●◐ HIGHLY RECOMMENDED
●●●●● OUTSTANDING / EXCEPTIONAL

BLOW JOB

●●●◐○

Glass: Shot
Garnish: Drop cherry into glass then float cream
Method: **SHAKE** all ingredients with ice and fine strain into chilled glass.

1/2	shot(s)	**Grand Marnier**
1/2	shot(s)	**Crème de bananes liqueur**
1/2	shot(s)	**Kahlúa coffee liqueur**

Comment: A juvenile but pleasant tasting sweet shot.

BLUE ANGEL

●●●○○

Glass: Martini
Garnish: Orange zest twist
Method: **SHAKE** all ingredients with ice and fine strain into chilled glass.

3/4	shot(s)	**Blue curaçao liqueur**
3/4	shot(s)	**Parfait Amour liqueur**
3/4	shot(s)	**Rémy Martin cognac**
3/4	shot(s)	**Freshly squeezed lemon juice**
3/4	shot(s)	**Double (heavy) cream**

Comment: This baby blue cocktail is sweet, creamy and floral.

BLUE BIRD

●●●○○

Glass: Martini
Garnish: Orange zest twist
Method: **SHAKE** all ingredients with ice and fine strain into chilled glass.

2	shot(s)	**Plymouth gin**
1	shot(s)	**Blue curaçao liqueur**
3/4	shot(s)	**Freshly squeezed lemon juice**
1/4	shot(s)	**Almond (orgeat) syrup**

Origin: Thought to have been created in the late 1950s in Montmartre, Paris, France.
Comment: A blue rinsed, orange washed, gin based 'tini' that benefits from being sweetened with almond rather than plain syrup.

BLUE BLAZER

●●●○○

Glass: Two old-fashioned glasses
Method: **STIR** honey with boiling water until honey dissolves. Add Scotch and peel. **FLAME** the mixture and stir with a long handled bar spoon. If still alight, extinguish flame and strain into second glass.

2	spoons	**Runny honey**
3/4	shot(s)	**Boiling water**
3	shot(s)	**The Famous Grouse Scotch**
6	twists	**Lemon peel**

Variant: This drink was originally mixed by pouring the ingredients from one metal mug to another while ignited.
Origin: Created by 'Professor' Jerry Thomas, inventor of many famous cocktails in the 19th century. Thomas toured the world like a travelling showman, displaying this and other drinks.
Comment: Only attempt to make this the original way if you're very experienced or very stupid.

A B C D E F G H I J K L M N N P Q R S T U V W X Y Z

BLUE CHAMPAGNE

Glass: Flute
Method: SHAKE first four ingredients with ice and strain into glass. **TOP** with champagne.

3/4	shot(s)	**Ketel One vodka**
1/8	shot(s)	**Cointreau / triple sec**
1/4	shot(s)	**Blue curaçao liqueur**
1/4	shot(s)	**Freshly squeezed lemon juice**
Top up with		**Piper-Heidsieck brut champagne**

Variant: With gin in place of vodka.
Comment: Fortified, citrussy champagne.

BLUE HEAVEN

Glass: Collins
Garnish: Pineapple wedge & cherry sail
Method: SHAKE all ingredients with ice and strain into ice-filled glass.

2	shot(s)	**Light white rum**
1	shot(s)	**Blue curaçao liqueur**
1/2	shot(s)	**Luxardo Amaretto di Saschira**
1/2	shot(s)	**Rose's lime cordial**
4	shot(s)	**Pressed pineapple juice**

Comment: Actually more aqua than blue, this sweet concoction includes orange, almond, lime cordial and pineapple.

BLUE COSMO

Glass: Martini
Garnish: Orange zest twist
Method: SHAKE all ingredients with ice and fine strain into chilled glass.

2	shot(s)	**Ketel One Citroen vodka**
3/4	shot(s)	**Blue curaçao liqueur**
1 1/2	shot(s)	**White cranberry & grape drink**
1/4	shot(s)	**Freshly squeezed lime juice**

Variant: Purple Cosmo
Comment: This blue rinsed drink may have sales appeal but sadly is not quite as good as a traditional red Cosmo.

BLUE KAMIKAZE

Glass: Shot
Method: SHAKE all ingredients with ice and fine strain into chilled glass.

1/2	shot(s)	**Ketel One vodka**
1/2	shot(s)	**Blue curaçao liqueur**
1/2	shot(s)	**Freshly squeezed lime juice**

Comment: Tangy orange - but it's blue.

BLUE FIN [NEW]

Glass: Martini
Garnish: Gummy fish
Method: SHAKE all ingredients with ice and fine strain into chilled glass.

2	shot(s)	**Ketel One Citroen vodka**
1	shot(s)	**Hpnotiq tropical liqueur**
1 1/2	shot(s)	**White cranberry & grape juice**

Origin: Created in 2003 at The Blue Fin, W Hotel, Times Square, New York, USA.
Comment: Citrussy, reminiscent of a blue Cosmo.

BLUE LADY

Glass: Martini
Garnish: Orange zest twist
Method: SHAKE all ingredients with ice and fine strain into chilled glass.

1	shot(s)	**Plymouth gin**
2	shot(s)	**Blue curaçao liqueur**
1	shot(s)	**Freshly squeezed lemon juice**
1/2	fresh	**Egg white**

Comment: Quite sweet with an orange, citrus finish.

BLUE HAWAIIAN

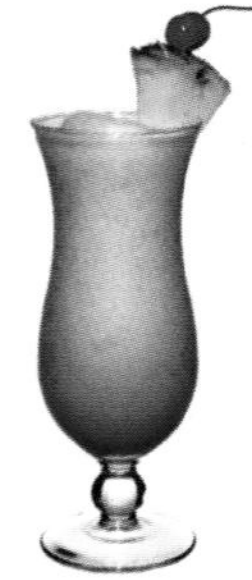

Glass: Hurricane
Garnish: Pineapple wedge & cherry on rim
Method: BLEND ingredients with 12oz scoop of crushed ice. Pour into glass and serve with straws.

2	shot(s)	**Light white rum**
1	shot(s)	**Blue curaçao liqueur**
1 1/2	shot(s)	**Coco López cream of coconut**
3	shot(s)	**Pressed pineapple juice**
1/4	shot(s)	**Freshly squeezed lemon juice**

Origin: Probably created by Don the Beachcomber in Los Angeles, USA.
Comment: A blue rinsed Piña Colada.

BLUE LAGOON

Glass: Collins
Garnish: Orange slice
Method: BLEND ingredients with 18oz scoop of crushed ice. Pour into glass and serve with straws.

1	shot(s)	**Plymouth gin**
1	shot(s)	**Ketel One vodka**
1	shot(s)	**Blue curaçao liqueur**
1	shot(s)	**Freshly squeezed lime juice**
1	shot(s)	**Sugar (gomme) syrup**

Variant: Vodka, blue curaçao and lemonade on the rocks.
Origin: Created in 1972 by Andy MacElhone (son of Harry) at Harry's New York Bar, Paris, France.
Comment: Better than the film – not hard!

BLUE MARGARITA

Glass: Coupette
Garnish: Salt rim & lime wedge on rim
Method: **SHAKE** all ingredients with ice and fine strain into chilled glass.

2	shot(s)	**Sauza Hornitos tequila**
1	shot(s)	**Blue curaçao liqueur**
1	shot(s)	**Freshly squeezed lime juice**
1/4	shot(s)	**Sugar (gomme) syrup**

Variant: Blend with crushed ice.
Comment: As the name suggests, a Margarita, only blue.

BLUE MONDAY [UPDATED]

Glass: Old-fashioned
Garnish: Orange slice
Method: **SHAKE** all ingredients with ice and strain into ice-filled glass.

1	shot(s)	**Orange flavoured vodka**
1	shot(s)	**Cointreau / triple sec**
1/4	shot(s)	**Blue curaçao liqueur**
1	shot(s)	**Freshly squeezed lemon juice**
1/4	shot(s)	**Sugar (gomme) syrup**
3	dashes	**Fee Brothers orange bitters**

Origin: Created in 2003 by yours truly.
Comment: Disco blue but refreshingly bittersweet orange in taste.

BLUE MOON [NEW]

Glass: Martini
Garnish: Orange zest twist
Method: **SHAKE** all ingredients with ice and fine strain into chilled glass.

2	shot(s)	**Plymouth gin**
1	shot(s)	**Serres liqueur de violette**
1/4	shot(s)	**Freshly squeezed lemon juice**
1/2	shot(s)	**Chilled mineral water (omit if wet ice)**

Origin: A long lost relation to the Aviation, originally made with the now extinct Crème Yvette liqueur. This recipe uses the best substitute, 'Serres Liqueur de Violette', and is adapted from one in Ted Haigh's 'Vintage Spirits & Forgotten Cocktails'.
Comment: Grey sky rather than blue but a must for Aviation lovers whatever the colour.

BLUE PASSION

Glass: Old-fashioned
Garnish: Orange zest twist
Method: **SHAKE** all ingredients with ice and strain into glass filled with crushed ice.

1	shot(s)	**Light white rum**
1	shot(s)	**Blue curaçao liqueur**
1 3/4	shot(s)	**Freshly squeezed lime juice**
1	shot(s)	**Sugar (gomme) syrup**

Comment: This sweet and sour tangy drink is surprisingly good.

BLUE RASPBERRY MARTINI

Glass: Martini
Garnish: Raspberries
Method: **SHAKE** all ingredients with ice and fine strain into chilled glass.

2	shot(s)	**Raspberry flavoured vodka**
1/2	shot(s)	**Blue curaçao liqueur**
3/4	shot(s)	**Freshly squeezed lime juice**
1/2	shot(s)	**Sugar (gomme) syrup**
3/4	shot(s)	**Chilled mineral water (omit if wet ice)**

Origin: Discovered in 2002 at The Sky Bar, Sunset Boulevard, Los Angeles, USA, where sour mix is used instead of fresh lime juice and sugar.
Comment: As turquoise-blue drinks go this one is surprisingly adult and tasty.

BLUE RIBAND

Glass: Martini
Garnish: Cherry dropped into glass
Method: **STIR** all ingredients with ice and strain into chilled glass.

2	shot(s)	**Plymouth gin**
1	shot(s)	**Cointreau / triple sec**
1	shot(s)	**Blue curaçao liqueur**

Origin: The 'Blue Riband' was awarded to the liner that made the fastest Atlantic crossing. This cocktail is thought to have been created on one of these ships.
Comment: A sweetened, blue rinsed, orange and gin Martini.

BLUE STAR

Glass: Martini
Garnish: Orange zest twist
Method: **SHAKE** all ingredients with ice and fine strain into chilled glass.

1 1/2	shot(s)	**Plymouth gin**
3/4	shot(s)	**Dry vermouth**
3/4	shot(s)	**Freshly squeezed orange juice**
1 1/2	shot(s)	**Blue curaçao liqueur**

Comment: Gin, orange and a kick.

BLUE VELVET MARGARITA [NEW]

Glass: Coupette
Garnish: Lime wedge on rim
Method: **SHAKE** all ingredients with ice and fine strain into chilled glass.

2	shot(s)	**Sauza Hornitos tequila**
1/2	shot(s)	**Cointreau / triple sec**
1/2	shot(s)	**Blue curaçao liqueur**
1	shot(s)	**Freshly squeezed lime juice**

Origin: Discovered in 2005 at Velvet Margarita Cantina, Los Angeles, USA.
Comment: May look lurid but is a surprisingly tasty Margarita.

A

B

C

D

E

F

G

H

I

J

K

L

M

N

N

P

Q

R

S

T

U

V

W

X

Y

Z

BLUE WAVE

Glass: Hurricane
Garnish: Pineapple wedge on rim
Method: **SHAKE** ingredients with ice and strain into ice-filled glass.

1	shot(s)	**Plymouth gin**
1	shot(s)	**Light white rum**
1/2	shot(s)	**Blue curaçao liqueur**
3	shot(s)	**Pressed pineapple juice**
1 3/4	shot(s)	**Freshly squeezed lime juice**
3/4	shot(s)	**Sugar (gomme) syrup**

Comment: A fruity holiday drink.

BLUEBERRY DAIQUIRI

Glass: Martini
Garnish: Float blueberries
Method: **MUDDLE** blueberries in base of shaker. Add other ingredients, **SHAKE** with ice and fine strain into chilled glass.

20	fresh	**Blueberries**
1 1/2	shot(s)	**Light white rum**
1	shot(s)	**Blueberry liqueur (crème de myrtilles)**
1/4	shot(s)	**Freshly squeezed lime juice**
1/4	shot(s)	**Vanilla sugar syrup**
3/4	shot(s)	**Chilled mineral water**

Origin: I created this drink in December 2002.
Comment: If you like blueberry pie then give this liquid version a try.

BLUEBERRY MARTINI #1

Glass: Martini
Garnish: Blueberries on stick
Method: **MUDDLE** blueberries in base of shaker. Add other ingredients, **SHAKE** with ice and fine strain into chilled glass.

30	fresh	**Blueberries**
2	shot(s)	**Ketel One vodka**
1	shot(s)	**Blueberry liqueur (crème de myrtilles)**
3/4	shot(s)	**Chilled mineral water**

Comment: Rich blueberry fruit fortified with vodka.

BLUEBERRY MARTINI #2 (SIMPLE)

Glass: Martini
Garnish: Blueberries on stick.
Method: **MUDDLE** blueberries in base of shaker. Add other ingredients, **SHAKE** with ice and fine strain into chilled glass.

30	fresh	**Blueberries**
2	shot(s)	**Ketel One vodka**
1/4	shot(s)	**Sugar (gomme) syrup**
3/4	shot(s)	**Sauvignon Blanc wine**

Comment: Rich blueberry fruit fortified with vodka – much more interesting with the additional splash of wine.

BLUEBERRY TEA

Glass: Toddy
Garnish: Lemon slice & cinnamon stick
Method: **POUR** first two ingredients into glass, top up with tea and stir.

3/4	shot(s)	**Luxardo Amaretto di Saschira**
3/4	shot(s)	**Grand Marnier**
Top up with		**Black breakfast tea (hot)**

Comment: This does indeed taste just as described on the tin.

BLUSH MARTINI

Glass: Martini
Garnish: Dust with cinnamon powder
Method: **SHAKE** all ingredients with ice and fine strain into chilled glass.

1	shot(s)	**Ketel One vodka**
3/4	shot(s)	**Vanilla schnapps liqueur**
1/2	shot(s)	**Luxardo Amaretto di Saschira**
3/4	shot(s)	**Milk**
3/4	shot(s)	**Double (heavy) cream**
1/4	shot(s)	**Cranberry juice**

Origin: Created by Colin William Crowden, Mashed Bar, Leicester, England.
Comment: Drier than it looks, but still one to follow the dessert trolley.

BLUSHIN' RUSSIAN [UPDATED]

Glass: Martini
Garnish: Float three coffee beans
Method: **SHAKE** all ingredients with ice and fine strain into chilled glass.

1	shot(s)	**Ketel One vodka**
1	shot(s)	**Kahlúa coffee liqueur**
1/2	shot(s)	**Luxardo Amaretto di Saschira**
3/4	shot(s)	**Double (heavy) cream**
3/4	shot(s)	**Milk**

Comment: White Russian with a hint of almond.

BOBBY BURNS

Glass: Martini
Garnish: Maraschino cherry in drink
Method: **SHAKE** all ingredients with ice and fine strain into chilled glass.

1 1/2	shot(s)	**The Famous Grouse Scotch whisky**
1 1/2	shot(s)	**Rosso (sweet) vermouth**
1/4	shot(s)	**Bénédictine D.O.M. liqueur**

Comment: Strictly speaking this drink should be stirred, but I prefer mine shaken so that's how it appears here.

BOHEMIAN ICED TEA

Glass: Old-fashioned
Garnish: Lemon zest twist
Method: **STIR** all ingredients with ice and strain into ice-filled glass.

$1^1/_2$	shot(s)	**Becherovka liqueur**
$^1/_2$	shot(s)	**Ketel One Citroen vodka**
$^1/_2$	shot(s)	**Krupnik honey liqueur**
$^1/_2$	shot(s)	**Peach schnapps liqueur**
$2^1/_2$	shot(s)	**Chilled Earl Grey lemon tea**

Origin: Created by Alex Kammerling at Detroit, London, England. Originally stirred in a tea pot and served in tea cups.
Comment: A fruity and refreshing drink with surprising flavours.

BOILER MAKER [NEW]

Glass: Boston & shot
Method: Fill shot glass with whiskey and Boston glass with cold beer. Down bourbon in one and then consume beer at a more leisurely pace.

1	shot(s)	**Bourbon whiskey**
1	pint	**Beer (well chilled)**

Origin: Unknown but in his book The Joy of Mixology Gary Regan credits steelworkers in western Pennsylvania.
Comment: More a ritualistic way of drinking than a cocktail but there are times when a shot of whiskey chased by a long cold beer is preferable to any cocktail.

BOLERO [NEW]

Glass: Martini
Garnish: Float apple slice
Method: **STIR** all ingredients with ice and strain into chilled glass.

$1^1/_2$	shot(s)	**Light white rum**
$^3/_4$	shot(s)	**Calvados (or applejack brandy)**
$^1/_4$	shot(s)	**Rosso (sweet) vermouth**

Origin: A classic of unknown origins.
Comment: A dry, challenging drink for modern palates. Be sure to stir well as dilution is key.

BOLERO SOUR [NEW]

Glass: Old-fashioned
Garnish: Orange & lime zest twists (discarded)
Method: **SHAKE** all ingredients with ice and strain into an ice-filled glass.

1	shot(s)	**Appleton V/X aged rum**
1	shot(s)	**Rémy Martin cognac**
$^1/_2$	shot(s)	**Freshly squeezed orange juice**
1	shot(s)	**Freshly squeezed lime juice**
$^1/_2$	shot(s)	**Sugar (gomme) syrup**
$^1/_2$	fresh	**Egg white**

Origin: Adapted from a 1950s recipe found in David Embury's The Fine Art of Mixing Drinks.
Comment: A beautifully balanced, flavoursome medley of sweet and sour.

BOLSHOI PUNCH

Glass: Old-fashioned
Method: **SHAKE** all ingredients with ice and strain into glass filled with crushed ice.

$1^1/_2$	shot(s)	**Wray & Nephew white overproof rum**
1	shot(s)	**Sisca crème de cassis**
$^3/_4$	shot(s)	**Freshly squeezed lime juice**
$^1/_2$	shot(s)	**Sugar (gomme) syrup**

Comment: Innocuous-seeming pink classic – richly flavoured and easy to drink.

BOMBAY

Glass: Martini
Garnish: Orange zest twist
Method: **STIR** all ingredients with ice and strain into chilled glass.

$1^3/_4$	shot(s)	**Rémy Martin cognac**
$1^1/_2$	shot(s)	**Cinzano Rosso sweet vermouth**
$^3/_4$	shot(s)	**Grand Marnier**
$^1/_2$	shot(s)	**Chilled mineral water (omit if wet ice)**
$^1/_4$	shot(s)	**Pernod anis**

Origin: My adaptation of a classic.
Comment: A smooth, complex, Sazerac-style Martini.

BOMBER

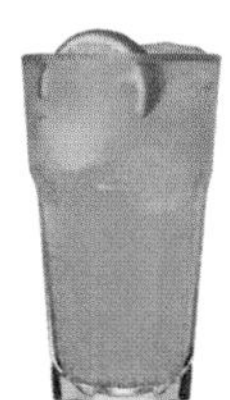

Glass: Collins
Garnish: Lime squeeze
Method: **SHAKE** first three ingredients with ice and strain into ice-filled glass. **TOP** with ginger beer, stir and serve with straws.

1	shot(s)	**Light white rum**
1	shot(s)	**Spiced rum**
1	shot(s)	**Freshly squeezed lime juice**
Top up with		**Ginger beer**

Origin: Created in 1998 by the B. Bar crew at The Reading Festival, England.
Comment: Cross between a Moscow Mule and a Cuba Libre.

BON BON MARTINI

Glass: Martini
Garnish: Lemon zest twist (or a Bon Bon)
Method: **SHAKE** all ingredients with ice and fine strain into chilled glass.

1	shot(s)	**Vanilla flavoured vodka**
$^1/_2$	shot(s)	**Butterscotch schnapps liqueur**
$^3/_4$	shot(s)	**Luxardo limoncello liqueur**
$^3/_4$	shot(s)	**Freshly squeezed lemon juice**
$^1/_4$	shot(s)	**Vanilla sugar syrup**
1	shot(s)	**Chilled mineral water (reduce if wet ice)**

Origin: Discovered in 2001 at Lab Bar, London, England.
Comment: Relive your youth and the taste of those big round sweets in this Martini.

BOOMERANG [UPDATED]

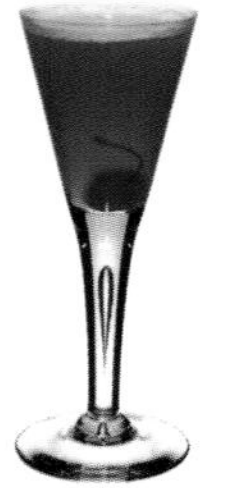

Glass: Martini
Garnish: Maraschino cherry
Method: **SHAKE** all ingredients with ice and fine strain into chilled glass.

$1\frac{1}{2}$	shot(s)	**Bourbon whiskey**
$\frac{3}{4}$	shot(s)	**Dry vermouth**
$\frac{3}{4}$	shot(s)	**Rosso (sweet) vermouth**
$\frac{1}{4}$	shot(s)	**Luxardo maraschino liqueur**
$\frac{1}{2}$	shot(s)	**Freshly squeezed lemon juice**
$\frac{1}{2}$	shot(s)	**Sugar (gomme) syrup**
4	dashes	**Angostura aromatic bitters**

Comment: A very Sweet Manhattan with lemon juice.

BORA BORA BREW | MOCKTAIL [UPDATED]

Glass: Collins
Garnish: Pineapple wedge
Method: **SHAKE** first two ingredients with ice and strain into ice-filled glass.

3	shot(s)	**Pressed pineapple juice**
$\frac{1}{8}$	shot(s)	**Pomegranate (grenadine) syrup**
Top up with		**Ginger ale**

Comment: Fruity and frothy ginger beer.

BORDERLINE [NEW]

Glass: Martini
Garnish: Orange twist
Method: **SHAKE** all ingredients with ice and fine strain into chilled glass.

2	shot(s)	**Bourbon whiskey**
$\frac{1}{2}$	shot(s)	**Maple syrup**
$\frac{1}{2}$	shot(s)	**Freshly squeezed lemon juice**
$\frac{3}{4}$	shot(s)	**Punt E Mes**

Origin: Created in 2004 by James Mellor at Mint Leaf, London, England.
Comment: Bourbon sweetened with maple syrup, soured by lemon and made more complex by vermouth.

BOSOM CARESSER [UPDATED]

Glass: Martini
Garnish: Orange peel twist (discarded)
Method: **SHAKE** all ingredients with ice and fine strain into chilled glass.

2	shot(s)	**Rémy Martin cognac**
$\frac{1}{2}$	shot(s)	**Grand Marnier**
$\frac{1}{2}$	shot(s)	**Malmsey Madeira**
$\frac{1}{4}$	shot(s)	**Pomegranate (grenadine) syrup**
1	fresh	**Egg yolk**

Comment: No bosoms to hand, then caress your throat.

BOSSA NOVA #1 [UPDATED]

Glass: Collins
Garnish: Lime wheel
Method: **SHAKE** all ingredients with ice and strain into ice-filled glass.

2	shot(s)	**Mount Gay Eclipse golden rum**
$\frac{3}{4}$	shot(s)	**Galliano liqueur**
$\frac{3}{4}$	shot(s)	**Apricot brandy liqueur**
2	shot(s)	**Pressed apple juice**
$\frac{3}{4}$	shot(s)	**Freshly squeezed lime juice**

Origin: Named after the Brazilian dance which in turn comes from the Portuguese 'bossa', meaning 'tendency', and 'nova', meaning 'new'.
Comment: Apple with the added zing of rum, Galliano, apricot and lime juice.

BOSSA NOVA #2 [UPDATED]

Glass: Collins
Garnish: Pineapple wedge
Method: **SHAKE** all ingredients with ice and strain into ice-filled glass.

2	shot(s)	**Mount Gay Eclipse golden rum**
$\frac{1}{2}$	shot(s)	**Galliano liqueur**
$\frac{1}{2}$	shot(s)	**Apricot brandy liqueur**
2	shot(s)	**Pressed pineapple juice**
$\frac{1}{2}$	shot(s)	**Freshly squeezed lemon juice**

Comment: Long and frothy with fruity rum and subtle anis notes. Not too sweet.

BOSTON [UPDATED]

Glass: Martini
Garnish: Apricot slice on rim
Method: **SHAKE** all ingredients with ice and fine strain into chilled glass.

$1\frac{3}{4}$	shot(s)	**Plymouth gin**
1	shot(s)	**Apricot brandy liqueur**
1	shot(s)	**Freshly squeezed lemon juice**
$\frac{1}{4}$	shot(s)	**Sugar (gomme) syrup**
$\frac{1}{8}$	shot(s)	**Pomegranate (grenadine) syrup**

Comment: Gin laced tangy fruit.

BOSTON FLIP

Glass: Wine goblet
Garnish: Dust with freshly grated nutmeg
Method: **SHAKE** all ingredients with ice and fine strain into chilled glass.

2	shot(s)	**Bourbon whiskey**
2	shot(s)	**Blandy's Alvada Madeira**
1	fresh	**Egg yolk**
$\frac{1}{4}$	shot(s)	**Sugar (gomme) syrup**

Comment: A good dusting of freshly grated nutmeg makes this old school drink.

●●●○○

BOSTON TEA PARTY [UPDATED]

Glass: Collins
Garnish: Orange slice
Method: **SHAKE** first ten ingredients with ice and strain into ice-filled glass. **TOP** with cola and serve with straws.

1/2	shot(s)	**Ketel One vodka**
1/2	shot(s)	**The Famous Grouse Scotch**
1/2	shot(s)	**Dry vermouth**
1/2	shot(s)	**Cointreau / triple sec**
1/2	shot(s)	**Pusser's navy rum**
1/2	shot(s)	**Plymouth gin**
1/2	shot(s)	**Sauza Hornitos tequila**
1/2	shot(s)	**Freshly squeezed orange juice**
1	shot(s)	**Freshly squeezed lime juice**
1/2	shot(s)	**Sugar (gomme) syrup**
Top up with		**Cola**

Origin: Named after the revolt by early US settlers against the imposition of tax by the British Crown, which became the War of Independence.
Comment: Just about every spirit from the speedrail plus a splash of orange, lime and coke.

●●●●◐

BOURBON BLUSH

Glass: Martini
Garnish: Strawberry on rim
Method: **MUDDLE** strawberries in base of shaker. Add other ingredients, **SHAKE** with ice and fine strain into chilled glass.

3	fresh	**Strawberries**
2	shot(s)	**Bourbon whiskey**
3/4	shot(s)	**Crème de fraise (strawberry) liqueur**
1/4	shot(s)	**Maple syrup**

Origin: Created in 2003 by Simon King at MJU @ Millennium Hotel, London, England.
Comment: Strawberry and maple syrup combine brilliantly with bourbon in this drink.

●●●●○

BOURBON COOKIE

Glass: Old-fashioned
Garnish: Dust with cinnamon powder
Method: **SHAKE** all ingredients with ice and fine strain into ice-filled glass.

2	shot(s)	**Bourbon whiskey**
1/2	shot(s)	**Double (heavy) cream**
1/2	shot(s)	**Milk**
1/2	shot(s)	**Mango or passion fruit sugar syrup**
1/2	shot(s)	**Butterscotch schnapps liqueur**

Origin: Created in 2002 by Andres Masso, London, England.
Comment: Looks tame but packs a flavoursome punch.

DRINKS ARE GRADED AS FOLLOWS:

● DISGUSTING ●◐ PRETTY AWFUL ●● BEST AVOIDED
●●◐ DISAPPOINTING ●●● ACCEPTABLE ●●●◐ GOOD
●●●● RECOMMENDED ●●●●◐ HIGHLY RECOMMENDED
●●●●● OUTSTANDING / EXCEPTIONAL

●●●◐○

BOURBON MILK PUNCH

Glass: Martini
Garnish: Dust with freshly grated nutmeg
Method: **SHAKE** all ingredients with ice and fine strain into chilled glass.

1 1/2	shot(s)	**Bourbon whiskey**
1/2	shot(s)	**Galliano liqueur**
1	shot(s)	**Double (heavy) cream**
1	shot(s)	**Milk**
1/4	shot(s)	**Sugar (gomme) syrup**

Comment: The character of bourbon shines through in this creamy number.

●●●◐○

BOURBON SMASH

Glass: Collins
Garnish: Lime wheel
Method: **MUDDLE** raspberries in base of shaker. Add other ingredients, **SHAKE** with ice and fine strain into ice-filled glass.

12	fresh	**Raspberries**
4	fresh	**Torn mint leaves**
2 1/2	shot(s)	**Bourbon whiskey**
3	shot(s)	**Cranberry juice**
1	shot(s)	**Freshly squeezed lime juice**
1/2	shot(s)	**Sugar (gomme) syrup**
2	dashes	**Angostura aromatic bitters**

Comment: This refreshing long drink has a sharp edge that adds to its appeal.

●●●●○

BOURBONELLA [UPDATED]

Glass: Martini
Garnish: Stemmed cherry on rim
Method: **STIR** all ingredients with ice and fine strain into chilled glass.

1 3/4	shot(s)	**Bourbon whiskey**
3/4	shot(s)	**Dry vermouth**
3/4	shot(s)	**Cointreau / triple sec**
1/4	shot(s)	**Pomegranate (grenadine) syrup**
3	dashes	**Peychaud's aromatic bitters**

Comment: If you like bourbon, you'll love this fruity Manhattan.

●●●●○

BRADFORD

Glass: Martini
Garnish: Olive on stick or lemon zest twist
Method: **SHAKE** all ingredients with ice and fine strain into chilled glass.

2 1/2	shot(s)	**Plymouth gin**
1/2	shot(s)	**Dry vermouth**
3	dashes	**Fee Brothers orange bitters (optional)**

Origin: A Bradford is a Martini which is shaken rather than stirred. Like the Martini itself, the origin of the Bradford is lost in time.
Comment: More approachable than a stirred Traditional Dry Martini and downright soft compared to a Naked Martini.

A B C D E F G H I J K L M N N P Q R S T U V W X Y Z

BRAINSTORM

Glass: Martini
Garnish: Orange zest twist
Method: **STIR** all ingredients with ice and strain into chilled glass.

1½	shot(s)	**Bourbon whiskey**
1	shot(s)	**Dry vermouth**
¾	shot(s)	**Bénédictine D.O.M. liqueur**
¾	shot(s)	**Chilled mineral water (omit if wet ice)**

Origin: Another long lost classic.
Comment: Spiced and slightly sweetened bourbon.

BRAMBLE

Glass: Old-fashioned
Garnish: Blackberry & lemon slice
Method: **SHAKE** first three ingredients with ice and strain into glass filled with crushed ice. **DRIZZLE** liqueur over drink to create a 'bleeding' effect in the glass. Serve with short straws.

2	shot(s)	**Plymouth gin**
1½	shot(s)	**Freshly squeezed lemon juice**
½	shot(s)	**Sugar (gomme) syrup**
½	shot(s)	**Crème de mûre (blackberry) liqueur**

Origin: Created in the mid-80s by Dick Bradsell at Fred's Club, Soho, London, England.
Comment: One of the best and most popular drinks created in the 1980s.

BRAMBLETTE

Glass: Martini
Garnish: Orange zest twist
Method: **SHAKE** all ingredients with ice and fine strain into chilled glass.

2	shot(s)	**Plymouth gin**
1	shot(s)	**Serres liqueur de violette**
¾	shot(s)	**Freshly squeezed lemon juice**
¼	shot(s)	**Sugar (gomme) syrup**

Comment: A martini style drink with a floral, gin laced palate.

BRANDY ALEXANDER

Glass: Martini
Garnish: Dust with freshly grated nutmeg
Method: **SHAKE** all ingredients with ice and fine strain into chilled glass.

2	shot(s)	**Rémy Martin cognac**
½	shot(s)	**Dark crème de cacao liqueur**
½	shot(s)	**White crème de cacao liqueur**
½	shot(s)	**Double (heavy) cream**
½	shot(s)	**Milk**

AKA: The Panama
Origin: Created prior to 1930, this classic blend of brandy and chocolate smoothed with cream is based on the original Alexander which calls for gin as its base.
Comment: This after dinner classic is rich, creamy and spicy.

BRANDY BLAZER [UPDATED]

Glass: Snifter & old-fashioned
Garnish: Lemon & orange zest twists
Method: **POUR** cognac into a warmed glass and rest the bowl of the glass on an old-fashioned glass so it lies on its side supported by the rim. **FLAME** the cognac and carefully move the glass back to an upright position sitting normally on your work surface. **POUR** in hot water (this will extinguish any remaining flame) and sugar. Stir, garnish and serve.

2	shot(s)	**Rémy Martin cognac**
2	shot(s)	**Hot water**
¼	shot(s)	**Sugar (gomme) syrup**

Origin: A variation on 'Professor' Jerry Thomas' Blue Blazer which involved theatrically pouring ignited brandy between two mugs. Please don't try this at home, kids.
Comment: One way to warm your winter nights.

BRANDY BUCK

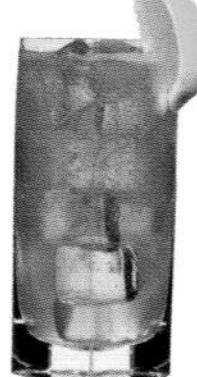

Glass: Collins
Garnish: Lemon wedge
Method: **SHAKE** first three ingredients with ice and strain into ice-filled glass. **TOP** with ginger ale and serve with straws.

2½	shot(s)	**Rémy Martin cognac**
¼	shot(s)	**Grand Marnier**
¼	shot(s)	**Freshly squeezed lemon juice**
Top up with		**Ginger ale**

Comment: Lemon juice adds balance to the sweet ginger ale. Cognac provides the backbone.

BRANDY CRUSTA

Glass: Flute
Garnish: Sugar rim & whole spiral of lemon peel in glass
Method: **SHAKE** all ingredients with ice and fine strain into chilled glass.

2	shot(s)	**Rémy Martin cognac**
½	shot(s)	**Cointreau / triple sec**
½	shot(s)	**Luxardo maraschino liqueur**
½	shot(s)	**Freshly squeezed lemon juice**
¾	shot(s)	**Chilled mineral water**
4	dashes	**Angostura aromatic bitters**

Origin: Created in 1852 by Joseph Santina at Jewel of the South, Gravier Street, New Orleans, USA. The name refers to the crust of sugar around the rim.
Comment: This old classic zings with fresh lemon and the sweetness of maraschino, which is beautifully balanced by the rich strong cognac base.

DRINKS ARE GRADED AS FOLLOWS:

● DISGUSTING ●◐ PRETTY AWFUL ●● BEST AVOIDED
●●◐ DISAPPOINTING ●●● ACCEPTABLE ●●●◐ GOOD
●●●● RECOMMENDED ●●●●◐ HIGHLY RECOMMENDED
●●●●● OUTSTANDING / EXCEPTIONAL

BRANDY FIX [UPDATED]

Glass: Old-fashioned
Garnish: Lemon zest twist
Method: **SHAKE** all ingredients with ice and strain into ice-filled glass.

2	shot(s)	**Rémy Martin cognac**
1/2	shot(s)	**Pressed pineapple juice**
1/2	shot(s)	**Freshly squeezed lemon juice**
1/4	shot(s)	**Sugar (gomme) syrup**
1/8	shot(s)	**Yellow Chartreuse**

Comment: This wonderful classic is on the tart side of well balanced.

BRANDY FIZZ

Glass: Collins
Garnish: Lemon wheel
Method: **SHAKE** first three ingredients with ice and strain into ice-filled glass. **TOP** with soda, stir and serve with straws.

1 1/2	shot(s)	**Rémy Martin cognac**
3/4	shot(s)	**Freshly squeezed lemon juice**
1	shot(s)	**Sugar (gomme) syrup**
Top up with		**Soda water**

Comment: A long, refreshing and tasty dry drink that combines cognac with lemon.

BRANDY FLIP

Glass: Wine goblet
Garnish: Dust with freshly ground nutmeg
Method: **SHAKE** all ingredients with ice and fine strain into chilled glass.

2	shot(s)	**Rémy Martin cognac**
1/2	shot(s)	**Sugar (gomme) syrup**
1	fresh	**Egg yolk**

Comment: A serious alternative to advocaat for those without raw egg inhibitions.

BRANDY MILK PUNCH [UPDATED]

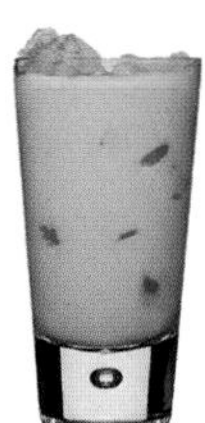

Glass: Collins
Garnish: Dust with freshly grated nutmeg
Method: **SHAKE** all ingredients with ice and strain into glass filled with crushed ice.

2	shot(s)	**Rémy Martin cognac**
3	shot(s)	**Milk**
1	shot(s)	**Double (heavy) cream**
1/4	shot(s)	**Sugar (gomme) syrup**
1/8	shot(s)	**Vanilla extract**

Origin: A New Orleans variant of the drink that enjoyed nationwide popularity during Prohibition.
Comment: This traditional New Orleans hangover cure beats your bog-standard vanilla milkshake.

BRANDY SMASH [NEW]

Glass: Old-fashioned
Garnish: Mint sprig
Method: Lightly **MUDDLE** mint in base of shaker just enough to bruise. Add other ingredients, **SHAKE** with ice and fine strain into ice-filled glass.

7	fresh	**Mint leaves**
2	shot(s)	**Rémy Martin cognac**
1/4	shot(s)	**Sugar (gomme) syrup**

Origin: A classic from the 1850s.
Comment: Sweetened cognac flavoured with mint. Simple but beautiful.

BRANDY SOUR

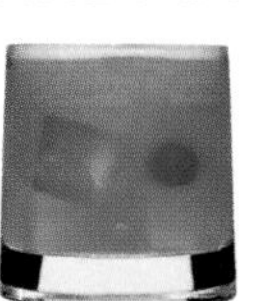

Glass: Old-fashioned
Garnish: Maraschino cherry
Method: **SHAKE** all ingredients with ice and strain into ice-filled glass.

2	shot(s)	**Rémy Martin cognac**
1	shot(s)	**Freshly squeezed lemon juice**
1/2	shot(s)	**Sugar (gomme) syrup**
1/2	fresh	**Egg white**
3	dashes	**Angostura aromatic bitters**

Comment: After the Whiskey Sour, this is the most requested sour. Try it and you'll see why – but don't omit the egg white.

BRAZEN MARTINI

Glass: Martini
Garnish: Frozen blueberries
Method: **STIR** all ingredients with ice and strain into chilled glass.

3	shot(s)	**Zubrówka bison vodka**
1/2	shot(s)	**Parfait Amour**

Comment: Not for the faint hearted – a great combination of strawy bison vodka with violet Parfait Amour.

BRAZILIAN BERRY

Glass: Old-fashioned
Garnish: Mint sprig
Method: **MUDDLE** fruit in base of shaker. Add other ingredients, **SHAKE** with ice and fine strain into glass filled with crushed ice. Serve with straws.

4	fresh	**Blackcurrants**
3	fresh	**Raspberries**
1 1/2	shot(s)	**Sauvignon Blanc wine**
1	shot(s)	**Sagatiba cachaça**
1	shot(s)	**Sisca crème de cassis**

Origin: Created in 2002 by Dan Spink at Browns, St Martin's Lane, London, England.
Comment: This drink combines wine, cachaça and rich berry fruits.

A **B** C D E F G H I J K L M N O P Q R S T U V W X Y Z

BRAZILIAN COFFEE

Glass: Toddy
Garnish: Float 3 coffee beans
Method: **BLEND** ingredients with 6oz scoop of crushed ice. Pour into glass and serve with straws.

1 shot(s) **Sagatiba cachaça**
1 shot(s) **Double (heavy) cream**
¾ shot(s) **Sugar (gomme) syrup**
2 shot(s) **Espresso coffee (cold)**

Comment: Strong coffee and plenty of sugar are essential in this Brazilian number.

BRAZILIAN MONK

Glass: Hurricane
Garnish: Cadbury's Flake in drink
Method: **BLEND** ingredients with two 12oz scoops of crushed ice. Pour into glass and serve with straws.

1 shot(s) **Hazelnut (crème de noisette) liqueur**
1 shot(s) **Kahlúa coffee liqueur**
1 shot(s) **Dark crème de cacao liqueur**
3 scoops **Vanilla ice cream**

Comment: Nutty and rich dessert in a glass.

BREAKFAST AT TERRELL'S [UPDATED]

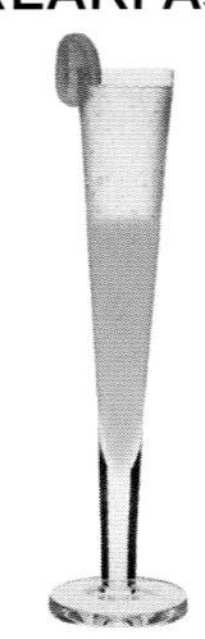

Glass: Flute
Garnish: Kumquat half
Method: **SHAKE** first four ingredients with ice and strain into chilled glass. **TOP** with champagne.

¾ shot(s) **Mandarine Napoléon liqueur**
¾ shot(s) **Freshly squeezed orange juice**
¾ shot(s) **Double (heavy) cream**
⅛ shot(s) **Sugar (gomme) syrup**
Top up with **Piper-Heidsieck brut champagne**

Origin: Created by Jamie Terrell for Philip Holzberg at Vinexpo, Bordeaux, France, 1999.
Comment: This creamy orange champagne cocktail is almost as smooth as a Sgroppino.

BREAKFAST MARTINI

Glass: Martini
Garnish: Slice of toast on rim
Method: **STIR** marmalade with gin in base of shaker until it dissolves. Add other ingredients, **SHAKE** with ice and fine strain into chilled glass.

1 spoon **Orange marmalade (rindless)**
1¾ shot(s) **Plymouth gin**
¾ shot(s) **Cointreau / triple sec**
¾ shot(s) **Freshly squeezed lemon juice**
¾ shot(s) **Sugar (gomme) syrup**

Origin: Created in the late 1990s by Salvatore Calabrese at the Library Bar, London, England. This is very similar to the Marmalade Cocktail created in the 1920s by Harry Craddock and published in The Savoy Cocktail Book.
Comment: The success or failure of this tangy drink is partly reliant on the quality of marmalade used.

BRIGHTON PUNCH [NEW]

Glass: Collins
Garnish: Pineapple wedge
Method: **SHAKE** all ingredients with ice and strain into ice-filled glass.

1½ shot(s) **Rémy Martin cognac**
1½ shot(s) **Bourbon whiskey**
1½ shot(s) **Bénédictine D.O.M. liqueur**
2½ shot(s) **Pressed pineapple juice**
2 shot(s) **Freshly squeezed lemon juice**

Variant: With orange juice in place of pineapple juice.
Origin: Popular in the bars of Berlin, Germany.
Comment: Don't bother trying the version with orange juice but do try halving the quantities and serving up. Served long or short this is beautifully balanced.

THE BROADMOOR

Glass: Martini
Garnish: Flamed orange zest twist
Method: **SHAKE** all ingredients with ice and fine strain into chilled glass.

2 shot(s) **The Famous Grouse Scotch**
½ shot(s) **Green Chartreuse**
½ shot(s) **Sugar (gomme) syrup**
4 dashes **Fee Brothers orange bitters**

Origin: Created in 2001 by Andreas Noren at The Player, London, and popularised at Milk & Honey, London, England.
Comment: Beautifully simple and seriously complex.

BRONX

Glass: Martini
Garnish: Cherry on rim
Method: **SHAKE** all ingredients with ice and fine strain into chilled glass.

1½ shot(s) **Plymouth gin**
¾ shot(s) **Dry vermouth**
¾ shot(s) **Rosso (sweet) vermouth**
1½ shot(s) **Freshly squeezed orange juice**
2 dashes **Angostura aromatic bitters (optional)**

Variant: 1/ Bloody Bronx – made with the juice of a blood orange. 2/ Golden Bronx – with the addition of an egg yolk. 3/ Silver Bronx - with the addition of egg white. Also see the Abbey Martini.
Origin: Created in 1906 by Johnny Solon, a bartender at New York's Waldorf-Astoria Hotel (the Empire State Building occupies the site today), and named after the newly opened Bronx Zoo. Reputedly the first cocktail to use fruit juice.
Comment: A serious, dry, complex cocktail – less bitter than many of its era, but even with the modern formula above, still quite challenging to today's palate.

BROOKLYN #1 [NEW]

Glass: Martini
Garnish: Maraschino cherry
Method: STIR all ingredients with ice and strain into chilled glass.

2 1/2	shot(s)	**Bourbon whiskey**
1/2	shot(s)	**Dry vermouth**
1/2	shot(s)	**Rosso (sweet) vermouth**
1/4	shot(s)	**Luxardo maraschino liqueur**
3	dashes	**Angostura aromatic bitters**

Origin: Though to have originated at the St George Hotel, Brooklyn, New York City, USA.
Comment: A Perfect Manhattan with maraschino liqueur.

BROOKLYN #2 [NEW]

Glass: Martini
Garnish: Maraschino cherry
Method: STIR all ingredients with ice and strain into chilled glass.

2	shot(s)	**Bourbon whiskey**
3/4	shot(s)	**Dry vermouth**
1/2	shot(s)	**Luxardo Amaretto di Saschira**

Comment: A simple, very approachable Manhattan.

BRUBAKER OLD-FASHIONED

Glass: Old-fashioned
Garnish: Two lemon zest twists
Method: STIR malt extract in glass with Scotch until malt extract dissolves. Add ice and one shot of Scotch and stir. Add remaining Scotch, sugar and Angostura and stir some more. Add more ice and keep stirring so that ice dilutes the drink.

2	spoons	**Malt Extract (available in health-food shops)**
2	shot(s)	**The Famous Grouse Scotch whisky**
1/4	shot(s)	**Sugar (gomme) syrup**
3	dashes	**Angostura aromatic bitters**

Origin: Created in 2003 by Shelim Islam at the GE Club, London, England. Shelim named this drink after a horse in the sports section of a paper (also a film made in the seventies starring Robert Redford).
Comment: If you like Scotch you should try this extra malty dram. After all that stirring you'll deserve one.

BUBBLEGUM SHOT

Glass: Shot
Method: SHAKE all ingredients with ice and fine strain into chilled glass.

1/2	shot(s)	**Midori melon liqueur**
1/2	shot(s)	**Luxardo Amaretto di Saschira**
1/4	shot(s)	**Double (heavy) cream**

Comment: As the name suggests, this tastes a little like bubble gum.

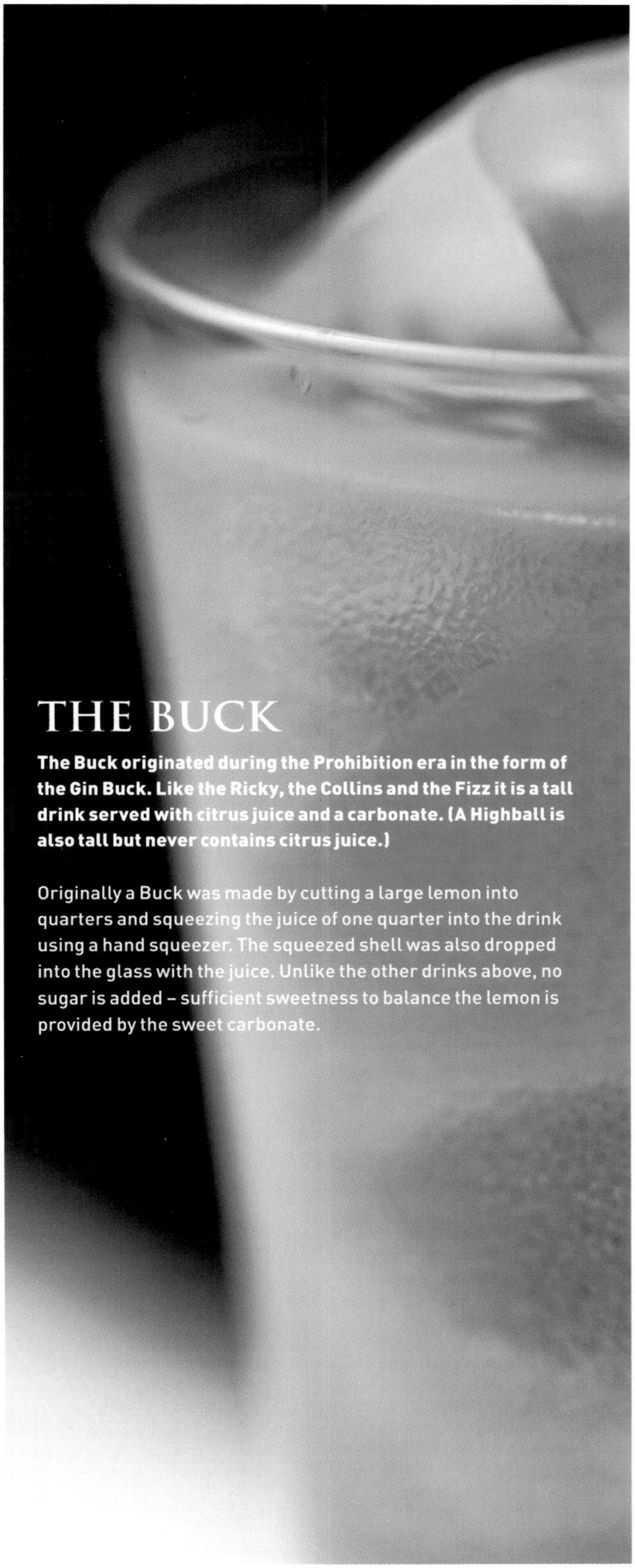

THE BUCK

The Buck originated during the Prohibition era in the form of the Gin Buck. Like the Ricky, the Collins and the Fizz it is a tall drink served with citrus juice and a carbonate. (A Highball is also tall but never contains citrus juice.)

Originally a Buck was made by cutting a large lemon into quarters and squeezing the juice of one quarter into the drink using a hand squeezer. The squeezed shell was also dropped into the glass with the juice. Unlike the other drinks above, no sugar is added – sufficient sweetness to balance the lemon is provided by the sweet carbonate.

A B C D E F G H I J K L M N N P Q R S T U V W X Y Z

●●●◐○

THE BUCK

Glass: Collins
Garnish: Lemon wedge
Method: POUR first two ingredients into ice-filled glass and top up with ginger ale. Stir and serve with straws.

2½ shot(s) **Plymouth gin** (or other spirit)
½ shot(s) **Freshly squeezed lemon juice**
Top up with **Ginger ale**

Variant: The recipe above is for a Gin Buck, but this drink can also be based on brandy, calvados, rum, whiskey, vodka etc.
Comment: The Buck can be improved by adding a dash of liqueur appropriate to the spirit base. E.g. add a dash of Grand Marnier to a Brandy Buck.

●●●○○

BUCK'S FIZZ

Glass: Flute
Method: POUR ingredients into chilled glass and gently stir.

2 shot(s) **Freshly squeezed orange juice**
Top up with **Piper-Heidsieck brut champagne**

AKA: Mimosa
Origin: Created in 1921 by Mr McGarry, first bartender at the Buck's Club, London.
Comment: Not really a cocktail and not that challenging, but great for brunch.

●●●●◐

BUENA VIDA

Glass: Old-fashioned
Garnish: Pineapple wedge on rim
Method: SHAKE all ingredients with ice and strain into glass filled with crushed ice.

2 shot(s) **Sauza Hornitos tequila**
1¾ shot(s) **Squeezed pink grapefruit juice**
¾ shot(s) **Pressed pineapple juice**
½ shot(s) **Vanilla sugar syrup**
3 dashes **Angostura aromatic bitters**

Comment: The fruits combine brilliantly with the tequila and spice comes courtesy of Angostura.

●●●◐○

BUG JUICE

Glass: Collins
Garnish: Orange wheel in drink
Method: SHAKE all ingredients with ice and fine strain into ice-filled glass.

2 shot(s) **Orange flavoured vodka**
1 shot(s) **Passoã passion fruit liqueur**
3 shot(s) **Pressed pineapple juice**

Origin: Created in 2003 by yours truly.
Comment: Named after its orange colour rather than its orange, passion and pineapple taste.

●●●◐○

BULLDOG

Glass: Collins
Method: SHAKE first four ingredients with ice and strain into ice-filled glass. **TOP** with cola, stir and serve with straws.

1 shot(s) **Light white rum**
1 shot(s) **Kahlúa coffee liqueur**
1½ shot(s) **Double (heavy) cream**
1½ shot(s) **Milk**
Top up with **Cola**

Comment: Surprisingly nice – cola cuts through the cream.

●●◐○○

BULLFROG

Glass: Old-fashioned
Garnish: Maraschino cherry
Method: SHAKE all ingredients with ice and strain into glass filled with crushed ice.

1½ shot(s) **Ketel One vodka**
¾ shot(s) **White crème de menthe liqueur**
1 shot(s) **Double (heavy) cream**
1 shot(s) **Milk**

Comment: Mint ice cream.

●●●◐○

BULL'S BLOOD

Glass: Martini
Garnish: Orange zest twist
Method: SHAKE all ingredients with ice and fine strain into chilled glass.

½ shot(s) **Light white rum**
1 shot(s) **Rémy Martin cognac**
1 shot(s) **Grand Marnier**
1½ shot(s) **Freshly squeezed orange juice**

Comment: This beautifully balanced fruity cocktail has a dry finish.

●●●◐○

BULL'S MILK [NEW]

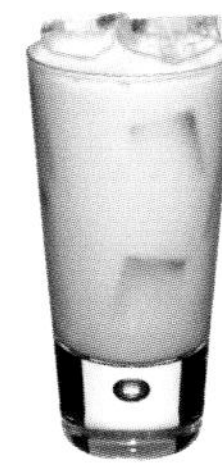

Glass: Collins
Method: SHAKE all ingredients with ice and strain into ice-filled glass.

1 shot(s) **Gosling's Black Seal rum**
1½ shot(s) **Rémy Martin cognac**
4 shot(s) **Milk**
½ shot(s) **Maple syrup**

Comment: Dark spirits tamed by thick maple syrup and milk.

DRINKS ARE GRADED AS FOLLOWS:

● DISGUSTING ●◐ PRETTY AWFUL ●● BEST AVOIDED
●●◐ DISAPPOINTING ●●● ACCEPTABLE ●●●◐ GOOD
●●●● RECOMMENDED ●●●●◐ HIGHLY RECOMMENDED
●●●●● OUTSTANDING / EXCEPTIONAL

●●●◐○

BUMBLE BEE

Glass: Shot
Method: Refrigerate ingredients then **LAYER** in chilled glass by carefully pouring in the following order.

- 1/2 shot(s) **Kahlúa coffee liqueur**
- 1/2 shot(s) **Luxardo Sambuca dei Cesari**
- 1/2 shot(s) **Baileys Irish cream liqueur**

Comment: A B-52 with a liquorice kick.

●●●◐○

BUONA SERA SHOT

Glass: Shot
Method: SHAKE all ingredients with ice and fine strain into chilled glass.

- 1/2 shot(s) **Kahlúa coffee liqueur**
- 1/2 shot(s) **Luxardo Amaretto di Saschira**
- 1/2 shot(s) **Vanilla-infused light white rum**

Comment: As sweet shots go this is one of my favourites.

●●○○○

BURNING BUSH SHOT

Glass: Shot
Method: POUR ingredients into chilled glass.

- 1 shot(s) **Sauza Hornitos tequila**
- 6 drops **Tabasco pepper sauce**

AKA: Prairie Dog, Prairie Fire
Comment: Hold onto your bowels!

●●●○○

BURNT TOASTED ALMOND

Glass: Martini
Garnish: Dust with freshly grated nutmeg
Method: SHAKE all ingredients with ice and fine strain into chilled glass.

- 1 shot(s) **Ketel One vodka**
- 1/2 shot(s) **Baileys Irish cream liqueur**
- 1/2 shot(s) **Kahlúa coffee liqueur**
- 1 shot(s) **Luxardo Amaretto di Saschira**
- 1 shot(s) **Double (heavy) cream**
- 1 shot(s) **Milk**

Variant: Toasted Almond
Comment: There's more than just almond to this sweety.

DRINKS ARE GRADED AS FOLLOWS:

● DISGUSTING ●◐ PRETTY AWFUL ●● BEST AVOIDED
●●◐ DISAPPOINTING ●●● ACCEPTABLE ●●●◐ GOOD
●●●● RECOMMENDED ●●●●◐ HIGHLY RECOMMENDED
●●●●● OUTSTANDING / EXCEPTIONAL

●●●◐○

BUTTERFLY'S KISS

Glass: Martini
Garnish: Cinnamon stick
Method: STIR all ingredients with ice and strain into chilled glass.

- 2 shot(s) **Vanilla-infused Ketel One vodka**
- 1 shot(s) **Hazelnut (crème de noisette) liqueur**
- 1/2 shot(s) **Goldschläger cinnamon schnapps**
- 1/2 shot(s) **Sugar (gomme) syrup**
- 1/2 shot(s) **Chilled mineral water (omit if wet ice)**

Origin: Adapted from a drink I discovered in 2003 at Bar Marmont, Los Angeles, USA.
Comment: Golden coloured Martini style drink complete with the odd gold flake and a hazelnut cinnamon twang.

●●●◐○

BUTTERSCOTCH DAIQUIRI [UPDATED]

Glass: Martini
Garnish: Butterscotch sweet in drink
Method: SHAKE all ingredients with ice and fine strain into chilled glass.

- 2 shot(s) **Light white rum**
- 1 shot(s) **Butterscotch schnapps liqueur**
- 1/2 shot(s) **Freshly squeezed lime juice**
- 1/2 shot(s) **Chilled mineral water (omit if wet ice)**

Comment: A candified Daiquiri.

●●●◐○

BUTTERSCOTCH DELIGHT

Glass: Shot
Method: Refrigerate ingredients then **LAYER** in chilled glass by carefully pouring in the following order.

- 3/4 shot(s) **Butterscotch schnapps liqueur**
- 3/4 shot(s) **Baileys Irish cream liqueur**

Origin: The origin of this drink is unknown but it is very popular in the bars in and around Seattle, USA.
Comment: Sweet connotations!

●●●●○

BUTTERSCOTCH MARTINI

Glass: Martini
Garnish: Butterscotch sweet
Method: SHAKE all ingredients with ice and fine strain into chilled glass.

- 2 shot(s) **Mount Gay Eclipse golden rum**
- 3/4 shot(s) **Butterscotch schnapps liqueur**
- 3/4 shot(s) **White crème de cacao liqueur**
- 1/8 shot(s) **Sugar (gomme) syrup**
- 1/2 shot(s) **Chilled mineral water (omit if wet ice)**

Comment: Sweet and suckable.

A B C D E F G H I J K L M N N P Q R S T U V W X Y Z

A
B
C
D
E
F
G
H
I
J
K
L
M
N
N
P
Q
R
S
T
U
V
W
X
Y
Z

BUZZARD'S BREATH [UPDATED]

Glass: Hurricane
Garnish: Pineapple wedge on rim
Method: **BLEND** ingredients with 12oz scoop of crushed ice. Pour into glass and serve with straws.

2½	shot(s)	**Sagatiba cachaça**
1	shot(s)	**Coco López cream of coconut**
2	shot(s)	**Pressed pineapple juice**
¼	shot(s)	**Double (heavy) cream**

Comment: A Piña Colada made with cachaça.

BYZANTINE

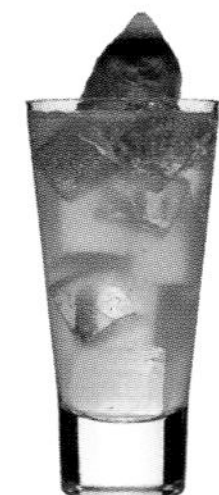

Glass: Collins
Garnish: Basil leaf
Method: **MUDDLE** basil in base of shaker. Add other ingredients apart from tonic water, **SHAKE** with ice and strain into ice-filled glass. **TOP** with tonic water.

6	fresh	**Basil leaves**
1½	shot(s)	**Plymouth gin**
½	shot(s)	**Passion fruit sugar syrup**
2	shot(s)	**Pressed pineapple juice**
½	shot(s)	**Lime & lemongrass cordial**
Top up with		**Tonic water**

Origin: Created in 2001 by Douglas Ankrah for Akbar, Soho, London, England.
Comment: This fruity, herbal drink is even better made the way Douglas originally intended, with basil infused gin instead of muddled leaves.

C C KAZI [UPDATED]

Glass: Martini
Garnish: Lime wedge on rim
Method: **SHAKE** all ingredients with ice and fine strain into chilled glass.

1¾	shot(s)	**Sauza Hornitos tequila**
1¾	shot(s)	**Cranberry juice**
½	shot(s)	**Freshly squeezed lime juice**
¼	shot(s)	**Sugar (gomme) syrup**

Comment: A Rude Cosmo without the liqueur.

CABLE CAR

Glass: Martini
Garnish: Lemon zest twist
Method: **SHAKE** all ingredients with ice and fine strain into chilled glass.

2	shot(s)	**Spiced rum**
1	shot(s)	**Cointreau / triple sec**
½	shot(s)	**Freshly squeezed lemon juice**
¼	shot(s)	**Sugar (gomme) syrup**
½	fresh	**Egg white**

Origin: Created by Tony Abou-Ganim in 1996 at the Starlight Room, in San Francisco's Sir Francis Drake Hotel. Positioned atop the hotel, the bar is passed by the Nob Hill cable cars, earning the bar the catchphrase 'Between the stars and the cable cars'.
Comment: Vanilla and spice from the rum interact with the orange liqueur in this balanced, Daiquiri style drink.

CACHAÇA DAIQUIRI

Glass: Martini
Garnish: Lime wedge on rim
Method: **SHAKE** all ingredients with ice and fine strain into chilled glass.

2	shot(s)	**Sagatiba cachaça**
½	shot(s)	**Freshly squeezed lime juice**
¼	shot(s)	**Sugar (gomme) syrup**
½	shot(s)	**Chilled mineral water**

Comment: Might be in a Martini glass but it tastes like a Caipirinha.

CACTUS BANGER

Glass: Martini
Garnish: Lime wedge on rim
Method: **SHAKE** all ingredients with ice and fine strain into chilled glass.

1	shot(s)	**Sauza Hornitos tequila**
1	shot(s)	**Grand Marnier**
2	shot(s)	**Freshly squeezed orange juice**
½	shot(s)	**Freshly squeezed lime juice**

Comment: A golden, sunny looking and sunny tasting drink.

CACTUS JACK

Glass: Martini
Garnish: Pineapple leaf
Method: **SHAKE** all ingredients with ice and fine strain into chilled glass.

1	shot(s)	**Sauza Hornitos tequila**
¾	shot(s)	**Blue curaçao liqueur**
1¼	shot(s)	**Freshly squeezed orange juice**
1	shot(s)	**Pressed pineapple juice**
½	shot(s)	**Freshly squeezed lemon juice**

Comment: Vivid in colour, this orange led, tequila based drink has a balanced sweet and sourness.

CAFÉ GATES

Glass: Toddy
Garnish: Three coffee beans
Method: Place bar spoon in glass, **POUR** first three ingredients and top up with coffee, then **FLOAT** cream by pouring over the back of a spoon.

¾	shot(s)	**Grand Marnier**
¾	shot(s)	**Kahlúa coffee liqueur**
¾	shot(s)	**Dark crème de cacao liqueur**
Top up with		**Filter coffee (hot)**
¾	shot(s)	**Double (heavy) cream**

Comment: Chocolate orange with coffee and cream.

CAIPIRINHA

Glass: Old-fashioned
Method: **MUDDLE** lime in base of glass to release the juices and oils in its skin. **Pour** cachaça and sugar into glass, add crushed ice and **CHURN** (stir) with bar spoon. Serve with straws.

3/4	fresh	**Lime cut into wedges**
2	shot(s)	**Sagatiba cachaça**
3/4	shot(s)	**Sugar (gomme) syrup**

Origin: A traditional Brazilian drink
Comment: Those who enjoy chewing on undissolved sugar should use granulated sugar in place of syrup.

CAIPIRISSIMA

Glass: Old-fashioned
Method: **MUDDLE** lime in base of glass. Add other ingredients and fill glass with crushed ice. **CHURN** (stir) drink with bar spoon and serve with straws.

3/4	fresh	**Lime cut into wedges**
2	shot(s)	**Light white rum**
3/4	shot(s)	**Sugar (gomme) syrup**

Comment: A Daiquiri style drink made like a Caipirinha to give that rustic edge.

CAIPIROVSKA

Glass: Old-fashioned
Method: **MUDDLE** lime in base of glass. Add other ingredients and fill glass with crushed ice. **CHURN** (stir) drink with bar spoon and serve with straws.

3/4	fresh	**Lime cut into wedges**
2	shot(s)	**Ketel One vodka**
3/4	shot(s)	**Sugar (gomme) syrup**

Comment: Lacks the character of a cachaça-based Caipirinha.

CAIPIRUVA

Glass: Old-fashioned
Method: **MUDDLE** grapes in base of shaker. Add other ingredients, **SHAKE** with ice and fine strain into glass filled with crushed ice.

10	fresh	**Seedless grapes**
2	shot(s)	**Sagatiba cachaça**
3/4	shot(s)	**Freshly squeezed lime juice**
3/4	shot(s)	**Sugar (gomme) syrup**

Comment: A grape juice laced twist on the Caipirinha.

CAIPIRINHA

Pronounced 'Kie-Pur-Reen-Yah', the name of this traditional Brazilian cocktail means 'little countryside drink'. It is made by muddling green lemons known as 'limon subtil', which are native to Brazil (limes are the best substitute when these are not available), and mixing with sugar and cachaça. Be sure to muddle in a sturdy, non-breakable glass.

There is much debate among bartenders as to whether granulated sugar or syrup should be used to make this drink. Those who favour granulated sugar argue that muddling with the abrasive crystals helps extract the oils from the lime's skin. Personally, I hate the crunch of sugar as inevitably not all the granulated sugar dissolves. Whether you should use brown or white sugar to make your syrup is another question! Either way, this is a refreshing drink.

Cachaça, a spirit distilled from fermented sugar cane juice, is the national spirit of Brazil - and Brazilians consume an astonishing 2,000,000,000 litres of it a year.

Capirinhas and variations on the theme are staples in cachaçerias, Brazilian bars which specialise in cachaça.

Caipirinha variations include
Berry Caipirinha
Black 'N' Blue Caipirovska
Caipirissima
Caipirovska
Caipiruva
Citrus Caipirovska
Grapefruit & Ginger Caipirinha
Passionate Caipirinha
Pineapple & Basil Caipirinha

A B **C** D E F G H I J K L M N N P Q R S T U V W X Y Z

CAJUN MARTINI

Glass: Martini
Garnish: Chilli pepper
Method: **STIR** vermouth with ice. Strain to discard vermouth to leave only a coating on the ice. Pour pepper vodka into mixing glass, stir with coated ice and strain into chilled glass.

1/2	shot(s)	**Dry vermouth**
2 1/2	shot(s)	**Pepper flavoured vodka**

Comment: A very hot vodka Martini. I dare you!

CALIFORNIA ROOT BEER [NEW]

Glass: Sling
Garnish: Lime wedge
Method: **SHAKE** first three ingredients with ice and strain into ice-filled glass. **TOP** with soda.

1	shot(s)	**Ketel One vodka**
1/2	shot(s)	**Kahlúa coffee liqueur**
3/4	shot(s)	**Galliano liqueur**
Top up with		**Soda water (club soda)**

Variant: Bartender's Root Beer
Comment: Does indeed taste like root beer.

CALL ME OLD-FASHIONED

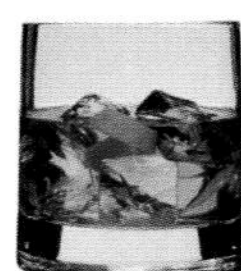

Glass: Old-fashioned
Garnish: Orange peel twist
Method: **STIR** sugar syrup and bitters with two ice cubes in a glass. Add one shot of cognac and two more ice cubes. Stir some more and add another two ice cubes and another shot of cognac. Stir lots more and add more ice.

2	shot(s)	**Rémy Martin cognac**
1/4	shot(s)	**Sugar (gomme) syrup**
2	dashes	**Angostura aromatic bitters**

Origin: Created in 2001 by yours truly.
Comment: An Old-Fashioned made with cognac instead of whiskey – works well.

CALVADOS COCKTAIL [NEW]

Glass: Martini
Garnish: Lemon twist
Method: **SHAKE** all ingredients with ice and fine strain into chilled glass.

2	shot(s)	**Calvados (or applejack brandy)**
3/4	shot(s)	**Cointreau / triple sec**
1 1/2	shot(s)	**Freshly squeezed orange juice**

Origin: Adapted from a recipe originally published in 1930 in the Savoy Cocktail Book.
Comment: Tangy orange with a sharp apple bite.

CAMERON'TINI

Glass: Martini
Garnish: Lemon twist
Method: **SHAKE** all ingredients with ice and fine strain into chilled glass.

1 3/4	shot(s)	**The Famous Grouse Scotch whisky**
1 1/4	shot(s)	**Freshly squeezed lemon juice**
1 1/4	shot(s)	**Almond (orgeat) syrup**
1/2	shot(s)	**Chilled mineral water (omit if wet ice)**

Origin: Adapted from a recipe in the 1947 edition of Trader Vic's Bartender's Guide. The drink first appeared as 'Cameron's Kick' in the 1930 Savoy Cocktail Book.
Comment: Rich, honeyed and balanced, but most emphatically rich.

CAMOMILE & BLACKTHORN BREEZE

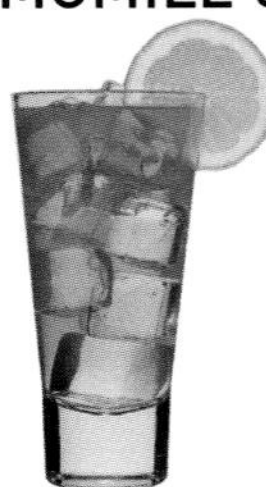

Glass: Collins
Garnish: Lemon wheel on rim
Method: **SHAKE** all ingredients with cubed ice and strain into ice-filled glass.

2	shot(s)	**Lime flavoured vodka**
2	shot(s)	**Lapponia Tyrni (blackthorn berry) liqueur**
4	shot(s)	**Cold camomile tea**

Origin: I created this in 2002 after a trip to Finland with Finlandia vodka.
Comment: Adult, clean and subtle in flavour with a distinctive blackthorn bite.

CANARIE

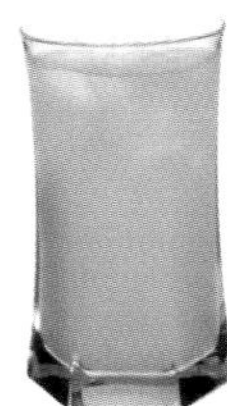

Glass: Collins (10oz/290ml max)
Method: **POUR** pastis and lemon syrup into glass. Serve iced water separately in a small jug (known in France as a 'broc') so the customer can dilute to their own taste (I recommend five shots). Lastly, add ice to fill glass.

1	shot(s)	**Ricard pastis**
1/2	shot(s)	**Lemon (citron) sugar syrup**
Top up with		**Chilled mineral water**

Origin: Very popular throughout France, this drink is fittingly named after the bird, which is typically bred for its bright yellow plumage.
Comment: The traditional French café drink with a twist of lemon sweetness.

CANARIES [UPDATED]

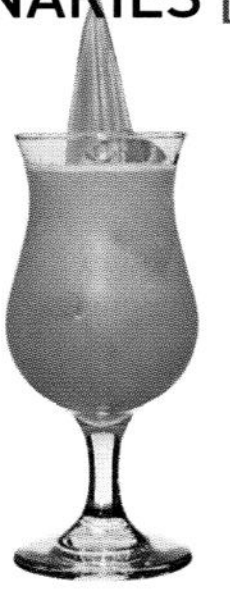

Glass: Hurricane
Garnish: Pineapple wedge on rim
Method: **SHAKE** ingredients with ice and strain into ice-filled glass.

3/4	shot(s)	**Light white rum**
3/4	shot(s)	**Cointreau / triple sec**
3/4	shot(s)	**Crème de bananes liqueur**
3/4	shot(s)	**Cherry (brandy) liqueur**
2	shot(s)	**Pressed pineapple juice**
2	shot(s)	**Freshly squeezed orange juice**

Comment: A long, fruity sweet drink that's only fit for consumption on a tropical beach.

CANARY FLIP

Glass: Martini
Garnish: Lemon zest twist
Method: **SHAKE** all ingredients with ice and fine strain into chilled glass.

- 2 shot(s) **Advocaat liqueur**
- 2 shot(s) **Sauvignon Blanc wine**
- ¾ shot(s) **Freshly squeezed lemon juice**

Origin: Created in 2002 by Alex Kammerling, London, England.
Comment: A delightful balance of egg, brandy and wine.

CANTEEN MARTINI

Glass: Martini
Garnish: Cherry in drink
Method: **SHAKE** all ingredients with ice and fine strain into chilled glass.

- 1½ shot(s) **Light white rum**
- 1½ shot(s) **Southern Comfort**
- ½ shot(s) **Luxardo Amaretto di Saschira**
- ½ shot(s) **Freshly squeezed lime juice**

Origin: Originally created by Joey Guerra at Canteen, New York City, and adapted by author and columnist Gary Regan.
Comment: Tangy, sweet and sour – Southern Comfort drinkers will love this.

CAPE CODDER

Glass: Old-fashioned
Garnish: Lime wedge
Method: **SHAKE** all ingredients with ice and strain into ice-filled glass.

- 2 shot(s) **Ketel One vodka**
- 3 shot(s) **Cranberry juice**
- ¼ shot(s) **Freshly squeezed lime juice**

Variant: Without lime juice this is a Cape Cod. Lengthened with soda becomes the Cape Cod Cooler.
Origin: Named after the resort on the Massachusetts coast. This fish shaped piece of land is where some of the first Europeans settled in the US. Here they found cranberries, the indigenous North American berry on which this drink is based.
Comment: Dry and refreshing but not particularly interesting.

DRINKS ARE GRADED AS FOLLOWS:

● DISGUSTING ●◐ PRETTY AWFUL ●● BEST AVOIDED
●●◐ DISAPPOINTING ●●● ACCEPTABLE ●●●◐ GOOD
●●●● RECOMMENDED ●●●●◐ HIGHLY RECOMMENDED
●●●●● OUTSTANDING / EXCEPTIONAL

CAPPERCAILLE [NEW]

Glass: Martini
Garnish: Pineapple wedge on rim
Method: **STIR** honey with whisky until honey dissolves. Add other ingredients, **SHAKE** with ice and fine strain into chilled glass.

- 2 spoons **Runny honey**
- 2 shot(s) **The Famous Grouse Scotch**
- ½ shot(s) **Cointreau / triple sec**
- ½ shot(s) **Apricot brandy liqueur**
- 1 shot(s) **Pressed pineapple juice**
- ½ shot(s) **Freshly squeezed lemon juice**

Origin: Created by Wayne Collins for Maxxium UK.
Comment: Wonderfully tangy, fruity Scotch.

CAPTAIN COLLINS

Glass: Collins
Garnish: Orange slice & cherry on stick (sail)
Method: **SHAKE** first three ingredients with ice and strain into ice-filled glass. **TOP** with soda, stir and serve with straws.

- 2 shot(s) **Canadian whiskey**
- 1 shot(s) **Freshly squeezed lemon juice**
- ½ shot(s) **Sugar (gomme) syrup**
- Top up with **Soda water (club soda)**

Origin: Classic Collins variation.
Comment: Sweetened, soured and diluted whiskey.

CARAMEL MANHATTAN

Glass: Martini
Garnish: Lemon twist (discarded) & pineapple wedge on rim
Method: **SHAKE** all ingredients with ice and fine strain into chilled glass.

- 1½ shot(s) **Bourbon whiskey**
- ¾ shot(s) **Cartron Caramel liqueur**
- ½ shot(s) **Rosso (sweet) vermouth**
- 1 shot(s) **Pressed pineapple juice**
- 2 dashes **Peychaud's aromatic bitters**

Origin: Adapted from a drink created in 2002 by Nick Strangeway, London, England.
Comment: Flavours combine harmoniously with the character of the bourbon still evident.

CARAMELISED APPLE MARTINI [NEW]

Glass: Martini
Garnish: Float apple slice
Method: **SHAKE** all ingredients with ice and fine strain into chilled glass.

- 2 shot(s) **Almond flavoured vodka**
- 1 shot(s) **Freshly pressed apple juice**
- ½ shot(s) **Freshly squeezed lemon juice**
- ½ shot(s) **Sugar (gomme) syrup**
- ½ shot(s) **Chilled mineral water (omit if wet ice)**

Origin: Created in 2005 by yours truly.
Comment: Appropriately if not imaginatively named.

A B C D E F G H I J K L M N N P Q R S T U V W X Y Z

CARAVAN

Glass: Collins
Garnish: Cherries
Method: **POUR** ingredients into ice-filled glass. Stir and serve with straws.

3	shot(s)	**Red wine**
1/2	shot(s)	**Grand Marnier**
Top up with		**Cola**

Origin: Popular in the French Alpine ski resorts.
Comment: A punch-like long drink.

CARDINAL PUNCH

Glass: Old-fashioned
Method: **POUR** cassis into ice-filled glass and top up with wine. Stir and serve with straws.

1	shot(s)	**Sisca crème de cassis**
Top up with		**Red wine**

Comment: A particularly fruity red.

CARIBBEAN BREEZE

Glass: Collins
Garnish: Pineapple wedge on rim
Method: **SHAKE** all ingredients with ice and strain into ice-filled glass.

1 1/4	shot(s)	**Pusser's navy rum**
1/2	shot(s)	**Crème de bananes liqueur**
2 1/2	shot(s)	**Pressed pineapple juice**
2	shot(s)	**Cranberry juice**
1/2	shot(s)	**Rose's lime cordial**

Comment: A long drink with bags of tangy fruit flavours.

CARIBBEAN CRUISE

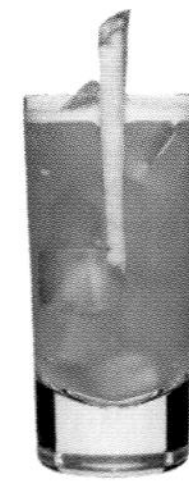

Glass: Collins
Garnish: Pineapple wedge on rim
Method: **SHAKE** all ingredients with ice and strain into ice-filled glass.

1 1/2	shot(s)	**Light white rum**
1 1/2	shot(s)	**Malibu coconut rum liqueur**
4	shot(s)	**Pressed pineapple juice**
1	spoon	**Pomegranate (grenadine) syrup**

Comment: Long, frothy and fruity - one for the beach bar.

DRINKS ARE GRADED AS FOLLOWS:

● DISGUSTING ●◐ PRETTY AWFUL ●● BEST AVOIDED
●●◐ DISAPPOINTING ●●● ACCEPTABLE ●●●◐ GOOD
●●●● RECOMMENDED ●●●●◐ HIGHLY RECOMMENDED
●●●●● OUTSTANDING / EXCEPTIONAL

CARIBBEAN PIÑA COLADA

Glass: Hurricane
Garnish: Pineapple wedge with cherry on stick.
Method: **BLEND** ingredients with 12oz scoop of crushed ice. Pour into glass and serve with straws.

2	shot(s)	**Light white rum**
3	shot(s)	**Pressed pineapple juice**
1/2	shot(s)	**Coco López cream of coconut**
4	dashes	**Angostura aromatic bitters**
1	pinch	**Salt**

Comment: Angostura and salt make this a less sticky Colada.

CARIBBEAN PUNCH

Glass: Collins
Method: **SHAKE** all ingredients with ice and strain into glass filled with crushed ice.

2 1/4	shot(s)	**Wray & Nephew overproof rum**
1/2	shot(s)	**Luxardo Amaretto di Saschira**
1/2	shot(s)	**Malibu coconut rum liqueur**
1/4	shot(s)	**Galliano liqueur**
1/4	shot(s)	**Pomegranate (grenadine) syrup**
3/4	shot(s)	**Freshly squeezed lemon juice**
3	shot(s)	**Pressed pineapple juice**

Comment: Red in colour and innocent looking, this flavoursome drink sure packs a punch.

CARNEVAL BATIDA [NEW]

Glass: Collins
Garnish: Mango slice on rim
Method: **SHAKE** all ingredients with ice and strain into glass filled with crushed ice.

2 1/2	shot(s)	**Sagatiba cachaça**
1 1/2	shot(s)	**Mango purée**
1 1/2	shot(s)	**Freshly squeezed orange juice**
1/2	shot(s)	**Freshly squeezed lime juice**
1/2	shot(s)	**Sugar (gomme) syrup**

Origin: The Batida is a traditional Brazilian drink.
Comment: Long, rich, refreshing and strangely filling.

CAROL CHANNING

Glass: Flute
Garnish: Raspberries
Method: **SHAKE** first three ingredients with ice and strain into chilled glass. **TOP** with champagne.

1/4	shot(s)	**Crème de framboise (raspberry) liqueur**
1/4	shot(s)	**Framboise eau de vie**
1/8	shot(s)	**Sugar (gomme) syrup**
Top up with		**Piper-Heidsieck brut champagne**

Origin: Created by Dick Bradsell in 1984 with the milliner Stephen Jones. Named after the famously large mouthed American comedienne Carol Channing because of her appearance in the film 'Thoroughly Modern Milly', where, for some unknown reason, she spends much of the time running around shouting 'raspberries'.
Comment: Fortified raspberry and champagne.

CARROT CAKE

Glass: Martini
Garnish: Dust with cinnamon powder
Method: SHAKE all ingredients with ice and fine strain into chilled glass.

2	shot(s)	**Baileys Irish cream liqueur**
3/4	shot(s)	**Goldschläger cinnamon schnapps**
1 1/2	shot(s)	**Kahlúa coffee liqueur**

Comment: Tastes nothing like carrot cake - surely that's a good thing.

CASABLANCA

Glass: Martini
Garnish: Dust with freshly grated nutmeg
Method: SHAKE all ingredients with ice and fine strain into chilled glass.

1	shot(s)	**Ketel One vodka**
1/4	shot(s)	**Galliano liqueur**
1 1/4	shot(s)	**Advocaat liqueur**
1/4	shot(s)	**Freshly squeezed lemon juice**
1 1/4	shot(s)	**Freshly squeezed orange juice**

Comment: Creamy, fruity, alcoholic custard. Different!

CASANOVA

Glass: Martini
Garnish: Crumble Cadbury's Flake bar over drink
Method: SHAKE all ingredients with ice and fine strain into chilled glass.

1 1/2	shot(s)	**Bourbon whiskey**
3/4	shot(s)	**Blandy's Alvada madeira**
3/4	shot(s)	**Kahlúa coffee liqueur**
3/4	shot(s)	**Double (heavy) cream**
3/4	shot(s)	**Milk**
1/8	shot(s)	**Sugar (gomme) syrup**

Comment: Rich, medium-sweet and creamy with a mocha coffee finish.

CASCADE MARTINI

Glass: Martini
Garnish: Raspberries on stick
Method: SHAKE all ingredients with ice and fine strain into chilled glass.

8	fresh	**Raspberries**
1 1/2	shot(s)	**Raspberry flavoured vodka**
2 1/2	shot(s)	**Cranberry juice**
1/2	shot(s)	**Freshly squeezed lemon juice**
1/4	shot(s)	**Chambord black raspberry liqueur**
1/4	shot(s)	**Vanilla sugar syrup**

Comment: Rich raspberry with hints of citrus and vanilla.

CASINO [UPDATED]

Glass: Martini
Garnish: Maraschino cherry
Method: SHAKE all ingredients with ice and fine strain into chilled glass.

2 1/2	shot(s)	**Plymouth gin**
1/2	shot(s)	**Luxardo maraschino liqueur**
1/2	shot(s)	**Freshly squeezed lemon juice**
1/2	shot(s)	**Chilled mineral water (omit if wet ice)**
3	dashes	**Fee Brothers orange bitters**

Variant: Bee's Knees, Blue Moon
Comment: Basically an Aviation dried with orange bitters.

CASSINI

Glass: Martini
Garnish: Three blackberries
Method: SHAKE all ingredients with ice and fine strain into chilled glass.

2	shot(s)	**Ketel One vodka**
2	shot(s)	**Cranberry juice**
1/4	shot(s)	**Sisca crème de cassis**

Origin: Created in 1998 by yours truly.
Comment: A simple but pleasant berry drink.

CASTRO [UPDATED]

Glass: Martini
Garnish: Lime wedge on rim
Method: SHAKE all ingredients with ice and fine strain into chilled glass.

1 1/2	shot(s)	**Appleton Estate V/X aged rum**
3/4	shot(s)	**Calvados (or applejack brandy)**
1/4	shot(s)	**Freshly squeezed orange juice**
1/2	shot(s)	**Freshly squeezed lime juice**
1/4	shot(s)	**Rose's lime cordial**
1/4	shot(s)	**Sugar (gomme) syrup**

Origin: Named after the Cuban.
Comment: Tangy and fruity.

CAUSEWAY

Glass: Collins
Method: SHAKE first five ingredients with ice and strain into ice-filled glass, TOP with ginger ale.

2	shot(s)	**Black Bush Irish whiskey**
1	shot(s)	**Drambuie liqueur**
4	dashes	**Angostura aromatic bitters**
2	dashes	**Fee Brothers orange bitters**
1/4	shot(s)	**Freshly squeezed lemon juice**
Top up with		**Ginger ale**

Origin: Created by David Myers at Titanic, London, England.
Comment: Dry aromatic long whiskey drink.

CELERY MARTINI [UPDATED]

Glass: Martini
Garnish: Salt rim & celery
Method: **SHAKE** all ingredients with ice and fine strain into chilled glass.

$1^{3}/_{4}$	shot(s)	**Freshly extracted celery juice**
2	shot(s)	**Ketel One vodka**
$^{1}/_{4}$	shot(s)	**Sugar (gomme) syrup**

Origin: Created by Andreas Tsanos at Momos, London, England in 2001.
Comment: I only usually like celery when loaded with blue cheese - but I love this Martini.

CELTIC MARGARITA [NEW]

Glass: Coupette
Garnish: Salt rim & lemon wedge
Method: **SHAKE** all ingredients with ice and fine strain into chilled glass.

2	shot(s)	**The Famous Grouse Scotch**
1	shot(s)	**Cointreau / triple sec**
1	shot(s)	**Freshly squeezed lemon juice**

Origin: Discovered in 2004 at Milk & Honey, London, England.
Comment: A Scotch Margarita – try it, it works.

CHAM 69 #1 [UPDATED]

Glass: Sling
Garnish: Berries
Method: **SHAKE** first four ingredients with ice and strain into ice-filled glass. **TOP** with 7-Up, stir and serve with straws.

2	shot(s)	**Ketel One vodka**
$^{3}/_{4}$	shot(s)	**Chambord black raspberry liqueur**
$^{3}/_{4}$	shot(s)	**Luxardo Amaretto di Saschira**
$^{3}/_{4}$	shot(s)	**Freshly squeezed lime juice**
Top up with		**7-Up (or lemonade)**

Origin: I created this drink back in 1998 and I've noticed it on cocktail menus across Europe. I was something of a beginner with a sweet tooth at the time but this new formulation is better balanced.
Comment: Medium sweet, long and fruity.

CHAM 69 #2 [NEW]

Glass: Sling
Garnish: Berries
Method: **SHAKE** first four ingredients with ice and strain into ice-filled glass. **TOP** with champagne, stir and serve with straws.

1	shot(s)	**Ketel One vodka**
$^{1}/_{2}$	shot(s)	**Chambord black raspberry liqueur**
$^{1}/_{2}$	shot(s)	**Luxardo Amaretto di Saschira**
$^{1}/_{4}$	shot(s)	**Freshly squeezed lime juice**
Top up with		**Piper-Heidsieck brut champagne**

Origin: While re-examining my old creation in 2005 I decided champagne would be more appropriate considering the name.
Comment: Long, fruity and refreshing.

CHAM CHAM

Glass: Flute
Garnish: Berries
Method: **POUR** liqueur into chilled glass and top with champagne.

$^{1}/_{2}$	shot(s)	**Chambord black raspberry liqueur**
Top up with		**Piper-Heidsieck brut champagne**

Comment: A pleasing blend of fruit and champagne to rival the Kir Royale.

CHAMPAGNE COCKTAIL

Glass: Flute
Garnish: Lemon peel twist
Method: Rub sugar cube with lemon peel, coat with bitters and drop into glass. Cover soaked cube with cognac, then **POUR** champagne.

1	cube	**Brown sugar**
3	dashes	**Angostura aromatic bitters**
1	shot(s)	**Rémy Martin cognac**
Top up with		**Piper-Heidsieck brut champagne**

Origin: First recorded in Jerry Thomas's 1862 book 'How To Mix Drinks', or 'The Bon Vivant's Companion', where he almost certainly mistakenly specifies this as a shaken drink. That would be explosive. It's thought the drink found popularity after a bartender named John Dougherty won an 1899 New York cocktail competition with a similar drink named Business Brace.
Comment: An over hyped classic cocktail that gets sweeter as you reach the dissolving cube at the bottom.

HOW TO MAKE SUGAR SYRUP

To make your own sugar syrup, gradually pour **TWO cups of granulated sugar into a saucepan containing ONE cup of hot water.** Stir as you pour and carry on stirring and simmering until the sugar is dissolved. Do not let the water even come close to boiling and only simmer for as long as it takes to dissolve the sugar. Allow syrup to cool and pour into an empty bottle. Ideally, you should finely strain your syrup into the bottle to remove any undissolved crystals which could otherwise encourage crystallisation. If kept in a refrigerator this mixture will last for a couple of months.

CHAMPAGNE CUP

Glass: Flute
Garnish: Maraschino cherry
Method: **STIR** first three ingredients with ice and strain into chilled glass. **TOP** with champagne and gently stir.

¾	shot(s)	**Rémy Martin cognac**
½	shot(s)	**Grand Marnier**
¼	shot(s)	**Maraschino syrup (from cherry jar)**
Top up with		**Piper-Heidsieck brut champagne**

Comment: Sweet maraschino helps balance this dry drink.

CHAMPAGNE DAISY

Glass: Flute
Garnish: Pomegranate wedge
Method: **SHAKE** first three ingredients with ice and fine strain into chilled glass, **TOP** with champagne.

1	shot(s)	**Yellow Chartreuse**
⅛	shot(s)	**Pomegranate (grenadine) syrup**
1	shot(s)	**Freshly squeezed lemon juice**
Top up with		**Piper-Heidsieck brut champagne**

Comment: You'll need to like Chartreuse and citrus champagne to appreciate this drink.

CHAMPS-ELYSÉES

Glass: Martini
Garnish: Lemon zest twist
Method: **SHAKE** all ingredients with ice and fine strain into chilled glass.

1¾	shot(s)	**Rémy Martin cognac**
¼	shot(s)	**Green Chartreuse**
½	shot(s)	**Freshly squeezed lemon juice**
½	shot(s)	**Sugar (gomme) syrup**
3	dashes	**Angostura aromatic bitters**
¾	shot(s)	**Chilled mineral water (omit if wet ice)**
½	fresh	**Egg white (optional)**

Origin: Named after the touristy Parisian boulevard where (coincidentally) Rémy Cointreau have their offices.
Comment: A great after dinner drink for lovers of cognac and Chartreuse.

CHARLES DAIQUIRI [NEW]

Glass: Martini
Garnish: Lime wedge on rim
Method: **SHAKE** all ingredients with ice and fine strain into chilled glass.

1	shot(s)	**Light white rum**
1	shot(s)	**Pusser's navy rum**
½	shot(s)	**Cointreau / triple sec**
½	shot(s)	**Freshly squeezed lime juice**
⅛	shot(s)	**Sugar (gomme) syrup**
½	shot(s)	**Chilled mineral water (omit if wet ice)**

Comment: Navy rum and triple sec add special interest to this Daiquiri.

CHARLIE CHAPLIN

Glass: Old-fashioned
Garnish: Lemon zest twist
Method: **SHAKE** all ingredients with ice and strain into ice-filled glass.

1½	shot(s)	**Plymouth sloe gin liqueur**
1½	shot(s)	**Apricot brandy liqueur**
1	shot(s)	**Freshly squeezed lemon juice**

Comment: This fruity number was originally served 'up' but is better over ice.

CHARLIE LYCHEE'TINI

Glass: Martini
Garnish: Whole lychee from tin in drink
Method: **STIR** all ingredients with ice and strain into chilled glass.

1	shot(s)	**Tio Pepe fino sherry**
1	shot(s)	**Pisco**
1	shot(s)	**Sake**
1	shot(s)	**Lychee syrup from tinned fruit**
⅛	shot(s)	**Elderflower cordial**

Origin: I created this drink in 2002 and named it for Charlie Rouse, who loves sherry.
Comment: Subtle with an interesting salty edge, this tastes almost like a wine.

CHAS

Glass: Martini
Garnish: Orange zest twist
Method: **SHAKE** all ingredients with ice and fine strain into chilled glass.

1¾	shot(s)	**Bourbon whiskey**
½	shot(s)	**Bénédictine D.O.M. liqueur**
½	shot(s)	**Luxardo Amaretto di Saschira**
½	shot(s)	**Cointreau / triple sec**
½	shot(s)	**Grand Marnier**

Origin: Created in 2003 by Murray Stenson at Zig Zag Café, Seattle, USA.
Comment: A wonderfully tangy cocktail with great bourbon personality and hints of almond and orange.

CHEEKY MONKEY

Glass: Martini
Method: **SHAKE** all ingredients with ice and fine strain into chilled glass.

1	shot(s)	**Ketel One Citroen vodka**
1	shot(s)	**Yellow Chartreuse**
2	shot(s)	**Freshly squeezed orange juice**
½	shot(s)	**Sugar (gomme) syrup**
4	dashes	**Fee Brothers orange bitters**

Origin: Adapted from a recipe created by Tony Conigliaro in 2001 at Isola, Knightsbridge, London, England.
Comment: Fire yellow in colour, this drink features the distinctive flavour of Chartreuse with a citrus supporting cast.

A B C D E F G H I J K L M N N P Q R S T U V W X Y Z

CHELSEA SIDECAR [UPDATED]

Glass: Martini
Garnish: Lemon zest twist
Method: **SHAKE** all ingredients with ice and fine strain into chilled glass.

1½	shot(s)	**Plymouth gin**
1	shot(s)	**Cointreau / triple sec**
1	shot(s)	**Freshly squeezed lemon juice**
¼	shot(s)	**Sugar (gomme) syrup**

Comment: Gin replaces cognac in this variation on the classic Sidecar.

CHERRUTE

Glass: Martini
Garnish: Maraschino cherry in drink
Method: **SHAKE** all ingredients with ice and fine strain into chilled glass.

2	shot(s)	**Ketel One vodka**
¾	shot(s)	**Cherry (brandy) liqueur**
1½	shot(s)	**Freshly squeezed golden grapefruit juice**

Comment: Sweet cherry brandy balanced by the fruity acidity of grapefruit, laced with vodka.

CHERRY ALEXANDER [NEW]

Glass: Martini
Garnish: Maraschino cherry
Method: **SHAKE** all ingredients with ice and fine strain into chilled glass.

1	shot(s)	**Vanilla flavoured vodka**
½	shot(s)	**Cherry (brandy) liqueur**
½	shot(s)	**White crème de cacao liqueur**
1	shot(s)	**Double (heavy) cream**
1	shot(s)	**Milk**

Origin: Created by Wayne Collins for Maxxium UK.
Comment: A fruity twist on the creamy classic.

CHERRY & HAZELNUT DAIQUIRI

Glass: Martini
Garnish: Cherry on rim
Method: **SHAKE** all ingredients with ice and fine strain into chilled glass.

2	shot(s)	**Light white rum**
¾	shot(s)	**Luxardo maraschino liqueur**
1½	shot(s)	**Hazelnut (crème de noisette) liqueur**
½	shot(s)	**Freshly squeezed lime juice**
½	shot(s)	**Chilled mineral water**

Origin: Adam Wyartt and I created this in 2003.
Comment: Nutty and surprisingly tangy.

CHERRY BLOSSOM [UPDATED]

Glass: Martini
Garnish: Maraschino cherry in drink
Method: **SHAKE** all ingredients with ice and fine strain into chilled glass.

¾	shot(s)	**Cherry (brandy) liqueur**
¾	shot(s)	**Kirsch eau de vie**
½	shot(s)	**Cointreau / triple sec**
1¼	shot(s)	**Freshly squeezed lemon juice**
¼	shot(s)	**Maraschino syrup (from cherry jar)**

Comment: Bundles of flavour – tangy and moreish.

CHERRY DAIQUIRI

Glass: Martini
Garnish: Cherry on rim
Method: **MUDDLE** cherries in base of shaker. Add other ingredients, **SHAKE** with ice and fine strain into chilled glass.

8	fresh	**Stoned cherries**
2	shot(s)	**Vanilla-infused rum**
1	shot(s)	**Cherry (brandy) liqueur**
⅛	shot(s)	**Maraschino syrup (from cherry jar)**
½	shot(s)	**Freshly squeezed lime juice**
½	shot(s)	**Chilled mineral water**

Origin: Created in 2003 by yours truly.
Comment: Cherry sweetness paired with Daiquiri sharpness.

CHERRY MARTINI

Glass: Martini
Garnish: Stemmed cherry
Method: **SHAKE** all ingredients with ice and fine strain into chilled glass.

2	shot(s)	**Wisniówka cherry vodka**
¾	shot(s)	**Cherry (brandy) liqueur**
1	shot(s)	**Freshly squeezed lemon juice**
½	shot(s)	**Sugar (gomme) syrup**

Comment: Exactly what the name promises.

CHERRY MASH SOUR

Glass: Old-fashioned
Garnish: Lemon twist & cherry
Method: **SHAKE** all ingredients with ice and strain into ice-filled glass.

2	shot(s)	**Jack Daniel's Tennessee whiskey**
½	shot(s)	**Cherry (brandy) liqueur**
¾	shot(s)	**Freshly squeezed lemon juice**
½	shot(s)	**Sugar (gomme) syrup**

Origin: Created by Dale DeGroff when Beverage Manager at the Rainbow Room Promenade Bar, New York City, USA.
Comment: The rich flavour of Tennessee whiskey soured with lemon and sweetened with cherry liqueur.

CHE'S REVOLUTION

Glass: Martini
Garnish: Pineapple wedge on rim
Method: **MUDDLE** mint with rum in base of shaker. Add other ingredients, **SHAKE** with ice and fine strain into chilled glass.

4	fresh	**Mint leaves**
2	shot(s)	**Light white rum**
1/4	shot(s)	**Maple syrup**
2	shot(s)	**Pressed pineapple juice**

Origin: Created in 2003 by Ben Reed for the launch party of MJU Bar @ Millennium Hotel, London, England.
Comment: Complex and smooth with hints of maple syrup and mint amongst the pineapple and rum.

CHICLET DAIQUIRI

Glass: Martini
Garnish: Banana slice on rim
Method: **BLEND** ingredients with a 12oz scoop of crushed ice and serve in large chilled glass.

2 1/2	shot(s)	**Light white rum**
1/2	shot(s)	**Crème de bananes liqueur**
1/8	shot(s)	**White crème de menthe liqueur**
1/2	shot(s)	**Freshly squeezed lime juice**
1/4	shot(s)	**Sugar (gomme) syrup**

Origin: Often found on Cuban bar menus, this was created at La Floridita, Havana.
Comment: A wonderfully refreshing drink on a summer's day with surprisingly subtle flavours.

CHIHUAHUA MAGARITA

Glass: Martini
Method: **SHAKE** all ingredients with ice and fine strain into chilled glass.

2	shot(s)	**Sauza Hornitos tequila**
2	shot(s)	**Freshly squeezed golden grapefruit juice**
1/8	shot(s)	**Agave syrup** (from health food shop)
3	dashes	**Angostura aromatic bitters**

Comment: Tequila and grapefruit juice pepped up with Angostura.

CHILL BREEZE [UPDATED]

Glass: Collins
Garnish: Lime wheel
Method: **SHAKE** all ingredients with ice and strain into ice-filled glass.

2	shot(s)	**Ketel One vodka**
1/2	shot(s)	**Passoã passion fruit liqueur**
1/2	shot(s)	**Cherry (brandy) liqueur**
3	shot(s)	**Cranberry juice**

Comment: A medium dry red fruity number for summer afternoons.

CHILL-OUT MARTINI

Glass: Martini
Garnish: Pineapple wedge on rim
Method: **SHAKE** all ingredients with ice and fine strain into chilled glass.

1 1/2	shot(s)	**Orange flavoured vodka**
1 1/2	shot(s)	**Malibu coconut rum**
1 1/2	shot(s)	**Baileys Irish cream liqueur**
1 1/2	shot(s)	**Freshly squeezed orange juice**

Comment: Smooth, creamy sweet orange and surprisingly strong.

CHIMAYO

Glass: Martini
Garnish: Float apple slice
Method: **SHAKE** all ingredients with ice and fine strain into chilled glass.

2	shot(s)	**Sauza Hornitos tequila**
3/4	shot(s)	**Sisca crème de cassis**
1 1/2	shot(s)	**Pressed apple juice**

Origin: Created by Adewale at the Arts Café, Leeds, England.
Comment: Medium sweet - apple juice and cassis take the sting off tequila.

CHIN CHIN

Glass: Flute
Method: **SHAKE** first three ingredients with ice and strain into glass. **TOP** up with champagne.

2	shot(s)	**The Famous Grouse Scotch whisky**
1	shot(s)	**Honey syrup**
1	shot(s)	**Pressed apple juice**
Top up with		**Piper-Heidsieck brut champagne**

Origin: Created by Tony Conigliaro at Isola, Knightsbridge, London, England.
Comment: Golden honey in colour and also in flavour. An unusual and great tasting Champagne cocktail.

CHINA BEACH

Glass: Martini
Garnish: Ginger slice on rim
Method: **SHAKE** all ingredients with ice and fine strain into chilled glass.

1	shot(s)	**Ketel One vodka**
1	shot(s)	**King's ginger liqueur**
2	shot(s)	**Cranberry juice**

Comment: Dry and lightly spiced.

A B C D E F G H I J K L M N N P Q R S T U V W X Y Z

CHINA BLUE

Glass: Collins
Garnish: Orange slice in drink
Method: **SHAKE** all ingredients with ice and strain into ice-filled glass.

1	shot(s)	**Blue curaçao liqueur**
1	shot(s)	**Soho lychee liqueur**
4	shot(s)	**Freshly squeezed grapefruit juice**

Origin: Emerged in Japan in the late 1990s and still popular along the Pacific Rim.
Comment: Looks sweet, but due to a generous splash of grapefruit is actually balanced and refreshing.

CHINA BLUE MARTINI

Glass: Martini
Garnish: Peeled lychee in drink
Method: **SHAKE** all ingredients with ice and fine strain into chilled glass.

1	shot(s)	**Blue curaçao liqueur**
1	shot(s)	**Soho lychee liqueur**
2	shot(s)	**Freshly squeezed grapefruit juice**
1/4	shot(s)	**Freshly squeezed lemon juice**

Origin: An almost inevitable short adaptation of the original long drink above.
Comment: This simple cocktail with its turquoise colour tastes more adult and interesting than its colour might suggest.

CHINA MARTINI [NEW]

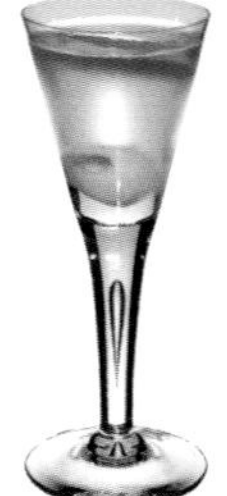

Glass: Martini
Garnish: Orange zest twist & lychee in glass
Method: **STIR** all ingredients with ice and fine strain into chilled glass.

1 1/2	shot(s)	**Plymouth gin**
1/2	shot(s)	**Soho lychee liqueur**
1/4	shot(s)	**Cointreau / triple sec**
1/2	shot(s)	**Dry vermouth**

Origin: Created in 2004 by Wayne Collins for Maxxium UK.
Comment: A complex, not too sweet lychee Martini.

CHINESE COSMOPOLITAN

Glass: Martini
Garnish: Flamed orange zest twist
Method: **SHAKE** all ingredients with ice and fine strain into chilled glass.

2	shot(s)	**Krupnik honey liqueur**
3/4	shot(s)	**Soho lychee liqueur**
1/2	shot(s)	**Freshly squeezed lime juice**
1	shot(s)	**Cranberry juice**

Origin: Discovered in 2003 at Raoul's Bar, Oxford, England.
Comment: Oriental in name and style – perhaps a tad sweeter than your standard Cosmo.

CHINESE PASSION

Glass: Sling
Garnish: Orange slice in glass
Method: **SHAKE** all ingredients with ice and strain into glass filled with crushed ice.

3/4	shot(s)	**Passoã passion fruit liqueur**
1 1/2	shot(s)	**Bourbon whiskey**
3/4	shot(s)	**Peach schnapps liqueur**
2 1/2	shot(s)	**Freshly squeezed orange juice**

Comment: Bizarrely, an element of Chinese flavour.

CHINESE WHISPER MARTINI

Glass: Martini
Garnish: Lemon zest twist
Method: **MUDDLE** ginger in base of shaker. Add other ingredients, **SHAKE** with ice and fine strain into chilled glass.

2	slices	**Fresh root ginger (thumbnail sized)**
2	shot(s)	**Ketel One Citroen vodka**
1	shot(s)	**Soho lychee liqueur**
1/2	shot(s)	**Freshly squeezed lime juice**
1/4	shot(s)	**Ginger syrup**

Origin: Adapted from a recipe discovered in 2003 at Oxo Tower Bar, London, England.
Comment: There's more than a whisper of ginger in this spicy Martini.

CHOC & NUT MARTINI

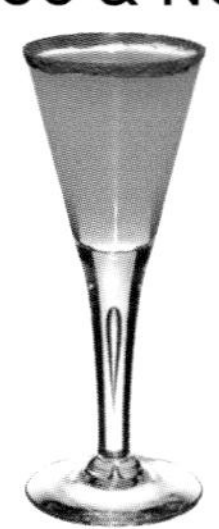

Glass: Martini
Garnish: Wipe rim with orange and dust with cocoa powder.
Method: **SHAKE** all ingredients with ice and fine strain into chilled glass.

2	shot(s)	**Ketel One vodka**
1	shot(s)	**Hazelnut (crème de noisette) liqueur**
1	shot(s)	**White crème de cacao liqueur**
1/4	shot(s)	**Chilled mineral water**

Comment: Surprise, surprise - it's sweet chocolate and hazelnut.

CHOCOLATE & CRANBERRY MARTINI

Glass: Martini
Garnish: Wipe rim with cacao liqueur & dust with cocoa powder
Method: **SHAKE** all ingredients with ice and fine strain into chilled, rimmed glass.

1	shot(s)	**Cranberry flavoured vodka**
1	shot(s)	**Vanilla flavoured vodka**
1/2	shot(s)	**White crème de cacao liqueur**
1	shot(s)	**Dry vermouth**
1	shot(s)	**Cranberry juice**

Origin: I created this drink in 2003 for Finlandia.
Comment: The chocolate rim makes this vanilla and cranberry vodka laced drink.

CHOCOLATE BISCUIT [UPDATED]

Glass: Martini
Garnish: Bourbon cream biscuit on rim
Method: **SHAKE** all ingredients with ice and fine strain into chilled glass.

2	shot(s)	**Rémy Martin cognac**
1	shot(s)	**Kahlúa coffee liqueur**
1	shot(s)	**Dark crème de cacao liqueur**

Origin: Created in 1999 by Gillian Stanfield at The Atlantic Bar & Grill, London, England.
Comment: Sweet and rich, with coffee and chocolate – one to chase dessert.

CHOCOLATE MARTINI

Glass: Martini
Garnish: Wipe rim with cacao liqueur & dust with cocoa powder
Method: **SHAKE** all ingredients with ice and fine strain into chilled glass.

2	shot(s)	**Ketel One vodka**
1	shot(s)	**White crème de cacao liqueur**
1	shot(s)	**Dry vermouth**

Comment: Vodka and chocolate made more interesting with a hint of vermouth.

CHOCOLATE MINT MARTINI

Glass: Martini
Garnish: Wipe rim with cacao liqueur & dust with cocoa powder
Method: **STIR** all ingredients with ice and strain into chilled glass.

2	shot(s)	**Ketel One vodka**
1/2	shot(s)	**White crème de menthe liqueur**
1/2	shot(s)	**White crème de cacao liqueur**
1/2	shot(s)	**Dry vermouth**

Comment: An after dinner sweety that tastes of chocolate mints.

CHOCOLATE PUFF

Glass: Old-fashioned
Garnish: Crumbled Cadbury's Flake bar
Method: **SHAKE** all ingredients with ice and fine strain into chilled glass.

1	shot(s)	**Mount Gay Eclipse golden rum**
1	shot(s)	**Dark crème de cacao liqueur**
6	spoons	**Natural yoghurt**
2	zests	**Fresh orange**
1/4	shot(s)	**Sugar (gomme) syrup**

Origin: Created by Wayne Collins in 2002 for Maxxium UK.
Comment: Smooth as you like. The orange is surprisingly evident.

CHOCOLATE SAZERAC [NEW]

Glass: Old-fashioned
Garnish: Lemon twist (discarded) & apple wedge
Method: Fill glass with ice, **pour** in absinthe, top up with water and leave the mixture to stand in the glass. Separately **SHAKE** bourbon, cacao, sugar and bitters with ice. Finally discard contents of glass (absinthe, water and ice) and strain contents of shaker into empty absinthe-coated glass.

1/2	shot(s)	**La Fée Parisian (68%) absinthe**
2	shot(s)	**Bourbon whiskey**
1/2	shot(s)	**White crème de cacao liqueur**
1/4	shot(s)	**Sugar (gomme) syrup**
2	dashes	**Peychaud's aromatic bitters**

Origin: Created in 2005 by Tonin Kacaj at Maze, London, England.
Comment: This twist on the classic Sazerac pairs absinthe, bourbon and chocolate to great effect.

CHOCOLATE SIDECAR [NEW]

Glass: Martini
Garnish: Wipe rim with cacao liqueur & dust with cocoa powder
Method: **SHAKE** all ingredients with ice and fine strain into chilled glass.

1	shot(s)	**Rémy Martin cognac**
1	shot(s)	**Dark crème de cacao liqueur**
1	shot(s)	**Ruby port**
1	shot(s)	**Freshly squeezed lime juice**
1/2	shot(s)	**Sugar (gomme) syrup**

Origin: Created in 2005 by Wayne Collins for Maxxium UK.

CICADA COCKTAIL

Glass: Martini
Garnish: Dust with freshly grated nutmeg
Method: **SHAKE** all ingredients with ice and fine strain into chilled glass.

2	shot(s)	**Jack Daniel's Tennessee whiskey**
1	shot(s)	**Luxardo Amaretto di Saschira**
1/2	shot(s)	**Double (heavy) cream**
3/4	shot(s)	**Sugar (gomme) syrup**

Origin: Those familiar with the Grasshopper cocktail (named for its green colour) will understand why this one is called the Cicada (they're a bit browner).
Comment: Smoothed whisky with more than a hint of almond.

CIDER APPLE COOLER

Glass: Collins
Method: **SHAKE** all ingredients with ice and strain into ice-filled glass.

2	shot(s)	**Calvados (or applejack brandy)**
1	shot(s)	**Apple schnapps liqueur**
4 1/2	shot(s)	**Pressed apple juice**

Comment: Not unlike the taste of strong dry cider.

A B C D E F G H I J K L M N O P Q R S T U V W X Y Z

CIDER APPLE MARTINI

Glass: Martini
Garnish: Apple wedge
Method: **SHAKE** all ingredients with ice and fine strain into chilled glass.

$1\frac{1}{2}$	shot(s)	**Calvados (or applejack brandy)**
$\frac{3}{4}$	shot(s)	**Apple schnapps liqueur**
$\frac{3}{4}$	shot(s)	**Freshly squeezed lemon juice**
1	shot(s)	**Pressed apple juice**
$\frac{1}{4}$	shot(s)	**Sugar (gomme) syrup**

Origin: Created in 1998 by Jamie Terrell at Lab, London, England.
Comment: As the name suggests, rich cider flavours with a sharp finish.

CINDERELLA

Glass: Collins
Garnish: Lemon wheel
Method: **SHAKE** first five ingredients with ice and strain into ice-filled glass. **TOP** with soda water.

2	shot(s)	**Freshly squeezed orange juice**
$1\frac{1}{2}$	shot(s)	**Pressed pineapple juice**
$\frac{3}{4}$	shot(s)	**Freshly squeezed lemon juice**
$\frac{1}{8}$	shot(s)	**Pomegranate (grenadine) syrup**
3	dashes	**Angostura aromatic bitters**
Top up with		**Soda water (club soda)**

Comment: Long, fresh and fruity.

CINNAMON DAIQUIRI

Glass: Martini
Garnish: Dust with cinnamon powder
Method: **SHAKE** all ingredients with ice and fine strain into chilled glass.

2	shot(s)	**Light white rum**
$\frac{1}{2}$	shot(s)	**Goldschläger cinnamon schnapps**
$\frac{1}{2}$	shot(s)	**Freshly squeezed lime juice**

Origin: Created in 1999 by Porik at Che, London, England.
Comment: A subtle spicy cinnamon taste with tangy length.

CITRUS CAIPIROVSKA

Glass: Old-fashioned
Method: **MUDDLE** lemon in base of glass. Add other ingredients and fill glass with crushed ice. **CHURN** drink with bar spoon and serve with short straws.

$\frac{3}{4}$	fresh	**Lemon cut into wedges**
2	shot(s)	**Ketel One Citroen vodka**
$\frac{3}{4}$	shot(s)	**Sugar (gomme) syrup**

Comment: Superbly refreshing balance of sweet and citrus sourness.

CITRUS MARTINI

Glass: Martini
Garnish: Orange zest twist
Method: **SHAKE** all ingredients with ice and fine strain into chilled glass.

$1\frac{1}{2}$	shot(s)	**Ketel One Citroen vodka**
1	shot(s)	**Freshly squeezed lemon juice**
$\frac{1}{4}$	shot(s)	**Sugar (gomme) syrup**
$\frac{1}{4}$	shot(s)	**Cointreau / triple sec**
3	dashes	**Fee Brothers orange bitters**

AKA: Lemon Martini
Origin: Created by Dick Bradsell at Fred's, London, England, in the late 80s.
Comment: Orange undertones add citrus depth to the lemon explosion.

CLARET COBBLER [NEW]

Glass: Goblet
Garnish: Mint sprig
Method: **SHAKE** all ingredients with ice and fine strain into glass filled with crushed ice. Serve with straws.

$1\frac{1}{2}$	shot(s)	**Rémy Martin cognac**
1	shot(s)	**Grand Marnier**
$2\frac{1}{2}$	shot(s)	**Red wine**

Origin: My version of an old classic.
Comment: Fortified and slightly sweetened wine cooled and lengthened by ice.

CLARIDGE

Glass: Martini
Garnish: Lemon zest twist
Method: **SHAKE** all ingredients with ice and fine strain into chilled glass.

$1\frac{1}{2}$	shot(s)	**Plymouth gin**
$1\frac{1}{2}$	shot(s)	**Dry vermouth**
$\frac{1}{2}$	shot(s)	**Cointreau / triple sec**
$\frac{1}{2}$	shot(s)	**Apricot brandy liqueur**

Origin: An old classic.
Comment: Gin for the strength, vermouth for dryness and liqueur to sweeten – an interesting combination.

CLASSIC [UPDATED]

Glass: Martini
Garnish: Lemon zest twist
Method: **SHAKE** all ingredients with ice and fine strain into chilled glass.

2	shot(s)	**Rémy Martin cognac**
$\frac{1}{2}$	shot(s)	**Freshly squeezed lemon juice**
$\frac{1}{2}$	shot(s)	**Grand Marnier**
$\frac{1}{2}$	shot(s)	**Luxardo maraschino liqueur**
$\frac{1}{2}$	shot(s)	**Chilled mineral water (omit if wet ice)**

Comment: Reminiscent of a Sidecar with Maraschino.

CLASSIC DAIQUIRI

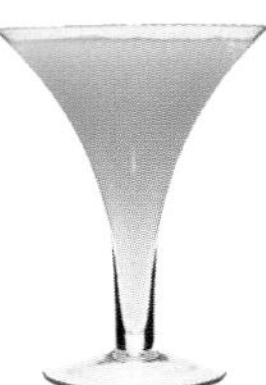

Glass: Martini
Garnish: Lime wedge on rim
Method: **SHAKE** all ingredients with ice and fine strain into chilled glass.

2	shot(s)	**Light white rum**
1/2	shot(s)	**Freshly squeezed lime juice**
1/4	shot(s)	**Sugar (gomme) syrup**
1/2	shot(s)	**Chilled mineral water (omit if wet ice)**

Variant: With aged rum
Origin: The creation of this drink is attributed to Mr Jennings Cox, an American engineer who was working at a mine near Santiago, Cuba in 1896.
Comment: This 'classic' Daiquiri is more properly titled a 'Natural' Daiquiri, but both terms are generally recognised as denoting that the drink should be shaken and served 'up' rather than blended with crushed ice. It also indicates that lime is the only fruit flavouring. My favourite cocktail.

CLEMENTINE [NEW]

Glass: Shot
Garnish: Sugar coated orange wedge
Method: Refrigerate ingredients then **LAYER** in chilled glass by carefully pouring in the following order. Instruct drinker to down in one and bite into the wedge.

1/2	shot(s)	**Luxardo limoncello liqueur**
1/2	shot(s)	**Mandarine Napoléon liqueur**

Comment: Short, sweet and very fruity.

CLIPPER COCKTAIL

Glass: Martini
Garnish: Lemon peel knot
Method: **SHAKE** all ingredients and fine strain into glass filled with crushed ice.

2	shot(s)	**Light white rum**
2	shot(s)	**Dry vermouth**
1/2	shot(s)	**Pomegranate (grenadine) syrup**

Origin: Peggy Guggenheim's biography mentions that this cocktail was served during the 1940s on the Boeing flying boats known as Clippers.
Comment: Light, easy drinking and very refreshing.

CLOCKWORK ORANGE

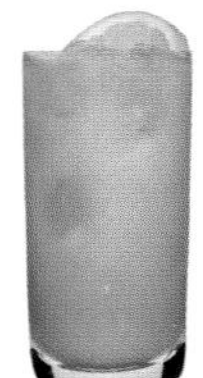

Glass: Collins
Garnish: Orange wheel in glass
Method: **SHAKE** all ingredients with ice and strain into ice-filled glass.

1 1/2	shot(s)	**Rémy Martin cognac**
1 1/2	shot(s)	**Grand Marnier**
4	shot(s)	**Freshly squeezed orange juice**

Comment: Not as memorable as the film but a pleasant orange drink all the same.

CLOVER LEAF MARTINI

Glass: Martini
Garnish: Clover/mint leaf
Method: **MUDDLE** raspberries in base of shaker. Add other ingredients, **SHAKE** with ice and fine strain into chilled glass.

10	fresh	**Raspberries**
2 1/2	shot(s)	**Plymouth gin**
3/4	shot(s)	**Freshly squeezed lemon juice**
1/4	shot(s)	**Pomegranate (grenadine) syrup**
1/4	shot(s)	**Sugar (gomme) syrup**
1/2	fresh	**Egg white**

Variant: 1./ Traditionally made with raspberry syrup and neither pomegranate syrup nor fresh raspberries.
2./ Muddle some mint with the raspberries in this recipe to add interest.
AKA: Without the mint garnish this drink called a 'Clover Club'.
Origin: This classic cocktail is thought to have been created at the Bellevue-Stratford Hotel in Philadelphia.
Comment: Carpet scaring red, this drink is fruity, strong and recommended.

CLUB COCKTAIL

Glass: Martini
Garnish: Maraschino cherry in drink
Method: **STIR** all ingredients with ice and fine strain into chilled glass.

2	shot(s)	**Mount Gay Eclipse golden rum**
1/2	shot(s)	**Rosso (sweet) vermouth**
1/2	shot(s)	**Dry vermouth**
1/2	shot(s)	**Maraschino syrup (from cherry jar)**
4	dashes	**Angostura aromatic bitters**
3/4	shot(s)	**Chilled mineral water (omit if wet ice)**

Origin: David Embury once wrote, "There are as many Club Cocktails as there are clubs." I based this one on a drink created by Michael Butt in 2002 at Milk & Honey, London, England.
Comment: An aromatic, spirited, classical cocktail.

COBBLED RASPBERRY MARTINI

Glass: Martini
Garnish: Mint leaf/raspberries on stick
Method: **MUDDLE** raspberries in base of shaker. Add other ingredients, **SHAKE** with ice and fine strain into chilled glass.

12	fresh	**Raspberries**
2	shot(s)	**Ketel One vodka**
1	shot(s)	**Red wine**
1/2	shot(s)	**Sugar (gomme) syrup**

Origin: Created in 2004 by yours truly.
Comment: The addition of a splash of wine to a simple Raspberry Martini adds another level of complexity.

COBBLERS

Cobblers emerged in the mid 1800s and circa 1880 the bartender Harry Johnson said of the Sherry Cobbler, "This drink is without doubt the most popular beverage in this country, with ladies as well as with gentlemen. It is a very refreshing drink for old and young."

Cobblers are served with straws in a goblet filled with crushed ice and decorated with fruit and a sprig or two of mint. They are based on spirits and/or wine sweetened with sugar syrup or sweet liqueur. Classically Cobblers contain little or no citrus but modern variations often call for citrus and other fruits to be muddled. Personally I believe it's the lack of citrus that sets Cobblers apart. The best examples of these use the tannin and acidity in the wine to bitter and so balance.

Cobblers are also classically built in the glass. I prefer to shake mine to properly cool and mix them before straining over fresh crushed ice and stirring (see my recipe for the Claret Cobbler). I've also recently taken to calling neo-Martinis which use wine in place of citrus 'Cobbled Martinis' (see Cobbled Raspberry Martini).

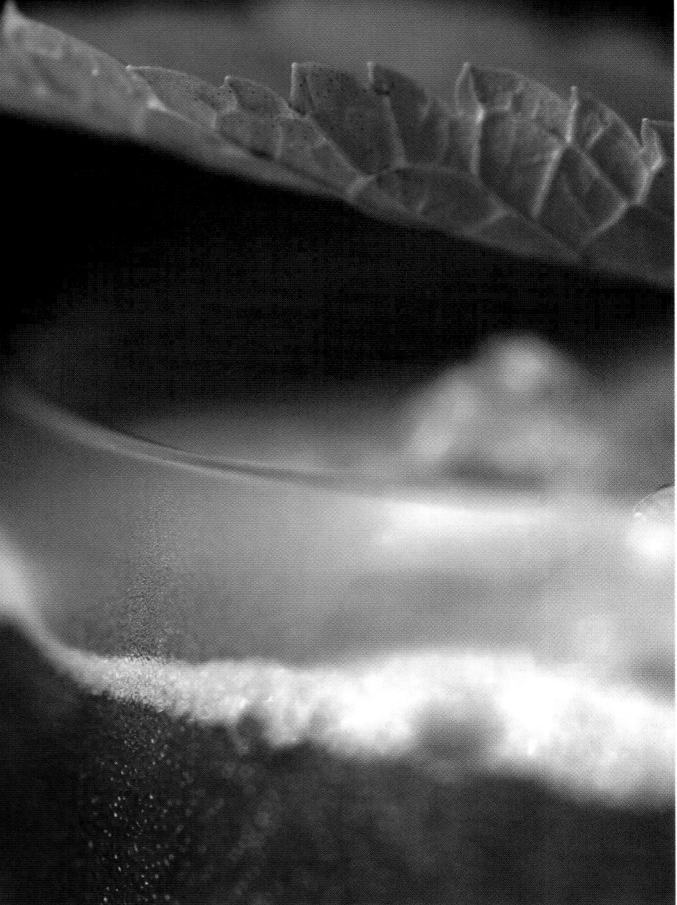

COCO CABANA

Glass: Martini
Garnish: Pineapple wedge on rim
Method: SHAKE all ingredients with ice and fine strain into chilled glass.

1½ shot(s) **Malibu coconut rum liqueur**
½ shot(s) **Midori melon liqueur**
2 shot(s) **Pressed pineapple juice**
¾ shot(s) **Double (heavy) cream**
¾ shot(s) **Milk**

Comment: A sweet, creamy tropical number for Barry Manilow fans.

COCO NAUT

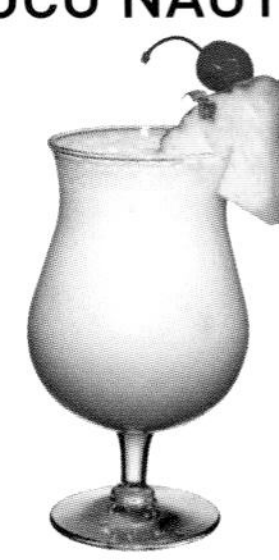

Glass: Hurricane
Garnish: Pineapple wedge on rim
Method: BLEND ingredients with 12oz scoop of crushed ice. Pour into glass and serve with straws.

2 shot(s) **Wray & Nephew overproof rum**
1½ shot(s) **Coco López cream of coconut**
1 shot(s) **Freshly squeezed lime juice**

Comment: This snow-white drink is hardly innocent with a double shot of overproof rum masked by the sweet coconut.

COCONUT DAIQUIRI

Glass: Martini
Method: SHAKE all ingredients with ice and fine strain into chilled glass.

2 shot(s) **Light white rum**
1 shot(s) **Malibu coconut rum liqueur**
½ shot(s) **Freshly squeezed lime juice**
½ shot(s) **Coconut syrup**
¾ shot(s) **Chilled mineral water (omit if wet ice)**

Variant: Blend with a 12oz scoop of crushed ice and a tad more coconut syrup.
Comment: That special Daiquiri flavour with a pleasing tropical touch.

COCONUT WATER

Glass: Martini
Method: STIR all ingredients with ice and fine strain into chilled glass.

2¼ shot(s) **Malibu coconut rum liqueur**
1 shot(s) **Ketel One vodka**
⅛ shot(s) **Coconut syrup**
1¼ shot(s) **Chilled mineral water (reduce if wet ice)**

Origin: Created in 2003 by yours truly.
Comment: Have you ever drunk from a fresh coconut in the Caribbean? Well, this is the alcoholic equivalent.

COFFEE & VANILLA DAIQUIRI

Glass: Martini
Garnish: Float three coffee beans
Method: **SHAKE** all ingredients with ice and fine strain into chilled glass.

2	shot(s)	**Vanilla-infused Havana Club rum**
1	shot(s)	**Kahlúa coffee liqueur**
1/2	shot(s)	**Freshly squeezed lime juice**
1/8	shot(s)	**Sugar (gomme) syrup**
3/4	shot(s)	**Chilled mineral water (omit if wet ice)**

Origin: Created in 2002 by yours truly.
Comment: Coffee, vanilla, sweetness and sourness all in harmony.

COLA DE MONO

Glass: Martini
Garnish: Dust with cinnamon powder
Method: **MUDDLE** cinnamon stick and pisco in base of shaker. Add other ingredients, **SHAKE** with ice and fine strain into a chilled glass.

1	inch	**Cinnamon stick**
2	shot(s)	**Pisco**
1	shot(s)	**Espresso coffee (cold)**
1	shot(s)	**Kahlúa coffee liqueur**

Origin: I based this on a Chilean drink traditionally consumed at Christmas, the name of which literally translates as 'Tail of Monkey'. The original uses milk and sugar instead of coffee liqueur.
Comment: Coffee and cinnamon – a drink to be savoured.

COLD COMFORT

Glass: Old-fashioned
Method: **SHAKE** all ingredients with ice and strain into ice-filled glass.

2	shot(s)	**Wray & Nephew overproof rum**
6	spoons	**Runny honey**
1	shot(s)	**Freshly squeezed lime juice**

Origin: I discovered this while in Jamaica in 2001.
Comment: Take at the first sign of a cold, and then retreat under your bedcovers. Repeat dose regularly while symptoms persist. Warning – do not consume with other forms of medication.

COLLAR & CUFF

Glass: Toddy
Method: Place bar spoon in glass, add ingredients and **STIR**.

2	spoons	**Runny honey**
1	shot(s)	**The Famous Grouse Scotch**
1	shot(s)	**King's ginger liqueur**
1	shot(s)	**Freshly squeezed lemon juice**
Top up with		**Boiling water**

Origin: Created in 2003 by yours truly.
Comment: Warming both due to the hot water and also to the flavour of ginger. One for a cold winter's night.

COLLINS

The Collins is thought to have been created by John Collins, a bartender at Limmer's Hotel, Conduit Street, London, circa 1800. However, others claim that the drink was invented around the same time in New Jersey, USA, by a different Mr Collins, an Irish immigrant who named it after his brother.

There is also debate as to whether Old Tom gin or Dutch Jenever was the original spirit base. Other spirits have since spawned an entire family of variants.

Collins variations include
Captain Collins (with Canadian whiskey)
Colonel Collins (with bourbon)
Jack Collins (with applejack)
Joe Collins (with vodka)
John Collins (with London dry gin)
Mike Collins (with Irish whiskey)
Pedro Collins (with rum)
Pepito Collins (with tequila)
Pierre Collins (with cognac/brandy)
Raspberry Collins
Sandy or Jock Collins (with Scotch whisky)
Tom Collins (with Old Tom gin)
Vodka Collins (AKA Joe Collins)

A
B
C
D
E
F
G
H
I
J
K
L
M
N
O
P
Q
R
S
T
U
V
W
X
Y
Z

COLLECTION MARTINI

Glass: Martini
Garnish: Lime wedge
Method: SHAKE all ingredients with ice and fine strain into chilled glass.

3/4	shot(s)	**Ketel One vodka**
3/4	shot(s)	**Ketel One Citroen vodka**
3/4	shot(s)	**Bénédictine D.O.M liqueur**
3/4	shot(s)	**Crème de mûre (blackberry) liqueur**
1/2	shot(s)	**Freshly squeezed lime juice**

Origin: Originally created by Matthew Randall whilst at The Collection, London, England.
Comment: Honey, spice and vodka enhanced by blackberries, with a very alcoholic edge.

COLLINS

Glass: Collins
Garnish: Orange slice & cherry on stick (sail)
Method: SHAKE first three ingredients with ice and strain into ice-filled glass. **TOP** with soda, stir and serve with straws.

2	shot(s)	**Jonge jenever**
1	shot(s)	**Freshly squeezed lemon juice**
1/2	shot(s)	**Sugar (gomme) syrup**
Top up with		**Soda water (club soda)**

Comment: A refreshing combination of spirit, lemon and sugar.

COLONEL COLLINS

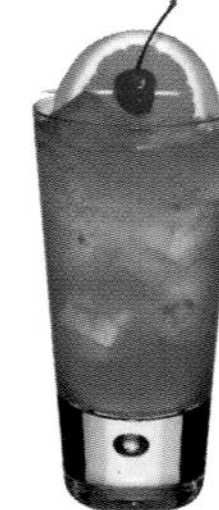

Glass: Collins
Garnish: Orange slice & cherry on stick (sail)
Method: SHAKE first three ingredients with ice and strain into ice-filled glass. **TOP** with soda, stir and serve with straws.

2	shot(s)	**Bourbon whiskey**
1	shot(s)	**Freshly squeezed lemon juice**
1/2	shot(s)	**Sugar (gomme) syrup**
Top up with		**Soda water (club soda)**

Origin: Classic Collins variation.
Comment: Sweetened, soured and diluted bourbon.

COLONEL T

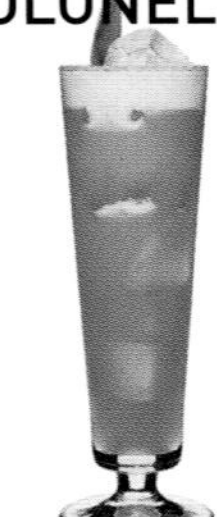

Glass: Sling
Garnish: Pineapple wedge
Method: SHAKE all ingredients with ice and strain into ice-filled glass.

2	shot(s)	**Bourbon whiskey**
1	shot(s)	**Apricot brandy liqueur**
2 1/2	shot(s)	**Pressed pineapple juice**

Comment: Mellow and long with pineapple, apricot and bourbon.

COLONIAL ROT

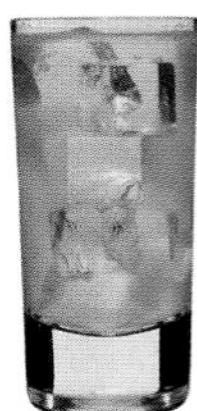

Glass: Collins
Garnish: Mint sprig
Method: Lightly **MUDDLE** mint in base of shaker just enough to bruise. Add next four ingredients, **SHAKE** with ice and fine strain into ice-filled glass. **TOP** up with half soda and half lemonade.

7	fresh	**Mint leaves**
1/2	shot(s)	**La Fée Parisian (68%) absinthe**
1	shot(s)	**Ketel One Citroen vodka**
1/2	shot(s)	**Sugar (gomme) syrup**
1/2	shot(s)	**Freshly squeezed lime juice**
Top up with		**Half soda and half lemonade**

Comment: Long and green with more than a touch of the green fairy.

COLORADO BULLDOG

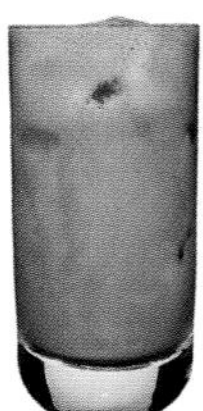

Glass: Collins
Method: SHAKE first four ingredients with ice and strain into ice-filled glass. **TOP** with cola.

1 1/2	shot(s)	**Ketel One vodka**
1	shot(s)	**Kahlúa coffee liqueur**
1	shot(s)	**Double (heavy) cream**
1	shot(s)	**Milk**
Top up with		**Cola**

Variant: Colorado Mother (with tequila in place of vodka).
Comment: This dog's bite is hidden by cream.

CONGO BLUE

Glass: Martini
Garnish: Lemon zest twist
Method: SHAKE all ingredients with ice and fine strain into chilled glass.

1 1/4	shot(s)	**Zubrówka bison vodka**
1/2	shot(s)	**Midori melon liqueur**
1	shot(s)	**Pressed apple juice**
1/2	shot(s)	**Crème de mûre (blackberry) liqueur**
1/4	shot(s)	**Freshly squeezed lemon juice**

Origin: Created in 1999 by Marc Dietrich at Atlantic Bar & Grill, London and apparently named after the beauty of the Congo sunset.
Comment: Flavoursome and sweet.

COOL MARTINI [UPDATED]

Glass: Martini
Garnish: Apple slice chevron
Method: SHAKE all ingredients with ice and fine strain into chilled glass.

1 1/2	shot(s)	**Midori melon liqueur**
1	shot(s)	**Sauza Hornitos tequila**
1 1/2	shot(s)	**Cranberry juice**

Comment: Tastes nothing like the ingredients - which include melon, tequila and cranberry juice. Try it and see if you taste toffee.

●●●●○

COOL ORCHARD

Glass: Old-fashioned
Garnish: Pineapple wedge & cherry
Method: **MUDDLE** ginger in base of shaker. Add other ingredients, **SHAKE** with ice and fine strain into ice-filled glass.

2	slices	**Fresh root ginger (thumbnail sized)**
1 1/2	shot(s)	**Appleton Estate V/X aged rum**
1/2	shot(s)	**Ginger sugar syrup**
1/4	shot(s)	**Almond (orgeat) sugar syrup**
1	shot(s)	**Pressed pineapple juice**
1/2	shot(s)	**Vanilla schnapps liqueur**
1/4	shot(s)	**Freshly squeezed lime juice**

Origin: Created in 2001 by Douglas Ankrah for Akbar, Soho, London, England.
Comment: An unusual line up of cocktail ingredients combine to make a great drink.

●●●●◐

COOLMAN MARTINI

Glass: Martini
Garnish: Orange zest twist
Method: **SHAKE** all ingredients with ice and fine strain into chilled glass.

1 3/4	shot(s)	**Zubrówka bison vodka**
1/2	shot(s)	**Cointreau / triple sec**
2	shot(s)	**Pressed apple juice**
1/4	shot(s)	**Freshly squeezed lemon juice**

Origin: Created in 2001 by Jack Coleman at The Library Bar, Lanesborough Hotel, London, England.
Comment: Fragrant and complex. Integrated hints of apple and orange are laced with grassy vodka.

●●●●○

COPPER ILLUSION [NEW]

Glass: Old-fashioned
Garnish: Orange zest twist
Method: **STIR** all ingredients with ice and strain into ice-filled glass.

1 1/2	shot(s)	**Plymouth gin**
3/4	shot(s)	**Campari**
3/4	shot(s)	**Cointreau / triple sec**

Variant: Negroni
Origin: Unknown but brought to my attention in 2005 courtesy of Angus Winchester and www.alconomics.com.
Comment: Basically a Negroni with liqueur replacing sweet vermouth. Like the Italian classic this is both bitter and sweet.

DRINKS ARE GRADED AS FOLLOWS:

● DISGUSTING ●◐ PRETTY AWFUL ●● BEST AVOIDED
●●◐ DISAPPOINTING ●●● ACCEPTABLE ●●●◐ GOOD
●●●● RECOMMENDED ●●●●◐ HIGHLY RECOMMENDED
●●●●● OUTSTANDING / EXCEPTIONAL

●●●○○

CORDLESS SCREWDRIVER

Glass: Shot
Garnish: Sugar coated half orange slice
Method: **POUR** vodka and champagne into glass and serve. Instruct drinker to down in one and then bite into the orange wedge.

1	shot(s)	**Orange flavoured vodka**
Top up with		**Piper-Heidsieck brut champagne**

Comment: A slammer style drink for those looking for a fruity alternative to tequila.

●●●○○

CORONATION

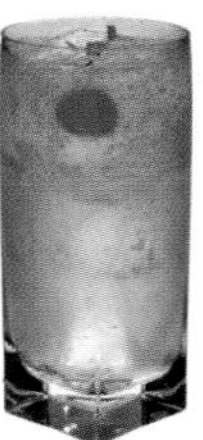

Glass: Collins
Garnish: Maraschino cherry
Method: **STIR** first five ingredients with ice and strain into ice-filled glass. **TOP** with soda, stir and serve with straws.

1	shot(s)	**Tio Pepe fino sherry**
1	shot(s)	**Dry vermouth**
2	shot(s)	**Sauvignon Blanc / unoaked Chardonnay wine**
1/4	shot(s)	**Luxardo maraschino liqueur**
2	dashes	**Angostura aromatic bitters**
Top up with		**Soda water (club soda)**

Comment: Light and aromatic.

●●●◐○

CORONATION MARTINI [NEW]

Glass: Martini
Garnish: Orange zest twist
Martini: **STIR** all ingredients with ice and strain into chilled glass.

1 3/4	shot(s)	**Tio Pepe fino sherry**
1 3/4	shot(s)	**Dry vermouth**
1/4	shot(s)	**Luxardo maraschino liqueur**
2	dashes	**Fee Brothers orange bitters**

Origin: A long lost classic from the 1930s.
Comment: Medium dry and aromatic.

●●●●○

CORPSE REVIVER

Glass: Martini
Garnish: Orange zest twist
Method: **STIR** ingredients with ice and strain into chilled glass.

1 1/2	shot(s)	**Rémy Martin cognac**
1	shot(s)	**Calvados (or applejack brandy)**
1	shot(s)	**Rosso (sweet) vermouth**
1/4	shot(s)	**Chilled mineral water**

Origin: Created by Frank Meier, Ritz Bar, Paris, France.
Comment: Pick-me-up hangover cure – or possibly put-you-right-back-down!

COSMOPOLITAN

The Cosmopolitan was, until recently, thought to have derived from a drink called the Harpoon, promoted by Ocean Spray during the 1960s. This consisted of vodka, cranberry juice and a squeeze of fresh lime. However, the latest research suggests that the cocktail was created by Cheryl Cook in the latter half of the 1980s while head bartender at The Strand on Washington Avenue, South Beach, Miami. She based her drink on the newly available Absolut Citron vodka and added a splash of triple sec, a dash of Rose's lime and, in her own words, "just enough cranberry to make it oh so pretty in pink".

The drink is believed to have travelled by way of San Francisco to Manhattan where Toby Cecchini is credited with first using fresh lime juice in place of Rose's at his Passerby bar. Whatever the origin, however, it is Sex And The City's Carrie Bradshaw who popularised the drink when she swapped Martinis for Cosmos.

Cosmopolitan variations include
Apricot Cosmo
Blue Cosmo
Blue Fin
Chinese Cosmopolitan
Cosmopolitan #1 (simple version)
Cosmopolitan # 2 (complex version
Ginger Cosmo
Grand Cosmopolitan
Hawaiian Cosmopolitan
Limey Cosmo
Metropolitan
Raspberry Cosmo
Royal Cosmopolitan
Rude Cosmopolitan
Rude Ginger Cosmopolitan
Sake'politan
Strawberry Cosmo
Watermelon Cosmo
White Cosmo
The Windsor Rose

COSMOPOLITAN #1 (SIMPLE) [UPDATED]

Glass: Martini
Garnish: Flamed orange zest twist
Method: **SHAKE** all ingredients with ice and fine strain into chilled glass.

1 shot(s) **Ketel One Citroen vodka**
1 shot(s) **Cointreau / triple sec**
1½ shot(s) **Cranberry juice**
½ shot(s) **Freshly squeezed lime juice**

Origin: My latest (2005), and apart from the drink below, I think best formula for this modern day classic.
Comment: When a quality juice with at least 24% cranberry is used, the balance of citrus, berry fruit and sweetness is perfect.

COSMOPOLITAN #2 (COMPLEX) [UPDATED]

Glass: Martini
Garnish: Flamed orange zest twist
Method: **SHAKE** all ingredients with ice and fine strain into chilled glass.

1 shot(s) **Ketel One Citroen vodka**
1 shot(s) **Cointreau / triple sec**
1½ shot(s) **Cranberry juice**
½ shot(s) **Freshly squeezed lime juice**
¼ shot(s) **Rose's lime cordial**
4 dashes **Fee Brothers orange bitters**

Origin: Formula by yours truly in 2005.
Comment: For those who are not content with simplicity.

COSMOPOLITAN DELIGHT

Glass: Martini
Garnish: Flamed orange zest twist
Method: **SHAKE** all ingredients with ice and fine strain into chilled glass.

1½ shot(s) **Rémy Martin cognac**
½ shot(s) **Grand Marnier**
1¼ shot(s) **Shiraz red wine**
¾ shot(s) **Freshly squeezed lemon juice**
¼ shot(s) **Almond (orgeat) syrup**
¼ shot(s) **Sugar (gomme) syrup**

Origin: Adapted from Dale DeGroff's book, 'The Craft of the Cocktail'. He credits the original recipe to a 1902 book by Charlie Paul.
Comment: No relation to the modern Cosmopolitan, this is a mellow, balanced blend of citrus, brandy and red wine.

COUNTRY BREEZE [NEW]

Glass: Collins
Garnish: Berries
Method: **SHAKE** all ingredients with ice and strain into ice-filled glass.

2 shot(s) **Plymouth gin**
½ shot(s) **Sisca crème de cassis**
3½ shot(s) **Pressed apple juice**

Comment: Not too sweet. The gin character shines through the fruit.

COWBOY MARTINI

Glass: Martini
Garnish: Orange zest twist
Method: Lightly **MUDDLE** mint in base of shaker just enough to bruise. Add other ingredients, **SHAKE** with ice and fine strain into chilled glass.

7	fresh	**Mint leaves**
3	shot(s)	**Plymouth gin**
1/2	shot(s)	**Sugar (gomme) syrup**
3	dashes	**Fee Brothers orange bitters (optional)**

AKA: The Cooperstown Cocktail
Origin: Created in the early 90s by Dick Bradsell at Detroit, London, England.
Comment: Sweetened gin shaken with fresh mint.

COX'S DAIQUIRI

Glass: Martini
Garnish: Cox's apple ring (in memory of Jennings Cox)
Method: SHAKE all ingredients with ice and fine strain into chilled glass.

2 1/2	shot(s)	**Vanilla-infused Havana Club rum**
1/2	shot(s)	**Freshly squeezed lime juice**
1/4	shot(s)	**Vanilla sugar syrup**
1	shot(s)	**Freshly pressed pineapple juice**

Origin: One of two cocktails with which I won 'The Best Daiquiri in London Competition' in 2002. It is named after Jennings Cox, the American mining engineer credited with first creating the Daiquiri.
Comment: Vanilla and pineapple bring out the sweetness of the rum against a citrus background.

CRANAPPLE BREEZE

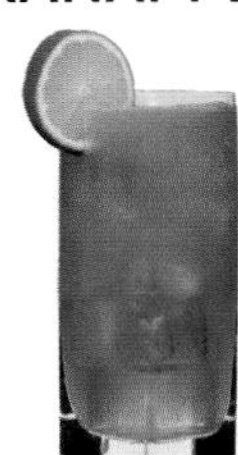

Glass: Collins
Garnish: Lime wheel on rim
Method: SHAKE first five ingredients with ice and strain into ice-filled glass. **TOP** with ginger ale and stir.

1	shot(s)	**Ketel One Citroen vodka**
1	shot(s)	**Cointreau / triple sec**
1	shot(s)	**Cranberry juice**
1	shot(s)	**Pressed apple juice**
1/2	shot(s)	**Freshly squeezed lime juice**
Top up with		**Ginger ale**

Origin: Created in 2002 by Wayne Collins.
Comment: A refreshing cooler for a hot day by the pool.

CRANBERRY COOLER

Glass: Collins
Garnish: Orange slice
Method: SHAKE all ingredients with ice and strain into ice-filled glass.

2	shot(s)	**Luxardo Amaretto di Saschira**
2	shot(s)	**Cranberry juice**
2	shot(s)	**Freshly squeezed orange juice**

Comment: Easy drinking for those with a sweet tooth.

CRANBERRY & MINT MARTINI

Glass: Martini
Garnish: Float mint leaf
Method: Lightly **MUDDLE** mint in base of shaker just enough to bruise. Add other ingredients, **SHAKE** with ice and fine strain into chilled glass.

8	fresh	**Mint leaves**
2	shot(s)	**Cranberry flavoured vodka**
2	shot(s)	**Cranberry juice**
1/4	shot(s)	**Pomegranate (grenadine) syrup**

Origin: Created in 2003 by yours truly.
Comment: This little red number combines the dryness of cranberry, the sweetness of grenadine and the fragrance of mint.

CRANBERRY MARTINI

Glass: Martini
Garnish: Redcurrants
Method: SHAKE all ingredients with ice and fine strain into chilled glass.

2	shot(s)	**Cranberry flavoured vodka**
1/4	shot(s)	**Dry vermouth**
1/8	shot(s)	**Campari**
1 1/2	shot(s)	**Cranberry juice**
1/4	shot(s)	**Sugar (gomme) syrup**

Origin: Created in 2003 by yours truly.
Comment: Full on cranberry with that characteristic dry edge.

CRANBERRY SAUCE

Glass: Martini
Garnish: Dried cranberries in base of glass
Method: SHAKE all ingredients with ice and fine strain into chilled glass.

2	shot(s)	**Cranberry flavoured vodka**
2	shot(s)	**Cranberry juice**
1	shot(s)	**Lapponia cranberry liqueur**

Origin: Created in 2003 by yours truly.
Comment: Rich, fruity flavour but with that customary dry cranberry finish.

CREAMSICLE

Glass: Martini
Garnish: Orange zest twist
Method: SHAKE all ingredients with ice and fine strain into chilled glass.

1 1/2	shot(s)	**Orange flavoured vodka**
1	shot(s)	**Grand Marnier**
3/4	shot(s)	**Double cream**
3/4	shot(s)	**Milk**
1/4	shot(s)	**Sugar (gomme) syrup**

Origin: Adapted from a cocktail discovered in 1999 at Lot 61, New York City, USA.
Comment: A milky orange number with a surprisingly pleasant taste.

CREAMY BEE

Glass: Martini
Garnish: Cinnamon rim & raspberry
Method: **SHAKE** all ingredients with ice and fine strain into chilled glass.

1½	shot(s)	**Krupnik honey liqueur**
½	shot(s)	**Baileys Irish cream liqueur**
½	shot(s)	**Chambord black raspberry liqueur**
½	shot(s)	**Hazelnut (crème de noisette) liqueur**
¼	shot(s)	**Goldschläger cinnamon schnapps**

Origin: Created in 2002 at Hush, London, England and originally made with cinnamon syrup in place of Goldschläger.
Comment: Creamy cinnamon with hints of honey, nuts and berries.

CREAMY CREAMSICLE

Glass: Martini
Method: **SHAKE** all ingredients with ice and fine strain into chilled glass.

½	shot(s)	**Orange flavoured vodka**
1¼	shot(s)	**Luxardo Amaretto di Saschira**
1	shot(s)	**Freshly squeezed orange juice**
¾	shot(s)	**Double (heavy) cream**
¾	shot(s)	**Milk**

Comment: Almond and orange smoothed with cream.

CREAM CAKE

Glass: Martini
Garnish: Crumbled Cadbury's Flake bar
Method: **SHAKE** all ingredients with ice and fine strain into chilled glass.

1¼	shot(s)	**Baileys Irish cream liqueur**
1¼	shot(s)	**Peach schnapps liqueur**
1¼	shot(s)	**Luxardo Amaretto di Saschira**
1	shot(s)	**Double (heavy) cream**

Comment: Creamy pleasure for the sweet of tooth.

CRÈME ANGLAISE MARTINI [NEW]

Glass: Martini
Garnish: Dust with cocoa powder
Method: **SHAKE** all ingredients with ice and fine strain into chilled glass.

1	shot(s)	**Vanilla-infused Ketel One vodka**
2	shot(s)	**Advocaat liqueur**
1	shot(s)	**Milk**

Origin: Created in 2004 by yours truly.
Comment: Very reminiscent of alcoholic crème anglaise.

CRÈME BRÛLÉE MARTINI

Glass: Martini
Garnish: Dust with cinnamon powder
Method: **SHAKE** all ingredients with ice and fine strain into chilled glass.

2	shot(s)	**Vanilla flavoured vodka**
½	shot(s)	**Cartron caramel liqueur**
¾	shot(s)	**Licor 43 (Cuarenta Y Tres) liqueur**
1	shot(s)	**Double (heavy) cream**
½	fresh	**Egg yolk**

Origin: Adapted from a drink created in 2002 by Yannick Miseriaux at the Fifth Floor Bar, London, England.
Comment: OK, so there's no crust, but this does contain egg yolk, caramel, vanilla, sugar and cream. Due to the cinnamon, it even has a brown top.

CRÈME DE CAFÉ

Glass: Old-fashioned
Method: **SHAKE** ingredients with ice and strain into ice-filled glass.

1	shot(s)	**Kahlúa coffee liqueur**
¾	shot(s)	**Mount Gay Eclipse golden rum**
¾	shot(s)	**Luxardo Sambuca dei Cesari**
1	shot(s)	**Double (heavy) cream**
1	shot(s)	**Milk**

Comment: Coffee predominates over the creaminess with hints of aniseed and rum.

CRIME OF PASSION SHOT

Glass: Shot
Method: **SHAKE** all ingredients with ice and fine strain into chilled glass.

½	shot(s)	**Cherry (brandy) liqueur**
½	shot(s)	**Passoã passion fruit liqueur**
½	shot(s)	**Ketel One vodka**

Comment: Passion, cherry and vodka - hardly criminal.

CRIMSON BLUSH [NEW]

Glass: Martini
Garnish: Berries
Method: **SHAKE** all ingredients with ice and fine strain into chilled glass.

2	shot(s)	**Ketel One Citroen vodka**
½	shot(s)	**Chambord black raspberry liqueur**
2	shot(s)	**Squeezed golden grapefruit juice**
¼	shot(s)	**Sugar (gomme) syrup**

Origin: Created in 2004 by Jonathan Lamm at The Admirable Crichton, London, England.
Comment: Well balanced, fruity sweet and sour.

A B C D E F G H I J K L M N O P Q R S T U V W X Y Z

CRIMSON TIDE

Glass: Old-fashioned
Garnish: Raspberries
Method: **MUDDLE** raspberries in base of shaker. Add other ingredients, **SHAKE** with ice and strain into glass filled with crushed ice.

7 fresh **Raspberries**
1¼ shot(s) **Raspberry flavoured vodka**
1 shot(s) **Hazelnut (crème de noisette) liqueur**
½ shot(s) **Chambord black raspberry liqueur**
¼ shot(s) **Freshly squeezed lime juice**

Comment: A medium-sweet tidal wave of flavours.

CROUCHING TIGER [NEW]

Glass: Shot
Method: **SHAKE** all ingredients with ice and fine strain into chilled glass.

¾ shot(s) **Sauza Hornitos tequila**
½ shot(s) **Soho lychee liqueur**

Comment: Tequila and lychee combine harmoniously in this semi –sweet shot.

CROWN STAG

Glass: Old-fashioned
Garnish: Slice of lemon
Method: **SHAKE** ingredients with ice and strain into ice-filled glass.

1½ shot(s) **Ketel One vodka**
1½ shot(s) **Jägermeister liqueur**
1 shot(s) **Chambord black raspberry liqueur**

Comment: A surprisingly workable combination.

CUBA LIBRE

Glass: Collins
Garnish: Lime wedge
Method: **POUR** ingredients into ice-filled glass, stir and serve with straws.

2 shot(s) **Light white rum**
½ shot(s) **Freshly squeezed lime juice**
Top up with **Cola**

Origin: This classic mix was allegedly so named in the early 1890s when a group of off-duty American soldiers were gathered in a bar in old Havana drinking rum and the soft drink, Coca Cola. The Captain raised his glass and sang out the battle cry that had inspired Cuba's victorious soldiers at war, Cuba Libre. But, nice although this story is, Coca Cola was not available in Havana in the early 90s.

The Cuba Libre peaked in popularity during the 1940s. During the war, all spirits production went over to industrial alcohol - in the absence of whiskey and gin, Americans turned to imported rum. Some think the drink was named for the Andrews Sisters song, Cuba Libre.
Comment: Basically a rum and cola with a squeeze of lime – Cuba Libre sounds better though!

CUBAN MASTER [UPDATED]

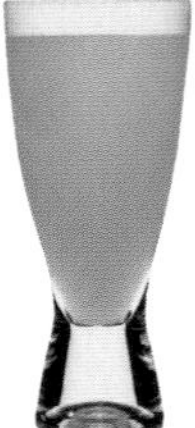

Glass: Collins
Garnish: Pineapple wedge
Method: **SHAKE** all ingredients with ice and strain into ice-filled glass.

1½ shot(s) **Light white rum**
1 shot(s) **Rémy Martin cognac**
1½ shot(s) **Freshly squeezed orange juice**
1½ shot(s) **Pressed pineapple juice**
½ shot(s) **Freshly squeezed lemon juice**
¼ shot(s) **Sugar (gomme) syrup**

Origin: A classic cocktail I discovered in 1999 during a trip to Cuba.
Comment: Well balanced, wonderfully fruity.

CUBAN SPECIAL [UPDATED]

Glass: Old-fashioned
Garnish: Orange zest twist
Method: **SHAKE** ingredients with ice and strain into ice-filled glass.

1½ shot(s) **Light white rum**
¾ shot(s) **Cointreau / triple sec**
2 shot(s) **Pressed pineapple juice**
¼ shot(s) **Freshly squeezed lime juice**

Comment: Not that special, but certainly OK.

CUBANITA

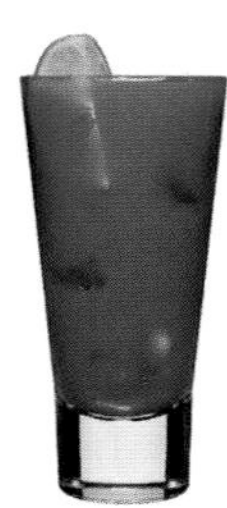

Glass: Collins
Garnish: Lime wedge
Method: **SHAKE** all ingredients with ice and strain into ice-filled glass.

2 shot(s) **Light white rum**
4 shot(s) **Pressed tomato juice**
½ shot(s) **Freshly squeezed lemon juice**
8 drops **Tabasco pepper sauce**
4 dashes **Lea & Perrins Worcestershire sauce**
½ spoon **Horseradish sauce**
2 pinch **Celery salt**
2 pinch **Black pepper**

Comment: The Bloody Mary returns - this time with rum.

CUCUMBER MARTINI

Glass: Martini
Garnish: Strip of cucumber
Method: **MUDDLE** cucumber in base of shaker. Add other ingredients, **SHAKE** with ice and strain into glass.

2 inches **Peeled chopped cucumber**
1 shot(s) **Zubrówka bison vodka**
1 shot(s) **Ketel One vodka**
½ shot(s) **Sugar (gomme) syrup**

Origin: There are many different Cucumber Martini recipes; this is mine.
Comment: Cucumber has never tasted so good.

CUCUMBER & MINT MARTINI [NEW]

Glass: Martini
Garnish: Cucumber wheel
Method: MUDDLE cucumber and mint in base of shaker. Add other ingredients, **SHAKE** with ice and fine strain into chilled glass.

2	inches	**Peeled diced cucumber**
7	fresh	**Mint leaves**
2	shot(s)	**Ketel One vodka**
1	shot(s)	**Pressed apple juice**
$\frac{1}{4}$	shot(s)	**Sugar (gomme) syrup**

Origin: Created in 2004 by David Ramos in the Netherlands.
Comment: A well balanced fortified salad in a glass – almost healthy.

CUCUMBER SAKE-TINI

Glass: Martini
Garnish: Three cucumber slices
Method: MUDDLE cucumber in base of shaker. Add other ingredients, **SHAKE** with ice and fine strain into chilled glass.

$1\frac{1}{2}$	inch	**Peeled diced cucumber**
$1\frac{1}{2}$	shot(s)	**Ketel One vodka**
$1\frac{1}{2}$	shot(s)	**Sake**
$\frac{1}{4}$	shot(s)	**Sugar (gomme) syrup**

Origin: Created in 2004 by Lisa Ball, London, England.
Comment: Subtle and dry. Cucumber and sake are made for each other.

CUMBERSOME

Glass: Martini
Garnish: Physalis (Cape gooseberry) on rim
Method: MUDDLE cucumber in base of shaker. Add other ingredients, **SHAKE** with ice and strain into a chilled Martini glass.

4	inch	**Fresh chopped peeled cucumber**
2	shot(s)	**Plymouth gin**
$\frac{1}{2}$	shot(s)	**Campari**
1	shot(s)	**Freshly squeezed orange juice**
$\frac{1}{2}$	shot(s)	**Sugar (gomme) syrup**

Origin: Created in 2002 by Shelim Islam at the GE Club, London, England.
Comment: Interesting and fresh as you like with a pleasant bitterness.

CUPPA JOE

Glass: Martini
Garnish: Lemon zest twist
Method: SHAKE all ingredients with ice and fine strain into chilled glass.

$1\frac{1}{2}$	shot(s)	**Ketel One vodka**
$1\frac{1}{2}$	shot(s)	**Hazelnut (crème de noisette) liqueur**
$1\frac{1}{2}$	shot(s)	**Espresso coffee (cold)**

Origin: Created in 2003 at Cellar Bar, New York City, USA.
Comment: Nutty coffee fortified with vodka – well balanced.

CURDISH MARTINI [UPDATED]

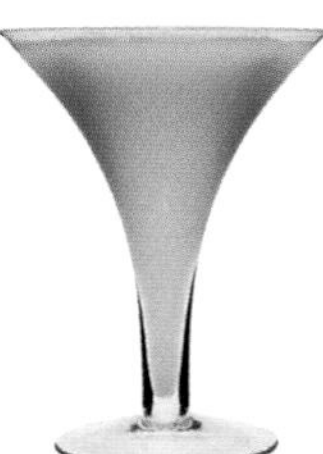

Glass: Martini
Garnish: Lemon zest twist
Method: SHAKE all ingredients with ice and fine strain into chilled glass.

2	shot(s)	**Plymouth gin**
$\frac{1}{2}$	shot(s)	**Sour apple liqueur**
$\frac{3}{4}$	shot(s)	**Freshly squeezed lime juice**
2	spoons	**Lemon curd**

Origin: Created in 2001 by Tadgh Ryan at West Street, London, England.
Comment: Beautifully balanced with the tang of lemon curd.

CUSTARD TART

Glass: Shot
Garnish: Physalis (Cape gooseberry) on rim
Method: MUDDLE physalis fruits in base of shaker can. Add other ingredients, **SHAKE** with ice and strain.

3	fresh	**Physalis fruits**
$\frac{3}{4}$	shot(s)	**Light white rum**
$\frac{1}{2}$	shot(s)	**Peach schnapps liqueur**
$\frac{1}{4}$	shot(s)	**Freshly squeezed lime juice**
$\frac{1}{2}$	shot(s)	**Advocaat liqueur**

Origin: Created by Alex Kammerling in 2001.
Comment: Custardy, strangely enough.

HOW TO MAKE SUGAR SYRUP

To make your own sugar syrup, gradually pour **TWO cups of granulated sugar into a saucepan containing ONE cup of hot water.** Stir as you pour and carry on stirring and simmering until the sugar is dissolved. Do not let the water even come close to boiling and only simmer for as long as it takes to dissolve the sugar. Allow syrup to cool and pour into an empty bottle. Ideally, you should finely strain your syrup into the bottle to remove any undissolved crystals which could otherwise encourage crystallisation. If kept in a refrigerator this mixture will last for a couple of months.

DAIQUIRI

Pronounced 'Dye-Ker-Ree', this drink is thought to have been created by Jennings Cox, an American engineer who was working at a copper mine near Santiago, Cuba, in 1896.

The popular version of the drink's origin states that another engineer called Pagliuchi was viewing mines in the region and met with Cox. During their meeting they set about making a drink from the ingredients Cox had to hand: rum, limes and sugar. The concoction was exquisite and Cox named the drink Daiquiri after the nearby port.

According to Cox's granddaughter, however, Cox ran out of gin when entertaining American guests. Wary of serving them straight rum, he added lime and sugar.

The Daiquiri seems to have come to America with US Admiral Lucius Johnson, who fought in the Spanish-American war of 1898. He introduced the drink to the Army & Navy Club in Washington DC and a plaque in their Daiquiri Lounge records his place in cocktail history.

The classic proportions of a Daiquiri are 8 parts rum to 2 parts lime juice to 1 part sugar syrup. (This translates as two shots of rum, half a shot of lime juice and quarter of a shot of sugar syrup.) Most of the Daiquiri recipes in this guide are based on these proportions.

Daiquiris are classically shaken and served straight-up or on the rocks. The frozen, blended version is said to have first been produced by Emilio Gonzalez at the Plaza Hotel in Cuba. However, Constantino (Constante) Ribalaigua Vert of Havana's Floridita bar made the drink famous in 1912 and today the Floridita is known as 'the cradle of the Daiquiri'.

Ernest Hemingway, the hard-drinking, Nobel prize-winning author, lived in Cuba for years, indulging his passions for fishing, shooting and boozing. In the 30s and the 40s he would often work his way through twelve of the Floridita's frozen Daiquiris - often doubles, called Papa Dobles in his honour. The Hemingway Special Daiquiri, which includes grapefruit, was created for him and continues to bear his name.

In his book 'Islands in the Stream', Hemingway's hero stares deep into his frozen Daiquiri, and Hemingway observes, "It reminded him of the sea. The frappéd part of the drink was like the wake of a ship and the clear part was the way the water looked when the bow cut it when you were in shallow water over marl bottom. That was almost the exact colour." The great man's bar stool can still be seen at the Floridita today.

DAIQUIRI VARIANTS

Acapulco Daiquiri
Ace Of Clubs Daiquiri
Aged Honey Daiquiri
Apple Daiquiri
Bahamas Daiquiri
Banana Daiquiri
Basil & Honey Daiquiri
Bella Donna Daiquiri
Black & White Daiquiri
Blueberry Daiquiri
Blueberry Pie Daiquiri
Butterscotch Daiquiri
Cachaça Daiquiri
Charles Daiquiri
Cherry & Hazelnut Daiquiri
Cherry Daiquiri
Chiclet Daiquiri
Cinnamon Daiquiri
Classic Daiquiri
Coconut Daiquiri
Coffee & Vanilla Daiquiri
Cox's Daiquiri
Daiquiri De Luxe
Dark Daiquiri
Derby Daiquiri
Difford's Daiquiri
El Presidente Daiquiri
Epestone Daiquiri
Floridita Daiquiri
Four W Daiquiri
French Daiquiri
Fruit Tree Daiquiri
Fu Manchu Daiquiri
Grapefruit Daiquiri
Greta Garbo
Havanatheone
Hemingway Special Daiquiri
Honey Daiquiri
Honeysuckle Daiquiri
Lisa B's Daiquiri
Lux Daiquiri
Mango Daiquiri
Melon Daiquiri
Miami Daiquiri
Millionaire's Daiquiri
Mulata Daiquiri
Naranja Daiquiri
Natural Daiquiri
Nevada Daiquiri
Orange Daiquiri
Passion Fruit Daiquiri
Peach Daiquiri
Peach Daiquiri Frozen
Pineapple & Cardamom Daiquiri
Pirate Daiquiri
Plum Daiquiri
Snow White Daiquiri
Spiced Apple Daiquiri
Strawberry Daiquiri
Strawberry Frozen Daiquiri
Turquoise Daiquiri
Vanilla Daiquiri

●●●●●

DAIQUIRI (CLASSIC)

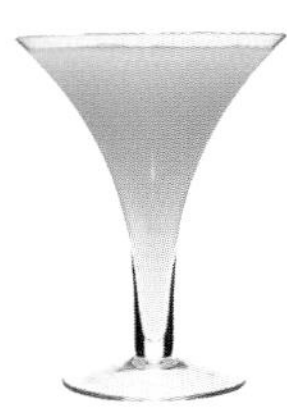

Glass: Martini
Garnish: Lime wedge on rim
Method: SHAKE all ingredients with ice and fine strain into chilled glass.

2	shot(s)	**Light or aged rum**
1/2	shot(s)	**Freshly squeezed lime juice**
1/4	shot(s)	**Sugar (gomme) syrup**
1/2	shot(s)	**Chilled mineral water (omit if wet ice)**

Origin: The creation of this drink is attributed to Mr Jennings Cox, an American engineer who was working at a mine near Santiago, Cuba in 1896.
Comment: This 'classic' Daiquiri is more properly titled a 'Natural' Daiquiri, but both terms are generally recognised as denoting that the drink should be shaken and served 'up' rather than blended with crushed ice.

●●●●○

DAIQUIRI DE LUXE [NEW]

Glass: Martini
Garnish: Lime wedge on rim
Method: SHAKE all ingredients with ice and fine strain into chilled glass.

2	shot(s)	**Light white rum**
1/4	shot(s)	**Rose's lime cordial**
1/2	shot(s)	**Freshly squeezed lime juice**
1/4	shot(s)	**Almond (orgeat) syrup**
1/4	shot(s)	**Chilled mineral water (omit if wet ice)**

Comment: A classic Daiquiri but with lime cordial and almond syrup replacing sugar as the sweetener.

●●●●●

DAIQUIRI ON THE ROCKS

Glass: Old-fashioned
Garnish: Lime wedge & maraschino cherry
Method: SHAKE all ingredients with ice and strain into ice-filled glass.

2	shot(s)	**Light white rum (or aged rum)**
1/2	shot(s)	**Freshly squeezed lime juice**
1/4	shot(s)	**Sugar (gomme) syrup**

Comment: Some hardened Daiquiri-philes prefer their tipple served over ice in an old-fashioned glass, arguing that a Martini glass is too dainty.

DRINKS ARE GRADED AS FOLLOWS:

● DISGUSTING ●◐ PRETTY AWFUL ●● BEST AVOIDED
●●◐ DISAPPOINTING ●●● ACCEPTABLE ●●●◐ GOOD
●●●● RECOMMENDED ●●●●◐ HIGHLY RECOMMENDED
●●●●● OUTSTANDING / EXCEPTIONAL

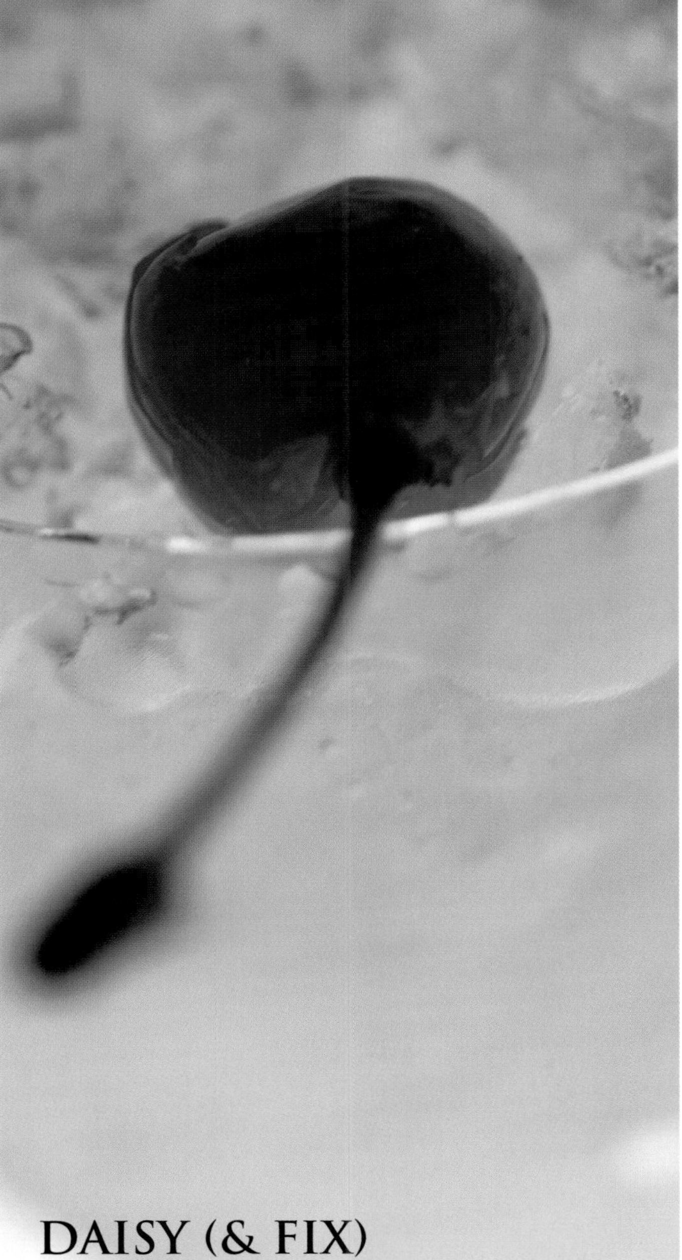

DAISY (& FIX)

There is little difference, if any, between a Daisy and a Fix. Both are very old drinks dating back to Victorian times and both terms are used fairly loosely. Both are of the Sour genre and consist of a citrus juice, sweetened with a syrup or liqueur, and fortified with a base spirit. However, Fixes tend to call for pineapple or sugar syrup while Daisies usually call for raspberry syrup or grenadine.

Daisies and Fixes are most commonly served in a goblet filled with crushed ice but Daisies can also be served straight-up or in a Collins glass.

Both drinks are traditionally garnished with seasonal fruit but modern tastes dictate simplicity.

DAISY DUKE [NEW]

Glass: Old-fashioned
Garnish: Berries
Method: SHAKE all ingredients with ice and strain into glass filled with crushed ice. Serve with straws.

2	shot(s)	**Bourbon whiskey**
1	shot(s)	**Freshly squeezed lemon juice**
½	shot(s)	**Pomegranate (grenadine) syrup**

Origin: Created in 2002 by Jake Burger at Townhouse, Leeds, England.
Comment: This bright red drink tastes more adult than it looks.

DAMN-THE-WEATHER

Glass: Martini
Method: SHAKE all ingredients with ice and fine strain into chilled glass.

1	shot(s)	**Plymouth gin**
1	shot(s)	**Sweet (rosso) vermouth**
½	shot(s)	**Cointreau / triple sec**
1½	shot(s)	**Freshly squeezed orange juice**

Comment: Gin and herbal notes emerge in this predominantly orange drink.

DAMSON IN DISTRESS

Glass: Shot
Method: SHAKE all ingredients with ice and fine strain into chilled glass.

1½	shot(s)	**Plymouth damson gin liqueur**
½	shot(s)	**Luxardo Amaretto di Saschira**
¼	shot(s)	**Freshly squeezed lemon juice**

Origin: Discovered in 2003 at Hush, London, England.
Comment: Damson and amaretto sharpened by lemon juice.

DANDY COCKTAIL [NEW]

Glass: Martini
Garnish: Lemon and orange zest twists
Method: STIR all ingredients with ice and strain into chilled glass.

1½	shot(s)	**Bourbon whiskey**
1½	shot(s)	**Dubonnet Red**
½	shot(s)	**Cointreau/triple sec**
3	dashes	**Angostura aromatic bitters**

Origin: A classic from the 1930s.
Comment: A complex, well balanced combo of spirit, liqueur and aromatic wine.

DARK DAIQUIRI

Glass: Martini
Garnish: Lime wedge
Method: SHAKE all ingredients with ice and fine strain into chilled glass.

1½	shot(s)	**Aged rum**
½	shot(s)	**Pusser's Navy rum**
½	shot(s)	**Freshly squeezed lime juice**
½	shot(s)	**Sugar (gomme) syrup**
¾	shot(s)	**Chilled mineral water (omit if wet ice)**

Comment: The fine sweet and sour balance of a great Daiquiri with hints of molasses.

DARK 'N' STORMY

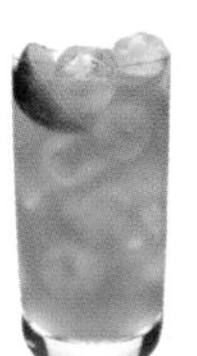

Glass: Collins
Garnish: Lime wedge
Method: SHAKE first three ingredients with ice and strain into ice-filled glass. **TOP** with ginger beer, stir and serve with straws.

2	shot(s)	**Gosling's Black Seal rum**
1	shot(s)	**Freshly squeezed lime juice**
½	shot(s)	**Sugar (gomme) syrup**
Top up with		**Ginger beer**

Origin: The national drink of Bermuda, where ginger beer and Gosling's rum are produced.
Comment: This deliciously spicy drink is part of the Mule family - but is distinctive due to the strong flavour of the rum.

DC MARTINI

Glass: Martini
Method: STIR all ingredients with ice and strain into chilled glass.

2	shot(s)	**Vanilla infused aged rum**
¼	shot(s)	**Hazelnut (crème de noisette) liqueur**
¼	shot(s)	**White crème de cacao liqueur**
¼	shot(s)	**Sugar (gomme) syrup**
½	shot(s)	**Chilled mineral water (omit if wet ice)**

Origin: Discovered in 2000 at Teatro, London, England.
Comment: Vanilla, chocolate and a hint of nut. Add more sugar to taste.

DEAD MAN'S MULE

Glass: Collins
Garnish: Lime wedge on rim
Method: SHAKE first four ingredients with ice and strain into ice-filled glass. **TOP** with ginger beer.

¾	shot(s)	**La Fée Parisian 68% absinthe**
¾	shot(s)	**Goldschläger cinnamon schnapps liqueur**
¾	shot(s)	**Almond (orgeat) syrup**
½	shot(s)	**Freshly squeezed lime juice**
Top up with		**Ginger beer**

Origin: Discovered in 2003 at the Met Bar, London, England.
Comment: Strong in every respect. Big, full-on flavours of aniseed, cinnamon and ginger.

DEAN'S GATE MARTINI

Glass: Martini
Garnish: Orange zest twist
Method: SHAKE all ingredients with ice and fine strain into chilled glass.

2	shot(s)	**Light white rum**
1	shot(s)	**Drambuie liqueur**
1	shot(s)	**Rose's lime cordial**
3/4	shot(s)	**Chilled mineral water (omit if wet ice)**

Comment: Rich and strong with a warm, honeyed citrus flavour.

DEATH BY CHOCOLATE

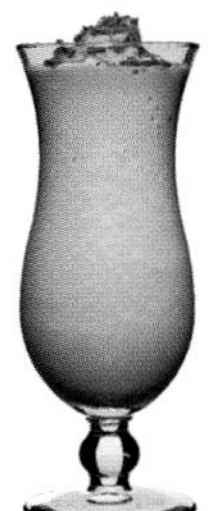

Glass: Hurricane
Garnish: Chocolate shavings (crumbled Cadbury's Flake bar)
Method: BLEND all ingredients with two 12oz scoops of crushed ice and serve with straws.

1	shot(s)	**Ketel One vodka**
1 1/2	shot(s)	**Baileys Irish Cream liqueur**
1	shot(s)	**Dark crème de cacao liqueur**
3	scoops	**Chocolate ice cream**

Comment: Unsophisticated but delicious. Don't be cheap – use deluxe ice cream

DEATH IN THE AFTERNOON

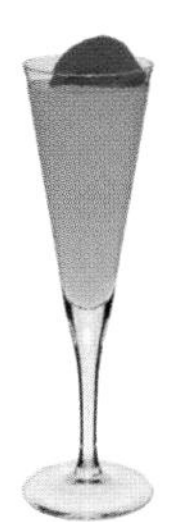

Glass: Flute
Garnish: Float rose petal
Method: SHAKE absinthe with ice (to chill and dilute) and fine strain into chilled glass. **TOP** with champagne.

1	shot(s)	**La Fée Parisian 68% absinthe**
Top up with		**Piper-Heidsieck brut champagne**

Origin: According to my 1949 copy of Esquire's 'Handbook For Hosts', this was created by Ernest Hemingway (not just named after his book). It re-emerged in London bars in 2002.
Comment: Bravado dominates this drink.

DEAUVILLE [NEW]

Glass: Martini
Garnish: Lemon zest twist
Method: SHAKE all ingredients with ice and fine strain into chilled glass.

1	shot(s)	**Calvados or applejack brandy**
1	shot(s)	**Rémy Martin cognac**
3/4	shot(s)	**Cointreau / triple sec**
1/2	shot(s)	**Freshly squeezed lemon juice**
1/8	shot(s)	**Sugar (gomme) syrup**
1/2	shot(s)	**Chilled mineral water (omit if wet ice)**

Variant: Apple Cart, Calvados Sidecar
Origin: A classic drink of unknown origin.
Comment: A well-balanced appley twist on the classic Sidecar.

DEEP SOUTH

Glass: Old-fashioned
Garnish: Lime wedge
Method: MUDDLE ginger in base of shaker. Add other ingredients, **SHAKE** with ice and fine strain into glass filled with crushed ice.

2	slices	**Fresh root ginger (thumbnail sized)**
1 1/2	shot(s)	**Clément Creole Shrubb liqueur**
1 1/2	shot(s)	**Freshly squeezed orange juice**
3/4	shot(s)	**Freshly squeezed lime juice**

Origin: Discovered in 1999 at AKA Bar, London, England.
Comment: Citrussy with delicate orange and ginger flavours.

THE DELICIOUS SOUR [NEW]

Glass: Old-fashioned
Garnish: Cherry & lemon slice on stick (sail)
Method: SHAKE all ingredients with ice and strain into ice-filled glass.

2	shot(s)	**Calvados or applejack brandy**
1	shot(s)	**Peach schnapps liqueur**
3/4	shot(s)	**Freshly squeezed lemon juice**
1/4	shot(s)	**Sugar (gomme) syrup**
1/2	fresh	**Egg white**

Origin: Adapted from a drink in Ted Haigh's book 'Vintage Spirits & Forgotten Cocktails'. Ted in turn credits an 1892 book, 'The Flowing Bowl' by William Schmidt.
Comment: Aptly named, this sour is tasty to say the least.

DELMONICO [NEW]

Glass: Martini
Garnish: Orange zest twist
Method: STIR all ingredients with ice and strain into chilled glass.

1 1/4	shot(s)	**Rémy Martin cognac**
1 1/2	shot(s)	**Sweet (rosso) vermouth**
1 1/4	shot(s)	**Dry vermouth**
3	dashes	**Angostura aromatic bitters**

Variant: If orange bitters are used in place of Angostura this becomes a Harvard.
Origin: A classic from the 1930s.
Comment: A Perfect Manhattan with cognac substituted for the whiskey.

DRINKS ARE GRADED AS FOLLOWS:

● DISGUSTING ●◐ PRETTY AWFUL ●● BEST AVOIDED
●●◐ DISAPPOINTING ●●● ACCEPTABLE ●●●◐ GOOD
●●●● RECOMMENDED ●●●●◐ HIGHLY RECOMMENDED
●●●●● OUTSTANDING / EXCEPTIONAL

DESSERT COCKTAILS

Dessert cocktails are a great way to end a meal, often even better than traditional desserts. They tend to fall into two camps. Either they are cocktails named after and tasting like actual desserts or they are simply sweet cocktails that befit the occasion. You might also consider a coffee-based cocktail in place of that after dinner coffee.

Examples of dessert cocktails:
Banoffee Martini
Caramel Sutra Martini
Casanova
Chocolate Martini
Crème Anglaise Martini
Crème Brûlée Martini
Death By Chocolate
Dreamsicle
Friar Tuck
Fruit & Nut Martini
Jaffa Martini
Jelly Belly Beany
Key Lime Pie
Lemon Chiffon Pie
Lemon Meringue Martini
Lemon Meringue Pie'tini
Lemon Sorbet
Mocha Martini
Russian Bride
Upside-down Raspberry Cheesecake
Zabaglione Martini

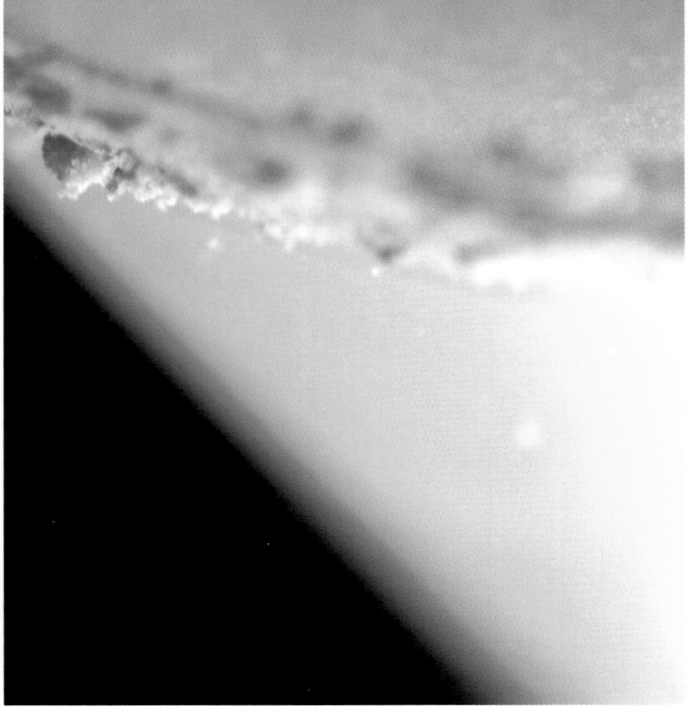

DELMONICO SPECIAL [NEW]

Glass: Martini
Garnish: Orange zest twist
Method: **STIR** all ingredients with ice and strain into chilled glass.

2¼	shot(s)	**Plymouth gin**
¼	shot(s)	**Rémy Martin cognac**
¾	shot(s)	**Dry vermouth**
3	dashes	**Angostura aromatic bitters**

Origin: A classic from the 1930s.
Comment: A Wet Martini dried with a splash of cognac.

DEMPSEY [NEW]

Glass: Martini
Garnish: Maraschino cherry
Method: **SHAKE** all ingredients with ice and fine strain into chilled glass.

1½	shot(s)	**Plymouth gin**
1½	shot(s)	**Calvados or applejack brandy**
¼	shot(s)	**Ricard pastis**
½	shot(s)	**Pomegranate (grenadine) syrup**

Origin: Forgotten classic.
Comment: Not sweet, not sour and not too strong. The pastis is well integrated.

DEPTH BOMB

Glass: Old-fashioned
Garnish: Lime wedge
Method: **SHAKE** all ingredients with ice and strain into glass filled with crushed ice.

1	shot(s)	**Calvados or applejack brandy**
1	shot(s)	**Rémy Martin cognac**
¾	shot(s)	**Freshly squeezed lime juice**
½	shot(s)	**Sugar (gomme) syrup**
¼	shot(s)	**Pomegranate (grenadine) syrup**

Comment: The lime, sugar and grenadine enhance the apple flavour of the apple brandy.

DEPTH CHARGE

Glass: Boston & shot
Method: **POUR** lager into Boston glass. **POUR** vodka into shot glass. **DROP** shot glass into lager and consume.

1	glass	**Pilsner lager**
1½	shot(s)	**Ketel One vodka**

Variant: Boilermaker
Comment: One way to ruin good beer.

DERBY DAIQUIRI

Glass: Martini
Garnish: Orange zest twist
Method: **SHAKE** all ingredients with ice and fine strain into chilled glass.

2	shot(s)	**Light white rum**
3/4	shot(s)	**Freshly squeezed orange juice**
1/2	shot(s)	**Freshly squeezed lime juice**
1/4	shot(s)	**Sugar (gomme) syrup**

Comment: A fruity twist on the Classic Daiquiri.

DERBY FIZZ [NEW]

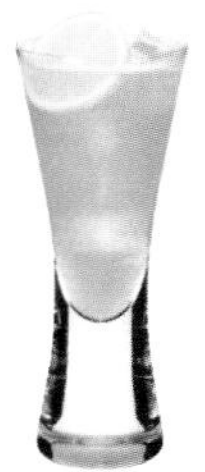

Glass: Collins (8oz max)
Garnish: Lemon slice
Method: **SHAKE** first six ingredients with ice and strain into chilled glass. **TOP** with soda.

1 3/4	shot(s)	**Bourbon whiskey**
1/2	shot(s)	**Light white rum**
1/4	shot(s)	**Grand Marnier liqueur**
1	shot(s)	**Freshly squeezed lemon juice**
1/2	shot(s)	**Sugar (gomme) syrup**
1/2		**Egg white (optional)**
Top up with		**Soda water (from siphon)**

Comment: An elongated sour with perfectly balanced strength, sweetness and sourness.

DESERT COOLER

Glass: Collins
Garnish: Orange slice
Method: **SHAKE** first three ingredients with ice and strain into ice-filled glass. **TOP** with ginger beer.

2	shot(s)	**Plymouth gin**
3/4	shot(s)	**Cherry (brandy) liqueur**
1 1/2	shot(s)	**Freshly squeezed orange juice**
Top up with		**Ginger beer**

Comment: Sandy in colour - as its name suggests - with a refreshing bite.

DETOX

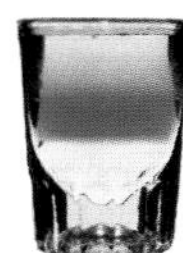

Glass: Shot
Garnish: Lime wedge on drink
Method: Refrigerate ingredients then **LAYER** in chilled glass by carefully pouring in the following order.

1/2	shot(s)	**Peach schnapps liqueur**
1/2	shot(s)	**Cranberry juice**
1/2	shot(s)	**Ketel One vodka**

Comment: Hardly a detox but tasty all the same.

DETROIT MARTINI

Glass: Martini
Garnish: Mint sprig
Method: Lightly **MUDDLE** mint in base of shaker (just to bruise). Add other ingredients, **SHAKE** with ice and fine strain into chilled glass.

7	fresh	**Mint leaves**
2 1/2	shot(s)	**Ketel One vodka**
1/2	shot(s)	**Sugar (gomme) syrup**
3/4	shot(s)	**Chilled mineral water**

Origin: Created by Dick Bradsell and based on the Cowboy Martini.
Comment: You can also add a splash of lime juice to this minty Martini.

DETROPOLITAN [NEW]

Glass: Martini
Garnish: Flamed orange zest
Method: **SHAKE** all ingredients with ice and fine strain into chilled glass.

1	shot(s)	**Ketel One vodka**
1/2	shot(s)	**Cointreau / triple sec**
1/4	shot(s)	**Sisca crème de cassis**
1 1/2	shot(s)	**Cranberry juice**
1/2	shot(s)	**Freshly squeezed lime juice**

Origin: Created at Detroit, London, England.
Comment: Yet another twist on the Cosmopolitan.

DEVIL [NEW]

Glass: Martini
Garnish: Lemon zest twist
Method: **SHAKE** all ingredients with ice and fine strain into chilled glass.

2	shot(s)	**Tawny port**
1 1/2	shot(s)	**Dry vermouth**
1/4	shot(s)	**Freshly squeezed lemon juice**

Comment: A devil to get out of your carpet but quite dry and aromatic on the palate.

DEVIL'S MANHATTAN

Glass: Martini
Garnish: Lemon zest twist
Method: **STIR** all ingredients with ice and strain into chilled glass.

2	shot(s)	**Bourbon whiskey**
1	shot(s)	**Southern Comfort liqueur**
1/2	shot(s)	**Sweet (rosso) vermouth**
3	dashes	**Peychaud's aromatic bitters**

Comment: A Sweet Manhattan with a hint of the south.

A B C **D** E F G H I J K L M N O P Q R S T U V W X Y Z

DIABLE ROUGE [UPDATED]

Glass: Martini
Garnish: Berries on stick
Method: **SHAKE** all ingredients with ice and fine strain into chilled glass.

2	shot(s)	**Ketel One vodka**
2	shot(s)	**Pressed pineapple juice**
1/4	shot(s)	**Sisca crème de cassis**

Comment: Not quite as rouge as the name would suggest. Hard to hate.

DIAMOND DOG [NEW]

Glass: Old-fashioned
Garnish: Orange slice
Method: **SHAKE** all ingredients with ice and strain into ice-filled glass.

1	shot(s)	**Campari**
1	shot(s)	**Dry vermouth**
1	shot(s)	**Rose's lime cordial**
1	shot(s)	**Freshly squeezed orange juice**

Origin: Discovered in 2005 at Four Seasons George V, Paris, France.
Comment: Bittersweet and refreshingly different.

DIAMOND FIZZ [NEW]

Glass: Collins (8oz max)
Garnish: Lemon slice
Method: **SHAKE** first three ingredients with ice and strain into chilled glass. **TOP** with champagne.

2	shot(s)	**Plymouth gin**
1	shot(s)	**Freshly squeezed lemon juice**
1/2	shot(s)	**Sugar (gomme) syrup**
Top up with		**Piper-Heidsieck brut champagne**

Origin: A long lost classic.
Comment: Why top a Fizz with soda when you can use champagne?

DIANA'S BITTER

Glass: Martini
Garnish: Split lime wedge
Method: **SHAKE** all ingredients with ice and fine strain into chilled glass.

2	shot(s)	**Plymouth gin**
1	shot(s)	**Campari**
1	shot(s)	**Freshly squeezed lime juice**
1/2	shot(s)	**Sugar (gomme) syrup**

Comment: A drink for the Campari aficionado: bittersweet and strong.

DICKENS' MARTINI

Glass: Martini
Method: **STIR** vermouth with ice and strain to **DISCARD** excess, leaving the mixing glass and ice coated with vermouth. **POUR** gin over vermouth coated ice, **STIR** and strain into chilled glass.

3/4	shot(s)	**Dry vermouth**
2 1/2	shot(s)	**Plymouth gin**

Comment: A Dry Martini served without a twist.

DIFFORD'S DAIQUIRI [NEW]

Glass: Old-fashioned
Garnish: Lime zest twist
Method: **SHAKE** all ingredients with ice and strain into ice-filled glass.

2 1/2	shot(s)	**Rum (must be 40% alc./vol.)**
1/2	shot(s)	**Freshly squeezed lime juice**
1	shot(s)	**Difford's Daiquiri Water**

Origin: Created in 2005 by yours truly.
Comment: The better the rum, the better the Daiquiri. However, this recipe can transform a Daiquiri made with light white rum into something that tastes like it's based on well aged rum.

DIFFORD'S OLD-FASHIONED [NEW]

Glass: Old-fashioned
Garnish: Orange zest twist
Method: **STIR** all ingredients with ice and strain into ice-filled glass.

2 1/2	shot(s)	**Bourbon whiskey**
1	shot(s)	**Difford's Daiquiri water**

Origin: Created in 2005 by yours truly.
Comment: Due to the use of Daiquiri water this tasty Old-fashioned doesn't require the arduous stirring and dilution traditionally associated with the drink.

DINO SOUR [NEW]

Glass: Old-fashioned
Garnish: Lemon slice & cherry on stick (flag)
Method: **SHAKE** all ingredients with ice and fine strain into chilled glass.

1	shot(s)	**Light white rum**
1	shot(s)	**Gosling's Black Seal rum**
1	shot(s)	**Freshly squeezed lemon juice**
1/2	shot(s)	**Sugar (gomme) syrup**
1/2	fresh	**Egg white**

Comment: Two diverse rums combine brilliantly in this classic sour.

DIPLOMAT [UPDATED]

Glass: Old-fashioned
Method: **STIR** all ingredients with ice and strain into ice-filled glass.

1½	shot(s)	**Dry vermouth**
1½	shot(s)	**Sweet (rosso) vermouth**
¼	shot(s)	**Luxardo Maraschino liqueur**
3	dashes	**Fee Brothers orange bitters**

Comment: Wonderfully aromatic.

DIRTY BANANA

Glass: Collins
Garnish: Banana slice on rim
Method: **BLEND** all ingredients with 12oz scoop crushed ice. Serve with straws.

1½	shot(s)	**Aged rum**
1	shot(s)	**Kahlúa coffee liqueur**
1	shot(s)	**Crème de bananes liqueur**
1	fresh	**Peeled banana**
1	shot(s)	**Double (heavy) cream**
1	shot(s)	**Milk**

Origin: A popular cocktail in Jamaica.
Comment: Long, creamy and filling banana drink with a 'dirty' flavour and colour courtesy of coffee liqueur.

DIRTY MARTINI

Glass: Martini
Garnish: Olive on stick
Method: **STIR** all ingredients with ice and strain into a chilled glass.

2½	shot(s)	**Plymouth gin**
¼	shot(s)	**Brine from cocktail olives**
¼	shot(s)	**Dry vermouth**

Variant: Substitute vodka for gin.
Comment: This drink varies from delicious to disgusting, depending on the liquid in your jar of olives. Oil will produce a revolting emulsion: make sure that your olives are packed in brine.

DIRTY SANCHEZ

Glass: Collins
Garnish: Lime wheel on rim
Method: **SHAKE** first four ingredients with ice and strain into ice-filled glass. **TOP** with ginger beer.

2	shot(s)	**Sauza Hornitos tequila**
¾	shot(s)	**Agavero tequila liqueur**
½	shot(s)	**Chambord black raspberry liqueur**
½	shot(s)	**Freshly squeezed lime juice**
Top up with		**Jamaican ginger beer**

Origin: Created in 2001 by Phillip Jeffrey and Ian Baldwin at the GE Club, London, England.
Comment: A wonderfully refreshing and complex long summer drink.

DIVINO'S [NEW]

Glass: Martini
Garnish: Chocolate shavings
Method: **SHAKE** all ingredients with ice and fine strain into chilled glass.

½	shot(s)	**Ketel One vodka**
2½	shot(s)	**Barolo wine**
1	shot(s)	**Dark crème de cacao liqueur**

Origin: Discovered in 2005 at DiVino, Hong Kong, China.
Comment: The chocolate liqueur takes the acidity off the wine without masking its flavour.

DIXIE DEW [NEW]

Glass: Martini
Garnish: Orange zest twist
Method: **SHAKE** all ingredients with ice and fine strain into chilled glass.

2	shot(s)	**Bourbon whiskey**
½	shot(s)	**White crème de menthe liqueur**
½	shot(s)	**Cointreau / triple sec**
¾	shot(s)	**Chilled mineral water (omit if wet ice)**

Comment: A peppermint fresh, bourbon laced drink.

DNA

Glass: Martini
Garnish: Orange zest twist
Method: **SHAKE** all ingredients with ice and fine strain into chilled glass.

1½	shot(s)	**Plymouth gin**
¾	shot(s)	**Apricot brandy liqueur**
¼	shot(s)	**Sugar (gomme) syrup**
1	shot(s)	**Freshly squeezed lemon juice**
4	drops	**Fee Brothers orange bitters (optional)**

Created by: Emmanuel Audermatte at The Atlantic Bar & Grill, London, England, in 1999.
Comment: Sharp and fruity.

DNA #2 [NEW]

Glass: Martini
Garnish: Lemon zest twist
Method: **SHAKE** all ingredients with ice and fine strain into chilled glass.

1	shot(s)	**Plymouth gin**
1	shot(s)	**Plymouth damson gin liqueur**
¾	shot(s)	**Apricot brandy liqueur**
½	shot(s)	**Freshly squeezed lime juice**
2	dashes	**Angostura aromatic bitters**
½	shot(s)	**Chilled mineral water (omit if wet ice)**

Origin: Created in 2005 by Tonin Kacaj at Maze, London, England.
Comment: Tangy, fruity and gin laced.

DOCTOR [NEW]

Glass: Martini
Garnish: Lime zest twist
Method: **SHAKE** all ingredients with ice and fine strain into chilled glass.

1½ shot(s) **Aged rum**
1½ shot(s) **Carlshamns Swedish Torr Flagg Punsch**
¾ shot(s) **Freshly squeezed lime juice**

Origin: In David Embury's classic, 'The Fine Art of Mixing Drinks', my hero lists four wildly different drinks using Swedish Punch. Trader Vic's 'Bartender's Guide' lists two variations of a single drink, for which the above is my own recipe.
Comment: Retitled 'Swedish Daiquiri', this could be a hit.

DOCTOR FUNK [NEW]

Glass: Sling
Garnish: Lime wedge
Method: **SHAKE** first six ingredients with ice and strain into glass filled with crushed ice. **TOP** with soda and serve with straws.

2½ shot(s) **Gosling's Black Seal rum**
¼ shot(s) **Pernod anis**
½ shot(s) **Freshly squeezed lemon juice**
¼ shot(s) **Freshly squeezed lime juice**
¼ shot(s) **Pomegranate (grenadine) syrup**
¼ shot(s) **Sugar (gomme) syrup**
Top up with **Soda water (club soda)**

Origin: A Tiki drink adapted from one created circa 1937 by Don The Beachcomber.
Comment: Too many and you'll need your very own doctor.

DOLCE-AMARO

Glass: Martini
Garnish: Orange zest twist
Method: **STIR** all ingredients with ice and strain into chilled glass.

1½ shot(s) **Campari**
1½ shot(s) **Bianco vermouth**
¾ shot(s) **Luxardo Amaretto di Saschira**

Comment: The very apt name translates as 'bittersweet'.

DOLCE HAVANA

Glass: Martini
Method: **SHAKE** all ingredients with ice and fine strain into chilled glass.

1¼ shot(s) **Light white rum**
½ shot(s) **Campari**
½ shot(s) **Cointreau / triple sec**
1¼ shot(s) **Freshly squeezed orange juice**
1¼ shot(s) **Freshly squeezed lime juice**
⅛ shot(s) **Sugar (gomme) syrup**

Origin: Created by Fabrizio Musorella in 2000 at the Library Bar, Lanesborough Hotel, London, England.
Comment: A melange of Mediterranean fruit.

DOLORES [NEW]

Glass: Martini
Garnish: Lemon zest twist
Method: **SHAKE** all ingredients with ice and fine strain into chilled glass.

2 shot(s) **Aged rum**
2 shot(s) **Dubonnet Red**
1 shot(s) **Tio Pepe fino sherry**

Origin: A classic. Some recipes include a splash of orange juice.
Comment: Aromatic and well balanced, provided you use French-made Dubonnet.

DONEGAL [NEW]

Glass: Martini
Garnish: Orange zest twist
Method: **SHAKE** all ingredients with ice and fine strain into chilled glass.

1½ shot(s) **Irish whiskey**
1¼ shot(s) **Dry vermouth**
½ shot(s) **Luxardo maraschino liqueur**
½ shot(s) **Mandarine Napoléon liqueur**

Comment: Aromatised Irish whiskey with cherry and orange.

DON JUAN

Glass: Martini
Garnish: Orange zest twist
Method: **SHAKE** all ingredients with ice and fine strain into chilled glass.

1¾ shot(s) **Rémy Martin cognac**
1 shot(s) **Licor 43 (Cuarenta Y Tres) liqueur**
1 shot(s) **Freshly squeezed orange juice**
½ shot(s) **Double (heavy) cream**
½ shot(s) **Milk**

Comment: A lightly creamy orange affair with vanilla spice.

DONNA'S CREAMY'TINI

Glass: Martini
Garnish: Cherry on rim
Method: **SHAKE** all ingredients with ice and fine strain into chilled glass.

1 shot(s) **Luxardo Amaretto di Saschira**
1 shot(s) **Cherry (brandy) liqueur**
1 shot(s) **Dark crème de cacao liqueur**
1 shot(s) **Double (heavy) cream**

Origin: Adapted from a drink created in 2002 by Yannick Miseriaux at the Fifth Floor Bar, London, England.
Comment: A fine example of an alcoholic liquid pudding.

DORIAN GRAY

Glass: Martini
Garnish: Orange zest twist
Method: **SHAKE** all ingredients with ice and fine strain into chilled glass.

1½	shot(s)	**Light white rum**
¾	shot(s)	**Grand Marnier liqueur**
1	shot(s)	**Freshly squeezed orange juice**
¾	shot(s)	**Cranberry juice**

Origin: Discovered in 1999 at One Aldwych, London, England. This cocktail takes its name from Oscar Wilde's novel, in which a socialite's wish to remain as young and charming as his own portrait is granted. Allured by his depraved friend Lord Henry Wotton, Dorian Gray assumes a life of perversion and sin. But every time he sins the painting ages, while Gray stays young and healthy.
Comment: Fruity and rum laced, not overly sweet.

DOUBLE GRAPE MARTINI

Glass: Martini
Garnish: Grapes on stick
Method: **MUDDLE** grapes in base of shaker. Add other ingredients, **SHAKE** with ice and fine strain into chilled glass.

12	fresh	**Seedless white grapes**
2	shot(s)	**Ketel One vodka**
¾	shot(s)	**Sauvignon Blanc wine**
½	shot(s)	**Sugar (gomme) syrup**

Origin: Created by yours truly in 2004.
Comment: The wine adds complexity to a simple Grape Martini.

DOUBLE VISION [UPDATED]

Glass: Martini
Garnish: Blackcurrants on stick
Method: **SHAKE** all ingredients with ice and fine strain into chilled glass.

1	shot(s)	**Ketel One Citroen vodka**
1	shot(s)	**Raspberry flavoured vodka**
1	shot(s)	**Pressed apple juice**
½	shot(s)	**Freshly squeezed lime juice**
¼	shot(s)	**Sugar (gomme) syrup**
3	dashes	**Angostura aromatic bitters**

Comment: Citrus fresh with strong hints of apple and red berries.

DOUGHNUT MARTINI

Glass: Martini
Garnish: Segment of doughnut
Method: **SHAKE** all ingredients with ice and fine strain into chilled glass.

1½	shot(s)	**Light white rum**
¾	shot(s)	**Bourbon whiskey**
½	shot(s)	**Vanilla schnapps liqueur**
½	shot(s)	**Licor 43 (Cuarenta Y Tres) liqueur**
⅛	shot(s)	**Butterscotch schnapps liqueur**
¾	shot(s)	**Chilled mineral water (omit if wet ice)**

Origin: Created in 2003 by yours truly.
Comment: My attempt at mimicking the taste of a Krispy Kreme Original Glazed doughnut without ending up with an overly sweet cocktail.

DOWA

Glass: Old-fashioned
Garnish: Lime wedge
Method: **STIR** honey and vodka in base of shaker until honey dissolves. Add lime juice, **SHAKE** with ice and strain into glass filled with crushed ice. Serve with straws.

4	spoons	**Runny honey**
2½	shot(s)	**Ketel One vodka**
¼	shot(s)	**Freshly squeezed lime juice**

Origin: This cocktail is particularly popular in upscale hotel bars in Kenya where it is enjoyed by the safari set. The name translates as 'medicine'.
Comment: Very similar to the Caipirovska in its use of vodka, lime and crushed ice: the honey makes the difference.

DOWNHILL RACER

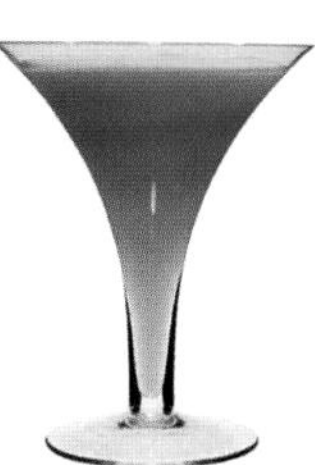

Glass: Martini
Garnish: Pineapple wedge on rim
Method: **SHAKE** all ingredients with ice and fine strain into chilled glass.

1¾	shot(s)	**Aged rum**
¾	shot(s)	**Luxardo Amaretto di Saschira**
1¾	shot(s)	**Pressed pineapple juice**

Comment: Aged rum sweetened, softened and flavoured with pineapple and amaretto.

To make your own sugar syrup, gradually pour TWO cups of granulated sugar into a saucepan containing ONE cup of hot water. Stir as you pour and carry on stirring and simmering until the sugar is dissolved. Do not let the water even come close to boiling and only simmer for as long as it takes to dissolve the sugar. Allow syrup to cool and pour into an empty bottle. Ideally, you should finely strain your syrup into the bottle to remove any undissolved crystals which could otherwise encourage crystallisation. If kept in a refrigerator this mixture will last for a couple of months.

DRY MARTINI

Although it is common for Martini & Rossi vermouth to be used in the preparation of this drink, the name is coincidental. Some say that the Martini was invented in 1911 by Martini di Arma di Taggia, the head bartender at New York's Knickerbocker Hotel, and that he used French vermouth and orange bitters.

Others claim that the name came from the Californian town of Martinez where in 1849 a passing gold miner imbibed the first Martinez Special (3 parts gin and 1 part dry sauterne garnished with an olive).

The truth is that no one knows where the Martini was created. It most probably evolved from the Manhattan, initially into the Martinez, a Manhattan made with gin instead of whiskey. In the last years of the 1800s the name Martinez changed to Martini. Both these drinks were originally mixed with Old Tom sweet gin, sweet vermouth, sugar and bitters - very different to the 'Dry' Martini we enjoy today.

However, a book published in 1906 by Louis Muckenstrum includes a 'Dry Martini Cocktail', made with dry vermouth, dry gin, orange bitters and a dash of curaçao. Despite the new dryness, bitters remained a usual ingredient until the 1940s.

By the 1950s what we now know as the 'Naked Martini' started to appear in cocktail books. Traditionally the (sweet or dry) vermouth and gin had been stirred with ice. Here they were combined by dosing a well chilled glass with a hint of vermouth and then simply pouring frozen gin into the vermouth coated glass.

There is some debate as to whether a Martini should be shaken or stirred. It should be stirred. If shaken, it becomes a 'Bradford'. Shaking the drink increases the dilution and introduces air bubbles into the drink, making it taste different and colder.

The 'Oliver Twist' choice between an olive (stuffed or otherwise) or a lemon zest twist is traditional and these are the two most common garnishes for a Dry Martini. There are, however, a number of variants. A 'Dickens' is a Martini without a twist, a 'Gibson' is a Martini with two onions instead of an olive or a twist and a 'Franklin Martini' is named after Franklin Roosevelt and has two olives. Please also see Martini om page 191.

DR ZEUS

Glass: Old-fashioned
Method: **POUR** Fernet Branca into ice-filled glass, **TOP** with chilled mineral water and leave to stand. Separately **MUDDLE** raisins in base of shaker, add other ingredients and **SHAKE** with ice. Finally **DISCARD** contents of glass and strain contents of shaker into the Fernet Branca coated glass.

1	shot(s)	**Fernet Branca**
20		**Raisins**
2	shot(s)	**Rémy Martin cognac**
1/4	shot(s)	**Sugar (gomme) syrup**
1/8	shot(s)	**Kahlúa coffee liqueur**
1	dash	**Fee Brothers orange bitters**

Origin: Created by Adam Ennis in 2001 at Isola, Knightsbridge, London, England.
Comment: Not that far removed from a Sazerac cocktail, this is innovative and great tasting.

DRAGON BLOSSOM [NEW]

Glass: Martini
Garnish: Maraschino cherry in drink
Method: **SHAKE** all ingredients with ice and fine strain into chilled glass.

1 3/4	shot(s)	**Rose petal vodka**
1/4	shot(s)	**Soho lychee liqueur**
1/4	shot(s)	**Maraschino syrup**
1 3/4	shot(s)	**Cranberry juice**

Comment: Light, aromatic, semi-sweet and distinctly oriental in style.

DRAMATIC MARTINI

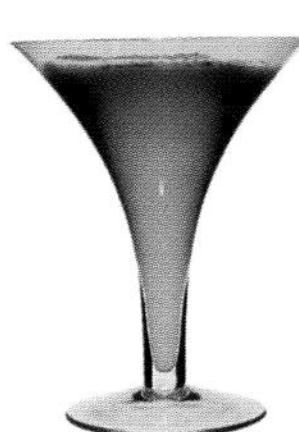

Glass: Martini
Garnish: Grate nutmeg over drink
Method: **SHAKE** all ingredients with ice and fine strain into chilled glass.

1	shot(s)	**Tuaca Italian liqueur**
1	shot(s)	**Grand Marnier liqueur**
1	shot(s)	**Baileys Irish Cream liqueur**
1	shot(s)	**Milk**

Comment: Creamy and sweet with orangey, herbal notes.

DREAMSICLE

Glass: Martini
Method: **SHAKE** first three ingredients with ice and fine strain into chilled glass. **FLOAT** cream.

1 1/2	shot(s)	**Kahlúa coffee liqueur**
3/4	shot(s)	**Cointreau / triple sec**
1	shot(s)	**Freshly squeezed orange juice**
3/4	shot(s)	**Double (heavy) cream**

Comment: Sweet coffee and orange smoothed by a creamy top. A veritable dessert in a glass.

DROWNED OUT

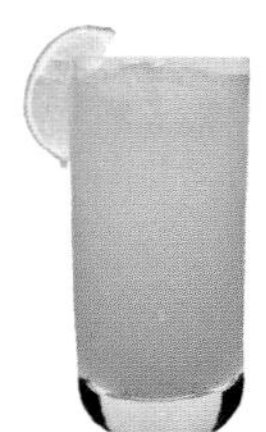

Glass: Collins
Garnish: Lime wedge
Method: POUR ingredients into ice-filled glass, stir and serve with straws.

2	shot(s)	**Pernod anis**
1	shot(s)	**Freshly squeezed lime juice**
Top up with		**Ginger ale**

Comment: Ginger combines with aniseed rather than drowning it.

DRY ICE MARTINI

Glass: Martini
Garnish: Lemon zest twist
Method: STIR all ingredients with ice and strain into chilled glass.

2	shot(s)	**Ketel One vodka**
1/2	shot(s)	**Dry vermouth**
3/4	shot(s)	**Icewine**

Origin: Created by yours truly in 2004.
Comment: Despite the name, this is slightly honeyed rather than dry.

DRY MARTINI #1 (TRADITIONAL)

Glass: Martini
Garnish: Chilled olive on stick or lemon zest twist
Method: STIR vermouth with ice and strain to discard excess, leaving the glass and ice coated with vermouth. **POUR** gin over vermouth coated ice, **STIR** and strain into a chilled glass.

3/4	shot(s)	**Dry vermouth**
2 1/2	shot(s)	**Plymouth gin**
2	dashes	**Fee Brothers orange bitters (optional)**

Variant: The proportion of gin to vermouth is a matter of taste, some say 7 to 1, others that one drop is sufficient. I recommend you ask the drinker how they would like their Martini, in the same manner that you might ask how they have their steak. If the drinker orders a 'Sweet Martini', use sweet red vermouth rather than dry and use a cherry as garnish instead of an olive.
Comment: This drink is an acquired taste, but all too easy to acquire.

DRY MARTINI #2 (NAKED)

Glass: Martini
Garnish: Chilled olive on stick or lemon zest twist
Method: POUR vermouth into frozen glass. Swirl glass to coat inside with vermouth and then shake out excess. Take bottle of gin from the freezer and **POUR** into glass.

1/4	shot(s)	**Dry vermouth**
2 1/2	shot(s)	**Plymouth gin**

Variant: Coat glass with vermouth by use of an atomiser.
Comment: The key to the success of this drink is for both glass and gin to be freezing cold. Consume quickly whilst still cold. The temperature masks the strength of the alcohol – be warned.

DRY ORANGE MARTINI [NEW]

Glass: Martini
Garnish: Grapefruit twist
Method: STIR all ingredients with ice and strain into chilled glass.

2	shot(s)	**Plymouth gin**
3/4	shot(s)	**Dry vermouth**
1/4	shot(s)	**Cointreau / triple sec**
2	dashes	**Fee Brothers orange bitters**

Origin: Created in 2003 by Wayne Collins for Maxxium UK.
Comment: Bone dry, orangey, aptly named Martini.

DULCHIN [NEW]

Glass: Martini
Garnish: Orange zest twist
Method: SHAKE all ingredients with ice and fine strain into chilled glass.

2	shot(s)	**Pisco**
1/2	shot(s)	**Grand Marnier liqueur**
1/2	shot(s)	**Apricot brandy liqueur**
1/4	shot(s)	**Rose's lime cordial**
1/4	shot(s)	**Pomegranate (grenadine) syrup**
3/4	shot(s)	**Chilled mineral water (omit if wet ice)**

Comment: This dry, amber coloured, fruity cocktail carries a pisco punch.

DURANGO [NEW]

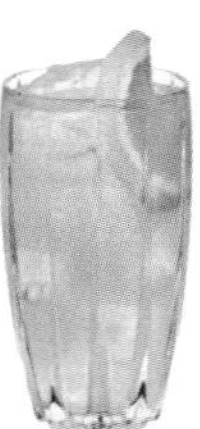

Glass: Collins
Garnish: Orange wheel
Method: SHAKE first three ingredients with ice and strain into ice filled glass. **TOP** with soda.

2	shot(s)	**Sauza Hornitos tequila**
3/4	shot(s)	**Luxardo Amaretto di Saschira**
1	shot(s)	**Freshly squeezed grapefruit juice**
Top up with		**Soda water (club soda)**

Comment: This sandy coloured drink makes tequila, amaretto and grapefruit juice into unlikely but harmonious bedfellows.

DUTCH BREAKFAST MARTINI

Glass: Martini
Garnish: Orange zest twist
Method: SHAKE all ingredients with ice and fine strain into chilled glass.

1 1/2	shot(s)	**Plymouth gin**
1 1/2	shot(s)	**Advocaat liqueur**
1	shot(s)	**Freshly squeezed lemon juice**
1/4	shot(s)	**Sugar (gomme) syrup**
1/8	shot(s)	**Galliano liqueur**

Origin: Created in 2002 by Alex Kammerling, London, England.
Comment: A tasty, aromatic, almost creamy alternative to a fry-up.

A B C D E F G H I J K L M N O P Q R S T U V W X Y Z

DUTCH COURAGE

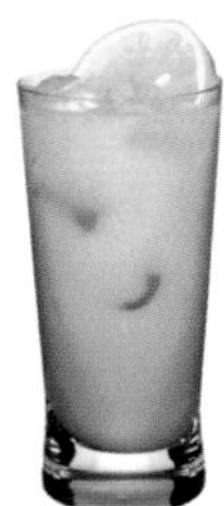

Glass: Collins
Garnish: Lemon slice
Method: **SHAKE** all ingredients with ice and strain into ice-filled glass.

1	shot(s)	**Plymouth gin**
1	shot(s)	**Advocaat liqueur**
3/4	shot(s)	**Freshly squeezed lemon juice**
3	shot(s)	**Pressed apple juice**

Origin: Created in 2002 by Alex Kammerling, London, England.
Comment: A refreshing alternative to a traditional English lemonade.

EARL GREY MAR-TEA-NI

Glass: Martini
Garnish: Lemon zest twist
Method: **SHAKE** all ingredients with ice and fine strain into chilled glass.

2	shot(s)	**Plymouth gin**
1 1/4	shot(s)	**Strong cold Earl Grey tea**
3/4	shot(s)	**Freshly squeezed lemon juice**
1/2	shot(s)	**Sugar (gomme) syrup**
1/2	fresh	**Egg white**

Origin: Adapted from a drink created in 2000 by Audrey Saunders at Bemelmans Bar at The Carlyle, New York City.
Comment: A fantastic and very English drink created by a New Yorker. The botanicals of gin combine wonderfully with the flavours and tannins of the tea.

DYEVITCHKA [UPDATED]

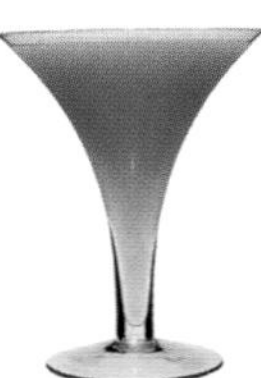

Glass: Martini
Garnish: Orange zest twist
Method: **SHAKE** all ingredients with ice and fine strain into chilled glass.

1	shot(s)	**Ketel One vodka**
1	shot(s)	**Cointreau / triple sec**
1/2	shot(s)	**Freshly squeezed lime juice**
1/4	shot(s)	**Sugar (gomme) syrup**
1 1/2	shot(s)	**Pressed pineapple juice**

Comment: Pineapple replaces cranberry in this Cosmo-like cocktail.

EAST INDIA #1 [NEW]

Glass: Martini
Garnish: Orange zest twist
Method: **SHAKE** all ingredients with ice and fine strain into chilled glass.

2 1/2	shot(s)	**Rémy Martin cognac**
1/8	shot(s)	**Grand Marnier liqueur**
1/8	shot(s)	**Luxardo maraschino liqueur**
1/4	shot(s)	**Pomegranate (grenadine) or raspberry syrup**
1	dash	**Angostura aromatic bitters**

Origin: An old classic. This recipe is adapted from one in Ted Haigh's book 'Vintage Spirits & Forgotten Cocktails'.
Comment: Cognac tamed and given an additional hint of fruit.

EARL GREY FIZZ

Glass: Flute
Garnish: Lemon knot
Method: **SHAKE** first three ingredients with ice and strain into chilled glass. **TOP** with champagne.

1	shot(s)	**Zubrówka bison vodka**
1/2	shot(s)	**Strong cold Earl Grey tea**
1/4	shot(s)	**Sugar (gomme) syrup**
Top up with		**Piper-Heidsieck brut champagne**

Origin: Created in 2002 by Henry Besant at Lonsdale House, London, England.
Comment: Looks like a glass of champagne but has a well judged little extra something.

EAST INDIA #2

Glass: Martini
Garnish: Orange zest twist & nutmeg dust
Method: **SHAKE** all ingredients with ice and fine strain into chilled glass.

1 1/2	shot(s)	**Rémy Martin cognac**
1	shot(s)	**Grand Marnier liqueur**
2	shot(s)	**Pressed pineapple juice**
2	dashes	**Angostura aromatic bitters**

Origin: Another version of the East India classic, thought to originate with Frank Meier at the Ritz Bar, Paris.
Comment: A rich but bitter short drink based on cognac.

HOW TO MAKE SUGAR SYRUP

To make your own sugar syrup, gradually pour TWO cups of granulated sugar into a saucepan containing ONE cup of hot water. Stir as you pour and carry on stirring and simmering until the sugar is dissolved. Do not let the water even come close to boiling and only simmer for as long as it takes to dissolve the sugar. Allow syrup to cool and pour into an empty bottle. Ideally, you should finely strain your syrup into the bottle to remove any undissolved crystals which could otherwise encourage crystallisation. If kept in a refrigerator this mixture will last for a couple of months.

EAST INDIAN

Glass: Martini
Garnish: Olive on stick
Method: **STIR** all ingredients with ice and strain into chilled glass.

2	shot(s)	**Tio Pepe fino sherry**
2	shot(s)	**Dry vermouth**
1/4	shot(s)	**Sugar (gomme) syrup**
3	dashes	**Fee Brothers orange bitters**

Variant: Bamboo
Comment: Dry and pretty flat (like much of India) but perfectly balanced with subtle hints of orange zest.

DRINKS ARE GRADED AS FOLLOWS:

● DISGUSTING ●◐ PRETTY AWFUL ●● BEST AVOIDED
●●◐ DISAPPOINTING ●●● ACCEPTABLE ●●●◐ GOOD
●●●● RECOMMENDED ●●●●◐ HIGHLY RECOMMENDED
●●●●● OUTSTANDING / EXCEPTIONAL

EASTER MARTINI

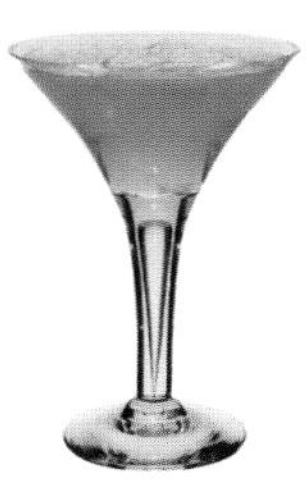

Glass: Martini
Garnish: Grated chocolate (crumbled Cadbury's Flake bar)
Method: **MUDDLE** cardamom pods in base of shaker. Add other ingredients, **SHAKE** with ice and fine strain into chilled glass.

4	pods	**Green cardamom**
2	shot(s)	**Vanilla flavoured vodka**
1	shot(s)	**White crème de cacao liqueur**
1/4	shot(s)	**Sugar (gomme) syrup**
1/2	shot(s)	**Chilled mineral water (omit if wet ice)**
1/2	fresh	**Egg white**

Origin: Created in 2003 by Simon King at MJU Bar, Millennium Hotel, London, England.
Comment: A standard Chocolate Martini with extra interest thanks to the clever use of vanilla and cardamom. The egg white was my own addition. It seemed appropriate given the Easter in the title.

EASTERN MARTINI

Glass: Martini
Garnish: Japanese ume plum in drink
Method: **SHAKE** all ingredients with ice and fine strain into chilled glass.

2	shot(s)	**Ketel One vodka**
1 1/2	shot(s)	**Choya Umeshu plum liqueur**
1	shot(s)	**Pressed apple juice**

Origin: Created in 2003 by Chris Langan, Barnomadics, Scotland.
Comment: Light, fragrant and fruity – distinctly oriental.

EASTERN PROMISE [NEW]

Glass: Martini
Garnish: Lemon zest twist
Method: **SHAKE** all ingredients with ice and fine strain into chilled glass.

2	shot(s)	**Orange flavoured vodka**
1/4	shot(s)	**Apricot brandy liqueur**
1/2	shot(s)	**Rose syrup**
1/2	shot(s)	**Freshly squeezed lemon juice**
1/2	shot(s)	**Chilled mineral water (omit if wet ice)**

Origin: Adapted from a drink discovered in 2004 at Oxo Tower Bar, London, England.
Comment: Citrus dominates this drink but the result is floral rather than tart.

EASY TIGER

Glass: Martini
Garnish: Orange zest twist
Comment: **MUDDLE** ginger in base of shaker. Add honey and tequila, and **STIR** until honey is dissolved. Add other ingredients, **SHAKE** with ice and fine strain into chilled glass.

2	slices	**Fresh ginger (thumb nail sized)**
2	spoons	**Runny honey**
2	shot(s)	**Sauza Hornitos tequila**
1	shot(s)	**Freshly squeezed lime juice**
3/4	shot(s)	**Chilled mineral water (omit if wet ice)**

Origin: Created in 1999 by Alex Kammerling.
Comment: Tangy and zesty with rich honey and ginger.

ECLIPSE

Glass: Collins
Garnish: Mint leaf & raspberry
Method: **MUDDLE** raspberries in base of shaker. Add other ingredients, **SHAKE** with ice and strain into glass filled with crushed ice. Serve with straws.

12	fresh	**Raspberries**
2	shot(s)	**Jack Daniel's Tennessee whiskey**
1	shot(s)	**Chambord black raspberry liqueur**
1/2	shot(s)	**Freshly squeezed lime juice**
2	shot(s)	**Cranberry juice**

Origin: Signature cocktail at the chain of Eclipse Bars, London, England.
Comment: A fruity summer cooler which I challenge anyone not to like.

EDEN

Glass: Collins
Garnish: Orange zest string
Method: **SHAKE** first three ingredients with ice and strain into ice-filled glass. **TOP** with tonic water.

2	shot(s)	**Orange flavoured vodka**
1/2	shot(s)	**Elderflower cordial**
1 1/2	shot(s)	**Pressed apple juice**
Top up with		**Tonic water**

Origin: Created in 2003 by Sylvain Solignac at Circus, London, England.
Comment: Orange zest predominates in this long refreshing drink.

A B C D **E** F G H I J K L M N O P Q R S T U V W X Y Z

EDEN MARTINI [NEW]

Glass: Martini
Garnish: Orange zest twist
Method: **SHAKE** all ingredients with ice and fine strain into chilled glass.

2½	shot(s)	**Plymouth gin**
½	shot(s)	**Parfait amour liqueur**
¼	shot(s)	**Rose water**
¼	shot(s)	**Freshly squeezed lemon juice**
¼	shot(s)	**Chilled mineral water (omit if wet ice)**

Origin: Adapted from a recipe discovered in 2003 at Oxo Tower Bar, London, England.
Comment: Rich purple in colour with rose, vanilla, almond, citrus and gin.

EGG CUSTARD MARTINI

Glass: Martini
Garnish: Dust with freshly ground nutmeg
Method: **SHAKE** all ingredients with ice and fine strain into chilled glass.

1½	shot(s)	**Ketel One vodka**
1	shot(s)	**Advocaat liqueur**
½	shot(s)	**Vanilla flavoured vodka**
½	shot(s)	**Bourbon whiskey**
¼	shot(s)	**Sugar (gomme) syrup**

Origin: Created in 2002 by Alex Kammerling, London, England.
Comment: As custardy as the name would suggest but surprisingly potent.

EGG NOG #1 (COLD)

Glass: Collins
Garnish: Dust with freshly grated nutmeg
Method: **SHAKE** all ingredients with ice and strain into ice-filled glass.

2½	shot(s)	**Rémy Martin cognac**
½	shot(s)	**Sugar (gomme) syrup**
½	shot(s)	**Double (heavy) cream**
1	fresh	**Egg**
2	shot(s)	**Milk**

Comment: Lightly flavoured alcoholic egg custard. Also try swapping dark rum for the cognac.

EGG NOG #2 (HOT) [NEW]

Glass: Toddy
Garnish: Dust with freshly grated nutmeg
Method: **POUR** ingredients into heatproof glass and **STIR** thoroughly. **HEAT** in microwave oven for a minute (adjust time as appropriate to your oven) and **STIR** again. Alternatively, mix and warm in pan over heat – do not boil.

2½	shot(s)	**Rémy Martin cognac**
½	shot(s)	**Sugar (gomme) syrup**
½	shot(s)	**Double (heavy) cream**
1	fresh	**Egg** (white & yolk)
2	shot(s)	**Milk**

Comment: A warming, spicy and filling meal in a glass.

EL BURRO [NEW]

Glass: Collins
Garnish: Lime slice
Method: **SHAKE** first four ingredients with ice and strain into ice-filled glass. **TOP** with ginger beer.

2	shot(s)	**Sauza Hornitos tequila**
½	shot(s)	**Freshly squeezed lime juice**
¼	shot(s)	**Sugar (gomme) syrup**
3	dashes	**Angostura aromatic bitters**
Top up with		**Ginger beer**

AKA: Mexican Mule
Origin: Created by Henry Besant and Andres Masso, London, England. The name of this Mexican version of the Moscow Mule translates from Spanish as 'The Donkey'.
Comment: Ginger spice and tequila soured with lime.

EL DIABLO [UPDATED]

Glass: Collins
Garnish: Lime wedge
Method: **SHAKE** first three ingredients with ice and strain into ice-filled glass. **TOP** with ginger beer.

2	shot(s)	**Sauza Hornitos tequila**
¾	shot(s)	**Sisca crème de cassis**
1	shot(s)	**Freshly squeezed lime juice**
Top up with		**Ginger beer**

Origin: Thought to have originated in California during the 1940s. The name translates as 'The Devil'.
Comment: In your face tequila, red fruit and ginger, but there's a time and place.

EL PRESIDENTE DAIQUIRI [NEW]

Glass: Martini
Garnish: Lime wedge on rim
Method: **SHAKE** all ingredients with ice and fine strain into chilled glass.

2	shot(s)	**Light white rum**
¾	shot(s)	**Pressed pineapple juice**
½	shot(s)	**Freshly squeezed lime juice**
¼	shot(s)	**Pomegranate (grenadine) syrup**

Origin: Classic variation on the Daiquiri, of unknown origin.
Comment: Rum and pineapple combine wonderfully and the Daiquiri is the king of cocktails.

EL TORADO [NEW]

Glass: Martini
Garnish: Float thin apple slice
Method: **SHAKE** all ingredients with ice and fine strain into chilled glass.

2	shot(s)	**Sauza Hornitos tequila**
½	shot(s)	**Dry vermouth**
1½	shot(s)	**Pressed apple juice**

Origin: Popular throughout Mexico.
Comment: Dry, sophisticated and fruity, with tequila body.

ELDERBUBBLE

Glass: Flute
Garnish: Cucumber slice
Method: **SHAKE** first three ingredients with ice and strain into chilled glass. **TOP** with champagne.

1	shot(s)	**Cucumber flavoured vodka**
3/4	shot(s)	**Elderflower cordial**
1/4	shot(s)	**Freshly squeezed lemon juice**
Top up with		**Piper-Heidsieck brut champagne**

Origin: Created in 2002 by Michael Mahe and popularised at Hush, London, England.
Comment: A summery champagne cocktail with elderflower and cucumber.

ELDERFLOWER COLLINS #1

Glass: Collins
Garnish: Physalis (cape gooseberry) on rim
Method: **SHAKE** first four ingredients with ice and strain into ice-filled glass. **TOP** with soda.

2	shot(s)	**Plymouth gin**
1/2	shot(s)	**Elderflower cordial**
1	shot(s)	**Freshly squeezed lemon juice**
1/8	shot(s)	**Sugar (gomme) syrup**
Top up with		**Soda water (club soda)**

Comment: Just as it says on the lid – a Collins with a hint of elderflower.

ELDERFLOWER COLLINS #2 [NEW]

Glass: Collins
Garnish: Lemon slice
Method: **SHAKE** first four ingredients with ice and strain into ice-filled glass. **TOP** with soda.

2	shot(s)	**Ketel One Citroen vodka**
1/8	shot(s)	**Luxardo maraschino liqueur**
3/4	shot(s)	**Elderflower cordial**
3/4	shot(s)	**Freshly squeezed lemon juice**
Top up with		**Soda water (club soda)**

Comment: Long and refreshing with a floral, cherry and citrus flavour.

ELDERFLOWER MARTINI

Glass: Martini
Garnish: Float rose petal
Method: **SHAKE** all ingredients with ice and fine strain into chilled glass.

1 1/2	shot(s)	**Zubrówka bison vodka**
1/2	shot(s)	**Dry vermouth**
1 1/2	shot(s)	**Elderflower cordial**

Comment: This veritable shrubbery is both floral and grassy with dry borders.

ELEGANTE MARGARITA

Glass: Coupette
Garnish: Lime wedge & salted rim (optional)
Method: **SHAKE** all ingredients with ice and fine strain into chilled glass.

1 1/2	shot(s)	**Sauza Hornitos tequila**
1/2	shot(s)	**Cointreau / triple sec**
1/2	shot(s)	**Rose's lime cordial**
3/4	shot(s)	**Freshly squeezed lime juice**
1/2	shot(s)	**Sugar (gomme) syrup**

Origin: Created in 1999 by Robert Plotkin and Raymon Flores of BarMedia, USA.
Comment: One of the best Margarita recipes around. Richly endowed with flavour.

ELISIAN [NEW]

Glass: Martini
Garnish: Float apple slice
Method: **STIR** all ingredients with ice and strain into chilled glass.

2	shot(s)	**Calvados or applejack brandy**
1/2	shot(s)	**Sweet (rosso) vermouth**
1/2	shot(s)	**Dry vermouth**
1/4	shot(s)	**Maple syrup**
3	dashes	**Angostura aromatic bitters**
3	dashes	**Peychaud's aromatic bitters**

Origin: Created in 2004 by Mickael Perror at Millbank Lounge Bar, London, England.
Comment: Dry and aromatic but not for all.

ELIXIR

Glass: Collins
Garnish: Mint sprig
Method: Lightly **MUDDLE** mint in base of shaker. Add next three ingredients, **SHAKE** with ice and strain into ice-filled glass. **TOP** with soda, stir and serve with straws.

7	fresh	**Mint leaves**
1 1/2	shot(s)	**Green Chartreuse**
1	shot(s)	**Sugar (gomme) syrup**
3/4	shot(s)	**Freshly squeezed lime juice**
Top up with		**Soda water (club soda)**

Origin: Created in 2003 by Gian Franco Pola for Capannina in Cremona and Coconuts in Rimini, Italy.
Comment: A minty, herbal, refreshing summer drink.

FOR MORE INFORMATION SEE OUR

A B C D **E** F G H I J K L M N O P Q R S T U V W X Y Z

ELLE FOR LEATHER

Glass: Collins
Garnish: Vanilla pod
Method: **SHAKE** first four ingredients with ice and strain into glass filled with crushed ice. **TOP** with champagne.

1½	shot(s)	**The Famous Grouse Scotch**
1	shot(s)	**Vanilla schnapps liqueur**
¼	shot(s)	**Freshly squeezed lemon juice**
⅛	shot(s)	**Sugar (gomme) syrup**
Top up with		**Piper-Heidsieck brut champagne**

Origin: Created in 2001 by Reece Clark at Hush Up, London, England.
Comment: A long, cool champagne cocktail pepped up with Scotch whisky and vanilla schnapps. Easy drinking - yet adult.

EMBASSY ROYAL

Glass: Martini
Garnish: Orange zest twist
Method: **SHAKE** all ingredients with ice and fine strain into chilled glass.

1¾	shot(s)	**Bourbon whiskey**
1	shot(s)	**Drambuie liqueur**
1	shot(s)	**Sweet (rosso) vermouth**
1	shot(s)	**Freshly squeezed orange juice**

Comment: An aromatic, herbal and altogether pleasant concoction.

EMERALD MARTINI [NEW]

Glass: Martini
Garnish: Sprayed and discarded lemon & lime zest twists plus mint leaf
Method: **STIR** all ingredients with ice and strain into chilled glass.

2	shot(s)	**Lime flavoured vodka**
1	shot(s)	**Green Chartreuse**
1	shot(s)	**Chilled mineral water**

Origin: Discovered in 2005 at Bugsy's, Prague, Czech Republic.
Comment: A serious drink that's rammed with alcohol and flavour.

EMPEROR'S MEMOIRS

Glass: Collins
Garnish: Orange & lemon zest twists
Method: **SHAKE** first four ingredients with ice and strain into ice-filled glass. **TOP** with ginger beer.

1	shot(s)	**Plymouth gin**
½	shot(s)	**Punt E Mes**
¼	shot(s)	**Ginger cordial (non-alcoholic)**
¼	shot(s)	**Freshly squeezed lemon juice**
Top up with		**Ginger beer**

Origin: Created in 2001 by Douglas Ankrah for Akbar, Soho, London, England.
Comment: Not particularly alcoholic, but strong in a gingery, spicy way.

ENCHANTED [NEW]

Glass: Collins
Garnish: Lychee/mint sprig
Method: **MUDDLE** grapes in base of shaker. Add next three ingredients, **SHAKE** with ice and fine strain into ice-filled glass. **TOP** with ginger ale.

7	fresh	**White seedless grapes**
1½	shot(s)	**Rémy Martin cognac**
½	shot(s)	**Soho lychee liqueur**
½	shot(s)	**Freshly squeezed lime juice**
Top up with		**Ginger ale**

Origin: Created by Wayne Collins, UK.
Comment: Light, fruity and easy drinking with lychee and ginger dominating.

ENGLISH GARDEN [NEW]

Glass: Collins
Garnish: Three slices of cucumber
Method: **SHAKE** all ingredients with ice and fine strain into ice-filled glass.

2	shot(s)	**Plymouth gin**
3	shot(s)	**Pressed apple juice**
½	shot(s)	**Elderflower cordial**
½	shot(s)	**Freshly squeezed lime juice**

Comment: Quintessentially English in flavour – anyone for tennis?

ENGLISH MARTINI

Glass: Martini
Garnish: Rosemary
Method: **MUDDLE** rosemary in base of shaker. Add other ingredients, **STIR** with ice and strain into chilled glass.

1	sprig	**Rosemary**
2½	shot(s)	**Plymouth gin**
¾	shot(s)	**Elderflower cordial**
½	shot(s)	**Sugar (gomme) syrup**

Origin: Adapted from a drink created in 2003 at MJU, Millennium Hotel, London, England.
Comment: Great served with roast lamb.

ENGLISH ROSE [NEW]

Glass: Martini
Garnish: Maraschino cherry
Method: **STIR** all ingredients with ice and strain into chilled glass.

1¾	shot(s)	**Plymouth gin**
¾	shot(s)	**Dry vermouth**
½	shot(s)	**Parfait Amour liqueur**
¼	shot(s)	**Freshly squeezed lemon juice**
⅛	shot(s)	**Pomegranate (grenadine) syrup**

Comment: A dry, complex, gin laced drink. Stir well.

●●●●○

ENVY

Glass: Martini
Garnish: Star fruit on rim
Method: SHAKE all ingredients with ice and fine strain into chilled glass.

1/2	shot(s)	**Ketel One vodka**
2	shot(s)	**Midori melon liqueur**
1	shot(s)	**Peach schnapps liqueur**
3/4	shot(s)	**Hazelnut (crème de noisette) liqueur**
1/4	shot(s)	**Freshly squeezed lime juice**

Comment: Green with ... melon, oh, and a hint of hazelnut. A tad on the sweet side.

●●●●○

EPESTONE DAIQUIRI [NEW]

Glass: Martini
Garnish: Lime wedge
Method: SHAKE all ingredients with ice and fine strain into chilled glass.

2	shot(s)	**Light white rum**
1/2	shot(s)	**Sisca crème de cassis**
1/2	shot(s)	**Freshly squeezed lime juice**
1/2	shot(s)	**Chilled mineral water (omit if wet ice)**

Comment: A pleasant, maroon coloured, black-currant flavoured Daiquiri.

●●●◐○

EPIPHANY [NEW]

Glass: Martini
Garnish: Berries on stick
Method: SHAKE all ingredients with ice and fine strain into chilled glass.

1 3/4	shot(s)	**Bourbon whiskey**
1/2	shot(s)	**Crème de mûre (blackberry) liqueur**
2	shot(s)	**Pressed apple juice**

Origin: Created in 2004 by Naomi Young at Match, London, England.
Comment: Not sure what a fruity bourbon drink has to do with the manifestation of Christ.

●●●●◐

EPISCOPAL [NEW]

Glass: Old-fashioned
Method: STIR ingredients with ice and fine strain into chilled glass.

1 1/2	shot(s)	**Green Chartreuse**
3/4	shot(s)	**Yellow Chartreuse**

Origin: A well-established drink promoted by the marketeers at Chartreuse and named after the devotees in the purple dresses.
Comment: My favourite way to enjoy Chartreuse. Especially good when made with V.E.P. Chartreuse.

●●●●●

ESCALATOR MARTINI

Glass: Martini
Garnish: Pear slice on rim
Method: SHAKE all ingredients with ice and fine strain into chilled glass.

1	shot(s)	**Poire William eau de vie**
1/2	shot(s)	**Zubrówka bison vodka**
2	shot(s)	**Pressed apple juice**
1/8	shot(s)	**Sugar (gomme) syrup**

Origin: Created in 2002 by Kevin Connelly, England. It's called an escalator because the 'apples and pears', rhyming slang for 'stairs', are shaken.
Comment: This orchard-fresh concoction was originally made with Korte Palinka (Hungarian pear schnapps) - if using that or Poire William liqueur in place of Poire William eau de vie, little or no sugar is necessary.

●●●●◐

ESPECIAL DAY [NEW]

Glass: Martini
Garnish: Blackberry & discarded lemon zest twist
Method: MUDDLE blackberries in base of shaker. Add other ingredients, **SHAKE** with ice and fine strain into chilled glass.

3	fresh	**Blackberries**
2	shot(s)	**Light white rum**
1/2	shot(s)	**Sweet (rosso) vermouth**
3/4	shot(s)	**Crème de mûre (blackberry) liqueur**
1/2	shot(s)	**Pressed pineapple juice**
3	dashes	**Peychaud's aromatic bitters**

Origin: Created in 2005 by Tonin Kacaj at Maze, London, England.
Comment: Beautifully balanced, aromatic, rum laced and fruity.

●●●●○

ESPRESSO DAIQUIRI [NEW]

Glass: Martini
Garnish: Float 3 coffee beans
Method: SHAKE all ingredients with ice and fine strain into chilled glass.

2	shot(s)	**Light white rum**
1 3/4	shot(s)	**Cold espresso coffee**
1/2	shot(s)	**Sugar (gomme) syrup**

Variant: Espresso Martini
Comment: Rum based twist on the ubiquitous Espresso Martini.

DRINKS ARE GRADED AS FOLLOWS:

● DISGUSTING ●◐ PRETTY AWFUL ●● BEST AVOIDED
●●◐ DISAPPOINTING ●●● ACCEPTABLE ●●●◐ GOOD
●●●● RECOMMENDED ●●●●◐ HIGHLY RECOMMENDED
●●●●● OUTSTANDING / EXCEPTIONAL

A B C D E F G H I J K L M N O P Q R S T U V W X Y Z

ESPRESSO MARTINI

Glass: Martini
Garnish: Float 3 coffee beans
Method: **SHAKE** all ingredients with ice and fine strain into chilled glass.

2	shot(s)	**Ketel One vodka**
1¾	shot(s)	**Cold espresso coffee**
½	shot(s)	**Sugar (gomme) syrup**

Variants: Espresso Daiquiri, Insomniac, Irish Coffee Martini, Jalisco Espresso, Jolt'ini.
Comment: Forget the vodka Red Bull, this is the connoisseur's way of combining caffeine and vodka.

ESQUIRE #1 [NEW]

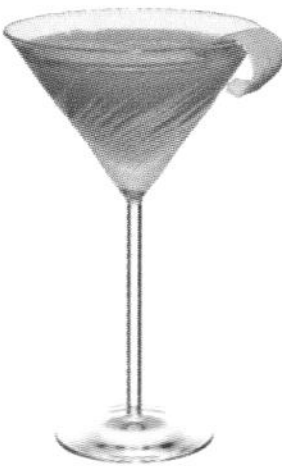

Glass: Martini
Garnish: Orange zest twist
Method: **SHAKE** all ingredients with ice and fine strain into chilled glass.

2	shot(s)	**Bourbon whiskey**
¾	shot(s)	**Grand Marnier liqueur**
¾	shot(s)	**Freshly squeezed orange juice**
1	dash	**Angostura aromatic bitters**
½	shot(s)	**Chilled mineral water (omit if wet ice)**

Comment: Spicy bourbon laden with orange fruit.

ESQUIRE #2

Glass: Martini
Garnish: Blackberry
Method: **STIR** all ingredients with ice and strain into chilled glass.

1½	shot(s)	**Ketel One vodka**
¾	shot(s)	**Raspberry flavoured vodka**
¾	shot(s)	**Parfait amour liqueur**

Origin: Created in the 1990s by Dick Bradsell for Esquire Magazine.
Comment: One for hardened Martini drinkers.

HOW TO MAKE SUGAR SYRUP

To make your own sugar syrup, gradually pour TWO cups of granulated sugar into a saucepan containing ONE cup of hot water. Stir as you pour and carry on stirring and simmering until the sugar is dissolved. Do not let the water even come close to boiling and only simmer for as long as it takes to dissolve the sugar. Allow syrup to cool and pour into an empty bottle. Ideally, you should finely strain your syrup into the bottle to remove any undissolved crystals which could otherwise encourage crystallisation. If kept in a refrigerator this mixture will last for a couple of months.

ESTES [NEW]

Glass: Collins
Garnish: Raspberry & thin strips of lime zest
Method: **MUDDLE** raspberries in base of shaker. Add other ingredients, **SHAKE** with ice and fine strain into glass filled with crushed ice.

7	fresh	**Raspberries**
1¾	shot(s)	**Sauza Hornitos tequila**
½	shot(s)	**Chambord black raspberry liqueur**
1¾	shot(s)	**Cranberry juice**
½	shot(s)	**Agave syrup (from health food shop)**
¾	shot(s)	**Freshly squeezed lime juice**

Origin: Created in 2005 by Henry Besant and Andres Masso, London, England, and named in honour of Tomas Estes, the official Tequila Ambassador in Europe.
Comment: This rich, fruity long drink is a real crowd pleaser.

ESTILO VIEJO [NEW]

Glass: Old-fashioned
Garnish: Lime zest twist
Method: **STIR** half of the tequila with two ice cubes in a glass. Add agave syrup and Angostura and two more ice cubes. Stir some more and add another two ice cubes and the rest of the tequila. Stir lots more and add more ice. The melting and stirring of the ice is essential to the dilution and taste of the drink.

2½	shot(s)	**Sauza Hornitos tequila**
½	shot(s)	**Agave syrup (from health food store)**
3	dashes	**Angostura aromatic bitters**

Origin: The name of this drink literally translates from Spanish as 'Old Style'. It is basically a Tequila Old-fashioned.
Comment: Even better when made with añejo tequila.

THE ESTRIBO [NEW]

Glass: Martini
Garnish: Berries on stick
Method: **SHAKE** all ingredients with ice and fine strain into chilled glass.

2	shot(s)	**Sauza Hornitos tequila**
¼	shot(s)	**Sisca crème de cassis**
1	shot(s)	**Pressed pineapple juice**
½	shot(s)	**Double (heavy) cream**
½	shot	**Milk**

Origin: The signature drink at El Estribo, Mexico City, which sadly closed in 2005. The drink and this once legendary tequila bar's name translate as 'The Stirrup'.
Comment: Pink and creamy but with a tequila kick.

E.T.

Glass: Shot
Method: Refrigerate ingredients and **LAYER** in chilled glass by carefully pouring in the following order.

1/2	shot(s)	**Midori melon liqueur**
1/2	shot(s)	**Baileys Irish Cream liqueur**
1/2	shot(s)	**Ketel One vodka**

Comment: Fortified creamy melon.

F-16 SHOT

Glass: Shot
Garnish: Split stemmed cherry on rim
Method: Refrigerate ingredients then **LAYER** in chilled glass by carefully pouring in the following order.

1/2	shot(s)	**Kahlúa coffee liqueur**
1/2	shot(s)	**Baileys Irish Cream liqueur**
1/2	shot(s)	**Light white rum**

Origin: Named for the F-16 jet and closely related to the B-52.
Comment: May not break the sound barrier but at least it layers well.

EVITA

Glass: Martini
Garnish: Orange zest twist
Method: SHAKE all ingredients with ice and fine strain into chilled glass.

2	shot(s)	**Ketel One vodka**
1/2	shot(s)	**Midori melon liqueur**
1	shot(s)	**Freshly squeezed orange juice**
1/2	shot(s)	**Freshly squeezed lime juice**

Comment: A tangy, lime green, medium-sweet combination of melon, orange and lime.

F. WILLY SHOT

Glass: Shot
Method: SHAKE all ingredients with ice and fine strain into chilled glass.

1/2	shot(s)	**Ketel One vodka**
1/2	shot(s)	**Light white rum**
1/2	shot(s)	**Luxardo Amaretto di Saschira**
1/2	shot(s)	**Cointreau / triple sec**
1/4	shot(s)	**Rose's lime cordial**

Comment: Not as bad as it looks or sounds.

EXOTIC PASSION

Glass: Collins
Garnish: Pineapple wedge & strawberry
Method: SHAKE all ingredients with ice and strain into ice-filled glass.

1 1/2	shot(s)	**Ketel One vodka**
3/4	shot(s)	**Passoã passion fruit liqueur**
3/4	shot(s)	**Crème de fraise (strawberry) liqueur**
1 1/2	shot(s)	**Pressed pineapple juice**
1 1/2	shot(s)	**Freshly squeezed golden grapefruit juice**

Comment: Bittersweet and floral - one for the poolside.

FANCY DRINK

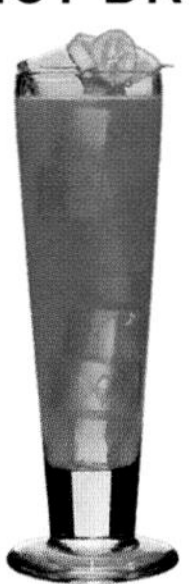

Glass: Sling
Garnish: Lemon slice & kumquat
Method: SHAKE first three ingredients with ice and strain into ice-filled glass. **TOP** with bitter lemon.

1	shot(s)	**Grand Marnier liqueur**
1	shot(s)	**Light white rum**
2	shot(s)	**Freshly squeezed grapefruit juice**
Top up with		**Bitter lemon**

Comment: Tasty tart! Refreshingly sour.

EXTRADITION

Glass: Old-fashioned
Garnish: Strawberry on rim
Method: MUDDLE strawberries in base of shaker. Add other ingredients, **SHAKE** with ice and fine strain into ice-filled glass.

3	fresh	**Hulled strawberries**
2	shot(s)	**Pisco**
2	shot(s)	**Pressed apple juice**
3/4	shot(s)	**Passion fruit sugar syrup**

Origin: Created in 2001 by Francis Timmons at Detroit, London, England.
Comment: A light, fruity drink for a summer afternoon.

FANCY FREE [NEW]

Glass: Martini
Garnish: Maraschino cherry
Method: SHAKE all ingredients with ice and fine strain into chilled glass.

2	shot(s)	**Bourbon whiskey**
1/2	shot(s)	**Luxardo maraschino liqueur**
2	dashes	**Angostura aromatic bitters**
2	dashes	**Fee Brothers orange bitters**
1/2	shot(s)	**Chilled mineral water (omit if wet ice)**

Comment: Aromatised, tamed bourbon.

FANTASIA [NEW]

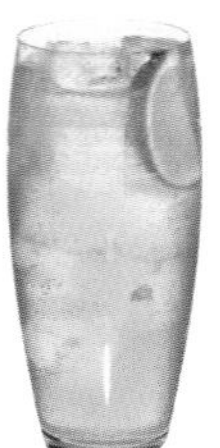

Glass: Collins
Garnish: Lime wedge
Method: **SHAKE** first four ingredients with ice and strain into ice-filled glass. **TOP** with 7-Up, stir and serve with straws.

1/4	shot(s)	**Freshly squeezed lime juice**
1/4	shot(s)	**Freshly squeezed lemon juice**
1/4	shot(s)	**Sugar (gomme) syrup**
5	dashes	**Angostura aromatic bitters**
Top up with		**7-Up / lemonade**

Origin: Discovered in 2004 at Claris Hotel, Barcelona, Spain.
Comment: A Spanish twist on the popular Australian LLB.

FAT SAILOR [NEW]

Glass: Old-fashioned
Garnish: Lime wedge
Method: **SHAKE** all ingredients with ice and strain into glass filled with crushed ice.

1 1/2	shot(s)	**Mount Gay Eclipse golden rum**
3/4	shot(s)	**Pusser's Navy rum (54.5% alc./vol.)**
1/4	shot(s)	**Kahlúa coffee liqueur**
1	shot(s)	**Rose's lime cordial**
1/2	shot(s)	**Freshly squeezed lime juice**

Origin: Tiki style drink of unknown origin.
Comment: A tasty, suitably calorie laden, rum concoction.

FBI

Glass: Collins
Garnish: Crumbled Cadbury's Flake bar
Method: **BLEND** all ingredients with 18oz scoop of crushed ice and serve with straws.

2	shot(s)	**Ketel One vodka**
1	shot(s)	**Baileys Irish Cream liqueur**
1	shot(s)	**Kahlúa coffee liqueur**
3	scoops	**Vanilla ice cream**

Comment: Yummy alcoholic milkshake with coffee and whiskey cream.

LA FEUILLE MORTE

Glass: Collins (10oz/290ml max)
Method: **POUR** first three ingredients into glass. Serve iced water separately in a small jug (known in France as a 'broc') so the customer can dilute to their own taste. (I recommend five shots.) Lastly, add ice to fill glass.

1	shot(s)	**Ricard pastis**
1/2	shot(s)	**Pomegranate (grenadine) syrup**
1/2	shot(s)	**Mint (menthe) syrup**
Top up with		**Chilled mineral water**

Origin: Pronounced 'Fueel-Mort', the name literally means 'The dead leaf', a reference to its colour.
Comment: A traditional French way to serve pastis.

FIESTA [NEW]

Glass: Martini
Garnish: Pomegranate seeds in drink
Method: **SHAKE** all ingredients with ice and fine strain into chilled glass.

1	shot(s)	**Light white rum**
1	shot(s)	**Calvados (applejack brandy)**
1	shot(s)	**Dry vermouth**
1/8	shot(s)	**Freshly squeezed lime juice**
1/8	shot(s)	**Pomegranate (grenadine) syrup**

Comment: With the right amount of quality pomegranate syrup, this is a great drink.

FIFTH AVENUE SHOT

Glass: Shot
Method: Refrigerate ingredients then **LAYER** in chilled glass by carefully pouring in the following order.

1/2	shot(s)	**Dark crème de cacao liqueur**
1/2	shot(s)	**Apricot brandy liqueur**
1/2	shot(s)	**Double (heavy) cream**

Comment: A sweet, apricot and chocolate creamy shot.

57 T-BIRD SHOT

Glass: Shot
Method: **SHAKE** all ingredients with ice and fine strain into chilled glass.

1/2	shot(s)	**Ketel One vodka**
1/2	shot(s)	**Grand Marnier liqueur**
1/2	shot(s)	**Luxardo Amaretto di Saschira**

Variants: With California Plates add 1/2 shot orange juice; with Cape Cod Plates add 1/2 shot cranberry juice; with Florida Plates add 1/2 shot grapefruit juice; with Hawaiian Plates add 1/2 shot pineapple juice.
Comment: A '57 T-bird, or 1957 Ford Thunderbird to give it its full title, immortalised in the Beach Boys' song 'Fun Fun Fun', was the classic car for any 1950s teenager. Top down, radio up, girl next to you...

FINE & DANDY [UPDATED]

Glass: Martini
Garnish: Lemon zest twist
Method: **SHAKE** all ingredients with ice and fine strain into chilled glass.

1 3/4	shot(s)	**Plymouth gin**
3/4	shot(s)	**Cointreau / triple sec**
1/2	shot(s)	**Freshly squeezed lemon juice**
1/8	shot(s)	**Sugar (gomme) syrup**
1/2	shot(s)	**Chilled mineral water (omit if wet ice)**
2	dashes	**Angostura aromatic bitters**

Comment: A challenging, gin based drink that's soured with lemon and sweetened with orange liqueur.

FINITALY

Glass: Martini
Garnish: Blueberries or raspberries.
Method: **SHAKE** all ingredients with ice and fine strain into chilled glass.

- $1\frac{1}{2}$ shot(s) **Cranberry flavoured vodka**
- $\frac{1}{2}$ shot(s) **Sweet (rosso) vermouth**
- $\frac{1}{2}$ shot(s) **Chambord black raspberry liqueur**
- $\frac{3}{4}$ shot(s) **Chilled mineral water (omit if wet ice)**

Origin: Created by Michael Mahe at Hush, London, England.
Comment: A simple, berry led Martini.

FINN ROUGE [NEW]

Glass: Martini
Garnish: Lemon zest twist
Method: **MUDDLE** raspberries in base of shaker. Add other ingredients, **SHAKE** with ice and fine strain into chilled glass.

- 5 fresh **Raspberries**
- $1\frac{3}{4}$ shot(s) **Cranberry flavoured vodka**
- $\frac{1}{2}$ shot(s) **Crème de framboise (raspberry) liqueur**
- $\frac{3}{4}$ shot(s) **Cranberry juice**
- $\frac{1}{4}$ shot(s) **Freshly squeezed lemon juice**
- $\frac{1}{8}$ shot(s) **Sugar (gomme) syrup**
- 1 pinch **Black pepper**

Origin: Adapted from a drink created in 2005 by Jamie Stephenson, Manchester, England.
Comment: A rather red, rasping, berry rich drink.

FINNBERRY MARTINI

Glass: Martini
Garnish: Cranberries
Method: **SHAKE** all ingredients with ice and fine strain into chilled glass.

- 2 shot(s) **Cranberry flavoured vodka**
- 2 shot(s) **Lingonberry or cranberry juice**
- 1 shot(s) **Lapponia cloudberry liqueur**

Origin: I created this in 2002 after a trip to Finland with Finlandia vodka.
Comment: This rich berry Martini can be varied by using other berry liqueurs in the Lapponia range – try using two with a half shot of each.

FIREBALL

Glass: Shot
Method: **SHAKE** all ingredients with ice and fine strain into chilled glass.

- 1 shot(s) **Cinnamon schnapps liqueur**
- 3 drops **Tabasco sauce**

Comment: Down this in one and be prepared for a sweet cinnamon palate quickly followed by a hot, spicy finish.

FIRST OF JULY

Glass: Martini
Garnish: Apple slice & blackberry on stick
Method: **MUDDLE** blackberries in base of shaker. Add other ingredients, **SHAKE** with ice and fine strain into chilled glass.

- 4 fresh **Blackberries**
- 2 shot(s) **Calvados or applejack brandy**
- 1 shot(s) **Chambord black raspberry liqueur**
- 2 shot(s) **Freshly squeezed pink grapefruit juice**

Origin: Created on 1st of July 2004 by David Guidi at Morton's, London, England.
Comment: Rich blackberry fruit with a hint of grapefruit acidity.

FISH HOUSE PUNCH #1 [NEW]

Glass: Collins
Garnish: Lemon wheel
Method: **SHAKE** all ingredients with ice and strain into ice-filled glass.

- 1 shot(s) **Rémy Martin cognac**
- 1 shot(s) **Mount Gay Eclipse golden rum**
- $\frac{3}{4}$ shot(s) **Peach schnapps liqueur**
- $\frac{3}{4}$ shot(s) **Freshly squeezed lemon juice**
- $\frac{1}{4}$ shot(s) **Sugar (gomme) syrup**
- 2 shot(s) **Chilled mineral water**

Origin: Probably the most famous of all punch recipes, this originated in 1732 at a Philadelphia fishing and social club called the 'State in Schuylkill'. As a punch the original was mixed in larger quantities and served from a punch bowl.

Many modern variations use soda water (club soda) in place of mineral water. The inclusion of peach liqueur is a modern substitute for the traditional peach brandy. However, it's believed the Schuylkill original omitted peach entirely.
Comment: This fruit laced mix is neither too sweet, nor too strong.

FISH HOUSE PUNCH #2 [UPDATED]

Glass: Collins
Garnish: Lemon wheel
Method: **SHAKE** all ingredients with ice and strain into ice-filled glass.

- 1 shot(s) **Rémy Martin cognac**
- 1 shot(s) **Light white rum**
- 1 shot(s) **Peach schnapps liqueur**
- 2 shot(s) **Strong cold tea (English Breakfast)**
- $1\frac{1}{2}$ shot(s) **Freshly squeezed lemon juice**
- $\frac{1}{4}$ shot(s) **Sugar (gomme) syrup**

Comment: Over the decades this recipe has constantly morphed. The inclusion of cold tea is the latest adaptation.

FIZZES

Like the Collins, this mid-19th century classic is basically a sour lengthened with charged water and at first glance there is little difference between a Fizz and a Collins. However, there are several distinguishing features. A Collins should be served in a fourteen ounce tall glass while that used for a Fizz should be no bigger than eight ounces. A Collins should be served in an ice-filled glass, while a Fizz should be served in a chilled glass without ice.

Ideally a Fizz should also be made using charged water from a siphon in preference to soda from bottles or cans. The burst of pressure from the siphon bulb generates tiny bubbles which give off carbonic acid, benefiting the flavour and the mouthfeel of the drink.

For the correct proportions I have once again turned to David Embury's seminal 'The Fine Art Of Mixing Drinks'. He recommends "1 - or a little less – sweet (sugar, fruit syrup, or liqueur), 2 sour (lime or lemon juice), 3 - or a little more - strong (spirituous liquor), and 4 weak (charged water and ice). I interpret this as follows: 2 shots spirit (gin, whiskey, vodka, brandy), 1 shot lemon or lime juice, 1/2 shot sugar syrup, topped up with soda. I also like to add half a fresh egg white, which technically makes the drink a 'Silver Fizz'.

●●●●○

FIZZ [NEW]

Glass: Collins (8oz max)
Garnish: Lemon slice
Method: **SHAKE** first four ingredients with ice and strain into chilled glass. **TOP** with soda.

2	shot(s)	**Spirit (gin, whiskey, vodka, brandy)**
1	shot(s)	**Freshly squeezed lemon or lime juice**
1/2	shot(s)	**Sugar (gomme) syrup**
1/2	fresh	**Egg white (optional)**
Top up with		**Soda water (from siphon)**

Origin: A mid-19th century classic.
Comment: I recommend the Derby Fizz with its combination of liqueur and spirits over these more traditional versions.

●●○○○

FLAMING DR PEPPER [NEW]

Glass: Shot & Boston
Method: **POUR** beer into Boston glass. **LAYER** amaretto and rum in chilled shot glass by carefully pouring amaretto and then rum. **IGNITE** the rum and carefully lift shot glass then drop (bottom first) into Boston glass.

1	bottle	**Lager beer**
1/2	shot(s)	**Luxardo Amaretto di Saschira**
1/2	shot(s)	**151° overproof rum**

Origin: So named as the end result resembles the taste of the proprietary Dr Pepper soft drink. This drink inspired an episode of The Simpsons featuring a similar drink titled the 'Flaming Homer' and later the 'Flaming Moe' (after the programme's bartender).
Comment: Please consider the likelihood of burning yourself while attempting to lift the flaming shot into the beer.

●●○○○

FLAMING FERRARI

This flaming drink (to be downed in one) requires an assistant to help the drinker consume the concoction.

Step 1.
Glass: Martini
Method: **LAYER** ingredients by carefully pouring in the following order.

1/2	shot(s)	**Pomegranate (grenadine) syrup**
1	shot(s)	**Galliano liqueur**
1	shot(s)	**Opal Nera black sambuca**
1	shot(s)	**Green Chartreuse**

Step 2.
Glass: Two shot glasses.
Method: **POUR** each ingredient into its own shot glass.

1	shot(s)	**Grand Marnier liqueur**
1	shot(s)	**Pusser's Navy rum**

Step 3.
Method: **IGNITE** the contents of the Martini glass. Give two long straws to the drinker and instruct them to drink the contents of the Martini glass in one go. As they do so, slowly **POUR** the contents of the two shot glasses into the flaming Martini glass.
Variant: Flaming Lamborghini with coffee liqueur and blue curaçao in the shot glasses.
Comment: Not recommended if you want to remember the rest of the evening and please be careful – alcohol and fire is a risky combination.

FLAMING HENRY

Glass: Shot
Method: **LAYER** by carefully pouring ingredients in the order below. Finally **IGNITE** bourbon. Extinguish flame prior to drinking and beware of hot glass rim.

1/2	shot(s)	**Luxardo Amaretto di Saschira**
1/2	shot(s)	**Baileys Irish Cream liqueur**
1/2	shot(s)	**Bourbon whiskey**

Origin: Created by Henry Smiff and friends in the South of France and popularised by one of their number, John Coe, the successful London drinks wholesaler.
Comment: Flaming good shot.

FLAMINGO #1

Glass: Martini
Garnish: Banana chunk on rim
Method: **SHAKE** all ingredients with ice and fine strain into chilled glass.

1	shot(s)	**Bourbon whiskey**
3/4	shot(s)	**Crème de bananes liqueur**
1 1/2	shot(s)	**Freshly squeezed orange juice**
3/4	shot(s)	**Freshly squeezed lemon juice**
1/2	fresh	**Egg white**

Comment: It's not pink but it has bourbon, banana, orange and lemon smoothed with egg white.

FLAMINGO #2

Glass: Martini
Garnish: Star fruit
Method: **SHAKE** all ingredients with ice and fine strain into chilled glass.

2	shot(s)	**Aged rum**
1 1/2	shot(s)	**Pressed pineapple juice**
1/2	shot(s)	**Freshly squeezed lime juice**
1/8	shot(s)	**Pomegranate (grenadine) syrup**

Origin: Classic of unknown origins.
Comment: A tasty, pink drink with a frothy top.

FLATLINER

Glass: Shot
Method: **POUR** sambuca into chilled glass. **LAYER** tequila by carefully pouring over sambuca. Lastly **DRIP** pepper sauce onto drink. This will sink through the tequila to form an orange line on top of the sambuca.

3/4	shot(s)	**Luxardo Sambuca dei Cesari**
3/4	shot(s)	**Sauza Hornitos tequila**
8	drops	**Tabasco pepper sauce**

Comment: A serious combination of sweetness, strength and heat. Looks great but tastes...

FLIPS

Flips basically consist of any fortified wine or liquor shaken with a whole egg and sweetened with sugar. They are typically garnished with a dusting of nutmeg and served in a sour glass or small Martini glass. Cream may sometimes be added to a Flip. In their day it was common for Flips to be served hot.

A B C D E **F** G H I J K L M N O P Q R S T U V W X Y Z

FLIP [NEW]

Glass: Sour or Martini
Garnish: Dust with freshly grated nutmeg
Method: **SHAKE** all ingredients with ice and fine strain into chilled glass.

2	shot(s)	**Spirit (brandy, gin, whiskey etc.)**
1	shot(s)	**Sugar (gomme) syrup**
1	fresh	**Egg (white & yolk)**
1/2	shot(s)	**Double (heavy) cream**

Variant: Served hot in a toddy glass. Heat in a microwave oven or mix in a pan over heat.
Comment: I favour creamy, spicy, bourbon based Flips.

THE FLIRT

Glass: Martini
Garnish: Lipstick on rim
Method: **SHAKE** all ingredients with ice and fine strain into chilled glass.

2	shot(s)	**Sauza Hornitos tequila**
3/4	shot(s)	**Apricot brandy liqueur**
3/4	shot(s)	**Freshly squeezed lime juice**
1	shot(s)	**Cranberry juice**

Origin: Created in 2002 by Dick Bradsell at Lonsdale House, London, England.
Comment: A fruity drink to upset glass washers throughout the land.

FLIRTINI #1 [NEW]

Glass: Martini
Garnish: Pineapple wedge on rim
Method: **SHAKE** all ingredients with ice and fine strain into chilled glass.

2	shot(s)	**Ketel One vodka**
1 1/2	shot(s)	**Pressed pineapple juice**
1/4	shot(s)	**Chambord black raspberry liqueur**

AKA: French Martini
Origin: Made famous on television's Sex And The City. Said to have been created in 2003 for Sarah Jessica Parker at Guastavinos, New York City, USA.
Comment: It's a French Martini! Hard not to like.

FLIRTINI #2

Glass: Martini
Garnish: Cherry on rim
Method: **SHAKE** first three ingredients with ice and fine strain into chilled glass. **TOP** with champagne.

3/4	shot(s)	**Ketel One vodka**
3/4	shot(s)	**Cointreau / triple sec**
2	shot(s)	**Pressed pineapple juice**
Top up with		**Piper-Heidsieck brut champagne**

Origin: Adapted from a recipe by the New York bartender Dale DeGroff.
Comment: A flirtatious little number that slips down easily.

FLORAL MARTINI [NEW]

Glass: Martini
Garnish: Edible flower petal
Method: **STIR** all ingredients with ice and fine strain into chilled glass.

2	shot(s)	**Plymouth gin**
1/2	shot(s)	**Elderflower cordial**
1/2	shot(s)	**Rosewater**
3/4	shot(s)	**Chilled mineral water (omit if wet ice)**

Origin: Adapted from a drink created in 2003 at Zander Bar, London, England.
Comment: An aptly named, gin based Martini.

FLORIDA COCKTAIL (MOCKTAIL) [NEW]

Glass: Collins
Garnish: Orange wheel & cherry on stick (sail)
Method: **SHAKE** first four ingredients with ice and strain into ice-filled glass, **TOP** with soda.

1	shot(s)	**Freshly squeezed pink grapefruit juice**
2	shot(s)	**Freshly squeezed orange juice**
1/2	shot(s)	**Freshly squeezed lemon juice**
1/4	shot(s)	**Sugar (gomme) syrup**
Top up with		**Soda water (club soda)**

Comment: The Florida sun shines through this fruity, refreshing drink.

FLORIDA DAIQUIRI

Glass: Martini
Garnish: Maraschino cherry
Method: **SHAKE** all ingredients with ice and fine strain into chilled glass.

2	shot(s)	**Light white rum**
1/2	shot(s)	**Freshly squeezed lime juice**
1/4	shot(s)	**Sugar (gomme) syrup**
1/2	shot(s)	**Freshly squeezed grapefruit juice**
1/8	shot(s)	**Maraschino liqueur**
3/4	shot(s)	**Chilled mineral water (omit if wet ice)**

Comment: The classic blend of rum, lime and sugar, but with a hint of freshly squeezed grapefruit juice and maraschino. A user-friendly version of a Hemingway Special.

FLORIDA SLING [UPDATED]

Glass: Sling
Garnish: Redcurrants/berries
Method: **SHAKE** all ingredients with ice and strain into ice-filled glass.

2	shot(s)	**Plymouth gin**
1/4	shot(s)	**Cherry (brandy) liqueur**
2	shot(s)	**Pressed pineapple juice**
3/4	shot(s)	**Freshly squeezed lemon juice**
1/4	shot(s)	**Pomegranate (grenadine) syrup**

Comment: A tall, pink, dumbed down Singapore Sling.

FLORIDITA DAIQUIRI

Glass: Martini
Garnish: Maraschino cherry
Method: **BLEND** all ingredients with 12oz scoop of crushed ice. Pour into glass and serve.

2 shot(s) **Light white rum**
1/2 shot(s) **Freshly squeezed lime juice**
1/2 shot(s) **Sugar (gomme) syrup**
1/8 shot(s) **Luxardo maraschino liqueur**

Variant: With fruit.
Origin: Emilio Gonzalez is said to have first adapted the Natural Daiquiri into this frozen version at the Plaza Hotel in Cuba. However, Constantino Ribalaigua Vert of Havana's Floridita bar made the drink famous in 1912 and today the Floridita is known as 'the cradle of the Daiquiri'.
Comment: Great on a hot day, but the coldness masks much of the flavour evident when this drink is served 'up' or natural.

FLORIDITA MARGARITA

Glass: Coupette
Garnish: Lime wedge & salted rim (optional)
Method: **SHAKE** all ingredients with ice and fine strain into chilled glass.

1 1/2 shot(s) **Sauza Hornitos tequila**
1/2 shot(s) **Cointreau / triple sec**
1/2 shot(s) **Cranberry juice**
1/4 shot(s) **Rose's lime cordial**
1 1/2 shot(s) **Freshly squeezed grapefruit juice**
3/4 shot(s) **Freshly squeezed lime juice**
1/2 shot(s) **Sugar (gomme) syrup**

Origin: Created in 1999 by Robert Plotkin and Raymon Flores of BarMedia, USA.
Comment: A blush coloured, Margarita-style drink with a well-matched amalgamation of flavours.

FLUFFY DUCK [NEW]

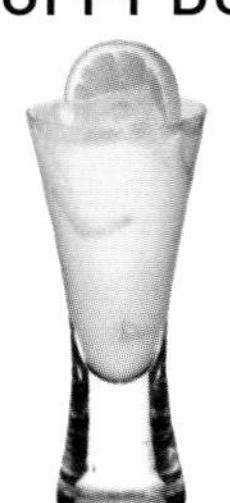

Glass: Collins
Garnish: Orange slice
Method: **SHAKE** first four ingredients with ice and strain into ice-filled glass. **TOP** with soda.

1 1/2 shot(s) **Plymouth gin**
1 shot(s) **Advocaat liqueur**
1/2 shot(s) **Cointreau / triple sec**
1 shot(s) **Freshly squeezed orange juice**
Top up with **Soda water (club soda)**

Comment: Light, creamy and easy drinking. The gin's character prevents it from being too fluffy.

FLUTTER

Glass: Martini
Garnish: Orange zest twist
Method: **SHAKE** all ingredients with ice and fine strain into chilled glass.

2 shot(s) **Sauza Hornitos tequila**
1 shot(s) **Kahlúa coffee liqueur**
1 1/4 shot(s) **Pressed pineapple juice**

Origin: Created in 2003 by Tony Conigliaro at Lonsdale House, London, England.
Comment: The three ingredients combine brilliantly.

FLY LIKE A BUTTERFLY

Glass: Martini
Garnish: Orange zest twist
Method: **SHAKE** all ingredients with ice and fine strain into chilled glass.

1 1/2 shot(s) **Dry vermouth**
1 1/2 shot(s) **Sweet (rosso) vermouth**
3/4 shot(s) **Dubonnet red**
3/4 shot(s) **Freshly squeezed orange juice**

Origin: My take on a classic called a 'Lovely Butterfly'.
Comment: This light, aromatic, sweet and sour beauty has a grown-up, quinine-rich flavour but lacks the 'sting like a bee' finish.

FLYING DUTCHMAN MARTINI

Glass: Martini
Garnish: Orange zest twist
Method: **STIR** all ingredients with ice and strain into chilled glass.

2 1/2 shot(s) **Oude jenever**
1/4 shot(s) **Cointreau / triple sec**
2 dashes **Fee Brothers orange bitters**
3/4 shot(s) **Chilled mineral water**

Comment: A Martini with more than a hint of orange.

FLYING GRASSHOPPER [UPDATED]

Glass: Martini
Garnish: Chocolate powder rim & mint leaf
Method: **SHAKE** all ingredients with ice and fine strain into chilled glass.

1 shot(s) **Ketel One vodka**
3/4 shot(s) **White crème de cacao liqueur**
1/2 shot(s) **White crème de menthe liqueur**
3/4 shot(s) **Double (heavy) cream**
3/4 shot(s) **Milk**

Comment: A Grasshopper with vodka – tastes like a choc mint ice cream.

FLYING SCOTSMAN

Glass: Old-fashioned
Method: **STIR** all ingredients with ice and strain into ice-filled glass.

2	shot(s)	**The Famous Grouse Scotch**
2	shot(s)	**Sweet (rosso) vermouth**
1/4	shot(s)	**Sugar (gomme) syrup**
3	dashes	**Angostura aromatic bitters**

Comment: Sweetened Scotch with plenty of spice: like a homemade whisky liqueur.

FLYING TIGRE COCTEL

Glass: Martini
Garnish: Orange zest twist
Method: **SHAKE** all ingredients with ice and fine strain into chilled glass.

1 3/4	shot(s)	**Light white rum**
3/4	shot(s)	**Plymouth gin**
1/4	shot(s)	**Sugar (gomme) syrup**
1/8	shot(s)	**Pomegranate (grenadine) syrup**
3	dashes	**Angostura aromatic bitters**
3/4	shot(s)	**Chilled mineral water (omit if wet ice)**

Origin: Adapted from a recipe in the 1949 edition of Esquire's 'Handbook For Hosts'. The drink is credited to an unnamed Captain serving in the US Marines, Amphibious Group Seven, at Santiago de Cuba in 1942.
Comment: Light, aromatic and complex – one to sip.

FOG CUTTER #1 [UPDATED]

Glass: Collins
Garnish: Orange slice
Method: **SHAKE** first six ingredients with ice and strain into ice-filled glass. **FLOAT** sherry on top of drink and serve without straws.

1 1/2	shot(s)	**Light white rum**
3/4	shot(s)	**Rémy Martin cognac**
1/2	shot(s)	**Plymouth gin**
2	shot(s)	**Freshly squeezed orange juice**
1/2	shot(s)	**Freshly squeezed lemon juice**
1/2	shot(s)	**Orgeat (almond) syrup**
1/2	shot(s)	**Amontillado sherry**

Origin: A version of what became a Tiki classic, sometimes credited to Trader Vic and/or Don the Beachcomber.
Comment: Looks like orange juice, but don't be fooled. It's long, fruity and strong.

FOG CUTTER #2 [UPDATED]

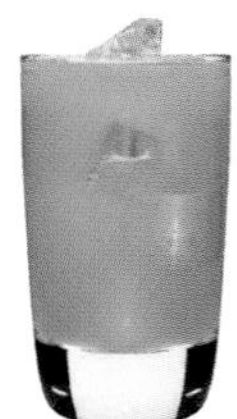

Glass: Old-fashioned
Garnish: Orange slice
Method: **SHAKE** first five ingredients with ice and strain into glass filled with crushed ice. **DRIZZLE** cherry brandy over drink and serve with straws.

1	shot(s)	**Light white rum**
1/2	shot(s)	**Rémy Martin cognac**
1/2	shot(s)	**Plymouth gin**
1/2	shot(s)	**Freshly squeezed lime juice**
1/4	shot(s)	**Sugar (gomme) syrup**
1/4	shot(s)	**Cherry brandy**

Comment: A well balanced (neither too strong nor too sweet), short, fruity drink.

FOG HORN

Glass: Old-fashioned
Garnish: Lime wedge
Method: **POUR** ingredients into ice-filled glass and stir.

2	shot(s)	**Plymouth gin**
1/2	shot(s)	**Rose's lime cordial**
Top up with		**Ginger ale**

Comment: Different! Almost flowery in taste with the spice of ginger beer.

FORBIDDEN FRUITS

Glass: Collins
Garnish: Berries on stick
Method: **MUDDLE** berries in base of shaker. Add next three ingredients, **SHAKE** with ice and strain into glass filled with crushed ice. **TOP** with ginger beer.

4	fresh	**Blackberries**
4	fresh	**Blueberries**
4	fresh	**Strawberries**
4	fresh	**Raspberries**
2	shot(s)	**Plymouth gin**
1	shot(s)	**Freshly squeezed lime juice**
1/2	shot(s)	**Sugar (gomme) syrup**
Top up with		**Ginger beer**

Origin: Created in 2001 by Andres Masso at Lab Bar, London, England.
Comment: Long and fruity with something of a bite.

To make your own sugar syrup, gradually pour TWO cups of granulated sugar into a saucepan containing ONE cup of hot water. Stir as you pour and carry on stirring and simmering until the sugar is dissolved. Do not let the water even come close to boiling and only simmer for as long as it takes to dissolve the sugar. Allow syrup to cool and pour into an empty bottle. Ideally, you should finely strain your syrup into the bottle to remove any undissolved crystals which could otherwise encourage crystallisation. If kept in a refrigerator this mixture will last for a couple of months.

FOSBURY FLIP

Glass: Collins
Garnish: Apricot slice on rim
Method: **SHAKE** all ingredients with ice and strain into ice-filled glass.

2	shot(s)	**Aged rum**
1	shot(s)	**Hazelnut (crème de noisette) liqueur**
1	shot(s)	**Apricot brandy liqueur**
2 1/2	shot(s)	**Freshly squeezed orange juice**
3/4	shot(s)	**Freshly squeezed lime juice**
1/8	shot(s)	**Pomegranate (grenadine) syrup**
1	fresh	**Egg yolk**

Origin: Created in 2002 by Salvatore Calabrese at the Library Bar, Lanesborough Hotel, London, England, for Kirsten Fosbury.
Comment: This richly flavoured, velvety drink is almost custardy in consistency.

FOUR W DAIQUIRI

Glass: Martini
Garnish: Grapefruit wedge on rim
Method: **SHAKE** all ingredients with ice and fine strain into chilled glass.

2	shot(s)	**Mount Gay Eclipse golden rum**
1 1/2	shot(s)	**Freshly squeezed grapefruit juice**
3/4	shot(s)	**Maple syrup**
2	dashes	**Angostura aromatic bitters**
1/2	shot(s)	**Chilled mineral water (omit if wet ice)**

Origin: My version of an old drink created by Herb Smith and popularised by his friend Oscar at the Waldorf, New York City. The drink was named in honour of the Duke of Windsor and his bride, formerly Wallis Warfield Simpson. The four 'W's stand for Wallis Warfield Windsor Wallop.
Comment: The oomph of rum, the sourness of grapefruit and the richness of maple syrup, all aromatised by bitters.

FOURTH OF JULY COCKTAIL

Glass: Martini
Garnish: Cinnamon dust
Method: **POUR** bourbon and Galliano into warm glass, **IGNITE** and sprinkle cinnamon while flaming. **SHAKE** last three ingredients with ice and strain into glass over extinguished bourbon and Galliano base.

---base---

1	shot(s)	**Bourbon whiskey**
1	shot(s)	**Galliano liqueur**
	dust	**Cinnamon over flame**

---top---

1	shot(s)	**Kahlúa coffee liqueur**
1	shot(s)	**Freshly squeezed orange juice**
1	shot(s)	**Double (heavy) cream**

Comment: More a stage show than a cocktail but rich and tasty all the same.

FOAMED DRINKS

These cocktails are served with a foam float, the aroma and flavour of which usually contrasts with that of the drink beneath, so adding complexity.

This foam is usually dispensed from a cream whipping siphon. Gelatin or egg white is added to the flavoured mixture so when the siphon is charged with nitrous oxide foam is produced.

Popular base ingredients include cold tea and fruit juice but the foam can be made using pretty much any liquid provided that it is not oily. Both the ingredients and the charged siphon should be stored in a refrigerator as the colder the foam, the thicker it will be when discharged and the longer it will last on the drink.

Nitrous oxide (N2O), the key to these foams, is commonly known as laughing gas and is a colourless non-flammable gas with a pleasant, slightly sweet smell. Its nickname refers to the stimulating effects of inhaling it, which include spontaneous laughter, slight hallucinations and an analgesic effect. It is used in motorsport to boost power (nitrous oxide kit), and in surgery and dentistry as an analgesic. A 50/50 mixture of nitrous oxide and oxygen ('gas and air') is commonly used during childbirth. Nitrous oxide is a powerful greenhouse gas and you add to its global warming effect when opening a bag of potato chips as the gas is used to displace staleness-inducing oxygen in snack food packaging.

WARNING

Inhaling nitrous oxide directly from a whipped cream charger or tank poses very serious health risks. These include potential lung collapse due to the high pressure and frostbite since the gas is very cold when released. I'm not suggesting you try this, but most recreational nitrous oxide users discharge the gas into a balloon before inhaling. Nitrous oxide can also cause mild nausea or dizziness and is unsafe to inhale while standing as you are likely to fall over. I should also add that the possession of and recreational use of nitrous oxide is a criminal offence in much of the US and other areas of the world.

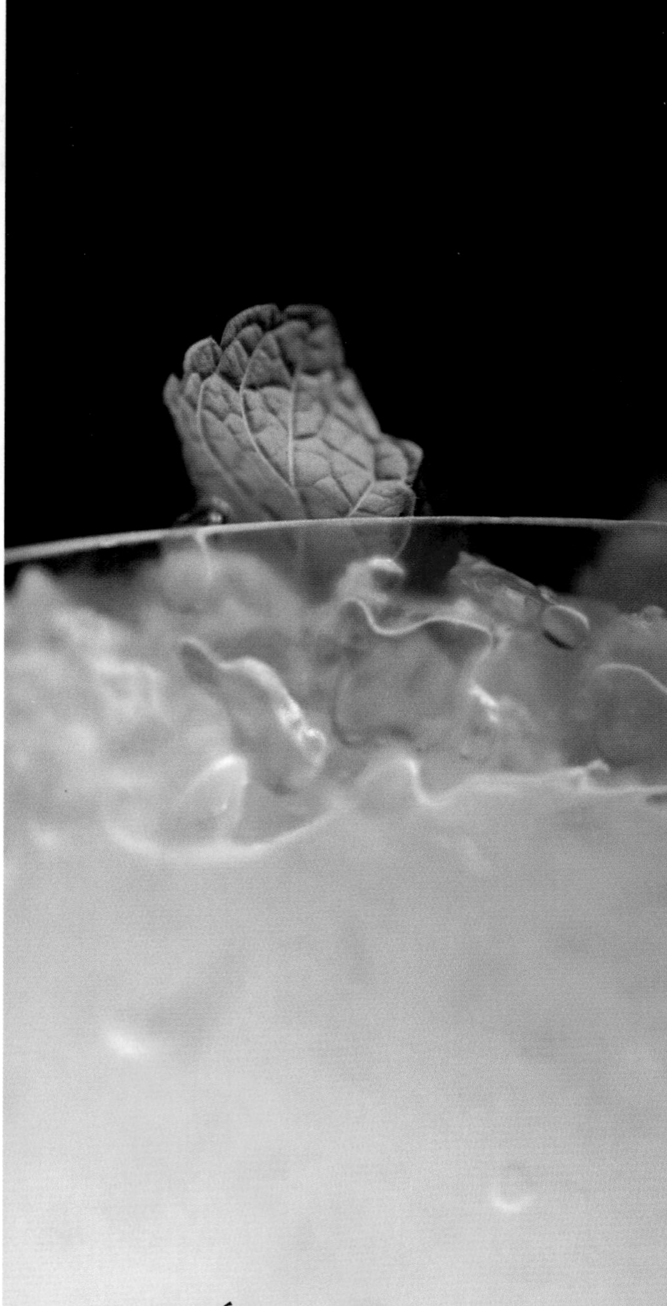

FRAPPÉS

To frappé is simply to chill with crushed ice and the term usually applies to a short drink where a spirit, a liqueur, or a combination of the two is simply poured over crushed ice. Any spirit or liqueur may be served Frappé but absinthe and crème de menthe are particularly identified with this serving style.

The Stinger, which calls for two shots of cognac to be poured over crushed ice with one shot of white crème de menthe, is probably the best known mixed Frappé.

FOURTH OF JULY SHOT

Glass: Shot
Method: Refrigerate ingredients then **LAYER** in chilled glass by carefully pouring in the following order.

1/4	shot(s)	**Pomegranate (grenadine) syrup**
1/2	shot(s)	**Blue curaçao liqueur**
1/2	shot(s)	**Ketel One vodka**

Comment: Looks cool... tastes less so!

FRANKENJACK [UPDATED]

Glass: Martini
Method: SHAKE all ingredients with ice and fine strain into chilled glass.

1 1/2	shot(s)	**Plymouth gin**
1	shot(s)	**Dry vermouth**
1/2	shot(s)	**Apricot brandy liqueur**
1/2	shot(s)	**Cointreau / triple sec**

Comment: Dry and sophisticated.

FRANKLIN MARTINI [NEW]

Glass: Martini
Garnish: Two olives
Method: STIR vermouth with ice and strain to **DISCARD** excess, leaving the glass and ice coated with vermouth. **POUR** gin over vermouth coated ice, **STIR** and strain into chilled glass.

3/4	shot(s)	**Dry vermouth**
2 1/2	shot(s)	**Plymouth gin**

Comment: A Dry Martini garnished with two olives.

FREDDY FUDPUCKER

Glass: Collins
Garnish: Orange slice
Method: SHAKE all ingredients with ice and strain into ice-filled glass.

2	shot(s)	**Sauza Hornitos tequila**
3 1/2	shot(s)	**Freshly squeezed orange juice**
1/2	shot(s)	**Galliano liqueur**

Variant: Harvey Wallbanger
Comment: A Harvey Wallbanger made with tequila in place of vodka. It's usual to build this drink and 'float' Galliano over the top. However, as the Galliano sinks anyway it is better shaken.

FREE TOWN

Glass: Martini
Garnish: Maraschino cherry
Method: **SHAKE** all ingredients with ice and fine strain into chilled glass.

2	shot(s)	**Light white rum**
1	shot(s)	**Tawny port**
1/2	shot(s)	**Sugar (gomme) syrup**
2	dashes	**Peychaud's aromatic bitters**

Origin: Created in 2004 by Alexandra Fiot at Lonsdale, London, England.
Comment: Great for sipping after dinner.

FRENCH 75

Glass: Flute
Garnish: Maraschino cherry
Method: **SHAKE** first three ingredients with ice and strain into chilled glass. **TOP** with champagne.

1	shot(s)	**Plymouth gin**
1/2	shot(s)	**Freshly squeezed lemon juice**
1/4	shot(s)	**Sugar (gomme) syrup**
Top up with		**Piper-Heidsieck brut champagne**

Origin: Legend has it that the drink was created by Harry MacElhone at his Harry's Bar, Paris, in 1925 and was named after the 75mm field gun used by the French army during the First World War. However, like other drinks in the first edition of Harry's own book, 'The ABC of Mixing Drinks', he credits the drink to MacGarry of Buck's Club, London, England.
Comment: Fresh, clean, sophisticated - very drinkable and hasn't dated.

FRENCH 76 [NEW]

Glass: Flute
Garnish: Maraschino cherry
Method: **SHAKE** first three ingredients with ice and strain into chilled glass. **TOP** with champagne.

1	shot(s)	**Ketel One vodka**
1/2	shot(s)	**Freshly squeezed lemon juice**
1/4	shot(s)	**Sugar (gomme) syrup**
Top up with		**Piper-Heidsieck brut champagne**

Variant: Diamond Fizz
Comment: A Vodka Sour topped with champagne. Works well.

FRENCH BISON-TINI [UPDATED]

Glass: Martini
Garnish: Raspberries on stick
Method: **SHAKE** all ingredients with ice and fine strain into chilled glass.

2	shot(s)	**Zubrówka bison vodka**
2	shot(s)	**Pressed pineapple juice**
1/4	shot(s)	**Chambord black raspberry liqueur**

Comment: A French Martini with the distinctive taste of Zubrówka.

FRENCH DAIQUIRI [NEW]

Glass: Martini
Garnish: Lime wedge on rim
Method: **SHAKE** all ingredients with ice and fine strain into chilled glass.

2	shot(s)	**Light white rum**
1	shot(s)	**Chambord black raspberry liqueur**
1/2	shot(s)	**Freshly squeezed lime juice**
3/4	shot(s)	**Chilled mineral water (omit if wet ice)**

Comment: A classic Daiquiri with a hint of berry fruit.

FRENCH DAISY [NEW]

Glass: Martini (champagne saucer)
Garnish: Lemon zest twist
Method: **SHAKE** first four ingredients with ice and fine strain into chilled glass. **TOP** with champagne.

1	shot(s)	**Rémy Martin cognac**
1/2	shot(s)	**Sisca crème de cassis**
1	shot(s)	**Freshly squeezed lemon juice**
1/2	shot(s)	**Elderflower cordial**
Top up with		**Piper Heidsieck brut champagne**

Origin: Created by Wayne Collins, UK.
Comment: Rich blackcurrant and elderflower with a hint of citrus and champagne.

FRENCH KISS #1 [NEW]

Glass: Martini
Garnish: Star anise
Method: **SHAKE** first three ingredients with ice and fine strain into chilled glass. **POUR** grenadine into centre of drink. (It should sink.)

1	shot(s)	**Ketel One vodka**
3/4	shot(s)	**Pernod anis**
2	shot(s)	**Freshly squeezed orange juice**
1/8	shot(s)	**Pomegranate (grenadine) syrup**

Comment: Looks like a Tequila Sunrise but tastes of anis and orange.

FRENCH KISS #2 [NEW]

Glass: Martini
Garnish: Raspberries on stick
Method: **SHAKE** all ingredients with ice and fine strain into chilled glass.

1 1/2	shot(s)	**Ketel One vodka**
1/2	shot(s)	**Chambord black raspberry liqueur**
1/2	shot(s)	**White crème de cacao liqueur**
1/2	shot(s)	**Milk**
1/2	shot(s)	**Double (heavy) cream**

Comment: Smooth creamy chocolate and raspberry.

A B C D E F G H I J K L M N O P Q R S T U V W X Y Z

FRENCH LEAVE [NEW]

Glass: Collins
Garnish: Orange slice
Method: **SHAKE** all ingredients with ice and strain into ice-filled glass.

1½	shot(s)	**Ketel One vodka**
½	shot(s)	**Pernod anis**
3½	shot(s)	**Freshly squeezed orange juice**

Comment: An easy drinking blend of vodka, anis and orange juice.

FRENCH MARTINI [UPDATED]

Glass: Martini
Garnish: Pineapple wedge on rim
Method: **SHAKE** all ingredients with ice and fine strain into chilled glass.

2	shot(s)	**Ketel One vodka**
1¾	shot(s)	**Pressed pineapple juice**
¼	shot(s)	**Chambord black raspberry liqueur**

AKA: Flirtini
Comment: Raspberry and pineapple laced with vodka. Easy drinking and very fruity.

FRENCH MOJITO [NEW]

Glass: Collins
Garnish: Raspberry & mint sprig
Method: Lightly **MUDDLE** mint in base of glass (just to bruise). Add rum, liqueur and lime juice. Half fill glass with crushed ice and **CHURN** (stir) with bar spoon. Continue to add crushed ice and churn until drink is level with glass rim.

12	fresh	**Mint leaves**
2	shot(s)	**Light white rum**
½	shot(s)	**Chambord black raspberry liqueur**
1	shot(s)	**Freshly squeezed lime juice**
¼	shot(s)	**Sugar (gomme) syrup**

Comment: A classic Mojito with a hint of berry fruit.

FRENCH MULE

Glass: Collins
Garnish: Sprig of mint
Method: **SHAKE** first four ingredients with ice and strain into ice-filled glass. **TOP** with ginger beer, stir and serve with straws.

2	shot(s)	**Rémy Martin cognac**
1	shot(s)	**Freshly squeezed lime juice**
1	shot(s)	**Sugar (gomme) syrup**
3	dashes	**Angostura aromatic bitters**
Top up with		**Ginger beer**

Comment: This French answer to the vodka based Moscow Mule uses cognac to make a more flavoursome, long, refreshing drink.

FRENCH SPRING PUNCH

Glass: Sling
Garnish: Strawberry
Method: **SHAKE** first four ingredients with ice and strain into ice-filled glass. **TOP** with champagne and serve with straws.

1	shot(s)	**Rémy Martin cognac**
¼	shot(s)	**Crème de fraise (strawberry) liqueur**
¼	shot(s)	**Freshly squeezed lemon juice**
¼	shot(s)	**Sugar (gomme) syrup**
Top up with		**Piper-Heidsieck brut champagne**

Origin: Created by Dick Bradsell and Rodolphe Sorel at Match EC1, London, England, during the late 1990s.
Comment: Not as popular as the Russian Spring Punch but still a modern day London classic.

FRENCH TEAR #1

Glass: Martini
Garnish: Pineapple wedge on rim
Method: **SHAKE** all ingredients with ice and fine strain into chilled glass.

1¾	shot(s)	**Spiced rum**
¾	shot(s)	**Grand Marnier liqueur**
2	shot(s)	**Pressed pineapple juice**

Origin: Discovered in 2000 at Quo Vadis, London, England.
Comment: Light, flavoursome, easy drinking. Altogether very gluggable.

FRESA BATIDA [NEW]

Glass: Collins
Garnish: Strawberry
Method: **MUDDLE** strawberries in base of shaker. Add other ingredients, **SHAKE** with ice and strain into glass filled with crushed ice.

7	fresh	**Strawberries**
2½	shot(s)	**Sagatiba cachaça**
½	shot(s)	**Freshly squeezed lemon juice**
½	shot(s)	**Sugar (gomme) syrup**

Origin: The Batida is a traditional Brazilian style of drink and 'Fresa' means strawberry in Portuguese, the official language of Brazil.
Comment: Strawberry flavoured, cachaça laced, long and very refreshing.

DRINKS ARE GRADED AS FOLLOWS:

DISGUSTING · PRETTY AWFUL · BEST AVOIDED · DISAPPOINTING · ACCEPTABLE · GOOD · RECOMMENDED · HIGHLY RECOMMENDED · OUTSTANDING / EXCEPTIONAL

FRESCA [NEW]

Glass: Martini
Garnish: Lemon zest twist
Method: **SHAKE** first four ingredients with ice and fine strain into chilled glass. **TOP** with 7-Up.

1½	shot(s)	**Ketel One Citroen vodka**
½	shot(s)	**Chambord black raspberry liqueur**
1	shot(s)	**Freshly squeezed pink grapefruit juice**
½	shot(s)	**Freshly squeezed lemon juice**
Top up with		**7-Up or lemonade**

Comment: The sweet, fizzy topping is essential to lengthen and balance this drink.

FRESCA NOVA

Glass: Flute
Method: **SHAKE** first four ingredients with ice and fine strain into chilled glass. **TOP** with champagne.

1½	shot(s)	**Grand Marnier liqueur**
¾	shot(s)	**Freshly squeezed orange juice**
¼	shot(s)	**Sugar (gomme) syrup**
1	shot(s)	**Double (heavy) cream**
Top up with		**Piper-Heidsieck brut champagne**

Origin: Created by Jamie Terrell for Philip Holzberg at Vinexpo 1999.
Comment: Cream, orange and champagne work surprisingly well. Be sure to add the champagne slowly.

FRIAR TUCK

Glass: Martini
Garnish: Dust with freshly ground nutmeg
Method: **SHAKE** all ingredients with ice and fine strain into chilled glass.

1	shot(s)	**Hazelnut (crème de noisette) liqueur**
1	shot(s)	**Dark crème de cacao liqueur**
1	shot(s)	**Double (heavy) cream**
1	shot(s)	**Milk**

Variant: With amaretto and ice cream.
Comment: Round, jolly and creamy with chocolate and hazelnut.

FRIDA'S BROW [NEW]

Glass: Martini
Garnish: Dust with cinnamon powder
Method: **SHAKE** all ingredients with ice and fine strain into chilled glass.

2	shot(s)	**Sauza Hornitos tequila**
½	shot(s)	**White crème de cacao liqueur**
¼	shot(s)	**Pomegranate (grenadine) syrup**
½	shot(s)	**Double (heavy) cream**
½	shot(s)	**Milk**

Origin: Discovered in 2005 at Velvet Margarita Cantina, Los Angeles, USA.
Comment: Creamy, sweetened tequila with hints of chocolate.

FROZEN COCKTAILS

These are cocktails blended with crushed ice. The ingredients are poured into an electric blender with an appropriate amount of crushed ice and then blended until a smooth, almost slushy consistency is achieved.

Frozen drinks are usually served heaped in large Martini glasses and should always be served with straws.

Practically any sour type drink can be adapted to be served frozen but the Frozen Daiquiri and Frozen Margarita are by far the best known examples. When adapting recipes be aware that drinks served frozen usually require more sugar than when served straight-up or on-the-rocks. Cocktails containing egg or cream do not usually make good frozen drinks.

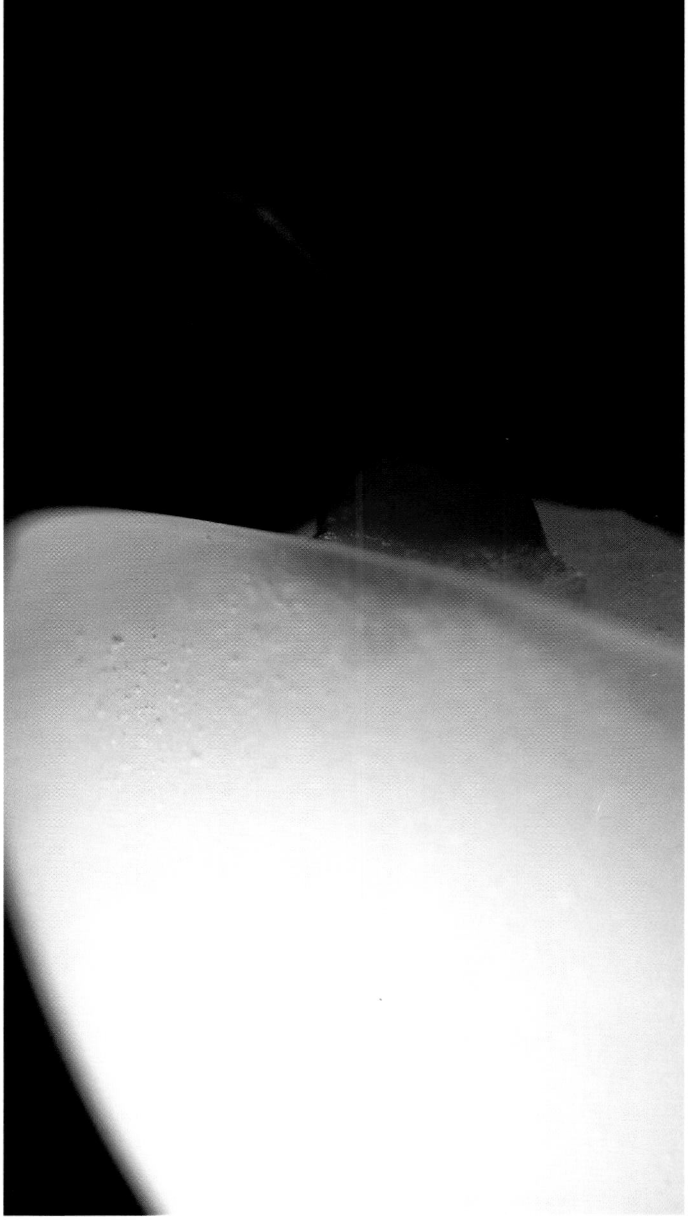

FRISKY BISON

Glass: Martini
Garnish: Float apple slice
Method: Lightly **MUDDLE** mint in base of shaker (just to bruise). Add other ingredients, **SHAKE** with ice and fine strain into chilled glass.

7	fresh	**Mint leaves**
2	shot(s)	**Zubrówka bison vodka**
1	shot(s)	**Apple schnapps liqueur**
1	shot(s)	**Pressed apple juice**
1/2	shot(s)	**Freshly squeezed lime juice**
1/4	shot(s)	**Sugar (gomme) syrup**

Origin: Created by Tony Kerr in 1999 at Mash & Air in Manchester.
Comment: Sweet 'n' sour, fruity, minty and fresh.

FRISKY LEMONADE

Glass: Collins
Garnish: Lime wedge
Method: **POUR** ingredients into ice-filled glass and stir.

2	shot(s)	**Lime flavoured vodka**
1/2	shot(s)	**Dry vermouth**
Top up with		**7-Up or lemonade**

Origin: Created by Aaron Rudd in 2002 at Home, London, England.
Comment: Reminiscent of alcoholic lemon barley water.

FROZEN DAIQUIRI [UPDATED]

Glass: Martini
Garnish: Maraschino cherry
Method: **BLEND** all ingredients with 12oz scoop of crushed ice. Serve heaped in the glass with straws.

2	shot(s)	**Light white rum**
1/2	shot(s)	**Freshly squeezed lime juice**
3/4	shot(s)	**Sugar (gomme) syrup**

Variant: Floridita Daiquiri or with fruit and/or fruit liqueurs.
Origin: Emilio Gonzalez is said to have first adapted the Natural Daiquiri into this frozen version at the Plaza Hotel in Cuba.
Comment: A superbly refreshing drink on a hot day.

DRINKS ARE GRADED AS FOLLOWS:

FROZEN MARGARITA [UPDATED]

Glass: Martini
Garnish: Maraschino cherry
Method: **BLEND** all ingredients with 12oz scoop of crushed ice. Serve heaped in the glass and with straws.

1 1/2	shot(s)	**Sauza Hornitos tequila**
3/4	shot(s)	**Cointreau / triple sec**
3/4	shot(s)	**Freshly squeezed lime juice**
1/2	shot(s)	**Sugar (gomme) syrup**

Variant: With fruit and/or fruit liqueurs.
Comment: Citrus freshness with the subtle agave of tequila served frozen.

FRU FRU

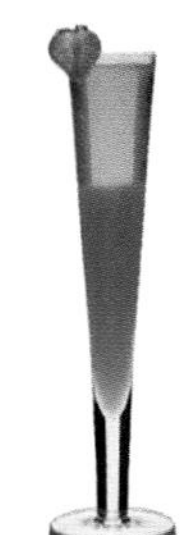

Glass: Flute
Garnish: Split strawberry
Method: **SHAKE** first three ingredients with ice and strain into glass. **TOP** with champagne.

3/4	shot(s)	**Passoã passion fruit liqueur**
3/4	shot(s)	**Crème de fraise (strawberry) liqueur**
3/4	shot(s)	**Freshly squeezed golden grapefruit juice**
Top up with		**Piper-Heidsieck brut champagne**

Comment: Dry, bitter grapefruit complimented by passion fruit and strawberry.

FRUIT & NUT CHOCOLATE MARTINI

Glass: Martini
Garnish: Crumbled Cadbury's Flake bar
Method: **SHAKE** all ingredients with ice and fine strain into chilled glass.

1	shot(s)	**Raspberry flavoured vodka**
1/2	shot(s)	**Hazelnut (crème de noisette) liqueur**
1/2	shot(s)	**White crème de cacao liqueur**
1/2	shot(s)	**Chambord black raspberry liqueur**
1/2	shot(s)	**Baileys Irish Cream liqueur**
3/4	shot(s)	**Double (heavy) cream**
3/4	shot(s)	**Milk**

Comment: Naughty but nice – one for confectionery lovers.

FRUIT & NUT MARTINI

Glass: Martini
Garnish: Orange zest twist & almond flakes
Method: **SHAKE** all ingredients with ice and fine strain into chilled glass.

1	shot(s)	**Vanilla flavoured vodka**
1	shot(s)	**Hazelnut (crème de noisette) liqueur**
1/2	shot(s)	**Pedro Ximénez sherry**
1	shot(s)	**Cranberry juice**
1/2	shot(s)	**Freshly squeezed orange juice**

Origin: Created by yours truly in 2004.
Comment: A rich Christmas pudding of a Martini.

FRUIT SALAD [UPDATED]

Glass: Sling
Garnish: Fruit Salad chewy sweet / banana slice
Method: **SHAKE** all ingredients with ice and strain into ice-filled glass.

2	shot(s)	**Ketel One vodka**
1/2	shot(s)	**Crème de bananes**
2 1/2	shot(s)	**Freshly squeezed orange juice**
1/2	shot(s)	**Galliano liqueur**
1/4	shot(s)	**Pomegranate (grenadine) syrup**

Comment: This variation on the Harvey Wallbanger tastes like Fruit Salad 'penny chew' sweets.

FRUIT SOUR

Glass: Old-fashioned
Garnish: Lemon zest twist
Method: **SHAKE** all ingredients with ice and strain into ice-filled glass.

1	shot(s)	**Bourbon whiskey**
1	shot(s)	**Cointreau / triple sec**
1	shot(s)	**Freshly squeezed lemon juice**
1/2	fresh	**Egg white**

Comment: An orange influenced, sweet and sour whiskey cocktail.

FRUITS OF THE FOREST [NEW]

Glass: Martini
Garnish: Rasberries on stick
Method: **SHAKE** first five ingredients with ice and fine strain into chilled glass. **POUR** last ingredient. It should sink to the bottom of the drink.

2	shot(s)	**Zubrówka bison vodka**
1	shot(s)	**Freshly squeezed orange juice**
1/2	shot(s)	**Elderflower cordial**
1/2	shot(s)	**Freshly squeezed lime juice**
1/2	fresh	**Egg white**
1/4	shot(s)	**Chambord black raspberry liqueur**

Origin: Created in 2004 by Stuart Barnett at TGI Friday's, Reading, England.
Comment: Look out for the fruity bottom.

FRUIT TREE DAIQUIRI

Glass: Martini
Garnish: Grapefruit or apricot wedge on rim
Method: **SHAKE** all ingredients with ice and fine strain into chilled glass.

2	shot(s)	**Light white rum**
3/4	shot(s)	**Apricot brandy liqueur**
3/4	shot(s)	**Freshly squeezed pink grapefruit juice**
3/4	shot(s)	**Freshly squeezed lime juice**
1/4	shot(s)	**Maraschino syrup (from cherry jar)**
1/2	shot(s)	**Chilled mineral water (omit if wet ice)**

Comment: A restrained Papa Doble with apricot liqueur.

FULL CIRCLE [NEW]

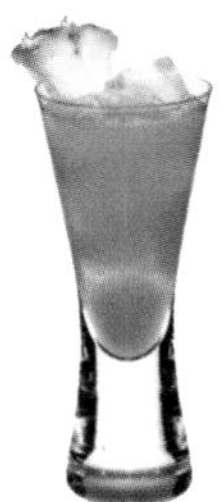

Glass: Collins
Garnish: Pineapple wedge on rim
Method: Cut pomegranate in half and juice with a spinning citrus juicer. **SHAKE** all ingredients with ice and strain into ice-filled glass.

3	shot(s)	**Freshly extracted pomegranate juice**
2	shot(s)	**Plymouth gin**
3/4	shot(s)	**Pressed pineapple juice**

Origin: Adapted from a drink discovered in 2004 at Mandarin Oriental, New York City, USA. The name is a reference to the bar's location - Columbus Circle, where the world's first one-way rotary system (roundabout) was implemented in 1904.
Comment: Fruity and easy drinking, yet with complexity from the gin.

FU MANCHU DAIQUIRI

Glass: Martini
Garnish: Pineapple wedge on rim
Method: **SHAKE** all ingredients with ice and fine strain into chilled glass.

2	shot(s)	**Light white rum**
1	shot(s)	**Freshly squeezed lime juice**
1/2	shot(s)	**Sugar (gomme) syrup**
1/4	shot(s)	**Cointreau / triple sec**
1/4	shot(s)	**White crème de menthe liqueur**
3/4	shot(s)	**Chilled mineral water (omit if wet ice)**

Origin: Adapted from a recipe by David Embury.
Comment: A natural Daiquiri with a refreshing, clean, citrussy, minty edge.

FUNKY MONKEY [NEW]

Glass: Goblet (or coconut shell)
Garnish: Toasted coconut strips
Method: **BLEND** all ingredients with 12oz scoop of crushed ice and serve with straws.

1	shot(s)	**Mount Gay Eclipse golden rum**
3/4	shot(s)	**Crème de bananes liqueur**
3/4	shot(s)	**White crème de cacao liqueur**
1	shot(s)	**Cream of coconut**
1	shot(s)	**Double (heavy) cream**
1	shot(s)	**Milk**
1	small	**Ripe banana (peeled)**

Origin: Created in 1998 by Tony Abou-Ganim, Las Vegas, USA.
Comment: Be sure to use a ripe or even over-ripe banana in this tropical style drink.

FOR MORE INFORMATION SEE OUR INGREDIENTS APPENDIX ON PAGE 322

●●◐○○

FUZZY NAVEL

Glass: Collins
Garnish: Lemon wheel in glass
Method: **SHAKE** all ingredients with ice and strain into ice-filled glass.

2	shot(s)	**Peach schnapps liqueur**
4	shot(s)	**Freshly squeezed orange juice**

Variant: Hairy Navel with the addition of a shot of vodka.
Origin: A not very well regarded but extremely well-known cocktail whose origins are lost.
Comment: The hairy version is a slightly more interesting, drier, less fluffy concoction. So why have a fluffy navel when you can have a hairy one?

●●●●○

GALVANISED NAIL

Glass: Martini
Garnish: Float apple slice
Method: **SHAKE** all ingredients with ice and fine strain into chilled glass.

$1\frac{1}{2}$	shot(s)	**Tuaca Italian liqueur**
$\frac{3}{4}$	shot(s)	**Drambuie liqueur**
$\frac{1}{4}$	shot(s)	**The Famous Grouse Scotch**
$\frac{1}{8}$	shot(s)	**Freshly squeezed lemon juice**
2	shot(s)	**Pressed apple juice**

Origin: Created in 2003 by yours truly, taking inspiration from the Rusty Nail.
Comment: Honey, vanilla, Scotch and apple with a hint of spice.

●●●●◐

THE GAME BIRD

Glass: Flute
Garnish: Lemon zest twist
Method: **SHAKE** first five ingredients with ice and strain into ice-filled glass. **TOP** with ginger ale.

2	shot(s)	**The Famous Grouse Scotch**
1	shot(s)	**Sour apple liqueur**
$\frac{1}{2}$	shot(s)	**Elderflower cordial**
$\frac{1}{2}$	shot(s)	**Freshly squeezed lemon juice**
$\frac{1}{4}$	shot(s)	**Sugar (gomme) syrup**
Top up with		**Ginger ale**

Origin: Created in 2002 by Wayne Collins, UK.
Comment: Fruity, spicy and well-balanced.

●●●○○

GARIBALDI [NEW]

Glass: Collins
Garnish: Orange slice
Method: **POUR** Campari into ice-filled glass. **TOP** with orange juice, stir and serve with straws.

2	shot(s)	**Campari**
Top up with		**Freshly squeezed orange juice**

Origin: Appears on cocktail lists throughout Italy. Named after the famous revolutionary general who helped liberate and reunify Italy.
Comment: Reminiscent of red grapefruit juice.

●●●◐○

GATOR BITE

Glass: Coupette
Garnish: Salt rim
Method: **SHAKE** all ingredients with ice and fine strain into chilled glass.

1	shot(s)	**Green Chartreuse**
$1\frac{1}{2}$	shot(s)	**Cointreau / triple sec**
1	shot(s)	**Freshly squeezed lime juice**
$\frac{3}{4}$	shot(s)	**Sugar (gomme) syrup**

Comment: Looks like a Margarita, but instead of tequila features the unique taste of Chartreuse. Yup, it bites.

●●●●◐

GE BLONDE

Glass: Martini
Garnish: Apple wedge
Method: **SHAKE** all ingredients with ice and fine strain into chilled glass.

$1\frac{3}{4}$	shot(s)	**The Famous Grouse Scotch**
$1\frac{1}{4}$	shot(s)	**Sauvignon Blanc wine**
1	shot(s)	**Pressed apple juice**
$\frac{1}{2}$	shot(s)	**Sugar (gomme) syrup**
$\frac{1}{4}$	shot(s)	**Freshly squeezed lemon juice**

Origin: A combined effort by the staff of London's GE Club in January 2002, this was named by Linda, a waitress at the club who happens to be blonde. She claimed the name was inspired by the cocktail's straw colour.
Comment: This delicate drink demands freshly pressed apple juice and a flavoursome Scotch with subtle peat.

●●●○○

GENTLE BREEZE (MOCKTAIL) [NEW]

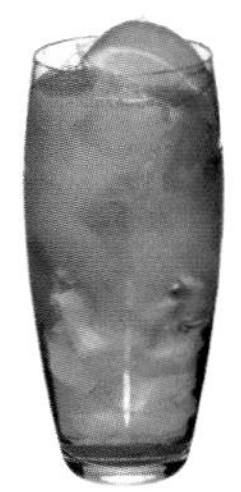

Glass: Collins
Garnish: Lime wedge
Method: **POUR** ingredients into ice-filled glass, stir and serve with straws.

4	shot(s)	**Cranberry juice**
2	shot(s)	**Freshy squeezed pink grapefruit juice**

Comment: A Seabreeze without the hard stuff.

DRINKS ARE GRADED AS FOLLOWS:

● DISGUSTING ●◐ PRETTY AWFUL ●● BEST AVOIDED
●●◐ DISAPPOINTING ●●● ACCEPTABLE ●●●◐ GOOD
●●●● RECOMMENDED ●●●●◐ HIGHLY RECOMMENDED
●●●●● OUTSTANDING / EXCEPTIONAL

GEORGIA MINT JULEP [NEW]

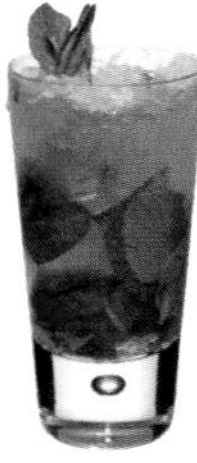

Glass: Collins
Garnish: Mint sprig
Method: Lightly **MUDDLE** (only to bruise) mint in base of shaker. Add other ingredients, **SHAKE** with ice and strain into chilled glass half filled with crushed ice. **CHURN** (stir) the drink using a bar spoon. Top up the glass with more crushed ice and churn again. Continue adding crushed ice and churning until the drink meets the rim of the glass. Serve with two long straws.

12	fresh	**Mint leaves**
2½	shot(s)	**Rémy Martin cognac**
1	shot(s)	**Peach schnapps liqueur**

Origin: This classic was originally made with peach brandy in place of peach liqueur, hence sugar is omitted from this recipe. May also be made with apricot brandy.
Comment: Bourbon, peach and mint are flavours that combine harmoniously.

GIBSON

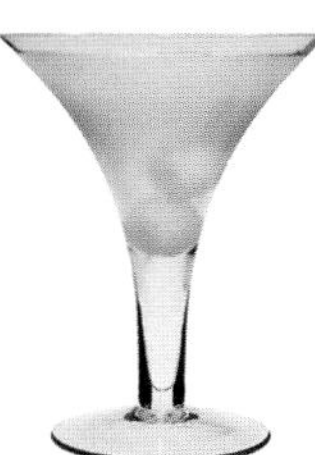

Glass: Martini
Garnish: Two chilled cocktail onions on stick
Method: **STIR** vermouth with ice in a mixing glass. Strain and discard excess vermouth to leave only a coating on the ice. **POUR** gin into mixing glass containing coated ice and STIR. Finally strain into chilled glass.

½	shot(s)	**Dry vermouth**
2½	shot(s)	**Plymouth gin**

Origin: This twist on the Dry Martini seems to have come into being early in the 20th century. During the 1890s and the first two decades of the 20th century the pen-and-ink drawings of Charles Dana Gibson were published in the glamour magazines of the day. His illustrations of girls were as iconic as the supermodels of today. It is said this drink was named after the well-endowed Gibson Girls - hence the two onions. However, cocktail books published at the time include a Martini-like drink named Gibson but without the onions. Gibson was a member of New York's The Players' club and a bartender there by the name of Charley Connolly is credited for at least adding the garnish, if not actually creating the drink.
Comment: A classic Dry Martini with cocktail onions in place of an olive or twist.

GIMLET #1

Glass: Martini
Garnish: Lime wedge or cherry
Method: **STIR** all ingredients with ice and strain into chilled glass.

2½	shot(s)	**Plymouth gin**
1¼	shot(s)	**Rose's lime cordial**

Variant: Other spirits, particularly vodka, may be substituted for gin.
Origin: Almost certainly originated in the British Navy.
Comment: A simple blend of gin and sweet lime.

GIMLET

In 1747, James Lind, a Scottish surgeon, discovered that consumption of citrus fruits helped prevent scurvy, one of the most common illnesses on board ship. (We now understand that scurvy is caused by a Vitamin C deficiency and that it is the vitamins in citrus fruit which help ward off the condition.) In 1867, the Merchant Shipping Act made it mandatory for all British ships to carry rations of lime juice for the crew.

Lauchlin Rose, the owner of a shipyard in Leith, Scotland, had been working to solve the problem of how to keep citrus juice fresh for months on board ship. In 1867 he patented a process for preserving fruit juice without alcohol. To give his product wider appeal he sweetened the mixture, packaged it in an attractive bottle and named it 'Rose's Lime Cordial'.

Once the benefits of drinking lime juice became more broadly known, British sailors consumed so much of the stuff, often mixed with their daily ration of rum and water ('grog'), that they became affectionately known as 'Limeys'. Naval officers mixed Rose's lime cordial with gin to make Gimlets.

A 'gimlet' was originally the name of a small tool used to tap the barrels of spirits which were carried on British Navy ships: this could be the origin of the drink's name. Another story cites a naval doctor, Rear-Admiral Sir Thomas Desmond Gimlette (1857-1943), who is said to have mixed gin with lime 'to help the medicine go down'. Although this is a credible story it is not substantiated in his obituary in The Times, 6 October 1943.

A B C D E F **G** H I J K L M N O P Q R S T U V W X Y Z

GIMLET #2 (SCHUMANN'S RECIPE) [NEW]

Glass: Martini
Garnish: Lime wedge or cherry
Method: SHAKE all ingredients with ice and fine strain into chilled glass.

2½ shot(s) **Plymouth gin**
¼ shot(s) **Freshly squeezed lime juice**
1¼ shot(s) **Rose's lime cordial**

Origin: A shaken twist on an already established drink by the famous bartender and cocktail author Charles Schumann of Munich, Germany.
Comment: Generously laced with gin and wonderfully tart.

GIN & IT

Glass: Old-fashioned
Garnish: Orange slice
Method: STIR all ingredients with ice and strain into ice-filled glass.

2 shot(s) **Plymouth gin**
1 shot(s) **Sweet (rosso) vermouth**

Origin: The name is short for 'Gin and Italian', a reference to the sweet vermouth, which was traditionally Italian while French vermouth was dry.
Comment: An old school version of the classic Martini. Simple but great.

GIN & SIN

Glass: Martini
Garnish: Orange zest twist
Method: SHAKE all ingredients with ice and fine strain into chilled glass.

2 shot(s) **Plymouth gin**
1 shot(s) **Freshly squeezed lemon juice**
¾ shot(s) **Freshly squeezed orange juice**
⅛ shot(s) **Pomegranate (grenadine) syrup**

Comment: Pleasant and fruity but lacking real personality.

FOR MORE INFORMATION SEE OUR
INGREDIENTS APPENDIX ON PAGE 322

GIN & TONIC

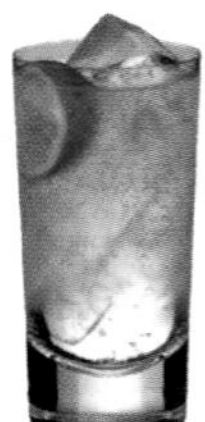

Glass: Collins
Garnish: Run lime wedge around rim of glass. Squeeze and drop into drink.
Method: POUR ingredients into ice-filled glass, stir and serve without straws.

2 shot(s) **Plymouth gin**
Top up with **Tonic water**

Origin: The precise origin of the G&T is lost in the mists of time. Gin (or at least a grain based juniper spirit) was drunk for medicinal reasons from the 1600s onwards. Quinine, the pungent bark extract which gives tonic its distinctive bitterness, had been used against malaria for even longer. The first known quinine-based tonics were marketed during the 1850s.

The popularity of tonic in the British colonies, especially India, is clear. Schweppes launched their first carbonated quinine tonic in 1870, branding it Indian Tonic Water. The ladies and gentlemen of the Raj also drank phenomenal quantities of gin. It is therefore accepted that gin and tonic emerged in India during the second half of the nineteenth century and was drunk partly to ward off malaria.
Comment: This might not be considered a cocktail by most, but it is actually classified as a Highball. Whatever, it's one of the simplest and best drinks ever devised, hence its lasting popularity.

GIN BERRY [NEW]

Glass: Martini
Garnish: Lime zest twist
Method: SHAKE all ingredients with ice and fine strain into chilled glass.

1½ shot(s) **Plymouth gin**
½ shot(s) **Chambord black raspberry liqueur**
½ shot(s) **Freshly squeezed lime juice**
1½ shot(s) **Cranberry juice**

Origin: Adapted from a drink created in 2004 by Chris Lacey, UK.
Comment: Berry flavours combine harmoniously with gin – what an appropriate name.

GIN DAISY [NEW]

Glass: Goblet
Garnish: Maraschino cherry
Method: SHAKE all ingredients with ice and strain into glass filled with crushed ice. **CHURN** (stir) drink with ice and serve with straws.

2½ shot(s) **Plymouth gin**
¼ shot(s) **Yellow Chartreuse liqueur**
¼ shot(s) **Pomegranate (grenadine) syrup**
¼ shot(s) **Freshly squeezed lemon juice**

Origin: A classic Daisy variation.
Comment: If correctly made this serious, gin dominated cocktail should be blush, not pink.

GIN FIX [UPDATED]

Glass: Goblet
Garnish: Lemon slice
Method: SHAKE all ingredients with ice and strain into glass filled with crushed ice. **CHURN** (stir) drink with ice and serve with straws.

2 shot(s) **Plymouth gin**
1 shot(s) **Freshly squeezed lemon juice**
1/2 shot(s) **Sugar (gomme) syrup**

Origin: The Fix is an old classic that's very similar to the Daisy.
Comment: A Gin Sour served over crushed ice in a goblet.

GIN FIXED [NEW]

Glass: Martini
Garnish: Lemon slice
Method: SHAKE all ingredients with ice and strain into glass filled with crushed ice. **CHURN** (stir) drink with ice and serve with straws.

2 shot(s) **Plymouth gin**
1/4 shot(s) **Cointreau / triple sec**
1 shot(s) **Pressed pineapple juice**
1/2 shot(s) **Freshly squeezed lemon juice**
1/4 shot(s) **Sugar (gomme) syrup**

Comment: Sweet and sour with a spirity pineapple twang.

GIN FIZZ

Glass: Collins (8oz max)
Garnish: Slice of lemon & mint
Method: SHAKE first three ingredients with ice and strain into chilled glass. **TOP** with soda.

2 shot(s) **Plymouth gin**
1 shot(s) **Freshly squeezed lemon juice**
1/2 shot(s) **Sugar (gomme) syrup**
Top up with **Soda water (from siphon)**

Variants: With the addition of egg white this drink becomes a 'Silver Fizz'; with egg yolk it becomes a 'Golden Fizz'. A Royal Fizz includes one whole egg, a Diamond Fizz uses champagne instead of charged water, a Green Fizz has a dash of green crème de menthe and a Purple Fizz uses equal parts of sloe gin and grapefruit juice in place of gin and lemon juice.
Origin: A mid-19th century classic.
Comment: Everyone has heard of this clean, refreshing, long drink but few have actually tried it.

GIN GARDEN

Glass: Martini
Garnish: Float cucumber slice
Method: MUDDLE cucumber in base of shaker. Add other ingredients, **SHAKE** with ice and fine strain into chilled glass.

1 inch **Chopped peeled cucumber**
2 shot(s) **Plymouth gin**
1 shot(s) **Pressed apple juice**
1/2 shot(s) **Elderflower cordial**

Origin: Created in 2001 through a collaboration between Daniel Warner at Zander and Tobias Blazquez Garcia at Steam, London, England.
Comment: The archetypal English spirit, fruit and vegetable combo.

GIN GENIE

Glass: Collins
Garnish: Mint sprig
Method: Lightly **MUDDLE** mint in base of shaker (just to bruise). Add other ingredients, **SHAKE** with ice and strain into glass filled with crushed ice.

8 fresh **Mint leaves**
1 1/2 shot(s) **Plymouth gin**
1 shot(s) **Plymouth sloe gin**
1 shot(s) **Freshly squeezed lemon juice**
1/2 shot(s) **Sugar (gomme) syrup**

Origin: Adapted from a drink created in 2002 by Wayne Collins, UK.
Comment: A fruit-led long drink for gin-loving Bowie fans.

GIN GIN MULE [NEW]

Glass: Collins
Garnish: Lime wedge
Method: MUDDLE ginger in base of shaker. Add next four ingredients, **SHAKE** with ice and fine strain into ice-filled glass. **TOP** with ginger beer.

2 slices **Fresh root ginger (thumbnail sized)**
2 shot(s) **Plymouth gin**
1/2 shot(s) **Freshly squeezed lime juice**
1/4 shot(s) **Sugar (gomme) syrup**
3 dashes **Angostura aromatic bitters**
Top up with **Ginger beer**

Origin: Adapted from a drink created in 2004 by Audrey Saunders, New York City, USA.
Comment: Spicy gin and ginger.

HOW TO MAKE SUGAR SYRUP

To make your own sugar syrup, gradually pour TWO cups of granulated sugar into a saucepan containing ONE cup of hot water. Stir as you pour and carry on stirring and simmering until the sugar is dissolved. Do not let the water even come close to boiling and only simmer for as long as it takes to dissolve the sugar. Allow syrup to cool and pour into an empty bottle. Ideally, you should finely strain your syrup into the bottle to remove any undissolved crystals which could otherwise encourage crystallisation. If kept in a refrigerator this mixture will last for a couple of months.

GIN SLING

Glass: Sling
Garnish: Lemon slice & cherry on stick (sail)
Method: SHAKE first three ingredients with ice and strain into ice-filled glass. **TOP** with soda water.

1½	shot(s)	**Plymouth gin**
1½	shot(s)	**Cherry (brandy) liqueur**
1	shot(s)	**Freshly squeezed lemon juice**
Top up with		**Soda water (club soda)**

Comment: Tangy cherry and gin.

GIN SOUR [UPDATED]

Glass: Old-fashioned
Garnish: Cherry & lemon slice on stick (sail)
Method: SHAKE all ingredients with ice and strain into ice-filled glass.

2	shot(s)	**Plymouth gin**
1	shot(s)	**Freshly squeezed lemon juice**
½	shot(s)	**Sugar (gomme) syrup**
½	fresh	**Egg white**
3	dashes	**Angostura aromatic bitters**

Comment: The juniper flavours in gin work well in this classic sour.

GINA

Glass: Sling
Garnish: Berries on stick
Method: SHAKE first three ingredients with ice and strain into ice-filled glass. **TOP** with soda.

2	shot(s)	**Plymouth gin**
½	shot(s)	**Sisca crème de cassis**
½	shot(s)	**Freshly squeezed lemon juice**
Top up with		**Soda water (club soda)**

AKA: Cassis Collins
Comment: The lemon and blackcurrant mask the character of the gin.

GINGER & LEMONGRASS MARTINI [NEW]

Glass: Martini
Garnish: Float thinly cut apple slice
Method: MUDDLE ginger and lemongrass in base of shaker. Add other ingredients and **STIR** until honey dissolves. **SHAKE** with ice and fine strain into chilled glass.

1	slice	**Fresh root ginger (thumbnail sized)**
½	stem	**Lemongrass (chopped)**
2	spoons	**Runny honey**
2	shot(s)	**Plymouth gin**
¼	shot(s)	**Dry vermouth**
¼	shot(s)	**Pressed apple juice**
¾	shot(s)	**STIR**

Origin: Created in 2005 by yours truly.
Comment: Consider infusing the lemongrass in gin instead of muddling.

GIN-GER & TONIC [NEW]

Glass: Collins
Garnish: Lime wedge
Method: MUDDLE ginger in base of shaker, add gin and sugar, **SHAKE** with ice and strain into ice-filled glass. **TOP** with tonic water.

2	slices	**Fresh root ginger (thumbnail sized)**
2	shot(s)	**Plymouth gin**
¼	shot(s)	**Sugar (gomme) syrup**
Top up with		**Tonic water**

Comment: A dry, refreshing long drink for those that like their G&Ts gingered.

GINGER COSMO

Glass: Martini
Garnish: Slice of ginger on rim
Method: SHAKE all ingredients with ice and fine strain into chilled glass.

2	shot(s)	**Ketel One Citroen vodka**
¾	shot(s)	**King's ginger liqueur**
1¼	shot(s)	**Cranberry juice**
¼	shot(s)	**Freshly squeezed lime juice**
⅛	shot(s)	**Sugar (gomme) syrup**

Origin: Emerged during 2002 in New York City.
Comment: Just what it says on the tin – your everyday Cosmo given extra vitality courtesy of a hint of ginger spice.

GINGER COSMOS [NEW]

Glass: Collins
Garnish: Basil leaf
Method: MUDDLE ginger and basil in base of shaker. Add other ingredients, **SHAKE** with ice and fine strain into glass filled with crushed ice. Stir and serve with straws.

2	slices	**Fresh root ginger (thumbnail sized)**
5	fresh	**Basil leaves**
2	shot(s)	**Plymouth gin**
1½	shot(s)	**Pressed pineapple juice**
1½	shot(s)	**Pressed apple juice**
¼	shot(s)	**Freshly squeezed lime juice**
¼	shot(s)	**Sugar syrup**

Origin: Created in 2003 by Massimiliano Greco at Zander, London, England. 'Cosmos' is a reference to the botanical name for pineapple, Ananas comosus.
Comment: Warming ginger spice in a very cooling, fruity drink.

GINGER MARGARITA [NEW]

Glass: Coupette
Garnish: Lime wedge on rim
Method: SHAKE all ingredients with ice and fine strain into chilled glass.

2	shot(s)	**Sauza Hornitos tequila**
1	shot(s)	**King's ginger liqueur**
1	shot(s)	**Freshly squeezed lime juice**

Comment: A Margarita spiced with ginger.

GINGER MARTINI

Glass: Martini
Garnish: Brandy snap biscuit
Method: **MUDDLE** ginger in base of shaker. Add other ingredients, **SHAKE** with ice and fine strain into chilled glass.

2	slices	**Fresh root ginger (thumbnail sized)**
2	shot(s)	**Ketel One vodka**
3/4	shot(s)	**Stone's green ginger wine**
3/4	shot(s)	**Pressed apple juice**
1/2	shot(s)	**Freshly squeezed lime juice**
1/4	shot(s)	**Sugar (gomme) syrup**

Origin: Discovered in 2003 at Hurricane Bar and Grill, Edinburgh, Scotland.
Comment: This Martini may be served chilled but its flavour is distinctly warming.

GINGER MOJITO [NEW]

Glass: Collins
Garnish: Mint sprig
Method: **MUDDLE** ginger in base of shaker. Add mint and lightly **MUDDLE** (just to bruise). Add next three ingredients, **SHAKE** with ice and fine strain into glass filled with crushed ice. **TOP** with ginger ale.

3	slices	**Fresh root ginger (thumbnail sized)**
12	fresh	**Mint leaves**
2	shot(s)	**Light white rum**
1/2	shot(s)	**Freshly squeezed lime juice**
1/2	shot(s)	**Sugar (gomme) syrup**
Top up with		**Ginger ale**

Comment: A spiced variation on the classic Mojito.

GINGER NUT

Glass: Collins
Garnish: Lemon wedge
Method: **POUR** ingredients into ice-filled glass and stir.

1 1/2	shot(s)	**Hazelnut (crème de noisette) liqueur**
1 1/2	shot(s)	**Ketel One Citroen vodka**
Top up with		**Ginger beer**

Comment: A long, refreshing meld of strong flavours.

GINGER PUNCH [NEW]

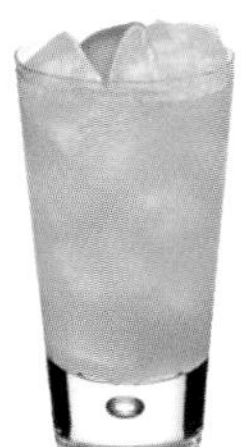

Glass: Collins
Garnish: Lime wedge
Method: **MUDDLE** ginger in base of shaker. Add honey and rum and **STIR** until honey is dissolved. Add lime juice and sugar, **SHAKE** with ice and fine strain into ice-filled glass. **TOP** with ginger ale.

2	slices	**Fresh root ginger (thumbnail sized)**
2	spoons	**Runny honey**
2 1/2	shot(s)	**Mount Gay Eclipse golden rum**
3/4	shot(s)	**Freshly squeezed lime juice**
1/4	shot(s)	**Sugar (gomme) syrup**
Top up with		**Ginger ale**

Comment: A ginger spiced rum punch.

GIN-GER TOM [UPDATED]

Glass: Collins
Garnish: Lime squeeze & mint sprig
Method: **MUDDLE** ginger in base of shaker. Add other ingredients, **SHAKE** with ice and fine strain into ice-filled glass.

2	slices	**Fresh root ginger (thumbnail sized)**
2	shot(s)	**Plymouth gin**
1	shot(s)	**Freshly squeezed lime juice**
1/2	shot(s)	**Sugar (gomme) syrup**
Top up with		**Soda water (club soda)**

Origin: Adapted from a drink created in 2003 by Jamie Terrell at Lab, London, England.
Comment: A Tom Collins with lime and ginger – very refreshing.

GINGERBREAD MARTINI

Glass: Martini
Garnish: Slice of root ginger
Method: **SHAKE** all ingredients with ice and fine strain into chilled glass.

1 1/2	shot(s)	**Bourbon whiskey**
3/4	shot(s)	**Butterscotch schnapps liqueur**
3/4	shot(s)	**Stone's green ginger wine**
2	shot(s)	**Pressed apple juice**

Origin: Created by yours truly in 2004.
Comment: Sticky, warming and spicy.

GINGERTINI

Glass: Martini
Garnish: Orange zest twist
Method: **SHAKE** all ingredients with ice and fine strain into chilled glass.

2	shot(s)	**Plymouth gin**
1/2	shot(s)	**King's ginger liqueur**
1/4	shot(s)	**Dry vermouth**
1/4	shot(s)	**Sugar (gomme) syrup**
1/2	shot(s)	**Chilled mineral water**

Origin: Created by yours truly in 2002.
Comment: A delicate Martini with a warming hint of ginger.

GIUSEPPE'S HABIT

Glass: Martini
Garnish: Star anise
Method: Spray the oils from two lemon zest twists into the cocktail shaker, wipe them around the rim of the glass and drop them into the shaker. Pour other ingredients into shaker. **SHAKE** with ice and fine strain into chilled glass.

2	twists	**Lemon zest**
1 1/2	shot(s)	**Galliano liqueur**
3/4	shot(s)	**Hazelnut (crème de noisette) liqueur**
3/4	shot(s)	**Cointreau / triple sec**
1 1/4	shot(s)	**Pressed apple juice**

Origin: Created in 2002 by Leon Stokes at Zinc Bar & Grill, Birmingham, England.
Comment: An intriguing drink that combines hazelnut, orange, apple, aniseed and peppermint.

A B C D E F **G** H I J K L M N O P Q R S T U V W X Y Z

GIVE ME A DIME

Glass: Martini
Garnish: Crumbled Cadbury's Flake bar
Method: **SHAKE** all ingredients with ice and fine strain into chilled glass.

$1\frac{1}{2}$	shot(s)	**White crème de cacao liqueur**
$1\frac{1}{2}$	shot(s)	**Butterscotch schnapps liqueur**
$1\frac{1}{2}$	shot(s)	**Double (heavy) cream**

Comment: Creamy, sweet and tasty.

GLASS TOWER

Glass: Collins
Method: **SHAKE** first five ingredients with ice and strain into ice-filled glass. **TOP** with 7-Up and stir.

1	shot(s)	**Ketel One vodka**
1	shot(s)	**Light white rum**
$\frac{1}{2}$	shot(s)	**Cointreau / triple sec**
$\frac{1}{2}$	shot(s)	**Peach schnapps liqueur**
$\frac{1}{4}$	shot(s)	**Luxardo Sambuca dei Cesari**
Top up with		**7-Up or lemonade**

Comment: A heady, slightly sweet combination of spirits and liqueurs.

GLOOM CHASER [UPDATED]

Glass: Martini
Garnish: Berries on stick
Method: **SHAKE** all ingredients with ice and fine strain into chilled glass.

1	shot(s)	**Grand Marnier liqueur**
1	shot(s)	**Mandarine Napoléon liqueur**
1	shot(s)	**Freshly squeezed lemon juice**
$\frac{1}{8}$	shot(s)	**Pomegranate (grenadine) syrup**

Comment: A sunny coloured drink for happy people: heavy on the orange.

GLOOM LIFTER

Glass: Martini
Garnish: Lime wedge
Method: **SHAKE** all ingredients with ice and fine strain into chilled glass.

$1\frac{1}{2}$	shot(s)	**Irish whiskey**
$\frac{1}{2}$	shot(s)	**Rémy Martin cognac**
1	shot(s)	**Freshly squeezed lime juice**
$\frac{1}{4}$	shot(s)	**Pomegranate (grenadine) syrup**
$\frac{1}{4}$	shot(s)	**Sugar (gomme) syrup**
$\frac{1}{2}$	fresh	**Egg white**

Comment: A whiskey and cognac sour with lime juice served straight-up.

GODFATHER

Glass: Old-fashioned
Method: **STIR** all ingredients with ice and strain into ice-filled glass.

2	shot(s)	**The Famous Grouse Scotch**
1	shot(s)	**Luxardo Amaretto di Saschira**

Variant: Based on vodka, this drink becomes a Godmother and when made with cognac it's known as a Godchild.
Comment: Scotch diluted and sweetened with almond – simple but good.

GODFREY

Glass: Old-fashioned
Garnish: Three blackberries on drink
Method: **MUDDLE** blackberries in base of shaker. Add other ingredients, **SHAKE** with ice and fine strain into glass filled with crushed ice.

6	fresh	**Blackberries**
$1\frac{1}{2}$	shot(s)	**Rémy Martin cognac**
$\frac{1}{2}$	shot(s)	**Grand Marnier liqueur**
$\frac{1}{4}$	shot(s)	**Crème de mûre (blackberry) liqueur**
$\frac{1}{4}$	shot(s)	**Freshly squeezed lemon juice**
$\frac{1}{4}$	shot(s)	**Sugar (gomme) syrup**

Origin: Created by Salvatore Calabrese at the Library Bar, Lanesborough Hotel, London, England.
Comment: Well balanced with a rich blackberry flavour.

GEORGETOWN PUNCH [NEW]

Glass: Collins
Garnish: Pineapple wedge
Method: **SHAKE** all ingredients with ice and fine strain into ice-filled glass.

1	shot(s)	**Light white rum**
$\frac{3}{4}$	shot(s)	**Gosling's Black Seal rum**
$1\frac{1}{2}$	shot(s)	**Malibu coconut rum liqueur**
1	shot(s)	**Cranberry juice**
1	shot(s)	**Pressed pineapple juice**
$\frac{3}{4}$	shot(s)	**Freshly squeezed lime juice**

Origin: Adapted from a drink discovered in 2005 at Degrees, Washington DC, USA.
Comment: A Tiki-style, fruity rum punch.

GOLD

Glass: Martini
Garnish: Orange zest twist
Method: **SHAKE** all ingredients with ice and fine strain into chilled glass.

$1\frac{1}{2}$	shot(s)	**The Famous Grouse Scotch**
1	shot(s)	**Cointreau / triple sec**
1	shot(s)	**Crème de bananes**
$\frac{3}{4}$	shot(s)	**Chilled mineral water (omit if wet ice)**

Comment: Sweet, ripe banana, Scotch and a hint of orange.

●●●◐○

GOLD MEDALLION [NEW]

Glass: Martini
Garnish: Flamed orange zest
Method: **SHAKE** all ingredients with ice and fine strain into chilled glass.

1½ shot(s) **Rémy Martin cognac**
1 shot(s) **Galliano liqueur**
1½ shot(s) **Freshly squeezed orange juice**
¼ shot(s) **Freshly squeezed lime juice**
½ fresh **Egg white (optional)**

Comment: Gold by name and golden in colour. Frothy, orange fresh and cognac based.

●●●●○

GOLD MEMBER

Glass: Martini
Garnish: Apple slice
Method: **SHAKE** all ingredients with ice and fine strain into chilled glass.

¾ shot(s) **Goldschläger cinnamon schnapps liqueur**
¾ shot(s) **Butterscotch schnapps liqueur**
¾ shot(s) **Apple schnapps liqueur**
2¼ shot(s) **Pressed apple juice**

Comment: Hints of cinnamon and apple – an interesting tipple, if a tad sweet.

●●●○○

GOLD RUSH SLAMMER [NEW]

Glass: Shot
Method: **SHAKE** first two ingredients with ice and fine strain into chilled glass. **TOP** with champagne.

½ shot(s) **Goldschläger cinnamon schnapps liqueur**
½ shot(s) **Sauza Hornitos tequila**
Top up with **Piper-Heidsieck brut champagne**

Origin: Discovered in 2003 at Oxo Tower Bar, London, England.
Comment: Flakes of gold dance with the champagne's bubbles.

●●●◐○

GOLDEN BIRD

Glass: Martini
Garnish: Orange beak on rim
Method: **SHAKE** all ingredients with ice and fine strain into chilled glass.

1 shot(s) **Light white rum**
1 shot(s) **Grand Marnier liqueur**
½ shot(s) **Crème de bananes**
1½ shot(s) **Freshly squeezed orange juice**
1 shot(s) **Pressed pineapple juice**

Comment: Fruity and sweet – an after dinner cocktail.

●●●◐○

GOLDEN CADILLAC [UPDATED]

Glass: Martini
Garnish: Dust with freshly ground nutmeg
Method: **SHAKE** all ingredients with ice and fine strain into chilled glass.

1 shot(s) **White crème de cacao liqueur**
½ shot(s) **Galliano liqueur**
1½ shot(s) **Freshly squeezed orange juice**
½ shot(s) **Double (heavy) cream**
½ shot(s) **Milk**
2 dashes **Fee Brothers orange bitters**

Origin: Adapted from a drink reputedly created in the late sixties at Poor Red's, a barbecue joint favoured by 'sportbike pilots' in El Dorado, California.
Comment: A silky smooth but not very potent cocktail.

●●●●○

GOLDEN DAWN [UPDATED]

Glass: Martini
Method: **SHAKE** first five ingredients with ice and fine strain into chilled glass. Carefully **POUR** grenadine into centre of drink so that it sinks to create a sunrise effect.

¾ shot(s) **Plymouth gin**
1 shot(s) **Calvados or applejack brandy**
1 shot(s) **Apricot brandy liqueur**
1 shot(s) **Freshly squeezed orange juice**
2 dashes **Angostura aromatic bitters**
¼ shot(s) **Pomegranate (grenadine) syrup**

Origin: Created in 1930 by Tom Buttery at the Berkshire Hotel, London, England. There are now many versions of this classic drink (David Embury's 'The Fine Art of Mixing Drinks' lists three) but this is my favourite.
Comment: If the syrup lying on the bottom is not stirred into the drink (or better still included when shaking) you may find this a little tart.

●●●◐○

GOLDEN DRAGON

Glass: Collins
Garnish: Green apple wedge
Method: **SHAKE** all ingredients with ice and strain into ice-filled glass.

2 shot(s) **Sauza Hornitos tequila**
¾ shot(s) **Pisang Ambon liqueur**
2 shot(s) **Pressed apple juice**
1 shot(s) **Freshly squeezed lime juice**
½ shot(s) **Passion fruit sugar syrup**

Comment: Bright green, tangy and tropical.

DRINKS ARE GRADED AS FOLLOWS:

● DISGUSTING ●◐ PRETTY AWFUL ●● BEST AVOIDED
●●◐ DISAPPOINTING ●●● ACCEPTABLE ●●●◐ GOOD
●●●● RECOMMENDED ●●●●◐ HIGHLY RECOMMENDED
●●●●● OUTSTANDING / EXCEPTIONAL

A B C D E F **G** H I J K L M N O P Q R S T U V W X Y Z

GOLDEN DREAM

Glass: Martini
Garnish: Sponge biscuit on rim
Method: SHAKE all ingredients with ice and fine strain into chilled glass.

1	shot(s)	**Cointreau / triple sec**
1	shot(s)	**Galliano liqueur**
2	shot(s)	**Freshly squeezed orange juice**
1	shot(s)	**Double (heavy) cream**

Comment: Tastes remarkably like syllabub.

GOLDEN FIZZ #1 [UPDATED]

Glass: Collins (8oz max)
Garnish: Lemon slice & mint
Method: SHAKE first four ingredients with ice and fine strain into chilled glass. **TOP** with soda.

2	shot(s)	**Plymouth gin**
1	shot(s)	**Freshly squeezed lemon juice**
1/2	shot(s)	**Sugar (gomme) syrup**
1	fresh	**Egg yolk**
Top up with		**Soda water (from siphon)**

Variant: Gin Fizz
Origin: Mid-19th century classic.
Comment: You may have some raw egg inhibitions to conquer before you can enjoy this drink.

GOLDEN FIZZ #2 [NEW]

Glass: Collins
Garnish: Orange slice/mint sprig
Method: STIR honey with gin in base of shaker until honey dissolves. Add next three ingredients, **SHAKE** with ice and strain into ice-filled glass. **TOP** with 7-Up.

2	spoons	**Runny honey**
1 1/2	shot(s)	**Plymouth gin**
1	shot(s)	**Cointreau / triple sec**
1	shot(s)	**Freshly squeezed golden grapefruit juice**
1/4	shot(s)	**Freshly squeezed lemon juice**
Top up with		**7-Up / lemonade**

Origin: Adapted from a drink created by Wayne Collins, UK.
Comment: More cloudy white than golden but a pleasant, refreshing long drink all the same.

GOLDEN GIRL

Glass: Martini
Garnish: Grated orange zest
Method: SHAKE all ingredients with ice and fine strain into chilled glass.

1 1/4	shot(s)	**Aged rum**
1	shot(s)	**Pressed pineapple juice**
1	shot(s)	**Tawny port**
1/4	shot(s)	**Sugar (gomme) syrup**
1	fresh	**Egg**

Origin: Created by Dale DeGroff, New York City, USA. I've slightly increased the proportions of rum and port from Dale's original recipe.
Comment: This appropriately named velvety drink is a refined dessert in a glass.

GOLDEN MAC [NEW]

Glass: Old-fashioned
Garnish: Orange zest twist
Method: MUDDLE ginger in base of shaker. Add honey and Scotch and **STIR** until honey dissolves. Add other ingredients, **SHAKE** with ice and fine strain into ice-filled glass.

2	slices	**Fresh root ginger (thumbnail sized)**
2	spoons	**Runny honey**
2	shot(s)	**The Famous Grouse Scotch**
1/4	shot(s)	**Butterscotch schnapps liqueur**
1/4	shot(s)	**Hazelnut (crème de noisette) liqueur**

Origin: Adapted from a drink discovered in 2003 at Golden Mac, Glasgow, Scotland.
Comment: Looks, and even tastes golden.

GOLDEN NAIL [NEW]

Glass: Old-fashioned
Garnish: Orange zest twist
Method: STIR all ingredients with ice and strain into ice-filled glass.

1 1/2	shot(s)	**Bourbon whiskey**
3/4	shot(s)	**Southern Comfort liqueur**
2	dashes	**Peychaud's aromatic bitters**

Comment: A warming taste of southern hospitality.

GOLDEN RETRIEVER

Glass: Martini
Garnish: Orange zest twist
Method: STIR all ingredients with ice and strain into chilled glass.

1	shot(s)	**Light white rum**
1	shot(s)	**Green Chartreuse**
1	shot(s)	**Licor 43 (Cuarenta Y Tres) liqueur**
1	shot(s)	**Chilled mineral water (omit if wet ice)**

Origin: Created in 2002 by Dick Bradsell at Alfred's, London, England.
Comment: The simple drinks are the best and this straw yellow cocktail subtly offers a myriad of flavours.

GOLDEN SCREW

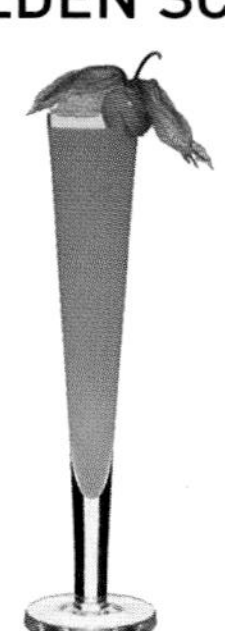

Glass: Flute
Garnish: Physalis fruit
Method: POUR all ingredients into chilled glass and lightly stir.

1/2	shot(s)	**Rémy Martin cognac**
1/2	shot(s)	**Apricot brandy liqueur**
1	shot(s)	**Freshly squeezed orange juice**
Top up with		**Piper-Heidsieck brut champagne**

Variant: With gin in place of brandy.
Comment: A favourite with Midas and others whose budgets extend beyond a Buck's Fizz or a Mimosa.

GOLDEN SHOT

Glass: Shot
Method: Refrigerate ingredients then **LAYER** in chilled glass by carefully pouring in the following order.

1/2	shot(s)	**Drambuie liqueur**
1/2	shot(s)	**Baileys Irish Cream liqueur**
1/2	shot(s)	**The Famous Grouse Scotch**

Comment: A whiskey based layered shot with plenty of character.

GOLDEN SLIPPER

Glass: Martini
Garnish: Apricot slice on rim
Method: **SHAKE** all ingredients with ice and fine strain into chilled glass.

1 1/2	shot(s)	**Yellow Chartreuse**
1 1/2	shot(s)	**Apricot brandy liqueur**
1	fresh	**Egg yolk**

Comment: Rich in colour and equally rich in flavour. A dessert with a punch.

GOLDEN WAVE [NEW]

Glass: Sling
Garnish: Pineapple wedge
Method: **BLEND** all ingredients with a 12oz scoop of crushed ice and serve with straws.

1	shot(s)	**Light white rum**
1	shot(s)	**Cointreau / triple sec**
1/2	shot(s)	**Velvet Falernum**
1	shot(s)	**Pressed pineapple juice**
3/4	shot(s)	**Freshly squeezed lemon juice**

Origin: A Tiki drink created in 1969 by Jose 'Joe' Yatco at China Trader, California, USA.
Comment: Rum laced fruit served long and cold with crushed ice.

GOLF COCKTAIL [UPDATED]

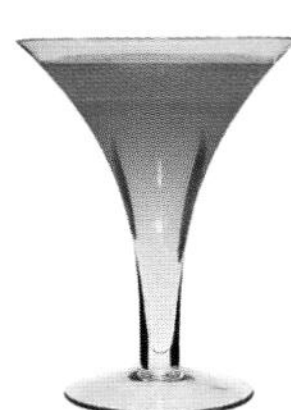

Glass: Martini
Garnish: Orange zest twist
Method: **STIR** all ingredients with ice and strain into chilled glass.

2	shot(s)	**Plymouth gin**
1	shot(s)	**Dry vermouth**
1	dash	**Angostura aromatic bitters**

Comment: A 'wet' Martini with bitters.

GOOMBAY SMASH

Glass: Collins
Garnish: Lime wedge
Method: **SHAKE** all ingredients with ice and strain into ice filled glass.

2	shot(s)	**Pusser's Navy rum**
3/4	shot(s)	**Malibu coconut rum liqueur**
3	shot(s)	**Pressed pineapple juice**
1/4	shot(s)	**Freshly squeezed lime juice**
1/2	shot(s)	**Cointreau / triple sec**

Comment: Smashes are usually short drinks that include muddled mint. Whatever's in a name, this Tiki-style drink is bound to get you smashed.

GRAND COSMOPOLITAN [UPDATED]

Glass: Martini
Garnish: Flamed orange zest twist
Method: **SHAKE** all ingredients with ice and fine strain into chilled glass.

1	shot(s)	**Ketel One Citroen vodka**
1	shot(s)	**Grand Marnier liqueur**
1 1/2	shot(s)	**Cranberry juice**
3/4	shot(s)	**Freshly squeezed lime juice**
2	dashes	**Fee Brothers orange bitters (optional)**

Comment: A 'grand' Cosmo indeed.

GRAND MARGARITA [NEW]

Glass: Coupette
Garnish: Salt rim & lime wedge
Method: **SHAKE** all ingredients with ice and fine strain into chilled glass.

2	shot(s)	**Sauza Hornitos Tequila**
1	shot(s)	**Grand Marnier liqueur**
1	shot(s)	**Freshly squeezed lime juice**

Comment: A wonderfully balanced and flavoursome Margarita that's far removed from those sweet disco drinks often peddled as Margaritas.

GRAND MIMOSA

Glass: Flute
Garnish: Strawberry on rim
Method: **SHAKE** first two ingredients with ice and strain into chilled glass. **TOP** with champagne.

1	shot(s)	**Grand Marnier liqueur**
2	shot(s)	**Freshly squeezed orange juice**
Top up with		**Piper-Heidsieck brut champagne**

Origin: The Mimosa was created in 1925 at the Ritz Hotel, Paris, and named after the Mimosa plant - probably because of its trembling leaves, rather like the gentle fizz of this mixture. The Grand Mimosa as shown here benefits from the addition of Grand Marnier liqueur.
Comment: As the name suggests, the orange of Grand Marnier heavily influences this drink. Basically a Buck's Fizz with more oomph.

GRAND SAZERAC [NEW]

Glass: Old-fashioned
Method: POUR absinthe into ice-filled glass and **TOP** with water. Leave the mixture to stand in the glass. Separately, **SHAKE** liqueur, bourbon and bitters with ice. Finally discard contents of absinthe-coated glass and fine strain contents of shaker into absinthe washed glass. (Note that there is no ice in the finished drink.)

1/2	shot(s)	**La Fée Parisian 68% absinthe**
Top up with		**Chilled mineral water**
1 1/2	shot(s)	**Grand Marnier liqueur**
1 1/2	shot(s)	**Bourbon whiskey**
2	dashes	**Angostura aromatic bitters**
3	dashes	**Peychaud's aromatic bitters**

Origin: Created in 2004 by yours truly.
Comment: An orange twist on the classic Sazerac.

GRAND SIDECAR [NEW]

Glass: Martini
Garnish: Orange zest twist
Method: SHAKE all ingredients with ice and fine strain into chilled glass.

2 1/2	shot(s)	**Grand Marnier liqueur**
1	shot(s)	**Freshly squeezed lemon juice**
1/2	shot(s)	**Chilled mineral water (omit if wet ice)**

Origin: Created by yours truly in June 2005.
Comment: A twist on the classic, simple but very tasty. Also works well shaken and strained into an ice-filled old-fashioned glass.

GRANDE CHAMPAGNE COSMO [UPDATED]

Glass: Martini
Garnish: Flamed orange zest twist
Method: SHAKE all ingredients with ice and fine strain into chilled glass.

1 1/2	shot(s)	**Rémy Martin cognac**
3/4	shot(s)	**Grand Marnier liqueur**
1/2	shot(s)	**Freshly squeezed lemon juice**
1	shot(s)	**Cranberry juice**
1/2	fresh	**Egg white**

Comment: 'Grande Champagne' refers to the top cru of the Cognac region: this drink is suitably elite.

GRANNY'S [UPDATED]

Glass: Martini
Garnish: Apple wedge on rim
Method: SHAKE all ingredients with ice and fine strain into chilled glass.

1 3/4	shot(s)	**Light white rum**
1/4	shot(s)	**Goldschläger cinnamon schnapps**
1/2	shot(s)	**Apple schnapps liqueur**
1 1/2	shot(s)	**Pressed apple juice**

Comment: Apple, rum and cinnamon were made for each other.

GRANNY'S MARTINI [NEW]

Glass: Martini
Garnish: Dust with ground nutmeg
Method: SHAKE all ingredients with ice and fine strain into chilled glass.

1	shot(s)	**Plymouth gin**
1/2	shot(s)	**Tio Pepe fino sherry**
2	shot(s)	**Advocaat liqueur**

Origin: I have to own up to creating and naming this drink after three drink categories often identified with a stereotypical English granny. Sorry, mum.
Comment: Creamy, Christmassy drink just for nana.

GRAPE DELIGHT [UPDATED]

Glass: Martini
Garnish: Grapes on stick
Method: MUDDLE grapes in base of shaker. Add rest of ingredients, **SHAKE** with ice and fine strain into chilled glass.

12	fresh	**Seedless red grapes**
2	shot(s)	**Plymouth gin**
1/2	shot(s)	**Plymouth sloe gin**
1/2	shot(s)	**Pressed apple juice**
1/4	shot(s)	**Sugar (gomme) syrup**
1/4	shot(s)	**Freshly squeezed lime juice**
1	dash	**Angostura aromatic bitters**

Comment: This rust coloured drink is fruity and delicate.

GRAPE EFFECT

Glass: Martini
Garnish: Grapes on stick
Method: MUDDLE grapes in base of shaker. Add other ingredients, **SHAKE** with ice and fine strain into chilled glass.

12	fresh	**Seedless white grapes**
2	shot(s)	**Light white rum**
1/2	shot(s)	**Elderflower cordial**

Comment: Delicately flavoured and heavily laced with rum.

GRAPE ESCAPE

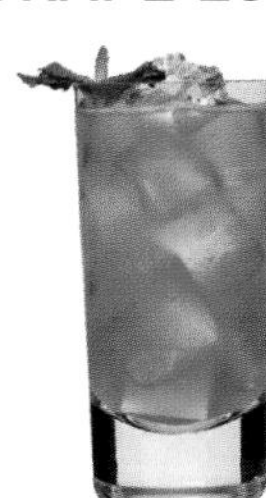

Glass: Collins
Garnish: Mint sprig
Method: MUDDLE grapes and mint in base of shaker. Add cognac and sugar, **SHAKE** with ice and strain into glass filled with crushed ice. **TOP** with champagne, stir and serve with straws.

8	fresh	**Seedless white grapes**
5	fresh	**Mint leaves**
2	shot(s)	**Rémy Martin cognac**
1/2	shot(s)	**Sugar (gomme) syrup**
Top up with		**Piper-Heidsieck brut champagne**

Origin: Created in 2000 by Brian Lucas and Max Warner at Long Bar @ Sanderson, London, England.
Comment: A cracking drink – subtle and refreshing.

A B C D E F **G** H I J K L M N O P Q R S T U V W X Y Z

GRAPE MARTINI

Glass: Martini
Garnish: Grapes on stick
Method: MUDDLE grapes in base of shaker. Add other ingredients, **SHAKE** with ice and fine strain into chilled glass.

12 fresh **Seedless white grapes**
2 shot(s) **Ketel One vodka**
1/2 shot(s) **Sugar (gomme) syrup**

Origin: Formula by yours truly in 2004.
Comment: Simple but remarkably tasty.

GRAPEFRUIT DAIQUIRI

Glass: Martini
Garnish: Cherry
Method: SHAKE all ingredients with ice and fine strain into chilled glass.

2 shot(s) **Aged rum**
1 1/2 shot(s) **Freshly squeezed grapefruit juice**
3/4 shot(s) **Sugar (gomme) syrup or Passion fruit sugar syrup**

Comment: The flavours of rum and grapefruit combine perfectly – clean and fresh.

GRAPEFRUIT JULEP [NEW]

Glass: Collins
Garnish: Mint sprig
Method: STIR honey with vodka in base of shaker until honey dissolves. Add other ingredients, **SHAKE** with ice and strain into glass filled with crushed ice.

1 spoon **Runny honey**
2 shot(s) **Ketel One vodka**
4 fresh **Mint leaves**
1/2 shot(s) **Freshly squeezed lime juice**
1/2 shot(s) **Pomegranate (grenadine) syrup**
3/4 shot(s) **Freshly squeezed pink grapefruit juice**

Origin: Created by Dale DeGroff, New York City, USA.
Comment: Wonderfully refreshing. Bring on the sun.

GRAPPA MANHATTAN

Glass: Martini
Garnish: Stemmed cherry on rim
Method: STIR all ingredients with ice and strain into chilled glass.

2 shot(s) **Grappa (moscato)**
1 1/2 shot(s) **Sweet (rosso) vermouth**
1/4 shot(s) **Maraschino syrup**
2 dashes **Angostura aromatic bitters**

Comment: Now that quality grappa is more widely available more aromatic cocktails such as this are bound to follow.

GRAPPARITA [NEW]

Glass: Coupette
Garnish: Lime wedge on rim
Method: SHAKE all ingredients with ice and fine strain into chilled glass.

2 shot(s) **Grappa**
1 shot(s) **Luxardo Limoncello liqueur**
1 shot(s) **Freshly squeezed lemon juice**
1/2 fresh **Egg white**

Origin: Adapted from a drink discovered in 2005 at Alfredo's of Rome, New York City, USA. The original called for sour mix.
Comment: Grappa replaces tequila and lemon liqueur triple sec in this Italian twist on the classic Margarita.

GRAPPLE MARTINI

Glass: Martini
Garnish: Grapes on stick
Method: MUDDLE grapes in base of shaker. Add other ingredients, **SHAKE** with ice and fine strain into chilled glass.

7 fresh **Seedless white grapes**
2 shot(s) **Ketel One vodka**
3/4 shot(s) **Sauvignon Blanc or unoaked Chardonnay wine**
1 shot(s) **Pressed apple juice**
1/4 shot(s) **Sugar (gomme) syrup**

Origin: Adapted from a recipe created in 2003 by Chris Setchell at Las Iguanas, UK.
Comment: A rounded, fruity Martini-style drink.

GRASSY FINNISH

Glass: Martini
Garnish: Lemongrass
Method: MUDDLE lemongrass in base of shaker. Add other ingredients, **SHAKE** with ice and fine strain into chilled glass.

1 stem **Fresh lemongrass (chopped)**
2 shot(s) **Lime flavoured vodka**
1 shot(s) **Krupnik honey liqueur**
1/4 shot(s) **Sugar (gomme) syrup**

Origin: Created in 2003 by Gerard McCurry at Revolution, UK.
Comment: Like Finland, this drink is clean, green, wooded and safe, but deep down there's plenty of spice.

FOR MORE INFORMATION SEE OUR

GRATEFUL DEAD

Glass: Sling
Garnish: Lime wedge
Method: **SHAKE** first seven ingredients with ice and strain into ice-filled glass. **TOP** with soda and serve with straws.

1/2	shot(s)	**Ketel One vodka**
1/2	shot(s)	**Plymouth gin**
1/2	shot(s)	**Light white rum**
1/2	shot(s)	**Cointreau / triple sec**
1/2	shot(s)	**Midori melon liqueur**
1	shot(s)	**Freshly squeezed lime juice**
1/2	shot(s)	**Sugar (gomme) syrup**
Top up with		**Soda water (club soda)**

Origin: LA Iced Tea with Midori in place of Chambord liqueur.
Comment: Don't be put off by the lime green colour. This fruity, sweet 'n' sour drink is actually quite pleasant.

GREAT MUGHAL MARTINI

Glass: Martini
Garnish: Lemon zest twist
Method: **MUDDLE** raisins in base of shaker. Add other ingredients, **SHAKE** with ice and fine strain into chilled glass.

20		**Raisins**
1 1/2	shot(s)	**Bourbon whiskey**
1/4	shot(s)	**Sugar (gomme) syrup**
3/4	shot(s)	**Passion fruit sugar syrup**
1/4	shot(s)	**Freshly squeezed lime juice**
3	drops	**Rosewater**
1	shot(s)	**Lime & lemongrass cordial**

Origin: Created in 2001 by Douglas Ankrah for Red Fort, Soho, London, England.
Comment: Douglas' original recipe called for raisin infused bourbon and I'd recommend you make this drink that way if time permits.

GREEN APPLE & CUCUMBER MARTINI [NEW]

Glass: Martini
Garnish: Float three cucumber slices
Method: **MUDDLE** cucumber in base of shaker. Add other ingredients, **SHAKE** with ice and fine strain into chilled glass.

1	inch	**Chopped peeled cucumber**
2	shot(s)	**Cucumber flavoured vodka**
1/2	shot(s)	**Sour apple liqueur**
1/2	shot(s)	**Pressed apple juice**
1/8	shot(s)	**Sugar (gomme) syrup**

Origin: Adapted from a recipe discovered in 2003 at Oxo Tower Bar, London, England.
Comment: Archetypal English flavours. Clean, green and refreshing.

GREEN DESTINY [NEW]

Glass: Old-fashioned
Garnish: Kiwi slice
Method: **MUDDLE** cucumber and kiwi in base of shaker. Add other ingredients, **SHAKE** with ice and fine strain into glass filled with crushed ice.

1	inch	**Chopped peeled cucumber**
1/2	fresh	**Kiwi fruit**
2	shot(s)	**Zubrówka bison vodka**
1 1/2	shot(s)	**Pressed apple juice**
1/4	shot(s)	**Sugar (gomme) syrup**

Origin: Created in 2001 by Andrew Tounos @ Hakk, Warsaw, Poland.
Comment: Looks green and even tastes green, but pleasantly so.

GREEN EYES [UPDATED]

Glass: Martini
Garnish: Lime wedge on rim
Method: **SHAKE** all ingredients with ice and fine strain into chilled glass.

2	shot(s)	**Ketel One Citroen vodka**
1/2	shot(s)	**Blue curaçao liqueur**
1	shot(s)	**Freshly squeezed orange juice**
1/2	shot(s)	**Freshly squeezed lemon juice**
1/4	shot(s)	**Almond (orgeat) syrup**

Comment: A cross between a Blue Cosmo and a short Screwdriver.

GREEN FAIRY

Glass: Martini
Method: **SHAKE** all ingredients with ice and fine strain into chilled glass.

1	shot(s)	**La Fée Parisian 68% absinthe**
1	shot(s)	**Freshly squeezed lemon juice**
3/4	shot(s)	**Sugar (gomme) syrup**
1	shot(s)	**Chilled mineral water (reduce if wet ice)**
1	dash	**Angostura aromatic bitters**
1/2	fresh	**Egg white**

Origin: Created by Dick Bradsell.
Comment: An Absinthe Sour style drink served straight-up.

GREEN FIZZ [NEW]

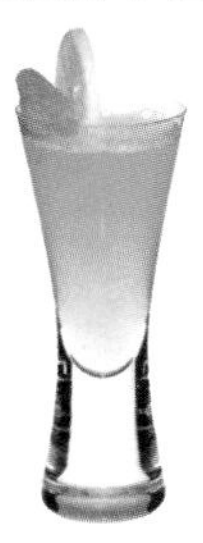

Glass: Collins (8oz max)
Garnish: Slice of lemon & mint
Method: **SHAKE** first four ingredients with ice and strain into chilled glass. **TOP** with soda.

2	shot(s)	**Plymouth gin**
1/2	shot(s)	**White crème de menthe liqueur**
1	shot(s)	**Freshly squeezed lemon juice**
1/4	shot(s)	**Sugar (gomme) syrup**
Top up with		**Soda water (from siphon)**

Variant: Gin Fizz
Origin: A mid-19th century classic.
Comment: Fresh, cleansing and refreshing - as only a minty Fizz can be.

A B C D E F **G** H I J K L M N O P Q R S T U V W X Y Z

GREEN FLY

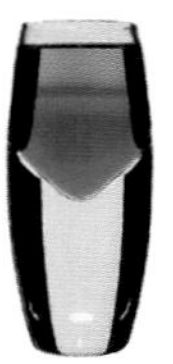

Glass: Shot
Method: Refrigerate ingredients then **LAYER** in chilled glass by carefully pouring in the following order.

1/2	shot(s)	**Midori melon liqueur**
1/2	shot(s)	**White crème de menthe liqueur**
1/2	shot(s)	**Green Chartreuse**

Origin: Created by Alex Turner at Circus, London, England.
Comment: A strong shot comprising three layers of different green liqueurs.

GREEN HORNET

Glass: Shot
Method: **SHAKE** all ingredients with ice and fine strain into chilled glass.

3/4	shot(s)	**Ketel One vodka**
1/8	shot(s)	**La Fée Parisian 68% absinthe**
3/4	shot(s)	**Pisang Ambon liqueur**
1/2	shot(s)	**Rose's lime cordial**

Comment: A surprisingly palatable and balanced shot.

GREEN SWIZZLE [NEW]

Glass: Old-fashioned
Method: **POUR** all ingredients into glass. Fill glass with crushed ice and **SWIZZLE** (stir) with bar spoon or swizzle stick to mix. Serve with straws.

2	shot(s)	**Light white rum**
1/2	shot(s)	**Freshly squeezed lime juice**
1/4	shot(s)	**White crème de menthe liqueur**
1/4	shot(s)	**Sugar (gomme) syrup**
1	dash	**Angostura aromatic bitters**

Variant: With gin in place of rum
Origin: This 1940s classic features in 'The Rummy Affair Of Old Biffy' by P.G. Wodehouse. Bertie Wooster sings its praises after enjoying a few at the Panters' Bar of the West Indian stand at the 1924 Empire Exhibition.
Comment: A Daiquiri-like drink with a hint of peppermint.

GREEN TEA MARTINI

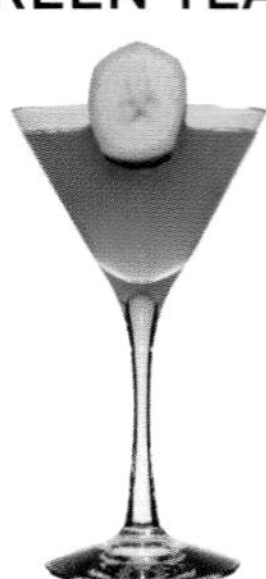

Glass: Martini
Garnish: Banana slice on rim
Method: **SHAKE** all ingredients with ice and fine strain into chilled glass.

2	shot(s)	**Zubrówka bison vodka**
1/4	shot(s)	**Pisang Ambon liqueur**
1/8	shot(s)	**White crème de menthe liqueur**
2	shot(s)	**Pressed apple juice**

Comment: It's green and, although it doesn't actually contain any tea, has something of the flavour of alcoholic peppermint tea.

GRETA GARBO

Glass: Martini
Garnish: Star anise
Method: **SHAKE** all ingredients with ice and fine strain into chilled glass.

2	shot(s)	**Light white rum**
1/4	shot(s)	**Luxardo Maraschino liqueur**
1/2	shot(s)	**Sugar (gomme) syrup**
1	shot(s)	**Freshly squeezed lime juice**
1/8	shot(s)	**Pernod anis**

Comment: A most unusual Daiquiri.

GREY MOUSE [NEW]

Glass: Shot
Method: **SHAKE** all ingredients with ice and fine strain into chilled glass.

1	shot(s)	**Baileys Irish Cream liqueur**
1/2	shot(s)	**Opal Nera black sambuca**

Comment: Aniseed and whiskey cream.

GREYHOUND [NEW]

Glass: Collins
Garnish: Orange slice
Method: **POUR** ingredients into ice-filled glass and stir.

2	shot(s)	**Ketel One vodka**
Top up with		**Freshly squeezed pink grapefruit juice**

Comment: A sour Screwdriver.

GROG [NEW]

Glass: Old-fashioned
Garnish: Lime wedge
Method: **STIR** honey with rum in base of shaker until honey dissolves. Add other ingredients, **SHAKE** with ice and strain into ice-filled glass.

2	spoons	**Runny honey**
1 1/2	shot(s)	**Pusser's Navy rum (54.4%)**
1/4	shot(s)	**Freshly squeezed lime juice**
2 1/2	shot(s)	**Chilled mineral water**
3	dashes	**Angostura aromatic bitters**

Variant: Hot Grog
Origin: For over 300 years the British Navy issued a daily 'tot' of rum. In 1740, as an attempt to combat drunkenness, Admiral Vernon gave orders that the standard daily issue of half a pint of neat, high-proof rum be replaced with two servings of a quarter of a pint, diluted 4:1 with water. The Admiral was nicknamed 'Old Grogram' due to the waterproof grogram cloak he wore, so the mixture he introduced became known as 'grog'. Lime juice was often added to the grog in an attempt to prevent scurvy. The 'tot' tradition, which started in Jamaica in 1665, was finally broken on 31st July 1970.
Comment: Strong, flavoursome Navy rum with a splash of scurvy-inhibiting lime. Too many and you'll be groggy in the morning.

THE GTO COCKTAIL [NEW]

Glass: Collins
Garnish: Pineapple wedge on rim
Method: **SHAKE** all ingredients with ice and strain into ice-filled glass.

2	shot(s)	**Jack Daniel's Tennessee whiskey**
1/2	shot(s)	**Luxardo Amaretto di Saschira**
1/2	shot(s)	**Freshly squeezed lemon juice**
3	shot(s)	**Pressed pineapple juice**

Origin: Adapted from a recipe discovered in 2004 at Jones, Los Angeles, USA.
Comment: A fruity, punch-like drink.

GUILLOTINE [NEW]

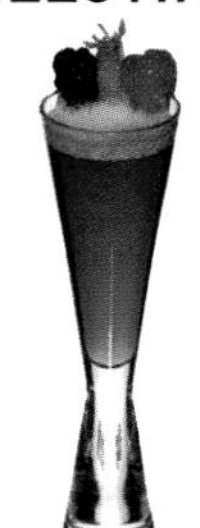

Glass: Flute
Garnish: Berries on rim
Method: **POUR** first two ingredients into glass and **TOP** with champagne.

1/2	shot(s)	**Sisca crème de cassis**
1/2	shot(s)	**Poire William eau de vie**
Top up with		**Piper-Heidsieck brut champagne**

Comment: Add some life to your bubbly.

GULF COAST SEX ON THE BEACH

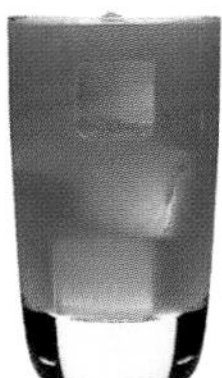

Glass: Collins
Method: **SHAKE** all ingredients with ice and strain into ice-filled glass.

1 1/2	shot(s)	**Light white rum**
3/4	shot(s)	**Midori melon liqueur**
3/4	shot(s)	**Crème de bananes**
1 1/2	shot(s)	**Pressed pineapple juice**
1 1/2	shot(s)	**Cranberry juice**
1/4	shot(s)	**Freshly squeezed lime juice**

Origin: Created in 1997 by Roberto Canino and Wayne Collins at Navajo Joe, London, England.
Comment: Golden tan in colour and tropical in flavour, complete with frothy top.

GUSTO [NEW]

Glass: Collins
Garnish: Apple slice
Method: **MUDDLE** grapes in base of shaker. Add other ingredients, **SHAKE** with ice and fine strain into ice-filled glass.

7	fresh	**Seedless green grapes**
2	shot(s)	**Sauza Hornitos tequila**
3/4	shot(s)	**Agavero tequila liqueur**
2	shot(s)	**Pressed apple juice**

Origin: Created in 2003 by Thomas Gillgren at The Kingly Club, London, England.
Comment: A pleasing long drink flavoured with apple, grape and tequila.

GYPSY MARTINI

Glass: Martini
Garnish: Rosemary
Method: **MUDDLE** rosemary and raisins in base of shaker. Add other ingredients, **SHAKE** with ice and fine strain into chilled glass.

1	sprig	**Fresh rosemary (remove stalk)**
10		**Raisins**
2	shot(s)	**Plymouth gin**
1/2	shot(s)	**Sugar (gomme) syrup**
1	shot(s)	**Chilled mineral water (reduce if wet ice)**

Origin: Adapted from a recipe created by Jason Fendick in 2002 for Steam, London, England.
Comment: Jason's original recipe called for raisin infused gin and I'd recommend you make this drink that way if time permits.

GYPSY QUEEN [NEW]

Glass: Martini
Garnish: Orange zest twist
Method: **STIR** all ingredients with ice and strain into chilled glass.

1 1/2	shot(s)	**Ketel One vodka**
3/4	shot(s)	**Bénédictine D.O.M. liqueur**
3/4	shot(s)	**Freshly squeezed orange juice**
1/4	shot(s)	**Freshly squeezed lemon juice**

Origin: A long lost classic.
Comment: Tangy, herbal, predominantly orange and not overly sweet.

HAIR OF THE DOG

Glass: Martini
Garnish: Grate fresh nutmeg
Method: **STIR** honey with Scotch until honey dissolves. Add other ingredients, **SHAKE** with ice and fine strain into chilled glass.

3	spoons	**Runny honey**
2	shot(s)	**The Famous Grouse Scotch**
1	shot(s)	**Double (heavy) cream**
1	shot(s)	**Milk**

Origin: Traditionally drunk as a pick-me-up hangover cure.
Comment: This drink's name and reputation as a hangover cure may lead you to assume it tastes unpleasant. In fact, honey, whisky and cream combine wonderfully.

HAKKATINI [NEW]

Glass: Martini
Garnish: Orange zest twist
Method: **SHAKE** all ingredients with ice and fine strain into chilled glass.

1	shot(s)	**Orange flavoured vodka**
1	shot(s)	**Grand Marnier**
1/4	shot(s)	**Campari**
3/4	shot(s)	**Pressed apple juice**

Origin: Adapted from a drink discovered in 2003 at Hakkasan, London, England.
Comment: Balanced bitter sweet orange and apple.

A B C D E F G **H** I J K L M N O P Q R S T U V W X Y Z

HAMMER OF THE GODS [NEW]

Glass: Shot & pint glass
Method: **LAYER** ingredients by carefully pouring into shot glass in the following order. **IGNITE** and hold pint glass upside down a few inches above the flame. Allow the drink to burn for thirty seconds or so before killing the flame, being sure to keep the pint glass in place. Instruct your subject to suck the alcohol vapour from the inverted pint glass using a bendy straw. Finally, remove the pint glass and let your subject consume the drink through the straw.

1	shot(s)	**Tuaca Italian liqueur**
1/2	shot(s)	**La Fée Parisian 68% absinthe**

Origin: Created by Dick Bradsell at The Player, London, UK.
Comment: Killjoys would point out the dangers of fire and alcohol and observe that this is hardly 'responsible drinking'.

HANKY-PANKY MARTINI [NEW]

Glass: Martini
Garnish: Orange zest twist
Method: **STIR** all ingredients with ice and strain into chilled glass.

1 3/4	shot(s)	**Plymouth gin**
1 3/4	shot(s)	**Sweet (rosso) vermouth**
1/8	shot(s)	**Fernet Branca**

Origin: Created in the early 1900s by Ada 'Coley' Coleman at The Savoy's American Bar, London, for actor Charles Hawtrey. He often said to Coley, "I am tired. Give me something with a bit of punch in it." This drink was her answer. After finishing his first one, Charles told Coley, "By Jove! That is the real hanky-panky!" And so it has since been named.
Comment: A Sweet Martini made bitter and aromatic by Fernet Branca.

HAPPY NEW YEAR [NEW]

Glass: Flute
Garnish: Orange slice on rim
Method: **SHAKE** first three ingredients with ice and fine strain into chilled glass. **TOP** with champagne.

1/4	shot(s)	**Rémy Martin cognac**
3/4	shot(s)	**Tawny port**
3/4	shot(s)	**Freshly squeezed orange juice**
Top up with		**Piper-Heidsieck brut champagne**

Origin: Created in 1981 by Charles Schumann, Munich, Germany.
Comment: Reminiscent of fizzy, fruity claret.

HARD LEMONADE

Glass: Collins
Garnish: Lemon wheel in glass
Method: **SHAKE** first three ingredients with ice and strain into ice-filled glass. **TOP** with soda and serve with straws.

2	shot(s)	**Ketel One vodka**
2	shot(s)	**Freshly squeezed lemon juice**
1	shot(s)	**Sugar (gomme) syrup**
Top up with		**Soda water (club soda)**

Variants: Vodka Collins, Ray's Hard Lemonade
Origin: Discovered in 2004 at Spring Street Natural Restaurant, New York City, USA.
Comment: Refreshing lemonade with a kick. Great for a hot afternoon.

THE HARLEM

Glass: Martini
Garnish: Cherry in drink
Method: **SHAKE** all ingredients with ice and fine strain into chilled glass.

2	shot(s)	**Plymouth gin**
1/4	shot(s)	**Luxardo Maraschino liqueur**
2	shot(s)	**Pressed pineapple juice**

Origin: Thought to date back to the Prohibition era and the Cotton Club in Harlem.
Comment: Soft and fruity. Careful, it's harder than you think.

HARVARD [NEW]

Glass: Martini
Garnish: Lemon zest twist
Method: **STIR** all ingredients with ice and strain into chilled glass.

1 1/4	shot(s)	**Rémy Martin cognac**
1 1/2	shot(s)	**Sweet (rosso) vermouth**
1 1/4	shot(s)	**Dry vermouth**
3	dashes	**Fee Brothers orange bitters**

Origin: A classic from the 1930s.
Comment: A Delmonico with orange bitters in place of Angostura. Rather like a Brandy Manhattan.

HARVARD COOLER

Glass: Collins
Garnish: Lime wedge
Method: **SHAKE** first three ingredients with ice and strain into ice-filled glass. **TOP** with soda, stir and serve with straws.

2	shot(s)	**Calvados or applejack brandy**
1	shot(s)	**Freshly squeezed lime juice**
1/2	shot(s)	**Sugar (gomme) syrup**
Top up with		**Soda water (club soda)**

Comment: Refreshing and not too sweet. Lime and sugar enhance the appley spirit.

HARVEY WALLBANGER

Glass: Collins
Garnish: Orange slice
Method: **SHAKE** all ingredients with ice and strain into ice-filled glass.

2	shot(s)	**Ketel One vodka**
3½	shot(s)	**Freshly squeezed orange juice**
½	shot(s)	**Galliano liqueur**

Variant: Freddie Fudpucker
Origin: Legend has it that 'Harvey' was a surfer at Manhattan Beach, California. His favourite drink was a Screwdriver with added Galliano. One day in the late sixties, while celebrating winning a surfing competition, he staggered from bar to bar, banging his surfboard on the walls, and so a contemporary classic gained its name.

However, an article in Bartender Magazine credits the creation to Bill Doner, the host of a house party held in the mid-sixties in Newport Beach, California. One of the guests, Harvey, was found banging his head the next morning, complaining of the hangover this drink induced.
Comment: It's usual to build this drink and 'float' Galliano over the built drink. However, as the Galliano sinks anyway it is better shaken.

HAVANA COBBLER

Glass: Old-fashioned
Garnish: Lime zest twist
Method: **SHAKE** all ingredients with ice and strain into glass filled with crushed ice.

2	shot(s)	**Light white rum**
1	shot(s)	**Tawny port**
½	shot(s)	**Stone's green ginger wine**
¼	shot(s)	**Sugar (gomme) syrup**

Comment: An unusual, spiced, Daiquiri-like drink.

HAVANA SPECIAL [NEW]

Glass: Old-fashioned
Garnish: Lime zest twist
Method: **SHAKE** all ingredients with ice and strain into glass filled with crushed ice.

2	shot(s)	**Light white rum**
1¾	shot(s)	**Pressed pineapple juice**
½	shot(s)	**Luxardo maraschino liqueur**

Comment: Daiquiri-like without the sourness. Fragrant and all too easy to drink.

FOR MORE INFORMATION SEE OUR
INGREDIENTS APPENDIX ON PAGE 322

HAVANATHEONE

Glass: Martini
Garnish: Mint leaf
Method: Lightly **MUDDLE** mint (just to bruise) in base of shaker. Add rum and honey and **STIR** until honey dissolves. Add other ingredients, **SHAKE** with ice and fine strain into chilled glass.

10	fresh	**Mint leaves**
2	spoons	**Runny honey**
2	shot(s)	**Light white rum**
½	shot(s)	**Freshly squeezed lime juice**
1	shot(s)	**Pressed apple juice**

Origin: Discovered in 2003 at Hush, London, England.
Comment: A flavoursome Daiquiri featuring honey, apple and mint.

HAWAIIAN

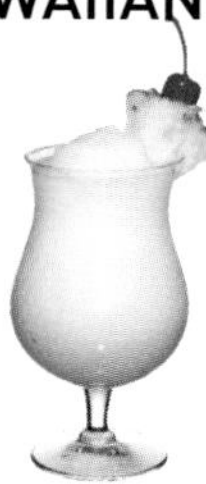

Glass: Hurricane
Garnish: Pineapple wedge & cherry
Method: **BLEND** all ingredients with two 12oz scoops crushed ice and serve with straws.

2	shot(s)	**Malibu coconut rum liqueur**
½	shot(s)	**Cointreau / triple sec**
½	shot(s)	**Light white rum**
1½	shot(s)	**Freshly squeezed orange juice**
1½	shot(s)	**Pressed pineapple juice**
1	shot(s)	**Freshly squeezed lime juice**
½	shot(s)	**Sugar (gomme) syrup**
1	shot(s)	**Coco López cream of coconut**

Comment: Coconut, rum and fruit juice. Aloha.

HAWAIIAN COCKTAIL

Glass: Martini
Garnish: Pineapple wedge & cherry on rim
Method: **SHAKE** all ingredients with ice and fine strain into chilled glass.

1½	shot(s)	**Light white rum**
½	shot(s)	**Southern Comfort liqueur**
½	shot(s)	**Luxardo Amaretto di Saschira**
¾	shot(s)	**Freshly squeezed orange juice**
1½	shot(s)	**Pressed pineapple juice**

Origin: Discovered in Las Vegas in 2004.
Comment: Sweet, tangy and fruity.

HAWAIIAN COSMOPOLITAN

Glass: Martini
Garnish: Pineapple wedge on rim
Method: **SHAKE** all ingredients with ice and fine strain into chilled glass.

2	shot(s)	**Ketel One Citroen vodka**
1	shot(s)	**Sour pineapple liqueur**
1	shot(s)	**Pressed apple juice**
½	shot(s)	**Freshly squeezed lime juice**

Origin: Created in 2002 by Wayne Collins, UK.
Comment: Fresh, tangy and distinctly tropical.

●●●●◐○

HAWAIIAN EYE [NEW]

Glass: Collins
Garnish: Pineapple wedge & cherry
Method: **BLEND** all ingredients with two 12oz scoops of crushed ice. Serve with straws.

1	shot(s)	**Light white rum**
1	shot(s)	**Mount Gay Eclipse golden rum**
½	shot(s)	**Velvet Falernum**
½	shot(s)	**Freshly squeezed lime juice**
½	shot(s)	**Sugar (gomme) syrup**

Origin: A Tiki drink created in 1963 by Tony Ramos at China Trader, California, USA, for the cast of the TV series of the same name.
Comment: Tropical, rum laced cooler.

●●●●○

HAWAIIAN MARTINI [NEW]

Glass: Martini
Garnish: Pineapple wedge & cherry
Method: **SHAKE** all ingredients with ice and fine strain into chilled glass.

1½	shot(s)	**Plymouth gin**
½	shot(s)	**Dry vermouth**
½	shot(s)	**Sweet (rosso) vermouth**
1½	shot(s)	**Pressed pineapple juice**

Origin: Adapted from a drink discovered in 2005 at the Four Seasons, Milan, Italy.
Comment: An aptly named fruity twist on the classic Martini.

●●●◐○

HAWAIIAN SEABREEZE [UPDATED]

Glass: Collins
Garnish: Pineapple wedge on rim
Method: **SHAKE** all ingredients with ice and strain into ice-filled glass.

2	shot(s)	**Mango flavoured vodka**
2½	shot(s)	**Cranberry juice**
1½	shot(s)	**Pressed pineapple juice**

Variant: Bay Breeze
Comment: Easygoing, foam topped relative of the Seabreeze.

●●●●◐

HAZEL'ITO

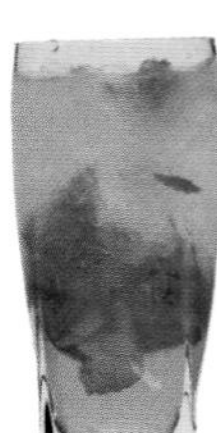

Glass: Collins
Method: Lightly **MUDDLE** mint in base of glass (just to bruise). Add other ingredients, fill glass with crushed ice and **CHURN** (stir) with bar spoon to mix.

12	fresh	**Mint leaves**
2	shot(s)	**Light white rum**
2	shot(s)	**Hazelnut (crème de noisette) liqueur**
1	shot(s)	**Freshly squeezed lime juice**
½	shot(s)	**Sugar (gomme) syrup**

Origin: Created in January 2002 by Adam Wyartt, London, England.
Comment: Looks like a Mojito but has a nutty twang courtesy of the hazelnut liqueur.

●●●●○

HAZELNUT ALEXANDER [NEW]

Glass: Martini
Garnish: Dust with cacao powder
Method: **SHAKE** all ingredients with ice and fine strain into chilled glass.

1¾	shot(s)	**Rémy Martin cognac**
¾	shot(s)	**Hazelnut (crème de noisette) liqueur**
½	shot(s)	**Dark crème de cacao liqueur**
½	shot(s)	**Double (heavy) cream**
½	shot(s)	**Milk**
2	dashes	**Angostura aromatic bitters**

Origin: Created in 2005 by James Mellnor at Maze, London, England.
Comment: Great twist on a classic – the use of bitters is inspired.

●●●◐○

HAZELNUT MARTINI [UPDATED]

Glass: Martini
Garnish: Hazelnut in drink
Method: **STIR** all ingredients with ice and strain into chilled glass.

2	shot(s)	**Ketel One vodka**
½	shot(s)	**Hazelnut (crème de noisette) liqueur**
½	shot(s)	**White crème de cacao liqueur**
¾	shot(s)	**Chilled mineral water (omit if wet ice)**

Comment: A hazelnut Vodkatini with a hint of chocolate.

●●●●◐

HEATHER JULEP

Glass: Collins
Garnish: Mint sprig
Method: Lightly **MUDDLE** mint in base of shaker (just to bruise). Add other ingredients, **SHAKE** with ice and strain into glass filled with crushed ice. **CHURN** (stir) the drink using a bar spoon. Top the glass with more crushed ice so as to fill it and churn again. Serve with straws.

12	fresh	**Mint leaves**
2½	shot(s)	**The Famous Grouse Scotch**
½	shot(s)	**Drambuie liqueur**
¾	shot(s)	**Sugar (gomme) syrup**

Origin: Adapted from a drink discovered in 2001 at Teatro, London, England.
Comment: A Scottish twist on the classic bourbon based Mint Julep.

DRINKS ARE GRADED AS FOLLOWS:

● DISGUSTING ●◐ PRETTY AWFUL ●● BEST AVOIDED
●●◐ DISAPPOINTING ●●● ACCEPTABLE ●●●◐ GOOD
●●●● RECOMMENDED ●●●●◐ HIGHLY RECOMMENDED
●●●●● OUTSTANDING / EXCEPTIONAL

HEAVEN SCENT

Glass: Martini
Garnish: Orange zest twist
Method: **SHAKE** all ingredients with ice and fine strain into chilled glass.

1½	shot(s)	**Vanilla flavoured vodka**
1½	shot(s)	**Krupnik honey liqueur**
½	shot(s)	**Freshly squeezed lemon juice**
¾	shot(s)	**Chilled mineral water (omit if wet ice)**

Origin: Discovered in 2003 at Oxo Tower Bar, London, England.
Comment: Honey, vanilla and lemon – reminiscent of a chilled, straight-up toddy.

HEAVENS ABOVE [NEW]

Glass: Collins
Garnish: Pineapple wedge on rim
Method: **SHAKE** all ingredients with ice and strain into glass filled with crushed ice.

2	shot(s)	**Mount Gay Eclipse golden rum**
¼	shot(s)	**Coffee liqueur**
¼	shot(s)	**Dark crème de cacao liqueur**
3	shot(s)	**Pressed pineapple juice**

Origin: A Tiki style drink adapted from a drink featured in Jeff Berry's 'Intoxica' and originally created circa 1970 at Top of Toronto, CN Tower, Toronto, Canada.
Comment: Slightly sweet, fruity rum – hard not to like.

HEDGEROW SLING [UPDATED]

Glass: Sling
Garnish: Seasonal berries & lemon slice
Method: **SHAKE** first three ingredients with ice and strain into ice-filled glass. **TOP** with soda, stir and serve with straws.

2	shot(s)	**Plymouth sloe gin**
1	shot(s)	**Freshly squeezed lemon juice**
½	shot(s)	**Crème de mûre (blackberry) liqueur**
Top up with		**Soda water (club soda)**

Origin: Created by Brian Duell at Detroit, London, England.
Comment: Rich, long, berry drink.

HEMINGWAY

Glass: Flute
Garnish: Freshly ground liquorice
Method: **POUR** anis into chilled glass. Top with champagne.

1	shot(s)	**Pernod anis**
Top up with		**Piper-Heidsieck brut champagne**

AKA: Corpse Reviver #2
Origin: Created at Cantineros' Club, the famous Cuban bar school.
Comment: Why dilute your anis with water when you can use champagne?

HEMINGWAY SPECIAL DAIQUIRI

Glass: 10oz Martini (huge)
Garnish: Lime wedge on rim
Method: **SHAKE** all ingredients with ice and fine strain into chilled glass.

3½	shot(s)	**Light white rum**
1	shot(s)	**Freshly squeezed grapefruit juice**
¾	shot(s)	**Luxardo Maraschino liqueur**
1	shot(s)	**Freshly squeezed lime juice**
½	shot(s)	**Sugar (gomme) syrup**

AKA: Papa Doble Daiquiri
Origin: Created by Constante Ribailagua, the legendary owner of La Floridita, Havana, Cuba for Ernest Hemingway, after the great man wandered into the bar to use the toilet. When Hemingway tried the Floridita's standard frozen Daiquiri, he is quoted as saying, "That's good but I prefer it without sugar and with double rum," – so the Hemingway Special was born.
Comment: A true Hemingway Special (also known as a Papa Doble) should be served without the addition of sugar. However, Hemingway had a hardened palate and an aversion to sugar - more delicate drinkers may prefer the recipe above.

HENRY VIII [NEW]

Glass: Flute
Garnish: Orange zest twist
Method: Soak sugar cube with absinthe and drop into chilled glass. **POUR** other ingredients over sugar cube and serve.

1	cube	**Sugar**
⅛	shot(s)	**La Fée Parisian 68% absinthe**
½	shot(s)	**Ketel One Citroen vodka**
½	shot(s)	**Pepper flavoured vodka**
Top up with		**Piper-Heidsieck brut champagne**

Origin: Created in 2004 by Henry Besant, London, England.
Comment: A contemporary twist on the classic Champagne Cocktail.

HIGHLAND SLING

Glass: Sling
Garnish: Apple wedge
Method: **SHAKE** all ingredients with ice and strain into ice-filled glass.

1½	shot(s)	**The Famous Grouse Scotch**
½	shot(s)	**Galliano liqueur**
1	shot(s)	**Cranberry juice**
½	shot(s)	**Apricot brandy liqueur**
2	shot(s)	**Pressed apple juice**

Comment: A surprisingly good combination of diverse flavours.

HIGHBALL

A highball is a type of simple cocktail with only two ingredients, normally a spirit and a carbonate, served in a tall ice-filled glass (often referred to as a highball glass). Unlike Rickeys, Collinses and Fizzes, highballs do not contain citrus fruit juice.

To make: pour two shots of your chosen spirit (Scotch, bourbon, cognac etc.) into a tall, ice-filled glass. Top up with a carbonated soft drink (ginger ale, soda or tonic water) and stir gently so as not to kill the fizz. Garnish with a slice of orange, lime or lemon as appropriate to the spirit and the carbonate.

THE HIVE [NEW]

Glass: Martini
Garnish: Orange zest twist
Method: STIR honey with vodka until honey dissolves. Add other ingredients, **SHAKE** with ice and fine strain into chilled glass.

2 spoons **Runny honey**
1 shot(s) **Ketel One vodka**
1 shot(s) **Krupnik honey liqueur**
2 shot(s) **Freshly squeezed golden grapefruit juice**

Origin: Discovered in 2004 at Circus, London, England.
Comment: Sour grapefruit balanced by sweet honey.

HOA SUA [NEW]

Glass: Martini
Garnish: Pineapple wedge on rim
Method: Cut pomegranate in half and juice using a spinning citrus juicer. **SHAKE** all ingredients with ice and fine strain into chilled glass.

1½ shot(s) **Freshly squeezed pomegranate juice**
1½ shot(s) **Light white rum**
¾ shot(s) **Sake**
⅛ shot(s) **Sugar (gomme) syrup**
1 dash **Angostura aromatic bitters**

Origin: Created in 2005 by yours truly for Hoa Sua catering school in Vietnam using locally available products.
Comment: Light and easy drinking – the rum flavour shines through.

HOBSON'S CHOICE (MOCKTAIL)

Glass: Collins
Garnish: Lime wedge on rim
Method: SHAKE all ingredients with ice and strain into ice-filled glass.

2½ shot(s) **Freshly squeezed orange juice**
2½ shot(s) **Pressed apple juice**
1 shot(s) **Freshly squeezed lime juice**
¼ shot(s) **Pomegranate (grenadine) syrup**

Comment: A fruity, non-alcoholic cocktail.

HONEY & MARMALADE DRAM'TINI

Glass: Martini
Garnish: Strips of orange peel
Method: STIR honey with Scotch in base of shaker until honey dissolves. Add other ingredients, **SHAKE** with ice and fine strain into chilled glass.

2 shot(s) **The Famous Grouse Scotch**
4 spoons **Runny honey**
1 shot(s) **Freshly squeezed lemon juice**
1 shot(s) **Freshly squeezed orange juice**

Origin: I adapted this recipe from the Honeysuckle Daiquiri.
Comment: This citrussy drink seems to enrich and enhance the flavour of Scotch.

HONEY APPLE MARTINI [NEW]

Glass: Martini
Garnish: Lemon zest twist
Method: SHAKE all ingredients with ice and fine strain into chilled glass.

1½	shot(s)	**Zubrówka bison vodka**
¾	shot(s)	**Krupnik honey liqueur**
1¼	shot(s)	**Pressed apple juice**
¼	shot(s)	**Freshly squeezed lemon juice**

Variant: Polish Martini
Comment: A classically Polish blend of flavours.

HONEY BEE

Glass: Martini
Garnish: Lemon zest twist
Method: STIR honey with vodka in base of shaker until honey dissolves. Add other ingredients, **SHAKE** with ice and fine strain into chilled glass.

2	shot(s)	**Light white rum**
2	spoons	**Runny honey**
½	shot(s)	**Freshly squeezed lemon juice**
¾	shot(s)	**Chilled mineral water (omit if wet ice)**

Origin: Adapted from a recipe in my 1949 copy of Esquire's 'Handbook For Hosts'.
Comment: Basically a honey Daiquiri – nice, though.

HONEY BERRY SOUR

Glass: Old-fashioned
Garnish: Lemon wedge
Method: SHAKE all ingredients with ice and strain into ice-filled glass.

1½	shot(s)	**Krupnik honey vodka**
¾	shot(s)	**Chambord black raspberry liqueur**
1	shot(s)	**Freshly squeezed lemon juice**
¼	shot(s)	**Sugar (gomme) syrup**
½	fresh	**Egg white**

Origin: Created by Tim Hallilaj.
Comment: More sweet than sour but berry nice.

HONEY BLOSSOM [NEW]

Glass: Old-fashioned
Garnish: Pineapple wedge on rim
Method: SHAKE all ingredients with ice and fine strain into ice-filled glass.

3	shot(s)	**Pressed pineapple juice**
1	shot(s)	**Freshly squeezed lemon juice**
¼	shot(s)	**Vanilla syrup**
½	fresh	**Egg white**
3	dashes	**Angostura aromatic bitters**

Origin: Created in 2003 by Tim Phillips at the GE Club, London, England.
Comment: Soft, fruity, yet adult. Note: contains trace amounts of alcohol.

HONEY DAIQUIRI [NEW]

Glass: Martini
Garnish: Lime wedge on rim
Method: STIR honey with rum in base of shaker until honey dissolves. Add other ingredients, **SHAKE** with ice and fine strain into chilled glass.

2	spoons	**Runny honey**
2	shot(s)	**Light white rum**
½	shot(s)	**Freshly squeezed lime juice**
½	shot(s)	**Chilled mineral water (omit if wet ice)**

Comment: Sweet honey replaces sugar syrup in this natural Daiquiri. Try experimenting with different honeys. I favour orange blossom honey.

HONEY LIMEAID (MOCKTAIL) [NEW]

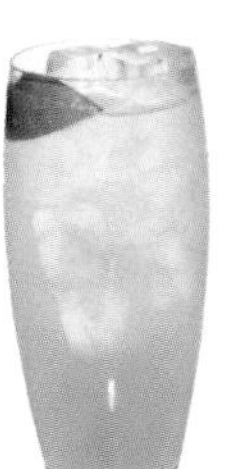

Glass: Collins
Garnish: Lime wedge
Method: STIR honey with lime juice in base of shaker until honey dissolves. **SHAKE** with ice and strain into ice-filled glass. **TOP** with soda.

1½	shot(s)	**Freshly squeezed lime juice**
7	spoons	**Runny honey**
Top up with		**Soda water (club soda)**

Origin: Discovered in 2005 at Hotel Quinta Real, Guadalajara, Mexico.
Comment: A refreshing Mexican variation on Real Lemonade.

HONEY VODKA SOUR

Glass: Old-fashioned
Garnish: Lemon wedge
Method: SHAKE all ingredients with ice and strain into ice-filled glass.

2	shot(s)	**Krupnik honey** vodka
1½	shot(s)	**Freshly squeezed lemon juice**
½	shot(s)	**Sugar (gomme) syrup**
½	fresh	**Egg white**
3	dashes	**Angostura aromatic bitters**

Comment: A vodka sour with true honey character.

HONEY WALL

Glass: Martini
Garnish: Flamed orange zest twist
Method: STIR all ingredients with ice and strain into chilled glass.

1¼	shot(s)	**Aged rum**
1¼	shot(s)	**Tuaca Italian liqueur**
1¼	shot(s)	**Kikor (or dark crème de cacao) liqueur**

Origin: Adapted from a drink created in 2002 by Dick Bradsell at Downstairs at Alfred's, London, England.
Comment: Strong, rich and chocolatey.

A B C D E F G **H** I J K L M N O P Q R S T U V W X Y Z

HONEYMOON

Glass: Martini
Garnish: Orange zest twist
Method: SHAKE all ingredients with ice and fine strain into chilled glass.

1¼	shot(s)	**Bénédictine D.O.M. liqueur**
1¼	shot(s)	**Calvados or applejack brandy**
¾	shot(s)	**Freshly squeezed lemon juice**
½	shot(s)	**Grand Marnier liqueur**
½	fresh	**Egg white**

Comment: A romantic combination of apple, orange, lemon and herbs.

HONEYSUCKLE DAIQUIRI

Glass: Martini
Garnish: Mint leaf
Method: STIR honey with rum in base of shaker until honey dissolves. Add lemon and orange juice, **SHAKE** with ice and fine strain into chilled glass.

2	shot(s)	**Light white rum**
4	spoons	**Runny honey**
1	shot(s)	**Freshly squeezed lemon juice**
1	shot(s)	**Freshly squeezed orange juice**

Variant: Made with gin in place of rum this drink becomes the 'Bee's Knees Martini'.
Origin: Adapted from a recipe in David Embury's 'The Fine Art Of Mixing Drinks'.
Comment: Honey – I love it!

THE HONEYSUCKLE ORCHARD [NEW]

Glass: Martini
Garnish: Lemon wedge on rim
Method: STIR honey with vodka in base of shaker until honey dissolves. Add other ingredients, **SHAKE** with ice and fine strain into chilled glass.

1	spoon	**Runny honey**
2	shot(s)	**Zubrówka bison vodka**
1½	shot(s)	**Pressed apple juice**
¼	shot(s)	**Freshly squeezed lemon juice**

Origin: Discovered in 2005 at The Stanton Social, New York City, USA.
Comment: A back to nature Polish Martini - all the better for it.

HONG KONG FUEY

Glass: Collins
Garnish: Orange slice & lime slice
Method: SHAKE first eight ingredients with ice and strain into ice-filled glass. **TOP** with 7-Up, stir and serve with straws.

½	shot(s)	**Ketel One vodka**
½	shot(s)	**Plymouth gin**
½	shot(s)	**Light white rum**
½	shot(s)	**Sauza Hornitos tequila**
½	shot(s)	**Midori melon liqueur**
¼	shot(s)	**Freshly squeezed lemon juice**
¼	shot(s)	**Rose's lime cordial**
½	shot(s)	**Green Chartreuse**
Top up with		**7-Up / lemonade**

Comment: Readers may recall Hong Kong Phooey, the children's TV series featuring the mild-mannered janitor Penry and his superhero alter ego. This drink is no better than Penry's kung fu but deadly all the same.

HONOLULU

Glass: Martini
Garnish: Pineapple wedge & cherry on rim
Method: SHAKE all ingredients with ice and fine strain into chilled glass.

2½	shot(s)	**Plymouth gin**
½	shot(s)	**Freshly squeezed orange juice**
½	shot(s)	**Pressed pineapple juice**
¾	shot(s)	**Freshly squeezed lime juice**
½	shot(s)	**Sugar (gomme) syrup**

Comment: Gin is hardly Hawaiian, but its bite works well in this tropically fruity cocktail.

HONOLULU JUICER [NEW]

Glass: Collins
Garnish: Pineapple wedge & cherry
Method: SHAKE all ingredients with ice and strain into glass filled with crushed ice.

1	shot(s)	**Gosling's Black Seal rum**
1½	shot(s)	**Southern Comfort**
2	shot(s)	**Pressed pineapple juice**
¾	shot(s)	**Rose's lime cordial**
¾	shot(s)	**Freshly squeezed lemon juice**
¼	shot(s)	**Sugar (gomme) syrup**

Origin: A classic Tiki drink.
Comment: A practically tropical, rum laced, fruity number.

HOW TO MAKE SUGAR SYRUP

To make your own sugar syrup, gradually pour TWO cups of granulated sugar into a saucepan containing ONE cup of hot water. Stir as you pour and carry on stirring and simmering until the sugar is dissolved. Do not let the water even come close to boiling and only simmer for as long as it takes to dissolve the sugar. Allow syrup to cool and pour into an empty bottle. Ideally, you should finely strain your syrup into the bottle to remove any undissolved crystals which could otherwise encourage crystallisation. If kept in a refrigerator this mixture will last for a couple of months.

HOOPLA

Glass: Martini
Garnish: Orange zest twist
Method: SHAKE all ingredients with ice and fine strain into chilled glass.

1	shot(s)	**Rémy Martin cognac**
1	shot(s)	**Cointreau / triple sec**
3/4	shot(s)	**Dry vermouth**
3/4	shot(s)	**Freshly squeezed lemon juice**
1/2	fresh	**Egg white**

Comment: Not far removed from a Sidecar.

HOP TOAD #1 [NEW]

Glass: Martini
Garnish: Apricot wedge on rim
Method: SHAKE all ingredients with ice and fine strain into chilled glass.

1 1/4	shot(s)	**Light white rum**
1 1/4	shot(s)	**Apricot brandy liqueur**
1 1/4	shot(s)	**Freshly squeezed lime juice**
1/2	shot(s)	**Chilled mineral water (omit if wet ice)**

Variant: Made with brandy this is sometimes known as a Bullfrog.
Origin: First published in Tom Bullock's 'Ideal Bartender', circa 1917.
Comment: Resembles an apricot Daiquiri that's heavy on the lime yet balanced.

HOP TOAD #2 [UPDATED]

Glass: Martini
Garnish: Apricot wedge on rim
Method: SHAKE all ingredients with ice and fine strain into chilled glass.

1 3/4	shot(s)	**Aged rum**
1	shot(s)	**Apricot brandy liqueur**
3/4	shot(s)	**Freshly squeezed lime juice**
1/2	shot(s)	**Chilled mineral water (omit if wet ice)**

Comment: Alcoholic apricot jam with a lovely twang of aged rum.

HORNITOS LAU [NEW]

Glass: Collins
Garnish: Mint sprig
Method: Lightly MUDDLE mint (just to bruise) in base of shaker. Add other ingredients, SHAKE with ice and strain into glass filled with crushed ice. CHURN (stir) drink and add more crushed ice so drink meets rim of glass.

12	fresh	**Mint leaves**
2	shot(s)	**Sauza Hornitos tequila**
1 1/2	shot(s)	**Licor 43 (Cuarenta Y Tres) liqueur**
1/2	shot(s)	**Freshly squeezed lime juice**

Origin: Created in 2005 by Jaspar Eyears at Bar Tiki, Mexico City, Mexico.
Comment: Jaspar recommends making a batch in their glasses and refreezing them with the straws already in the glass, like the old colonels and their julep freezers in Kentucky.

HORSE'S NECK WITH A KICK

Glass: Collins
Garnish: Peel rind of a large lemon in a spiral and place in glass with end hanging over rim.
Method: POUR ingredients into ice-filled glass and stir.

2	shot(s)	**Bourbon whiskey**
3	dashes	**Angostura aromatic bitters**
Top up with		**Ginger ale**

Variant: A Horse's Neck without a kick is simply ginger ale and bitters.
Comment: Whiskey and ginger with added shrubbery.

HOT BUTTERED JACK

Glass: Toddy
Garnish: Grate nutmeg over drink
Method: Place bar spoon in warmed glass. Add ingredients and STIR until butter dissolves.

1	large	**Knob (pat) unsalted butter**
2	shot(s)	**Jack Daniel's Tennessee whiskey**
3/4	shot(s)	**Sugar (gomme) syrup**
Top up with		**Boiling water**

Comment: Warming and smooth – great on a cold day or whenever you fancy a warming treat.

HOT BUTTERED RUM

Glass: Toddy
Garnish: Cinnamon stick and slice of lemon studded with cloves
Method: Place bar spoon loaded with honey in warmed glass. Add other ingredients and STIR until honey and butter are dissolved.

2	spoons	**Runny honey**
1	large	**Knob (pat) unsalted butter**
2	shot(s)	**Mount Gay Eclipse golden rum**
1/4	spoon	**Freshly grated nutmeg**
Top up with		**Boiling water (or hot cider)**

Comment: In 'The Fine Art of Mixing Drinks', David Embury says, "The Hot Spiced Rum is bad enough, but the lump of butter is the final insult. It blends with the hot rum just about as satisfactorily as warm olive oil blends with champagne!" It's rare for me to question Embury but I rather like this slightly oily, warming, spicy toddy.

HOT GROG [NEW]

Glass: Toddy
Garnish: Lemon peel twist
Method: Place bar spoon loaded with honey in warmed glass. Add other ingredients and STIR until honey dissolves.

3	spoons	**Runny honey**
1	shot(s)	**Pusser's Navy rum (54.5% alc./vol.)**
1/4	shot(s)	**Freshly squeezed lime juice**
2 1/2	shot(s)	**Boiling water**

Variant: Black Stripe, with molasses replacing the honey.
Comment: Warming, honeyed, pungent rum with a hint of lime.

HOT COCKTAILS

On a cold winter's night there is nothing that warms the cockles more than a piping hot, spirit laced drink. Such winter warmers transcend the ubiquitous Irish Coffee. In the 1930s cocktail heyday there were a number of recognised categories of popular hot drinks. These include:

Possets - Sweetened and spiced milk mixed with hot ale or wine. If eggs are substituted for the milk, the mixture becomes an Egg Posset.

Mull – A Mull or 'Mulled Wine' is simply spiced and sweetened wine served hot. Traditionally these drinks were heated by dipping a white-hot poker from the fire into the drink. Today the kitchen hob or microwave oven are less spectacular but equally effective.

Negus – A sweetened, spiced wine (usually port) served with hot water. While similar to a Mull, the Negus differs in that it is warmed by the addition of hot water rather than by being heated. The Negus is thought to have been invented by Colonel Francis Negus during the reign of Queen Anne (1702-1714).

Wassail Bowl – An old English hot drink traditionally served on Christmas Eve. It may be made from wine, cider, beer or any combination of the three. Mixed in bulk over a slow heat, flavourings include baked apples, nutmeg, cloves and cinnamon, and it is often thickened with eggs. The Swedes have a similar drink served at Christmas called Glogg, while the Danes call theirs Øgge.

Bishops – Similar to the Wassail Bowl above, except that beer is never used and baked oranges are used instead of apples.

Many other cocktails including the Grog and Punch are more familiarly mixed with ice and served cold but also have hot variations. Other famous hot cocktails include the Blue Blazer, Hot Buttered Rum and Hot Toddy.

International Coffees - The most popular hot, alcohol-laced drink, Irish Coffee was created more recently in 1942. It has since spawned a number of variations, loosely categorised as 'International Coffees'. These include: American Coffee (with bourbon or Southern Comfort), Caribbean Coffee (with rum), French Coffee (with cognac &/or liqueur such as Grand Marnier), Gaelic Coffee (with Scotch &/or Drambuie) and the Italian Coffee (with amaretto). Café noir is a simpler after-dinner coffee drink, where spirits or liqueurs are served to accompany a coffee or simply poured into the coffee.

When serving hot drinks in glassware be sure to use heatproof glasses, pre-warm each glass and place a bar spoon in the glass to help absorb the shock of the heat when the drink is poured.

HOT PASSION [UPDATED]

Glass: Collins
Garnish: Maraschino cherry
Method: **SHAKE** all ingredients with ice and strain into ice-filled glass.

1	shot(s)	**Passoã passion fruit liqueur**
1	shot(s)	**Ketel One vodka**
2	shot(s)	**Cranberry juice**
2	shot(s)	**Freshly squeezed orange juice**

Comment: A fruity, slightly sweet twist on a Madras.

HOT RED BLOODED FRENCHMAN [NEW]

Glass: Toddy
Garnish: Orange zest twists
Method: Place bar spoon in warmed glass. Add other ingredients and **STIR.**

1	shot(s)	**Grand Marnier liqueur**
2	shot(s)	**Red wine (Claret)**
½	shot(s)	**Freshly squeezed orange juice**
½	shot(s)	**Freshly squeezed lemon juice**
¼	shot(s)	**Sugar (gomme) syrup**
Top up with		**Boiling water**

Comment: Warm, fruity red wine – great on a cold night.

HOT RUM PUNCH

Glass: Toddy
Garnish: Ground nutmeg
Method: Place bar spoon in warmed glass. Add ingredients and **STIR.**

1	shot(s)	**Mount Gay Eclipse golden rum**
1	shot(s)	**Rémy Martin cognac**
½	shot(s)	**Tio Pepe fino sherry**
¼	shot(s)	**Sugar (gomme) syrup**
1	shot(s)	**Freshly squeezed lime juice**
Top up with		**Boiling water**

Origin: Punch was one of many rum-based drinks popular in the 18th century, when taverns would serve cold punch and warm it upon request by dunking a red-hot iron in it. This version is said to have been a favourite drink of Mozart the composer.
Comment: A great winter warmer.

HOT SHOT

Glass: Shot
Method: **LAYER** by carefully pouring ingredients in the following order.

¾	shot(s)	**Galliano liqueur**
¾	shot(s)	**Hot espresso coffee**
½	shot(s)	**Double (heavy) cream**

Origin: A huge drink in Scandinavia during the early nineties.
Comment: The Scandinavian answer to Irish coffee.

HOT TODDY #1

Glass: Toddy
Garnish: Cinnamon stick
Method: Place bar spoon loaded with honey in warmed glass. Add other ingredients and **STIR** until honey dissolves.

1	spoon	**Runny honey**
2	shot(s)	**The Famous Grouse Scotch**
1/2	shot(s)	**Freshly squeezed lemon juice**
1/2	shot(s)	**Sugar (gomme) syrup**
3	dried	**Cloves**
Top up with		**Boiling water**

Origin: Lost in time but Dickens refers to a "Whisky Toddy" in 'The Pickwick Papers'.
Comment: The smoky flavours in the Scotch add spice to this warming drink that's great when you're feeling down with a cold or the flu.

HOT TODDY #2 [NEW]

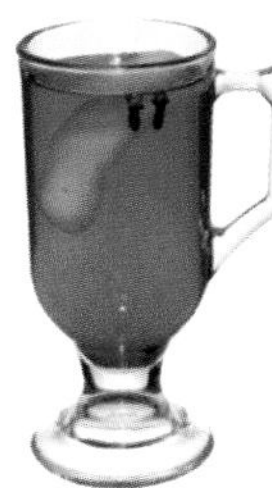

Glass: Toddy
Garnish: Lemon zest twist
Method: Place bar spoon loaded with honey in warmed glass. Add other ingredients and **STIR** until honey dissolves.

1	spoon	**Runny honey**
2	shot(s)	**The Famous Grouse Scotch**
3	dried	**Cloves**
1/4	spoon	**Freshly grated nutmeg**
Top up with		**Hot black English breakfast tea**

Comment: Tea and Scotch combine wonderfully in this hot and spicy winter warmer.

HOT TUB

Glass: Martini
Garnish: Pineapple wedge on rim
Method: **SHAKE** first three ingredients with ice and fine strain into chilled glass. **TOP** with Prosecco.

1 1/2	shot(s)	**Ketel One vodka**
1/4	shot(s)	**Chambord black raspberry liqueur**
1	shot(s)	**Pressed pineapple juice**
Top up with		**Prosecco sparkling wine**

Origin: Adapted from a drink discovered in 2004 at Teatro, Boston, USA.
Comment: Basically a French Martini with bubbles.

HULK [NEW]

Glass: Old-fashioned
Method: **LAYER** ingredients in ice-filled glass by carefully pouring in the following order.

2	shot(s)	**Hpnotiq liqueur**
1	shot(s)	**Rémy Martin cognac**

Comment: Turns green when mixed. A crying waste of good cognac.

HUNK MARTINI

Glass: Martini
Garnish: Maraschino cherry in drink
Method: **SHAKE** all ingredients with ice and fine strain into chilled glass.

2	shot(s)	**Vanilla flavoured vodka**
1 3/4	shot(s)	**Pressed pineapple juice**
1/2	shot(s)	**Freshly squeezed lime juice**
1/4	shot(s)	**Sugar (gomme) syrup**

Origin: The drink Carrie and co discovered in the summer of 2003. In this series the Sex And The City stars dropped Cosmopolitans in favour of Hunks – no change there then!
Comment: Pineapple and vanilla combine wonderfully. American readers may notice more than a passing resemblance to a Key Lime Pie served without the Graham Cracker rim.

HURRICANE #1 [UPDATED]

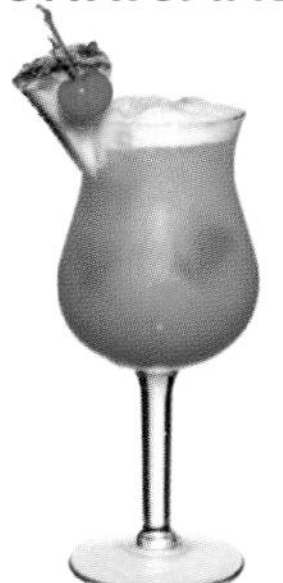

Glass: Hurricane
Garnish: Pineapple wedge & cherry on rim
Method: **SHAKE** all ingredients with ice and strain into ice-filled glass.

1 1/2	shot(s)	**Light white rum**
1	shot(s)	**Pusser's Navy rum**
1	shot(s)	**Freshly squeezed orange juice**
1	shot(s)	**Pressed pineapple juice**
3/4	shot(s)	**Rose's lime cordial**
1/2	shot(s)	**Freshly squeezed lime juice**
1/4	shot(s)	**Passion fruit sugar syrup**

Origin: Named after the shape of a hurricane lamp and served in the tall, shapely glass of the same name. Thought to have originated in 1939 at The Hurricane Bar, New York City, but made famous at Pat O'Brien's in New Orleans. Some old cocktail books list a much earlier Hurricane made with cognac, absinthe and vodka.
Comment: A strong, tangy, refreshing drink packed with fruit and laced with rum.

HURRICANE #2 [NEW]

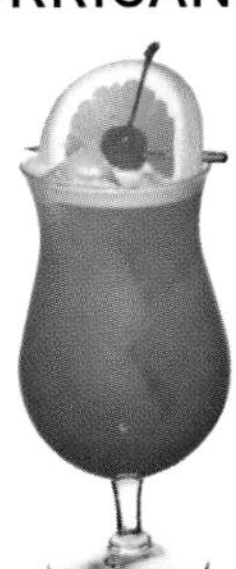

Glass: Hurricane
Garnish: Orange slice & cherry on stick (sail)
Method: Cut passion fruit in half and scoop flesh into shaker. Add other ingredients, **SHAKE** with ice and strain into ice-filled glass.

1	fresh	**Passion fruit**
1 1/2	shot(s)	**Gosling's Black Seal rum**
1 1/2	shot(s)	**Light white rum**
1	shot(s)	**Freshly squeezed orange juice**
1	shot(s)	**Pressed pineapple juice**
1/2	shot(s)	**Freshly squeezed lime juice**
1/4	shot(s)	**Passion fruit sugar syrup**
1/4	shot(s)	**Grenadine syrup**

Comment: Sweet, tangy and potentially dangerous.

I B DAMM'D

Glass: Martini
Garnish: Peach wedge
Method: SHAKE all ingredients with ice and fine strain into chilled glass.

2½ shot(s) **Oude jenever**
¼ shot(s) **Elderflower cordial**
1¾ shot(s) **Pressed apple juice**
¼ shot(s) **Peach schnapps liqueur**

Origin: Discovered in 2003 at Oxo Tower Bar, London, England.
Comment: Subtle combination of fruit and floral flavours.

ICE MAIDEN MARTINI

Glass: Martini
Garnish: Orange zest twist
Method: STIR all ingredients with ice and strain into chilled glass.

1½ shot(s) **Plymouth gin**
1 shot(s) **Icewine**
¾ shot(s) **Sauvignon Blanc or unoaked Chardonnay wine**
¾ shot(s) **Chilled mineral water**

Origin: Created in 2004 by yours truly.
Comment: A subtle Martini with the honeyed flavours of icewine melding with botanicals in the gin and balanced by the acidity of the white wine.

ICE 'T' KNEE

Glass: Martini
Garnish: Lemon zest twist
Method: STIR all ingredients with ice and strain into chilled glass.

2 shot(s) **Ketel One vodka**
1½ shot(s) **Jasmine tea (cold)**
¾ shot(s) **Icewine**

Origin: Created by yours truly in 2004.
Comment: Honeyed palate topped off with tannin and jasmine.

ICE WHITE COSMO

Glass: Martini
Garnish: Flamed orange zest twist
Method: SHAKE all ingredients with ice and fine strain into chilled glass.

2 shot(s) **Ketel One vodka**
¾ shot(s) **Icewine**
1¼ shot(s) **White cranberry juice**
¼ shot(s) **Freshly squeezed lime juice**

Origin: Created by yours truly in 2004.
Comment: Recognisably from the Cosmo family but wonderfully different.

ICED SAKE MARTINI

Glass: Martini
Garnish: Float 3 slices cucumber
Method: STIR all ingredients with ice and strain into chilled glass.

2 shot(s) **Ketel One vodka**
2 shot(s) **Sake**
¼ shot(s) **Icewine**

Origin: Created in 2004 by yours truly.
Comment: The icewine adds interest and wonderfully honeyed notes to this Sake Martini.

ICED TEA [NEW]

Glass: Collins
Garnish: Lime wedge
Method: SHAKE first six ingredients with ice and strain into glass filled with crushed ice. **TOP** with cola.

½ shot(s) **Rémy Martin cognac**
½ shot(s) **Gosling's Black Seal rum**
½ shot(s) **Cointreau / triple sec**
½ shot(s) **Freshly squeezed orange juice**
½ shot(s) **Freshly squeezed lime juice**
2 shot(s) **Cold breakfast tea**
Top up with **Cola**

Origin: Created in 1990 by Charles Schumann, Munich, Germany.
Comment: Sweetened and fortified fruity cola.

ICEWINE MARTINI

Glass: Martini
Garnish: Orange zest twist
Method: STIR all ingredients with ice and strain into chilled glass.

1½ shot(s) **Ketel One vodka**
1½ shot(s) **Icewine**
1½ shot(s) **Pressed apple juice**

Origin: Created in 2004 by yours truly.
Comment: Delicate with subtle flavours.

ICY PINK LEMONADE [NEW]

Glass: Collins
Garnish: Lemon wheel
Method: SHAKE first four ingredients with ice and strain into ice-filled glass. **TOP** with soda.

2 shot(s) **Ketel One vodka**
½ shot(s) **Chambord black raspberry liqueur**
2 shot(s) **Freshly squeezed lemon juice**
½ shot(s) **Sugar (gomme) syrup**
Top up with **Soda water (club soda)**

Comment: Tangy, citrussy, fruity and refreshing - just not that butch.

A B C D E F G H **I** J K L M N O P Q R S T U V W X Y Z

IGNORANCE IS BLISS [NEW]

Glass: Collins
Garnish: Half passion fruit
Method: **SHAKE** all ingredients with ice and strain into ice-filled glass.

2	shot(s)	**Ketel One Citroen vodka**
1/2	shot(s)	**Campari**
3	shot(s)	**Pressed apple juice**
1/4	shot(s)	**Passion fruit sugar syrup**

Comment: This long drink has a bitter bite.

IGUANA

Glass: Shot
Method: **SHAKE** all ingredients with ice and fine strain into chilled glass.

1/2	shot(s)	**Ketel One vodka**
1/2	shot(s)	**Sauza Hornitos tequila**
1/2	shot(s)	**Kahlúa coffee liqueur**

Comment: Coffee and tequila's successful relationship is enhanced by the introduction of vodka.

IGUANA WANA

Glass: Old-fashioned
Garnish: Orange slice
Method: **SHAKE** all ingredients with ice and strain into ice-filled glass.

1	shot(s)	**Ketel One vodka**
3/4	shot(s)	**Peach schnapps liqueur**
2 1/2	shot(s)	**Freshly squeezed orange juice**

Comment: Orange juice and peach schnapps, laced with vodka.

I'LL TAKE MANHATTAN [NEW]

Glass: Martini
Garnish: Maraschino cherry
Method: **STIR** all ingredients with ice and strain into chilled glass.

2	shot(s)	**Bourbon whiskey**
1	shot(s)	**Sweet (rosso) vermouth**
1/2	shot(s)	**Cherry (brandy) liqueur**
2	dashes	**Angostura aromatic bitters**

Origin: Adapted from a drink discovered in 2005 at The Stanton Social, New York City, USA.
Comment: Cherry is more than a garnish in this twist on the classic Manhattan.

ILLICIT AFFAIR

Glass: Old-fashioned
Garnish: Orange slice
Method: **SHAKE** all ingredients with ice and strain into ice-filled glass.

2	shot(s)	**Raspberry flavoured vodka**
1 3/4	shot(s)	**Freshly squeezed orange juice**
1 3/4	shot(s)	**Cranberry juice**

Comment: Fruity, easy drinking.

ILLUSION

Glass: Collins
Garnish: Watermelon wedge on rim
Method: **SHAKE** all ingredients with ice and strain into ice-filled glass.

2	shot(s)	**Ketel One vodka**
3/4	shot(s)	**Cointreau / triple sec**
3/4	shot(s)	**Midori melon liqueur**
2 1/2	shot(s)	**Freshly pressed pineapple juice**

Comment: This medium-sweet, lime green drink is one for a summer's day by the pool.

IMPERIAL MARTINI

Glass: Martini
Garnish: Maraschino cherry
Method: **STIR** all ingredients with ice and strain into chilled glass.

1 1/2	shot(s)	**Plymouth gin**
1 1/2	shot(s)	**Dry vermouth**
3	dashes	**Angostura aromatic bitters**
1/8	shot(s)	**Luxardo Maraschino liqueur**

Comment: This rust coloured Martini is very dry despite the inclusion of maraschino liqueur – not for everyone.

INCOGNITO

Glass: Martini
Garnish: Apricot slice on rim
Method: **SHAKE** all ingredients with ice and fine strain into chilled glass.

1 1/2	shot(s)	**Rémy Martin cognac**
1 1/2	shot(s)	**Dry vermouth**
1	shot(s)	**Apricot brandy liqueur**
3	dashes	**Angostura aromatic bitters**

Comment: Dry with hints of sweet apricot – most unusual.

INCOME TAX COCKTAIL [NEW]

Glass: Martini
Garnish: Orange zest twist
Method: **SHAKE** all ingredients with ice and fine strain into chilled glass.

1	shot(s)	**Plymouth gin**
1	shot(s)	**Dry vermouth**
1	shot(s)	**Sweet (rosso) vermouth**
1	shot(s)	**Freshly squeezed orange juice**
1	dash	**Angostura aromatic bitters**

Origin: Classic of unknown origin.
Comment: Income tax should be scrapped in favour of purchase tax but the cocktail is rather good. Dry and aromatic.

INDIAN ROSE [NEW]

Glass: Martini
Garnish: Edible rose petal
Method: **SHAKE** all ingredients with ice and fine strain into chilled glass.

$2\frac{1}{2}$	shot(s)	**Plymouth gin**
$\frac{1}{4}$	shot(s)	**Apricot brandy liqueur**
$\frac{1}{4}$	shot(s)	**Rosewater**
$\frac{1}{4}$	shot(s)	**Rose syrup**
$\frac{1}{2}$	shot(s)	**Chilled mineral water (omit if wet ice)**

Origin: Adapted from a drink discovered in 2005 at Mie N Yu, Washington DC, USA.
Comment: Subtle rose hue and flavour.

INGA FROM SWEDEN

Glass: Collins
Garnish: Strawberry
Method: **MUDDLE** strawberries in base of shaker. Add other ingredients, **SHAKE** with ice and fine strain into ice-filled glass.

2	fresh	**Strawberries**
$1\frac{1}{2}$	shot(s)	**Xanté pear liqueur**
$\frac{1}{2}$	shot(s)	**Campari**
2	shot(s)	**Cranberry juice**
$\frac{1}{4}$	shot(s)	**Sugar (gomme) syrup**
$\frac{1}{4}$	shot(s)	**Freshly squeezed lime juice**

Comment: Inga must like a touch of bitter Italian with her fruit.

INK MARTINI #1

Glass: Martini
Garnish: Orange zest twist
Method: **SHAKE** all ingredients with ice and fine strain into chilled glass.

$1\frac{1}{4}$	shot(s)	**Plymouth gin**
$\frac{1}{2}$	shot(s)	**Blue curaçao liqueur**
$\frac{1}{2}$	shot(s)	**Peach schnapps liqueur**
2	shot(s)	**Cranberry juice**

Origin: Created in 2002 by Gentian Naci at Bar Epernay, Birmingham, England.
Comment: This simple, appropriately named drink is surprisingly quaffable.

INK MARTINI #2 [NEW]

Glass: Martini
Garnish: Orange zest twist
Method: **SHAKE** all ingredients with ice and fine strain into chilled glass.

2	shot(s)	**Ketel One vodka**
$\frac{1}{2}$	shot(s)	**Blue curaçao liqueur**
$1\frac{1}{2}$	shot(s)	**Cranberry juice**

Origin: Discovered in 2005 at Halo, Atlanta, USA.
Comment: Surprisingly subtle and pleasant in flavour.

INSOMNIAC [NEW]

Glass: Martini
Garnish: Float three coffee beans
Method: **SHAKE** all ingredients with ice and fine strain into chilled glass.

$\frac{3}{4}$	shot(s)	**Ketel One vodka**
$\frac{3}{4}$	shot(s)	**Hazelnut (crème de noisette) liqueur**
$\frac{3}{4}$	shot(s)	**Kahlúa coffee liqueur**
1	shot(s)	**Cold espresso coffee**
$\frac{1}{2}$	shot(s)	**Double cream**
$\frac{1}{2}$	shot(s)	**Milk**

Variant: Espresso Martini
Comment: Wonderfully balanced, creamy and caffeine laced.

INTERNATIONAL INCIDENT

Glass: Martini
Garnish: Dust with freshly grated nutmeg
Method: **SHAKE** all ingredients with ice and fine strain into chilled glass.

$\frac{3}{4}$	shot(s)	**Ketel One vodka**
$\frac{3}{4}$	shot(s)	**Kahlúa coffee liqueur**
$\frac{3}{4}$	shot(s)	**Luxardo Amaretto di Saschira**
$\frac{3}{4}$	shot(s)	**Hazelnut (crème de noisette) liqueur**
$1\frac{1}{2}$	shot(s)	**Baileys Irish Cream liqueur**

Comment: Rich and creamy.

INTIMATE MARTINI

Glass: Martini
Garnish: Orange zest twist
Method: **STIR** all ingredients with ice and strain into chilled glass.

2	shot(s)	**Ketel One vodka**
$\frac{1}{2}$	shot(s)	**Dry vermouth**
1	shot(s)	**Apricot brandy liqueur**
3	dashes	**Fee Brothers orange bitters**

Comment: Sweet apricot dried and balanced by vermouth and bitters. Surprisingly complex and pleasant.

IRISH ALEXANDER

Glass: Martini
Garnish: Crumbled Cadbury's Flake bar
Method: **SHAKE** all ingredients with ice and fine strain into chilled glass.

$1^1/_2$	shot(s)	**Baileys Irish Cream liqueur**
$1^1/_2$	shot(s)	**Rémy Martin cognac**
1	shot(s)	**Double (heavy) cream**

Comment: Rich, thick, creamy and yummy.

IRISH CHARLIE

Glass: Shot
Method: **SHAKE** all ingredients with ice and fine strain into chilled glass.

$^3/_4$	shot(s)	**Baileys Irish Cream liqueur**
$^3/_4$	shot(s)	**White crème de menthe liqueur**

Variant: Float Baileys on crème de menthe
Comment: The ingredients go surprisingly well together.

IRISH CHOCOLATE ORANJ'TINI

Glass: Martini
Garnish: Crumbled Cadbury's Flake bar
Method: **SHAKE** all ingredients with ice and fine strain into chilled glass.

$1^1/_2$	shot(s)	**Baileys Irish Cream liqueur**
$1^1/_2$	shot(s)	**Kahlúa coffee liqueur**
$1^1/_2$	shot(s)	**Grand Marnier liqueur**

Comment: A B-52 served 'up'.

IRISH COFFEE

Glass: Toddy
Garnish: Three coffee beans
Method: Place bar spoon in glass. **POUR** whiskey into glass, top with coffee and stir. **FLOAT** cream.

1	shot(s)	**Irish whiskey**
Top up with		**Hot filter coffee**
Float		**Lightly whipped cream**

Variation: Add sugar syrup to taste prior to floating cream. Alternatively sweeten with a liqueur.
AKA: Gaelic Coffee
Tip: Lightly whip or simply shake cream in container before pouring over the bowl of a spoon. It also helps if the cream is gently warmed.
Origin: Created in 1942 by Joe Sheridan, a bartender at Foynes Airport (near the present-day Shannon airport). In 1947, at the end of a trip to Ireland, an American journalist, Stan Delaphane, visited Joe Sheridan's bar and tried his Irish Coffee. Delaphane was so impressed that on returning home he passed the recipe on to the bartender at his local bar, the Buena Vista Café, in San Francisco. So the recipe spread and the drink became a classic.
Comment: Coffee with a whiskey kick - a simple but great idea.

IRISH COFFEE MARTINI

Glass: Martini
Garnish: Float three coffee beans
Method: **SHAKE** all ingredients with ice and fine strain into chilled glass.

$1^1/_2$	shot(s)	**Irish whiskey**
2	shot(s)	**Cold espresso coffee**
$^1/_2$	shot(s)	**Sugar (gomme) syrup**
1	shot(s)	**Double (heavy) cream**

Origin: Created in 2003 by yours truly.
Comment: Forget sipping warm java through a cold head of cream. This Martini version of the classic Irish Coffee offers all the flavour without the moustache.

IRISH ESPRESSO'TINI

Glass: Martini
Garnish: Float three coffee beans
Method: **SHAKE** all ingredients with ice and fine strain into chilled glass.

2	shot(s)	**Baileys Irish Cream liqueur**
$1^1/_4$	shot(s)	**Vanilla-infused Ketel One vodka**
$1^1/_4$	shot(s)	**Cold espresso coffee**

Comment: Richly flavoured with a pleasingly bitter finish.

IRISH FLAG

Glass: Shot
Method: Refrigerate ingredients and **LAYER** in chilled glass by carefully pouring in the following order.

$^1/_2$	shot(s)	**White crème de menthe liqueur**
$^1/_2$	shot(s)	**Bailey's Irish Cream liqueur**
$^1/_2$	shot(s)	**Grand Marnier liqueur**

Origin: The Irish tricolour is the national flag of the Republic of Ireland. Its three equal stripes represent the political landscape. Orange stands for the Protestants because of William of Orange, the Protestant king of England who defeated the Roman Catholic James II in 1690. Green stands for the Catholic nationalists of the south and white for the hope for peace between Catholics and Protestants.
Comment: Tricoloured orange and mint smoothed with cream liqueur.

IRISH FRAPPÉ

Glass: Hurricane
Garnish: Float three coffee beans
Method: **BLEND** all ingredients with two 12oz scoops of crushed ice and serve with straws.

3	shot(s)	**Baileys Irish Cream liqueur**
2	shot(s)	**Cold espresso coffee**
2	scoops	**Coffee ice cream**

Comment: A tasty frappé with coffee, cream and a hint of whiskey.

A B C D E F G H I J K L M N O P Q R S T U V W X Y Z

IRISH LATTE

Glass: Toddy
Method: **POUR** ingredients into warmed glass in the following order.

1 shot(s) **Hot espresso coffee**
1½ shot(s) **Baileys Irish Cream liqueur**
Top up with **Steamed semi-skimmed foaming milk**

Comment: A latte with extra interest and flavour courtesy of Irish cream liqueur.

IRISH MANHATTAN

Glass: Martini
Garnish: Shamrock
Method: **STIR** all ingredients with ice and strain into chilled glass.

1½ shot(s) **Bourbon whiskey**
1 shot(s) **Tuaca Italian liqueur**
½ shot(s) **Grand Marnier liqueur**
¼ shot(s) **Vanilla sugar syrup**

Origin: Adapted from a drink discovered in 2001 at Detroit, London, England.
Comment: There's nothing Irish about this drink, but it's good all the same.

ISLAND BREEZE

Glass: Collins
Garnish: Grapefruit wedge on rim
Method: **SHAKE** all ingredients with ice and strain into ice-filled glass.

2 shot(s) **Malibu coconut rum liqueur**
2½ shot(s) **Cranberry juice**
1½ shot(s) **Freshly squeezed grapefruit juice**

Origin: Named after the Twelve Islands Shipping Company, the Caribbean producers of Malibu.
Comment: Great balance of sweet and sour flavours.

ITALIAN JOB # 1

Glass: Collins
Garnish: Orange slice
Method: **SHAKE** first six ingredients with ice and strain into ice-filled glass. **TOP** with tonic water, stir and serve with straws.

¾ shot(s) **Monasterium liqueur**
¾ shot(s) **Campari**
¾ shot(s) **Mandarine Napoléon liqueur**
1½ shot(s) **Freshly squeezed golden grapefruit juice**
½ shot(s) **Freshly squeezed lemon juice**
¼ shot(s) **Sugar (gomme) syrup**
Top up with **Tonic water**

Origin: Created by Tony Conigliaro in 2001 at Isola, Knightsbridge, London, England.
Comment: This orange coloured drink combines sweet and sour flavours in a most interesting and grown up way.

ITALIAN JOB #2

Glass: Sling
Garnish: Orange peel twist
Method: **SHAKE** first three ingredients with ice and strain into glass filled with crushed ice. **TOP** with wine and serve with straws.

1 shot(s) **Tuaca Italian liqueur**
1 shot(s) **Luxardo Amaretto di Saschira**
1 shot(s) **Cranberry juice**
Top up with **Red wine (Shiraz)**

Origin: Discovered in 2002 at Rapscallion, London, England.
Comment: Mix layers with straw prior to drinking for vanillaed, almond, fruity wine.

ITALIAN SUN

Glass: Martini
Garnish: Lemon zest twist
Method: **SHAKE** all ingredients with ice and fine strain into chilled glass.

2 shot(s) **Sauvignon Blanc wine**
1½ shot(s) **Luxardo Limoncello liqueur**
¾ shot(s) **Hazelnut (crème de noisette) liqueur**
½ shot(s) **Freshly squeezed lemon juice**

Origin: Created in 2002 by Dan Spink at Browns, St Martin's Lane, London, England.
Comment: Tastes rather like a bon bon (a round, sugar coated, lemon flavoured sweet).

ITALIAN SURFER WITH A RUSSIAN ATTITUDE

Glass: Martini
Method: **SHAKE** all ingredients with ice and fine strain into chilled glass.

1½ shot(s) **Ketel One vodka**
½ shot(s) **Luxardo Amaretto di Saschira**
½ shot(s) **Malibu coconut rum liqueur**
¾ shot(s) **Pressed pineapple juice**
¾ shot(s) **Cranberry juice**

Variant: Served as a long drink, over ice in a Collins glass.
Comment: Fruity and easy drinking but a tad sweet.

I.V.F. MARTINI

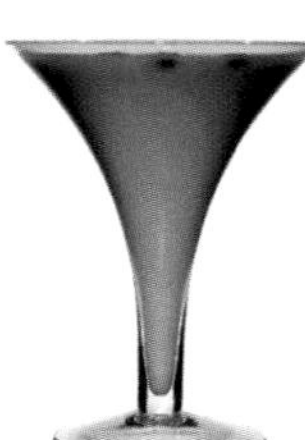

Glass: Martini
Garnish: Float three coffee beans
Method: **SHAKE** first four ingredients with ice and strain into glass. **FLOAT** cream on drink.

1 shot(s) **La Fée Parisian 68% absinthe**
½ shot(s) **Kahlúa coffee liqueur**
½ shot(s) **Tuaca Italian liqueur**
2 shot(s) **Cold espresso coffee**
1 shot(s) **Double (heavy) cream**

Origin: Created by Giovanni Burdi, London, England. In this case I.V.F. stands for 'Italy v France' not 'in vitro fertilisation'.
Comment: Creamy, sweetened absinthe and coffee – hardcore but tasty.

JACK COLLINS [NEW]

Glass: Collins
Garnish: Lemon slice
Method: SHAKE first three ingredients with ice and strain into ice-filled glass. **TOP** with soda, stir and serve with straws.

2	shot(s)	**Calvados or applejack brandy**
1	shot(s)	**Freshly squeezed lemon juice**
1/2	shot(s)	**Sugar (gomme) syrup**
Top up with		**Soda water (club soda)**

Origin: A Collins named after its applejack (apple brandy) base.
Comment: Apple brandy make a great base spirit in this refreshing classic.

JACK DEMPSEY [NEW]

Glass: Martini
Garnish: Maraschino cherry
Method: SHAKE all ingredients with ice and fine strain into chilled glass.

1 1/2	shot(s)	**Light white rum**
1 1/2	shot(s)	**Plymouth gin**
1/4	shot(s)	**Freshly squeezed lemon juice**
1/4	shot(s)	**Sugar (gomme) syrup**
3/4	shot(s)	**Chilled mineral water (omit if wet ice)**

Comment: Dilution makes or breaks this subtle, gin laced drink.

JACK FROST [NEW]

Glass: Old-fashioned
Garnish: Orange zest twist
Method: SHAKE all ingredients with ice and strain into ice-filled glass.

2	shot(s)	**Jack Daniel's Tennessee whiskey**
1/2	shot(s)	**Drambuie liqueur**
3/4	shot(s)	**Freshly squeezed orange juice**
1/2	shot(s)	**Freshly squeezed lemon juice**
1/4	shot(s)	**Pomegranate (grenadine) syrup**

Comment: Tangy and fruity with the whiskey base dominating.

JACK-IN-THE-BOX

Glass: Martini
Garnish: Pineapple wedge on rim
Method: SHAKE all ingredients with ice and fine strain into chilled glass.

2	shot(s)	**Calvados or applejack brandy**
2	shot(s)	**Pressed pineapple juice**
1/4	shot(s)	**Sugar (gomme) syrup**
3	dashes	**Angostura aromatic bitters**

AKA: Jersey City
Variant: Pineapple Blossom
Origin: My adaptation of a classic cocktail.
Comment: Apple and pineapple with a spirity spice.

JACK PUNCH

Glass: Collins
Garnish: Pineapple wedge on rim
Method: Cut passion fruit in half and scoop flesh into shaker. Add other ingredients, **SHAKE** with ice and strain into ice-filled glass.

1	fresh	**Passion fruit**
2	shot(s)	**Jack Daniel's Tennessee whiskey**
1/2	shot(s)	**Licor 43 (Cuarenta Y Tres) liqueur**
3	shot(s)	**Pressed pineapple juice**
1/8	shot(s)	**Sugar (gomme) syrup**
3	dashes	**Angostura aromatic bitters**

Origin: Adapted from a recipe created in 2002 at Townhouse, London, England.
Comment: Vanilla hints in the whiskey and liqueur combine to dominate this fruity long drink.

JACK ROSE

Glass: Martini
Garnish: Lemon wedge on rim
Method: SHAKE all ingredients with ice and fine strain into chilled glass.

2	shot(s)	**Calvados or applejack brandy**
1/2	shot(s)	**Freshly squeezed lemon juice**
1/2	shot(s)	**Pomegranate (grenadine) syrup**
1/2	fresh	**Egg white**

Origin: Some claim this classic drink is named after the Jacqueminot rose which takes its own name from the French general, Jean-François Jacqueminot. Another theory traces the drink to a 1920s New York gangster called Jack Rose, whose favourite beverage was allegedly applejack brandy. Of course 'Jack' could simply refer to the drink's base spirit (applejack) and 'Rose' to its reddish hue.
Comment: An apple brandy sour sweetened with grenadine. Rose-coloured, tart and appley.

JACKIE O'S ROSE

Glass: Martini
Garnish: Lime wedge on rim
Method: SHAKE all ingredients with ice and fine strain into chilled glass.

2	shot(s)	**Light white rum**
1	shot(s)	**Freshly squeezed lime juice**
1/2	shot(s)	**Cointreau / triple sec**
1/2	shot(s)	**Sugar (gomme) syrup**
1/2	spoon	**Rosewater (optional)**

Comment: In its simplest form this is a Daiquiri with added liqueur - or a Margarita with rum. Whatever, it's a good balance of sweet and sour.

JACKTINI

Glass: Martini
Method: **SHAKE** all ingredients with ice and fine strain into chilled glass.

1	shot(s)	**Jack Daniel's Tennessee whiskey**
1	shot(s)	**Mandarine Napoléon liqueur**
1¾	shot(s)	**Freshly squeezed lemon juice**
½	shot(s)	**Sugar (gomme) syrup**

Comment: A citrus bite and a smooth Tennessee whiskey draw enhanced with rich mandarin liqueur.

JACUZZI

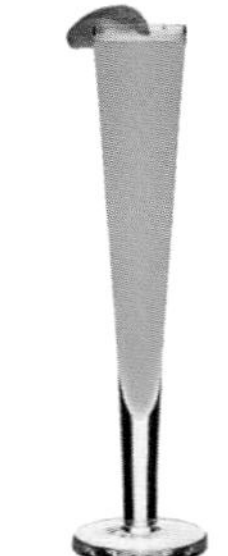

Glass: Flute
Garnish: Orange slice on rim
Method: **SHAKE** first three ingredients with ice and fine strain into chilled glass. **TOP** with champagne.

1	shot(s)	**Peach schnapps liqueur**
½	shot(s)	**Plymouth gin**
1	shot(s)	**Freshly squeezed orange juice**
Top up with		**Piper-Heidsieck brut champagne**

Comment: A sweet, peachy champagne cocktail.

JADE DAIQUIRI [NEW]

Glass: Martini
Garnish: Mint leaf
Method: **SHAKE** all ingredients with ice and fine strain into chilled glass.

2	shot(s)	**Light white rum**
¼	shot(s)	**Cointreau / triple sec**
¼	shot(s)	**White crème de menthe liqueur**
½	shot(s)	**Freshly squeezed lime juice**
¼	shot(s)	**Sugar (gomme) syrup**

Comment: A Daiquiri with a splash of orange and mint liqueurs. Fresh breath enhancing.

JADE GARDEN [NEW]

Glass: Collins
Garnish: Lemon slice
Method: **SHAKE** all ingredients with ice and strain into ice-filled glass.

2	shot(s)	**Ketel One vodka**
1	shot(s)	**Cold strong jasmine tea**
½	shot(s)	**Elderflower cordial**
1½	shot(s)	**Pressed apple juice**
½	shot(s)	**Freshly squeezed lemon juice**
¼	shot(s)	**Sugar (gomme) syrup**

Origin: Adapted from drink created in 2004 by Michael Butt and Giles Looker of Soulshakers, England.
Comment: Not too dry, nor too sweet, but tasty, balanced and refreshing.

JADED LADY [UPDATED]

Glass: Martini
Garnish: Orange zest twist (discarded)
Method: **SHAKE** all ingredients with ice and fine strain into chilled glass.

1	shot(s)	**Plymouth gin**
¾	shot(s)	**Blue curaçao liqueur**
¾	shot(s)	**Advocaat liqueur**
1	shot(s)	**Freshly squeezed orange juice**
3	dashes	**Fee Brothers orange bitters**

Origin: Created by yours truly in 1996.
Comment: Thick and creamy with orange, vanilla and a hint of gin.

JAFFA MARTINI

Glass: Martini
Garnish: Float mini Jaffa Cake
Method: **SHAKE** all ingredients with ice and fine strain into chilled glass.

1	shot(s)	**Cointreau / triple sec**
1	shot(s)	**Dark crème de cacao liqueur**
½	shot(s)	**Orange flavoured vodka**
½	shot(s)	**Freshly squeezed lemon juice**
1	shot(s)	**Freshly squeezed orange juice**
3	dashes	**Fee Brothers orange bitters (optional)**
1	whole	**Egg**

Origin: Created by yours truly in 2004. McVitie's Jaffa Cakes have a tangy orange jelly centre on a hardish sponge base, covered in dark chocolate. Back in 1991 these tasty little snacks beat off UK Customs & Excise who sought to reclassify them as chocolate biscuits, which, unlike cakes, are categorised as luxuries and so subjected to Value Added Tax.
Comment: Sweet, dessert-style cocktail.

JALISCO

Glass: Martini
Garnish: Grapes on stick
Method: **MUDDLE** grapes in base of shaker. Add other ingredients, **SHAKE** with ice and fine strain into chilled glass.

12	fresh	**Seedless white grapes**
2½	shot(s)	**Sauza Hornitos tequila**
½	shot(s)	**Sugar (gomme) syrup**
3	dashes	**Fee Brothers orange bitters**

Origin: Created in 2003 by Shelim Islam at GE Club, London, England. Pronounced 'Hal-is-co', this cocktail takes its name from the Mexican state that is home to the town of Tequila and the spirit of the same name.
Comment: It's amazing how well grapes combine with tequila.

JALISCO ESPRESSO [NEW]

Glass: Martini
Garnish: Float 3 coffee beans
Method: **SHAKE** all ingredients with ice and fine strain into chilled glass.

2	shot(s)	**Sauza Hornitos tequila**
1	shot(s)	**Cold espresso coffee**
1	shot(s)	**Kahlúa coffee liqueur**

Origin: Adapted from a drink created in 2005 by Henry Besant & Andres Masso, London, England, and named after the Mexican state where the tequila industry is centred.
Comment: A tequila laced wake up call.

JAM ROLL

Glass: Shot
Method: Refrigerate ingredients then **LAYER** in chilled glass by carefully pouring in the following order.

1/2	shot(s)	**Chambord black raspberry liqueur**
1/2	shot(s)	**Hazelnut (crème de noisette) liqueur**
1/2	shot(s)	**Baileys Irish Cream liqueur**

Origin: Created in 2003 at Liquid Lounge, Marbella, Spain.
Comment: A very sweet jam roll laced with alcohol.

JAMAICAN MULE

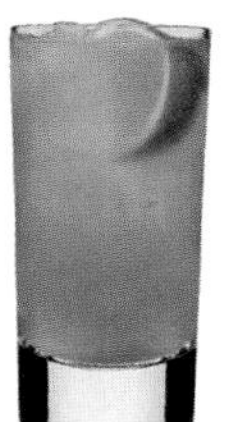

Glass: Collins
Garnish: Lime wedge
Method: **POUR** ingredients into ice-filled glass and lightly stir.

2	shot(s)	**Spiced rum**
1/2	shot(s)	**Freshly squeezed lime juice**
1/2	shot(s)	**Sugar (gomme) syrup**
Top up with		**Ginger beer**

Comment: A long, rum based drink with a spicy ginger taste.

JAMAICAN SUNSET

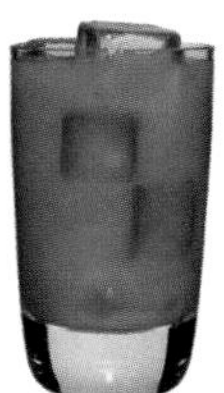

Glass: Collins
Garnish: Orange slice
Method: **SHAKE** all ingredients with ice and strain into ice-filled glass.

1 1/2	shot(s)	**Wray & Nephew overproof rum**
1 1/2	shot(s)	**Cranberry juice**
3	shot(s)	**Freshly squeezed orange juice**

Comment: Made with vodka as a base this drink would be called a Madras. Overproof rum adds both strength and flavour.

JAMBOUREE [NEW]

Glass: Martini
Garnish: Orange zest twist
Method: **STIR** preserve with bourbon in base of shaker until mostly dissolved. Add other ingredients, **SHAKE** with ice and fine strain into chilled glass.

2	spoons	**Apricot preserve (jam)**
2	shot(s)	**Bourbon whiskey**
1/2	shot(s)	**Grand Marnier liqueur**
1/2	shot(s)	**Freshly squeezed lemon juice**
3/4	shot(s)	**Chilled mineral water**

Comment: Rich and jammy flavours balanced by bourbon and lemon juice.

JAMES JOYCE [NEW]

Glass: Martini
Garnish: Maraschino cherry
Method: **SHAKE** all ingredients with ice and fine strain into chilled glass.

1 1/2	shot(s)	**Irish whiskey**
3/4	shot(s)	**Sweet (rosso) vermouth**
3/4	shot(s)	**Cointreau / triple sec**
1/2	shot(s)	**Freshly squeezed lime juice**

Origin: Created in 2001 by the American drinks author Gary Regan. This recipe is taken from his book, 'The Joy of Mixology'.
Comment: A balanced adult sour blend.

JA-MORA

Glass: Flute
Garnish: Float single raspberry
Method: **SHAKE** first four ingredients with ice and fine strain into chilled glass. **TOP** with champagne.

1	shot(s)	**Ketel One vodka**
1/2	shot(s)	**Chambord black raspberry liqueur**
1/2	shot(s)	**Freshly squeezed orange juice**
1/2	shot(s)	**Pressed apple juice**
Top up with		**Piper-Heidsieck brut champagne**

Origin: Created by Jamie Terrell and Andres Masso in 1998. Named after 'mora', the Spanish for raspberry. The 'j' and 'a' stand for the names of its two creators.
Comment: Ja-more of this fruity champagne cocktail you drink, ja-more you'll like it.

JAPANESE COCKTAIL

Glass: Martini
Garnish: Lemon zest twist
Method: **SHAKE** all ingredients with ice and fine strain into chilled glass.

2 1/2	shot(s)	**Rémy Martin cognac**
1/2	shot(s)	**Almond (orgeat) syrup**
3	dashes	**Angostura aromatic bitters**
3/4	shot(s)	**Chilled mineral water (omit if wet ice)**

Origin: A classic cocktail which features in Jerry Thomas' 1887 cocktail book.
Comment: Lightly sweetened and diluted cognac flavoured with almond and a hint of spice.

A B C D E F G H I **J** K L M N O P Q R S T U V W X Y Z

JAPANESE PEAR

Glass: Martini
Garnish: Pear slice on rim
Method: **SHAKE** all ingredients with ice and fine strain into chilled glass.

1½	shot(s)	**Ketel One vodka**
1	shot(s)	**Sake**
½	shot(s)	**Poire William eau de vie**
¼	shot(s)	**Sugar (gomme) syrup**

Origin: Adapted in 2002 from a recipe from Grand Pacific Blue Room, Sydney, Australia.
Comment: Originally made with Poire William liqueur, hence this version calls for a little sugar.

JAPANESE SLIPPER

Glass: Martini
Garnish: Salt rim
Method: **SHAKE** all ingredients with ice and fine strain into chilled glass.

2	shot(s)	**Sauza Hornitos tequila**
1	shot(s)	**Midori melon liqueur**
1	shot(s)	**Freshly squeezed lime juice**

Comment: A Melon Margarita.

JASMINE

Glass: Martini
Garnish: Lemon zest twist
Method: **SHAKE** all ingredients with ice and fine strain into chilled glass.

1	shot(s)	**Plymouth gin**
½	shot(s)	**Campari**
½	shot(s)	**Cointreau / triple sec**
1	shot(s)	**Freshly squeezed lemon juice**
½	shot(s)	**Sugar (gomme) syrup**
¾	shot(s)	**Chilled mineral water (omit if wet ice)**

Origin: Created in 1999 by Paul Harrington, Berkeley, California, USA.
Comment: The distinctive flavour of Campari is enhanced by lemon and orange.

JAYNE MANSFIELD

Glass: Flute
Garnish: Strawberry on rim
Method: **MUDDLE** strawberries in base of shaker. Add next three ingredients, **SHAKE** with ice and fine strain into glass. **TOP** with champagne.

4	fresh	**Hulled strawberries**
1	shot(s)	**Light white rum**
1	shot(s)	**Crème de fraise (strawberry) liqueur**
¼	shot(s)	**Sugar (gomme) syrup**
Top up with		**Piper-Heidsieck brut champagne**

Origin: Named after the Hollywood actress.
Comment: Champagne is made to go with strawberries.

JEAN GABIN [NEW]

Glass: Toddy
Garnish: Dust with freshly grated nutmeg
Method: **POUR** first three ingredients into glass. Add maple syrup and **STIR** until maple syrup dissolves.

1½	shot(s)	**Gosling's Black Seal rum**
¾	shot(s)	**Calvados or applejack brandy**
5	shot(s)	**Hot milk**
1	spoon	**Maple syrup**

Origin: Created in 1986 by Charles Schumann, Munich, Germany.
Comment: Beats hot chocolate as a nightcap.

JEAN MARC

Glass: Collins
Garnish: Mint sprig
Method: **MUDDLE** mint and ginger in base of shaker. Add next two ingredients, **SHAKE** with ice and fine strain into ice-filled glass. **TOP** with Appletiser, stir and serve with straws.

2	slices	**Fresh root ginger (thumbnail sized)**
4	fresh	**Mint leaves**
1½	shot(s)	**Green Chartreuse**
¼	shot(s)	**Apple schnapps liqueur**
Top up with		**Appletiser**

Origin: Created in 2003 by yours truly after judging a Chartreuse cocktail competition in London and realising which flavours best combine with Chartreuse. Named after my friend the President Directeur General of Chartreuse.
Comment: Chartreuse combines well with apple, ginger and mint – they're all in this long, refreshing, summertime drink.

JELLY BELLY BEANY

Glass: Martini
Garnish: Jelly beans
Method: **SHAKE** all ingredients with ice and fine strain into chilled glass.

1½	shot(s)	**Light white rum**
1	shot(s)	**Peach schnapps liqueur**
1	shot(s)	**Malibu coconut rum liqueur**
2	dashes	**Fee Brothers orange bitters**
½	shot(s)	**Chilled mineral water**

Origin: Created in 2002 at Hush, London, England.
Comment: It's a sweetie but you're going to enjoy chewing on it.

JENEVER SOUR [NEW]

Glass: Old-fashioned
Garnish: Maraschino cherry
Method: **SHAKE** all ingredients with ice and strain into ice-filled glass.

2	shot(s)	**Oude jenever**
1	shot(s)	**Freshly squeezed lemon juice**
½	shot(s)	**Sugar (gomme) syrup**
½	fresh	**Egg white**

Comment: One of the more delicately flavoured sours.

JEREZ

Glass: Old-fashioned
Method: **STIR** all ingredients with ice and strain into ice-filled glass.

- ½ shot(s) **Tio Pepe Fino sherry**
- ½ shot(s) **Pedro Ximénez sherry**
- 1 shot(s) **Peach schnapps liqueur**
- 1 shot(s) **Sauvignon Blanc wine**
- 1 shot(s) **La Vieille Prune (prunelle)**
- 1 dash **Angostura aromatic bitters**

Origin: This drink heralds from one of the noble houses of Spain – well that's what the sherry PR told me, anyway. I've changed the recipe slightly.
Comment: Sherry depth and stoned fruit flavours.

JERSEY SOUR [NEW]

Glass: Old-fashioned
Garnish: Lemon zest twist
Method: **SHAKE** all ingredients with ice and fine strain into chilled glass.

- 2 shot(s) **Calvados or applejack brandy**
- 1 shot(s) **Freshly squeezed lemon juice**
- ½ shot(s) **Sugar (gomme) syrup**
- ½ fresh **Egg white**

Origin: The classic name for an Applejack sour.
Comment: Apple brandy is possibly the best spirit on which to base a sour.

JOAN BENNETT [NEW]

Glass: Collins
Garnish: Pineapple wedge on rim
Method: **SHAKE** all ingredients with ice and strain into glass filled with crushed ice.

- 2 shot(s) **Light white rum**
- 1 shot(s) **Parfait amour**
- 2½ shot(s) **Pressed pineapple juice**

Origin: Adapted from a Tiki drink featured in Jeff Berry's 'Intoxica' and originally created in 1932 at Sloppy Joe's Bar, Havana, Cuba. Named after Hollywood ingénue, Joan Bennett, who in the same year starred in Fox's Careless Lady. Years later she hit the news when her husband, producer Walter Wanger, shot her agent in the crotch after catching them in bed together. Ooerr!
Comment: Fruity and floral, but an unfortunate colour.

JOCKEY CLUB [NEW]

Glass: Martini
Garnish: Orange zest twist
Method: **SHAKE** all ingredients with ice and fine strain into chilled glass.

- 2 shot(s) **Plymouth gin**
- ½ shot(s) **Luxardo Amaretto di Saschira**
- ½ shot(s) **Freshly squeezed lemon juice**
- ¾ shot(s) **Chilled mineral water (omit if wet ice)**
- 1 dash **Fee Brothers orange bitters**
- 1 dash **Angostura aromatic bitters**

Variant: Some old books, including 'The Fine Art of Mixing Drinks', describe the Jockey Club as a Manhattan with maraschino.
Origin: This classic drink from the 1930s originally called for crème de noyaux, a liqueur similar in flavour to amaretto.
Comment: Peachy almond and gin with citrus overtones.

JODI MAY [NEW]

Glass: Collins
Garnish: Orange wheel
Method: **SHAKE** all ingredients with ice and fine strain into chilled glass.

- 1½ shot(s) **Jack Daniel's Tennessee whiskey**
- ½ shot(s) **Cointreau / triple sec**
- 2½ shot(s) **Freshly squeezed orange juice**
- 1½ shot(s) **Cranberry juice**
- ¼ shot(s) **Freshly squeezed lime juice**

Origin: Adapted from a drink discovered in 2003 at World Service, Nottingham, England.
Comment: Long, fruity and laced with whiskey.

JOHN COLLINS [NEW]

Glass: Collins
Garnish: Orange slice & cherry on stick (sail)
Method: **SHAKE** first three ingredients with ice and strain into ice-filled glass. **TOP** with soda, stir and serve with straws.

- 2 shot(s) **Plymouth gin**
- 1 shot(s) **Freshly squeezed lemon juice**
- ½ shot(s) **Sugar (gomme) syrup**
- Top up with **Soda water (club soda)**

Origin: Thought to have been created by John Collins, a bartender at Limmer's Hotel, Conduit Street, London, circa 1800.
Comment: A refreshing balance of sour lemon and sugar, laced with gin.

HOW TO MAKE SUGAR SYRUP

To make your own sugar syrup, gradually pour TWO cups of granulated sugar into a saucepan containing ONE cup of hot water. Stir as you pour and carry on stirring and simmering until the sugar is dissolved. Do not let the water even come close to boiling and only simmer for as long as it takes to dissolve the sugar. Allow syrup to cool and pour into an empty bottle. Ideally, you should finely strain your syrup into the bottle to remove any undissolved crystals which could otherwise encourage crystallisation. If kept in a refrigerator this mixture will last for a couple of months.

●●●●○

JOLT'INI [NEW]

Glass: Martini
Garnish: Float 3 coffee beans
Method: **SHAKE** all ingredients with ice and fine strain into chilled glass.

2	shot(s)	**Vanilla flavoured vodka**
1/2	shot(s)	**Kahlúa coffee liqueur**
1	shot(s)	**Cold espresso coffee**

Origin: Discovered in 2005 at Degrees, Washington DC, USA.
Comment: A flavoursome wake up call of espresso coffee laced with vanilla vodka.

●●●●○

JOSE COLLINS [NEW]

Glass: Collins
Garnish: Orange slice & cherry on stick (sail)
Method: **SHAKE** first three ingredients with ice and strain into ice-filled glass. **TOP** with soda, stir and serve with straws.

2	shot(s)	**Sauza Hornitos tequila**
1	shot(s)	**Freshly squeezed lemon juice**
1/2	shot(s)	**Sugar (gomme) syrup**
Top up with		**Soda water (club soda)**

AKA: Juan Collins
Comment: The classic long balance of sweet and sour with tequila adding Mexican spirit.

●●●●○

THE JOURNALIST [NEW]

Glass: Martini
Garnish: Maraschino cherry in drink
Method: **SHAKE** all ingredients with ice and fine strain into chilled glass.

2	shot(s)	**Plymouth gin**
1/2	shot(s)	**Dry vermouth**
1/2	shot(s)	**Sweet (rosso) vermouth**
1/4	shot(s)	**Cointreau / triple sec**
1/4	shot(s)	**Freshly squeezed lemon juice**
2	dashes	**Angostura aromatic bitters**

Origin: An old classic that remains popular in San Francisco.
Comment: Like some journalists I've met, this gin Martini is bitter and sour.

●●●●◐

JUBILANT [NEW]

Glass: Martini
Garnish: Orange slice on rim
Method: **SHAKE** all ingredients with ice and fine strain into chilled glass.

1 1/2	shot(s)	**Plymouth gin**
3/4	shot(s)	**Bénédictine D.O.M. liqueur**
1/2	shot(s)	**Freshly squeezed lemon juice**
1/2	shot(s)	**Freshly squeezed orange juice**
1/2	fresh	**Egg white**

Origin: A long lost classic.
Comment: Wonderfully balanced, aromatic, herbal and fruity.

●●●◐○

JUDY (MOCKTAIL) [NEW]

Glass: Collins
Garnish: Lime wedge
Method: **SHAKE** all ingredients with ice and strain into ice-filled glass.

2	shot(s)	**Freshly squeezed golden grapefruit juice**
3	shot(s)	**Pressed pineapple juice**
1/2	shot(s)	**Freshly squeezed lemon juice**
1/2	shot(s)	**Rose's lime cordial**

Comment: A refreshing, not sweet, driver's option. Consider adding a couple of dashes of Angostura aromatic bitters, although be aware that these contain some alcohol.

●●●●●

JULEP [UPDATED]

Glass: Collins
Garnish: Mint sprig
Method: Lightly **MUDDLE** mint leaves with spirit in base of shaker (just enough to bruise). (At this stage, if time allows, you should refrigerate the shaker, mint and spirit, and the glass in which the drink is to be served, for at least two hours.) Add other ingredients to shaker, **SHAKE** with ice and strain into glass filled with crushed ice. **CHURN** (stir) the drink with the crushed ice using a bar spoon. Top with more crushed ice to fill glass and churn again. Serve with straws.

12	fresh	**Mint leaves**
2 1/2	shot(s)	**Spirit (bourbon, rye, rum, gin, brandy or calvados/applejack)**
3/4	shot(s)	**Sugar (gomme) syrup**
3	dashes	**Angostura aromatic bitters**

Comment: Adjust sugar to balance if using a fortified wine in place of a spirit.

●●●●◐

JULEP MARTINI

Glass: Martini
Garnish: Mint leaf
Method: Lightly **MUDDLE** mint in base of shaker (just to bruise). Add other ingredients, **SHAKE** with ice and fine strain into chilled glass.

8	fresh	**Mint leaves**
2 1/2	shot(s)	**Bourbon whiskey**
1/2	shot(s)	**Sugar (gomme) syrup**
3/4	shot(s)	**Chilled mineral water (omit if wet ice)**

Origin: Adapted from a recipe created in the mid 1990s by Dick Bradsell. **Comment:** A short variation on the classic Julep: sweetened bourbon and mint.

DRINKS ARE GRADED AS FOLLOWS:

● DISGUSTING ●◐ PRETTY AWFUL ●● BEST AVOIDED
●●◐ DISAPPOINTING ●●● ACCEPTABLE ●●●◐ GOOD
●●●● RECOMMENDED ●●●●◐ HIGHLY RECOMMENDED
●●●●● OUTSTANDING / EXCEPTIONAL

●●●●○

JULES DELIGHT [NEW]

Glass: Martini
Garnish: Strawberry
Method: MUDDLE strawberries in base of shaker. Add other ingredients, **SHAKE** with ice and fine strain into chilled glass.

3	fresh	**Strawberries**
2	shot(s)	**Ketel One vodka**
1/4	shot(s)	**White balsamic vinegar**
3/4	shot(s)	**Pressed apple juice**
1/4	shot(s)	**Freshly squeezed lemon juice**
1/2	shot(s)	**Sugar (gomme) syrup**

Origin: Created in 2005 by Julian Gauldonie at Trailer Happiness, London, England.
Comment: Sweet fortified strawberries with a cleansing balsamic vinegar bite.

●●●○○

JULIETTE [NEW]

Glass: Collins
Garnish: Pineapple wedge & cherry
Method: SHAKE all ingredients with ice and strain into ice-filled glass.

1	shot(s)	**Rémy Martin cognac**
1	shot(s)	**Xanté pear liqueur**
1/4	shot(s)	**Chambord black raspberry liqueur**
2 1/2	shot(s)	**Cranberry juice**
1	shot(s)	**Pressed pineapple juice**

Comment: Fruity, medium sweet, cognac laced cooler.

●●●◐○

JUMBLED FRUIT JULEP [NEW]

Glass: Collins
Garnish: Strawberry & mint sprig
Method: MUDDLE strawberries and then mint in base of shaker (just to bruise mint). Add other ingredients, **SHAKE** with ice and strain into glass filled with crushed ice.

4	fresh	**Mint leaves**
3	fresh	**Strawberries (hulled)**
2	shot(s)	**Mango flavoured vodka**
1	shot(s)	**Pressed apple juice**
1/2	shot(s)	**Passion fruit sugar syrup**
1/2	shot(s)	**Freshly squeezed lime juice**

Origin: Created in 2005 by Michael Butt and Giles Looker of Soulshakers, England.
Comment: A fruity twist on the classic Julep.

●●●●○

JUMPING JACK FLASH [UPDATED]

Glass: Martini
Glass: Pineapple wedge on rim
Method: SHAKE all ingredients with ice and fine strain into chilled glass.

1 1/2	shot(s)	**Jack Daniel's Tennessee whiskey**
1/2	shot(s)	**Crème de bananes liqueur**
1/2	shot(s)	**Galliano liqueur**
3/4	shot(s)	**Freshly squeezed orange juice**
3/4	shot(s)	**Pressed pineapple juice**

Comment: Whiskey further mellowed and sweetened by a tasty combo of liqueurs and juices.

JULEPS

Juleps are tall drinks generally served in Collins glasses but originally served in Julep Cups and based on a spirit, liqueur or fortified wine. They are most often served with fresh mint over crushed ice.

The name derives from the Arabic word 'julab', meaning rosewater, and the Mint Julep has become the ultimate Deep South American cocktail, famously served at the Kentucky Derby. The first known written reference is in 1803, when a julep could be made with rum, brandy or whiskey, but by 1900 whiskey had become the normal base.

The Mint Julep reached Britain in 1837, thanks to the novelist Captain Frederick Marryat, who complained of being woken at 7am by a slave brandishing a Julep. He popularised it through his descriptions of American Fourth of July celebrations.

The key to this drink is serving it ice cold and giving the flavours in the mint time to marry with the spirit. Hence, Juleps are ideally prepared hours in advance of serving.

Julep Variations
Georgia Mint Julep
Grapefruit Julep
Heather Julep
Jumbled Fruit Julep
Mint Julep

JUNE BUG

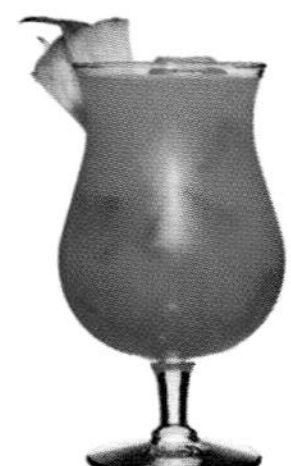

Glass: Hurricane
Garnish: Pineapple wedge & cherry on rim
Method: **SHAKE** all ingredients with ice and strain into glass filled with crushed ice. Serve with straws.

1	shot(s)	**Midori melon liqueur**
1	shot(s)	**Malibu coconut rum liqueur**
1	shot(s)	**Crème de bananes liqueur**
4	shot(s)	**Pressed pineapple juice**
1	shot(s)	**Freshly squeezed lime juice**

Comment: Sweet, fruity and lime green in colour.

JUNGLE BIRD [NEW]

Glass: Old-fashioned (or Tiki mug)
Garnish: Orange slice & cherry on stick (flag)
Method: **SHAKE** all ingredients with ice and strain into glass filled with crushed ice.

1½	shot(s)	**Gosling's Black Seal rum**
½	shot(s)	**Campari**
½	shot(s)	**Freshly squeezed lime juice**
½	shot(s)	**Sugar (gomme) syrup**
2	shot(s)	**Pressed pineapple juice**

Origin: Adapted from a drink featured in Jeff Berry's 'Intoxica' and originally created circa 1978 at the Aviary Bar, Kuala Lumpur, Malaysia.
Comment: Bittersweet and fruity with good rum notes.

JUNGLE FIRE SLING

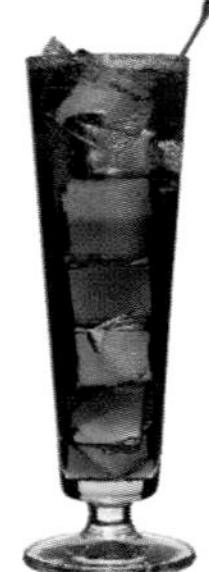

Glass: Sling
Garnish: Orange slice & cherry on stick (sail)
Method: **SHAKE** first four ingredients with ice and strain into ice-filled glass. **TOP** with ginger ale, stir and serve with straws.

1	shot(s)	**Rémy Martin cognac**
1	shot(s)	**Cherry (brandy) liqueur**
½	shot(s)	**Parfait amour liqueur**
½	shot(s)	**Bénédictine D.O.M. liqueur**
Top up with		**Ginger ale**

Comment: Hardly the most refined of drinks, but it does have the refreshing zing of ginger with a soupcon of sticky fruit, herbs and cognac in the background.

JUNGLE JUICE

Glass: Collins
Garnish: Orange slice
Method: **SHAKE** all ingredients with ice and strain into ice-filled glass.

1	shot(s)	**Ketel One vodka**
1	shot(s)	**Light white rum**
½	shot(s)	**Cointreau / triple sec**
1	shot(s)	**Cranberry juice**
1	shot(s)	**Freshly squeezed orange juice**
1	shot(s)	**Pressed pineapple juice**
¾	shot(s)	**Freshly squeezed lime juice**
¼	shot(s)	**Sugar (gomme) syrup**

Comment: If this is the juice of the jungle, I'm a monkey's uncle. That said, as fruity long drinks go this is not bad at all.

JUPITER MARTINI [NEW]

Glass: Martini
Garnish: Orange zest twist
Method: **SHAKE** all ingredients with ice and fine strain into chilled glass.

2	shot(s)	**Plymouth gin**
1	shot(s)	**Dry vermouth**
¼	shot(s)	**Parfait amour liqueur**
¼	shot(s)	**Freshly squeezed orange juice**

Origin: A classic which is thought to have originated sometime in the 1920s.
Comment: Bone dry and aromatic, this drink's colour is the grey hue of an overcast sky.

THE JUXTAPOSITION

Glass: Martini
Garnish: Two pineapple wedges on rim
Method: **STIR** honey with vodka in base of shaker until honey dissolves. Add other ingredients, **SHAKE** with ice and fine strain into chilled glass.

2	spoons	**Runny honey**
2	shot(s)	**Cranberry flavoured vodka**
1	shot(s)	**Pressed pineapple juice**
¾	shot(s)	**Freshly squeezed lime juice**
3	dashes	**Angostura aromatic bitters**

Origin: Adapted from a long drink created in 2003 by Michael Butt and Giles Looker of Soulshakers, England.
Comment: Tangy, complex and smoothed by foaming pineapple.

KAMIKAZE

Glass: Shot
Method: **SHAKE** all ingredients with ice and fine strain into chilled glass.

1	shot(s)	**Sauza Hornitos tequila**
½	shot(s)	**Cointreau / triple sec**
½	shot(s)	**Freshly squeezed lime juice**

Variant: With vodka in place of tequila.
Comment: A bite-sized Margarita.

KAMANIWANALAYA

Glass: Collins
Garnish: Pineapple wedge & cherry
Method: **SHAKE** all ingredients with ice and strain into ice-filled glass.

1½	shot(s)	**Light white rum**
½	shot(s)	**Pusser's Navy rum**
1	shot(s)	**Luxardo Amaretto di Saschira**
3	shot(s)	**Pressed pineapple juice**

Comment: Try saying the name after a few of these rum laced, tropical pineapple concoctions.

KARAMEL SUTRA MARTINI

Glass: Martini
Garnish: Fudge on rim
Method: **SHAKE** all ingredients with ice and fine strain into chilled glass.

1½	shot(s)	**Vanilla flavoured vodka**
1½	shot(s)	**Tuaca Italian liqueur**
1	shot(s)	**Toffee liqueur**

Origin: Adapted from a drink discovered in 2003 at the Bellagio, Las Vegas, USA.
Comment: Liquid confectionery that bites back.

KATINKA

Glass: Martini
Garnish: Split lime wedge
Method: **SHAKE** all ingredients with ice and fine strain into chilled glass.

1½	shot(s)	**Ketel One vodka**
1	shot(s)	**Apricot brandy liqueur**
1	shot(s)	**Freshly squeezed lime juice**
½	shot(s)	**Sugar (gomme) syrup**

Comment: Medium sweet, yet also tart and tangy.

KAVA [NEW]

Glass: Collins
Garnish: Pineapple wedge & cherry
Method: **SHAKE** all ingredients with ice and strain into glass filled with crushed ice.

1½	shot(s)	**Light white rum**
½	shot(s)	**Mount Gay Eclipse golden rum**
1	shot(s)	**Pressed pineapple juice**
1	shot(s)	**Freshly squeezed lemon juice**
¼	shot(s)	**Pomegranate (grenadine) syrup**
¼	shot(s)	**Sugar (gomme) syrup**

Variant: Multiply ingredients by a factor of four to make a Kava Bowl and serve in an ice-filled Tiki bowl.
Origin: Adapted from a drink featured in Jeff Berry's 'Intoxica' and originally created circa 1942 by Trader Vic.
Comment: A wonderfully fruity, fluffy and kitsch Tiki drink.

KEE-WEE MARTINI

Glass: Martini
Garnish: Kiwi slice on rim
Method: Cut kiwi fruit in half, scoop out flesh into base of shaker and **MUDDLE**. Add other ingredients, **SHAKE** with ice and fine strain into chilled glass.

1	fresh	**Kiwi fruit**
2	shot(s)	**Plymouth gin**
¼	shot(s)	**Freshly squeezed lemon juice**
½	shot(s)	**Sugar (gomme) syrup**

Origin: My version of this ubiquitous drink.
Comment: The citrus hints in the kiwi combine brilliantly with those in the gin and fresh lemon juice.

KENTUCKY COLONEL

Glass: Old-fashioned
Garnish: Peach slice & mint sprig
Method: **SHAKE** all ingredients with ice and strain into glass filled with crushed ice.

1½	shot(s)	**Bourbon whiskey**
¼	shot(s)	**Southern Comfort liqueur**
¼	shot(s)	**Cointreau / triple sec**
1	shot(s)	**Freshly extracted peach juice**
½	shot(s)	**Freshly squeezed lemon juice**
½	shot(s)	**Sugar (gomme) syrup**

Origin: Created by Morgan Watson of Apartment, Belfast, Northern Ireland.
Comment: Peach and bourbon with hints of orange and spice.

KENTUCKY DREAM

Glass: Old-fashioned
Garnish: Lemon zest twist
Method: **STIR** vanilla liqueur and bitters with two ice cubes in a glass. Add half the bourbon and two more ice cubes. Stir some more and add another two ice cubes and the rest of the bourbon. Add the last two ingredients and more ice cubes, and stir lots more. The melting and stirring in of ice cubes is essential to the dilution and taste of the drink.

½	shot(s)	**Vanilla schnapps liqueur**
2	dashes	**Angostura aromatic bitters**
2	shot(s)	**Bourbon whiskey**
½	shot(s)	**Apricot brandy liqueur**
1	shot(s)	**Pressed apple juice**

Origin: Created in 2002 by Wayne Collins for Maxxium UK.
Comment: Tames bourbon and adds hints of apricot, vanilla and apple.

KENTUCKY JEWEL [NEW]

Glass: Martini
Garnish: Berries on stick
Method: **SHAKE** all ingredients with ice and fine strain into chilled glass.

1½	shot(s)	**Bourbon whiskey**
¼	shot(s)	**Chambord black raspberry liqueur**
¼	shot(s)	**Cointreau / triple sec**
2	shot(s)	**Cranberry juice**

Origin: Adapted from a drink created in 2004 by Jonathan Lamm, The Admirable Crichton, London, England.
Comment: Easy sipping, fruity bourbon.

FOR MORE INFORMATION SEE OUR INGREDIENTS APPENDIX ON PAGE 322

A B C D E F G H I J **K** L M N O P Q R S T U V W X Y Z

KENTUCKY MAC

Glass: Old-fashioned
Garnish: Mint sprig
Method: **MUDDLE** ginger and mint in base of shaker. Add other ingredients, **SHAKE** with ice and strain into glass filled with crushed ice.

2	slices	**Fresh root ginger (thumbnail sized)**
2	fresh	**Mint leaves**
1½	shot(s)	**Bourbon whiskey**
1	shot(s)	**Stone's green ginger wine**
2	shot(s)	**Pressed apple juice**

Origin: Created in 1999 by Jamie Terrell, London, England.
Comment: Spicy, yet smooth and easy to sip.

KENTUCKY MUFFIN

Glass: Old-fashioned
Garnish: Blueberries
Method: **MUDDLE** blueberries in base of shaker. Add other ingredients, **SHAKE** with ice and strain into glass filled with crushed ice. Stir and serve with straws.

12	fresh	**Blueberries**
2	shot(s)	**Bourbon whiskey**
1	shot(s)	**Pressed apple juice**
½	shot(s)	**Freshly squeezed lime juice**
½	shot(s)	**Sugar (gomme) syrup**

Origin: Created in 2000 at Mash, London, England.
Comment: Blueberries, lime and apple combine with and are fortified by bourbon.

KENTUCKY PEAR

Glass: Martini
Garnish: Pear slice on rim
Method: **SHAKE** all ingredients with ice and fine strain into chilled glass.

1	shot(s)	**Bourbon whiskey**
1	shot(s)	**Xanté pear liqueur**
1	shot(s)	**Freshly extracted pear juice**
1	shot(s)	**Pressed apple juice**

Origin: Created in 2003 by Jes at The Cinnamon Club, London, England.
Comment: Pear, apple, vanilla and whiskey are partners in this richly flavoured drink.

KENTUCKY TEA

Glass: Collins
Garnish: Lime wedge
Method: **SHAKE** first four ingredients with ice and strain into ice-filled glass. **TOP** with ginger ale.

2	shot(s)	**Bourbon whiskey**
1	shot(s)	**Cointreau / triple sec**
1	shot(s)	**Freshly squeezed lime juice**
½	shot(s)	**Sugar (gomme) syrup**
Top up with		**Ginger ale**

Comment: Spicy whiskey and ginger.

KEY LIME

Glass: Coupette
Garnish: Lime wedge on rim
Method: **BLEND** all ingredients without ice and serve.

1½	shot(s)	**Vanilla flavoured vodka**
1½	shot(s)	**Lime flavoured vodka**
½	shot(s)	**Sugar (gomme) syrup**
½	shot(s)	**Rose's lime cordial**
3	scoops	**Vanilla ice cream**

Comment: Tangy, smooth and rich! Alcoholic ice cream for the grown-up palate.

KEY LIME PIE #1

Glass: Martini
Garnish: Pie rim (wipe with cream mix and dip into crushed Graham Crackers or digestive biscuits)
Method: **SHAKE** first three ingredients with ice and fine strain into chilled, rimmed glass. **SHAKE** cream and Licor 43 without ice so as to mix and whip. **FLOAT** cream mix on surface of drink.

2	shot(s)	**Malibu coconut rum liqueur**
1	shot(s)	**Cointreau / triple sec**
1	shot(s)	**Freshly squeezed lime juice**
2	shot(s)	**Double (heavy) cream**
½	shot(s)	**Licor 43 (Cuarenta Y Tres) liqueur**

Origin: Created by Michael Waterhouse, owner of Dylan Prime, New York City, USA.
Comment: This extremely rich drink is great when served as a dessert alternative.

KEY LIME PIE #2

Glass: Martini
Garnish: Pie rim (wipe with cream mix and dip into crushed Graham Crackers or digestive biscuits)
Method: **SHAKE** all ingredients with ice and fine strain into chilled, rimmed glass.

2	shot(s)	**Vanilla flavoured vodka**
1¾	shot(s)	**Pressed pineapple juice**
½	shot(s)	**Freshly squeezed lime juice**
¼	shot(s)	**Rose's lime cordial**

Comment: Beautiful balance of pineapple, vanilla, sweet and sour.

KEY LIME PIE #3 [NEW]

Glass: Martini
Garnish: Pie rim (wipe with cream mix and dip into crushed Graham Crackers or digestive biscuits)
Method: **SHAKE** all ingredients with ice and fine strain into chilled, rimmed glass.

2	shot(s)	**Ketel One Citroen vodka**
½	shot(s)	**Vanilla schnapps liqueur**
1½	shot(s)	**Pressed pineapple juice**
½	shot(s)	**Freshly squeezed lime juice**
¼	shot(s)	**Rose's lime cordial**

Origin: Recipe adapted from one by Claire Smith in 2005, London, England.
Comment: My favourite rendition of this dessert-in-a-glass cocktail.

●●●◐○

KEY WEST COOLER

Glass: Collins
Garnish: Lime wedge on rim
Method: **SHAKE** all ingredients with ice and strain into ice-filled glass.

1½	shot(s)	**Ketel One vodka**
1	shot(s)	**Malibu coconut rum liqueur**
2	shot(s)	**Cranberry juice**
2	shot(s)	**Freshly squeezed orange juice**

Comment: A coconut laced Breeze that's perfectly suited to the poolside.

●●◐○○

K.G.B.

Glass: Shot
Method: **LAYER** in glass by pouring carefully in the following order.

½	shot(s)	**Kahlúa coffee liqueur**
½	shot(s)	**Galliano liqueur**
½	shot(s)	**Rémy Martin cognac**

Comment: The initials of this simple peppermint and coffee shooter stand for Kahlúa, Galliano and brandy.

●●●◐○

KILLER PUNCH

Glass: Collins
Garnish: Lime wedge
Method: **SHAKE** all ingredients with ice and strain into ice-filled glass.

1	shot(s)	**Ketel One vodka**
½	shot(s)	**Midori melon liqueur**
½	shot(s)	**Luxardo Amaretto di Saschira**
½	shot(s)	**Freshly squeezed lime juice**
3½	shot(s)	**Cranberry juice**

Comment: Pretty soft, sweet and fruity as killers go.

●●●◐○

KIR

Glass: Goblet
Method: **POUR** cassis into glass and top with chilled wine.

½	shot(s)	**Sisca crème de cassis**
Top up with		**Dry white wine**

Variant: Kir Royale
Origin: This drink takes its name from a colourful politician and WWII resistance hero by the name of Canon Felix Kir, who served as the Mayor of Dijon, France, between 1945 and 1965. In order to promote local products, at receptions he served an aperitif made with crème de cassis and Bourgogne Aligoté white wine. The concoction quickly became known as Canon Kir's aperitif, then Father Kir's aperitif and finally as the 'Kir' aperitif.
Comment: Blackcurrant wine - clean, crisp and not too sweet.

●●●◐○

KIR MARTINI

Glass: Martini
Garnish: Berries on stick
Method: **STIR** all ingredients with ice and strain into chilled glass.

2	shot(s)	**Ketel One vodka**
1	shot(s)	**Sauvignon Blanc wine**
1	shot(s)	**Sisca crème de cassis**

Origin: Created by yours truly in 2004.
Comment: The Canon's traditional white wine and cassis aperitif with added oomph.

●●●◐○

KIR ROYALE

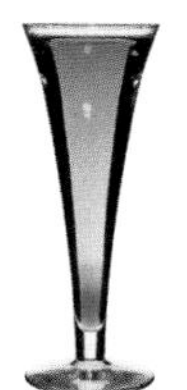

Glass: Flute
Method: **POUR** cassis into glass and **TOP** with champagne.

½	shot(s)	**Sisca crème de cassis**
Top up with		**Piper-Heidsieck brut champagne**

Variant: Kir
Comment: Easy to make, easy to drink.

●●◐○○

KISS OF DEATH [NEW]

Glass: Shot
Method: Take sambuca from freezer and Galliano from refrigerator then **LAYER** in chilled glass by carefully pouring in the following order.

¾	shot(s)	**Luxardo Sambuca dei Cesari**
¾	shot(s)	**Galliano liqueur**

Comment: Will give you fresh breath with which to apply that kiss.

●●●○○

KIWI BATIDA [NEW]

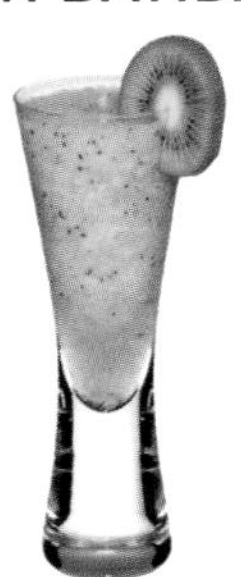

Glass: Collins
Garnish: Kiwi slice
Method: Cut kiwi in half and scoop flesh into blender. Add other ingredients and **BLEND** with 18oz scoop crushed ice until smooth. Serve with straws.

1	fresh	**Kiwi**
2½	shot(s)	**Sagatiba cachaça**
1	shot(s)	**Sugar (gomme) syrup**

Comment: The kiwi fruit flavour is a little lacking so this drink is improved by using kiwi-flavoured sugar syrup.

DRINKS ARE GRADED AS FOLLOWS:

● DISGUSTING ●◐ PRETTY AWFUL ●● BEST AVOIDED
●●◐ DISAPPOINTING ●●● ACCEPTABLE ●●●◐ GOOD
●●●● RECOMMENDED ●●●●◐ HIGHLY RECOMMENDED
●●●●● OUTSTANDING / EXCEPTIONAL

A B C D E F G H I J **K** L M N O P Q R S T U V W X Y Z

KIWI BELLINI

Glass: Flute
Garnish: Kiwi slice on rim
Method: Cut kiwi fruit in half, scoop out flesh into base of shaker and **MUDDLE**. Add next three ingredients, **SHAKE** with ice and fine strain into chilled glass. **TOP** with Prosecco.

1	fresh	**Kiwi fruit**
1¼	shot(s)	**Ketel One vodka**
¼	shot(s)	**Freshly squeezed lemon juice**
¼	shot(s)	**Sugar (gomme) syrup**
Top up with		**Prosecco**

Origin: Adapted from a drink discovered at Zuma, London, England, in 2004.
Comment: Lemon fresh kiwi, fortified with vodka and charged with Prosecco.

KIWI COLLINS

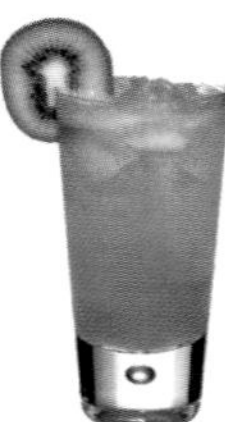

Glass: Collins
Garnish: Kiwi slice
Method: Cut kiwi fruit in half, scoop out flesh into base of shaker and **MUDDLE**. Add next three ingredients, **SHAKE** with ice and fine strain into ice-filled glass. **TOP** with soda water.

1	fresh	**Kiwi fruit**
2	shot(s)	**Ketel One vodka**
1½	shot(s)	**Freshly squeezed lemon juice**
½	shot(s)	**Sugar (gomme) syrup**
Top up with		**Soda water (club soda)**

Origin: Formula by yours truly.
Comment: A fruity adaptation of a Vodka Collins.

KIWI CRUSH [NEW]

Glass: Martini
Garnish: Kiwi slice
Method: Cut kiwi fruit in half, scoop out flesh into base of shaker and **MUDDLE**. Add other ingredients, **SHAKE** with ice and fine strain into chilled glass.

1	fresh	**Kiwi fruit**
2	shot(s)	**Ketel One Citroen vodka**
1	shot(s)	**Pressed apple juice**
½	shot(s)	**Freshly squeezed lemon juice**
¼	shot(s)	**Almond (orgeat) sugar syrup**

Origin: Recipe adapted from one by Claire Smith in 2005, London, England.
Comment: Spirit laced kiwi, citrus and almond.

DRINKS ARE GRADED AS FOLLOWS:

● DISGUSTING ●◐ PRETTY AWFUL ●● BEST AVOIDED
●●◐ DISAPPOINTING ●●● ACCEPTABLE ●●●◐ GOOD
●●●● RECOMMENDED ●●●●◐ HIGHLY RECOMMENDED
●●●●● OUTSTANDING / EXCEPTIONAL

KIWI MARTINI (SIMPLE)

Glass: Martini
Garnish: Kiwi slice on rim
Method: Cut kiwi fruit in half, scoop out flesh into base of shaker and **MUDDLE**. Add other ingredients, **SHAKE** with ice and fine strain into chilled glass.

1	fresh	**Kiwi fruit**
2	shot(s)	**Ketel One vodka**
½	shot(s)	**Sugar (gomme) syrup**

Origin: Formula by yours truly in 2004.
Comment: You may need to adjust the sugar depending on the ripeness of your fruit.

KLONDIKE [NEW]

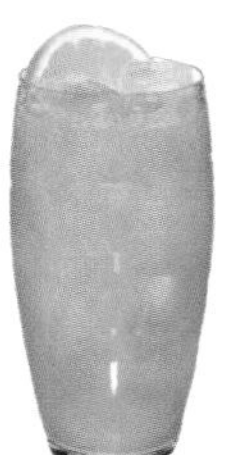

Glass: Collins
Garnish: Orange slice
Method: **POUR** ingredients into ice-filled glass and stir.

2	shot(s)	**Bourbon whiskey**
2	shot(s)	**Freshly squeezed orange juice**
Top up with		**Ginger ale**

Comment: A simple drink but the three ingredients combine well.

KNICKERBOCKER MARTINI [UPDATED]

Glass: Martini
Garnish: Orange zest twist
Method: **STIR** all ingredients with ice and strain into chilled glass.

1¾	shot(s)	**Plymouth gin**
¾	shot(s)	**Dry vermouth**
½	shot(s)	**Sweet (rosso) vermouth**

Origin: Thought to have been created at the Knickerbocker Hotel, New York City, USA.
Comment: Aromatic vermouth dominates this flavoursome Martini variant.

KNICKERBOCKER SPECIAL [NEW]

Glass: Martini
Garnish: Pineapple wedge & cherry on rim
Method: **SHAKE** all ingredients with ice and fine strain into chilled glass.

2	shot(s)	**Light white rum**
½	shot(s)	**Grand Marnier liqueur**
½	shot(s)	**Pressed pineapple juice**
½	shot(s)	**Freshly squeezed orange juice**
½	shot(s)	**Freshly squeezed lemon juice**
¼	shot(s)	**Raspberry or strawberry sugar syrup**

Comment: A bit fluffy but fans of French Martinis will love it.

KNICKER DROPPER GLORY

Glass: Shot
Method: **SHAKE** all ingredients with ice and fine strain into chilled glass.

1	shot(s)	**Hazelnut (crème de noisette) liqueur**
1/2	shot(s)	**Freshly squeezed lemon juice**

Origin: Created circa 2000 by Jason Fendick, London, England.
Comment: Nutty sweetness sharpened with lemon.

KNOCKOUT MARTINI [NEW]

Glass: Martini
Garnish: Float star anise
Method: **STIR** all ingredients with ice and strain into chilled glass.

1 1/2	shot(s)	**Plymouth gin**
1 1/2	shot(s)	**Dry vermouth**
1/4	shot(s)	**Pernod anis**
1/8	shot(s)	**White crème de menthe liqueur**

Comment: A Wet Martini with hints of aniseed and mint. Stir well as it benefits from dilution.

KOI YELLOW

Glass: Martini
Garnish: Float rose petal
Method: **SHAKE** all ingredients with ice and fine strain into chilled glass.

2	shot(s)	**Raspberry flavoured vodka**
1/2	shot(s)	**Cointreau / triple sec**
1	shot(s)	**Freshly squeezed lemon juice**
1/2	shot(s)	**Sugar (gomme) syrup**

Origin: The signature drink at Koi Restaurant, Los Angeles, USA.
Comment: Sherbet / raspberry Martini with a sweet and citrus sour finish.

KOOL HAND LUKE

Glass: Rocks
Method: **MUDDLE** lime in base of glass to release its juices. Pour rum and sugar syrup into glass, add crushed ice and **CHURN**. Serve with straws.

1	fresh	**Lime cut into eighths**
2	shot(s)	**Myers's Planters' Punch rum**
1	shot(s)	**Sugar (gomme) syrup**
2	dashes	**Angostura aromatic bitters**

Comment: This looks like a Caipirinha and has a similar balance of sweet, sour and spirit. The bitters bring out the spice in the rum, which is every bit as pungent as cachaça.

KOOLAID

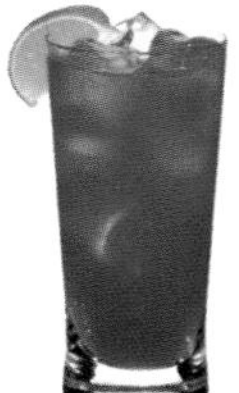

Glass: Collins
Garnish: Lime wedge
Method: **SHAKE** all ingredients with ice and strain into ice-filled glass.

1 1/2	shot(s)	**Ketel One vodka**
3/4	shot(s)	**Midori melon liqueur**
3/4	shot(s)	**Luxardo Amaretto di Saschira**
1/2	shot(s)	**Freshly squeezed lime juice**
2	shot(s)	**Cranberry juice**
1	shot(s)	**Freshly squeezed orange juice**

Origin: A drink with unknown origins that emerged and morphed during the 1990s.
Comment: Tangy liquid marzipan with hints of melon, cranberry and orange juice.

KRAKOW TEA

Glass: Collins
Garnish: Mint sprig & lime wedge
Method: Lightly **MUDDLE** mint in base of shaker (just to bruise). **SHAKE** all ingredients with ice and fine strain into ice-filled glass.

12	fresh	**Mint leaves**
2	shot(s)	**Zubrówka bison vodka**
1	shot(s)	**Strong cold camomile tea**
3 1/2	shot(s)	**Pressed apple juice**
1/4	shot(s)	**Freshly squeezed lime juice**
1/4	shot(s)	**Sugar (gomme) syrup**

Origin: Created in 2002 by Domhnall Carlin at Apartment, Belfast, Northern Ireland.
Comment: Refreshing and floral with a dry, citrus finish.

KRETCHMA [NEW]

Glass: Martini
Garnish: Dust with cocoa powder
Method: **SHAKE** all ingredients with ice and fine strain into chilled glass.

2	shot(s)	**Ketel One vodka**
3/4	shot(s)	**White crème de cacao liqueur**
1/2	shot(s)	**Freshly squeezed lemon juice**
1/8	shot(s)	**Pomegranate (grenadine) syrup**

Variant: Without grenadine this is a 'Ninitchka'.
Origin: Adapted from a recipe in David Embury's 'The Fine Art Of Mixing Drinks'.
Comment: Fortified Turkish Delight.

KURRANT AFFAIR

Glass: Collins
Garnish: Lemon wheel
Method: **SHAKE** all ingredients with ice and strain into ice-filled glass.

1 1/2	shot(s)	**Ketel One Citroen vodka**
3/4	shot(s)	**Raspberry flavoured vodka**
3	shot(s)	**Pressed apple juice**

Comment: Berry and citrus vodka combine with apple in this tall, refreshing summery drink.

A B C D E F G H I J K L M N O P Q R S T U V W X Y Z

L.A. ICED TEA

Glass: Sling
Garnish: Split lime wedge
Method: **SHAKE** first seven ingredients with ice and strain into ice-filled glass. **TOP** with soda.

1/2	shot(s)	**Ketel One vodka**
1/2	shot(s)	**Plymouth gin**
1/2	shot(s)	**Light white rum**
1/2	shot(s)	**Cointreau / triple sec**
1/2	shot(s)	**Midori melon liqueur**
1	shot(s)	**Freshly squeezed lime juice**
1/2	shot(s)	**Sugar (gomme) syrup**
Top up with		**Soda water (club soda)**

Comment: Long and lime green with subtle notes of melon and fresh lime.

LAVENDER & BLACK PEPPER MARTINI [NEW]

Glass: Martini
Method: Pour the syrup into an ice filled mixing glass. Add the vodka and black pepper. **STIR** and super-fine strain into chilled glass.

2 1/2	shot(s)	**Ketel One vodka**
1/4	shot(s)	**Sonoma Lavender sugar syrup**
2	grinds	**Freshly ground black pepper**

Origin: Adapted from a recipe created in 2006 by Richard Gillam at The Kenilworth Hotel, Warwickshire, England.
Comment: Subtly sweetened and lavender flavoured vodka with a bump and grind of spicy pepper.

LAVENDER MARTINI [NEW]

Glass: Martini
Garnish: Lemon zest twist
Method: **STIR** all ingredients with ice and strain into chilled glass.

2 1/2	shot(s)	**Lavender infused Ketel One vodka**
3/4	shot(s)	**Parfait amour liqueur**
1/4	shot(s)	**Dry vermouth**

Origin: Created in 2006 by yours truly.
Comment: Infusing lavender in vodka tends to make it bitter but the parfait amour adds sweetness as well as flavour and colour.

LAVENDER MARGARITA [NEW]

Glass: Coupette
Garnish: Lime wedge
Method: **SHAKE** all ingredients with ice and fine strain into chilled glass.

2	shot(s)	**Sauza Hornitos tequila**
1	shot(s)	**Freshly squeezed lime juice**
1/2	shot(s)	**Sonoma lavender infused sugar syrup**

Origin: Created in 2006 by yours truly.
Comment: Lavender lime and tequila combine harmoniously.

LAGO COSMO

Glass: Martini
Garnish: Orange zest twist
Method: **SHAKE** all ingredients with ice and fine strain into chilled glass.

1 1/2	shot(s)	**Cranberry flavoured vodka**
3/4	shot(s)	**Cointreau / triple sec**
1 3/4	shot(s)	**Freshly squeezed orange juice**
1/4	shot(s)	**Freshly squeezed lime juice**
1/2	shot(s)	**Sugar (gomme) syrup**

Origin: Discovered in 2003 at Nectar @ Bellagio, Las Vegas, USA.
Comment: A Cosmo with cranberry vodka in place of citrus vodka and orange juice in place of cranberry juice.

LANDSLIDE

Glass: Shot
Method: Refrigerate ingredients then **LAYER** in chilled glass by carefully **pour**ing in the following order.

1/2	shot(s)	**Luxardo Amaretto di Saschira liqueur**
1/2	shot(s)	**Crème de bananes liqueur**
1/2	shot(s)	**Baileys Irish Cream liqueur**

Comment: A sweet but pleasant combination of banana, almond and Irish cream liqueur.

THE LAST WORD [NEW]

Glass: Martini
Garnish: Lime wedge on rim
Method: **SHAKE** all ingredients with ice and fine strain into chilled glass.

3/4	shot(s)	**Plymouth gin**
3/4	shot(s)	**Green Chartreuse**
3/4	shot(s)	**Luxardo maraschino liqueur**
3/4	shot(s)	**Freshly squeezed lime juice**
1/2	shot(s)	**Chilled mineral water (omit if wet ice)**

Origin: An old classic championed in 2005 by the team at Pegu Club, New York City, USA.
Comment: Chartreuse devotees will love this balanced, tangy drink. I'm one.

LAZARUS

Glass: Martini
Garnish: Float three coffee beans
Method: **SHAKE** all ingredients with ice and fine strain into chilled glass.

1	shot(s)	**Ketel One vodka**
1	shot(s)	**Kahlúa coffee liqueur**
1/2	shot(s)	**Rémy Martin cognac**
1	shot(s)	**Espresso coffee (cold)**

Origin: Created in 2000 by David Whitehead at Atrium, Leeds, England.
Comment: A flavoursome combination of spirit and coffee.

LCB MARTINI

Glass: Martini
Garnish: Lemon zest twist
Method: SHAKE all ingredients with ice and fine strain into chilled glass.

2	shot(s)	**Ketel One vodka**
3/4	shot(s)	**Sauvignon Blanc/unoaked Chardonnay wine**
2	shot(s)	**Freshly squeezed pink grapefruit juice**
1/4	shot(s)	**Sugar (gomme) syrup**

Origin: Created by yours truly in 2004 and named after Lisa Clare Ball, who loves both Sauvignon and pink grapefruit juice.
Comment: A sweet and sour, citrus fresh Martini.

LEAP YEAR MARTINI [NEW]

Glass: Martini
Garnish: Lemon peel twist
Method: SHAKE all ingredients with ice and fine strain into chilled glass.

2	shot(s)	**Plymouth gin**
1/2	shot(s)	**Grand Marnier liqueur**
1/2	shot(s)	**Sweet (rosso) vermouth**
1/4	shot(s)	**Freshly squeezed lemon juice**

Origin: Harry Craddock created this drink for the Leap Year celebrations at the Savoy Hotel, London, on 29th February 1928 and recorded it in his 1930 Savoy Cocktail Book.
Comment: This drink, which is on the dry side, needs to be served ice-cold.

LEAVE IT TO ME MARTINI [NEW]

Glass: Martini
Garnish: Lemon zest twist
Method: SHAKE all ingredients with ice and fine strain into chilled glass.

1 1/2	shot(s)	**Plymouth gin**
1/2	shot(s)	**Apricot brandy liqueur**
3/4	shot(s)	**Sweet (rosso) vermouth**
1/2	shot(s)	**Freshly squeezed lemon juice**
1/4	shot(s)	**Sonoma pomegranate (grenadine) syrup**

Origin: Adapted from a recipe in Harry Craddock's 1930 Savoy Cocktail Book.
Comment: Gin, apricot, vermouth and lemon create an old fashioned but well balanced drink.

THE LEGEND

Glass: Martini
Garnish: Blackberries on stick
Method: SHAKE all ingredients with ice and fine strain into chilled glass.

2	shot(s)	**Ketel One vodka**
1	shot(s)	**Freshly squeezed lime juice**
1/4	shot(s)	**Crème de mûre (blackberry) liqueur**
1/4	shot(s)	**Sugar (gomme) syrup**
4	dashes	**Fee Brothers orange bitters**

Origin: Created in the late 1990s by Dick Bradsell for Karen Hampsen at Legends, London, England.
Comment: The quality of orange bitters and blackberry liqueur used dramatically affect the flavour of this blush coloured cocktail.

LEMON BEAT

Glass: Rocks
Garnish: Lemon slice
Method: STIR honey with cachaça in the base of shaker to dissolve honey. Add other ingredients, **SHAKE** with ice and strain into ice-filled glass.

2	spoons	**Clear runny honey**
2	shot(s)	**Cachaça**
1	shot(s)	**Freshly squeezed lemon juice**

Comment: Simple but effective. Use quality cachaça and honey and you'll have a great drink.

LEMON BUTTER COOKIE

Glass: Old-fashioned
Garnish: Lemon zest twist
Method: SHAKE all ingredients with ice and strain into glass filled with crushed ice.

3/4	shot(s)	**Zubrówka bison vodka**
3/4	shot(s)	**Ketel One vodka**
3/4	shot(s)	**Krupnik honey liqueur**
2	shot(s)	**Pressed apple juice**
1/2	shot(s)	**Almond (orgeat) syrup**
1/8	shot(s)	**Freshly squeezed lemon juice**

Origin: Created in 2002 by Mark 'Q-Ball' Linnie and Martin Oliver at The Mixing Tin, Leeds, England.
Comment: An appropriate name for a most unusually flavoured drink modelled on the Polish Martini.

LEMON CHIFFON PIE

Glass: Coupette
Garnish: Grated lemon zest
Method: BLEND all ingredients with crushed ice and serve with straws.

1	shot(s)	**Light white rum**
1	shot(s)	**White crème de cacao liqueur**
1	shot(s)	**Freshly squeezed lemon juice**
2	scoops	**Vanilla ice cream**

Comment: Creamy and tangy – like a lemon pie. Consume in place of dessert.

LEMON CURD MARTINI [NEW]

Glass: Martini
Garnish: Lemon wedge on rim
Method: SHAKE all ingredients with ice and fine strain into chilled glass.

3	spoons	**Lemon curd**
2	shot(s)	**Ketel One Citroen vodka**
1/2	shot(s)	**Freshly squeezed lemon juice**

Origin: Created by yours truly.
Comment: This almost creamy cocktail is named after and tastes like its primary ingredient. Martini purists may justifiably baulk at the absence of vermouth and the presence of fruit.

LEMON DROP

Glass: Shot
Garnish: Sugar coated slice of lemon
Method: **SHAKE** all ingredients with ice and fine strain into chilled glass.

1/2	shot(s)	**Ketel One vodka**
1/2	shot(s)	**Cointreau / triple sec**
1/2	shot(s)	**Freshly squeezed lemon juice**

Comment: Lemon and orange combine to make a fresh tasting citrus shot.

LEMON DROP MARTINI [NEW]

Glass: Martini
Garnish: Lemon zest twist
Method: **SHAKE** all ingredients with ice and fine strain into chilled glass.

2	shot(s)	**Ketel One Citroen vodka**
1	shot(s)	**Cointreau / triple sec**
3/4	shot(s)	**Freshly squeezed lemon juice**
1/2	shot(s)	**Sugar (gomme) syrup**

Comment: Sherbety lemon.

LEMON LIME & BITTERS

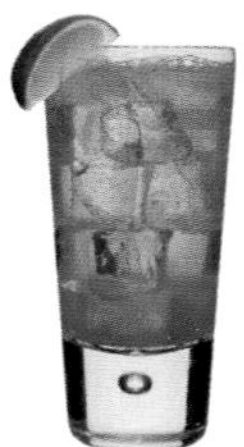

Glass: Collins
Garnish: Lime wedge
Method: Squeeze lime wedges and drop into glass. **ADD** Angostura bitters and fill glass with ice. **TOP** with lemonade, stir and serve with straws.

4	fresh	**Lime wedges**
5	dashes	**Angostura aromatic bitters**
Top up with		**7-Up**

AKA: LLB
Origin: Very popular in its homeland, Australia.
Comment: If you're unlucky enough to be the driver, this refreshing long drink is a good low alcohol option.

LEMON MARTINI [NEW]

Glass: Martini
Garnish: Lemon zest twist
Method: **MUDDLE** lemongrass in base of shaker. Add other ingredients, **SHAKE** with ice and fine strain into chilled glass.

1	inch	**Lemongrass chopped**
2	shot(s)	**Ketel One vodka**
1/4	shot(s)	**Dry vermouth**
1	shot(s)	**Freshly squeezed lemon juice**
1/2	shot(s)	**Sugar (gomme) syrup**

Origin: Created in 2006 by yours truly.
Comment: A complex, delicately lemon Vodkatini.

LEMON MERINGUE MARTINI [UPDATED]

Glass: Martini
Garnish: Lemon zest twist
Method: **SHAKE** all ingredients with ice and fine strain into chilled glass.

2	shot(s)	**Ketel One Citroen vodka**
1	shot(s)	**Baileys Irish Cream liqueur**
1	shot(s)	**Freshly squeezed lemon juice**
1/4	shot(s)	**Sugar (gomme) syrup**

Origin: Adapted from a drink created in 2000 by Ben Reed, London, England.
Comment: Slightly creamy in consistency, this tangy lemon drink is indeed reminiscent of the eponymous dessert.

LEMON MERINGUE PIE'TINI

Glass: Martini
Garnish: Pie rim (wipe outside edge of rim with cream mix and dip into crunched up Graham Cracker or digestive biscuits)
Method: **SHAKE** first three ingredients with ice and fine strain into chilled and rimmed glass. **SHAKE** cream and Licor 43 without ice so as to mix and whip. **FLOAT** cream mix by pouring over back of a spoon.

1	shot(s)	**Luxardo limoncello liqueur**
1	shot(s)	**Sugar (gomme) syrup**
1	shot(s)	**Freshly squeezed lemon juice**
2	shot(s)	**Double (heavy) cream**
1/2	shot(s)	**Cuarenta Y Tres (Licor 43) liqueur**

Origin: Created by Michael Waterhouse at Dylan Prime, New York City.
Comment: Rich and syrupy base sipped through a vanilla cream topping.

LEMON SORBET

Glass: Martini (saucer)
Garnish: Strips of lemon rind
Method: Heat water in pan and add sugar. Simmer and stir until sugar dissolves, add lemon juice and grated lemon rind and continue to simmer and stir for a few minutes. Take off the heat and allow to cool. Fine strain into a shallow container and stir in liqueur and orange bitters. Beat egg whites and fold into mix. Place in freezer and store for up to 3-4 days before use.

3/4	cup(s)	**Mineral water**
1	cup(s)	**Granulated white sugar**
1/2	cup(s)	**Freshly squeezed lemon juice**
5	rinds	**Fresh lemon**
		(avoid the pith when grating)
1/4	cup(s)	**Luxardo limoncello liqueur**
2	spoons	**Fee Brothers orange bitters**
2	fresh	**Egg whites**

Variant: To make any other citrus flavour sorbet, simply substitute the juice and peel of another fruit such as grapefruit, lime or orange.
Comment: My favourite recipe for this dessert and occasional cocktail ingredient.

LEMONY [NEW]

Glass: Martini
Garnish: Maraschino cherry
Method: **SHAKE** all ingredients with ice and fine strain into chilled glass.

2	shot(s)	**Plymouth gin**
½	shot(s)	**Yellow Chartreuse liqueur**
½	shot(s)	**Luxardo limoncello liqueur**
½	shot(s)	**Freshly squeezed lemon juice**
½	shot(s)	**Chilled mineral water (omit if wet ice)**

Comment: Lemon subtly dominates this complex, herbal drink.

LEMONGRAD

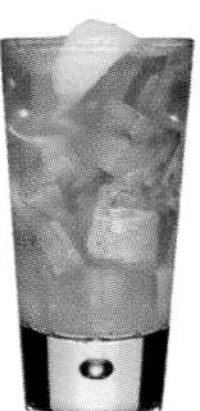

Glass: Collins
Garnish: Lemon wedge squeezed over drink
Method: **SHAKE** first three ingredients with ice and strain into ice-filled glass. **TOP** with tonic and lightly stir.

2	shot(s)	**Ketel One Citroen vodka**
1	shot(s)	**Elderflower cordial**
½	shot(s)	**Freshly squeezed lemon juice**
Top up with		**Tonic water**

Origin: Created in 2002 by Alex Kammerling, London, England.
Comment: A great summer afternoon drink. Fresh lemon with elderflower and quinine.

LEMONGRASS COSMO [NEW]

Glass: Martini
Garnish: Lemon zest twist
Method: **MUDDLE** lemongrass in base of shaker. **ADD** other ingredients, **SHAKE** with ice and fine strain into chilled glass.

¼	stem	**Fresh lemongrass (finely chopped)**
1	shot(s)	**Ketel One Citroen vodka**
1	shot(s)	**Cointreau / triple sec**
1½	shot(s)	**Cranberry juice**
½	shot(s)	**Freshly squeezed lemon juice**

Origin: Adapted from a drink discovered in 2005 at Opia, Hong Kong, China
Comment: Lemongrass adds complexity to this balanced Cosmo.

LENINADE

Glass: Martini
Garnish: Orange zest twist
Method: **SHAKE** all ingredients with ice and fine strain into chilled glass.

1½	shot(s)	**Ketel One Citroen vodka**
1	shot(s)	**Freshly squeezed lemon juice**
¼	shot(s)	**Sugar (gomme) syrup**
¼	shot(s)	**Cointreau / triple sec**
3	dashes	**Fee Brothers orange bitters**

Origin: Created by Dick Bradsell at Fred's, London, England, in the late 80s.
Comment: Orange undertones add citrus depth to the lemon explosion.

LIFE (LOVE IN THE FUTURE ECSTASY)

Glass: Old-fashioned
Garnish: Mint leaf
Method: **MUDDLE** mint in base of shaker. Add next three ingredients, **SHAKE** with ice and fine strain into glass filled with crushed ice. **DRIZZLE** tea liqueur over drink.

7	leaves	**Fresh mint**
1½	shot(s)	**Ketel One vodka**
1	shot(s)	**Freshly squeezed lime juice**
½	shot(s)	**Sugar (gomme) syrup**
1	shot(s)	**Tea liqueur**

Origin: Adapted from a drink created in 1999 by Nick Strangeway at Ché, London, England, for Martin Sexton (writer and artistic entrepreneur).
Comment: Refreshing tea and mint.

LIGHT BREEZE

Glass: Collins
Garnish: Lemon slice
Method: **POUR** all ingredients into ice-filled glass. Stir and serve with straws.

3	shot(s)	**Cranberry juice**
2	shot(s)	**Freshly squeezed golden grapefruit juice**
2	shot(s)	**Pernod anis**

Origin: Created in 2000 by yours truly at the Light Bar, London, England (hence the name).
Comment: A Seabreeze based on anis rather than vodka, with aniseed depth and sweetness.

LIGHTER BREEZE

Glass: Collins
Garnish: Apple wedge on rim
Method: **POUR** all ingredients into ice-filled glass. Stir and serve with straws.

3	shot(s)	**Pressed apple juice**
2	shot(s)	**Cranberry juice**
½	shot(s)	**Elderflower cordial**
2	shot(s)	**Pernod anis**

Comment: Long, fragrant and refreshing.

LIMA SOUR [NEW]

Glass: Old-fashioned
Garnish: Lemon zest string
Method: **BLEND** all ingredients with one 12oz scoop of crushed ice. Serve with straws.

2	shot(s)	**Pisco**
½	shot(s)	**Luxardo maraschino liqueur**
¾	shot(s)	**Freshly squeezed golden grapefruit juice**
¾	shot(s)	**Freshly squeezed lime juice**
¾	shot(s)	**Sugar (gomme) syrup**

Origin: Created before 1947 by Jerry Hooker.
Comment: A refreshing blend of pisco, maraschino and citrus.

LIME BLUSH (MOCKTAIL) [NEW]

Glass: Old-fashioned
Garnish: Lime wedge
Method: SHAKE all ingredients with ice and strain into glass filled with crushed ice.

2 shot(s) **Freshly squeezed lime juice**
1/2 shot(s) **Rose's lime cordial**
1/2 shot(s) **Sonoma pomegranate (grenadine) syrup**
1/2 shot(s) **Sugar (gomme) syrup**

Origin: Adapted from a drink discovered in 2005 at Blue Bar, Four Seasons Hotel, Hong Kong, China.
Comment: Refreshingly sweet and sour.

LIME BREEZE

Glass: Collins
Garnish: Lime wedge
Method: SHAKE all ingredients with ice and fine strain into ice-filled glass.

2 shot(s) **Lime flavoured vodka**
3 shot(s) **Cranberry juice**
1 1/2 shot(s) **Freshly squeezed golden grapefruit juice**

Comment: A lime driven Sea Breeze.

LIME SOUR

Glass: Old-fashioned
Garnish: Lime wedge on rim
Method: SHAKE all ingredients with ice and strain into ice-filled glass.

2 shot(s) **Lime flavoured vodka**
1 1/4 shot(s) **Freshly squeezed lime juice**
1/4 shot(s) **Sugar (gomme) syrup**
1/2 fresh **Egg white**

Comment: Fresh egg white gives this drink a wonderfully frothy top and smoothes the alcohol and lime juice.

LIMEADE (MOCKTAIL) [NEW]

Glass: Collins
Garnish: Lime wedge
Method: SHAKE all ingredients with ice and fine strain into ice filled glass.

2 shot(s) **Freshly squeezed lime juice**
1 shot(s) **Sugar (gomme) syrup**
3 shot(s) **Chilled mineral water**

Variant: Shake first two ingredients & top with sparkling water.
Comment: A superbly refreshing alternative to lemonade.

LIMELITE

Glass: Collins
Garnish: Lime wedge
Method: SHAKE first four ingredients with ice and strain into ice-filled glass. **TOP** with 7-Up.

2 shot(s) **Lime flavoured vodka**
1/2 shot(s) **Cointreau / triple sec**
1/2 shot(s) **Freshly squeezed lime juice**
1/4 shot(s) **Sugar (gomme) syrup**
Top up with **7-Up**

Comment: Long and citrussy.

LIMEOSA

Glass: Flute
Method: SHAKE first two ingredients with ice and fine strain into chilled glass. **TOP** with champagne and gently stir.

1 shot(s) **Lime flavoured vodka**
2 shot(s) **Freshly squeezed orange juice**
Top up with **Piper-Heidsieck brut champagne**

Comment: Why settle for a plain old Buck's Fizz when you could add a shot of lime-flavoured vodka?

LIMERICK

Glass: Collins
Garnish: Lime wedge squeezed over drink
Method: SHAKE first three ingredients with ice and strain into ice-filled glass. **TOP** with soda water and lightly stir.

2 shot(s) **Lime flavoured vodka**
1 shot(s) **Freshly squeezed lime juice**
1/2 shot(s) **Sugar (gomme) syrup**
Top up with **Soda water (club soda)**

Origin: I created this twist on the classic Vodka Rickey in 2002.
Comment: A refreshing lime cooler.

LIMEY

Glass: Martini
Garnish: Lime zest twist
Method: SHAKE all ingredients with ice and fine strain into chilled glass.

2 shot(s) **Lime flavoured vodka**
1/2 shot(s) **Freshly squeezed lime juice**
1/2 shot(s) **Sugar (gomme) syrup**
1/8 shot(s) **Rose's lime cordial**
3 dashes **Angostura aromatic bitters**
1/2 shot(s) **Chilled mineral water (omit if wet ice)**

Origin: I created and named this drink after the British naval tradition of mixing lime juice with spirits in an attempt to prevent scurvy. This practice gained British sailors the nickname 'limeys'.
Comment: A rust coloured drink with a delicately sour flavour.

LIMEY COSMO

Glass: Martini
Garnish: Lime wedge on rim
Method: **SHAKE** all ingredients with ice and fine strain into chilled glass.

1½	shot(s)	**Lime flavoured vodka**
1	shot(s)	**Cointreau / triple sec**
1¼	shot(s)	**Cranberry juice**
¼	shot(s)	**Freshly squeezed lime juice**
½	shot(s)	**Rose's lime cordial**

Comment: If you like Cosmopolitans, you'll love this zesty alternative.

LIMNOLOGY

Glass: Martini
Garnish: Lime zest twist
Method: **STIR** all ingredients with ice and fine strain into chilled glass.

2	shot(s)	**Lime flavoured vodka**
1	shot(s)	**Rose's lime cordial**
¾	shot(s)	**Chilled water (reduceif wet ice)**

Origin: The name means the study of the physical phenomena of lakes and other fresh waters – appropriate for this fresh green drink.
Comment: A vodka Gimlet made with lime flavoured vodka.

LIMEY MULE

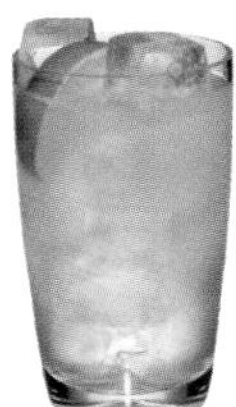

Glass: Collins
Garnish: Lime wedge
Method: **SHAKE** first three ingredients with ice and strain into ice-filled glass. **TOP** with ginger ale, lightly stir and serve with straws.

2	shot(s)	**Lime flavoured vodka**
1	shot(s)	**Freshly squeezed lime juice**
½	shot(s)	**Sugar (gomme) syrup**
Top up with		**Ginger ale**

Comment: Made with plain vodka this drink is a Moscow Mule. This variant uses lime flavoured vodka.

LIMONCELLO MARTINI [NEW]

Glass: Martini
Garnish: Lemon zest twist
Method: **SHAKE** all ingredients with ice and fine strain into chilled glass.

1½	shot(s)	**Ketel One vodka**
1½	shot(s)	**Luxardo limoncello liqueur**
1	shot(s)	**Freshly squeezed lemon juice**

Origin: Adapted from a drink created in 2005 by Francesco at Mix, New York City, USA.
Comment: If you like the liqueur you'll love the cocktail.

LIMINAL SHOT

Glass: Shot
Method: Refrigerate ingredients then **LAYER** in chilled glass by carefully pouring in the following order.

½	shot(s)	**Sonoma pomegranate (grenadine) syrup**
½	shot(s)	**Blue curaçao liqueur**
¾	shot(s)	**Lime flavoured vodka**

Comment: The name means transitional, marginal, a boundary or a threshold. Appropriate since the layers border each other.

LIMOUSINE

Glass: Old-fashioned
Method: Place bar spoon in glass. **POUR** ingredients into glass and stir.

2	shot(s)	**Lime flavoured vodka**
1	shot(s)	**Honey liqueur**
4	shot(s)	**Hot camomile tea**

Origin: Created in 2002 by yours truly.
Comment: In winter this hot drink is a warming treat. In summer serve cold over ice, as pictured.

LIMITED LIABILITY

Glass: Old-fashioned
Method: **SHAKE** all ingredients with ice and strain into ice-filled glass.

2	shot(s)	**Lime flavoured vodka**
¾	shot(s)	**Freshly squeezed lime juice**
1	shot(s)	**Honey liqueur**

Origin: Created in 2002 by yours truly.
Comment: A sour and flavoursome short - honey and lime work well together.

LINSTEAD

Glass: Martini
Garnish: Lemon zest twist
Method: **SHAKE** all ingredients with ice and fine strain into chilled glass.

2	shot(s)	**The Famous Grouse Scotch whisky**
2	shot(s)	**Pressed pineapple juice**
¼	shot(s)	**Sugar (gomme) syrup**
⅛	shot(s)	**La Fée Parisian 68% absinthe**

Comment: Absinthe and pineapple come through first, with Scotch last. A great medley of flavours.

A B C D E F G H I J K L M N O P Q R S T U V W X Y Z

A B C D E F G H I J K **L** M N O P Q R S T U V W X Y Z

LIQUORICE ALL SORT

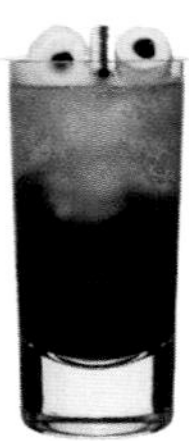

Glass: Collins
Garnish: Liquorice Allsort sweet
Method: SHAKE first four ingredients with ice and strain into ice-filled glass. **TOP** with lemonade.

1	shot(s)	**Opal Nera black sambuca**
1	shot(s)	**Crème de bananes liqueur**
1	shot(s)	**Crème de fraise (strawberry) liqueur**
1	shot(s)	**Blue curaçao liqueur**
Top up with		**7-Up / lemonade**

Origin: George Bassett (1818-1886), a manufacturer of liquorice sweets, did not invent the Liquorice Allsort that carries his name. That happened 15 years after George died when a salesman accidentally dropped a tray of sweets, they fell in a muddle and the famous sweet was born.
Comment: This aptly named, semi-sweet drink has a strong liquorice flavour with hints of fruit.

LIQUORICE MARTINI

Glass: Martini
Garnish: Piece of liquorice
Method: STIR all ingredients with ice and strain into chilled glass.

2	shot(s)	**Plymouth gin**
1/4	shot(s)	**Opal Nera black sambuca**
1/8	shot(s)	**Sugar (gomme) syrup**

Origin: Created in 2003 by Jason Fendick, London, England.
Comment: Gin tinted violet, flavoured with liquorice and slightly sweetened.

LIQUORICE SHOT

Glass: Shot
Method: SHAKE all ingredients with ice and fine strain into chilled glass.

1/2	shot(s)	**Ketel One vodka**
1/2	shot(s)	**Luxardo white sambuca**
1/2	shot(s)	**Crème de cassis**

Comment: For liquorice fans.

LIQUORICE WHISKY SOUR

Glass: Old-fashioned
Garnish: Cherry & lemon slice (sail)
Method: SHAKE all ingredients with ice and strain into ice-filled glass.

2	shot(s)	**The Famous Grouse Scotch whisky**
1/2	shot(s)	**Ricard pastis**
1	shot(s)	**Freshly squeezed lemon juice**
1/2	shot(s)	**Sugar (gomme) syrup**
1/2	fresh	**Egg white**
3	dashes	**Angostura aromatic bitters**

Origin: Created in 2006 by yours truly.
Comment: Pastis adds a pleasing hint of liquorice to the classic Whisky Sour.

LISA B'S DAIQUIRI

Glass: Martini
Garnish: Grapefruit zest twist
Method: SHAKE all ingredients with ice and fine strain into chilled glass.

2 1/2	shot(s)	**Vanilla infused Light rum**
1/2	shot(s)	**Freshly squeezed lime juice**
1/2	shot(s)	**Sonoma vanilla bean sugar syrup**
1	shot(s)	**Freshly squeezed pink grapefruit juice**

Origin: Created in 2003 by yours truly for a gorgeous fan of both Daiquiris and pink grapefruit juice.
Comment: Reminiscent of a Hemingway Special, this flavoursome, vanilla laced Daiquiri has a wonderfully tangy bitter-sweet finish.

LITTLE ITALY [NEW]

Glass: Martini
Garnish: Orange zest twist
Method: STIR all ingredients with ice and fine strain into chilled glass.

2	shot(s)	**Bourbon whiskey**
1	shot(s)	**Sweet (rosso) vermouth**
1/2	shot(s)	**Cynar liqueur**

Origin: Adapted from a drink discovered in 2006 at Pegu Club, New York City, USA.
Comment: A sweet, Manhattan-style drink, bittered with Cynar.

LIVINGSTONE [NEW]

Glass: Martini
Garnish: Lemon peel twist
Method: SHAKE all ingredients with ice and fine strain into chilled glass.

2	shot(s)	**Plymouth gin**
1	shot(s)	**Dry vermouth**
1/4	shot(s)	**Sugar (gomme) syrup**

Variant: Use pomegranate syrup in place of sugar and you have a Red Livingstone, named after London's 'lefty' mayor, Ken.
Origin: This 1930s classic was named after Doctor Livingstone, the famous African missionary.
Comment: The classic gin and vermouth Martini made more approachable with a dash of sugar.

LOCH ALMOND

Glass: Collins
Garnish: Float amaretti biscuit
Method: POUR all ingredients into ice-filled glass, stir and serve with straws.

1 1/2	shot(s)	**The Famous Grouse Scotch whisky**
1 1/2	shot(s)	**Luxardo Amaretto di Saschira liqueur**
Top up with		**Ginger ale**

Comment: If you haven't got to grips with Scotch but like amaretto, try this spicy almond combination.

LOLA

Glass: Martini
Garnish: Orange zest twist
Method: SHAKE all ingredients with ice and fine strain into chilled glass.

1½ shot(s) **Mount Gay Eclipse golden rum**
½ shot(s) **Mandarine Napoléon liqueur**
½ shot(s) **White crème de cacao liqueur**
1 shot(s) **Freshly squeezed orange juice**
½ shot(s) **Double (heavy) cream**

Origin: Created in 1999 by Jamie Terrell, London, England.
Comment: Strong, creamy orange.

LOLITA MARGARITA [NEW]

Glass: Coupette
Garnish: Lime wedge on rim
Method: STIR honey with tequila in base of shaker to dissolve honey. Add other ingredients, SHAKE with ice and fine strain into chilled glass.

2 spoons **Runny honey**
2 shot(s) **Sauza Hornitos tequila**
1 shot(s) **Freshly squeezed lime juice**
2 dashes **Angostura aromatic bitters**

Origin: Named after the novel by Vladimir Nabokov which chronicles a middle-aged man's infatuation with a 12 year old girl. Nabokov invented the word 'nymphet' to describe her seductive qualities.
Comment: A fittingly seductive Margarita.

LONDON CALLING

Glass: Martini
Garnish: Orange zest twist
Method: STIR all ingredients with ice and strain into chilled glass.

2 shot(s) **Plymouth gin**
1¼ shot(s) **Plymouth sloe gin liqueur**
½ shot(s) **Sweet (rosso) vermouth**
2 dashes **Fee Brothers orange bitters**

Origin: Discovered in 2003 at Oxo Tower Bar & Brasserie, London, England.
Comment: A traditionally styled sweet Martini with a dry, fruity finish.

LONDON COCKTAIL [NEW]

Glass: Martini
Garnish: Orange zest twist
Method: SHAKE all ingredients with ice and fine strain into chilled glass.

2½ shot(s) **Plymouth gin**
⅛ shot(s) **La Fée Parisian 68% absinthe**
⅛ shot(s) **Sugar (gomme) syrup**
2 dashes **Fee Brothers orange bitters**
½ shot(s) **Chilled mineral water (omit if wet ice)**

Origin: Adapted from a recipe in Harry Craddock's 1930 Savoy Cocktail Book.
Comment: Chilled, diluted and sweetened gin invigorated by a hint of absinthe.

LONDON FOG [NEW]

Glass: Old-fashioned
Garnish: Orange zest twist
Method: Fill glass with ice. Add ingredients in the following order and STIR. Add more ice to fill.

1 shot(s) **Plymouth gin**
2 shot(s) **Chilled mineral water**
1 shot(s) **Pernod anis**

Comment: Dry liquorice and aniseed.

LONELY BULL

Glass: Old-fashioned
Garnish: Dust with freshly grated nutmeg
Method: SHAKE all ingredients with ice and strain into ice-filled glass.

1½ shot(s) **Sauza Hornitos tequila**
1½ shot(s) **Kahlúa coffee liqueur**
¾ shot(s) **Double (heavy) cream**
¾ shot(s) **Milk**

Comment: Like a creamy iced coffee – yum.

LONG BEACH ICED TEA [UPDATED]

Glass: Sling
Garnish: Lemon slice
Method: SHAKE all ingredients with ice and strain into ice-filled glass. Serve with straws.

½ shot(s) **Kahlúa coffee liqueur**
½ shot(s) **Sauza Hornitos tequila**
½ shot(s) **Light white rum**
½ shot(s) **Plymouth gin**
½ shot(s) **Ketel One vodka**
1 shot(s) **Freshly squeezed lime juice**
½ shot(s) **Sugar (gomme) syrup**
2 shot(s) **Cranberry juice**

Comment: One of the more grown-up 'Iced Tea' cocktails.

LONG FLIGHT OF STAIRS [NEW]

Glass: Collins
Garnish: Apple or pear slice
Method: SHAKE all ingredients with ice and strain into ice-filled glass. Serve with straws.

1 shot(s) **Pear flavoured vodka**
1 shot(s) **Calvados or applejack brandy**
1 shot(s) **Pear & cognac liqueur**
2½ shot(s) **Pressed apple juice**

Origin: Created in 2005 by yours truly as a homage to the G.E. Club's 'Stairs Martini'.
Comment: A seriously tasty, strong, long drink. The name is a reversal of the London rhyming slang 'apples and pears' (stairs).

A B C D E F G H I J K L M N O P Q R S T U V W X Y Z

LONG ISLAND ICED TEA

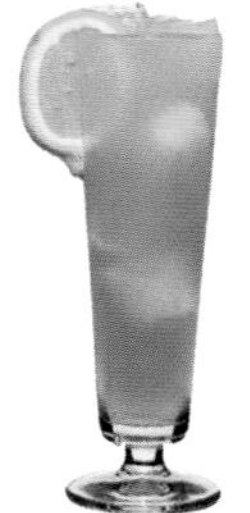

Glass: Sling
Garnish: Lemon slice
Method: **SHAKE** first seven ingredients with ice and strain into ice-filled glass. **TOP** with cola, stir and serve with straws.

1/2	shot(s)	**Light white rum**
1/2	shot(s)	**Plymouth gin**
1/2	shot(s)	**Ketel One vodka**
1/2	shot(s)	**Sauza Hornitos tequila**
1/2	shot(s)	**Cointreau / triple sec**
1	shot(s)	**Freshly squeezed lime juice**
1/2	shot(s)	**Sugar (gomme) syrup**
Top up with		**Cola**

Origin: This infamous drink reached the height of its popularity in the early 1980s. It looks like iced tea disguising its contents - hence the name.
Comment: A cooling combination of five different spirits with a hint of lime and a splash of cola.

LONG ISLAND SPICED TEA

Glass: Collins
Method: **SHAKE** first seven ingredients with ice and strain into ice-filled glass. **TOP** with cola, lightly stir and serve with straws.

1/2	shot(s)	**Spiced rum**
1/2	shot(s)	**Ketel One vodka**
1/2	shot(s)	**Plymouth gin**
1/2	shot(s)	**Sauza Hornitos tequila**
1/2	shot(s)	**Cointreau / triple sec**
1	shot(s)	**Freshly squeezed lime juice**
1/2	shot(s)	**Sugar (gomme) syrup**
Top up with		**Cola**

Comment: A contemporary spicy twist on an American classic.

LOTUS ESPRESSO [NEW]

Glass: Martini
Garnish: Float three coffee beans
Method: **SHAKE** all ingredients with ice and fine strain into chilled glass.

2	shot(s)	**Ketel One vodka**
1/2	shot(s)	**Kahlúa coffee liqueur**
1/2	shot(s)	**Maple syrup**
1	shot(s)	**Espresso coffee (cold)**

Origin: Adapted from a drink discovered in 2005 at Lotus Bar, Sydney, Australia.
Comment: Coffee to the fore but with complex, earthy bitter-sweet notes.

LOTUS MARTINI

Glass: Martini
Garnish: Mint leaf
Method: Lightly **MUDDLE** mint (just to bruise) in base of shaker. Add other ingredients, **SHAKE** with ice and fine strain into chilled glass.

7	fresh	**Fresh mint leaves**
2	shot(s)	**Plymouth gin**
1/4	shot(s)	**Blue curaçao liqueur**
1 1/2	shot(s)	**Lychee syrup from tinned fruit**
1/4	shot(s)	**Sonoma pomegranate (grenadine) syrup**

Origin: Created in 2001 by Martin Walander at Match Bar, London, England.
Comment: This violet coloured drink may have an unlikely list of ingredients, but – boy! - does it look and taste good.

LOUD SPEAKER MARTINI [NEW]

Glass: Martini
Garnish: Lemon peel twist
Method: **SHAKE** all ingredients with ice and fine strain into chilled glass.

1 1/2	shot(s)	**Plymouth gin**
1 1/2	shot(s)	**Rémy Martin cognac**
1/2	shot(s)	**Sweet (rosso) vermouth**
1/4	shot(s)	**Freshly squeezed lemon juice**
1/4	shot(s)	**Sugar (gomme) syrup**

Origin: Adapted from a recipe in the 1930 Savoy Cocktail Book by Harry Craddock. He says, "This it is that gives Radio Announcers their peculiar enunciation. Three of them will produce oscillation, and after five it is possible to reach the osculation stage."
Comment: I've added a dash of sugar to the original recipe which I found too dry.

LOUISIANA TRADE

Glass: Old-fashioned
Garnish: Lime wedge
Method: **SHAKE** all ingredients with ice and strain into glass filled with crushed ice.

2	shot(s)	**Southern Comfort**
1/2	shot(s)	**Maple syrup**
1	shot(s)	**Freshly squeezed lime juice**
1/4	shot(s)	**Sugar (gomme) syrup**

Origin: Created in 2001 by Mehdi Otmann at Zeta, London, England.
Comment: Peach and apricot with the freshness of lime and the dense sweetness of maple syrup.

HOW TO MAKE SUGAR SYRUP

To make your own sugar syrup, gradually pour TWO cups of granulated sugar into a saucepan containing ONE cup of hot water. Stir as you pour and carry on stirring and simmering until the sugar is dissolved. Do not let the water even come close to boiling and only simmer for as long as it takes to dissolve the sugar. Allow syrup to cool and pour into an empty bottle. Ideally, you should finely strain your syrup into the bottle to remove any undissolved crystals which could otherwise encourage crystallisation. If kept in a refrigerator this mixture will last for a couple of months.

●●●●◐○

LOVE JUNK

Glass: Old-fashioned
Garnish: Apple wedge
Method: **SHAKE** all ingredients with ice and strain into ice-filled glass.

2	shot(s)	**Ketel One vodka**
$\frac{1}{2}$	shot(s)	**Midori melon liqueur**
$\frac{1}{2}$	shot(s)	**Peach schnapps liqueur**
$1\frac{1}{2}$	shot(s)	**Pressed apple juice**

Comment: A light, crisp, refreshing blend of peach, melon and apple juice, laced with vodka.

●●●●◐○

LOVED UP

Glass: Martini
Garnish: Berries on stick
Method: **SHAKE** all ingredients with ice and fine strain into chilled glass.

$1\frac{1}{2}$	shot(s)	**Sauza Hornitos tequila**
$\frac{1}{2}$	shot(s)	**Cointreau / triple sec**
$\frac{1}{2}$	shot(s)	**Chambord black raspberry liqueur**
$\frac{1}{2}$	shot(s)	**Freshly squeezed lime juice**
1	shot(s)	**Freshly squeezed orange juice**
$\frac{1}{4}$	shot(s)	**Sugar (gomme) syrup**

Origin: Adapted from a cocktail discovered in 2002 at the Merc Bar, New York City, where the original name was listed as simply 'Love'.
Comment: Tequila predominates in this rusty coloured drink, which also features orange and berry fruit.

●●●●●◐

LUCKY LILY MARGARITA [NEW]

Glass: Coupette
Garnish: Pineapple wedge dusted with pepper on rim
Method: **STIR** honey with tequila in base of shaker to dissolve honey. **ADD** other ingredients, **SHAKE** with ice and fine strain into chilled glass.

2	spoons	**Runny honey**
2	shot(s)	**Sauza Hornitos tequila**
1	shot(s)	**Pressed pineapple juice**
$\frac{3}{4}$	shot(s)	**Freshly squeezed lime juice**
5	grinds	**Black pepper**

Origin: Adapted from a drink discovered in 2006 at All Star Lanes, London, England.
Comment: Spicy tequila and pineapple tingle with balance and flavour.

●●●●◐○

LUCKY LINDY

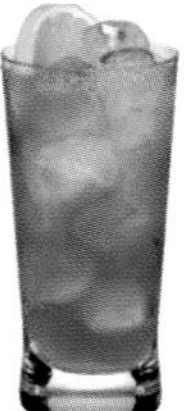

Glass: Collins
Garnish: Lemon wheel
Method: **STIR** honey with bourbon in base of shaker so as to dissolve honey. Add lemon juice, **SHAKE** with ice and strain into ice-filled glass. **TOP** with 7-Up, lightly stir and serve with straws.

3	spoon(s)	**Runny honey**
2	shot(s)	**Bourbon whiskey**
$\frac{1}{2}$	shot(s)	**Freshly squeezed lemon juice**
Top up with		**7-Up**

Origin: Adapted from a drink discovered in 2003 at The Grange Hall, New York City, USA.
Comment: A long refreshing drink that combines whisky, citrus and honey – a long chilled toddy without the spice.

●●●●◐○

LUSH

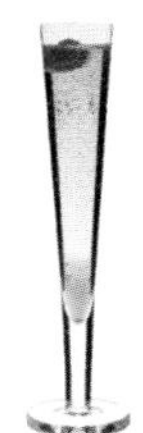

Glass: Flute
Garnish: Raspberry in glass
Method: **POUR** vodka and liqueur into chilled glass, top with champagne and lightly stir.

1	shot(s)	**Ketel One vodka**
$\frac{1}{2}$	shot(s)	**Chambord black raspberry liqueur**
Top up with		**Piper-Heidsieck brut champagne**

Origin: Created in 1999 by Spike Marchant at Alphabet, London, England.
Comment: It is, are you?

●●●●◐○

LUTKINS SPECIAL MARTINI [NEW]

Glass: Martini
Garnish: Orange zest twist
Method: **SHAKE** all ingredients with ice and fine strain into chilled glass.

$1\frac{1}{2}$	shot(s)	**Plymouth gin**
1	shot(s)	**Dry vermouth**
$\frac{1}{2}$	shot(s)	**Apricot brandy liqueur**
$\frac{3}{4}$	shot(s)	**Freshly squeezed orange juice**

Origin: Adapted from a recipe in Harry Craddock's 1930 Savoy Cocktail Book.
Comment: I've tried many variations on the above formula and none are that special.

FOR MORE INFORMATION SEE OUR
INGREDIENTS APPENDIX ON PAGE 320

DRINKS ARE GRADED AS FOLLOWS:
● DISGUSTING ●◐ PRETTY AWFUL ●● BEST AVOIDED
●●◐ DISAPPOINTING ●●● ACCEPTABLE ●●●◐ GOOD
●●●● RECOMMENDED ●●●●◐ HIGHLY RECOMMENDED
●●●●● OUTSTANDING / EXCEPTIONAL

LUX DAIQUIRI

Glass: Martini (large)
Garnish: Maraschino cherry
Method: **BLEND** all ingredients with one 12oz scoop of crushed ice and serve in chilled glass.

3	shot(s)	**Light white rum**
3/4	shot(s)	**Freshly squeezed lime juice**
1/2	shot(s)	**Luxardo maraschino liqueur**
1/4	shot(s)	**Sugar (gomme) syrup**
1/4	shot(s)	**Maraschino syrup (from cherry jar)**

Origin: This was one of two cocktails with which I won a Havana Club Daiquiri competition in 2002. I named it after Girolamo Luxardo, creator of the now famous liqueur, 'Luxardo Maraschino'. My educated sub also informs me Lux is Latin for light.
Comment: A classic frozen Daiquiri heavily laced with maraschino cherry.

LUXURY COCKTAIL [UPDATED]

Glass: Martini
Method: **SHAKE** all ingredients with ice and fine strain into chilled glass.

2	shot(s)	**Plymouth gin**
3/4	shot(s)	**Pimm's No.1 Cup**
1/2	shot(s)	**Crème de bananes liqueur**
3/4	shot(s)	**Sweet (rosso) vermouth**
1/4	shot(s)	**Rose's lime cordial**
3	dashes	**Angostura aromatic bitters**

Comment: Sticky banana followed by a bitter, refined aftertaste.

LUXURY MOJITO

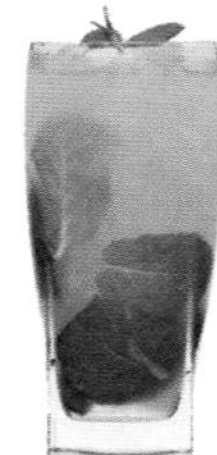

Glass: Collins
Garnish: Mint sprig
Method: **MUDDLE** mint in glass with sugar and lime juice. Fill glass with crushed ice, add rum, Angostura and champagne , then stir.

12	fresh	**Mint leaves**
1/4	shot(s)	**Sugar (gomme) syrup**
1	shot(s)	**Freshly squeezed lime juice**
2	shot(s)	**Appleton Estate V/X aged rum**
3	dashes	**Angostura aromatic bitters**
Top up with		**Piper-Heidsieck brut champagne**

Comment: A Mojito made with aged rum and topped with champagne instead of soda water: more complex than the original.

LYCHEE & BLACKCURRANT MARTINI

Glass: Martini
Garnish: Peeled lychee in glass
Method: **SHAKE** all ingredients with ice and fine strain into chilled glass.

2	shot(s)	**Plymouth gin**
1/2	shot(s)	**Soho lychee liqueur**
1/4	shot(s)	**Crème de cassis**
1/4	shot(s)	**Rose's lime cordial**
3/4	shot(s)	**Chilled mineral water (omit if wet ice)**

Origin: Created by yours truly in 2004.
Comment: Light, fragrant and laced with gin.

LYCHEE & ROSE PETAL MARTINI

Glass: Martini
Garnish: Float rose petal
Method: **STIR** all ingredients with ice and strain into chilled glass.

2	shot(s)	**Plymouth gin**
1	shot(s)	**Rose petal vodka liqueur**
1	shot(s)	**Lychee syrup from tinned fruit**
2	dashes	**Peychaud's aromatic bitters**

Origin: Created in 2002 by Dick Bradsell for Opium, London, England.
Comment: Light pink in colour and subtle in flavour.

LYCHEE & SAKE MARTINI

Glass: Martini
Garnish: Peeled lychee in glass
Method: **STIR** all ingredients with ice and strain into chilled glass.

1 1/2	shot(s)	**Plymouth gin**
2	shot(s)	**Sake**
3/4	shot(s)	**Soho lychee liqueur**

Origin: Created in 2004 by yours truly.
Comment: A soft, Martini styled drink with subtle hints of sake and lychee.

LYCHEE MAC

Glass: Old-fashioned
Garnish: Peeled lychee in drink
Method: **SHAKE** all ingredients with ice and strain into ice-filled glass.

2 1/4	shot(s)	**The Famous Grouse Scotch whisky**
1	shot(s)	**Soho lychee liqueur**
3/4	shot(s)	**Stone's green ginger wine**

Origin: Created by yours truly in 2004.
Comment: Peaty Scotch with sweet lychee and hot ginger.

LYCHEE MARTINI

Glass: Martini
Garnish: Whole lychee from tin
Method: **STIR** all ingredients with ice and fine strain into chilled glass.

2	shot(s)	**Ketel One vodka**
1/2	shot(s)	**Soho lychee liqueur**
1/2	shot(s)	**Dry vermouth**
1	shot(s)	**Lychee syrup from tinned fruit**

Origin: Thought to have been first made in 2001 at Clay, a Korean restaurant in New York City, USA.
Comment: If you like lychee you'll love this delicate Martini.

LYCHEE RICKEY [NEW]

Glass: Collins (small 8oz)
Garnish: Immerse length of lime peel in drink.
Method: **SHAKE** first three ingredients with ice and strain into ice-filled glass. **TOP** with soda water.

2	shot(s)	**Plymouth gin**
1	shot(s)	**Soho lychee liqueur**
1/2	shot(s)	**Freshly squeezed lime juice**
Top up with		**Soda water (club soda)**

Origin: Adapted from a drink discovered in 2005 at Club 97, Hong Kong, China.
Comment: The lychee liqueur dominates this surprisingly dry Rickey.

LYNCHBURG LEMONADE

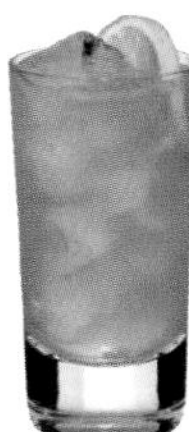

Glass: Collins
Garnish: Lemon slice
Method: **SHAKE** first three ingredients with ice and strain into ice-filled glass. **TOP** with 7-Up.

1 1/2	shot(s)	**Jack Daniel's Tennessee whiskey**
1	shot(s)	**Cointreau / triple sec**
1	shot(s)	**Freshly squeezed lemon juice**
Top up with		**7-Up**

Variant: With three dashes Angostura aromatic bitters.
Origin: Created for the Jack Daniel's distillery in - yep, you guessed it - Lynchburg, Tennessee.
Comment: Tangy, light and very easy to drink.

M.G.F.

Glass: Martini
Garnish: Orange zest twist
Method: **SHAKE** all ingredients with ice and fine strain into chilled glass.

1	shot(s)	**Orange flavoured vodka**
1	shot(s)	**Ketel One Citroen vodka**
1	shot(s)	**Pressed pink grapefruit juice**
1	shot(s)	**Freshly squeezed lemon juice**
1/2	shot(s)	**Sugar (gomme) syrup**

Origin: Discovered in 2003 at Claridge's Bar, London, England.
Comment: Short and sharp.

MAC ORANGE [UPDATED]

Glass: Old-fashioned
Garnish: Orange zest twist
Method: **SHAKE** all ingredients with ice and fine strain into chilled glass.

2	shot(s)	**The Famous Grouse Scotch whisky**
1	shot(s)	**Stone's ginger wine**
1	shot(s)	**Freshly squeezed orange juice**
1/4	shot(s)	**Sugar (gomme) syrup**
3	dashes	**Fee Brothers orange bitters**

Comment: A Whisky Mac with orange topping off the ginger.

MACKA [NEW]

Glass: Collins
Garnish: Lemon slice
Method: **SHAKE** first four ingredients with ice and strain into ice-filled glass. **TOP** with soda.

2	shot(s)	**Plymouth gin**
1/2	shot(s)	**Dry vermouth**
1/2	shot(s)	**Sweet (rosso) vermouth**
1/2	shot(s)	**Crème de cassis**
Top up with		**Soda water (club soda)**

Comment: A long fruity drink for parched palates.

MAD MONK MILKSHAKE

Glass: Collins
Garnish: Tie cord around glass
Method: **SHAKE** all ingredients with ice and strain into ice-filled glass.

2	shot(s)	**Frangelico hazelnut liqueur**
1	shot(s)	**Baileys Irish Cream liqueur**
1/4	shot(s)	**Kahlúa coffee liqueur**
1	shot(s)	**Double (heavy) cream**
2	shot(s)	**Milk**

Variant: Blend instead of shaking and serve frozen.
Comment: Long, creamy and slightly sweet with hazelnut and coffee.

MADRAS

Glass: Collins
Garnish: Orange slice
Method: **SHAKE** all ingredients with ice and strain into ice-filled glass.

2	shot(s)	**Ketel One vodka**
3	shot(s)	**Cranberry juice**
2	shot(s)	**Freshly squeezed orange juice**

Comment: A Seabreeze with orange juice in place of grapefruit juice, making it slightly sweeter.

MADROSKA

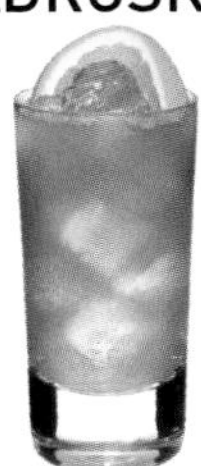

Glass: Collins
Garnish: Orange slice
Method: **SHAKE** all ingredients with ice and strain into ice-filled glass.

2	shot(s)	**Ketel One vodka**
2 1/2	shot(s)	**Pressed apple juice**
1 1/2	shot(s)	**Cranberry juice**
1	shot(s)	**Freshly squeezed orange juice**

Origin: Created in 1998 by Jamie Terrell, London, England.
Comment: A Madras with more than a hint of apple juice.

MAE WEST MARTINI

Glass: Martini
Garnish: Melon wedge on rim
Method: SHAKE all ingredients with ice and fine strain into chilled glass.

2	shot(s)	**Ketel One vodka**
1/2	shot(s)	**Luxardo Amaretto di Saschira liqueur**
1/4	shot(s)	**Midori melon liqueur**
1 1/2	shot(s)	**Cranberry juice**

Comment: A rosé coloured, semi-sweet concoction with a cherry-chocolate flavour.

VIC'S ORIGINAL 1944 MAI TAI

Glass: Mai Tai (16oz old-fashioned)
Garnish: Half spent lime shell, mint sprig, pineapple cube & cherry on stick
Method: "Cut lime in half; squeeze juice over shaved ice in a Mai Tai (double old-fashioned) glass; save one spent shell. Add remaining ingredients and enough shaved ice to fill glass. Hand shake. Decorate with spent lime shell, fresh mint, and a fruit stick."

1	fresh	**Lime**
2	shot(s)	**17yo Wray & Nephew Jamaican rum**
1/2	shot(s)	**Dutch orange curaçao liqueur**
1/4	shot(s)	**Orgeat (almond) sugar syrup**
1/4	shot(s)	**Rock candy syrup**

Comment: In the words of the master, from his Bartender's Guide.

MAI TAI #2 (BEAUMONT-GANTT'S FORMULA)

Glass: Old-fashioned
Garnish: Mint sprig
Method: Lightly muddle mint in base of shaker (just to bruise). Add other ingredients, **SHAKE** with ice and strain glass filled with crushed ice.

12	fresh	**Mint leaves**
1 1/2	shot(s)	**Myers's Planters' Punch rum**
1	shot(s)	**Light white rum**
3/4	shot(s)	**Cointreau / triple sec**
1/2	shot(s)	**Velvet Falernum syrup**
1	shot(s)	**Freshly squeezed lime juice**
1	shot(s)	**Freshly squeezed pink grapefruit juice**
2	dashes	**Angostura aromatic bitters**

Origin: It is claimed that Ernest Raymond Beaumont-Gantt first served this drink in 1933 at his Don The Beachcomber's bar in Hollywood, California. This is some ten years earlier than Bergeron's Mai Tai-Roa Aé moment in cocktail history.
Comment: Whichever of the two created the drink; it is Trader Vic that made it famous and it is his recipe that endures.

DRINKS ARE GRADED AS FOLLOWS:

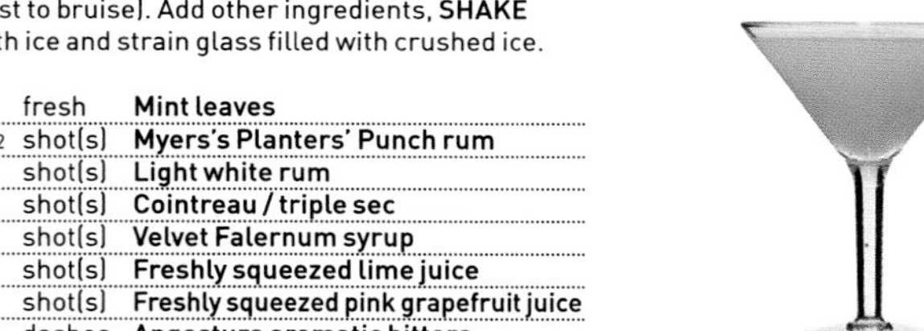

MAI TAI #3 (DIFFORD'S FORMULA)

Glass: Old-fashioned
Garnish: Mint sprig & lime wedge
Method: SHAKE all ingredients with ice and strain into glass filled with crushed ice.

2	shot(s)	**Aged rum**
1/2	shot(s)	**Cointreau / triple sec**
3/4	shot(s)	**Freshly squeezed lime juice**
1/2	shot(s)	**Orgeat (almond) syrup**
1/4	shot(s)	**Sugar (gomme) syrup**

Origin: My adaptation of Victor Bergeron's (Trader Vic's) 1944 classic.
Comment: I love Daiquiris and this is basically a classic Daiquiri with a few bells and whistles.

MAIDEN'S BLUSH [NEW]

Glass: Martini
Garnish: Lemon peel twist
Method: SHAKE all ingredients with ice and fine strain into chilled glass.

2	shot(s)	**Plymouth gin**
1/2	shot(s)	**Cointreau / triple sec**
1/2	shot(s)	**Sonoma pomegranate (grenadine) syrup**
1/4	shot(s)	**Freshly squeezed lemon juice**
1/2	shot(s)	**Chilled mineral water (omit if wet ice)**

Origin: Adapted from a recipe in Harry Craddock's 1930 Savoy Cocktail Book.
Comment: Pale pink, subtle and light.

MAIDEN'S PRAYER [UPDATED]

Glass: Martini
Garnish: Orange zest twist
Method: SHAKE all ingredients with ice and fine strain into chilled glass.

1 1/2	shot(s)	**Plymouth gin**
1	shot(s)	**Cointreau / triple sec**
1	shot(s)	**Freshly squeezed orange juice**
1/2	shot(s)	**Freshly squeezed lemon juice**

Origin: Adapted from a recipe in Harry Craddock's 1930 Savoy Cocktail Book.
Comment: Fresh, zesty orange with a pleasing twang of alcohol.

MAINBRACE

Glass: Martini
Garnish: Orange zest twist
Method: SHAKE all ingredients with ice and fine strain into chilled glass.

1 1/2	shot(s)	**Plymouth gin**
1 1/2	shot(s)	**Cointreau / triple sec**
1 1/2	shot(s)	**Freshly squeezed golden grapefruit juice**

Comment: Full-on grapefruit laced with gin and a hint of orange. Tart finish.

MAI TAI

In 1934, Victor Jules Bergeron, or Trader Vic as he became known, opened his first restaurant in Oakland, San Francisco. He served Polynesian food with a mix of Chinese, French and American dishes cooked in wood-fired ovens. But he is best known for the rum based cocktails he created.

One evening in 1944 he tested a new drink on two friends from Tahiti, Ham and Carrie Guild. After the first sip, Carrie exclaimed,"Mai Tai-Roa Aé", which in Tahitian means 'Out of this world - the best!'.

So Bergeron named his drink the Mai Tai. The original was based on 17 year old Jamaican J.Wray & Nephew rum which Vic in his own guide describes as being "surprisingly golden in colour, medium bodied, but with the rich pungent flavour particular to the Jamaican blends". Vic states he used "rock candy" syrup. This is an old term for the type of strong sugar syrup I prescribe in this guide. You could dangle a piece of string in it to encourage crystallisation and make rock candy.

When supplies of the Jamaican 17-year-old rum dwindled, Vic started using a combination of dark Jamaican rum and Martinique rum to achieve the desired flavour. Sheer demand in his chain of restaurants later necessitated the introduction of a Mai Tai pre-mix (still available from www.tradervics.com).

Others, particularly Ernest Raymond Beaumont-Gantt, then owner of a Hollywood bar called Don the Beachcomber's, have also laid claim to the creation of this drink. But as Vic says in his own Bartender's Guide, "Anybody who says I didn't create this drink is a dirty stinker."

A B C D E F G H I J K L **M** N O P Q R S T U V W X Y Z

MAJOR BAILEY #1 [NEW]

Glass: Sling
Garnish: Mint sprig
Method: Lightly **MUDDLE** (only bruise) mint with gin in base of shaker. Add other ingredients, **SHAKE** with ice and fine strain into glass half filled with crushed ice. **CHURN** (stir) drink with the ice using a barspoon. Top the glass to the brim with more crushed ice and churn again. Serve with straws.

12	fresh	**Mint leaves**
2	shot(s)	**Plymouth gin**
1/4	shot(s)	**Freshly squeezed lime juice**
1/4	shot(s)	**Freshly squeezed lemon juice**
1/2	shot(s)	**Sugar (gomme) syrup**

Origin: Adapted from a recipe in the 1947 Trader Vic's Bartender's Guide by Victor Bergeron.
Comment: As Victor says of this gin based Julep, "This is a hell of a drink."

MAJOR BAILEY #2 [NEW]

Glass: Sling
Garnish: Mint sprig
Method: **BLEND** all ingredients with one 12oz scoop of crushed ice and serve with straws.

2	shot(s)	**Light white rum**
1	shot(s)	**Cointreau / triple sec**
1	shot(s)	**Pressed pineapple juice**
1/2	shot(s)	**Freshly squeezed lemon juice**
1/4	shot(s)	**Sugar (gomme) syrup**

Origin: Adapted from a drink created by Victor Bergeron.
Comment: Made well, this is a long, fruity, brilliant frozen Daiquiri.

MAGIC BUS

Glass: Martini
Garnish: Lime wedge on rim
Method: **SHAKE** all ingredients with ice and fine strain into chilled glass.

1	shot(s)	**Sauza Hornitos tequila**
1	shot(s)	**Cointreau / triple sec**
1	shot(s)	**Cranberry juice**
1	shot(s)	**Freshly squeezed orange juice**

Comment: Orange and cranberry laced with tequila.

MALCOLM LOWRY [NEW]

Glass: Old-fashioned
Garnish: Lime wedge
Method: **SHAKE** all ingredients with ice and strain into ice-filled glass.

1	shot(s)	**Sauza Hornitos tequila**
1/2	shot(s)	**Wray & Nephew overproof white rum**
1/4	shot(s)	**Cointreau / triple sec**
1/2	shot(s)	**Freshly squeezed lime juice**
1/4	shot(s)	**Sugar (gomme) syrup**

Origin: Created by drinks author David Broom. Named after Malcolm Lowry's 1947 novel 'Under the Volcano' which explores a man's battle with alcoholism in Mexico.
Comment: A suitably 'hard' and flavoursome Daiquiri-like drink.

MAMBO

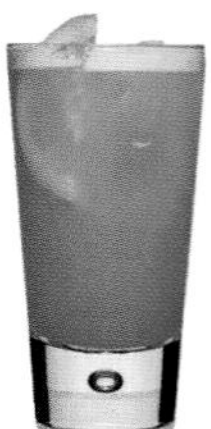

Glass: Collins
Garnish: Orange slice
Method: **SHAKE** all ingredients with ice and strain into ice-filled glass.

1	shot(s)	**Ketel One vodka**
1	shot(s)	**Cointreau / triple sec**
1	shot(s)	**Apricot brandy liqueur**
1/4	shot(s)	**Campari**
3	shot(s)	**Freshly squeezed orange juice**

Origin: Created by Nichole Colella.
Comment: A slightly bitter, tangy, orange, cooling drink.

MAN-BOUR-TINI

Glass: Martini
Garnish: Orange zest twist
Method: **SHAKE** all ingredients with ice and fine strain into chilled glass.

1	shot(s)	**Mandarine Napoléon liqueur**
3/4	shot(s)	**Bourbon whiskey**
1/2	shot(s)	**Freshly squeezed lime juice**
2	shot(s)	**Cranberry juice**
1/4	shot(s)	**Sugar (gomme) syrup**

Origin: Created in 1999 by yours truly.
Comment: A rounded, fruity, bourbon based drink with mandarin and lime sourness.

MANDARINE COLLINS

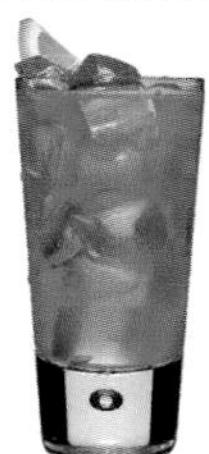

Glass: Collins
Garnish: Half orange slice
Method: **SHAKE** first three ingredients with ice and strain into ice-filled glass. **TOP** with soda.

1 1/2	shot(s)	**Plymouth gin**
1	shot(s)	**Mandarine Napoléon liqueur**
1	shot(s)	**Freshly squeezed lemon juice**
Top up with		**Soda water (club soda)**

Comment: A tangy, long refreshing drink with an intense mandarin flavour.

MANDARINE SIDECAR [NEW]

Glass: Martini
Garnish: Sugar rim (optional) & lemon zest twist
Method: **SHAKE** all ingredients with ice and fine strain into chilled glass.

1 1/2	shot(s)	**Rémy Martin cognac**
1	shot(s)	**Mandarine Napoléon liqueur**
1	shot(s)	**Freshly squeezed lemon juice**
3/4	shot(s)	**Chilled mineral water (omit if wet ice)**
1/8	shot(s)	**Sugar (gomme) syrup**

Comment: Wonderfully tart and strong in flavour.

MANDARINE SONGBIRD [NEW]

Glass: Collins
Garnish: Orange slice
Method: SHAKE first three ingredients with ice and fine strain into ice-filled glass. **TOP** with ginger beer.

2	shot(s)	**Mandarine Napoléon liqueur**
1/2	shot(s)	**Freshly squeezed lemon juice**
3/4	shot(s)	**Freshly squeezed orange juice**
Top up with		**Ginger beer**

Comment: Long, spicy orange.

MANDARINE SOUR

Glass: Old-fashioned
Garnish: Lemon slice
Method: SHAKE all ingredients with ice and strain into ice-filled glass.

2	shot(s)	**Mandarine Napoléon liqueur**
1	shot(s)	**Freshly squeezed lemon juice**
1/4	shot(s)	**Sugar (gomme) syrup**
1/2	fresh	**Egg white**

Comment: Sour, but with a strong mandarin sweetness.

MANDARINTINI [NEW]

Glass: Martini
Garnish: Orange slice on rim
Method: SHAKE all ingredients with ice and fine strain into chilled glass.

1 1/2	shot(s)	**Orange flavoured vodka**
1/2	shot(s)	**Campari**
1/2	shot(s)	**Grand Marnier liqueur**
1 1/2	shot(s)	**Pressed apple juice**

Origin: Adapted from a drink discovered in 2005 at Aqua Spirit, Hong Kong, China.
Comment: This bittersweet palate cleanser looks like pink grapefruit juice.

MANDARITO [UPDATED]

Glass: Collins
Garnish: Mint sprig
Method: Lightly **MUDDLE** mint (just to bruise) in base of glass. Add next four ingredients, half fill glass with crushed ice and **CHURN** (stir). Fill glass to brim with more crushed ice and churn some more. **TOP** with soda, stir and serve with straws.

12	fresh	**Mint leaves**
1 1/2	shot(s)	**Mandarine Napoléon liqueur**
1	shot(s)	**Ketel One vodka**
1	shot(s)	**Freshly squeezed lime juice**
1/8	shot(s)	**Sugar (gomme) syrup**
Top up with		**Soda water (club soda)**

Comment: A vodka Mojito with mandarin accents.

MANGO BATIDA

Glass: Collins
Garnish: Mango slice
Method: SHAKE all ingredients with ice and strain into ice-filled glass.

2 1/2	shot(s)	**Cachaça**
2	shot(s)	**Sweetened mango purée**
1	shot(s)	**Freshly squeezed lemon juice**

Origin: Formula by yours truly in 2004.
Comment: Depending on the sweetness of the mango purée, this drink may benefit from the addition of a dash of sugar syrup.

MANGO COLLINS

Glass: Collins
Garnish: Lemon slice
Method: SHAKE first three ingredients with ice and strain into ice-filled glass. **TOP** with soda, stir and serve with straws.

2	shot(s)	**Plymouth gin**
2	shot(s)	**Sweetened mango purée**
1 1/2	shot(s)	**Freshly squeezed lemon juice**
Top up with		**Soda water (club soda)**

Origin: Formula by yours truly in 2004.
Comment: Lemon juice and gin combine with mango in this refreshing tall drink.

MANGO DAIQUIRI

Glass: Martini
Garnish: Lime wedge on rim
Method: SHAKE all ingredients with ice and fine strain into chilled glass.

2	shot(s)	**Light white rum**
2	shot(s)	**Sweetened mango purée**
1/2	shot(s)	**Freshly squeezed lime juice**

Origin: Formula by yours truly in 2004.
Variant: Blended with 12oz scoop crushed ice and an additional half shot of sugar syrup.
Comment: Tropical yet potent and refreshing.

MANGO MARGARITA #1 (SERVED 'UP')

Glass: Coupette
Garnish: Lime wedge on rim
Method: SHAKE all ingredients with ice and fine strain into chilled glass.

2	shot(s)	**Sauza Hornitos tequila**
1	shot(s)	**Sweetened mango purée**
1	shot(s)	**Cointreau / triple sec**
1	shot(s)	**Freshly squeezed lime juice**

Origin: Formula by yours truly in 2004.
Comment: The character of the tequila is not overwhelmed by the fruit.

A B C D E F G H I J K L M N O P Q R S T U V W X Y Z

MANGO MARGARITA #2 (FROZEN) [NEW]

Glass: Coupette
Garnish: Mango slice on rim
Method: BLEND all ingredients with 12oz scoop crushed ice. Serve with straws.

2	shot(s)	**Sauza Hornitos tequila**
3/4	shot(s)	**Sweetened mango purée**
1	shot(s)	**Cointreau / triple sec**
1/2	shot(s)	**Freshly squeezed lime juice**
1/4	shot(s)	**Sugar (gomme) syrup**

Origin: Formula by yours truly in 2006.
Comment: Mango first and Margarita second.

MANGO MARTINI

Glass: Martini
Garnish: Mango slice on rim
Method: SHAKE all ingredients with ice and fine strain into chilled glass.

2 1/2	shot(s)	**Ketel One Citroen vodka**
2	shot(s)	**Sweetened mango purée**

Origin: Formula by yours truly in 2004.
Comment: This drink doesn't work nearly so well with plain vodka - if citrus vodka is not available, try using gin.

MANGO PUNCH

Glass: Collins
Garnish: Mango slice (dried or fresh)
Method: SHAKE all ingredients with ice and fine strain into glass filled with crushed ice.

2	shot(s)	**Wray & Nephew overproof rum**
3	shot(s)	**Sweetened mango purée**
3/4	shot(s)	**Freshly squeezed lime juice**
3/4	shot(s)	**Sugar (gomme) syrup**

Origin: Created in 2004 by yours truly.
Comment: A distinctly tropical cocktail flavoured with mango.

MANGO RUM COOLER

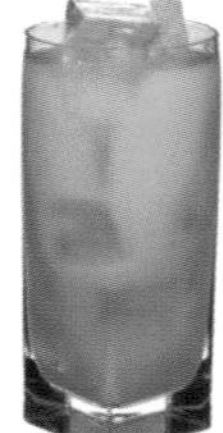

Glass: Collins
Garnish: Mango slice (dried or fresh)
Method: SHAKE all ingredients with ice and strain into ice-filled glass.

2 1/2	shot(s)	**Light white rum**
1 1/2	shot(s)	**Sweetened mango purée**
1	shot(s)	**Pressed apple juice**
1 1/2	shot(s)	**Freshly squeezed lemon juice**

Origin: Created in 2004 by yours truly.
Comment: Long, fruity and cooling.

MANHATTAN DRY

Glass: Martini
Garnish: Twist of orange (discarded) & two maraschino cherries
Method: STIR all ingredients with ice and strain into chilled glass.

2 1/2	shot(s)	**Bourbon whiskey**
1	shot(s)	**Dry vermouth**
3	dashes	**Angostura aromatic bitters**

Variant: Served over ice in an old-fashioned glass.
Comment: A bone dry Manhattan for those with dry palates.

MANHATTAN PERFECT

Glass: Martini
Garnish: Twist of orange (discarded) & two maraschino cherries
Method: STIR all ingredients with ice and strain into chilled glass.

2 1/2	shot(s)	**Bourbon whiskey**
1/2	shot(s)	**Sweet (rosso) vermouth**
1/2	shot(s)	**Dry vermouth**
3	dashes	**Angostura aromatic bitters**

Variant: Served over ice in an old-fashioned glass.
Comment: The Manhattan version most popularly served - medium dry.

MANHATTAN SWEET

Glass: Martini
Garnish: Twist of orange (discarded) & two maraschino cherries
Method: STIR all ingredients with ice and strain into chilled glass.

2 1/2	shot(s)	**Bourbon whiskey**
1	shot(s)	**Sweet (rosso) vermouth**
1/8	shot(s)	**Syrup from jar of maraschino cherries**
3	dashes	**Angostura aromatic bitters**

Variant: Served over ice in an old-fashioned glass.
Comment: I must confess to preferring my Manhattans served sweet, or perfect at a push. The Manhattan is complex, challenging and moreish. Best of all, it's available in a style to suit every palate.

MANHATTAN ISLAND

Glass: Martini
Garnish: Maraschino cherry
Method: STIR all ingredients with ice and fine strain into chilled glass.

2	shot(s)	**Rémy Martin cognac**
1	shot(s)	**Sweet (rosso) vermouth**
3	dashes	**Angostura aromatic bitters**
1/8	shot(s)	**Luxardo maraschino liqueur**

Comment: A twist on the classic Harvard, or brandy based Manhattan.

MANHATTAN

Like so many cocktails, the origins of the Manhattan are lost in time. The drink started appearing in cocktail books around the 1880s and popular legend states that it was created on 18 November 1874 at the Manhattan Club in New York City for Lady Randolph Churchill, American mother of Winston. She was at a party to celebrate the successful gubernatorial campaign of Samuel Jones Tilden. (The celebrated Manhattan Club was opposite the site that is now the Empire State Building). Others claim it was invented in the 1860s by a man called Black who ran a saloon on Broadway.

The Manhattan was originally made with rye whiskey but it is now common to use bourbon. When Scotch is substituted it becomes a Rob Roy, with brandy (cognac) it is a Harvard and it is a Star Cocktail when made with applejack.

Some time in 2005 it became conventional in some bars to garnish a Manhattan with two cherries as a 9/11 tribute.

MARGARITA

Basically a Sidecar made with tequila in place of cognac, there are many people who claim to have invented the Margarita. The following are just a few of the more plausible stories: the last is most widely regarded as fact.

Pancho Morales, a bartender from Juarez, Mexico, was asked to make a 'Magnolia' but couldn't remember the ingredients, so threw something together. Although it was not what the customer ordered, she loved it. Her name was Margarita.

Carlos Herrera created the cocktail for a lady called Marjorie who drank no spirit but tequila. He added Cointreau and lime and the unique salt rim which caught people's attention at the bar.

Daniel (Danny) Negrete created the drink in 1936 for his girlfriend, called Margarita, when he was the manager of Garci Crespo Hotel in Puebla, Mexico.

Vernon Underwood was president of Young's Market Company, who in the 1930s had started distributing Cuervo tequila. He went to Johnny Durlesser, head bartender of the Tail O' The Cock in LA, and asked him to create something using his spirit. He named it after his wife Margaret and hispanicised her name to Margarita.

Sara Morales, an expert in Mexican folklore, claimed the Margarita was created in 1930 by Doña Bertha, owner of Bertha's Bar in Taxco, Mexico.

The drink could be named after Margarita Island, located in the Caribbean north of Venezuela, two-and-a-half hours from Miami. Margarita is also the Spanish equivalent of the girl's name 'Margaret', and the Spanish word for daisy.

In 1948 a socialite called Margaret Sames was hosting a party at her cliff-side house in Acapulco, Mexico. Among her guests was Nicky Hilton of the famous hotel family (and one of Liz Taylor's many ex-husbands). Looking for something to pep up the party, Margaret began to experiment at the bar and created the first Margarita. She thought nothing of it until, when flying home to San Antonio from Acapulco airport, she saw a bar advertising 'Margarita's Drink', a cocktail with exactly the same ingredients as her own.

MAPLE OLD-FASHIONED

Glass: Martini
Garnish: Orange zest twist
Method: **STIR** one shot of the bourbon with two ice cubes in a glass. Add maple syrup and Angostura and two more ice cubes. Stir some more and add another two ice cubes and the rest of the bourbon. Stir lots more so as to melt the ice, then add fresh ice to complete the drink. The melting and stirring in of ice cubes is essential to the dilution and taste of this drink.

2	shot(s)	**Bourbon whiskey**
1/2	shot(s)	**Maple syrup**
2	dashes	**Angostura aromatic bitters**

Origin: Discovered in 2004 at Indigo Yard, Edinburgh, Scotland.
Comment: Maple syrup replaces sugar in this reworking of the classic Old-fashioned.

MAPLE LEAF [NEW]

Glass: Old-fashioned
Garnish: Lemon zest twist
Method: **SHAKE** all ingredients with ice and strain into ice-filled glass.

2	shot(s)	**Bourbon whiskey**
1/2	shot(s)	**Freshly squeezed lemon juice**
1/4	shot(s)	**Maple syrup**

Comment: This trio combine wonderfully with maple to the fore.

MAPLE POMME [NEW]

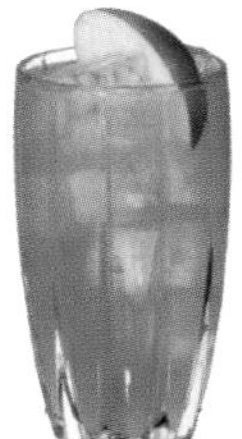

Glass: Collins
Garnish: Apple wedge
Method: **SHAKE** first four ingredients with ice and strain into ice-filled glass. **TOP** with ginger ale, lightly stir and serve with straws.

2	shot(s)	**The Famous Grouse Scotch whisky**
1/2	shot(s)	**Freshly squeezed lemon juice**
1	shot(s)	**Pressed apple juice**
1/2	shot(s)	**Maple syrup**
Top up with		**Ginger ale**

Origin: Adapted from a short drink created in 2005 by Tonin Kacaj at Maze, London, England.
Comment: Scotch based drink for warm weather.

MARACUJA BATIDA [NEW]

Glass: Collins
Garnish: Lemon slice
Method: Cut passion fruit in half and scoop out flesh into shaker. Add other ingredients, **SHAKE** with ice and fine strain into ice-filled glass.

2	fresh	**Passion fruit**
2	shot(s)	**Cachaça**
3/4	shot(s)	**Freshly squeezed lemon juice**
3/4	shot(s)	**Sugar (gomme) syrup**

Variant: Serve blended with crushed ice (add half a shot of passion fruit syrup to the above recipe).
Origin: The Batida is a traditional Brazilian drink and 'maracuja' means passion fruit in Portuguese.
Comment: Cachaça combines with passion fruit.

MARAMA RUM PUNCH [NEW]

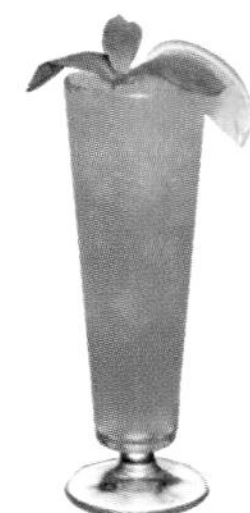

Glass: Sling
Garnish: Mint sprig & lime wedge
Method: Lightly **MUDDLE** mint (just to bruise). Add next five ingredients, **SHAKE** with ice and strain into ice-filled glass. **TOP** with 7-Up, lightly stir and serve with straws.

12	fresh	**Mint leaves**
1 1/2	shot(s)	**Wray & Nephew overproof rum**
1/2	shot(s)	**Cointreau / triple sec**
1/2	shot(s)	**Freshly squeezed lime juice**
1/2	shot(s)	**Almond (orgeat) syrup**
3	dashes	**Angostura aromatic bitters**
Top up with		**7-Up**

Comment: A tangy, well-balanced punch.

MARGARITA #1 (STRAIGHT-UP)

Glass: Coupette
Garnish: Salt rim & lime wedge
Method: **SHAKE** all ingredients with ice and fine strain into chilled glass.

2	shot(s)	**Sauza Hornitos tequila**
1	shot(s)	**Cointreau / triple sec**
1	shot(s)	**Freshly squeezed lime juice**

Variant: Margaritas made with premium tequilas are sometimes referred to as 'Deluxe' or 'Cadillac' Margaritas.
Tip: For the perfect salt rim, liquidise sea salt to make it finer, then run a lime wedge around the outside edge of the glass before dipping the rim in salt. Rimming only half the glass with salt gives the drinker the option of enjoying the cocktail with or without salt.
Comment: One of the great classics.

MARGARITA #2 (ON THE ROCKS)

Glass: Old-fashioned
Garnish: Salt rim & lime wedge
Method: **SHAKE** all ingredients with ice and strain into ice-filled glass.

2	shot(s)	**Sauza Hornitos tequila**
1	shot(s)	**Cointreau / triple sec**
1	shot(s)	**Freshly squeezed lime juice**

Comment: Tangy citrus, tequila and salt.

MARGARITA #3 (FROZEN) [UPDATED]

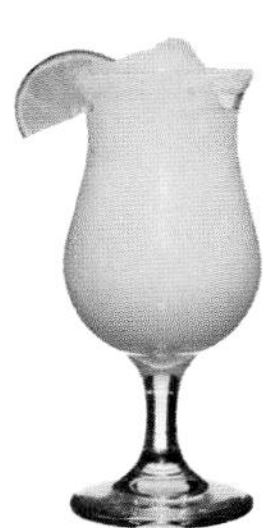

Glass: Martini
Garnish: Maraschino cherry
Method: **BLEND** all ingredients with 12oz scoop of crushed ice. Serve heaped in the glass and with straws.

1 1/2	shot(s)	**Sauza Hornitos tequila**
3/4	shot(s)	**Cointreau / triple sec**
3/4	shot(s)	**Freshly squeezed lime juice**
1/2	shot(s)	**Sugar (gomme) syrup**

Variant: With fruit and/or fruit liqueurs.
Comment: Citrus freshness with the subtle agave of tequila served frozen.

MARGARITA #4 (SALT FOAM FLOAT) [NEW]

Glass: Coupette
Garnish: Lime wedge on rim
Method: Combine first three ingredients, **POUR** into cream whipping siphon and **CHARGE** with nitrous oxide. Shake and place siphon in a refrigerator for one hour prior to making drink. **SHAKE** next three ingredients with ice and fine strain into chilled glass. **SQUIRT** salt foam over surface of drink from siphon.

4 spoons **Sea salt**
1 pint **Chilled mineral water**
2 fresh **Egg whites**
2 shot(s) **Sauza Hornitos tequila**
1 shot(s) **Cointreau / triple sec**
1 shot(s) **Freshly squeezed lime juice**

Comment: Classic Margarita with a salty foam topping.

MARGUERITE MARTINI [NEW]

Glass: Martini
Garnish: Orange zest twist
Method: **SHAKE** all ingredients with ice and fine strain into chilled glass.

2 shot(s) **Plymouth gin**
½ shot(s) **Dry vermouth**
1 dash **Fee Brothers orange bitters**

Origin: Adapted from a recipe in Harry Craddock's 1930 Savoy Cocktail Book.
Comment: A slightly wet yet bone dry classic Martini with a hint of orange.

MARIA THERESA MARGARITA [NEW]

Glass: Martini
Garnish: Lime wedge on rim
Method: **STIR** honey with tequila in base of shaker to dissolve honey. **ADD** other ingredients, **SHAKE** with ice and fine strain into chilled glass.

2 spoons **Runny honey**
2 shot(s) **Sauza Hornitos tequila**
1 shot(s) **Cranberry juice**
½ shot(s) **Freshly squeezed lime juice**

Origin: Adapted from a Tiki drink created by Victor Bergeron (Trader Vic).
Comment: Originally sweetened with sugar syrup, this is better smoothed with honey.

MARMALADE MARTINI [NEW]

Glass: Martini
Garnish: Orange zest twist
Method: **SHAKE** all ingredients with ice and fine strain into chilled glass.

4 spoons **Orange marmalade**
2 shot(s) **Plymouth gin**
½ shot(s) **Freshly squeezed lemon juice**

Origin: Adapted from a recipe in the 1930 Savoy Cocktail Book by Harry Craddock (the original recipe serves six people).
Comment: Harry wrote of his own drink, "By its bitter-sweet taste this cocktail is especially suited to be a luncheon aperitif."

MARMARITA [NEW]

Glass: Coupette
Garnish: Wipe Marmite (yeast extract) around rim
Method: **SHAKE** all ingredients with ice and fine strain into chilled glass.

2 shot(s) **Sauza Hornitos tequila**
1 shot(s) **Cointreau**
1 shot(s) **Freshly squeezed lime juice**

Origin: Created in 2005 by Simon (Ginger) at Blanch House, Brighton, England.
Comment: A Margarita with a Marmite rim. After all, yeast extract is slightly salty.

MARNY COCKTAIL [NEW]

Glass: Martini
Garnish: Orange zest twist
Method: **SHAKE** all ingredients with ice and fine strain into chilled glass.

2 shot(s) **Plymouth gin**
1 shot(s) **Grand Marnier liqueur**
2 dashes **Fee Brothers orange bitters (optional)**

Origin: Adapted from a recipe in Harry Craddock's 1930 Savoy Cocktail Book.
Comment: Spirit and liqueur in harmony.

MARQUEE [UPDATED]

Glass: Martini
Garnish: Raspberries on stick
Method: **SHAKE** all ingredients with ice and fine strain into chilled glass.

1½ shot(s) **Bourbon whiskey**
1½ shot(s) **Cranberry juice**
½ shot(s) **Chambord black raspberry liqueur**
½ shot(s) **Freshly squeezed lemon juice**
¼ shot(s) **Sugar (gomme) syrup**

Origin: Created in 1998 by Giovanni Burdi at Match EC1, London, England.
Comment: Raspberry and bourbon combine perfectly in this short, slightly sweet, fruity drink.

MARTINEZ [UPDATED]

Glass: Martini
Garnish: Lemon zest twist
Method: **STIR** all ingredients with ice and strain into chilled glass.

1½ shot(s) **Plymouth gin**
1½ shot(s) **Sweet (rosso) vermouth**
¼ shot(s) **Cointreau / triple sec**
2 dashes **Fee Brothers orange bitters (optional)**

Variant: Use maraschino liqueur in place of orange liqueur.
Origin: Supposedly the forerunner of the modern Dry Martini, this was created in 1870 by 'Professor' Jerry Thomas using a sweet style of gin known as 'Old Tom'.
Comment: This medium dry Martini is somewhat more approachable than a Dry Martini.

THE MARTINI

The origin of the classic Martini is disputed and shrouded in mystery. Many books have been written on the subject, and it's a topic which can raise temperatures among drinks aficionados. Most agree that it was created some time around the turn of the last century.

When or wherever the Martini was actually invented, and however it acquired its name, for several decades the name was only applied to a drink containing gin and vermouth in varying proportions. Then came the Vodkatini which extended the meaning of the name. But even then, if a drink didn't contain gin and/or vodka and vermouth it simply wasn't a Martini. Purists hold to this definition today.

Language and the meaning of words are changing faster than ever, and today pretty much any drink served in a V-shaped glass is popularly termed a 'Martini' regardless of its contents. These contemporary, non-traditional Martinis are sometimes referred to as Neo-martinis or Alternatinis and the pages of this guide are filled with such drinks.

I believe a drink should at least be based on gin or vodka to properly be termed a Martini, and ideally should also include vermouth. However, you'll find plenty of drinks in my guides called 'Something' Martini containing all manner of fruits and liqueurs and not a single drop of vermouth – their only claim to the name is the V-shaped glass they are served in.

Even the name of the iconic glass has changed. The old guard of bartending still insist on referring to it as a 'Cocktail Glass'. To my understanding that's now a generic term for glasses designed to hold cocktails, a term which also encompasses the likes of Hurricanes, Slings and Coupettes. Today a V-shaped glass is commonly known as a Martini glass.

For those seeking traditional Martinis based on gin and/or vodka with vermouth and without muddled fruit and suchlike, here are a few classic variations.

Dickens Martini – without a twist.
Dirty Martini – with the brine from an olive jar.
Dry Martini (Traditional) – stirred with gin/vodka.
Dry Martini (Naked) – frozen gin/vodka poured into a frozen glass coated with vermouth.
Franklin Martini - named after Franklin Roosevelt and served with two olives.
Gibson Martini – with two onions instead of an olive or a twist.
Martinez – said to be the original Martini.
Medium Martini – A wet Martini with dry sweet vermouth.
Vesper Martini – James Bond's Martini, with gin and vodka.
Vodkatini – very dry, vodka based Martini.
Wet Martini – heavy on the vermouth.

Please see relevant entries in this guide and my account of the Dry Martini on page 102.

A B C D E F G H I J K L M N O P Q R S T U V W X Y Z

●●●●◐○

MARTINI ROYALE

Glass: Martini
Garnish: Lemon zest twist
Method: **STIR** vodka and crème de cassis with ice and strain into chilled glass. **TOP** with chilled champagne.

1½ shot(s)	**Ketel One vodka**
½ shot(s)	**Crème de cassis liqueur**
Top up with	**Piper-Heidsieck brut champagne**

Origin: Created in 2001 by Dick Bradsell at Monte's, London, England.
Comment: The Kir Royale meets the vodkatini in this pink but powerful drink.

●●●●●◐

MARTINI SPECIAL [NEW]

Glass: Martini
Garnish: Orange zest twist
Method: Fill glass with ice and **POUR** absinthe and Angostura over ice. Top with chilled mineral water and leave to stand. **SHAKE** gin, vermouth and orange water with ice. **DISCARD** contents of standing glass and fine strain shaken drink into washed glass.

¼ shot(s)	**La Fée Parisian 68% absinthe**
4 dashes	**Angostura aromatic bitters**
Top up with	**Chilled mineral water**
2 shot(s)	**Plymouth gin**
¾ shot(s)	**Sweet (rosso) vermouth**
⅛ shot(s)	**Orange flower water**

Origin: Adapted from a recipe in Harry Craddock's 1930 Savoy Cocktail Book.
Comment: Aromatic, very dry and very serious – yet it has a frothy head.

●●●●○

MARTINI THYME

Glass: Martini
Garnish: Thread three green olives onto thyme sprig
Method: **MUDDLE** thyme in base of shaker. **ADD** other ingredients, **SHAKE** with ice and fine strain into chilled glass.

2 sprigs	**Lemon thyme (remove stalks)**
1 shot(s)	**Plymouth gin**
¾ shot(s)	**Green Chartreuse**
¼ shot(s)	**Sugar (gomme) syrup**

Origin: A combination of two very similar drinks, that both originally called for thyme infused gin. The first I discovered at The Lobby Bar (One Aldwych, London) and the other came from Tony Conigliaro at Isola, London, England.
Comment: A wonderfully fresh herbal Martini with the distinctive taste of Chartreuse. You'll either love it or hate it.

DRINKS ARE GRADED AS FOLLOWS:

● DISGUSTING ●◐ PRETTY AWFUL ●● BEST AVOIDED
●●◐ DISAPPOINTING ●●● ACCEPTABLE ●●●◐ GOOD
●●●● RECOMMENDED ●●●●◐ HIGHLY RECOMMENDED
●●●●● OUTSTANDING / EXCEPTIONAL

●●●●●

MARY PICKFORD

Glass: Martini
Garnish: Maraschino cherry
Method: **SHAKE** all ingredients with ice and fine strain into chilled glass.

2 shot(s)	**Light white rum**
1½ shot(s)	**Pressed pineapple juice**
¼ shot(s)	**Sonoma pomegranate (grenadine) syrup**
⅛ shot(s)	**Luxardo maraschino liqueur**

Origin: Created in the 1920s (during prohibition) by Fred Kaufman at the Hotel Nacîonal de Cuba, Havana, for the silent movie star. She was in Cuba filming a movie with her husband Douglas Fairbanks and Charlie Chaplin.
Comment: When made correctly, this pale pink cocktail has a perfect balance between the fruit flavours and the spirit of the rum.

●●●●◐

MARY QUEEN OF SCOTS [NEW]

Glass: Martini
Garnish: Sugar rim & maraschino cherry
Method: **SHAKE** all ingredients with ice and fine strain into chilled glass.

1½ shot(s)	**The Famous Grouse Scotch whisky**
¾ shot(s)	**Drambuie liqueur**
¾ shot(s)	**Green Chartreuse**

Origin: Discovered in 2006 on Kyle Branch's Cocktail Hotel blog (www.cocktailhotel.blogspot.com). Mary Stuart, Mary Queen of Scots, was born on December 8th 1542 at Linlithgow Palace in West Lothian. On February 8th 1587, she was executed in the Great Hall of Fotheringhay.
Comment: Slightly sweet but herbal, serious and strong.

●●●●○

MARY ROSE

Glass: Martini
Garnish: Lime twist (discard) & rosemary sprig
Method: **MUDDLE** rosemary in base of shaker. Add other ingredients, **SHAKE** with ice and fine strain into chilled glass.

1 sprig	**Fresh rosemary**
2 shot(s)	**Plymouth gin**
1 shot(s)	**Green Chartreuse liqueur**
½ shot(s)	**Sugar (gomme) syrup**
½ shot(s)	**Chilled mineral water (omit if wet ice)**

Origin: Created in 1999 by Philip Jeffrey at the Great Eastern Hotel, London, England. Named after King Henry VIII's warship, sunk during an engagement with the French fleet in 1545 and now on display in Portsmouth.
Comment: Herbal, herbal and herbal with a hint of spice.

MAURICE MARTINI [NEW]

Glass: Martini
Garnish: Orange zest twist
Method: **SHAKE** all ingredients with ice and fine strain into chilled glass.

1½	shot(s)	**Plymouth gin**
¾	shot(s)	**Dry vermouth**
¾	shot(s)	**Sweet (rosso) vermouth**
¼	shot(s)	**La Fée Parisian 68% absinthe**
¾	shot(s)	**Freshly squeezed orange juice**

Origin: Adapted from a recipe in Harry Craddock's 1930 Savoy Cocktail Book.
Comment: A perfect Martini with an aromatic burst of absinthe and a hint of orange.

MAT THE RAT

Glass: Collins
Garnish: Lime wedge
Method: **SHAKE** first four ingredients with ice and strain into ice-filled glass. **TOP** with 7-Up, lightly stir and serve with straws.

2	shot(s)	**Spiced rum**
½	shot(s)	**Cointreau / triple sec**
1½	shot(s)	**Freshly squeezed orange juice**
½	shot(s)	**Freshly squeezed lime juice**
Top up with		**7-Up**

Origin: A popular drink in UK branches of TGI Friday's, where it was created.
Comment: Whether or not Mat was a rat, we shall never know. However, the drink that's named after him is long and thirst-quenching.

MATADOR

Glass: Collins
Garnish: Pineapple wedge on rim
Method: **SHAKE** all ingredients with ice and strain into ice-filled glass.

2	shot(s)	**Sauza Hornitos tequila**
1	shot(s)	**Cointreau / triple sec**
1	shot(s)	**Freshly squeezed lime juice**
2	shot(s)	**Pressed pineapple juice**

Comment: A long Margarita with pineapple juice. The lime and tequila work wonders with the sweet pineapple.

MAURESQUE

Glass: Collins (10oz max)
Method: **POUR** pastis and almond syrup into glass. Serve iced water separately in a small jug (known in France as a 'broc') so the customer can dilute to their own taste (I recommend five shots). Lastly, add ice to fill glass.

1	shot(s)	**Ricard pastis**
½	shot(s)	**Almond (orgeat) syrup**
Top up with		**Chilled mineral water**

Origin: Pronounced 'Mor-Esk', this drink is very popular in the South of France.
Comment: Long, refreshing aniseed, liquorice and almond.

MAYAN

Glass: Old-fashioned
Garnish: Float 3 coffee beans
Method: **SHAKE** all ingredients with ice and strain into ice-filled glass.

1½	shot(s)	**Sauza Hornitos tequila**
½	shot(s)	**Kahlúa coffee liqueur**
2½	shot(s)	**Pressed pineapple juice**

Comment: Tequila, coffee and pineapple juice combine in this medium dry short drink.

MAYAN WHORE

Glass: Sling
Garnish: Split pineapple wedge
Method: **SHAKE** first three ingredients with ice and strain into ice-filled glass. **TOP** with soda, **DO NOT STIR** and serve with straws.

2	shot(s)	**Sauza Hornitos tequila**
1½	shot(s)	**Pressed pineapple juice**
¾	shot(s)	**Kahlúa coffee liqueur**
Top up with		**Soda water (club soda)**

Comment: An implausible ménage à trois: coffee, tequila and pineapple, served long.

MAYFAIR COCKTAIL [NEW]

Glass: Martini
Garnish: Orange zest twist
Method: **MUDDLE** cloves in base of shaker. Add other ingredients, **SHAKE** with ice and fine strain into chilled glass.

2	dried	**Cloves**
2	shot(s)	**Plymouth gin**
1	shot(s)	**Apricot brandy liqueur**
1	shot(s)	**Freshly squeezed orange juice**
¼	shot(s)	**Sugar (gomme) syrup**

Variant: With World's End Pimento Dram liqueur in place of sugar.
Origin: Adapted from a recipe in Harry Craddock's 1930 Savoy Cocktail Book.
Comment: The kind of spiced drink you'd usually expect to be served hot.

THE MAYFLOWER MARTINI

Glass: Martini
Garnish: Edible flower petal
Method: **SHAKE** all ingredients with ice and fine strain into chilled glass.

1½	shot(s)	**Plymouth gin**
½	shot(s)	**Apricot brandy liqueur**
1	shot(s)	**Pressed apple juice**
¼	shot(s)	**Elderflower cordial**
½	shot(s)	**Freshly squeezed lemon juice**

Origin: Created in 2002 by Wayne Collins for Maxxium UK.
Comment: Fragrant balance of English fruits and flowers.

MAXIM'S COFFEE (HOT) [NEW]

Glass: Toddy
Garnish: Float 3 coffee beans
Method: **POUR** all ingredients into warmed glass and **STIR**.

1	shot(s)	**Rémy Martin cognac**
1/2	shot(s)	**Bénédictine D.O.M. liqueur**
1/4	shot(s)	**Galliano liqueur**
Top up with		**Hot filter coffee**

Comment: An interesting herbal cognac laced coffee.

MELON BALL

Glass: Shot
Method: **SHAKE** all ingredients with ice and fine strain into chilled glass.

1/2	shot(s)	**Ketel One vodka**
1/2	shot(s)	**Midori melon liqueur**
3/4	shot(s)	**Freshly squeezed orange juice**

Comment: A vivid green combination of vodka, melon and orange.

M.C. MARTINI [UPDATED]

Glass: Martini
Garnish: Lime zest twist
Method: **SHAKE** all ingredients with ice and fine strain into chilled glass.

2	shot(s)	**Plymouth gin**
1	shot(s)	**Sauvignon Blanc wine**
1/2	shot(s)	**Elderflower cordial**

Origin: Created in 2003 by yours truly for Marie Claire magazine.
Comment: If you're an "independent, stylish and image-conscious woman who wants to get the best out of her life", then this drink was created for you. If you're not, drink this floral Martini and dream of meeting (or being) such a woman.

MELON COLLIE MARTINI

Glass: Martini
Garnish: Crumbled Cadbury's Flake bar
Method: **SHAKE** all ingredients with ice and fine strain into chilled glass.

1	shot(s)	**Light white rum**
1/2	shot(s)	**Malibu coconut rum**
3/4	shot(s)	**Midori melon liqueur**
1/4	shot(s)	**White crème de cacao liqueur**
3/4	shot(s)	**Double (heavy) cream**
3/4	shot(s)	**Milk**

Origin: Created in 2003 by Simon King at MJU, Millennium Hotel, London, England.
Comment: Something of a holiday disco drink but tasty all the same.

MEDICINAL SOLUTION [NEW]

Glass: Collins
Garnish: Lime wedge
Method: **SHAKE** first five ingredients with ice and strain into ice-filled glass. **TOP** with tonic water, lightly stir and serve with straws.

1 1/2	shot(s)	**Oude jenever**
1/2	shot(s)	**Green Chartreuse liqueur**
1/2	shot(s)	**Freshly squeezed lime juice**
1/4	shot(s)	**Sugar (gomme) syrup**
3	dashes	**Angostura aromatic bitters**
Top up with		**Tonic water**

Origin: Created in 2006 by yours truly.
Comment: Every ingredient, apart from the sugar, has at some time been consumed for its medicinal qualities. Even the sugar is still used to make bitter tasting medicine more palatable. Some might say that's just what I've done here.

MELON DAIQUIRI #1 (SERVED 'UP')

Glass: Martini
Garnish: Melon slice or melon balls
Method: Cut melon into 8 segments and deseed. Cut cubes of flesh from skin of one segment and **MUDDLE** in base of shaker. Add other ingredients, **SHAKE** with ice and fine strain into chilled glass.

1/8	fresh	**Cantaloupe / Galia melon**
2	shot(s)	**Light white rum**
1/2	shot(s)	**Midori melon liqueur**
1/2	shot(s)	**Freshly squeezed lime juice**
1/8	shot(s)	**Sugar (gomme) syrup**

Comment: A classic Daiquiri with the gentle touch of melon.

MEDIUM MARTINI [NEW]

Glass: Martini
Garnish: Orange zest twist
Method: **STIR** all ingredients with ice and strain into chilled glass.

1 1/2	shot(s)	**Plymouth gin**
3/4	shot(s)	**Dry vermouth**
3/4	shot(s)	**Sweet (rosso) vermouth**

Origin: Adapted from a recipe in Harry Craddock's 1930 Savoy Cocktail Book.
Comment: A classic Martini served perfect and very wet. I prefer mine shaken which is the method Harry specifies in his guide.

MELON DAIQUIRI #2 (SERVED FROZEN)

Glass: Martini (large 10oz)
Garnish: Melon slice or melon balls
Method: Cut melon into 8 segments and deseed. Cut cubes of flesh from skin of one segment and place in blender. Add other ingredients and **BLEND** with half scoop crushed ice. Serve with straws.

1/8	fresh	**Cantaloupe / Galia melon**
2	shot(s)	**Light white rum**
1/2	shot(s)	**Midori melon liqueur**
1/2	shot(s)	**Freshly squeezed lime juice**
1/4	shot(s)	**Sugar (gomme) syrup**

Comment: A cooling, fruity Daiquiri.

MELON MARGARITA #1 (SERVED 'UP')

Glass: Coupette
Garnish: Melon slice or melon balls
Method: Cut melon into 8 segments and deseed. Cut cubes of flesh from skin of one segment and **MUDDLE** in base of shaker. Add other ingredients, **SHAKE** with ice and fine strain into chilled glass.

1/8	fresh	**Cantaloupe / Galia melon**
2	shot(s)	**Sauza Hornitos tequila**
1	shot(s)	**Midori melon liqueur**
1	shot(s)	**Freshly squeezed lime juice**

Comment: Looks like stagnant pond water but tastes fantastic.

MELON MARGARITA #2 (SERVED FROZEN)

Glass: Coupette
Garnish: Melon slice or melon balls
Method: Cut melon into 8 segments and deseed. Cut cubes of flesh from skin of one segment and place in blender. Add other ingredients and **BLEND** with 6oz scoop crushed ice. Serve with straws.

1/8	fresh	**Cantaloupe / Galia melon**
2	shot(s)	**Sauza Hornitos tequila**
1	shot(s)	**Midori melon liqueur**
1/2	shot(s)	**Freshly squeezed lime juice**

Comment: Melon and tequila always combine well - here in a frozen Margarita.

MELON MARTINI #1

Glass: Martini
Garnish: Split lime wedge
Method: **SHAKE** all ingredients with ice and fine strain into chilled glass.

2 1/4	shot(s)	**Ketel One vodka**
1	shot(s)	**Midori melon liqueur**
1/2	shot(s)	**Freshly squeezed lime juice**
1/4	shot(s)	**Sugar (gomme) syrup**

Comment: Bright green, lime and melon with more than a hint of vodka. Do it properly - have a fresh one.

MELON MARTINI #2 (FRESH FRUIT)

Glass: Martini
Garnish: Melon wedge on rim
Method: Cut melon into 8 segments and deseed. Cut cubes of flesh from skinof one segment and **MUDDLE** in base of shaker. Add other ingredients, **SHAKE** with ice and fine strain into chilled glass.

1/8	fresh	**Cantaloupe / Galia melon**
2	shot(s)	**Ketel One vodka**
1/4	shot(s)	**Sugar (gomme) syrup**

Variant: Substitute Midori melon liqueur for sugar syrup.
Comment: Probably the most popular of all the fresh fruit martinis.

MELONCHOLY MARTINI

Glass: Martini
Garnish: Mint sprig
Method: **SHAKE** all ingredients with ice and fine strain into chilled glass.

1	shot(s)	**Ketel One vodka**
1	shot(s)	**Midori melon liqueur**
1/2	shot(s)	**Cointreau / triple sec**
1/2	shot(s)	**Malibu coconut rum liqueur**
1	shot(s)	**Pressed pineapple juice**
3/4	shot(s)	**Double (heavy) cream**
1/4	shot(s)	**Freshly squeezed lime juice**

Origin: Created in 2002 by Daniel O'Brien at Ocean Bar, Edinburgh, Scotland.
Comment: Sweet, but the flavours in this smooth, tangy, lime-green drink combine surprisingly well.

MELLOW MARTINI

Glass: Martini
Garnish: Fresh lychee on a stick
Method: **SHAKE** all ingredients with ice and fine strain into chilled glass.

1 1/2	shot(s)	**Ketel One vodka**
1/2	shot(s)	**Soho lychee liqueur**
1/2	shot(s)	**Crème de bananes liqueur liqueur**
1 1/2	shot(s)	**Pressed pineapple juice**

Comment: A fruity, tropical drink with a frothy head. Too fluffy to be a Martini.

MENEHUNE JUICE [NEW]

Glass: Old-fashioned
Garnish: Lime wedge, mint & Menehune
Method: **SHAKE** all ingredients with ice and strain into glass filled with crushed ice. Serve with straws.

2	shot(s)	**Light white rum**
1/2	shot(s)	**Cointreau / triple sec**
3/4	shot(s)	**Freshly squeezed lime juice**
1/4	shot(s)	**Almond (orgeat) sugar syrup**
1/4	shot(s)	**Sugar (gomme) syrup**

Origin: Adapted from a recipe in the 1947-72 Trader Vic's Bartender's Guide by Victor Bergeron.
Comment: Slightly sweet and strong. According to Vic, "One sip and you may see a Menehune."

MERRY WIDOW #1 [NEW]

Glass: Martini
Garnish: Lemon zest twist
Method: **STIR** all ingredients with ice and strain into chilled glass.

1 1/2	shot(s)	**Plymouth gin**
1 1/2	shot(s)	**Dry vermouth**
1/4	shot(s)	**La Fée Parisian 68% absinthe**
1/4	shot(s)	**Bénédictine D.O.M. liqueur**
3	dashes	**Angostura aromatic bitters**
1/2	shot(s)	**Chilled minera water (omit if wet ice)**

Origin: Adapted from a recipe in Harry Craddock's 1930 Savoy Cocktail Book.
Comment: Aromatic, complex, strong and bitter.

MERRY WIDOW #2

Glass: Martini
Garnish: Orange zest twist
Method: **STIR** all ingredients with ice and strain into chilled glass.

$1^1/_4$	shot(s)	**Ketel One vodka**
$1^1/_4$	shot(s)	**Dubonnet Red**
$1^1/_4$	shot(s)	**Dry vermouth**
1	dash	**Fee Brothers orange bitters**

Comment: Aromatic and complex - for toughened palates.

MESA FRESCA [NEW]

Glass: Collins
Garnish: Lime wheel
Method: **SHAKE** all ingredients with ice and strain into ice-filled glass.

2	shot(s)	**Sauza Hornitos tequila**
3	shot(s)	**Freshly squeezed pink grapefruit juice**
1	shot(s)	**Freshly squeeezed lime juice**
$^1/_2$	shot(s)	**Sugar (gomme) syrup**

Origin: Discovered in 2005 at Mesa Grill, New York City, USA.
Comment: Sweet and sour tequila and grapefruit.

MET MANHATTAN

Glass: Martini
Garnish: Orange zest twist
Method: **SHAKE** all ingredients with ice and fine strain into chilled glass.

2	shot(s)	**Bourbon whiskey**
1	shot(s)	**Grand Marnier liqueur**
$^1/_2$	shot(s)	**Butterscotch schnapps liqueur**
2	dashes	**Fee Brothers orange bitters**

Origin: The Met Bar, Metropolitan Hotel, London, England.
Comment: Smooth and rounded bourbon with a hint of orange toffee.

METROPOLITAN

Glass: Martini
Garnish: Flamed orange twist
Method: **SHAKE** all ingredients with ice and fine strain into chilled glass.

2	shot(s)	**Raspberry flavoured vodka**
$^1/_2$	shot(s)	**Cointreau / triple sec**
1	shot(s)	**Cranberry juice**
$^1/_2$	shot(s)	**Freshly squeezed lime juice**
$^1/_4$	shot(s)	**Rose's lime cordial**

Origin: Created in 1993 by Chuck Coggins at Marion's Continental Restaurant & Lounge, New York City. Marion's was originally opened in 1950 by fashion model Marion Nagy, who came to the States after seeking asylum while swimming for Hungary in the Paris Peace Games after WWII.
Comment: A Cosmo with more than a hint of blackcurrant.

MERRY-GO-ROUND MARTINI [NEW]

Glass: Martini
Garnish: Olive & lemon zest twist
Method: **STIR** all ingredients with ice and fine strain into chilled glass.

2	shot(s)	**Plymouth gin**
$^1/_2$	shot(s)	**Dry vermouth**
$^1/_2$	shot(s)	**Sweet (rosso) vermouth**

Origin: Long lost classic variation on the Dry Martini.
Comment: Stir this 'perfect' Martini around and then get merry.

MEXICAN [NEW]

Glass: Martini
Garnish: Pineapple wedge on rim
Method: **SHAKE** all ingredients with ice and fine strain into chilled glass.

2	shot(s)	**Sauza Hornitos tequila**
$1^1/_2$	shot(s)	**Pressed pineapple juice**
$^1/_4$	shot(s)	**Sonoma pomegranate (grenadine) syrup**

Variant: Substitute sugar syrup for pomegranate syrup.
Comment: Fresh pineapple makes this drink.

MEXICAN 55 [NEW]

Glass: Collins
Garnish: Lime wedge
Method: **SHAKE** first four ingredients with ice and strain into ice-filled glass. **TOP** with champagne.

$1^1/_2$	shot(s)	**Sauza Hornitos tequila**
1	shot(s)	**Freshly squeezed lemon juice**
$^1/_2$	shot(s)	**Sugar (gomme) syrup**
2	dashes	**Angostura aromatic bitters**
Top up with		**Piper-Heidsieck brut champagne**

Origin: An adaptation of the classic French '75 created in 1988 at La Perla, Paris, France. The name comes from Fidel Castro's statement that bullets, like wine, came in vintages and Mexican '55 was a good year (for bullets).
Comment: Suitably hard, yet surprisingly refreshing and sophisticated.

MEXICAN COFFEE (HOT) [NEW]

Glass: Toddy
Garnish: Three coffee beans
Method: Place bar spoon in glass. **POUR** first three ingrediuents into glass and stir. **FLOAT** cream.

1	shot(s)	**Sauza Hornitos tequila**
$^1/_4$	shot(s)	**Sugar (gomme) syrup**
Top up with		**Hot filter coffee**
Float		**Double (heavy) cream**

Tip: Lightly whip or simply shake cream in container before pouring over the bowl of a spoon. It also helps if the cream is gently warmed.
Comment: Tequila's answer to the Irish Coffee.

MEXICAN MANHATTAN [NEW]

Glass: Martini
Garnish: Maraschino cherry
Method: **STIR** all ingredients with ice and strain into chilled glass.

2	shot(s)	**Sauza Hornitos tequila**
1	shot(s)	**Red (rosso) vermouth**
3	dashes	**Angostura aromatic bitters**

Comment: You've tried this with bourbon, now surprise yourself with an aged tequila.

MEXICAN MARTINI

Glass: Martini
Garnish: Pineapple leaf on rim
Method: **SHAKE** all ingredients with ice and fine strain into chilled glass.

2	shot(s)	**Sauza Hornitos tequila**
1/4	shot(s)	**Crème de cassis**
2	shot(s)	**Pressed pineapple juice**

Origin: Discovered in 2004 at Indigo Yard, Edinburgh, Scotland.
Comment: Tequila, pineapple and blackcurrant combine in this medium dry cocktail.

MEXICAN MELON BALL [NEW]

Glass: Collins
Garnish: Melon balls on stick
Method: Cut melon into 8 segments and deseed. Cut cubes of flesh from skin of one segment and **MUDDLE** in base of shaker. Add other ingredients, **SHAKE** with ice and fine strain into ice-filled glass.

1/8	fresh	**Cantaloupe / Galia melon**
2	shot(s)	**Sauza Hornitos tequila**
2	shot(s)	**Freshly squeezed orange juice**
1/4	shot(s)	**Sugar (gomme) syrup**

Origin: Adapted from a drink discovered at the Flying V Bar & Grill, Tucson, Arizona, USA.
Comment: Orange and melon laced with tequila.

MEXICAN MULE

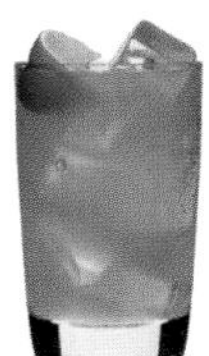

Glass: Collins
Garnish: Lime wedge
Method: **SHAKE** first three ingredients with ice and strain into ice-filled glass. **TOP** with ginger beer, lightly stir and serve with straws.

1 1/2	shot(s)	**Sauza Hornitos tequila**
3/4	shot(s)	**Freshly squeezed lime juice**
1/4	shot(s)	**Sugar (gomme) syrup**
Top up with		**Ginger beer**

AKA: El Burro
Comment: A tequila based version of the Moscow Mule.

MEXICAN SURFER

Glass: Martini
Garnish: Lime wedge on rim
Method: **SHAKE** all ingredients with ice and fine strain into chilled glass.

2	shot(s)	**Sauza Hornitos tequila**
1 1/2	shot(s)	**Pressed pineapple juice**
1/2	shot(s)	**Rose's lime cordial**

Comment: Frothy topped, easy to make, and all too easy to drink.

MEXICAN TEA (HOT) [NEW]

Glass: Toddy
Garnish: Lime slice
Method: Place bar spoon in warmed glass. **POUR** all ingredients into glass and stir.

2	shot(s)	**Sauza Hornitos tequila**
1/2	shot(s)	**Sugar (gomme) syrup**
Top up with		**Hot black breakfast tea**

Comment: Tiffin will never be the same again.

MEXICO CITY

Glass: Coupette
Garnish: Lime wedge on rim
Method: **SHAKE** all ingredients with ice and fine strain into chilled glass.

1 1/2	shot(s)	**Sauza Hornitos tequila**
3/4	shot(s)	**Grand Marnier liqueur**
1/2	shot(s)	**Freshly squeezed lime juice**
1/2	shot(s)	**Cranberry juice**
1/4	shot(s)	**Sugar (gomme) syrup**

Origin: Adapted from a cocktail discovered in 2002 at the Merc Bar, New York City.
Comment: This pinky-red Margarita benefits from a hint of cranberry.

MEXICANO (HOT) [NEW]

Glass: Toddy
Garnish: Dust with nutmeg & cinnamon
Method: **POUR** tequila and liqueur into warmed glass and top with coffee. **FLOAT** cream over drink.

1	shot(s)	**Sauza Hornitos tequila**
1/2	shot(s)	**Grand Marnier liqueur**
Top up with		**Hot filter coffee**
Float		**Double (heavy) cream**

Tip: Lightly whip or simply shake cream in container before pouring over the bowl of a spoon. It also helps if the cream is gently warmed.
Comment: A spicy, flavour-packed hot coffee.

MIAMI BEACH [NEW]

Glass: Martini
Garnish: Pineapple wedge & cherry
Method: **SHAKE** all ingredients with ice and fine strain into chilled glass.

2	shot(s)	**Plymouth gin**
1½	shot(s)	**Pressed pineapple juice**
¼	shot(s)	**Sugar (gomme) syrup**

Comment: Fruity and well proportioned – like the babes on Miami Beach. Sorry.

MIAMI DAIQUIRI

Glass: Martini
Garnish: Mint leaf
Method: **SHAKE** all ingredients with ice and fine strain into chilled glass.

2	shot(s)	**Light white rum**
¼	shot(s)	**White crème de menthe**
½	shot(s)	**Freshly squeezed lime juice**
⅛	shot(s)	**Sugar (gomme) syrup**
¾	shot(s)	**Chilled mineral water (omit if wet ice)**

Origin: My adaptation of a classic.
Comment: The merest hint of mint in a refreshing Daiquiri with a dry finish.

MICHELADA [NEW]

Glass: Collins
Garnish: Lime wedge
Method: **STIR** first six ingredients in bottom of glass. Fill glass with ice and **TOP** with beer.

¾	shot(s)	**Freshly squeezed lime juice**
⅛	shot(s)	**Soy sauce**
3	drops	**Tabasco pepper sauce**
2	dashes	**Worcestershire sauce**
1	pinch	**Celery salt**
1	pinch	**Black pepper**
Top up with		**Beer**

Origin: A Mexican classic.
Comment: Made with lager this spicy drink is sometimes called a White Mary. It's best made with a dark, flavoursome beer.

MILANO [NEW]

Glass: Old-fashioned
Garnish: Orange slice
Method: **STIR** all ingredients with ice and strain into ice-filled glass.

1	shot(s)	**Ketel One vodka**
1	shot(s)	**Campari**
1	shot(s)	**Sweet (rosso) vermouth**

AKA: Negrosky
Comment: A Negroni with vodka in place of gin.

MILANO SOUR [NEW]

Glass: Old-fashioned
Garnish: Lemon slice & maraschino cherry (sail)
Method: **SHAKE** all ingredients with ice and fine strain into ice-filled glass.

1½	shot(s)	**Plymouth gin**
1	shot(s)	**Galliano liqueur**
1	shot(s)	**Freshly squeezed lemon juice**
½	fresh	**Egg white**

Origin: Created in 2006 by your truly.
Comment: Delicate anise and peppermint with citrus freshness.

MILHO VERDE BATIDA [NEW]

Glass: Collins
Garnish: Cinnamon dust
Method: **BLEND** all ingredients with 12oz scoop crushed ice. Serve with straws.

2½	shot(s)	**Cachaça**
70	grams	**Sweetcorn (canned)**
1½	shot(s)	**Sweetened condensed milk**

Origin: A classic Brazilian drink.
Comment: Quite possibly your first sweetcorn cocktail.

MILK & HONEY MARTINI

Glass: Martini
Garnish: Grate fresh nutmeg over drink
Method: **STIR** Scotch with honey in base of shaker to dissolve honey. Add other ingredients, **SHAKE** with ice and fine strain into chilled glass.

2	shot(s)	**The Famous Grouse Scotch whisky**
3	spoons	**Runny honey**
½	shot(s)	**Honey liqueur**
¾	shot(s)	**Double (heavy) cream**
¾	shot(s)	**Milk**

Origin: Created in 2002 by yours truly.
Comment: The rich flavour of Scotch is tamed by honey and cream.

MILK PUNCH [UPDATED]

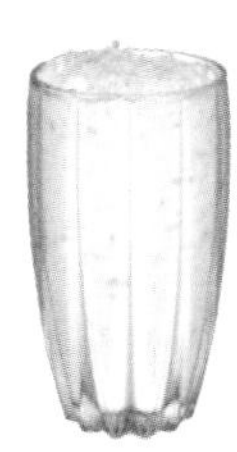

Glass: Collins
Garnish: Dust with freshly grated nutmeg
Method: **SHAKE** all ingredients with ice and strain into glass filled with crushed ice.

1	shot(s)	**Rémy Martin cognac**
½	shot(s)	**Goslings Black Seal rum**
½	shot(s)	**Sonoma vanilla bean sugar syrup**
2	shot(s)	**Milk**
1	shot(s)	**Double (heavy) cream**

Comment: The cream, vanilla and sugar tame the cognac and rum.

MINT JULEP

This is the ultimate Deep South cocktail, famously served at the Kentucky Derby. The name derives from the Arabic word 'julab', meaning rosewater, and the first known written reference dates back to 1803. At that time it could be made with rum, brandy or whiskey, but by 1900 whiskey had become the preferred ingredient.

The Mint Julep reached Britain in 1837, thanks to the novelist Captain Frederick Marryat, who complained of being woken at 7am by a slave brandishing a Julep. He popularised it through his descriptions of American Fourth of July celebrations.

When making a Mint Julep it is important to only bruise the mint as crushing the leaves releases the bitter, inner juices. Also be sure to discard the stems, which are also bitter.

It is imperative that the drink is served ice cold. Cocktail etiquette dictates that the shaker containing the mint and other ingredients should be placed in a refrigerator with the serving glass for at least two hours prior to adding ice, shaking and serving.

Variations on the Mint Julep include substituting the bourbon for rye whiskey, rum, gin, brandy, calvados or applejack brandy. Another variation calls for half a shot of aged rum to be floated on top of the bourbon-based julep.

MOJITO

Between the wars, and especially during Prohibition, Cuba had a thriving international bar culture. In fact, when Prohibition was announced, numerous companies outfitted ferries for the overnight booze cruise to the island. At the heart of this bar culture were Cuba's bartenders, many of them trained at the Association Cantineros Cuba - the legendary Havana bar school.

A classic, long blend of rum, lime and mint, the Mojito was probably invented after Americans introduced the locals to the Mint Julep. Bodeguita del Medio is usually credited with the first Mojito and this is apparently where Hemingway went for his.

In January 2003 the Mojito had something of a boost when the newly released Bond film, Die Another Day, saw James visit Cuba and order a Mojito in preference to his more usual Vodka Martini.

MOJITO VARIATIONS

Apple Mojito
Apple Virgin Mojito
Bajan Mojito
Bajito
French Mojito
Ginger Mojito
Rude Mojito
Luxury Mojito
Milky Mojito
Mojito
Mojito de Casa
Momo Special
Orange Mojito
Pineapple Mojito
Strawberry & Balsamic Mojito

●●●●◐○

MILKY MOJITO

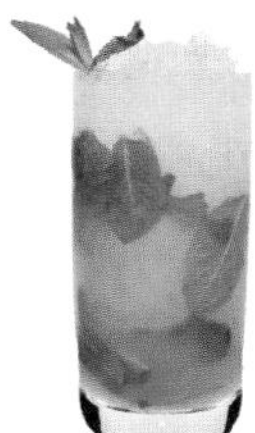

Glass: Collins
Garnish: Mint spring
Method: Lightly **MUDDLE** (just to bruise) mint in glass. Fill glass with crushed ice, add other ingredients. **TOP** with soda, stir and serve with straws.

12	fresh	**Mint leaves**
1	shot(s)	**Freshly squeezed lime juice**
$\frac{3}{4}$	shot(s)	**Sugar (gomme) syrup**
2	shot(s)	**Pernod anis**
Top up with		**Soda water (club soda)**

Comment: An anise laced alternative to a Mojito. The name refers to the opaque white colour of the drink after soda is added to the anis.

●●●●●◐

THE MILLION DOLLAR COCKTAIL

Glass: Martini
Garnish: Lemon zest twist (round like an egg yolk in the foam)
Method: **SHAKE** all ingredients with ice and fine strain into chilled glass.

2	shot(s)	**Plymouth gin**
1	shot(s)	**Sweet (rosso) vermouth**
$\frac{1}{2}$	shot(s)	**Pressed pineapple juice**
$\frac{1}{4}$	shot(s)	**Sonoma pomegranate (grenadine) syrup**
$\frac{1}{2}$	fresh	**Egg white**

Origin: This classic cocktail is thought to have been created around 1910 by Ngiam Tong Boon at The Long Bar, Raffles Hotel, Singapore. Boon is more famous for the Singapore Sling.
Comment: Serious, yet superbly smooth and a bit fluffy.

●●●●●◐

MILLION DOLLAR MARGARITA [NEW]

Glass: Old-fashioned
Garnish: Lime wedge
Method: **SHAKE** all ingredients with ice and strain into ice-filled glass.

1$\frac{1}{2}$	shot(s)	**Sauza Hornitos tequila**
1$\frac{1}{2}$	shot(s)	**Grand Marnier (Cuvée du Centenaire)**
$\frac{1}{2}$	shot(s)	**Freshly squeezed lime juice**

Origin: Discovered in 2006 at Maison 140 Hotel, Los Angeles, USA where I paid a mere $41.14 plus tip for the drink.
Comment: The proportions of this Margarita accentuate the liqueur.

●●●●●○

MILLIONAIRE [NEW]

Glass: Martini
Garnish: Quarter orange slice on rim
Method: **SHAKE** all ingredients with ice and fine strain into chilled glass.

2	shot(s)	**Bourbon whiskey**
$\frac{1}{2}$	shot(s)	**Cointreau/ triple sec**
$\frac{1}{2}$	shot(s)	**Freshly squeezed lemon juice**
$\frac{1}{4}$	shot(s)	**Sonoma pomegranate (grenadine) syrup**
$\frac{1}{2}$	fresh	**Egg white**

Comment: Rust coloured tangy citrus smoothed and served straight-up.

●●●●◐○

MILLIONAIRE'S DAIQUIRI

Glass: Martini
Garnish: Star fruit
Method: **SHAKE** all ingredients with ice and fine strain into chilled glass.

1$\frac{3}{4}$	shot(s)	**Light white rum**
$\frac{3}{4}$	shot(s)	**Plymouth sloe gin**
$\frac{3}{4}$	shot(s)	**Apricot brandy liqueur**
$\frac{3}{4}$	shot(s)	**Freshly squeezed lime juice**
$\frac{1}{4}$	shot(s)	**Sonoma pomegranate (grenadine) syrup**

Origin: This heralds from a classic cocktail known simply as the Millionaire. Originally sloe gin was the main base ingredient, but David Embury once wrote, "Since the sloe gin, which is a liqueur, predominates in this drink, I do not regard it as a true cocktail." Thus above is my modern adaptation.
Comment: The colour of this cocktail, due to sloe liqueur and grenadine, belies a surprisingly dry finish.

●●●●●○

MILLY MARTINI

Glass: Martini
Garnish: Pineapple wedge on rim
Method: Lightly **MUDDLE** basil (just to bruise) in base of shaker. Add other ingredients, **SHAKE** with ice and fine strain into chilled glass.

5	fresh	**Basil leaves**
2	shot(s)	**Plymouth gin**
2	shot(s)	**Pressed pineapple juice**
$\frac{1}{2}$	shot(s)	**Sugar (gomme) syrup**
2	dashes	**Fee Brothers orange bitters**

Origin: Created in 2003 by Shelim Islam at the GE Club, London, England.
Comment: Gin and pineapple with a pleasing hint of basil.

●●●●◐○

MIMOSA

Glass: Flute
Garnish: Orange zest twist
Method: **POUR** ingredients into chilled glass and gently stir.

$\frac{1}{2}$	shot(s)	**Grand Marnier liqueur**
1$\frac{3}{4}$	shot(s)	**Freshly squeezed orange juice**
Top up with		**Piper-Heidsieck brut champagne**

Variant: When made with mandarin juice this becomes a Puccini.
Origin: Created in 1925 at the Ritz Hotel in Paris and named after the tropical flowering shrub.
Comment: The British version of this drink was invented by a Mr. McGarry, barman at Buck's Club, in the early 20th century, using grenadine in place of orange liqueur. Naturally enough, he called it the Buck's Fizz.

DRINKS ARE GRADED AS FOLLOWS:

● DISGUSTING ●◐ PRETTY AWFUL ●● BEST AVOIDED
●●◐ DISAPPOINTING ●●● ACCEPTABLE ●●●◐ GOOD
●●●● RECOMMENDED ●●●●◐ HIGHLY RECOMMENDED
●●●●● OUTSTANDING / EXCEPTIONAL

●●●●◐

MINT COCKTAIL [NEW]

Glass: Martini
Garnish: Mint leaf
Method: Lightly **MUDDLE** (just to bruise) mint in base of shaker. Add other ingredients, **SHAKE** with ice and fine strain into chilled glass.

12	fresh	**Mint leaves**
2	shot(s)	**Plymouth gin**
1	shot(s)	**Sauvignon Blanc wine**
1/4	shot(s)	**White crème de menthe liqueur**
1/4	shot(s)	**Sugar (gomme) syrup**

Origin: Adapted from a recipe in Harry Craddock's 1930 Savoy Cocktail Book.
Comment: A great grassy, minty digestif with a good balance between acidity and sweetness.

●●●●○

MINT COLLINS [NEW]

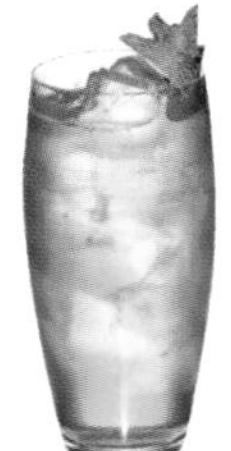

Glass: Collins
Garnish: Mint sprig
Method: Lightly **MUDDLE** (just to bruise) mint in base of shaker. Add next three ingredients, **SHAKE** with ice and fine strain into chilled glass. **TOP** with soda, lightly stir and serve with straws.

12	fresh	**Mint leaves**
2	shot(s)	**Plymouth gin**
1	shot(s)	**Freshly squeezed lemon juice**
1/2	shot(s)	**Sugar (gomme) syrup**
Top up with		**Soda water (club soda)**

Origin: Adapted from a recipe in the 1947-72 Trader Vic's Bartender's Guide by Victor Bergeron.
Comment: Exactly what the name promises.

●●●●●

MINT DAIQUIRI [NEW]

Glass: Martini
Garnish: Mint leaf
Method: Lightly **MUDDLE** (just to bruise) mint in base of shaker. Add other ingredients, **SHAKE** with ice and fine strain into chilled glass.

12	fresh	**Mint leaves**
2	shot(s)	**Light white rum**
1/2	shot(s)	**Freshly squeezed lime juice**
1/4	shot(s)	**Sugar (gomme) syrup**
1/2	shot(s)	**Chilled mineral water (omit if wet ice)**

Origin: Created in 2006 by yours truly.
Comment: A short, concentrated Mojito.

●●●◐○

MINT FIZZ

Glass: Collins
Garnish: Mint sprig
Method: Lightly **MUDDLE** mint (just to bruise) in base of shaker. Add other ingredients apart from soda, **SHAKE** with ice and fine strain into ice-filled glass. **TOP** with soda, lightly stir and serve with straws.

7	fresh	**Mint leaves**
2	shot(s)	**Plymouth gin**
1	shot(s)	**Freshly squeezed lime juice**
1/4	shot(s)	**White crème de menthe**
1/2	shot(s)	**Sugar (gomme) syrup**
Top up with		**Soda (from siphon)**

Comment: Long, refreshing citrus and mint fizz.

●●●●●

MINT JULEP

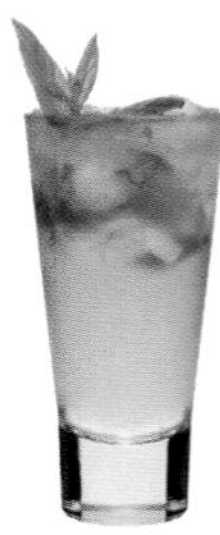

Glass: Collins
Garnish: Mint sprig and slice of lemon
Method: Lightly **MUDDLE** (only bruise) mint in base of shaker. Add other ingredients, **SHAKE** with ice and strain into glass half filled with crushed ice. **CHURN** (stir) the drink with the crushed ice using a bar spoon. Top up the glass with more crushed ice and **CHURN** again. Repeat this process until the drink fills the glass and serve with straws.

12	fresh	**Mint leaves**
2 1/2	shot(s)	**Bourbon whiskey**
3/4	shot(s)	**Sugar (gomme) syrup**
3	dashes	**Angostura aromatic bitters**

Comment: This superb drink is better if the shaker and its contents are placed in the refrigerator for several hours prior to mixing, allowing the mint flavours to infuse in the bourbon.

●●●●◐

MINT LIMEADE (MOCKTAIL) [NEW]

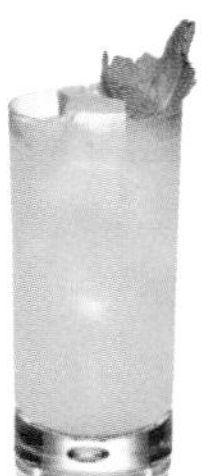

Glass: Collins
Garnish: Mint sprig
Method: Lightly **MUDDLE** (just to bruise) mint in base of shaker. Add next three ingredients, **SHAKE** with ice and fine strain into ice-filled glass. **TOP** with 7-Up, lightly stir and serve with straws.

12	fresh	**Mint leaves**
1 1/2	shot(s)	**Freshly squeezed lime juice**
1	shot(s)	**Pressed apple juice**
3/4	shot(s)	**Sugar (gomme) syrup**
Top up with		**7-Up**

Origin: Created in 2006 by yours truly.
Comment: Superbly refreshing - mint and lime served long.

●●●●◐

MINT MARTINI [NEW]

Glass: Martini
Garnish: Mint leaf
Method: Lightly **MUDDLE** (just to bruise) mint in base of shaker. Add other ingredients, **SHAKE** with ice and fine strain into chilled glass.

12	fresh	**Mint leaves**
1 1/2	shot(s)	**Ketel One vodka**
1/2	shot(s)	**Dry vermouth**
1/4	shot(s)	**White crème de menthe liqueur**
1 1/2	shot(s)	**Sauvignon Blanc wine**
1/4	shot(s)	**Sugar (gomme) syrup**

Origin: Created in 2005 by yours truly.
Comment: An after dinner palate cleanser.

DRINKS ARE GRADED AS FOLLOWS:

● DISGUSTING ●◐ PRETTY AWFUL ●● BEST AVOIDED
●●◐ DISAPPOINTING ●●● ACCEPTABLE ●●●◐ GOOD
●●●● RECOMMENDED ●●●●◐ HIGHLY RECOMMENDED
●●●●● OUTSTANDING / EXCEPTIONAL

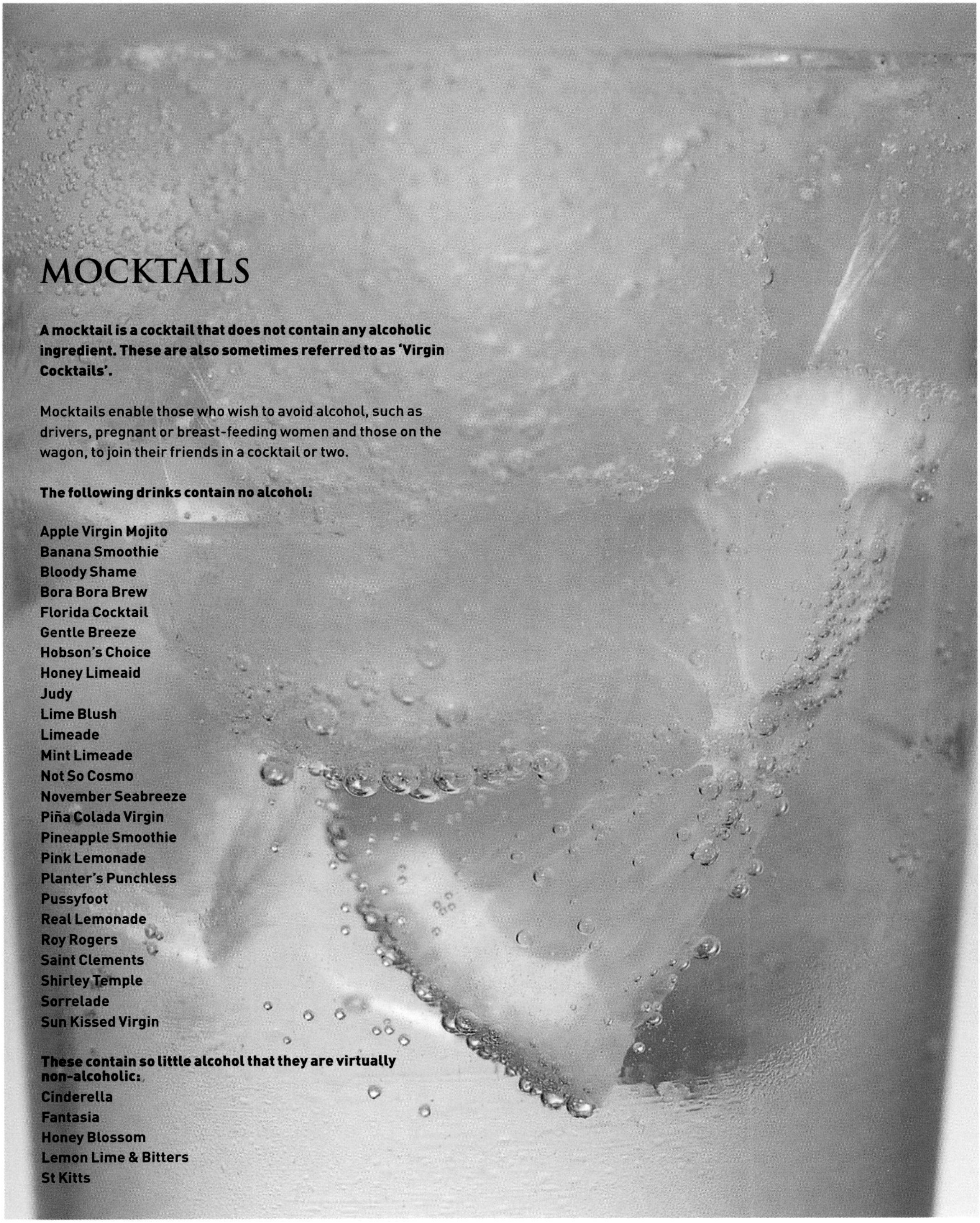

MOCKTAILS

A mocktail is a cocktail that does not contain any alcoholic ingredient. These are also sometimes referred to as 'Virgin Cocktails'.

Mocktails enable those who wish to avoid alcohol, such as drivers, pregnant or breast-feeding women and those on the wagon, to join their friends in a cocktail or two.

The following drinks contain no alcohol:

Apple Virgin Mojito
Banana Smoothie
Bloody Shame
Bora Bora Brew
Florida Cocktail
Gentle Breeze
Hobson's Choice
Honey Limeaid
Judy
Lime Blush
Limeade
Mint Limeade
Not So Cosmo
November Seabreeze
Piña Colada Virgin
Pineapple Smoothie
Pink Lemonade
Planter's Punchless
Pussyfoot
Real Lemonade
Roy Rogers
Saint Clements
Shirley Temple
Sorrelade
Sun Kissed Virgin

These contain so little alcohol that they are virtually non-alcoholic:
Cinderella
Fantasia
Honey Blossom
Lemon Lime & Bitters
St Kitts

MISS MARTINI

Glass: Martini
Garnish: Raspberries on stick
Method: MUDDLE raspberries in base of shaker. Add other ingredients, **SHAKE** with ice and fine strain into chilled glass.

7	fresh	**Raspberries**
2	shot(s)	**Ketel One vodka**
½	shot(s)	**Chambord black raspberry liqueur**
¼	shot(s)	**Double (heavy) cream**
¼	shot(s)	**Milk**
⅛	shot(s)	**Sugar (gomme) syrup**

Origin: Created in 1997 by Giovanni Burdi at Match EC1, London, England.
Comment: A pink, fruity and creamy concoction.

MISSIONARY'S DOWNFALL [NEW]

Glass: Collins
Garnish: Mint sprig
Method: Lightly **MUDDLE** mint (just to bruise) in base of shaker. Add other ingredients, **SHAKE** with ice and strain into glass filled with crushed ice.

12	fresh	**Mint leaves**
2	shot(s)	**Light white rum**
½	shot(s)	**Peach schnapps liqueur**
1½	shot(s)	**Freshly squeezed lime juice**
½	shot(s)	**Sugar (gomme) syrup**
2	shot(s)	**Freshly squeezed pineapple juice**

Origin: Created in the 1930s by Don The Beachcomber at his restaurant in Hollywood, California, USA.
Comment: Superbly balanced and refreshing rum, lime, mint and a hint of peach.

MISSISSIPPI PUNCH [UPDATED]

Glass: Collins
Garnish: Lemon slice
Method: SHAKE all ingredients with ice and strain into glass filled with crushed ice.

1½	shot(s)	**Bourbon whiskey**
¾	shot(s)	**Rémy Martin cognac**
¾	shot(s)	**Freshly squeezed lemon juice**
1	shot(s)	**Sugar (gomme) syrup**
2	shot(s)	**Chilled mineral water**

Comment: Balanced and refreshing.

MISSISSIPPI SCHNAPPER

Glass: Martini
Garnish: Orange zest twist
Method: SHAKE all ingredients with ice and fine strain into chilled glass.

2	shot(s)	**Jack Daniel's Tennessee whiskey**
¾	shot(s)	**Peach schnapps liqueur**
½	shot(s)	**Cointreau / triple sec**
¼	shot(s)	**Freshly squeezed lime juice**
¼	shot(s)	**Sugar (gomme) syrup**

Origin: Created in 1999 by Dan Cottle at Velvet, Manchester, England.
Comment: Orange predominates with peach sweetness balanced by whiskey and lime.

MISTER STU

Glass: Collins
Garnish: Pineapple wedge on rim
Method: SHAKE all ingredients with ice and strain into ice-filled glass. Serve with straws.

2	shot(s)	**Sauza Hornitos tequila**
½	shot(s)	**Luxardo Amaretto di Saschira liqueur**
½	shot(s)	**Malibu coconut rum liqueur**
1½	shot(s)	**Pressed pineapple juice**
1½	shot(s)	**Freshly squeezed orange juice**

Comment: There's a touch of the disco about this foamy drink, but it is still complex and interesting.

MITCH MARTINI

Glass: Martini
Garnish: Lemon zest twist
Method: SHAKE all ingredients with ice and fine strain into chilled glass.

2	shot(s)	**Zubrowka bison vodka**
2	shot(s)	**Pressed apple juice**
½	shot(s)	**Freshly squeezed lemon juice**
¼	shot(s)	**Passion fruit syrup**

Origin: Created in 1997 by Giovanni Burdi at Match EC1, London, England.
Comment: One of London's most popular contemporary classics.

MOCHA MARTINI

Glass: Martini
Garnish: Dust with cocoa powder
Method: SHAKE first four ingredients with ice and fine strain into chilled glass. **FLOAT** cream in centre of drink.

1½	shot(s)	**Bourbon whiskey**
1	shot(s)	**Cold espresso coffee**
½	shot(s)	**Baileys Irish Cream liqueur**
½	shot(s)	**Dark crème de cacao liqueur**
½	shot(s)	**Double (heavy) cream**

Comment: Made with great espresso, this drink is a superb, richly flavoured balance of sweet and bitter.

MODERNISTA [NEW]

Glass: Martini
Garnish: Lemon zest twist
Method: SHAKE all ingredients with ice and fine strain into chilled glass.

2	shot(s)	**Plymouth gin**
½	shot(s)	**Goslings Black Seal rum**
¼	shot(s)	**Pernod anis**
1	shot(s)	**Carlshamns Swedish Torr Flaggpunsch**
¼	shot(s)	**Freshly squeezed lemon juice**
1	dash	**Fee Brothers orange bitters**

Origin: Adapted from a drink created by Ted Haigh (AKA Dr. Cocktail) and derived from the 'Modern Cocktail'. See Ted's book, 'Vintage Spirits & Forgotten Cocktails'.
Comment: A massive flavour hit to awaken your taste buds.

A B C D E F G H I J K L **M** N O P Q R S T U V W X Y Z

MOJITO

Glass: Collins
Garnish: Mint sprig
Method: Lightly **MUDDLE** mint (just to bruise) in base of glass. Add rum, lime juice and sugar. Half fill glass with crushed ice and **CHURN** (stir) with bar spoon. Fill glass with more crushed ice and **CHURN** some more. **TOP** with soda, stir and serve with straws.

12	fresh	**Mint leaves**
2	shot(s)	**Light white rum**
3/4	shot(s)	**Freshly squeezed lime juice**
1/4	shot(s)	**Sugar (gomme) syrup**
Top up with		**Soda water (club soda)**

Variant: Add a dash or two of Angostura aromatic bitters.
Comment: When well made, this Cuban cousin of the Mint Julep is one of the world's greatest and most refreshing cocktails.

MOJITO DE CASA [NEW]

Glass: Collins
Garnish: Mint sprig
Method: Lightly **MUDDLE** mint (just to bruise) in base of glass. Add tequila, lime juice and sugar. Half fill glass with crushed ice and **CHURN** (stir) with bar spoon. Fill glass with more crushed ice and **CHURN** some more. **TOP** with soda, stir and serve with straws.

12	fresh	**Mint leaves**
2	shot(s)	**Sauza Hornitos tequila**
3/4	shot(s)	**Freshly squeezed lime juice**
1/2	shot(s)	**Sugar (gomme) syrup**
Top up with		**Soda water (club soda)**

Origin: Created at Mercadito, New York City, USA.
Comment: A tequila based Mojito.

MOLOTOV COCKTAIL

Glass: Martini
Garnish: Lemon zest
Method: SHAKE all ingredients with ice and fine strain into chilled glass.

1 1/2	shot(s)	**Lime flavoured vodka**
1 1/4	shot(s)	**Parfait Amour liqueur**
1/2	shot(s)	**Freshly squeezed lemon juice**
1/2	shot(s)	**Opal Nera black sambuca**

Origin: I created this drink after a visit to the Rajamäki distillery in Finland. At the start of the Second World War the plant was used to produce Molotov cocktails, inflammatory bombs with which the Finns put hundreds of Soviet tanks out of action.
Comment: I selected the ingredients to represent the four liquids used in the wartime weapon. Vodka, which is clear, stands for alcohol, parfait amour shares the purple hue of paraffin, lemon juice represents gasoline and black sambuca replaces tar.

LA MOMIE

Glass: Shot
Method: POUR pastis into chilled glass and top with chilled water.

1/2	shot(s)	**Ricard pastis**
Top up with		**Chilled water**

Origin: Pronounced 'Mom-Ee', this shot is very popular in the South of France.
Comment: A bite-sized aniseed tipple.

MOMISETTE

Glass: Collins (10oz max)
Method: POUR pastis and almond syrup into glass. Serve with bottle of sparkling water so the customer can dilute to their own taste. (I recommend five shots.) Lastly, add ice to fill glass.

1	shot(s)	**Ricard pastis**
1/4	shot(s)	**Almond (orgeat) syrup**
Top up with		**Sparkling mineral water**

Origin: A traditional French drink, the name of which literally translates as 'tiny mummy'.
Comment: Complex balance of anis, almond and liquorice.

MOMO SPECIAL

Glass: Collins
Garnish: Mint sprig
Method: Lightly **MUDDLE** mint (just to bruise) in base of shaker. Add next three ingredients, **SHAKE** with ice and strain into ice-filled glass. **TOP** with soda, lightly stir and serve with straws.

12	fresh	**Mint leaves**
2	shot(s)	**Ketel One vodka**
1/2	shot(s)	**Freshly squeezed lime juice**
1/2	shot(s)	**Sugar (gomme) syrup**
Top up with		**Soda water (club soda)**

Origin: Created in 1998 by Simon Mainoo at Momo, London, England.
Comment: Enrich the minty flavour by macerating the mint in the vodka some hours before making.

MONA LISA

Glass: Collins
Garnish: Orange slice
Method: SHAKE first three ingredients with ice and strain into ice-filled glass. **TOP** with tonic water.

1	shot(s)	**Green Chartreuse liqueur**
3	shot(s)	**Freshly squeezed orange juice**
2	dashes	**Angostura aromatic bitters**
Top up with		**Tonic water**

Comment: Chartreuse fans will appreciate this drink, which is also an approachable way for novices to acquire a taste for the green stuff.

●●●●○

MONARCH MARTINI

Glass: Martini
Garnish: Lemon zest twist
Method: Lightly **MUDDLE** mint (just to bruise) in base of shaker. Add other ingredients, **SHAKE** with ice and fine strain into chilled glass.

7	fresh	**Mint leaves**
1½	shot(s)	**Plymouth gin**
½	shot(s)	**Freshly squeezed lemon juice**
¾	shot(s)	**Elderflower cordial**
½	shot(s)	**Sugar (gomme) syrup**
½	shot(s)	**Chilled mineral water (omit if wet ice)**

Origin: Created in 2003 by Douglas Ankrah at Townhouse, London, England. Doug's original recipe omitted water and included a dash of peach bitters.
Comment: Wonderfully floral and minty – worthy of a right royal drinker.

●●●●○

MONKEY GLAND #1

Glass: Martini
Garnish: Orange zest twist
Method: **SHAKE** all ingredients with ice and fine strain into chilled glass.

2	shot(s)	**Plymouth gin**
¼	shot(s)	**La Fée Parisian 68% absinthe**
1½	shot(s)	**Freshly squeezed orange juice**
¼	shot(s)	**Sonoma pomegranate (grenadine) syrup**

Origin: Created in the 1920s by Harry MacElhone at his Harry's New York Bar in Paris. The Monkey Gland takes its name from the work of Dr Serge Voronoff, who attempted to delay the ageing process by transplanting monkey testicles.
Comment: Approach with caution. Due diligence reveals a dangerous base of gin and absinthe.

●●●●○

MONKEY GLAND #2

Glass: Old-fashioned
Garnish: Orange slice
Method: **SHAKE** all ingredients with ice and strain into ice-filled glass.

2	shot(s)	**Plymouth gin**
1¼	shot(s)	**Freshly squeezed orange juice**
½	shot(s)	**Bénédictine D.O.M. liqueur**
¼	shot(s)	**Sonoma pomegranate (grenadine) syrup**

Comment: A somewhat off-putting name for a very palatable cocktail.

●●●●○

MONKEY SHINE

Glass: Martini
Garnish: Cinnamon rim
Method: **SHAKE** all ingredients with ice and fine strain into chilled glass.

2	shot(s)	**Mount Gay Eclipse golden rum**
1	shot(s)	**Malibu coconut rum liqueur**
1	shot(s)	**Pressed pineapple juice**

Origin: An adaptation of a drink discovered in 2003 at the Bellagio Resort & Casino, Las Vegas.
Comment: The sweet, tropical fruitiness of this drink is set off by the spicy rim.

●●●◐○

MONKEY WRENCH

Glass: Collins
Method: **POUR** rum into ice-filled glass. Top with grapefruit juice, stir and serve with straws.

2	shot(s)	**Mount Gay Eclipse golden rum**
Top up with		**Freshly squeezed pink grapefruit juice**

Comment: Simple but pleasant.

●●●○○

MONK'S CANDY BAR

Glass: Martini
Garnish: Sprinkle with nutmeg
Method: **SHAKE** all ingredients with ice and fine strain into chilled glass.

1	shot(s)	**Frangelico hazelnut liqueur**
½	shot(s)	**Butterscotch schnapps liqueur**
½	shot(s)	**Kahlúa coffee liqueur**
1	shot(s)	**Double (heavy) cream**
1	shot(s)	**Milk**

Comment: Creamy and sweet, with hazelnut, butterscotch and coffee.

●●●○○

MONK'S HABIT

Glass: Collins
Garnish: Orange slice
Method: **SHAKE** all ingredients with ice and strain into ice-filled glass.

1½	shot(s)	**Light white rum**
½	shot(s)	**Cointreau / triple sec**
1	shot(s)	**Frangelico hazelnut liqueur**
3	shot(s)	**Pressed pineapple juice**
¼	shot(s)	**Sonoma pomegranate (grenadine) syrup**

Comment: Fruit and nut laced with rum. Slightly sweet.

●●●◐○

MONTE CARLO

Glass: Collins
Garnish: Maraschino cherry
Method: **POUR** first three ingredients into empty glass. **ADD** soda water to half fill glass. Fill glass with ice and then top up with more soda. (This avoids 'shocking' the anis with the ice.) Serve with straws.

1	shot(s)	**Pernod anis**
½	shot(s)	**Luxardo maraschino liqueur**
¾	shot(s)	**Freshly squeezed lime juice**
Top up with		**Soda water (club soda)**

Origin: An adaptation of a Martini style drink created in 2002 by Alex Turner, London, England.
Comment: A long, fragrant, almost floral summer cooler with lots of aniseed.

DRINKS ARE GRADED AS FOLLOWS:

● DISGUSTING ●◐ PRETTY AWFUL ●● BEST AVOIDED
●●◐ DISAPPOINTING ●●● ACCEPTABLE ●●●◐ GOOD
●●●● RECOMMENDED ●●●●◐ HIGHLY RECOMMENDED
●●●●● OUTSTANDING / EXCEPTIONAL

MOSCOW MULE

This classic combination was born in 1941. John G. Martin had acquired the rights to Smirnoff vodka for Heublein, a small Connecticut based liquor and food distributor. Jack Morgan, the owner of Hollywood's famous Cock'n'Bull Saloon, was trying to launch his own brand of ginger beer. The two men met at New York City's Chatham Bar and hit on the idea of mixing Martin's vodka with Morgan's ginger beer and adding a dash of lime to create a new cocktail, the Moscow Mule.

To help promote the drink, and hence their respective products, Morgan had the idea of marketing the Moscow Mule using specially engraved mugs. The five ounce mugs were embossed with a kicking mule and made at a copper factory a friend of his had recently inherited. The promotion helped turn Smirnoff into a major brand.

MONTE CARLO IMPERIAL [NEW]

Glass: Martini
Garnish: Mint leaf
Method: **SHAKE** first three ingredients with ice and fine strain into chilled glass. **TOP** with champagne.

1½	shot(s)	**Plymouth gin**
½	shot(s)	**Freshly squeezed lemon juice**
½	shot(s)	**White crème de menthe liqueur**
Top up with		**Piper-Heidsieck brut champagne**

Origin: Adapted from a recipe in Harry Craddock's 1930 Savoy Cocktail Book.
Comment: A classic, minty digestif.

MONTEGO BAY [NEW]

Glass: Old-fashioned
Garnish: Lime wedge
Method: **SHAKE** all ingredients with ice and strain into ice-filled glass.

1½	shot(s)	**Martinique agricole rum (50% alc./vol.)**
½	shot(s)	**Freshly squeezed lime juice**
½	shot(s)	**Cointreau / triple sec**
¼	shot(s)	**Sugar (gomme) syrup**
2	dashes	**Angostura aromatic bitters**

Origin: Adapted from a recipe in the 1947-72 Trader Vic's Bartender's Guide by Victor Bergeron.
Comment: The name suggests Jamaica but the recipe requires agricole rum. This pungent style of rum is not Jamaican.

MONZA

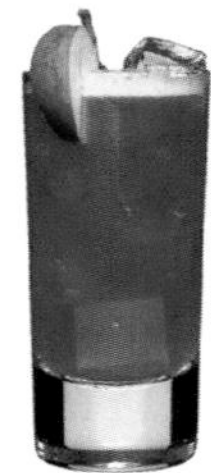

Glass: Collins
Garnish: Slice of apple
Method: Cut passion fruit in half and scoop flesh into shaker. Add other ingredients, **SHAKE** with ice and strain into ice-filled glass.

1	fresh	**Passion fruit**
2	shot(s)	**Ketel One vodka**
2	shot(s)	**Campari**
2	shot(s)	**Pressed apple juice**
¼	shot(s)	**Sugar (gomme) syrup**

Origin: A classic cocktail promoted by Campari and named after the Italian Grand Prix circuit.
Comment: If you like Campari you'll love this.

MOONRAKER [NEW]

Glass: Martini
Garnish: Maraschino cherry
Method: **SHAKE** all ingredients with ice and fine strain into chilled glass.

1½	shot(s)	**Rémy Martin cognac**
1½	shot(s)	**Dubonnet red**
¾	shot(s)	**Peach schnapps liqueur**
¼	shot(s)	**Pernod anis**

Origin: Adapted from a recipe in the 1947-72 Trader Vic's Bartender's Guide by Victor Bergeron.
Comment: A diverse range of flavours come together surprisingly well.

MOON RIVER [NEW]

Glass: Martini
Garnish: Mint leaf
Method: **SHAKE** all ingredients with ice and fine strain into chilled glass.

1½	shot(s)	**Plymouth gin**
½	shot(s)	**Apricot brandy liqueur**
½	shot(s)	**Cointreau / triple sec**
¼	shot(s)	**Galliano liqueur**
½	shot(s)	**Freshly squeezed lemon juice**
½	shot(s)	**Chilled mineral water (omit if wet ice)**

Origin: Adapted from a drink discovered in 2005 at Bar Opiume, Singapore.
Comment: There's a hint of aniseed in this fruity, sweet and sour drink.

MOONLIGHT MARTINI [NEW]

Glass: Martini
Garnish: Lemon zest twist
Method: **SHAKE** all ingredients with ice and fine strain into chilled glass.

1½	shot(s)	**Plymouth gin**
¼	shot(s)	**Kirsch eau de vie**
1	shot(s)	**Sauvignon Blanc wine**
1¼	shot(s)	**Freshly squeezed pink grapefruit juice**

Origin: Adapted from a recipe in Harry Craddock's 1930 Savoy Cocktail Book.
Comment: Craddock describes this as "a very dry cocktail". It is, but pleasantly so.

MOONSHINE MARTINI [NEW]

Glass: Martini
Garnish: Maraschino cherry
Method: **SHAKE** all ingredients with ice and fine strain into chilled glass.

1½	shot(s)	**Plymouth gin**
1	shot(s)	**Dry vermouth**
½	shot(s)	**Luxardo maraschino liqueur**
⅛	shot(s)	**La Fée Parisian 68% absinthe**

Origin: Adapted from a recipe in the 1930 Savoy Cocktail Book by Harry Craddock.
Comment: A wet Martini with balanced hints of maraschino and absinthe.

MORAVIAN COCKTAIL [NEW]

Glass: Old-fashioned
Garnish: Orange slice & cherry
Method: **SHAKE** all ingredients with ice and strain into ice-filled glass.

¾	shot(s)	**Slivovitz plum brandy**
¾	shot(s)	**Becherovka Czech liqueur**
1½	shot(s)	**Rosso (sweet) vermouth**

Origin: Discovered in 2005 at Be Bop Bar, Prague, Czech Republic.
Comment: The hardcore, Czech answer to the Italian Negroni.

●●●●○

MORNING GLORY

Glass: Old-fashioned
Garnish: Lemon zest twist
Method: **SHAKE** all ingredients with ice and strain into ice-filled glass.

1	shot(s)	**Rémy Martin cognac**
3/4	shot(s)	**Grand Marnier liqueur**
1/8	shot(s)	**La Fée Parisian 68% absinthe**
1/2	shot(s)	**Freshly squeezed lemon juice**
1/4	shot(s)	**Sugar (gomme) syrup**
2	dashes	**Angostura aromatic bitters**
1/2	shot(s)	**Chilled mineral water (omit if wet ice)**

Origin: My interpretation of a classic.
Comment: Sophisticated and complex – one for sipping.

●●●●○

MORNING GLORY FIZZ

Glass: Old-fashioned
Garnish: Lime wheel
Method: **SHAKE** first six ingredients with ice and strain into ice-filled glass. **TOP** with soda water from a siphon.

1	shot(s)	**The Famous Grouse Scotch whisky**
1/4	shot(s)	**La Fée Parisian 68% absinthe**
3/4	shot(s)	**Freshly squeezed lime juice**
3/4	shot(s)	**Freshly squeezed lemon juice**
1/4	shot(s)	**Sugar (gomme) syrup**
1/2	fresh	**Egg white**
Top up with		**Soda water from a siphon**

Comment: Considered a morning after pick-me-up but is great at any time.

●●●○○

MOSCOW LASSI

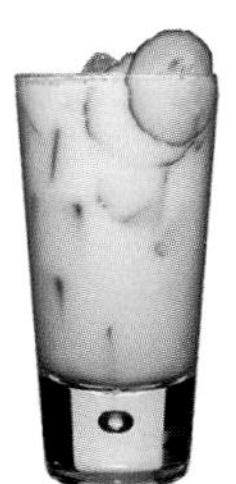

Glass: Collins
Garnish: Cucumber slices
Method: **MUDDLE** cucumber in base of shaker. Add other ingredients. **SHAKE** with ice and fine strain into ice-filled glass.

2	inches	**Chopped & peeled cucumber**
1	shot(s)	**Sweetened mango purée**
1 1/2	shot(s)	**Ketel One vodka**
2	shot(s)	**Pressed apple juice**
3	spoon(s)	**Natural yoghurt**
1/4	shot(s)	**Sugar (gomme) syrup**

Origin: Created in 2001 by Jamie Stephenson at Gaucho Grill, Manchester, England.
Comment: One to serve with your Indian takeaway.

●●●●○

MOSCOW MULE [UPDATED]

Glass: Collins (or copper mug)
Garnish: Lime wedge & mint sprig
Method: **SHAKE** first four ingredients with ice and strain into ice-filled glass. **TOP** with ginger beer and stir.

2	shot(s)	**Ketel One vodka**
1/2	shot(s)	**Freshly squeezed lime juice**
1/4	shot(s)	**Sugar (gomme) syrup**
3	dashes	**Angostura aromatic bitters**
Top up with		**Ginger beer**

Origin: My take on the drink created in 1941 by John G. Martin and Jack Morgan.
Comment: A long, vodka based drink with spice provided by ginger beer and Angostura.

●●●●○

MOTOX [NEW]

Glass: Martini
Garnish: Coriander leaf
Method: **MUDDLE** ginger and coriander in base of shaker. Add other ingredients, **SHAKE** with ice and fine strain into chilled glass.

1	slice	**Root ginger (thumbnail sized)**
10	fresh	**Coriander leaves**
1 1/2	shot(s)	**Ketel One Citroen vodka**
1/2	shot(s)	**Luxardo limoncello liqueur**
1	shot(s)	**Pressed pineapple juice**
1	shot(s)	**Pressed apple juice**

Origin: Adapted from a drink discovered in 2005 at Mo Bar, Landmark Mandarin Oriental Hotel, Hong Kong.
Comment: Each sip is fruity, lemon fresh and followed by a hot ginger hit.

●●●◐○

MOUNTAIN [NEW]

Glass: Martini
Garnish: Maraschino cherry
Method: **SHAKE** all ingredients with ice and fine strain into chilled glass.

2	shot(s)	**Bourbon whiskey**
3/4	shot(s)	**Dry vermouth**
3/4	shot(s)	**Sweet (rosso) vermouth**
1/2	fresh	**Egg white**

Comment: A perfect Manhattan smoothed by egg white.

●●●◐○

MOUNTAIN SIPPER

Glass: Old-fashioned
Garnish: Orange zest twist
Method: **SHAKE** all ingredients with ice and strain into ice-filled glass.

2	shot(s)	**Jack Daniel's Tennessee whiskey**
1	shot(s)	**Cointreau / triple sec**
1	shot(s)	**Cranberry juice**
1	shot(s)	**Freshly squeezed grapefruit juice**
1/8	shot(s)	**Sugar (gomme) syrup**

Comment: Fruity citrus flavours balance the richness of the whiskey.

●●●●○

MRS ROBINSON #1

Glass: Old-fashioned
Garnish: Three raspberries
Method: **MUDDLE** raspberries in base of shaker. Add next four ingredients, **SHAKE** with ice and strain into ice-filled glass. **TOP** with soda, lightly stir and serve with straws.

8	fresh	**Raspberries**
2	shot(s)	**Bourbon whiskey**
1	shot(s)	**Crème de framboise (raspberry) liqueur**
1/4	shot(s)	**Freshly squeezed lemon juice**
1/4	shot(s)	**Sugar (gomme) syrup**
Top up with		**Soda water (club soda)**

Origin: Created in 2000 by Max Warner at Long Bar, Sanderson, London, England.
Comment: Rich raspberry fruit laced with bourbon.

MRS. ROBINSON #2 [NEW]

●●●◐○

Glass: Martini
Garnish: Quarter orange slice on rim
Method: SHAKE all ingredients with ice and fine strain into chilled glass.

- 2½ shot(s) **Ketel One vodka**
- 1 shot(s) **Freshly squeezed orange juice**
- ½ shot(s) **Galliano liqueur**

Origin: Discovered in 2006 on Kyle Branch's Cocktail Hotel blog. (www.cocktailhotel.blogspot.com).
Comment: A short Harvey Wallbanger.

MUDDY WATER

●●●◐○

Glass: Old-fashioned
Garnish: Float 3 coffee beans
Method: SHAKE all ingredients with ice and strain into ice-filled glass.

- 1 shot(s) **Ketel One vodka**
- 1 shot(s) **Kahlúa coffee liqueur**
- 1 shot(s) **Baileys Irish Cream liqueur**

Comment: Coffee and whiskey cream with added vodka.

MUDSLIDE

●●●●○

Glass: Hurricane
Garnish: Crumbled Cadbury's Flake bar
Method: BLEND all ingredients with two 12oz scoops of crushed ice and serve with straws.

- 1½ shot(s) **Baileys Irish Cream liqueur**
- 1½ shot(s) **Kahlúa coffee liqueur**
- 1½ shot(s) **Ketel One vodka**
- 3 scoops **Vanilla ice cream**

Comment: A simply scrumptious dessert drink with whiskey cream and coffee.

MULATA DAIQUIRI

●●●●◐

Glass: Martini
Garnish: Lime wedge on rim
Method: SHAKE all ingredients with ice and fine strain into chilled glass.

- 2 shot(s) **Appleton Estate V/X aged rum**
- ½ shot(s) **Dark crème de cacao liqueur**
- ½ shot(s) **Freshly squeezed lime juice**
- ¼ shot(s) **Sugar (gomme) syrup**

Comment: A classic Daiquiri with aged rum and a hint of chocolate.

MUCKY BOTTOM [NEW]

●●●◐○

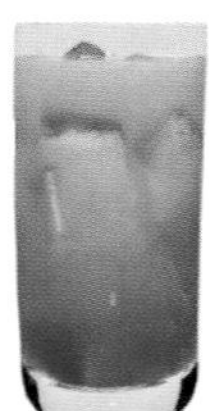

Glass: Collins
Method: SHAKE first three ingredients with ice and strain into ice-filled glass. **POUR** coffee liqueur around top of drink - this will fall to the base of the glass and create the mucky bottom.

- 2 shot(s) **Malibu coconut rum liqueur**
- 1 shot(s) **Pernod anis**
- 3 shot(s) **Freshly squeezed grapefruit juice**
- ¾ shot(s) **Kahlúa coffee liqueur**

Origin: Created in 2003 by yours truly. (Formerly named Red Haze.)
Comment: Four very strong and distinctive flavours somehow tone each other down.

MUJER VERDE [NEW]

●●●●○

Glass: Martini
Garnish: Lime zest twist
Method: SHAKE all ingredients with ice and fine strain into chilled glass.

- 1 shot(s) **Plymouth gin**
- ½ shot(s) **Green Chartreuse liqueur**
- ½ shot(s) **Yellow Chartreuse liqueur**
- ½ shot(s) **Freshly squeezed lime juice**
- ¼ shot(s) **Sugar (gomme) syrup**
- ¾ shot(s) **Chilled mineral water (omit if wet ice)**

Origin: Discovered in 2006 at Absinthe, San Francisco, where 'D Mexican' resurrected this drink from his hometown of Guadalajara.
Comment: The name means 'Green Lady'... and she packs a Chartreuse punch.

MULE'S HIND LEG

●●●●◐

Glass: Martini
Garnish: Apricot slice on rim
Method: SHAKE all ingredients with ice and fine strain into chilled glass.

- 1 shot(s) **Plymouth gin**
- 1 shot(s) **Bénédictine D.O.M. liqueur**
- 1 shot(s) **Calvados or applejack brandy**
- ¼ shot(s) **Maple syrup**
- ¾ shot(s) **Apricot brandy liqueur**
- ½ shot(s) **Chilled mineral water (omit if wet ice)**

Origin: My version of a classic 1920s recipe.
Comment: Apricot and maple syrup dominate this medium sweet drink.

HOW TO MAKE SUGAR SYRUP

To make your own sugar syrup, gradually pour TWO cups of granulated sugar into a saucepan containing ONE cup of hot water. Stir as you pour and carry on stirring and simmering until the sugar is dissolved. Do not let the water even come close to boiling and only simmer for as long as it takes to dissolve the sugar. Allow syrup to cool and pour into an empty bottle. Ideally, you should finely strain your syrup into the bottle to remove any undissolved crystals which could otherwise encourage crystallisation. If kept in a refrigerator this mixture will last for a couple of months.

MULLED WINE

Glass: Toddy
Garnish: Cinnamon stick
Method: **MUDDLE** cloves in base of mixing glass. Add rest of ingredients apart from boiling water, **STIR** and fine strain into warmed glass. **TOP** with boiling water and **STIR**.

5	whole	**Dried cloves**
1	pinch	**Freshly grated nutmeg**
1	pinch	**Ground cinnamon**
1½	shot(s)	**Warre's Otima Tawny Port**
1½	shot(s)	**Red wine**
¼	shot(s)	**Grand Marnier liqueur**
½	shot(s)	**Freshly squeezed lemon juice**
Top up with		**Boiling water**

Variant: Better if several servings are made and the ingredients warmed in a saucepan.
Comment: Warming, soothing and potent.

MYRTLE MARTINI

Glass: Martini
Garnish: Sugar rim
Method: **SHAKE** all ingredients with ice and fine strain into chilled glass.

2	shot(s)	**Ketel One vodka**
½	shot(s)	**Crème de myrtille (bilberry) liqueur**
2	shot(s)	**Pressed apple juice**
¼	shot(s)	**Sugar (gomme) syrup**
¼	shot(s)	**Freshly squeezed lime juice**

Origin: Created in 2003 at Cheyne Walk Brasserie & Salon, London, England.
Comment: A fruity concoction to remember should you find yourself with a bottle of crème de myrtille.

MYSTIQUE

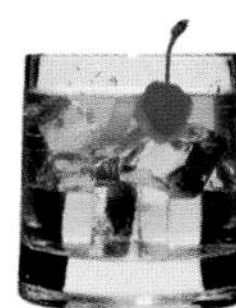

Glass: Old-fashioned
Garnish: Orange zest twist
Method: **SHAKE** all ingredients with ice and strain into ice-filled glass.

½	shot(s)	**The Famous Grouse Scotch whisky**
¾	shot(s)	**Drambuie liqueur**
½	shot(s)	**Peach schnapps liqueur**
¼	shot(s)	**Luxardo maraschino liqueur**
3	dashes	**Fee Brothers orange bitters**

Origin: Created by Greg Pearson at Mystique, Manchester, England in 1999. Joint winner of the Manchester Food & Drink Festival cocktail competition.
Comment: Honeyed, peachy, orange Scotch.

MYSTIQUE MARTINI

Glass: Martini
Garnish: Raspberries on stick
Method: **STIR** all ingredients with ice and fine strain into chilled glass.

2	shot(s)	**The Famous Grouse Scotch whisky**
1	shot(s)	**Tuaca Italian liqueur**
¾	shot(s)	**Chambord black raspberry liqueur**

Origin: Created in 2002 by Tim Halilaj, Albania.
Comment: Rust coloured and fruit charged.

NACIONAL DAIQUIRI #1 [NEW]

Glass: Martini
Garnish: Maraschino cherry
Method: **SHAKE** all ingredients with ice and fine strain into chilled glass.

2	shot(s)	**Light white rum**
¾	shot(s)	**Apricot brandy liqueur**
½	shot(s)	**Freshly squeezed lime juice**
¾	shot(s)	**Chilled mineral water (omit if wet ice)**

Origin: An old classic named after the Hotel Nacional, Havana, Cuba, where it was created.
Comment: A sophisticated complex apricot Daiquiri.

NACIONAL DAIQUIRI #2 [NEW]

Glass: Martini
Garnish: Maraschino cherry
Method: **SHAKE** all ingredients with ice and fine strain into chilled glass.

2	shot(s)	**Light white rum**
½	shot(s)	**Apricot brandy liqueur**
1½	shot(s)	**Pressed pineapple juice**
½	shot(s)	**Freshly squeezed lime juice**

Comment: An apricot Daiquiri with extra interest courtesy of pineapple.

NANTUCKET

Glass: Collins
Garnish: Lime wedge
Method: **SHAKE** all ingredients with ice and strain into ice-filled glass.

2	shot(s)	**Light white rum**
3	shot(s)	**Cranberry juice**
2	shot(s)	**Freshly squeezed golden grapefruit juice**

Origin: Popularised by the Cheers bar chain, this is named after the beautiful island off Cape Cod.
Comment: Essentially a Seabreeze with rum in place of vodka.

NAPOLEON MARTINI [NEW]

Glass: Martini
Garnish: Lemon peel twist
Method: **SHAKE** all ingredients with ice and fine strain into chilled glass.

2	shot(s)	**Plymouth gin**
¼	shot(s)	**Cointreau / triple sec**
½	shot(s)	**Dubonnet Red**
¼	shot(s)	**Fernet Branca**
½	shot(s)	**Chilled mineral water (omit if wet ice)**

Origin: Adapted from a recipe in Harry Craddock's 1930 Savoy Cocktail Book.
Comment: A beautifully balanced, very approachable, rust coloured Martini.

NARANJA DAIQUIRI

Glass: Martini
Garnish: Orange slice on rim
Method: **SHAKE** all ingredients with ice and fine strain into chilled glass.

1¾	shot(s)	**Light white rum**
¾	shot(s)	**Grand Marnier liqueur**
1	shot(s)	**Freshly squeezed orange juice**
½	shot(s)	**Freshly squeezed lime juice**
⅛	shot(s)	**Sugar (gomme) syrup**

Comment: The Latino version of an orange Daiquiri.

NATURAL DAIQUIRI

Glass: Martini
Garnish: Lime wedge
Method: **SHAKE** all ingredients with ice and fine strain into chilled glass.

2	shot(s)	**Light white rum (or aged rum)**
½	shot(s)	**Freshly squeezed lime juice**
¼	shot(s)	**Sugar (gomme) syrup**
½	shot(s)	**Chilled mineral water (omit if wet ice)**

Variant: Flavoured syrups may be substituted for sugar syrup. Alternatively you can use flavoured rum (see Vanilla Daiquiri) or add fresh fruit and/or fruit juice and/or fruit liqueur (see Melon Daiquiri etc.).
Origin: Created in 1896 by Jennings Cox, an American engineer who was working at a mine near Santiago, Cuba.
Comment: A deliciously simple, clean, refreshing sour drink.

NAUTILUS [NEW]

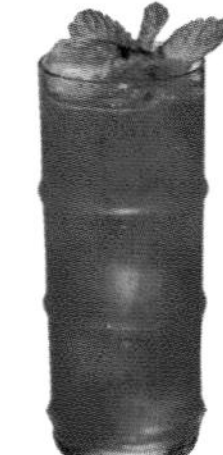

Glass: Collins (or Nautilus seashell)
Garnish: Mint sprig
Method: **SHAKE** all ingredients with ice and strain into ice-filled glass. Serve with straws.

2	shot(s)	**Sauza Hornitos tequila**
2	shot(s)	**Cranberry juice**
1	shot(s)	**Freshly squeezed lime juice**
½	shot(s)	**Sugar (gomme) syrup**

Origin: Adapted from a drink created by Victor Bergeron (Trader Vic).
Comment: Basically a Margarita lengthened with cranberry juice.

NAVIGATOR [NEW]

Glass: Martini
Garnish: Lemon zest twist
Method: **SHAKE** all ingredients with ice and fine strain into chilled glass.

2	shot(s)	**Plymouth gin**
1	shot(s)	**Luxardo limoncello liqueur**
1	shot(s)	**Freshly squeezed pink grapefruit juice**

Origin: Created in 2005 by Jamie Terrell, London, England.
Comment: This fruity, grapefruit-led drink is pleasantly bitter and sour.

NAVY GROG

Glass: Old-fashioned
Garnish: Lemon wedge
Method: **STIR** honey with rum in base of shaker to dissolve honey. Add next three ingredients, **SHAKE** with ice and strain into ice-filled glass.

3	spoons	**Runny honey**
1½	shot(s)	**Pusser's Navy rum**
¼	shot(s)	**Freshly squeezed lime juice**
2½	shot(s)	**Chilled mineral water**
2	dashes	**Angostura aromatic bitters**

Variant: Also great served hot. Top with boiling water and garnish with a cinnamon stick.
Comment: An extremely drinkable, honeyed cocktail.

NEGRONI

Glass: Old-fashioned
Garnish: Orange zest twist
Method: **STIR** all ingredients with ice and strain into ice-filled glass.

1	shot(s)	**Plymouth gin**
1	shot(s)	**Campari**
1	shot(s)	**Sweet (rosso) vermouth**

Variant: Serve in a Collins glass topped with soda water (club soda).
Origin: This drink takes its name from Count Camillo Negroni. In the mid-1920s, while drinking at the Casoni Bar in Florence, Italy, he is said to have asked for an Americano 'with a bit more kick'.
Comment: Bitter and dry, but very tasty.

NEGUS (HOT)

Glass: Toddy
Garnish: Dust with freshly ground nutmeg
Method: Place bar spoon in warmed glass. **POUR** all ingredients into glass and **STIR**.

3	shot(s)	**Warre's Otima Tawny Port**
1	shot(s)	**Freshly squeezed lemon juice**
½	shot(s)	**Sugar (gomme) syrup**
Top up with		**Boiling water**

Variant: Bishop
Origin: Colonel Francis Negus was the MP for Ipswich from 1717 to 1732. He created this diluted version of the original Bishop.
Comment: A tangy, citrussy hot drink.

NEVADA DAIQUIRI

Glass: Martini
Garnish: Lime wedge on rim
Method: **SHAKE** all ingredients with ice and fine strain into chilled glass.

2	shot(s)	**Pusser's Navy rum**
1	shot(s)	**Freshly squeezed grapefruit juice**
½	shot(s)	**Freshly squeezed lime juice**
½	shot(s)	**Sugar (gomme) syrup**

Comment: A pungent Daiquiri with the intense flavour of Navy rum.

NEW ORLEANS MULE [NEW]

Glass: Collins
Garnish: Lime wedge
Method: SHAKE first four ingredients with ice and fine strain into ice-filled glass. **TOP** with ginger beer.

2	shot(s)	**Bourbon whiskey**
1	shot(s)	**Kahlúa coffee liqueur**
1	shot(s)	**Pressed pineapple juice**
1/2	shot(s)	**Freshly squeezed lime juice**
Top up with		**Ginger beer**

Comment: A spicy, full-flavoured taste of the South.

NEW ORLEANS PUNCH

Glass: Collins
Garnish: Lemon slice
Method: SHAKE all ingredients with ice and strain into glass filled with crushed ice. Serve with straws.

1 1/2	shot(s)	**Bourbon whiskey**
3/4	shot(s)	**Aged rum**
1 1/2	shot(s)	**Chambord black raspberry liqueur**
3/4	shot(s)	**Freshly squeezed lemon juice**
3	shot(s)	**Cold black camomile tea**

Comment: Raspberry is the predominant flavour in this long drink.

NEW YEAR'S ABSOLUTION [NEW]

Glass: Old-fashioned
Garnish: Mint sprig
Method: STIR honey with absinthe in base of shaker until honey dissolves. Add apple juice, **SHAKE** with ice and strain into ice-filled glass. **TOP** with ginger ale and stir.

2	spoons	**Runny honey**
1	shot(s)	**La Fée Parisian 68% absinthe**
1	shot(s)	**Pressed apple juice**
Top up with		**Ginger ale**

Comment: The green fairy, tamed with honey and spiced with ginger.

NEW YORKER

Glass: Martini
Garnish: Orange zest twist
Method: SHAKE all ingredients with ice and fine strain into chilled glass.

2	shot(s)	**Bourbon whiskey**
1	shot(s)	**Claret (red wine)**
1/2	shot(s)	**Freshly squeezed lemon juice**
1/2	shot(s)	**Sugar (gomme) syrup**

Comment: Sweet 'n' sour whiskey and wine.

NEW PORT CODEBREAKER

Glass: Collins
Method: SHAKE all ingredients with ice and strain into ice-filled glass.

1	shot(s)	**Sauza Hornitos tequila**
1	shot(s)	**Pusser's Navy rum**
1/2	shot(s)	**Warninks advocaat**
1/2	shot(s)	**Coco López cream of coconut**
4	shot(s)	**Freshly squeezed orange juice**

Origin: Adapted from a cocktail discovered in 1999 at Porter's Bar, Covent Garden, London.
Comment: This straw yellow drink is a most unusual mix of ingredients.

NIAGARA FALLS

Glass: Flute
Garnish: Physalis
Method: SHAKE first four ingredients with ice and strain into chilled glass. **TOP** with ginger ale and lightly stir.

1	shot(s)	**Ketel One vodka**
1	shot(s)	**Grand Marnier liqueur**
1/2	shot(s)	**Freshly squeezed lemon juice**
1/4	shot(s)	**Sugar (gomme) syrup**
Top up with		**Ginger ale**

Comment: Ginger ale and orange complement each other, fortified by vodka.

NICE PEAR-TINI

Glass: Martini
Garnish: Pear slice on rim
Method: SHAKE all ingredients with ice and fine strain into chilled glass.

1	shot(s)	**Rémy Martin cognac**
1/2	shot(s)	**Pear & cognac liqueur**
1/2	shot(s)	**Poire William eau de vie**
2	shot(s)	**Freshly extracted pear juice**
1/4	shot(s)	**Sugar (gomme) syrup**

Origin: Created in 2002 by yours truly.
Comment: Spirited, rich and fruity.

NICKY FINN [NEW]

Glass: Martini
Garnish: Lemon zest twist
Method: SHAKE all ingredients with ice and fine strain into chilled glass.

1	shot(s)	**Rémy Martin cognac**
1	shot(s)	**Cointreau / triple sec**
1	shot(s)	**Freshly squeezed lemon juice**
1/4	shot(s)	**Pernod anis**

Origin: Adapted from a recipe in 'Cocktail: The Drinks Bible for the 21st Century' by Paul Harrington and Laura Moorhead.
Comment: Basically a Sidecar spiked with an aniseedy dash of Pernod.

NICKY'S FIZZ [NEW]

Glass: Collins
Garnish: Orange slice
Method: SHAKE first two ingredients with ice and strain into ice-filled glass. **TOP** with soda, lightly stir and serve with straws.

2	shot(s)	**Plymouth gin**
2	shot(s)	**Freshly squeezed grapefruit juice**
Top up with		**Soda water (from siphon)**

Comment: A dry, refreshing, long drink.

NIGHT & DAY [NEW]

Glass: Flute
Garnish: Orange zest twist
Method: POUR ingredients into chilled glass.

1/2	shot(s)	**Campari**
1/2	shot(s)	**Grand Marnier liqueur**
Top up with		**Piper-Heidsieck brut champagne**

Comment: Dry, aromatic, orange champagne.

NIGHTMARE MARTINI

Glass: Martini
Garnish: Maraschino cherry
Method: SHAKE all ingredients with ice and fine strain into chilled glass.

1	shot(s)	**Plymouth gin**
1	shot(s)	**Dubonnet Red**
1/2	shot(s)	**Cherry (brandy) liqueur**
2	shot(s)	**Freshly squeezed orange juice**

Comment: Pleasant enough, with hints of cherry. Hardly a nightmare.

NINE-20-SEVEN

Glass: Flute
Method: POUR ingredients into chilled glass and lightly stir.

1/4	shot(s)	**Vanilla flavoured vodka**
1/4	shot(s)	**Cuarenta Y Tres (Licor 43)**
Top up with		**Piper-Heidsieck brut champagne**

Origin: Created in 2002 by Damian Caldwell at Home Bar, London, England. Damian was lost for a name until a customer asked the time.
Comment: Champagne with a hint of vanilla.

FOR MORE INFORMATION SEE OUR
INGREDIENTS APPENDIX ON PAGE 320

NOBLE EUROPE

Glass: Old-fashioned
Garnish: Orange slice in glass
Method: SHAKE all ingredients with ice and strain into glass filled with crushed ice.

1 1/2	shot(s)	**Tokaji Hungarian wine**
1	shot(s)	**Ketel One vodka**
1	shot(s)	**Freshly squeezed orange juice**
1	dash	**Vanilla essence**

Origin: Created in 2002 by Dan Spink at Browns, St Martin's Lane, London, England.
Variant: Also great served 'up' in a Martini glass.
Comment: A delicious cocktail that harnesses the rich, sweet flavours of Tokaji and delivers them very approachably.

NOME

Glass: Martini
Garnish: Mint leaf
Method: STIR all ingredients with ice and strain into chilled glass.

1 1/2	shot(s)	**Plymouth gin**
1	shot(s)	**Yellow Chartreuse**
1 1/2	shot(s)	**Tio Pepe Fino sherry**

AKA: Alaska Martini
Origin: A classic cocktail whose origin is unknown.
Comment: This dyslexic gnome is dry and interesting.

NOON [NEW]

Glass: Martini
Garnish: Orange zest twist
Method: SHAKE all ingredients with ice and strain into chilled glass.

1 1/2	shot(s)	**Plymouth gin**
3/4	shot(s)	**Dry vermouth**
3/4	shot(s)	**Sweet (rosso) vermouth**
3/4	shot(s)	**Freshly squeezed orange juice**
2	dashes	**Angostura aromatic bitters**
1/2	fresh	**Egg white**

Comment: This classic cocktail is smooth and aromatic.

NORTHERN LIGHTS

Glass: Martini
Garnish: Star anise
Method: SHAKE all ingredients with ice and fine strain into chilled glass.

1 1/2	shot(s)	**Zubrówka bison vodka**
3/4	shot(s)	**Apple schnapps liqueur**
1	shot(s)	**Pressed apple juice**
1/2	shot(s)	**Freshly squeezed lime juice**
1/2	shot(s)	**Pernod anis**
1/2	shot(s)	**Sugar (gomme) syrup**

Origin: Created in 2003 by Stewart Hudson at MJU Bar, Millennium Hotel, London, England.
Comment: Wonderfully refreshing: apple and anis served up on a grassy vodka base.

NORTH POLE MARTINI [NEW]

Glass: Martini
Method: SHAKE first four ingredients with ice and fine strain into chilled glass. **FLOAT** cream over drink.

2	shot(s)	**Plymouth gin**
1	shot(s)	**Luxardo maraschino liqueur**
1/2	shot(s)	**Freshly squeezed lemon juice**
1/2	fresh	**Egg white**
Float		**Double (heavy) cream**

Origin: Adapted from a recipe in the 1947-72 Trader Vic's Bartender's Guide by Victor Bergeron.
Comment: An Aviation smoothed by egg white and cream.

NOT SO COSMO (MOCKTAIL)

Glass: Martini
Garnish: Orange zest twist
Method: SHAKE all ingredients with ice and fine strain into chilled glass.

1	shot(s)	**Freshly squeezed orange juice**
1	shot(s)	**Cranberry juice**
1	shot(s)	**Freshly squeezed lime juice**
1	shot(s)	**Freshly squeezed lemon juice**

Origin: Discovered in 2003 at Claridge's Bar, London, England.
Comment: This non-alcoholic cocktail may look like a Cosmo but it doesn't taste like one.

NOVEMBER SEABREEZE (MOCKTAIL)

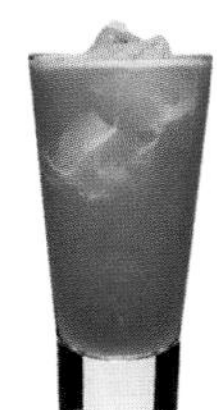

Glass: Collins
Garnish: Lime wedge
Method: SHAKE first three ingredients with ice and strain into ice-filled glass. **TOP** with soda, gently stir and serve with straws.

2	shot(s)	**Cranberry juice**
2	shot(s)	**Pressed apple juice**
1	shot(s)	**Freshly squeezed lime juice**
Top up with		**Soda water (club soda)**

Comment: A superbly refreshing fruity drink, whatever the time of year.

NO. 10 LEMONADE [NEW]

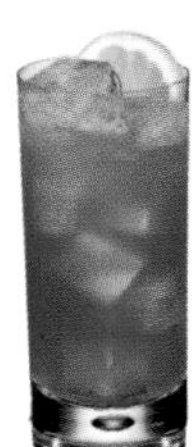

Glass: Collins
Garnish: Lemon slice
Method: MUDDLE blueberries in base of shaker. Add next three ingredients, **SHAKE** with ice and fine strain into ice filled glass. **TOP** with soda, lightly stir and serve with straws.

12	fresh	**Blueberries**
2	shot(s)	**Light white rum**
1 1/2	shot(s)	**Freshly squeezed lemon juice**
3/4	shot(s)	**Sugar (gomme) syrup**
Top up with		**Soda water (club soda)**

Origin: Adapted from a drink discovered in 2006 at Double Seven, New York City, USA.
Comment: Basically a long blueberry Daiquiri.

NUTCRACKER SWEET [NEW]

Glass: Martini
Garnish: Dust with cocoa powder
Method: SHAKE all ingredients with ice and fine strain into chilled glass.

2	shot(s)	**Ketel One vodka**
1	shot(s)	**White crème de cacao liqueur**
3/4	shot(s)	**Luxardo Amaretto di Saschira liqueur**

Comment: After dinner, fortified almond and chocolate.

NUTS & BERRIES

Glass: Martini
Garnish: Float raspberry and almond flake
Method: STIR all ingredients with ice and strain into chilled glass.

1	shot(s)	**Raspberry flavoured vodka**
1	shot(s)	**Almond flavoured vodka**
1/4	shot(s)	**Frangelico hazelnut liqueur**
1/4	shot(s)	**Chambord black raspberry liqueur**
1	shot(s)	**7-Up**

Origin: Created in 2004 by yours truly.
Comment: The inclusion of a carbonate (7-Up) may annoy some classical bartenders but it adds flavour, sweetness and dilution.

NUTTY BERRY'TINI

Glass: Martini
Garnish: Float mint leaf
Method: SHAKE all ingredients with ice and fine strain into chilled glass.

2	shot(s)	**Cranberry flavoured vodka**
1/2	shot(s)	**Cherry (brandy) liqueur**
1/2	shot(s)	**Frangelico hazelnut liqueur**
1/4	shot(s)	**Luxardo maraschino liqueur**
1	shot(s)	**Cranberry juice**
1/2	shot(s)	**Freshly squeezed lime juice**

Origin: Created by yours truly in 2003.
Comment: Cranberry vodka and juice, sweetened with cherry liqueur, dried with lime juice and flavoured with hazelnut.

NUTTY NASHVILLE

Glass: Martini
Garnish: Lemon zest twist
Method: STIR honey with bourbon in base of shaker to dissolve honey. Add other ingredients, **SHAKE** with ice and fine strain into chilled glass.

2	spoon(s)	**Runny honey**
2	shot(s)	**Bourbon whiskey**
1	shot(s)	**Frangelico hazelnut liqueur**
1	shot(s)	**Krupnik honey liqueur**

Origin: Created in 2001 by Jason Fendick at Rockwell, Trafalgar Hotel, London, England.
Comment: Bourbon and hazelnut smoothed and rounded by honey.

NUTTY RUSSIAN

Glass: Old-fashioned
Method: SHAKE all ingredients with ice and strain into ice-filled glass.

1 1/2	shot(s)	**Ketel One vodka**
3/4	shot(s)	**Frangelico hazelnut liqueur**
3/4	shot(s)	**Kahlúa coffee liqueur**

Comment: A Black Russian with hazelnut liqueur.

NUTTY SUMMER

Glass: Martini
Garnish: Drop three dashes of Angostura aromatic bitters onto surface of drink and stir around with a cocktail stick - essential to both the look and flavour.
Method: SHAKE all ingredients with ice and fine strain into chilled glass.

1 1/2	shot(s)	**Warninks advocaat**
3/4	shot(s)	**Luxardo Amaretto di Saschira liqueur**
3/4	shot(s)	**Malibu coconut rum liqueur**
3/4	shot(s)	**Pressed pineapple juice**
1/2	shot(s)	**Double (heavy) cream**

Origin: Created in 2001 by Daniel Spink at Hush Up, London, England.
Comment: This subtle, dessert style cocktail is packed with flavour. A superb after dinner tipple for summer.

OATMEAL COOKIE

Glass: Shot
Method: SHAKE all ingredients with ice and fine strain into chilled glass.

1/2	shot(s)	**Butterscotch schnapps liqueur**
1/4	shot(s)	**Goldschläger cinnamon schnapps**
3/4	shot(s)	**Baileys Irish Cream liqueur**

Comment: A well balanced, creamy shot with hints of butterscotch and cinnamon.

OÁZA [NEW]

Glass: Old-fashioned
Garnish: Lime wedge
Method: SHAKE all ingredients with ice and strain into ice-filled glass.

2	shot(s)	**Becherovka**
3/4	shot(s)	**Freshly squeezed lime juice**
1/4	shot(s)	**Sugar (gomme) syrup**

Origin: A popular drink in the Czech Republic where Becherovka, a herbal liquor, is the national drink.
Comment: Herbal and bittersweet. Not for everyone.

ODDBALL MANHATTAN DRY [NEW]

Glass: Martini
Garnish: Two maraschino cherries
Method: STIR all ingredients with ice and strain into chilled glass.

2 1/2	shot(s)	**Bourbon whiskey**
1	shot(s)	**Dry vermouth**
1/2	shot(s)	**Yellow Chartreuse liqueur**
3	dashes	**Angostura aromatic bitters**

Comment: Not as oddball as it sounds, the Chartreuse combines harmoniously.

O'HENRY [NEW]

Glass: Collins
Garnish: Lemon slice
Method: SHAKE first two ingredients with ice and strain into ice-filled glass. **TOP** with ginger ale, lightly stir and serve with straws.

2	shot(s)	**Bourbon whiskey**
1	shot(s)	**Bénédictine D.O.M. liqueur**
Top up with		**Ginger ale**

Origin: Discovered in 2006 at Brandy Library, New York City, USA.
Comment: Herbal whiskey and ginger.

OH GOSH!

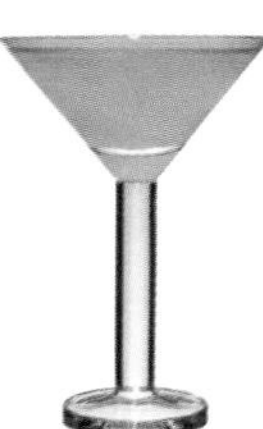

Glass: Martini
Garnish: Lemon zest twist
Method: SHAKE all ingredients with ice and fine strain into chilled glass.

1 1/2	shot(s)	**Light white rum**
1	shot(s)	**Cointreau / triple sec**
1/2	shot(s)	**Freshly squeezed lime juice**
1/4	shot(s)	**Sugar (gomme) syrup**
1/2	shot(s)	**Chilled mineral water (omit if wet ice)**

Origin: Created by Tony Conigliaro in 2001 at Isola, London, England. A customer requested a Daiquiri with a difference – when this was served he took one sip and exclaimed "Oh gosh!".
Comment: A very subtle orange twist on the classic Daiquiri.

OIL SLICK

Glass: Shot
Method: Refrigerate ingredients then **LAYER** in chilled glass by carefully pouring in the following order.

3/4	shot(s)	**Opal Nera black sambuca**
3/4	shot(s)	**Baileys Irish Cream liqueur**

Comment: Whiskey cream and liquorice.

OLD FASHIONED #1 (CLASSIC VERSION)

Glass: Old-fashioned
Garnish: Orange (or lemon) twist
Method: STIR one shot of bourbon with two ice cubes in a glass. Add sugar syrup and Angostura and two more ice cubes. Stir some more and add another two ice cubes and the rest of the bourbon. Stir lots more and add more ice.

2½	shot(s)	**Bourbon whiskey**
½	shot(s)	**Sugar (gomme) syrup**
3	dashes	**Angostura aromatic bitters**

Origin: Said to have been created between 1900 and 1907, at the Pendennis Club, Louisville, Kentucky, USA.
Comment: The melting and stirring in of ice cubes is essential to the dilution and taste of this classic.

OLD FASHIONED #2 (US VERSION)

Glass: Old-fashioned
Garnish: Orange zest twist & maraschino cherry
Method: MUDDLE orange and cherries in base of shaker. Add other ingredients, **SHAKE** with ice and fine strain into ice-filled glass.

2	whole	**Maraschino cherries**
1	fresh	**Orange slice (cut into eight segments)**
2	shot(s)	**Bourbon whiskey**
⅛	shot(s)	**Maraschino syrup (from the cherry jar)**
2	dashes	**Angostura aromatic bitters**

Comment: This drink is often mixed in the glass in which it is to be served. Shaking better incorporates the flavours produced by muddling and fine straining removes the orange peel and cherry skin.

OLD FASHIONED CADDY [NEW]

Glass: Old-fashioned
Garnish: Orange slice & cherry (sail)
Method: SHAKE all ingredients with ice and strain into ice-filled glass.

2	shot(s)	**The Famous Grouse Scotch whisky**
½	shot(s)	**Cherry (brandy) liqueur**
½	shot(s)	**Sweet (rosso) vermouth**
2	dashes	**Angostura aromatic bitters**

Origin: Created in 2005 by Wayne Collins, London, England.
Comment: Rich, red and packed with flavour.

OLD PAL [UPDATED]

Glass: Old-fashioned
Garnish: Orange slice
Method: STIR all ingredients with ice and strain into ice-filled glass.

1¼	shot(s)	**Bourbon whiskey**
1¼	shot(s)	**Dry vermouth**
1¼	shot(s)	**Campari**

Comment: Dry and bitter.

OLE

Glass: Martini
Garnish: Orange wheel on rim
Method: SHAKE all ingredients with ice and fine strain into chilled glass.

2	shot(s)	**Rémy Martin cognac**
¾	shot(s)	**Cuarenta Y Tres (Licor 43) liqueur**
1½	shot(s)	**Freshly squeezed orange juice**

Comment: Vanilla, orange and brandy combine well.

OLYMPIC [NEW]

Glass: Martini
Garnish: Orange zest twist
Method: SHAKE all ingredients with ice and fine strain into chilled glass.

1¼	shot(s)	**Rémy Martin cognac**
1¼	shot(s)	**Grand Marnier liqueur**
1¼	shot(s)	**Freshly squeezed orange juice**

Origin: Adapted from a recipe in Harry Craddock's 1930 Savoy Cocktail Book.
Comment: The perfect balance of cognac and orange juice. One to celebrate the 2012 Games perhaps.

ONION RING MARTINI

Glass: Martini
Garnish: Onion ring
Method: MUDDLE onion in base of shaker. Add other ingredients, **SHAKE** with ice and fine strain into chilled glass.

2	ring(s)	**Fresh red onion**
1	shot(s)	**Sake**
2	shot(s)	**Plymouth gin**
3	dashes	**Fee Brothers orange bitters**
⅛	shot(s)	**Sugar (gomme) syrup**

Origin: Reputed to have been created at the Bamboo Bar, Bangkok, Thailand.
Comment: Certainly one of the most obscure Martini variations – drinkable, but leaves you with onion breath.

OPAL [UPDATED]

Glass: Martini
Garnish: Orange zest twist
Method: SHAKE all ingredients with ice and fine strain into chilled glass.

2	shot(s)	**Plymouth gin**
½	shot(s)	**Cointreau / triple sec**
1¼	shot(s)	**Freshly squeezed orange juice**
¼	shot(s)	**Sugar (gomme) syrup**
⅛	shot(s)	**Orange flower water (optional)**

Origin: Adapted from the 1920s recipe.
Comment: Fresh, fragrant flavours of orange zest and gin.

A B C D E F G H I J K L M N **O** P Q R S T U V W X Y Z

OPAL CAFÉ

Glass: Shot
Method: SHAKE first two ingredients with ice and fine strain into chilled glass. **FLOAT** thin layer of cream over drink.

1/2	shot(s)	**Opal Nera black sambuca**
1/2	shot(s)	**Cold espresso coffee**
Float		**Double (heavy) cream**

Comment: A great liquorice and coffee drink to sip or shoot.

ORANGE BLOOM MARTINI [NEW]

Glass: Martini
Garnish: Maraschino cherry
Method: SHAKE all ingredients with ice and fine strain into chilled glass.

2	shot(s)	**Plymouth gin**
1	shot(s)	**Cointreau / triple sec**
1	shot(s)	**Sweet (rosso) vermouth**

Origin: Adapted from a recipe in the 1930s edition of the Savoy Cocktail Book by Harry Craddock.
Comment: Strong, fruity zesty orange laced with gin.

OPENING SHOT

Glass: Shot
Method: SHAKE all ingredients with ice and fine strain into chilled glass.

1	shot(s)	**Bourbon whiskey**
1/2	shot(s)	**Sweet (rosso) vermouth**
1/8	shot(s)	**Sonoma pomegranate (grenadine) syrup**

Variant: Double the quantities and strain into a Martini glass and you have the 1920s classic I based this drink on.
Comment: Basically a miserly Sweet Manhattan.

ORANGE BLOSSOM

Glass: Old-fashioned
Garnish: Orange zest twist
Method: SHAKE all ingredients with ice and strain into ice-filled glass.

1 1/2	shot(s)	**Plymouth gin**
1/2	shot(s)	**Cointreau / triple sec**
1 1/2	shot(s)	**Freshly squeezed orange juice**
1/2	shot(s)	**Freshly squeezed lime juice**
1/8	shot(s)	**Sonoma pomegranate (grenadine) syrup**

Variant: Served long in a Collins glass this becomes a Harvester.
Comment: Gin sweetened with liqueur and grenadine, and soured with lime.

OPERA

Glass: Martini
Garnish: Orange zest twist
Method: SHAKE all ingredients with ice and fine strain into chilled glass.

2	shot(s)	**Plymouth gin**
2	shot(s)	**Dubonnet Red**
1/4	shot(s)	**Luxardo maraschino liqueur**
3	dashes	**Fee Brothers orange bitters**

Origin: Adapted from the classic 1920s cocktail.
Comment: Dubonnet smoothes the gin while maraschino adds floral notes.

ORANGE BRÛLÉE [NEW]

Glass: Martini
Garnish: Dust with cocoa powder
Method: SHAKE first three ingredients with ice and fine strain into chilled glass. **FLOAT** thin layer of cream over drink and turn glass to spread evenly.

1 1/2	shot(s)	**Luxardo Amaretto di Saschira liqueur**
1 1/2	shot(s)	**Grand Marnier liqueur**
3/4	shot(s)	**Rémy Martin cognac**
1/4	shot(s)	**Double (heavy) cream**

Origin: Created in 2005 by Xavier Laigle at Bar Le Forum, Paris, France.
Comment: A great looking, beautifully balanced after-dinner drink.

ORANG-A-TANG [UPDATED]

Glass: Sling
Garnish: Orange slice on rim
Method: SHAKE first five ingredients with ice and strain into ice-filled glass. **FLOAT** layer of rum over drink.

1 1/2	shot(s)	**Ketel One vodka**
3/4	shot(s)	**Cointreau / triple sec**
2	shot(s)	**Freshly squeezed orange juice**
1/2	shot(s)	**Freshly squeezed lime juice**
1/4	shot(s)	**Sonoma pomegranate (grenadine) syrup**
1/2	shot(s)	**Wood's 100 old navy rum**

Comment: Orange predominates in this long, tangy, tropical cooler.

ORANGE CUSTARD MARTINI

Glass: Martini
Garnish: Orange zest twist
Method: SHAKE all ingredients with ice and fine strain into chilled glass.

2	shot(s)	**Warninks advocaat**
1	shot(s)	**Tuaca Italian liqueur**
1/2	shot(s)	**Grand Marnier liqueur**
1/4	shot(s)	**Vanilla syrup**

Origin: I created this drink in 2002 after rediscovering advocaat on a trip to Amsterdam.
Comment: A smooth, creamy orangey dessert cocktail.

ORANGE DAIQUIRI #1 [NEW]

Glass: Old-fashioned
Garnish: Orange zest twist
Method: **SHAKE** all ingredients with ice and fine strain into ice-filled glass.

2	shot(s)	**Aged rum**
3/4	shot(s)	**Freshly squeezed orange juice**
1/2	shot(s)	**Freshly squeezed lime juice**
1/4	shot(s)	**Sugar (gomme) syrup**

AKA: Bolo
Origin: My take on a popular drink.
Comment: Far more serious than it looks. Sweet and sour in harmony.

ORANGE DAIQUIRI #2

Glass: Martini
Garnish: Orange zest twist
Method: **SHAKE** all ingredients with ice and fine strain into chilled glass.

2	shot(s)	**Clément Créole Shrubb liqueur**
1/2	shot(s)	**Freshly squeezed lime juice**
3/4	shot(s)	**Chilled mineral water (omit if wet ice)**

Variant: Derby Daiquiri
Origin: I conceived this drink in 1998, after visiting the company which was then importing Créole Shrubb. I took a bottle to London's Met Bar and Ben Reed made me my first Orange Daiquiri.
Comment: Créole Shrubb is an unusual liqueur made by infusing orange peel in casks of mature Martinique rum.

ORANGE MARTINI [NEW]

Glass: Martini
Garnish: Orange zest twist
Method: **SHAKE** all ingredients with ice and fine strain into chilled glass.

2	shot(s)	**Plymouth gin**
1	shot(s)	**Freshly squeezed orange juice**
1/2	shot(s)	**Sweet (rosso) vermouth**
1/4	shot(s)	**Sugar (gomme) syrup**
3	dashes	**Fee Brothers orange bitters**

Origin: Adapted from the Orange Cocktail and Orange Martini Cocktail in the 1930s edition of the Savoy Cocktail Book by Harry Craddock.
Comment: A sophisticated, complex balance of orange and gin.

ORANGE MOJITO

Glass: Collins
Garnish: Mint sprig
Method: Lightly **MUDDLE** mint (just to bruise) in base of glass. Add other ingredients and half fill glass with crushed ice. **CHURN** (stir) with bar spoon. Fill with more crushed ice and churn some more. **TOP** with soda, stir and serve with straws.

8	fresh	**Mint leaves**
1 1/2	shot(s)	**Orange flavoured vodka**
1/2	shot(s)	**Mandarine Napoléon liqueur**
1/2	shot(s)	**Light white rum**
1	shot(s)	**Freshly squeezed lime juice**
1/2	shot(s)	**Sugar (gomme) syrup**
Top up with		**Soda water (club soda)**

Origin: Created in 2001 by Jamie MacDonald while working in Sydney, Australia.
Comment: Mint and orange combine to make a wonderfully fresh drink.

ORANJINIHA

Glass: Collins
Garnish: Orange slice in glass
Method: **SHAKE** all ingredients with ice and strain into glass filled with crushed ice.

2	shot(s)	**Orange flavoured vodka**
3	shot(s)	**Freshly squeezed orange juice**
1	shot(s)	**Freshly squeezed lemon juice**
1	shot(s)	**Sugar (gomme) syrup**

Origin: Created in 2002 by Alex Kammerling, London, England.
Comment: A tall, richly flavoured orange drink.

ORCHARD BREEZE

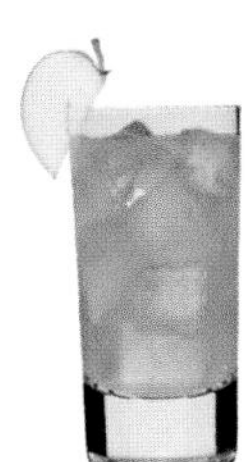

Glass: Collins
Garnish: Apple slice on rim
Method: **SHAKE** all ingredients with ice and strain into ice-filled glass.

2	shot(s)	**Ketel One vodka**
2 1/2	shot(s)	**Pressed apple juice**
1 1/2	shot(s)	**Sauvignon Blanc wine**
3/4	shot(s)	**Elderflower cordial**
1/4	shot(s)	**Freshly squeezed lime juice**

Origin: Created in 2002 by Wayne Collins for Maxxium UK.
Comment: A refreshing, summery combination of white wine, apple, lime and elderflower laced with vodka.

HOW TO MAKE SUGAR SYRUP

To make your own sugar syrup, gradually pour TWO cups of granulated sugar into a saucepan containing ONE cup of hot water. Stir as you pour and carry on stirring and simmering until the sugar is dissolved. Do not let the water even come close to boiling and only simmer for as long as it takes to dissolve the sugar. Allow syrup to cool and pour into an empty bottle. Ideally, you should finely strain your syrup into the bottle to remove any undissolved crystals which could otherwise encourage crystallisation. If kept in a refrigerator this mixture will last for a couple of months.

ORIENTAL GRAPE MARTINI

Glass: Martini
Garnish: Grapes on stick
Method: **MUDDLE** grapes in base of shaker. Add other ingredients, **SHAKE** with ice and fine strain into chilled glass.

12	fresh	**Seedless white grapes**
1½	shot(s)	**Ketel One vodka**
1½	shot(s)	**Sake**
¼	shot(s)	**Sugar (gomme) syrup**

Variants: Double Grape Martini, Grape Martini, Grapple.
Origin: Created by yours truly in 2004.
Comment: Sake adds some oriental intrigue to what would otherwise be a plain old Grape Martini.

ORIENTAL TART

Glass: Martini
Garnish: Peeled lychee in drink
Method: **SHAKE** all ingredients with ice and fine strain into chilled glass.

1½	shot(s)	**Plymouth gin**
1	shot(s)	**Soho lychee liqueur**
2	shot(s)	**Freshly squeezed golden grapefruit juice**

Origin: Created in 2004 by yours truly.
Comment: A sour, tart, fruity Martini with more than a hint of lychee.

OSMO [NEW]

Glass: Martini
Garnish: Orange zest twist
Method: **SHAKE** all ingredients with ice and fine strain into chilled glass.

2	shot(s)	**Sake**
½	shot(s)	**Cointreau / triple sec**
¼	shot(s)	**Freshly squeezed lime juice**
1½	shot(s)	**Cranberry juice**
⅛	shot(s)	**Sugar (gomme) syrup**

Origin: Adapted from a drink discovered in 2005 at Mo Bar, Landmark Mandarin Oriental Hotel, Hong Kong, China.
Comment: A sake based Cosmopolitan.

OUZI

Glass: Shot
Method: **SHAKE** all ingredients with ice and fine strain into chilled glass.

¾	shot(s)	**Ketel One vodka**
½	shot(s)	**Ouzo**
¼	shot(s)	**Sugar (gomme) syrup**
¼	shot(s)	**Freshly squeezed lemon juice**

Comment: A lemon and liquorice shooter.

PAGO PAGO [NEW]

Glass: Martini
Garnish: Lime wedge on rim
Method: **SHAKE** all ingredients with ice and fine strain into chilled glass.

2	shot(s)	**Mount Gay golden rum**
¼	shot(s)	**Green Chartreuse liqueur**
½	shot(s)	**White crème de cacao liqueur**
½	shot(s)	**Freshly squeezed lime juice**
⅛	shot(s)	**Sugar (gomme) syrup**
½	shot(s)	**Chilled mineral water (omit if wet ice)**

Comment: A Daiquiri with a liqueur twist.

PAINKILLER

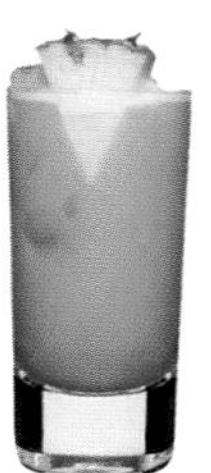

Glass: Collins
Garnish: Pineapple wedge & cherry
Method: **SHAKE** all ingredients with ice and strain into ice-filled glass.

2	shot(s)	**Pusser's Navy rum**
2	shot(s)	**Pressed pineapple juice**
1	shot(s)	**Freshly squeezed orange juice**
1	shot(s)	**Coco López cream of coconut**

Origin: From the Soggy Dollar Bar on the island of Jost Van Dyke in the British Virgin Islands. The bar's name is logical, as most of the clientele are sailors and there is no dock. Hence they have to swim ashore, often paying for drinks with wet dollars.
Comment: Full-flavoured and fruity.

PAISLEY MARTINI

Glass: Martini
Garnish: Lemon zest twist
Method: **STIR** all ingredients with ice and strain into chilled glass.

2½	shot(s)	**Plymouth gin**
½	shot(s)	**Dry vermouth**
¼	shot(s)	**The Famous Grouse Scotch whisky**

Comment: A dry Martini for those with a penchant for Scotch.

PALOMA [NEW]

Glass: Collins
Garnish: Lime wedge & salt rim
Method: **SHAKE** first four ingredients with ice and strain into ice-filled glass. **TOP** with soda, lightly stir and serve with straws.

2	shot(s)	**Sauza Hornitos tequila**
3	shot(s)	**Freshly squeezed pink grapefruit juice**
½	shot(s)	**Freshly squeezed lime juice**
¼	shot(s)	**Agave syrup (from health food shop)**
Top up with		**Soda water (club soda)**

Origin: The name is Spanish for 'dove' and the cocktail is well-known in Mexico.
Comment: A long, fruity, Margarita.

PALE RIDER

Glass: Collins
Garnish: Lime wedge
Method: **SHAKE** all ingredients with ice and strain into ice-filled glass.

2	shot(s)	**Raspberry flavoured vodka**
1/2	shot(s)	**Peach schnapps liqueur**
2	shot(s)	**Cranberry juice**
1	shot(s)	**Pressed pineapple juice**
1	shot(s)	**Freshly squeezed lime juice**
1/2	shot(s)	**Sugar (gomme) syrup**

Origin: Created in 1997 by Wayne Collins at Navajo Joe, London, England.
Comment: Sweet and fruity.

PALL MALL MARTINI [NEW]

Glass: Martini
Garnish: Orange zest twist
Method: **SHAKE** all ingredients with ice and fine strain into chilled glass.

1	shot(s)	**Plymouth gin**
1	shot(s)	**Dry vermouth**
1	shot(s)	**Sweet (rosso) vermouth**
1/4	shot(s)	**White crème de cacao liqueur**
1	dashes	**Fee Brothers orange bitters**

Comment: A classic Martini served 'perfect' with the tiniest hint of chocolate.

PALOOKAVILLE

Glass: Collins
Garnish: Lemon wedge
Method: **SHAKE** all ingredients with ice and strain into ice-filled glass.

2	shot(s)	**Zubrowka bison vodka**
3/4	shot(s)	**Apple schnapps liqueur**
2	shot(s)	**Pressed apple juice**
3/4	shot(s)	**Freshly squeezed lemon juice**
3/4	shot(s)	**Elderflower cordial**

Origin: Adapted from a cocktail Chris Edwardes created for Norman Cook, AKA Fatboy Slim, at Blanch House, Brighton, England and named after Cook's 2004 album, which is named in turn after a place mentioned by Marlon Brando in On The Waterfront.
Comment: The Polish combo of zubrówka and apple benefits from a distinctly English touch of elderflower.

PALERMO

Glass: Martini
Garnish: Vanilla pod
Method: **SHAKE** all ingredients with ice and fine strain into chilled glass.

1 1/2	shot(s)	**Vanilla infused light white rum**
1	shot(s)	**Sauvignon Blanc wine**
1 1/4	shot(s)	**Pressed pineapple juice**
1/4	shot(s)	**Sugar (gomme) syrup**

Origin: Adapted from a cocktail discovered in 2001 at Hotel du Vin, Bristol, England.
Comment: This smooth cocktail beautifully combines vanilla rum with tart wine and the sweetness of the pineapple juice.

PALM BEACH [NEW]

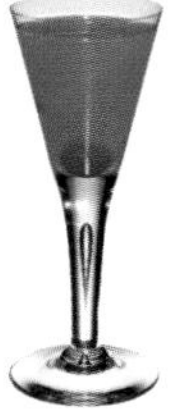

Glass: Martini
Garnish: Maraschino cherry
Method: **SHAKE** all ingredients with ice and fine strain into chilled glass.

2 1/2	shot(s)	**Plymouth gin**
1/2	shot(s)	**Sweet (rosso) vermouth**
1	shot(s)	**Freshly squeezed pink grapefruit juice**

Origin: A classic from the 1940s.
Comment: Dry, aromatic and packs one hell of a punch.

PALM SPRINGS

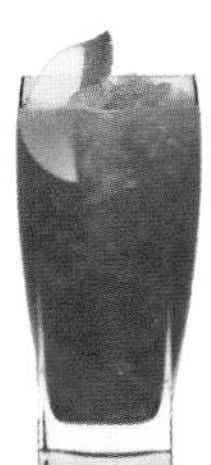

Glass: Collins
Garnish: Apple slice & mint sprig
Method: **SHAKE** all ingredients with ice and strain into glass filled with crushed ice.

4	fresh	**Mint leaves**
1	shot(s)	**Passoã passion fruit liqueur**
1	shot(s)	**Mount Gay Eclipse golden rum**
1/4	shot(s)	**Freshly squeezed lime juice**
1	shot(s)	**Pressed apple juice**
2	shot(s)	**Cranberry juice**

Comment: Sweet and aromatic.

PALMA VIOLET MARTINI

Glass: Martini
Garnish: Parma Violet sweets
Method: **SHAKE** all ingredients with ice and fine strain into chilled glass.

1 1/2	shot(s)	**Ketel One vodka**
1/4	shot(s)	**Peach schnapps liqueur**
1/2	shot(s)	**Freshly squeezed lemon juice**
1	shot(s)	**Benoit Serres violet liqueur**
1/4	shot(s)	**Sugar (gomme) syrup**
1	dash	**Fee Brothers orange bitters**
1/2	shot(s)	**Chilled mineral water (omit if wet ice)**

Origin: Created in 2001 by Jamie Terrell at LAB, London, England.
Comment: A subtly floral drink with a delicate colour.

PANCHO VILLA [NEW]

Glass: Martini (saucer)
Garnish: Pineapple wedge on rim
Method: **SHAKE** all ingredients with ice and fine strain into chilled glass.

1	shot(s)	**Light white rum**
1	shot(s)	**Plymouth gin**
1	shot(s)	**Apricot brandy liqueur**
1/4	shot(s)	**Cherry (brandy) liqueur**
1/4	shot(s)	**Pressed pineapple juice**
1/2	shot(s)	**Chilled mineral water (omit if wet ice)**

Origin: Adapted from a recipe in the 1947-72 Trader Vic's Bartender's Guide by Victor Bergeron.
Comment: To quote Victor Bergeron, "This'll tuck you away neatly – and pick you up and throw you right on the floor".

PAPPY HONEYSUCKLE

Glass: Martini
Garnish: Physalis fruit
Method: **STIR** honey with whiskey in base of shaker to dissolve honey. Add other ingredients, **SHAKE** with ice and fine strain into chilled glass.

- 1 1/2 shot(s) **Black Bush Irish whiskey**
- 2 spoons **Runny honey**
- 1 1/4 shot(s) **Sauvignon Blanc wine**
- 1 1/2 shot(s) **Pressed apple juice**
- 1/4 shot(s) **Passion fruit syrup**
- 1/4 shot(s) **Freshly squeezed lemon juice**

Origin: Created in 2002 by Shelim Islam at the GE Club, London, England.
Comment: Fresh and fruity with honeyed sweetness.

PARADISE #1 [NEW]

Glass: Martini
Garnish: Orange zest twist
Method: **SHAKE** all ingredients with ice and fine strain into chilled glass.

- 2 shot(s) **Plymouth gin**
- 1 shot(s) **Apricot brandy liqueur**
- 1 shot(s) **Freshly squeezed orange juice**
- 1/4 shot(s) **Freshly squeezed lemon juice**

Origin: Proportioned according to a recipe in the 1930 edition of the Savoy Cocktail Book by Harry Craddock.
Comment: Orange predominates in this strong complex cocktail.

PARADISE #2

Glass: Martini
Garnish: Orange zest twist
Method: **SHAKE** all ingredients with ice and fine strain into chilled glass.

- 2 shot(s) **Plymouth gin**
- 3/4 shot(s) **Apricot brandy liqueur**
- 1 3/4 shot(s) **Freshly squeezed orange juice**
- 3 dashes **Fee Brothers orange bitters (optional)**

Origin: This 1920s recipe has recently been revitalised by Dale DeGroff.
Comment: When well made, this wonderfully fruity cocktail beautifully harnesses and balances its ingredients.

PARADISE #3 [NEW]

Glass: Martini
Garnish: Orange zest twist
Method: Cut passion fruit in half and scoop flesh into shaker. Add other ingredients, **SHAKE** with ice and fine strain into chilled glass.

- 1 fresh **Passion fruit**
- 2 shot(s) **Plymouth gin**
- 3/4 shot(s) **Apricot brandy liqueur**
- 3/4 shot(s) **Freshly squeezed orange juice**

Comment: Thick, almost syrupy. Rich and fruity.

PARIS SOUR [NEW]

Glass: Old-fashioned
Garnish: Lemon zest twist
Method: **SHAKE** all ingredients with ice and strain into ice-filled glass.

- 2 shot(s) **Bourbon whiskey**
- 1 1/4 shot(s) **Dubonnet Red**
- 1/4 shot(s) **Sugar (gomme) syrup**
- 1/2 shot(s) **Freshly squeezed lemon juice**
- 1/2 fresh **Egg white**

Origin: Created in 2005 by Mark at Match Bar, London, England.
Comment: A wonderfully accommodating whiskey sour – it's easy to make and a pleasure to drink.

PARISIAN MARTINI [NEW]

Glass: Martini
Garnish: Lemon peel twist
Method: **SHAKE** all ingredients with ice and fine strain into chilled glass.

- 1 1/4 shot(s) **Plymouth gin**
- 1 1/4 shot(s) **Crème de cassis**
- 1 1/4 shot(s) **Dry vermouth**

Origin: A drink created in the 1920s to promote crème de cassis. This recipe is adapted from one in Harry Craddock's Savoy Cocktail Book.
Comment: Full-on rich cassis is barely tempered by gin and dry vermouth.

PARISIAN SPRING PUNCH

Glass: Collins
Garnish: Lemon zest knot
Method: **SHAKE** first four ingredients with ice and strain into ice-filled glass. **TOP** with champagne and serve with straws.

- 1 shot(s) **Calvados or applejack brandy**
- 1/2 shot(s) **Dry vermouth**
- 1/4 shot(s) **Freshly squeezed lemon juice**
- 1/4 shot(s) **Sugar (gomme) syrup**
- Top up with **Piper-Heidsieck brut champagne**

Comment: Dry apple and champagne – like upmarket cider.

PARK AVENUE [NEW]

Glass: Martini
Garnish: Maraschino cherry
Method: **SHAKE** all ingredients with ice and fine strain into chilled glass.

- 2 shot(s) **Plymouth gin**
- 1/2 shot(s) **Grand Marnier liqueur**
- 1/2 shot(s) **Sweet (rosso) vermouth**
- 1 shot(s) **Pressed pineapple juice**

Origin: A classic from the 1940s.
Comment: Very fruity and well-balanced rather than dry or sweet.

PARK LANE

Glass: Martini
Garnish: Orange zest twist
Method: **SHAKE** all ingredients with ice and strain into chilled glass.

2	shot(s)	**Plymouth gin**
3/4	shot(s)	**Apricot brandy liqueur**
3/4	shot(s)	**Freshly squeezed orange juice**
1/8	shot(s)	**Sonoma pomegranate (grenadine) syrup**
1/2	fresh	**Egg white**

Comment: This smooth, frothy concoction hides a mean kick.

PARLAY PUNCH [NEW]

Glass: Collins
Garnish: Lime wedge
Method: **SHAKE** all ingredients with ice and strain into ice-filled glass.

1 1/2	shot(s)	**Bourbon whiskey**
1	shot(s)	**Southern Comfort**
1	shot(s)	**Pressed pineapple juice**
1	shot(s)	**Cranberry juice**
1/2	shot(s)	**Freshly squeezed orange juice**
1/2	shot(s)	**Freshly squeezed lime juice**

Origin: Adapted from a recipe discovered at Vortex Bar, Atlanta, USA.
Comment: Too many of these tangy punches and you'll be parlaying till dawn.

PARMA NEGRONI [NEW]

Glass: Collins
Garnish: Orange slice
Method: **SHAKE** first five ingredients with ice and strain into ice-filled glass. **TOP** with tonic water, lightly stir and serve with straws.

1	shot(s)	**Plymouth gin**
1	shot(s)	**Campari**
1	shot(s)	**Freshly squeezed pink grapefruit juice**
2	dashes	**Angostura aromatic bitters**
1/2	shot(s)	**Sugar (gomme) syrup**
Top up with		**Tonic water**

Origin: Discovered in 2005 at Club 97, Hong Kong, China.
Comment: Negroni drinkers will love this fruity adaptation.

PASS-ON-THAT

Glass: Collins
Garnish: Crown with passion fruit half
Method: Cut passion fruit in half and scoop flesh into shaker. Add other ingredients, **SHAKE** with ice and fine strain into ice-filled glass.

1	fresh	**Passion fruit**
1	shot(s)	**Ketel One vodka**
1	shot(s)	**Passoã passion fruit liqueur**
3	shot(s)	**Cranberry juice**

Comment: Full-on passion fruit and berries.

PASSBOUR COOLER

Glass: Collins
Garnish: Orange slice in glass
Method: **SHAKE** all ingredients with ice and strain into ice-filled glass.

1 1/2	shot(s)	**Bourbon whiskey**
3/4	shot(s)	**Passoã passion fruit liqueur**
3/4	shot(s)	**Cherry (brandy) liqueur**
3	shot(s)	**Cranberry juice**

Comment: Cherry and bourbon with passion fruit.

PASSION FRUIT CAIPIRINHA

Glass: Old-fashioned
Method: **MUDDLE** lime wedges in the base of sturdy glass (being careful not to break the glass). Cut the passion fruit in half and scoop out the flesh into the glass. **POUR** cachaça and sugar syrup into glass, add crushed ice and **CHURN** (stir) with barspoon. Serve with straws.

1	fresh	**Passion fruit**
3/4	fresh	**Lime cut into wedges**
2	shot(s)	**Cachaça**
3/4	shot(s)	**Sugar (gomme) syrup**

Comment: A tasty fruit Caipirinha. You may end up sipping this from the glass as the passion fruit pips tend to clog straws.

PASSION FRUIT COLLINS

Glass: Collins
Garnish: Lemon slice
Method: Cut passion fruit in half and scoop out flesh into shaker. Add next three ingredients, **SHAKE** with ice and fine strain into ice-filled glass. **TOP** with soda, stir and serve with straws.

2	fresh	**Passion fruit**
2	shot(s)	**Plymouth gin**
1 1/2	shot(s)	**Freshly squeezed lemon juice**
1/2	shot(s)	**Passion fruit syrup**
Top up with		**Soda water (club soda)**

Origin: Formula by yours truly in 2004.
Comment: This fruity adaptation of the classic Collins may be a tad sharp for some: if so, add a dash more sugar.

PASSION FRUIT DAIQUIRI

Glass: Martini
Garnish: Lime wedge on rim
Method: Cut passion fruit in half and scoop out flesh into shaker. Add other ingredients, **SHAKE** with ice and fine strain into chilled glass.

2	fresh	**Passion fruit**
2	shot(s)	**Light white rum**
1/2	shot(s)	**Freshly squeezed lime juice**
1/2	shot(s)	**Sugar (gomme) syrup**

Origin: Formula by yours truly in 2004.
Comment: The rum character comes through in this fruity cocktail.

A B C D E F G H I J K L M N N **P** Q R S T U V W X Y Z

PIMM'S CUP

This quintessential English summer tipple is usually accredited to James Pimm, who in 1823-4 began trading as a shellfish-monger in London's Lombard Street. He later moved to nearby number 3 Poultry, also in the City of London, where he established Pimm's Oyster Warehouse. It is here, in 1840, that he is said to have first served this drink.

Others dispute this, maintaining that James Pimm only unwittingly lent his name to the drink. They say the true credit lies with his successor, Samuel Morey, who is recorded as having taken out a retail liquor licence in 1860. This would appear to be when the oyster bar first offered its customers spirits. Many establishments of the day mixed house spirits to serve with liqueurs and juices as 'cups', in reference to the tankards in which they were sold. Naturally the 'cup' made at Pimm's Oyster Bar was named after the establishment which retained the goodwill of its founder.

Pimm's restaurant became very popular and changed hands a couple more times. Eventually Horatio David Davies, a wine merchant and owner of cafes in London bought the business. He became Sir Horatio, a Member of Parliament and between 1897-1898, Lord Mayor of London. He formed Pimm's into a private company in 1906, which was controlled by family trusts for another 57 years after his death.

The precise date that the drink Pimm's was first sold outside restaurants and bars controlled by the Pimm's company is unknown. However, it is certain that the original product, No.1, was based on gin and flavoured with numerous botanicals including quinine. A second Pimm's product based on Scotch (Pimm's No.2 Cup) was launched and a third (Pimm's No.3 Cup) was based on brandy. Pimm's became popular in Britain in the 1920s and took off internationally after the Second World War. Other versions were then introduced: Pimm's No.4 based on rum, Pimm's No.6 on vodka and Pimm's No.7 on rye whiskey.

PASSION FRUIT MARGARITA

Glass: Coupette
Garnish: Salt & lime wedge rim
Method: Cut passion fruit in half and scoop out flesh into shaker. Add other ingredients, **SHAKE** with ice and fine strain into chilled glass.

1 fresh **Passion fruit**
2 shot(s) **Sauza Hornitos tequila**
1 shot(s) **Cointreau / triple sec**
1 shot(s) **Freshly squeezed lime juice**
¼ shot(s) **Passion fruit syrup**

Origin: Formula by yours truly in 2004.
Comment: The flavour of tequila is very evident in this fruity adaptation.

PASSION FRUIT MARTINI #1

Glass: Martini
Garnish: Physalis (cape gooseberry)
Method: Cut passion fruit in half and scoop out flesh into shaker. Add other ingredients, **SHAKE** with ice and fine strain into chilled glass.

1 fresh **Passion fruit**
2 shot(s) **Ketel One vodka**
½ shot(s) **Sugar (gomme) syrup**

Origin: Formula by yours truly in 2004.
Comment: A simple but tasty cocktail that wonderfully harnesses the flavour of passion fruit.

PASSION FRUIT MARTINI #2

Glass: Martini
Garnish: Physalis (Cape gooseberry)
Method: Cut passion fruit in half and scoop out flesh into shaker. Add other ingredients, **SHAKE** with ice and fine strain into chilled glass.

2 fresh **Passion fruit**
2 shot(s) **Ketel One vodka**
½ shot(s) **Passion fruit syrup**

Origin: Formula by yours truly in 2004.
Comment: Not for Martini purists, but a fruity, easy drinking concoction for everyone else.

PASSION FRUIT MARTINI #3

Glass: Martini
Garnish: Float passion fruit half
Method: Cut passion fruit in half and scoop out flesh into shaker. Add other ingredients, **SHAKE** with ice and fine strain into chilled glass.

2 fresh **Passion fruit**
2 shot(s) **Plymouth gin**
½ shot(s) **Cointreau / triple sec**
¼ shot(s) **Freshly squeezed lemon juice**
½ shot(s) **Passion fruit syrup**
½ fresh **Egg white**

Origin: Formula by yours truly in 2004.
Comment: Full-on passion fruit with gin and citrus hints.

PASSION KILLER

Glass: Shot
Method: Refrigerate ingredients then **LAYER** in chilled glass by carefully pouring in the following order.

½ shot(s) **Midori melon liqueur**
½ shot(s) **Passoã passion fruit liqueur**
½ shot(s) **Sauza Hornitos tequila**

Comment: Tropical fruit and tequila.

PASSION PUNCH [NEW]

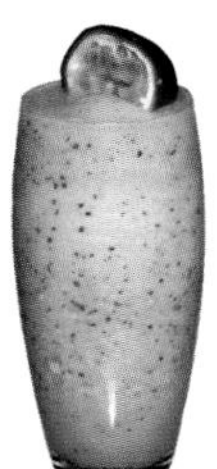

Glass: Collins (or individual scorpion bowl)
Garnish: Half passion fruit
Method: Cut passion fruit in half and scoop flesh into blender. Add other ingredients and **BLEND** with 12oz scoop crushed ice. Serve with straws.

1 fresh **Passion fruit**
2 shot(s) **Plymouth gin**
¼ shot(s) **Rémy Martin cognac**
¾ shot(s) **Freshly squeezed lime juice**
¾ shot(s) **Sugar (gomme) syrup**
2 dashes **Angostura aromatic bitters**

Origin: Adapted from a recipe in the 1947-72 Trader Vic's Bartender's Guide by Victor Bergeron.
Comment: To quote the Trader, "A robust libation with the opulence of 'down under'."

PASSIONATE RUM PUNCH

Glass: Collins
Garnish: Passion fruit quarter
Method: Cut passion fruit in half and scoop out flesh into shaker. Add other ingredients, **SHAKE** with ice and fine strain into glass filled with crushed ice.

3 fresh **Passion fruit**
2¼ shot(s) **Wray & Nephew overproof rum**
¾ shot(s) **Freshly squeezed lime juice**
1 shot(s) **Sugar (gomme) syrup**
½ shot(s) **Passion fruit syrup**

Origin: Formula by yours truly in 2004.
Comment: Rum and fruit combine brilliantly in this tropical punch style drink.

PASSOVER

Glass: Collins
Garnish: Orange slice
Method: **SHAKE** all ingredients with ice and strain into ice-filled glass.

2 shot(s) **Ketel One vodka**
1 shot(s) **Passoã passion fruit liqueur**
3 shot(s) **Freshly squeezed pink grapefruit juice**

Comment: Tropical and sweet.

PIÑA COLADA

Three Puerto Rican bartenders contest the ownership of this drink. Ramón Marrero Pérez claims to have first made it at the Caribe Hilton hotel's Beachcomber Bar in San Juan on 15th August 1954 using the then newly available Coco López cream of coconut. Ricardo Garcia, who also worked at the Caribe, says that it was he who invented the drink. But Ramón Portas Mingot says he created it in 1963 at the Barrachina Bar in Old San Juan.

It is commonly accepted that the Piña Colada was created and heavily promoted at the Caribe Hilton Hotel and the hotel credits Ramón Marrero Pérez with the invention. Opening in 1949 at a prime beachfront location, the Caribe was the first luxury hotel in San Juan and became a popular destination for the rich and famous who helped spread the popularity of the drink.

The name 'Piña Colada' literally means 'strained pineapple', a reference to the freshly pressed and strained pineapple juice used in the drink's preparation. Another essential ingredient, 'cream of coconut', is a canned, non-alcoholic, thick, syrup-like blend of coconut juice, sugar, emulsifier, cellulose, thickeners, citric acid and salt. The original brand, Coco López, was created in the early 1950s by Don Ramón López-Irizarry after receiving a development grant from the Puerto Rican government. Cream of coconut had previously been made but López-Irizarry mechanised the labour intensive process. The brand was launched in 1954 and is directly linked to the creation of the Piña Colada at the Caribe.

PAVLOVA SHOT

Glass: Shot
Method: Refrigerate ingredients then **LAYER** in chilled glass by carefully pouring in the following order.

- 3/4 shot(s) **Chambord black raspberry liqueur**
- 3/4 shot(s) **Ketel One vodka**

Comment: Pleasant, sweet shot.

PEACH DAIQUIRI

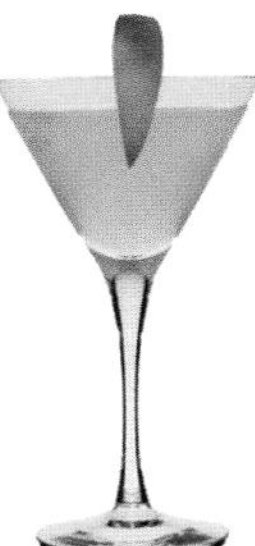

Glass: Martini
Garnish: Peach wedge on rim
Method: SHAKE all ingredients with ice and fine strain into chilled glass.

- 2 shot(s) **Light white rum**
- 1 shot(s) **Peach schnapps liqueur**
- 1/2 shot(s) **Freshly squeezed lime juice**
- 1/2 shot(s) **Chilled mineral water (omit if wet ice)**

Origin: My take on the Cuban Daiquiri de Melocoton.
Comment: A classic Daiquiri with a hint of peach liqueur.

PEACH MELBA MARTINI

Glass: Martini
Garnish: Float flaked almonds
Method: SHAKE all ingredients with ice and fine strain into chilled glass.

- 1 1/2 shot(s) **Vanilla flavoured vodka**
- 3/4 shot(s) **Peach schnapps liqueur**
- 3/4 shot(s) **Chambord black raspberry liqueur**
- 1 shot(s) **Double (heavy) cream**
- 1 shot(s) **Milk**

Origin: Melba is a name given to various dishes dedicated to Dame Nellie Melba, the 19th century Australian opera singer. Peach Melba was created in 1892 by the world famous chef Georges-Auguste Escoffier, who was the business partner of César Ritz.
Comment: Not quite Peach Melba dessert, but rich and tasty all the same.

PEANUT BUTTER & JELLY SHOT

Glass: Shot
Method: SHAKE all ingredients with ice and fine strain into chilled glass.

- 1/2 shot(s) **Chambord black raspberry liqueur**
- 1/2 shot(s) **Frangelico hazelnut liqueur**
- 1/2 shot(s) **Baileys Irish Cream liqueur**

Comment: Does indeed taste a little like peanut butter and jelly (jam in the UK).

PEAR & CARDAMOM SIDECAR

Glass: Martini
Garnish: Pear slice on rim
Method: MUDDLE cardamom in base of shaker. Add other ingredients, **SHAKE** with ice and fine strain into chilled glass.

- 2 pods **Green cardamom**
- 1 shot(s) **Rémy Martin cognac**
- 3/4 shot(s) **Cointreau / triple sec**
- 3/4 shot(s) **Pear & cognac liqueur**
- 3/4 shot(s) **Freshly squeezed lemon juice**
- 1/8 shot(s) **Sugar (gomme) syrup**
- 1/2 shot(s) **Chilled mineral water (omit if wet ice)**

Origin: Adapted from a drink created in 2002 by Jason Scott at Oloroso, Edinburgh, Scotland.
Comment: A wonderful meld of aromatic ingredients.

PEAR & ELDERFLOWER MARTINI

Glass: Martini
Garnish: Pear slice on rim
Method: SHAKE all ingredients with ice and fine strain into chilled glass.

- 2 shot(s) **Ketel One vodka**
- 2 shot(s) **Freshly extracted pear juice**
- 1/2 shot(s) **Elderflower cordial**

Origin: Created in 2001 by Angelo Vieira at St. Martins, London, England.
Comment: Pear and elderflower are a match made in St Martins Lane.

PEAR & VANILLA RICKEY

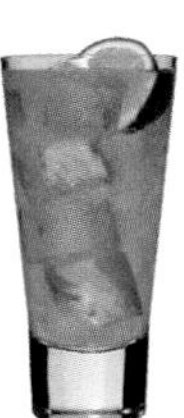

Glass: Collins
Garnish: Lime wedge
Method: SHAKE first three ingredients with ice and strain into ice-filled glass. **TOP** with 7-Up, lightly stir and serve with straws.

- 1 shot(s) **Vanilla flavoured vodka**
- 1 shot(s) **Pear & cognac liqueur**
- 1 shot(s) **Freshly squeezed lime juice**
- Top up with **7-Up**

Comment: Vanilla and pear create a creamy mouthful cut by lime juice.

PEAR DROP

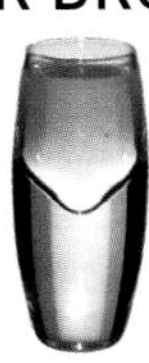

Glass: Shot
Method: SHAKE all ingredients with ice and fine strain into chilled glass.

- 1/2 shot(s) **Ketel One Citroen vodka**
- 1/2 shot(s) **Soho lychee liqueur**
- 1/2 shot(s) **Pear & cognac liqueur**

Comment: Sweet, sticky and strong.

PEAR DROP MARTINI

Glass: Martini
Garnish: Pear drop sweet in drink
Method: **SHAKE** all ingredients with ice and fine strain into chilled glass.

1¼	shot(s)	**Pear & cognac liqueur**
1	shot(s)	**Luxardo limoncello liqueur**
1	shot(s)	**Poire William eau de vie**
1	shot(s)	**Freshly extracted pear juice**

Origin: Created in 2002 by yours truly.
Comment: Not as sticky as the sweet it takes its name from but full-on tangy pear.

PEAR SHAPED #1 (DELUXE VERSION)

Glass: Martini
Garnish: Pear slice on rim
Method: Cut passion fruit in half and scoop out flesh into base of shaker. Add other ingredients, **SHAKE** with ice and fine strain into chilled glass.

1	fresh	**Passion fruit**
1½	shot(s)	**The Famous Grouse Scotch whisky**
1	shot(s)	**Pear & cognac liqueur**
1	shot(s)	**Freshly extracted pear juice**
1	shot(s)	**Pressed apple juice**
¼	shot(s)	**Freshly squeezed lime juice**

Comment: Wonderful balance of flavours but pear predominates with a dry yet floral finish.

PEAR SHAPED #2 (POPULAR VERSION)

Glass: Collins
Glass: Pear wedge on rim
Method: **SHAKE** all ingredients with ice and strain into ice-filled glass.

2	shot(s)	**The Famous Grouse Scotch whisky**
1	shot(s)	**Pear & cognac liqueur**
3	shot(s)	**Pressed apple juice**
½	shot(s)	**Freshly squeezed lime juice**
¼	shot(s)	**Sonoma vanilla bean sugar syrup**

Origin: Adapted from a drink created in 2003 by Jamie Terrell at Dick's Bar, Atlantic, London, England.
Comment: Scotch, pear and apple combine wonderfully in this medium-sweet long drink.

PEDRO COLLINS

Glass: Collins
Garnish: Orange slice & cherry on stick (sail)
Method: **SHAKE** first three ingredients with ice and strain into ice-filled glass. **TOP** with soda, lightly stir and serve with straws.

2	shot(s)	**Light white rum**
1	shot(s)	**Freshly squeezed lime juice**
½	shot(s)	**Sugar (gomme) syrup**
Top up with		**Soda water (club soda)**

Comment: This rum based Tom Collins is basically a long Daiquiri with soda.

PEGGY MARTINI [NEW]

Glass: Martini
Garnish: Orange zest twist
Method: **SHAKE** all ingredients with ice and fine strain into chilled glass.

2	shot(s)	**Plymouth gin**
1	shot(s)	**Dry vermouth**
¼	shot(s)	**La Fée Parisian 68% absinthe**
¼	shot(s)	**Dubonnet Red**
½	shot(s)	**Chilled mineral water (omit if wet ice)**

Origin: Adapted from a recipe in the 1930s edition of the Savoy Cocktail Book by Harry Craddock.
Comment: Very dry and aromatic. Sadly this will appeal to few palates.

PEGU CLUB [NEW]

Glass: Martini
Garnish: Lime wedge on rim
Method: **SHAKE** all ingredients with ice and fine strain into chilled glass.

2	shot(s)	**Plymouth gin**
1	shot(s)	**Cointreau / triple sec**
½	shot(s)	**Freshly squeezed lime juice**
¼	shot(s)	**Sugar (gomme) syrup**
1	dash	**Angostura aromatic bitters**
1	dash	**Fee Brothers orange bitters**
½	shot(s)	**Chilled mineral water (omit if wet ice)**

Origin: Created in the 1920s at the Pegu Club, an expat gentlemen's club in British colonial Rangoon, Burma.
The recipe was first published in Harry MacElhone's 1927 'Barflies and Cocktails'. In his seminal 1930 Savoy Cocktail Book, Harry Craddock notes of this drink, "The favourite cocktail of the Pegu Club, Burma, and one that has travelled, and is asked for, round the world."
Comment: I've added a dash of sugar to the original recipe to reduce the tartness of this gin based Margarita-like concoction.

PENDENNIS COCKTAIL [NEW]

Glass: Martini
Garnish: Maraschino cherry
Method: **SHAKE** all ingredients with ice and fine strain into chilled glass.

2	shot(s)	**Plymouth gin**
1	shot(s)	**Apricot brandy liqueur**
½	shot(s)	**Freshly squeezed lime juice**
1	dash	**Peychaud's aromatic bitters**
¾	shot(s)	**Chilled mineral water (omit if wet ice)**

Origin: This classic is named after the Pendennis Club in Louisville, Kentucky, which is popularly supposed to be the birthplace of the Old-Fashioned.
Comment: Tangy, subtle, sweet and sour.

A B C D E F G H I J K L M N N P Q R S T U V W X Y Z

PISCO PUNCH

The creation of the Pisco Punch is usually credited to Professor Jerry Burns of San Francisco's Bank Exchange. However, its origin could lie in the late 1800s, when the drink was served aboard steamships stopping in Chile en route to San Francisco. The following story of the Pisco Punch and the Bank Exchange comes from the 1973 edition of the California Historical Quarterly and Robert O'Brien's book, 'This Was San Francisco'.

The Bank Exchange was a ballroom that opened in 1854 and survived the earthquake and fire of 1906. Its popularity never waned and only Prohibition brought about its demise. Much of the Bank Exchange's notoriety was due to the Pisco Punch, so much so that the establishment gained the nickname 'Pisco John's' after one of its original owners.

The recipe was handed down from owner to owner in absolute secrecy. Duncan Nichol, the Scottish immigrant who owned the bar from the late 1870s until it closed, inherited it from the previous owners, Orrin Dorman and John Torrence, and is thought to have carried it to his grave.

A B C D E F G H I J K L M N N **P** Q R S T U V W X Y Z

PEPPER & VANILLA'TINI

Glass: Martini
Garnish: Strip yellow pepper
Method: SHAKE all ingredients with ice and fine strain into chilled glass.

1	shot(s)	**Vanilla-infused Ketel One vodka**
3/4	shot(s)	**Pepper vodka**
1	shot(s)	**Cuarenta Y Tres (Licor 43) liqueur**
3/4	shot(s)	**Tuaca liqueur**
1	shot(s)	**Freshly extracted yellow bell pepper juice**

Origin: Created in 2002 by yours truly.
Comment: Vanilla and pepper seem to complement each other in a sweet and sour kind of way.

PEPPERED MARY

Glass: Collins
Garnish: Peppered rim & cherry tomato
Method: SHAKE all ingredients with ice and fine strain into chilled glass.

2	shot(s)	**Pepper vodka**
2	shot(s)	**Freshly extracted yellow bell pepper juice**
2	shot(s)	**Pressed tomato juice**
1/2	shot(s)	**Freshly squeezed lemon juice**
7	drops	**Tabasco hot pepper sauce**
1	spoon	**Lea & Perrins Worcestershire sauce**

Origin: Created in 2003 by yours truly.
Comment: Hot and sweet pepper spice this Bloody Mary.

PERFECT ALIBI

Glass: Collins
Garnish: Mint leaf & lime squeeze
Method: MUDDLE ginger in base of shaker. Add other ingredients, **SHAKE** with ice and fine strain into ice-filled glass.

2	fresh	**Thumb-nail sized slices root ginger**
1/2	shot(s)	**Sugar (gomme) syrup**
1 1/2	shot(s)	**Krupnik honey liqueur**
1/2	shot(s)	**Bärenjäger honey liqueur**
3	shot(s)	**Cold black jasmine tea (fairly weak)**

Origin: Created in 2001 by Douglas Ankrah for Akbar, London, England.
Comment: A very unusual and pleasant mix of flavours.

PERFECT JOHN

Glass: Martini
Garnish: Orange zest twist
Method: SHAKE all ingredients with ice and fine strain into chilled glass.

1	shot(s)	**Ketel One vodka**
3/4	shot(s)	**Cointreau / triple sec**
1 1/2	shot(s)	**Freshly squeezed orange juice**
1/4	shot(s)	**Galliano liqueur**

Comment: A straight-up Harvey Wallbanger with Cointreau.

PERFECT MARTINI [NEW]

Glass: Martini
Garnish: Orange zest twist
Method: SHAKE all ingredients with ice and fine strain into chilled glass.

1 1/4	shot(s)	**Plymouth gin**
1 1/4	shot(s)	**Dry vermouth**
1 1/4	shot(s)	**Sweet (rosso) vermouth**
1	dash	**Fee Brothers orange bitters (optional)**

Variant: Merry-Go-Round Martini
Origin: Adapted from a recipe in the 1930 edition of the Savoy Cocktail Book by Harry Craddock.
Comment: The high proportion of vermouth makes this Martini almost sherry-like.

PERIODISTA DAIQUIRI [NEW]

Glass: Martini
Garnish: Lime wedge
Method: SHAKE all ingredients with ice and fine strain into chilled glass.

1 1/2	shot(s)	**Light white rum**
1/2	shot(s)	**Freshly squeezed lime juice**
1/2	shot(s)	**Grand Marnier liqueur**
1/2	shot(s)	**Apricot brandy liqueur**
1/2	shot(s)	**Chilled mineral water (omit if wet ice)**

Comment: Basically an orange and apricot Daiquiri.

PERNOD & BLACK MARTINI

Glass: Martini
Garnish: Blackberries
Method: MUDDLE blackberries in base of shaker. Add other ingredients, **SHAKE** with ice and fine strain into chilled glass.

7	fresh	**Blackberries**
1/2	shot(s)	**Pernod anis**
1 1/2	shot(s)	**Ketel One vodka**
1/2	shot(s)	**Crème de mûre (blackberry) liqueur**
1	shot(s)	**Freshly squeezed lime juice**
1/8	shot(s)	**Sonoma vanilla bean sugar syrup**
3/4	shot(s)	**Chilled mineral water (omit if wet ice)**

Origin: Created in 2003 by yours truly.
Comment: Pernod enhances the rich, tart flavours of blackberry.

PERROQUET

Glass: Collins (10oz / 290ml max)
Method: POUR pastis and mint syrup into glass. Serve iced water separately in a small jug (known in France as a 'broc') so the customer can dilute to their own taste (I recommend five shots). Lastly, add ice to fill glass.

1	shot(s)	**Ricard pastis**
1/4	shot(s)	**Green mint (menthe) syrup**
Top up with		**Chilled mineral water**

Origin: Very popular throughout France, this drink is named after the parrot due to the bird's brightly coloured plumage.
Comment: The traditional French café drink with a hint of sweet mint.

PERRY-TINI

Glass: Martini
Garnish: Pear slice on rim
Method: **SHAKE** first three ingredients with ice and fine strain into chilled glass. **TOP** with champagne.

1	shot(s)	**Poire William eau de vie**
1	shot(s)	**Pear & cognac liqueur**
2	shot(s)	**Freshly extracted pear juice**
Top up with		**Piper-Heidsieck brut champagne**

Origin: Created in 2002 by yours truly.
Comment: Pear with a hint of sparkle.

PETER PAN MARTINI [NEW]

Glass: Martini
Garnish: Orange zest twist
Method: **SHAKE** all ingredients with ice and fine strain into chilled glass.

2	shot(s)	**Plymouth gin**
1	shot(s)	**Dry vermouth**
1	shot(s)	**Freshly squeezed orange juice**
3	dashes	**Fee Brothers peach bitters**

Origin: Adapted from a recipe in the 1930 edition of the Savoy Cocktail Book by Harry Craddock.
Comment: Orange predominates in this complex cocktail.

PETTO MARTINI [NEW]

Glass: Martini
Garnish: Orange zest twist
Method: **SHAKE** all ingredients with ice and fine strain into chilled glass.

2	shot(s)	**Plymouth gin**
1	shot(s)	**Dry vermouth**
1	shot(s)	**Sweet (rosso) vermouth**
1/4	shot(s)	**Freshly squeezed orange juice**
1/8	shot(s)	**Luxardo maraschino liqueur**

Origin: Adapted from a recipe in the 1930 edition of the Savoy Cocktail Book by Harry Craddock.
Comment: A wonderfully aromatic classic Martini served 'perfect' with a hint of orange juice and maraschino.

PHARMACEUTICAL STIMULANT

Glass: Old-fashioned
Garnish: Float three coffee beans
Method: **SHAKE** all ingredients with ice and strain into ice-filled glass.

2	shot(s)	**Ketel One vodka**
1/2	shot(s)	**Kahlúa coffee liqueur**
2	shot(s)	**Espresso coffee (cold)**
1/4	shot(s)	**Sugar (gomme) syrup**

Origin: Created in 1998 by Dick Bradsell at The Pharmacy, London, England.
Comment: A real wake-up call and the drink that led to many an Espresso Martini.

PICCA

Glass: Martini
Garnish: Maraschino cherry
Method: **SHAKE** all ingredients with ice and fine strain into chilled glass.

1 1/2	shot(s)	**The Famous Grouse Scotch whisky**
1	shot(s)	**Galliano liqueur**
1	shot(s)	**Sweet (rosso) vermouth**
3/4	shot(s)	**Chilled mineral water (omit if wet ice)**

Comment: Bittersweet whisky.

PICCADILLY MARTINI [NEW]

Glass: Martini
Garnish: Lemon zest twist
Method: **SHAKE** all ingredients with ice and fine strain into chilled glass.

2	shot(s)	**Plymouth gin**
1	shot(s)	**Dry vermouth**
1/8	shot(s)	**La Fée Parisian 68% absinthe**
1/8	shot(s)	**Sonoma pomegranate (grenadine) syrup**

Origin: Adapted from a recipe in Harry Craddock's 1930 Savoy Cocktail Book.
Comment: A classic Martini tempered by a hint of pomegranate and absinthe.

PICHUNCHO MARTINI

Glass: Martini
Garnish: Orange zest twist
Method: **SHAKE** all ingredients with ice and fine strain into a chilled glass.

2 1/4	shot(s)	**Pisco**
1 1/2	shot(s)	**Sweet (rosso) vermouth**
1/4	shot(s)	**Sugar (gomme) syrup**

Origin: Based on a traditional Chilean drink: pisco and vermouth served on the rocks.
Comment: This drink craves the best pisco and the best sweet vermouth. Find those and measure carefully and it's sublime.

PIERRE COLLINS

Glass: Collins
Garnish: Orange slice & cherry on stick (sail)
Method: **SHAKE** first three ingredients with ice and strain into ice-filled glass. **TOP** with soda, lightly stir and serve with straws.

2	shot(s)	**Rémy Martin cognac**
1	shot(s)	**Freshly squeezed lemon juice**
1/2	shot(s)	**Sugar (gomme) syrup**
Top up with		**Soda water (club soda)**

Comment: A Tom Collins made with cognac. The cognac's character shines through.

A B C D E F G H I J K L M N Ñ **P** Q R S T U V W X Y Z

PILGRIM COCKTAIL

Glass: Martini
Garnish: Dust with grated nutmeg
Method: **SHAKE** all ingredients with ice and fine strain into chilled glass.

1½ shot(s) **Mount Gay Eclipse golden rum**
½ shot(s) **Grand Marnier liqueur**
1 shot(s) **Freshly squeezed orange juice**
¾ shot(s) **Freshly squeezed lime juice**
¼ shot(s) **World's End Pimento Dram liqueur**
3 dashes **Angostura aromatic bitters**

Variant: Can also be served hot by simmering ingredients gently in a saucepan.
Comment: Whether you serve this hot or cold, it's a delicately spiced drink to warm the cockles.

PIMM'S COCKTAIL

Glass: Martini
Garnish: Lemon & orange zest twist
Method: **SHAKE** first four ingredients with ice and strain into chilled glass. **TOP** with champagne.

2 shot(s) **Pimm's No.1 Cup**
½ shot(s) **Plymouth gin**
¼ shot(s) **Freshly squeezed lemon juice**
¼ shot(s) **Sugar (gomme) syrup**
Top up with **Piper-Heidsieck brut champagne**

Comment: Luxuriate in this quintessentially English tipple.

PIMM'S CUP (OR CLASSIC) [UPDATED]

Glass: Collins
Garnish: Mint sprig
Method: **POUR** Pimm's into glass half filled with ice. Add fruit and fill glass with more ice. Top with 7-Up (or ginger ale), lightly stir and serve with straws.

2 shot(s) **Pimm's No. 1 Cup**
1 slice **Lemon**
1 slice **Orange**
2 slices **Cucumber**
1 sliced **Strawberry**
Top up with **7-Up (or ginger ale)**

Origin: Usually credited to James Pimm in 1840 but more likely to have been first made by Samuel Morey in the 1860s.
Comment: You've not properly experienced an English summer until you've drunk one of these whilst sheltering from the rain.

PIMM'S ROYALE

Glass: Flute
Garnish: Berries on stick with cucumber peel
Method: **POUR** Pimm's into chilled glass and **TOP** with champagne.

1 shot(s) **Pimm's No.1 Cup**
Top up with **Piper-Heidsieck brut champagne**

Comment: Dry, subtle and refreshing.

PIÑA MARTINI [NEW]

Glass: Martini
Garnish: Pineapple wedge on rim
Method: **SHAKE** all ingredients with ice and fine strain into chilled glass.

2 shot(s) **Ketel One vodka**
1¾ shot(s) **Pressed pineapple juice**
¼ shot(s) **Freshly squeezed lime juice**
⅛ shot(s) **Sugar (gomme) syrup**

Origin: Created in 2005 by yours truly.
Comment: Rich pineapple but not too sweet.

PIÑA COLADA

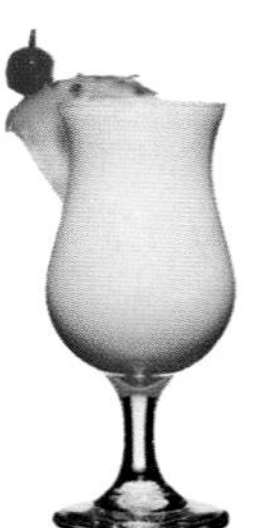

Glass: Hurricane (or hollowed out pineapple)
Garnish: Pineapple wedge & cherry
Method: **BLEND** all ingredients with one 12oz scoop crushed ice and serve with straws.

2 shot(s) **Mount Gay golden rum**
3 shot(s) **Pressed pineapple juice**
2 shot(s) **Coco López cream of coconut**
½ shot(s) **Double (heavy) cream**

Variant: Made with dark rums.
Comment: A wonderful creamy, fruity concoction that's not half as sticky as the world would have you believe. Too much ice will detract from the creaminess and kill the drink.

PIÑA COLADA VIRGIN (MOCKTAIL)

Glass: Hurricane
Garnish: Pineapple wedge & cherry on rim
Method: **BLEND** all ingredients with 18oz of crushed ice and serve with straws.

6 shot(s) **Pressed pineapple juice**
¾ shot(s) **Double (heavy) cream**
¾ shot(s) **Milk**
2 shot(s) **Coco López cream of coconut**

AKA: Snow White
Comment: A Piña Colada with its guts ripped out.

PINEAPPLE & CARDAMOM DAIQUIRI

Glass: Martini
Garnish: Pineapple wedge on rim
Method: **MUDDLE** cardamom in base of shaker. Add other ingredients, **SHAKE** with ice and fine strain into chilled glass.

4 pods **Green cardamom**
2 shot(s) **Light white rum**
1¾ shot(s) **Pressed pineapple juice**
¼ shot(s) **Freshly squeezed lime juice**
¼ shot(s) **Sugar (gomme) syrup**

Origin: Adapted from Henry Besant's Pineapple & Cardamom Martini.
Comment: One of the tastiest Daiquiris I've tried.

PINEAPPLE & CARDAMOM MARTINI

Glass: Martini
Garnish: Pineapple wedge on rim
Method: **MUDDLE** cardamom in base of shaker. Add other ingredients, **SHAKE** with ice and fine strain into chilled glass.

4	pods	**Green cardamom**
2	shot(s)	**Ketel One vodka**
2	shot(s)	**Pressed pineapple juice**
1/4	shot(s)	**Sugar (gomme) syrup**

Origin: Created in 2002 by Henry Besant at Lonsdale House, London, England.
Comment: This is about as good as it gets: a spectacular pairing of fruit and spice.

PINEAPPLE DAIQUIRI #1 (ON-THE-ROCKS) [NEW]

Glass: Old-fashioned
Garnish: Pineapple wedge & cherry
Method: **SHAKE** all ingredients with ice and fine strain into ice-filled glass.

2	shot(s)	**Light white rum**
1	shot(s)	**Pressed pineapple juice**
1/2	shot(s)	**Freshly squeezed lime juice**
1/4	shot(s)	**Sugar (gomme) syrup**

Origin: Formula by yours truly.
Comment: Rum and pineapple are just meant to go together.

PINEAPPLE & GINGER MARTINI

Glass: Martini
Garnish: Pineapple wedge on rim
Method: **MUDDLE** ginger in base of shaker. Add other ingredients, **SHAKE** with ice and fine strain into chilled glass.

2	slices	**Fresh root ginger (thumbnail sized)**
2	shot(s)	**Ketel One vodka**
2	shot(s)	**Pressed pineapple juice**
1/8	shot(s)	**Sugar (gomme) syrup**

Comment: Smooth, rich pineapple flavour with hints of vodka and ginger.

PINEAPPLE DAIQUIRI #2 (FROZEN) [NEW]

Glass: Martini (Large)
Garnish: Pineapple wedge & cherry
Method: **BLEND** all ingredients with two 12oz scoops crushed ice and serve with straws.

2	shot(s)	**Light white rum**
1 1/2	shot(s)	**Pressed pineapple juice**
1/2	shot(s)	**Freshly squeezed lime juice**
3/4	shot(s)	**Sugar (gomme) syrup**

Origin: Formula by yours truly.
Comment: Fluffy but very tasty.

PINEAPPLE & SAGE MARGARITA [NEW]

Glass: Coupette
Garnish: Pineapple wedge on rim
Method: Lightly **MUDDLE** sage in base of shaker. Add other ingredients, **SHAKE** with ice and fine strain into chilled glass.

5	fresh	**Sage leaves**
2	shot(s)	**Sauza Hornitos tequila**
1	shot(s)	**Pressed pineapple juice**
1/2	shot(s)	**Freshly squeezed lime juice**
1/4	shot(s)	**Agave syrup (from health food store)**

Origin: Adapted from a drink created in 2005 at Green & Red Bar, London, England.
Comment: Herbal tequila and sweet pineapple in harmony.

PINEAPPLE FIZZ

Glass: Collins
Garnish: Lime wedge & cherry
Method: **SHAKE** first four ingredients with ice and strain into ice-filled glass. **TOP** with soda, lightly stir and serve with straws.

2	shot(s)	**Mount Gay Eclipse golden rum**
1 1/2	shot(s)	**Pressed pineapple juice**
1	shot(s)	**Freshly squeezed lime juice**
1/2	shot(s)	**Sugar (gomme) syrup**
Top up with		**Soda water (club soda)**

Comment: A Pineapple Daiquiri lengthened with soda. Surprisingly tasty and refreshing.

PINEAPPLE BLOSSOM

Glass: Martini
Garnish: Pineapple wedge on rim
Method: **SHAKE** all ingredients with ice and fine strain into chilled glass.

2	shot(s)	**The Famous Grouse Scotch whisky**
1	shot(s)	**Pressed pineapple juice**
1/2	shot(s)	**Freshly squeezed lemon juice**
1/2	shot(s)	**Sugar (gomme) syrup**

Origin: My interpretation of a classic.
Comment: Richly flavoured but drier than you might expect.

PINEAPPLE MARGARITA

Glass: Coupette
Garnish: Pineapple wedge on rim
Method: **SHAKE** all ingredients with ice and fine strain into chilled glass.

2	shot(s)	**Sauza Hornitos tequila**
3/4	shot(s)	**Cointreau / triple sec**
1 1/2	shot(s)	**Pressed pineapple juice**

Variant: Add half a shot of pineapple syrup, blend with 12oz scoop of crushed ice and serve frozen.
Comment: A Tequila Margarita with a pineapple fruit kick.

PINEAPPLE MOJITO

Glass: Collins
Method: Lightly **MUDDLE** mint (just to bruise) in glass. **POUR** other ingredients into glass and half fill with crushed ice. **CHURN** (stir) with barspoon. Fill glass with more crushed ice, churn and serve with straws.

12	fresh	**Mint leaves**
2	shot(s)	**Light white rum**
3/4	shot(s)	**Cuarenta Y Tres (Licor 43) liqueur**
2	shot(s)	**Pressed pineapple juice**
1	shot(s)	**Freshly squeezed lime juice**

Origin: Discovered in 2003 at Apartment 195, London, England.
Comment: A fruity, vanilla-ed twist on the classic Mojito.

PINEAPPLE SMOOTHIE (MOCKTAIL) [NEW]

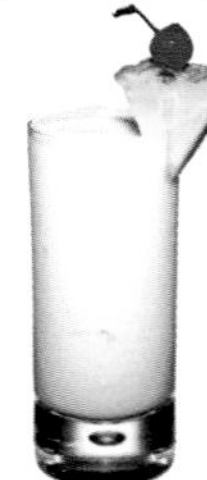

Glass: Collins
Garnish: Pineapple wedge
Method: **BLEND** all ingredients with 12oz scoop crushed ice. Serve with straws.

2 tblspoon		**Natural yoghurt**
2 tblspoon		**Runny honey**
4	shot(s)	**Pressed pineapple juice**

Comment: Fluffy in every sense of the word.

PINI [NEW]

Glass: Martini
Garnish: Maraschino cherry
Method: **SHAKE** all ingredients with ice and fine strain into chilled glass.

2	shot(s)	**Pisco**
1/2	shot(s)	**Rémy Martin cognac**
1/4	shot(s)	**White crème de cacao liqueur**
1/4	shot(s)	**Sugar (gomme) syrup**
1/2	shot(s)	**Chilled mineral water (omit if wet ice)**

Comment: Use a great pisco and you'll have a wonderfully complex drink.

PINK CLOUD [NEW]

Glass: Martini
Method: **SHAKE** all ingredients with ice and fine strain into chilled glass.

1	shot(s)	**Luxardo Amaretto di Saschira liqueur**
1	shot(s)	**Sonoma pomegranate (grenadine) syrup**
1	shot(s)	**White crème de cacao liqueur**
3/4	shot(s)	**Evaporated milk (sweetened)**

Origin: Adapted from a recipe in the 1947-72 Trader Vic's Bartender's Guide by Victor Bergeron.
Comment: To make this sweet after dinner drink I've used amaretto and pomegranate syrup in place of crème de noyaux. This almond flavoured liqueur made from apricot and peach stones is not currently available in the UK. US readers should use 2 shots of crème de noyaux in place of the first two ingredients.

PINK DAIQUIRI [NEW]

Glass: Martini
Garnish: Lime wedge on rim
Method: **SHAKE** all ingredients with ice and fine strain into chilled glass.

2	shot(s)	**Light white rum**
1/2	shot(s)	**Freshly squeezed lime juice**
1/2	shot(s)	**Sonoma pomegranate (grenadine) syrup**
1/4	shot(s)	**Luxardo maraschino liqueur**
3	dashes	**Angostura aromatic bitters**
1/2	shot(s)	**Chilled mineral water (omit if wet ice)**

AKA: Daiquiri No.5
Origin: A classic from the 1930s.
Comment: The quality of pomegranate syrup will make or break this delicate Daiquiri.

PINK FLAMINGO

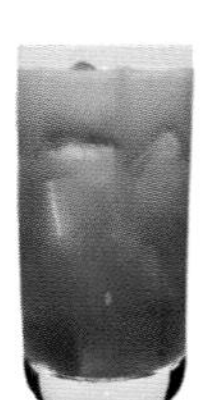

Glass: Collins
Garnish: Apple wheel
Method: **SHAKE** all ingredients with ice and fine strain into chilled glass.

2	shot(s)	**Orange flavoured vodka**
1	shot(s)	**Sour apple liqueur**
1/2	shot(s)	**Freshly squeezed lime juice**
1	shot(s)	**Cranberry juice**

Origin: Created in 2002 by Wayne Collins for Maxxium UK.
Comment: Soapy and citrus flavoured – but in a nice way.

PINK GIN #1 (TRADITIONAL) [UPDATED]

Glass: Martini
Garnish: Lemon zest twist
Method: **RINSE** chilled glass with Angostura bitters. **POUR** gin and water into rinsed glass and stir.

2	dashes	**Angostura aromatic bitters**
2	shot(s)	**Plymouth gin (from freezer)**
2	shot(s)	**Chilled mineral water**

Origin: Gin was a favourite of the Royal Navy – along with rum, which was served as a daily ration right up until the 70s. It was often mixed with healthy ingredients to make them more palatable. Pink gin was originally used against stomach upsets, as Angostura aromatic bitters were considered medicinal.
Comment: A traditionally made Pink Gin without ice.

PINK GIN #2 (MODERN)

Glass: Martini
Garnish: Lemon zest twist
Method: **STIR** all ingredients with ice and strain into chilled glass.

2	shot(s)	**Plymouth gin**
2	shot(s)	**Chilled mineral water**
1	dash	**Angostura aromatic bitters**

Comment: Normally I'd advocate liberal use of Angostura bitters but this refined and subtle drink benefits from frugality.

PINK GIN & TONIC

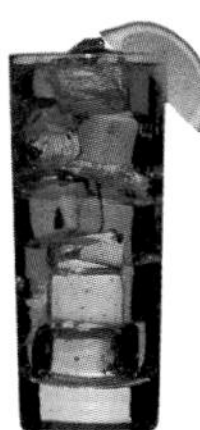

Glass: Collins
Garnish: Lime slice
Method: **POUR** gin and Angostura bitters into ice-filled glass, top with tonic, lightly stir and serve with straws.

2	shot(s)	**Plymouth gin**
4	dashes	**Angostura aromatic bitters**
Top up with		**Tonic water**

Comment: Basically a G&T with an extra pep of flavour from Angostura, this has a wider appeal than the original Pink Gin.

PINK GRAPEFRUIT MARGARITA [NEW]

Glass: Coupette
Garnish: Lime wedge on rim
Method: **SHAKE** all ingredients with ice and fine strain into chilled glass.

2	shot(s)	**Sauza Hornitos tequila**
1	shot(s)	**Freshly squeezed pink grapefruit juice**
1/2	shot(s)	**Freshly squeezed lime juice**
1/4	shot(s)	**Sugar (gomme) syrup**

Comment: Delivers exactly what the name promises.

PINK HOUND

Glass: Martini
Garnish: Lemon zest twist
Method: **SHAKE** all ingredients with ice and fine strain into chilled glass.

2	shot(s)	**Plymouth gin**
1 3/4	shot(s)	**Freshly squeezed pink grapefruit juice**
1/4	shot(s)	**Sugar (gomme) syrup**

Comment: A flavoursome balance of sweet and sour.

PINK LADY [UPDATED]

Glass: Martini
Garnish: Lemon zest twist
Method: **SHAKE** all ingredients with ice and fine strain into chilled glass.

2	shot(s)	**Plymouth gin**
1/2	shot(s)	**Freshly squeezed lemon juice**
1/2	shot(s)	**Sonoma pomegranate (grenadine) syrup**
1/2	fresh	**Egg white (optional)**

Variant: With the addition of half a shot apple brandy.
Origin: A classic cocktail named after a successful 1912 stage play.
Comment: Despite the colour, this is sharp and alcoholic.

PINK LEMONADE (MOCKTAIL)

Glass: Collins
Garnish: Lemon slice
Method: **SHAKE** first three ingredients with ice and strain into ice-filled glass. **TOP** with soda and serve with straws.

2	shot(s)	**Freshly squeezed lemon juice**
1/2	shot(s)	**Sonoma pomegranate (grenadine) syrup**
1/4	shot(s)	**Sugar (gomme) syrup**
Top up with		**Soda water (club soda)**

Origin: Discovered in 2004 in New York City.
Comment: A tall, pink, tangy, alcohol free cocktail.

PINK PALACE [NEW]

Glass: Martini
Garnish: Lemon twist
Method: **SHAKE** all ingredients with ice and fine strain into chilled glass.

2	shot(s)	**Plymouth gin**
1/2	shot(s)	**Grand Marnier**
1/2	shot(s)	**Freshly squeezed lemon juice**
1/4	shot(s)	**Sonoma pomegranate (grenadine) syrup**

Origin: The signature drink at The Polo Lounge, Beverly Hills Hotel, Los Angeles, USA. The hotel, which is lovingly termed the 'Pink Palace', inspired The Eagles' Hotel California and graces the album cover.
Comment: A great drink but rarely done justice at the Polo Lounge.

PINK SIN MARTINI

Glass: Martini
Garnish: Dust with cinnamon powder
Method: **SHAKE** all ingredients with ice and fine strain into chilled glass.

1 1/2	shot(s)	**Ketel One vodka**
1	shot(s)	**White crème de cacao liqueur**
3/4	shot(s)	**Goldschläger cinnamon schnapps liqueur**
1	shot(s)	**Cranberry juice**

Comment: This looks a little like a Cosmo but delivers sweet cinnamon and chocolate.

PINK TUTU

Glass: Old-fashioned
Garnish: Orange slice
Method: **SHAKE** all ingredients with ice and strain into ice-filled glass.

1	shot(s)	**Peach schnapps liqueur**
1/2	shot(s)	**Ketel One vodka**
1/2	shot(s)	**Campari**
2	shot(s)	**Freshly squeezed grapefruit juice**
1/4	shot(s)	**Sugar (gomme) syrup**

Origin: Created in 1999 by Dominique of Café Rouge, Leeds, England.
Comment: A cocktail that's both bitter and sweet.

A B C D E F G H I J K L M N N **P** Q R S T U V W X Y Z

●●●●○

PINKY PINCHER [NEW]

Glass: Old-fashioned
Garnish: Mint sprig, orange & lemon slice
Method: **SHAKE** all ingredients with ice and strain into ice-filled glass.

2	shot(s)	**Bourbon whiskey**
1	shot(s)	**Freshly squeezed orange juice**
1	shot(s)	**Freshly squeezed lemon juice**
1/4	shot(s)	**Orgeat (almond) sugar syrup**
1/4	shot(s)	**Sugar (gomme) syrup**

Origin: Adapted from a drink created by Victor Bergeron (Trader Vic).
Comment: Fruity, sweetened bourbon.

●●●●○

PINO PEPE [NEW]

Glass: Sling (or pineapple shell)
Garnish: Mint sprig
Method: **BLEND** all ingredients with 12oz scoop crushed ice. Pour into glass (or pineapple shell) and serve with straws. If using a pineapple shell, serve with ice cubes.

1	shot(s)	**Light white rum**
1	shot(s)	**Ketel One vodka**
1/2	shot(s)	**Cointreau /triple sec**
2	shot(s)	**Pressed pineapple juice**
1/2	shot(s)	**Freshly squeezed lime juice**
1/4	shot(s)	**Freshly squeezed lemon juice**
1/2	shot(s)	**Sugar (gomme) syrup**

Origin: Adapted from a recipe in the 1947-72 Trader Vic's Bartender's Guide by Victor Bergeron.
Comment: To quote Trader Vic, "Lethal but smooth – pineapple at its best".

●●●●○

PIRATE DAIQUIRI

Glass: Martini
Garnish: Lime wedge on rim
Method: **SHAKE** all ingredients with ice and fine strain into chilled glass.

3/4	shot(s)	**Wray & Nephew overproof rum**
3/4	shot(s)	**Pusser's Navy rum**
1/2	shot(s)	**Goldschläger cinnamon schnapps liqueur**
1/2	shot(s)	**Freshly squeezed lime juice**
1/4	shot(s)	**Sonoma pomegranate (grenadine) syrup**
3/4	shot(s)	**Chilled mineral water (omit if wet ice)**

Origin: Created in 2004 by yours truly.
Comment: Why the name? Well, the rums are hard and nautical, the lime protects against scurvy, the liqueur contains gold and the syrup is red as blood.

DRINKS ARE GRADED AS FOLLOWS:

● DISGUSTING ●◐ PRETTY AWFUL ●● BEST AVOIDED
●●◐ DISAPPOINTING ●●● ACCEPTABLE ●●●◐ GOOD
●●●● RECOMMENDED ●●●●◐ HIGHLY RECOMMENDED
●●●●● OUTSTANDING / EXCEPTIONAL

●●●●○

PISCO COLLINS

Glass: Collins
Garnish: Orange slice & cherry on stick (sail)
Method: **SHAKE** first three ingredients with ice and strain into ice-filled glass. **TOP** with soda, lightly stir and serve with straws.

2	shot(s)	**Pisco**
1	shot(s)	**Freshly squeezed lime juice**
1/2	shot(s)	**Sugar (gomme) syrup**
Top up with		**Soda water (club soda)**

Comment: The most aromatic and flavoursome of the Collins family.

●●●●◐

PISCO PUNCH #1 (DIFFORD'S FORMULA)

Glass: Collins
Garnish: Pineapple wedge on rim
Method: **MUDDLE** cloves in base of shaker. Add other ingredients except for champagne, **SHAKE** with ice and strain into ice-filled glass. **TOP** with champagne.

4	dried	**Cloves**
2 1/4	shot(s)	**Pisco**
1 3/4	shot(s)	**Pressed pineapple juice**
1/4	shot(s)	**Freshly squeezed orange juice**
1/2	shot(s)	**Freshly squeezed lemon juice**
1/2	shot(s)	**Sugar (gomme) syrup**
Top up with		**Piper-Heidsieck brut champagne**

Origin: Created in 2003 by yours truly.
Variant: This recipe is improved by using the marinade prescribed in Alfredo Micheli's Pisco Punch in place of sugar syrup. If using the marinade drop one of the marinated pineapple wedges and cloves into the drink as the garnish.
Comment: A tangy, balanced combination of rich flavours. The quality of pisco used is crucial to the success of a Pisco Punch.

●●●●●

PISCO PUNCH #2 (ALFREDO MICHELI'S FORMULA)

Glass: Goblet
Garnish: Pineapple wedge on rim
Method: **MUDDLE** orange and pineapple in base of shaker. Add pisco and pineapple marinade, **SHAKE** with ice and fine strain into ice-filled glass. **TOP** with no more than 2 shots of soda water.

2	fresh	**Orange slices**
3		**Marinaded pineapple wedges**
2	shot(s)	**Pisco**
3/4	shot(s)	**Pineapple marinade**
Top up with		**Soda water (club soda)**

Recipe for marinade: Core and remove the rind from one ripe pineapple. Cut the pineapple into rings and then into wedges and place in a deep container. Add 30 cloves and one litre of sugar syrup and marinate for 24 hours.
Origin: Alfredo Micheli (who went by the nickname Mike) was employed at the Bank Exchange and spied on Duncan Nichol to learn how to make this legendary drink. After he believed he'd learnt the secret he left to start serving at a newly opened competitor to the Bank Exchange, Paoli's on Montgomery Street.
Comment: This subtly flavoured drink is justifiably legendary.

PUNCH

Long before the Martini, the V-shaped glass and the cocktail shaker, the drink of choice at society gatherings was punch and the punch bowl was the centre of activity at every party. Punch had existed in India for centuries before colonialists brought it back to Europe some time in the latter half of the 1600s. The name derives from the Hindi word for five, 'panch', and refers to the five key ingredients: alcohol, citrus, sugar, water and spices.

In India, it was made with arrack (the Arabic word for liquor and a local spirit distilled from palm sap or sugar cane). Back in Britain it was common for punches to be spiced with nutmeg or tea.

The classic proportions of a punch follow a mnemonic, 'one of sour, two of sweet, three of strong and four of weak.' It refers to lime juice, sugar, rum and water: the fifth element, spice, was added to taste. To fill a Collins glass I translate it as follows - all shaken with ice, strained and served over crushed ice.

1 sour =	3/4 shot(s)	**Freshly squeezed lemon or lime juice**
2 sweet =	1 1/2 shot(s)	**Sugar (gomme) syrup (sweet)**
3 strong =	2 1/4 shot(s)	**Spirit (preferably overproof)**
4 weak =	3 shot(s)	**Chilled mineral water (or fruit juice)**
5 spice =	3 dashes	**Angostura aromatic bitters**

The basic punch principle of balancing sweet and sour with spirit and dilution remains key to making a good cocktail to this day. Indeed, the essential punch ingredients - spirit, citrus, sugar and water - lie at the centre of most modern day cocktails including the Daiquiri, Sour, Margarita, Caipirinha and Sidecar. Today's hip bartenders are now also reintroducing the fifth punch ingredient by muddling or macerating herbs and spices in their cocktails.

Two traditional punches remain on today's cocktail lists, the 'Rum Punch' and the 'Hot Whisky Punch', now better known as the 'Hot Toddy'. Also bear in mind that the Gin Punch probably led to the creation of the Collins.

PISCO PUNCH #3 (LANES' FORMULA) [UPDATED]

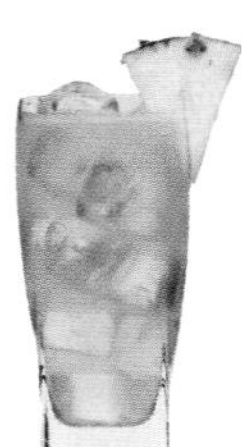

Glass: Collins
Garnish: Pineapple wedge on rim
Method: **SHAKE** first four ingredients with ice and strain into glass filled with crushed ice. **TOP** with soda, lightly stir and serve with straws.

$2\frac{1}{2}$	shot(s)	**Pisco**
$\frac{1}{2}$	shot(s)	**Freshly squeezed lemon juice**
1	shot(s)	**Pressed pineapple juice**
$\frac{1}{2}$	shot(s)	**Sugar (gomme) syrup**
Top up with		**Soda water (club soda)**

Origin: This recipe is said to herald from John Lanes, manager of the famous Bank Exchange when it closed in 1919.
Comment: Pisco's character comes through the fruit in this long, refreshing classic.

PISCO PUNCH #4 (PROSSER'S FORMULA)

Glass: Martini
Garnish: Grapes on rim
Method: **MUDDLE** grapes in base of shaker. Add other ingredients, **SHAKE** with ice and fine strain into chilled glass.

20	fresh	**Seedless white grapes**
$2\frac{1}{2}$	shot(s)	**Pisco**
1	shot(s)	**Pressed pineapple juice**
$\frac{1}{8}$	shot(s)	**La Fée Parisian 68% absinthe**

Origin: Jack Koeppler, the bartender at the Buena Vista Café in San Francisco who's also famous for being the first bartender in America to serve Irish Coffee, was given this recipe by the son of its creator, a fellow San Franciscan by the name of Mr Prosser. I've adapted this recipe from his, which originally comprised: 2 shots white grape juice, 2 shots pisco, 1 spoon pineapple juice and 1 spoon absinthe.
Comment: An aromatic take on the Pisco Punch.

PISCO NARANJA

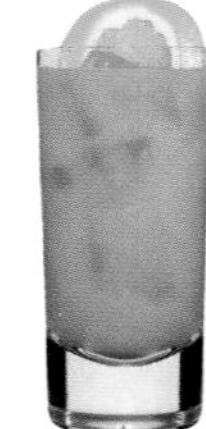

Glass: Collins
Garnish: Orange slice
Method: **SHAKE** all ingredients with ice and strain into ice-filled glass.

2	shot(s)	**Pisco**
3	shot(s)	**Freshly squeezed orange juice**
1	shot(s)	**Grand Marnier liqueur**

Origin: I based this recipe on the traditional Chilean combination of pisco and orange juice.
Comment: Aromatic brandy and orange juice pepped up and sweetened with a slug of orange liqueur.

FOR MORE INFORMATION SEE OUR
INGREDIENTS APPENDIX
ON PAGE 320

PISCO SOUR (TRADITIONAL RECIPE) [NEW]

Glass: Goblet
Garnish: Three drops of Angostura bitters
Method: **BLEND** all ingredients with 12oz scoop crushed ice and serve with straws.

2	shot(s)	**Pisco**
1	shot(s)	**Freshly squeezed lime juice**
1	shot(s)	**Sugar (gomme) syrup**
$\frac{1}{2}$	fresh	**Egg white**

Variant: Dust with cinnamon powder.
Origin: Believed to have first been created in the 1920s, the Pisco Sour has since become the national drink of both Chile and Peru.
Comment: One of the few really brilliant blended drinks.

PISCO SOUR (DIFFORD'S VERSION)

Glass: Old-fashioned
Garnish: Three drops of Angostura bitters
Method: **SHAKE** all ingredients with ice and fine strain into chilled glass.

$2\frac{1}{2}$	shot(s)	**Pisco**
1	shot(s)	**Freshly squeezed lime juice**
$\frac{1}{2}$	shot(s)	**Sugar (gomme) syrup**
$\frac{1}{2}$	fresh	**Egg white**

Origin: My adaptation of the Chilean and Peruvian classic.
Comment: Traditionally this drink is blended with crushed ice, but I prefer it served straight-up. Be sure to drink it quickly while it's cold.

PISCOLA

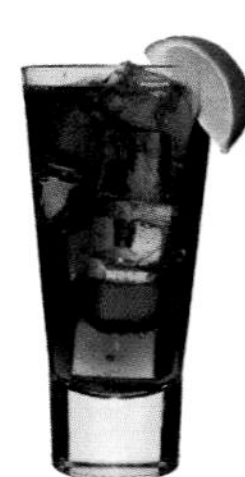

Glass: Collins
Garnish: Lime wedge
Method: **POUR** pisco and bitters into ice-filled glass, top with cola, stir and serve with straws.

$2\frac{1}{2}$	shot(s)	**Pisco**
3	dashes	**Angostura aromatic bitters**
Top up with		**Cola**

Origin: A popular long drink in its native Chile.
Comment: A 'brandy' and cola with a hint of angostura. Try it and see why the Chileans enjoy it.

PLANTATION PUNCH [NEW]

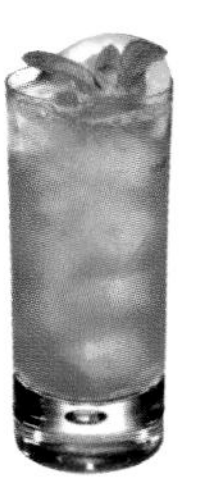

Glass: Collins
Garnish: Orange slice & mint sprig
Method: **SHAKE** first five ingredients with ice and strain into ice-filled glass. **TOP** with soda.

$1\frac{1}{2}$	shot(s)	**Southern Comfort**
1	shot(s)	**Light white rum**
$\frac{3}{4}$	shot(s)	**Freshly squeezed lemon juice**
$\frac{1}{4}$	shot(s)	**Sugar (gomme) syrup**
2	dashes	**Angostura aromatic bitters**
Top up with		**Soda water (club soda)**

Comment: Southern Comfort drives this tropical punch.

PLANTER'S PUNCH

Glass: Collins
Garnish: Orange slice & mint sprig
Method: **SHAKE** all ingredients with ice and strain into ice-filled glass.

1½	shot(s)	**Myers's Planters' Punch rum**
1	shot(s)	**Freshly squeezed lime juice**
½	shot(s)	**Sugar (gomme) syrup**
2	shot(s)	**Chilled mineral water**
3	dashes	**Angostura aromatic bitters**

Origin: Invented in the late 19th century by the founder of Myers's rum, Fred L. Myers. The recipe on the back of each bottle is known as the 'Old Plantation formula' and uses the classic rum punch proportions of 1 sour (lime), 2 sweet (sugar), 3 strong (rum) and 4 weak (water). Rather than this or the American formula (1 sweet, 2 sour, 3 weak and 4 strong), I've followed David A. Embury's recommendation of 1 sweet, 2 sour, 3 strong and 4 weak.
Comment: A twangy punch which harnesses the rich flavours of Myers's rum.

PLANTER'S PUNCHLESS (MOCKTAIL) [NEW]

Glass: Collins
Garnish: Lime wedge
Method: **SHAKE** first three ingredients with ice and strain into ice-filled glass. **TOP** with 7-Up, lightly stir and serve with straws.

2	shot(s)	**Pressed apple juice**
¾	shot(s)	**Freshly squeezed lime juice**
¼	shot(s)	**Sonoma pomegranate (grenadine) syrup**
Top up with		**7-Up**

Comment: A pleasant, if uninspiring, driver's option.

PLANTEUR [NEW]

Glass: Collins
Garnish: Orange slice
Method: **SHAKE** all ingredients with ice and strain into ice-filled glass.

2	shot(s)	**Martinique blanc agricole rum (50% alc./vol.)**
3½	shot(s)	**Freshly squeezed orange juice**
¼	shot(s)	**Sonoma pomegranate (grenadine) syrup**

Comment: Handle with extreme care.

PLATINUM BLONDE [NEW]

Glass: Martini
Garnish: Freshly grated nutmeg
Method: **SHAKE** all ingredients with ice and fine strain into chilled glass.

1½	shot(s)	**Aged rum**
1½	shot(s)	**Grand Marnier liqueur**
½	shot(s)	**Double (heavy) cream**
½	shot(s)	**Milk**

Comment: An after dinner sipper.

PLAYA DEL MAR [UPDATED]

Glass: Martini
Garnish: Pineapple wedge on rim
Method: **SHAKE** all ingredients with ice and fine strain into chilled glass.

1	shot(s)	**Sauza Hornitos tequila**
½	shot(s)	**Cointreau / triple sec**
1	shot(s)	**Cranberry juice**
¾	shot(s)	**Pressed pineapple juice**
½	shot(s)	**Freshly squeezed lime juice**
¼	shot(s)	**Sugar (gomme) syrup**

Origin: This cocktail was created in 1997 by Wayne Collins at Navajo Joe, London, England. The name translates as 'Beach of the Sea'.
Comment: A fruity complex taste with a hint of tequila.

PLAYMATE MARTINI

Glass: Martini
Garnish: Orange zest twist
Method: **SHAKE** all ingredients with ice and fine strain into chilled glass.

1	shot(s)	**Rémy Martin cognac**
1	shot(s)	**Grand Marnier liqueur**
1	shot(s)	**Apricot brandy liqueur**
1	shot(s)	**Freshly squeezed orange juice**
½	fresh	**Egg white**
3	dashes	**Angostura aromatic bitters**

Comment: Smooth and easy drinking.

PLUM COCKTAIL

Glass: Martini
Garnish: Plum quarter on rim
Method: Cut plum into quarters, remove stone and peel. **MUDDLE** plum in base of shaker. Add other ingredients, **SHAKE** with ice and fine strain into chilled glass.

1	fresh	**Plum (stoned and peeled)**
2	shot(s)	**Zuta Osa Slivovitz plum brandy**
¼	shot(s)	**Dry vermouth**
¼	shot(s)	**Sugar (gomme) syrup**

Origin: Formula by yours truly in 2004.
Comment: The slivovitz adds woody, brandied notes to the plum.

PLUM DAIQUIRI

Glass: Martini
Garnish: Lime wedge on rim
Method: Cut plum into quarters, remove stone and peel. **MUDDLE** plum pieces in base of shaker. Add other ingredients, **SHAKE** with ice and fine strain into chilled glass.

1	fresh	**Plum (stoned and peeled)**
2	shot(s)	**Light white rum**
½	shot(s)	**Freshly squeezed lime juice**
½	shot(s)	**Sugar (gomme) syrup**

Origin: Formula by yours truly in 2004.
Comment: Depending on the ripeness of the plums, you may need to adjust the quantity of sugar.

A B C D E F G H I J K L M N N **P** Q R S T U V W X Y Z

PLUM MARTINI

Glass: Martini
Garnish: Plum quarter on rim (unpeeled)
Method: Cut plum into quarters, remove stone and peel. **MUDDLE** plum pieces in base of shaker. Add other ingredients, **SHAKE** with ice and fine strain into chilled glass.

1	fresh	**Plum (stoned and peeled)**
2	shot(s)	**Ketel One vodka**
3/4	shot(s)	**Dry vermouth**
1/2	shot(s)	**Sugar (gomme) syrup**

Origin: Formula by yours truly in 2004.
Variant: Substitute vanilla sugar syrup for plain sugar syrup.
Comment: Fortified plum juice in a Martini glass.

PLUM PUDDING MARTINI

Glass: Martini
Garnish: Grate fresh nutmeg over drink
Method: Cut plum into quarters, remove stone and peel. **MUDDLE** plum pieces in base of shaker. Add other ingredients, **SHAKE** with ice and fine strain into chilled glass.

1	fresh	**Plum (stoned, peeled & chopped)**
1	shot(s)	**Raspberry flavoured vodka**
1	shot(s)	**Vanilla flavoured vodka**
1/2	shot(s)	**Luxardo Amaretto di Saschira liqueur**
1/8	shot(s)	**Goldschläger cinnamon liqueur**

Origin: Created in 2004 by yours truly.
Comment: Spicy and fruity.

PLUM SOUR [NEW]

Glass: Old-fashioned
Garnish: Orange zest twist
Method: **MUDDLE** plum in base of shaker. Add other ingredients, **SHAKE** with ice and fine strain into ice-filled glass.

1	fresh	**Plum (peeled stoned and chopped)**
2	shot(s)	**Ketel One vodka**
1	shot(s)	**Freshly squeezed lemon juice**
1/2	shot(s)	**Sugar (gomme) syrup**
1/2	fresh	**Egg white**

Comment: Soft, ripe plums are key to this fruity sour.

POET'S DREAM

Glass: Martini
Garnish: Squeezed lemon zest twist
Method: **STIR** all ingredients with ice and strain into chilled glass.

1	shot(s)	**Plymouth gin**
1	shot(s)	**Bénédictine D.O.M. liqueur**
1	shot(s)	**Dry vermouth**
3/4	shot(s)	**Chilled mineral water (omit if wet ice)**

Origin: Adapted from a recipe in the 1949 edition of Esquire's Handbook for Hosts.
Comment: Subtle, honeyed and herbal.

POGO STICK [NEW]

Glass: Martini (large)
Garnish: Mint sprig
Method: **BLEND** all ingredients with 12oz scoop crushed ice. Serve with straws.

2	shot(s)	**Plymouth gin**
1/2	shot(s)	**Pressed pineapple juice**
1/2	shot(s)	**Freshly squeezed pink grapefruit juice**
1/2	shot(s)	**Freshly squeezed lime juice**
1/2	shot(s)	**Sugar (gomme) syrup**

Origin: Adapted from a recipe in the 1947-72 Trader Vic's Bartender's Guide by Victor Bergeron.
Comment: To quote Trader Vic, "A refreshing blend of gin with pineapple and grapefruit juice... a real romper".

POINSETTIA [UPDATED]

Glass: Flute
Garnish: Quarter slice of orange on rim
Method: **POUR** first two ingredients into chilled glass. **TOP** with champagne.

1/2	shot(s)	**Cointreau / triple sec**
1	shot(s)	**Cranberry juice**
Top up with		**Piper-Heidsieck brut champagne**

Comment: Fruity champagne.

POLISH MARTINI [UPDATED]

Glass: Martini
Garnish: Lemon zest twist
Method: **SHAKE** all ingredients with ice and fine strain into chilled glass.

1	shot(s)	**Ketel One vodka**
1	shot(s)	**Zubrówka bison vodka**
3/4	shot(s)	**Krupnik honey liqueur**
1 1/2	shot(s)	**Pressed apple juice**

Origin: Created by Dick Bradsell, for his (Polish) father-in-law, Victor Sarge.
Comment: A round, smooth and very tasty alternatini.

POLLY'S SPECIAL

Glass: Martini
Garnish: Grapefruit wedge on rim
Method: **SHAKE** all ingredients with ice and fine strain into chilled glass.

1 3/4	shot(s)	**The Famous Grouse Scotch whisky**
1	shot(s)	**Freshly squeezed grapefruit juice**
1	shot(s)	**Grand Marnier liqueur**
1/4	shot(s)	**Sugar (gomme) syrup**

Origin: I adapted this recipe from a 1947 edition of Trader Vic's Bartender's Guide.
Comment: Sweet, sour, flavoursome and balanced – for grown-ups who like the taste of alcohol.

●●●◐○

POMEGRANATE BELLINI [NEW]

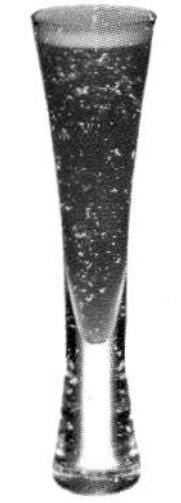

Glass: Flute
Method: Cut pomegranate in half and juice using a citrus juicer. **SHAKE** first three ingredients with ice and fine strain into chilled glass. **TOP** with sparkling wine.

1	shot(s)	Freshly squeezed pomegranate juice
1/2	shot(s)	Cuarenta Y Tres (Licor 43) liqueur
1/8	shot(s)	Freshly squeezed lemon juice
Top up with		Prosecco sparkling wine

Origin: Created in 2005 by yours truly.
Comment: This red drink is drier and more adult than it looks.

●●●●◐

POMEGRANATE MARGARITA [NEW]

Glass: Coupette
Garnish: Lime wedge on rim
Method: Cut pomegranate in half and juice using a citrus juicer. **SHAKE** all ingredients with ice and fine strain into chilled glass.

2	shot(s)	Sauza Hornitos tequila
1	shot(s)	Freshly squeezed pomegranate juice
1/2	shot(s)	Freshly squeezed lime juice
1/4	shot(s)	Sonoma pomegranate (grenadine) syrup

Origin: Recipe by yours truly in 2006.
Comment: Pomegranate and tequila combine harmoniously in this Margarita.

●●●●◐

POMEGRANATE MARTINI [NEW]

Glass: Martini
Garnish: Orange zest twist
Method: Cut pomegranate in half and juice using a citrus juicer. **SHAKE** all ingredients with ice and fine strain into chilled glass.

2	shot(s)	Ketel One vodka
1 1/2	shot(s)	Freshly squeezed pomegranate juice
1/2	shot(s)	Sonoma pomegranate (grenadine) syrup

Origin: Adapted from a drink discovered in 2005 at Lotus Bar, Sydney, Australia.
Comment: This drink was originally based on gin but I find that juniper and pomegranate clash.

●●●●○

POMPANSKI MARTINI

Glass: Martini
Garnish: Orange zest twist
Method: **SHAKE** all ingredients with ice and fine strain into chilled glass.

1 3/4	shot(s)	Ketel One vodka
1/2	shot(s)	Cointreau / triple sec
1 1/2	shot(s)	Freshly squeezed grapefruit juice
1/4	shot(s)	Sugar (gomme) syrup
1	spoon	Dry vermouth

Comment: Dry and zesty with the sharp freshness of grapefruit and a hint of orange.

●●●◐○

PONCHE DE ALGARROBINA [NEW]

Glass: Goblet
Garnish: Dust with cinnamon
Method: **BLEND** all ingredients with 12oz scoop crushed ice. Serve with straws.

2	shot(s)	Pisco
1	fresh	Egg yolk
1	shot(s)	Condensed milk
1	spoon	Algarrobo extract (or malt extract from healthfood shops)

Tip: It pays to add the condensed milk and Algarrobo (or malt extract) after starting the blender.
Origin: A traditional Peruvian drink I discovered at Tito's Restaurant, London, England. Algarrobo is extracted from the fruits of the tree of the same name. It is a sticky honey-like liquid which I find tastes a little like malt extract.
Comment: A creamy frozen drink with real character.

●●●●○

PONCE DE LEON [NEW]

Glass: Flute
Method: **SHAKE** first four ingredients with ice and fine strain into chilled glass. **TOP** with champagne.

1/2	shot(s)	Mount Gay golden rum
1/2	shot(s)	Rémy Martin cognac
1/2	shot(s)	Cointreau /triple sec
1/2	shot(s)	Freshly squeezed pink grapefruit juice
Top up with		Piper-Heidsieck brut champagne

Origin: A long lost classic.
Comment: A well-balanced classic champagne cocktail.

●●●●○

PONCHA

Glass: Collins
Garnish: Orange wedge
Method: **STIR** honey with aguardiente in base of shaker to dissolve honey. Add other ingredients, **SHAKE** with ice and strain into ice filled glass.

2	spoons	Runny honey
2 1/2	shot(s)	Aguardiente (Torres Aqua d'Or)
1	shot(s)	Freshly squeezed lemon juice
1/4	shot(s)	Sugar (gomme) syrup
1 1/2	shot(s)	Freshly squeezed orange juice
1 1/2	shot(s)	Freshly squeezed grapefruit juice

Origin: My adaptation of a tradtitional drink from the island of Madeira.
Comment: This citrus refresher is reputedly an excellent cold remedy.

DRINKS ARE GRADED AS FOLLOWS:

● DISGUSTING ●◐ PRETTY AWFUL ●● BEST AVOIDED
●●◐ DISAPPOINTING ●●● ACCEPTABLE ●●●◐ GOOD
●●●● RECOMMENDED ●●●●◐ HIGHLY RECOMMENDED
●●●●● OUTSTANDING / EXCEPTIONAL

PONTBERRY MARTINI

Glass: Martini
Garnish: Blackberries
Method: **SHAKE** all ingredients with ice and fine strain into chilled glass.

- 1 1/2 shot(s) **Ketel One vodka**
- 1/2 shot(s) **Crème de mûre (blackberry) liqueur**
- 2 shot(s) **Cranberry juice**

Origin: Created by Dick Bradsell in the late 90s for the opening of Agent Provocateur in Pont Street, London, England.
Comment: A light, fruity, easy drinking cocktail.

POOH'TINI

Glass: Martini
Garnish: Lemon zest twist
Method: **STIR** honey with vodka in base of shaker to dissolve honey. Add other ingredients, **SHAKE** with ice and fine strain into chilled glass.

- 2 spoon(s) **Runny honey**
- 2 shot(s) **Zubrówka bison grass vodka**
- 1/2 shot(s) **Krupnik honey liqueur**
- 1 1/2 shot(s) **Cold black camomile tea**

Origin: Adapted from a drink discovered in 1999 at Lot 61, New York City.
Comment: Grassy honey with a spicy, slightly tannic, camomile finish.

PORT & MELON MARTINI

Glass: Martini
Garnish: Melon wedge on rim
Method: Cut melon into eight segments and deseed. Cut cubes of flesh from skin of one segment and **MUDDLE** in base of shaker. Add other ingredients, **SHAKE** with ice and fine strain into chilled glass.

- 1/8 fresh **Cantaloupe / Galia melon**
- 1 1/2 shot(s) **Ketel One vodka**
- 1 1/2 shot(s) **Dry white port (e.g. Dow's Fine White)**
- 1 pinch **Ground ginger**

Origin: Created in 2004 by yours truly.
Comment: The classic seventies starter served as a Martini.

PORT & STARBOARD [NEW]

Glass: Shot
Method: Refrigerate ingredients then **LAYER** in chilled glass by carefully pouring in the following order.

- 1/2 shot(s) **Sonoma pomegranate (grenadine) syrup**
- 1/2 shot(s) **White crème de menthe liqueur**

Origin: Named after and inspired by the red and green running lights which respectively mark the 'Port' (left-hand) and 'Starboard' (right-hand) sides of a ship. The red light is called the Port side because port wine is red. The original name for the opposite side was Larboard, but over the years it was corrupted to Starboard.
Comment: Easy to layer but hard to drink. Very sweet.

PORT LIGHT [NEW]

Glass: Martini
Garnish: Passion fruit half
Method: **STIR** honey with bourbon in base of shaker to dissolve honey. Cut passion fruit in half and scoop flesh into shaker. Add other ingredients, **SHAKE** with ice and fine strain into ice-filled glass.

- 2 spoons **Runny honey**
- 2 shot(s) **Bourbon whiskey**
- 1 fresh **Passion fruit**
- 1 shot(s) **Freshly squeezed lemon juice**
- 1/2 shot(s) **Sonoma pomegranate (grenadine) syrup**
- 1/2 fresh **Egg white**

Origin: Adapted from a drink created by Victor Bergeron (Trader Vic).
Comment: Strong and very fruity. Too many will put your lights out.

PORT WINE COCKTAIL

Glass: Martini
Garnish: Orange zest twist
Method: **STIR** all ingredients with ice and strain into chilled glass.

- 3 shot(s) **Warre's Otima Tawny Port**
- 1 shot(s) **Rémy Martin cognac**

Origin: A classic from the early 1900s.
Comment: Port and brandy served straight-up and dressed up.

POTTED PARROT [NEW]

Glass: Sling
Garnish: Parrot on stick & mint sprig
Method: **SHAKE** all ingredients with ice and strain into glass filled with crushed ice.

- 2 shot(s) **Light white rum**
- 1/2 shot(s) **Cointreau / triple sec**
- 2 shot(s) **Freshly squeezed orange juice**
- 1 shot(s) **Freshly squeezed lemon juice**
- 1/4 shot(s) **Almond (orgeat) sugar syrup**
- 1/4 shot(s) **Sugar (gomme) syrup**

Origin: Adapted from a recipe in the 1947-72 Trader Vic's Bartender's Guide by Victor Bergeron. Popular in Trader Vic's restaurants.
Comment: Tangy orange, not too sweet.

POUSSE-CAFÉ

Glass: Shot
Method: Refrigerate ingredients then **LAYER** in chilled glass by carefully pouring in the following order.

- 1/4 shot(s) **Sonoma pomegranate (grenadine) syrup**
- 1/4 shot(s) **Kahlúa coffee liqueur**
- 1/4 shot(s) **Green crème de menthe**
- 1/4 shot(s) **Cointreau / triple sec**
- 1/4 shot(s) **Bourbon whiskey**
- 1/4 shot(s) **Wray & Nephew white overproof rum**

Origin: A pousse-café is a term for any multi-layered cocktail. (See 'Layer' in 'Bartending Basics'.)
Comment: More a test of patience and a steady hand than a drink.

●●●◐○

PRAIRIE OYSTER

Glass: Coupette
Method: Taking care not to break the egg yolk, **PLACE** it in the centre hollow of the glass. **SHAKE** the rest of the ingredients with ice and strain over egg. Instruct drinker to down in one.

1	raw	**Egg yolk**
1	shot(s)	**Rémy Martin cognac**
1/4	shot(s)	**Worcestershire sauce**
1/4	shot(s)	**Tomato juice**
5	drops	**Tabasco**
2	pinches	**Pepper**
2	pinches	**Salt**
1/2	spoon	**Malt vinegar**

Origin: Thought to have been created in Germany in the 1870s. Jeeves makes something similar for Bertie Wooster in a P.G. Wodehouse tale.
Comment: Like many supposed hangover cures, this works on the kill or... basis. It tastes better than it looks.

●●●●○

PRESIDENT [NEW]

Glass: Martini
Garnish: Orange zest twist
Method: **SHAKE** all ingredients with ice and fine strain into chilled glass.

2	shot(s)	**Light white rum**
1	shot(s)	**Freshly squeezed orange juice**
1/4	shot(s)	**Freshly squeezed lemon juice**
1/4	shot(s)	**Sonoma pomegranate (grenadine) syrup**
1/2	shot(s)	**Chilled mineral water (omit if wet ice)**

Origin: Adapted from a recipe in Harry Craddock's 1930 Savoy Cocktail Book.
Comment: A delicately fruity orange Daiquiri.

●●●●○

PRESIDENTE

Glass: Martini
Garnish: Orange zest twist
Method: **SHAKE** all ingredients with ice and fine strain into chilled glass.

1 1/2	shot(s)	**Light white rum**
3/4	shot(s)	**Cointreau / triple sec**
3/4	shot(s)	**Dry vermouth**
1/8	shot(s)	**Sonoma pomegranate (grenadine) syrup**
1/2	shot(s)	**Chilled mineral water (omit if wet ice)**

Origin: This classic was created during the 1920s in Vista Alegre, Cuba. The name refers to Mario Garcia Menocal, who was president of Cuba from 1912 to 1920.
Comment: A lightly flavoured classic cocktail.

DRINKS ARE GRADED AS FOLLOWS:

● DISGUSTING ●◐ PRETTY AWFUL ●● BEST AVOIDED
●●◐ DISAPPOINTING ●●● ACCEPTABLE ●●●◐ GOOD
●●●● RECOMMENDED ●●●●◐ HIGHLY RECOMMENDED
●●●●● OUTSTANDING / EXCEPTIONAL

●●●●○

PRICKLY PEAR MULE

Glass: Collins
Garnish: Pear slice on rim
Method: **SHAKE** first five ingredients with ice and strain into ice-filled glass. **TOP** with ginger beer.

1 1/4	shot(s)	**Pear & cognac liqueur**
1 1/4	shot(s)	**Poire William eau de vie**
3	shot(s)	**Freshly extracted pear juice**
1/4	shot(s)	**Freshly squeezed lemon juice**
2	dashes	**Angostura aromatic bitters**
Top up with		**Jamaican ginger beer**

Origin: Created in 2002 by yours truly.
Tip: Fill the glass with ice and go easy on the ginger beer which can predominate and overpower the pear.
Comment: Subtle pear with ginger spice.

●●●●○

PRINCE CHARLIE

Glass: Martini
Garnish: Lemon zest twist
Method: **SHAKE** all ingredients with ice and fine strain into chilled glass.

1	shot(s)	**Rémy Martin cognac**
1	shot(s)	**Drambuie liqueur**
1	shot(s)	**Freshly squeezed lemon juice**
3/4	shot(s)	**Chilled mineral water (omit if wet ice)**

Origin: A long lost classic.
Comment: Cognac and honey with sweet and sourness in harmony.

●●●◐○

PRINCE OF WALES [NEW]

Glass: Flute
Garnish: Lemon peel twist
Method: Rub sugar cube with lemon peel, coat with bitters and drop into glass. **POUR** cognac and liqueur over soaked cube and top with champagne.

1	cube	**Brown sugar**
2	dashes	**Angostura aromatic bitters**
1/2	shot(s)	**Rémy Martin cognac**
1/2	shot(s)	**Grand Marnier liqueur**
Top up with		**Piper-Heidsieck brut champagne**

Comment: More interesting than a classic Champagne Cocktail.

●●●●○

PRINCESS MARINA [NEW]

Glass: Martini
Garnish: Orange zest twist
Method: **SHAKE** all ingredients with ice and fine strain into chilled glass.

1	shot(s)	**Plymouth gin**
1/2	shot(s)	**Calvados or applejack brandy**
1/2	shot(s)	**Dubonnet Red**
1/2	shot(s)	**Cointreau / triple sec**
1/2	shot(s)	**Carlshamns Swedish Torr Flaggpunsch**
3/4	shot(s)	**Chilled mineral water (omit if wet ice)**

Origin: Created in the late 1920s/early 1930s and named after Princess Marina, the late mother of The Duke of Kent, Prince Michael of Kent and Princess Alexandra.
Comment: Delicate yet loaded with alcohol and flavour.

PRINCESS MARY [NEW]

Glass: Martini
Garnish: Dust with cocoa powder
Method: **SHAKE** all ingredients with ice and fine strain into chilled glass.

1½	shot(s)	**Plymouth gin**
1	shot(s)	**White crème de cacao liqueur**
¾	shot(s)	**Double (heavy) cream**
¾	shot(s)	**Milk**

Origin: Created in 1922 by Harry MacElhone to celebrate H.R.H. Princess Mary's marriage. The original recipe featured equal parts of all four ingredients.
Comment: Slightly sweet, very creamy - drink after dinner.

PRINCESS MARY'S PRIDE [NEW]

Glass: Martini
Garnish: Orange zest twist
Method: **SHAKE** all ingredients with ice and fine strain into chilled glass.

2	shot(s)	**Calvados / applejack brandy**
1	shot(s)	**Dubonnet Red**
1	shot(s)	**Dry vermouth**

Origin: Created by Harry Craddock on 28th February 1922 to mark the wedding celebrations of H.R.H. Princess Mary. Recipe from 1930's Savoy Cocktail Book.
Comment: Apple brandy to the fore, followed by aromatised wine.

PRINCESS PRIDE [NEW]

Glass: Martini
Garnish: Orange zest twist
Method: **SHAKE** all ingredients with ice and fine strain into chilled glass.

2	shot(s)	**Calvados or applejack brandy**
1	shot(s)	**Dubonnet Red**
1	shot(s)	**Sweet (rosso) vermouth**

Origin: Adapted from a recipe in the 1947-72 Trader Vic's Bartender's Guide by Victor Bergeron.
Comment: Vic's improved version of the drink above.

PRINCETON [UPDATED]

Glass: Martini
Garnish: Lemon zest twist
Method: **STIR** all ingredients with ice and strain into chilled glass.

2	shot(s)	**Plymouth gin**
1	shot(s)	**Warre's Otima Tawny Port**
¼	shot(s)	**Sugar (gomme) syrup**
2	dashes	**Fee Brothers orange bitters**

Origin: An old classic originally made with sweet 'Old Tom' gin and without the sugar syrup.
Comment: Overproof wine with a herbal orange garnish.

PRINCETON MARTINI [NEW]

Glass: Martini
Garnish: Lime zest twist
Method: **SHAKE** all ingredients with ice and fine strain into chilled glass.

2	shot(s)	**Plymouth gin**
½	shot(s)	**Dry vermouth**
¼	shot(s)	**Rose's lime cordial**
½	shot(s)	**Chilled mineral water (omit if wet ice)**

Comment: The Dry Martini meets the Gimlet. They should meet more often.

PRUNE FACE

Glass: Old-fashioned
Garnish: Orange zest twist
Method: **POUR** bourbon into glass with four ice cubes and **STIR** until ice has at least half melted. Add other ingredients and additional ice and stir some more.

2	shot(s)	**Bourbon whiskey**
¾	shot(s)	**Vieille de prune eau de vie**
¼	shot(s)	**Mandarine Napoléon liqueur**
¼	shot(s)	**Sugar (gomme) syrup**

Origin: Created in 2002 by Daniel Warner at Zander, London, England and named after my friend's nickname for his stepmother.
Comment: Why muddle cherries into your Old Fashioned when you can add a hint of prune?

PRUNEAUX [NEW]

Glass: Martini
Garnish: Prunes on stick
Method: **SHAKE** all ingredients with ice and fine strain into chilled glass.

1½	shot(s)	**Plymouth gin**
1	shot(s)	**Amontillado sherry**
½	shot(s)	**Pedro Ximenez sherry**
¾	shot(s)	**Freshly squeezed orange juice**
¾	shot(s)	**Syrup from tinned prunes**

Origin: Adapted from a recipe in Harry Craddock's 1930 Savoy Cocktail Book.
Comment: Sherried prunes further fortified by gin.

P.S. I LOVE YOU

Glass: Martini
Garnish: Crumbled Cadbury's Flake bar
Method: **SHAKE** all ingredients with ice and fine strain into chilled glass.

1¼	shot(s)	**Baileys Irish Cream liqueur**
1¼	shot(s)	**Luxardo Amaretto di Saschira liqueur**
¾	shot(s)	**Mount Gay Eclipse golden rum**
¾	shot(s)	**Kahlúa coffee liqueur**
1	shot(s)	**Double (heavy) cream**

Comment: P.S. You'll love this creamy flavoursome drink.

PUCCINI

Glass: Flute
Garnish: Mandarin (tangerine) segment
Method: **MUDDLE** segments in base of shaker. Add liqueur, **SHAKE** with ice and fine strain into chilled glass. **TOP** with champagne and lightly stir.

8 segments **Fresh mandarin (tangerine/clementine/satsuma)**
3/4 shot(s) **Mandarine Napoléon liqueur**
Top up with **Prosecco sparkling wine**

Origin: Named after the composer of Madame Butterfly, this cocktail is popular in Venice and other areas of northern Italy. It is often made without mandarin liqueur.
Comment: The use of mandarin (tangerine) instead of orange makes the Puccini slightly sharper than the similar Mimosa.

PULP FICTION

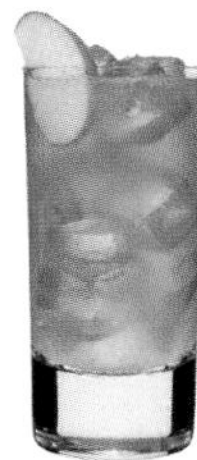

Glass: Collins
Method: **SHAKE** all ingredients with ice and strain into ice filled glass. **TOP** with 7-Up.

2 shot(s) **Pressed apple juice**
2 shot(s) **Rémy Martin cognac**
1 shot(s) **Apple schnapps liqueur**
Top up with **7-Up**

Origin: Discovered in 2001 at Teatro, London, England.
Comment: Originally made with apple pulp, this drink has a zingy apple taste.

PURPLE COSMO

Glass: Martini
Garnish: Orange zest twist
Method: **STIR** all ingredients with ice and strain into chilled glass.

2 shot(s) **Ketel One Citroen vodka**
3/4 shot(s) **Parfait Amour liqueur**
1 1/2 shot(s) **White cranberry & grape juice**
1/4 shot(s) **Freshly squeezed lime juice**

Variant: Blue Cosmo
Comment: If shaken this becomes more of a grey Cosmo. The flavour and colour make for an interesting twist.

PURPLE FLIRT #1

Glass: Martini
Garnish: Orange zest twist
Method: **SHAKE** all ingredients with ice and fine strain into chilled glass.

1 1/2 shot(s) **Ketel One vodka**
3/4 shot(s) **Opal Nera black sambuca**
2 shot(s) **Cranberry juice**

Comment: This purple drink is surprisingly balanced with subtle hints of liquorice.

PURPLE FLIRT #2

Glass: Old-fashioned
Garnish: Orange slice & cherry (sail)
Method: **SHAKE** all ingredients with ice and strain into ice-filled glass.

1 shot(s) **Goslings Black Seal rum**
1/4 shot(s) **Blue curaçao liqueur**
1 shot(s) **Pressed pineapple juice**
1/2 shot(s) **Freshly squeezed lemon juice**
1/4 shot(s) **Sonoma pomegranate (grenadine) syrup**
1/2 fresh **Egg white**

Comment: This popular drink is more brown than purple. It tastes OK, anyway.

PURPLE HAZE

Glass: Shot
Method: **SHAKE** first three ingredients with ice and strain into glass. **POUR** liqueur down the inside of the glass. This will fall to the bottom and form the purple haze.

1 1/2 shot(s) **Ketel One vodka**
1/2 shot(s) **Freshly squeezed lime juice**
1/4 shot(s) **Sugar (gomme) syrup**
1/8 shot(s) **Chambord black raspberry liqueur**

Comment: A sweet and sour shot with a sweet, berry base.

PURPLE HOOTER

Glass: Collins
Garnish: Lime wedge
Method: **SHAKE** first three ingredients with ice and strain into ice-filled glass. **TOP** with soda.

2 shot(s) **Ketel One vodka**
1 shot(s) **Chambord black raspberry liqueur**
1 shot(s) **Freshly squeezed lime juice**
Top up with **Soda water (club soda)**

Comment: Tangy, fruity, long and refreshing.

PURPLE PEAR MARTINI

Glass: Martini
Garnish: Pear slice on rim
Method: **SHAKE** all ingredients with ice and fine strain into chilled glass.

2 shot(s) **Poire William eau de vie**
2 shot(s) **Benoit Serres liqueur de violette**
1/2 shot(s) **Sugar (gomme) syrup**

Origin: Created in 2002 by yours truly.
Comment: This floral drink suits its name.

DRINKS ARE GRADED AS FOLLOWS:

● DISGUSTING ●◐ PRETTY AWFUL ●● BEST AVOIDED
●●◐ DISAPPOINTING ●●● ACCEPTABLE ●●●◐ GOOD
●●●● RECOMMENDED ●●●●◐ HIGHLY RECOMMENDED
●●●●● OUTSTANDING / EXCEPTIONAL

PURPLE TURTLE

Glass: Shot
Method: SHAKE all ingredients with ice and fine strain into chilled glass.

1/2	shot(s)	**Sauza Hornitos tequila**
1/2	shot(s)	**Blue curaçao liqueur**
1/2	shot(s)	**Plymouth sloe gin**

Comment: This aquamarine shooter goes down a treat.

PUSSYFOOT (MOCKTAIL) [UPDATED]

Glass: Collins
Garnish: Orange slice
Method: MUDDLE mint in base of shaker. Add other ingredients, **SHAKE** with ice and fine strain into ice-filled glass.

7	fresh	**Mint leaves**
4	shot(s)	**Freshly squeezed orange juice**
1/2	shot(s)	**Freshly squeezed lemon juice**
1/2	shot(s)	**Freshly squeezed lime juice**
1/2	shot(s)	**Sonoma pomegranate (grenadine) syrup**
1	fresh	**Egg yolk**

Origin: Created in 1920 by Robert Vermeire at the Embassy Club, London, England. This non-alcoholic cocktail is named after 'Pussyfoot' (William E.) Johnson who was an ardent supporter of Prohibition.
Comment: Probably the best non-alcoholic cocktail ever.

QUARTER DECK [NEW]

Glass: Martini
Garnish: Orange zest twist
Method: SHAKE all ingredients with ice and fine strain into chilled glass.

2	shot(s)	**Light white rum**
1	shot(s)	**Pedro Ximenez sherry**
1/4	shot(s)	**Freshly squeezed lemon juice**
3/4	shot(s)	**Chilled mineral water (omit if wet ice)**

Origin: Long lost classic.
Comment: Hints of prune, toffee and maple syrup. Very complex.

QUARTERBACK

Glass: Martini
Garnish: Orange zest twist
Method: SHAKE all ingredients with ice and fine strain into chilled glass.

1	shot(s)	**Yellow Chartreuse**
1	shot(s)	**Cointreau / triple sec**
1	shot(s)	**Double (heavy) cream**
1	shot(s)	**Milk**

Comment: This white, creamy drink has a flavoursome bite.

QUEBEC [NEW]

Glass: Martini
Garnish: Orange zest twist
Method: STIR all ingredients with ice and strain into chilled glass.

2	shot(s)	**Canadian whisky (or bourbon whiskey)**
2	shot(s)	**Dubonnet Red**
2	dashes	**Fee Brothers orange bitters**

Origin: Created in 2004 at Victoria Bar, Berlin, Germany.
Comment: Canadian whisky with French accents of aromatised wine – très Quebecois.

QUEEN MARTINI [NEW]

Glass: Martini
Garnish: Maraschino cherry
Method: SHAKE all ingredients with ice and fine strain into chilled glass.

1 1/2	shot(s)	**Plymouth gin**
1/2	shot(s)	**Dry vermouth**
1/2	shot(s)	**Red (rosso) vermouth**
1/2	shot(s)	**Freshly squeezed orange juice**
1/2	shot(s)	**Pressed pineapple juice**

Comment: A 'perfectly' fruity Martini that's fit for a...

QUELLE VIE [NEW]

Glass: Martini
Garnish: Orange zest twist
Method: STIR all ingredients with ice and fine strain into chilled glass.

2	shot(s)	**Rémy Martin cognac**
1/2	shot(s)	**Kummel**
3/4	shot(s)	**Chilled mineral water (omit if wet ice)**

Origin: Adapted from a recipe in the 1930 Savoy Cocktail Book by Harry Craddock.
Comment: In Craddock's words, "Brandy gives you courage and Kummel makes you cautious, thus giving you a perfect mixture of bravery and caution, with the bravery predominating."

QUINCE SOUR [NEW]

Glass: Old-fashioned
Garnish: Lemon slice & cherry (sail)
Method: STIR quince jam with vodka in base of shaker to dissolve jam. Add other ingredients, **SHAKE** with ice and fine strain into ice-filled glass.

3	spoons	**Quince jam /membrillo Spanish quince paste**
2	shot(s)	**Ketel One vodka**
1	shot(s)	**Freshly squeezed lemon juice**
1/2	fresh	**Egg white**

Comment: The sweet quince both flavours and balances this sour.

RAGING BULL

Glass: Shot
Method: Refrigerate ingredients then **LAYER** in chilled glass by carefully pouring in the following order.

1/2	shot(s)	**Kahlúa coffee liqueur**
1/2	shot(s)	**Luxardo Sambuca dei Cesari**
1/2	shot(s)	**Sauza Hornitos tequila**

Comment: Coffee and sambuca make a great combination, as do coffee and tequila.

RAMOS GIN FIZZ

Glass: Small Collins (8oz)
Method: Vigorously **SHAKE** first nine ingredients with ice and strain into chilled (empty) glass. **TOP** with soda water from a siphon.

2	shot(s)	**Plymouth gin**
3/4	shot(s)	**Milk**
3/4	shot(s)	**Double (heavy) cream**
1/2	shot(s)	**Freshly squeezed lemon juice**
1/2	shot(s)	**Freshly squeezed lime juice**
1/2	shot(s)	**Sugar (gomme) syrup**
1/8	shot(s)	**Orange flower water**
4	drops	**Vanilla extract (optional)**
1	fresh	**Egg white**
Top up with		**Soda water from siphon**

Origin: Created in 1888 by Henry C. Ramos when he opened his Imperial Cabinet Bar in New Orleans. The recipe was kept secret until the onset of Prohibition when his brother, Charles Henry Ramos, published it in a full-page advertisement. Since 1935, the Roosevelt (now named the Fairmont), New Orleans, has held the trademark on the name Ramos Gin Fizz.
Comment: Smooth, fluffy, sweet and sour.

RANDY

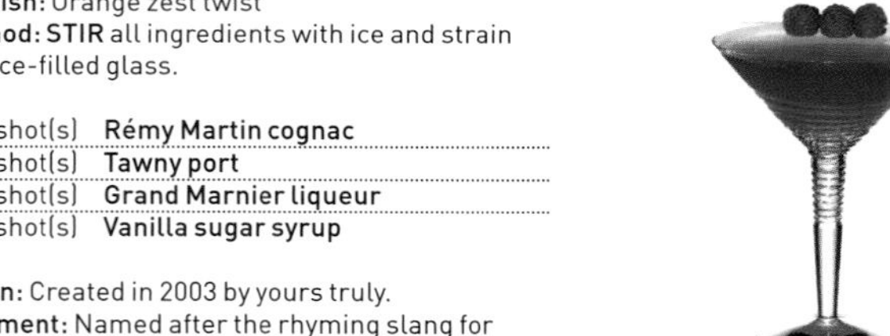

Glass: Old-fashioned
Garnish: Orange zest twist
Method: **STIR** all ingredients with ice and strain into ice-filled glass.

1 1/2	shot(s)	**Rémy Martin cognac**
1 1/2	shot(s)	**Tawny port**
1/2	shot(s)	**Grand Marnier liqueur**
1/4	shot(s)	**Vanilla sugar syrup**

Origin: Created in 2003 by yours truly.
Comment: Named after the rhyming slang for port and brandy, its base ingredients. Love interest comes courtesy of orange and vanilla.

RASPBERRY CAIPIRINHA

Glass: Old-fashioned
Method: **MUDDLE** lime and raspberries in base of glass. Add other ingredients and fill glass with crushed ice. **CHURN** drink with barspoon and serve with short straws.

3/4	fresh	**Lime cut into wedges**
8	fresh	**Raspberries**
2	shot(s)	**Sagatiba cachaça**
3/4	shot(s)	**Sugar (gomme) syrup**

Variants: Substitute other berries and fruits for raspberries. Add raspberry liqueur in place of sugar. Use rum in place of cachaça to make a Raspberry Caipirissima.
Comment: A fruity twist on the popular Caipirinha.

RASPBERRY COLLINS

Glass: Collins
Garnish: Three raspberries & lemon slice
Method: **MUDDLE** raspberries in base of shaker. Add next five ingredients, **SHAKE** with ice and strain into ice-filled glass. **TOP** with soda, lightly stir and serve with straws.

10	fresh	**Raspberries**
2	shot(s)	**Plymouth gin**
1 1/2	shot(s)	**Freshly squeezed lemon juice**
1/2	shot(s)	**Crème de framboise (raspberry) liqueur**
1/2	shot(s)	**Sugar (gomme) syrup**
3	dashes	**Fee Brothers orange bitters (optional)**
Top up with		**Soda water (club soda)**

Variant: Raspberry Debonnaire
Origin: Created in 1999 by Cairbry Hill, London, England.
Comment: This fruity drink is the most popular modern adaptation of the classic Collins.

RASPBERRY COSMO [UPDATED]

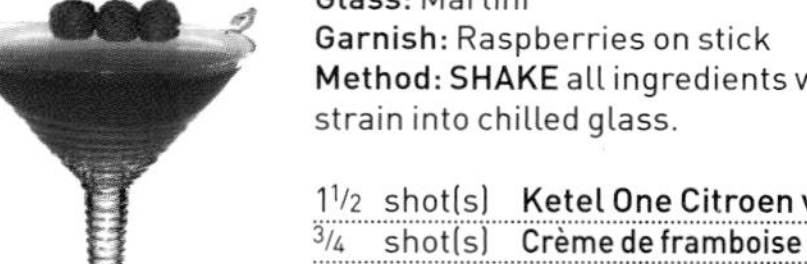

Glass: Martini
Garnish: Raspberries on stick
Method: **SHAKE** all ingredients with ice and fine strain into chilled glass.

1 1/2	shot(s)	**Ketel One Citroen vodka**
3/4	shot(s)	**Crème de framboise (raspberry) liqueur**
1	shot(s)	**Cranberry juice**
1/2	shot(s)	**Freshly squeezed lime juice**

Origin: Formula by yours truly in 2006.
Comment: Your classic Cosmo but with raspberry liqueur replacing orange liqueur.

HOW TO MAKE SUGAR SYRUP

To make your own sugar syrup, gradually pour TWO cups of granulated sugar into a saucepan containing ONE cup of hot water. Stir as you pour and carry on stirring and simmering until the sugar is dissolved. Do not let the water even come close to boiling and only simmer for as long as it takes to dissolve the sugar. Allow syrup to cool and pour into an empty bottle. Ideally, you should finely strain your syrup into the bottle to remove any undissolved crystals which could otherwise encourage crystallisation. If kept in a refrigerator this mixture will last for a couple of months.

A B C D E F G H I J K L M N O P Q **R** S T U V W X Y Z

RASPBERRY DEBONNAIRE

Glass: Collins
Garnish: Three raspberries & lemon slice
Method: **MUDDLE** raspberries in base of shaker. Add next five ingredients, **SHAKE** with ice and fine strain into ice-filled glass. **TOP** with soda, lightly stir and serve with straws.

10	fresh	**Raspberries**
2	shot(s)	**Ketel One vodka**
1½	shot(s)	**Freshly squeezed lemon juice**
½	shot(s)	**Crème de framboise (raspberry) liqueur**
½	shot(s)	**Sugar (gomme) syrup**
3	dashes	**Fee Brothers orange bitters (optional)**
Top up with		**Soda water (club soda)**

Variant: Raspberry Collins
Comment: If based on gin rather than vodka this would be a Raspberry Collins.

RASPBERRY LYNCHBURG

Glass: Collins
Garnish: Raspberries on drink
Method: **SHAKE** first three ingredients with ice and strain into ice-filled glass. **TOP** with 7-Up and **DRIZZLE** liqueur around surface of drink. It will fall through the drink, leaving coloured threads.

2	shot(s)	**Jack Daniel's Tennessee whiskey**
¾	shot(s)	**Freshly squeezed lime juice**
¼	shot(s)	**Sugar (gomme) syrup**
Top up with		**7-Up**
½	shot(s)	**Chambord black raspberry liqueur**

Origin: Created in 1992 by Wayne Collins at Roadhouse, London, England.
Comment: This variation on a Lynchburg Lemonade has a sweet and sour flavour laced with whiskey.

RASPBERRY MARGARITA

Glass: Coupette
Garnish: Lime wedge on rim
Method: **MUDDLE** raspberries in base of shaker. Add other ingredients, **SHAKE** with ice and fine strain into chilled glass.

7	fresh	**Raspberries**
2	shot(s)	**Sauza Hornitos tequila**
1	shot(s)	**Cointreau / triple sec**
1	shot(s)	**Freshly squeezed lime juice**
1/8	shot(s)	**Sugar (gomme) syrup**

Comment: Just as it says – a raspberry flavoured Margarita.

RASPBERRY MARTINI #1 [UPDATED]

Glass: Martini
Garnish: Three raspberries on stick
Method: **MUDDLE** raspberries in base of shaker. Add other ingredients, **SHAKE** with ice and fine strain into chilled glass.

10	fresh	**Raspberries**
2½	shot(s)	**Ketel One vodka**
½	shot(s)	**Sugar (gomme) syrup**

Comment: The simplest of raspberry Martinis but still tastes good.

RASPBERRY MARTINI #2 [UPDATED]

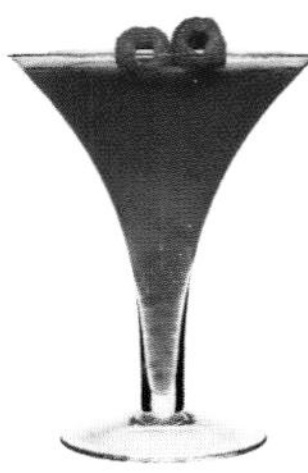

Glass: Martini
Garnish: Three raspberries on stick
Method: **MUDDLE** raspberries in base of shaker. Add other ingredients, **SHAKE** with ice and fine strain into chilled glass.

7	fresh	**Raspberries**
2	shot(s)	**Plymouth gin**
1	shot(s)	**Crème de framboise (raspberry) liqueur**
2	dashes	**Fee Brothers orange bitters (optional)**

Origin: Created in 1997 by Dick Bradsell, London, England.
Comment: Great raspberry flavour integrated with gin.

RASPBERRY MOCHA'TINI

Glass: Martini
Garnish: Three raspberries on stick
Method: **SHAKE** all ingredients with ice and fine strain into chilled glass.

1½	shot(s)	**Raspberry flavoured vodka**
¾	shot(s)	**Dark crème de cacao liqueur**
¾	shot(s)	**Crème de framboise (raspberry) liqueur**
1	shot(s)	**Cold espresso coffee**

Origin: Discovered in 2002 at Lot 61, New York City, USA.
Comment: Sweet chocolate and raspberry tempered by dry coffee and vodka.

RASPBERRY MULE

Glass: Collins
Garnish: Lime wedge
Method: **MUDDLE** raspberries in base of shaker. Add next three ingredients, **SHAKE** with ice and fine strain into ice-filled glass. **TOP** with ginger beer, lightly stir and serve with straws.

12	fresh	**Raspberries**
2	shot(s)	**Ketel One vodka**
1	shot(s)	**Freshly squeezed lime juice**
½	shot(s)	**Sugar (gomme) syrup**
Top up with		**Ginger beer**

Comment: The fruity alternative to a Moscow Mule.

RASPBERRY SAKE'TINI [UPDATED]

Glass: Martini
Garnish: Three raspberries.
Method: **SHAKE** all ingredients with ice and fine strain into chilled glass.

1½	shot(s)	**Raspberry flavoured vodka**
1½	shot(s)	**Sake**
½	shot(s)	**Chambord black raspberry liqueur**
½	shot(s)	**Pressed pineapple juice**

Comment: Fruity with wafts of sake – reminiscent of a French Martini.

RASPBERRY WATKINS [UPDATED]

Glass: Sling
Garnish: Three raspberries
Method: SHAKE first four ingredients with ice and strain into ice-filled glass. **TOP** with soda, lightly stir and serve with straws.

2	shot(s)	**Ketel One vodka**
1/2	shot(s)	**Chambord black raspberry liqueur**
1/2	shot(s)	**Freshly squeezed lime juice**
1/4	shot(s)	**Sonoma pomegranate (grenadine) syrup**
Top up with		**Soda water (club soda)**

Comment: A light, long, fizzy and refreshing drink.

RASPUTIN

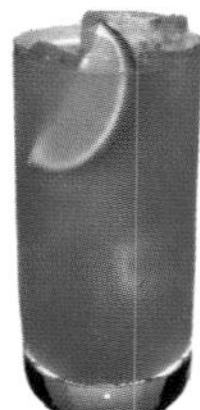

Glass: Collins
Garnish: Lime wedge
Method: SHAKE all ingredients with ice and strain into ice-filled glass.

2	shot(s)	**Raspberry flavoured vodka**
2 1/2	shot(s)	**Cranberry juice**
1 1/2	shot(s)	**Freshly squeezed grapefruit juice**

Comment: This fruity adaptation of an Arizona Breeze is raspberry rich.

RAT PACK MANHATTAN

Glass: Martini
Garnish: Orange zest twist & maraschino cherry
Method: Chill glass, add Grand Marnier, swirl to coat and then **DISCARD. STIR** other ingredients with ice and strain into liqueur coated glass.

1/2	shot(s)	**Grand Marnier liqueur**
1 1/2	shot(s)	**Bourbon whiskey**
3/4	shot(s)	**Sweet (rosso) vermouth**
3/4	shot(s)	**Dry vermouth**
3	dashes	**Angostura aromatic bitters**

Origin: Created in 2000 by Wayne Collins at High Holborn, London, England. Originally Wayne used different whiskies to represent each of the Rat Pack crooners. The wash of Grand Marnier was for Sammy Davis, the wild card of the bunch.
Comment: A twist on the classic Manhattan.

RATTLESNAKE [NEW]

Glass: Martini
Garnish: Lemon zest twist
Method: SHAKE all ingredients with ice and fine strain into chilled glass.

2	shot(s)	**Bourbon whiskey**
1/4	shot(s)	**Freshly squeezed lemon juice**
1/4	shot(s)	**Sugar (gomme) syrup**
1/8	shot(s)	**La Fée Parisian 68% absinthe**
1/2	fresh	**Egg white**
1/2	shot(s)	**Chilled mineral water (omit if wet ice)**

Origin: Adapted from a recipe purloined from a 1930 edition of The Savoy Cocktail Book by Harry Craddock.
Comment: To quote Craddock, "So called because it will either cure rattlesnake bite, or kill rattlesnakes, or make you see them."

RATTLESNAKE SHOT

Glass: Shot
Method: Refrigerate ingredients then **LAYER** in chilled glass by carefully pouring in the following order.

1/2	shot(s)	**Kahlúa coffee liqueur**
1/2	shot(s)	**White crème de cacao liqueur**
1/2	shot(s)	**Baileys Irish cream liqueur**

Comment: Tastes rather like a strong cappuccino.

RAY GUN

Glass: Flute
Garnish: Orange zest twist
Method: POUR Chartreuse and blue curaçao into chilled glass. Top with champagne.

1/2	shot(s)	**Green Chartreuse**
3/4	shot(s)	**Blue curaçao liqueur**
Top up with		**Piper-Heidsieck brut champagne**

Comment: Not for the faint-hearted.

RAY'S HARD LEMONADE

Glass: Collins
Garnish: Mint sprig
Method: Lightly **MUDDLE** (just to bruise) mint in base of shaker. Add next four ingredients, **SHAKE** with ice and fine strain into ice-filled glass. **TOP** with soda, lightly stir and serve with straws.

7	fresh	**Mint leaves**
2	shot(s)	**Ketel One vodka**
1	shot(s)	**Freshly squeezed lemon juice**
2	shot(s)	**Freshly squeezed lime juice**
1 1/2	shot(s)	**Sugar (gomme) syrup**
Top up with		**Soda water (club soda)**

Variant: Hard Lemonade
Origin: Discovered in 2004 at Spring Street Natural Restaurant, New York City, USA.
Comment: Alcoholic lemonade with mint? A vodka variation on the Mojito? However you describe it, it works.

RAZZITINI

Glass: Martini
Garnish: Lemon twist / raspberries on stick
Method: SHAKE first two ingredients with ice and fine strain into chilled glass. **TOP** with 7-Up.

2 1/2	shot(s)	**Ketel One Citroen vodka**
3/4	shot(s)	**Chambord black raspberry liqueur**
Top up with		**7-Up**

Origin: Discovered in 2003 at Paramount Hotel, New York City, USA.
Comment: This citrus and raspberry Martini is a tad on the sweet side.

RAZZMATAZZ [NEW]

Glass: Martini
Garnish: Float mint sprig
Method: **STIR** honey with vodka until honey is dissolved. Add other ingredients, **SHAKE** with ice and fine strain into chilled glass.

3 spoons **Runny honey**
1½ shot(s) **Raspberry flavoured vodka**
½ shot(s) **Cointreau / triple sec**
1 shot(s) **Pressed apple juice**
¼ shot(s) **Freshly squeezed lime juice**
6 fresh **Mint leaves (torn)**

Origin: Created by Wayne Collins, London, England.
Comment: Fruity with plenty of razzmatazz.

RAZZZZZBERRY MARTINI

Glass: Martini
Garnish: Three raspberries on stick
Method: **SHAKE** all ingredients with ice and fine strain into chilled glass.

2 shot(s) **Vanilla flavoured vodka**
½ shot(s) **Chambord black raspberry liqueur**
2 shot(s) **Cranberry juice**

Comment: Raspberry and vanilla with characteristic dry cranberry fruit.

REAL LEMONADE [MOCKTAIL]

Glass: Collins
Garnish: Lemon wheel in glass
Method: **POUR** ingredients into ice-filled glass and lightly **STIR**. Serve with straws.

2 shot(s) **Freshly squeezed lemon juice**
1 shot(s) **Sugar (gomme) syrup**
Top up with **Soda water (club soda)**

Comment: The classic English summertime refresher.

REDBACK

Glass: Shot
Garnish: Maraschino cherry on rim
Method: **POUR** sambuca into glass, then pour advocaat down the side of the glass.

1 shot(s) **Opal Nera black sambuca**
½ shot(s) **Warninks advocaat**

Comment: An impressive looking shot.

DRINKS ARE GRADED AS FOLLOWS:

● DISGUSTING ●◐ PRETTY AWFUL ●● BEST AVOIDED
●●◐ DISAPPOINTING ●●● ACCEPTABLE ●●●◐ GOOD
●●●● RECOMMENDED ●●●●◐ HIGHLY RECOMMENDED
●●●●● OUTSTANDING / EXCEPTIONAL

RED ANGEL

Glass: Martini
Garnish: Orange zest twist
Method: **SHAKE** all ingredients with ice and fine strain into chilled glass.

2 shot(s) **Shiraz red wine**
1 shot(s) **Grand Marnier liqueur**
¼ shot(s) **Luxardo maraschino liqueur**
¾ shot(s) **Chilled mineral water (omit if wet ice)**

Origin: Created in 2001 by Tony Conigliaro at Isola, Knightsbridge, London, England.
Comment: A subtly flavoured cocktail with a dry, almost tannic edge.

RED APPLE

Glass: Martini
Garnish: Maraschino cherry
Method: **SHAKE** all ingredients with ice and fine strain into chilled glass.

1½ shot(s) **Bourbon whiskey**
½ shot(s) **Sour apple liqueur**
2 shot(s) **Cranberry juice**

Variant: Sour Apple Martini
Comment: As Apple Martinis go, this one is rather good.

THE RED ARMY [UPDATED]

Glass: Old-fashioned
Garnish: Two raspberries
Method: **MUDDLE** raspberries in base of shaker. Add other ingredients, **SHAKE** with ice and fine strain into a glass filled with crushed ice.

12 fresh **Raspberries**
2 shot(s) **Raspberry flavoured vodka**
1 shot(s) **Freshly squeezed lime juice**
½ shot(s) **Sugar (gomme) syrup**
½ shot(s) **Cointreau / triple sec**
½ shot(s) **Crème de framboise (raspberry) liqueur**

Origin: Created in 2002 by Alex Kammerling, London, England.
Comment: Rather red and rather fruity.

RED BREAST [NEW]

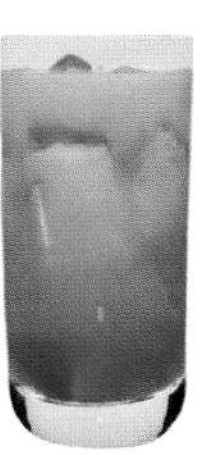

Glass: Collins
Garnish: Raspberry
Method: **POUR** first three ingredients into ice-filled glass and lightly stir. **DRIZZLE** raspberry liqueur over surface of drink.

2 shot(s) **The Famous Grouse Scotch whisky**
½ shot(s) **Freshly squeezed lime juice**
Top up with **Ginger beer**
½ shot(s) **Crème de framboise (raspberry) liqueur**

Origin: Created in 2004 by Wayne Collins, England.
Comment: Long and a tad pink but packs a tasty punch.

RED HOOKER [UPDATED]

Glass: Martini
Garnish: Peach slice on rim
Method: **SHAKE** all ingredients with ice and fine strain into chilled glass.

1	shot(s)	**White peach puree (sweetened)**
2	shot(s)	**Sauza Hornitos tequila**
3/4	shot(s)	**Crème de framboise (raspberry) liqueur**
3/4	shot(s)	**Freshly squeezed lemon juice**

Comment: An appropriately named red, fruity drink with more than a hint of tequila.

RED LION #1 (MODERN FORMULA)

Glass: Martini
Garnish: Orange slice on rim
Method: **SHAKE** all ingredients with ice and fine strain into chilled glass.

1 1/4	shot(s)	**Plymouth gin**
1 1/4	shot(s)	**Grand Marnier liqueur**
1	shot(s)	**Freshly squeezed orange juice**
1	shot(s)	**Freshly squeezed lemon juice**
1/8	shot(s)	**Sonoma pomegranate (grenadine) syrup**

Origin: This classic drink is said to have been created for the Chicago World Fair in 1933. However, it won the British Empire Cocktail Competition that year and was more likely created by W J Tarling for Booth's gin and named after the brand's Red Lion Distillery in London.
Comment: The colour of a summer's twilight with a rich tangy orange flavour.

RED LION #2 (EMBURY'S FORMULA)

Glass: Martini
Garnish: Orange slice on rim
Method: **SHAKE** all ingredients with ice and fine strain into chilled glass.

2	shot(s)	**Plymouth gin**
1/4	shot(s)	**Grand Marnier liqueur**
1/2	shot(s)	**Freshly squeezed lime juice**
1/4	shot(s)	**Sonoma pomegranate (grenadine) syrup**
3/4	shot(s)	**Chilled mineral water (reduce if wet ice)**

Origin: Recipe adapted from one originally published in The Fine Art of Mixing Drinks by David Embury.
Comment: Embury is a Daiquiri fan and this is reminiscent of a Daiquiri in both style and proportions.

RED MARAUDER

Glass: Martini
Garnish: Raspberries on stick
Method: **SHAKE** all ingredients with ice and fine strain into chilled glass.

2	shot(s)	**Rémy Martin cognac**
1 1/2	shot(s)	**Cranberry juice**
1/2	shot(s)	**Chambord black raspberry liqueur**
1/4	shot(s)	**Freshly squeezed lime juice**

Origin: Originally created for Martell, long term sponsors of the Grand National, this is named after the horse that won in 2001.
Comment: Slightly sweet and fruity with a hint of raspberry and cognac's distinctive flavour.

RED MELON'TINI

Glass: Martini
Garnish: Watermelon wedge on rim
Method: Cut watermelon into 16 segments, chop the flesh from one segment into cubes and **MUDDLE** in base of shaker. Add other ingredients, **SHAKE** with ice and fine strain into chilled glass.

1/16	fresh	**Watermelon (diced)**
2	shot(s)	**Pepper flavoured vodka**
1/4	shot(s)	**Sugar (gomme) syrup**
4	grinds	**Black pepper**

Origin: Discovered in 2002 at the Fifth Floor Bar, London, England.
Comment: Watermelon pepped up with vodka and the subtlest peppery finish.

RED NECK MARTINI

Glass: Martini
Garnish: Orange zest twist
Method: **SHAKE** all ingredients with ice and fine strain into chilled glass.

2	shot(s)	**The Famous Grouse Scotch whisky**
1	shot(s)	**Dubonnet Red**
1	shot(s)	**Cherry (brandy) liqueur**

Origin: Created by Sylvain Solignac in 2002 at Circus Bar, London, England.
Comment: Nicely balanced, aromatic and not too sweet – the flavour of the Scotch shines through.

RED OR DEAD

Glass: Collins
Garnish: Lime wedge
Method: **SHAKE** all ingredients with ice and strain into ice-filled glass.

1 1/2	shot(s)	**Southern Comfort liqueur**
3/4	shot(s)	**Campari**
3/4	shot(s)	**Freshly squeezed lime juice**
3	shot(s)	**Cranberry juice**

Comment: This long, ruby drink balances sweetness, sourness and bitterness.

RED ROVER

Glass: Old-fashioned
Garnish: Orange slice in glass
Method: **SHAKE** all ingredients with ice and strain into ice-filled glass.

3	shot(s)	**Red wine**
1	shot(s)	**Pusser's Navy rum**
1/2	shot(s)	**Chambord black raspberry liqueur**

Comment: Carpet-scaring red with the body of red wine but the palate of a cocktail.

RED RUM MARTINI

Glass: Martini
Garnish: Redcurrants draped over rim
Method: **MUDDLE** redcurrants in base of shaker. Add other ingredients, **SHAKE** with ice and fine strain into chilled glass.

24	fresh	**Redcurrants**
2	shot(s)	**Aged rum**
1/2	shot(s)	**Plymouth sloe gin liqueur**
1/2	shot(s)	**Freshly squeezed lemon juice**
1/2	shot(s)	**Vanilla sugar syrup**

Origin: Created by Jason Scott in 2002 at Oloroso, Edinburgh, Scotland. This cocktail, which is red and contains rum, is named after 'Red Rum', the only horse in history to win the Grand National three times (on his other two attempts he came second). He became a British hero, made an appearance on the BBC Sports Personality of the Year show and paraded right up until his death at the age of 30 in 1995.
Comment: A beautifully fruity, adult balance of bittersweet flavours.

RED SNAPPER

Glass: Collins
Garnish: Rim the glass with black pepper and celery salt, add cherry tomato on a stick
Method: **SHAKE** all ingredients with ice and strain into ice-filled glass. Serve with straws.

2	shot(s)	**Plymouth gin**
4	shot(s)	**Pressed tomato juice**
1/2	shot(s)	**Freshly squeezed lemon juice**
7	drops	**Tabasco pepper sauce**
4	dashes	**Lea & Perrins Worcestershire sauce**
1/2	shot(s)	**Tawny port**
2	pinch	**Celery salt**
2	grinds	**Black pepper**

Variant: Bloody Mary
Origin: A gin-based Bloody Mary, derived from Fernand Petiot's original.
Comment: Looks like a Bloody Mary but features gin's aromatic botanicals.

REEF JUICE

Glass: Collins
Garnish: Split pineapple wedge
Method: **SHAKE** all ingredients with ice and strain into ice-filled glass.

1 1/2	shot(s)	**Pusser's Navy rum**
1/2	shot(s)	**Ketel One vodka**
1	shot(s)	**Crème de bananes liqueur**
1/2	shot(s)	**Freshly squeezed lime juice**
2 1/2	shot(s)	**Pressed pineapple juice**
1/2	shot(s)	**Sonoma pomegranate (grenadine) syrup**

Origin: Charles Tobias, proprietor of Pusser's, created this drink at the Beach Bar in Fort Lauderdale, Florida. It was a favourite of a friend who crashed his boat on the reef.
Comment: Tangy, fruity and dangerously moreish.

RED SNAPPER

In 1920, at Harry's New York Bar in Paris, the French bartender Fernand Petiot created the Bloody Mary – then a plain mix of vodka and tomato juice. He moved to the States and became bartender at the King Cole Bar in Manhattan's St. Regis Hotel. Here he mixed the drink for Serge Obolansky, the president of the hotel, who found it a bit flat, so Petiot added salt, pepper, lemon and Worcestershire sauce.

Sadly, Vincent Astor, who owned the hotel, found the name a little crude for his clientele and the drink was officially renamed the Red Snapper – although customers continued to order Bloody Marys. Nowadays a Red Snapper is a Bloody Mary made with gin instead of vodka.

REGGAE RUM PUNCH [UPDATED]

Glass: Collins
Garnish: Pineapple & cherry on rim
Method: **SHAKE** all ingredients with ice and strain into a glass filled with crushed ice.

$1\frac{3}{4}$	shot(s)	**Wray & Nephew overproof rum**
$\frac{1}{2}$	shot(s)	**Crème de fraise (strawberry) liqueur**
$\frac{3}{4}$	shot(s)	**Freshly squeezed lime juice**
$\frac{3}{4}$	shot(s)	**Sonoma pomegranate (grenadine) syrup**
$\frac{3}{4}$	shot(s)	**Pressed pineapple juice**
$1\frac{1}{2}$	shot(s)	**Freshly squeezed orange juice**

Origin: The most popular punch in Jamaica, where it is sold under different names with slightly varying ingredients. It always contains orange, pineapple and, most importantly, overproof rum.
Comment: Jamaicans have a sweet tooth and love their rum. This drink combines sweetness, strength and a generous amount of fruit.

REMEMBER THE MAINE

Glass: Old-fashioned
Garnish: Lemon peel twist
Method: **POUR** absinthe into ice-filled glass, top up with water and set to one side. Separately, **POUR** other ingredients into an ice-filled mixing glass and **STIR** well. **DISCARD** absinthe, water and ice from serving glass. Finally strain contents of mixing glass into the absinthe rinsed glass.

1	shot(s)	**La Fée Parisian 68% absinthe**
Top up with		**Chilled mineral water**
2	shot(s)	**Bourbon whiskey**
$\frac{3}{4}$	shot(s)	**Cherry (brandy) liqueur**
$\frac{3}{4}$	shot(s)	**Sweet (rosso) vermouth**

Origin: Adapted from a recipe created by Charles H. Baker Jr. in "memory of a night in Havana during the Unpleasantnesses of 1933" and named after the press slogan which allegedly provoked the 1898 Spanish-American War.
Comment: A twist on the Sazerac.

REMSEN COOLER [NEW]

Glass: Collins
Garnish: Whole lemon peel
Method: **POUR** ingredients into ice-filled glass and serve with straws.

$2\frac{1}{2}$	shot(s)	**The Famous Grouse Scotch whisky**
Top up with		**Soda (fom siphon)**

Origin: Adapted from a recipe purloined from David Embury's classic book, The Fine Art of Mixing Drinks, and so named because it was originally made with the now defunct Remsen Scotch whisky. Embury claims this is "the original cooler".
Comment: Scotch and soda for the sophisticate.

RESOLUTE [UPDATED]

Glass: Martini
Garnish: Lemon zest twist
Method: **SHAKE** all ingredients with ice and fine strain into chilled glass.

2	shot(s)	**Plymouth gin**
1	shot(s)	**Apricot brandy liqueur**
$\frac{1}{2}$	shot(s)	**Freshly squeezed lemon juice**
$\frac{3}{4}$	shot(s)	**Chilled mineral water (omit if wet ice)**

Origin: Adapted from a recipe purloined from a 1930 edition of The Savoy Cocktail Book by Harry Craddock.
Comment: Simple but tasty. All three flavours work in harmony.

RHETT BUTLER

Glass: Old-fashioned
Garnish: Lime wedge
Method: **SHAKE** all ingredients with ice and fine strain into ice-filled glass.

1	shot(s)	**Grand Marnier liqueur**
1	shot(s)	**Southern Comfort liqueur**
2	shot(s)	**Cranberry juice**
1	shot(s)	**Freshly squeezed lime juice**

Comment: A simple and well-balanced classic drink.

RHUBARB & CUSTARD MARTINI

Glass: Martini
Garnish: Grate fresh nutmeg over drink
Method: **SHAKE** all ingredients with ice and fine strain into chilled glass.

$1\frac{1}{4}$	shot(s)	**Plymouth gin**
$1\frac{1}{4}$	shot(s)	**Warninks advocaat**
$1\frac{1}{4}$	shot(s)	**Syrup from tinned rhubarb**

Origin: I created this drink in 2002. Rhubarb and Custard is a great British dessert and was a cult children's TV cartoon in the 1970s. It featured a naughty pink cat called Custard and a dog named Rhubarb who, like many British men, spent a lot of time in his garden shed.
Comment: As sharp, sweet, creamy and flavourful as the dessert it imitates.

RHUBARB & HONEY BELLINI

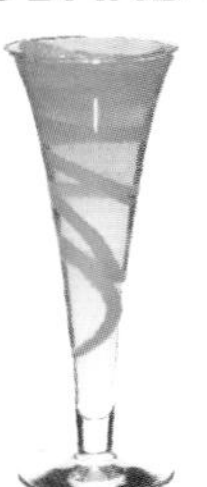

Glass: Flute
Garnish: Orange zest string
Method: **SHAKE** rhubarb syrup and honey liqueur with ice and fine strain into chilled glass. **TOP** with Prosecco and gently stir.

$1\frac{1}{4}$	shot(s)	**Syrup from tinned rhubarb**
$1\frac{1}{4}$	shot(s)	**Krupnik honey liqueur**
Top up with		**Prosecco sparkling wine**

Origin: A simplified adaptation of a drink created in 2003 by Tony Conigliaro at London's Shumi.
Comment: This implausible combination works surprisingly well.

●●●●○

RHUBARB & LEMONGRASS MARTINI

Glass: Martini
Garnish: Stick of lemongrass in drink
Method: **MUDDLE** lemongrass in base of shaker. Add other ingredients, **SHAKE** with ice and fine strain into chilled glass.

4	inches	**Fresh lemongrass (chopped)**
2	shot(s)	**Plymouth gin**
2	shot(s)	**Syrup from tinned rhubarb**
1/8	shot(s)	**Sugar (gomme) syrup**

Origin: I based this drink on one I discovered in 2003 at Zuma, London, England.
Comment: Fragrant exotic lemon flavours combine with, well, rhubarb to make a surprisingly refreshing long drink.

●●●●○

RIBALAIGUA DAIQUIRI #3 [NEW]

Glass: Martini
Garnish: Mint leaf
Method: **SHAKE** all ingredients with ice and fine strain into chilled glass.

2	shot(s)	**Light white rum**
½	shot(s)	**Luxardo maraschino liqueur**
1	shot(s)	**Freshly squeezed pink grapefruit juice**
½	shot(s)	**Chilled mineral water (omit if wet ice)**

Variant: With gin in place of rum this becomes Seventh Heaven No. 2.
Origin: Named for Constantino Ribalaigua, who introduced Hemingway to the Daiquiri at El Floridita, Havana, Cuba.
Comment: This unusual Daiquiri leads with sweet maraschino and finishes with sour grapefruit.

●●●●○

RICKEY (GIN RICKEY)

Glass: Collins (small 8oz)
Garnish: Immerse length of lime peel in drink.
Method: **SHAKE** first three ingredients with ice and strain into ice-filled glass. **TOP** with soda.

2	shot(s)	**Plymouth gin**
½	shot(s)	**Freshly squeezed lime juice**
¼	shot(s)	**Sugar (gomme) syrup**
Top up with		**Soda water**

Origin: Believed to have been created at the Shoemaker's restaurant in Washington, circa 1900, and named after Colonel Joe Rickey.
Comment: Clean, sharp and refreshing.

FOR MORE INFORMATION SEE OUR INGREDIENTS APPENDIX ON PAGE 322

RICKEYS

The Rickey is believed to have been created at the Shoemaker's restaurant in Washington, circa 1900, and named after Colonel Joe Rickey, for whom it was invented.

Many confuse the Rickey and the Collins. For the record, a Rickey is made with lime juice and a Collins with lemon juice. A Rickey is also usually served in a shorter glass than a Collins but this difference is secondary.

The best-known Rickey is the Gin Rickey but these drinks can be based on any liquor and the Vodka Rickey is also popular. Liqueurs also work brilliantly: try substituting apricot brandy for the base spirit to make an Apricot Rickey. (You will need to adjust the amount of sugar in the recipe according to the sweetness of the liqueur.)

THE RITZ COCKTAIL

Glass: Martini
Garnish: Orange zest twist
Method: **STIR** first four ingredients with ice and strain into chilled glass. **TOP** with a splash of champagne.

1	shot(s)	**Rémy Martin cognac**
1/2	shot(s)	**Cointreau / triple sec**
1/4	shot(s)	**Luxardo maraschino liqueur**
1/4	shot(s)	**Freshly squeezed lemon juice**
Top up with		**Piper-Heidsieck brut champagne**

Origin: Created in the mid-1980s by Dale DeGroff at Aurora, New York City, USA.
Comment: This combination of spirit, liqueurs, fruit and champagne tastes like alcoholic lemon tea.

RIVIERA BREEZE

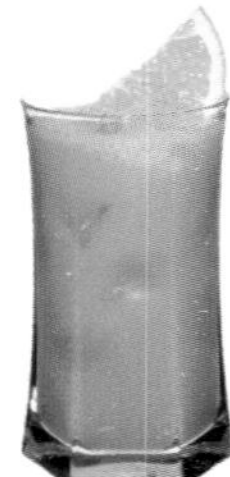

Glass: Old-fashioned
Garnish: Orange slice in glass
Method: **POUR** pastis and orange juice into glass and then fill with ice. **TOP** with ginger ale and stir.

1 1/2	shot(s)	**Ricard pastis**
2	shot(s)	**Freshly squeezed orange juice**
Top up with		**Ginger ale**

Origin: Created in 2003 by Roo Buckley at Café Lebowitz, New York City, USA.
Comment: An aniseed-rich summertime cooler.

ROA AÉ

Glass: Collins
Garnish: Pineapple wedge on rim
Method: **SHAKE** all ingredients with ice and strain into ice-filled glass.

1 1/2	shot(s)	**Light white rum**
1/2	shot(s)	**Apricot brandy liqueur**
1/2	shot(s)	**Grand Marnier liqueur**
1/2	shot(s)	**Pear & cognac liqueur**
3	shot(s)	**Pressed pineapple juice**
3/4	shot(s)	**Freshly squeezed lime juice**

Origin: Discovered in 2003 at Booly Mardy's, Glasgow, Scotland. Cocktail aficionados will be familiar with the Tahitian phrase 'Mai Tai – Roa Aé'. or 'out of this world – the best', which gave the Mai Tai its name. This cocktail means simply 'the best'.
Comment: Not quite the best, but this long, fruity thirst-quencher isn't half bad.

THE ROADRUNNER [NEW]

Glass: Martini
Garnish: Lemon zest twist
Method: **SHAKE** all ingredients with ice and fine strain into chilled glass.

2	shot(s)	**Vanilla infused Sauza Hornitos tequila**
3/4	shot(s)	**Freshly squeezed lemon juice**
1/2	shot(s)	**Maple syrup**
2	dashes	**Angostura aromatic bitters**
1/2	fresh	**Egg white**

Origin: Discovered in 2005 at The Cuckoo Club, London, England.
Comment: Citrus and tequila with a hint of maple and vanilla, smoothed with egg white.

ROB ROY #1

Glass: Martini
Garnish: Cherry & lemon zest twist (discard twist)
Method: **STIR** all ingredients with ice and strain into chilled glass.

2	shot(s)	**The Famous Grouse Scotch whisky**
1	shot(s)	**Sweet (rosso) vermouth**
2	dashes	**Angostura aromatic bitters**
1/8	shot(s)	**Maraschino syrup (optional)**

Variant: 'Highland', made with orange bitters in place of Angostura.
Origin: Created in 1894 at New York's Waldorf-Astoria Hotel (the Empire State Building occupies the site today), and named after a Broadway show playing at the time.
Comment: A Sweet Manhattan made with Scotch in place of bourbon. The dry, peaty whisky and bitters ensure it's not too sweet.

ROB ROY #2 [NEW]

Glass: Martini
Garnish: Cherry & orange zest twist (discard twist)
Method: **STIR** all ingredients with ice and strain into chilled glass.

2	shot(s)	**The Famous Grouse Scotch whisky**
1	shot(s)	**Sweet (rosso) vermouth**
2	dashes	**Peychaud's aromatic bitters**
1/2	shot(s)	**Chilled mineral water (omit if wet ice)**

Origin: This variation on the classic Rob Roy is recommended by author David Embury in his influential Fine Art of Mixing Drinks.
Comment: The Scotch answer to the Manhattan with added complexity courtesy of Peychaud's aromatic bitters.

HOW TO MAKE SUGAR SYRUP

To make your own sugar syrup, gradually pour TWO cups of granulated sugar into a saucepan containing ONE cup of hot water. Stir as you pour and carry on stirring and simmering until the sugar is dissolved. Do not let the water even come close to boiling and only simmer for as long as it takes to dissolve the sugar. Allow syrup to cool and pour into an empty bottle. Ideally, you should finely strain your syrup into the bottle to remove any undissolved crystals which could otherwise encourage crystallisation. If kept in a refrigerator this mixture will last for a couple of months.

ROBIN HOOD #1

Glass: Martini
Garnish: Apple wedge on rim
Method: **SHAKE** all ingredients with ice and fine strain into chilled glass.

1¾	shot(s)	**Light white rum**
1¼	shot(s)	**Apple schnapps liqueur**
¾	shot(s)	**Rose's lime cordial**
½	shot(s)	**Freshly squeezed lime juice**

Origin: Adapted from a drink created in 2002 by Tony Conigliaro at Lonsdale House, London, England.
Comment: American readers might consider this an Apple Martini based on rum.

ROC-A-COE [NEW]

Glass: Martini
Garnish: Maraschino cherry
Method: **STIR** all ingredients with ice and strain into chilled glass.

1½	shot(s)	**Plymouth gin**
2	shot(s)	**Amontillado sherry**
1/8	shot(s)	**Sugar (gomme) syrup**
½	shot(s)	**Chilled mineral water (omit if wet ice)**

Origin: Adapted from a recipe purloined from a 1930 edition of The Savoy Cocktail Book by Harry Craddock.
Comment: Aromatic and balanced.

ROCKY MOUNTAIN ROOTBEER

Glass: Collins
Garnish: Lime wedge
Method: **POUR** vodka and liqueur into ice-filled glass, top up with cola and lightly stir.

2	shot(s)	**Ketel One vodka**
¾	shot(s)	**Galliano liqueur**
Top up with		**Cola**

Comment: Does indeed taste reminiscent of alcoholic root beer.

THE ROFFIGNAC [NEW]

Glass: Collins
Garnish: Lime wedge
Method: **SHAKE** first two ingredients with ice and strain into ice-filled glass. **TOP** with soda, lightly stir and serve with straws.

2	shot(s)	**Rémy Martin cognac**
1	shot(s)	**Crème de framboise (raspberry) liqueur**
Top up with		**Soda water (club soda)**

Origin: Discovered in 2005 at the Sazerac Bar, New Orleans, USA, and named after Count Louis Philippe Joseph de Roffignac, Mayor of New Orleans 1820-1828. Roffignac is noted for introducing street lights to the city and laying cobblestones on the roads in the French Quarter.
Comment: This bright red, fruity drink is simple but moreish.

ROGER

Glass: Martini
Garnish: Peach slice on rim
Method: **SHAKE** all ingredients with ice and fine strain into chilled glass.

2	shot(s)	**Ketel One vodka**
2	shot(s)	**White peach purée**
½	shot(s)	**Freshly squeezed lemon juice**
¼	shot(s)	**Sugar (gomme) syrup**

Origin: A popular drink in Venice, where it is made using the peach purée mix prepared for Bellinis.
Comment: Thick and very fruity – one for a summer's afternoon.

ROMAN PUNCH

Glass: Collins
Garnish: Lemon slice
Method: **SHAKE** all ingredients with ice and strain into glass filled with crushed ice. Serve with straws.

1½	shot(s)	**Bénédictine D.O.M. liqueur**
¾	shot(s)	**Freshly squeezed lemon juice**
1½	shot(s)	**Rémy Martin cognac**
¾	shot(s)	**Wray & Nephew overproof rum**
2	shot(s)	**Chilled mineral water**

Comment: Spirited and refreshing with herbal notes.

LA ROSA MARGARITA [NEW]

Glass: Coupette
Garnish: Lime wedge on rim
Method: **SHAKE** all ingredients with ice and fine strain ino chilled glass.

2	shot(s)	**Sauza Hornitos tequila**
¾	shot(s)	**Blackberry (mûre) liqueur**
1	shot(s)	**Cold hibiscus tea (strong brewed)**
½	shot(s)	**Freshly squeezed lime juice**

Comment: A fruity yet dry crimson-coloured Margarita.

ROSARITA MARGARITA [UPDATED]

Glass: Coupette
Garnish: Lime wedge & optional salted rim
Method: **SHAKE** all ingredients with ice and fine strain into chilled glass.

1½	shot(s)	**Sauza Hornitos tequila**
¾	shot(s)	**Grand Marnier liqueur**
½	shot(s)	**Cranberry juice**
½	shot(s)	**Rose's lime cordial**
¾	shot(s)	**Freshly squeezed lime juice**
½	shot(s)	**Sugar (gomme) syrup**

Origin: Created in 1999 by Robert Plotkin and Raymon Flores of BarMedia, USA.
Comment: This peachy coloured Margarita is well balanced and flavoursome.

A B C D E F G H I J K L M N O P Q R S T U V W X Y Z

THE ROSE #1 (ORIGINAL) [NEW]

Glass: Martini
Garnish: Maraschino cherry
Method: **STIR** all ingredients with ice and fine strain into chilled glass.

2	shot(s)	**Dry vermouth**
1	shot(s)	**Kirsch eau de vie**
1/2	shot(s)	**Raspberry (or pomegranate) syrup**

Origin: Created in 1920 by Johnny Milta at the Chatham Hotel, Paris. This recipe is adapted from one in The Fine Art of Mixing Drinks by David Embury.
Comment: This salmon pink drink is wonderfully aromatic.

THE ROSE #2 [NEW]

Glass: Martini
Garnish: Maraschino cherry
Method: **STIR** all ingredients with ice and fine strain into chilled glass.

2	shot(s)	**Plymouth gin**
1	shot(s)	**Cherry (brandy) liqueur**
1	shot(s)	**Dry vermouth**

Origin: Adapted from a recipe in Harry Craddock's 1930 Savoy Cocktail Book.
Comment: Cherry and gin dried with vermouth.

THE ROSE #3 [NEW]

Glass: Martini
Garnish: Maraschino cherry
Method: **SHAKE** all ingredients with ice and fine strain into chilled glass.

1 1/2	shot(s)	**Kirsch eau de vie**
1 1/2	shot(s)	**Dry vermouth**
1/2	shot(s)	**Sonoma pomegranate (grenadine) syrup**

Origin: Adapted from a recipe in Harry Craddock's 1930 Savoy Cocktail Book.
Comment: Delicate, aromatic cherry – not too sweet.

ROSE PETALINI [NEW]

Glass: Martini
Garnish: Float red rose petal
Method: **STIR** all ingredients with ice and strain into chilled glass.

1 1/2	shot(s)	**Rose vodka**
1 1/2	shot(s)	**Plymouth gin**
1	shot(s)	**Lychee syrup (from tinned lychees)**
3	shot(s)	**Peychaud's aromatic bitters**

Origin: Discovered in 2005 at Rain, Amsterdam, The Netherlands.
Comment: Peychaud's bitters give this fragrant cocktail a delicate pink hue.

ROSELYN MARTINI [NEW]

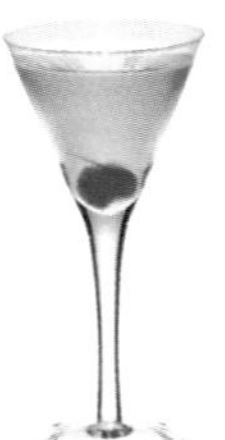

Glass: Martini
Garnish: Maraschino cherry
Method: **SHAKE** all ingredients with ice and fine strain into chilled glass.

2	shot(s)	**Plymouth gin**
1	shot(s)	**Dry vermouth**
1/4	shot(s)	**Sonoma pomegranate (grenadine) syrup**

Origin: Adapted from a recipe in Harry Craddock's 1930 Savoy Cocktail Book.
Comment: Subtle and beautifully balanced. A wet Martini made 'easy' by a dash of pomegranate syrup.

ROSITA [NEW]

Glass: Old-fashioned
Garnish: Orange zest twist
Method: **STIR** all ingredients with ice and strain into ice-filled glass.

2	shot(s)	**Sauza Hornitos tequila**
3/4	shot(s)	**Campari**
3/4	shot(s)	**Dry vermouth**
3/4	shot(s)	**Sweet (rosso) vermouth**
2	dashes	**Angostura aromatic bitters**

Comment: A bittersweet, tequila based, Negroni-like drink.

ROSSINI

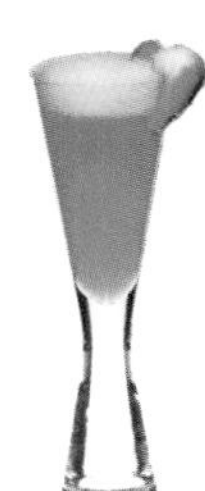

Glass: Flute
Garnish: Strawberry on rim
Method: **MUDDLE** strawberries in base of shaker. Add strawberry liqueur, **SHAKE** with ice and fine strain into chilled glass. **TOP** with Prosecco and gently stir.

4	fresh	**Strawberries**
3/4	shot(s)	**Crème de fraise (strawberry) liqueur**
Top up with		**Prosecco sparkling wine**

Origin: Named for the 19th century opera composer, this is one of the most popular Bellini variants in Venice.
Comment: Strawberries seem to complement Prosecco even better than white peaches.

ROSY MARTINI

Glass: Martini
Garnish: Orange zest twist
Method: **STIR** all ingredients with ice and strain into chilled glass.

2	shot(s)	**Ketel One Citroen vodka**
3/4	shot(s)	**Cointreau / triple sec**
3/4	shot(s)	**Dubonnet Red**

Comment: An aptly named drink with hints of spice, citrus peel, honey and mulled wine.

ROULETTE [NEW]

Glass: Martini
Garnish: Orange zest twist
Method: **SHAKE** all ingredients with ice and fine strain into chilled glass.

1½	shot(s)	**Calvados or applejack brandy**
¾	shot(s)	**Light white rum**
¾	shot(s)	**Carlshamns Swedish Torr Flaggpunsch**
½	shot(s)	**Chilled mineral water (omit if wet ice)**

Origin: Adapted from a recipe in Harry Craddock's 1930 Savoy Cocktail Book.
Comment: Balanced apple and spice.

ROY ROGERS (MOCKTAIL)

Glass: Collins
Garnish: Lime wedge
Method: **POUR** grenadine and cola into ice-filled glass and stir. Serve with straws.

¼	shot(s)	**Sonoma pomegranate (grenadine) syrup**
Top up with		**Cola**

Comment: I wouldn't bother.

ROYAL BERMUDA YACHT CLUB DAIQUIRI [NEW]

Glass: Martini
Garnish: Lime wedge on rim
Method: **SHAKE** all ingredients with ice and fine strain into chilled glass.

2½	shot(s)	**Mount Gay golden rum**
¾	shot(s)	**Freshly squeezed lime juice**
½	shot(s)	**Velvet Falernum liqueur**
¼	shot(s)	**Cointreau / triple sec**

Origin: Created at the eponymous club, established in Bermuda in 1844 and largely frequented by British Army officers.
This recipe is adapted from one in Trader Vic's Bartender's Guide.
Comment: A full-flavoured, tangy Daiquiri.

ROYAL COSMOPOLITAN

Glass: Martini
Garnish: Orange zest twist
Method: **SHAKE** first four ingredients with ice and fine strain into chilled glass. **TOP** with champagne.

1	shot(s)	**Ketel One Citroen vodka**
½	shot(s)	**Cointreau / triple sec**
1	shot(s)	**Cranberry juice**
¼	shot(s)	**Freshly squeezed lime juice**
Top up with		**Piper-Heidsieck brut champagne**

Origin: Created in 2003 by Wayne Collins, London, UK.
Comment: The classic Cosmopolitan with a layer of fizz on top adding a biscuity complexity. Sex And The City meets Ab Fab.

ROYAL MOJITO [NEW]

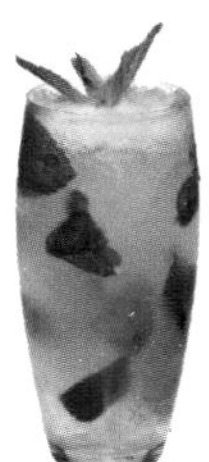

Glass: Collins
Garnish: Mint sprig
Method: Lightly **MUDDLE** mint (just to bruise) in base of glass. Add rum, lime juice and sugar. Half fill glass with crushed ice and **CHURN** (stir) with bar spoon. Fill glass with more crushed ice and **CHURN** some more. **TOP** with champagne, lightly stir and serve with straws.

12	fresh	**Mint leaves**
2	shot(s)	**Light white rum**
¾	shot(s)	**Freshly squeezed lime juice**
¼	shot(s)	**Sugar (gomme) syrup**
Top up with		**Piper-Heidsieck brut champagne**

AKA: Luxury Mojito
Comment: A Mojito topped with champagne instead of soda water. There's posh!

ROYAL SMILE [NEW]

Glass: Martini
Garnish: Lemon zest twist
Method: **SHAKE** all ingredients with ice and fine strain into chilled glass.

1	shot(s)	**Plymouth gin**
1	shot(s)	**Calvados or applejack brandy**
½	shot(s)	**Freshly squeezed lemon juice**
¼	shot(s)	**Sonoma pomegranate (grenadine) syrup**
½	shot(s)	**Chilled mineral water (omit if wet ice)**

Origin: Purloined from David Embury's classic book, The Fine Art of Mixing Drinks.
Comment: This balanced sweet and sour could put a smile on anyone's face. Unless one is not amused!

ROYAL VELVET MARGARITA [NEW]

Glass: Coupette (or fresh pineapple shell)
Garnish: Lime wedge
Method: **SHAKE** all ingredients with ice and fine strain into chilled glass.

2	shot(s)	**Sauza Hornitos tequila**
½	shot(s)	**Chambord black raspberry liqueur**
½	shot(s)	**Luxardo Amaretto di Saschira liqueur**
1	shot(s)	**Freshly squeezed lime juice**

Origin: Discovered in 2005 at Velvet Margarita Cantina, Los Angeles, USA.
Comment: An almond and berry flavoured Margarita.

R U BOBBY MOORE?

Glass: Martini
Garnish: Apple wedge on rim
Method: STIR honey with Scotch and vodka in base of shaker until honey dissolves. Add other ingredients, **SHAKE** with ice and fine strain into chilled glass.

3	spoons	**Runny honey**
1	shot(s)	**The Famous Grouse Scotch whisky**
1	shot(s)	**Zubrówka (bison grass) vodka**
¾	shot(s)	**Sauvignon Blanc wine**
1	shot(s)	**Pressed apple juice**

Origin: Created in 2002 by yours truly and named after the rhyming slang for 'are you bloody sure?' Bobby Moore was the 60s England football captain and West Ham United defender who regrettably died young in 1993. My dictionary of rhyming slang claims 'Bobby Moore' means 'door' – well, not in East London it doesn't.
Comment: It's common to pair both Scotch and zubrówka with apple, but combining all three together with wine and honey really works.

RUBY MARTINI #1

Glass: Martini
Garnish: Lemon wedge on rim
Method: SHAKE all ingredients with ice and fine strain into chilled glass.

1½	shot(s)	**Ketel One Citroen vodka**
1	shot(s)	**Cointreau / triple sec**
1	shot(s)	**Freshly squeezed pink grapefruit juice**
¼	shot(s)	**Sugar (gomme) syrup**

Origin: Several appearances in episodes of the hit US TV series, Sex And The City, helped this drink become fashionable in 2002, particularly in New York City. It is thought to have originated at the Wave restaurant in Chicago's W Hotel.
Comment: A sour, citrus-led variation on the Cosmopolitan.

RUBY MARTINI #2 [NEW]

Glass: Martini
Garnish: Raspberry & lemon twist
Method: SHAKE all ingredients with ice and fine strain into chilled glass.

1½	shot(s)	**Rémy Martin cognac**
½	shot(s)	**Cointreau / triple sec**
½	shot(s)	**Crème de framboise (raspberry) liqueur**
½	shot(s)	**Sweet (rosso) vermouth**

Origin: Created by Wayne Collins, London, England.
Comment: Fruity and slightly sweet.

RUDE COSMOPOLITAN

Glass: Martini
Garnish: Orange zest twist
Method: SHAKE all ingredients with ice and fine strain into chilled glass.

1	shot(s)	**Sauza Hornitos tequila**
1	shot(s)	**Cointreau / triple sec**
1½	shot(s)	**Cranberry juice**
½	shot(s)	**Freshly squeezed lime juice**
2	dashes	**Fee Brothers orange bitters (optional)**

AKA: Mexico City
Comment: Don't let the pink appearance of this Cosmopolitan (made with tequila in place of vodka) fool you into thinking it's a fluffy cocktail. It's both serious and superb.

RUDE GINGER COSMOPOLITAN

Glass: Martini
Garnish: Orange zest twist
Method: MUDDLE ginger in base of shaker. Add other ingredients, **SHAKE** with ice and fine strain into chilled glass.

2	slices	**Fresh root ginger (thumbnail sized)**
1½	shot(s)	**Sauza Hornitos tequila**
1	shot(s)	**Cointreau / triple sec**
1	shot(s)	**Cranberry juice**
½	shot(s)	**Freshly squeezed lime juice**
¼	shot(s)	**Rose's lime cordial**

Origin: Created in 2003 by Jeremy Adderley at Halo, Edinburgh, Scotland.
Comment: To quote Halo's list, "Looks like a Cosmo, goes like a Mexican!"

RUM & RAISIN ALEXANDRA

Glass: Martini
Garnish: Three red grapes on stick
Method: MUDDLE grapes in base of shaker. Add other ingredients, **SHAKE** with ice and fine strain into chilled glass.

7	fresh	**Red seedless grapes**
1½	shot(s)	**Aged rum**
½	shot(s)	**Sisca crème de cassis**
½	shot(s)	**Double (heavy) cream**
½	shot(s)	**Milk**
¼	shot(s)	**Sugar (gomme) syrup**

Origin: Created in 2003 by Ian Morgan, England.
Comment: Forgo the ice cream and try this creamy, quaffable, alcoholic dessert.

To make your own sugar syrup, gradually pour TWO cups of granulated sugar into a saucepan containing ONE cup of hot water. Stir as you pour and carry on stirring and simmering until the sugar is dissolved. Do not let the water even come close to boiling and only simmer for as long as it takes to dissolve the sugar. Allow syrup to cool and pour into an empty bottle. Ideally, you should finely strain your syrup into the bottle to remove any undissolved crystals which could otherwise encourage crystallisation. If kept in a refrigerator this mixture will last for a couple of months.

●●●●●

RUM PUNCH

Glass: Collins
Garnish: Orange slice & cherry (sail)
Method: **SHAKE** all ingredients with ice and strain into glass filled with crushed ice.

3/4	shot(s)	**Freshly squeezed lime juice**
1 1/2	shot(s)	**Sugar (gomme) syrup**
2 1/4	shot(s)	**Wray & Nephew overproof rum**
3	shot(s)	**Chilled mineral water**
3	dashes	**Angostura aromatic bitters**

Comment: The classic proportions of this drink (followed above) are 'one of sour, two of sweet, three of strong and four of weak' – referring to lime juice, sugar syrup, rum and water respectively. In Jamaica, the spiritual home of the Rum Punch, they like their rum overproof (more than 57% alc./vol.) and serving over crushed ice dilutes and tames this very strong drink.

●●●●◐

RUM PUNCH-UP [NEW]

Glass: Martini
Garnish: Lime wedge on rim
Method: **SHAKE** all ingredients with ice and fine strain into chilled glass.

1 1/2	shot(s)	**Wray & Nephew overproof rum**
1/2	shot(s)	**Freshly squeezed lime juice**
1/2	shot(s)	**Sugar (gomme) syrup**
1	shot(s)	**Chilled mineral water (reduce if wet ice)**
2	dashes	**Angostura aromatic bitters**

Origin: Adapted from a drink discovered in 2006 at Albannach, London, England.
Comment: Exactly what the name promises – a rum punch served straight-up, Daiquiri style.

●●●●○

RUMBA [NEW]

Glass: Old-fashioned
Garnish: Lime wedge
Method: **SHAKE** all ingredients with ice and strain into glass filled with crushed ice. Serve with straws.

3/4	shot(s)	**Wray & Nephew overproof rum**
1	shot(s)	**Plymouth gin**
1	shot(s)	**Freshly squeezed lime juice**
1/2	shot(s)	**Sonoma pomegranate (grenadine) syrup**
1/4	shot(s)	**Sugar (gomme) syrup**
1/2	shot(s)	**Chilled mineral water (omit if wet ice)**

Origin: Recipe adapted from David Embury's classic book, The Fine Art of Mixing Drinks.
Comment: To quote Embury, "Whoever thought up this snootful of liquid dynamite certainly liked his liquor hard!"

DRINKS ARE GRADED AS FOLLOWS:

● DISGUSTING ●◐ PRETTY AWFUL ●● BEST AVOIDED
●●◐ DISAPPOINTING ●●● ACCEPTABLE ●●●◐ GOOD
●●●● RECOMMENDED ●●●●◐ HIGHLY RECOMMENDED
●●●●● OUTSTANDING / EXCEPTIONAL

●●●●○

RUM RUNNER

Glass: Hurricane
Garnish: Pineapple wedge & cherry
Method: **SHAKE** all ingredients with ice and strain into glass filled with crushed ice.

1 1/2	shot(s)	**Pusser's Navy rum**
1/2	shot(s)	**Crème de mûre (blackberry) liqueur**
1	shot(s)	**Crème de bananes liqueur**
1	shot(s)	**Freshly squeezed lime juice**
2	shot(s)	**Pressed pineapple juice**
1/2	shot(s)	**Sonoma pomegranate (grenadine) syrup**

Comment: Fruity, sharp and rounded.

●●●●○

RUM SOUR

Glass: Old-fashioned
Garnish: Orange zest twist
Method: **SHAKE** all ingredients with ice and strain into ice-filled glass.

2	shot(s)	**Aged rum**
1	shot(s)	**Freshly squeezed orange juice**
1	shot(s)	**Freshly squeezed lime juice**
1/2	shot(s)	**Sugar (gomme) syrup**
1/2	fresh	**Egg white**

Comment: Smooth and sour – well balanced.

●●●◐○

RUSSIAN [NEW]

Glass: Martini
Garnish: Orange zest twist
Method: **SHAKE** all ingredients with ice and fine strain into chilled glass.

1 1/2	shot(s)	**Plymouth gin**
1	shot(s)	**Ketel One vodka**
1	shot(s)	**White crème de cacao liqueur**

Origin: Adapted from a recipe in Harry Craddock's 1930 Savoy Cocktail Book.
Comment: Gin and vodka with a sweet hint of chocolate.

●●●●○

RUSSIAN BRIDE

Glass: Martini
Garnish: Dust with cocoa powder
Method: **SHAKE** all ingredients with ice and fine strain into chilled glass.

2	shot(s)	**Vanilla flavoured vodka**
3/4	shot(s)	**Kahlúa coffee liqueur**
1/4	shot(s)	**White crème de cacao liqueur**
1/2	shot(s)	**Double (heavy) cream**
1/2	shot(s)	**Milk**

Origin: Created in 2002 by Miranda Dickson, A.K.A. the Vodka Princess, for the UK's Revolution bar chain, where some 500,000 are sold each year.
Comment: A little on the sweet side for some but vanilla, coffee and chocolate smoothed with cream is a tasty combination.

RUSSIAN QUALUUDE SHOT

Glass: Shot
Method: Refrigerate ingredients then **LAYER** in chilled glass by carefully pouring in the following order.

1/2 shot(s) **Galliano liqueur**
1/2 shot(s) **Green Chartreuse**
1/2 shot(s) **Ketel One vodka**

Comment: An explosive herb and peppermint shot.

RUSSIAN SPRING PUNCH

Glass: Sling
Garnish: Lemon slice & berries
Method: SHAKE first four ingredients with ice and strain into glass filled with crushed ice. **TOP** with champagne, lightly stir and serve with straws.

1 shot(s) **Ketel One vodka**
1/4 shot(s) **Sisca crème de cassis**
1 shot(s) **Freshly squeezed lemon juice**
1/4 shot(s) **Sugar (gomme) syrup**
Top up with **Champagne**

Origin: My version of a drink created in the 1990s by Dick Bradsell, London, England.
Comment: Well balanced, complex and refreshing.

RUSTY NAIL

Glass: Old-fashioned
Garnish: Lemon zest twist
Method: STIR ingredients with ice and strain into ice-filled glass.

2 shot(s) **The Famous Grouse Scotch whisky**
3/4 shot(s) **Drambuie liqueur**

Origin: Created in 1942 at a Hawaiian bar for the artist Theodore Anderson.
Comment: The liqueur smoothes and wonderfully combines with the Scotch.

SAGE MARGARITA [NEW]

Glass: Coupette
Garnish: Float sage leaf
Method: Lightly **MUDDLE** (just to bruise) sage in base of shaker. Add other ingredients, **SHAKE** with ice and fine strain into chilled glass.

3 fresh **Sage leaves**
2 shot(s) **Sauza Hornitos tequila**
1 shot(s) **Cointreau / triple sec**
1 shot(s) **Freshly squeezed lime juice**
1/8 shot(s) **Sugar (gomme) syrup**

Comment: Exactly as promised – a sage flavoured Margarita.

SAGE MARTINI [NEW]

Glass: Martini
Garnish: Float sage leaf
Method: Lightly **MUDDLE** (just to bruise) sage in base of shaker. Add other ingredients, **SHAKE** with ice and fine strain into chilled glass.

3 fresh **Sage leaves**
1 1/2 shot(s) **Ketel One vodka**
1 1/2 shot(s) **Dry vermouth**
3/4 shot(s) **Pressed apple juice**

Comment: Delicate sage and a hint of apple, dried with vermouth and fortified with vodka.

SAIGON COOLER

Glass: Collins
Garnish: Three raspberries
Method: MUDDLE raspberries in base of shaker. Add other ingredients, **SHAKE** with ice and fine strain into ice-filled glass.

7 fresh **Raspberries**
2 shot(s) **Plymouth gin**
1/2 shot(s) **Chambord black raspberry liqueur**
3 shot(s) **Cranberry juice**
3/4 shot(s) **Freshly squeezed lime juice**

Origin: Created at Bam-Bou, London, England.
Comment: Well balanced sweet 'n' sour with a rich fruity flavour.

SAIGON SLING

Glass: Sling
Garnish: Pineapple wedge & cherry on rim
Method: SHAKE first seven ingredients with ice and strain into ice-filled glass. **TOP** with ginger ale.

1 1/2 shot(s) **Plymouth gin**
3/4 shot(s) **Ginger & lemongrass cordial**
1/2 shot(s) **Krupnik honey liqueur**
3/4 shot(s) **Freshly squeezed lime juice**
1 shot(s) **Pressed pineapple juice**
1/4 shot(s) **Passoã passion fruit liqueur**
2 dashes **Peychaud's aromatic bitters**
Top up with **Ginger ale**

Origin: Created in 2001 by Rodolphe Manor for a London bartending competition.
Comment: A fusion of unusual flavours.

SAILOR'S COMFORT

Glass: Old-fashioned
Garnish: Lime wedge
Method: SHAKE first four ingredients with ice and strain into ice-filled glass. **TOP** with soda, lightly stir and serve with straws.

1 shot(s) **Plymouth sloe gin liqueur**
1 shot(s) **Southern Comfort liqueur**
1 shot(s) **Rose's lime cordial**
3 dashes **Angostura aromatic bitters**
Top up with **Soda water (club soda)**

Origin: Discovered in 2002 at Lightship Ten, London.
Comment: Lime, peach and hints of berry make a light, easy drink.

SAINT CLEMENTS (MOCKTAIL)

Glass: Collins
Garnish: Lime wedge
Method: **POUR** ingredients into ice-filled glass, lightly stir and serve with straws.

3	shot(s)	**Freshly squeezed orange juice**
Top up with		**Bitter lemon**

Comment: Only slightly more interesting than orange juice.

ST KITTS (MOCKTAIL)

Glass: Collins
Garnish: Lime wedge
Method: **SHAKE** first three ingredients with ice and strain into ice-filled glass. **TOP** with ginger ale, lightly stir and serve with straws.

3	shot(s)	**Pineapple juice**
1/2	shot(s)	**Freshly squeezed lime juice**
1/4	shot(s)	**Sonoma pomegranate (grenadine) syrup**
Top up with		**Ginger ale**

Variant: Add 3 dashes Angostura aromatic bitters. This adds a tiny amount of alcohol but greatly improves the drink.
Comment: Rust coloured and refreshing.

ST. PATRICK'S DAY

Glass: Old-fashioned
Garnish: Mint sprig/shamrock
Method: **STIR** all ingredients with ice and strain into ice-filled glass.

2	shot(s)	**Irish whiskey**
1	shot(s)	**Green Chartreuse**
1	shot(s)	**Green crème de menthe**
1	dash	**Angostura aromatic bitters.**

Origin: Created in 2006 by your truly.
Comment: Minty, herbal whiskey – a helluva craic.

SAKE'POLITAN [UPDATED]

Glass: Martini
Garnish: Orange zest twist
Method: **SHAKE** all ingredients with ice and fine strain into chilled glass.

2 1/4	shot(s)	**Sake**
3/4	shot(s)	**Cointreau / triple sec**
3/4	shot(s)	**Cranberry juice**
1/4	shot(s)	**Freshly squeezed lime juice**
2	dashes	**Fee Brothers orange bitters (optional)**

Comment: A Cosmo with more than a hint of sake.

SAKE-TINI #1

Glass: Martini
Garnish: Three thin slices of cucumber
Method: **STIR** all ingredients with ice and strain into chilled glass.

1	shot(s)	**Plymouth gin**
2 1/2	shot(s)	**Sake**
1/2	shot(s)	**Grand Marnier liqueur**

Comment: Sake and a hint of orange liqueur add the perfect aromatic edge to this Martini-style drink.

SAKE-TINI #2 [NEW]

Glass: Martini
Garnish: Orange zest twist
Method: **SHAKE** all ingredients with ice and fine strain into chilled glass.

1 1/2	shot(s)	**Ketel One vodka**
1	shot(s)	**Plum wine**
1/2	shot(s)	**Sake**
1	shot(s)	**Cranberry juice**

Origin: Discovered in 2005 at Nobu Berkeley, London, England.
Comment: Salmon-coloured, light and fragrant with plum wine and sake to the fore.

SAKINI

Glass: Martini
Garnish: Olives on stick
Method: **STIR** all ingredients with ice and strain into chilled glass.

1	shot(s)	**Sake**
2 1/2	shot(s)	**Ketel One vodka**

Comment: Very dry. The sake creates an almost wine-like delicacy.

SALTECCA

Glass: Martini
Garnish: Lemon zest twist
Method: **STIR** all ingredients with ice and fine strain into chilled glass.

2	shot(s)	**Sauza Hornitos tequila**
1/2	shot(s)	**Fino sherry**
1/8	shot(s)	**Brine from jar of salted capers**
1/8	shot(s)	**Sugar (gomme) syrup**
1/2	shot(s)	**Chilled mineral water (omit if wet ice)**

Comment: Reminiscent of salted water after boiling vegetables but you've got to try these things.

SALTY DOG

Glass: Martini
Garnish: Salt rim
Method: **SHAKE** all ingredients with ice and fine strain into chilled glass.

2	shot(s)	**Ketel One vodka**
2¼	shot(s)	**Freshly squeezed grapefruit juice**
1/8	shot(s)	**Luxardo maraschino liqueur (optional)**

Origin: Created in the 1960s.
Comment: For a more interesting drink, try basing this classic on gin rather than vodka.

SALTY LYCHEE MARTINI

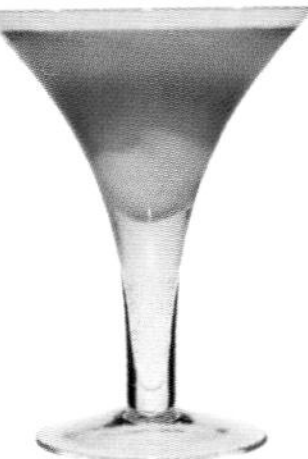

Glass: Martini
Garnish: Lychee from tin
Method: **STIR** all ingredients with ice and strain into chilled glass.

2	shot(s)	**Fino sherry**
1	shot(s)	**Lanique rose petal liqueur**
1	shot(s)	**Lychee syrup from tinned fruit**

Origin: I created this drink in 2002 after trying Dick Bradsell's Lychee & Rose Petal Martini (also in this guide).
Comment: Light pink in colour and subtle in flavour with the salty tang of Fino sherry.

SAN FRANCISCO [UPDATED]

Glass: Collins
Garnish: Pineapple wedge on rim
Method: **SHAKE** all ingredients with ice and strain into ice-filled glass.

2	shot(s)	**Ketel One vodka**
½	shot(s)	**Cointreau / triple sec**
½	shot(s)	**Crème de bananes liqueur**
1½	shot(s)	**Freshly squeezed orange juice**
1½	shot(s)	**Pressed pineapple juice**
¼	shot(s)	**Sonoma pomegranate (grenadine) syrup**

Comment: Long, fruity, slightly sweet and laced with vodka.

SANDSTORM

Glass: Collins
Garnish: Pineapple wedge on rim
Method: **SHAKE** all ingredients with ice and strain into ice-filled glass.

1½	shot(s)	**Plymouth gin**
1	shot(s)	**Grand Marnier liqueur**
½	shot(s)	**Vanilla schnapps liqueur**
1½	shot(s)	**Freshly squeezed grapefruit juice**
1½	shot(s)	**Pressed pineapple juice**
¼	shot(s)	**Sugar (gomme) syrup**
¼	shot(s)	**Freshly squeezed lime juice**
¼	shot(s)	**Rose's lime cordial**

Origin: Created in 2003 by James Cunningham at Zinc, Glasgow, Scotland, and named for its cloudy yellow colour.
Comment: A long, fruity drink featuring well-balanced sweet and sourness.

SANDY GAFF [NEW]

Glass: Boston
Method: **POUR** ale into glass, top with ginger ale and lightly stir.

2/3rds fill	**Dark beer**
Top up with	**Ginger ale**

AKA: Shandy Gaff
Origin: Adapted from a recipe purloined from David Embury's classic book, The Fine Art of Mixing Drinks.
Comment: Better than your average lager shandy.

LA SANG

Glass: Collins
Garnish: Chopped fruit
Method: **SHAKE** all ingredients with ice and strain into ice-filled glass.

2	shot(s)	**Rémy Martin cognac**
2	shot(s)	**Red wine**
2	shot(s)	**Freshly squeezed orange juice**
¼	shot(s)	**Sugar (gomme) syrup**

Origin: French for 'blood', this cocktail is a twist on the classic Spanish Sangria, which also means 'blood'.
Comment: The tannin in the wine balances the fruit and sweetness nicely.

SANGAREE [NEW]

Glass: Collins
Garnish: Dust grated nutmeg
Method: **SHAKE** all ingredients with ice and strain into ice-filled glass.

1	shot(s)	**Rémy Martin cognac**
2	shot(s)	**Red wine**
½	shot(s)	**Grand Marnier liqueur**
1	shot(s)	**Freshly squeezed orange juice**
¼	shot(s)	**Freshly squeezed lemon juice**
¼	shot(s)	**Sugar (gomme) syrup**
1	shot(s)	**Chilled mineral water (reduce if wet ice)**

Origin: This version of the Sangria was popular in 19th century America.
Comment: Basically red wine and orange liqueur, diluted with water, lemon juice and sugar.

SANGRIA

Glass: Collins
Garnish: Chopped fruit
Method: **SHAKE** all ingredients with ice and strain into ice-filled glass.

1	shot(s)	**Rémy Martin cognac**
2	shot(s)	**Shiraz red wine**
½	shot(s)	**Grand Marnier liqueur**
2	shot(s)	**Freshly squeezed orange juice**

Comment: This party classic from Spain suits serving in jugs or punch bowls.

SANGRIA MARTINI

Glass: Martini
Garnish: Quarter orange slice
Method: SHAKE all ingredients with ice and fine strain into chilled glass.

1	shot(s)	Red wine
3/4	shot(s)	Freshly squeezed orange juice
1 1/2	shot(s)	Rémy Martin cognac
1/2	shot(s)	Apple schnapps liqueur
1/2	shot(s)	Crème de framboise (raspberry) liqueur

Origin: Created in 2003 by Angelo Vieira at Light Bar, St. Martins Hotel, London, England.
Comment: Brandy based and fruit laced – just like its namesake.

SANGRITA [UPDATED]

Glass: Shot
Method: SHAKE ingredients with ice and strain into shot glass. Serve with a shot of tequila. The drinker can either down the tequila and chase it with sangrita or sip the two drinks alternately.

1/2	shot(s)	Tomato juice
1/2	shot(s)	Freshly squeezed lime juice
1/2	shot(s)	Pomegranate juice
1/4	shot(s)	Freshly squeezed orange juice
1/4	spoon	Sonoma pomegranate (grenadine) syrup
6	drops	Tabasco
3	dashes	Worcestershire sauce
1	pinch	Cellery salt
1	grind	Black pepper

Origin: The name means 'little blood' in Spanish and the drink is served with tequila in every bar in Mexico.
Comment: In Mexico the quality of the homemade Sangrita can make or break a bar. This recipe is spicy and slightly sweet and perfect for chasing tequila.

SANTIAGO

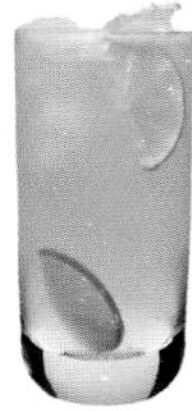

Glass: Collins
Garnish: Lime slices
Method: SHAKE first five ingredients with ice and strain into ice-filled glass. TOP with 7-Up, lightly stir and serve with straws.

1	shot(s)	Light white rum
1	shot(s)	Spiced rum
1/2	shot(s)	Freshly squeezed lime juice
1/2	shot(s)	Freshly squeezed orange juice
3	dashes	Angostura aromatic bitters
Top up with		7-Up

Comment: Light, refreshing and slightly spicy.

DRINKS ARE GRADED AS FOLLOWS:

● DISGUSTING ●◐ PRETTY AWFUL ●● BEST AVOIDED
●●◐ DISAPPOINTING ●●● ACCEPTABLE ●●●◐ GOOD
●●●● RECOMMENDED ●●●●◐ HIGHLY RECOMMENDED
●●●●● OUTSTANDING / EXCEPTIONAL

SAZERAC

The rounded, distinctive flavour of this classic New Orleans cocktail is reliant on one essential ingredient: Peychaud's aromatic bitters.

Antoine Amedee Peychaud's father was forced to flee the island of San Domingo, where his family owned a coffee plantation, after the slaves rebelled. He arrived in New Orleans as a refugee in 1795.

His son became a pharmacist and bought his own Drug and Apothecary Store at what was then No. 123 Royal Street in 1834. There he created an 'American Aromatic Bitter Cordial' and marketed it as a medicinal tonic. Such potions were fashionable and there were many similar products.

Antoine also served his bitters mixed with brandy and other liquors. (It is often falsely claimed that the word 'cocktail' originated with Antoine, from a measure known as a 'coquetier' he used to prepare drinks. But it is undisputed that the term appeared in print in an upstate New York newspaper in 1806, when Antoine was only a child.)

Antoine Peychaud advertised his bitters in local newspapers and many New Orleans bars served drinks prepared with them. One such bar was the Sazerac Coffee House at 13 Exchange Alley, owned by John B. Schiller, who was also the local agent for a French cognac company called Sazerac-du-Forge et Fils of Limoges. It was here, in 1858, that a bartender called Leon Lamothe is thought to have created the Sazerac, probably using Peychaud's aromatic bitters, Sazerac cognac and sugar.

A decade or so later, one Thomas H Handy took over the coffee house and Antoine Peychaud fell upon hard times and sold his pharmacy store, along with the formula and brand name of his bitters. A combination of the phylloxera aphid (which devastated French vineyards) and the American Civil War made cognac hard to obtain and Handy was forced to change the recipe of the bar's now established house cocktail. He still used the all-important Peychaud's bitters but substituted Maryland Club rye whiskey, retaining a dash of cognac and adding a splash of the newly fashionable absinthe.

The Sazerac was further adapted in 1912 when absinthe was banned in the US and Herbsaint from Louisiana was substituted. Today the name Sazerac is owned by the Sazerac Company, who license it to the Sazerac Bar at the Fairmont Hotel.

SANTIAGO DAIQUIRI [NEW]

Glass: Martini
Garnish: Maraschino cherry
Method: **SHAKE** all ingredients with ice and fine strain into chilled glass.

2	shot(s)	**Light white rum**
1	shot(s)	**Freshly squeezed lemon juice**
1/2	shot(s)	**Sonoma pomegranate (grenadine) syrup**
1/2	shot(s)	**Chilled mineral water (omit if wet ice)**

Origin: Adapted from a recipe in Harry Craddock's 1930 Savoy Cocktail Book. Made with Bacardi rum this becomes the Bacardi Cocktail.
Comment: This Daiquiri is particularly delicate in its balance between sweet and sour.

SATSUMA MARTINI

Glass: Martini
Garnish: Orange zest twist
Method: **SHAKE** all ingredients with ice and fine strain into chilled glass.

1 1/2	shot(s)	**Orange flavoured vodka**
3/4	shot(s)	**Grand Marnier liqueur**
2	shot(s)	**Pressed apple juice**
2	dashes	**Fee Brothers orange bitters**

Origin: Discovered in 2002 at the Fifth Floor Bar, London, England.
Comment: Tastes like its namesake – hard to believe it's almost half apple.

SATAN'S WHISKERS (STRAIGHT) [NEW]

Glass: Martini
Garnish: Orange zest twist
Method: **SHAKE** all ingredients with ice and fine strain into chilled glass.

1	shot(s)	**Plymouth gin**
1	shot(s)	**Dry vermouth**
1	shot(s)	**Sweet vermouth**
1/2	shot(s)	**Grand Marnier liqueur**
1	shot(s)	**Freshly squeezed orange juice**
1	dash	**Fee Brothers orange bitters (optional)**

Variant: To serve 'Curled' use triple sec in place of Grand Marnier.
Origin: Adapted from a recipe in Harry Craddock's 1930 Savoy Cocktail Book.
Comment: A variation on the Bronx. Perfectly balanced tangy orange.

SATURN MARTINI

Glass: Martini
Garnish: Grapes on stick
Method: **MUDDLE** grapes in base of shaker. **STIR** honey with vodka and grapes to dissolve honey. Add wine, **SHAKE** with ice and fine strain into chilled glass.

7	fresh	**Seedless white grapes**
1 1/2	shot(s)	**Ketel One Citroen vodka**
2	shot(s)	**Runny honey**
1 1/2	shot(s)	**Sauvignon Blanc wine**

Origin: Created in 2001 by Tony Conigliaro at Isola, Knightsbridge, London, England.
Comment: Delicate, beautifully balanced and subtly flavoured.

SAVANNAH

Glass: Martini
Garnish: Orange zest twist
Method: **SHAKE** all ingredients with ice and fine strain into chilled glass.

2 1/2	shot(s)	**Plymouth gin**
3/4	shot(s)	**Freshly squeezed orange juice**
1/2	shot(s)	**White crème de cacao liqueur**
1/2	fresh	**Egg white**

Origin: Adapted from a recipe in the 1949 edition of Esquire's Handbook for Hosts.
Comment: Gin and orange with a hint of chocolate – smoothed by egg white.

SAVOY SPECIAL #1 [NEW]

Glass: Martini
Garnish: Orange zest twist
Method: **SHAKE** all ingredients with ice and fine strain into chilled glass.

2	shot(s)	**Plymouth gin**
1	shot(s)	**Dry vermouth**
1/4	shot(s)	**Sonoma pomegranate (grenadine) syrup**
1/8	shot(s)	**La Fée Parisian 68% absinthe**
1/2	shot(s)	**Chilled mineral water (omit if wet ice)**

Origin: Adapted from a recipe in Harry Craddock's 1930 Savoy Cocktail Book.
Comment: Wonderfully dry and aromatic.

HOW TO MAKE SUGAR SYRUP

To make your own sugar syrup, gradually pour TWO cups of granulated sugar into a saucepan containing ONE cup of hot water. Stir as you pour and carry on stirring and simmering until the sugar is dissolved. Do not let the water even come close to boiling and only simmer for as long as it takes to dissolve the sugar. Allow syrup to cool and pour into an empty bottle. Ideally, you should finely strain your syrup into the bottle to remove any undissolved crystals which could otherwise encourage crystallisation. If kept in a refrigerator this mixture will last for a couple of months.

●●●●○

SAZERAC

Glass: Old-fashioned
Garnish: Lemon zest twist
Method: **POUR** absinthe into ice-filled glass, top with water and leave to stand. Separately **SHAKE** bourbon, cognac, sugar and bitters with ice. **DISCARD** contents of glass (absinthe, water and ice) and **STRAIN** contents of shaker into absinthe-coated glass.

In glass

3/4	shot(s)	**La Fée Parisian 68% absinthe**
Top up with		**Chilled mineral water**

In shaker

1	shot(s)	**Bourbon whiskey**
1	shot(s)	**Rémy Martin cognac**
1/2	shot(s)	**Sugar (gomme) syrup**
3	dashes	**Angostura aromatic bitters**
3	dashes	**Peychaud's bitters**

Comment: Don't be concerned about chucking expensive absinthe down the drain - its flavour will be very evident in the finished drink. Classically this drink is stirred but it is much better shaken.

●●●◐◐

SCANDINAVIAN POP [NEW]

Glass: Collins
Garnish: Lime wedge
Method: **SHAKE** first three ingredients with ice and strain into ice-filled glass. **TOP** up with ginger ale.

2	shot(s)	**Raspberry flavoured vodka**
2	shot(s)	**Cranberry juice**
1/2	shot(s)	**Freshly squeezed lime juice**
Top up with		**Ginger ale**

Origin: Created by Wayne Collins, London, England.
Comment: Berry fruit with a spicy splash of ginger.

●●●○○

SCARLETT O'HARA

Glass: Martini
Garnish: Cranberries or lime wedge
Method: **SHAKE** all ingredients with ice and fine strain into chilled glass.

2	shot(s)	**Southern Comfort liqueur**
1	shot(s)	**Cranberry juice**
1	shot(s)	**Freshly squeezed lime juice**

Origin: Created in 1939 and named after the heroine of Gone With The Wind, the Scarlett O'Hara is said to have put Southern Comfort on the proverbial drink map.
Comment: The tang of lime and the dryness of cranberry balance the apricot sweetness of Southern Comfort.

●●●●○

SCOFFLAW [NEW]

Glass: Martini
Garnish: Lemon zest twist
Method: **SHAKE** all ingredients with ice and fine strain into chilled glass.

1 1/2	shot(s)	**Bourbon whiskey**
1 1/2	shot(s)	**Dry vermouth**
1/2	shot(s)	**Freshly squeezed lemon juice**
1/4	shot(s)	**Pomegranate (grenadine) syrup**
1	dash	**Fee Brothers orange bitters**

Origin: During the height of Prohibition The Boston Herald ran a competition asking readers to coin a new word for "a lawless drinker of illegally made or illegally obtained liquor". Out of 25,000 entries, 'Scofflaw' was chosen and on 15th January 1924 the $200 prize was shared between the two people who had submitted the word. This cocktail was created by Jock at Harry's American Bar, Paris, to celebrate the new term.
Comment: This rust-coloured drink is made or broken by the quality of pomegranate syrup used.

●●●●○

SCORPION

Glass: Collins
Garnish: Gardenia or orange slice & mint
Method: **BLEND** all ingredients with 12oz crushed ice and serve with straws.

1 1/2	shot(s)	**Light white rum**
3/4	shot(s)	**Rémy Martin cognac**
2	shot(s)	**Freshly squeezed orange juice**
1	shot(s)	**Freshly squeezed lemon juice**
1/2	shot(s)	**Almond (orgeat) sugar syrup**

Variant: With pisco in place of brandy.
Origin: Adapted from a recipe purloined from Trader Vic's Bartender's Guide.
Comment: Well balanced, refreshing spirit and orange. Not sweet.

●●●◐○

SCOTCH BOUNTY MARTINI [UPDATED]

Glass: Martini
Garnish: Orange zest twist
Method: **SHAKE** all ingredients with ice and fine strain into chilled glass.

1 1/2	shot(s)	**The Famous Grouse Scotch whisky**
1/2	shot(s)	**White crème de cacao liqueur**
1/2	shot(s)	**Malibu coconut rum liqueur**
1 1/2	shot(s)	**Freshly squeezed orange juice**
1/8	shot(s)	**Sonoma pomegranate (grenadine) syrup**

Comment: A medium-sweet combination of Scotch, coconut and orange.

A B C D E F G H I J K L M N O P Q R **S** T U V W X Y Z

SCOTCH MILK PUNCH

Glass: Martini
Garnish: Grate nutmeg over drink
Method: **SHAKE** all ingredients with ice and fine strain into chilled glass.

2	shot(s)	**The Famous Grouse Scotch whisky**
½	shot(s)	**Sugar (gomme) syrup**
¾	shot(s)	**Double (heavy) cream**
¾	shot(s)	**Milk**

Comment: A creamy, malty affair.

SCOTCH NEGRONI [NEW]

Glass: Old-fashioned
Garnish: Orange slice
Method: **STIR** all ingredients with ice and strain into ice-filled glass.

1	shot(s)	**The Famous Grouse Scotch whisky**
1	shot(s)	**Sweet (rosso) vermouth**
1	shot(s)	**Campari**

Comment: Dry, slightly smoky – for palates that appreciate bitterness.

THE SCOTT [NEW]

Glass: Martini
Garnish: Lemon zest twist
Method: **STIR** all ingredients with ice and strain into chilled glass.

2	shot(s)	**The Famous Grouse Scotch whisky**
1	shot(s)	**Dry vermouth**
½	shot(s)	**Drambuie liqueur**

Origin: Discovered in 2006 at The Clift Hotel, San Francisco, USA.
Comment: This golden drink is dry and sophisticated, yet honeyed and approachable.

SCREAMING BANANA BANSHEE [UPDATED]

Glass: Hurricane
Garnish: Banana chunk on rim
Method: **BLEND** all ingredients with 12oz scoop of crushed ice and serve with straws.

2	shot(s)	**Ketel One vodka**
1	shot(s)	**Crème de bananes liqueur**
1	shot(s)	**White crème de cacao liqueur**
1½	shot(s)	**Double (heavy) cream**
1½	shot(s)	**Milk**
½	fresh	**Peeled banana**

Origin: Without the vodka this is a plain 'Banana Banshee'.
Comment: An alcoholic milkshake – not too sweet.

SCREWDRIVER

Glass: Collins
Garnish: Orange slice
Method: **POUR** vodka into ice-filled glass and top with orange juice. Lightly stir and serve with straws.

2	shot(s)	**Ketel One vodka**
Top up with		**Freshly squeezed orange juice**

Origin: This cocktail first appeared in the 1950s in the Middle East. Parched US engineers working in the desert supposedly added orange juice to their vodka and stirred it with the nearest thing to hand, usually a screwdriver.
Comment: The temperature at which this drink is served and the freshness of the orange juice makes or breaks it.

SEABREEZE #1 (SIMPLE)

Glass: Collins
Garnish: Lime slice
Method: **SHAKE** all ingredients with ice and strain into ice-filled glass.

2	shot(s)	**Ketel One vodka**
3	shot(s)	**Cranberry juice**
1½	shot(s)	**Freshly squeezed grapefruit juice**

Origin: Thought to have originated in the early 1990s in New York City.
Comment: Few bartenders bother to shake this simple drink, instead simply pouring and stirring in the glass.

SEABREEZE #2 (LAYERED)

Glass: Collins
Garnish: Lime wedge
Method: **POUR** cranberry juice into ice-filled glass. **SHAKE** other ingredients with ice and carefully strain into glass to **LAYER** over the cranberry juice.

3	shot(s)	**Cranberry juice**
2	shot(s)	**Ketel One vodka**
1½	shot(s)	**Freshly squeezed pink grapefruit juice**
½	shot(s)	**Freshly squeezed lime juice**

Comment: This layered version requires mixing with straws prior to drinking.

SEELBACH

Glass: Flute
Garnish: Orange zest twist
Method: **POUR** first four ingredients into chilled glass. Top with champagne.

¾	shot(s)	**Bourbon whiskey**
½	shot(s)	**Cointreau / triple sec**
1	dash	**Angostura aromatic bitters**
1	dash	**Peychaud's aromatic bitters**
Top up with		**Piper-Heidsieck brut champagne**

Origin: Created in 1917 and named after its place of origin, the Seelbach Hotel, Louisville, Kentucky, USA.
Comment: This champagne cocktail is fortified with bourbon and orange liqueur.

SENSATION [NEW]

Glass: Martini
Garnish: Maraschino cherry
Method: Lightly **MUDDLE** mint (just to bruise) in base of shaker. Add other ingredients, **SHAKE** with ice and fine strain into chilled glass.

12	fresh	**Mint leaves**
2	shot(s)	**Plymouth gin**
3/4	shot(s)	**Freshly squeezed lemon juice**
3/4	shot(s)	**Luxardo maraschino liqueur**
1/8	shot(s)	**Sugar (gomme) syrup**
1/2	shot(s)	**Chilled mineral water (omit if wet ice)**

Origin: Adapted from a recipe in Harry Craddock's 1930 Savoy Cocktail Book.
Comment: Fresh, fragrant and balanced.

SERENDIPITY

Glass: Collins
Garnish: Slice of lemon
Method: **MUDDLE** blackberries in base of shaker. Add other ingredients, **SHAKE** with ice and strain into glass filled with crushed ice.

6	fresh	**Blackberries**
1	shot(s)	**Plymouth gin**
1/2	shot(s)	**Vanilla schnapps liqueur**
1/2	shot(s)	**Sisca crème de cassis**
3	shot(s)	**Cranberry juice**
1/4	shot(s)	**Freshly squeezed lemon juice**
1/4	shot(s)	**Sugar (gomme) syrup**

Origin: Created in 2002 by Jamie Stephenson, Manchester, England.
Comment: Long, red, fruity, vanilla.

SETTLE PETAL

Glass: Martini
Garnish: Float rose petal
Method: **STIR** all ingredients with ice and strain into chilled glass.

2	shot(s)	**Plymouth gin**
1	shot(s)	**Cucumber flavoured vodka**
1/2	shot(s)	**Rosewater**
1/2	shot(s)	**Vanilla syrup**

Origin: Created in 2003 by Andy Fitzmorris at Eclipse, Notting Hill, London, England.
Comment: An aptly named floral Martini.

SEVENTH HEAVEN #2 [NEW]

Glass: Martini
Garnish: Mint leaf
Method: **SHAKE** all ingredients with ice and fine strain into chilled glass.

2 1/4	shot(s)	**Plymouth gin**
3/4	shot(s)	**Luxardo maraschino liqueur**
1 1/2	shot(s)	**Freshly squeezed pink grapefruit juice**

Origin: Adapted from the Seventh Heaven No. 2 recipe in Harry Craddock's 1930 Savoy Cocktail Book.
Comment: Drink this and you'll be there.

THE 75 [NEW]

Glass: Martini
Garnish: Float star anise
Method: **SHAKE** all ingredients with ice and fine strain into chilled glass.

2	shot(s)	**Calvados or applejack brandy**
1	shot(s)	**Plymouth gin**
1/4	shot(s)	**La Fée Parisian 68% absinthe**
1/4	shot(s)	**Sonoma pomegranate (grenadine) syrup**
1/2	shot(s)	**Chilled mineral water (omit if wet ice)**

Origin: Along with its sister drink, the French 75, this was named after the 75mm field gun used by the French army during the First World War. Both drinks are thought to have been created in 1925 by Harry MacElhone at his Harry's American Bar, Paris, France.
Comment: Dry, aromatic and complex - best appreciated by spirit hardened palates.

SEX ON THE BEACH #1

Glass: Collins
Garnish: Orange slice & cherry (sail)
Method: **SHAKE** all ingredients with ice and strain into ice-filled glass.

2	shot(s)	**Ketel One vodka**
1/2	shot(s)	**Chambord black raspberry liqueur**
1/2	shot(s)	**Butterscotch schnapps liqueur**
1 1/2	shot(s)	**Freshly squeezed orange juice**
1 1/2	shot(s)	**Cranberry juice**

Variant: With melon liqueur in place of peach schnapps.
Origin: An infamous cocktail during the 1980s.
Comment: Sweet fruit laced with vodka.

SEX ON THE BEACH #2

Glass: Old-fashioned
Garnish: Orange slice & cherry (sail)
Method: **SHAKE** all ingredients with ice and strain into ice-filled glass.

2	shot(s)	**Ketel One vodka**
1/2	shot(s)	**Chambord black raspberry liqueur**
1/2	shot(s)	**Midori melon liqueur**
1 1/2	shot(s)	**Pressed pineapple juice**

Comment: Sweeter than most.

SEX ON THE BEACH #3

Glass: Shot
Method: Refrigerate ingredients then **LAYER** in chilled glass by carefully pouring in the following order.

1/2	shot(s)	**Chambord black raspberry liqueur**
1/2	shot(s)	**Midori melon liqueur**
1/2	shot(s)	**Freshly squeezed lime juice**
1/2	shot(s)	**Pressed pineapple juice**

Comment: A sweet and sour shot, combining raspberry, melon, lime and pineapple.

SGROPPINO

Glass: Flute
Garnish: Lemon zest twist
Method: **BLEND** all ingredients without additional ice and serve in chilled glass.

½	shot(s)	**Ketel One vodka**
¼	shot(s)	**Double (heavy) cream**
1½	shot(s)	**Prosecco sparkling wine**
2	scoop(s)	**Lemon sorbet (see recipe under L)**

AKA: Sorbetto
Origin: Pronounced 'scroe-pee-noe', this hybrid of cocktail and dessert is often served after meals in Venice. The name comes from a vernacular word meaning 'untie', a reference to the belief that it relaxes your stomach after a hearty meal.
Comment: Smooth and all too easy to quaff. A great dessert.

SHADY GROVE COOLER

Glass: Collins
Garnish: Lime wedge on rim
Method: **SHAKE** first three ingredients with ice and strain into ice-filled glass. **TOP** with ginger ale, lightly stir and serve with straws.

2	shot(s)	**Plymouth gin**
1	shot(s)	**Freshly squeezed lime juice**
½	shot(s)	**Sugar (gomme) syrup**
Top up with		**Ginger ale**

Comment: Long and refreshing with lime freshness and a hint of ginger.

SHAKERATO [NEW]

Glass: Martini
Garnish: Lemon zest twist
Method: **SHAKE** all ingredients with ice and fine strain into chilled glass.

1½	shot(s)	**Campari**
¼	shot(s)	**Freshly squeezed lemon juice**
¼	shot(s)	**Sugar (gomme) syrup**
1½	shot(s)	**Chilled mineral water**

Comment: Campari lovers only need apply.

SHAMROCK #1 [NEW]

Glass: Martini
Garnish: Twist of orange (discarded)
Method: **STIR** all ingredients with ice and strain into chilled glass.

2½	shot(s)	**Bourbon whiskey**
1	shot(s)	**Sweet (rosso) vermouth**
¼	shot(s)	**Green crème de menthe**
2	dashes	**Angostura aromatic bitters**

Origin: Purloined from David Embury's classic book, The Fine Art of Mixing Drinks.
Comment: Basically a Sweet Manhattan with a dash of green crème de menthe.

SHAMROCK #2 [NEW]

Glass: Martini
Garnish: Mint leaf
Method: **SHAKE** all ingredients with ice and fine strain into chilled glass.

1½	shot(s)	**Irish whiskey**
1½	shot(s)	**Dry vermouth**
½	shot(s)	**Green Chartreuse**
½	shot(s)	**Green crème de menthe**
½	shot(s)	**Chilled mineral water (omit if wet ice)**

Origin: Adapted from a recipe in Harry Craddock's 1930 Savoy Cocktail Book.
Comment: A great drink for St. Patrick's Day.

SHAMROCK EXPRESS

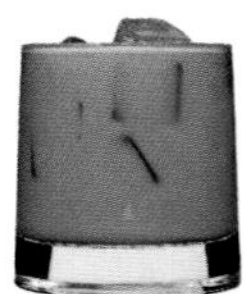

Glass: Old-fashioned
Method: **SHAKE** all ingredients with ice and strain into ice-filled glass.

1½	shot(s)	**Espresso coffee (cold)**
¾	shot(s)	**Butterscotch schnapps liqueur**
1	shot(s)	**Ketel One vodka**
1	shot(s)	**Baileys Irish cream liqueur**
¼	shot(s)	**Sugar (gomme) syrup**

Origin: Created in 1999 by Greg Pearson at Mystique, Manchester, England.
Comment: Creamy coffee with the sweetness of butterscotch.

SHARK BITE

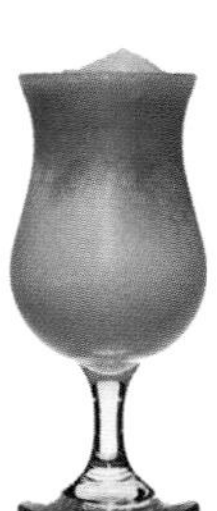

Glass: Hurricane
Method: **BLEND** first three ingredients with 18oz scoop crushed ice and pour into glass. **POUR** grenadine around edge of the drink. Do not stir before serving.

2	shot(s)	**Pusser's Navy rum**
3	shot(s)	**Freshly squeezed orange juice**
½	shot(s)	**Freshly squeezed lime juice**
¾	shot(s)	**Sonoma pomegranate (grenadine) syrup**

Comment: Strong rum and orange juice. A tad sweet but easy to drink.

SHIRLEY TEMPLE (MOCKTAIL)

Glass: Collins
Garnish: Maraschino cherry & lemon slice
Method: **POUR** ingredients into ice-filled glass, lightly stir and serve with straws.

¼	shot(s)	**Sonoma pomegranate (grenadine) syrup**
¼	shot(s)	**Freshly squeezed lemon juice**
Top up with		**Ginger ale**

Comment: I've added a splash of lemon juice to the usual recipe. It's still not that exciting.

SHOWBIZ

Glass: Martini
Garnish: Blackcurrants on stick
Method: **SHAKE** all ingredients with ice and fine strain into chilled glass.

1¾	shot(s)	**Ketel One vodka**
1	shot(s)	**Sisca crème de cassis**
1¾	shot(s)	**Freshly squeezed grapefruit juice**

Comment: Sweet cassis soured with grapefruit and fortified with vodka.

SICILIAN NEGRONI [NEW]

Glass: Old-fashioned
Garnish: Orange slice
Method: **SHAKE** all ingredients with ice and strain into ice-filled glass.

1½	shot(s)	**Plymouth gin**
1½	shot(s)	**Campari**
1½	shot(s)	**Blood orange juice**

Origin: Discovered in 2006 at The Last Supper Club, San Francisco, USA.
Comment: Blood orange juice replaces sweet vermouth in this fruity Negroni.

SIDECAR #1 (EQUAL PARTS CLASSIC FORMULA)

Glass: Martini
Garnish: Lemon zest twist
Method: **SHAKE** all ingredients with ice and fine strain into chilled glass.

1¼	shot(s)	**Rémy Martin cognac**
1¼	shot(s)	**Cointreau / triple sec**
1¼	shot(s)	**Freshly squeezed lemon juice**

Variant: Apple Cart
Comment: Dry and tart but beautifully balanced and refined.

SIDECAR #2 (DIFFORD'S FORMULA)

Glass: Martini
Garnish: Lemon zest twist
Method: **SHAKE** all ingredients with ice and fine strain into chilled glass.

1½	shot(s)	**Rémy Martin cognac**
1	shot(s)	**Cointreau / triple sec**
1	shot(s)	**Freshly squeezed lemon juice**
½	shot(s)	**Chilled mineral water (omit if wet ice)**

Origin: My take on the classic.
Comment: This formula helps the cognac rise above the liqueur and lemon juice.

SIDECAR

In his classic Fine Art of Mixing Drinks, David Embury writes of the Sidecar: "It was invented by a friend of mine at a bar in Paris during World War I and was named after the motorcycle sidecar in which the good captain customarily was driven to and from the little bistro where the drink was born and christened."

Embury doesn't name the bar but it's commonly assumed that he meant Harry's New York Bar and that the cocktail was created by its owner, Harry MacElhone. However, in Harry's own book he credits the drink to MacGarry of Buck's Club, London.

There have been periods when it has been fashionable to coat the rim of the glass in which this drink is to be served with sugar. Thankfully sugar rims are now out of vogue and, as Embury writes in his book, "A twist of lemon may be used if desired and the peel dropped into the glass. Otherwise no decoration."

SINGAPORE SLING

This drink was created some time between 1911 and 1915 by Chinese-born Ngiam Tong Boon at the Long Bar in Raffles Hotel, Singapore.

Raffles Hotel is named after the colonial founder of Singapore, Sir Stamford Raffles, and was the Near East's expat central. As Charles H. Baker Jr. wrote in his 1946 Gentleman's Companion, "Just looking around the terrace porch we've seen Frank Buck, the Sultan of Johor, Aimee Semple McPherson, Somerset Maugham, Dick Halliburton, Doug Fairbanks, Bob Ripley, Ruth Elder and Walker Camp – not that this is any wonder". It still sticks out of modern-day Singapore like a vast, colonial Christmas cake.

Although there is little controversy as to who created the Singapore Sling, where he created it and (roughly) when, there is huge debate over the original name and ingredients. Singapore and the locality was colonially known as the 'Straits Settlements' and it seems certain that Boon's drink was similarly named the 'Straits Sling'. The name appears to have changed some time between 1922 and 1930.

Not even the Raffles Hotel itself is sure of the original recipe and visiting the present day Long Bar in search of enlightenment is hopless. Sadly, the Singapore Slings now served there are made from a powdered pre-mix, which is also available in the gift shop below.

Great debate rages over the type of cherry brandy used. Was it a cherry 'brandy' liqueur or actually a cherry eau de vie? Did fruit juice feature in the original recipe at all? We shall probably never know, so I've listed several versions which are generally accepted to pass for a Singapore Sling today. Please also see the entry for 'Straits Sling'.

SIDECAR #3 (EMBURY'S FORMULA)

Glass: Martini
Garnish: Lemon zest twist
Method: **SHAKE** all ingredients with ice and fine strain into chilled glass.

2 shot(s) **Rémy Martin cognac**
1/2 shot(s) **Freshly squeezed lemon juice**
1/2 shot(s) **Cointreau / triple sec**
1/2 shot(s) **Chilled mineral water (omit if wet ice)**

Origin: In The Fine Art of Mixing Drinks, David Embury writes of the 'equal parts' Sidecar, "This is the most perfect example of a magnificent drink gone wrong". He argues that "Essentially the Sidecar is nothing but a Daiquiri with brandy in the place of rum and Cointreau in the place of sugar syrup" and so the Daiquiri formula should be followed as above.
Comment: A Sidecar for those with a dry palate.

SIDECAR NAMED DESIRE [UPDATED]

Glass: Martini
Garnish: Lemon zest twist
Method: **SHAKE** all ingredients with ice and fine strain into chilled glass.

2 shot(s) **Calvados or applejack brandy**
1 shot(s) **Apple schnapps liqueur**
1 shot(s) **Freshly squeezed lemon juice**

Comment: Take a classic Sidecar and add some love interest – apple!

SIDEKICK

Glass: Martini
Garnish: Quarter orange slice on rim
Method: **SHAKE** all ingredients with ice and fine strain into chilled glass.

2 shot(s) **Pear & cognac liqueur**
3/4 shot(s) **Cointreau / triple sec**
1 shot(s) **Freshly squeezed orange juice**
1/2 shot(s) **Freshly squeezed lime juice**

Origin: Adapted from a drink discovered in 2003 at Temple Bar, New York City.
Comment: Rich pear and orange with a stabilising hint of sour lime.

SILENT THIRD

Glass: Martini
Garnish: Lemon zest twist
Method: **SHAKE** all ingredients with ice and fine strain into chilled glass.

2 shot(s) **The Famous Grouse Scotch whisky**
1/2 shot(s) **Cointreau / triple sec**
3/4 shot(s) **Freshly squeezed lemon juice**
3/4 shot(s) **Chilled mineral water**

Comment: A sour, sharp whisky drink.

●●●◐○

SILK STOCKINGS [NEW]

Glass: Martini
Garnish: Cinamon dust
Method: **SHAKE** all ingredients with ice and fine strain into chilled glass.

2	shot(s)	**Sauza Hornitos tequila**
3/4	shot(s)	**White crème de cacao liqueur**
3/4	shot(s)	**Sonoma pomegranate (grenadine) syrup**
1/2	shot(s)	**Double (heavy) cream**
1/2	shot(s)	**Milk**

Comment: Smoothed and sweetened tequila with a hint of chocolate and fruit.

●●●●○

SILVER BULLET MARTINI

Glass: Martini
Garnish: Lemon zest twist
Method: **SHAKE** all ingredients with ice and fine strain into chilled glass.

2	shot(s)	**Plymouth gin**
1	shot(s)	**Kümmel liqueur**
1	shot(s)	**Freshly squeezed lemon juice**
1/4	shot(s)	**Sugar (gomme) syrup**

Variant: A modern variation is to substitute sambuca for kümmel.
Origin: Thought to have been created in the 1920s.
Comment: Caraway and fennel flavour this unusual sweet 'n' sour drink.

●●●●○

SILVER FIZZ

Glass: Collins (8oz max)
Garnish: Lemon slice
Method: **SHAKE** first four ingredients with ice and strain into chilled glass (no ice). **TOP** with soda from siphon.

2	shot(s)	**Spirit (gin, whiskey, vodka, brandy)**
1	shot(s)	**Freshly squeezed lemon or lime juice**
1/2	shot(s)	**Sugar (gomme) syrup**
1/2	fresh	**Egg white (optional)**
Top up with		**Soda water (from siphon)**

Origin: A mid-19th century classic.
Variant: Omit the egg white and this is a mere Fizz.
Comment: I prefer my Fizzes with the addition of egg white. Why not also try a Derby Fizz, which combines liqueur and spirits?

●●●◐○

SILVER MARTINI [NEW]

Glass: Martini
Garnish: Maraschino cherry
Method: **SHAKE** all ingredients with ice and fine strain into chilled glass.

1 1/2	shot(s)	**Plymouth gin**
1 1/2	shot(s)	**Dry vermouth**
1/4	shot(s)	**Luxardo maraschino liqueur**
2	dashes	**Fee Brothers orange bitters**

Origin: Adapted from a recipe in Harry Craddock's 1930 Savoy Cocktail Book.
Comment: Dry and aromatic – for serious imbibers only.

●●●◐○

SINGAPORE SLING #1 (BAKER'S FORMULA) [NEW]

Glass: Collins (10oz max)
Garnish: Lemon slice & cherry (sail)
Method: **SHAKE** first three ingredients with ice and strain into ice-filled glass. **TOP** with soda, lightly stir and serve with straws.

1 1/2	shot(s)	**Plymouth gin**
3/4	shot(s)	**Bénédictine D.O.M. liqueur**
3/4	shot(s)	**Cherry (brandy) liqueur**
Top up with		**Soda water (club soda)**

Variant: Straits Sling
Origin: Adapted from a recipe by Charles H. Baker Jr. and published in his 1946 Gentleman's Companion. He originally called for Old Tom gin.
Comment: Lacks the citrus of other Singapore Slings but dilution cuts and so balances the sweetness of the liqueurs.

●●●●○

SINGAPORE SLING #2 [UPDATED]

Glass: Sling
Garnish: Lemon slice & cherry (sail)
Method: **SHAKE** first six ingredients with ice and strain into ice-filled glass. **TOP** with soda, lightly stir and serve with straws.

2	shot(s)	**Plymouth gin**
1/2	shot(s)	**Bénédictine D.O.M. liqueur**
1/2	shot(s)	**Cherry (brandy) liqueur**
1	shot(s)	**Freshly squeezed lemon juice**
2	dashes	**Fee Brothers orange bitters**
2	dashes	**Angostura aromatic bitters**
Top up with		**Soda water (club soda)**

Comment: On the sour side of dry, this is decidedly more complex than most Singapore Sling recipes.

●●●◐○

SINGAPORE SLING #3 [UPDATED]

Glass: Sling
Garnish: Orange slice & cherry (flag)
Method: **SHAKE** first eight ingredients with ice and strain into ice-filled glass. **TOP** with soda, lightly stir and serve with straws.

2	shot(s)	**Plymouth gin**
1/2	shot(s)	**Cherry (brandy) liqueur**
1/4	shot(s)	**Bénédictine D.O.M. liqueur**
1/4	shot(s)	**Cointreau / triple sec**
1 1/2	shot(s)	**Pressed pineapple juice**
1/2	shot(s)	**Freshly squeezed lime juice**
1/4	shot(s)	**Sonoma pomegranate (grenadine) syrup**
2	dashes	**Angostura aromatic bitters**
Top up with		**Soda water (club soda)**

Comment: Foaming, tangy and very fruity.

DRINKS ARE GRADED AS FOLLOWS:

● DISGUSTING ●◐ PRETTY AWFUL ●● BEST AVOIDED
●●◐ DISAPPOINTING ●●● ACCEPTABLE ●●●◐ GOOD
●●●● RECOMMENDED ●●●●◐ HIGHLY RECOMMENDED
●●●●● OUTSTANDING / EXCEPTIONAL

SLINGS

The word 'Sling' comes from the German 'schlingen', meaning 'to swallow', and Slings based on a spirit mixed with sugar and water were popularly drunk in the late 1800s.

Slings are similar to Toddies and like Toddies can be served hot. (Toddies, however, are never served cold.) The main difference between a Toddy and a Sling is that Slings are not flavoured by the addition of spices. Also, Toddies tend to be made with plain water, while Slings are charged with water, soda water or ginger ale.

SIR CHARLES PUNCH

Glass: Old-fashioned
Garnish: Orange zest twist
Method: **STIR** all ingredients with ice and strain into ice-filled glass.

1 shot(s) **Tawny port**
$^1/_2$ shot(s) **Rémy Martin cognac**
$^1/_2$ shot(s) **Grand Marnier liqueur**
1/8 shot(s) **Sugar (gomme) syrup**

Origin: Adapted from a recipe in the 1949 edition of Esquire's Handbook for Hosts, which suggests serving it at Christmas.
Comment: Short but full of personality - like Kyle Minogue.

SIR THOMAS [NEW]

Glass: Martini
Garnish: Maraschino cherry
Method: **STIR** all ingredients with ice and strain into chilled glass.

2 shot(s) **Bourbon whiskey**
$^1/_2$ shot(s) **Cointreau / triple sec**
$^1/_2$ shot(s) **Cherry (brandy) liqueur**
$^1/_2$ shot(s) **Sweet (rosso) vermouth**

Origin: Created in 2005 by Tom Ward, England.
Comment: Akin to a fruit laced Sweet Manhattan.

SKI BREEZE

Glass: Collins
Garnish: Apple slice
Method: **POUR** ingredients into ice-filled glass, lightly stir and serve with straws.

2 shot(s) **Raspberry flavoured vodka**
3 shot(s) **Pressed apple juice**
3 shot(s) **Ginger ale**

Comment: A meld of apple and berries with hint of ginger.

SLEEPING BISON-TINI

Glass: Martini
Garnish: Pear slice on rim
Method: **SHAKE** all ingredients with ice and fine strain into chilled glass.

$1^1/_2$ shot(s) **Zubrówka bison vodka**
$^1/_4$ shot(s) **Apricot brandy liqueur**
$^1/_4$ shot(s) **Pear & cognac liqueur**
1 shot(s) **Freshly extracted pear juice**
1 shot(s) **Pressed apple juice**
1 shot(s) **Strong cold camomile tea**

Comment: A light cocktail featuring a melange of subtle flavours.

SLEEPY HOLLOW [NEW]

Glass: Old-fashioned
Garnish: Lemon slice
Method: Lightly **MUDDLE** mint in base of shaker (just to bruise). Add other ingredients, **SHAKE** with ice and fine strain into glass filled with crushed ice. Serve with straws.

10	fresh	**Mint leaves**
2	shot(s)	**Plymouth gin**
1/2	shot(s)	**Apricot brandy liqueur**
1	shot(s)	**Freshly squeezed lemon juice**
1/2	shot(s)	**Sugar (gomme) syrup**

Origin: An adaption of a drink created in the early 1930s and named after Washington Irving's novel and its enchanted valley with ghosts, goblins and headless horseman.
Comment: Hints of lemon and mint with gin and apricot fruit. Very refreshing.

SLING [NEW]

Glass: Sling
Garnish: Lemon slice
Method: **SHAKE** first three ingredients with ice and strain into ice-filled glass. Top up with soda or ginger ale.

2	shot(s)	**Liquor (gin, rum, scotch, whisky etc.)**
1/2	shot(s)	**Freshly squeezed lemon juice**
1/4	shot(s)	**Sugar (gomme) syrup**
Top with		**Soda or ginger ale**

Origin: 'Sling' comes from the German word 'schlingen', meaning 'to swallow' and is a style of drink which was popular in the late 1800s.
Comment: Sugar balances the citrus juice, the spirit fortifies and the carbonate lengthens.

SLIPPERY NIPPLE

Glass: Shot
Method: **LAYER** in glass by carefully pouring ingredients in the following order.

1/4	shot(s)	**Sonoma pomegranate (grenadine) syrup**
3/4	shot(s)	**Luxardo Sambuca dei Cesari**
3/4	shot(s)	**Baileys Irish cream liqueur**

Comment: The infamous red, clear and brown shot. Very sweet.

SLOE GIN FIZZ

Glass: Sling
Garnish: Lemon slice or cucumber slice
Method: **SHAKE** first five ingredients with ice and strain into ice-filled glass. **TOP** with soda, stir and serve with straws.

1	shot(s)	**Plymouth gin**
1 1/2	shot(s)	**Plymouth sloe gin liqueur**
1	shot(s)	**Freshly squeezed lime juice**
1/4	shot(s)	**Sugar (gomme) syrup**
1/2	fresh	**Egg white**
Top up with		**Soda water (club soda)**

Comment: A sour gin fizz with dark, rich sloe gin.

SLOE MOTION

Glass: Flute
Garnish: Lemon zest
Method: **POUR** liqueur into chilled glass and top with champagne.

3/4	shot(s)	**Plymouth sloe gin liqueur**
Top up with		**Piper-Heidsieck brut champagne**

Comment: Sloe gin proves to be an excellent complement to champagne.

SLOE TEQUILA

Glass: Old-fashioned
Garnish: Lime wedge
Method: **SHAKE** all ingredients with ice and strain into ice-filled glass.

1	shot(s)	**Plymouth sloe gin liqueur**
1	shot(s)	**Sauza Hornitos tequila**
1	shot(s)	**Rose's lime cordial**

Comment: Berry fruit and tequila with a surprisingly tart, bitter finish.

SLOPPY JOE

Glass: Martini
Garnish: Lime wedge
Method: **SHAKE** all ingredients with ice and fine strain into chilled glass.

1	shot(s)	**Light white rum**
1	shot(s)	**Dry vermouth**
1/4	shot(s)	**Cointreau / triple sec**
1	shot(s)	**Freshly squeezed lime juice**
1/2	shot(s)	**Sugar (gomme) syrup**
1/4	shot(s)	**Sonoma pomegranate (grenadine) syrup**

Comment: Nicely balanced sweet and sourness.

SLOW SCREW

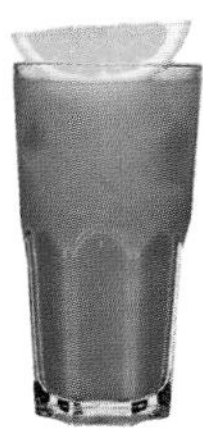

Glass: Collins
Garnish: Orange slice
Method: **SHAKE** all ingredients with ice and strain into ice-filled glass.

1	shot(s)	**Plymouth sloe gin liqueur**
1	shot(s)	**Ketel One vodka**
4	shot(s)	**Freshly squeezed orange juice**

Comment: A Screwdriver with sloe gin.

DRINKS ARE GRADED AS FOLLOWS:

● DISGUSTING ●◐ PRETTY AWFUL ●● BEST AVOIDED
●●◐ DISAPPOINTING ●●● ACCEPTABLE ●●●◐ GOOD
●●●● RECOMMENDED ●●●●◐ HIGHLY RECOMMENDED
●●●●● OUTSTANDING / EXCEPTIONAL

A B C D E F G H I J K L M N O P Q R S T U V W X Y Z

SLOW COMFORTABLE SCREW

Glass: Collins
Garnish: Half orange slice
Method: **SHAKE** all ingredients with ice and strain into ice-filled glass.

1	shot(s)	**Ketel One vodka**
1	shot(s)	**Plymouth sloe gin liqueur**
1	shot(s)	**Southern Comfort liqueur**
3	shot(s)	**Freshly squeezed orange juice**

Comment: A Screwdriver with sloe gin and Southern Comfort. Fruity and fairly sweet.

SLOW COMFORTABLE SCREW AGAINST THE WALL

Glass: Collins
Method: **SHAKE** first four ingredients with ice and strain into ice-filled glass. Lastly **FLOAT** Galliano.

1	shot(s)	**Ketel One vodka**
1	shot(s)	**Plymouth sloe gin liqueur**
1	shot(s)	**Southern Comfort liqueur**
3	shot(s)	**Freshly squeezed orange juice**
1/2	shot(s)	**Galliano liqueur**

Comment: Galliano adds the wall (as in Harvey Wallbanger) and some herbal peppermint to this Slow Comfortable Screw.

SMARTINI

Glass: Martini
Garnish: Three Smarties in drink
Method: **SHAKE** all ingredients with ice and fine strain into chilled glass.

2	shot(s)	**Ketel One Citroen vodka**
1	shot(s)	**White crème de cacao liqueur**
1/4	shot(s)	**Sugar (gomme) syrup**
3/4	shot(s)	**Chilled mineral water (omit if wet ice)**
3	dashes	**Fee Brothers orange bitters**

Comment: Citrus with a crispy chocolate edge. A sweetie.

SMOKY APPLE MARTINI [NEW]

Glass: Martini
Garnish: Maraschino cherry
Method: **SHAKE** all ingredients with ice and fine strain into chilled glass.

2 1/2	shot(s)	**The Famous Grouse Scotch whisky**
1	shot(s)	**Sour apple liqueur**
1/2	shot(s)	**Rose's lime cordial**

Comment: Scotch adds some peaty character to this twist on the Sour Apple Martini.

SMOKY MARTINI #1

Glass: Martini
Garnish: Lemon zest twist
Method: **STIR** all ingredients with ice and strain into chilled glass.

2 1/2	shot(s)	**Plymouth gin**
1/2	shot(s)	**Dry vermouth**
1/4	shot(s)	**The Famous Grouse Scotch whisky**

Variant: Substitute vodka for gin.
Comment: A pleasant variation on the classic Dry Martini.

SMOKY MARTINI #2

Glass: Martini
Garnish: Orange zest twist
Method: **STIR** all ingredients with ice and strain into chilled glass.

2	shot(s)	**Plymouth gin**
1	shot(s)	**Plymouth sloe gin liqueur**
1/4	shot(s)	**Dry vermouth**
2	dashes	**Fee Brothers orange bitters**

Origin: Created in 1997 by Giovanni Burdi at Match EC1, London, England.
Comment: The basic Martini formula (gin plus vermouth) is enhanced with sloe gin and the traditional orange bitters variation, delivering a distinctive 'smoky' character.

SMOOTH & CREAMY'TINI

Glass: Martini
Garnish: Dust with grated nutmeg
Method: **SHAKE** all ingredients with ice and fine strain into chilled glass.

1 1/2	shot(s)	**Mount Gay Eclipse golden rum**
1	shot(s)	**Malibu coconut rum liqueur**
1/4	shot(s)	**Crème de bananes liqueur**
3/4	shot(s)	**Double (heavy) cream**
3/4	shot(s)	**Milk**

Comment: Creamy and moreish.

SNAKEBITE

Glass: Collins
Method: **POUR** lager into glass and top with cider.

Half fill with	**Lager**
Top up with	**Cider**

Variant: Add a dash of blackcurrant cordial to make a 'Snakebite & Black'.
Comment: The students' special.

SNOOD MURDEKIN

Glass: Shot
Method: **SHAKE** first three ingredients with ice and strain into chilled glass. **FLOAT** cream over drink.

1/2	shot(s)	**Ketel One vodka**
1/2	shot(s)	**Chambord black raspberry liqueur**
1/2	shot(s)	**Kahlúa coffee liqueur**
1/4	shot(s)	**Double (heavy) cream**

Origin: Created in the late 90s by Dick Bradsell at Detroit, London, England, for Karin Wiklund, and named for the sad, flute-playing Moomin Troll.
Comment: Moreish combination of coffee and raspberries topped by cream.

SNOOPY [NEW]

Glass: Old-fashioned
Garnish: Orange zest twist
Method: **SHAKE** all ingredients with ice and fine strain into ice-filled glass.

1	shot(s)	**Galliano liqueur**
1 1/2	shot(s)	**Bourbon whiskey**
1/2	shot(s)	**Campari**
3/4	shot(s)	**Grand Marnier liqueur**
1/4	shot(s)	**Freshly squeezed lemon juice**

Comment: Tangy fruit with a balancing hint of citrus and bitterness.

SNOW FALL MARTINI

Glass: Martini
Garnish: Vanilla pod
Method: **MUDDLE** vanilla pod in base of shaker. Add other ingredients, **SHAKE** with ice and fine strain into chilled glass.

1/4	pod	**Vanilla**
2	shot(s)	**Vanilla flavoured vodka**
1 1/4	shot(s)	**Double (heavy) cream**
1 1/4	shot(s)	**Milk**
1/4	shot(s)	**Sugar (gomme) syrup**

Origin: Discovered in 2002 at Lot 61, New York City.
Comment: An alcoholic version of a vanilla milkshake.

SNOW ON EARTH

Glass: Shot
Method: **SHAKE** first three ingredients with ice and strain into chilled glass. Carefully **FLOAT** cream on drink.

1/2	shot(s)	**Kahlúa coffee liqueur**
1/2	shot(s)	**Chambord black raspberry liqueur**
1/2	shot(s)	**Krupnik honey liqueur**
1/2	shot(s)	**Double (heavy) cream**

Comment: A sweet, flavoursome shot.

SNOW WHITE DAIQUIRI

Glass: Martini
Garnish: Pineapple wedge on rim
Method: **SHAKE** all ingredients with ice and fine strain into chilled glass.

2	shot(s)	**Light white rum**
1/2	shot(s)	**Pressed pineapple juice**
1/2	shot(s)	**Freshly squeezed lime juice**
1/4	shot(s)	**Sugar (gomme) syrup**
1/2	fresh	**Egg white**

Origin: My adaptation of a classic cocktail.
Comment: The pineapple and albumen ensure that this delightful Daiquiri has an appropriately white frothy head.

SNOWBALL

Glass: Collins
Garnish: Lime slice on rim
Method: **SHAKE** first three ingredients with ice and strain into ice-filled glass. **TOP** with 7-Up, lightly stir and serve with straws.

2	shot(s)	**Warninks advocaat liqueur**
1	shot(s)	**Tio Pepe fino sherry**
3/4	shot(s)	**Rose's lime cordial**
Top up with		**7-Up**

Origin: This is thought to have originated in Britain in the late 1940s or early 1950s, reaching its peak of popularity in the 1970s.
Comment: The classic light, fluffy concoction. Try it, you may like it.

SNYDER MARTINI [NEW]

Glass: Martini
Garnish: Orange zest twist
Method: **SHAKE** all ingredients with ice and fine strain into chilled glass.

2	shot(s)	**Plymouth gin**
1	shot(s)	**Dry vermouth**
1/4	shot(s)	**Grand Marnier liqueur**

Origin: Adapted from a recipe in Harry Craddock's 1930 Savoy Cocktail Book.
Comment: Dry, hardcore and yet mellow.

SOCIALITE

Glass: Old-fashioned
Method: **SHAKE** all ingredients with ice and strain into glass filled with crushed ice.

1	shot(s)	**Freshly squeezed lemon juice**
1/2	shot(s)	**Vanilla sugar syrup**
1	shot(s)	**Grand Marnier liqueur**
1	shot(s)	**Vanilla flavoured vodka**
1	shot(s)	**Luxardo limoncello liqueur**

Origin: Discovered in 2001 at Lab Bar, London, England.
Comment: Rich citrus with lashings of vanilla.

A B C D E F G H I J K L M N O P Q R **S** T U V W X Y Z

●●●●○

SODDEN GRAPE MARTINI

Glass: Martini
Garnish: Three grapes on stick
Method: **MUDDLE** grapes in base of shaker. Add other ingredients, **SHAKE** with ice and fine strain into chilled glass.

7	fresh	**Seedless white grapes**
2	shot(s)	**Zubrówka bison vodka**
3/4	shot(s)	**Icewine**

Origin: Created by yours truly in 2004.
Comment: A 'sod' is a piece of turf. Here 'sodden' refers to the bison grass, the flavour of which combines well with the grapes and icewine.

●●●●○

SOLENT SUNSET

Glass: Collins
Garnish: Pineapple wedge & cherry on rim
Method: **SHAKE** all ingredients with ice and fine strain into ice-filled glass.

2	shot(s)	**Pusser's Navy rum**
3/4	shot(s)	**Freshly squeezed lime juice**
3	shot(s)	**Pressed pineapple juice**
1/4	shot(s)	**Sonoma pomegranate (grenadine) syrup**

Comment: A Naval style tropical rum punch for those occasional hot sunny days on the Solent (the stretch of sea which separates the Isle of Wight from mainland Britain).

●●●◐○

SOPHISTICATED SAVAGE

Glass: Old-fashioned
Garnish: Lime wedge
Method: **SHAKE** all ingredients with ice and strain into ice-filled glass.

2	shot(s)	**Tuaca liqueur**
1	shot(s)	**Sagatiba cachaça**
1/2	shot(s)	**Freshly squeezed lime juice**
1/2	fresh	**Egg white**

Created by: Poul Jensen, Brighton, England.
Comment: A sour drink with a horse's kick leading into a smooth subtle finish.

FOR MORE INFORMATION SEE OUR
INGREDIENTS APPENDIX ON PAGE 322

●●●◐○

SORRELADE (MOCKTAIL) [NEW]

Glass: Collins
Garnish: Lime wedge
Method: (This is a bulk recipe.) **SOAK** dried sorrel in water with ginger, ground cloves and honey for 12 hours. Bring this mixture to the **BOIL** then leave to cool and **SOAK** for a further 12 hours **STRAIN** and then keep refrigerated.

70g	dried	**Sorrel (hibiscus flowers)**
1.25	litres	**Mineral water**
30g	fresh	**Root ginger (sliced)**
1/2	spoon	**Ground cloves**
3	spoons	**Runny honey**

Origin: Jamaican sorrel, also known by its scientific name 'Hibiscus Sabdariffa', is a plant propagated for its red petals. In Jamaica these are used to make this refreshing drink. (Jamaican sorrel is not related to the English garden herb of the same name.)
Comment: Sorrelade looks a little like cranberry juice and like cranberry juice has a bittersweet, slightly spicy taste.

●●●●◐

SORREL RUM PUNCH

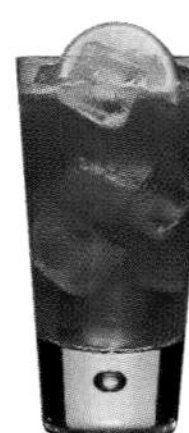

Glass: Collins
Garnish: Lime wedge
Method: **SHAKE** all ingredients with ice and strain into glass filled with crushed glass. Serve with straws.

2 1/4	shot(s)	**Wray & Nephew overproof rum**
3	shot(s)	**Sorrelade (see recipe above)**
3/4	shot(s)	**Freshly squeezed lime juice**
1 1/2	shot(s)	**Sugar (gomme) syrup**

Origin: A classic Jamaican punch using the classic proportions of 'one of sour, two of sweet, three of strong and four of weak'.
Comment: This drink harnesses the flavour of sorrelade and combines it with the traditional strength and bittersweetness of rum punch. Jamaica in a glass.

●●●●●

SO-SO MARTINI [NEW]

Glass: Martini
Garnish: Float wafer thin apple slice
Method: **SHAKE** all ingredients with ice and fine strain into chilled glass.

1 1/2	shot(s)	**Plymouth gin**
1 1/2	shot(s)	**Dry vermouth**
3/4	shot(s)	**Calvados or applejack brandy**
1/2	shot(s)	**Sonoma pomegranate (grenadine) syrup**

Origin: Adapted from a recipe in Harry Craddock's 1930 Savoy Cocktail Book.
Comment: This beautifully balanced, appley drink is so much more than so-so.

DRINKS ARE GRADED AS FOLLOWS:

● DISGUSTING ●◐ PRETTY AWFUL ●● BEST AVOIDED
●●◐ DISAPPOINTING ●●● ACCEPTABLE ●●●◐ GOOD
●●●● RECOMMENDED ●●●●◐ HIGHLY RECOMMENDED
●●●●● OUTSTANDING / EXCEPTIONAL

SOUR

Glass: Old-fashioned
Garnish: Cherry & lemon slice sail
Method: SHAKE all ingredients with ice and strain into ice-filled glass

2	shot(s)	Spirit (whiskey, gin, rum or brandy etc.)
3/4	shot(s)	Freshly squeezed lemon juice
1	shot(s)	Sugar (gomme) syrup
1/2	fresh	Egg white
3	dashes	Angostura aromatic bitters

Comment: This recipe follows the classic sour proportions: three quarter part of the sour ingredient (lemon juice), one part of the sweet ingredient (sugar syrup) and two parts of the strong ingredient (spirit) - 3:4:8. I prefer mine sourer with one part lemon juice and half a part sugar (4:2:8) and that's the formula I've tended to use in other sour drinks in this guide.

SOUR APPLE MARTINI #1 (POPULAR US VERSION)

Glass: Martini
Garnish: Cherry in glass
Method: SHAKE all ingredients with ice and fine strain into chilled glass.

2	shot(s)	Ketel One vodka
1 1/2	shot(s)	Sour apple liqueur
1/4	shot(s)	Rose's lime cordial

Variant: Some bars add sour mix in place of Rose's, others add a dash of fresh lime and sugar.
Comment: A hugely popular drink across North America.

SOUR APPLE MARTINI #2 (DELUXE US VERSION)

Glass: Martini
Garnish: Float wafer thin apple slice
Method: SHAKE all ingredients with ice and fine strain into chilled glass.

2	shot(s)	Ketel One vodka
1	shot(s)	Sour apple liqueur
1/2	shot(s)	Freshly squeezed lime juice
1/4	shot(s)	Sugar (gomme) syrup
1/2	fresh	Egg white

Comment: A sophisticated version of the contemporary classic.

SOURPUSS MARTINI

Glass: Martini
Garnish: Physalis (Cape gooseberry) on rim
Method: SHAKE all ingredients with ice and fine strain into chilled glass.

1	shot(s)	Ketel One Citroen vodka
1/2	shot(s)	Midori melon liqueur
1/2	shot(s)	Sour apple liqueur
2	shot(s)	Pressed apple juice

Origin: Created in 2001 by Colin 'Big Col' Crowden at Time, Leicester, England.
Comment: A lime-green, flavoursome cocktail that balances sweet and sour.

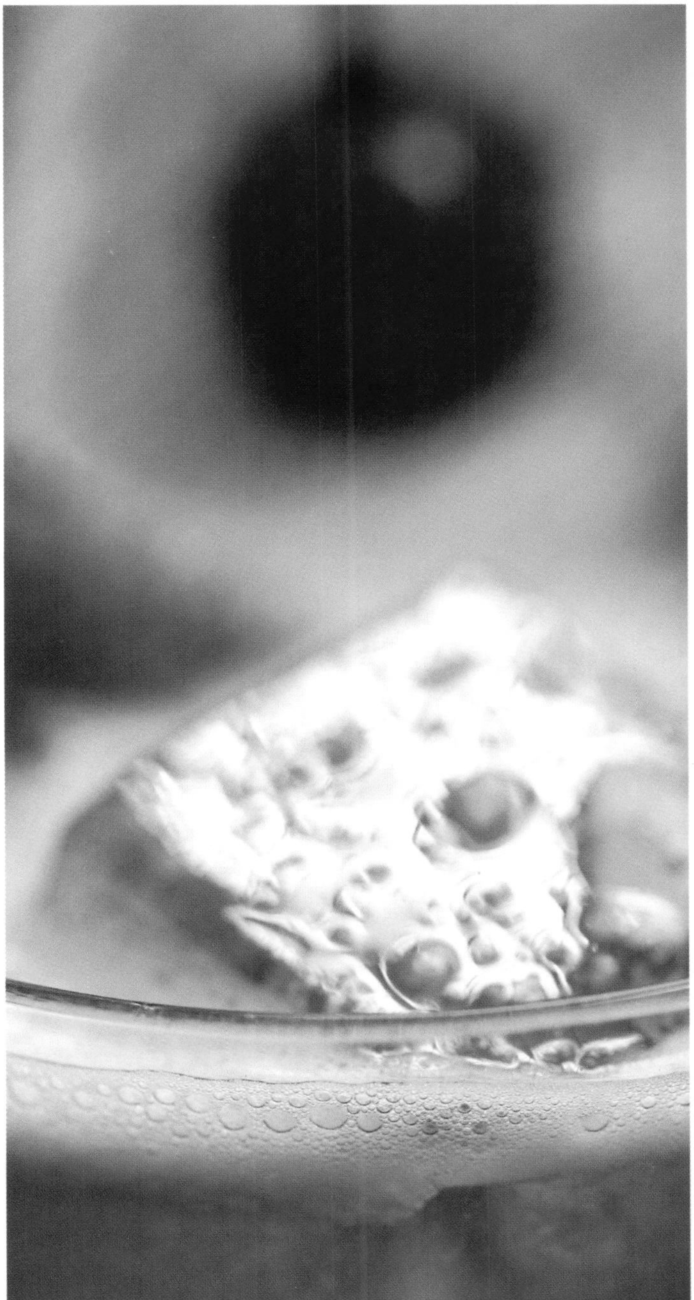

SOURS

Sours are aptly named drinks. Their flavour comes from either lemon or lime juice, which is balanced with sugar. Sours can be based on practically any spirit but the bourbon based Whiskey Sour is by far the most popular. Many (including myself) believe this drink is only properly made when smoothed with a little egg white.

Sours are served either straight-up in a Sour glass (rather like a small flute) or on the rocks in an old-fashioned glass. They are traditionally garnished with a cherry and an orange slice, or sometimes a lemon slice.

SOUTH BEACH

Glass: Martini
Garnish: Orange zest twist
Method: **SHAKE** all ingredients with ice and fine strain into chilled glass.

1	shot(s)	**Campari**
1	shot(s)	**Luxardo Amaretto di Saschira liqueur**
2½	shot(s)	**Freshly squeezed orange juice**
¼	shot(s)	**Sugar (gomme) syrup**

Origin: Created in 1992 by Dale DeGroff, New York City, USA.
Comment: An unusual, bittersweet combination with a strong orange and almond flavour.

SOUTH CHINA BREEZE

Glass: Collins
Garnish: Orange slice
Method: **SHAKE** all ingredients with ice and strain into ice-filled glass.

2	shot(s)	**Orange flavoured vodka**
3	shot(s)	**Freshly squeezed grapefruit juice**
1½	shot(s)	**Lychee syrup from tinned fruit**
3	dashes	**Angostura aromatic bitters**

Comment: Orange and grapefruit with an oriental influence by way of lychee.

SOUTH OF THE BORDER

Glass: Martini
Garnish: Three coffee beans
Method: **SHAKE** all ingredients with ice and fine strain into chilled glass.

2	shot(s)	**Sauza Hornitos tequila**
1	shot(s)	**Kahlúa coffee liqueur**
¾	shot(s)	**Freshly squeezed lime juice**
½	fresh	**Egg white**

Comment: A strange mix of lime and coffee.

SOUTH PACIFIC [NEW]

Glass: Martini
Garnish: Pineapple wedge on rim
Method: Cut passion fruit in half and scoop flesh into shaker. Add other ingredients, **SHAKE** with ice and fine strain into chilled glass.

1	fresh	**Passion fruit**
1	shot(s)	**Soho lychee liqueur**
1	shot(s)	**Ketel One Citroen vodka**
1	shot(s)	**Pressed pineapple juice**
½	shot(s)	**Freshly squeezed lime juice**

Origin: Adapted from a recipe created by Wayne Collins, London, England.

SOUTH PACIFIC BREEZE

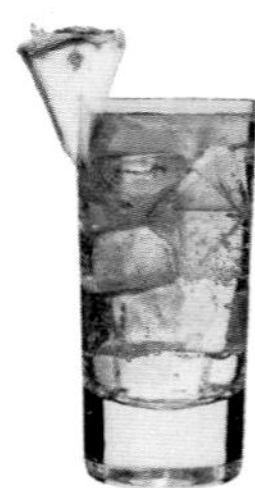

Glass: Collins
Garnish: Pineapple wedge on rim
Method: **POUR** gin and Galliano into ice-filled glass. **TOP** with 7-Up to just below the rim. **DRIZZLE** blue curaçao around top of drink (it will sink leaving strings of blue). Serve with straws.

1½	shot(s)	**Plymouth gin**
¾	shot(s)	**Galliano liqueur**
Top up with		**7-Up**
¾	shot(s)	**Blue curaçao liqueur**

Comment: Quite sweet but flavoursome – looks great.

SOUTHERN CIDER

Glass: Martini
Garnish: Lime wedge
Method: **SHAKE** all ingredients with ice and fine strain into chilled glass.

2	shot(s)	**Southern Comfort liqueur**
1	shot(s)	**Freshly squeezed lime juice**
1½	shot(s)	**Cranberry juice**

Origin: Discovered at Opryland Hotel, Nashville, USA.
Comment: Strangely, this cocktail does have a cidery taste.

SOUTHERN MANHATTAN [NEW]

Glass: Martini
Garnish: Orange zest twist
Method: **STIR** all ingredients with ice and strain into chilled glass.

2	shot(s)	**Bourbon whiskey**
1	shot(s)	**Southern Comfort liqueur**
1	shot(s)	**Sweet (rosso) vermouth**
3	dashes	**Peychaud's aromatic bitters**

Origin: Created in by yours truly in August 2005 for Tales of the Cocktail, New Orleans, USA.
Comment: A Manhattan with Southern Comfort and Peychaud's adding a hint of southern flavour.

SOUTHERN MINT COBBLER [NEW]

Glass: Old-fashioned
Garnish: Mint sprig
Method: Lightly **MUDDLE** mint (just to bruise) in base of shaker. Add other ingredients, **SHAKE** with ice and fine strain into glass filled with crushed ice. Serve with straws.

7	fresh	**Mint leaves**
2	shot(s)	**Southern Comfort liqueur**
1	shot(s)	**White peach puree (sweetened)**
½	shot(s)	**Freshly squeezed lemon juice**

Comment: Very fruity and very easy to drink.

SOUTHERN MULE [NEW]

Glass: Collins
Garnish: Lime wedge
Method: SHAKE first three ingredients with ice and strain into ice-filled glass. **TOP** with ginger beer, lightly stir and serve with straws.

2	shot(s)	**Southern Comfort**
1/2	shot(s)	**Freshly squeezed lime juice**
3	dashes	**Angostura aromatic bitters**
Top up with		**ginger beer**

Comment: Tangy, fruity and spiced with ginger.

SOUTHERN PEACH

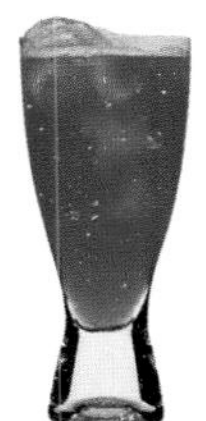

Glass: Collins
Garnish: Lime wedge
Method: SHAKE all ingredients with ice and strain into ice-filled glass. Serve with straws.

1	shot(s)	**Southern Comfort liqueur**
1	shot(s)	**Peach schnapps liqueur**
3	shot(s)	**Cranberry juice**
1	shot(s)	**Freshly squeezed lime juice**

Comment: Fruity and slightly sweet but far from offensive.

SOUTHERN PUNCH

Glass: Collins
Garnish: Pineapple wedge on rim
Method: SHAKE all ingredients with ice and strain into ice-filled glass.

1 1/2	shot(s)	**Southern Comfort liqueur**
1/2	shot(s)	**Jack Daniel's Tennessee whiskey**
2	shot(s)	**Pressed pineapple juice**
1	shot(s)	**Freshly squeezed lemon juice**
1/2	shot(s)	**Sugar (gomme) syrup**
1/2	shot(s)	**Sonoma pomegranate (grenadine) syrup**

Comment: Tropical flavours with the warmth of the liquor trailed by a fresh lemon finish.

SOUTHERN TEA-KNEE

Glass: Martini
Garnish: Apricot slice on rim
Method: SHAKE all ingredients with ice and fine strain into chilled glass.

1	shot(s)	**Southern Comfort liqueur**
1/2	shot(s)	**Plymouth gin**
1/2	shot(s)	**Apricot brandy liqueur**
1/2	shot(s)	**Crème de bananes liqueur**
2	shot(s)	**Strong cold Earl Grey tea**

Origin: Created by yours truly in 2002.
Comment: Sweet fruity flavours balanced by tannic bitterness in the tea.

SOUTHSIDE ROYALE [NEW]

Glass: Martini
Garnish: Mint leaf
Method: Lightly **MUDDLE** (just to bruise) mint in base of shaker. Add next three ingredients, **SHAKE** with ice and fine strain into chilled glass. **TOP** with a splash of champagne.

7	fresh	**Mint leaves**
2	shot(s)	**Plymouth gin**
1	shot(s)	**Freshly squeezed lemon juice**
1/2	shot(s)	**Sugar (gomme) syrup**
Top up with		**Piper-Heidsieck brut champagne**

Variant: Topped with soda (from a siphon, please) in place of champagne this becomes a mere 'Southside'.
Origin: Created during Prohibition, either at a New York City speakeasy called Jack & Charlie's, or at Manhattan's Stork Club, or by Chicago's Southside gang to make their bootleg liquor more palatable.
Comment: A White Lady with fresh mint and champagne.

SOYER AU CHAMPAGNE

Glass: Martini (Parfait glass)
Method: PLACE scoop of ice cream in base of glass. **SHAKE** next three ingredients with ice and strain over ice cream. **TOP** with champagne and serve while foaming with straws that the drinker should use to mix.

1	scoop	**Vanilla ice cream**
1/2	shot(s)	**Rémy Martin cognac**
1/2	shot(s)	**Luxardo maraschino liqueur**
1/2	shot(s)	**Grand Marnier liqueur**
Top up with		**Piper-Heidsieck brut champagne**

Origin: Adapted from a recipe in the 1949 edition of Esquire's Handbook For Hosts. Apparently this was "one of the most popular drinks at Christmas in the continental cafés".
Comment: A unique dessert of a drink.

SPARKLING PERRY

Glass: Flute
Garnish: Pear slice on rim
Method: SHAKE first three ingredients with ice and fine strain into chilled glass. **TOP** with champagne and lightly stir.

3/4	shot(s)	**Poire William eau de vie**
3/4	shot(s)	**Pear & cognac liqueur**
1	shot(s)	**Freshly extracted pear juice**
Top up with		**Piper-Heidsieck brut champagne**

Origin: Created in December 2002 by yours truly.
Comment: Reminiscent of perry (pear cider).

SPENCER COCKTAIL [NEW]

Glass: Martini
Garnish: Orange zest twist (discarded) & maraschino cherry
Method: SHAKE all ingredients with ice and fine strain into chilled glass.

2	shot(s)	Plymouth gin
1	shot(s)	Apricot brandy liqueur
1/4	shot(s)	Freshly squeezed orange juice
1	dash	Angostura aromatic bitters

Origin: Adapted from a recipe in Harry Craddock's 1930 Savoy Cocktail Book.
Comment: To quote Craddock, "Very mellifluous: has a fine and rapid action: for morning work."

SPEYSIDE MARTINI

Glass: Martini
Garnish: Lemon zest twist
Method: MUDDLE grapes in base of shaker. Add other ingredients, **SHAKE** with ice and fine strain into chilled glass.

7	fresh	Seedless white grapes
2	shot(s)	The Famous Grouse Scotch whisky
3/4	shot(s)	Apricot brandy liqueur
3/4	shot(s)	Freshly squeezed grapefruit juice

Origin: Discovered in 2004 at Indigo Yard, Edinburgh, Scotland.
Comment: Scotch, grape juice, apricot liqueur and grapefruit may seem an unlikely combo but they get on well together.

SPICED APPLE DAIQUIRI

Glass: Martini
Garnish: Apple wedge on rim
Method: SHAKE all ingredients with ice and fine strain into chilled glass.

2	shot(s)	Light white rum
1/2	shot(s)	Apple schnapps liqueur
1/4	shot(s)	Goldschläger cinnamon schnapps liqueur
1/2	shot(s)	Freshly squeezed lime juice
3/4	shot(s)	Pressed apple juice

Origin: Created in 1999 by yours truly.
Comment: Sour apple and cinnamon laced with rum.

SPICED CRANBERRY MARTINI

Glass: Martini
Garnish: Cranberry juice & cinnamon rim
Method: MUDDLE cloves in base of shaker. Add other ingredients, **SHAKE** with ice and fine strain into chilled glass.

7	dried	Cloves
1	shot(s)	Cranberry flavoured vodka
1	shot(s)	Pusser's Navy rum
2	shot(s)	Cranberry juice
1/2	shot(s)	Sugar (gomme) syrup

Origin: Created in 2003 by yours truly.
Comment: The cloves and the colour add a festive note to this notional Martini.

SPICED PEAR

Glass: Old-fashioned
Garnish: Pear slice
Method: SHAKE all ingredients with ice and strain into ice-filled glass.

1	shot(s)	Pear & cognac liqueur
1	shot(s)	Spiced rum
1	shot(s)	Freshly extracted pear juice
1/2	shot(s)	Freshly squeezed lime juice
1/2	shot(s)	Sugar (gomme) syrup

Origin: Created in 2002 by James Stewart, Edinburgh, Scotland.
Comment: Just as it says on the tin – spiced pear.

SPICY FINN

Glass: Martini
Garnish: Blueberry or raspberry on rim
Method: MUDDLE ginger in base of shaker. Add other ingredients, **SHAKE** with ice and fine strain into chilled glass.

3	slices	Root ginger (thumb nail sized)
2	shot(s)	Cranberry flavoured vodka
1/2	shot(s)	Campari
1/2	shot(s)	Sugar (gomme) syrup
1	shot(s)	Chilled mineral water (reduce if wet ice)

Origin: Created by Michael Mahe at Hush, London.
Comment: Cranberry vodka, Campari and ginger with a dash of gomme to sweeten things up.

SPICY VEGGY

Glass: Martini
Garnish: Chunk of carrot on rim
Method: MUDDLE coriander seeds in base of shaker. Add other ingredients, **SHAKE** with ice and fine strain into chilled glass.

2	dozen	Coriander seeds
2	shot(s)	Plymouth gin
2	shot(s)	Freshly extracted carrot juice
1/4	shot(s)	Sugar (gomme) syrup
1	pinch	Black pepper
1	pinch	Salt

Origin: Created in 2002 by yours truly.
Comment: Reminiscent of alcoholic carrot and coriander soup.

SPIKED APPLE CIDER (HOT) [NEW]

Glass: Toddy
Garnish: Cinnamon dust
Method: MUDDLE cloves in base of shaker. Add cognac and apple juice, **SHAKE** without ice and fine strain into glass. **WARM** in microwave then **FLOAT** double cream over drink.

2	dried	Cloves
2	shot(s)	Rémy Martin cognac
3	shot(s)	Pressed apple juice
Float		Double (heavy) cream

Origin: Adapted from a drink discovered in 2006 at Double Seven, New York City, USA.
Comment: Warming and lightly spiced under a creamy head.

SPORRAN BREEZE

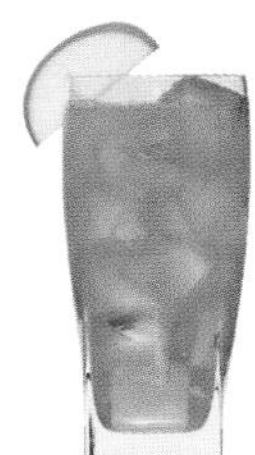

Glass: Collins
Garnish: Apple slice on rim
Method: **SHAKE** all ingredients with ice and strain into ice-filled glass. Serve with straws.

2	shot(s)	**The Famous Grouse Scotch whisky**
1/2	shot(s)	**Passion fruit syrup**
4	shot(s)	**Pressed apple juice**

Origin: Phillip Jeffrey created this drink for me in 2002 at the GE Club, London, England. I take credit (if any's due) for the name.
Comment: As with all simple drinks, the quality and flavour of the three ingredients used greatly affects the end product – choose wisely and you'll have a deliciously fresh blend of malty fruit.

SPRITZ AL BITTER

Glass: Old-fashioned
Garnish: Orange zest twist
Method: **POUR** ingredients into ice-filled glass and lightly stir.

1 1/2	shot(s)	**Campari**
1 1/2	shot(s)	**White wine**
Top up with		**Soda water (club soda)**

Origin: The origins of this Venetian speciality date back to the end of the 19th century when the Austrians ruled the city.
Comment: Basically a Spritzer with a generous splash of Campari – dry and very refreshing.

SPRITZER

Glass: Goblet
Garnish: Lemon zest twist
Method: **POUR** ingredients into chilled glass and lightly stir. No ice!

3	shot(s)	**Chilled dry white wine**
Top up with		**Soda water (club soda)**

Comment: The ultimate 'girlie' drink. To avoid ridicule when diluting a glass of white wine try adding a couple of ice cubes instead.

SPUTNIK

Glass: Martini
Garnish: Orange zest twist
Method: **SHAKE** all ingredients with ice and fine strain into chilled glass.

1	shot(s)	**Ketel One vodka**
1	shot(s)	**Peach schnapps liqueur**
1 1/2	shot(s)	**Freshly squeezed orange juice**
1	shot(s)	**Double (heavy) cream**

Comment: Blasts of fruit cut through this soft creamy drink.

SPUTNIK #2

Glass: Old-fashioned
Garnish: Orange slice
Method: **SHAKE** all ingredients with ice and strain into ice-filled glass.

1	shot(s)	**Light white rum**
1	shot(s)	**Rémy Martin cognac**
2	shot(s)	**Freshly squeezed orange juice**
1/2	shot(s)	**Sugar (gomme) syrup**

Origin: A cocktail served in underground clubs all over the former Eastern Bloc. It was originally made with cheap Cuban rum, Georgian brandy and tinned orange juice.
Comment: Orange, cognac and rum meld well.

SQUASHED FROG

Glass: Shot
Method: Refrigerate ingredients then **LAYER** in chilled glass by carefully pouring in the following order.

1/2	shot(s)	**Sonoma pomegranate (grenadine) syrup**
1/2	shot(s)	**Midori melon liqueur**
1/2	shot(s)	**Warninks advocaat**

Comment: Very sweet. However, the taste is not as offensive as the name might suggest.

STAIRS MARTINI

Glass: Martini
Garnish: Pear slice on rim
Method: **SHAKE** all ingredients with ice and fine strain into chilled glass.

2	shot(s)	**Ketel One vodka**
1	shot(s)	**Freshly extracted pear juice**
1	shot(s)	**Pressed apple juice**
1/4	shot(s)	**Freshly squeezed lemon juice**
1/4	shot(s)	**Sugar (gomme) syrup**
2	dashes	**Fee Brothers orange bitters**

Origin: Created in 2000 by Ian Baldwin at the GE Club, London, England.
Comment: In London's cockney rhyming slang 'apples and pears' means stairs. So this tasty cocktail is appropriately named.

STANLEY COCKTAIL [NEW]

Glass: Martini
Garnish: Lemon zest twist
Method: **SHAKE** all ingredients with ice and fine strain into chilled glass.

1 1/2	shot(s)	**Plymouth gin**
1 1/2	shot(s)	**Light white rum**
1/2	shot(s)	**Freshly squeezed lemon juice**
1/2	shot(s)	**Sonoma pomegranate (grenadine) syrup**

Origin: Adapted from a recipe in Harry Craddock's 1930 Savoy Cocktail Book.
Comment: Salmon pink and reminiscent of a Daiquiri with a splash of gin.

THE STAR #1 [NEW]

Glass: Martini
Garnish: Olive on stick
Method: STIR all ingredients with ice and fine strain into chilled glass.

1½	shot(s)	**Calvados or applejack brandy**
1½	shot(s)	**Sweet (rosso) vermouth**
1	dash	**Angostura aromatic bitters**

Variant: T.N.T. Special - with the addition of a dash of sugar.
Origin: Recipe from Harry Craddock's 1930 Savoy Cocktail Book. Created in the 1870s by a bartender at the legendary Manhattan Club, which once stood at the north corner of 34th Street and 5th Avenue, New York City.
Comment: Like many old classics, this drink needs dilution so stir until you're bored and thirsty.

STARS & STRIPES SHOT [NEW]

Glass: Shot
Method: Refrigerate ingredients then **LAYER** in chilled glass by carefully pouring in the following order.

½	shot(s)	**Sisca crème de cassis**
½	shot(s)	**Luxardo maraschino liqueur**
½	shot(s)	**Green Chartreuse**

Origin: Adapted from a recipe in Harry Craddock's 1930 Savoy Cocktail Book.
Comment: The taste is too sweet and the colours aren't quite right. A shame.

STEALTH

Glass: Shot
Method: Refrigerate ingredients then **LAYER** in chilled glass by carefully pouring in the following order.

½	shot(s)	**Kahlúa coffee liqueur**
½	shot(s)	**Tuaca Italian liqueur**
½	shot(s)	**Baileys Irish cream liqueur**

Origin: Created by Poul Jensen, at St. James', Brighton, England. Another of the B-52 family of drinks, but named after Stealth bombers instead.
Comment: Reminiscent of a vanilla cappuccino.

STEEL BOTTOM

Glass: Collins
Method: POUR ingredients into glass, lightly stir and serve with straws.

1	shot(s)	**Wray & Nephew overproof rum**
Top up with		**Red Stripe beer**

Origin: A very popular drink in Jamaica.
Comment: For those who like their beer turbo charged.

STEEP FLIGHT

Glass: Collins
Garnish: Apple or pear slice
Method: SHAKE all ingredients with ice and fine strain into ice-filled glass.

1	shot(s)	**Calvados (or applejack brandy)**
1	shot(s)	**Pear flavoured vodka**
1	shot(s)	**Pear & cognac liqueur**
3	shot(s)	**Pressed apple juice**

Origin: Created in 2005 by yours truly. Awarded a Gold in Long Drink category at the Drinks International Bartender's Challenge on 31st May 2006.
Comment: 'Apples and pears' is the cockney rhyming slang for stairs, hence the flavours in this particular flight.

STILETTO

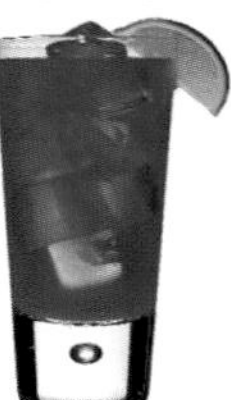

Glass: Collins
Garnish: Lime wedge
Method: SHAKE all ingredients with ice and strain into ice-filled glass.

2	shot(s)	**Bourbon whiskey**
1	shot(s)	**Luxardo Amaretto di Saschira liqueur**
2½	shot(s)	**Cranberry juice**
½	shot(s)	**Freshly squeezed lime juice**
¼	shot(s)	**Sugar (gomme) syrup**

Comment: Long and fruity with a hint of bourbon and almond.

STINGER [UPDATED]

Glass: Old-fashioned
Garnish: Mint sprig
Method: SHAKE all ingredients with ice and strain into glass filled with crushed ice. Serve with straws.

2	shot(s)	**Rémy Martin cognac**
¾	shot(s)	**White crème de menthe**

Origin: In the classic film 'High Society', Bing Crosby explains to Grace Kelly how the Stinger gained its name: "It's a Stinger. It removes the sting."
Comment: A refreshing, peppermint and cognac digestif.

STONE & GRAVEL

Glass: Old-fashioned
Method: POUR ingredients into glass filled with crushed ice and stir.

1	shot(s)	**Wray & Nephew overproof rum**
3	shot(s)	**Stone's green ginger wine**

Origin: A popular drink in Jamaica.
Comment: Simple, strong and surprisingly good.

●●●●○

STONEY POINT MEADOW

Glass: Martini
Garnish: Lemon zest twist
Method: **SHAKE** all ingredients with ice and fine strain into chilled glass.

2½	shot(s)	**Bourbon whiskey**
¾	shot(s)	**Elderflower cordial**
¾	shot(s)	**Vanilla sugar syrup**
½	fresh	**Egg white**

Origin: Created in 2002 by Marie-Claire Rose at Blue Bar, Edinburgh, Scotland, and named after Albert Blanton, a nineteenth-century bourbon distiller who built a house called Stoney Point Mansion.
Comment: Bourbon tamed and smoothed with vanilla and floral flavours.

●●●●○

STORK CLUB

Glass: Martini
Garnish: Orange zest twist
Method: **SHAKE** all ingredients with ice and fine strain into chilled glass.

1	shot(s)	**Plymouth gin**
1	shot(s)	**Cointreau / triple sec**
1	shot(s)	**Freshly squeezed orange juice**
½	shot(s)	**Freshly squeezed lime juice**
2	dashes	**Fee Brothers orange bitters (optional)**

Comment: Orange and gin with a souring splash of lime juice.

●●●●○

STRAITS SLING [NEW]

Glass: Sling
Garnish: Orange slice & cherry (sail)
Method: **SHAKE** first six ingredients with ice and strain into ice-filled glass. **TOP** with soda, lightly stir and serve with straws.

2	shot(s)	**Plymouth gin**
½	shot(s)	**Bénédictine D.O.M. liqueur**
½	shot(s)	**Kirsch eau de vie**
1	shot(s)	**Freshly squeezed lemon juice**
2	dashes	**Fee Brothers orange bitters**
2	dashes	**Angostura aromatic bitters**
Top up with		**Soda water (club soda)**

Origin: Thought to be the original name of the Singapore Sling. Conjecture, partly based on a reference to 'Kirsch' in Embury's Fine Art of Mixing Drinks, has it that the drink was originally based on cherry eau de vie and not the cherry liqueur used in most Singapore Sling recipes today.
Comment: Dry cherry and gin come to the fore in this long, refreshing drink.

DRINKS ARE GRADED AS FOLLOWS:

● DISGUSTING ●◐ PRETTY AWFUL ●● BEST AVOIDED
●●◐ DISAPPOINTING ●●● ACCEPTABLE ●●●◐ GOOD
●●●● RECOMMENDED ●●●●◐ HIGHLY RECOMMENDED
●●●●● OUTSTANDING / EXCEPTIONAL

●●●◐○

STRASBERI SLING

Glass: Sling
Garnish: Mint sprig
Method: **SHAKE** all ingredients with ice and strain into ice-filled glass.

1½	shot(s)	**Raspberry flavoured vodka**
1	shot(s)	**Pimm's No. 1 Cup**
½	shot(s)	**Sugar (gomme) syrup**
1	shot(s)	**Freshly squeezed lime juice**
3	shot(s)	**Pressed apple juice**

Origin: Created in 2002 by Alex Kammerling, London, England.
Comment: Raspberry and apple combine beautifully in this refreshing drink with its clean citrus tang.

●●●●○

STRAWBERRY & BALSAMIC MOJITO [NEW]

Glass: Collins
Garnish: Strawberry & lime wedge
Method: **MUDDLE** strawberries in base of shaker. Add next five ingredients, **SHAKE** with ice and fine strain into chilled glass. **TOP** with soda.

7	fresh	**Strawberries**
2	shot(s)	**Light white rum**
¾	shot(s)	**Freshly squeezed lime juice**
¼	shot(s)	**White balsamic vinegar**
½	shot(s)	**Sugar (gomme) syrup**
12	fresh	**Mint leaves (torn)**
Top up with		**Soda water**

Origin: Adapted from a drink created in 2005 by Simon Warneford at Blanch House, Brighton, England.
Comment: A fruity twist on the classic Mojito.

●●●◐○

STRAWBERRY BLONDE MARTINI

Glass: Martini
Garnish: Float basil leaf
Method: **MUDDLE** basil in mixing glass. Add other ingredients, **STIR** with ice and fine strain into chilled glass.

4	fresh	**Basil leaves**
2½	shot(s)	**Raspberry flavoured vodka**
½	shot(s)	**Dry vermouth**
½	shot(s)	**Crème de fraise (strawberry) liqueur**
1/8	shot(s)	**Sugar (gomme) syrup**

Origin: Adapted from a recipe discovered in 2003 at Oxo Tower Bar, London, England.
Comment: Berry vodka dominates with hints of strawberry and basil.

●●●◐○

STRAWBERRY COSMO

Glass: Martini
Garnish: Strawberry on rim
Method: **SHAKE** all ingredients with ice and fine strain into chilled glass.

2	shot(s)	**Ketel One Citroen vodka**
¾	shot(s)	**Crème de fraise (strawberry) liqueur**
1¼	shot(s)	**Cranberry juice**
½	shot(s)	**Freshly squeezed lime juice**

Origin: Formula by yours truly in 2004.
Comment: Strawberry liqueur replaces the usual orange liqueur in this contemporary classic.

STRAWBERRY DAIQUIRI

Glass: Martini
Garnish: Strawberry on rim
Method: **MUDDLE** strawberries in base of shaker. Add other ingredients, **SHAKE** with ice and fine strain into chilled glass.

7	fresh	**Hulled strawberries**
2	shot(s)	**Light white rum**
1/2	shot(s)	**Freshly squeezed lime juice**
1/4	shot(s)	**Sugar (gomme) syrup**

Origin: A popular drink in Cuba where it is known as a Daiquiri de Fresa.
Comment: Makes strawberries and cream appear very dull.

THE STRAWBERRY ÉCLAIR

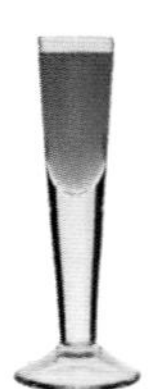

Glass: Shot
Method: **SHAKE** all ingredients with ice and fine strain into chilled glass.

1/2	shot(s)	**Frangelico hazelnut liqueur**
1/2	shot(s)	**Crème de fraise (strawberry) liqueur**
1/4	shot(s)	**Freshly squeezed lime juice**

Origin: This drink heralds from Australia where it is a popular shot.
Comment: Far from sophisticated (some would say like Australia) but very appropriately named..

STRAWBERRY FROZEN DAIQUIRI

Glass: Martini
Garnish: Split strawberry
Method: **BLEND** all ingredients with 6oz scoop of crushed ice.

2	shot(s)	**Light white rum**
3/4	shot(s)	**Freshly squeezed lime juice**
1/2	shot(s)	**Sugar (gomme) syrup**
5	fresh	**Hulled strawberries (chopped)**

Comment: A delicious twist on a classic – Strawberry Mivvi for grown-ups.

STRAWBERRY MARGARITA

Glass: Martini
Garnish: Strawberry on rim
Method: **MUDDLE** strawberries in base of shaker. Add other ingredients, **SHAKE** with ice and fine strain into chilled glass.

5	fresh	**Hulled strawberries**
2	shot(s)	**Sauza Hornitos tequila**
1	shot(s)	**Freshly squeezed lime juice**
3/4	shot(s)	**Sugar (gomme) syrup**

Origin: Formula by yours truly in 2004.
Comment: Fresh strawberries combine well with tequila in this fruit margarita.

STRAWBERRY MARTINI

Glass: Martini
Garnish: Strawberry on rim
Method: **MUDDLE** strawberries in base of shaker. Add other ingredients, **SHAKE** with ice and fine strain into chilled glass.

5	fresh	**Hulled strawberries (chopped)**
2 1/2	shot(s)	**Ketel One vodka**
1/2	shot(s)	**Sugar (gomme) syrup**
2	grinds	**Black pepper**

Origin: Created by yours truly in 2004.
Comment: Rich strawberries fortified with vodka and a hint of pepper spice.

STRAWBERRY 'N' BALSAMIC MARTINI

Glass: Martini
Garnish: Strawberry on rim
Method: **MUDDLE** strawberries in base of shaker. Add other ingredients, **SHAKE** with ice and fine strain into chilled glass.

5	fresh	**Hulled strawberries (chopped)**
2 1/2	shot(s)	**Ketel One vodka**
1/8	shot(s)	**Balsamic vinegar**
1/2	shot(s)	**Sugar (gomme) syrup**

Origin: My version of a drink that became popular in London in 2002 and I believe originated in Che.
Comment: The balsamic adds a little extra interest to the fortified strawberries.

STRUDEL MARTINI

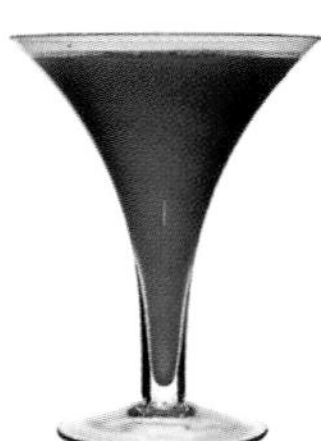

Glass: Martini
Garnish: Dust with cinnamon powder
Method: **SHAKE** all ingredients with ice and fine strain into chilled glass.

1 1/2	shot(s)	**Ketel One vodka**
1/2	shot(s)	**Pedro Ximénez sherry**
3/4	shot(s)	**Pressed apple juice**
1/2	shot(s)	**Double (heavy) cream**
1/2	shot(s)	**Milk**

Origin: Created in 2002 by Jason Borthwick, Tiles, Edinburgh, Scotland.
Comment: Still think sherry is just for Granny?

STUPID CUPID

Glass: Martini
Garnish: Lemon zest twist
Method: **SHAKE** all ingredients with ice and fine strain into chilled glass.

2	shot(s)	**Ketel One Citroen vodka**
1/2	shot(s)	**Plymouth sloe gin liqueur**
1	shot(s)	**Freshly squeezed lime juice**
1/2	shot(s)	**Sugar (gomme) syrup**

Comment: Citrussy with subtle sloe gin.

SUBURBAN [NEW]

Glass: Old-fashioned
Garnish: Orange zest twist
Method: **STIR** all ingredients with ice and strain into ice-filled glass.

$1^1/_2$	shot(s)	**Bourbon whiskey**
$^3/_4$	shot(s)	**Aged rum**
$^3/_4$	shot(s)	**Tawny port**
1	dash	**Fee Brothers orange bitters**
1	dash	**Angostura aromatic bitters**

Origin: Created at New York's old Waldorf-Astoria Hotel (the Empire State Building occupies the site today) for James R Keene, a racehorse owner whose steeds ran in the Suburban Handicap at Brooklyn's Sheepshead Bay track.
Comment: An interesting alternative to an Old-fashioned.

SUITABLY FRANK

Glass: Shot
Method: Refrigerate ingredients then **LAYER** in chilled glass by carefully pouring in the following order.

$^1/_2$	shot(s)	**Cuarenta Y Tres (Licor 43) liqueur**
$^1/_2$	shot(s)	**Cherry (brandy) liqueur**
$^1/_2$	shot(s)	**Ketel One vodka**

Comment: Frankly – it's a good shot.

SUMMER BREEZE

Glass: Collins
Garnish: Half slice orange
Method: **SHAKE** all ingredients with ice and strain into ice-filled glass.

2	shot(s)	**Ketel One vodka**
2	shot(s)	**Cranberry juice**
2	shot(s)	**Pressed apple juice**
$^1/_2$	shot(s)	**Elderflower cordial**
1/8	shot(s)	**Freshly squeezed lime juice**

Origin: Created in 1998 by Dick Bradsell, London, England.
Comment: Cranberry, apple and elderflower fortified with vodka.

SUMMER ROSE MARTINI

Glass: Martini
Garnish: Red rose petal (edible)
Method: **STIR** first three ingredients with ice and strain into chilled glass. **POUR** grenadine into the centre of the drink. This should sink and settle to form a red layer in the base of the glass.

$1^1/_2$	shot(s)	**Ketel One vodka**
$^3/_4$	shot(s)	**White crème de cacao liqueur**
$^1/_2$	shot(s)	**Soho lychee liqueur**
$^1/_2$	shot(s)	**Sonoma pomegranate (grenadine) syrup**

Origin: Created in 2003 by Davide Lovison at Isola Bar, London, England.
Comment: This red and white layered drink could have been named War of the Roses. Unless you've a sweet tooth don't mix the factions – sip from the chocolate and lychee top and stop when you hit red.

SUMMER TIME MARTINI

Glass: Martini
Garnish: Kumquat
Method: **SHAKE** all ingredients with ice and fine strain into chilled glass.

$1^1/_2$	shot(s)	**Plymouth gin**
1	shot(s)	**Grand Marnier liqueur**
$1^1/_2$	shot(s)	**Freshly squeezed orange juice**
$^1/_4$	shot(s)	**Sonoma pomegranate (grenadine) syrup**

Comment: Smooth, gin laced fruit for a summer's day.

SUMO IN A SIDECAR [NEW]

Glass: Martini
Garnish: Orange zest twist
Method: **SHAKE** all ingredients with ice and fine strain into chilled glass.

$2^1/_2$	shot(s)	**Sake**
1	shot(s)	**Apricot brandy liqueur**
$^1/_2$	shot(s)	**Freshly squeezed lemon juice**

Comment: Hints of sake but retains the Sidecar style.

SUN KISSED VIRGIN (MOCKTAIL)

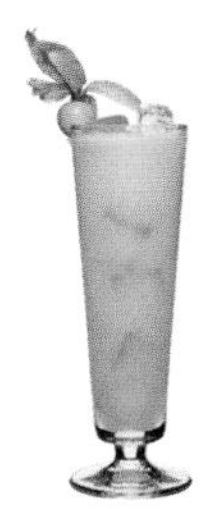

Glass: Sling
Garnish: Physalis (cape gooseberry) on rim
Method: **SHAKE** all ingredients with ice and strain into ice-filled glass.

2	shot(s)	**Freshly squeezed orange juice**
2	shot(s)	**Pressed pineapple juice**
1	shot(s)	**Freshly squeezed lime juice**
$^1/_2$	shot(s)	**Almond (orgeat) sugar syrup**

Comment: Golden, slightly sweet and very fruity – just like a Sun Kissed Virgin should be. Sorry.

THE SUN SALUTATION [NEW]

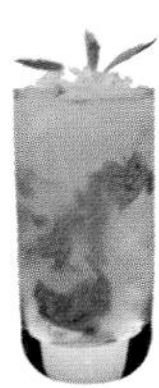

Glass: Collins
Garnish: Berries & mint sprig
Method: **MUDDLE** mint in base of shaker. Add next three ingredients, **SHAKE** with ice and fine strain into ice-filled glass. **TOP** with soda.

10	fresh	**Mint leaves**
1	shot(s)	**Ketel One vodka**
$1^1/_2$	shot(s)	**Soho lychee liqueur**
$^3/_4$	shot(s)	**Freshly squeezed lemon juice**
Top up with		**Soda (club soda)**

Origin: Adapted from a recipe by David Nepove, Enrico's Bar & Restaurant, San Francisco.
Comment: Mint with a hint of lychee – long and refreshing.

SUNDOWNER #1

Glass: Martini
Garnish: Orange zest twist
Method: **SHAKE** all ingredients with ice and fine strain into chilled glass.

2 shot(s) **Rémy Martin cognac**
1/2 shot(s) **Grand Marnier liqueur**
1/2 shot(s) **Freshly squeezed orange juice**
1/4 shot(s) **Freshly squeezed lemon juice**
3/4 shot(s) **Chilled mineral water (omit if wet ice)**

Variant: Red Lion
Origin: This cocktail is popular in South Africa where it is made with locally produced brandy and a local orange liqueur called Van der Hum.
Comment: Cognac and orange served 'up'.

SUNDOWNER #2 [UPDATED]

Glass: Old-fashioned
Garnish: Mint sprig
Method: **SHAKE** all ingredients with ice and strain into ice-filled glass.

1 1/2 shot(s) **Southern Comfort liqueur**
3/4 shot(s) **Grand Marnier liqueur**
2 shot(s) **Sauvignon Blanc wine**

Origin: Adapted from a cocktail created in 2002 by Gary Regis at Bed Bar, London, England.
Comment: Subtle meld of summer and citrus flavours.

SUNNY BREEZE

Glass: Collins
Garnish: Half orange slice
Method: **SHAKE** all ingredients with ice and strain into glass filled with crushed ice.

1 1/2 shot(s) **Pernod anis**
1/2 shot(s) **Cointreau / triple sec**
1/2 shot(s) **Grand Marnier liqueur**
3 shot(s) **Freshly squeezed pink grapefruit juice**

Origin: Created in 2003 by yours truly.
Comment: A suitably named refreshing long drink with an adult dry edge and kick.

SUNSHINE COCKTAIL #1

Glass: Martini
Garnish: Pineapple wedge on rim
Method: **SHAKE** all ingredients with ice and fine strain into chilled glass.

1 1/2 shot(s) **Light white rum**
1 1/2 shot(s) **Dry vermouth**
1 1/2 shot(s) **Pressed pineapple juice**
1/8 shot(s) **Sonoma pomegranate (grenadine) syrup**

Origin: Adapted from a recipe in my 1949 copy of Esquire's Handbook For Hosts.
Comment: Light, fruity and a tad on the sweet side, but could well brighten your day.

SUNSHINE COCKTAIL #2 [NEW]

Glass: Martini
Garnish: Lemon zest twist
Method: **SHAKE** all ingredients with ice and fine strain into chilled glass.

1 1/2 shot(s) **Light white rum**
1 1/2 shot(s) **Dry vermouth**
1/4 shot(s) **Sisca crème de cassis**
1/4 shot(s) **Freshly squeezed lemon juice**

Origin: Adapted from a recipe in Harry Craddock's 1930 Savoy Cocktail Book.
Comment: More a sunset but fruity, flavoursome and well-balanced all the same.

SUNSTROKE [UPDATED]

Glass: Martini
Garnish: Orange zest twist (round to make sun)
Method: **SHAKE** all ingredients with ice and fine strain into chilled glass.

1 shot(s) **Ketel One vodka**
1 shot(s) **Cointreau / triple sec**
2 shot(s) **Freshly squeezed pink grapefruit juice**

Comment: Fruity but balanced. One to sip in the shade.

SUPERMINTY-CHOCOLATINI

Glass: Martini
Garnish: Chocolate powder rim
Method: **SHAKE** all ingredients with ice and fine strain into chilled glass.

2 shot(s) **Ketel One vodka**
1 shot(s) **White crème de cacao liqueur**
1 shot(s) **White crème de menthe**

Comment: Obvious but nicely flavoured.

SURFER ON A.C.D.

Glass: Shot
Method: **SHAKE** first two ingredients with ice and fine strain into chilled glass. **FLOAT** Jägermeister.

1/2 shot(s) **Malibu coconut rum liqueur**
3/4 shot(s) **Pressed pineapple juice**
1/4 shot(s) **Jägermeister liqueur**

Comment: The spirity herbal topping counters the sweet coconut and pineapple base.

DRINKS ARE GRADED AS FOLLOWS:

● DISGUSTING ●◐ PRETTY AWFUL ●● BEST AVOIDED
●●◐ DISAPPOINTING ●●● ACCEPTABLE ●●●◐ GOOD
●●●● RECOMMENDED ●●●●◐ HIGHLY RECOMMENDED
●●●●● OUTSTANDING / EXCEPTIONAL

THE SUZY WONG MARTINI [NEW]

Glass: Martini
Garnish: Orange zest twist
Method: MUDDLE basil in base of shaker. Add other ingredients, **SHAKE** with ice and fine strain into chilled glass.

7	fresh	**Basil leaves**
2	shot(s)	**Orange flavoured vodka**
1/2	shot(s)	**Grand Marnier liqueur**
1	shot(s)	**Freshly squeezed orange juice**
1/2	shot(s)	**Freshly squeezed lime juice**
1/4	shot(s)	**Sugar (gomme) syrup**

Origin: Discovered in 2005 at Suzy Wong, Amsterdam, The Netherlands.
Comment: Fresh tasting orange with a hint of basil.

SWAMP WATER

Glass: Collins
Garnish: Lime wedge & mint leaf
Method: SHAKE all ingredients with ice and strain into ice-filled glass.

1 1/2	shot(s)	**Green Chartreuse**
4	shot(s)	**Pressed pineapple juice**
1/2	shot(s)	**Freshly squeezed lime juice**

Comment: Long and refreshing - the herbal taste of Chartreuse combined with the fruitiness of pineapple.

SWEDISH BLUE MARTINI

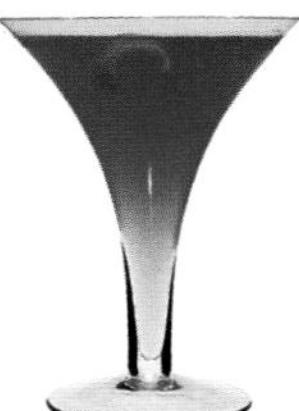

Glass: Martini
Garnish: Orange peel twist
Method: SHAKE all ingredients with ice and fine strain into chilled glass.

2	shot(s)	**Ketel One vodka**
1/2	shot(s)	**Blue curaçao liqueur**
1/2	shot(s)	**Peach schnapps liqueur**
1/4	shot(s)	**Freshly squeezed lime juice**
1/4	shot(s)	**Sugar (gomme) syrup**
2	dashes	**Fee Brothers orange bitters**
1/2	shot(s)	**Chilled mineral water (omit if wet ice)**

Origin: Created in 1999 by Timothy Schofield at Teatro, London, England.
Comment: A fruity, blue concoction laced with vodka. Slightly sweet.

FOR MORE INFORMATION SEE OUR INGREDIENTS APPENDIX ON PAGE 322

SWIZZLE

Swizzles originated in the Caribbean. They are sour style drinks that, distinctively, must be churned with a swizzle stick.

Originally a twig with a few forked branches, today swizzle sticks are usually made of metal or plastic and have several blades or fingers attached to the base at right angles to the shaft. To use one, simply immerse the blades in the drink, hold the shaft between the palms of both hands and rotate the stick rapidly by sliding your hands back and forth against it. If you do not have a bona fide swizzle stick, use a barspoon in the same manner.

Swizzles can be served as short drinks or lengthened with mineral water.

SWEET LOUISE [UPDATED]

Glass: Martini
Garnish: Blackberry
Method: Cut passion fruit in half and scoop out flesh into shaker. Add other ingredients, **SHAKE** with ice and fine strain into chilled glass.

1	fresh	**Passion fruit**
1	shot(s)	**Raspberry flavoured vodka**
½	shot(s)	**Chambord black raspberry liqueur**
½	shot(s)	**Luxardo Amaretto di Saschira liqueur**
¾	shot(s)	**Freshly squeezed lime juice.**
¼	shot(s)	**Sonoma pomegranate (grenadine) syrup**

Origin: Created in 2000 at Monte's Club, London, England
Comment: Lots of contrasting flavours but she's a sweet girl.

SWEET SCIENCE

Glass: Martini
Garnish: Orange zest twist
Method: SHAKE all ingredients with ice and fine strain into chilled glass.

2	shot(s)	**The Famous Grouse Scotch whisky**
¾	shot(s)	**Drambuie liqueur**
1½	shot(s)	**Freshly squeezed orange juice**

Origin: Created by Charles Schumann, Munich, Germany.
Comment: Herbal Scotch and orange.

SWEET TART

Glass: Sling
Garnish: Sugar rim & redcurrants
Method: SHAKE first four ingredients with ice and strain into ice-filled glass. **TOP** with 7-Up.

2	shot(s)	**Ketel One vodka**
¾	shot(s)	**Chambord black raspberry liqueur**
¾	shot(s)	**Luxardo Amaretto di Saschira liqueur**
1	shot(s)	**Freshly squeezed lime juice**
Top up with		**7-Up**

Comment: As the name suggests, a fruity combination of sweet and sour.

SWIZZLE [NEW]

Glass: Old-fashioned
Garnish: Fruit or mint sprigs
Method: POUR ingredients into glass filled with crushed ice. **SWIZZLE** with a swizzle stick and serve with straws.

2	shot(s)	**Liquor (rum, brandy, gin or whiskey etc.)**
½	shot(s)	**Fresh lemon or lime juice**
½	shot(s)	**Sugar (gomme) syrup or liqueur**

Variants: With rum try orgeat syrup or Velvet Falernum in place of the sugar syrup. With whiskey try Chartreuse.
Origin: Adapted from a recipe purloined from David Embury's classic book, The Fine Art of Mixing Drinks.
Comment: Match the appropriate citrus juice and sweetener to your spirit and you'll have a superb drink.

TAILOR MADE [NEW]

Glass: Martini
Garnish: Grapefruit zest twist
Method: STIR honey with bourbon in base of shaker to dissolve honey. Add other ingredients, **SHAKE** with ice and fine strain into chilled glass.

1	spoon	**Runny honey**
1½	shot(s)	**Bourbon whiskey**
¼	shot(s)	**Velvet Falernum liqueur**
1	shot(s)	**Freshly squeezed pink grapefruit juice**
1	shot(s)	**Cranberry juice**

Origin: Created by Dale DeGroff, New York City, USA.
Comment: Light, balanced fruit and bourbon.

TAINTED CHERRY

Glass: Martini
Garnish: Maraschino cherry
Method: SHAKE all ingredients with ice and fine strain into chilled glass.

1¾	shot(s)	**Ketel One vodka**
¾	shot(s)	**Cherry (brandy) liqueur**
1¾	shot(s)	**Freshly squeezed orange juice**

Comment: Orange and cherry combine to produce a flavour rather like amaretto.

TANGO MARTINI #1 [UPDATED]

Glass: Martini
Garnish: Orange zest twist
Method: SHAKE all ingredients with ice and fine strain into chilled glass.

1½	shot(s)	**Plymouth gin**
½	shot(s)	**Sweet (rosso) vermouth**
½	shot(s)	**Dry vermouth**
½	shot(s)	**Cointreau/triple sec**
1	shot(s)	**Freshly squeezed orange juice**

Origin: Adapted from a recipe in Harry Craddock's 1930 Savoy Cocktail Book.
Comment: Balanced and complex with hints of gin and orange.

TANGO MARTINI #2

Glass: Martini
Garnish: Orange zest twist
Method: SHAKE all ingredients with ice and fine strain into chilled glass.

1¾	shot(s)	**Plymouth gin**
¾	shot(s)	**Passoã passion fruit liqueur**
2	shot(s)	**Freshly squeezed grapefruit juice**
¼	shot(s)	**Sugar (gomme) syrup**

Origin: Adapted from a drink discovered in 2003 at the Bellagio, Las Vegas, USA.
Comment: Floral and balanced.

TANTRIS SIDECAR

Glass: Martini
Garnish: Lemon zest twist
Method: SHAKE all ingredients with ice and fine strain into chilled glass.

1½	shot(s)	**Calvados or applejack brandy**
¼	shot(s)	**Cointreau / triple sec**
½	shot(s)	**Green Chartreuse**
¼	shot(s)	**Freshly squeezed lemon juice**
2	shot(s)	**Pressed pineapple juice**

Origin: Adapted from a drink created by Audrey Saunders at Bemelmans Bar at The Carlyle Hotel, New York City, USA.
Comment: A Sidecar with extra interest courtesy of Chartreuse, pineapple and Calvados.

TARRABERRY'TINI

Glass: Martini
Garnish: Tarragon sprig
Method: MUDDLE tarragon in base of shaker. Add other ingredients, **SHAKE** with ice and fine strain into chilled glass.

2	sprigs	**Fresh tarragon**
1½	shot(s)	**Cranberry flavoured vodka**
¼	shot(s)	**Pernod anis**
2	shot(s)	**Cranberry juice**
¼	shot(s)	**Freshly squeezed lemon juice**

Origin: Created in 2003 by yours truly.
Comment: Cranberry with subtle hints of tarragon and lemon.

TARTE AUX POMMES

Glass: Collins
Garnish: Apple chevron
Method: SHAKE all ingredients with ice and strain into ice-filled glass.

1	shot(s)	**Calvados or applejack brandy**
½	shot(s)	**Sisca crème de cassis**
¼	shot(s)	**Goldschläger cinnamon schnapps**
4	shot(s)	**Cranberry juice**
3	dashes	**Angostura aromatic bitters**

Origin: Created in 2001 by Jamie Stephenson at The Lock, Manchester, England.
Comment: Rich in flavour and well balanced.

TARTE TATIN MARTINI

Glass: Martini
Garnish: Cinnamon dust
Method: SHAKE first three ingredients with ice and strain into chilled glass. **SHAKE** cream with ice and carefully pour so as to **LAYER** over drink.

2	shot(s)	**Vanilla flavoured vodka**
¾	shot(s)	**Apple schnapps liqueur**
¾	shot(s)	**Cartron caramel liqueur**
2	shot(s)	**Double (heavy) cream**

Origin: Created in 2003 by yours truly. The name means a tart of caramelised apples cooked under a pastry lid, a dish created by the Tatin sisters.
Comment: A creamy top hides a vanilla, apple and caramel combo.

TARTINI

Glass: Martini
Garnish: Raspberry
Method: MUDDLE raspberries in base of shaker. Add other ingredients, **SHAKE** with ice and fine strain into chilled glass.

12	fresh	**Raspberries**
2	shot(s)	**Raspberry flavoured vodka**
½	shot(s)	**Chambord black raspberry liqueur**
1½	shot(s)	**Cranberry juice**

Origin: Adapted from a cocktail I found at Soho Grand, New York City, USA.
Comment: Rich raspberry flavour, well balanced with bite.

TATANKA

Glass: Old-fashioned
Garnish: Apple slice
Method: SHAKE all ingredients with ice and strain into ice-filled glass.

2	shot(s)	**Zubrówka bison vodka**
2½	shot(s)	**Pressed apple juice**

Origin: This Polish drink takes its name from the film 'Dances with Wolves'. Tatanka is a Native American word for buffalo and refers to the bison grass flavoured vodka the cocktail is based on.
Comment: The taste of this excellent drink (which is equally good served straight-up) is a little reminiscent of Earl Grey tea.

TATANKA ROYALE

Glass: Flute
Garnish: Apple slice
Method: SHAKE first two ingredients with ice and fine strain into chilled glass. **TOP** with champagne.

1	shot(s)	**Zubrówka bison vodka**
1	shot(s)	**Pressed apple juice**
Top up with		**Piper-Heidsieck brut champagne**

Origin: Discovered in 2004 at Indigo Yard, Edinburgh, Scotland.
Comment: Champagne with a subtle, grassy hint of apple.

TAWNY-TINI

Glass: Martini
Garnish: Orange zest twist
Method: SHAKE all ingredients with ice and fine strain into chilled glass.

2	shot(s)	**Ketel One vodka**
2	shot(s)	**Tawny port**
¼	shot(s)	**Maple syrup**

Comment: Dry yet rich. Port combines wonderfully with the maple syrup and is further fortified by the grainy vodka.

A B C D E F G H I J K L M N O P Q R S **T** U V W X Y Z

TEDDY BEAR'TINI

Glass: Martini
Garnish: Pear slice
Method: SHAKE all ingredients with ice and fine strain into chilled glass.

1½ shot(s) **Pear & cognac liqueur**
¾ shot(s) **Apple schnapps liqueur**
1½ shot(s) **Pressed apple juice**
1 pinch **Ground cinnamon**

Origin: Created in 2002 at The Borough, Edinburgh, Scotland. Originally named after a well-known cockney duo but renamed after the rhyming slang for pear.
Comment: Beautifully balanced apple and pear with a hint of cinnamon spice.

TENNESSEE BERRY MULE

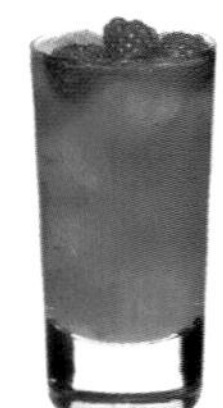

Glass: Collins
Garnish: Three raspberries
Method: MUDDLE raspberries in base of shaker. Add next four ingredients, **SHAKE** with ice and strain into ice-filled glass. **TOP** with ginger beer, lightly stir and serve with straws.

8 fresh **Raspberries**
1½ shot(s) **Jack Daniel's Tennessee whiskey**
1 shot(s) **Luxardo Amaretto di Saschira liqueur**
1½ shot(s) **Cranberry juice**
½ shot(s) **Freshly squeezed lime juice**
Top up with **Ginger beer**

Origin: Adapted in 2003 from a recipe Alex Kammerling created for TGI Friday's UK. Named partly for the ingredients and partly as a reference to Jack Daniel's proprietor (and nephew), Lemuel Motlow, who took up mule trading during Prohibition.
Comment: A berry rich cocktail laced with whiskey, flavoured with amaretto and topped with ginger beer.

TENNESSEE ICED TEA

Glass: Sling
Garnish: Lemon wedge on rim
Method: SHAKE first six ingredients with ice and strain into ice-filled glass. **TOP** with cola and serve with straws.

1 shot(s) **Jack Daniel's Tennessee whiskey**
½ shot(s) **Light white rum**
½ shot(s) **Ketel One vodka**
½ shot(s) **Cointreau / triple sec**
¾ shot(s) **Freshly squeezed lemon juice**
¼ shot(s) **Sugar (gomme) syrup**
Top up with **Cola**

Comment: JD and cola with extra interest courtesy of several other spirits and lemon juice.

DRINKS ARE GRADED AS FOLLOWS:

● DISGUSTING ●◐ PRETTY AWFUL ●● BEST AVOIDED
●●◐ DISAPPOINTING ●●● ACCEPTABLE ●●●◐ GOOD
●●●● RECOMMENDED ●●●●◐ HIGHLY RECOMMENDED
●●●●● OUTSTANDING / EXCEPTIONAL

TENNESSEE RUSH

Glass: Collins
Garnish: Lime wedge
Method: SHAKE all ingredients with ice and strain into ice-filled glass.

2 shot(s) **Jack Daniel's Tennessee whiskey**
1 shot(s) **Mandarine Napoléon liqueur**
2½ shot(s) **Cranberry juice**
½ shot(s) **Freshly squeezed lime juice**

Comment: This ruby red cocktail is long, fruity, refreshing and not too sweet.

TEQUILA FIZZ

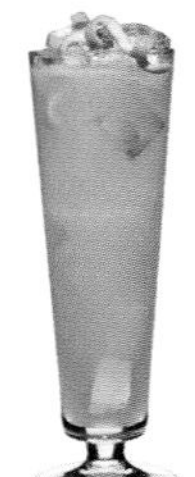

Glass: Sling
Garnish: Orange zest twist
Method: SHAKE first four ingredients with ice and strain into ice-filled glass. **TOP** with 7-Up.

2 shot(s) **Sauza Hornitos tequila**
1 shot(s) **Freshly squeezed orange juice**
1 shot(s) **Freshly squeezed lime juice**
½ shot(s) **Sugar (gomme) syrup**
Top up with **7-Up**

Comment: Refreshing with lingering lime.

TEQUILA MOCKINGBIRD [NEW]

Glass: Martini
Garnish: Mint leaf
Method: SHAKE all ingredients with ice and fine strain into chilled glass.

2 shot(s) **Sauza Hornitos tequila**
½ shot(s) **Green crème de menthe**
¼ shot(s) **Freshly squeezed lime juice**
1/8 shot(s) **Sugar (gomme) syrup**
½ shot(s) **Chilled mineral water (omit if wet ice)**

Comment: Minty tequila.

TEQUILA SLAMMER

Glass: Shot
Method: POUR tequila into glass and then carefully **LAYER** with champagne. The drinker should hold and cover the top of the glass with the palm of their hand so as to grip it firmly and seal the contents inside. Then they should briskly pick the glass up and slam it down (not so hard as to break the glass), then quickly gulp the drink down in one while it is still fizzing.

1 shot(s) **Sauza Hornitos tequila**
1 shot(s) **Piper-Heidsieck brut champagne**

Variants: With cream soda or ginger ale.
Comment: Seems a waste of good tequila and champagne but there's a time and a place.

TEQUILA SMASH [NEW]

Glass: Old-fashioned
Garnish: Mint sprig
Method: **SHAKE** all ingredients with ice and fine strain into ice-filled glass.

7	fresh	**Mint leaves**
2	shot(s)	**Sauza Hornitos tequila**
1/4	shot(s)	**Agave syrup**

Origin: Adapted from the classic Brandy Smash.
Comment: Simple, not sweet: a great way to appreciate quality tequila.

TEQUILA SOUR

Glass: Old-fashioned
Garnish: Lime zest twist
Method: **SHAKE** all ingredients with ice and fine strain into ice-filled glass.

2	shot(s)	**Sauza Hornitos tequila**
1	shot(s)	**Freshly squeezed lime juice**
1/2	shot(s)	**Sugar (gomme) syrup**
1/2	fresh	**Egg white**

Comment: A standard sour but with tequila zing.

TEQUILA SUNRISE

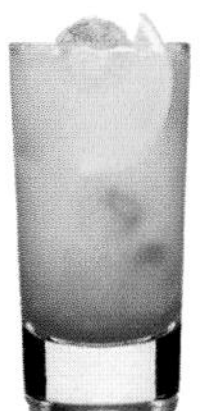

Glass: Collins
Garnish: Orange wheel & cherry
Method: **SHAKE** first two ingredients with ice and strain into ice-filled glass. **POUR** grenadine in a circle around the top of the drink. (It will sink to create a sunrise effect.)

2	shot(s)	**Sauza Hornitos tequila**
3	shot(s)	**Freshly squeezed orange juice**
3/4	shot(s)	**Sonoma pomegranate (grenadine) syrup**

Comment: Everyone has heard of this drink, but those who have tried it will wonder why it's so famous.

TEQUILA SUNSET

Glass: Sling
Garnish: Lemon slice
Method: **STIR** honey with tequila in base of shaker until honey dissolves. Add other ingredients, **SHAKE** with ice and strain into ice-filled glass.

7	spoons	**Runny honey**
2	shot(s)	**Sauza Hornitos tequila**
2	shot(s)	**Freshly squeezed lemon juice**

Comment: A good sweet and sour balance with subtle honey hints.

TEQUILA SLAMMER

Originally topped with ginger ale and not champagne, this infamous libation is thought to have started out as a Hell's Angel drink – it needs no ice and can be carried in a bike bag.

The simplest slammer is a lick of salt, a shot of tequila and then a bite of lemon (or lime). A Bermuda Slammer involves straight tequila, salt, a slice of lemon and a partner: one has to lick the salt off the other one's neck and bite the lemon (held between their partner's teeth) before downing a shot of tequila.

To quote Victor Bergeron (Trader Vic), "You know, this rigmarole with a pinch of salt and lemon juice and tequila - in whatever order - was originally for a purpose: It's hot in Mexico. People dehydrate themselves. And they need more salt. Here, it's not so hot, and we don't need salt in the same way. So you can drink tequila straight right out of the bottle, if you want to."

TEQUILA'TINI

Glass: Martini
Garnish: Lime zest twist
Method: **SHAKE** all ingredients with ice and fine strain into chilled glass.

2	shot(s)	**Sauza Hornitos tequila**
1	shot(s)	**Dry vermouth**
3	dashes	**Angostura aromatic bitters**
1/2	shot(s)	**Sugar (gomme) syrup**

Comment: If you like tequila and strong drinks – this is for you.

TERESA [NEW]

Glass: Martini
Garnish: Lime wedge on rim
Method: **SHAKE** all ingredients with ice and fine strain into chilled glass.

2	shot(s)	**Campari**
3/4	shot(s)	**Sisca crème de cassis**
1	shot(s)	**Freshly squeezed lime juice**

Origin: Created by Rafael Ballesteros of Spain, this recipe is taken from The Joy of Mixology by Gary Regan.
Comment: Bold, sweet and sour.

TESTAROSSA

Glass: Collins
Garnish: Orange wheel
Method: **POUR** all ingredients into ice-filled glass, lightly stir and serve with straws.

1 1/2	shot(s)	**Campari**
1 1/2	shot(s)	**Ketel One vodka**
Top up with		**Soda water (club soda)**

Comment: Campari and soda with some oomph.

TEST PILOT

Glass: Old-fashioned
Garnish: Lime zest twist
Method: **SHAKE** all ingredients with ice and fine strain into ice-filled glass.

1 1/2	shot(s)	**Aged rum**
3/4	shot(s)	**Light white rum**
1/4	shot(s)	**Cointreau / triple sec**
1/4	shot(s)	**Velvet Falernum liqueur**
1/4	shot(s)	**Freshly squeezed lemon juice**

Origin: Adapted from a recipe in the 1947-72 Trader Vic's Bartender's Guide by Victor Bergeron.
Comment: A fruity, sophisticated Daiquiri with hints of almond and spicy clove, served short over ice.

TEX COLLINS

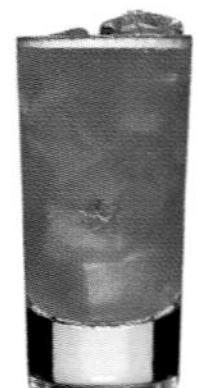

Glass: Collins
Garnish: Lemon slice
Method: **STIR** honey with gin in base of shaker to dissolve honey. Add grapefruit juice, **SHAKE** with ice and strain into ice-filled glass. **TOP** with soda water.

2	shot(s)	**Plymouth gin**
2	spoons	**Runny honey**
2	shot(s)	**Freshly squeezed grapefruit juice**
Top up with		**Soda water (club soda)**

Origin: Adapted from a recipe in the 1949 edition of Esquire's Handbook For Hosts.
Comment: A dry, tart blend of grapefruit and gin.

TEXAS ICED TEA

Glass: Sling
Garnish: Lemon wedge on rim
Method: **SHAKE** first six ingredients with ice and strain into ice-filled glass. **TOP** with cola.

1	shot(s)	**Sauza Hornitos tequila**
1/2	shot(s)	**Light white rum**
1/2	shot(s)	**Ketel One vodka**
1/2	shot(s)	**Cointreau / triple sec**
3/4	shot(s)	**Freshly squeezed lemon juice**
1/4	shot(s)	**Sugar (gomme) syrup**
Top up with		**Cola**

Comment: My favourite of the Iced Tea family of drinks. The tequila shines through.

TEXSUN

Glass: Martini
Garnish: Lemon zest twist
Method: **SHAKE** all ingredients with ice and fine strain into chilled glass.

1 1/2	shot(s)	**Bourbon whiskey**
1 1/2	shot(s)	**Dry vermouth**
1 1/2	shot(s)	**Freshly squeezed pink grapefruit juice**

Origin: Adapted from a recipe in the 1949 edition of Esquire's Handbook for Hosts.
Comment: Bone dry with fruity herbal hints.

THAI LADY [NEW]

Glass: Martini
Garnish: Lemon zest twist
Method: **MUDDLE** lemongrass in base of shaker. Add other ingredients, **SHAKE** with ice and fine strain into chilled glass.

2	inches	**fresh lemongrass (chopped)**
2	shot(s)	**Plymouth gin**
1/2	shot(s)	**Cointreau / triple sec**
1	shot(s)	**Freshly squeezed lemon juice**
1/4	shot(s)	**Sugar (gomme) syrup**

Origin: Adapted from a recipe created by Jamie Terrell, London, England.
Comment: A White Lady with the added flavour of lemongrass.

THAI LEMONADE [NEW] [MOCKTAIL]

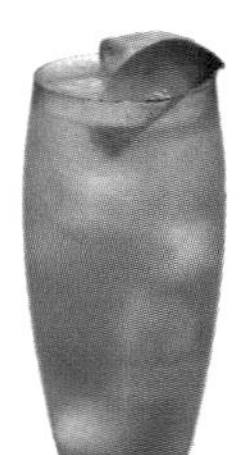

Glass: Collins
Garnish: Lime wedge
Method: **MUDDLE** coriander in base of shaker. Add next two ingredients, **SHAKE** with ice and fine strain into ice-filled glass. **TOP** with ginger beer.

5	sprigs	**fresh coriander**
2	shot(s)	**Freshly squeezed lime juice**
1/2	shot(s)	**Almond (orgeat) sugar syrup**
Top up with		**Ginger beer**

Origin: Adapted from a drink created in 2005 by Charlotte Voisey, London, England.
Comment: Lime lemonade with Thai influences courtesy of ginger, almond and coriander.

THOMAS BLOOD MARTINI

Glass: Martini
Garnish: Apple wedge on rim
Method: **STIR** honey with vodka in base of shaker until honey dissolves. Add other ingredients, **SHAKE** with ice and fine strain into chilled glass.

2	spoons	**Runny honey**
1	shot(s)	**Ketel One vodka**
1	shot(s)	**Krupnik honey liqueur**
1	shot(s)	**Apple schnapps liqueur**
1	shot(s)	**Freshly squeezed lemon juice**

Comment: An appealing, honey led mélange of sweet and sour.

THREE MILER

Glass: Martini
Garnish: Lemon zest twist
Method: **SHAKE** all ingredients with ice and fine strain into chilled glass.

1 1/2	shot(s)	**Rémy Martin cognac**
1 1/2	shot(s)	**Light white rum**
1/2	shot(s)	**Freshly squeezed lemon juice**
1/2	shot(s)	**Sonoma pomegranate (grenadine) syrup**

Origin: Adapted from the Three Miller Cocktail in the 1930 Savoy Cocktail Book. Most other cocktail books spell it with one 'l' as I have here.
Comment: A seriously strong drink, in flavour and in alcohol.

THREESOME

Glass: Martini
Garnish: Pineapple wedge on rim
Method: **SHAKE** all ingredients with ice and fine strain into chilled glass.

1 1/2	shot(s)	**Calvados or applejack brandy**
1	shot(s)	**Cointreau / triple sec**
1/2	shot(s)	**Pernod anis**
1 1/2	shot(s)	**Pressed pineapple juice**

Origin: Adapted from a drink discovered in 2002 at Circus Bar, London, England.
Comment: Why stop at three when you can have a foursome? An interesting meld of apple, orange, anise and pineapple.

THRILLER MARTINI

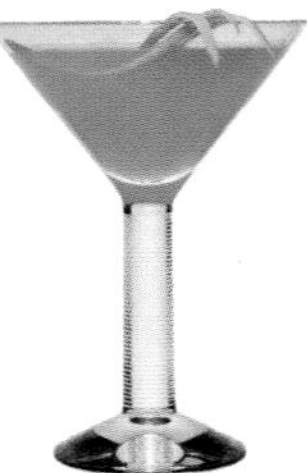

Glass: Martini
Garnish: Orange zest twist
Method: **SHAKE** all ingredients with ice and fine strain into chilled glass.

2 1/2	shot(s)	**The Famous Grouse Scotch whisky**
3/4	shot(s)	**Stone's green ginger wine**
3/4	shot(s)	**Freshly squeezed orange juice**
1/8	shot(s)	**Sugar (gomme) syrup**

Comment: Spiced Scotch with a hint of orange.

THRILLER FROM VANILLA

Glass: Martini
Garnish: Half vanilla pod
Method: **SHAKE** all ingredients with ice and fine strain into chilled glass.

3/4	shot(s)	**Vanilla infused Ketel One vodka**
3/4	shot(s)	**Plymouth gin**
1/2	shot(s)	**Cointreau / triple sec**
2	shot(s)	**Freshly squeezed orange juice**

Origin: Adapted from a drink discovered in 2003 at Oporto, Leeds, England. The 'Thriller in Manila' was the name given to the 1975 heavyweight fight between Muhammad Ali and Smokin' Joe Frazier.
Comment: Orange and creamy vanilla fortified with a hint of gin.

THUNDERBIRD

Glass: Martini
Garnish: Pineapple wedge on rim
Method: **SHAKE** all ingredients with ice and fine strain into chilled glass.

1 1/2	shot(s)	**Bourbon whiskey**
3/4	shot(s)	**Luxardo Amaretto di Saschira liqueur**
1	shot(s)	**Pressed pineapple juice**
1	shot(s)	**Freshly squeezed orange juice**

Comment: Tangy bourbon with fruity almond.

TI PUNCH

Glass: Old-fashioned
Garnish: Lime zest twist
Method: **POUR** all ingredients into glass with three cubes of ice. Serve with teaspoon so the drinker can tease some juice from the lime wedge if desired.

1	wedge	**Lime**
1 1/2	shot(s)	**Rhum Agricole**
1/4	shot(s)	**Cane juice syrup (not gomme)**

Origin: Named Ti from the French word 'Petit', this is literally a small rum punch: unlike most rum punches, it is not lengthened with water or juice. It is popular in the French islands of Martinique, Guadeloupe, Réunion and Maurice where it's often drunk straight down followed by a large glass of chilled water (called a 'crase' in Martinique). These islands are also home to Rhum Agricole (a style of rum distilled only from sugar cane juice and usually bottled at 50% alc./vol.)
Comment: This drink only works with authentic agricole rum.

TICK-TACK MARTINI

Glass: Martini
Garnish: Three Tic-Tac mints
Method: **STIR** all ingredients with ice and strain into chilled glass.

2	shot(s)	**Ketel One vodka**
1/2	shot(s)	**Luxardo Sambuca dei Cesari**
1/2	shot(s)	**White crème de menthe**

Origin: Created in 2001 by Rodolphe Sorel.
Comment: Strangely enough, tastes like a Tic-Tac mint.

TIGER'S MILK

Glass: Old-fashioned
Garnish: Grate nutmeg over drink
Method: **SHAKE** all ingredients with ice and strain into ice-filled glass.

2	shot(s)	**Rémy Martin cognac**
2	drops	**Vanilla essence**
1	pinch	**Ground cinnamon**
1/4	shot(s)	**Sugar (gomme) syrup**
3/4	shot(s)	**Double cream**
3/4	shot(s)	**Milk**
1/2	fresh	**Egg white**

Origin: Adapted from a recipe purloined from Charles H. Baker Jr's classic book, The Gentleman's Companion. He first discovered this drink in April 1931 at Gerber's Snug Bar, Peking, China.
Comment: Creamy cognac and spice.

TIKI BAR MARGARITA [NEW]

Glass: Old-fashioned
Garnish: Mint leaf, pineapple wedge & lime wedge
Method: **SHAKE** all ingredients with ice and strain into glass filled with crushed ice.

2	shot(s)	**Sauza Hornitos tequila**
1	shot(s)	**Freshly squeezed lime juice**
1/2	shot(s)	**Almond (orgeat) syrup**

Origin: Created in 2005 by Crispin Somerville and Jaspar Eyears at Bar Tiki, Mexico City.
Comment: A simple almond twist on the classic Margarita – fantastic.

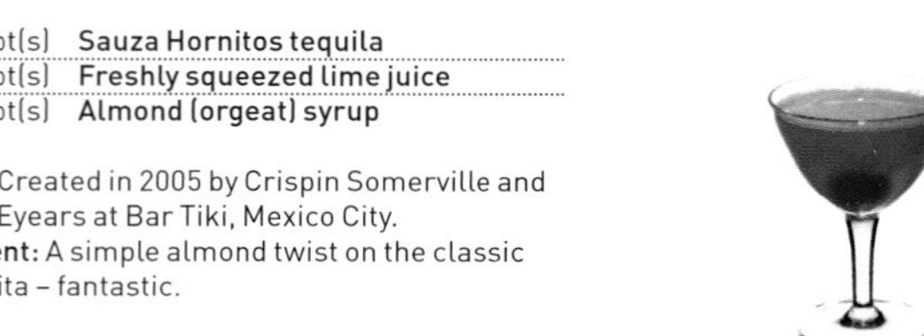

TIKI MAX

Glass: Old-fashioned
Garnish: Mint sprig & lime wedge
Method: **SHAKE** first nine ingredients with ice and strain into glass filled with crushed ice. **FLOAT** overproof Navy rum on drink.

1	shot(s)	**Pusser's Navy rum**
1/2	shot(s)	**Myers's rum**
1/2	shot(s)	**Grand Marnier liqueur**
1/2	shot(s)	**Apricot brandy liqueur**
3/4	shot(s)	**Freshly squeezed lime juice**
1	shot(s)	**Orgeat (almond) syrup**
1 1/2	shot(s)	**Pressed pineapple juice**
1/2	shot(s)	**Freshly squeezed orange juice**
6	dashes	**Angostura aromatic bitters**
1/2	shot(s)	**Woods 100 overproof navy rum**

Origin: Created by yours truly.
Comment: This drink breaks the golden rule – simple is beautiful. However, it's tasty and very dangerous.

TILT

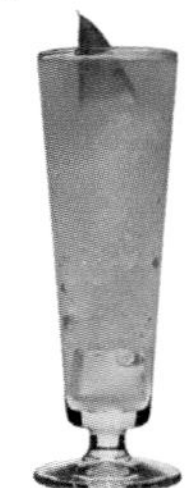

Glass: Sling
Garnish: Pineapple leaf garnish
Method: **SHAKE** first five ingredients with ice and strain into glass filled with crushed ice. **TOP** with bitter lemon.

1 1/2	shot(s)	**Pineapple vodka**
1/2	shot(s)	**Malibu coconut rum liqueur**
1 1/2	shot(s)	**Pressed pineapple juice**
1	shot(s)	**Freshly squeezed pink grapefruit juice**
1/4	shot(s)	**Vanilla sugar syrup**
Top up with		**Bitter lemon**

Comment: Totally tropical taste.

TIPPERARY #1 [NEW]

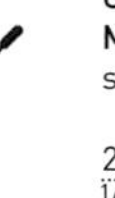

Glass: Martini
Garnish: Cherries on stick
Method: **SHAKE** all ingredients with ice and fine strain into chilled glass.

2	shot(s)	**Irish whiskey**
1/2	shot(s)	**Green Chartreuse liqueur**
1	shot(s)	**Sweet (rosso) vermouth**
1/2	shot(s)	**Chilled mineral water (omit if wet ice)**

Origin: Adapted from a recipe in Harry Craddock's 1930 Savoy Cocktail Book, which called for equal parts.
Comment: Chartreuse fans will love this serious drink. The uninitiated will hate it.

HOW TO MAKE SUGAR SYRUP

To make your own sugar syrup, gradually pour TWO cups of granulated sugar into a saucepan containing ONE cup of hot water. Stir as you pour and carry on stirring and simmering until the sugar is dissolved. Do not let the water even come close to boiling and only simmer for as long as it takes to dissolve the sugar. Allow syrup to cool and pour into an empty bottle. Ideally, you should finely strain your syrup into the bottle to remove any undissolved crystals which could otherwise encourage crystallisation. If kept in a refrigerator this mixture will last for a couple of months.

A B C D E F G H I J K L M N O P Q R S T U V W X Y Z

TIPPERARY #2 [NEW]

Glass: Martini
Garnish: Mint leaf
Method: Lightly **MUDDLE** mint in base of shaker (just to bruise). Add other ingredients, **SHAKE** with ice and fine strain into chilled glass.

7	fresh	**Mint leaves**
2	shot(s)	**Plymouth gin**
1	shot(s)	**Dry vermouth**
1/4	shot(s)	**Freshly squeezed orange juice**
1/4	shot(s)	**Sonoma pomegranate (grenadine) syrup**

Origin: Adapted from a drink purloined from David Embury's classic book, The Fine Art of Mixing Drinks.
Comment: Delicate with subtle hints of mint, orange and gin.

TIRAMISU MARTINI

Glass: Martini
Garnish: Chocolate powder dust
Method: **SHAKE** all ingredients with ice and fine strain into chilled glass.

1	shot(s)	**Rémy Martin cognac**
1/2	shot(s)	**Kahlúa coffee liqueur**
1/2	shot(s)	**Dark crème de cacao liqueur**
1/2	shot(s)	**Double (heavy) cream**
1/2	shot(s)	**Milk**
1	fresh	**Egg yolk**
1	spoon	**Mascarpone cheese**

Origin: Created by Adam Ennis in 2001 at Isola, London, England.
Comment: The chef meets the bartender in this rich dessert cocktail.

TIZIANO

Glass: Flute
Garnish: Grapes on rim
Method: **MUDDLE** grapes in base of shaker. Add Dubonnet, **SHAKE** with ice and fine strain into chilled glass. Slowly **TOP** with Prosecco and lightly stir.

10	fresh	**Seedless red grapes**
1	shot(s)	**Dubonnet Red**
Top up with		**Prosecco sparkling wine**

Origin: Named for the 15th century Venetian painter Titian, who was celebrated for his use of auburn red, this cocktail is commonplace in his home town, where it is made without Dubonnet.
Comment: Not dissimilar to a sparkling Shiraz wine.

TOAST & ORANGE MARTINI

Glass: Martini (small)
Garnish: Orange zest twist
Method: **SHAKE** all ingredients with ice and fine strain into chilled glass.

2	shot(s)	**Bourbon whiskey**
1	spoon	**Orange marmalade**
3	dashes	**Peychaud's aromatic bitters**
1/8	shot(s)	**Sugar (gomme) syrup**

Comment: Bourbon rounded and enhanced by bitter orange and Peychaud's bitters.

TIKI CULTURE & COCKTAILS

The word Tiki originally meant the procreative power and sexual organ of the Polynesian god Tane, often referred to as the 'first man', and also refers to carved totem pole-like statues like the huge stone heads discovered on Easter Island. In this context, however, it refers to a style of bars, drinks and kitsch that reached its apex in 50s and 60s America and is undergoing a quiet revival.

The repeal of Prohibition, cheap rum, America's need to escape the Depression and American troops returning with souvenirs from the Pacific after the WWII all contributed to the explosion of Tiki culture. But its creation is attributed to two men.

In 1934 Ernest Beaumont-Gantt, a New Orleans native who had travelled the Caribbean, opened his Don the Beachcomber bar and assumed the persona of Donn Beach. He created cocktails based on rum and decorated his bar like the rum shacks he'd come across in Jamaica.

A few hundred miles north, in Oakland, San Francisco, another character, Victor Jules Bergeron, launched Hinky Dink's restaurant. Like Donn Beach, he based his cocktails substantially on rum and by 1936 he had also assumed an alter ego, The Trader, and renamed his restaurant Trader Vic's. He decorated the interior with fishing nets, stuffed fish and carved Tiki poles. It proved an overnight hit, and Tiki bars decked out like beach huts with grass skirted waitresses sprung up across America.

In 1959, Hawaii became a state, further fuelling Tiki culture. At suburban luau parties men dressed in Hawaiian shirts and women as hula girls. The craze lasted into the late 60s, when it was sidelined by the hippie scene and the Vietnam War.

Thankfully a few Tiki bars, led by the Trader Vic's chain, kept Tiki culture alive to be rediscovered by a new generation. While full-blown Tiki may be too kitsch for today's style setters, Tiki drinks based on rum mixed with tropical juices and served in ceramic Tiki mugs are once again available in the most fashionable bars in London, New York and San Francisco.

There are numerous Tiki cocktails in this guide but perhaps the best known are the Mai Tai, Zombie and Suffering Bastard.

A B C D E F G H I J K L M N O P Q R S **T** U V W X Y Z

TOASTED ALMOND

Glass: Martini
Garnish: Dust with chocolate powder
Method: SHAKE all ingredients with ice and fine strain into chilled glass.

1	shot(s)	**Ketel One vodka**
1	shot(s)	**Luxardo Amaretto di Saschira liqueur**
$\frac{3}{4}$	shot(s)	**Kahlúa coffee liqueur**
$\frac{3}{4}$	shot(s)	**Double (heavy) cream**
$\frac{3}{4}$	shot(s)	**Milk**

Comment: Slightly sweet but smooth, creamy and definitely toasted.

TODDY MARTINI

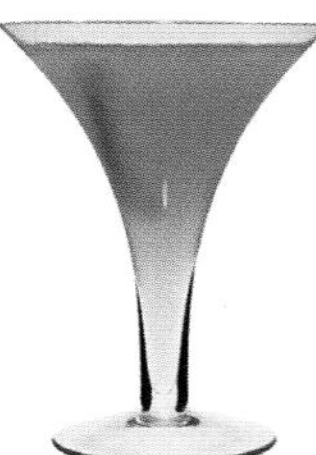

Glass: Martini
Garnish: Lemon zest twist
Method: SHAKE all ingredients with ice and fine strain into chilled glass.

$1\frac{1}{2}$	shot(s)	**The Famous Grouse Scotch whisky**
1	shot(s)	**Honey liqueur**
$\frac{3}{4}$	shot(s)	**Freshly squeezed lemon juice**

Origin: Created in 2001 by Jamie Terrell at LAB, London, England.
Comment: An ice cold but warming combo of Scotch, honey and lemon.

TOFFEE APPLE

Glass: Sling
Garnish: Apple wedge on rim
Method: SHAKE all ingredients with ice and strain into ice-filled glass.

1	shot(s)	**Calvados or applejack brandy**
2	shot(s)	**Cartron caramel liqueur**
1	shot(s)	**Apple schnapps liqueur**
1	shot(s)	**Freshly pressed apple juice**
$\frac{1}{4}$	shot(s)	**Freshly squeezed lime juice**

Origin: Created in 2002 by Nick Strangeway, London, England.
Comment: The taste is just as the name suggests.

TOFFEE APPLE MARTINI

Glass: Martini
Garnish: Apple and fudge on rim
Method: SHAKE all ingredients with ice and fine strain into chilled glass.

1	shot(s)	**Calvados or applejack brandy**
1	shot(s)	**Apple vodka**
$1\frac{1}{2}$	shot(s)	**Pressed apple juice**
1	shot(s)	**Clear toffee liqueur**

Origin: Created in 2003 by yours truly.
Comment: This amber, liquid toffee apple is almost creamy on the palate.

TOKYO BLOODY MARY

Glass: Collins
Garnish: Stick of celery
Method: SHAKE all ingredients with ice and strain into ice-filled glass.

2	shot(s)	**Sake**
$3\frac{1}{2}$	shot(s)	**Tomato juice**
$\frac{1}{2}$	shot(s)	**Freshly squeezed lemon juice**
$\frac{1}{4}$	shot(s)	**Tawny port**
7	drops	**Tabasco sauce**
3	dashes	**Worcestershire sauce**
1	pinch	**Celery salt**
1	grind	**Black pepper**

Comment: Sake adds an interesting dimension to the traditionally vodka based Bloody Mary.

TOKYO ICED TEA

Glass: Sling
Garnish: Lemon slice
Method: SHAKE first seven ingredients with ice and strain into ice-filled glass. **TOP** with 7-Up, lightly stir and serve with straws.

$\frac{1}{2}$	shot(s)	**Light white rum**
$\frac{1}{2}$	shot(s)	**Plymouth gin**
$\frac{1}{2}$	shot(s)	**Ketel One vodka**
$\frac{1}{2}$	shot(s)	**Sauza Hornitos tequila**
$\frac{1}{2}$	shot(s)	**Cointreau / triple sec**
1	shot(s)	**Freshly squeezed lime juice**
$\frac{1}{2}$	shot(s)	**Midori melon liqueur**
Top up with		**7-Up**

Comment: You will be surprised how the half shot of melon liqueur shows through the other ingredients.

TOKYO TEA

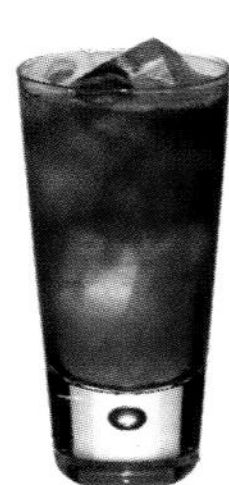

Glass: Collins
Garnish: Peeled lychee in drink
Method: SHAKE first three ingredients with ice and fine strain into ice-filled glass. **TOP** with cola, lightly stir and serve with straws.

2	shot(s)	**Plymouth gin**
$1\frac{1}{2}$	shot(s)	**Soho lychee liqueur**
1	shot(s)	**Jasmine tea (strong & cold)**
Top up with		**Cola**

Origin: Created by yours truly in 2004
Comment: Light, floral and, due to the tannins in the jasmine tea, refreshingly dry.

FOR MORE INFORMATION SEE OUR

TOLLEYTOWN PUNCH

Glass: Collins
Garnish: Cranberries, orange & lemon slices
Method: SHAKE first four ingredients with ice and strain into ice-filled glass. TOP with ginger ale.

2	shot(s)	Jack Daniel's Tennessee whiskey
2	shot(s)	Cranberry juice
1/2	shot(s)	Pressed pineapple juice
1/2	shot(s)	Freshly squeezed orange juice
Top up with		Ginger ale

Origin: A drink promoted by Jack Daniel's. Tolleytown lies just down the road from Lynchburg.
Comment: A fruity long drink with a dry edge that also works well made in bulk and served from a punch bowl.

TOM & JERRY [NEW]

Glass: Toddy
Garnish: Grate nutmeg over drink
Method: Separately BEAT egg white until stiff and frothy and yolk until as liquid as water, then MIX together and pour into glass. Add rum, cognac, sugar and spices and STIR mixture together. TOP with boiling water, STIR and serve.

1	fresh	Egg white
1	fresh	Egg yolk
1 1/2	shot(s)	Mount Gay golden rum
1 1/2	shot(s)	Rémy Martin cognac
1/4	shot(s)	Sugar (gomme) syrup
1	pinch	Ground cloves
1	pinch	Ground cinnamon
Top up with		Boiling water

Origin: Created in the early 19th century and attributed to Jerry Thomas. This recipe is adapted from Harry Craddock's 1930 Savoy Cocktail Book.
Comment: To quote Craddock, "The Tom and Jerry and the Blue Blazer – the latter a powerful concoction of burning whisky and boiling water – were the greatest cold weather beverages of that era."

TOM COLLINS

Glass: Collins
Garnish: Orange slice & cherry (flag)
Method: SHAKE first three ingredients with ice and strain into ice-filled glass. TOP with soda, lightly stir and serve with straws.

2	shot(s)	Plymouth gin
1	shot(s)	Freshly squeezed lemon juice
3/4	shot(s)	Sugar (gomme) syrup
Top up with		Soda water (club soda)

Origin: Thought to have been created circa 1800 by John Collins, a bartender at Limmer's Hotel, Conduit Street, London. It was originally made using sweet Old Tom gin, which is now very difficult to obtain.
Comment: A medium-sweet gin Collins.

TOMAHAWK

Glass: Collins
Garnish: Pineapple wedge
Method: SHAKE all ingredients with ice and strain into ice-filled glass.

1	shot(s)	Sauza Hornitos tequila
1	shot(s)	Cointreau / triple sec
2	shot(s)	Cranberry juice
2	shot(s)	Pressed pineapple juice

Comment: A simple recipe, and an effective drink.

TOMATE

Glass: Collins (10oz / 290ml max)
Method: POUR pastis and grenadine into glass. SERVE iced water separately in a small jug (known in France as a 'broc') so the customer can dilute to their own taste (I recommend five shots). Lastly, ADD ICE to fill glass.

1	shot(s)	Ricard pastis
1/4	shot(s)	Sonoma pomegranate (grenadine) syrup
Top up with		Chilled water

Origin: Very popular throughout France. Pronounced 'Toh-Maht', the name literally means 'tomato' and refers to the drink's colour.
Comment: The traditional aniseed and liquorice French café drink with a sweet hint of fruit.

TOMMY'S MARGARITA

Glass: Margarita
Garnish: Lime wedge on half salted rim
Method: SHAKE all ingredients with ice and fine strain into chilled glass.

2	shot(s)	Sauza Hornitos tequila
1	shot(s)	Freshly squeezed lime juice
1/2	shot(s)	Agave syrup (from health food shop)

Origin: Created by Julio Bermejo and named after his family's Mexican restaurant and bar in San Francisco. Julio is legendary for his Margaritas and knowledge of tequila.
Comment: The flavour of agave is king in this simple Margarita, made without the traditional orange liqueur.

TONGUE TWISTER [NEW]

Glass: Old-fashioned
Garnish: Maraschino cherry
Method: SHAKE all ingredients with ice and strain into glass filled with crushed ice.

3/4	shot(s)	Light white rum
3/4	shot(s)	Sauza Hornitos tequila
3/4	shot(s)	Ketel One vodka
1/2	shot(s)	Coco López cream of coconut
3	shot(s)	Pressed pineapple juice
1/2	shot(s)	Double (heavy) cream
1/2	shot(s)	Milk
1/4	shot(s)	Sonoma pomegranate (grenadine) syrup

Origin: Adapted from a drink featured in May 2006 on www.tikibartv.com.
Comment: This creamy, sweet Tiki number is laced with three different spirits.

TOO CLOSE FOR COMFORT [NEW]

Glass: Martini
Garnish: Lemon zest twist
Method: **SHAKE** all ingredients with ice and fine strain into chilled glass.

1½	shot(s)	**Ketel One vodka**
1	shot(s)	**Southern Comfort liqueur**
1	shot(s)	**Freshly squeezed lemon juice**
½	shot(s)	**Sugar (gomme) syrup**

Origin: Adapted from a drink discovered in 2005 at Mezza9, Singapore.
Comment: Sweet and sour with the distinctive flavour of Southern Comfort.

TOOTIE FRUITY LIFESAVER [UPDATED]

Glass: Collins
Garnish: Pineapple wedge & cherry
Method: **SHAKE** all ingredients with ice and strain into ice-filled glass. Serve with straws.

1½	shot(s)	**Ketel One vodka**
¾	shot(s)	**Crème de bananes liqueur**
¾	shot(s)	**Galliano liqueur**
1	shot(s)	**Cranberry juice**
1	shot(s)	**Pressed pineapple juice**
1	shot(s)	**Freshly squeezed orange juice**

Comment: Aptly named fruity drink.

TOP BANANA SHOT

Glass: Shot
Method: Refrigerate ingredients then **LAYER** in chilled glass by carefully pouring in the following order.

½	shot(s)	**Kahlúa coffee liqueur**
½	shot(s)	**White crème de cacao liqueur**
½	shot(s)	**Crème de bananes liqueur**
½	shot(s)	**Ketel One vodka**

Comment: Banana, chocolate and coffee.

TOTAL RECALL

Glass: Collins
Garnish: Lime wedge liqueur
Method: **SHAKE** all ingredients with ice and strain into ice-filled glass.

¾	shot(s)	**Southern Comfort liqueur**
¾	shot(s)	**Sauza Hornitos tequila**
¾	shot(s)	**Mount Gay Eclipse gold rum**
1½	shot(s)	**Cranberry juice**
1½	shot(s)	**Freshly squeezed orange juice**
¾	shot(s)	**Freshly squeezed lime juice**

Comment: A long, burgundy coloured drink with a taste reminiscent of blood orange.

TRANSYLVANIAN MARTINI

Glass: Martini
Garnish: Pineapple wedge
Method: **SHAKE** ingredients with ice and fine strain into chilled glass.

2	shot(s)	**Ketel One vodka**
1	shot(s)	**Passoã passion fruit liqueur**
1	shot(s)	**Pressed pineapple juice**

Origin: Created for the 1994 International Bartenders cocktail competition.
Comment: A tad sweet and a tad dull.

TRE MARTINI

Glass: Martini
Garnish: Lemon zest twist
Method: **SHAKE** all ingredients with ice and fine strain into chilled glass.

2	shot(s)	**Light white rum**
½	shot(s)	**Chambord black raspberry liqueur**
1½	shot(s)	**Freshly pressed apple juice**

Origin: Created in 2002 by Åsa Nevestveit at Sosho, London, England.
Comment: A simple, well balanced, fruity drink laced with rum.

TREACLE

Glass: Old-fashioned
Garnish: Lemon zest twist
Method: **STIR** sugar syrup and bitters with two ice cubes in glass. Add one shot of rum and two more ice cubes. **STIR** some more and add another two ice cubes and another shot of rum. **STIR** lots more and add more ice if required. Finally **FLOAT** apple juice.

¼	shot(s)	**Sugar (gomme) syrup**
2	dashes	**Angostura aromatic bitters**
2	shot(s)	**Myers's Planters' Punch rum**
½	shot(s)	**Pressed apple juice**

Origin: This twist on the Old-Fashioned was created by Dick Bradsell. Like the original, it takes about five minutes to make and there are no shortcuts.
Comment: Almost like molasses – very dark flavour.

TRES COMPADRES MARGARITA

Glass: Coupette
Garnish: Lime wedge & salted rim (optional)
Method: **SHAKE** all ingredients with ice and fine strain into chilled glass.

1¼	shot(s)	**Sauza Hornitos tequila**
½	shot(s)	**Cointreau / triple sec**
½	shot(s)	**Chambord black raspberry liqueur**
½	shot(s)	**Rose's lime cordial**
¾	shot(s)	**Freshly squeezed lime juice**
¾	shot(s)	**Freshly squeezed orange juice**
¾	shot(s)	**Freshly squeezed grapefruit juice**

Origin: Created in 1999 by Robert Plotkin and Raymon Flores of BarMedia, USA.
Comment: A well balanced, tasty twist on the standard Margarita.

TRIANGULAR MARTINI

Glass: Martini
Garnish: Toblerone chocolate on rim
Method: **STIR** honey with vodka in base of shaker until honey dissolves. Add other ingredients, **SHAKE** with ice and fine strain into chilled glass.

2	spoons	**Runny honey**
1½	shot(s)	**Vanilla flavoured vodka**
½	shot(s)	**Luxardo Amaretto di Saschira liqueur**
1¼	shot(s)	**Dark crème de cacao liqueur**
¾	shot(s)	**Double (heavy) cream**
½	fresh	**Egg white**

Origin: Created by yours truly in 2003. The famous triangular Toblerone chocolate bar was invented in 1908 by the Swiss chocolate maker Theodor Tobler. The name is a blend of Tobler with Torrone, the Italian word for honey-almond nougat, one of its main ingredients.
Comment: Nibble at the garnish as you sip honeyed, chocolate and almond flavoured liquid candy.

TRIBBBLE

Glass: Shot
Method: Refrigerate ingredients then **LAYER** in chilled glass by carefully pouring in the following order.

½	shot(s)	**Butterscotch schnapps liqueur**
½	shot(s)	**Crème de bananes liqueur**
½	shot(s)	**Baileys Irish cream liqueur**

Origin: A drink created by bartenders at TGI Friday's UK in 2002.
Comment: Named 'Tribbble' with three 'Bs' due to its three layers: butterscotch, banana and Baileys.

TRIFLE MARTINI

Glass: Martini
Garnish: Hundreds & thousands
Method: **SHAKE** all ingredients with ice and fine strain into chilled glass.

2	shot(s)	**Raspberry flavoured vodka**
½	shot(s)	**Chambord black raspberry liqueur**
2	shot(s)	**Drambuie cream liqueur**

Origin: Created by Ian Baldwin at GE Club, London, England.
Comment: A cocktail that tastes like its namesake.

FOR MORE INFORMATION SEE OUR
INGREDIENTS APPENDIX ON PAGE 322

TRIFLE'TINI

Glass: Martini
Garnish: Crumbled Cadbury's Flake bar
Method: **MUDDLE** raspberries and strawberries in base of shaker. Add next four ingredients, **SHAKE** with ice and fine strain into chilled glass. Lightly **WHIP** cream and **FLOAT** over drink.

10	fresh	**Raspberries**
2	fresh	**Strawberries**
2	shot(s)	**Rémy Martin cognac**
¾	shot(s)	**Luxardo Amaretto di Saschira liqueur**
½	shot(s)	**Crème de fraise (strawberry) liqueur**
1	shot(s)	**Pedro Ximénez sherry**
1½	shot(s)	**Double (heavy) cream**

Origin: Created in 2000 by Ian Baldwin at the GE Club, London, England.
Comment: Very rich – looks and tastes like a trifle.

TRILBY

Glass: Martini
Garnish: Orange zest twist
Method: **STIR** all ingredients with ice and strain into chilled glass.

1	shot(s)	**The Famous Grouse Scotch whisky**
1	shot(s)	**Parfait Amour**
1	shot(s)	**Cinzano Rosso vermouth**
1/8	shot(s)	**La Fée Parisian 68% absinthe**
¾	shot(s)	**Chilled mineral water (omit if wet ice)**
2	dashes	**Fee Brothers orange bitters**

Comment: An aromatic old classic of unknown origin.

TRINITY [NEW]

Glass: Martini
Garnish: Orange twist (discarded) & two maraschino cherries
Method: **STIR** all ingredients with ice and strain into chilled glass.

2½	shot(s)	**The Famous Grouse Scotch whisky**
1	shot(s)	**Dry vermouth**
¼	shot(s)	**Apricot brandy liqueur**
¼	shot(s)	**White crème de menthe liqueur**
1	dash	**Fee Brothers orange bitters**

Origin: Recipe purloined from David Embury's classic book, The Fine Art of Mixing Drinks.
Comment: A Dry Manhattan based on Scotch with a dash of apricot liqueur and a touch of crème de menthe.

TRIPLE 'C' MARTINI [NEW]

Glass: Martini
Garnish: Dark chocolate on rim
Method: **SHAKE** all ingredients with ice and fine strain into chilled glass.

2	shot(s)	**Vanilla-infused Ketel One vodka**
1	shot(s)	**Dark crème de cacao liqueur**
1¼	shot(s)	**Cranberry juice**

Origin: I created this drink in 2004 and originally called it the Chocolate Covered Cranberry Martini.
Comment: Rich vanilla, dark chocolate and cranberry juice.

TRIPLE ORANGE MARTINI

Glass: Martini
Garnish: Orange zest twist
Method: **SHAKE** all ingredients with ice and fine strain into chilled glass.

1	shot(s)	**Ketel One vodka**
1	shot(s)	**Grand Marnier liqueur**
1/4	shot(s)	**Campari**
2	shot(s)	**Freshly squeezed orange juice**
1/2	fresh	**Egg white**

Origin: Created in 1998 by yours truly.
Comment: A trio of orange flavours. The bitter orange of Campari adds character and balance.

TRIPLEBERRY [NEW]

Glass: Martini
Garnish: Berries on stick
Method: **MUDDLE** raspberries in base of shaker. Add other ingredients, **SHAKE** with ice and fine strain into chilled glass.

7	fresh	**Raspberries**
2	shot(s)	**Ketel One vodka**
1/2	shot(s)	**Sisca crème de cassis**
1/2	shot(s)	**Crème de fraise (strawberry) liqueur**
1/4	shot(s)	**Red wine**

Origin: Created in 2006 by yours truly.
Comment: Rich berry fruit fortified with vodka and tamed by the tannins in a splash of red wine.

TROPIC

Glass: Collins
Garnish: Lemon slice
Method: **SHAKE** all ingredients with ice and strain into ice-filled glass.

1	shot(s)	**Bénédictine D.O.M. liqueur**
2	shot(s)	**Sauvignon Blanc wine**
2	shot(s)	**Freshly squeezed grapefruit juice**
1/2	shot(s)	**Freshly squeezed lemon juice**

Origin: Based on a recipe believed to date back to the 1950s.
Comment: A light, satisfying cooler.

TROPICAL BREEZE

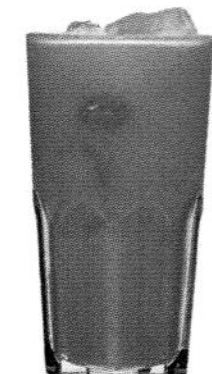

Glass: Collins
Garnish: Lime wedge
Method: **SHAKE** all ingredients with ice and strain into ice-filled glass.

1	shot(s)	**Passoã passion fruit liqueur**
1 1/2	shot(s)	**Ketel One vodka**
2 1/2	shot(s)	**Cranberry juice**
1 1/2	shot(s)	**Freshly squeezed pink grapefruit juice**

Comment: A sweet, fruity Seabreeze.

TROPICAL CAIPIRINHA

Glass: Old-fashioned
Garnish: Two squeezed lime wedges in drink
Method: **SHAKE** all ingredients with ice and strain into glass filled with crushed ice.

1	shot(s)	**Sagatiba cachaça**
1	shot(s)	**Malibu coconut rum liqueur**
1	shot(s)	**Pressed pineapple juice**
1	shot(s)	**Freshly squeezed lime juice**
1/4	shot(s)	**Sugar (gomme) syrup**

Origin: Created by yours truly in 2003.
Comment: In drink circles, tropical usually spells sweet. This drink has a tropical flavour but an adult sourness.

TROPICAL DAIQUIRI [NEW]

Glass: Martini
Garnish: Pineapple wedge on rim
Method: **SHAKE** all ingredients with ice and fine strain into chilled glass.

2	shot(s)	**Goslings Black Seal rum**
1	shot(s)	**Pressed pineapple juice**
1/2	shot(s)	**Freshly squeezed lime juice**
1/4	shot(s)	**Sonoma pomegranate (grenadine) syrup**

Origin: Adapted from a recipe in David Embury's classic book, The Fine Art of Mixing Drinks.
Comment: A seriously twangy Daiquiri.

TULIP COCKTAIL [NEW]

Glass: Martini
Garnish: Lemon zest twist
Method: **SHAKE** all ingredients with ice and fine strain into chilled glass.

1	shot(s)	**Calvados or applejack brandy**
1	shot(s)	**Sweet (rosso) vermouth**
1/2	shot(s)	**Freshly squeezed lemon juice**
1/2	shot(s)	**Apricot brandy liqueur**
1/2	shot(s)	**Chilled mineral water (omit if wet ice)**

Origin: Adapted from a recipe in Harry Craddock's 1930 Savoy Cocktail Book.
Comment: Rich but balanced with bags of fruit: apple, apricot and lemon.

TURF MARTINI [NEW]

Glass: Martini
Garnish: Orange zest twist
Method: **SHAKE** all ingredients with ice and fine strain into chilled glass.

1 1/2	shot(s)	**Plymouth gin**
1 1/2	shot(s)	**Sweet (rosso) vermouth**
1/8	shot(s)	**Luxardo maraschino liqueur**
1/8	shot(s)	**La Fée Parisian 68% absinthe**
2	dashes	**Fee Brothers orange bitters**

Origin: Created before 1900 at the Ritz Hotel, Paris, France.
Comment: Old-school, full flavoured, aromatic and dry.

TURKISH COFFEE MARTINI

Glass: Martini
Garnish: Float three coffee beans
Method: **MUDDLE** cardamom pods in base of shaker. Add other ingredients, **SHAKE** with ice and fine strain into chilled glass.

9	pods	**Green cardamom**
2	shot(s)	**Ketel One vodka**
2	shot(s)	**Espresso coffee (cold)**
1/2	shot(s)	**Sugar (gomme) syrup**

Origin: I created this in 2003.
Comment: Coffee is often made with cardamom in Arab countries. This drink harnesses the aromatic, eucalyptus, citrus flavour of cardamom coffee and adds a little vodka zing.

TURKISH DELIGHT

Glass: Martini
Garnish: Turkish Delight on rim
Method: **STIR** honey and vodka in base of shaker until honey dissolves. Add other ingredients, **SHAKE** with ice and fine strain into chilled glass.

2	spoons	**Runny honey**
1	shot(s)	**Ketel One vodka**
1	shot(s)	**Vanilla flavoured vodka**
1/2	shot(s)	**White crème de cacao liqueur**
1/8	shot(s)	**Rosewater**
3/4	shot(s)	**Chilled water (omit if wet ice)**
1/2	fresh	**Egg white**

Origin: Created in 2003 by yours truly.
Comment: Rosewater, honey, chocolate and vanilla provide a distinct flavour of Turkish Delight - fortified with vodka.

TURQUOISE DAIQUIRI

Glass: Martini
Garnish: Lime wedge on rim
Method: **SHAKE** all ingredients with ice and fine strain into chilled glass.

1 1/2	shot(s)	**Light white rum**
1/2	shot(s)	**Cointreau / triple sec**
1/2	shot(s)	**Blue curaçao liqueur**
3/4	shot(s)	**Freshly squeezed lime juice**
1	shot(s)	**Pressed pineapple juice**

Comment: A blue-rinsed Daiquiri with orange and pineapple – with tequila instead of rum it would be a twisted Margarita.

TUSCAN MULE

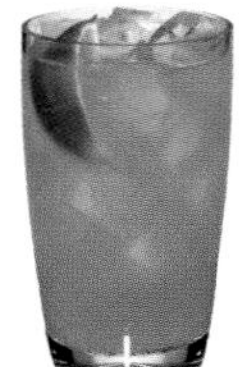

Glass: Collins
Garnish: Lime wedge
Method: **SHAKE** first two ingredients with ice and strain into ice-filled glass. **TOP** with ginger beer, lightly stir and serve with straws.

2	shot(s)	**Tuaca Italian liqueur**
3/4	shot(s)	**Freshly squeezed lime juice**
Top up with		**Jamaican ginger beer**

Origin: Adapted from drink created in 2003 by Sammy Berry, Brighton, England.
Comment: A spicy long drink smoothed with vanilla.

TUTTI FRUTTI

Glass: Collins
Garnish: Split lime wedge
Method: **SHAKE** all ingredients with ice and strain into ice-filled glass.

1	shot(s)	**Sauza Hornitos tequila**
1	shot(s)	**Passoã passion fruit liqueur**
1	shot(s)	**Midori melon liqueur**
3	shot(s)	**Cranberry juice**

Comment: A berry drink with a tropical tinge.

TUXEDO MARTINI [UPDATED]

Glass: Martini
Garnish: Orange zest twist
Method: **STIR** all ingredients with ice and fine strain into chilled glass.

1 1/2	shot(s)	**Plymouth gin**
1 1/2	shot(s)	**Dry vermouth**
1/2	shot(s)	**Fino sherry**
1	dash	**Fee Brothers orange bitters**

Origin: Created at the Tuxedo Club, New York, circa 1885. A year later this was the birthplace of the tuxedo, when a tobacco magnate, Griswold Lorillard, wore the first ever tailless dinner jacket and named the style after the club.
Comment: Fino adds a nutty saltiness to this very wet, aromatic Martini.

TVR

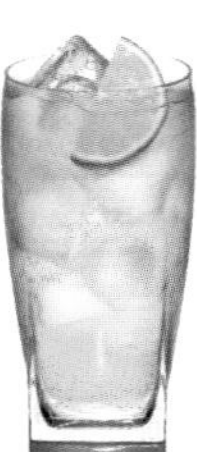

Glass: Collins
Garnish: Lime wedge in drink
Method: **POUR** ingredients into ice-filled glass. Lightly stir and serve with straws.

1	shot(s)	**Sauza Hornitos tequila**
1	shot(s)	**Ketel One vodka**
Top up with		**Red Bull**

Variant: Served as a shot.
Origin: A 90s drink named after its ingredients (tequila, vodka and Red Bull), which is also the name of a British sports car.
Comment: While I personally find the smell of Red Bull reminiscent of perfumed puke, this drink could be far worse.

TWENTIETH CENTURY MARTINI [UPDATED]

Glass: Martini
Garnish: Lemon zest twist
Method: **SHAKE** all ingredients with ice and fine strain into chilled glass.

1 1/2	shot(s)	**Plymouth gin**
3/4	shot(s)	**Dry vermouth**
1/2	shot(s)	**White crème de cacao liqueur**
1/2	shot(s)	**Freshly squeezed lemon juice**

Origin: Thought to have been created in 1939 by one C. A. Tuck and named after the express train that travelled between New York City and Chicago.
Comment: Chocolate and lemon juice. 21st century tastes have moved on.

A B C D E F G H I J K L M N O P Q R S **T** U V W X Y Z

TWINKLE

Glass: Martini
Garnish: Lemon zest twist
Method: **SHAKE** first two ingredients with ice and fine strain into chilled glass. **TOP** with Prosecco (or champagne).

3	shot(s)	**Ketel One vodka**
$^{3}/_{4}$	shot(s)	**Elderflower cordial**
Top up with		**Prosecco (or Piper-Heidsieck brut champagne)**

Origin: Created in 2002 by Tony Conigliaro at Lonsdale House, London, England.
Comment: It's hard to believe this floral, dry, golden tipple contains three whole shots of vodka.

TWISTED SOBRIETY

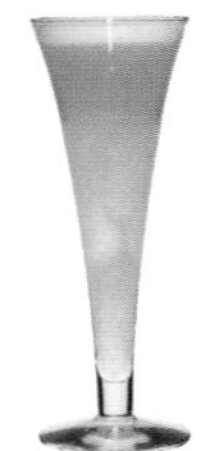

Glass: Flute
Method: **SHAKE** first two ingredients with ice and fine strain into chilled glass. **TOP** with champagne.

1	shot(s)	**Rémy Martin cognac**
1	shot(s)	**Poire William liqueur**
Top up with		**Piper-Heidsieck brut champagne**

Comment: Fortified champagne with a hint of pear.

TWO 'T' FRUITY MARTINI

Glass: Martini
Garnish: Tooty Frooties
Method: **SHAKE** all ingredients with ice and fine strain into chilled glass.

$2^{1}/_{2}$	shot(s)	**Ketel One vodka**
$^{3}/_{4}$	shot(s)	**Passion fruit syrup**
3	dashes	**Fee Brothers orange bitters**

Origin: Created in 2002 at Hush, London, England.
Comment: Simple is beautiful – this drink is both. The rawness of vodka is balanced with sweet passion fruit and hints of orange bitterness.

TYPHOON

Glass: Old-fashioned
Method: **STIR** all ingredients with ice and strain into ice-filled glass.

$1^{3}/_{4}$	shot(s)	**Plymouth gin**
$^{1}/_{2}$	shot(s)	**Luxardo Sambuca dei Cesari**
$^{1}/_{2}$	shot(s)	**Rose's lime cordial**

Comment: Great if you love sambuca.

UGURUNDU [NEW]

Glass: Shot
Method: Lightly **MUDDLE** mint in base of shaker (just to bruise). Add other ingredients, **SHAKE** with ice and fine strain into chilled glass.

3	fresh	**Mint leaves**
$^{1}/_{2}$	shot(s)	**Cranberry flavoured vodka**
$^{1}/_{2}$	shot(s)	**Rose's lime cordial**

Origin: Created in 2004 by Peter Kubista at Bugsy's Bar, Prague, Czech Republic.
Comment: Fresh tasting and all too easy to knock back.

UMBONGO

Glass: Collins
Garnish: Orange slice in glass
Method: Cut passion fruit in half and scoop out flesh into shaker. Add next three ingredients, **SHAKE** with ice and fine strain into ice-filled glass. **TOP** with ginger ale.

1	fresh	**Passion fruit**
1	shot(s)	**Passoã passion fruit liqueur**
1	shot(s)	**Ketel One vodka**
1	shot(s)	**Freshly squeezed orange juice**
Top up with		**Ginger ale**

Comment: Pleasant, light and medium sweet tropical style drink.

UNCLE VANYA

Glass: Martini
Garnish: Lime wedge on rim
Method: **SHAKE** all ingredients with ice and fine strain into chilled glass.

$1^{3}/_{4}$	shot(s)	**Ketel One vodka**
1	shot(s)	**Crème de mûre (blackberry) liqueur**
1	shot(s)	**Freshly squeezed lime juice**
$^{1}/_{2}$	shot(s)	**Sugar (gomme) syrup**
$^{1}/_{2}$	fresh	**Egg white**

Origin: Named after Anton Chekhov's greatest play – a cheery tale of envy and despair. A popular drink in Britain's TGI Friday's bars, its origins are unknown.
Comment: Simple but great – smooth, sweet 'n' sour blackberry, although possibly a tad on the sweet side for some.

UNION CLUB [NEW]

Glass: Martini
Garnish: Orange zest twist
Method: **SHAKE** all ingredients with ice and fine strain into chilled glass.

2	shot(s)	**Bourbon whiskey**
$^{1}/_{4}$	shot(s)	**Cointreau / triple sec**
$^{1}/_{2}$	shot(s)	**Freshly squeezed lime juice**
1/8	shot(s)	**Orgeat sugar syrup**
1/8	shot(s)	**Sonoma pomegranate (grenadine) syrup**
$^{1}/_{2}$	fresh	**Egg white**

Origin: Adapted from a recipe purloined from David Embury's classic book, The Fine Art of Mixing Drinks.
Comment: Balanced sweet and sour with bourbon to the fore.

●●●○○

UNIVERSAL SHOT

Glass: Shot
Method: Refrigerate ingredients then **LAYER** in chilled glass by carefully pouring in the following order.

1/2	shot(s)	**Midori melon liqueur**
1/2	shot(s)	**Freshly squeezed pink grapefruit juice**
1/2	shot(s)	**Ketel One vodka**

Comment: Sweet melon liqueur toned down by grapefruit and fortified by vodka.

●●●●○

UPSIDE-DOWN RASPBERRY CHEESECAKE

Glass: Martini
Garnish: Sprinkle crunched Graham Cracker or digestive biscuits
Method: First layer: **MUDDLE** raspberries in base of shaker. Add Chambord, **SHAKE** with ice and fine strain into centre of glass. Second layer: Grate lemon zest into shaker. Add rest of ingredients, **SHAKE** all ingredients with ice and strain into glass over spoon so as to **LAYER** over raspberry base.

4	fresh	**Raspberries**
1/2	shot(s)	**Chambord black raspberry liqueur**

NEXT **LAYER**

1/2	fresh	**Lemon zest (grated)**
2	shot(s)	**Vanilla flavoured vodka**
1/2	shot(s)	**Vanilla liqueur**
1/2	shot(s)	**Sugar (gomme) syrup**
5	spoons	**Mascarpone cheese**
1	shot(s)	**Double (heavy) cream**

Origin: I created this in 2003 after adapting Wayne Collins' original cheesecake recipe.
Comment: Surprisingly, the biscuity top continues to float as you sip the vanilla cream layer right down to the point when you hit the raspberry topping – sorry, base.

●●●◐○

URBAN HOLISTIC [NEW]

Glass: Martini
Garnish: Lemon zest twist
Method: **SHAKE** first two ingredients with ice and fine strain into chilled glass. **TOP** with ginger ale.

2	shot(s)	**Sake**
1	shot(s)	**Dry vermouth**
Top up with		**Ginger ale**

Origin: Adapted from a drink discovered in 2005 at Mo Bar, Landmark Mandarin Oriental Hotel, Hong Kong, China.
Comment: East meets west in this dry refreshing cocktail.

●●●●○

URBAN OASIS

Glass: Martini
Garnish: Orange zest twist
Method: **SHAKE** all ingredients with ice and fine strain into chilled glass.

1 1/2	shot(s)	**Orange flavoured vodka**
1/2	shot(s)	**Raspberry flavoured vodka**
1/4	shot(s)	**Chambord black raspberry liqueur**
2	shot(s)	**Pressed pineapple juice**

Origin: Discovered in 2003 at Paramount Hotel, New York City, USA.
Comment: Alcoholic orange sherbet – how bad is that?

●●●●●

U.S. MARTINI

Glass: Martini
Garnish: Vanilla pod
Method: **SHAKE** all ingredients with ice and fine strain into chilled glass.

1 1/2	shot(s)	**Vanilla infused Rémy Martin cognac**
1 1/4	shot(s)	**Sauvignon Blanc wine**
1 1/2	shot(s)	**Pressed pineapple juice**
1/4	shot(s)	**Sugar (gomme) syrup**

Origin: Adapted from the Palermo cocktail discovered in 2001 at Hotel du Vin, Bristol, England. I created this drink in 2003 and named it after the grape varieties Ugni and Sauvignon. Ugni Blanc is the most common grape in Cognac, and Sauvignon Blanc is the grape used in the wine.
Comment: A relatively dry cocktail where the vanilla combines beautifully with the cognac and the acidity of the wine balances the sweetness of the pineapple juice.

●●●◐○

UTTERLY BUTTERLY

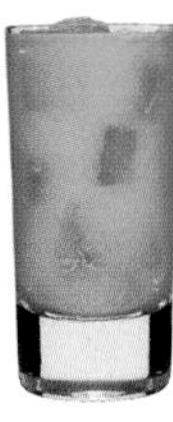

Glass: Collins
Garnish: Apple wedge
Method: **STIR** peanut butter with vodka in base of shaker. Add other ingredients, **SHAKE** with ice and fine strain into ice-filled glass.

1	spoon	**Smooth peanut butter**
2	shot(s)	**Ketel One vodka**
1/4	shot(s)	**Goldschläger cinnamon schnapps**
1/2	shot(s)	**Malibu coconut rum liqueur**
1 1/2	shot(s)	**Pressed apple juice**
1 1/2	shot(s)	**Pressed pineapple juice**
3/4	shot(s)	**Freshly squeezed lime juice**

Comment: Yup, your eyes are not deceiving you and nor will your taste buds – it's made with peanut butter. Refreshingly different.

DRINKS ARE GRADED AS FOLLOWS:

● DISGUSTING ●◐ PRETTY AWFUL ●● BEST AVOIDED
●●◐ DISAPPOINTING ●●● ACCEPTABLE ●●●◐ GOOD
●●●● RECOMMENDED ●●●●◐ HIGHLY RECOMMENDED
●●●●● OUTSTANDING / EXCEPTIONAL

●●●◐○

VACATION

Glass: Martini
Garnish: Pineapple wedge or orange slice on rim
Method: This drink can be finished with your choice of three different coloured and flavoured liqueurs. **SHAKE** first five ingredients with ice and fine strain into chilled glass. Then **POUR** your favoured final ingredient into the centre of the drink. It should sink.

2 shot(s) **Vanilla flavoured vodka**
1/2 shot(s) **Malibu coconut rum liqueur**
1/2 shot(s) **Freshly squeezed lime juice**
1 shot(s) **Pressed pineapple juice**
1/4 fresh **Egg white**
1/4 shot(s) **Chambord (red) or Midori (green) or Blue curaçao liqueur (blue)**

Origin: My adaptation (in 2003) of the signature drink at the Merc Bar, New York City, USA.
Comment: A great looking, fairly sweet cocktail with hints of vanilla, coconut and pineapple.

●●●●○

VALENCIA

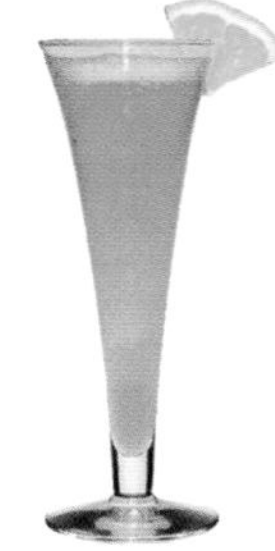

Glass: Flute
Garnish: Orange zest twist
Method: **POUR** first three ingredients into chilled glass. **TOP** with champagne.

1/2 shot(s) **Apricot brandy liqueur**
1/4 shot(s) **Freshly squeezed orange juice**
4 dashes **Fee Brothers orange bitters (optional)**
Top up with **Piper-Heidsieck brut champagne**

Variant: Also served as a Martini with gin in place of champagne.
Origin: Adapted from the Valencia Cocktail No. 2 in The Savoy Cocktail Book.
Comment: Floral and fruity – makes Bucks Fizz look a tad sad.

●●●◐○

VALKYRIE

Glass: Old-fashioned
Garnish: Lemon zest twist
Method: **SHAKE** all ingredients with ice and strain into glass filled with crushed ice. Serve with straws.

2 shot(s) **Vanilla flavoured vodka**
1/2 shot(s) **Freshly squeezed lemon juice**
1/2 shot(s) **Vanilla sugar syrup**

Origin: Created in 2003 by yours truly. The name comes from Norse mythology and literally translates as 'chooser of the slain'.
Comment: This sipping drink has a rich vanilla, sweet 'n' sour flavour.

DRINKS ARE GRADED AS FOLLOWS:

● DISGUSTING ●◐ PRETTY AWFUL ●● BEST AVOIDED
●●◐ DISAPPOINTING ●●● ACCEPTABLE ●●●◐ GOOD
●●●● RECOMMENDED ●●●●◐ HIGHLY RECOMMENDED
●●●●● OUTSTANDING / EXCEPTIONAL

●●●●○

VAMPIRO

Glass: Old-fashioned
Garnish: Lime wedge
Method: **SHAKE** all ingredients with ice and strain into ice-filled glass.

2 shot(s) **Sauza Hornitos tequila**
1 shot(s) **Pressed tomato juice**
1 shot(s) **Freshly squeezed orange juice**
1/2 shot(s) **Freshly squeezed lime juice**
1/2 shot(s) **Sonoma pomegranate (grenadine) syrup**
7 drops **Hot pepper sauce**
1 pinch **Celery salt**
1 pinch **Freshly ground black pepper**

Origin: The national drink of Mexico where it's often made with pomegranate juice in place of tomato juice and without the grenadine.
Comment: Something of a supercharged Bloody Mary with tequila and a hint of sweet grenadine.

●●●●◐

VANDERBILT [UPDATED]

Glass: Martini
Garnish: Lemon zest twist
Method: **SHAKE** all ingredients with ice and fine strain into chilled glass.

2 1/4 shot(s) **Rémy Martin cognac**
3/4 shot(s) **Cherry (brandy) liqueur**
1/8 shot(s) **Sugar (gomme) syrup**
2 dashes **Angostura aromatic bitters**

Origin: Adapted from a recipe in Harry Craddock's 1930 Savoy Cocktail Book.
Comment: Tangy, rich cherry and hints of vanilla fortified with brandy.

●●●●◐

VANILLA & GRAPEFRUIT DAIQUIRI

Glass: Martini
Garnish: Grapefruit zest twist (discarded) & vanilla pod
Method: **SHAKE** all ingredients with ice and fine strain into chilled glass.

2 1/2 shot(s) **Vanilla infused light white rum**
1/2 shot(s) **Freshly squeezed lime juice**
1/2 shot(s) **Sonoma vanilla bean sugar syrup**
1 shot(s) **Freshly squeezed pink grapefruit juice**

Origin: Created in 2003 by yours truly.
Comment: Reminiscent of a Hemingway Special, this flavoursome, vanilla laced Daiquiri has a wonderfully tangy bittersweet finish.

●●●●○

VANILLA & RASPBERRY MARTINI [NEW]

Glass: Martini
Garnish: Raspberries on stick
Method: **MUDDLE** raspberries in base of shaker. Add other ingredients, **SHAKE** with ice and fine strain into chilled glass.

12 fresh **Raspberries**
2 shot(s) **Vanilia infused Ketel One vodka**
1/4 shot(s) **Red wine**
1/4 shot(s) **Sugar (gomme) syrup**
1/2 shot(s) **Chilled mineral water (omit if wet ice)**

Origin: Created in 2006 by yours truly.
Comment: Exactly that – vanilla and raspberry.

VANILLA DAIQUIRI

Glass: Martini
Garnish: Lime wedge on rim
Method: **SHAKE** all ingredients with ice and fine strain into chilled glass.

2	shot(s)	**Vanilla infused light white rum**
1/2	shot(s)	**Freshly squeezed lime juice**
1/4	shot(s)	**Sugar (gomme) syrup**
3/4	shot(s)	**Chilled mineral water (omit if wet ice)**

Comment: The classic 'Natural Daiquiri' with a hint of vanilla.

VANILLA LAIKA

Glass: Collins
Garnish: Berries
Method: **SHAKE** all ingredients with ice and strain into glass filled with crushed ice.

1 1/2	shot(s)	**Vanilla flavoured vodka**
3/4	shot(s)	**Crème de mûre (blackberry) liqueur**
1/4	shot(s)	**Freshly squeezed lemon juice**
3/4	shot(s)	**Sugar (gomme) syrup**
4	shot(s)	**Pressed apple juice**

Origin: Created by Jake Burger in 2002 at Townhouse, Leeds, England. Laika was a Russian dog and the first canine in space.
Comment: Vanilla berry fruit in a tall, refreshing drink.

VANILLA MARGARITA

Glass: Old-fashioned
Garnish: Lime wedge
Method: **SHAKE** all ingredients with ice and fine strain into ice filled chilled glass.

2	shot(s)	**Vanilla infused Sauza Hornitos tequila**
1	shot(s)	**Freshly squeezed lemon juice**
1	shot(s)	**Cointreau / triple sec**

Origin: I first discovered this drink in 1998 at Café Pacifico, London, England.
Comment: A classic Margarita with a hint of vanilla.

VANILLA SENSATION

Glass: Martini
Garnish: Float wafer thin apple slice
Method: **SHAKE** all ingredients with ice and fine strain into chilled glass.

2	shot(s)	**Vanilla flavoured vodka**
1	shot(s)	**Sour apple liqueur**
1/2	shot(s)	**Dry vermouth**

Origin: Created in 2003 but by whom is unknown.
Comment: A pleasing vanilla twist on an Apple Martini.

VANILLA VODKA SOUR

Glass: Flute
Garnish: Lemon & orange zest twists
Method: **SHAKE** all ingredients with ice and fine strain into chilled glass.

2	shot(s)	**Vanilla flavoured vodka**
3/4	shot(s)	**Cuarenta Y Tres (Licor 43) liqueur**
3/4	shot(s)	**Freshly squeezed lemon juice**
1/2	fresh	**Egg white**

Comment: A Vodka Sour with a blast of spicy vanilla.

VANILLA'TINI

Glass: Martini
Garnish: Half vanilla pod
Method: **STIR** all ingredients with ice and strain into chilled glass.

2 1/2	shot(s)	**Vanilla flavoured vodka**
1/2	shot(s)	**Frangelico hazelnut liqueur**
1 1/2	shot(s)	**7-Up**

Origin: Discovered in 2003 at Paramount Hotel, New York City.
Comment: Vanilla, hazelnut and a hint of creamy citrus.

VANITINI

Glass: Martini
Garnish: Pineapple wedge on rim
Method: **SHAKE** all ingredients with ice and fine strain into chilled glass.

2	shot(s)	**Vanilla flavoured vodka**
2	shot(s)	**Sauvignon Blanc wine**
3/4	shot(s)	**Sour pineapple liqueur**
1/4	shot(s)	**Crème de mûre (blackberry) liqueur**

Comment: Vanilla and pineapple dried by the acidity of the wine, and sweetened and flavoured by blackberry liqueur.

VAN'S THE MAN

Glass: Collins
Garnish: Lime wedge
Method: **SHAKE** first three ingredients with ice and strain into ice-filled glass. **TOP** with ginger beer.

1 1/2	shot(s)	**La Fée Parisian 68% absinthe**
1	shot(s)	**Rose's lime cordial**
1	shot(s)	**Elderflower cordial**
Top up with		**Ginger beer**

Origin: From a recipe created by Giovanni Burdi, London, England.
Comment: Named not after the musician, but after Van Gogh who cut off one of his ears, reputedly as a direct result of over-consumption of absinthe.

A B C D E F G H I J K L M N O P Q R S T U V W X Y Z

VANTE MARTINI

Glass: Martini
Garnish: Orange zest twist
Method: **MUDDLE** cardamom in base of shaker. Add other ingredients, **SHAKE** with ice and fine strain into chilled glass.

4	pods	**Cardamom**
1½	shot(s)	**Vanilla flavoured vodka**
1½	shot(s)	**Sauvignon Blanc wine**
1	shot(s)	**Cuarenta Y Tres (Licor 43) liqueur**
¼	shot(s)	**Pressed pineapple juice**

Origin: Created in 2003 by yours truly.
Comment: Bold, aromatic and complex flavours.

VAVAVOOM

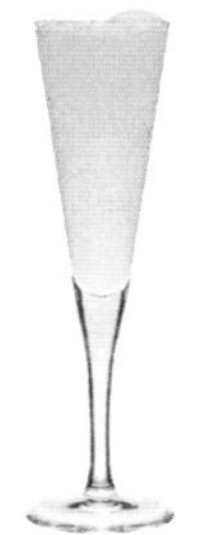

Glass: Flute
Method: **POUR** ingredients into chilled glass.

½	shot(s)	**Freshly squeezed lemon juice**
½	shot(s)	**Cointreau / triple sec**
½	shot(s)	**Sugar (gomme) syrup**
Top up with		**Piper-Heidsieck brut champagne**

Origin: Adapted from a drink created in 2002 by Yannick Miseriaux at The Fifth Floor Bar, London, England, and named after the Renault television advertisements.
Comment: This drink does indeed give champagne vavavoom.

VELVET FOG [NEW]

Glass: Martini
Garnish: Orange peel twist (discarded) & freshly grated nutmeg
Method: **SHAKE** all ingredients with ice and fine strain into chilled glass.

1½	shot(s)	**Ketel One vodka**
1¼	shot(s)	**Freshly squeezed lime juice**
¾	shot(s)	**Velvet Falernum liqueur**
¾	shot(s)	**Freshly squeezed orange juice**
2	dashes	**Angostura aromatic bitters**

Origin: Created by Dale DeGroff, New York City, USA.
Comment: Tangy, freshand bittersweet.

VELVET HAMMER [UPDATED]

Glass: Martini
Garnish: Grate nutmeg over drink
Method: **SHAKE** all ingredients with ice and fine strain into chilled glass.

1	shot(s)	**Ketel One vodka**
¾	shot(s)	**Cointreau / triple sec**
¾	shot(s)	**White crème de cacao liqueur**
¾	shot(s)	**Double (heavy) cream**
¾	shot(s)	**Milk**
¼	shot(s)	**Sonoma pomegranate (grenadine) syrup**

Variant: With apricot brandy and coffee liqueur in place of cacao and grenadine.
Comment: Lots of velvet with a little bit of hammer courtesy of a shot of vodka.

VENETO

Glass: Martini
Garnish: Lemon zest twist
Method: **SHAKE** all ingredients with ice and fine strain into chilled glass.

2	shot(s)	**Rémy Martin cognac**
½	shot(s)	**Luxardo Sambuca dei Cesari**
½	shot(s)	**Freshly squeezed lemon juice**
1/8	shot(s)	**Sugar (gomme) syrup**
½	shot(s)	**Egg white**

Comment: A serious, Stinger-like drink.

VENUS IN FURS

Glass: Collins
Garnish: Berries & lemon wheel in glass
Method: **SHAKE** all ingredients with ice and strain into ice-filled glass.

1	shot(s)	**Raspberry flavoured vodka**
1	shot(s)	**Ketel One Citroen vodka**
3½	shot(s)	**Pressed apple juice**
3	dashes	**Angostura aromatic bitters**

Origin: A cocktail which emerged in London's bars early in 2002.
Comment: Juicy flavours with a hint of spice make for a refreshing, quaffable drink.

VENUS MARTINI

Glass: Martini
Garnish: Raspberry in drink
Method: **MUDDLE** raspberries in base of shaker. Add other ingredients, **SHAKE** with ice and fine strain into chilled glass.

7	fresh	**Raspberries**
2	shot(s)	**Plymouth gin**
1	shot(s)	**Cointreau / triple sec**
¼	shot(s)	**Sugar (gomme) syrup**
3	dashes	**Peychaud's aromatic bitters (optional)**

Comment: Raspberry with hints of bitter orange and gin – surprisingly dry.

VERDANT MARTINI

Glass: Martini
Garnish: Float mint leaf
Method: **SHAKE** all ingredients with ice and fine strain into chilled glass.

2	shot(s)	**Zubrówka bison vodka**
1/8	shot(s)	**Green Chartreuse**
2	shot(s)	**Pressed apple juice**
½	shot(s)	**Freshly squeezed lime juice**

Origin: I created this drink in 2003 and named it after the hue of its ingredients.
Comment: A herbal apple pie of a drink.

VERDI MARTINI

Glass: Martini
Garnish: Pineapple wedge on rim
Method: **SHAKE** all ingredients with ice and fine strain into chilled glass.

$1^3/_4$	shot(s)	**Raspberry flavoured vodka**
$^1/_2$	shot(s)	**Midori melon liqueur**
$^1/_2$	shot(s)	**Peach schnapps liqueur**
1	shot(s)	**Pressed pineapple juice**
1	shot(s)	**Pressed apple juice**
$^1/_4$	shot(s)	**Freshly squeezed lime juice**

Origin: Adapted from a drink discovered in 2002 at the Fifth Floor Bar, London, England.
Comment: A melange of fruits combine in a gluggable short drink.

VERT'ICAL BREEZE

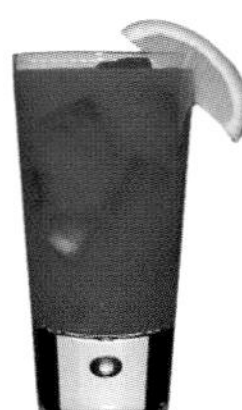

Glass: Collins
Garnish: Lemon wedge
Method: **SHAKE** all ingredients with ice and strain into ice-filled glass.

$1^1/_2$	shot(s)	**La Fée Parisian 68% absinthe**
3	shot(s)	**Cranberry juice**
3	shot(s)	**Freshly squeezed grapefruit juice**

Comment: For those who don't speak French, 'vert' means green – the colour of absinthe. Vertical suggests takeoff – try it and see.

THE VESPER MARTINI

Glass: Martini
Garnish: Lemon zest twist
Method: **SHAKE** all ingredients with ice and fine strain into chilled glass.

3	shot(s)	**Plymouth gin**
1	shot(s)	**Ketel One vodka**
$^1/_2$	shot(s)	**Dry vermouth**

Origin: 007's original 'shaken not stirred' Martini as chronicled in the first James Bond novel, Casino Royale.
Comment: Enough alcohol to drop a rhino – licensed to kill.

VIAGRA FALLS

Glass: Martini
Garnish: Orange zest twist
Method: **SHAKE** all ingredients with ice and fine strain into chilled glass.

$^3/_4$	shot(s)	**La Fée Parisian 68% absinthe**
$1^1/_2$	shot(s)	**Sour apple liqueur**
$1^3/_4$	shot(s)	**Chilled mineral water**
2	dashes	**Fee Brothers orange bitters**

Origin: Created by Jack Leuwens, London, England.
Comment: Aniseed and apple – sure to get your pecker up.

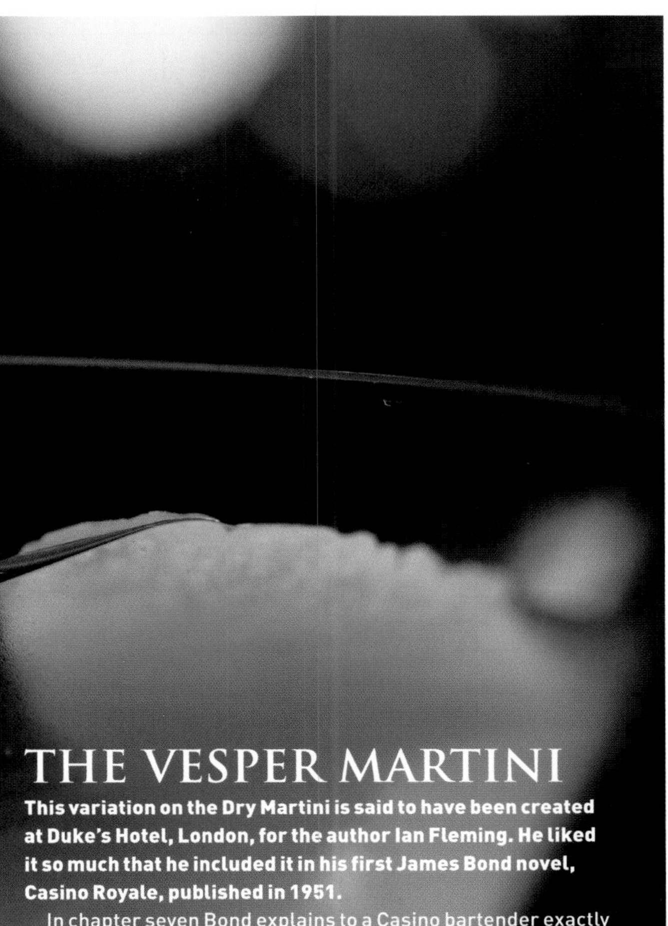

THE VESPER MARTINI

This variation on the Dry Martini is said to have been created at Duke's Hotel, London, for the author Ian Fleming. He liked it so much that he included it in his first James Bond novel, Casino Royale, published in 1951.

In chapter seven Bond explains to a Casino bartender exactly how to make and serve the drink: "In a deep champagne goblet. Three measures of Gordon's, one of vodka, half a measure of Kina Lillet [now called Lillet Blanc]. Shake it very well until it's ice-cold, then add a large slice of lemon peel."

When made, 007 compliments the bartender, but tells him it would be better made with a grain-based vodka. He also explains his Martini to Felix Leiter, the CIA man, saying, "This drink's my own invention. I'm going to patent it when I can think of a good name."

In chapter eight, Bond meets the beautiful agent Vesper Lynd. She explains why her parents named her Vesper and Bond asks if she'd mind if he called his favourite Martini after her. Like so many of Bond's love interests Vesper turns out to be a double agent and the book closes with his words, "The bitch is dead now."

Many bartenders advocate that a Martini should be stirred and not shaken, some citing the ridiculous argument that shaking will "bruise the gin". If you like your Martinis shaken (as I do) then avoid the possible look of distaste from your server and order a Vesper. This Martini is always shaken, an action that aerates the drink, and makes it colder and more dilute than simply stirring. It also gives the drink a slightly clouded appearance and can leave small shards of ice on the surface of the drink. This is easily prevented by the use of a fine strainer when pouring.

VIEUX CARRÉ COCKTAIL [NEW]

Glass: Old-fashioned
Garnish: Lemon zest twist
Method: **STIR** all ingredients with ice and strain into ice-filled glass.

1	shot(s)	**Bourbon whiskey**
1	shot(s)	**Rémy Martin cognac**
3/4	shot(s)	**Sweet (rosso) vermouth**
1/4	shot(s)	**Bénédictine D.O.M. liqueur**
2	dashes	**Peychaud's aromatic bitters**
2	dashes	**Angostura aromatic bitters**

Origin: Created in 1938 by Walter Bergeron, the head bartender at what is now the Carousel bar at the Monteleone Hotel, New Orleans, USA. Pronounced 'Voo-Ka-Ray', it is named after the French term for New Orlean's French Quarter and literally translates as 'old square'.
Comment: Like an ultra-smooth and complex Sweet Manhattan served on the rocks.

VIOLET AFFINITY

Glass: Martini
Garnish: Lemon zest twist
Method: **STIR** all ingredients with ice and strain into chilled glass.

2	shot(s)	**Benoit Serres liqueur de violette**
1	shot(s)	**Sweet (rosso) vermouth**
1	shot(s)	**Dry vermouth**

Origin: An adaptation of the classic Affinity.
Comment: Amazingly delicate and complex for such a simple drink.

VODKA COLLINS

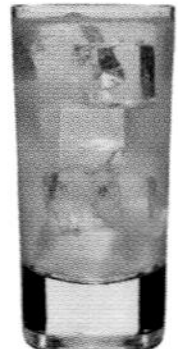

Glass: Collins
Garnish: Orange slice & cherry on stick (sail)
Method: **SHAKE** first three ingredients with ice and strain into ice-filled glass. **TOP** with soda, lightly stir and serve with straws.

2	shot(s)	**Ketel One vodka**
1	shot(s)	**Freshly squeezed lemon juice**
1/2	shot(s)	**Sugar (gomme) syrup**
Top up with		**Soda water (club soda)**

AKA: Joe Collins
Comment: A Tom Collins with vodka – a refreshing balance of sweet and sour.

VODKA ESPRESSO

Glass: Old-fashioned
Garnish: Three coffee beans
Method: **SHAKE** all ingredients with ice and strain into ice-filled glass.

2	shot(s)	**Ketel One vodka**
1 1/2	shot(s)	**Cold espresso coffee**
1/2	shot(s)	**Kahlúa coffee liqueur**
1/4	shot(s)	**Sugar (gomme) syrup**

Origin: Created in 1983 by Dick Bradsell at the Soho Brasserie, London, England.
Comment: Vodka and coffee combine in this tasty wake up call.

VODKA GIMLET

Glass: Martini
Garnish: Lime wedge or cherry
Method: **STIR** all ingredients with ice and strain into chilled glass.

2 1/2	shot(s)	**Ketel One vodka**
1 1/4	shot(s)	**Rose's lime cordial**

Variants: Shaken. The original Gimlet is based on gin.
Comment: Sweetened lime fortified with vodka.

VODKA SOUR

Glass: Old-fashioned
Garnish: Lemon wheel & cherry on stick (sail)
Method: **SHAKE** all ingredients with ice and strain into ice-filled glass.

2	shot(s)	**Ketel One vodka**
1	shot(s)	**Freshly squeezed lemon juice**
1/2	shot(s)	**Sugar (gomme) syrup**
3	dashes	**Angostura aromatic bitters**
1/2	fresh	**Egg white**

Comment: A great vodka based drink balancing sweet and sour.

VODKATINI

Glass: Martini
Garnish: Lemon zest twist / olives
Method: **STIR** vermouth with ice in a mixing glass and strain to **DISCARD** excess vermouth, leaving only a coating on the ice. **POUR** vodka into mixing glass containing coated ice, **STIR** and strain into chilled glass.

1/2	shot(s)	**Dry vermouth**
2 1/2	shot(s)	**Ketel One vodka**

Variant: Various flavours may be steeped in the vodka such as cardamom, fennel, ginger, lavender, mint and star anise.
Comment: Consuming while still ice cold is key to the enjoyment of this modern classic.

VOLGA BOATMAN [UPDATED]

Glass: Martini
Garnish: Orange zest twist
Method: **SHAKE** all ingredients with ice and fine strain into chilled glass.

1 1/2	shot(s)	**Ketel One vodka**
3/4	shot(s)	**Kirsch eau de vie**
1 1/2	shot(s)	**Freshly squeezed orange juice**

Origin: Recipe adapted from David Embury's classic Fine Art of Mixing Drinks. Named after the epic (and somewhat camp) Cecil B. De Mille movie, which took its name from a Russian folksong hymning the Volga, Europe's longest river.
Comment: A Screwdriver served straight-up with a twist of cherry.

VOODOO

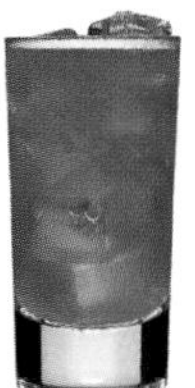

Glass: Collins
Garnish: Dust with cinnamon sprinkled through flame
Method: **SHAKE** all ingredients with ice and strain into ice-filled glass.

2	shot(s)	**Aged rum**
¾	shot(s)	**Sweet (rosso) vermouth**
2½	shot(s)	**Pressed apple juice**
½	shot(s)	**Freshly squeezed lime juice**
¼	shot(s)	**Sugar (gomme) syrup**

Origin: Created in 2002 by Alex Kammerling, London, England.
Comment: The rich flavour of the aged rum marries well with apple and lime juice.

VOWEL COCKTAIL

Glass: Martini
Garnish: Orange zest twist
Method: **SHAKE** all ingredients with ice and fine strain into chilled glass.

1¼	shot(s)	**The Famous Grouse Scotch whisky**
1	shot(s)	**Kümmel liqueur**
1	shot(s)	**Sweet (rosso) vermouth**
¾	shot(s)	**Freshly squeezed orange juice**
2	dashes	**Angostura bitters**

Origin: Adapted from a recipe in Vintage Spirits & Forgotten Cocktails by Ted Haigh (AKA Dr. Cocktail).
Comment: Caraway from the Kümmel subtly dominates this aromatic drink.

WAGON WHEEL

Glass: Old-fashioned
Garnish: Lemon slice in drink
Method: **SHAKE** all ingredients with ice and fine strain into glass filled with crushed ice.

1½	shot(s)	**Southern Comfort liqueur**
1½	shot(s)	**Rémy Martin cognac**
¾	shot(s)	**Freshly squeezed lemon juice**
¼	shot(s)	**Sonoma pomegranate (grenadine) syrup**

Origin: Adapted from a recipe purloined from David Embury's Fine Art of Mixing Drinks.
Comment: This classic cocktail will be best appreciated by lovers of Southern Comfort.

WALNUT MARTINI

Glass: Martini
Garnish: Float walnut half
Method: **STIR** all ingredients with ice and strain into chilled glass.

2	shot(s)	**Ketel One vodka**
¾	shot(s)	**Tuaca Italian liqueur**
¾	shot(s)	**Toschi Nocello walnut liqueur**
¾	shot(s)	**Dry vermouth**

Origin: Created in 2005 by yours truly.
Comment: Nutty but nice.

WALTZING MATILDA [UPDATED]

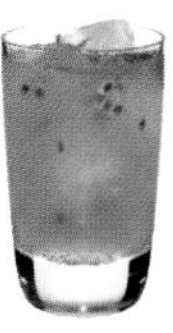

Glass: Collins
Garnish: Half orange slice
Method: Cut passion fruit in half and scoop out flesh into shaker. Add next three ingredients, **SHAKE** with ice and fine strain into ice-filled glass. **TOP** with ginger ale.

1	fresh	**Passion fruit**
1	shot(s)	**Plymouth gin**
2	shot(s)	**Sauvignon Blanc wine**
1/8	shot(s)	**Grand Marnier liqueur**
Top up with		**Ginger ale**

Origin: Adapted from a recipe from David Embury's classic book, The Fine Art of Mixing Drinks.
Comment: Passion fruit, gin, wine and ginger ale all combine well in this refreshing drink.

WANTON ABANDON [NEW]

Glass: Martini
Garnish: Strawberry on rim
Method: **MUDDLE** strawberries in base of shaker. Add next three ingredients, **SHAKE** with ice and fine strain into chilled glass. **TOP** with champagne.

5	fresh	**Strawberries**
2	shot(s)	**Ketel One vodka**
¾	shot(s)	**Freshly squeezed lemon juice**
½	shot(s)	**Sugar (gomme) syrup**
Top up with		**Piper-Heidsieck brut champagne**

Comment: A crowd pleaser – looks great and its fruity, balanced flavour will offend few.

WARD EIGHT

Glass: Martini
Garnish: Orange slice & cherry (sail)
Method: **SHAKE** all ingredients with ice and fine strain into chilled glass.

2¼	shot(s)	**Bourbon whiskey**
¾	shot(s)	**Freshly squeezed lemon juice**
¾	shot(s)	**Freshly squeezed orange juice**
¼	shot(s)	**Sonoma pomegranate (grenadine) syrup**
½	shot(s)	**Chilled mineral water (omit if wet ice)**

Origin: Ward Eight was a voting district of Boston and famed for its political corruption. This drink was first served by Tom Hussion in November 1898 at Boston's Locke-Ober Café, in honour of Martin Lomasney, who owned the café and was running for election in Ward Eight.
Comment: This is a spirited, sweet and sour combination – like most politicians.

FOR MORE INFORMATION SEE OUR INGREDIENTS APPENDIX ON PAGE 322

●●●◐○

WARSAW

Glass: Martini
Garnish: Orange zest twist
Method: **STIR** all ingredients with ice and strain into chilled glass.

- 2 shot(s) **Ketel One vodka**
- 1/2 shot(s) **Polska Wisniówka cherry liqueur**
- 1/4 shot(s) **Cointreau / triple sec**
- 2 dashes **Angostura aromatic bitters**
- 3/4 shot(s) **Chilled mineral water (omit if wet ice)**

Comment: Subtle cherry notes with orange.

●●●●◐

WARSAW COOLER

Glass: Collins
Garnish: Mint sprig & orange zest
Method: **STIR** honey with vodka in base of shaker until honey dissolves. Add other ingredients, **SHAKE** with ice and strain into ice-filled glass.

- 2 spoons **Runny honey**
- 1 1/2 shot(s) **Zubrówka bison vodka**
- 1/2 shot(s) **Spiced rum**
- 1/4 shot(s) **Cointreau / triple sec**
- 1/2 shot(s) **Sugar (gomme) syrup**
- 3/4 shot(s) **Freshly squeezed lemon juice**
- 2 shot(s) **Pressed apple juice**

Origin: Created in 2002 by Morgan Watson of Apartment, Belfast, Northern Ireland.
Comment: Orange, honey, apple and spice laced with Polish bison grass vodka.

●●●●◐

WASABI MARTINI

Glass: Martini
Garnish: Float strips of yaki nori seaweed.
Method: Squeeze a pea-sized quantity of wasabi paste onto a barspoon and **STIR** with vodka until wasabi dissolves. Add other ingredients, **SHAKE** with ice and fine strain into chilled glass.

- 2 shot(s) **Ketel One vodka**
- 1 pea **Wasabi paste**
- 3/4 shot(s) **Freshly squeezed lemon juice**
- 1/2 shot(s) **Sugar (gomme) syrup**

Origin: Created in 2004 by Philippe Guidi at Morton's, London, England.
Comment: Wonderfully balanced with spicy heat and a zesty finish.

●●●●◐

WASHINGTON APPLE [NEW]

Glass: Collins
Garnish: Apple slice
Method: **SHAKE** first four ingredients with ice and fine strain into ice-filled glass. **DRIZZLE** grenadine over drink. Serve with straws.

- 2 shot(s) **Ketel One vodka**
- 3 shot(s) **Pressed apple juice**
- 1/4 shot(s) **Freshly squeezed lime juice**
- 1/2 shot(s) **Sour apple liqueur**
- 1/4 shot(s) **Sonoma pomegranate (grenadine) syrup**

Origin: Created by Wayne Collins, London, England.
Comment: A long version of the popular Sour Apple Martini.

●●●●○

WATERMELON & BASIL MARTINI

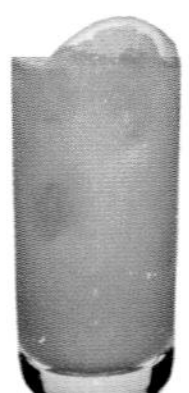

Glass: Martini
Garnish: Watermelon wedge on rim
Method: Cut watermelon into 16 segments, chop the flesh from one segment into cubes and **MUDDLE** in base of shaker. Add other ingredients, **SHAKE** with ice and fine strain into chilled glass.

- 1/16 fresh **Watermelon (diced)**
- 7 fresh **Basil leaves (torn)**
- 2 shot(s) **Plymouth gin**
- 1/2 shot(s) **Sugar (gomme) syrup**

Comment: Refreshing watermelon with interesting herbal hints from the basil and gin.

●●●●○

WATERMELON & BASIL SMASH

Glass: Collins
Garnish: Watermelon wedge on rim
Method: Cut watermelon into 16 segments, chop the flesh from one segment into cubes and **MUDDLE** in base of shaker. Add next three ingredients, **SHAKE** with ice and fine strain into ice-filled glass. **TOP** with ginger ale.

- 1/16 fresh **Watermelon (diced)**
- 8 fresh **Torn basil leaves**
- 2 shot(s) **Sauza Hornitos tequila**
- 3/4 shot(s) **Luxardo limoncello liqueur**
- Top up with **Ginger ale**

Comment: Sweet and sour, long and refreshing with subtle hints of basil, ginger and tequila amongst the fruit.

●●●◐○

WATERMELON COSMO

Glass: Martini (large)
Garnish: Watermelon wedge on rim
Method: Cut watermelon into 16 segments, chop the flesh from one segment into cubes and **MUDDLE** in base of shaker. Add other ingredients, **SHAKE** with ice and fine strain into chilled glass.

- 1/16 fresh **Watermelon (diced)**
- 2 shot(s) **Ketel One Citroen vodka**
- 3/4 shot(s) **Freshly squeezed lime juice**
- 3/4 shot(s) **Cranberry juice**
- 1/2 shot(s) **Midori melon liqueur**
- 1/8 shot(s) **Rose's lime cordial**
- 2 dashes **Fee Brothers orange bitters**

Origin: Created in 2003 by Eric Fossard at Cecconi's, London, England.
Comment: Looks like a standard Cosmo but tastes just as the name suggests.

DRINKS ARE GRADED AS FOLLOWS:

● DISGUSTING ●◐ PRETTY AWFUL ●● BEST AVOIDED
●●◐ DISAPPOINTING ●●● ACCEPTABLE ●●●◐ GOOD
●●●● RECOMMENDED ●●●●◐ HIGHLY RECOMMENDED
●●●●● OUTSTANDING / EXCEPTIONAL

WATERMELON MAN [NEW]

Glass: Collins
Garnish: Lime wedge
Method: **SHAKE** first four ingredients with ice and strain into ice-filled glass. **TOP** with 7-Up and serve with straws.

2	shot(s)	**Ketel One vodka**
1/2	shot(s)	**Watermelon liquer**
1/4	shot(s)	**Passion fruit sugar syrup**
1/2	shot(s)	**Freshly squeezed lime juice**
Top up with		**7-Up**

Origin: This cocktail is popular in Berlin, Germany, and is named after the Herbie Hancock track which was a top ten hit for the Latin jazzster Mongo Santamaria in 1963.
Comment: Fruity and sweet.

WATERMELON MARTINI

Glass: Martini
Garnish: Watermelon wedge on rim
Method: Cut watermelon into 16 segments, chop the flesh from one segment into cubes and **MUDDLE** in base of shaker. Add other ingredients, **SHAKE** with ice and fine strain into chilled glass.

1/16	fresh	**Watermelon (diced)**
2	shot(s)	**Ketel One vodka**
1/2	shot(s)	**Sugar (gomme) syrup**

Comment: So fruity, you can almost convince yourself this is a health drink!

WEBSTER MARTINI [NEW]

Glass: Martini
Garnish: Lime zest twist
Method: **SHAKE** all ingredients with ice and fine strain into chilled glass.

2	shot(s)	**Plymouth gin**
1	shot(s)	**Dry vermouth**
1/2	shot(s)	**Apricot brandy liqueur**
1/2	shot(s)	**Freshly squeezed lime juice**

Origin: Adapted from a recipe in Harry Craddock's 1930 Savoy Cocktail Book. Craddock writes of this drink, "A favourite cocktail at the bar of the S.S. Mauretania."
Comment: Balanced rather than sweet. The old-school Dry Martini meets the contemporary fruit driven Martini.

WEEPING JESUS

Glass: Old-fashioned
Method: **SHAKE** first three ingredients with ice and strain into glass filled with crushed ice. **TOP** with 7-Up.

1	shot(s)	**La Fée Parisian 68% absinthe**
1	shot(s)	**Peach schnapps liqueur**
1	shot(s)	**Sonoma pomegranate (grenadine) syrup**
Top up with		**7-Up**

Origin: Created in 2002 by Andy Jones at Yates's, London, England.
Comment: This bright red cocktail makes the strong aniseed flavours of absinthe approachable.

THE WENTWORTH

Glass: Martini
Garnish: Orange zest twist
Method: **SHAKE** all ingredients with ice and fine strain into chilled glass.

1 1/4	shot(s)	**Bourbon whiskey**
1 1/4	shot(s)	**Dubonnet Red**
1 1/4	shot(s)	**Cranberry juice**

Origin: Created in 2003 by Sharon Cooper at the Harvest Restaurant, Pomfret, Connecticut, USA.
Comment: The pleasing tang of bourbon adds backbone to this fruity herbal cocktail.

WET MARTINI

Glass: Martini
Garnish: Olive or twist?
Method: **STIR** all ingredients with ice and strain into chilled glass.

3	shot(s)	**Plymouth gin**
1 1/2	shot(s)	**Dry vermouth**

Origin: A generous measure of vermouth to two of gin, hence the name 'Wet' Martini.
Comment: Reputed to be a favourite of HRH Prince Charles.

THE WET SPOT [NEW]

Glass: Martini
Garnish: Lemon zest twist
Method: **SHAKE** all ingredients with ice and fine strain into chilled glass.

1 1/2	shot(s)	**Plymouth gin**
1/2	shot(s)	**Apricot brandy liqueur**
1/2	shot(s)	**Elderflower cordial**
1	shot(s)	**Pressed apple juice**
3/4	shot(s)	**Freshly squeezed lemon juice**

Origin: Adapted from a drink created by Willy Shine and Aisha Sharpe at Bed Bar, New York City, USA.
Comment: Sharp but fresh tasting and moreish.

WHAT THE HELL [UPDATED]

Glass: Martini
Garnish: Lime wedge on rim
Method: **SHAKE** all ingredients with ice and fine strain into chilled glass.

2	shot(s)	**Plymouth gin**
1	shot(s)	**Apricot brandy liqueur**
3/4	shot(s)	**Dry vermouth**
1/4	shot(s)	**Freshly squeezed lime juice**
1/8	shot(s)	**Sugar (gomme) syrup**

Comment: Gin and dry apricots.

WHIP ME & BEAT ME

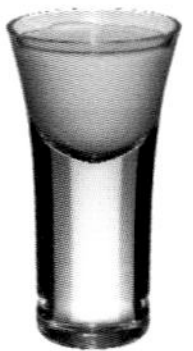

Glass: Shot
Method: SHAKE all ingredients with ice and fine strain into chilled glass.

1/2	shot(s)	**La Fée Parisian 68% absinthe**
1/2	shot(s)	**Malibu coconut rum liqueur**
1/2	shot(s)	**Double (heavy) cream**
1/2	shot(s)	**Milk**

Comment: A creamy, coconut, absinthe laden shot.

WHISKEY COBBLER

Glass: Goblet
Garnish: Lemon slice & mint sprig
Method: SHAKE all ingredients with ice and strain into glass filled with crushed ice.

2	shot(s)	**The Famous Grouse Scotch whisky**
1/2	shot(s)	**Rémy Martin cognac**
1/2	shot(s)	**Grand Marnier liqueur**

Comment: A hardcore yet sophisticated drink.

WHISKEY COLLINS

Glass: Collins
Garnish: Orange slice & cherry (sail)
Method: SHAKE first four ingredients with ice and strain into ice-filled glass. TOP with soda water, lightly stir and serve with straws.

2	shot(s)	**Bourbon whiskey**
3/4	shot(s)	**Freshly squeezed lemon juice**
1/2	shot(s)	**Sugar (gomme) syrup**
3	dashes	**Angostura aromatic bitters**
Top up with		**Soda water (club soda)**

Comment: A whiskey based twist on the classic Tom Collins.

WHISKEY DAISY

Glass: Martini
Garnish: Lemon zest twist
Method: SHAKE all ingredients with ice and fine strain into chilled glass.

1 3/4	shot(s)	**Bourbon whiskey**
3/4	shot(s)	**Freshly squeezed lemon juice**
1/2	shot(s)	**Cointreau / triple sec**
1/4	shot(s)	**Sonoma pomegranate (grenadine) syrup**

Comment: This venerable, bourbon led classic has a strong citrus flavour.

WHISKEY SOUR #1 (CLASSIC FORMULA)

Glass: Old-fashioned
Garnish: Lemon slice & cherry (sail)
Method: SHAKE all ingredients with ice and strain into ice-filled glass.

2	shot(s)	**Bourbon whiskey**
3/4	shot(s)	**Freshly squeezed lemon juice**
1	shot(s)	**Sugar (gomme) syrup**
3	dashes	**Angostura aromatic bitters**
1/2	fresh	**Egg white**

Origin: This recipe follows the classic sour proportions (3:4:8): three quarter part of the sour ingredient (lemon juice), one part of the sweet ingredient (sugar syrup) and two parts of the strong ingredient (whiskey).
Comment: I find the classic formulation more sweet than sour and prefer the 4:2:8 ratio below.

WHISKEY SOUR #2 (DIFFORD'S FORMULA) [NEW]

Glass: Old-fashioned
Garnish: Lemon slice & cherry (sail)
Method: SHAKE all ingredients with ice and strain into ice-filled glass.

2	shot(s)	**Bourbon whiskey**
1	shot(s)	**Freshly squeezed lemon juice**
1/2	shot(s)	**Sugar (gomme) syrup**
3	dashes	**Angostura aromatic bitters**
1/2	fresh	**Egg white**

Origin: My 4:2:8 sour formula.
Comment: Smooth with a hint of citrus sourness and an invigorating blast of whiskey.

WHISKEY SQUIRT [NEW]

Glass: Collins
Garnish: Peach slice
Method: SHAKE first three ingredients with ice and strain into ice-filled glass. TOP with soda from a siphon. Serve with straws.

2	shot(s)	**Peach puree (sweetened)**
2	shot(s)	**Bourbon whiskey**
1/4	shot(s)	**Grand Marnier liqueur**
Top up with		**Soda (from siphon)**

Origin: Adapted from a recipe purloined from David Embury's classic book, The Fine Art of Mixing Drinks.
Comment: Peach combines wonderfully with bourbon and this drink benefits from that marriage.

DRINKS ARE GRADED AS FOLLOWS:

● DISGUSTING ●◐ PRETTY AWFUL ●● BEST AVOIDED
●●◐ DISAPPOINTING ●●● ACCEPTABLE ●●●◐ GOOD
●●●● RECOMMENDED ●●●●◐ HIGHLY RECOMMENDED
●●●●● OUTSTANDING / EXCEPTIONAL

WHISKY FIZZ

Glass: Collins
Garnish: Lemon slice
Method: **SHAKE** first three ingredients with ice and strain into ice-filled glass. **TOP** with soda, lightly stir and serve with straws.

2	shot(s)	**The Famous Grouse Scotch whisky**
1	shot(s)	**Freshly squeezed lemon juice**
1/2	shot(s)	**Sugar (gomme) syrup**
Top up with		**Soda from siphon**

Comment: The character of the whisky shines through this refreshing, balanced, sweet and sour drink.

WHISKY MAC

Glass: Old-fashioned
Method: **POUR** ingredients into ice-filled glass and lightly stir.

2	shot(s)	**The Famous Grouse Scotch whisky**
1	shot(s)	**Stone's green ginger wine**

Comment: Ginger wine smoothes and spices Scotch.

WHITE COSMO

Glass: Martini
Garnish: Orange zest twist
Method: **SHAKE** all ingredients with ice and fine strain into chilled glass.

1	shot(s)	**Ketel One Citroen vodka**
1	shot(s)	**Cointreau / triple sec**
1 1/2	shot(s)	**White cranberry & grape juice**
1/2	shot(s)	**Freshly squeezed lime juice**

AKA: Cosmo Blanco
Origin: Emerged during 2002 in New York City.
Comment: Just what it says on the tin.

WHITE ELEPHANT

Glass: Martini
Garnish: Dust with cocoa powder
Method: **SHAKE** all ingredients with ice and fine strain into chilled glass.

2	shot(s)	**Ketel One vodka**
3/4	shot(s)	**White crème de cacao liqueur**
3/4	shot(s)	**Double (heavy) cream**
3/4	shot(s)	**Milk**

AKA: White Beach
Comment: Smooth and creamy with a hint of chocolate.

WHITE GIN FIZZ

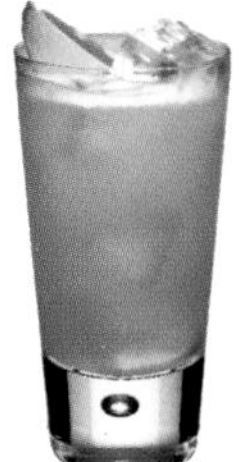

Glass: Collins
Garnish: Lemon wedge in drink
Method: **SHAKE** first four ingredients with ice and strain into ice-filled glass. **TOP** with soda from a siphon.

2	shot(s)	**Plymouth gin**
1	shot(s)	**Freshly squeezed lemon juice**
1/4	shot(s)	**Sugar (gomme) syrup**
2	scoops	**Lemon sorbet (see recipe under 'L')**
Top up with		**Soda water (from siphon)**

Origin: Created in 2003 by Tony Conigliaro at Shumi, London, England.
Comment: Almost creamy in consistency, this gin fizz reminds me of the Sgroppino found in Venice.

WHITE KNIGHT

Glass: Martini
Method: **SHAKE** all ingredients with ice and fine strain into chilled glass.

3/4	shot(s)	**The Famous Grouse Scotch whisky**
3/4	shot(s)	**Kahlúa coffee liqueur**
3/4	shot(s)	**Drambuie liqueur**
3/4	shot(s)	**Double (heavy) cream**
3/4	shot(s)	**Milk**

Comment: This creamy after-dinner drink features Scotch and honey with a hint of coffee. Not too sweet.

WHITE LADY [UPDATED]

Glass: Martini
Garnish: Lemon zest twist
Method: **SHAKE** all ingredients with ice and fine strain into chilled glass.

2	shot(s)	**Plymouth gin**
3/4	shot(s)	**Cointreau / triple sec**
3/4	shot(s)	**Freshly squeezed lemon juice**
1	fresh	**Egg white**

Origin: In 1919 Harry MacElhone, while working at Ciro's Club, London, England, created his first White Lady with 2 shots triple sec, 1 shot white crème de menthe and 1 shot lemon juice. In 1923, he created the White Lady above at his own Harry's New York Bar in Paris, France.
Comment: A simple but lovely classic drink with a sour finish.

WHITE LION [NEW]

Glass: Martini
Garnish: Lime wedge on rim
Method: **SHAKE** all ingredients with ice and fine strain into chilled glass.

2	shot(s)	**Light white rum**
1/4	shot(s)	**Cointreau / triple sec**
1/2	shot(s)	**Freshly squeezed lime juice**
1/4	shot(s)	**Sonoma pomegranate (grenadine) syrup**

Origin: Adapted from a recipe purloined from David Embury's classic book, The Fine Art of Mixing Drinks.
Comment: This fruity Daiquiri is superb when made with quality pomegranate syrup and rum.

WHITE RUSSIAN

Glass: Old-fashioned
Garnish: Dust with grated nutmeg
Method: SHAKE all ingredients with ice and strain into ice-filled glass.

2	shot(s)	**Ketel One vodka**
1	shot(s)	**Kahlúa coffee liqueur**
3/4	shot(s)	**Double (heavy) cream**
3/4	shot(s)	**Milk**

Variant: Shake and strain vodka and coffee liqueur, then float cream.
Comment: A Black Russian smoothed with cream.

WHITE SANGRIA

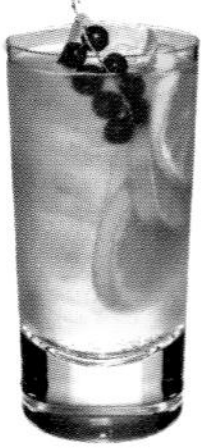

Glass: Old-fashioned
Garnish: Fruit slices
Method: SHAKE first three ingredients with ice and strain into ice-filled glass. **TOP** with 7-Up.

1	shot(s)	**Grand Marnier liqueur**
2	shot(s)	**Sauvignon Blanc wine**
1	shot(s)	**White cranberry & grape drink**
Top up with		**7-Up**

Comment: A twist on the traditional Spanish and Portugese punch.

WHITE SATIN

Glass: Martini
Garnish: Cocoa dust
Method: SHAKE all ingredients with ice and fine strain into chilled glass.

1 1/2	shot(s)	**Galliano liqueur**
1	shot(s)	**Kahlúa coffee liqueur**
3/4	shot(s)	**Double (heavy) cream**
3/4	shot(s)	**Milk**

Comment: Smoother than a cashmere codpiece!

WHITE STINGER

Glass: Old-fashioned
Method: SHAKE all ingredients with ice and strain into ice-filled glass.

2	shot(s)	**Ketel One vodka**
1/2	shot(s)	**White crème de menthe**
1/2	shot(s)	**White crème de cacao liqueur**

Comment: Liquid After Eights.

WIBBLE

Glass: Martini
Garnish: Lemon zest twist
Method: SHAKE all ingredients with ice and fine strain into chilled glass.

1	shot(s)	**Plymouth gin**
1	shot(s)	**Plymouth sloe gin liqueur**
1	shot(s)	**Freshly squeezed grapefruit juice**
1/4	shot(s)	**Freshly squeezed lemon juice**
1/8	shot(s)	**Sugar (gomme) syrup**
1/8	shot(s)	**Crème de mûre (blackberry) liqueur**

Origin: Created in 1999 by Dick Bradsell at The Player, London, England, for Nick Blacknell, a conspicuous lover of gin.
Comment: As Dick once said to me, "It may make you wobble, but it won't make you fall down." Complex and balanced.

WIDOW'S KISS [UPDATED]

Glass: Martini
Garnish: Mint leaf
Method: SHAKE all ingredients with ice and fine strain into chilled glass.

1 1/2	shot(s)	**Calvados or applejack brandy**
3/4	shot(s)	**Bénédictine D.O.M. liqueur**
3/4	shot(s)	**Yellow Chartreuse**
3/4	shot(s)	**Chilled water (omit if ice wet)**
2	dashes	**Angostura aromatic bitters**

Origin: Created before 1895 by George Kappeler at New York City's Holland House. This classic was originally made with green Chartreuse but is better with yellow.
Comment: Fantastically herbal with hints of apple, mint and eucalyptus.

WILD HONEY

Glass: Martini
Garnish: Grate nutmeg over drink
Method: SHAKE all ingredients with ice and fine strain into chilled glass.

1 1/2	shot(s)	**The Famous Grouse Scotch whisky**
3/4	shot(s)	**Vanilla flavoured vodka**
1	shot(s)	**Drambuie liqueur**
1/2	shot(s)	**Galliano liqueur**
1/2	shot(s)	**Double (heavy) cream**
1/2	shot(s)	**Milk**

Origin: Created in 2001 by James Price at Bar Red, London, England.
Comment: A serious yet creamy after dinner cocktail with whisky and honey.

HOW TO MAKE SUGAR SYRUP

To make your own sugar syrup, gradually pour TWO cups of granulated sugar into a saucepan containing ONE cup of hot water. Stir as you pour and carry on stirring and simmering until the sugar is dissolved. Do not let the water even come close to boiling and only simmer for as long as it takes to dissolve the sugar. Allow syrup to cool and pour into an empty bottle. Ideally, you should finely strain your syrup into the bottle to remove any undissolved crystals which could otherwise encourage crystallisation. If kept in a refrigerator this mixture will last for a couple of months.

WILD PROMENADE MARTINI

Glass: Martini
Garnish: Float 3 raspberries
Method: MUDDLE cucumber and raspberries in base of shaker. Add other ingredients, **SHAKE** with ice and fine strain into ice-filled glass.

2	inch	**Chopped cucumber**
5	fresh	**Raspberries**
1½	shot(s)	**Ketel One vodka**
½	shot(s)	**Raspberry flavoured vodka**
½	shot(s)	**Crème de framboise (raspberry) liqueur**
¼	shot(s)	**Sugar (gomme) syrup**

Origin: Created in 2002 by Mehdi Otmann at The Player, London, England.
Comment: Rich raspberry with green hints of cucumber.

WILTON MARTINI

Glass: Martini
Garnish: Float cinnamon dusted apple slice
Method: SHAKE all ingredients with ice and fine strain into chilled glass.

1	shot(s)	**Ketel One vodka**
1	shot(s)	**Calvados or applejack brandy**
½	shot(s)	**Apple schnapps liqueur**
1/8	shot(s)	**Goldschläger cinnamon schnapps**
1½	shot(s)	**Pressed apple juice**

Origin: An adaptation (2003) of the signature cocktail at The Blue Bar, London, England.
Comment: Refined cinnamon and apple.

WIMBLEDON MARTINI

Glass: Martini
Garnish: Strawberry on rim
Method: MUDDLE strawberries in base of shaker. Add other ingredients, **SHAKE** with ice and fine strain into chilled glass.

6	fresh	**Hulled strawberries**
1½	shot(s)	**Light white rum**
1½	shot(s)	**Crème de fraise (strawberry) liqueur**
¼	shot(s)	**Sugar (gomme) syrup**
½	shot(s)	**Double (heavy) cream**
½	shot(s)	**Milk**

Comment: Takes some getting through the strainer, but when you do it's simply strawberries and cream.

THE WINDSOR ROSE [NEW]

Glass: Martini
Garnish: Float rose petal
Method: SHAKE all ingredients with ice and fine strain into chilled glass.

1	shot(s)	**Orange flavoured vodka**
1	shot(s)	**Cointreau / triple sec**
1½	shot(s)	**Cranberry juice**
½	shot(s)	**Freshly squeezed lime juice**
1/8	shot(s)	**Rosewater**

Origin: Discovered in 2005 at The Polo Club Lounge, New Orleans, USA.
Comment: An range vodka and rosewater Cosmo.

WINDY MILLER

Glass: Collins
Garnish: Thin slices of lemon
Method: SHAKE first three ingredients with ice and strain into glass filled with crushed ice. **TOP** with 7-Up.

1	shot(s)	**Ketel One Citroen vodka**
1	shot(s)	**Mandarine Napoléon liqueur**
½	shot(s)	**La Fée Parisian 68% absinthe**
Top up with		**7-Up**

Origin: Discovered in 2000 at Teatro, London, England.
Comment: British readers over 40 may remember the children's TV series Trumpton, Chigley and Camberwick Green. If you do, then sing between sips, 'Pugh, Pugh, Barney McGrew, Cuthbert, Dibble and Grubb.'

WINE COOLER

Glass: Collins
Method: POUR first four ingredients into ice-filled glass. **TOP** with 7-Up, lightly stir and serve with straws.

4	shot(s)	**Sauvignon Blanc wine**
½	shot(s)	**Ketel One Citroen vodka**
½	shot(s)	**Freshly squeezed lemon juice**
½	shot(s)	**Freshly squeezed orange juice**
Top up with		**7-Up**

Comment: Like a citrussy white wine Spritzer.

WINK

Glass: Old-fashioned
Garnish: Wink as you serve
Method: POUR absinthe into ice-filled glass. **TOP** with chilled water and leave to stand. Separately **SHAKE** other ingredients with ice. **DISCARD** contents of glass and strain contents of shaker into empty (absinthe washed) glass.

½	shot(s)	**La Fée Parisian 68% absinthe**
2	shot(s)	**Plymouth gin**
½	shot(s)	**Sugar (gomme) syrup**
¼	shot(s)	**Cointreau / triple sec**
2	dashes	**Peychaud's aromatic bitters**
½	shot(s)	**Chilled mineral water (omit if wet ice)**

Origin: Created in 2002 by Tony Conigliaro at Lonsdale House, London, England.
Comment: A pink rinsed drink with a wonderfully aromatic flavour.

WINTER MARTINI [NEW]

Glass: Martini
Garnish: Lemon zest twist
Method: STIR all ingredients with ice and strain into chilled glass.

2	shot(s)	**Rémy Martin cognac**
½	shot(s)	**Sour apple liqueur**
½	shot(s)	**Dry vermouth**
1/8	shot(s)	**Sugar (gomme) syrup**

Comment: Reminiscent of an Apple Cart (a Calvados Sidecar), this is simple, balanced and tastes great.

WONKY MARTINI

Glass: Martini
Garnish: Orange zest twist
Method: **STIR** all ingredients with ice and strain into chilled glass.

1½ shot(s) **Vanilla flavoured vodka**
1½ shot(s) **Tuaca Italian liqueur**
1½ shot(s) **Sweet (rosso) vermouth**
2 dashes **Fee Brothers orange bitters**

Origin: Created in 2003 by yours truly.
Comment: A sweet, wet Vodkatini invigorated with orange and vanilla.

WOODLAND PUNCH [NEW]

Glass: Collins
Garnish: Lime wedge
Method: **SHAKE** first four ingredients with ice and strain into ice-filled glass. **TOP** with soda, lightly stir and serve with straws.

2 shot(s) **Southern Comfort liqueur**
¼ shot(s) **Cherry (brandy) liqueur**
½ shot(s) **Freshly squeezed lime juice**
2 shot(s) **Pressed pineapple juice**
Top up with **Soda water**

Origin: Adapted from a drink created in 1997 by Foster Creppel. This is the signature drink at his Woodland Plantation, the great house on the west bank of the Mississippi that features on every bottle of Southern Comfort.
Comment: Tart, tangy and refreshing.

WOO WOO [UPDATED]

Glass: Old-fashioned
Garnish: Split lime wedge
Method: **SHAKE** all ingredients with ice and strain into ice-filled glass.

2 shot(s) **Ketel One vodka**
1 shot(s) **Peach schnapps liqueur**
3 shot(s) **Cranberry juice**

Comment: Fruity, dry cranberry laced with vodka and peach. Not nearly as bad as its reputation but still lost in the eighties.

YACHT CLUB [NEW]

Glass: Martini
Garnish: Lemon zest twist
Method: **STIR** all ingredients with ice and strain into chilled glass.

2 shot(s) **Mount Gay golden rum**
1 shot(s) **Sweet (rosso) vermouth**
¼ shot(s) **Apricot brandy liqueur**

Origin: Adapted from a recipe purloined from David Embury's classic book, The Fine Art of Mixing Drinks.
Comment: Rich and slightly sweet with hints of apricot fruit.

YELLOW BELLY MARTINI

Glass: Martini
Garnish: Lemon zest twist
Method: **SHAKE** all ingredients with ice and fine strain into chilled glass.

1 shot(s) **Ketel One Citroen vodka**
1 shot(s) **Freshly squeezed lemon juice**
1 shot(s) **Luxardo limoncello liqueur**
1/8 shot(s) **Sugar (gomme) syrup**
½ shot(s) **Chilled mineral water (omit if wet ice)**

Comment: Lemon, lemon, lemon. Nice, though...

YELLOW BIRD

Glass: Martini
Garnish: Banana slice on rim
Method: **SHAKE** all ingredients with ice and fine strain into chilled glass.

1½ shot(s) **Mount Gay Eclipse golden rum**
½ shot(s) **Crème de bananes liqueur**
¼ shot(s) **Apricot brandy liqueur**
2 shot(s) **Pressed pineapple juice**
½ shot(s) **Freshly squeezed lime juice**
½ shot(s) **Sugar (gomme) syrup**
¼ shot(s) **Galliano liqueur**

Comment: A sweet and sour cocktail with four different fruits, rum and a splash of Galliano.

YELLOW FEVER MARTINI

Glass: Martini
Garnish: Pineapple wedge on rim
Method: **SHAKE** all ingredients with ice and fine strain into chilled glass.

2½ shot(s) **Ketel One vodka**
½ shot(s) **Galliano liqueur**
1½ shot(s) **Pressed pineapple juice**
½ shot(s) **Freshly squeezed lime juice**
1/8 shot(s) **Sugar (gomme) syrup**

Comment: Fortified pineapple with a subtle hint of cooling peppermint.

YELLOW PARROT

Glass: Martini
Garnish: Orange zest twist
Method: **SHAKE** all ingredients with ice and fine strain into chilled glass.

¼ shot(s) **La Fée Parisian 68% absinthe**
1 shot(s) **Yellow Chartreuse**
1 shot(s) **Apricot brandy liqueur**
1½ shot(s) **Chilled mineral water (reduce if wet ice)**

Origin: Some say this was created in 1935 by Albert Coleman at The Stork Club, New York City, but the drink featured in Harry Craddock's Savoy Cocktail Book five years before that.
Comment: The aniseed of the absinthe combines well with the other ingredients. A bit of a sweety but a strong old bird.

YULE LUVIT

Glass: Shot
Garnish: Grate nutmeg over drink
Method: Refrigerate ingredients then **LAYER** in chilled glass by carefully pouring in the following order.

3/4	shot(s)	**Hazelnut liqueur**
3/4	shot(s)	**Bourbon whiskey**

Comment: Actually, you'll find it strongly nutty and sweet.

YUM

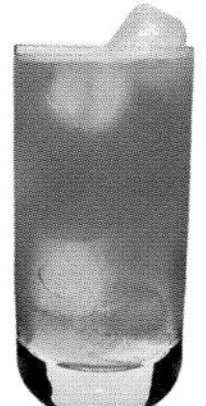

Glass: Collins
Garnish: Lemon wedge
Method: **SHAKE** all ingredients with ice and strain into ice-filled glass.

1 1/2	shot(s)	**Mandarine Napoléon liqueur**
1/2	shot(s)	**Peach schnapps liqueur**
1/4	shot(s)	**Chambord black raspberry liqueur**
1	shot(s)	**Freshly squeezed lemon juice**
3	shot(s)	**Pressed apple juice**

Comment: If you like sweet, fruity 'disco drinks' then this is indeed yummy.

Z MARTINI

Glass: Martini
Garnish: Hand stuffed blue cheese olives
Method: **STIR** all ingredients with ice and strain into chilled glass.

2 1/2	shot(s)	**Ketel One vodka**
1 1/4	shot(s)	**Dry white port (e.g. Dow's Fine White)**

Origin: Discovered in 2004 at Les Zygomates, Boston, USA.
Comment: Grainy vodka with dry, wine-like notes. Top marks for the garnish alone.

ZABAGLIONE MARTINI

Glass: Martini
Method: Separately **BEAT** egg white until stiff and frothy and yolk until this is as liquid as water, then pour into shaker. Add other ingredients, **SHAKE** with ice and fine strain into chilled glass.

1	fresh	**Egg yolk**
1	fresh	**Egg white**
1 1/2	shot(s)	**Warninks advocaat**
1/2	shot(s)	**Rémy Martin cognac**
1	shot(s)	**Marsala**
3/4	shot(s)	**Freshly squeezed lemon juice**

Origin: I created this drink in 2003 after the classic Italian dessert, which incidentally derives its name from the Neapolitan dialect word 'zapillare', meaning 'to foam'.
Comment: Like the dessert, this is sweet and rich with flavours of egg and fortified wine.

ZAKUSKI MARTINI

Glass: Martini
Garnish: Lemon zest & cucumber peel
Method: **MUDDLE** cucumber in base of shaker. Add other ingredients, **SHAKE** with ice and fine strain into chilled glass.

1	inch	**Peeled cucumber (chopped)**
2	shot(s)	**Ketel One Citroen vodka**
1/2	shot(s)	**Cointreau / triple sec**
1/2	shot(s)	**Freshly squeezed lemon juice**
1/4	shot(s)	**Sugar (gomme) syrup**

Origin: Created in 2002 by Alex Kammerling, London, England.
Comment: Appropriately named after the Russian snack.

THE ZAMBOANGA 'ZEINIE' COCKTAIL [NEW]

Glass: Martini
Garnish: Lime zest twist (discarded) & cherry
Method: **SHAKE** all ingredients with ice and fine strain into chilled glass.

2	shot(s)	**Rémy Martin cognac**
1	shot(s)	**Pressed pineapple juice**
1/2	shot(s)	**Freshly squeezed lime juice**
1/4	shot(s)	**Maraschino syrup (from cherries)**
2	dashes	**Angostura aromatic bitters**

Origin: Adapted from a recipe purloined from Charles H. Baker Jr's classic book, The Gentleman's Companion. He describes this as "another palate twister from the land where the Monkeys Have No Tails. This drink found its way down through the islands to Mindanao from Manila...".
Comment: Reminiscent of a tropical Sidecar.

ZANZIBAR [NEW]

Glass: Old-fashioned
Garnish: Lime zest twist
Method: **SHAKE** all ingredients with ice and strain into glass filled with crushed ice.

2	shot(s)	**Goslings Black Seal rum**
1/4	shot(s)	**Apricot brandy liqueur**
1/4	shot(s)	**Grand Marnier liqueur**
1/2	shot(s)	**Freshly squeezed orange juice**
1/2	shot(s)	**Freshly squeezed lime juice**
1/8	shot(s)	**Almond (orgeat) syrup**

Origin: Discovered in 2005 at Zanzi Bar, Prague, Czech Republic.
Comment: Tangy rum and citrus with fruit and hints of almond.

DRINKS ARE GRADED AS FOLLOWS:

● DISGUSTING ●◐ PRETTY AWFUL ●● BEST AVOIDED
●●◐ DISAPPOINTING ●●● ACCEPTABLE ●●●◐ GOOD
●●●● RECOMMENDED ●●●●◐ HIGHLY RECOMMENDED
●●●●● OUTSTANDING / EXCEPTIONAL

ZA-ZA

Glass: Martini
Garnish: Orange zest twist
Method: **SHAKE** all ingredients with ice and fine strain into ice filled glass.

2	shot(s)	**Plymouth gin**
2	shot(s)	**Dubonnet Red**

AKA: Dubonnet Cocktail
Variant: Substitute sloe gin or Fino sherry in place of gin.
Origin: Adapted from a recipe in the 1930s Savoy Cocktail Book by Harry Craddock. This classic cocktail was created for and named after Zsa Zsa Gabor.
Comment: Classically this drink is stirred but it is better with the dilution and aeration achieved by shaking. (US readers - beware of non-French Dubonnet.)

ZELDA MARTINI

Glass: Martini
Garnish: Mint sprig
Method: Lightly **MUDDLE** mint (just to bruise) in base of shaker. Add other ingredients, **SHAKE** with ice and fine strain into chilled glass.

5	fresh	**Mint leaves**
2	shot(s)	**Zubrówka bison vodka**
1	shot(s)	**Freshly squeezed lime juice**
¾	shot(s)	**Almond (orgeat) syrup**
½	shot(s)	**Chilled mineral water (omit if wet ice)**

Origin: Created in May 2002 by Phillip Jeffrey at the GE Club, London, England. He made it for a friend called Zelda – and the name really wouldn't have worked if she'd been called Tracy.
Comment: Bison grass vodka combines brilliantly with mint and almond.

ZESTY

Glass: Old-fashioned
Garnish: Lime zest twist
Method: **SHAKE** all ingredients with ice and strain into glass filled with crushed ice.

2	shot(s)	**Frangelico hazelnut liqueur**
½	shot(s)	**Freshly squeezed lime juice**

Comment: Citrus fresh with a nutty touch.

ZEUS MARTINI

Glass: Martini
Garnish: Float three coffee beans
Method: **POUR** Fernet Branca into frozen glass, swirl round and **DISCARD. MUDDLE** raisins with cognac in base of shaker. Add other ingredients, **SHAKE** with ice and fine strain into chilled glass.

1	shot(s)	**Fernet Branca**
25	dried	**Raisins**
2	shot(s)	**Rémy Martin cognac**
¼	shot(s)	**Maple syrup**
1/8	shot(s)	**Kahlúa coffee liqueur**
1	shot(s)	**Chilled mineral water (reduce if wet ice)**

Origin: Adapted from Dr Zeus, a cocktail created by Adam Ennis in 2001 at Isola, London, England.
Comment: Rich, pungent and not sweet.

ZHIVAGO MARTINI

Glass: Martini
Garnish: Float wafer thin apple slice
Method: **SHAKE** all ingredients with ice and fine strain into chilled glass.

1½	shot(s)	**Vanilla flavoured vodka**
½	shot(s)	**Bourbon whiskey**
½	shot(s)	**Sour apple liqueur**
1	shot(s)	**Freshly squeezed lime juice**
¾	shot(s)	**Sugar (gomme) syrup**

Origin: Created in 2002 by Alex Kammerling, London, England.
Comment: Perfectly balanced sweet and sour – sweet apple, vanilla and bourbon balanced by lime juice.

ZINGY GINGER MARTINI

Glass: Martini
Garnish: Lemon zest twist
Method: **SHAKE** all ingredients with ice and fine strain into chilled glass.

2½	shot(s)	**Ketel One Citroen vodka**
½	shot(s)	**Freshly squeezed lemon juice**
½	shot(s)	**Ginger cordial**
½	shot(s)	**Chilled mineral water (omit if wet ice)**

Origin: Created in 2001 by Reece Clark at Hush Up, London, England.
Comment: It sure is both zingy and gingery.

ZOMBIE #1 (INTOXICA! RECIPE)

Glass: Hurricane
Garnish: Mint sprig
Method: **STIR** brown sugar with lemon juice in base of shaker until it dissolves. Add other ingredients, **SHAKE** with ice and strain into ice-filled glass.

1	teaspoon	**Brown sugar**
1	shot(s)	**Freshly squeezed lemon juice**
1	shot(s)	**Light white rum**
1	shot(s)	**Mount Gay golden rum**
1	shot(s)	**Demerara 151° overproof rum**
1	shot(s)	**Pressed pineapple juice**
1	shot(s)	**Freshly squeezed lime juice**
1	shot(s)	**Passion fruit syrup**
1	dash	**Angostura aromatic bitters**

Origin: The above recipe for Don the Beachcomber's classic cocktail is based on one published in Intoxica! by Jeff Berry. It is claimed Don contributed it to a 1950s barbeque manual published by his friend Louis Spievak.
Comment: Plenty of flavour and alcohol with tangy rum and fruit.

DRINKS ARE GRADED AS FOLLOWS:

● DISGUSTING ●◐ PRETTY AWFUL ●● BEST AVOIDED
●●◐ DISAPPOINTING ●●● ACCEPTABLE ●●●◐ GOOD
●●●● RECOMMENDED ●●●●◐ HIGHLY RECOMMENDED
●●●●● OUTSTANDING / EXCEPTIONAL

ZOMBIE #2 (VIC'S FORMULA)

Glass: Collins (14oz)
Garnish: Mint sprig
Method: BLEND all ingredients with one 12oz scoop crushed ice. Serve with straws.

3/4	shot(s)	Light white rum
3/4	shot(s)	Aged Jamaican rum
1/2	shot(s)	Grand Marnier liqueur
1 1/2	shot(s)	Freshly squeezed orange juice
2 1/2	shot(s)	Pressed pineapple juice
1	shot(s)	Freshly squeezed lemon juice
1/2	shot(s)	Freshly squeezed lime juice
1/4	shot(s)	Sonoma pomegranate (grenadine) syrup

Origin: Adapted from a recipe in the 1947-72 Trader Vic's Bartender's Guide by Victor Bergeron.
Comment: More fruit than alcohol but tangy not sweet.

ZOMBIE #3 (MODERN FORMULA)

Glass: Hurricane
Garnish: Pineapple wedge
Method: SHAKE first nine ingredients with ice and strain into glass filled with crushed ice. FLOAT rum.

3/4	shot(s)	Light white rum
3/4	shot(s)	Pusser's Navy rum
3/4	shot(s)	Mount Gay Eclipse golden rum
1/2	shot(s)	Apricot brandy liqueur
1/2	shot(s)	Grand Marnier liqueur
2 1/2	shot(s)	Freshly squeezed orange juice
2 1/2	shot(s)	Pressed pineapple juice
1	shot(s)	Freshly squeezed lime juice
1/2	shot(s)	Sonoma pomegranate (grenadine) syrup
1/2	shot(s)	Wray & Nephew overproof rum

Comment: A heady mix of four different rums with pineapple, orange, lime and grenadine.

ZOOM

Glass: Martini
Garnish: Dust with cocoa powder
Method: SHAKE all ingredients with ice and fine strain into chilled glass.

2 1/2	shot(s)	Rémy Martin cognac
3	spoons	Runny honey
1/2	shot(s)	Double (heavy) cream
1/2	shot(s)	Milk

Variant: Base on other spirits or add a dash of cacao.
Comment: Cognac is smoothed with honey and softened with milk and cream in this classic cocktail.

ZUB-WAY

Glass: Collins
Garnish: Three raspberries
Method: Chop watermelon and MUDDLE in base of shaker with raspberries. Add other ingredients, SHAKE with ice and fine strain into ice-filled glass.

1/16	fresh	Watermelon (diced)
2 1/2	shot(s)	Zubrówka bison vodka
1/2	shot(s)	Sugar (gomme) syrup

Origin: Created in 1999 by Jamie Terrell, London.
Comment: Few ingredients, but loads of flavour.

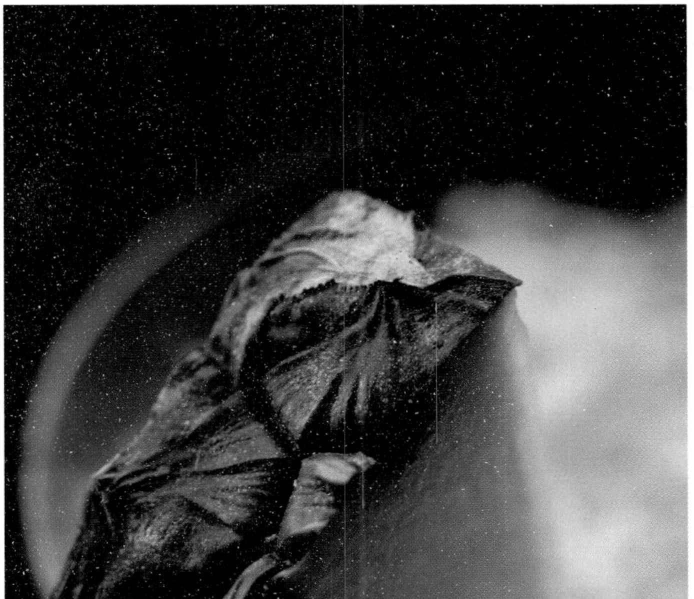

ZOMBIE

This cocktail is thought to have been created in 1934 by Don the Beachcomber at his Beachcomber restaurant in Hollywood. However, Charles H Baker claimed that a man named Christopher Clark invented a Zombie cocktail in 1935 after returning from Haiti. And Joseph Lanza claims that a Zombie cocktail debuted at the 1939 World's Fair in Flushing, New York. Whatever the truth of the matter, the recipes here derive from Don the Beachcomber's Zombie.

In The Fine Art of Mixing Drinks David Embury describes the Zombie as the "grandfather of all pixies, and great-uncle to the gremlins". And Trader Vic, with Beach the founding father of Tiki drinks, wrote of this drink on his menus, "a real dirty stinker".

DON'S ORIGINAL ZOMBIE FORMULA

Glass: 14 oz
Garnish: Pineapple wedge, orange slice, cherry & mint sprig
Method: BLEND all ingredients with crushed ice and pour into a glass with three or four ice cubes.

1 1/4	shot(s)	Puerto Rican Ramirez Royal rum
1	shot(s)	Demerara 151° overproof rum
1	shot(s)	Cuban Palau 30 year old rum
1	shot(s)	Jamaican 32 year old rum
1	shot(s)	Myers's Planter's Punch rum
3/4	shot(s)	Maraschino liqueur
1/2	shot(s)	Velvet Falernum liqueur
1/2	shot(s)	Freshly squeezed grapefruit juice
3/4	shot(s)	Freshly squeezed lime juice
1/2	shot(s)	Sugar (gomme) syrup
2	dashes	Pernod anis
2	dashes	Angostura aromatic bitters
3	dashes	Grenadine syrup

Origin: The above recipe is from a book called Hawai'i: Tropical Rum Drinks & Cuisine by Don The Beachcomber, written by Arnold Bitner & Phoebe Beach (Don's widow).

Maker's
Mark

INGREDIENTS APPENDIX

INGREDIENTS APPENDIX

ABSINTHE

There are two basic styles of absinthe commonly available – French and Czech. French styles, which are mostly still banned in their country of origin, have a full-bodied aniseed flavour and a deep green colour. When served with water the colour should change and eventually go cloudy. This process of precipitation is known as the louche.

Czech absinth (spelt without the 'e') usually has a bluer tinge to its green colour. The aniseed flavour is more subtle than in its French counterpart and it is not usual for it to turn cloudy with the addition of water.

Absinthe Cocktail ●●●◐○
Absinthe Frappé ●●●◐○
Absinthe Sour ●●●◐○
Absinthe Suisesse ●●●○○
Absinthe Without Leave ●●◐○○
Applesinth ●●●●○
B-55 Shot ●●●○○
Chocolate Sazerac ●●●●○
Colonial Rot ●●●○○
Dead Man's Mule ●●●◐○
Death In The Afternoon ●●◐○○
Grand Sazerac ●●●●○
Green Fairy ●●●●○
Green Hornet ●●●●○
Hammer Of The Gods ●●◐○○
Henry VIII ●●●◐○
I.V.F. Martini ●●●◐○
Linstead ●●●●◐
London Cocktail ●●●○○
Martini Special ●●●●◐
Maurice Martini ●●●◐○
Merry Widow #1 ●●●◐○
Monkey Gland #1 ●●●●○
Moonshine Martini ●●●●◐
Morning Glory ●●●●○
Morning Glory Fizz ●●●●○
New Year's Absolution ●●●◐○
Peggy Martini ●●●○○
Piccadilly Martini ●●●●◐
Pisco Punch #4
(Prosser's Formula) ●●●●●
Rattlesnake ●●●◐○
Remember The Maine ●●●●◐
Savoy Special #1 ●●●●○
Sazerac ●●●●●
The 75 ●●●●◐
Trilby ●●●●○
Turf Martini ●●●●○
Van's The Man ●●●●○
Vert'ical Breeze ●●●●○
Viagra Falls ●●●◐○
Weeping Jesus ●●●◐○
Whip Me & Beat Me ●●●○○
Windy Miller ●●●●○
Wink ●●●●○
Yellow Parrot ●●●●○

ADVOCAAT LIQUEUR

This Dutch liqueur is derived from an alcoholic drink that colonists in South Africa made from the yellowish pulp of the abacate fruit. In Holland, egg yolks took the place of abacate and the name, already evolved into 'avocado' by Portuguese colonists, became Advocaat in Dutch.

The best advocaat liqueurs are entirely natural products, made exclusively from brandy, egg yolks, sugar and vanilla, without any preservatives or artificial thickeners. They have a thick, indulgent, luscious custardy consistency. The palate features subtle, creamy vanilla, cocoa powder and a hint of cooked egg yolk.

Ambrosia'tini ●●●◐○
Apple & Custard Martini ●●●◐○
Beach Blonde ●●●●○
Bessie & Jessie ●●●◐○
Canary Flip ●●●●◐
Casablanca ●●●○○
Crème Anglaise Martini ●●●●○
Custard Tart ●●●●○
Dutch Breakfast Martini ●●●●○
Dutch Courage ●●●●○
Egg Custard Martini ●●●◐○
Fluffy Duck ●●●◐○
Granny's Martini ●●●○○
Jaded Lady ●●●○○
New Port Codebreaker ●●●◐○
Nutty Summer ●●●●◐
Orange Custard Martini ●●●◐○
Redback ●●●○○
Rhubarb & Custard Martini ●●●●○
Snowball ●●●◐○
Squashed Frog ●●●○○
Zabaglione Martini ●●●◐○

AMARETTO LIQUEUR

See 'Luxardo Amaretto di Saschira Liqueur'

AMONTILLADO

See 'Sherry Amontillado'

ANGOSTURA AROMATIC BITTERS

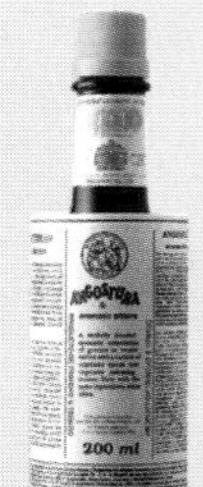

44.7% alc./vol. (89.4°proof)

www.angostura.com

Producer: Angostura Ltd, Laventille, Port of Spain, Trinidad, West Indies.

These famous bitters were first made in 1824 by the German Surgeon-General of a military hospital in the town of Angostura, Venezuela, to help treat stomach disorders and indigestion. In 1875, due to unrest in Venezuela, production was moved to Trinidad. It was here that the laid-back Caribbean attitude affected Angostura's packaging. One day a new batch of labels was ordered and a simple mistake led to them being too big for the bottles. The error was spotted in time but everyone thought somebody else would deal with the problem. No one did, so they simply stuck the labels on the bottles, intending to fix the next batch. No one quite got round to it and the oversized label became a trademark of the brand.

One of the smallest bottles on any bar, Angostura is packed with flavour: Turkish coffee, jasmine, dried mint, fruit poached with cloves and cinnamon, cherry, orange and lemon zest. A dash adds that indefinable something which brings cocktails to life.

Abbey Martini ●●●◐○
Adam and Eve ●●●●○
Affinity ●●●◐○
The Alamagoozlum Cocktail ●●●●◐
Alfonso ●●●◐○
Almond & Apricot Martini ●●●●○
Amaretto Sour ●●●◐○
Americana ●●●◐○
Apple Brandy Sour ●●●●◐
Apple Virgin Mojito ●●●●○
Apricot Martini ●●●○○
Aunt Agatha ●●●◐○
Bahama Mama ●●●●○
Barbara West ●●●◐○
Barnum ●●●◐○
Biarritz ●●●◐○
Bitter Elder ●●●◐○
Blackthorn Irish ●●●◐○

Boomerang ●●●●○
Bourbon Smash ●●●◐○
Brandy Crusta ●●●●○
Brandy Sour ●●●●◐
Bronx ●●●◐○
Brooklyn #1 ●●●●○
Brubaker Old-Fashioned ●●●●○
Buena Vida ●●●●◐
Call Me Old-Fashioned ●●●●◐
Caribbean Piña Colada ●●●◐○
Causeway ●●●◐○
Champagne Cocktail ●●●○○
Champs-Elysées ●●●●◐
Chihuahua Magarita ●●●◐○
Cinderella ●●◐○○
Club Cocktail ●●●●○
Coronation ●●●○○
Dandy Cocktail ●●●●○
Delmonico ●●●◐○
Delmonico Special ●●●◐○
DNA #2 ●●●○○
Double Vision ●●●○○
East India #1 ●●●●◐
East India #2 ●●●●○
El Burro ●●●●○
Elisian ●●●●○
Esquire #1 ●●●●○
Estilo Viejo ●●●●◐
Fancy Free ●●●●○
Fantasia ●●●◐○
Fine & Dandy ●●●◐○
Flying Scotsman ●●●●○
Flying Tigre Coctel ●●●●○
Four W Daiquiri ●●●●○
French Mule ●●●●○
Gin Gin Mule ●●●●○
Gin Sour ●●●●○
Golden Dawn ●●●●○
Grand Sazerac ●●●●○
Grape Delight ●●●◐○
Grappa Manhattan ●●●●○
Green Fairy ●●●●○
Green Swizzle ●●●●○
Grog ●●●●○
Hazelnut Alexander ●●●●○
Hoa Sua ●●●●○
Honey Blossom ●●●○○
Honey Vodka Sour ●●●●○
Horse's Neck With A Kick ●●●○○
I'll Take Manhattan ●●●●○
Imperial Martini ●●●○○
Incognito ●●●◐○
Income Tax Cocktail ●●●●○
Jack-In-The-Box ●●●●○
Jack Punch ●●●●○
Japanese Cocktail ●●●●○
Jerez ●●●●○
Jockey Club ●●●◐○
The Journalist ●●●●○
Julep ●●●●●
The Juxtaposition ●●●●○
Kentucky Dream ●●●●○
Kool Hand Luke ●●●●○
Lemon Lime & Bitters ●●●◐○
Limey ●●●◐○
Liquorice Whiskey Sour ●●●●◐
Lolita Margarita ●●●●◐
Luxury Cocktail ●●●◐○
Luxury Mojito ●●●●○
Mai Tai #2
(Beaumont-Gantt's Formula) ●●●●○
Manhattan Dry ●●●●◐
Manhattan Perfect ●●●●●
Manhattan Sweet ●●●●●
Manhattan Island ●●●●○
Maple Old-Fashioned ●●●●○
Marama Rum Punch ●●●●○
Martini Special ●●●●◐
Medicinal Solution ●●●◐○
Merry Widow #1 ●●●◐○
Mexican 55 ●●●●○
Mexican Manhattan ●●●●○
Mint Julep ●●●●●
Mona Lisa ●●●●○
Montego Bay ●●●◐○
Morning Glory ●●●●○
Moscow Mule ●●●●○
Navy Grog ●●●●○
Noon ●●●●○
Oddball Manhattan Dry ●●●●○
Old Fashioned #1
(Classic Version) ●●●●●
Old Fashioned #2
(US Version) ●●●●◐
Old Fashioned Caddy ●●●●○
Parma Negroni ●●●●○
Passion Punch ●●●◐○
Pegu Club ●●●●○
Pilgrim Cocktail ●●●●○
Pink Daiquiri ●●●●○
Pink Gin #1 (Traditional) ●●●●○
Pink Gin #2 (Modern) ●●●●○
Pink Gin & Tonic ●●●●○
Piscola ●●●◐○
Plantation Punch ●●●◐○
Planter's Punch ●●●●○
Playmate Martini ●●●●◐
Prickly Pear Mule ●●●●○
Prince Of Wales ●●●◐○
Rat Pack Manhattan ●●●●○
The Roadrunner ●●●●○
Rob Roy #1 ●●●●○
Rosita ●●●●○
Rum Punch ●●●●●
Rum Punch-Up ●●●●◐
Sailor's Comfort ●●●○○
St Patrick's Day ●●●●○
Santiago ●●●○○
Sazerac ●●●●●
Seelbach ●●●○○
Shamrock #1 ●●●○○
Singapore Sling #2 ●●●●○
Singapore Sling #3 ●●●◐○
Sour ●●●◐○
South China Breeze ●●●●○
Southern Mule ●●●◐○
Spencer Cocktail ●●●●○
The Star #1 ●●●●○
Straits Sling ●●●●○
Suburban ●●●●○
Tarte Aux Pommes ●●●●○
Tequila'tini ●●●◐○
Tiki Max ●●●●○
Treacle ●●●●◐
Vanderbilt ●●●●◐
Velvet Fog ●●●●◐
Venus in Furs ●●●◐○
Vieux Carré Cocktail ●●●●◐
Vodka Sour ●●●●○
Vowel Cocktail ●●●●◐
Warsaw ●●●◐○
Whiskey Collins ●●●●◐
Whiskey Sour #1
(Classic Formula) ●●●●○
Whiskey Sour #2
(Difford's Formula) ●●●●●
Widow's Kiss ●●●●●
The Zamboanga
'Zeinie' Cocktail ●●●●○
Zombie #1
(Intoxica! Recipe) ●●●●○

ANIS

See 'Pernod Anis'

ANISETTE LIQUEUR

This sweet, aniseed-flavoured liqueur with coriander and various other herbs is popular throughout the Mediterranean - in France, Spain and North Africa.

Absinthe Frappé ●●●◐○

APPLEJACK BRANDY

See 'Calvados'

APPLE JUICE

Apples are a good source of dietary fibre, vitamin C and vitamin B5, plus minerals such as copper, iron and potassium. Choose a flavoursome variety like Bramley over more bland types like Washington Red or Golden Delicious.

The best way to use apples in cocktails is as a juice. You can make your own in a standard electric juice extractor. There is no need to peel or core apples, as the skin and core contain over half the fruit's nutrients. Simply remove the stalks and chop the fruit into small enough chunks to fit through the feeder.

Unchecked, the juice will quickly oxidise and discolour but a splash of lime juice helps prevent this without too much effect on the flavour. You'll find that crisper apples yield clearer juice.

Most supermarkets carry at least one quality pressed apple juice and the best of these cloudy juices make DIY juicing unnecessary. Avoid the packaged 'pure', clear apple juices as these tend to be overly sweet and artificial tasting.

Achilles Heel ●●●●○
Alan's Apple Breeze ●●●◐○
Almond Martini #1 ●●●●○
Amber ●●●●◐
American Pie Martini ●●●●○
Aphrodisiac ●●●●○
Apple & Blackberry Pie ●●●◐○
Apple & Elderflower Collins ●●●●○
Apple Breeze ●●●●○
Apple Buck ●●●●○
Apple Crumble Martini #1 ●●●◐○
Apple Crumble Martini #2 ●●●●○
Apple Daiquiri ●●●●○
Apple Mac ●●●●○
Apple Martini ●●●●○
Apple Martini #1 (simple version) ●●●●○
Apple Martini #2 ●●●●○
Apple Martini #3 ●●●●○
Apple Of My Eire ●●●●○
Apple Of One's Eye ●●●●◐
Apple Pie Martini ●●●●○
Appleissimo ●●●●○
Apple Strudel Martini ●●●◐○
Apple Strudel Martini #2 ●●●●◐
Apple Virgin Mojito (Mocktail) ●●●●○
Applesinth ●●●●○
Apple 'N' Pears ●●●●◐
Applily Married ●●●●◐
Apricot Sour ●●●●○
Artlantic ●●●○○
Auntie's Hot Xmas Punch ●●●●○
Autumn Martini ●●●●○
Azure Martini ●●●●○
Baltic Breeze ●●●◐○
Banana Smoothie (Mocktail) ●●●●◐
Bee Sting ●●●●○
Beetle Jeuse ●●●●○
Bitter Elder ●●●◐○
Black Bison Martini ●●●●◐
Black Bison Martini #2 ●●●●○
Bossa Nova # 1 ●●●●○
Caramelised Apple Martini ●●●●○
Chimayo ●●●◐○
Chin Chin ●●●●○
Cider Apple Cooler ●●●●○
Congo Blue ●●●◐○
Coolman Martini ●●●●◐
Country Breeze ●●●◐○
Cranapple Breeze ●●●◐○
Cucumber & Mint Martini ●●●●○
Double Vision ●●●○○
Dutch Courage ●●●●○
Eastern Martini ●●●●◐
Eden ●●●●○
El Torado ●●●●◐
English Garden ●●●●○
Epiphany ●●●●○
Escalator Martini ●●●●●
Extradition ●●●●○
Frisky Bison ●●●●◐
GE Blonde ●●●●◐
Gin Garden ●●●●○
Ginger & Lemongrass Martini ●●●●○
Ginger Cosmos ●●●◐○
Ginger Martini ●●●●○
Gingerbread Martini ●●●●○
Giuseppe's Habit ●●●●○
Gold Member ●●●●○
Golden Dragon ●●●◐○
Granny's ●●●●○
Grape Delight ●●●◐○
Grapple Martini ●●●●○
Green Apple & Cucumber Martini ●●●●○
Green Destiny ●●●◐○
Green Tea Martini ●●●●○
Hakkatini ●●●●○
Havanatheone ●●●●●
Hawaiian Cosmoplitan ●●●●○
Highland Sling ●●●●○
Hobson's Choice ●●◐○○ (Mocktail)
Honey Apple Martini ●●●●○
The Honeysuckle Orchard ●●●●○
I B Damm'd ●●●●◐
Icewine Martini ●●●●◐
Ignorance Is Bliss ●●●◐○
Jade Garden ●●●●○
Ja-Mora ●●●●○
Jules Delight ●●●●○
Jumbled Fruit Julep ●●●◐○
Kentucky Dream ●●●●○
Kentucky Mac ●●●◐○
Kentucky Muffin ●●●●○
Kentucky Pear ●●●●◐
Kiwi Crush ●●●●○
Krakow Tea ●●●●○
Kurrant Affair ●●●○○
Lemon Butter Cookie ●●●●○
Lighter Breeze ●●●◐○
Long Flight of Stairs ●●●●◐
Love Junk ●●●◐○
Madroska ●●●○○
Mandarinitini ●●●○○
Mango Rum Cooler ●●●◐○
Maple Pomme ●●●●○
The Mayflower Martini ●●●●○
Mint Limeade (Mocktail) ●●●●◐
Mitch Martini ●●●●○
Monza ●●●◐○
Moscow Lassi ●●●○○
Motox ●●●●○
Myrtle Martini ●●●◐○
New Year's Absolution ●●●◐○
Northern Lights ●●●●○
November Seabreeze (Mocktail) ●●●◐○
Orchard Breeze ●●●●◐
Palookaville ●●●●○
Palm Springs ●●●◐○
Pappy Honeysuckle ●●●●◐
Pear Shaped #1 (Deluxe Version) ●●●●◐
Pear Shaped #2 (Popular Version) ●●●●◐
Planter's Punchless (Mocktail) ●●●○○
Polish Martini ●●●●●
Pulp Fiction ●●●●○
Razzmatazz ●●●○○
R U Bobby Moore? ●●●●◐
Sage Martini ●●●●○
Satsuma Martini ●●●◐○
Ski Breeze ●●●○○
Sleeping Bison-tini ●●●●○
Sourpuss Martini ●●●●○
Spiced Apple Daiquiri ●●●●○
Spiked Apple Cider (Hot) ●●●●○
Sporran Breeze ●●●●◐
Stairs Martini ●●●●●
Steep Flight ●●●●●
Strasberi Sling ●●●◐○
Strudel Martini ●●●●◐
Summer Breeze ●●●●○
Tatanka ●●●●◐
Tatanka Royale ●●●●○
Teddy Bear'tini ●●●●○
Toffee Apple ●●●●○
Toffee Apple Martini ●●●●○
Tre Martini ●●●●○
Treacle ●●●●◐
Utterly Butterly ●●●◐○
Vanilla Laika ●●●◐○
Venus in Furs ●●●◐○
Verdi Martini ●●●●○
Voodoo ●●●●○
Warsaw Cooler ●●●●◐
Washington Apple ●●●●◐
The Wet Spot ●●●●○
Wilton Martini ●●●●○
Yum ●●●○○

APPLE SCHNAPPS LIQUEUR

The term schnapps traditionally suggests a clear strong spirit. However, in recent years the term has come to refer to sweet liqueurs of only 20-24% alc./vol., bearing no resemblance to the strong dry schnapps from which they take their name. I call such drinks 'schnapps liqueurs' to avoid confusion.

Amber ●●●●◐
American Beauty ●●●●◐
Apple & Cranberry Pie ●●●●○
Apple & Custard Martini ●●●◐○
Apple Manhattan ●●●●○
Apple Martini #2 ●●●●○
Apple Martini #3 ●●●●○
Apple Mojito ●●●●○
Apple Pie Shot ●●●●○
Appleissimo ●●●●○
Apple Spritz ●●●●○
Apple Strudel Martini ●●●◐○
Apple Strudel Martini #2 ●●●●◐
Big Apple Martini ●●●◐○
Black Bison Martini ●●●●◐
Cider Apple Cooler ●●●●○
Frisky Bison ●●●●◐
Gold Member ●●●●○
Granny's ●●●●○
Jean Marc ●●●●○
Northern Lights ●●●●○
Palookaville ●●●●○
Pulp Fiction ●●●●○
Robin Hood #1 ●●●●○
Sangria Martini ●●●●○
Sidecar Named Desire ●●●●○
Spiced Apple Daiquiri ●●●●○
Tarte Tatin Martini ●●●●○
Teddy Bear'tini ●●●●○
Thomas Blood Martini ●●●◐○
Toffee Apple ●●●●○
Wilton Martini ●●●●○

APRICOT BRANDY LIQUEUR

This amber coloured liqueur is sometimes also known as 'apry'. It is a liqueur produced by infusing apricots in brandy and flavouring the infusion with various herbs.

Alan's Apple Breeze ●●●◐○
Almond & Apricot Martini ●●●●○
Apricot Fizz ●●●◐○
Apricot Lady Sour ●●●◐○
Apricot Mango Martini ●●●●○
Apricot Martini ●●●○○
Apricot Sour ●●●●○
Atlantic Breeze ●●●○○
Aunt Emily ●●●●○
Bajan Passion ●●●●○
Baltic Breeze ●●●◐○
Banana Boomer ●●●●○
Barnum ●●●◐○
Bingo ●●●○○
Bitter Sweet Symphony ●●●◐○
Bossa Nova #1 ●●●●○
Bossa Nova #2 ●●●◐○
Boston ●●●◐○
Cappercaille ●●●●○
Charlie Chaplin ●●●◐○
Claridge ●●●●○
Colonel T ●●●◐○

DNA ●●●◐○
DNA #2 ●●●○○
Dulchin ●●●●○
Eastern Promise ●●●●○
Fifth Avenue Shot ●●◐○○
The Flirt ●●●◐○
Fosbury Flip ●●●●◐
Frankenjack ●●●●○
Fruit Tree Daiquiri ●●●●○
Golden Dawn ●●●●○
Golden Screw ●●●◐○
Golden Slipper ●●●◐○
Highland Sling ●●●●○
Hop Toad #1 ●●●●○
Hop Toad #2 ●●●●○
Incognito ●●●◐○
Indian Rose ●●●●○
Intimate Martini ●●●●○
Katinka ●●●◐○
Kentucky Dream ●●●●○
Leave It To Me Martini ●●●◐○
Lutkins Special Martini ●●●◐○
Mambo ●●●◐○
Mayfair Cocktail ●●●●○
The Mayflower Martini ●●●●○
Millionaire's Daiquiri ●●●◐○
Moon River ●●●◐○
Mule's Hind Leg ●●●●◐
Nacional Daiquiri #1 ●●●●◐
Nacional Daiquiri #2 ●●●●◐
Pancho Villa ●●●●○
Paradise #1 ●●●◐○
Paradise #2 ●●●●◐
Paradise #3 ●●●◐○
Park Lane ●●●●◐
Pendennis Cocktail ●●●●○
Periodista Daiquiri ●●●●○
Playmate Martini ●●●●◐
Resolute ●●●●○
Roa Aé ●●●◐○
Sleeping Bison-tini ●●●●○
Sleepy Hollow ●●●●○
Southern Tea-Knee ●●●●◐
Spencer Cocktail ●●●●○
Speyside Martini ●●●●○
Sumo in a Sidecar ●●●●◐
Tiki Max ●●●●○
Trinity ●●●○○
Tulip Cocktail ●●●●○
Valencia ●●●●○
Webster Martini ●●●◐○
The Wet Spot ●●●●○
What The Hell ●●●●○
Yacht Club ●●●◐○
Yellow Bird ●●●○○
Yellow Parrot ●●●●○
Zanzibar ●●●◐○
Zombie #3
(Modern Formula) ●●●●○

BANANA

A rich source of potassium and vitamin B6, bananas also contain malic acid, which makes them refreshing when eaten raw. Bananas are transported green and ripened prior to sale in dedicated ripening warehouses. They should not be stored in refrigerators as exposure to low temperatures turns the fruit black.

Avalanche ●●●○○
Banana Batida ●●●◐○
Banana Colada ●●●●○
Banana Daiquiri ●●●◐○
Banana Smoothie (Mocktail)
●●●●◐
Banoffee Martini ●●●●○
Beach Blonde ●●●●○
Dirty Banana ●●●●○
Funky Monkey ●●●●○
Screaming Banana Banshee
●●●◐○

BASIL LEAVES

This aromatic herb has a strong lemon and jasmine flavour.

Bajito ●●●●◐
Basil & Honey Daiquiri ●●●●●
Basil Beauty ●●●●○
Basil Bramble Sling ●●●●○
Basil Grande ●●●●○
Basil Mary ●●●●○
Basilico ●●●◐○
Byzantine ●●●●○
Ginger Cosmos ●●●◐○
Milly Martini ●●●●○
Strawberry Blonde Martini ●●●◐○
The Suzy Wong Martini ●●●◐○
Watermelon & Basil Martini ●●●●○
Watermelon & Basil Smash ●●●●○

BECHEROVKA (CARLSBAD BECHER)

The Czech national liqueur.

Be-ton ●●●◐○
Bohemian Iced Tea ●●●●◐

BEER

Although beer is one of the widely consumed alcoholic beverages, sadly it does not greatly feature in the world of cocktails. At least, not yet! Suggestions to simon@diffordsguide.com please.

Black & Tan ●●●◐○
Boiler Maker ●●●◐○
Depth Charge ●●○○○
Flaming Dr Pepper ●●○○○
Michelada ●●●○○
Steel Bottom ●●●○○
Sandy Gaff ●●●◐○
Snakebite ●●●○○

BÉNÉDICTINE D.O.M. LIQUEUR

A legendary herbal liqueur produced by Benedictine monks.

April Shower ●●●●○
B2C2 ●●●◐○
B & B ●●●●○
BBC ●●●◐○
Bobby Burns ●●●●○
Brainstorm ●●●●◐
Brighton Punch ●●●●◐
Chas ●●●●○
Collection Martini ●●●○○
Gypsy Queen ●●●●○
Honeymoon ●●●●○
Jubilant ●●●●◐
Jungle Fire Sling ●●●○○
Maxim's Coffee (Hot) ●●●●○
Merry Widow #1 ●●●◐○
Monkey Gland #2 ●●●●○
Mule's Hind Leg ●●●●◐
O'Henry ●●●◐○
Poet's Dream ●●●●◐
Roman Punch ●●●●○
Singapore Sling #1
(Baker's Formula) ●●●◐○
Singapore Sling #2 ●●●●○
Singapore Sling #3 ●●●◐○
Straits Sling ●●●●○
Tropic ●●●●◐
Vieux Carré Cocktail ●●●●◐
Widow's Kiss ●●●●●

BLACKBERRIES

See 'Raspberries & Blackberries'

BLACKCURRANTS

The fruit of a native northern European shrub that is now widely cultivated in France, Germany, The Netherlands and Belgium. Cultivation began in the French Côte d'Or where blackcurrants are heavily used in the production of cassis liqueur.

Brazilian Berry ●●●●○

BLUEBERRIES

Blueberry pie is as much an American icon as the Stars and Stripes. This bushy shrub, which is related to the bilberry, is native to the States and many different types grow there – not all of them blue. The lowbush blueberry, which is called the 'bleuet' in Quebec, tends to be smaller and sweeter than other varieties and is often marketed as 'wild blueberry'. The larger, highbush blueberry is the variety most cultivated in the US.

These soft berries are best muddled in the base of your shaker or glass. Recipes in this guide specify the number required for each drink. Alternatively, you can make a purée. Just stick them in the blender and add a touch of sugar syrup. Fresh blueberries should not be stored in the refrigerator.

Black & Blue Caipirovska ●●●●○
Blueberry Daiquiri ●●●●○
Blueberry Martini #1 ●●●●○
Blueberry Martini #2
(simple) ●●●●○
Forbidden Fruits ●●●●○
Kentucky Muffin ●●●●○
No. 10 Lemonade ●●●●◐

BLUE CURAÇAO LIQUEUR

Blue curaçao liqueur is traditionally flavoured with bitter Curaçao oranges and a touch of spice. While the flavour may be natural the colour is most certainly not.

Alexander's Big Brother ●●●○○
Artlantic ●●●○○
Baby Blue Martini ●●●◐○
Bazooka Joe ●●◐○○
Bikini Martini ●●●●○
Black Mussel ●●●◐○
Blue Angel ●●●○○
Blue Bird ●●●○○
Blue Champagne ●●●○○
Blue Cosmo ●●●◐○
Blue Hawaiian ●●●○○
Blue Heaven ●●◐○○
Blue Kamikaze ●●●◐○
Blue Lady ●●●○○
Blue Lagoon ●●●○○
Blue Margarita ●●●◐○
Blue Monday ●●●◐○
Blue Passion ●●●●○
Blue Raspberry Martini ●●●●○
Blue Riband ●●●○○
Blue Star ●●●○○
Blue Velvet Margarita ●●●●○
Blue Wave ●●●○○
Cactus Jack ●●●◐○
China Blue ●●●◐○
Fourth Of July Shot ●●◐○○
Green Eyes ●●●◐○
Ink Martini #1 ●●●◐○
Ink Martini #2 ●●●◐○

Jaded Lady ●●●○○
Liminal Shot ●●●○○
Liquorice All Sort ●●●◐○
Lotus Martini ●●●●○
Purple Flirt #2 ●●●○○
Purple Turtle ●●●◐○
Ray Gun ●●●○○
South Pacific Breeze ●●●◐○
Swedish Blue Martini ●●●◐○
Turquoise Daiquiri ●●●◐○
Vacation ●●●◐○

BOURBON

See 'Whiskey – Bourbon'

BUTTERSCOTCH SCHNAPPS LIQUEUR

Butterscotch is one of those indulgent flavours that take us back to our youth, a world of cookies, ice-cream toppings and candies. Sweet and creamy, it also has a wonderfully tangy bite.

The name has nothing to do with Scotch whisky, or anything Scottish at all. It comes from the term 'scotch', meaning to cut or score a surface, and 'butter' for the butter in the candy. When butterscotch candy is poured out to cool, it is scotched to make it easier to break into pieces later.

Apple Cart ●●●●○
Banoffee Martini ●●●●○
Bit-O-Honey ●●●○○
Bon Bon Martini ●●●●○
Bourbon Cookie ●●●●○
Butterscotch Daiquiri ●●●◐○
Butterscotch Delight ●●●◐○
Butterscotch Martini ●●●●○
Doughnut Martini ●●●◐○
Gingerbread Martini ●●●●○
Give Me A Dime ●●●●○
Gold Member ●●●●○
Golden Mac ●●●◐○
Met Manhattan ●●●●○
Monk's Candy Bar ●●●○○
Shamrock Express ●●●◐○
Tribbble ●●●●○

CACHAÇA

Pronounced 'Ka-Shah-Sa', cachaça is the spirit of Brazil. As it is based on sugar cane, it is very similar to a rum. However, maize meal is traditionally used to start the fermentation, so many brands of cachaça are not strictly rums. Further, most rums are produced from molasses, a by-product of sugar refining, but the best cachaça is distilled from fermented sugar cane juice. (Many bigger brands, however, use molasses, which ferments more quickly as the sugars break down faster after they have been burnt. And a lot of smaller distillers use sugar cane syrup.)

Cachaça is distilled to a maximum of 75% alcoholic strength, unlike most light rums which are usually distilled to 96% strength. This lower distillation strength means cachaça retains more of the aroma and flavour of the sugar cane and is less refined than most rums.

Abaci Batida ●●●●○
Azure Martini ●●●●○
Banana Batida ●●●◐○
Batida De Coco ●●●○○
Beja Flor ●●●●○
Berry Caipirinha ●●●●○
Brazilian Berry ●●●●○
Brazilian Coffee ●●●◐○
Buzzard's Breath ●●●◐○
Cachaca Daiquiri ●●●◐○
Caipirinha ●●●●●
Caipiruva ●●●●○
Carneval Batida ●●●●○
Fresa Batida ●●●◐○
Kiwi Batida ●●●○○
Lemon Beat ●●●●○
Mango Batida ●●●●○
Maracuja Batida ●●●●○
Milho Verde Batida ●●●◐○
Passion Fruit Caipirinha ●●●●○
Raspberry Caipirinha ●●●●○
Sophisticated Savage ●●●◐○
Tropical Caipirinha ●●●●◐

CALVADOS

Calvados is a French brandy made from apples, although some styles also contain pears. The name is an appellation contrôlée, meaning that Calvados can only be produced in defined areas of north-west France.

Like Cognac and Armagnac, the Calvados-making district is divided into smaller areas. Two of these sub-regions have their own appellations contrôlées: Pays d'Auge and Domfront.

Pays d'Auge, the area around the villages of Orne and Eure, is generally considered to produce the best Calvados and by law all AOC Pays d'Auge Calvados must be double-distilled in pot stills.

Domfront Calvados, which acquired its AOC at the end of 1997, must contain at least 30% perry pears.

A.J. ●●●●○
Ambrosia ●●●●○
Apple & Custard Martini ●●●◐○
Apple & Spice ●●●○○
Apple Brandy Sour ●●●●◐
Apple Buck ●●●●○
Apple Cart ●●●●○
Apple Sunrise ●●●○○
Apples 'N' Pears ●●●●◐
Aunt Emily ●●●●○
Avenue ●●●◐○
Bentley ●●●●○
Bolero ●●●◐○
Calvados Cocktail ●●●●○
Castro ●●●◐○
Cider Apple Cooler ●●●●○
Corpse Reviver ●●●●○
Deauville ●●●●○
The Delicious Sour ●●●●○
Dempsey ●●●●○
Depth Bomb ●●●◐○
Elisian ●●●●○
Fiesta ●●●●○
First Of July ●●●●○
Golden Dawn ●●●●○
Harvard Cooler ●●●●◐
Honeymoon ●●●●○
Jack Collins ●●●●◐
Jack-In-The-Box ●●●●○
Jack Rose ●●●●○
Jean Gabin ●●●●○
Jersey Sour ●●●●●
Julep ●●●●●
Long Flight of Stairs ●●●●◐
Mule's Hind Leg ●●●●◐
Parisian Spring Punch ●●●●○
Princess Marina ●●●●○
Princess Mary's Pride ●●●○○
Princess Pride ●●●◐○
Roulette ●●●●○
Royal Smile ●●●●○
The 75 ●●●●◐
Sidecar Named Desire ●●●●○
So-So Martini ●●●●●
The Star #1 ●●●●○
Steep Flight ●●●●●
Tantris Sidecar ●●●●○
Tarte Aux Pommes ●●●●○
Threesome ●●●◐○
Toffee Apple ●●●●○
Toffee Apple Martini ●●●●○
Tulip Cocktail ●●●●○
Widow's Kiss ●●●●●
Wilton Martini ●●●●○

CAMPARI

Amaro Dolce ●●●◐○
Americano ●●●●○
Bellissimo ●●●○○
Bitterest Pill ●●●◐○
Bloodhound ●●●◐○
Copper Illusion ●●●●○
Cranberry Martini ●●●◐○
Cumbersome ●●●●○
Diamond Dog ●●●◐○
Diana's Bitter ●●●○○
Dolce-Amaro ●●●◐○
Dolce Havana ●●●●○
Garibaldi ●●●○○
Hakkatini ●●●●○
Ignorance Is Bliss ●●●◐○
Inga From Sweden ●●●●○
Italian Job #1 ●●●◐○
Jasmine ●●●●○
Jungle Bird ●●●●○
Mambo ●●●◐○
Mandarinitini ●●●○○
Milano ●●●●◐
Monza ●●●◐○
Negroni ●●●●◐
Night & Day ●●●◐○
Old Pal ●●●◐○
Parma Negroni ●●●●○
Pink Tutu ●●●◐○
Red or Dead ●●●○○
Rosita ●●●●○
Scotch Negroni ●●●●○
Shakerato ●●●◐○
Sicilian Negroni ●●●●○
Snoopy ●●●●○
South Beach ●●●●○
Spicy Finn ●●●●○
Spritz al Bitter ●●●◐○
Teresa ●●●○○
Testarossa ●●●◐○
Triple Orange Martini ●●●●○

CARAMEL LIQUEUR

Derived from the Latin 'cannamella' for sugar cane, caramel means melted sugar that has been browned by heating. Tiny amounts of caramel have long been used to colour spirits and liqueurs but caramel flavoured liqueurs are a relatively recent phenomenon.

Caramel Manhattan ●●●●◐
Crème Brûlée Martini ●●●●○
Tarte Tatin Martini ●●●●○
Toffee Apple ●●●●○

CHAMBORD

16.5% alc./vol. (33°proof)

www.chambord online.com

Producer: Chambord et Cie, Chambord, France.

Chambord Liqueur Royale de France, to use its full name, is believed to have been created in the time of Louis XIV, when hunting parties visited Chambord, the largest chateau in the French Loire Valley. It is a rich Framboise-style liqueur made from small black raspberries and herbs combined with honey and high quality neutral alcohol.

Chambord is popularly mixed as a Kir-like drink with champagne – the Cham Cham. Its distinctive orb shaped bottle is easily recognised and a 'must stock' in most cocktail bars. Although there are other raspberry liqueurs, it is Chambord that graces our shelves and those of some of the world's most noted cocktail bars.

Chambord's rich flavour is ideally suited to a variety of cocktail recipes and has a taste that includes raspberry fool, black-currant jam, cherry jam, honeyed vanilla, sloe and damson, plus a hint of raisins and stewed prunes.

Achilles Heel ●●●●○
Basil Grande ●●●●○
Berry Nice ●●●◐○
Black Forest Gateau Martini ●●●●◐
Cascade Martini ●●●●○
Cham 69 #1 ●●●◐○
Cham 69 #2 ●●●◐○
Cham Cham ●●●◐○
Creamy Bee ●●●●○
Crimson Blush ●●●●○
Crimson Tide ●●●●○
Crown Stag ●●●◐○
Dirty Sanchez ●●●●○
Eclipse ●●●●◐
Estes ●●●●○
Finitaly ●●●●○
First of July ●●●●○
Flirtini #1 ●●●●○
French Bison-tini ●●●●○
French Daiquiri ●●●●○
French Kiss #2 ●●●◐○
French Martini ●●●●○
French Mojito ●●●●◐
Fresca ●●●◐○
Fruit & Nut Chocolate Martini ●●●●○
Fruits Of The Forest ●●●◐○
Gin Berry ●●●◐○
Honey Berry Sour ●●●●○
Hot Tub ●●●●○
Icy Pink Lemonade ●●●◐○
Jam Roll ●●◐○○
Ja-Mora ●●●●○
Juliette ●●●○○
Kentucky Jewel ●●●●○
Loved Up ●●●◐○
Lush ●●●◐○
Marquee ●●●●○
Miss Martini ●●●◐○
Mystique Martini ●●●●○
New Orleans Punch ●●●◐○
Nuts & Berries ●●●●○
Pavlova Shot ●●●◐○
Peach Melba Martini ●●●◐○
Peanut Butter & Jelly Shot ●●●◐○
Purple Haze ●●●◐○
Purple Hooter ●●●◐○
Raspberry Sake'tini ●●●◐○
Raspberry Watkins ●●◐○○
Razzintini ●●●◐○
Razzzzzberry Martini ●●●◐○
Red Marauder ●●●●◐
Red Rover ●●●●○
Royal Velvet Margarita ●●●◐○
Saigon Cooler ●●●◐○
Sex On The Beach #1 ●●◐○○
Sex On The Beach #2 ●●◐○○
Sex On The Beach #3 ●●◐○○
Snood Murdekin ●●●◐○
Snow on Earth ●●●○○
Sweet Louise ●●●○○
Sweet Tart ●●●◐○
Tartini ●●●●○
Tre Martini ●●●●○
Tres Compadres Margarita ●●●●◐
Trifle Martini ●●●◐○
Urban Oasis ●●●●○
Vacation ●●●◐○
Yum ●●●○○

CHAMPAGNE

The vineyards of the Champagne region are the most northerly in France, lying north-east of Paris, on either side of the River Marne. Most of the champagne houses are based in one of two towns: Epernay and Reims.

Champagne, surprisingly, is made predominantly from black grapes. The three grape varieties used are Pinot Noir (the red grape of Burgundy), Pinot Meunier (a fruitier relative of Pinot Noir) and Chardonnay. Pinot Meunier is the most commonly used of these three varieties with Chardonnay, the only white grape, accounting for less than 30% of vines in the Champagne region. Pinot Meunier buds late and ripens early so can be relied upon to ripen throughout the Champagne region, which probably explains its domination..

Air Mail ●●●●◐
Alfonso ●●●◐○
Ambrosia ●●●●○
Americana ●●●◐○
Anita's Attitude Adjuster ●●●◐○
Apple Spritz ●●●●○
Atomic Cocktail ●●●○○
Autumn Punch ●●●●◐
B2C2 ●●●◐○
Baltic Spring Punch ●●●●○
Beverly Hills Iced Tea ●●●◐○
Black Magic ●●●○○
Black Mussel ●●●◐○
Black Velvet ●●●◐○
Bling! Bling! ●●●●◐
Blue Champagne ●●●○○
Breakfast At Terrell's ●●●●○
Buck's Fizz ●●●○○
Carol Channing ●●●○○
Cham 69 #2 ●●●◐○
Cham Cham ●●●◐○
Champagne Cocktail ●●●○○
Champagne Cup ●●●◐○
Champagne Daisy ●●●○○
Chin Chin ●●●●○
Cordless Screwdriver ●●●○○
Death In The Afternoon ●●◐○○
Diamond Fizz ●●●●○
Earl Grey Fizz ●●●●○
Elderbubble ●●●◐○
Elle For Leather ●●●●◐
Flirtini #2 ●●●●○
French 75 ●●●◐○
French 76 ●●●●○
French Daisy ●●●◐○
French Spring Punch ●●●●○
Fresca Nova ●●●◐○
Fru Fru ●●●◐○
Gold Rush Slammer ●●●○○
Golden Screw ●●●◐○
Grand Mimosa ●●●◐○
Grape Escape ●●●●◐
Guillotine ●●●◐○
Happy New Year ●●●○○
Hemingway ●●●○○
Henry VIII ●●●◐○
Jacuzzi ●●●◐○
Ja-Mora ●●●●○
Jayne Mansfield ●●●●○
Kir Royale ●●●◐○
Limeosa ●●●◐○
Lush ●●●◐○
Luxury Mojito ●●●●○
Martini Royale ●●●◐○
Mexican 55 ●●●●○
Mimosa ●●●◐○
Monte Carlo Imperial ●●●○○
Night & Day ●●●◐○
Nine-20-Seven ●●●●○
Parisian Spring Punch ●●●●○
Perry-tini ●●●●○
Pimm's Cocktail ●●●●◐
Pimm's Royale ●●●◐○
Pisco Punch #1
(Difford's Formula) ●●●●◐
Poinsettia ●●●◐○
Ponce de Leon ●●●●○
Prince Of Wales ●●●◐○
Ray Gun ●●●○○
The Ritz Cocktail ●●●●○
Royal Cosmopolitan ●●●●○
Royal Mojito ●●●●●
Russian Spring Punch ●●●●◐
Seelbach ●●●○○
Sloe Motion ●●●◐○
Southside Royalee ●●●●○
Soyer Au Champagne ●●●◐○
Sparkling Perry ●●●●○
Tatanka Royale ●●●●○
Tequila Slammer ●●●○○
Twinkle ●●●●○
Twisted Sobriety ●●●●○
Valencia ●●●●○
Vavavoom ●●●●○
Wanton Abandon ●●●●○

CHARTREUSE - GREEN

Beetle Jeuse ●●●●○
The Broadmoor ●●●●◐
Champs-Elysées ●●●●◐
Elixir ●●●●○
Emerald Martini ●●●●○
Episcopal ●●●●◐
Flaming Ferrari ●●○○○
Gator Bite ●●●◐○
Golden Retriever ●●●●◐
Green Fly ●●●◐○
Hong Kong Fuey ●●●○○
Jean Marc ●●●●○
The Last Word ●●●●◐
Martini Thyme ●●●●○
Mary Queen of Scots ●●●●◐
Mary Rose ●●●●○
Medicinal Solution ●●●◐○
Mona Lisa ●●●●○
Mujer Verde ●●●●○
Pago Pago ●●●◐○
Ray Gun ●●●○○
Russian Qualuude Shot ●●●○○
St Patrick's Day ●●●●○
Shamrock #2 ●●●●○
Stars & Stripes Shot ●●◐○○
Swamp Water ●●●●○
Tantris Sidecar ●●●●○
Tipperary #1 ●●●●◐

CHARTREUSE - YELLOW

The Alamagoozlum Cocktail ●●●●◐
Alaska Martini ●●●●○
Ambrosia'tini ●●●◐○
Apache ●●●○○
Barnacle Bill ●●●○○
Brandy Fix ●●●●◐
Champagne Daisy ●●●○○
Cheeky Monkey ●●●●○
Episcopal ●●●●◐
Gin Daisy ●●●●○
Golden Slipper ●●●◐○
Lemony ●●●●○
Mujer Verde ●●●●○
Nome ●●●●○
Oddball Manhattan Dry ●●●●○
Quarterback ●●●●○
Widow's Kiss ●●●●●
Yellow Parrot ●●●●○

CHERRY BRANDY LIQUEUR

This richly flavoured liqueur is made from the juice of ripe, dark red cherries. The best liqueurs are made by crushing the kernels while pressing the cherries as this enhances almond notes. It is typical for herbs and spices such as cinnamon and cloves to also be added to cherry brandy liqueurs.

Aquarius ●●●◐○
Banana Boomer ●●●●○
Blood & Sand ●●●●◐
Canaries ●●●○○
Cherrute ●●●●○
Cherry Alexander ●●●●○
Cherry Blossom ●●●◐○
Cherry Daiquiri ●●●●○
Cherry Martini ●●●●○
Cherry Mash Sour ●●●◐○
Chill Breeze ●●●○○
Crime Of Passion Shot ●●●○○
Desert Cooler ●●●◐○
Donna's Creamy'tini ●●●◐○
Florida Sling ●●●○○
Fog Cutter # 2 ●●●●○
Gin Sling ●●●●○
I'll Take Manhattan ●●●●○
Jungle Fire Sling ●●●○○
Nightmare Martini ●●●○○
Nutty Berry'tini ●●●◐○
Old Fashioned Caddy ●●●●○
Pancho Villa ●●●●○
Passbour Cooler ●●●○○
Red Neck Martini ●●●●○
Remember The Maine ●●●●◐
The Rose #2 ●●●◐○
Singapore Sling #1
(Baker's Formula) ●●●◐○
Singapore Sling #2 ●●●●○
Singapore Sling #3 ●●●◐○
Sir Thomas ●●●●○
Suitably Frank ●●●◐○
Tainted Cherry ●●●○○
Vanderbilt ●●●●◐
Woodland Punch ●●●◐○

CINNAMON SCHNAPPS LIQUEUR

Cinnamon is obtained from the bark of several tropical trees. Sri Lanka and China are the largest producers. Cinnamon liqueurs have a warm, sweet, spicy flavour.

Apple Pie Martini ●●●●○
Apple Strudel Martini ●●●◐○
Azure Martini ●●●●○
Butterfly's Kiss ●●●◐○
Carrot Cake ●●●◐○
Cinnamon Daiquiri ●●●◐○
Creamy Bee ●●●●○
Dead Man's Mule ●●●◐○
Fireball ●●○○○
Gold Member ●●●●○
Gold Rush Slammer ●●●○○
Oatmeal Cookie ●●●◐○
Pink Sin Martini ●●●○○
Pirate Daiquiri ●●●●○
Plum Pudding Martini ●●●◐○
Spiced Apple Daiquiri ●●●●○
Tarte Aux Pommes ●●●●○
Utterly Butterly ●●●◐○
Wilton Martini ●●●●○

COCONUT RUM LIQUEUR

Coconut rums are mostly made in the Caribbean but are also common in France and Spain. They are made by blending rectified white rum with coconut extracts and tend to be presented in opaque white bottles.

Atomic Dog ●●●○○
Bahama Mama ●●●●○
Bahamas Daiquiri ●●●●◐
Black & White Daiquiri ●●●●◐
Black Widow ●●●○○
Caribbean Cruise ●●●◐○
Caribbean Punch ●●●●○
Chill-Out Martini ●●●○○
Coco Cabana ●●●◐○
Coconut Daiquiri ●●●●○
Coconut Water ●●●●○
Georgetown Punch ●●●●○
Goombay Smash ●●●●◐
Hawaiian ●●●○○
Island Breeze ●●●◐○
Italian Surfer With
A Russian Attitude ●●●○○
Jelly Belly Beany ●●●●○
June Bug ●●●◐○
Key Lime Pie #1 ●●●●○
Key West Cooler ●●●◐○
Melon Collie Martini ●●●●○
Meloncholy Martini ●●●●○
Mister Stu ●●●◐○
Monkey Shine ●●●●○
Mucky Bottom ●●●◐○
Nutty Summer ●●●●◐
Scotch Bounty Martini ●●●◐○
Smooth & Creamy'tini ●●●●○
Surfer on A.C.D. ●●●◐○
Tilt ●●●●○
Tropical Caipirinha ●●●●◐
Utterly Butterly ●●●◐○
Vacation ●●●◐○
Whip Me & Beat Me ●●●○○

COFFEE (ESPRESSO)

Coffee beans are the dried and roasted seed of a cherry which grows on a bush in the tropics. There are two main species of coffee plant: Coffea Arabica and Coffea Canephora. These are commonly known as Arabica and Robusta. Arabica is relatively low in caffeine, more delicate and requires more intensive cultivation. Robusta is higher in caffeine, more tolerant of climate and parasites, and can be grown fairly cheaply. Robusta beans tend to be woody and bitter while Arabica beans have well-rounded, subtle flavours.

Most of the recipes in this guide which use coffee call for espresso and, as with other ingredients, the quality of this will greatly affect the finished drink. I strongly recommend using an Arabica coffee brewed in an espresso machine or a moka pot.

Black Martini ●●●●◐
Brazilian Coffee ●●●◐○
Café Gates (filter coffee) ●●●◐○
Cola De Mono ●●●●◐
Cuppa Joe ●●●●○
Espresso Daiquiri ●●●●○
Espresso Martini ●●●●○
Hot Shot ●●●○○
Insomniac ●●●●◐
Irish Coffee (filter coffee) ●●●●○
Irish Coffee Martini ●●●●◐
Irish Espresso'tini ●●●●◐
Irish Frappé ●●●◐○
Irish Latte ●●●◐○
I.V.F. Martini ●●●◐○
Jalisco Espresso ●●●●◐
Jolt'ini ●●●●○
Lazarus ●●●●◐
Lotus Espresso ●●●●◐
Mocha Martini ●●●●◐
Opal Café ●●●●○
Pharmaceutical Stimulant ●●●●○
Raspberry Mocha'tini ●●●●○
Shamrock Express ●●●◐○
Turkish Coffee Martini ●●●●○
Vodka Espresso ●●●●◐

COFFEE LIQUEUR

Coffee flavoured liqueurs are made by infusing coffee beans in alcohol or by infusing beans in hot water and then blending with alcohol. Look for brands made using Arabica coffee beans.

Adios ●●●◐○
After Six Shot ●●◐○○
Afterburner ●●●○○
Aggravation ●●●●○
Alexander The Great ●●●◐○
Alexandra ●●●◐○
Alice From Dallas ●●●◐○
All Fall Down ●●●◐○
Apache ●●●○○
Attitude Adjuster ●●●○○
Avalanche Shot ●●◐○○
B5200 ●●●○○
B-52 Shot ●●●◐○
B-53 Shot ●●●○○
B-54 Shot ●●●○○
B-55 Shot ●●●○○
B-52 Frozen ●●●◐○
Baby Guinness ●●●◐○
Bahamas Daiquiri ●●●●◐
Bartender's Root Beer ●●●●○
Beam-Me-Up Scotty ●●●○○
Black Irish ●●●○○
Black Russian ●●●○○
Blow Job ●●●◐○
Blushin' Russian ●●●●○
Brazilian Monk ●●●◐○
Bulldog ●●●◐○
Bumble Bee ●●●◐○
Buona Sera Shot ●●●◐○
Burnt Toasted Almond ●●●○○
Café Gates ●●●◐○
California Root Beer ●●●◐○
Carrot Cake ●●●◐○
Casanova ●●●●○
Chocolate Biscuit ●●●◐○
Coffee & Vanilla Daiquiri ●●●●○
Cola De Mono ●●●●◐
Colorado Bulldog ●●◐○○
Crème De Café ●●●◐○
Dirty Banana ●●●●○
Dr Zeus ●●●●◐
Dreamsicle ●●●◐○
F-16 Shot ●●●○○
Fat Sailor ●●●●○
FBI ●●●●○
Flutter ●●●●◐
Fourth Of July Cocktail ●●●○○
Heavens Above ●●●◐○
Iguana ●●●◐○
Insomniac ●●●●◐
International Incident ●●●●○
Irish Chocolate Oranj'tini ●●●◐○
I.V.F. Martini ●●●◐○
Jalisco Espresso ●●●●◐
Jolt'ini ●●●●○
K.G.B. ●●◐○○
Lazarus ●●●●◐
Lonely Bull ●●●◐○
Long Beach Iced Tea ●●●◐○
Lotus Espresso ●●●●◐
Mad Monk Milkshake ●●●◐○
Mayan ●●●◐○
Mayan Whore ●●●●○
Monk's Candy Bar ●●●○○
Muddy Water ●●●◐○
Mudslide ●●●●○
Mucky Bottom ●●●◐○
New Orleans Mule ●●●◐○
Nutty Russian ●●●◐○
Pharmaceutical Stimulant ●●●●○
Pousse-café ●●◐○○
P.S. I Love You ●●●●○
Raging Bull ●●●◐○
Rattlesnake Shot ●●●○○
Russian Bride ●●●●○
Snood Murdekin ●●●◐○
Snow on Earth ●●●○○
South Of The Border ●●●○○
Stealth ●●●◐○
Tiramisu Martini ●●●●○
Toasted Almond ●●●●○
Top Banana Shot ●●●◐○
Vodka Espresso ●●●●◐
White Knight ●●●◐○
White Russian ●●●◐○
White Satin ●●●○○
Zeus Martini ●●●●◐

COGNAC

Cognac is a fine French brandy from the region around the little town of Cognac in south-west France, recognised with its own appellation contrôlée. With its rolling countryside, groves of trees and the Charente River, the area is picturesque. It is divided into six sub-regions, reflecting variations in climate and soil. As a general rule, the best soil is the chalkiest. The most regarded (and most central) region, Grande Champagne, has only a very thin layer of top soil over solid chalk. The biggest houses only use grapes from the best four sub-regions to produce their cognacs.

A.B.C. ●●●◐○
Ambrosia ●●●●○
Ambrosia'tini ●●●◐○
American Beauty ●●●●◐
Apple Of One's Eye ●●●●◐
April Shower ●●●●○
Atomic Cocktail ●●●○○
Auntie's Hot Xmas Punch ●●●●○
B2C2 ●●●◐○
B & B ●●●●○
Baltimore Egg Nog ●●●○○
Banana Bliss ●●●○○
BBC ●●●◐○
Between The Sheets ●●●●◐
Biarritz ●●●◐○
Blue Angel ●●●○○
Bolero Sour ●●●●●
Bombay ●●●●◐
Bosom Caresser ●●●●○
Brandy Alexander ●●●●○
Brandy Blazer ●●●◐○
Brandy Buck ●●●◐○
Brandy Crusta ●●●●○
Brandy Fix ●●●●◐
Brandy Fizz ●●●●○
Brandy Flip ●●●●◐
Brandy Milk Punch ●●●◐○
Brandy Smash ●●●●○
Brandy Sour ●●●●◐
Brighton Punch ●●●●◐
Bull's Blood ●●●◐○
Bull's Milk ●●●◐○
Call Me Old-Fashioned ●●●●◐
Champagne Cocktail ●●●○○
Champagne Cup ●●●◐○
Champs-Elysées ●●●●◐
Chocolate Biscuit ●●●◐○
Chocolate Sidecar ●●●●○
Claret Cobbler ●●●●○
Classic ●●●●●
Clockwork Orange ●●●◐○
Corpse Reviver ●●●●○
Cosmopolitan Delight ●●●●◐
Cuban Master ●●●○○
Deauville ●●●●○
Delmonico ●●●◐○
Delmonico Special ●●●◐○
Depth Bomb ●●●◐○

Don Juan ●●●◐○
East India #1 ●●●●◐
East India #2 ●●●●○
Egg Nog #1 ●●●○○ (Cold)
Egg Nog #2 ●●●●○ (Hot)
Enchanted ●●●◐○
Fish House Punch #1 ●●●●○
Fish House Punch #2 ●●●●○
Fizz ●●●●○
Flip ●●●●◐
Fog Cutter #1 ●●●●○
Fog Cutter # 2 ●●●●○
French Daisy ●●●◐○
French Mule ●●●●○
French Spring Punch ●●●●○
Georgia Mint Julep ●●●●◐
Gloom Lifter ●●●●○
Godfrey ●●●●○
Gold Medallion ●●●◐○
Golden Screw ●●●◐○
Grande Champagne Cosmo ●●●●○
Grape Escape ●●●●◐
Happy New Year ●●●○○
Harvard ●●●◐○
Hazelnut Alexander ●●●●○
Hoopla ●●●●○
Hot Rum Punch ●●●◐○
Hulk ●●◐○○
Iced Tea ●●●◐○
Incognito ●●●◐○
Irish Alexander ●●●◐○
Japanese Cocktail ●●●●○
Julep ●●●●●
Juliette ●●●○○
Jungle Fire Sling ●●●○○
K.G.B. ●●◐○○
Lazarus ●●●●◐
Loud Speaker Martini ●●●◐○
Mandarine Sidecar ●●●●○
Manhattan Island ●●●●○
Maxim's Coffee (Hot) ●●●●○
Milk Punch ●●●●○
Mississippi Punch ●●●●○
Moonraker ●●●●○
Morning Glory ●●●●○
Nice Pear-tini ●●●●◐
Nicky Finn ●●●●○
Ole ●●●◐○
Olympic ●●●●◐
Orange Brûlée ●●●●●
Passion Punch ●●●◐○
Pear & Cardamom Sidecar ●●●●◐
Pierre Collins ●●●●○
Pini ●●●●◐
Playmate Martini ●●●●◐
Ponce de Leon ●●●●○
Port Wine Cocktail ●●●◐○
Prairie Oyster ●●●◐○
Prince Charlie ●●●●○
Prince Of Wales ●●●◐○
Pulp Fiction ●●●●○
Quelle Vie ●●●◐○
Randy ●●●●○
Red Marauder ●●●●◐
The Ritz Cocktail ●●●●○
The Roffignac ●●●●○
Roman Punch ●●●●○
Ruby Martini #2 ●●●◐○
La Sang ●●●●○
Sangaree ●●●●○
Sangria ●●●◐○
Sangria Martini ●●●●○
Sazerac ●●●●●
Scorpion ●●●●○
Sidecar #1 (Equal parts classic formula) ●●●●◐
Sidecar #2 (Difford's formula) ●●●●●
Sidecar #3 (Embury's formula) ●●●◐○
Sir Charles Punch ●●●●○
Soyer Au Champagne ●●●◐○
Spiked Apple Cider (Hot) ●●●●○
Sputnik #2 ●●●●○
Stinger ●●●●○
Sundowner #1 ●●●●○
Three Miler ●●●●○
Tiger's Milk ●●●◐○
Tiramisu Martini ●●●●○
Tom & Jerry ●●●○○
Trifle'tini ●●●◐○
Twisted Sobriety ●●●●○
Vanderbilt ●●●●◐
Veneto ●●●◐○
Vieux Carré Cocktail ●●●●◐
Wagon Wheel ●●●○○
Whiskey Cobbler ●●●○○
Winter Martini ●●●●◐
The Zamboanga 'Zeinie' Cocktail ●●●●○
Zeus Martini ●●●●◐
Zoom ●●●●◐

COINTREAU LIQUEUR

40% alc./vol. (80°proof)

www.cointreau.com

Producer: Rémy Cointreau, Angers, France

The distilling firm of Cointreau was started in 1849 by two brothers, Adolphe and Edouard-Jean Cointreau, who were confectioners in Angers. The liqueur we know today was created by Edouard Cointreau, the son of Edouard-Jean, and first marketed in the 1870s. Cointreau should not be confused with other liqueurs labelled mere 'triple sec'. This term is a confusing one as it means 'triple dry' and they tend to be very sweet.

Where cocktail recipes call for the use of triple sec, we recommend Cointreau, which is made from the fragrant peels of bitter and sweet oranges, carefully grown and meticulously selected for their quality. A versatile cocktail

ingredient, Cointreau can also be served straight over ice, or mixed with fruit juices, tonic or lemonade.

The mainstay of many classic recipes, Cointreau has a luscious, ripe taste featuring bitter orange, zesty, citrus hints, a splash of orange juice and a hint of spice.

Acapulco Daiquiri ●●●●○
Agent Orange ●●●●○
Alexander's Big Brother ●●●○○
Ambrosia ●●●●○
Anita's Attitude Adjuster ●●●◐○
Apple Cart ●●●●○
Attitude Adjuster ●●●○○
B2C2 ●●●◐○
Balalaika ●●●●○
Bamboo ●●●●◐
Beach Iced Tea ●●●◐○
Beachcomber ●●●●○
Beja Flor ●●●●○
Between The Sheets ●●●●◐
Beverly Hills Iced Tea ●●●◐○
The Big Easy ●●●●○
Bitter Sweet Symphony ●●●◐○
Blue Champagne ●●●○○
Blue Monday ●●●◐○
Blue Riband ●●●○○
Blue Velvet Margarita ●●●●○
Boston Tea Party ●●●○○
Bourbonella ●●●●○
Brandy Crusta ●●●●○
Breakfast Martini ●●●●◐
Cable Car ●●●●○
Call Me Old-Fashioned ●●●●◐
Canaries ●●●○○
Cappercaille ●●●●○
Celtic Margarita ●●●●◐
Charles Daiquiri ●●●●◐
Chas ●●●●○
Chelsea Sidecar ●●●●◐
Cherry Blossom ●●●◐○
China Martini ●●●◐○
Citrus Martini ●●●●○
Claridge ●●●●○
Coolman Martini ●●●●◐
Copper Illusion ●●●●○
Cosmopolitan #1 (simple version) ●●●●◐
Cosmopolitan #2 (complex version) ●●●●●
Cranapple Breeze ●●●◐○
Cuban Special ●●●○○
Damn-The-Weather ●●●◐○
Dandy Cocktail ●●●●○
Deauville ●●●●○
Detropolitan ●●●●○
Dixie Dew ●●●●○
Dolce Havana ●●●●○
Dreamsicle ●●●◐○
Dry Orange Martini ●●●●◐
Dyevitchka ●●●●○
Elegante Margarita ●●●●◐
F. Willy Shot ●●●◐○
Fine & Dandy ●●●◐○
Flirtini #2 ●●●●○
Floridita Margarita ●●●●○
Fluffy Duck ●●●◐○
Flying Dutchman Martini ●●●●○
Frankenjack ●●●●○
Frozen Margarita ●●●●○
Fruit Sour ●●●●○
Fu Manchu Daiquiri ●●●●○
Gator Bite ●●●◐○
Gin Fixed ●●●●○
Giuseppe's Habit ●●●●○
Glass Tower ●●●○○
Gold ●●●○○
Golden Dream ●●●●○
Golden Fizz #2 ●●●●◐
Golden Wave ●●●◐○
Goombay Smash ●●●●◐
Grateful Dead ●●●◐○
Hawaiian ●●●○○
Hoopla ●●●●○
Iced Tea ●●●◐○
Illusion ●●●●○
Jackie O's Rose ●●●●○
Jade Daiquiri ●●●●○
Jaffa Martini ●●●◐○
James Joyce ●●●●○
Jasmine ●●●●○
Jodi May ●●●◐○
The Journalist ●●●●○
Jungle Juice ●●●◐○
Kamikaze ●●●●○
Kentucky Colonel ●●●●○
Kentucky Jewel ●●●●○
Kentucky Tea ●●●◐○
Key Lime Pie #1 ●●●●○
Koi Yellow ●●●●○
L.A. Iced Tea ●●●◐○
Lago Cosmo ●●●◐○
Lemon Drop Martini ●●●◐○
Lemongrass Cosmo ●●●●◐
Leninade ●●●●○
Limelite ●●●○○
Limey Cosmo ●●●●○
Long Island Iced Tea ●●●◐○
Long Island Spiced Tea ●●●◐○
Loved Up ●●●◐○
Lynchburg Lemonade ●●●●○
Mai Tai #2 (Beaumont-Gantt's Formula) ●●●●○
Mai Tai #3 (Difford's Formula) ●●●●●
Maiden's Blush ●●●●◐
Maiden's Prayer ●●●◐○
Mainbrace ●●●●○
Major Bailey #2 ●●●●◐
Magic Bus ●●●◐○
Malcolm Lowry ●●●●○
Mambo ●●●◐○
Mango Margarita #1 (Served 'Up') ●●●●○
Mango Margarita #2 (Frozen) ●●●●○
Marama Rum Punch ●●●●○
Margarita #1 (Straight-up) ●●●●◐
Margarita #2 (On the Rocks) ●●●●◐
Margarita #3 (Frozen) ●●●●○
Margarita #4 (Salt Foam Float) ●●●◐○
Marmarita ●●●●○
Martinez ●●●●●
Mat The Rat ●●●◐○
Matador ●●●●○
Meloncholy Martini ●●●●○
Menehune Juice ●●●●○
Metropolitan ●●●●○
Millionaire ●●●●○
Mississippi Schnapper ●●●◐○
Monk's Habit ●●●○○
Montego Bay ●●●◐○
Moon River ●●●◐○
Mountain Sipper ●●●◐○
Napoleon Martini ●●●●◐
Nicky Finn ●●●●○
Oh Gosh! ●●●●●
Opal ●●●●◐
Orang-A-Tang ●●●●○
Orange Bloom Martini ●●●●◐
Orange Blossom ●●●◐○
Osmo ●●●●○
Passion Fruit Margarita ●●●●○
Passion Fruit Martini #3 ●●●●○
Pear & Cardamom Sidecar ●●●●◐
Pegu Club ●●●●○
Perfect John ●●●●○
Pineapple Margarita ●●●●○
Pino Pepe ●●●●○
Playa Del Mar ●●●●○
Poinsettia ●●●◐○
Pompanski Martini ●●●●○
Ponce de Leon ●●●●○
Potted Parrot ●●●◐○
Pousse-café ●●◐○○
Presidente ●●●●○
Princess Marina ●●●●○
Quarterback ●●●●○
Raspberry Margarita ●●●●○
Razzmatazz ●●●○○
The Red Army ●●●◐○
The Ritz Cocktail ●●●●○

Rosy Martini ●●●●○
Royal Bermuda Yacht Club Daiquiri ●●●●○
Royal Cosmopolitan ●●●●○
Ruby Martini #1 ●●●●○
Ruby Martini #2 ●●●◐○
Rude Cosmopolitan ●●●●◐
Rude Ginger Cosmopolitan ●●●●○
Sake'politan ●●●●○
San Fransisco ●●●◐○
Seelbach ●●●○○
Sidecar #1 (Equal parts classic formula) ●●●●◐
Sidecar #2 (Difford's formula) ●●●●●
Sidecar #3 (Embury's formula) ●●●◐○
Sidekick ●●●●○
Silent Third ●●●◐○
Singapore Sling #3 ●●●◐○
Sir Thomas ●●●●○
Sloppy Joe ●●●●○
Stork Club ●●●●○
Sunny Breeze ●●●◐○
Sunstroke ●●●●○
Tango Martini #1 ●●●●○
Tantris Sidecar ●●●●○
Tennessee Iced Tea ●●●●○
Test Pilot ●●●●○
Texas Iced Tea ●●●◐○
Thai Lady ●●●●○
Threesome ●●●◐○
Thriller From Vanilla ●●●●○
Tokyo Iced Tea ●●●◐○
Tomahawk ●●●◐○
Tres Compadres Margarita ●●●●◐
Turquoise Daiquiri ●●●◐○
Union Club ●●●●○
Vanilla Margarita ●●●●○
Vavavoom ●●●●○
Velvet Hammer ●●●◐○
Venus Martini ●●●●○
Warsaw ●●●◐○
Warsaw Cooler ●●●●◐
Whiskey Daisy ●●●◐○
White Cosmo ●●●●○
White Lady ●●●●○
White Lion ●●●●○
The Windsor Rose ●●●◐○
Wink ●●●●○
Zakuski Martini ●●●●○

CRANBERRY JUICE - RED

Cranberries are native to America and are grown in large, flooded fields, known as cranberry bogs. Experts say you can tell when a cranberry is ready to eat because it bounces. Cranberries are high in vitamin C and pectin, and a popular natural remedy for cystitis.

Cranberry is the exception which proves the 'fresh is best' rule. Don't even contemplate muddling fresh berries: pure cranberry juice is extremely sour and is normally sweetened and blended to make it more palatable.

Pick up a carton of cranberry juice from the refrigerated display of your local supermarket. As with other juices, avoid the non-refrigerated products and read the small print carefully – some products end up with barely any cranberry and taste far too sweet. Look for products containing at least 20% cranberry juice.

Absolutely Fabulous ●●●●○
Alan's Apple Breeze ●●●◐○
American Pie Martini ●●●●○
Apple & Cranberry Pie ●●●●○
Apple Breeze ●●●●○
Apple Of My Eire ●●●●○
Apple Pie Martini ●●●●○
Appleissimo ●●●●○
Apricot Cosmo ●●●●◐
Aquarius ●●●◐○
Arizona Breeze ●●●●○
Baby Woo Woo ●●●○○
Baltic Breeze ●●●◐○
Basil Grande ●●●●○
Bay Breeze ●●●○○
Bay Of Passion ●●●○○
Beach Iced Tea ●●●◐○
Blood Orange ●●●○○
Blush Martini ●●●◐○
Bourbon Smash ●●●◐○
C C Kazi ●●●●○
Cape Codder ●●●◐○
Caribbean Breeze ●●●●○
Cascade Martini ●●●●○
Cassini ●●●◐○
Chill Breeze ●●●○○
China Beach ●●●●○
Chinese Cosmopolitan ●●●●○
Chocolate & Cranberry Martini ●●●●○
Cool Martini ●●●◐○
Cosmopolitan #1 (simple version) ●●●●◐
Cosmopolitan #2 (complex version) ●●●●●
Cranapple Breeze ●●●◐○
Cranberry Cooler ●●●○○
Cranberry & Mint Martini ●●●●○
Cranberry Martini ●●●◐○
Cranberry Sauce ●●●○○
Detox ●●●○○
Detropolitan ●●●●○
Dorian Gray ●●●◐○
Dragon Blossom ●●●●○
Eclipse ●●●●◐
Estes ●●●●○
Finn Rouge ●●●◐○
Finnberry Martini ●●●●○
The Flirt ●●●◐○
Floridita Margarita ●●●●○
Fruit & Nut Martini ●●●●○
Gentle Breeze (Mocktail) ●●●○○
Gin Berry ●●●◐○
Ginger Cosmo ●●●●○
Georgetown Punch ●●●●○
Grand Cosmopolitan ●●●●◐
Grande Champagne Cosmo ●●●●○
Gulf Coast Sex On The Beach ●●●●○
Hawaiian Seabreeze ●●●◐○
Highland Sling ●●●●○
Hot Passion ●●●○○
Illicit Affair ●●●◐○
Inga From Sweden ●●●●○
Ink Martini #1 ●●●◐○
Ink Martini #2 ●●●◐○
Island Breeze ●●●◐○
Italian Job #2 ●●●●○
Italian Surfer With A Russian Attitude ●●●○○
Jamaican Sunset ●●●●○
Jodi May ●●●◐○
Juliette ●●●○○
Jungle Juice ●●●◐○
Kentucky Jewel ●●●●○
Key West Cooler ●●●◐○
Killer Punch ●●●◐○
Koolaid ●●●●○
Lemongrass Cosmo ●●●●◐
Light Breeze ●●●◐○
Lighter Breeze ●●●◐○
Lime Breeze ●●●◐○
Limey Cosmo ●●●●○
Long Beach Iced Tea ●●●◐○
Madras ●●●◐○
Madroska ●●●○○
Mae West Martini ●●●●○
Magic Bus ●●●◐○
Man-Bour-Tini ●●●●○
Maria Theresa Margarita ●●●●○
Marquee ●●●●○
Metropolitan ●●●●○
Mexican Tea (Hot) ●●●●◐
Mountain Sipper ●●●◐○
Nantucket ●●●◐○
Nautilus ●●●●◐
Not So Cosmo (Mocktail) ●●●◐○
November Seabreeze (Mocktail) ●●●◐○
Nutty Berry'tini ●●●◐○
Osmo ●●●●○
Pale Rider ●●●○○
Palm Springs ●●●◐○
Parlay Punch ●●●○○
Pass-on-that ●●●○○
Passbour Cooler ●●●○○
Pink Flamingo ●●●○○
Pink Sin Martini ●●●○○
Playa Del Mar ●●●●○
Poinsettia ●●●◐○
Pontberry Martini ●●●●○
Purple Flirt #1 ●●●●○
Seabreeze #2 (Layered) ●●●◐○
Sex On The Beach #1 ●●◐○○
Southern Cider ●●●○○
Southern Peach ●●●○○
Spiced Cranberry Martini ●●●●○
Stiletto ●●●◐○
Strawberry Cosmo ●●●◐○
Summer Breeze ●●●●○
Tailor Made ●●●●○
Tarraberry'tini ●●●●○
Tarte Aux Pommes ●●●●○
Tartini ●●●●○
Tennessee Berry Mule ●●●●○
Tennessee Rush ●●●◐○
Tolleytown Punch ●●●◐○
Tomahawk ●●●◐○
Tootie Fruity Lifesaver ●●●○○
Total Recall ●●●◐○
Triple 'C' Martini ●●●●◐
Tropical Breeze ●●●○○
Tutti Frutti ●●●○○
Vert'ical Breeze ●●●●○
Watermelon Cosmo ●●●◐○
The Wentworth ●●●●○
White Cosmo ●●●●○
White Sangria ●●●◐○
Woo Woo ●●●◐○

CRANBERRY (WHITE) & GRAPE DRINK

White cranberry juice drinks are made with white cranberries, harvested before they develop their familiar red colour. They tend to be less tart than red cranberry drinks.

Blue Cosmo ●●●◐○
Blue Fin ●●●◐○
Ice White Cosmo ●●●●○
Purple Cosmo ●●●●◐
Raspberry Cosmo ●●●◐○
Rasputin ●●●○○
Razzzzzberry Martini ●●●◐○
Red Apple ●●●●○
Red Marauder ●●●●◐
Red or Dead ●●●○○
Rhett Butler ●●●●○
Rosarita Margarita ●●●●○
Royal Cosmopolitan ●●●●○
Rude Cosmopolitan ●●●●◐
Rude Ginger Cosmopolitan ●●●●○
Saigon Cooler ●●●◐○
Sake'politan ●●●●○
Sake-tini #2 ●●●●○
Scandinavian Pop ●●●○○
Scarlett O'Hara ●●●○○
Seabreeze #1 (Simple) ●●●◐○

CRÈME DE MÛRE (BLACKBERRY) LIQUEUR

This blackberry flavoured liqueur is made by macerating fresh blackberries in alcohol. The name refers to 'mûre', the French for blackberry, and 'crème' as in the French phrase 'crème de la crème', meaning 'best of the best'.

Basil Bramble Sling ●●●●○
Black & White Daiquiri ●●●●◐
Bramble ●●●●◐
Collection Martini ●●●○○
Congo Blue ●●●◐○
Epiphany ●●●●○
Especial Day ●●●●◐
Godfrey ●●●●○
Hedgerow Sling ●●●◐○
La Rosa Margarita ●●●●○
Rum Runner ●●●●○
Uncle Vanya ●●●●○
Vanilla Laika ●●●◐○
Vanitini ●●●◐○
Wibble ●●●●◐

CUCUMBER

The fruit of a climbing plant originating from the foothills of the Himalayas, cucumbers should be used as fresh as possible, so look for firm, unwrinkled fruit. The skin can be quite bitter so cucumber is best

peeled before use in cocktails. Either muddle in the base of your shaker or juice using an extractor.

Cucumber Martini ●●●●◐
Cucumber & Mint Martini ●●●●○
Cucumber Sake-Tini ●●●●○
Cumbersome ●●●●○
Green Apple & Cucumber Martini ●●●●○
Green Destiny ●●●◐○
Moscow Lassi ●●●○○
Pimm's Cup (or Classic) ●●●◐○
Wild Promenade Martini ●●●●○
Zakuski Martini ●●●●○

DOUBLE (HEAVY) CREAM

I've specified 'double' or 'heavy cream' in preference to lighter creams. In many recipes this is diluted with an equal measure of milk – a combination known in the trade as 'half & half'.

Absinthe Suisesse ●●●○○
Ace ●●●◐○
Aggravation ●●●●○
Alessandro ●●●○○
Alexander ●●●◐○
Alexander's Big Brother ●●●○○
Alexander's Sister ●●●◐○
Alexander The Great ●●●◐○
Alexandra ●●●◐○
Apple & Cranberry Pie ●●●●○
Apple & Spice ●●●○○
Apple Pie Shot ●●●●○
Apple Strudel Martini ●●●◐○
Atholl Brose ●●●●○
Avalanche ●●●○○
Baltimore Egg Nog ●●●○○
Bananas & Cream ●●●●○
Banoffee Martini ●●●●○
Banshee ●●●○○
Barbara ●●●○○
Barbary Coast Highball ●●●◐○
Barnamint ●●●○○
Bazooka ●●◐○○
BBC ●●●◐○
Bee's Knees #1 ●●●●○
Bird Of Paradise ●●●●◐
Black Forest Gateau Martini ●●●●◐
Black Widow ●●●○○
Blue Angel ●●●○○
Blush Martini ●●●◐○
Blushin' Russian ●●●●○
Bourbon Cookie ●●●●○
Bourbon Milk Punch ●●●◐○
Brandy Alexander ●●●●○
Brandy Milk Punch ●●●◐○
Brazilian Coffee ●●●◐○
Breakfast At Terrell's ●●●●○
Bubblegum Shot ●●●○○
Bulldog ●●●◐○
Bullfrog ●●◐○○
Burnt Toasted Almond ●●●○○
Buzzard's Breath ●●●◐○
Café Gates ●●●◐○
Casanova ●●●●○
Cherry Alexander ●●●●○
Coco Cabana ●●●◐○
Colorado Bulldog ●●◐○○
Cream Cake ●●●◐○
Creamsicle ●●●●○
Creamy Creamsicle ●●●◐○
Crème Brûlée Martini ●●●●○
Créme De Cafè ●●●◐○
Dirty Banana ●●●●○
Don Juan ●●●◐○
Donna's Creamy'tini ●●●◐○
Dreamsicle ●●●◐○
Egg Nog #1 (Cold) ●●●○○
Egg Nog #2 (Hot) ●●●●○
The Estribo ●●●◐○
Fifth Avenue Shot ●●◐○○
Flip ●●●●◐
Flying Grasshopper ●●●◐○
Fourth Of July Cocktail ●●●○○
French Kiss #2 ●●●◐○
Fresca Nova ●●●◐○
Friar Tuck ●●●◐○
Frida's Brow ●●●●○
Fruit & Nut Chocolate Martini ●●●●○
Funky Monkey ●●●●○
Give Me A Dime ●●●●○
Golden Cadillac ●●●◐○
Golden Dream ●●●●○
Hair Of The Dog ●●●●○
Hazelnut Alexander ●●●●○
Hot Shot ●●●○○
Insomniac ●●●●◐
Irish Alexander ●●●◐○
Irish Coffee Martini ●●●●◐
I.V.F. Martini ●●●◐○
Key Lime Pie #1 ●●●●○
Lemon Meringue Pie'tini ●●●●○
Lola ●●●◐○
Lonely Bull ●●●◐○
Mad Monk Milkshake ●●●◐○
Melon Collie Martini ●●●●○
Meloncholy Martini ●●●●○
Mexican Coffee (Hot) ●●●◐○
Mexicano (Hot) ●●●●◐
Milk & Honey Martini ●●●●◐
Milk Punch ●●●●○
Miss Martini ●●●◐○
Mocha Martini ●●●●◐
Monk's Candy Bar ●●●○○
North Pole Martini ●●●●○
Nutty Summer ●●●●◐
Opal Café ●●●●○
Orange Brûlée ●●●●●
Peach Melba Martini ●●●◐○
Piña Colada ●●●●◐
Piña Colada Virgin (Mocktail) ●●●○○
Platinum Blonde ●●●◐○
Princess Mary ●●●○○
P.S. I Love You ●●●●○
Quarterback ●●●●○
Ramos Gin Fizz ●●●●○
Rum & Raisin Alexandra ●●●●○
Russian Bride ●●●●○
Scotch Milk Punch ●●●◐○
Screaming Banana Banshee ●●●◐○
Sgroppino ●●●●◐
Silk Stockings ●●●◐○
Smooth & Creamy'tini ●●●●○
Snood Murdekin ●●●◐○
Snow Fall Martini ●●●●○
Snow on Earth ●●●○○
Spiked Apple Cider (Hot) ●●●●○
Sputnik ●●●◐○
Strudel Martini ●●●●◐
Tarte Tatin Martini ●●●●○
Tick-Tack Martini ●●●○○
Tiramisu Martini ●●●●○
Toasted Almond ●●●●○
Tongue Twister ●●●○○
Triangular Martini ●●●●○
Trifle'tini ●●●◐○
Upside-Down Raspberry Cheesecake ●●●●○
Velvet Hammer ●●●◐○
Whip Me & Beat Me ●●●○○
White Elephant ●●●◐○
White Knight ●●●◐○
White Russian ●●●◐○
White Satin ●●●○○
Wild Honey ●●●◐○
Wimbledon Martini ●●●●○
Zoom ●●●●◐

CREAM OF COCONUT

This is a non-alcoholic, sticky blend of coconut juice, sugar, emulsifier, cellulose, thickeners, citric acid and salt. Fortunately it tastes better than it sounds and is an essential ingredient of a good Piña Colada. One 15oz/425ml can will make approximately 25 drinks. Once opened the contents should be transferred to a suitable container and stored in a refrigerator. This may thicken the product, so gentle warming may be required prior to use. Coconut milk is very different and cannot be substituted.

Banana Colada ●●●●○
Batida de Coco ●●●○○
Blue Hawaiian ●●●○○
Buzzard's Breath ●●●◐○
Coco Naut ●●◐○○
Funky Monkey ●●●●○
Hawaiian ●●●○○
New Port Codebreaker ●●●◐○
Painkiller ●●●●○
Piña Colada ●●●●◐
Piña Colada Virgin (Mocktail) ●●●○○
Tongue Twister ●●●○○

CRÈME DE BANANES LIQUEUR

The French term 'crème de' indicates that one particular flavour predominates in the liqueur - it does not imply that the liqueur contains cream. Many fruit liqueurs are described as 'crème de' followed by the name of a fruit. This refers to the liqueur's quality, as in the phrase 'crème de la crème'. Therefore crème de bananes is a banana flavoured liqueur made by infusion and maceration of the fruit in neutral spirit.

Crème de bananes liqueurs are clear yellow in clour with the flavour of ripe bananas, enhanced with a touch of soft vanilla and a hint of almond. Extracts of various other herbs and spices may also be added to enhance the liqueur's flavour.

Avalanche ●●●○○
Banana Batida ●●●◐○
Banana Bliss ●●●○○
Banana Boomer ●●●●○
Banana Colada ●●●●○
Banana Daiquiri ●●●◐○
Bananas & Cream ●●●●○
Banoffee Martini ●●●●○
Banshee ●●●○○
Bazooka ●●◐○○
Bazooka Joe ●●◐○○
Beam-Me-Up Scotty ●●●○○
Beja Flor ●●●●○
Blow Job ●●●◐○
Canaries ●●●○○
Caribbean Breeze ●●●●○
Chiclet Daiquiri ●●●◐○
Dirty Banana ●●●●○
Flamingo #1 ●●●◐○
Fruit Salad ●●●○○
Funky Monkey ●●●●○
Gold ●●●○○
Golden Bird ●●●◐○
Gulf Coast Sex On The Beach ●●●●○
Jumping Jack Flash ●●●●○
June Bug ●●●◐○
Landslide ●●●○○
Liquorice All Sort ●●●◐○
Luxury Cocktail ●●●◐○
Mellow Martini ●●●◐○
Reef Juice ●●●●○
Rum Runner ●●●●○
San Francisco ●●●◐○
Screaming Banana Banshee ●●●◐○
Smooth & Creamy'tini ●●●●○
Southern Tea-Knee ●●●●◐
Tootie Fruity Lifesaver ●●●○○
Top Banana Shot ●●●◐○
Tribbble ●●●●○
Yellow Bird ●●●○○

CRÈME DE CACAO LIQUEUR

See 'Brown Crème de Cacao' and 'White Crème de Cacao'

CRÈME DE CASSIS LIQUEUR

As with other 'crème de' liqueurs, this term does not mean the liqueur contains any cream. Crème de cassis is a blackcurrant liqueur which originated in France and can be made by infusion and/or maceration. The original recipe for a crème de cassis is thought to have been formulated by Denis Lagoute in 1841 in the French Dijon region. Many of the best examples are still produced in this region.

EEC law states that crème de cassis must have a minimum of 400g of sugar per litre and a minimum alcoholic strength of

15%. Unfortunately no minimum is set for the fruit content although the best brands will contain as much as 600g of black-currants per litre. Brands with a high fruit content will have a more fruity taste and a deeper colour than low-fruit brands.

Apple Sunrise ●●●○○
Arnaud Martini ●●●●○
Ballet Russe ●●●◐○
Black Forest Gateau Martini ●●●●◐
Black Mussel ●●●◐○
Blimey ●●●●○
Bolshoi Punch ●●●●○
Brazilian Berry ●●●●○
Cardinal Punch ●●●◐○
Cassini ●●●◐○
Chimayo ●●●◐○
Country Breeze ●●●◐○
Detropolitan ●●●●○
Diable Rouge ●●●◐○
El Diablo ●●●◐○
Epestone Daiquiri ●●●●○
The Estribo ●●●◐○
French Daisy ●●●◐○
Gina ●●●◐○
Guillotine ●●●◐○
Kir ●●●◐○
Kir Martini ●●●◐○
Kir Royale ●●●◐○
Liquorice Shot ●●●◐○
Lychee & Blackcurrant Martini ●●●●○
Macka ●●●◐○
Martini Royale ●●●◐○
Mexican Martini ●●●◐○
Parisian Martini ●●●●○
Rum & Raisin Alexandra ●●●●○
Russian Spring Punch ●●●●◐
Showbiz ●●●●○
Stars & Stripes Shot ●●◐○○
Sunshine Cocktail #2 ●●●●○
Tarte Aux Pommes ●●●●○
Teresa ●●●○○
Tripleberry ●●●●○

CRÈME DE FRAISE (STRAWBERRY) LIQUEUR

The French word for strawberry is 'fraise' and and these liqueurs should have a rich ripe strawberry flavour with light hints of citrus fruit.

Black Forest Gateau Martini ●●●●◐
Black Widow ●●●○○
Bourbon Blush ●●●●◐
Exotic Passion ●●●◐○
French Spring Punch ●●●●○
Fru Fru ●●●◐○
Jayne Mansfield ●●●●○
Liquorice All Sort ●●●◐○
Reggae Rum Punch ●●●●◐
Rossini ●●●●○
Strawberry Blonde Martini ●●●◐○
Strawberry Cosmo ●●●◐○
The Strawberry Éclair ●●●●○
Trifle'tini ●●●◐○
Tripleberry ●●●●○
Wimbledon Martini ●●●●○

CRÈME DE FRAMBOISE (RASPBERRY) LIQUEUR

Made by macerating fresh raspberries in neutral alcohol this dark red liqueur is named 'Framboise', the French name for raspberry.

Blood Orange ●●●○○
Carol Channing ●●●○○
Finn Rouge ●●●◐○
Mrs Robinson #1 ●●●●○
Raspberry Collins ●●●●○
Raspberry Cosmo ●●●◐○
Raspberry Debonnaire ●●●◐○
Raspberry Martini #2 ●●●●○
Raspberry Mocha'tini ●●●●○
The Red Army ●●●◐○
Red Breast ●●●◐○
The Roffignac ●●●●○
Ruby Martini #2 ●●●◐○
Sangria Martini ●●●●○

DARK CRÈME DE CACAO LIQUEUR

Flavoured with roasted cacao beans and herbs. Please note that 'dark crème de cacao' liqueurs are sometimes alternatively named 'brown crème de cacao'. See also 'white crème de cacao liqueur'.

Apple Strudel Martini ●●●◐○
Brandy Alexander ●●●●○
Brazilian Monk ●●●◐○
Café Gates ●●●◐○
Chocolate Biscuit ●●●◐○
Chocolate Puff ●●●●○
Chocolate Sidecar ●●●●○
Death By Chocolate ●●●●○
DiVino's ●●●●○
Donna's Creamy'tini ●●●◐○
Fifth Avenue Shot ●●◐○○
Friar Tuck ●●●◐○
Funky Monkey ●●●●○
Hazelnut Alexander ●●●●○
Honey Wall ●●●●○
Jaffa Martini ●●●◐○
Mocha Martini ●●●●◐
Mulata Daiquiri ●●●●◐
Raspberry Mocha'tini ●●●●○
Tiramisu Martini ●●●●○
Triangular Martini ●●●●○
Triple 'C' Martini ●●●●◐

DRAMBUIE LIQUEUR

Apple of My Eire ●●●●○
Atholl Brose ●●●●○
Auld Acquaintance ●●●○○
Causeway ●●●◐○
Dean's Gate Martini ●●●◐○
Embassy Royal ●●●◐○
Galvanised Nail ●●●●◐
Golden Shot ●●●○○
Heather Julep ●●●●◐
Jack Frost ●●●○○
Mary Queen of Scots ●●●●◐
Mystique ●●●◐○
Prince Charlie ●●●●○
Rusty Nail ●●●●○
The Scott ●●●●○
Sweet Science ●●●◐○
Trifle Martini ●●●◐○
White Knight ●●●◐○
Wild Honey ●●●◐○

DUBONNET RED

Alfonso ●●●◐○
Aviator ●●●●○
Bartender's Martini ●●●●○
Bentley ●●●●○
Dandy Cocktail ●●●●○
Dolores ●●●●○
Fly Like A Butterfly ●●●●○
Merry Widow #2 ●●●◐○
Moonraker ●●●●○
Napoleon Martini ●●●●◐
Nightmare Martini ●●●○○
Opera ●●●●○
Paris Sour ●●●●○
Peggy Martini ●●●○○
Princess Marina ●●●●○
Princess Mary's Pride ●●●○○
Princess Pride ●●●◐○
Quebec ●●●●○
Red Neck Martini ●●●●○
Rosy Martini ●●●●○
Tiziano ●●●◐○
The Wentworth ●●●●○
Za-Za ●●●●○

EGGS

Raw eggs can be hazardous to health so you may decide it is safer to use commercially produced pasteurised egg white, particularly if you are infirm or pregnant (but then you probably shouldn't be drinking cocktails anyway).

Many cocktails only taste their best when made with fresh eggs. I'm sure I've suffered more upset stomachs from drinking too much alcohol than I have as a result of bad eggs. That said, it's worth taking steps to reduce the risk of Salmonella poisoning and therefore I recommend you store small, free range eggs in a refrigerator and use them well before the sell-by-date.

Don't consume eggs if:

1. **You are uncertain about their freshness.**
2. **There is a crack or flaw in the shell.**
3. **They don't wobble when rolled across a flat surface.**
4. **The egg white is watery instead of gel-like.**
5. **The egg yolk is not convex and firm.**
6. **The egg yolk bursts easily.**
7. **They smell foul.**

Absinthe Sour ●●●◐○
Absinthe Suisesse ●●●○○
Acapulco Daiquiri ●●●●○
Ace ●●●◐○
The Alamagoozlum Cocktail ●●●●◐
Amaretto Sour ●●●◐○
Apple Brandy Sour ●●●●◐
Apricot Lady Sour ●●●○○
Autumn Martini ●●●●○
Biarritz ●●●◐○
Blue Lady ●●●○○
Bolero Sour ●●●●●
Brandy Sour ●●●●◐
Cable Car ●●●●○
Champs-Elysées ●●●●◐
Clover Leaf Martini ●●●●◐
The Delicious Sour ●●●●○
Derby Fizz ●●●●◐
Dino Sour ●●●●◐
Earl Grey Mar-tea-ni ●●●●◐
Easter Martini ●●●●◐
Egg Nog #1 (Cold) ●●●○○
Egg Nog #2 (Hot) ●●●●○
Fizz ●●●●○
Flamingo #1 ●●●◐○
Flip ●●●●◐
Fosbury Flip ●●●●◐
Fruit Sour ●●●●○
Fruits Of The Forest ●●●◐○
Gin Sour ●●●●○
Gloom Lifter ●●●●○
Gold Medallion ●●●◐○
Golden Fizz #1
Golden Girl ●●●●○
Golden Slipper ●●●◐○
Grande Champagne Cosmo ●●●●○
Grapparita ●●●◐○
Green Fairy ●●●●○
Honey Berry Sour ●●●●○
Honey Blossom ●●●○○
Honey Vodka Sour ●●●●○
Honeymoon ●●●●○
Hoopla ●●●●○
Jaffa Martini ●●●◐○
Jenever Sour ●●●●○
Jersey Sour ●●●●●
Jubilant ●●●●◐
Lemon Sorbet ●●●●○
Lime Sour ●●●●○
Liquorice Whiskey Sour ●●●●◐
Mandarine Sour ●●●◐○
Margarita #4
(Salt Foam Float) ●●●◐○
Milano Sour ●●●●○
The Million Dollar Cocktail ●●●●◐
Millionaire ●●●●○
Morning Glory Fizz ●●●●○
Mountain ●●●◐○
Noon ●●●●○
North Pole Martini ●●●●○
Paris Sour ●●●●○
Park Lane ●●●●◐
Passion Fruit Martini #3 ●●●●○
Pink Lady ●●●●◐
Pisco Sour
(Traditional Recipe) ●●●●◐
Pisco Sour

(Difford's Version) ●●●●●
Playmate Martini ●●●●◐
Plum Sour ●●●●○
Ponche de Algarrobina ●●●◐○
Port Light ●●●◐○
Prairie Oyster ●●●◐○
Purple Flirt #2 ●●●○○
Pussyfoot (Mocktail) ●●●●◐
Quince Sour ●●●●○
Ramos Gin Fizz ●●●●○
Rattlesnake ●●●◐○
The Roadrunner ●●●●○
Rum Sour ●●●●○
Savannah ●●●◐○
Silver Fizz ●●●●○
Sloe Gin Fizz ●●●◐○
Snow White Daiquiri ●●●●○
Sophisticated Savage ●●●◐○
Sour ●●●◐○
Sour Apple Martini #2 (Deluxe US version) ●●●●◐
South Of The Border ●●●○○
Stoney Point Meadow ●●●●○
Tequila Sour ●●●●◐
Tick-Tack Martini ●●●○○
Tiramisu Martini ●●●●○
Tom & Jerry ●●●○○
Triangular Martini ●●●●○
Triple Orange Martini ●●●●○
Turkish Delight ●●●●○
Uncle Vanya ●●●●○
Union Club ●●●●○
Vacation ●●●◐○
Vanilla Vodka Sour ●●●●○
Veneto ●●●◐○
Vodka Sour ●●●●○
Whiskey Sour #1 (Classic Formula) ●●●●○
Whiskey Sour #2 (Difford's Formula) ●●●●●
White Lady ●●●●○
Zabaglione Martini ●●●◐○

ELDERFLOWER CORDIAL

Elderflower cordial is a traditional Victorian British thirst quencher which found its way from the farmhouse kitchen to the supermarket shelf in the late 80s. It is made from the tiny white flowers which cover the elder bush, a common sight during early summer.

To make homemade elderflower cordial you'll need about 30 heads of elderflower, rinsed clean of dirt and bugs. Do not use the leaves or branches as they are poisonous and, if using wild flowers, be sure you have identified them correctly: a mistake could have serious consequences.

Pour 6 pints (3 litres) of boiling water over 900g (2lb) of sugar in a bowl, and stir until the sugar has dissolved. Leave to cool. Wash and slice 2 unwaxed oranges and 3 unwaxed lemons and add these along with 2 teaspoons of citric acid (available from chemists) and 30 elderflower heads. Leave in a cool place for 24 hours, stirring occasionally. Finally, strain through muslin and bottle. You can store this in a refrigerator for up to two weeks.

Apple & Elderflower Collins ●●●●○
Bitter Elder ●●●◐○
Charlie Lychee'tini ●●●●○
Eden ●●●●○
Elderbubble ●●●◐○
Elderflower Collins #1 ●●●●○
Elderflower Collins #2 ●●●●○
Elderflower Martini ●●●●○
English Garden ●●●●○
Floral Martini ●●●●○
French Daisy ●●●◐○
Fruits Of The Forest ●●●◐○
The Game Bird ●●●●◐
Gin Garden ●●●●○
Grape Effect ●●●●○
I B Damm'd ●●●●◐
Jade Garden ●●●●○
Lemongrad ●●●●◐
Lighter Breeze ●●●◐○
The Mayflower Martini ●●●●○
M.C. Martini ●●●●●
Monarch Martini ●●●●○
Orchard Breeze ●●●●◐
Palookaville ●●●●○
Pear & Elderflower Martini ●●●●○
Stoney Point Meadow ●●●●○
Summer Breeze ●●●●○
Twinkle ●●●●○
Van's The Man ●●●●○
The Wet Spot ●●●●○

FINO

See under 'Sherry – Fino'

GALLIANO LIQUEUR

A golden Italian liqueur flavoured with herbs.

Adam And Eve ●●●●○
Atlantic Breeze ●●●○○
Bartender's Root Beer ●●●●○
Bossa Nova #1 ●●●●○
Bossa Nova #2 ●●●◐○
Bourbon Milk Punch ●●●◐○
California Root Beer ●●●◐○
Caribbean Punch ●●●●○
Casablanca ●●●○○
Dutch Breakfast Martini ●●●●○
Flaming Ferrari ●●○○○
Fourth Of July Cocktail ●●●○○
Freddy Fudpucker ●●●◐○
Fruit Salad ●●●○○
Giuseppe's Habit ●●●●○
Gold Medallion ●●●◐○
Golden Cadillac ●●●◐○
Golden Dream ●●●●○
Harvey Wallbanger ●●●◐○
Highland Sling ●●●●○
Hot Shot ●●●○○
Jumping Jack Flash ●●●●○
K.G.B. ●●◐○○
Kiss of Death ●●◐○○
Maxim's Coffee (Hot) ●●●●○
Milano Sour ●●●●○
Moon River ●●●◐○
Mrs Robinson #2 ●●●◐○
Perfect John ●●●●○
Picca ●●●●○
Rocky Mountain Rootbeer ●●●◐○
Russian Qualuude Shot ●●●○○
Slow Comfortable Screw Against Wall ●●●◐○
Snoopy ●●●●○
South Pacific Breeze ●●●◐○
Tootie Fruity Lifesaver ●●●○○
White Satin ●●●○○
Wild Honey ●●●◐○
Yellow Bird ●●●○○
Yellow Fever Martini ●●●◐○

GIN

See 'Plymouth Gin'

GINGER ALE

A non-alcoholic drink made by adding ginger essence, colouring and sweeteners to aerated water. Not as powerful in flavour as ginger beer.

Apple Buck ●●●●○
The Big Easy ●●●●○
Bora Bora Brew (Mocktail) ●●●○○
Brandy Buck ●●●◐○
The Buck ●●●◐○
Causeway ●●●◐○
Cranapple Breeze ●●●◐○
Drowned Out ●●●◐○
Enchanted ●●●◐○
Fog Horn ●●●◐○
The Game Bird ●●●●◐
Ginger Mojito ●●●●○
Ginger Punch ●●●◐○
Horse's Neck With A Kick ●●●○○
Jungle Fire Sling ●●●○○
Kentucky Tea ●●●◐○
Klondike ●●●◐○
Limey Mule ●●●●○
Loch Almond ●●●●○
Maple Pomme ●●●●○
New Year's Absolution ●●●◐○
Niagara Falls ●●●◐○
O'Henry ●●●◐○
Riviera Breeze ●●●◐○
Saigon Sling ●●●◐○
St Kitts ●●●●○
Sandy Gaff ●●●◐○
Scandinavian Pop ●●●○○
Shady Grove Cooler ●●●◐○
Shirley Temple (Mocktail) ●●●○○
Ski Breeze ●●●○○
Sling ●●●●○
Tolleytown Punch ●●●◐○
Urban Holistic ●●●◐○
Waltzing Matilda ●●●●○
Watermelon & Basil Smash ●●●●○

GINGER BEER

A fizzy drink flavoured with ginger - either non-alcoholic or only mildly so. Buy a quality brand or brew your own as follows:

Combine 2oz/56 grams of peeled and crushed root ginger, two lemons sliced into thick rings, one teaspoon of cream of tartar, 1lb/450 grams sugar and 1 gallon/ 4 litres water in a large stainless steel saucepan and bring to the boil. Stir and leave to cool to blood temperature. Stir in 1 oz/ 28 grams of yeast and leave to ferment for 24 hours. Skim off the yeast from the surface and fine strain the liquid into four sterilised 1 litre plastic bottles with screw caps. (Leave at least 2 inches/5cm of air at the top of each bottle and ensure all utensils are scrupulously clean.). Place bottles upright and release excess pressure after 12 hours. Check again after another 12 hours. Once the bottles feel firm and under pressure, place them in the refrigerator and consume their contents within three days.

Apple Of One's Eye ●●●●◐
Berry Nice ●●●◐○
Bomber ●●●●○
Dark 'N' Stormy ●●●●○
Dead Man's Mule ●●●◐○
Desert Cooler ●●●◐○
Dirty Sanchez ●●●●○
El Burro ●●●●○
El Diablo ●●●◐○
Emperor's Memoirs ●●●●○
Forbidden Fruits ●●●●○
Gin Gin Mule ●●●●○
Ginger Nut ●●●◐○
Jamaican Mule ●●●◐○
Mandarine Songbird ●●●○○
Mexican Mule ●●●●◐
Moscow Mule ●●●●○
New Orleans Mule ●●●◐○
Prickly Pear Mule ●●●●○
Raspberry Mule ●●●●○
Red Breast ●●●◐○
Southern Mule ●●●◐○
Tennessee Berry Mule ●●●●○
Thai Lemonade ●●●◐○
Tuscan Mule ●●●◐○
Van's The Man ●●●●○

GRAND MARNIER

40% alc./vol. (80° proof)

www.grand-marnier.com

Producer: Marnier-Lapostolle (Société des Produits), Paris, France.

US distributor: Marnier-Lapostolle

Grand Marnier is one of the best known and most widely sold premium liqueurs in the world. With a cognac base, its unique flavour and aroma come from the maceration and distillation of natural, tropical orange peels.

Founded in 1827 by Jean Baptiste Lapostolle, Grand Marnier is still a family-run business and continues to use traditional production methods and the original Grand Marnier recipe. But despite its heritage, Grand Marnier is an essential cocktail ingredient in today's leading style bars.

Grand Marnier is silky rich with a zesty, juicy flavour. It has a good underlying bite of bitter orange and hints of marmalade and cognac richness at the edges, making it the perfect cocktail partner.

Grand Marnier also produce two special cuvées or blends, 'Grand Marnier Cuvée du Centenaire', created in 1927 by Louis-Alexandre Marnier-Lapostolle to celebrate the 100th anniversary of the company's foundation; and 'Grand Marnier Cuvée du Cent Cinquantenaire', an exceptional Grand Marnier created in 1977 by the chairman of the company, Jacques Marnier-Lapostolle, to celebrate its 150th anniversary.

A number of the cocktails in this guide which call for Grand Marnier benefit from the extra complexity provided by these exceptional cuvées. I've marked these drinks with an '*' in the list below and in the recipe after Grand Marnier.

Agent Orange ●●●●○
The Alamagoozlum Cocktail ●●●●◐
Alice From Dallas ●●●◐○
Alice In Wonderland ●●●○○
Apple Of My Eire ●●●●○
Attitude Adjuster ●●●○○
B-52 Shot ●●●◐○
B-52 Frozen ●●●◐○
B. J. Shot ●●●○○
Bartender's Martini ●●●●○
Basil Grande ●●●●○
Biarritz ●●●◐○
Bingo ●●●○○
Black Magic
Blow Job ●●●◐○
Blueberry Tea ●●●●○
Bombay ●●●●◐
Bosom Caresser ●●●●○
Brandy Buck ●●●◐○
Bull's Blood ●●●◐○
Cactus Banger ●●●●○
Café Gates ●●●◐○
Caravan ●●●○○
Champagne Cup ●●●◐○
Chas ●●●●○
Claret Cobbler ●●●●○
Classic ●●●●●
Clockwork Orange ●●●◐○
Cosmopolitan Delight ●●●●◐
Creamsicle ●●●●○
Derby Fizz ●●●●◐
Dorian Gray ●●●◐○
Dramatic Martini ●●●◐○
Dulchin ●●●●○
East India* #1 ●●●●◐
East India #2 ●●●●○
Esquire #1 ●●●●○
Fancy Drink ●●●◐○
57 T-Bird Shot ●●●●○
Flaming Ferrari ●●○○○
French Tear #1 ●●●●○
Fresca Nova ●●●◐○
Gloom Chaser ●●●◐○
Golden Bird ●●●◐○
Grand Cosmopolitan ●●●●◐
Grand Margarita* ●●●●●
Grand Mimosa ●●●◐○
Grand Sazerac* ●●●●○
Grand Sidecar* ●●●●○
Grande Champagne Cosmo ●●●●○
Hakkatini ●●●●○
Honeymoon ●●●●○
Hot Red Blooded Frenchman ●●●●○
Irish Chocolate Oranj'tini ●●●◐○
Irish Flag ●●●○○
Irish Manhattan ●●●●○
Jambouree ●●●●○
Knickerbocker Special ●●●●○
Leap Year Martini ●●●○○
Mandarinitini ●●●○○
Marny Cocktail* ●●●●◐
Met Manhattan ●●●●○
Mexican Tea (Hot) ●●●●◐
Mexicano (Hot) ●●●●◐
Million Dollar Margarita* ●●●●◐
Mimosa ●●●◐○
Morning Glory ●●●●○
Mulled Wine ●●●●○
Naranja Daiquiri ●●●●○
Niagara Falls ●●●◐○
Night & Day ●●●◐○
Olympic ●●●●◐
Orange Brûlée ●●●●●
Orange Custard Martini ●●●◐○
Park Avenue ●●●●○
Periodista Daiquiri ●●●●○
Pilgrim Cocktail ●●●●○
Pink Palace ●●●●◐
Pisco Naranja ●●●◐○
Platinum Blonde ●●●◐○
Playmate Martini* ●●●●◐
Polly's Special ●●●●○
Prince Of Wales* ●●●◐○
Randy ●●●●○
Rat Pack Manhattan ●●●●○
Red Angel ●●●●○
Red Lion #1 (Modern Formula) ●●●●◐
Red Lion #2 (Embury's Formula) ●●●●◐
Rhett Butler ●●●●○
Roa Aé ●●●◐○
Rosarita Margarita ●●●●○
Sake-tini #1 ●●●●○
Sandstorm ●●●●○
Sangaree ●●●●○
Sangria ●●●◐○
Satsuma Martini ●●●◐○
Satan's Whiskers (Straight) ●●●●◐
Sir Charles Punch ●●●●○
Snoopy ●●●●○
Snyder Martini ●●●●○
Socialite ●●●◐○
Soyer Au Champagne ●●●◐○
Summer Time Martini ●●●◐○
Sundowner #1 ●●●●○
Sundowner #2 ●●●●○
Sunny Breeze ●●●◐○
The Suzy Wong Martini ●●●◐○
Tiki Max ●●●●○
Triple Orange Martini ●●●●○
Waltzing Matilda ●●●●○
Whiskey Cobbler ●●●○○
Whiskey Squirt ●●●●○
White Sangria ●●●◐○
Zanzibar ●●●◐○
Zombie #2 (Vic's Formula) ●●●◐○
Zombie #3 (Modern Formula) ●●●●○

GRAPEFRUIT JUICE

This citrus fruit originated in Jamaica and may take its unusual name from the way the unripe fruit hangs in green clusters from the tree like bunches of grapes. Or then again, maybe some early botanist just got confused.

Grapefruit is a recognised antioxidant and pink grapefruit contains lycopene, which is thought to boost the body's immune system. Consuming large quantities of concentrated grapefruit juice can, however, produce reactions with certain prescription-only medicines.

As a rule of thumb – the darker the flesh, the sweeter the juice and the more beta-carotene and vitamins. But even the sweetest of grapefruits are wonderfully sharp and tart.

I must confess that I tend to use packaged 'freshly squeezed' grapefruit juice from the supermarket. However, this is a relatively easy fruit to juice yourself using a citrus press or an electric spinning juicer. Simply cut in half and juice away, taking care to avoid the pith, which can make the juice bitter. As with other citrus fruits, avoid storing in the refrigerator immediately prior to use as cold fruit yield less juice.

A.J. ●●●●○
Acapulco ●●●◐○
Arizona Breeze ●●●●○
Baby Blue Martini ●●●◐○
Bald Eagle Martini ●●●●◐
Bitter Sweet Symphony ●●●◐○
Blinker ●●●●○
Bloodhound ●●●◐○
Buena Vida ●●●●◐
Cherrute ●●●●○
Chihuahua Margarita ●●●◐○
China Blue ●●●◐○
China Blue Martini ●●●●○
Crimson Blush ●●●●○
Durango ●●●◐○
Exotic Passion ●●●◐○
Fancy Drink ●●●◐○
First of July ●●●●○
Florida Cocktail (Mocktail) ●●●○○
Florida Daiquiri ●●●●◐
Floridita Margarita ●●●●○
Four W Daiquiri ●●●●○
Fresca ●●●◐○
Fru Fru ●●●◐○
Fruit Tree Daiquiri ●●●●○
Gentle Breeze (Mocktail) ●●●○○
Golden Fizz #2 ●●●●◐
Grapefruit Daiquiri ●●●●○
Grapefruit Julep ●●●●◐
Greyhound ●●●○○
Hemingway Special Daiquiri ●●●●◐
The Hive ●●●●○
Island Breeze ●●●◐○
Italian Job #1 ●●●◐○
Judy (Mocktail)
LCB Martini ●●●●○
Light Breeze ●●●◐○
Lima Sour ●●●◐○
Lime Breeze ●●●◐○
Lisa B's Daiquiri ●●●●●
M.G.F. ●●●●○
Mai Tai #2 (Beaumont-Gantt's Formula) ●●●●○
Mainbrace ●●●●○
Mesa Fresca ●●●●○
Monkey Wrench ●●●◐○
Moonlight Martini ●●●●○
Mountain Sipper ●●●◐○
Mucky Bottom ●●●◐○
Nantucket ●●●◐○
Navigator ●●●●○
Nevada Daiquiri ●●●●○
Nicky's Fizz ●●●◐○
Oriental Tart ●●●●○
Paloma ●●●●◐
Palm Beach ●●●◐○
Parma Negroni ●●●●○
Passover ●●●○○
Pink Grapefruit Margarita ●●●●○
Pink Hound ●●●●○
Pink Tutu ●●●◐○
Pogo Stick ●●●●○
Polly's Special ●●●●○
Pompanski Martini ●●●●○
Ponce de Leon ●●●●○
Poncha ●●●●○
Rasputin ●●●○○
Ribalaigua Daiquiri #3 ●●●●○
Ruby Martini #1 ●●●●○
Salty Dog ●●●●○
Sandstorm ●●●●○
Seabreeze #1 (Simple) ●●●◐○
Seabreeze #2 (Layered) ●●●◐○
Seventh Heaven #2 ●●●●◐
Showbiz ●●●●○
South China Breeze ●●●●○
Speyside Martini ●●●●○
Sunny Breeze ●●●◐○
Sunstroke ●●●●○
Tailor Made ●●●●○
Tango Martini #2 ●●●●○
Tex Collins ●●●◐○
Texsun ●●●◐○
Tilt ●●●●○

Tres Compadres Margarita ●●●●◐
Tropic ●●●●◐
Tropical Breeze ●●●○○
Universal Shot ●●●○○
Vanilla & Grapefruit Daiquiri ●●●●◐
Vert'ical Breeze ●●●●○
Wibble ●●●●◐

GRAPES

Oddly, many of the grapes which are classically used for winemaking are not particularly good to eat. Only a few, like Gamay, Tokay, Zinfandel and Muscat, are used for both purposes.

The main commercially available table grapes are Concord, which gives a purple juice which is used for concentrates and jellies, Emperor, which is red and thick-skinned, and Thompson Seedless, which is green and sweet. Seedless grapes are easiest to use in cocktails. Fresh grape juice has a delicate, subtle flavour which is very different from the syrupy stuff in cartons.

The best way to extract juice is to muddle the required number of grapes in the base of your shaker. Recipes in this guide call for 'seedless red grapes' or 'seedless white grapes'. Obviously, if you've opted for a grape that has seeds you'll need to remove them yourself before you muddle the grapes. Crushing seeds releases bitter flavours which can spoil a drink.

Black Magic ●●●○○
Caipiruva ●●●●○
Double Grape Martini ●●●●◐
Enchanted ●●●◐○ (white grapes)
Grape Delight ●●●◐○ (red grapes)
Grape Effect ●●●●○ (white grapes)
Grape Escape ●●●●◐ (white grapes)
Grape Martini ●●●●○ (white grapes)
Grapple Martini ●●●●○ (white grapes)
Jalisco ●●●●○ (white grapes)
Oriental Grape Martini ●●●●◐
Pisco Punch #4 (Prosser's Formula) ●●●●●
Rum & Raisin Alexandra ●●●●○
Saturn Martini ●●●●◐
Sodden Grape Martini ●●●●○
Speyside Martini ●●●●○
Tiziano ●●●◐○

GREEN BANANA LIQUEUR

Absinthe Without Leave ●●◐○○
Bali Trader ●●●◐○

GREEN CRÈME DE MENTHE LIQUEUR

A mint-flavoured liqueur with a striking green colour.

After Eight ●●●○○
Alexander's Sister ●●●◐○
Barnamint ●●●○○
Bullfrog ●●◐○○
Flying Grasshopper ●●●◐○
Green Fizz ●●●◐○
Green Fly ●●●◐○
Green Swizzle ●●●●○
Green Tea Martini ●●●●○
Irish Flag ●●●○○
Jade Daiquiri ●●●●○
Miami Daiquiri ●●●●○
Mint Cocktail ●●●●◐
Mint Fizz ●●●◐○
Monte Carlo Imperial ●●●○○
St Patrick's Day ●●●●○
Shamrock #1 ●●●○○
Shamrock #2 ●●●●○
Tequila Mockingbird ●●●○○

GRENADINE

See 'Pomegranate (Grenadine) Syrup'

HALF AND HALF

This blend of 50% milk and 50% cream is relatively unknown in the UK. I've listed milk and cream as separate ingredients in this guide.

HAZELNUT LIQUEUR

French hazelnut liqueurs are known as crème de noisette. Edmond Briottet is one of the better producers.

Apple Pie Shot ●●●●○
Bellissimo ●●●○○
Black Nuts ●●◐○○
Brazilian Monk ●●●◐○
Butterfly's Kiss ●●●◐○
Cherry & Hazelnut Daiquiri ●●●●○
Choc & Nut Martini ●●●◐○
Creamy Bee ●●●●○
Crimson Tide ●●●●○
Cuppa Joe ●●●●○
DC Martini ●●●●○
Envy ●●●●○
Fosbury Flip ●●●●◐
Friar Tuck ●●●◐○
Fruit & Nut Chocolate Martini ●●●●○
Fruit & Nut Martini ●●●●○
Ginger Nut ●●●◐○
Giuseppe's Habit ●●●●○
Golden Mac ●●●◐○
Hazel'ito ●●●●◐
Hazelnut Alexander ●●●●○
Hazelnut Martini ●●●◐○
International Incident ●●●●○
Italian Sun ●●●●○
Jam Roll ●●◐○○
Knicker Dropper Glory ●●●●○
Mad Monk Milkshake ●●●◐○
Monk's Candy Bar ●●●○○
Monk's Habit ●●●○○
Nuts & Berries ●●●●○
Nutty Berry'tini ●●●◐○
Nutty Nashville ●●●●○
Nutty Russian ●●●◐○
Peanut Butter & Jelly Shot ●●●◐○
The Strawberry Éclair ●●●●○
Vanilla'tini ●●●◐○
Yule Luvit ●●●◐○
Zesty ●●●◐○

HONEY

Many bartenders dilute honey with equal parts of warm water to make it easier to mix. I prefer to use good quality runny honey (preferably orange blossom) and dissolve it by stirring into the cocktail's base spirit prior to adding the other ingredients. This may be a tad time consuming but it avoids unnecessary dilution. Decant your honey into a squeezy plastic bottle with a fine nozzle for easy dispensing.

Aged Honey Daiquiri ●●●●●
Air Mail ●●●●◐
Almond & Sake Martini ●●●●○
Applily Married ●●●●◐
Atholl Brose ●●●●○
Banana Smoothie (Mocktail) ●●●●◐
Basil & Honey Daiquiri ●●●●●
Bebbo ●●●●○
Bee Sting ●●●●○
Bee's Knees #1 ●●●●○
Bee's Knees #2 ●●●●◐
Blue Blazer ●●●○○
Cappercailie ●●●●○
Cold Comfort ●●●●○
Dowa ●●●●○
Easy Tiger ●●●●○
Ginger & Lemongrass Martini ●●●●○
Ginger Punch ●●●◐○
Golden Fizz #2 ●●●●◐
Golden Mac ●●●◐○
Grapefruit Julep ●●●●◐
Grog ●●●●○
Hair Of The Dog ●●●●○
Havanatheone ●●●●●
The Hive ●●●●○
Honey & Marmalade Dram'tini ●●●●◐
Honey Bee ●●●●○
Honey Daiquiri ●●●●◐
Honey Limeaid (Mocktail) ●●●●○
Honeysuckle Daiquiri ●●●●●
The Honeysuckle Orchard ●●●●○
Hot Buttered Rum ●●●●○
Hot Grog ●●●●○
Hot Toddy #1 ●●●●◐
Hot Toddy #2 ●●●●◐
The Juxtaposition ●●●●○
Lemon Beat ●●●●○
Lolita Margarita ●●●●◐
Lucky Lily Margarita ●●●●◐
Lucky Lindy ●●●◐○
Maria Theresa Margarita ●●●●○
Milk & Honey Martini ●●●●◐
Navy Grog ●●●●○
New Year's Absolution ●●●◐○
Nutty Nashville ●●●●○
Pappy Honeysuckle ●●●●◐
Pineapple Smoothie (Mocktail) ●●●◐○
Poncha ●●●●○
Pooh'tini ●●●●◐
Port Light ●●●◐○

HONEY LIQUEUR

There are many varieties of honey liqueur but the Polish brands claim the oldest heritage. Traditional Polish vodka-based honey liqueurs are thought to have originated in the 16th century. Besides the cocktails below, these liqueurs are worth enjoying neat and slightly warmed in a balloon glass – at London's Baltic they warm the bottle in a baby's bottle warmer.

Afternoon Tea-Ni ●●●●○
Bohemian Iced Tea ●●●●◐
Chinese Cosmopolitan ●●●●○
Creamy Bee ●●●●○
Grassy Finnish ●●●●○
Heaven Scent ●●●◐○
The Hive ●●●●○
Honey Apple Martini ●●●●○
Honey Berry Sour ●●●●○
Honey Vodka Sour ●●●●○
Lemon Butter Cookie ●●●●○
Limited Liability ●●●●◐
Limousine ●●●●○
Milk & Honey Martini ●●●●◐
Nutty Nashville ●●●●○
Perfect Alibi ●●●●○
Polish Martini ●●●●●
Pooh'tini ●●●●◐
Rhubarb & Honey Bellini ●●●●○
Saigon Sling ●●●◐○
Snow on Earth ●●●○○
Thomas Blood Martini ●●●◐○
Toddy Martini ●●●◐○

ICE CREAM (VANILLA)

Vanilla ice cream may not be exciting, but it is safe and almost universally liked. There are few people who can honestly say they hate the stuff, making it the obvious choice for a bar's freezer. Splash out on a decent brand. You'll taste the difference.

Barnamint ●●●○○
Black Irish ●●●○○
Brazilian Monk ●●●◐○
FBI ●●●●○
Key Lime ●●●●○
Lemon Chiffon Pie ●●●●○
Mudslide ●●●●○
Soyer Au Champagne ●●●◐○

INFUSIONS

Some recipes call for an infused spirit, such as vanilla-infused rum. You make this by putting three split vanilla pods in a bottle of rum and leaving it to stand for a fortnight. Warming and turning the bottle frequently can speed the infusion.

Other herbs, spices and even fruits can be infused in a similar manner in vodka, gin, rum, whiskey and tequila. Whatever spirit you decide to use, pick a brand that is at least 40% alcohol by volume.

Be aware that when the level of spirit in a bottle drops below the flavouring, the alcohol loses its preservative effect and the flavouring can start to rot. Also be careful not to load the spirit with too much flavour or leave it to infuse for too long. Sample the infusion every couple of days to ensure the taste is not becoming overpowering.

IRISH CREAM LIQUEUR

In November 1974 R&A Bailey perfected the technique of combining Irish whiskey, cocoa and fresh cream without souring the cream. Sales grew quickly and it is now the world's best selling liqueur. There are, however, many equally good alternatives.

A.B.C. ●●●◐○
Absinthe Without Leave ●●◐○○
After Six Shot ●●◐○○
Apache ●●●○○
B5200 ●●●○○
B-52 Shot ●●●◐○
B-53 Shot ●●●○○
B-54 Shot ●●●○○
B-55 Shot ●●●○○
B-52 Frozen ●●●◐○
B. J. Shot ●●●○○
Baby Guinness ●●●◐○
Bananas & Cream ●●●●○
Barnamint ●●●○○
Bazooka Joe ●●◐○○
Beam-Me-Up Scotty ●●●○○
Bit-O-Honey ●●●○○
Black Dream ●●●○○
Black Irish ●●●○○
Bumble Bee ●●●◐○
Burnt Toasted Almond ●●●○○
Butterscotch Delight ●●●◐○
Carrot Cake ●●●◐○
Chill-Out Martini ●●●○○
Creamy Bee ●●●●○
Cream Cake ●●●◐○
Death By Chocolate ●●●●○
Dramatic Martini ●●●◐○
E.T. ●●●●○
Extradition ●●●●○
FBI ●●●●○
Flaming Henry ●●●◐○
Fruit & Nut Chocolate Martini ●●●●○
Golden Shot ●●●○○
International Incident ●●●●○
Irish Alexander ●●●◐○
Irish Charlie ●●●○○
Irish Chocolate Oranj'tini ●●●◐○
Irish Espresso'tini ●●●●◐
Irish Flag ●●●○○
Irish Frappé ●●●◐○
Irish Latte ●●●◐○
Jam Roll ●●◐○○
Landslide ●●●○○
Lemon Meringue Martini ●●●●○
Mad Monk Milkshake ●●●◐○
Mocha Martini ●●●●◐
Muddy Water ●●●◐○
Mudslide ●●●●○
Oatmeal Cookie ●●●◐○
Oil Slick ●●◐○○
Peanut Butter & Jelly Shot ●●●◐○
P.S. I Love You ●●●●○
Rattlesnake Shot ●●●○○
Shamrock Express ●●●◐○
Slippery Nipple ●●○○○
Stealth ●●●◐○
Tribbble ●●●●○

JÄGERMEISTER

Assisted Suicide ●●●◐○
Crown Stag ●●●◐○
Surfer on A.C.D. ●●●◐○

JONGE JENEVER

Jenever (or genever) is a juniper-flavoured spirit from Holland and Belgium. The juniper means jenever is technically a gin and in fact it was the forerunner of the London dry gins popular today. There are three basic styles of jenever - 'oude' (literally, 'old'), 'jonge' ('young') and 'korenwijn' ('corn wine'). They differ according to the percentage of malt-wine (a kind of unaged whiskey) and botanicals contained.

Jonge jenever is so named because it is a modern, contemporary style. It was first developed in the 1950s in response to consumer demand for a lighter, more mixable jenever.

The Alamagoozlum Cocktail ●●●●◐
Collins ●●●●○
Flying Dutchman Martini ●●●●○
I B Damm'd ●●●●◐
Jenever Sour ●●●●○
Medicinal Solution ●●●◐○

KETEL ONE VODKA

40% alc./vol. (80°proof)

www.KetelOne.com

Producer: Nolet Distillery, Schiedam, The Netherlands.

US distributor: Nolet Spirits U.S.A.. 30 Journey, Aliso Viejo,CA 92656, Tel: 949 448 5700 / 800 243 3618

UK distributor: InSpirit Brands, Tel: 020 7739 1333

Ketel One vodka is the creation of one of Holland's oldest distilling families, the Nolet family of Schiedam, who have been distilling since 1691 when Joannes Nolet started his distillation business.

The Dutch refer to their pot stills as 'ketels', thus this vodka is named after the Nolets' original coal-fired pot still number one, still used today in the production of Ketel One. After distillation, this small batch distilled spirit is then slowly filtered through charcoal to ensure its purity.

Ten generations after Joannes, Carolus Nolet now runs the company with the help of his two sons, Carl and Bob. They introduced Ketel One to the US in 1991 where it has since enjoyed phenomenal growth. This looks as if it's being repeated in the UK where the brand was launched in 1999.

Ketel One's balanced and clean palate with its classic wheat character makes beautifully smooth Martinis while still showing the character of the grain from which it is made.

After Eight ●●●○○
Agent Orange ●●●●○
Alabama Slammer #1 ●●●◐○
Alexander The Great ●●●◐○
Almond Martini #1 ●●●●○
Anis'tini ●●●●○
Anita's Attitude Adjuster ●●●◐○
Apple & Melon Martini ●●●◐○
Apple Martini #1 (simple version) ●●●●○
Apple Martini #2 ●●●●○
Apricot Cosmo ●●●●◐
Asian Ginger Martini ●●●●○
Atomic Cocktail ●●●○○
Awol ●●●●○
B-53 Shot ●●●○○
Baby Woo Woo ●●●○○
Balalaika ●●●●○
Bali Trader ●●●◐○
Ballet Russe ●●●◐○
Baltic Breeze ●●●◐○
Banana Boomer ●●●●○
Barbara ●●●○○
Basil Grande ●●●●○
Basilico ●●●◐○
Bay Breeze ●●●○○
Bay Of Passion ●●●○○
Beach Iced Tea ●●●◐○
Bellini-Tini ●●●●○
Beverly Hills Iced Tea ●●●◐○
Big Apple Martini ●●●◐○
Bingo ●●●○○
Bitter Sweet Symphony ●●●◐○
Bitterest Pill ●●●◐○
Black Forest Gateau Martini ●●●●◐
Black Irish ●●●○○
Black 'N' Blue Caipirovska ●●●●○
Black Russian ●●●○○
Bling! Bling! ●●●●◐
Bloodhound ●●●◐○
Bloody Mary (modern recipe) ●●●●◐
Blue Champagne ●●●○○
Blue Kamikaze ●●●◐○
Blue Lagoon ●●●○○
Blueberry Martini #1 ●●●●○
Blueberry Martini #2 (simple) ●●●●○
Blush Martini ●●●◐○
Blushin' Russian ●●●●○
Boston Tea Party ●●●○○
Bullfrog ●●◐○○
Burnt Toasted Almond ●●●○○
Caipirovska ●●●◐○
California Root Beer ●●●◐○
Cape Codder ●●●◐○
Casablanca ●●●○○
Cassini ●●●◐○
Celery Martini ●●●●○
Cham 69 #1 ●●●◐○
Cham 69 #2 ●●●◐○
Cherrute ●●●●○
Chill Breeze ●●●○○
China Beach ●●●●○

Choc & Nut Martini ●●●◐○
Chocolate Martini ●●●●○
Chocolate Mint Martini ●●●●○
Cobbled Raspberry Martini ●●●●◐
Coconut Water ●●●●○
Collection Martini ●●●○○
Colorado Bulldog ●●◐○○
Crime Of Passion Shot ●●●○○
Crown Stag ●●●◐○
Cucumber Martini ●●●●◐
Cucumber & Mint Martini ●●●●○
Cucumber Sake-Tini ●●●●○
Cuppa Joe ●●●●○
Death By Chocolate ●●●●○
Depth Charge ●●○○○
Detox ●●●○○
Detroit Martini ●●●●○
Detropolitan ●●●●○
Diable Rouge ●●●◐○
DiVino's ●●●●○
Double Grape Martini ●●●●◐
Dowa ●●●●○
Dry Ice Martini ●●●●◐
Dyevitchka ●●●●○
Eastern Martini ●●●●◐
Egg Custard Martini ●●●◐○
Envy ●●●●○
Espresso Martini ●●●●○
Esquire #2 ●●●◐○
E.T. ●●●●○
Evita ●●●◐○
Exotic Passion ●●●◐○
F. Willy Shot ●●●◐○
FBI ●●●●○
57 T-Bird Shot ●●●●○
Fizz ●●●●○
Flip ●●●●◐
Flirtini #1 ●●●●○
Flirtini #2 ●●●●○
Flying Grasshopper ●●●◐○
Fourth Of July Shot ●●◐○○
French 76 ●●●●○
French Kiss #1 ●●●○○
French Kiss #2 ●●●◐○
French Leave ●●●○○
French Martini ●●●●○
Fruit Salad ●●●○○
Ginger Martini ●●●●○
Glass Tower ●●●○○
Grape Martini ●●●●○
Grapefruit Julep ●●●●◐
Grapple Martini ●●●●○
Grateful Dead ●●●◐○
Green Hornet ●●●●○
Greyhound ●●●○○
Gypsy Queen ●●●●○
Hard Lemonade ●●●●○
Harvey Wallbanger ●●●◐○
Hazelnut Martini ●●●◐○
The Hive ●●●●○
Hong Kong Fuey ●●●○○
Hot Passion ●●●○○
Hot Tub ●●●●○
Ice "T" Knee ●●●●◐
Ice White Cosmo ●●●●○
Iced Sake Martini ●●●●◐
Icewine Martini ●●●●◐
Icy Pink Lemonade ●●●◐○
Iguana ●●●◐○
Iguana Wana ●●●○○
Illusion ●●●●○
Ink Martini #2 ●●●◐○
Insomniac ●●●●◐
International Incident ●●●●○
Intimate Martini ●●●●○
Italian Surfer With A Russian Attitude ●●●○○
Jade Garden ●●●●○
Ja-Mora ●●●●○
Japanese Pear ●●●●○
Jules Delight ●●●●○
Jungle Juice ●●●◐○

Katinka ●●●◐○
Key Lime Pie #2 ●●●●○
Key West Cooler ●●●◐○
Killer Punch ●●●◐○
Kir Martini ●●●◐○
Kiwi Bellini ●●●●○
Kiwi Collins ●●●●○
Kiwi Crush ●●●●○
Kiwi Martini (simple) ●●●●○
Koolaid ●●●●○
Kretchma ●●●◐○
L.A. Iced Tea ●●●◐○
Lavender & Black Pepper Martini ●●●●○
Lazarus ●●●●◐
LCB Martini ●●●●○
The Legend ●●●●○
Lemon Butter Cookie ●●●●○
Lemon Drop Martini ●●●◐○
Lemon Martini ●●●●◐
Life (Love In the Future Ecstasy) ●●●◐○
Limoncello Martini ●●●◐○
Liquorice Shot ●●●◐○
Long Beach Iced Tea ●●●◐○
Long Island Iced Tea ●●●◐○
Long Island Spiced Tea ●●●◐○
Lotus Espresso ●●●●◐
Love Junk ●●●◐○
Lush ●●●◐○
Lychee Martini ●●●●○
Madras ●●●●○
Madroska ●●●○○
Mae West Martini ●●●●○
Mambo ●●●◐○
Mandarito ●●●●○
Martini Royale ●●●◐○
Melon Ball ●●●○○
Melon Martini #1 ●●●○○
Melon Martini #2 (Fresh Fruit) ●●●●○
Meloncholy Martini ●●●●○
Mellow Martini ●●●◐○
Merry Widow #2 ●●●◐○
Milano ●●●●◐
Mint Martini ●●●●◐
Miss Martini ●●●◐○
Momo Special ●●●●○
Monza ●●●◐○
Moscow Lassi ●●●○○
Moscow Mule ●●●●○
Mrs Robinson #2 ●●●◐○
Muddy Water ●●●◐○
Mudslide ●●●●○
Myrtle Martini ●●●◐○
Niagara Falls ●●●◐○
Noble Europe ●●●●◐
Nutcracker Sweet ●●●◐○
Nutty Russian ●●●◐○
Orang-A-Tang ●●●●○
Orchard Breeze ●●●●◐
Oriental Grape Martini ●●●●◐
Ouzi ●●●◐○
Palma Violet Martini ●●●◐○
Pass-on-that ●●●○○
Passion Fruit Martini #1 ●●●●○
Passion Fruit Martini #2 ●●●●○
Passover ●●●○○
Pavlova Shot ●●●◐○
Pear & Elderflower Martini ●●●●○
Perfect John ●●●●○
Pernod & Black Martini ●●●●○
Pharmaceutical Stimulant ●●●●○
Piña Martini ●●●●○
Pineapple & Cardamom Martini ●●●●●
Pineapple & Ginger Martini ●●●●○
Pink Sin Martini ●●●○○
Pink Tutu ●●●◐○
Pino Pepe ●●●●○
Plum Martini ●●●●○
Plum Sour ●●●●○
Polish Martini ●●●●●

Pomegranate Martini ●●●●◐
Pompanski Martini ●●●●○
Pontberry Martini ●●●●○
Port & Melon Martini ●●●●◐
Purple Flirt #1 ●●●●○
Purple Haze ●●●◐○
Purple Hooter ●●●◐○
Quince Sour ●●●●○
Raspberry Martini #1 ●●●◐○
Raspberry Mule ●●●●○
Raspberry Watkins ●●●○○
Ray's Hard Lemonade ●●●●○
Reef Juice ●●●●○
Rocky Mountain Rootbeer ●●●◐○
Roger ●●●◐○
Russian ●●●◐○
Russian Qualuude Shot ●●●○○
Russian Spring Punch ●●●●◐
Sage Martini ●●●●○
Sake-tini #2 ●●●●○
Sakini ●●●●○
Salty Dog ●●●●○
San Fransisco ●●●◐○
Screaming Banana Banshee ●●●◐○
Screwdriver ●●●◐○
Seabreeze #1 (Simple) ●●●◐○
Seabreeze #2 (Layered) ●●●◐○
Sex On The Beach #1 ●●◐○○
Sex On The Beach #2 ●●●○○
Sgroppino ●●●●◐
Shamrock Express ●●●◐○
Showbiz ●●●●○
Silver Fizz ●●●●○
Slow Screw ●●●○○
Slow Comfortable Screw ●●●◐○
Slow Comfortable Screw Against The Wall ●●●◐○
Snood Murdekin ●●●◐○
Sour Apple Martini #1 (Popular US version) ●●●●○
Sour Apple Martini #2 (Deluxe US version) ●●●●◐
Sputnik ●●●◐○
Stairs Martini ●●●●●
Strawberry Martini ●●●●○
Strawberry 'N' Balsamic Martini ●●●●◐
Strudel Martini ●●●●◐
Suitably Frank ●●●◐○
Summer Breeze ●●●●○
Summer Rose Martini ●●●●○
The Sun Salutation ●●●●○
Sunstroke ●●●●○
Superminty-Chocolatini ●●●◐○
Swedish Blue Martini ●●●◐○
Sweet Tart ●●●◐○
Tainted Cherry ●●●○○
Tawny-Tini ●●●●○
Tennessee Iced Tea ●●●●○
Testarossa ●●●◐○
Texas Iced Tea ●●●◐○
Thomas Blood Martini ●●●◐○
Tick-Tack Martini ●●●○○
Toasted Almond ●●●●○
Tokyo Iced Tea ●●●◐○
Tongue Twister ●●●○○
Too Close For Comfort ●●●◐○
Tootie Fruity Lifesaver ●●●○○
Top Banana Shot ●●●◐○
Transylvanian Martini ●●●○○
Triple Orange Martini ●●●●○
Tripleberry ●●●●○
Tropical Breeze ●●●○○
Turkish Coffee Martini ●●●●○
Turkish Delight ●●●●○
TVR ●●●○○
Twinkle ●●●●○
Two "T" Fruity Martini ●●●●○
Umbongo ●●●○○
Uncle Vanya ●●●●○
Universal Shot ●●●○○
Utterly Butterly ●●●◐○

Velvet Fog ●●●●◐
Velvet Hammer ●●●◐○
The Vesper Martini ●●●●●
Vodka Collins ●●●●○
Vodka Espresso ●●●●◐
Vodka Gimlet ●●●●○
Vodka Sour ●●●●○
Vodkatini ●●●●◐
Volga Boatman ●●●◐○
Walnut Martini ●●●●○
Wanton Abandon ●●●●○
Warsaw ●●●◐○
Wasabi Martini ●●●●◐
Washington Apple ●●●●◐
Watermelon Man ●●●◐○
Watermelon Martini ●●●●○
White Elephant ●●●◐○
White Russian ●●●◐○
White Stinger ●●●◐○
Wild Promenade Martini ●●●●○
Wilton Martini ●●●●○
Woo Woo ●●●◐○
Yellow Fever Martini ●●●◐○
Z Martini ●●●●●

KETEL ONE CITROEN VODKA

40% alc./vol. (80°proof)

www.**KetelOne.com**

Producer: **Nolet Distillery, Schiedam, The Netherlands.**

US distributor: **Nolet Spirits U.S.A. 30 Journey, Aliso Viejo, CA 92656.**

Tel: **949 448 5700 / 800 243 3618**

UK distributor: **InSpirit Brands,** Tel: **020 7739 1333**

Having already created what they and many top bartenders consider the perfect vodka for Martinis, the Nolet family wanted to create a flavoured vodka of equal excellence for making the ultimate Cosmopolitan. The family spent more than two years researching and evaluating different blending and infusion methods, before arriving at the costly but effective process of hand-crafting in small batches and infusing with natural citrus flavour until the perfect balance is reached.

Ketel One Citroen combines the smooth qualities of the original Ketel One Vodka with the refreshing natural essence of citrus fruit. To ensure continuity in the quality of Ketel One Citroen, a member of the Nolet family personally samples each batch produced prior to release.

There are few other citrus-flavoured vodkas with the rich, natural lemon peel oil flavours found in Ketel One Citroen. These combine with a clean grain character to make this vodka an ideal base for Cosmopolitans and other contemporary cocktails.

Asian Mary ●●●●○
Basil Beauty ●●●●○
Blue Cosmo ●●●◐○
Blue Fin ●●●◐○
Bohemian Iced Tea ●●●●◐
Cheeky Monkey ●●●●○
Chinese Whisper Martini ●●●●○
Citrus Caipirovska ●●●●○
Citrus Martini ●●●●○
Collection Martini ●●●○○
Colonial Rot ●●●○○
Cosmopolitan #1 (simple version) ●●●●◐
Cosmopolitan #2 (complex version) ●●●●●
Cranapple Breeze ●●●◐○
Crimson Blush ●●●●○
Double Vision ●●●○○
Elderflower Collins #2 ●●●●○
Fresca ●●●◐○
Ginger Cosmo ●●●●○
Ginger Nut ●●●◐○
Grand Cosmopolitan ●●●●◐
Green Eyes ●●●◐○
Hawaiian Cosmoplitan ●●●●○
Henry VIII ●●●◐○
Ignorance Is Bliss ●●●◐○
Key Lime Pie #3 ●●●●○
Kurrant Affair ●●●○○
Lemon Curd Martini ●●●●○
Lemon Meringue Martini ●●●●○
Lemongrad ●●●●◐
Lemongrass Cosmo ●●●●◐
Leninade ●●●●○
M.G.F. ●●●●○
Mango Martini ●●●●○
Motox ●●●●○
Pear Drop ●●●◐○
Purple Cosmo ●●●●◐
Raspberry Cosmo ●●●◐○
Razzintini ●●●◐○
Rosy Martini ●●●●○
Royal Cosmopolitan ●●●●○
Ruby Martini #1 ●●●●○
Saturn Martini ●●●●◐
Smartini ●●●●○
Sourpuss Martini ●●●●○
South Pacific ●●●◐○
Strawberry Cosmo ●●●◐○
Stupid Cupid ●●●○○
Venus in Furs ●●●◐○
Watermelon Cosmo ●●●◐○
White Cosmo ●●●●○
Windy Miller ●●●●○
Wine Cooler ●●●◐○
Yellow Belly Martini ●●●●○
Zakuski Martini ●●●●○
Zingy Ginger Martini ●●●●○

LEMONCELLO

See 'Luxardo Limoncello Liqueur'

LEMONS & LIMES

Originally from India or Malaysia, lemons are available throughout the year and in many different varieties, distinguishable by their shape, size and thickness of skin.

The smaller and more fragrant lime is closely related to the lemon. It is cultivated in tropical countries and is widely used in Caribbean and Brazilian cuisine.

Both these citrus fruits are bartender staples and their juice is used to balance sweetness and add depth to a bewildering range of cocktails. Lemon and lime juice will curdle cream and cream liqueurs but will happily mix with most other spirits and liqueurs. Limes generally pair well with rum while lemons are preferable in drinks based on whiskey or brandy.

Limes and lemons last longer if stored in the refrigerator. But you'll get more juice out of them if you let them warm up to room temperature and roll the fruit on a surface under the palm of your hand before you cut them. Save hard fruits for garnishing: soft fruits have more juice and flavour.

To juice, simply cut in half widthways and juice using a press, squeezer or spinning juicer, taking care not to grind the pith. Ideally you should juice your lemons and limes immediately prior to use as the juice will oxidise after a couple of hours.

I'd guess that, along with sugar syrup, these fruits are the most frequently used ingredients in this guide. Hence I've not even tried to index them.

LIME CORDIAL

Lauchlan Rose started importing lime juice from the West Indies to England in the 1860s, when ships were compelled to carry lime or lemon juice to prevent scurvy. In 1867 he devised a method for preserving juice without alcohol and created lime cordial, the world's first concentrated fruit drink. (What a spoilsport.) Thankfully all of the drinks in this guide that call for lime cordial are alcoholic.

Acapulco Daiquiri ●●●●○
Blue Heaven ●●◐○○
Caribbean Breeze ●●●●○
Castro ●●●◐○
Daiquiri De Luxe ●●●●○
Dean's Gate Martini ●●●◐○
Diamond Dog ●●●◐○
Dulchin ●●●●○
Elegante Margarita ●●●●◐
F. Willy Shot ●●●◐○
Fat Sailor ●●●●○
Floridita Margarita ●●●●○
Fog Horn ●●●◐○
Gimlet #1 ●●●●○
Gimlet #2 ●●●●◐
Green Hornet ●●●●○
Hong Kong Fuey ●●●○○
Honolulu Juicer ●●●◐○
Hurricane #1 ●●●●○
Judy (Mocktail) ●●●◐○
Key Lime ●●●●○
Key Lime Pie #2 ●●●●○
Key Lime Pie #3 ●●●●○
Lime Blush ●●●○○ (Mocktail)
Limey ●●●◐○
Limey Cosmo ●●●●○
Limnology ●●●◐○
Luxury Cocktail ●●●◐○
Lychee & Blackcurrant Martini ●●●●○
Metropolitan ●●●●○
Mexican Surfer ●●●●○
Princeton Martini ●●●●○
Robin Hood #1 ●●●●○
Rosarita Margarita ●●●●○
Rude Ginger Cosmopolitan ●●●●○
Sailor's Comfort ●●●○○
Sandstorm ●●●●○
Sloe Tequila ●●●◐○
Smoky Apple Martini ●●●◐○
Snowball ●●●◐○
Sour Apple Martini #1 (Popular US version) ●●●●○
Tres Compadres Margarita ●●●●◐
Typhoon ●●●○○
Ugurundu ●●●◐○
Van's The Man ●●●●○
Vodka Gimlet ●●●●○
Watermelon Cosmo ●●●◐○

LIMONCELLO LIQUEUR

See 'Luxardo Limoncello Liqueur'

LITCHI LIQUEUR

See 'Lychee Liqueur'

LUXARDO AMARETTO DI SASCHIRA LIQUEUR

28% alc./vol. (56°proof)

www.luxardo.it

Producer: Girolamo Luxardo SpA., Torreglia, Padova, Italy.

This delicate liqueur is an Italian classic, packed with the unique flavour of sweet almond, once sacred to the Greek goddess Cybele. The Luxardo family have been distilling fine liqueurs in the Veneto region of Italy for six generations now. They make their amaretto with the pure paste of the finest almonds, from Avola in southern Sicily, and age it for eight months in larch vats to impart its distinctive, well-rounded taste. Their very contemporary amaretto is a vital tool in any mixologist's flavour armoury, with its palate of almond and marzipan.

A.B.C. ●●●◐○
Alabama Slammer #2 ●●●◐○
Almond Martini #2 ●●●●○
Almond Old Fashioned ●●●●◐
Amaretto Sour ●●●◐○
Artlantic ●●●○○
Atholl Brose ●●●●○
Autumn Punch ●●●●◐
B-54 Shot ●●●○○
Bananas & Cream ●●●●○
Bella Donna Daiquiri ●●●●◐
Bird Of Paradise ●●●●◐
Blue Heaven ●●◐○○
Blueberry Tea ●●●●○
Blush Martini ●●●◐○
Blushin' Russian ●●●●○
Brooklyn #2 ●●●●○
Bubblegum Shot ●●●○○
Buona Sera Shot ●●●◐○
Burnt Toasted Almond ●●●○○
Canteen Martini ●●●◐○
Caribbean Punch ●●●●○
Cham 69 #1 ●●●◐○
Cham 69 #2 ●●●◐○
Chas ●●●●○
Cicada Cocktail ●●●◐○
Cranberry Cooler ●●●○○
Creamy Creamsicle ●●●◐○
Cream Cake ●●●◐○
Damson In Distress ●●●●○
Dolce-Amaro ●●●◐○
Donna's Creamy'tini ●●●◐○
Downhill Racer ●●●●○
Durango ●●●◐○
F. Willy Shot ●●●◐○
57 T-Bird Shot ●●●●○
Flaming Dr Pepper ●●○○○
Flaming Henry ●●●◐○
Godfather ●●●◐○
The GTO Cocktail ●●●◐○
Hawaiian Cocktail ●●●●○
International Incident ●●●●○

Italian Job #2 ●●●●○
Italian Surfer With A Russian
Attitude ●●●○○
Jockey Club ●●●◐○
Kamaniwanalaya ●●●◐○
Killer Punch ●●●◐○
Koolaid ●●●●○
Landslide ●●●○○
Loch Almond ●●●●○
Mae West Martini ●●●●○
Mister Stu ●●●◐○
Nutcracker Sweet ●●●◐○
Nutty Summer ●●●●◐
Orange Brûlée ●●●●●
Pink Cloud ●●●○○
Plum Pudding Martini ●●●◐○
P.S. I Love You ●●●●○
Royal Velvet Margarita ●●●◐○
South Beach ●●●●○
Stiletto ●●●◐○
Sweet Louise ●●●○○
Sweet Tart ●●●◐○
Tennessee Berry Mule ●●●●○
Thunderbird ●●●●○
Toasted Almond ●●●●○
Triangular Martini ●●●●○
Trifle'tini ●●●◐○

LUXARDO LIMONCELLO LIQUEUR

27% alc./vol. (54° proof)

www.luxardo.it

Producer: Girolamo Luxardo SpA., Torreglia, Padova, Italy.

Despite its vibrant yellow-green hue, this is an extremely traditional Italian liqueur – and, since the 90s, one of Italy's most popular. For generations, families have macerated lemon zest in spirit and sugar, encapsulating the mixologist's favourite combination of sour citrus, sweet and spirit: the formula at the heart of the Daiquiri, the Caipirinha and many more.

Luxardo Limoncello delivers a rich sweet lemon flavour in a blast of sour citrus, lemon zest and candied citrus, which somehow remain pure and balanced. It is increasingly popular among bartenders seeking new ways of delivering that vital citrus tang.

Basilico ●●●◐○
Bellissimo ●●●○○
Bon Bon Martini ●●●●○
Clementine ●●●○○
Grapparita ●●●◐○
Lemon Meringue Pie'tini ●●●●○
Lemon Sorbet ●●●●○
Lemony ●●●●○
Limoncello Martini ●●●◐○
Motox ●●●●○
Navigator ●●●●○
Pear Drop Martini ●●●●○
Socialite ●●●◐○
Watermelon & Basil Smash ●●●●○
Yellow Belly Martini ●●●●○

LUXARDO MARASCHINO ORIGINALE LIQUEUR

32% alc./vol. (64°proof)

www.luxardo.it

Producer: Girolamo Luxardo SpA., Torreglia, Padova, Italy.

Until well into the 20th century, the bitter Marasca cherry grew only on the Dalmatian coast. Now part of Croatia, Zara, Dalmatia, was Italian territory when Girolamo Luxardo's wife began producing a liqueur from the local cherries. So popular did her maraschino become that in 1821 Girolamo founded a distillery to mass-produce it. The business prospered until the disruption of the Second World War, after which the family moved production to Italy. Today the Luxardos base their liqueur on cherries from their own 200 acre orchard and age it for two years in white Finnish ashwood vats. The silky palate features hints of dark chocolate, vanilla and marmalade alongside subtle cherry notes, with an elegant white chocolate and cherry finish, making it essential to a range of classic and modern cocktails.

Aviation ●●●●●
Beachcomber ●●●●○
Boomerang ●●●●○
Brandy Crusta ●●●●○
Brooklyn #1 ●●●●○
Casino ●●●●○
Cherry & Hazelnut Daiquiri ●●●●○
Classic ●●●●●
Coronation ●●●○○
Coronation Martini ●●●◐○
Diplomat ●●●◐○
Donegal ●●●●○
East India #1 ●●●●◐
Elderflower Collins #2 ●●●●○
Fancy Free ●●●●○
Florida Daiquiri ●●●●◐
Floridita Daiquiri ●●●●○
Greta Garbo ●●●●○
The Harlem ●●●●○
Havana Special ●●●●○
Hemingway Special Daiquiri ●●●●◐
Imperial Martini ●●●○○
The Last Word ●●●●◐
Lima Sour ●●●◐○
Lux Daiquiri ●●●●○
Manhattan Island ●●●●○
Mary Pickford ●●●●●
Monte Carlo ●●●◐○
Moonshine Martini ●●●●◐
Mystique ●●●◐○
North Pole Martini ●●●●○
Nutty Berry'tini ●●●◐○
Opera ●●●●○
Petto Martini ●●●●◐
Pink Daiquiri ●●●●○
Red Angel ●●●●○
Ribalaigua Daiquiri #3 ●●●●○
The Ritz Cocktail ●●●●○
Salty Dog ●●●●○
Sensation ●●●●○
Seventh Heaven #2 ●●●●◐
Silver Martini ●●●◐○
Soyer Au Champagne ●●●◐○
Stars & Stripes Shot ●●◐○○
Turf Martini ●●●●○

LUXARDO SAMBUCA DEI CESARI

38% alc. /vol. (76°proof)

www.luxardo.it

Producer: Girolamo Luxardo SpA., Torreglia, Padova, Italy.

The elder bush, with its distinctive bunches of black berries, grows wild all over Europe. Along with anise, it is the vital ingredient in Luxardo sambuca, which takes its name from the Latin term for the plant.

This clear liqueur is crafted from green Sicilian aniseed and elder-berries grown in the Euganean hills. Uniquely, it is matured in Finnish ash wood vats.

The clean, rich aniseed palate is lighter and less syrupy than some other brands, with subtle hints of lemon zest. A star performer in a number of contemporary cocktails, it is also great served 'con mosca' – flamed in a glass with three floating coffee beans signifying health, wealth and happiness, to bestow good luck.

All White Frappé ●●●◐○
Anis'tini ●●●●○
Bumble Bee ●●●◐○
Crème De Café ●●●◐○
Flatliner ●●●◐○
Glass Tower ●●●○○
Kiss of Death ●●◐○○
Liquorice Shot ●●●◐○
Raging Bull ●●●◐○
Slippery Nipple ●●○○○
Tick-Tack Martini ●●●○○
Typhoon ●●●○○
Veneto ●●●◐○

LYCHEE LIQUEUR

Native to South China, the lychee's distinctive floral, fragrant flavour has a luscious delicacy which is distinctly Asian. Revered for over two thousand years as a symbol of love and romance, in part for its flavour and in part for its similarity to the heart, lychee is making waves in fusion food and cocktails around the world.

China Martini ●●●◐○
Chinese Cosmopolitan ●●●●○
Chinese Whisper Martini ●●●●○
Crouching Tiger ●●●○○
Dragon Blossom ●●●●○
Enchanted ●●●◐○
Lychee & Blackcurrant Martini ●●●●○
Lychee & Sake Martini ●●●●○
Lychee Mac ●●●◐○
Lychee Martini ●●●●○
Lychee Rickey ●●●◐○
Mellow Martini ●●●◐○
Oriental Tart ●●●●○
Pear Drop ●●●◐○
Summer Rose Martini ●●●●○
The Sun Salutation ●●●●○
Tokyo Tea ●●●●○

MADEIRA

Madeira is a fortified wine from the semi-tropical island of the same name in the Atlantic, 600km off the coast of Morocco. Until the opening of the Suez Canal, Madeira enjoyed a strategic position on the Atlantic shipping lanes and during the 17th and 18th centuries ships sailing from Britain carried the island's wine as ballast. The wine was slowly warmed during the voyage through the tropics, creating a mellow, baked flavour. This unusual, richly flavoured wine became popular. So the ships' effects were replicated on the island using a heating process called 'estufagem'.

There are four predominant styles of Madeira available: Sercial –(dry), Verdelho –(medium dryand traditionally referred to as 'Rainwater'), Bual –(medium sweet) and Malmsey (sweet).

Baltimore Egg Nog ●●●○○
Bosom Caresser ●●●●○
Boston Flip ●●●●○
Casanova ●●●●○
China Blue ●●●◐○

MANDARINE NAPOLÉON LIQUEUR

38% alc./vol. (76°proof)

www.mandarine-napoleon.com

Producer: Fourcroy S.A., Rue Steyls 119, B1020 Brussels, Belgium.

Emperor Napoléon Bonaparte's physician, Antoine-Francois de Fourcroy, created a special liqueur for the Emperor based on aged cognacs and exotic mandarine oranges. Mandarines, often known as tangerines, had been introduced into Europe from China in the 18th century and grew particularly well in Corsica, Bonaparte's birthplace.

Mandarine Napoléon was first commercially distilled in 1892, using the finest aged French cognacs and mandarine peels from the Mediterranean area blended with an infusion of herbs and spices. The distillate is aged for at least three years, until it acquires the rich mellow flavour which makes Mandarine Napoléon one of the great classic liqueurs of the world.

Mandarine Napoléon is brilliantly suited to cocktail mixing and distinctly different from other orange liqueurs on bartenders' shelves. Its luscious zesty tangerine flavour with a herbal backnote gives a sophisticated twist to a Cosmopolitan but is also superb on its own, long over ice with a splash of tonic.

Auld Acquaintance ●●●○○
Breakfast At Terrell's ●●●●○
Clementine ●●●○○
Donegal ●●●●○
Gloom Chaser ●●●◐○
Italian Job #1 ●●●◐○
Jacktini ●●●◐○
Lola ●●●◐○
Man-Bour-Tini ●●●●○
Mandarine Collins ●●●○○
Mandarine Sidecar ●●●●○
Mandarine Songbird ●●●○○
Mandarine Sour ●●●◐○
Mandarito ●●●●○
Orange Mojito ●●●●○
Prune Face ●●●●○
Puccini ●●●◐○
Tennessee Rush ●●●◐○
Windy Miller ●●●●○
Yum ●●●○○

MAPLE SYRUP

The boiled-down sap of the North American sugar maple, authentic maple syrup has a complex sweetness appreciated all over the world. Please be wary of synthetic imitations, which are nowhere near as good as the real thing. Maple syrups are graded A or B – grade B, which is dark and very strongly flavoured, is sometimes known as 'cooking syrup'. The A grade syrups are all of equal quality and divided into categories according to their hue and level of flavour, most generally 'light amber', 'medium amber' and 'dark amber'. Confusingly, some Canadian and US states have their own names for these categories. I favour a medium amber or light syrup.

Maple syrup should be stored in the refrigerator and consumed within 28 days of opening. To use in a cocktail, simply pour into a thimble measure and follow the recipe.

Banoffee Martini ●●●●○
Bourbon Blush ●●●●◐
Bull's Milk ●●●◐○
Che's Revolution ●●●●◐
Elisian ●●●●○
Four W Daiquiri ●●●●○
Jean Gabin ●●●●○
Lotus Espresso ●●●●◐
Louisiana Trade ●●●◐○
Maple Old-Fashioned ●●●●○
Maple Leaf ●●●●○
Maple Pomme ●●●●○
Mule's Hind Leg ●●●●◐
The Roadrunner ●●●●○
Tawny-Tini ●●●●○
Zeus Martini ●●●●◐

MARASCHINO LIQUEUR

'See Luxardo Maraschino Originale Liqueur'

MARASCHINO SYRUP

The sweet liquid from a jar of maraschino cherries.

Dragon Blossom ●●●●○
Fruit Tree Daiquiri ●●●●○
Grappa Manhattan ●●●●○
Lux Daiquiri ●●●●○
Manhattan Sweet ●●●●●
Old Fashioned #2 (US Version) ●●●●◐
Rob Roy #1 ●●●●○
The Zamboanga 'Zeinie' Cocktail ●●●●○

MIDORI MELON LIQUEUR

20% alc./vol. (40°proof)

www.midori-world.com

Producer: Suntory Limited, Japan.

Midori is flavoured with extracts of honeydew melons and can rightly claim to be the original melon liqueur. Midori's vibrant green colour, light melon taste and great versatility has ensured its demand in bars worldwide. Launched in 1978 at New York's famed Studio 54 nightclub, Midori was shaken within sight of the cast of Saturday Night Fever. That same year, Midori won first prize in the U.S. Bartenders' Guild Annual Championship.

The name 'Midori' is Japanese for green and it is owned by Suntory, Japan's leading producer and distributor of alcoholic beverages. Midori is one of the most noted modern day cocktail ingredients due to its vibrant colour and flavour, being: fruity, luscious, lightly syrupy while retaining freshness, with honeyed melon and a hint of green apple. It is also great simply served long with sparkling apple juice or cranberry juice.

Apache ●●●○○
Apple & Melon Martini ●●●◐○
Atomic Dog ●●●○○
Awol ●●●●○
Bubblegum Shot ●●●○○
Coco Cabana ●●●◐○
Congo Blue ●●●◐○
Cool Martini ●●●◐○
Envy ●●●●○
E.T. ●●●●○
Evita ●●●◐○
Grateful Dead ●●●◐○
Green Fly ●●●◐○
Gulf Coast Sex On The Beach ●●●●○
Hong Kong Fuey ●●●○○
Illusion ●●●●○
Japanese Slipper ●●●●○
June Bug ●●●◐○
Killer Punch ●●●◐○
Koolaid ●●●●○
L.A. Iced Tea ●●●◐○
Love Junk ●●●◐○
Mae West Martini ●●●●○
Melon Ball ●●●○○
Melon Collie Martini ●●●●○
Melon Daiquiri #1 (Served 'Up') ●●●●○
Melon Daiquiri #2 (Served Frozen) ●●●◐○
Melon Margarita #1 (Served 'Up') ●●●●○
Melon Margarita #2 (Served Frozen) ●●●◐○
Melon Martini #1 ●●●○○
Meloncholy Martini ●●●●○
Passion Killer ●●●○○
Sex On The Beach #2 ●●●○○
Sex On The Beach #3 ●●◐○○
Sourpuss Martini ●●●●○
Squashed Frog ●●●○○
Tokyo Iced Tea ●●●◐○
Tutti Frutti ●●●○○
Universal Shot ●●●○○
Vacation ●●●◐○
Verdi Martini ●●●●○
Watermelon Cosmo ●●●◐○

MINT LEAVES

This perennial herb grows in most temperate parts of the world. The varieties which non-botanists call 'mint' belong to the genus mentha. Mentha species include apple mint, curly mint, pennyroyal, peppermint, pineapple mint, spearmint and water or bog mint.

Spearmint, or garden mint, is the most common kind and you may well find it growing in your garden. It has a fruity aroma and flavour and, like peppermint, has bright green leaves and purple flowers. Spearmint is generally used for cooking savouries, such as mint sauce.

Peppermint is the second most common kind. Its leaves produce a pungent oil which is used to flavour confectionery, desserts and liqueurs such as crème de menthe.

The main visible difference between peppermint and spearmint is in the leaves. Spearmint leaves have a crinkly surface and seem to grow straight out of the plant's main stem, while peppermint leaves have smoother surfaces and individual stems. Peppermint can also tend towards purple. Which type of mint you choose to use in drinks is largely a matter of personal taste: some recommend mentha nemorosa for Mojitos.

Growing your own mint, be it spearmint, peppermint or otherwise is easy – but be sure to keep it in a container or it will overrun your garden. Either buy a plant or place a sprig in a glass of water. When it roots, pot it in a large, shallow tub with drainage holes. Place bricks under the tub to prevent the roots from growing through the holes.

Bajito ●●●●◐
Beetle Jeuse ●●●●○
Bourbon Smash ●●●◐○
Brandy Smash ●●●●○
Che's Revolution ●●●●◐
Colonial Rot ●●●○○
Cowboy Martini ●●●◐○
Cranberry & Mint Martini ●●●●○
Cucumber & Mint Martini ●●●●○
Detroit Martini ●●●●○
Elixir ●●●●○
French Mojito ●●●●◐
Frisky Bison ●●●●◐
Georgia Mint Julep ●●●●◐
Gin Genie ●●●●○
Ginger Mojito ●●●●○
Grape Escape ●●●●◐
Grapefruit Julep ●●●●◐
Havanatheone ●●●●●
Hazel'ito ●●●●◐
Heather Julep ●●●●◐
Hornitos Lau ●●●●○
Jean Marc ●●●●○
Julep ●●●●●
Julep Martini ●●●●◐
Jumbled Fruit Julep ●●●◐○
Kentucky Mac ●●●◐○
Krakow Tea ●●●●○
Life (Love In the Future Ecstasy) ●●●◐○
Lotus Martini ●●●●○
Luxury Mojito ●●●●○
Mai Tai #2 (Beaumont-Gantt's Formula) ●●●●○
Major Bailey #1 ●●●●◐
Mandarito ●●●●○
Marama Rum Punch ●●●●○
Milky Mojito ●●●◐○
Mint Cocktail ●●●●◐
Mint Collins ●●●●○
Mint Daiquiri ●●●●●
Mint Fizz ●●●◐○
Mint Julep ●●●●●
Mint Limeade (Mocktail) ●●●●◐
Mint Martini ●●●●◐
Missionary's Downfall ●●●●●
Mojito ●●●●●
Mojito de Casa ●●●●○
Momo Special ●●●●○
Monarch Martini ●●●●○
Orange Mojito ●●●●○
Palm Springs ●●●◐○
Pineapple Mojito ●●●●◐
Pussyfoot (Mocktail) ●●●●◐
Ray's Hard Lemonade ●●●●○
Razzmatazz ●●●○○
Royal Mojito ●●●●●
Sensation ●●●●○
Sleepy Hollow ●●●●○
Southern Mint Cobbler ●●●●○
Southside Royalee ●●●●○
Strawberry & Balsamic Mojito ●●●●○
The Sun Salutation ●●●●○
Tequila Smash ●●●●◐
Tipperary #2 ●●●●◐
Ugurundu ●●●◐○
Zelda Martini ●●●●○

OPAL NERA BLACK SAMBUCA

40% alc./vol. (80°proof)

www.opalnera.com

Producer: Fratelli Francoli S.p.A., Ghemme, Corso Romagnano, Italy.

In 1989 Alessandro Francoli was on honeymoon in America, when he took time out to present his company's traditional Italian grappas and sambucas to a potential buyer. He noticed the interest the buyer showed in a coffee sambuca, and this dark liqueur set Alessandro thinking. He experimented with different flavours and created Opal Nera, a black coloured sambuca with a hint of lemon. Opal Nera's seductive and unmistakable colour comes from elderberries, a key ingredient in all sambucas: Francoli macerate their purple-black skins.

Opal Nera Black Sambuca is a favourite with many bartenders due to its colour and flavour, which includes aniseed, soft black liquorice, light elderberry spice and lemon zest.

Alessandro ●●●○○
Black Dream ●●●○○
Black Jack ●●●○○
Black Nuts ●●◐○○
Black Widow ●●●○○
Flaming Ferrari ●●○○○
Liquorice All Sort ●●●◐○
Liquorice Martini ●●●◐○
Molotov Cocktail ●●●◐○
Opal Café ●●●●○
Purple Flirt #1 ●●●●○
Redback ●●●○○

ORANGE BITTERS

Sadly, this key cocktail ingredient is hard to find in modern liquor stores. There are a number of brands that profess to be 'orange bitters' but many hardly taste of orange and are more like sweet liqueurs than bitters. Search the internet for suitable brands or make your own. See www.drinkboy.com/LiquorCabinet/Flavorings/OrangeBitters.htm

Adonis ●●●●◐
Alaska Martini ●●●●○
Almond Old Fashioned ●●●●◐
Apricot Cosmo ●●●●◐
Bamboo ●●●●◐
Banana Bliss ●●●○○
Blackthorn English ●●●●○
Bradford ●●●●○
The Broadmoor ●●●●◐
Casino ●●●●○
Causeway ●●●◐○
Cheeky Monkey ●●●●○
Citrus Martini ●●●●○
Coronation Martini ●●●◐○
Cosmopolitan #2 (complex version) ●●●●●
Cowboy Martini ●●●◐○
Diplomat ●●●◐○
DNA ●●●◐○
Dr Zeus ●●●●◐
Dry Martini ●●●●●
Dry Orange Martini ●●●●◐
East Indian ●●●●◐
Fancy Free ●●●●○
Flying Dutchman Martini ●●●●○
Golden Cadillac ●●●◐○
Grand Cosmopolitan ●●●●◐
Harvard ●●●◐○
Intimate Martini ●●●●○
Jaded Lady ●●●○○
Jaffa Martini ●●●◐○
Jalisco ●●●●○
Jelly Belly Beany ●●●●○
Jockey Club ●●●◐○
The Legend ●●●●○
Lemon Sorbet ●●●●○
Leninade ●●●●○
London Calling ●●●◐○
London Cocktail ●●●○○
Mac Orange ●●●◐○
Marguerite Martini ●●●●○
Marny Cocktail ●●●●◐
Martinez ●●●●●
Merry Widow #2 ●●●◐○
Met Manhattan ●●●●○
Milly Martini ●●●●○
Modernista ●●●◐○
Mystique ●●●◐○
Oil Slick ●●◐○○
Onion Ring Martini ●●●○○
Opera ●●●●○
Orange Martini ●●●●○
Pall Mall Martini ●●●●○
Palma Violet Martini ●●●◐○
Paradise #2 ●●●●◐
Pegu Club ●●●●○
Perfect Martini ●●●◐○
Princeton ●●●●○
Quebec ●●●●○
Raspberry Collins ●●●●○
Raspberry Debonair ●●●◐○
Raspberry Martini #2 ●●●●○
Rude Cosmopolitan ●●●●◐
Sake'politan ●●●●○
Satsuma Martini ●●●◐○
Satan's Whiskers (Straight) ●●●●◐
Scofflaw ●●●●○
Silver Martini ●●●◐○
Singapore Sling #2 ●●●●○
Smartini ●●●●○
Smoky Martini #2 ●●●○○
Stairs Martini ●●●●●
Stork Club ●●●●○
Straits Sling ●●●●○
Suburban ●●●●○
Swedish Blue Martini ●●●◐○
Trilby ●●●●○
Trinity ●●●○○
Turf Martini ●●●●○
Tuxedo Martini ●●●●◐
Two "T" Fruity Martini ●●●●○
Valencia ●●●●○
Viagra Falls ●●●◐○
Watermelon Cosmo ●●●◐○
Wonky Martini ●●●●◐

ORANGE JUICE

The orange is now so commonly available in our shops and markets that it's hard to believe it was once an exotic and expensive luxury. Although native to China, its name originates from 'naranga' in the old Indian language of Sanskrit.

There are many different types of orange but the best ones for bartending purposes are Washington Navels, which are in season from the end of October. These have a firm, rough skin perfect for cutting twists from and are juicy and slightly sour.

Simply cut in half and juice with a hand press. If using an electric spinning citrus juicer take care not to grind the pith.

Oranges are so widely available and easy to juice that as I write this I'm wondering why I so often buy packaged juice from the supermarket. My only defence is that I always buy freshly squeezed, refrigerated juice.

Abbey Martini ●●●◐○
Agent Orange ●●●●○
Air Mail ●●●●◐
Alabama Slammer #1 ●●●◐○
Alabama Slammer #2 ●●●◐○
American Beauty ●●●●◐
Apple Sunrise ●●●○○
Apricot Fizz ●●●◐○
April Shower ●●●●○
Auld Acquaintance ●●●○○
Aunt Agatha ●●●◐○
Aunt Emily ●●●●○
Bahama Mama ●●●●○
Banana Boomer ●●●●○
Beach Blonde ●●●●○
Bebbo ●●●●○
Bee's Knees #1 ●●●●○
Bee's Knees #2 ●●●●◐
The Big Easy ●●●●○
Bishop ●●●◐○
Blood & Sand ●●●●◐
Blood Orange ●●●○○
Blue Star ●●●○○
Bolero Sour ●●●●●
Boston Tea Party ●●●○○
Breakfast At Terrell's ●●●●○
Bronx ●●●◐○
Buck's Fizz ●●●○○
Bull's Blood ●●●◐○
Cactus Banger ●●●●○
Cactus Jack ●●●◐○
Calvados Cocktail ●●●●○
Canaries ●●●○○
Carneval Batida ●●●●○
Casablanca ●●●○○
Castro ●●●◐○
Cheeky Monkey ●●●●○
Chill-Out Martini ●●●○○
Chinese Passion ●●●◐○
Chocolate Puff ●●●●○
Cinderella ●●◐○○
Classic ●●●●●
Cranberry Cooler ●●●○○
Creamy Creamsicle ●●●◐○
Cuban Master ●●●○○

Cumbersome ●●●●○
Damn-The-Weather ●●●◐○
Deep South ●●●○○
Derby Daiquiri ●●●●◐
Desert Cooler ●●●◐○
Diamond Dog ●●●◐○
Dolce Havana ●●●●○
Don Juan ●●●◐○
Dorian Gray ●●●◐○
Dreamsicle ●●●◐○
Embassy Royal ●●●◐○
Esquire #1 ●●●●○
Evita ●●●◐○
Flamingo #1 ●●●◐○
Florida Cocktail (Mocktail) ●●●○○
Fluffy Duck ●●●◐○
Fly Like A Butterfly ●●●●○
Fog Cutter #1 ●●●●○
Fosbury Flip ●●●●◐
Fourth Of July Cocktail ●●●○○
Freddy Fudpucker ●●●◐○
French Kiss #1 ●●●○○
French Leave ●●●○○
Fresca Nova ●●●◐○
Fruit & Nut Martini ●●●●○
Fruit Salad ●●●○○
Fruits Of The Forest ●●●◐○
Fuzzy Navel ●●◐○○
Garibaldi ●●●○○
Gin & Sin ●●●◐○
Gold Medallion ●●●◐○
Golden Bird ●●●◐○
Golden Cadillac ●●●◐○
Golden Dawn ●●●●○
Golden Dream ●●●●○
Golden Screw ●●●◐○
Grand Mimosa ●●●◐○
Green Eyes ●●●◐○
Gypsy Queen ●●●●○
Happy New Year ●●●○○
Harvey Wallbanger ●●●◐○
Hawaiian ●●●○○
Hawaiian Cocktail ●●●●○
Hobson's Choice (Mocktail) ●●◐○○
Honey & Marmalade Dram'tini ●●●●◐
Honeysuckle Daiquiri ●●●●●
Honolulu ●●●●○
Hot Passion ●●●○○
Hot Red Blooded Frenchman ●●●●○
Hurricane #1 ●●●●○
Hurricane #2 ●●●○○
Iced Tea ●●●◐○
Iguana Wana ●●●○○
Illicit Affair ●●●◐○
Income Tax Cocktail ●●●●○
Jack Frost ●●●○○
Jacuzzi ●●●◐○
Jaded Lady ●●●○○
Jaffa Martini ●●●◐○
Jamaican Sunset ●●●●○
Ja-Mora ●●●●○
Jodi May ●●●◐○
Jubilant ●●●●◐
Jumping Jack Flash ●●●●○
Jungle Juice ●●●◐○
Jupiter Martini ●●●◐○
Key West Cooler ●●●◐○
Klondike ●●●◐○
Knickerbocker Special ●●●●○
Koolaid ●●●●○
Lago Cosmo ●●●◐○
Limeosa ●●●◐○
Lola ●●●◐○
Loved Up ●●●◐○
Lutkins Special Martini ●●●◐○
Mac Orange ●●●◐○
Madras ●●●◐○
Madroska ●●●○○
Maiden's Prayer ●●●◐○
Magic Bus ●●●◐○
Mambo ●●●◐○
Mandarine Songbird ●●●○○
Maurice Martini ●●●◐○
Mat The Rat ●●●◐○
Mayfair Cocktail ●●●●○
Melon Ball ●●●○○
Mexican Melon Ball ●●●◐○
Mimosa ●●●◐○
Mister Stu ●●●◐○
Mona Lisa ●●●●○
Monkey Gland #1 ●●●●○
Monkey Gland #2 ●●●●○
Mrs Robinson #2 ●●●◐○
Naranja Daiquiri ●●●●○
New Port Codebreaker ●●●◐○
Nightmare Martini ●●●○○
Noble Europe ●●●●◐
Noon ●●●●○
Not So Cosmo (Mocktail) ●●●◐○
Ole ●●●◐○
Olympic ●●●●◐
Opal ●●●●◐
Orang-A-Tang ●●●●○
Orange Blossom ●●●◐○
Orange Daiquiri #1 ●●●●◐
Orange Martini ●●●●○
Oranjiniha ●●●●○
Painkiller ●●●●○
Paradise #1 ●●●◐○
Paradise #2 ●●●●◐
Paradise #3 ●●●◐○
Park Lane ●●●●◐
Parlay Punch ●●●○○
Perfect John ●●●●○
Peter Pan Martini ●●●●○
Petto Martini ●●●●◐
Pilgrim Cocktail ●●●●○
Pinky Pincher ●●●●○
Pisco Punch #1 (Difford's Formula) ●●●●◐
Pisco Naranja ●●●◐○
Planteur ●●●●○
Playmate Martini ●●●●◐
Poncha ●●●●○
Potted Parrot ●●●◐○
President ●●●●○
Pruneaux ●●●●○
Pussyfoot (Mocktail) ●●●●◐
Queen Martini ●●●●○
Red Lion #1 (Modern Formula) ●●●●◐
Reggae Rum Punch ●●●●◐
Riviera Breeze ●●●◐○
Rum Sour ●●●●○
Saint Clements (Mocktail) ●●●○○
San Fransisco ●●●◐○
La Sang ●●●●○
Sangaree ●●●●○
Sangria ●●●◐○
Sangria Martini ●●●●○
Sangrita ●●●●◐
Santiago ●●●○○
Satan's Whiskers (Straight) ●●●●◐
Savannah ●●●◐○
Scorpion ●●●●○
Scotch Bounty Martini ●●●◐○
Screwdriver ●●●◐○
Sex On The Beach #1 ●●◐○○
Shark Bite ●●●◐○
Sicilian Negroni ●●●●○
Sidekick ●●●●○
Slow Screw ●●●○○
Slow Comfortable Screw ●●●◐○
Slow Comfortable Screw Against the Wall ●●●◐○
South Beach ●●●●○
Spencer Cocktail ●●●●○
Sputnik ●●●◐○
Sputnik #2 ●●●●○
Stork Club ●●●●○
Summer Time Martini ●●●◐○
Sun Kissed Virgin (Mocktail) ●●●○○
Sundowner #1 ●●●●○
The Suzy Wong Martini ●●●◐○
Sweet Science ●●●◐○
Tainted Cherry ●●●○○
Tango Martini #1 ●●●●○
Tequila Fizz ●●●●○
Tequila Sunrise ●●●◐○
Thriller Martini ●●●●○
Thriller From Vanilla ●●●●○
Thunderbird ●●●●○
Tiki Max ●●●●○
Tipperary #2 ●●●●◐
Tolleytown Punch ●●●◐○
Tootie Fruity Lifesaver ●●●○○
Total Recall ●●●◐○
Tres Compadres Margarita ●●●●◐
Triple Orange Martini ●●●●○
Umbongo ●●●○○
Valencia ●●●●○
Vampiro ●●●●○
Velvet Fog ●●●●◐
Volga Boatman ●●●◐○
Vowel Cocktail ●●●●◐
Ward Eight ●●●●○
Wine Cooler ●●●◐○
Zanzibar ●●●◐○
Zombie #2 (Vic's Formula) ●●●◐○
Zombie #3 (Modern Formula) ●●●●○

PARFAIT AMOUR LIQUEUR

A French, lilac coloured curaçao liqueur flavoured with rose petals, vanilla pods and almonds. The name means 'perfect love'.

Barnacle Bill ●●●○○
Blue Angel ●●●○○
Brazen Martini ●●●●○
Eden Martini ●●●◐○
English Rose ●●●●○
Esquire #2 ●●●◐○
Joan Bennett ●●●○○
Jungle Fire Sling ●●●○○
Jupiter Martini ●●●◐○
Lavender Martini ●●●●○
Molotov Cocktail ●●●◐○
Purple Cosmo ●●●●◐
Trilby ●●●●○

PASSION FRUIT LIQUEUR

Apple Of My Eire ●●●●○
Bajan Mojito ●●●◐○
Bay Of Passion ●●●○○
Bug Juice ●●●◐○
Chill Breeze ●●●○○
Chinese Passion ●●●◐○
Crime Of Passion Shot ●●●○○
Exotic Passion ●●●◐○
Fru Fru ●●●◐○
Hot Passion ●●●○○
Palm Springs ●●●◐○
Pass-on-that ●●●○○
Passbour Cooler ●●●○○
Passion Killer ●●●○○
Passover ●●●○○
Saigon Sling ●●●◐○
Tango Martini #2 ●●●●○
Transylvanian Martini ●●●○○
Tropical Breeze ●●●○○
Tutti Frutti ●●●○○
Umbongo ●●●○○

PASTIS

See 'Ricard Pastis'

PEACH SCHNAPPS LIQUEUR

The peach originated in China, where the tree has been cultivated since the 5th century BC. It reached Europe by way of Alexander the Great and the Greeks and its sweet, succulent flavour has made it a favourite liqueur ingredient since time immemorial.

During the 80s, peach schnapps appeared on the scene, and rapidly ousted the more syrupy, heavier peach liqueurs of old.

Achilles Heel ●●●●○
Apple Spritz ●●●●○
Baby Woo Woo ●●●○○
Bellini #2 (Difford's formula) ●●●●○
Bellini-Tini ●●●●○
Bikini Martini ●●●●○
Bohemian Iced Tea ●●●●◐
Chinese Passion ●●●◐○
Cream Cake ●●●◐○
The Delicious Sour ●●●●○
Detox ●●●○○
Envy ●●●●○
Fish House Punch #1 ●●●●○
Fish House Punch #2 ●●●●○
Fuzzy Navel ●●◐○○
Georgia Mint Julep ●●●●◐
Glass Tower ●●●○○
I B Damm'd ●●●●◐
Iguana Wana ●●●○○
Ink Martini #1 ●●●◐○
Jacuzzi ●●●◐○
Jelly Belly Beany ●●●●○
Jerez ●●●●○
Love Junk ●●●◐○
Missionary's Downfall ●●●●●
Mississippi Schnapper ●●●◐○
Moonraker ●●●●○
Mystique ●●●◐○
Oatmeal Cookie ●●●◐○
Pale Rider ●●●○○
Palma Violet Martini ●●●◐○
Peach Daiquiri ●●●●○

Peach Melba Martini ●●●◐○
Pink Tutu ●●●◐○
Sex On The Beach #1 ●●◐○○
Southern Peach ●●●○○
Sputnik ●●●◐○
Swedish Blue Martini ●●●◐○
Verdi Martini ●●●●○
Weeping Jesus ●●●◐○
Woo Woo ●●●◐○
Yum ●●●○○

PEACHES

White peaches are preferable for use in cocktails. They have finer flesh and flavour, and produce more juice than yellow peaches, which generally mature later. When peeling peaches for muddling or pureeing, try plunging them into boiling water for thirty seconds first.

Bellini #1 (Original) ●●●●○
Bellini #2 (Difford's Formula) ●●●●○
Bellini-Tini ●●●●○
Kentucky Colonel ●●●●○

PEAR & COGNAC LIQUEUR

Apples 'N' Pears ●●●●◐
Asian Pear Martini ●●●●○
Inga From Sweden ●●●●○
Juliette ●●●○○
Kentucky Pear ●●●●◐
Long Flight of Stairs ●●●●◐
Nice Pear-tini ●●●●◐
Pear & Cardamom Sidecar ●●●●◐
Pear & Vanilla Rickey ●●●◐○
Pear Drop ●●●◐○
Pear Drop Martini ●●●●○
Pear Shaped #1 (Deluxe Version) ●●●●◐
Pear Shaped #2 (Popular Version) 4.5
Perry-tini ●●●●○
Prickly Pear Mule ●●●●○
Roa Aé ●●●◐○
Sidekick ●●●●○
Sleeping Bison-tini ●●●●○
Sparkling Perry ●●●●○
Spiced Pear ●●●●◐
Steep Flight ●●●●●
Teddy Bear'tini ●●●●○

PEAR JUICE

Western varieties of pear soften when ripe and tend to have quite a grainy texture; Asian types, such as the nashi pear, are crisp when ripe. Unless otherwise stated, pear in this guide means the Western varieties. Conference is widely available and works well in cocktails.

Pears will ripen after they are picked, but spoil quickly, so care is needed in storage.

The best way to extract the flavour of a pear is to use an electric juice extractor. Surprisingly, you'll find that beautifully ripe fruits yield little and much of that is in the form of slush. Instead, look for pears which are on their way to ripeness but still have a good crunch.

Remove the stalk but don't worry about peeling or removing the core. Cut the fruit into chunks small enough to push into the juicer. If you hate cleaning an electric juice extractor then use a blender or food processor.

Asian Pear Martini ●●●●○
Autumn Punch ●●●●◐
Kentucky Pear ●●●●◐
Nice Pear-tini ●●●●◐
Pear & Elderflower Martini ●●●●○
Pear Drop Martini ●●●●○
Pear Shaped #1 (Deluxe Version) ●●●●◐
Perry-tini ●●●●○
Prickly Pear Mule ●●●●○
Sleeping Bison-tini ●●●●○
Sparkling Perry ●●●●○
Spiced Pear ●●●●◐
Stairs Martini ●●●●●

PERNOD ANIS

40% alc./vol. (80°proof)

www.pernod.net

Producer: Pernod Enterprise, France

Pernod's story starts in 1789 when Dr Pierre Ordinaire first prescribed his pain relieving and reviving 'absinthe elixir' in Switzerland. Ten years later, Major Dubied bought the formula and set up an absinthe factory in Couvet, Switzerland, with his son-in-law, Henri-Louis Pernod. In 1805, Henri-Louis Pernod established Pernod Fils in Pontarlier, France. The authentic absinthe, the original Pernod was created from a recipe that included 'artemisia absinthium': the plant of absinthe.

Pernod quickly gained fame as THE absinthe of Parisian café society. But a prohibitionist propaganda movement sprang up and a massive press campaign blamed absinthe abuse as the cause of socially unacceptable behaviour, insanity, tuberculosis and even murder. On 7th January 1915, absinthe was banned and Pernod Fils was forced to close. But by 1920, anise liquors were legalised again, albeit in a more sober form, and in its new guise Pernod remained as popular as ever. The Pernod we enjoy today is an historic blend of 14 herbs including star anise, fennel, mint and coriander.

Pernod is best served long with cranberry juice, apple juice or bitter lemon, diluted five to one.

Anis'tini ●●●●○
Appleissimo ●●●●○
Barnacle Bill ●●●○○
Blackthorn Irish ●●●◐○
Bombay ●●●●◐
Doctor Funk ●●●○○
Drowned Out ●●●◐○
French Kiss #1 ●●●○○
French Leave ●●●○○
Greta Garbo ●●●●○
Hemingway ●●●○○
Knockout Martini ●●●◐○
Light Breeze ●●●◐○
Lighter Breeze ●●●◐○
London Fog ●●●○○
Milky Mojito ●●●◐○
Modernista ●●●◐○
Monte Carlo ●●●◐○
Moonraker ●●●●○
Mucky Bottom ●●●◐○
Nicky Finn ●●●●○
Northern Lights ●●●●○
Pernod & Black Martini ●●●●○
Sunny Breeze ●●●◐○
Tarraberry'tini ●●●●○
Threesome ●●●◐○

PEYCHAUD'S AROMATIC BITTERS

Algonquin ●●●●○
Auntie's Hot Xmas Punch ●●●●○
Behemoth ●●●●○
Bourbonella ●●●●○
Caramel Manhattan ●●●●◐
Chocolate Sazerac ●●●●○
Devil's Manhattan ●●●●○
Elisian ●●●●○
Especial Day ●●●●◐
Free Town ●●●●○
Golden Nail ●●●●○
Grand Sazerac ●●●●○
Lychee & Rose Petal Martini ●●●●○
Pendennis Cocktail ●●●●○
Rob Roy #2 ●●●●◐
Rose Petalini ●●●●○
Saigon Sling ●●●◐○
Sazerac ●●●●●
Seelbach ●●●○○
Southern Manhattan ●●●●○
Toast & Orange Martini ●●●●○
Venus Martini ●●●●○
Vieux Carré Cocktail ●●●●◐
Wink ●●●●○

PIMM'S NO. 1 CUP

Afternoon Tea-Ni ●●●●○
Luxury Cocktail ●●●◐○
Pimm's Cocktail ●●●●◐
Pimm's Cup (or Classic) ●●●◐○
Pimm's Royale ●●●◐○
Strasberi Sling ●●●◐○

PINEAPPLE JUICE

Pineapples are widely grown in the West Indies, Africa and Asia. There are many varieties which vary significantly in both size and flavour. When pineapples are ripe the skin changes colour from yellow-green to brown; over-ripe pineapples are yellow-brown.

Pineapples are tropical and tend to deteriorate at temperatures below 7°C (45°F) so are best left out of the refrigerator.

Pineapple is one of the most satisfying fruits to juice due to the quantity of liquid it yields. Chop the crown and bottom off, then slice the skin off, without worrying too much about the little brown dimples that remain. Finally slice the fruit along its length around the hard central core, and chop into pieces small enough to fit into your juice extractor. The base is the sweetest part of a pineapple, so if you are only juicing half be sure to divide the fruit lengthways.

For convenience I still often end up buying cartons of 'pressed pineapple juice' from the supermarket chill cabinet. As with all such juices, look for those labelled 'not from concentrate'. When buying supermarket own brand pineapple juice, read the label carefully to avoid stuff made from concentrate.

Abacaxi Ricaço ●●●●○
Abaci Batida ●●●●○
Acapulco ●●●◐○
Algonquin ●●●●○
Atlantic Breeze ●●●○○
Atomic Dog ●●●○○
Aunt Agatha ●●●◐○
Awol ●●●●○
Baby Blue Martini ●●●◐○
Bahama Mama ●●●●○
Bahamas Daiquiri ●●●●◐
Bali Trader ●●●◐○
Banana Boomer ●●●●○
Banana Colada ●●●●○
Basil Beauty ●●●●○
Bay Breeze ●●●○○
Bay Of Passion ●●●○○
Blue Hawaiian ●●●○○

Blue Heaven ●●◐○○
Blue Wave ●●●○○
Bossa Nova #2 ●●●◐○
Brandy Fix ●●●●◐
Brighton Punch ●●●●◐
Buena Vida ●●●●◐
Bug Juice ●●●◐○
Buzzard's Breath ●●●◐○
Byzantine ●●●●○
Cactus Jack ●●●◐○
Canaries ●●●○○
Cappercaille ●●●●○
Caramel Manhattan ●●●●◐
Caribbean Breeze ●●●●○
Caribbean Cruise ●●●◐○
Caribbean Piña Colada ●●●◐○
Caribbean Punch ●●●●○
Che's Revolution ●●●●◐
Cinderella ●●◐○○
Coco Cabana ●●●◐○
Colonel T ●●●◐○
Cool Orchard ●●●●○
Cox's Daiquiri ●●●●●
Cuban Master ●●●○○
Cuban Special ●●●○○
Diable Rouge ●●●◐○
Downhill Racer ●●●●○
Dyevitchka ●●●●○
East India #2 ●●●●○
El Presidente Daiquiri ●●●●◐
Especial Day ●●●●◐
The Estribo ●●●◐○
Exotic Passion ●●●◐○
Flamingo #2 ●●●◐○
Flirtini #1 ●●●●○
Flirtini #2 ●●●●○
Florida Sling ●●●○○
Flutter ●●●●◐
French Bison-tini ●●●●○
French Martini ●●●●○
French Tear #1 ●●●●○
Full Circle ●●●●○
Galvanised Nail ●●●●◐
Gin Fixed ●●●●○
Ginger Cosmos ●●●◐○
Georgetown Punch ●●●●○
Golden Bird ●●●◐○
Golden Girl ●●●●○
Golden Wave ●●●◐○
Goombay Smash ●●●●◐
The GTO Cocktail ●●●◐○
Gulf Coast Sex On The Beach ●●●●○
The Harlem ●●●●○
Havana Special ●●●●○
Hawaiian ●●●○○
Hawaiian Cocktail ●●●●○
Hawaiian Martini ●●●●○
Hawaiian Seabreeze ●●●◐○
Heavens Above ●●●◐○
Honey Blossom ●●●○○
Honolulu ●●●●○
Honolulu Juicer ●●●◐○
Hot Tub ●●●●○
Hunk Martini ●●●●◐
Hurricane #1 ●●●●○
Hurricane #2 ●●●○○
Illusion ●●●●○
Italian Surfer With A Russian Attitude ●●●○○
Jack-In-The-Box ●●●●○
Jack Punch ●●●●○
Joan Bennett ●●●○○
Judy (Mocktail) ●●●◐○
Juliette ●●●○○
Jumping Jack Flash ●●●●○
June Bug ●●●◐○
Jungle Bird ●●●●○
Jungle Juice ●●●◐○
The Juxtaposition ●●●●○
Kamaniwanalaya ●●●◐○
Kava ●●●●○
Key Lime Pie #2 ●●●●○
Key Lime Pie #3 ●●●●○
Knickerbocker Special ●●●●○
Linstead ●●●●◐
Lucky Lily Margarita ●●●●◐
Major Bailey #2 ●●●●◐
Mary Pickford ●●●●●
Matador ●●●●○
Mayan ●●●◐○
Mayan Whore ●●●●○
Meloncholy Martini ●●●●○
Mellow Martini ●●●◐○
Mexican ●●●●○
Mexican Martini ●●●◐○
Mexican Surfer ●●●●○
Miami Beach ●●●●○
The Million Dollar Cocktail ●●●●◐
Milly Martini ●●●●○
Missionary's Downfall ●●●●●
Mister Stu ●●●◐○
Monkey Shine ●●●●○
Monk's Habit ●●●○○
Motox ●●●●○
Nacional Daiquiri #2 ●●●●◐
New Orleans Mule ●●●◐○
New Year's Absolution ●●●◐○
Nutty Summer ●●●●◐
Painkiller ●●●●○
Palermo ●●●●◐
Pancho Villa ●●●●○
Park Avenue ●●●●○
Parlay Punch ●●●○○
Piña Martini ●●●●○
Piña Colada ●●●●◐
Piña Colada Virgin (Mocktail) ●●●○○
Pineapple & Cardamom Daiquiri ●●●●◐
Pineapple & Cardamom Martini ●●●●●
Pineapple & Ginger Martini ●●●●○
Pineapple & Sage Margarita ●●●●◐
Pineapple Blossom ●●●●○
Pineapple Daiquiri #1 (On-the-rocks) ●●●●◐
Pineapple Daiquiri #2 (Frozen) ●●●●◐
Pineapple Fizz ●●●●●
Pineapple Margarita ●●●●○
Pineapple Mojito ●●●●◐
Pineapple Smoothie (Mocktail) ●●●◐○
Pino Pepe ●●●●○
Pisco Punch #1 (Difford's Formula) ●●●●◐
Pisco Punch #3 (Lanes' Formula) ●●●●○
Pisco Punch #4 (Prosser's Formula) ●●●●●
Playa Del Mar ●●●●○
Pogo Stick ●●●●○
Purple Flirt #2 ●●●○○
Queen Martini ●●●●○
Raspberry Sake'tini ●●●◐○
Reef Juice ●●●●○
Reggae Rum Punch ●●●●◐
Roa Aé ●●●◐○
Rum Runner ●●●●○
Saigon Sling ●●●◐○
St Kitts ●●●●○
San Fransisco ●●●◐○
Sandstorm ●●●●○
Sex On The Beach #2 ●●●○○
Sex On The Beach #3 ●●◐○○
Singapore Sling #3 ●●●◐○
Snow White Daiquiri ●●●●○
Solent Sunset ●●●●○
South Pacific ●●●◐○
Southern Punch ●●●◐○
Sun Kissed Virgin (Mocktail) ●●●○○
Sunshine Cocktail #1 ●●●●◐
Surfer on A.C.D. ●●●◐○
Swamp Water ●●●●○
Tantris Sidecar ●●●●○
Threesome ●●●◐○
Thunderbird ●●●●○
Tiki Max ●●●●○
Tilt ●●●●○
Tolleytown Punch ●●●◐○
Tomahawk ●●●◐○
Tongue Twister ●●●○○
Tootie Fruity Lifesaver ●●●○○
Transylvanian Martini ●●●○○
Tropical Caipirinha ●●●●◐
Tropical Daiquiri ●●●●◐
Turquoise Daiquiri ●●●◐○
Urban Oasis ●●●●○
U.S. Martini ●●●●●
Utterly Butterly ●●●◐○
Vacation ●●●◐○
Vante Martini ●●●●◐
Verdi Martini ●●●●○
Woodland Punch ●●●◐○
Yellow Bird ●●●○○
Yellow Fever Martini ●●●◐○
The Zamboanga 'Zeinie' Cocktail ●●●●○
Zombie #1 (Intoxica! Recipe) ●●●●○
Zombie #2 (Vic's Formula) ●●●◐○
Zombie #3 (Modern Formula) ●●●●○

PISCO

A type of brandy and the national drink of both Chile and Peru, pisco probably takes its name from the port of Pisco in Peru.

The best pisco is made from the fermented juice of the Muscat grape, which grows in the Ica region of southwestern Peru and in Chile's Elqui Valley. There are many varieties of Muscat. The Quebranta grape is favoured in Peru where it is usually blended with one or two other varietals such as Italia, Moscatel, Albilla, Negra, Mollar and Torontel. In Chile Common Black, Mollar, Pink Muscat, Torontel, Pedro Jimenez and Muscat of Alexandria are all used.

Charlie Lychee'tini ●●●●○
Cola De Mono ●●●●◐
Extradition ●●●●○
Lima Sour ●●●◐○
Pichuncho Martini ●●●●◐
Pini ●●●●◐
Pisco Collins ●●●●○
Pisco Punch #1 (Difford's Formula) ●●●●◐
Pisco Punch #2 (Alfredo Micheli's Formula) ●●●●●
Pisco Punch #3 (Lanes' Formula) ●●●●○
Pisco Punch #4 (Prosser's Formula) ●●●●●
Pisco Naranja ●●●◐○
Pisco Sour (Traditional Recipe) ●●●●◐
Pisco Sour (Difford's Version) ●●●●●
Piscola ●●●◐○
Ponche de Algarrobina ●●●◐○

PLYMOUTH GIN

41.2% alc./vol. (82.4°proof)

www.plymouthgin.com

Producer: V&S Plymouth Ltd, Black Friars Distillery, Plymouth, England

US distributor: The Absolut Spirits Company Inc.. Tel: 212 641 8700

UK distributor: Maxxium UK Tel: 01786 430 500

Since 1793, Plymouth Gin has been hand-crafted in England's oldest working distillery – Black Friars in Plymouth. It is still bottled at the unique strength of 41.2% alc./vol., and is based on a recipe that is over 200 years old. Plymouth Gin, which can only be produced in Plymouth, differs from London gins due to the use of only sweet botanicals combined with soft Dartmoor water. The result is a wonderfully aromatic and smooth gin.

Plymouth has been used by bartenders in cocktails since 1896, when it was first mixed in the original Dry Martini, and is favoured by many top bartenders due to its fresh juniper, lemony bite with deeper earthy notes.

Abbey Martini ●●●◐○
Ace ●●●◐○
Alaska Martini ●●●●○
Alessandro ●●●○○
Alexander ●●●◐○
Alexander's Big Brother ●●●○○
Alexander's Sister ●●●◐○
Anita's Attitude Adjuster ●●●◐○
Apple & Elderflower Collins ●●●●○
Apricot Mango Martini ●●●●○
Apricot Martini ●●●○○
Arizona Breeze ●●●●○
Arnaud Martini ●●●●○
Attitude Adjuster ●●●○○
Aunt Emily ●●●●○
Aviation ●●●●●
Aviator ●●●●○
Baby Blue Martini ●●●◐○
Barbara West ●●●◐○
Barbary Coast Highball ●●●◐○
Barbary Coast Martini ●●●●○
Barnum ●●●◐○
Bartender's Martini ●●●●○
Basil Bramble Sling ●●●●○

Beach Iced Tea ●●●◐○
Bebbo ●●●●○
Bee's Knees Martini #2 ●●●●◐
Beverly Hills Iced Tea ●●●◐○
Bikini Martini ●●●●○
Bitter Elder ●●●◐○
Black Bison Martini ●●●●◐
Blackthorn English ●●●●○
Blue Bird ●●●○○
Blue Lady ●●●○○
Blue Lagoon ●●●○○
Blue Moon ●●●◐○
Blue Riband ●●●○○
Blue Star ●●●○○
Blue Wave ●●●○○
Boston ●●●◐○
Boston Tea Party ●●●○○
Bradford ●●●●○
Bramble ●●●●◐
Bramblette ●●●◐○
Breakfast Martini ●●●●◐
Bronx ●●●◐○
The Buck ●●●◐○
Byzantine ●●●●○
Casino ●●●●○
Chelsea Sidecar ●●●●◐
China Martini ●●●◐○
Claridge ●●●●○
Clover Leaf Martini ●●●●◐
Copper Illusion ●●●●○
Country Breeze ●●●◐○
Cowboy Martini ●●●◐○
Cumbersome ●●●●○
Curdish Martini ●●●●○
Damn-The-Weather ●●●◐○
Damson In Distress ●●●●○
Delmonico Special ●●●◐○
Dempsey ●●●●○
Desert Cooler ●●●◐○
Diamond Fizz ●●●●○
Diana's Bitter ●●●○○
Dickens' Martini ●●●●◐
Dirty Martini ●●●◐○
DNA ●●●◐○
DNA #2 ●●●○○
Dry Martini ●●●●●
Dry Martini #2 (Naked) ●●●●○
Dry Orange Martini ●●●●◐
Dutch Breakfast Martini ●●●●○
Dutch Courage ●●●●○
Earl Grey Mar-tea-ni ●●●●◐
Eden Martini ●●●◐○
Elderflower Collins #1 ●●●●○
Emperor's Memoirs ●●●●○
English Garden ●●●●○
English Rose ●●●●○
Fine & Dandy ●●●◐○
Fizz ●●●●○
Flip ●●●●◐
Floral Martini ●●●●○
Florida Sling ●●●○○
Fluffy Duck ●●●◐○
Flying Tigre Coctel ●●●●○
Fog Cutter #1 ●●●●○
Fog Cutter # 2 ●●●●○
Fog Horn ●●●◐○
Forbidden Fruits ●●●●○
Frankenjack ●●●●○
Franklin Martini ●●●●●
French 75 ●●●◐○
Full Circle ●●●●○
Gibson ●●●●◐
Gimlet #1 ●●●●○
Gimlet #2 ●●●●◐
Gin & It ●●●●○
Gin & Sin ●●●◐○
Gin & Tonic ●●●●●
Gin Berry ●●●◐○
Gin Daisy ●●●●○
Gin Fix ●●●●○
Gin Fixed ●●●●○
Gin Fizz ●●●●○
Gin Garden ●●●●○
Gin Genie ●●●●○
Gin Gin Mule ●●●●○
Gin Sling ●●●●○
Gin Sour ●●●●○
Gina ●●●◐○
Ginger & Lemongrass Martini ●●●●○
Gin-Ger & Tonic ●●●◐○
Ginger Cosmos ●●●◐○
Gin-Ger Tom ●●●●○
Gingertini ●●●●○
Golden Dawn ●●●●○
Golden Fizz #1 ●●●◐○
Golden Fizz #2 ●●●●◐
Golf Cocktail ●●●●○
Granny's Martini ●●●○○
Grape Delight ●●●◐○
Grateful Dead ●●●◐○
Green Fizz ●●●◐○
Gypsy Martini ●●●●○
Hanky-Panky Martini ●●●●○
The Harlem ●●●●○
Hawaiian Martini ●●●●○
Hong Kong Fuey ●●●○○
Honolulu ●●●●○
I B Damm'd ●●●●◐
Imperial Martini ●●●○○
Income Tax Cocktail ●●●●○
Indian Rose ●●●●○
Ink Martini #1 ●●●◐○
Jack Dempsey ●●●◐○
Jacuzzi ●●●◐○
Jaded Lady ●●●○○
Jasmine ●●●●○
Jockey Club ●●●◐○
John Collins ●●●●○
The Journalist ●●●●○
Jubilant ●●●●◐
Julep ●●●●●
Jupiter Martini ●●●◐○
Kee-Wee Martini ●●●●○
Knickerbocker Martini ●●●◐○
Knockout Martini ●●●◐○
L.A. Iced Tea ●●●◐○
The Last Word ●●●●◐
Leap Year Martini ●●●○○
Leave It To Me Martini ●●●◐○
Lemony ●●●●○
Liquorice Martini ●●●◐○
Livingstone ●●●●○
London Calling ●●●◐○
London Cocktail ●●●○○
London Fog ●●●○○
Long Beach Iced Tea ●●●◐○
Long Island Iced Tea ●●●◐○
Long Island Spiced Tea ●●●◐○
Lotus Martini ●●●●○
Loud Speaker Martini ●●●◐○
Lutkins Special Martini ●●●◐○
Luxury Cocktail ●●●◐○
Lychee & Blackcurrant Martini ●●●●○
Lychee & Rose Petal Martini ●●●●○
Lychee & Sake Martini ●●●●○
Lychee Rickey ●●●◐○
Macka ●●●◐○
Maiden's Blush ●●●●◐
Maiden's Prayer ●●●◐○
Mainbrace ●●●●○
Major Bailey #1 ●●●●◐
Mandarine Collins ●●●○○
Mango Collins ●●●●○
Marguerite Martini ●●●●○
Marmalade Martini ●●●●◐
Marny Cocktail ●●●●◐
Martinez ●●●●●
Martini Special ●●●●◐
Martini Thyme ●●●●○
Mary Rose ●●●●○
Maurice Martini ●●●◐○
Mayfair Cocktail ●●●●○
The Mayflower Martini ●●●●○
M.C. Martini ●●●●●
Medium Martini ●●●●◐
Merry Widow #1 ●●●◐○
Merry-Go-Round Martini ●●●●○
Miami Beach ●●●●○
Milano Sour ●●●●○
The Million Dollar Cocktail ●●●●◐
Milly Martini ●●●●○
Mint Cocktail ●●●●◐
Mint Collins ●●●●○
Mint Fizz ●●●◐○
Modernista ●●●◐○
Monarch Martini ●●●●○
Monkey Gland #1 ●●●●○
Monkey Gland #2 ●●●●○
Monte Carlo Imperial ●●●○○
Moon River ●●●◐○
Moonlight Martini ●●●●○
Moonshine Martini ●●●●◐
Mujer Verde ●●●●○
Mule's Hind Leg ●●●●◐
Napoleon Martini ●●●●◐
Navigator ●●●●○
Negroni ●●●●◐
Nicky's Fizz ●●●◐○
Nightmare Martini ●●●○○
Nome ●●●●○
Noon ●●●●○
North Pole Martini ●●●●○
Onion Ring Martini ●●●○○
Opal ●●●●◐
Opera ●●●●○
Orange Bloom Martini ●●●●◐
Orange Blossom ●●●◐○
Orange Martini ●●●●○
Oriental Tart ●●●●○
Paisley Martini ●●●●○
Pall Mall Martini ●●●●○
Palm Beach ●●●◐○
Pancho Villa ●●●●○
Paradise #1 ●●●◐○
Paradise #2 ●●●●◐
Paradise #3 ●●●◐○
Parisian Martini ●●●●○
Park Avenue ●●●●○
Park Lane ●●●●◐
Parma Negroni ●●●●○
Passion Fruit Collins ●●●●○
Passion Fruit Martini #3 ●●●●○
Passion Punch ●●●◐○
Peggy Martini ●●●○○
Pegu Club ●●●●○
Pendennis Cocktail ●●●●○
Perfect Martini ●●●◐○
Peter Pan Martini ●●●●○
Petto Martini ●●●●◐
Piccadilly Martini ●●●●◐
Pimm's Cocktail ●●●●◐
Pink Gin #1 (Traditional) ●●●●○
Pink Gin #2 (Modern) ●●●●○
Pink Gin & Tonic ●●●●○
Pink Hound ●●●●○
Pink Lady ●●●●◐
Pink Palace ●●●●◐
Poet's Dream ●●●●◐
Pogo Stick ●●●●○
Princess Marina ●●●●○
Princess Mary ●●●○○
Princeton ●●●●○
Princeton Martini ●●●●○
Pruneaux ●●●●○
Queen Martini ●●●●○
Raspberry Collins ●●●●○
Ramos Gin Fizz ●●●●○
Raspberry Martini #2 ●●●●○
Red Lion #1 (Modern Formula) ●●●●◐
Red Lion #2 (Embury's Formula) ●●●●◐
Red Snapper ●●●●○
Resolute ●●●●○
Rhubarb & Custard Martini ●●●●○
Rhubard & Lemongrass Martini ●●●●○
Rickey (Gin Rickey) ●●●●○
Roc-A-Coe ●●●◐○
The Rose #2 ●●●◐○
Rose Petalini ●●●●○
Roselyn Martini ●●●●◐
Royal Smile ●●●●○
Rumba ●●●●○
Russian ●●●◐○
Saigon Cooler ●●●◐○
Saigon Sling ●●●◐○
Sake-tini #1 ●●●●○
Sandstorm ●●●●○
Satan's Whiskers (Straight) ●●●●◐
Savannah ●●●◐○
Savoy Special #1 ●●●●○
Sensation ●●●●○
Serendipity ●●●●○
Seventh Heaven #2 ●●●●◐
The 75 ●●●●◐
Shady Grove Cooler ●●●◐○
Sicilian Negroni ●●●●○
Silver Bullet Martini ●●●●○
Silver Fizz ●●●●○
Silver Martini ●●●◐○
Singapore Sling #1 (Baker's Formula) ●●●◐○
Singapore Sling #2 ●●●●○
Singapore Sling #3 ●●●◐○
Sleepy Hollow ●●●●○
Sling ●●●●○
Sloe Gin Fizz ●●●◐○
Slow Comfortable Screw Against the Wall ●●●◐○
Smoky Martini #1 ●●●●○
Smoky Martini #2 ●●●○○
Snyder Martini ●●●●○
So-So Martini ●●●●●
Sour ●●●◐○
South Pacific Breeze ●●●◐○
Southern Tea-Knee ●●●●◐
Southside Royale ●●●●○
Spencer Cocktail ●●●●○
Spicy Veggy ●●●◐○
Stanley Cocktail ●●●●○
Stork Club ●●●●○
Straits Sling ●●●●○
Summer Time Martini ●●●◐○
Swizzle ●●●●◐
Tango Martini #1 ●●●●○
Tango Martini #2 ●●●●○
Tex Collins ●●●◐○
Thai Lady ●●●●○
Thriller From Vanilla ●●●●○
Tipperary #2 ●●●●◐
Tokyo Iced Tea ●●●◐○
Tokyo Tea ●●●●○
Tom Collins ●●●●○
Turf Martini ●●●●○
Tuxedo Martini ●●●●◐
Twentieth Century Martini ●●●◐○
Typhoon ●●●○○
Venus Martini ●●●●○
The Vesper Martini ●●●●●
Waltzing Matilda ●●●●○
Watermelon & Basil Martini ●●●●○
Webster Martini ●●●◐○
Wet Martini ●●●●◐
The Wet Spot ●●●●○
What The Hell ●●●●○
White Gin Fizz ●●●◐○
White Lady ●●●●○
Wibble ●●●●◐
Wink ●●●●○
Za-Za ●●●●○

PLYMOUTH SLOE GIN LIQUEUR

26% alc./vol. (52°proof)

www.plymouthgin.com

Producer: Coates & Co Ltd, Plymouth.

US distributor: The Absolut Spirits Company Inc..

Tel: 212 641 8700

UK distributor: Maxxium UK
Tel: 01786 430 500

The making of fruit liqueurs is a long tradition in the British countryside and Plymouth Gin stays true to a unique 1883 recipe. The sloe berries are slowly and gently steeped in high strength Plymouth gin, soft Dartmoor water and a further secret ingredient. It is an unhurried process and the drink is bottled only when the Head Distiller decides the perfect flavour has been reached. The result is an entirely natural product with no added flavouring or colourings.

This richly flavoured liqueur is initially dry but opens with smooth, sweet, lightly jammy, juicy cherry and raspberry notes alongside a complimentary mixture of figs, cloves, set honey and stewed fruits. The finish has strong almond notes.

Alabama Slammer #2 ●●●◐○
Blackthorn English ●●●●○
Charlie Chaplin ●●●◐○
Gin Genie ●●●●○
Grape Delight ●●●◐○
Hedgerow Sling ●●●◐○
London Calling ●●●◐○
Millionaire's Daiquiri ●●●◐○
Purple Turtle ●●●◐○
Red Rum Martini ●●●●◐
Sailor's Comfort ●●●○○
Sloe Gin Fizz ●●●◐○
Sloe Motion ●●●◐○
Sloe Tequila ●●●◐○
Slow Screw ●●●○○
Slow Comfortable Screw ●●●◐○
Smoky Martini #2 ●●●○○
Stupid Cupid ●●●○○
Wibble ●●●●◐

POMEGRANATE (GRENADINE) SYRUP

Originally grenadine was a syrup flavoured with pomegranate. Sadly most of today's commercially available grenadine syrups are flavoured with red berries and cherry juice. They may be blood red but they don't taste of pomegranate. Hunt out one of the few genuine commercially made pomegranate syrups or make your own.

Separate the seed cells of four pomegranates from the outer membranes and skin, then pulp them in a food processor. Simmer and stir the pulp in a saucepan with a quarter cup of honey for several minutes. Strain through a cheesecloth-layered sieve and store in a refrigerator.

Ace ●●●◐○
Alabama Slammer #1 ●●●◐○
American Beauty ●●●●◐
Apricot Martini ●●●○○
Aunt Emily ●●●●○
Avenue ●●●◐○
Bacardi Cocktail ●●●●○
Bazooka ●●◐○○
Blinker ●●●●○
Bora Bora Brew (Mocktail) ●●●○○
Bosom Caresser ●●●●○
Boston ●●●◐○
Bourbonella ●●●●○
Caribbean Cruise ●●●◐○
Caribbean Punch ●●●●○
Champagne Daisy ●●●○○
Cinderella ●●◐○○
Clipper Cocktail ●●●◐○
Clover Leaf Martini ●●●●◐
Cranberry & Mint Martini ●●●●○
Daisy Duke ●●●◐○
Dempsey ●●●●○
Depth Bomb ●●●◐○
Doctor Funk ●●●○○
Dulchin ●●●●○
East India #1 ●●●●◐
El Presidente Daiquiri ●●●●◐
English Rose ●●●●○
La Feuille Morte ●●●◐○
Fiesta ●●●●○
Flaming Ferrari ●●○○○
Flamingo #2 ●●●◐○
Florida Sling ●●●○○
Flying Tigre Coctel ●●●●○
Fosbury Flip ●●●●◐
Fourth Of July Shot ●●◐○○
French Kiss #1 ●●●○○
Frida's Brow ●●●●○
Fruit Salad ●●●○○
Gin & Sin ●●●◐○
Gin Daisy ●●●●○
Gloom Chaser ●●●◐○
Gloom Lifter ●●●●○
Golden Dawn ●●●●○
Grapefruit Julep ●●●●◐
Hobson's Choice (Mocktail) ●●◐○○
Hurricane #2 ●●●○○
Jack Frost ●●●○○
Jack Rose ●●●●○
Kava ●●●●○
Kretchma ●●●◐○
Leave It To Me Martini ●●●◐○
Lime Blush (Mocktail)(Mocktail)
Lotus Martini ●●●●○
Maiden's Blush ●●●●◐
Mary Pickford ●●●●●
Mexican ●●●●○
The Million Dollar Cocktail ●●●●◐
Millionaire ●●●●○
Millionaire's Daiquiri ●●●◐○
Monkey Gland #1 ●●●●○
Monkey Gland #2 ●●●●○
Monk's Habit ●●●○○
Opening Shot ●●●◐○
Orang-A-Tang ●●●●○
Orange Blossom ●●●◐○
Park Lane ●●●●◐
Piccadilly Martini ●●●●◐
Pink Cloud ●●●○○
Pink Daiquiri ●●●●○
Pink Lady ●●●●◐
Pink Lemonade (Mocktail) ●●●○○
Pink Palace ●●●●◐
Pirate Daiquiri ●●●●○
Planter's Punchless (Mocktail) ●●●○○
Planteur ●●●●○
Pomegranate Margarita ●●●●◐
Pomegranate Martini ●●●●◐
Port & Starboard ●●◐○○
Port Light ●●●◐○
Pousse-café ●●◐○○
President ●●●●○
Presidente ●●●●○
Purple Flirt #2 ●●●○○
Pussyfoot (Mocktail) ●●●●◐
Red Lion #1 (Modern Formula) ●●●●◐
Red Lion #2 (Embury's Formula) ●●●●◐
Reef Juice ●●●●○
Reggae Rum Punch ●●●●◐
The Rose #3 ●●●●◐
Roselyn Martini ●●●●◐
Roy Rogers (Mocktail) ●●◐○○
Royal Smile ●●●●○
Rumba ●●●●○
Rum Runner ●●●●○
St Kitts ●●●●○
San Fransisco ●●●◐○
Sangrita ●●●●◐
Santiago Daiquiri ●●●●●
Savoy Special #1 ●●●●○
Scofflaw ●●●●○
Scotch Bounty Martini ●●●◐○
The 75 ●●●●◐
Shark Bite ●●●◐○
Shirley Temple (Mocktail) ●●●○○
Silk Stockings ●●●◐○
Singapore Sling #3 ●●●◐○
Slippery Nipple ●●○○○
Sloppy Joe ●●●●○
Solent Sunset ●●●●○
So-So Martini ●●●●●
Southern Punch ●●●◐○
Squashed Frog ●●●○○
Stanley Cocktail ●●●●○
Summer Rose Martini ●●●●○
Summer Time Martini ●●●◐○
Sunshine Cocktail #1 ●●●●◐
Sweet Louise ●●●○○
Tequila Sunrise ●●●◐○
Three Miler ●●●●○
Tipperary #2 ●●●●◐
Tomate ●●●○○
Tongue Twister ●●●○○
Tropical Daiquiri ●●●●◐
Union Club ●●●●○
Vampiro ●●●●○
Velvet Hammer ●●●◐○
Wagon Wheel ●●●○○
Ward Eight ●●●●○
Washington Apple ●●●●◐
Weeping Jesus ●●●◐○
Whiskey Daisy ●●●◐○
White Lion ●●●●○
Zombie #2 (Vic's Formula) ●●●◐○
Zombie #3 (Modern Formula) ●●●●○

PORT (PORTO)

Port, or to give it its full name 'vinho do porto', is a Portuguese wine from the area known as the Upper Douro which starts 45 miles from the coast at the town of Oporto and stretches east to the Spanish border. Wine is fortified with grape brandy, which stops fermentation before it is complete by raising the alcoholic strength beyond that at which the fermenting yeasts can survive. This produces wines with residual sugars, giving port its inherently sweet style.

Chocolate Sidecar ●●●●○
Basil Mary ●●●●○
Bishop ●●●◐○
Bloody Joseph ●●●◐○
Bloody Maria ●●●●○
Bloody Mary (modern recipe) ●●●●◐
Devil ●●●◐○
Free Town ●●●●○
Golden Girl ●●●●○
Happy New Year ●●●○○
Havana Cobbler ●●●●○
Mulled Wine ●●●●○
Negus (Hot) ●●●●○
Port & Melon Martini ●●●●◐
Port Wine Cocktail ●●●◐○
Princeton ●●●●○
Randy ●●●●○
Red Snapper ●●●●○
Sir Charles Punch ●●●●○
Suburban ●●●●○
Tawny-Tini ●●●●○
Tokyo Bloody Mary ●●●●○

PUREES

Fruit purees are made from fresh fruit which has been chopped up and liquidised. When making your own puree add roughly five to ten percent sugar syrup to your pureed fruit depending on the fruit's ripeness. Commercially available purees contain differing amounts of added sugar and, if using such a product, you may have to adjust the balance of your drink to allow for the extra sweetness.

PROSECCO SPARKLING WINE

Prosecco is a wine produced around the towns of Conegliano and Valdobbiadene in the Italian

province of Treviso. It can be still, semi-sparkling or sparkling, dry, off-dry or sweet. The style called for in this guide, and the preferred style for export, is dry and sparkling. 'Frizzante' means 'semi-sparkling' and 'spumante' means 'sparkling'.

The better wines from hillside vineyards are labelled Prosecco di Conegliano-Valdobbiadene. The best are 'Prosecco Superiore di Cartizze' from the great hill of Cartizze in the Valdobbiadene sub-region.

Bellini #1 (original) ●●●●○
Bellini #2 (Difford's formula) ●●●●○
Hot Tub ●●●●○
Pomegranate Bellini ●●●◐○
Puccini ●●●◐○
Rhubarb & Honey Bellini ●●●●○
Rossini ●●●●○
Sgroppino ●●●●◐
Tiziano ●●●◐○
Twinkle ●●●●○

PUSSER'S NAVY RUM

47.75% alc./vol. (95.5°proof)

www.pussers.com

Producer: Pusser's Rum Limited, Tortola, British Virgin Islands.

The name 'Pusser' is slang in the Royal Navy for purser, the officer with responsibility for the issue of rum on board ship. For more than 300 years the British Navy issued a daily 'tot' of Pusser's rum, with a double issue before battle. This tradition, which started in Jamaica in 1665, was finally broken on 31st July 1970, a day now known as 'Black Tot Day'. In 1979 the Admiralty approved the re-blending of Pusser's rum to the original specifications by Charles Tobias in the British Virgin Islands. A significant donation from the sale of each bottle accrues to the benefit of The Royal Navy Sailor's Fund, a naval charity established to compensate sailors for their lost tot.

This Navy rum delivers a rich medley of flavours: molasses, treacle, vanilla, cinnamon, nutmeg, sticky toffee pudding, espresso and creamy tiramisu with subtle hints of oak.

Alexandra ●●●◐○
All Fall Down ●●●◐○
Aunt Agatha ●●●◐○
Bahama Mama ●●●●○
Baltimore Egg Nog ●●●○○
Bee's Knees #1 ●●●●○
Boston Tea Party ●●●○○
Caribbean Breeze ●●●●○
Charles Daiquiri ●●●●◐
Dark Daiquiri ●●●●◐
Fat Sailor ●●●●○
Flaming Ferrari ●●○○○
Goombay Smash ●●●●◐
Grog ●●●●○
Hot Grog ●●●●○
Hurricane #1 ●●●●○
Kamaniwanalaya ●●●◐○
Navy Grog ●●●●○
Nevada Daiquiri ●●●●○
New Port Codebreaker ●●●◐○
Painkiller ●●●●○
Pirate Daiquiri ●●●●○
Red Rover ●●●●○
Reef Juice ●●●●○
Rum Runner ●●●●○
Shark Bite ●●●◐○
Solent Sunset ●●●●○
Spiced Cranberry Martini ●●●●○
Tiki Max ●●●●○
Zombie #3 (Modern Formula) ●●●●○

RASPBERRIES & BLACKBERRIES

Both these berries grow on brambly bushes and are related to the rose. Both can be cultivated in a wide range of colours, from white or yellow to orange, pink or purple, as well as the more common red and black.

The loganberry is a cross between a blackberry and a raspberry and is named after its Californian creator, James H Logan. Other later hybrids of the two fruits include the tayberry (named after the Scottish river) and the boysenberry (named after its creator).

The juice of both raspberries and blackberries is intense and a little goes a long way. Which is just as well because there's precious little juice in each berry and you'll find putting them through an electric juicer a complete waste of time. Instead, either blend them into a puree or (as I do) muddle the fruits in the base of your shaker or in the glass. Recipes in this guide state how many fruits you should muddle for each drink.

Apple & Blackberry Pie ●●●◐○
Berry Caipirinha ●●●●○
Berry Nice ●●●◐○
Black & White Daiquiri ●●●●◐
Black & Blue Caipirovska ●●●●○
Blimey ●●●●○
Bling! Bling! ●●●●◐
Blood Orange ●●●○○
Bourbon Smash ●●●◐○
Brazilian Berry ●●●●○
Clover Leaf Martini ●●●●◐
Cobbled Raspberry Martini ●●●●◐
Eclipse ●●●●◐
Especial Day ●●●●◐
Estes ●●●●○
Finn Rouge ●●●◐○
First Of July ●●●●○
Forbidden Fruits ●●●●○
Godfrey ●●●●○
Miss Martini ●●●◐○
Mrs Robinson #1 ●●●●○
Pernod & Black Martini ●●●●○
Raspberry Caipirinha ●●●●○
Raspberry Collins ●●●●○
Raspberry Debonnaire ●●●◐○
Raspberry Margarita ●●●●○
Raspberry Martini #1 ●●●◐○
Raspberry Martini #2 ●●●●○
Raspberry Mule ●●●●○
The Red Army ●●●◐○
The Rose #1 (original) ●●●●◐
Saigon Cooler ●●●◐○
Serendipity ●●●●○
Tartini ●●●●○
Tennessee Berry Mule ●●●●○
Trifle'tini ●●●◐○
Tripleberry ●●●●○
Upside-Down Raspberry Cheesecake ●●●●○
Vanilla & Raspberry Martini ●●●●○
Venus Martini ●●●●○
Wild Promenade Martini ●●●●○

RICARD PASTIS

45% alc./vol. (90°proof)

Producer: Pernod (Group Pernod Ricard), Créteil, France.

A French classic, this liquorice based spirit is Europe's number one selling spirit brand and the third biggest brand worldwide. Created by Paul Ricard in Marseille in 1932, it is now produced in Bessan, Southern France. The unique flavour of this pastis derives from liquorice root, green anise, fennel and seven different aromatic herbs from Provence.

It is anethole, made from fennel and green anise, which produces Ricard's most distinctive effect: it turns milky on contact with water or ice.

Traditionally served over ice diluted with five parts of water, Ricard adds a rich aniseed flavour and distinctive cloudy appearance to a number of classic and modern cocktails. Besides the predominant aniseed, its dry palate features fennel, soft liquorice and a delicious minty lemon freshness.

Canarie ●●●◐○
Dempsey ●●●●○
La Feuille Morte ●●●◐○
Liquorice Whiskey Sour ●●●●◐
Mauresque ●●●●○
La Momie ●●●○○
Momisette ●●●●○
Perroquet ●●●○○
Riviera Breeze ●●●◐○
Tomate ●●●○○

RUM

Rum is a spirit made from sugar cane or its by-products. The recipes in this guide call for a number of styles of rum, as explained below.

RUM - AGED (AÑEJO)

Like other distillates, rum is clear when it condenses after distillation. The fact that ageing in oak barrels improved the raw rum was discovered when ships carried rum on the long passage to Europe: it arrived darker in colour and with an enhanced flavour.

Today, rum is aged in barrels from France or the United States which have previously been used to age cognac, bourbon or whiskey. They may be charred or scraped clean to remove any previous charring before receiving the rum: the treatment of the barrels is reflected in the character they impart to the finished rum.

Aged Honey Daiquiri ●●●●●
Bahama Mama ●●●●○
Bolero Sour ●●●●●
Castro ●●●◐○
Cool Orchard ●●●●○
Daiquiri (Classic) ●●●●●
Difford's Daiquiri ●●●●●
Dirty Banana ●●●●○
Doctor ●●●●○
Dolores ●●●●○
Downhill Racer ●●●●○
Flamingo #2 ●●●◐○
Fosbury Flip ●●●●◐
Golden Girl ●●●●○
Grapefruit Daiquiri ●●●●○
Honey Wall ●●●●○
Hop Toad #2 ●●●●○
Orange Daiquiri #1 ●●●●◐
Platinum Blonde ●●●◐○
Red Rum Martini ●●●●◐
Rum & Raisin Alexandra ●●●●○
Rum Sour ●●●●○
Suburban ●●●●○
Test Pilot ●●●●○
Voodoo ●●●●○

RUM - BERMUDAN DARK

A few recipes in this guide require the use of Bermudan rum, a distinctive dark blend.

Bella Donna Daiquiri ●●●●◐
Bull's Milk ●●●◐○
Dark 'N' Stormy ●●●●○
Dino Sour ●●●●◐
Doctor Funk ●●●○○
Georgetown Punch ●●●●○
Honolulu Juicer ●●●◐○
Hurricane #2 ●●●○○
Iced Tea ●●●◐○
Jean Gabin ●●●●○
Jungle Bird ●●●●○
Milk Punch ●●●●○
Modernista ●●●◐○
Purple Flirt #2 ●●●○○
Tropical Daiquiri ●●●●◐
Zanzibar ●●●◐○

RUM - GOLDEN

As the name would suggest, an amber coloured rum traditionaly aged in wood.

Abacaxi Ricaço ●●●●○
Acapulco ●●●◐○
Ace Of Clubs Daiquiri ●●●●◐
Air Mail ●●●●◐
Bajan Mojito ●●●◐○
Bajan Passion ●●●●○
Banana Colada ●●●●○
Bossa Nova #1 ●●●●○
Bossa Nova #2 ●●●◐○
Butterscotch Martini ●●●●○
Chocolate Puff ●●●●○
Club Cocktail ●●●●○
Crème De Café ●●●◐○
Difford's Daiquiri ●●●●●
Fat Sailor ●●●●○
Fish House Punch #1 ●●●●○
Four W Daiquiri ●●●●○
Funky Monkey ●●●●○
Ginger Punch ●●●◐○
Hawaiian Eye ●●●◐○
Heavens Above ●●●◐○
Hot Buttered Rum ●●●●○
Hot Rum Punch ●●●◐○
Julep ●●●●●
Kava ●●●●○
Lola ●●●◐○
Monkey Shine ●●●●○
Monkey Wrench ●●●◐○
Pago Pago ●●●◐○
Palm Springs ●●●◐○
Pilgrim Cocktail ●●●●○
Piña Colada ●●●●◐
Pineapple Fizz ●●●●●
Ponce de Leon ●●●●○
P.S. I Love You ●●●●○
Royal Bermuda Yacht Club Daiquiri ●●●●○
Smooth & Creamy'tini ●●●●○
Tom & Jerry ●●●○○
Total Recall ●●●◐○
Yacht Club ●●●◐○
Yellow Bird ●●●○○
Zombie #1 (Intoxica! Recipe) ●●●●○
Zombie #3 (Modern Formula) ●●●●○

RUM - JAMAICAN OVERPROOF

Originally gunpowder was used to determine the strength of a spirit. The tester would mix the spirit with gunpowder and attempt to light it. If the spirit did not ignite, it was underproof; if it burned steadily, it was proof; if it exploded, it was overproof.

Proof is measured differently in the UK and the US, but in the States 100°proof is double alcohol by volume (measured by the Gay-Lussac scale). Hence an overproof rum is over 100°proof or 50% alc./vol. in strength.

Afterburner ●●●○○
The Alamagoozlum Cocktail ●●●●◐
Assisted Suicide ●●●◐○
Awol ●●●●○
Beach Blonde ●●●●○
Bolshoi Punch ●●●●○
Caribbean Punch ●●●●○
Coco Naut ●●◐○○
Cold Comfort ●●●●○
Flaming Dr Pepper ●●○○○
Jamaican Sunset ●●●●○
Vic's Original 1944 Mai Tai ●●●●●
Mango Punch ●●●●○
Marama Rum Punch ●●●●○
Passionate Rum Punch ●●●●○
Pirate Daiquiri ●●●●○
Reggae Rum Punch ●●●●◐
Roman Punch ●●●●○
Rum Punch ●●●●●
Rum Punch-Up ●●●●◐
Rumba ●●●●○
Sorrel Rum Punch ●●●●◐
Steel Bottom ●●●○○
Stone & Gravel ●●●◐○
Zombie #2 (Vic's Formula) ●●●◐○
Zombie #3 (Modern Formula) ●●●●○

RUM - LIGHT/WHITE

Rum is termed 'light' or 'heavy', depending on the purity to which it was distilled. Essentially, the flavour of any spirit comes from 'congeners' – products of fermentation which are not ethyl alcohol. When alcohol is concentrated during distillation, the levels of congeners are reduced. The fewer congeners, the lighter the rum. The more congeners, the heavier.

The fermentation process also affects whether a rum is light or heavy. A longer, slower fermentation will result in a heavier rum.

The odour, texture and taste of light rums are more subtle and refined than those of heavy rums, which have a heavy, syrupy flavour to match their dark colour.

Light rums tend to originate from countries originally colonised by the Spanish, such as Cuba, the Dominican Republic, Puerto Rico and Venezuela.

Acapulco Daiquiri ●●●●○
Alan's Apple Breeze ●●●◐○
Anita's Attitude Adjuster ●●●◐○
Apple Daiquiri ●●●●○
Apple Mojito ●●●●○
Apricot Lady Sour ●●●◐○
Atlantic Breeze ●●●○○
Atomic Dog ●●●○○
Bajito ●●●●◐
Banana Daiquiri ●●●◐○
Basil & Honey Daiquiri ●●●●●
Beach Iced Tea ●●●◐○
Beachcomber ●●●●○
Bee's Knees #1 ●●●●○
Between The Sheets ●●●●◐
Black & White Daiquiri ●●●●◐
Black Martini ●●●●◐
Blue Hawaiian ●●●○○
Blue Heaven ●●◐○○
Blue Passion ●●●●○
Blue Wave ●●●○○
Blueberry Daiquiri ●●●●○
Bolero ●●●◐○
Bomber ●●●●○
Bulldog ●●●◐○
Bull's Blood ●●●◐○
Butterscotch Daiquiri ●●●◐○
Caipirissima ●●●●○
Canaries ●●●○○
Canteen Martini ●●●◐○
Caribbean Cruise ●●●◐○
Caribbean Piña Colada ●●●◐○
Charles Daiquiri ●●●●◐
Cherry & Hazelnut Daiquiri ●●●●○
Che's Revolution ●●●●◐
Chiclet Daiquiri ●●●◐○
Cinnamon Daiquiri ●●●◐○
Classic Daiquiri ●●●●●
Clipper Cocktail ●●●◐○
Coconut Daiquiri ●●●●○
Cuba Libre ●●●◐○
Cuban Master ●●●○○
Cuban Special ●●●○○
Cubanita ●●●●○
Custard Tart ●●●●○
Dean's Gate Martini ●●●◐○
Daiquiri (Classic) ●●●●●
Daiquiri De Luxe ●●●●○
Daiquiri On The Rocks ●●●●●
Derby Daiquiri ●●●●◐
Derby Fizz ●●●●◐
Difford's Daiquiri ●●●●●
Dino Sour ●●●●◐
Dolce Havana ●●●●○
Dorian Gray ●●●◐○
Doughnut Martini ●●●◐○
El Presidente Daiquiri ●●●●◐
Epestone Daiquiri ●●●●○
Especial Day ●●●●◐
Espresso Daiquiri ●●●●○
Extradition ●●●●○
F. Willy Shot ●●●◐○
Fancy Drink ●●●◐○
Fiesta ●●●●○
Fish House Punch #2 ●●●●○
Florida Daiquiri ●●●●◐
Floridita Daiquiri ●●●●○
Flying Tigre Coctel ●●●●○
Fog Cutter #1 ●●●●○
Fog Cutter # 2 ●●●●○
Free Town ●●●●○
French Daiquiri ●●●●○
French Mojito ●●●●◐
Frozen Daiquiri ●●●●○
Fruit Tree Daiquiri ●●●●○
Fu Manchu Daiquiri ●●●●○
Ginger Mojito ●●●●○
Glass Tower ●●●○○
Georgetown Punch ●●●●○
Golden Bird ●●●◐○
Golden Retriever ●●●●◐
Golden Wave ●●●◐○
Granny's ●●●●○
Grape Effect ●●●●○
Grateful Dead ●●●◐○
Green Swizzle ●●●●○
Greta Garbo ●●●●○
Gulf Coast Sex On The Beach ●●●●○
Havana Cobbler ●●●●○
Havana Special ●●●●○
Havanatheone ●●●●●
Hawaiian ●●●○○
Hawaiian Cocktail ●●●●○
Hawaiian Eye ●●●◐○
Hazel'ito ●●●●◐
Hemingway Special Daiquiri ●●●●◐
Hoa Sua ●●●●○
Honey Bee ●●●●○
Honey Daiquiri ●●●●◐
Honeysuckle Daiquiri ●●●●●
Hong Kong Fuey ●●●○○
Hop Toad #1 ●●●●○
Hurricane #1 ●●●●○
Hurricane #2 ●●●○○
Jack Dempsey ●●●◐○
Jackie O's Rose ●●●●○
Jade Daiquiri ●●●●○
Jayne Mansfield ●●●●○
Jelly Belly Beany ●●●●○
Joan Bennett ●●●○○
Jungle Juice ●●●◐○
Kamaniwanalaya ●●●◐○
Kava ●●●●○
Knickerbocker Special ●●●●○
L.A. Iced Tea ●●●◐○
Lemon Chiffon Pie ●●●●○
Long Beach Iced Tea ●●●◐○
Long Island Iced Tea ●●●◐○
Lux Daiquiri ●●●●○
Mai Tai #2 (Beaumont-Gantt's Formula) ●●●●○
Major Bailey #2 ●●●●◐
Mango Daiquiri ●●●●○
Mango Rum Cooler ●●●◐○
Mary Pickford ●●●●●
Melon Collie Martini ●●●●○
Melon Daiquiri #1 (Served 'Up') ●●●●○
Melon Daiquiri #2 (Served Frozen) ●●●◐○
Menehune Juice ●●●●○
Miami Daiquiri ●●●●○
Millionaire's Daiquiri ●●●◐○
Mint Daiquiri ●●●●●
Missionary's Downfall ●●●●●
Mojito ●●●●●
Monk's Habit ●●●○○
Nacional Daiquiri #1 ●●●●◐
Nacional Daiquiri #2 ●●●●◐
Nantucket ●●●◐○
Naranja Daiquiri ●●●●○

Natural Daiquiri ●●●●●
No. 10 Lemonade ●●●●◐
Oh Gosh! ●●●●●
Orange Mojito ●●●●○
Pancho Villa ●●●●○
Passion Fruit Daiquiri ●●●●○
Peach Daiquiri ●●●●○
Pedro Collins ●●●●○
Periodista Daiquiri ●●●●○
Pineapple & Cardamom Daiquiri ●●●●◐
Pineapple Daiquiri #1 (On-the-rocks) ●●●●◐
Pineapple Daiquiri #2 (Frozen) ●●●●◐
Pineapple Mojito ●●●●◐
Pink Daiquiri ●●●●○
Pino Pepe ●●●●○
Plantation Punch ●●●◐○
Plum Daiquiri ●●●●○
Potted Parrot ●●●◐○
President ●●●●○
Presidente ●●●●○
Quarter Deck ●●●●○
Ribalaigua Daiquiri #3 ●●●●○
Roa Aé ●●●◐○
Robin Hood #1 ●●●●○
Roulette ●●●●○
Royal Mojito ●●●●●
Santiago ●●●○○
Santiago Daiquiri ●●●●●
Scorpion ●●●●○
Sling ●●●●○
Sloppy Joe ●●●●○
Snow White Daiquiri ●●●●○
Sour ●●●◐○
Spiced Apple Daiquiri ●●●●○
Sputnik #2 ●●●●○
Stanley Cocktail ●●●●○
Strawberry & Balsamic Mojito ●●●●○
Strawberry Daiquiri ●●●●○
Strawberry Frozen Daiquiri ●●●◐○
Sunshine Cocktail #1 ●●●●◐
Sunshine Cocktail #2 ●●●●○
Swizzle ●●●●◐
Tennessee Iced Tea ●●●●○
Test Pilot ●●●◐○
Texas Iced Tea ●●●◐○
Three Miler ●●●◐○
Tokyo Iced Tea ●●●◐○
Tongue Twister ●●●○○
Tre Martini ●●●◐○
Turquoise Daiquiri ●●●◐○
White Lion ●●●●○
Wimbledon Martini ●●●●○
Zombie #1 (Intoxica! Recipe) ●●●●○
Zombie #2 (Vic's Formula) ●●●◐○
Zombie #3 (Modern Formula) ●●●●○

RUM - NAVY

See 'Pusser's Navy Rum'

RUM - SPICED

Spiced rums are continuously distilled light rums flavoured with spices including ginger, cinnamon, clove and vanilla.

Black Beard ●●●○○
Bomber ●●●●○
Cable Car ●●●●○
French Tear #1 ●●●●○
Jamaican Mule ●●●◐○
Long Island Spiced Tea ●●●◐○
Mat The Rat ●●●◐○
Santiago ●●●○○
Spiced Pear ●●●●◐
Warsaw Cooler ●●●●◐

RUM - VANILLA INFUSED

The pods of a tropical plant which belongs to the orchid family, vanilla has long been a prized flavouring. The vanilla orchid is cultivated in many different tropical regions. Bourbon vanilla is generally considered the finest kind, and Mexico and the Indian Ocean islands are popularly known as the best producers. Once the pods are harvested from the parent vine, they undergo months of curing to develop and refine their distinctive flavour.

In this guide, recipes utilise the flavour of vanilla by infusing it in a spirit, most often rum or vodka. Simply take two quality vanilla pods (roughly 6in/15cm long) and split them lengthwise with a sharp knife. Place them in the bottle of spirit you want to flavour and leave it to infuse for a fortnight, turning occasionally.

Buona Sera Shot ●●●◐○
Cherry Daiquiri ●●●●○
Coffee & Vanilla Daiquiri ●●●●○
Cox's Daiquiri ●●●●●
DC Martini ●●●●○
Lisa B's Daiquiri ●●●●●
Palermo ●●●●◐
Vanilla & Grapefruit Daiquiri ●●●●◐
Vanilla Daiquiri ●●●●◐

SAKE

Sometimes described as a rice wine, sometimes as a rice beer, sake shares qualities of both. It is fermented from specially developed rice and water by brewmasters ('toji'). But, although sake is brewed like a beer, it is served like a wine and, like a wine, can either be dry or sweet, heavy or light. But it is slightly more alcoholic than wine - 14-18% alc./vol..

Sake (pronounced Sar-Keh – heavy on the K!) is native to Japan (and parts of China). The basic outline of production has changed little since the 11th century, but complex and fragrant sake has only been generally available since the 1970s.

Almond & Sake Martini ●●●●○
Asian Ginger Martini ●●●●○
Bloody Maru ●●●◐○
Charlie Lychee'tini ●●●●○
Cucumber Sake-Tini ●●●●○
Hoa Sua ●●●●○
Iced Sake Martini ●●●●◐
Japanese Pear ●●●●○
Lychee & Sake Martini ●●●●○
Onion Ring Martini ●●●○○
Oriental Grape Martini ●●●●◐
Osmo ●●●●○
Raspberry Sake'tini ●●●◐○
Sake'politan ●●●●○
Sake-tini #1 ●●●●○
Sake-tini #2 ●●●●○
Sakini ●●●●○
Sumo in a Sidecar ●●●●◐
Tokyo Bloody Mary ●●●●○
Urban Holistic ●●●◐○

SAMBUCA BLACK

See 'Opal Nera Black Sambuca'

SAMBUCA WHITE

See 'Luxardo Sambuca dei Cesari'

SCOTCH

See 'Whisky – Scotch'

SHERRY

A fortified wine produced around the region of Jerez, Spain. See below for styles of sherry used in this guide.

SHERRY – AMONTILLADO

An Amontillado sherry begins as a Fino, a pale, dry sherry produced under a layer of a kind of yeast known as 'flor'. Once the flor dies, increasing the oxidisation and changing the flavour of the wine, the sherry becomes an Amontillado. There are two distinct Amontillado styles. One is naturally dry, while the other is sweetened. Recipes in this guide which call for Amontillado sherry require the better quality, dry style.

Atomic Cocktail ●●●○○
Barbara West ●●●◐○
Fog Cutter #1 ●●●●○
Pruneaux ●●●●○
Roc-A-Coe ●●●◐○

SHERRY – FINO

Pronounced 'Fee-No' this pale, dry style of sherry is best drunk young. It is produced under a layer of a kind of yeast known as 'flor' which protects the wine from oxidation.

Adonis ●●●●◐
Alaska Martini ●●●●○
Bamboo ●●●●◐
Bartender's Martini ●●●●○
Charlie Lychee'tini ●●●●○
Coronation ●●●○○
Coronation Martini ●●●◐○
Dolores ●●●●○
East Indian ●●●●◐
Granny's Martini ●●●○○
Hot Rum Punch ●●●◐○
Jerez ●●●●○
Nome ●●●●○
Saltecca ●●●○○
Salty Lychee Martini ●●●●○
Snowball ●●●◐○
Tuxedo Martini ●●●●◐

SHERRY - PEDRO XIMÉNEZ

A superbly rich dessert sherry made from sun-dried Pedro Ximénez (pronounced Hee-May-Neth) grapes.

Auntie's Hot Xmas Punch ●●●●○
Fruit & Nut Martini ●●●●○
Jerez ●●●●○
Pruneaux ●●●●○
Quarter Deck ●●●●○
Strudel Martini ●●●●◐
Trifle'tini ●●●◐○

SLOE GIN LIQUEUR

See 'Plymouth Sloe Gin Liqueur'

SOUR APPLE SCHNAPPS LIQUEUR

In the following recipes, a standard apple schnapps liqueur will not work: a sour version is required.

Apple & Melon Martini ●●●◐○
Apple Buck ●●●●○
Big Apple Martini ●●●◐○
Curdish Martini ●●●●○
The Game Bird ●●●●◐
Green Apple & Cucumber Martini ●●●●○
Pink Flamingo ●●●○○
Red Apple ●●●●○
Smoky Apple Martini ●●●◐○
Sour Apple Martini #1 (Popular US version) ●●●●○
Sour Apple Martini #2 (Deluxe US version) ●●●●◐
Vanilla Sensation ●●●●○
Viagra Falls ●●●◐○
Washington Apple ●●●●◐
Winter Martini ●●●●◐
Zhivago Martini ●●●●○

SOUR MIX

Sour mix is a term for a blend of lemon or lime juice mixed with sugar syrup. Commercial pre-mixed sour mix is available in a dried crystal or powdered form, often with the addition of pasteurised egg white. Margarita mix is a similar pre-mix, but with the addition of orange flavours. I strongly advocate the use of freshly squeezed juice and sugar syrup and in this guide they appear as separate ingredients.

SOUTHERN COMFORT

A whiskey-based spirit.

Alabama Slammer #1 ●●●◐○
Alabama Slammer #2 ●●●◐○
Avalanche Shot ●●◐○○
Bazooka ●●◐○○
The Big Easy ●●●●○
Canteen Martini ●●●◐○
Devil's Manhattan ●●●●○
Golden Nail ●●●●○
Hawaiian Cocktail ●●●●○
Honolulu Juicer ●●●◐○
Kentucky Colonel ●●●●○
Louisiana Trade ●●●◐○
Parlay Punch ●●●○○
Plantation Punch ●●●◐○
Red or Dead ●●●○○
Rhett Butler ●●●●○
Sailor's Comfort ●●●○○
Scarlett O'Hara ●●●○○
Slow Comfortable Screw ●●●◐○
Slow Comfortable Screw Against The Wall ●●●◐○
Southern Cider ●●●○○
Southern Manhattan ●●●●○
Southern Mint Cobbler ●●●●○
Southern Mule ●●●◐○
Southern Peach ●●●○○
Southern Punch ●●●◐○
Southern Tea-Knee ●●●●◐
Sundowner #2 ●●●●○
Too Close For Comfort ●●●◐○
Total Recall ●●●◐○
Wagon Wheel ●●●○○
Woodland Punch ●●●◐○

STRAWBERRY LIQUEUR

See 'Crème de Fraise (Strawberry) Liqueur'

SUGAR SYRUP

Many cocktails benefit from sweetening but granulated sugar does not dissolve easily in cold drinks. Hence pre-dissolved sugar syrup (also known as 'simple syrup') is used. Commercially made 'gomme sirop' (gum syrup) is sugar syrup with the addition of gum arabic, the crystallised sap of the acacia tree. Many bartenders don't like using gomme syrup but prefer to use simple or sugar syrup. Others prefer gomme as it adds mouth-feel and smoothness to some drinks.

Make your own sugar syrup by gradually pouring and stirring two cups of granulated sugar into a saucepan containing one cup of hot water and simmer until the sugar is dissolved. Do not let the water even come close to boiling and only simmer for as long as it takes to dissolve the sugar. Allow syrup to cool and pour into an empty bottle. Ideally, you should finely strain your syrup into the bottle to remove any undissolved crystals which could otherwise encourage crystallisation. If kept in a refrigerator this mixture will last for a couple of months.

A wide range of flavoured sugar syrups are commercially available. Orgeat (almond), passion fruit and vanilla are among the most popular. See also 'Pomegranate (Grenadine) Syrup'.

TEQUILA

Tequila is named after the town of the same name located about forty miles west of Guadalajara in the state of Jalisco, Mexico. Despite its lethal reputation, tequila is no stronger than other spirits and is usually bottled at 38% alc./vol. (76°proof). Another common misconception is that tequila sometimes has a worm in the bottle. This is not true. It is tequila's relation, mezcal, which comes with the 'worm' - which is in any case a moth larva. Mezcal is a very different spirit.

Tequila has a strong, herbal flavour with a slightly oily consistency. The best wood aged tequilas also have complex subtle flavours such as vanilla, a result of the ageing process.

Acapulco ●●●◐○
Adios ●●●◐○
Alice From Dallas ●●●◐○
Alice In Wonderland ●●●○○
All Fall Down ●●●◐○
Almond Old Fashioned ●●●●◐
Anita's Attitude Adjuster ●●●◐○
Bald Eagle Shot ●●◐○○
Bald Eagle Martini ●●●●◐
Beach Iced Tea ●●●◐○
Bee Sting ●●●●○
Bird Of Paradise ●●●●◐
Bloody Maria ●●●●○
Blue Margarita ●●●◐○
Blue Velvet Margarita ●●●●○
Boston Tea Party ●●●○○
Buena Vida ●●●●◐
Burning Bush Shot ●●○○○
C C Kazi ●●●●○
Cactus Banger ●●●●○
Cactus Jack ●●●◐○
Chihuahua Magarita ●●●◐○
Chimayo ●●●◐○
Cool Martini ●●●◐○
Crouching Tiger ●●●○○
Dirty Sanchez ●●●●○
Durango ●●●◐○
Easy Tiger ●●●●○
El Burro ●●●●○
El Diablo ●●●◐○
El Torado ●●●●◐
Elegante Margarita ●●●●◐
Estes ●●●●○
Estilo Viejo ●●●●◐
The Estribo ●●●◐○
Flatliner ●●●●●
The Flirt ●●●◐○
Floridita Margarita ●●●●○
Flutter ●●●●◐
Freddy Fudpucker ●●●◐○
Frida's Brow ●●●●○
Frozen Margarita ●●●●○
Ginger Margarita ●●●●○
Gold Rush Slammer ●●●○○
Golden Dragon ●●●◐○
Grand Margarita ●●●●●
Hong Kong Fuey ●●●○○
Hornitos Lau ●●●●○
Iguana ●●●◐○
Jalisco ●●●●○
Jalisco Espresso ●●●●◐
Japanese Slipper ●●●●○
Jose Collins ●●●●○
Kamikaze ●●●●○
Lavender Margarita ●●●●●
Lolita Margarita ●●●●◐
Lonely Bull ●●●◐○
Long Beach Iced Tea ●●●◐○
Long Island Iced Tea ●●●◐○
Long Island Spiced Tea ●●●◐○
Loved Up ●●●◐○
Lucky Lily Margarita ●●●●◐
Magic Bus ●●●◐○
Malcolm Lowry ●●●●○
Mango Margarita #1 (Served 'Up') ●●●●○
Mango Margarita #2 (Frozen) ●●●●○
Margarita #1 (Straight-up) ●●●●◐
Margarita #2 (On the Rocks) ●●●●◐
Margarita #3 (Frozen) ●●●●○
Margarita #4 (Salt Foam Float) ●●●◐○
Maria Theresa Margarita ●●●●○
Marmarita ●●●●○
Matador ●●●●○
Mayan ●●●◐○
Mayan Whore ●●●●○
Melon Margarita #1 (Served 'Up') ●●●●○
Melon Margarita #2 (Served Frozen) ●●●◐○
Mesa Fresca ●●●●○
Mexican ●●●●○
Mexican 55 ●●●●○
Mexican Coffee (Hot) ●●●◐○
Mexican Manhattan ●●●●○
Mexican Martini ●●●◐○
Mexican Melon Ball ●●●◐○
Mexican Mule ●●●●◐
Mexican Surfer ●●●●○
Mexican Tea (Hot) ●●●●◐
Mexican City ●●●●◐
Mexicano (Hot) ●●●●◐
Million Dollar Margarita ●●●●◐
Mister Stu ●●●◐○
Mojito de Casa ●●●●○
Nautilus ●●●●◐
New Port Codebreaker ●●●◐○
Paloma ●●●●◐
Passion Fruit Margarita ●●●●○
Passion Killer ●●●○○
Pineapple & Sage Margarita ●●●●◐
Pineapple Margarita ●●●●○
Pink Grapefruit Margarita ●●●●○
Playa Del Mar ●●●●○
Pomegranate Margarita ●●●●◐
Purple Turtle ●●●◐○
Raging Bull ●●●◐○
Raspberry Margarita ●●●●○
La Rosa Margarita ●●●●○
Rosarita Margarita ●●●●○
Rosita ●●●●○
Royal Velvet Margarita ●●●◐○
Rude Cosmopolitan ●●●●◐
Rude Ginger Cosmopolitan ●●●●○
Saltecca ●●●○○

Silk Stockings ●●●◐○
Sloe Tequila ●●●◐○
South Of The Border ●●●○○
Strawberry Margarita ●●●●○
Tequila Fizz ●●●●○
Tequila Mockingbird ●●●○○
Tequila Slammer ●●●○○
Tequila Smash ●●●●◐
Tequila Sour ●●●●◐
Tequila Sunrise ●●●◐○
Tequila Sunset ●●●●○
Tequila'tini ●●●◐○
Texas Iced Tea ●●●◐○
Tiki Bar Margarita ●●●●◐
Tokyo Iced Tea ●●●◐○
Tomahawk ●●●◐○
Tommy's Margarita ●●●●●
Tongue Twister ●●●○○
Total Recall ●●●◐○
Tres Compadres Margarita ●●●●◐
Tutti Frutti ●●●○○
TVR ●●●○○
Vampiro ●●●●○
Watermelon & Basil Smash ●●●●○

TOMATO JUICE

Originally from Peru, the tomato was imported into Spain in the 16th century.

Buy a quality, chilled, freshly pressed juice or make your own. Avoid sweet packaged juices made from concentrate.

Basil Mary ●●●●○
Bloody Joseph ●●●◐○
Bloody Maria ●●●●○
Bloody Maru ●●●◐○
Bloody Mary (1930s recipe) ●●◐○○
Bloody Mary (modern recipe) ●●●●◐
Bloody Shame (Mocktail) ●●●◐○
Cubanita ●●●●○
Peppered Mary ●●●●○
Prairie Oyster ●●●◐○
Red Snapper ●●●●○
Sangrita ●●●●◐
Tokyo Bloody Mary ●●●●○
Vampiro ●●●●○

TRIPLE SEC

An orange-flavoured liqueur often used in cocktails. Cointreau makes a good substitute.

TUACA LIQUEUR

Apple Crumble Martini #2 ●●●●○

Dramatic Martini ●●●◐○
Galvanised Nail ●●●●◐
Hammer Of The Gods ●●◐○○
Honey Wall ●●●●○
Irish Manhattan ●●●●○
Italian Job #2 ●●●●○
I.V.F. Martini ●●●◐○
Karamel Sutra Martini ●●●○○
Mystique Martini ●●●●○
Orange Custard Martini ●●●◐○
Pepper & Vanilla'tini ●●●●◐
Sophisticated Savage ●●●◐○
Stealth ●●●◐○
Tuscan Mule ●●●◐○
Walnut Martini ●●●●○
Wonky Martini ●●●●◐

VANILLA (SCHNAPPS) LIQUEUR

The term schnapps traditionally suggests a clear, strong spirit. However, in recent years the term has come to refer to sweet liqueurs of only 20-24% alc./vol., bearing no resemblance to the strong dry schnapps from which they take their name. I've added the term 'liqueur' in this guide to help make the type of vanilla schnapps called for more obvious.

Blush Martini ●●●◐○
Cool Martini ●●●◐○
Custard Tart ●●●●○
Doughnut Martini ●●●◐○
Elle For Leather ●●●●◐
Kentucky Dream ●●●●○
Key Lime Pie #3 ●●●●○

VERMOUTH - DRY

Vermouth as we know it today was invented during the 18th century in the ancient Kingdom of Savoy, which is now divided between north-west Italy and parts of southern and eastern France. At that time the region had an abundance of grapes and produced only very ordinary wines. As a result, enterprising types fortified wine, added herbs and spices, and created vermouth.

Affinity ●●●◐○
Algonquin ●●●●○
Almond & Apricot Martini ●●●●○
Almond & Coconut Martini ●●●◐○
Almond Martini #2 ●●●●○
American Beauty ●●●●◐
Apple Manhattan ●●●●○
Arnaud Martini ●●●●○
Aviator ●●●●○
Bamboo ●●●●◐
Bartender's Martini ●●●●○
Black Bison Martini ●●●●◐
Blackthorn English ●●●●○
Blackthorn Irish ●●●◐○
Blue Star ●●●○○
Bobby Burns ●●●●○
Boomerang ●●●●○
Boston Tea Party ●●●○○
Bourbonella ●●●●○
Bradford ●●●●○
Brainstorm ●●●●◐
Bronx ●●●◐○
Brooklyn #1 ●●●●○
Brooklyn #2 ●●●●○
Cajun Martini ●●●○○
China Martini ●●●◐○
Chocolate & Cranberry Martini ●●●●○
Chocolate Martini ●●●●○
Chocolate Mint Martini ●●●●○
Claridge ●●●●○
Clipper Cocktail ●●●◐○
Club Cocktail ●●●●○
Coronation ●●●○○
Coronation Martini ●●●◐○
Cranberry Martini ●●●◐○
Delmonico ●●●◐○
Delmonico Special ●●●◐○
Devil ●●●◐○
Diamond Dog ●●●◐○
Dickens' Martini ●●●●◐
Diplomat ●●●◐○
Dirty Martini ●●●◐○
Donegal ●●●●○
Dry Ice Martini ●●●●◐
Dry Martini ●●●●●
Dry Martini #2 (Naked) ●●●●○
Dry Orange Martini ●●●●◐
East Indian ●●●●◐
El Torado ●●●●◐
Elderflower Martini ●●●●○
Elisian ●●●●○
English Rose ●●●●○
Fiesta ●●●●○
Fly Like A Butterfly ●●●●○
Franklin Martini ●●●●●
Frisky Lemonade ●●●◐○
Gibson ●●●●◐
Ginger & Lemongrass Martini ●●●●○
Gingertini ●●●●○
Golf Cocktail ●●●●○
Harvard ●●●◐○
Hawaiian Martini ●●●●○
Hoopla ●●●●○
Imperial Martini ●●●○○
Incognito ●●●◐○
Income Tax Cocktail ●●●●○
Intimate Martini ●●●●○
The Journalist ●●●●○
Jupiter Martini ●●●◐○
Knickerbocker Martini ●●●◐○
Knockout Martini ●●●◐○
Lavender Martini ●●●●○
Lemon Martini ●●●●◐
Livingstone ●●●●○
Lutkins Special Martini ●●●◐○
Lychee Martini ●●●●○
Macka ●●●◐○
Manhattan Dry ●●●●◐
Manhattan Perfect ●●●●●
Marguerite Martini ●●●●○
Maurice Martini ●●●◐○
Medium Martini ●●●●◐
Merry Widow #1 ●●●◐○
Merry Widow #2 ●●●◐○
Merry-Go-Round Martini ●●●●○
Mint Martini ●●●●◐
Moonshine Martini ●●●●◐
Mountain ●●●◐○
Noon ●●●●○
Oddball Manhattan Dry ●●●●○
Old Pal ●●●◐○
Paisley Martini ●●●●○
Pall Mall Martini ●●●●○
Parisian Martini ●●●●○
Parisian Spring Punch ●●●●○
Peggy Martini ●●●○○
Perfect Martini ●●●◐○
Peter Pan Martini ●●●●○
Petto Martini ●●●●◐
Piccadilly Martini ●●●●◐
Plum Cocktail ●●●◐○
Plum Martini ●●●●○
Poet's Dream ●●●●◐
Pompanski Martini ●●●●○
Presidente ●●●●○
Princess Mary's Pride ●●●○○
Princeton Martini ●●●●○
Queen Martini ●●●●○
The Rose #1 (original) ●●●●◐
The Rose #2 ●●●◐○
The Rose #3 ●●●●◐
Roselyn Martini ●●●●◐
Rosita ●●●●○
Sage Martini ●●●●○
Satan's Whiskers (Straight) ●●●●◐
Savoy Special #1 ●●●●○
Scofflaw ●●●●○
The Scott ●●●●○
Shamrock #2 ●●●●○
Silver Martini ●●●◐○
Sloppy Joe ●●●●○
Smoky Martini #1 ●●●●○
Smoky Martini #2 ●●●○○
Snyder Martini ●●●●○
So-So Martini ●●●●●
Strawberry Blonde Martini ●●●◐○
Sunshine Cocktail #1 ●●●●◐
Sunshine Cocktail #2 ●●●●○
Tango Martini #1 ●●●●○
Tequila'tini ●●●◐○
Texsun ●●●◐○
Tipperary #2 ●●●●◐
Trinity ●●●○○
Tuxedo Martini ●●●●◐
Twentieth Century Martini ●●●◐○
Urban Holistic ●●●◐○
Vanilla Sensation ●●●●○
The Vesper Martini ●●●●●
Violet Affinity ●●●●◐
Vodkatini ●●●●◐
Walnut Martini ●●●●○
Webster Martini ●●●◐○
Wet Martini ●●●●◐
What The Hell ●●●●○
Winter Martini ●●●●◐

VERMOUTH - SWEET (ROSSO)

Popular belief has it that Italian vermouth was originally sweet and produced from red wine, while French vermouth was typically dry and white. Hence, many old cocktail books refer to 'French' for dry vermouth and 'Italian' where sweet vermouth is called for. The truth is that the division between the styles of the two countries was never that defined and producers in both countries now make both sweet

(rosso) and dry styles. Although red vermouth was initially based on red wine, now virtually all is made from white wine with caramel blended in to give an amber colour.

Abbey Martini ●●●◐○
Adonis ●●●●◐
Affinity ●●●◐○
Aviator ●●●●○
Behemoth ●●●●○
Blood & Sand ●●●●◐
Bolero ●●●◐○
Bombay ●●●●◐
Boomerang ●●●●○
Bronx ●●●◐○
Brooklyn #1 ●●●●○
Caramel Manhattan ●●●●◐
Club Cocktail ●●●●○
Corpse Reviver ●●●●○
Damn-The-Weather ●●●◐○
Delmonico ●●●◐○
Devil's Manhattan ●●●●○
Diplomat ●●●◐○
Elisian ●●●●○
Embassy Royal ●●●◐○
Especial Day ●●●●◐
Finitaly ●●●●○
Fly Like A Butterfly ●●●●○
Flying Scotsman ●●●●○
Gin & It ●●●●○
Grappa Manhattan ●●●●○
Hanky-Panky Martini ●●●●○
Harvard ●●●◐○
Hawaiian Martini ●●●●○
I'll Take Manhattan ●●●●○
Income Tax Cocktail ●●●●○
James Joyce ●●●●○
The Journalist ●●●●○
Knickerbocker Martini ●●●◐○
Leap Year Martini ●●●○○
Leave It To Me Martini ●●●◐○
Little Italy ●●●◐○
London Calling ●●●◐○
Loud Speaker Martini ●●●◐○
Luxury Cocktail ●●●◐○
Macka ●●●◐○
Manhattan Perfect ●●●●●
Manhattan Sweet ●●●●●
Manhattan Island ●●●●○
Martinez ●●●●●
Martini Special ●●●●◐
Maurice Martini ●●●◐○
Medium Martini ●●●●◐
Merry-Go-Round Martini ●●●●○
Mexican Manhattan ●●●●○
Milano ●●●●◐
The Million Dollar Cocktail ●●●●◐
Moravian Cocktail ●●●○○
Mountain ●●●◐○
Negroni ●●●●◐
Noon ●●●●○
Old Fashioned Caddy ●●●●○
Opening Shot ●●●◐○
Orange Bloom Martini ●●●●◐
Orange Martini ●●●●○
Pall Mall Martini ●●●●○
Palm Beach ●●●◐○
Park Avenue ●●●●○
Perfect Martini ●●●◐○
Petto Martini ●●●●◐
Picca ●●●●○
Pichuncho Martini ●●●●◐
Princess Pride ●●●◐○
Queen Martini ●●●●○
Rat Pack Manhattan ●●●●○
Remember The Maine ●●●●◐
Rob Roy #1 ●●●●○
Rob Roy #2 ●●●●◐
Rosita ●●●●○
Ruby Martini #2 ●●●◐○
Satan's Whiskers (Straight) ●●●●◐
Scotch Negroni ●●●●○
Shamrock #1 ●●●○○
Sir Thomas ●●●●○
Southern Manhattan ●●●●○
The Star #1 ●●●●○
Tango Martini #1 ●●●●○
Tipperary #1 ●●●●◐
Trilby ●●●●○
Tulip Cocktail ●●●●○
Turf Martini ●●●●○
Vieux Carré Cocktail ●●●●◐
Violet Affinity ●●●●◐
Voodoo ●●●●○
Vowel Cocktail ●●●●◐
Wonky Martini ●●●●◐
Yacht Club ●●●◐○

VIOLET LIQUEUR

A liqueur flavoured with the purple flowers from a small perennial plant. Usually from France, particularly Toulouse.

Blue Moon ●●●◐○
Bramblette ●●●◐○
Palma Violet Martini ●●●◐○
Purple Pear Martini ●●●●○
Violet Affinity ●●●●◐

VODKA – UNFLAVOURED GRAIN

See 'Ketel One Vodka'

VODKA – ALMOND FLAVOURED

Almond & Apricot Martini ●●●●○
Almond & Coconut Martini ●●●◐○
Almond & Sake Martini ●●●●○
Almond Collins ●●●●○
Almond Martini #2 ●●●●○
Caramelised Apple Martini ●●●●○

VODKA – APPLE FLAVOURED

Apple & Blackberry Pie ●●●◐○
Apple Martini #3 ●●●●○
Apple Mojito ●●●●○
Applily Married ●●●●◐
Toffee Apple Martini ●●●●○

VODKA – BISON GRASS FLAVOURED

See 'Zubrówka vodka'

VODKA – CHERRY FLAVOURED

Cherry Martini ●●●●○

VODKA – CITRUS FLAVOURED

See 'Ketel One Citroen'

VODKA – CRANBERRY FLAVOURED

Apple & Cranberry Pie ●●●●○
Chocolate & Cranberry Martini ●●●●○
Cranberry & Mint Martini ●●●●○
Cranberry Martini ●●●◐○
Cranberry Sauce ●●●●○
Finitaly ●●●●○
Finn Rouge ●●●◐○
Finnberry Martini ●●●●○
The Juxtaposition ●●●●○
Lago Cosmo ●●●◐○
Nutty Berry'tini ●●●◐○
Spiced Cranberry Martini ●●●●○
Spicy Finn ●●●●○
Tarraberry'tini ●●●●○
Ugurundu ●●●◐○

VODKA – LIME FLAVOURED

Blimey ●●●●○
Camomile & Blackthorn Breeze ●●●●◐
Emerald Martini ●●●●○
Frisky Lemonade ●●●◐○
Grassy Finnish ●●●●○
Key Lime ●●●●○
Lime Breeze ●●●◐○
Lime Sour ●●●●○
Limelite ●●●○○
Limeosa ●●●◐○
Limerick ●●●●○
Limey ●●●◐○
Limey Cosmo ●●●●○
Limey Mule ●●●●○
Liminal Shot ●●●○○
Limited Liability ●●●●◐
Limnology ●●●◐○
Limousine ●●●●○
Molotov Cocktail ●●●◐○

VODKA – MANGO

Hawaiian Seabreeze ●●●◐○
Jumbled Fruit Julep ●●●◐○

VODKA – ORANGE FLAVOURED

Blood Orange ●●●○○
Blue Monday ●●●◐○
Bug Juice ●●●◐○
Chill-Out Martini ●●●○○
Cordless Screwdriver ●●●○○
Creamsicle ●●●●○
Creamy Creamsicle ●●●◐○
Eastern Promise ●●●●○
Eden ●●●●○
Hakkatini ●●●●○
Jaffa Martini ●●●◐○
M.G.F. ●●●●○
Mandarinitini ●●●○○
Orange Mojito ●●●●○
Oranjiniha ●●●●○
Pink Flamingo ●●●○○
Satsuma Martini ●●●◐○
South China Breeze ●●●●○
The Suzy Wong Martini ●●●◐○
Urban Oasis ●●●●○
The Windsor Rose ●●●◐○

VODKA – PEAR FLAVOURED

Apples 'N' Pears ●●●●◐
Steep Flight ●●●●●

VODKA – PEPPER FLAVOURED

Red Marauder ●●●●◐

VODKA - RASPBERRY FLAVOURED

Amaro Dolce ●●●◐○
Berry Nice ●●●◐○
Blue Raspberry Martini ●●●●○
Cascade Martini ●●●●○
Crimson Tide ●●●●○
Double Vision ●●●○○
Esquire #2 ●●●◐○
Fruit & Nut Chocolate Martini ●●●●○
Illicit Affair ●●●◐○
Koi Yellow ●●●●○
Kurrant Affair ●●●○○
Metropolitan ●●●●○
Nuts & Berries ●●●●○
Pale Rider ●●●○○
Plum Pudding Martini ●●●◐○
Raspberry Mocha'tini ●●●●○
Raspberry Sake'tini ●●●◐○
Rasputin ●●●○○
Razzmatazz ●●●○○
The Red Army ●●●◐○
Scandinavian Pop ●●●○○
Ski Breeze ●●●○○
Strasberi Sling ●●●◐○
Strawberry Blonde Martini ●●●◐○
Sweet Louise ●●●○○
Tartini ●●●●○
Trifle Martini ●●●◐○
Urban Oasis ●●●●○
Venus in Furs ●●●◐○
Verdi Martini ●●●●○
Wild Promenade Martini ●●●●○

VODKA - VANILLA FLAVOURED

Aphrodisiac ●●●●○
Apple Strudel Martini #2 ●●●●◐
Banoffee Martini ●●●●○
Bon Bon Martini ●●●●○
Butterfly's Kiss ●●●◐○
Cherry Alexander ●●●●○
Chocolate & Cranberry Martini ●●●●○
Crème Anglaise Martini ●●●●○
Crème Brûlée Martini ●●●●○
Easter Martini ●●●●◐
Egg Custard Martini ●●●◐○
Fruit & Nut Martini ●●●●○
Heaven Scent ●●●◐○
Hunk Martini ●●●●◐
Irish Espresso'tini ●●●●◐
Jolt'ini ●●●●○
Karamel Sutra Martini ●●●○○
Key Lime ●●●●○
Nine-20-Seven ●●●●○
Peach Melba Martini ●●●◐○
Pear & Vanilla Rickey ●●●◐○
Pepper & Vanilla'tini ●●●●◐
Plum Pudding Martini ●●●◐○
Razzzzzberry Martini ●●●◐○
Russian Bride ●●●●○
Snow Fall Martini ●●●●○
Socialite ●●●◐○
Tarte Tatin Martini ●●●●○
Thriller From Vanilla ●●●●○
Triangular Martini ●●●●○
Triple 'C' Martini ●●●●◐
Turkish Delight ●●●●○
Upside-Down Raspberry Cheesecake ●●●●○
Vacation ●●●◐○
Valkyrie ●●●◐○
Vanilla & Raspberry Martini ●●●●○
Vanilla Laika ●●●◐○
Vanilla Sensation ●●●●○
Vanilla Vodka Sour ●●●●○
Vanilla'tini ●●●◐○
Vanitini ●●●◐○
Vante Martini ●●●●◐
Wild Honey ●●●◐○
Wonky Martini ●●●●◐
Zhivago Martini ●●●●○

WATER

The dilution of a cocktail is key to achieving the right balance. This varies according to how hard you shake, how cold your ice is and how much ice you use. Even if a recipe doesn't call for a splash of water, don't be scared to add some if you feel it needs it. Use spring or filtered water and keep a bottle in your refrigerator next to the bottle of sugar syrup.

WHISKEY - BOURBON

Bourbon can be made anywhere in the USA, but it is native to the South, and only Kentucky bourbon can advertise the state where it is made. Thus, there is no bourbon with Tennessee on the label.

Bourbons are produced in a specific way. A bourbon must contain at least 51% corn (but not more than 80%), be distilled to a strength of not more than 80% alc./vol., be stored in charred new white oak barrels at a strength no higher than 62.5% alc./vol. and aged for at least two years, and be reduced at the time of bottling to no lower than 40% alc./vol..

Straight bourbon whiskey must be aged for a minimum of two years in new, charred oak casks. Any whiskey which has been aged for less than four years must state its age on the label. Generally, two to four year old whiskies are best avoided. No colouring or flavouring may be added to straight whiskey.

Adam And Eve ●●●●○
American Pie Martini ●●●●○
Americana ●●●◐○
Apple Manhattan ●●●●○
Apricot Sour ●●●●○
Avenue ●●●◐○
Barbary Coast Highball ●●●◐○
Behemoth ●●●●○
Blinker ●●●●○
Boiler Maker ●●●◐○
Boomerang ●●●●○
Borderline ●●●◐○
Boston Flip ●●●●○
Bourbon Blush ●●●●◐
Bourbon Cookie ●●●●○
Bourbon Milk Punch ●●●◐○
Bourbon Smash ●●●◐○
Bourbonella ●●●●○
Brainstorm ●●●●◐
Brighton Punch ●●●●◐
Brooklyn #1 ●●●●○
Brooklyn #2 ●●●●○
Caramel Manhattan ●●●●◐
Casanova ●●●●○
Chas ●●●●○
Chinese Passion ●●●◐○
Chocolate Sazerac ●●●●○
Colonel Collins ●●●●○
Colonel T ●●●◐○
Daisy Duke ●●●◐○
Dandy Cocktail ●●●●○
Derby Fizz ●●●●◐
Devil's Manhattan ●●●●○
Difford's Old-Fashioned ●●●●◐
Dixie Dew ●●●●○
Doughnut Martini ●●●◐○
Egg Custard Martini ●●●◐○
Embassy Royal ●●●◐○
Epiphany ●●●●○
Esquire #1 ●●●●○
Fancy Free ●●●●○
Fizz ●●●●○
Flaming Henry ●●●◐○
Flamingo #1 ●●●◐○
Flip ●●●●◐
Fourth Of July Cocktail ●●●○○
Fruit Sour ●●●●○
Gingerbread Martini ●●●●○
Golden Nail ●●●●○
Grand Sazerac ●●●●○
Mughal Martini ●●●●○
Horse's Neck With A Kick ●●●○○
I'll Take Manhattan ●●●●○
Irish Manhattan ●●●●○
Jambouree ●●●●○
Julep ●●●●●
Julep Martini ●●●●◐
Kentucky Colonel ●●●●○
Kentucky Dream ●●●●○
Kentucky Jewel ●●●●○
Kentucky Mac ●●●◐○
Kentucky Muffin ●●●●○
Kentucky Pear ●●●●◐
Kentucky Tea ●●●◐○
Klondike ●●●◐○
Little Italy ●●●◐○
Lucky Lindy ●●●◐○
Man-Bour-Tini ●●●●○
Manhattan Dry ●●●●◐
Manhattan Perfect ●●●●●
Manhattan Sweet ●●●●●
Maple Old-Fashioned ●●●●○
Maple Leaf ●●●●○
Marquee ●●●●○
Met Manhattan ●●●●○
Millionaire ●●●●○
Mint Julep ●●●●●
Mississippi Punch ●●●●○
Mocha Martini ●●●●◐
Mountain ●●●◐○
Mrs Robinson #1 ●●●●○
New Orleans Mule ●●●◐○
New Orleans Punch ●●●◐○
New Yorker ●●●●○
Nutty Nashville ●●●●○
Oddball Manhattan Dry ●●●●○
O'Henry ●●●◐○
Old Fashioned #1 (Classic Version) ●●●●●
Old Fashioned #2 (US Version) ●●●●◐
Old Pal ●●●◐○
Opening Shot ●●●◐○
Paris Sour ●●●●○
Parlay Punch ●●●○○
Passbour Cooler ●●●○○
Pinky Pincher ●●●●○
Port Light ●●●◐○
Pousse-café ●●◐○○
Prune Face ●●●●○
Quebec ●●●●○
Rat Pack Manhattan ●●●●○
Rattlesnake ●●●◐○
Red Apple ●●●●○
Remember The Maine ●●●●◐
Sazerac ●●●●●
Scofflaw ●●●●○
Seelbach ●●●○○
Shamrock #1 ●●●○○
Sir Thomas ●●●●○
Snoopy ●●●●○
Southern Manhattan ●●●●○
Stiletto ●●●◐○
Stoney Point Meadow ●●●●○
Suburban ●●●●○
Tailor Made ●●●●○
Texsun ●●●◐○
Thunderbird ●●●●○
Toast & Orange Martini ●●●●○
Union Club ●●●●○
Vieux Carré Cocktail ●●●●◐
Ward Eight ●●●●○
The Wentworth ●●●●○
Whiskey Collins ●●●●◐
Whiskey Daisy ●●●◐○
Whiskey Sour #1 (Classic Formula) ●●●●○
Whiskey Sour #2 (Difford's Formula) ●●●●●
Whiskey Squirt ●●●●○
Yule Luvit ●●●◐○
Zhivago Martini ●●●●○

WHISKEY - IRISH

Due to the domination of Irish Distillers, the producers' group now owned by Pernod-Ricard, as a rule Irish whiskey is triple-distilled and not peated and hence light and smooth. (The independent Cooley Distillery produces some notable exceptions to these rules.)

Blackthorn Irish ●●●◐○
Causeway ●●●◐○
Donegal ●●●●○
Gloom Lifter ●●●●○
Irish Coffee ●●●●○
Irish Coffee Martini ●●●●◐
James Joyce ●●●●○
Pappy Honeysuckle ●●●●◐
St Patrick's Day ●●●●○
Shamrock #2 ●●●●○
Tipperary #1 ●●●●◐

WHISKEY - TENNESSEE

The main difference between bourbon and Tennessee whiskey lies in the Lincoln County Process, a form of charcoal filtration. In the 1820s someone (possibly Alfred Eaton) started filtering whiskey through maple charcoal. Tennessee whiskeys are now filtered through 10-12 feet of maple charcoal before they are bottled, removing impurities and giving a 'sooty' sweetness to the finished spirit. A Tennessee whiskey must be made from at least 51% of one particular grain. This could be rye or wheat, but most often, as with bourbon, corn is the favoured base.

Bee Sting ●●●●○
Black Jack ●●●○○
Cherry Mash Sour ●●●◐○
Cicada Cocktail ●●●◐○
Eclipse ●●●●◐
The GTO Cocktail ●●●◐○
Hot Buttered Jack ●●●●○
Jack Frost ●●●○○
Jack Punch ●●●●○
Jacktini ●●●◐○
Jodi May ●●●◐○
Jumping Jack Flash ●●●●○
Lynchburg Lemonade ●●●●○
Mississippi Schnapper ●●●◐○
Mountain Sipper ●●●◐○
Raspberry Lynchburg ●●●◐○
Southern Punch ●●●◐○
Tennessee Berry Mule ●●●●○
Tennessee Iced Tea ●●●●○
Tennessee Rush ●●●◐○
Tolleytown Punch ●●●◐○

WHISKY – CANADIAN

John Molson, though better known for brewing, is credited with first introducing whisky to Canada in 1799. His lead was followed by Scottish emigrants who found their new home had plentiful and cheap grain. Whisky production started at Kingston, on Lake Ontario, and spread as farming developed. However, barley was not common, so they reduced the amount of barley and added corn, wheat and rye instead.

In 1875, government regulation specified that Canadian whisky must be made from cereal grains in Canada, using continuous distillation. The rules also state that Canadian whisky must be aged a minimum of 3 years and a maximum of 18 years in charred oak barrels.

Captain Collins ●●●◐○
Quebec ●●●●○

WHISKY - SCOTCH

For whisky to be called 'Scotch whisky' it must be a) made in Scotland and b) aged in oak casks for a minimum of three years. Malt whisky – based on malted barley - was the original Scottish whisky and is at the core of all decent Scotch. But, although it has recently become extremely popular, the majority of pot still malt whisky is sold in blends (which include non-malt whiskies), not as single malt whiskies (which do not). Blended Scotch whisky, or 'Scotch' for short is the world's most popular whisky and accounts for well over 85% of all Scottish whisky.

A standard blended whisky will probably contain 15-40% malt and have no age statement (though every whisky in it will have been aged at least three years). Some blends describe themselves as 'deluxe' - this is a reference to the percentage of malt whisky in the blend and the average age of the whisky. A deluxe brand will usually contain more than 45% pot-still malt and will show an age statement of 12 years or more.

Affinity ●●●◐○
Aggravation ●●●●○
Apple Crumble Martini #1 ●●●◐○
Apple Mac ●●●●○
Aquarius ●●●◐○
Atholl Brose ●●●●○
Auld Acquaintance ●●●○○
Barbary Coast Martini ●●●●○
Bessie & Jessie ●●●◐○
Blood & Sand ●●●●◐
Bloody Joseph ●●●◐○
Blue Blazer ●●●○○
Bobby Burns ●●●●○
Boston Tea Party ●●●○○
The Broadmoor ●●●●◐
Brubaker Old-Fashioned ●●●●○
Cameron'tini ●●●●◐
Cappercaille ●●●●○
Celtic Margarita ●●●●◐
Chin Chin ●●●●○
Collar & Cuff ●●●●○
Elle For Leather ●●●●◐
Flying Scotsman ●●●●○
Galvanised Nail ●●●●◐
The Game Bird ●●●●◐
GE Blonde ●●●●◐
Godfather ●●●◐○
Gold ●●●○○
Golden Mac ●●●◐○
Golden Shot ●●●○○
Hair Of The Dog ●●●●○
Heather Julep ●●●●◐
Highland Sling ●●●●○
Honey & Marmalade Dram'tini ●●●●◐
Hot Toddy #1 ●●●●◐
Hot Toddy #2 ●●●●◐
Linstead ●●●●◐
Liquorice Whiskey Sour ●●●●◐
Loch Almond ●●●●○
Lychee Mac ●●●◐○
Mac Orange ●●●◐○
Maple Pomme ●●●●○
Mary Queen of Scots ●●●●◐
Milk & Honey Martini ●●●●◐
Morning Glory Fizz ●●●●○
Mystique ●●●◐○
Mystique Martini ●●●●○
Old Fashioned Caddy ●●●●○
Paisley Martini ●●●●○
Pear Shaped #1 (Deluxe Version) ●●●●◐
Pear Shaped #2 (Popular Version) ●●●●◐
Picca ●●●●○
Pineapple Blossom ●●●●○
Polly's Special ●●●●○
Red Breast ●●●◐○
Red Neck Martini ●●●●○
Remsen Cooler ●●●●○
Rob Roy #1 ●●●●◐
Rob Roy #2 ●●●●◐
R U Bobby Moore? ●●●●◐
Rusty Nail ●●●●○
Scotch Bounty Martini ●●●◐○
Scotch Milk Punch ●●●◐○
Scotch Negroni ●●●●○
The Scott ●●●●○
Silent Third ●●●◐○
Silver Fizz ●●●●○
Sling ●●●●○
Smoky Apple Martini ●●●◐○
Smoky Martini #1 ●●●●○
Sour ●●●◐○
Speyside Martini ●●●●○
Sporran Breeze ●●●●◐
Sweet Science ●●●◐○
Swizzle ●●●●◐
Thriller Martini ●●●●○
Toddy Martini ●●●◐○
Trilby ●●●●○
Trinity ●●●○○
Vowel Cocktail ●●●●◐
Whiskey Cobbler ●●●○○
Whisky Fizz ●●●●○
Whisky Mac ●●●◐○
White Knight ●●●◐○
Wild Honey ●●●◐○

WHITE CRÈME DE CACAO LIQUEUR

A number of recipes require the chocolate flavour of crème de cacao but without the dark brown colour. White crème de cacao liqueurs are made by extracting the flavour of roasted cacao beans by distillation instead of percolation. This also typically gives white crème de cacao liqueurs a lighter flavour than their dark counterparts.

Ace of Clubs Daiquiri ●●●●◐
After Eight ●●●○○
Alexander ●●●◐○
Alexander the Great ●●●◐○
All White Frappé ●●●◐○
Apple Strudel Martini ●●●◐○
Autumn Punch ●●●●◐
Avalanche Shot ●●◐○○
Banshee ●●●○○
Barbara ●●●○○
Barbary Coast Highball ●●●◐○
Barbary Coast Martini ●●●●○
Behemoth ●●●●○
Bird of Paradise ●●●●◐
Black Martini ●●●●◐
Brandy Alexander ●●●●○
Butterscotch Martini ●●●●○
Cherry Alexander ●●●●○
Choc & Nut Martini ●●●◐○
Chocolate & Cranberry Martini ●●●●○
Chocolate Martini ●●●●○
Chocolate Mint Martini ●●●●○
Chocolate Sazerac ●●●●○
DC Martini ●●●●○
Easter Martini ●●●●◐
Flying Grasshopper ●●●◐○
French Kiss #2 ●●●◐○
Frida's Brow ●●●●○
Fruit & Nut Chocolate Martini ●●●●○
Fu Manchu Daiquiri ●●●●○
Give Me A Dime ●●●●○
Golden Cadillac ●●●◐○
Hazelnut Martini ●●●◐○
Heavens Above ●●●◐○
Kretchma ●●●◐○
Lemon Chiffon Pie ●●●●○
Lola ●●●◐○
Melon Collie Martini ●●●●○
Nutcracker Sweet ●●●◐○
Pago Pago ●●●◐○
Pall Mall Martini ●●●●○
Pini ●●●●◐
Pink Cloud ●●●○○
Pink Sin Martini ●●●○○
Princess Mary ●●●○○
Rattlesnake Shot ●●●○○
Russian ●●●◐○
Russian Bride ●●●●○
Savannah ●●●◐○
Scotch Bounty Martini ●●●◐○
Screaming Banana Banshee ●●●◐○
Silk Stockings ●●●◐○
Smartini ●●●●○
Summer Rose Martini ●●●●○
Superminty-Chocolatini ●●●◐○
Top Banana Shot ●●●◐○
Turkish Delight ●●●●○
Twentieth Century Martini ●●●◐○
Velvet Hammer ●●●◐○
White Elephant ●●●◐○
White Stinger ●●●◐○

WHITE CRÈME DE MENTHE LIQUEUR

White crème de menthe is an aromatic liqueur that's flavoured with oil extracted from fresh mint leaves. Its is great served over ice (preferably crushed) as a digestif or blended in a range of cocktails.

After Six Shot ●●◐○○
Afterburner ●●●○○
All White Frappé ●●●◐○
American Beauty ●●●●◐
Bald Eagle Shot ●●◐○○
Chiclet Daiquiri ●●●◐○
Chocolate Mint Martini ●●●●○
Dixie Dew ●●●●○
Irish Charlie ●●●○○
Knockout Martini ●●●◐○
Miami Daiquiri ●●●●○
Mint Cocktail ●●●●◐
Mint Fizz ●●●◐○
Monte Carlo Imperial ●●●○○
Stinger ●●●●○
Superminty-Chocolatini ●●●◐○
Tick-Tack Martini ●●●○○
Trinity ●●●○○
White Stinger ●●●◐○

WINE - RED

The acidity in table wine can balance a cocktail in a similar way to citrus juice. Avoid heavily oaked wines.

American Beauty ●●●●◐
Caravan ●●●○○
Cardinal Punch ●●●◐○
Claret Cobbler ●●●●○
Cobbled Raspberry Martini ●●●●◐
Cosmopolitan Delight ●●●●◐
DiVino's ●●●●○
Hot Red Blooded Frenchman ●●●●○
Italian Job #2 ●●●●○ (Shiraz)
Mulled Wine ●●●●○
New Yorker ●●●●○
Red Angel ●●●●○
Red Rover ●●●●○
La Sang ●●●●○
Sangaree ●●●●○
Sangria ●●●◐○
Sangria Martini ●●●●○
Tripleberry ●●●●○
Vanilla & Raspberry Martini ●●●●○

WINE - WHITE

The acidity in table wine can balance a cocktail in a similar way to citrus juice. The grassy notes in Sauvignon Blanc make this grape varietal particularly suitable for cocktail use.

Apache ●●●○○
Blueberry Martini #2 (simple) ●●●●○
Brazilian Berry ●●●●○
Canary Flip ●●●●◐
Coronation ●●●○○
Double Grape Martini ●●●●◐
GE Blonde ●●●●◐
Grapple Martini ●●●●○
I B Damm'd ●●●●◐
Italian Sun ●●●●○
Jerez ●●●●○
Kir ●●●◐○
Kir Martini ●●●◐○
LCB Martini ●●●●○
M.C. Martini ●●●●●
Mint Cocktail ●●●●◐
Mint Martini ●●●●◐
Moonlight Martini ●●●●○
Orchard Breeze ●●●●◐
Palermo ●●●●◐
Pappy Honeysuckle ●●●●◐
R U Bobby Moore? ●●●●◐
Saturn Martini ●●●●◐
Spritz al Bitter ●●●◐○
Spritzer ●●●○○
Sundowner #2 ●●●●○
Tropic ●●●●◐
U.S. Martini ●●●●●
Vanitini ●●●◐○
Vante Martini ●●●●◐
Waltzing Matilda ●●●●○
White Sangria ●●●◐○
Wine Cooler ●●●◐○

ZUBRÓWKA BISON VODKA

A Polish vodka flavoured with bison grass.

Achilles Heel ●●●●○
Amber ●●●●◐
Apple Breeze ●●●●○
Apple Pie Martini ●●●●○
Autumn Martini ●●●●○
Autumn Punch ●●●●◐
Beetle Jeuse ●●●●○
Brazen Martini ●●●●○
Congo Blue ●●●◐○
Coolman Martini ●●●●◐
Cucumber Martini ●●●●◐
Earl Grey Fizz ●●●●○
Elderflower Martini ●●●●○
Escalator Martini ●●●●●
French Bison-tini ●●●●○
Frisky Bison ●●●●◐
Fruits Of The Forest ●●●◐○
Green Destiny ●●●◐○
Green Tea Martini ●●●●○
Honey Apple Martini ●●●●○
The Honeysuckle Orchard ●●●●○
Krakow Tea ●●●●○
Lemon Butter Cookie ●●●●○
Mitch Martini ●●●●○
Northern Lights ●●●●○
Palookaville ●●●●○
Polish Martini ●●●●●
Pooh'tini ●●●●◐
R U Bobby Moore? ●●●●◐
Sleeping Bison-tini ●●●●○
Sodden Grape Martini ●●●●○
Tatanka ●●●●◐
Tatanka Royale ●●●●○
Warsaw Cooler ●●●●◐
Zelda Martini ●●●●○
Zub-Way ●●●●○

GREAT COCKTAIL BARS OF THE WORLD

These are my personal favourite bars in just a few of the cities I've visited since writing the last volume of this cocktail guide. For more great bars in the world's greatest cities check out our quarterly guide: every issue includes reviews from six or more cities.

AMSTERDAM, THE NETHERLANDS

THE MANSION

2 Hobbemastraat (@ Vossiusstraat), Amsterdam, 1071 ZA, The Netherlands
***Tel:** +31 (0)20 616 6664,*
***www.**the-mansion.nl*

This multi-layered venue packs in four bars, a relaxed lounge, a restaurant and a basement club. A keen bunch of bartenders produce some of the best drinks in The Netherlands.

THE ODEON

460 Singel (btwn Beulingstraat & Koningsplein), Amsterdam, 1000 AB, The Netherlands
***Tel:** +31 (0)20 521 8555,*
***www.**odeontheater.nl*

The club with VIP gallery in the huge, ornate old theatre must rank as the most stunning nightclub space in the world; the tiny bar with original 17th century cherubs offers amazing drinks from bartender Marty Billsborough.

DI GIOIA

45 Korte Leidese Dwarsstraat, Amsterdam, 1017 PW, The Netherlands
***Tel:** +31 20 626 6769,*
***www.**tao-group.nl*

Formerly Suzy Wong, this is an oasis of sophisticated civilisation on a busy, tacky street. The eponymous mixologist Andrea di Gioia serves good cocktails to a hip, upscale, 30-something crowd.

The Odeon

The Mansion

Halo

ATLANTA, USA

HALO LOUNGE

817 West Peachtree Street NW (entrance on 6th St), Midtown, Atlanta, GA 30308, USA
***Tel:** +1 404 962 7333,*
***www.**halolounge.com*

This concrete bunker of a space lies below what was once the grand 1920s Biltmore Hotel. Part nightclub, part chilled cocktail lounge, Halo attracts a stylish mixed gay & straight crowd. The short cocktail list is the most innovative I've found in Atlanta.

VICKERY'S BAR & GRILL

1106 Crescent Avenue NE (btwn 12th & 13th Sts), Midtown, Atlanta, Georgia, GA 30309, USA
***Tel:** +1 404 881 1106,*
***www.**vickerys.com*

This well-run, homely bar and restaurant is warmly lit and intimate, with a large patio for sunny days. The gay and straight hipsters who come here appreciate the premium spirits and good wine list.

AUCKLAND NEW ZEALAND

COCO CLUB

***3 Fort Lane, Central, Auckland, New Zealand. Tel:** +64 (0)9 309 3848*

Buzz to enter this speakeasy-styled venue set down an authentically grotty alley: inside is a luxurious, sophisticated lounge where cocktails are lovingly made by experienced bartenders and even the pool tables ooze class.

CROW BAR

26 Wyndham Street, Central, Auckland, New Zealand
***Tel:** +64 (0)9 366 0398*

Arguably the first cocktail lounge in Auckland, this moodily lit basement space offers well made classic drinks dispensed by bartenders in white shirts and black waistcoats: some locals sadly prefer the Heineken available on draught.

S.P.Q.R. CAFÉ & BAR

150 Ponsonby Road, Ponsonby, Auckland, New Zealand
***Tel:** + 64 (0)9 360 1710*

This predominantly gay venue is café styled and attracts a truly diverse range of friendly locals. The wine list is extensive and the signature SPQR Martini is a must-try.

BARCELONA, SPAIN

BOADAS COCKTAIL BAR

1 Tallers (@ Rambla), Barcelona, Catalonia, 08001, Spain
***Tel:** +34 93 318 8826*

Delightfully tatty, this tiny place dates back to 1933 and is still family-owned. Flamboyant bartenders confidently mix a range of old school cocktails: go for a Daiquiri or the cocktail of the day, which is chalked on a board behind the bar.

DRY MARTINI

●●●●◐

162-166 Carrer Aribau, Barcelona, Catalunya, 08036, Spain
***Tel:** +34 93 217 5072,*
***www.**drymartinibcn.com*

Dry Martini is something of a relic from a bygone era with its long wooden bar and panelling. Old-school bartenders in white jackets produce an array of classic cocktails with a touch of theatre and some considerable style.

BERLIN, GERMANY

DIE HAIFISCH BAR

●●●●◐

25 Arndtstrasse, Kreuzberg, West Berlin, 10965, Germany
***Tel:** +49 (0)30 691 1352*

The name translates as 'The Shark Bar' and the space-age interior is white, almost clinical, but with subtle art deco and Gaudiesque flourishes. You'll find an impressive, classically led cocktail list, incredibly friendly and attentive staff, plus a sushi bar.

GREEN DOOR

●●●●○

***50 Winterfeldstrasse, Schoeneberg, Berlin, 10781, Germany Tel:** +49 (0)30 215 2515,*
***www.**greendoor.de*

Stylish 30-somethings enjoy expertly made drinks from an impressively hefty cocktail list: the mixes take no prisoners but the accompanying glasses of water tame them. Credit cards are not accepted so cash is a must.

BAR AM LÜTZOWPLATZ

●●●●○

7 Lützowplatz, Tiergarten, West Berlin, Germany
***Tel:** +49 (0)30 262 6807,*
***www.**baramLuetzowplatz.com*

Cocktails from the inspiring list are brilliantly made, the choice of champagnes and spirits pleases and the young, moneyed clientele look good. However, poor air-con can make the long, narrow room feel rather like a smoking carriage.

REINGOLD

●●●●◐

11 Novalisstrasse, Mitte, East Berlin, 10115, Germany
***Tel:** +49 (0)30 2838 7676,*
***www.**reingold.de*

Images of the Côte d'Azure and rich old soaks enjoying the sun adorn the walls of this slick lounge. The monster cocktail list appears to include every classic one could name.

VICTORIA BAR

●●●●◐

102 Potsdamer Strasse (btwn Lützowstrasse & Pohlstrasse), Tiegarten, West Berlin, 10785, Germany
***Tel:** +49 (0)30 2575 9977,*
***www.**victoriabar.de*

One of the very best cocktail lounges in a city that is full of them, this attracts an older, in-the-know crowd. The impressive menu lists some 180 cocktails by base spirit; the décor is modern; the atmosphere is laid-back and smoky.

Malmaison

BIRMINGHAM, ENGLAND

MALMAISON BAR

●●●●○

Malmaison Hotel, Royal Mail Street, Birmingham, B1 1RD, England
Tel: *+44 (0)121 246 5000*

Incredibly affable staff lovingly mix cocktails from a 56 strong list, which includes all the popular classics plus plenty of contemporary drinks. The vast, bold space is comfortable rather than cosy but the rooms above make for an easy ride home.

BOSTON, USA

NO. 9 PARK

●●●●○

9 Park Street (btwn Beacon & Tremont Sts), Beacon Hill, Boston, Massachusetts, MA 02108, USA
***Tel:** +1 617 742 9991,*
***www.**no9park.com*

Like many of Boston's best bars, No. 9 Park is part of an esteemed restaurant, this one owned by chef Barbara Lynch. While the décor may disappoint, the welcome, service, food and drinks will not and the after-workers come in droves.

TROQUET

140 Boylston Street (btwn South Charles & Tremont Sts.), Back Bay, Boston, Massachusetts, MA 02116, USA
***Tel:** +1 617 695 9463,*
***www.**troquetboston.com*

Aptly described as a 'food and wine boutique', Troquet is a paradise for oenophiles and foodies. Cocktail lovers are also well catered for in a comfortable, modern space populated by a mixed bunch of friendly Bostonites.

BRIGHTON, ENGLAND

BLANCH HOUSE

17 Atlingworth Street, Kemptown, Brighton, East Sussex, BN2 1PL, England
***Tel:** +44 (0)127 3603 504,*
***www.**blanchhouse.co.uk*

A mere forty drinkers fill this intimate little hotel bar. Superb classic and contemporary cocktails are consumed by a decadent crowd of hotel residents, locals and restaurant guests.

KOBA

●●●●○

135 Western Road (@ Preston St), Brighton, East Sussex, BN1 2LA, England
***Tel:** +44 (0)127 3270 059,*
***www.**kobauk.com*

This small, relaxed and innovative bar features stunning members' spaces out back. Opt for The Gods, with its high ceiling, plush furnishings and copper panelling, where your choice of 80 cocktails will be delivered to your table.

PINTXO PEOPLE

●●●●◐

95-99 Western Road, Brighton, BN1 2LB
***Tel:** 01273 732 323,*
***www.**pintxopeople.co.uk*

The first venture from top mixologist Jason Fendick combines Catalan food with substantially classic cocktails: the upstairs bar offers some great drinks, among them the innovative Canapé Cocktails, served in undersized glassware.

Koba

Hallion

EDINBURGH, SCOTLAND

DRAGONFLY

●●●●○

52 West Port, Edinburgh, EH1 2LD, Scotland
***Tel:** +44 (0)131 228 4543,*
***www.**dragonflycocktailbar.com*

Housed in what was originally a fire station, this eclectically styled bar is part seventies, part nineties, with comfy chairs and elaborate chandeliers. The broadsheet cocktail list successfully covers all the classic bases.

HALLION

●●●●◐

12 Picardy Place, Edinburgh, EH1 3JT, Scotland
***Tel:** +44 (0)131 523 1523,*
***www.**thehallion.com*

This exclusive, stylish and elegant club occupies a grand Georgian townhouse. Members congregate around its island bar to appreciate the marvellous cocktails.

HALO

●●●●◐

3 Melville Place, Edinburgh, EH3 7PR, Scotland
***Tel:** +44 (0)131 539 8500,*
***www.**halobar.co.uk*

Halo combines the warm welcome of a local pub with the décor and liquid refreshments of an upscale lounge. Start an evening with a couple of cocktails from the evolving and adventurous list, plus a plate of their incredible fish and chips.

TIGERLILY

●●●●◐

125 George Street, New Town, Edinburgh
***Tel:** +44 (0)131 225 5005,*
***www.**tigerlilyedinburgh.co.uk*

This listed Georgian townhouse contains a restaurant, a bar, a club and a hotel. Soon after opening its modern, confident style made it a landmark on the upscale Edinburgh scene.

TONIC

●●●●◐

34a North Castle Street, New Town, Edinburgh, Midlothian, EH2 3BN, Scotland
***Tel:** +44 (0)131 225 6431*

Visually unremarkable, Tonic is effectively a social club for members of the Edinburgh bar industry: the extensive cocktail menu includes Scotland's best list of classics, the frozen drinks are very popular, and the atmosphere is as lively as you'd expect.

VILLAGER

●●●●○

49-50 George IV Bridge, Edinburgh, Midlothian, EH1 1EJ, Scotland
***Tel:** +44 (0)131 226 2781,*
***www.**villager-e.com*

This funky little place on George IV Bridge is effortlessly cool with its part-classic, part-quirky interior. The buzz is great and the cocktails even better.

Malmaison

Blanch House

GLASGOW, SCOTLAND

SALTY DOG

●●●●○

2nd Floor Terrace, Princes Square (off Buchanan St), Glasgow, G1 3JN, Scotland
***Tel:** + 44 (0)141 221 7800,*
***www.**salty-dog.info*

Salty Dog exudes a café bar feel and sits under the glazed roof of an upscale shopping mall. The extensive, leather bound bar menu includes reams of contemporary and classic cocktails. All are made to a high standard, as is the food.

HELSINKI, FINLAND

KÄMP BAR & LIBRARY

●●●●○

Hotel Kämp, 29 Pohjoiseplanadi, Helsinki, 00100, Finland
***Tel:** +358 (0)9 576 111,*
***www.**hotelkamp.fi*

This classic bar lies on the ground floor of the historic, luxury Hotel Kämp. It is a civilised, informal and relaxing place, serving morning coffee, afternoon tea and, of course, well-made cocktails.

HONG KONG, CHINA

AQUA SPIRIT

●●●●○

29th & 30th Floors, One Peking Road, Tsim Sha Tsui (Kowloon side), Hong Kong, China
***Tel:** +852 3427 2288,*
***www.**aqua.com.hk*

The soaring walls of glass around this über-glam bar and restaurant offer incredible views over Hong Kong island and Kowloon Park. Besides the spectacular décor there's an impressive range of sakes and grappas.

DROP BAR

●●●●○

Basement, On Lok Mansion, 39-43 Hollywood Road, (entrance off Cochrine St), Hong Kong
***Tel:** +852 2543 8856*

DJ-owned and DJ led, this high energy place serves excellent and unique Martinis, or it does when you can get to the bar. Arrive before 11pm or you may face a door challenge, although the party doesn't really start till after midnight.

FEATHER BOA

●●●●○

38 Staunton Street, Soho, Central, Hong Kong, China
***Tel:** +852 2857 2586*

This intimate, renaissance-styled lounge offers great cocktails: try a fruit Daiquiri or an Espresso Martini. It's discreet enough to pull a truly groovy crowd: mainly media, models and fashionistas.

FINDS

●●●●○

2nd Floor, LKF Tower, 33 Wyndham Street, Lan Kwai Fong, Central, Hong Kong
***Tel:** +852 2522 9318,*
***www.**finds.com.hk*

This handsome, snow white restaurant-cum-bar is a real escape from the heat of the streets. The extensive cocktail list includes many original creations, and the food is brilliant too.

Salty Dog

Tabú

LAS VEGAS, USA

SENSI

Bellagio Via Foire Promenade, 3600 Las Vegas Boulevard South, Las Vegas, Nevada, NV89109, USA
***Tel:** +1 877 234 6358,*
***www.**bellagio.com*

This restaurant not only boasts some of the most fantastic food in Vegas but a bar with fabulous cocktails. The zen-like interior houses relaxing water features, 80 tonnes of hand-carved stone, a glass encased kitchen and a wine list to die for.

TABÚ ULTRA LOUNGE

●●●●○

Ground Floor, MGM Grand Hotel, 3799 Las Vegas Boulevard, Las Vegas, Nevada, NV 89109, USA
***Tel:** +1 702 891 7129,*
***www.**mgmgrand.com*

Situated on the ground floor of the monster MGM Grand, this is a surprisingly glamorous space populated by the beautiful and well-heeled. Book to score a table and enjoy some of the better drinks in Sin City.

43 South Moulton

LONDON, ENGLAND

43 SOUTH MOLTON

●●●●○

43 South Molton Street, Mayfair, London, W1K 5RS, England
***Tel:** +44 (0)20 7647 4343,*
***www.**43southmolton.com*

The posh address draws a suitably high net worth crowd to this members club, themed like an eccentric country house. The cocktails are sublime, the service is great and out of the four floors the basement is the best.

ALL STAR LANES

●●●●◐

Victoria House, Bloomsbury Place (off Southampton Row), Holborn, London, WC1 4DA, England
***Tel:** +44 (0)20 7025 2676,*
***www.**allstarlanes.co.uk*

This decidedly boutique bowling alley houses an equally slick lounge bar and draws a fashionable 20-30-something crowd. Cocktails are beautifully balanced, beer drinkers are well served and non-drinkers will love their iced teas, shakes and malts.

AURORA BAR

●●●●○

Great Eastern Hotel, Liverpool Street, London, EC2M 7QN, England
***Tel:** +44 (0)20 7618 7000,*
***www.**aurora-restaurant.co.uk*

First opened in 1884, in the landmark (now refurbed) Great Eastern Hotel, this is an oasis amid the bustle of the City. Join the suited City folk to enjoy the peace, plus a fine Armagnac, a Cognac, or one of the excellent classic cocktails.

43 South Moulton

All Star Lanes

43 South Moulton

Cocoon

B@1

●●●●○

85 Battersea Rise (nr Northcote Rd), Battersea, London, SW11 1HW, England
***Tel:** +44 (0)20 7978 6595,*
***www.**beatone.co.uk*

This tiny, downbeat, bartender-owned venue is usually filled to bursting point with sweaty, frisky locals. The thick cocktail menu covers all the bases, the athletic bartenders impress and the place can be a real blast.

COCOON

●●●●◐

65 Regent Street (entrance on Air Street), London, W1B 4EA, England
***Tel:** +44 (0)20 7494 7600,*
***www.**cocoon-restaurants.com*

This space age, Asian-influenced bar and restaurant inhabits a series of spherical pods. Classic and fusion cocktails are superb, the wine list has some interesting bins, and the shochu and sake selections are exceptional.

THE DORCHESTER BAR

●●●●◐

53 Park Lane, Mayfair, London, W1A 2HJ, England
***Tel:** +44 (0)20 7629 8888,*
***www.**thedorchester.com*

This blingy, modern bar in a majestic, old school hotel may surprise many: but tradition survives in the drinks. One of the oldest cocktails of all, the Martinez, heads up a classic list based around the UK's largest range of vermouths.

The Dorchester Bar

Cocoon

Green & Red Bar & Cantina

Dusk

Hawksmoor

DUSK BAR, KITCHEN & LOUNGE

●●●◐○

339 Battersea Park Road, London, SW11 4LS, England
Tel: +44 (0)20 7622 2112,
www.duskbar.co.uk

Some way off the beaten track, even for Battersea residents, this cool lounge bar transforms into a major party venue at weekends. The warm, welcoming interior, well-made drinks and motivated staff make the place.

GREEN & RED BAR & CANTINA

51 Bethnal Green Road, Shoreditch, London, E1 6LA, England
Tel: +44 (0)20 7749 9670,
www.greenred.co.uk

This unpromising building houses London's foremost tequila bar and the huge range of 100% agave offerings feature prominently in the excellent cocktail list. The TARDIS-like basement provides DJ-driven madness at weekends.

HAWKSMOOR

157 Commercial Street, Spitalfields, London, E1 6BJ, England
Tel: +44 (0)20 7247 7392,
www.thehawksmoor.com

As befits a steakhouse, this cocktail bar offers a superb range of bourbons, while the informative list provides an extensive selection of well-made Juleps and Sours. There are some fantastic Spanish wines and phenomenal super Tuscans.

Green & Red Bar & Cantina

Lonsdale

LONSDALE

●●●●◐

44-48 Lonsdale Road, Notting Hill, London, W11 2DE, England
***Tel:** +44 (0)20 7727 4080*

On a residential street in deepest Notting Hill lies one of London's best bars. Beautiful people drink balanced, imaginative cocktails and nibble on tasty bar snacks amid quirkily stylish design.

LOST SOCIETY

●●●●◐

697 Wandsworth Road, Clapham, London, SW8 3JF, England
***Tel:** +44 (0)20 7652 6526,*
***www.**lostsociety.co.uk*

The many intimate rooms and spaces in this converted 16th century barn vary wildly in style but are always beautiful. The comprehensive cocktail list is perfectly rendered, the clientele are gorgeous and the atmosphere pure party.

Lost Society

MATCHBAR

●●●●○

37-38 Margaret Street
(nr Oxford Circus),
London, W1G 0JF, England
***Tel:** +44 (0)20 7499 3443,*
***www.**matchbar.com*

Of the three excellent Match bars in London, this is the most central. Like the others, it is primarily about good drinks, particularly cocktails: a number of contemporary classics are Match creations.

DYNAMITE
BOOGALOO
OLD SCH
vs.
NEW SCHOOL
WE PHOTOGRAPH THEM AND
THEY BEAT US UP
GARDEN
OF
EARTHLY
DELIGHTS

MILK & HONEY

●●●●◐

61 Poland Street, Soho, London, W1F 7NU, England
Tel: 07000 655 469,
www.mlkhny.com

A larger copy of the famously secretive Manhattan club, the three floors feel like a 30s speakeasy. The comfortably moody surroundings, discreet location and calm atmosphere, coupled with the best classic cocktails in London, make this a very special place.

Salvatore

MONTGOMERY PLACE

●●●●◐

31 Kensington Park Road, Notting Hill, London, W11 2EU, England
***Tel:** +44 (0)20 7792 3921,*
***www.**montgomeryplace.co.uk*

This tiny but very serious cocktail bar offers a truly extraordinary list of once-forgotten Prohibition classics: short, very adult drinks served (and priced) with the reverence they deserve.

SALVATORE

●●●●◐

Ground Floor, Fifty, 50 St James' Street, London, SW1A 1JT, England
***Tel:** +44 (0)8704 155 050,*
***www.**fiftylondon.com*

Part of London's most opulent casino, this is named for and run by Salvatore Calabrese, once manager of the Lanesborough's Library Bar. The list features his fifty favourite cocktails and high rollers can enjoy 1788 cognac at £1500 a pop.

TRAILER HAPPINESS

●●●●◐

Basement, 177 Portobello Road (corner of Elgin Crescent), Notting Hill, London, W11 2DY, England
***Tel:** +44 (0)20 7727 2700,*
***www.**trailerh.com*

Themed like a mid-60s, California valley bachelor pad, Trailer H is a celebration of Tiki culture. An extremely able bar crew generate fabulous cocktails, both Tiki and new era.

Trailer Happiness

Trailer Happiness

LOS ANGELES, USA

VERMONT BAR

1714 North Vermont Avenue (@ Sunset), Silver Lake, West Hollywood, Los Angeles, California, CA 90027, USA
***Tel:** +1 323 661 6163*

This bright and airy space, with white vaulted ceilings and pine tables, attracts what a friend described as a 'fabulous clientele, half straight and half gay'. The cocktails are good and the food is great.

TIKI-TI

*4427 West Sunset Boulevard (btwn Virtgil Pl & N Hoover St), Silverlake, Los Angeles, CA 90027, USA **Tel:** +1 323 669 9381, **www.**tiki-ti.com*

A must-visit for any serious cocktail aficionado, this is one of the best surviving examples of a classic Tiki interior. The drinks are not especially outstanding but this tiny, family-owned shack is wonderfully, authentically kitsch. Bring cash as cards are not accepted.

TRADER VIC'S

*Beverly Hilton Hotel, 9876 Wilshire Boulevard, Beverly Hills, CA 90210, USA **Tel:** +1 310 274 7777, **www.**tradervics.com*

The oldest and probably the best of the legendary Tiki chain, this is primarily a restaurant: however, a Mai Tai is de rigeur. Expect 5* treatment from manager Chai Rojana, who was hired by Trader Vic himself.

MEXICO CITY, MEXICO

CAFEINA

73 Nuevo Leon, Condesa, Mexico City, 06140, Mexico
***Tel:** +52 55 5212 0090*

This DJ led lounge mixes antique and modern furnishings to good effect. Bar staff produce some well balanced drinks from a cocktail menu where Martinis are listed under headings such as "Martini Classico" and "Popsicle Martini".

MIAMI, USA

THE RALEIGH LOBBY BAR

Raleigh Hotel, 1775 Collins Avenue (@ 22nd St), South Beach, Miami Beach, Florida, FL 33139, USA
***Tel:** +1 305 534 6300,*
***www.**raleighhotel.com*

The elegant, Art Deco Raleigh Hotel is one of the most beautiful on the Collins' Avenue beachfront. The hidden, intimate, wood panelled 1940s lobby bar is warm and loungy, and the small selection of cocktails is the best on the beach.

MILAN, ITALY

MARTINI BAR

Dolce & Gabbana Menswear Boutique, 15 Corso Venezia, Fashion District, Milan, Lombardy, 20121, Italy
***Tel:** +39 (0)2 7601 1154*

Hidden behind the shirts and suits of Dolce & Gabbana's menswear store lies this slick, black and red, oriental-styled bar. The short cocktail list is dominated by classic Martini variations such as the Vesper and the Gibson.

NASHVILLE, USA

THE BOUND'RY RESTAURANT

●●●●◐

911 Twentieth Avenue South, Nashville, Tennessee, TN 37212, USA
***Tel:** +1 615 321 3043,*
***www.**pansouth.net*

This large, two-tiered restaurant with conservatory bar and outdoor seating is famed for its beer selection. Cocktails from the 16 strong Martini list are also brilliant and arrive with half in your glass and half chilling in a miniature carafe.

Martini Bar

INDI
UNIVER
SANTA CLARA
UNIVERSITY
Le Monde

Harry's New York Bar

NEW YORK, USA

ANGEL'S SHARE

●●●●◐

8 Stuyvesant Street (@ 9th St & Third Ave), East Village, Manhattan, New York City, NY 10003, USA. ***Tel:*** *+1 212 777 5415*

Behind an unmarked door above a very ordinary Japanese restaurant is this Eastern-influenced lounge. The perfectly made classic cocktails make it legendary.

BRANDY LIBRARY

●●●●◐

25 North Moore Street (@ Varick St), Tribeca, Manhattan, New York, NY 10013, USA
Tel: *+1 212 226 5545,*
www.*brandylibrary.com*

This bar's name hints at what to expect: wooden floor to ceiling shelves lined with brandies from around the world. The "Librarians" tasked with dispensing the bottles also mix great cocktails.

DOUBLE SEVEN

●●●●◐

418 West 14th Street (btwn Ninth & Tenth Aves), Meatpacking District, New York City, NY 10014, USA. ***Tel:*** *+1 212 981 9099*

This stylish lounge is noted for its cocktails and the daily changing menu is overseen by Sasha Petraske of Milk & Honey fame. Drinks are made with fresh juices and served with Debauve & Gallais chocolates. Arrive before 10pm at weekends to avoid disappointment on the door.

EAST SIDE COMPANY BAR

●●●●○

49 Essex Street (btwn Grand & Hester Sts), Lower East Side, Manhattan, New York City, NY 10002, USA. ***Tel:*** *+1 212 614 7408*

Sasha Petraske's second speakeasy-styled bar is almost as discreet but, fortunately, less exclusive than Milk & Honey. There is no cocktail list but the discerning local crowd enjoy beautifully made classics.

EMPLOYEES ONLY

●●●●○

510 Hudson Street, Tribeca, Manhattan, New York, NY 10014, USA. ***Tel:*** *+1 212 242 3021,*
www.*employeesonlynyc.com*

A fortune teller sits in the vestibule of this art deco lounge with a classic tin ceiling, carved wood panelled walls, marble floors and a long, welcoming bar. The bartenders sport Savoia white jackets and have a justified reputation for mixology.

FLATIRON LOUNGE

●●●●◐

37 West 19th Street (btwn 5th & 6th Aves), Flatiron District, New York City, NY 10011, USA
Tel: *+1 212 727 7741,*
www.*flatironlounge.com*

Both this lounge and its locale take their name from the landmark Flatiron Building. The centrepiece of the art deco-styled lounge is the 30-foot mahogany bar where expert bartenders serve flights of taster size Martinis.

LITTLE BRANCH

●●●●○

22 Seventh Avenue South), Greenwich Village, Manhattan, New York City, NY 10014, USA
Tel: *+1 212 929 4360*

Sasha Petraske's third bar repeats his winning formula of upscale speakeasy style and classic cocktails. While fairly discreet, however, this bar is open to all, and the distinctly old school cocktails are consistently good.

MILK & HONEY

●●●●◐

134 Eldridge Street (just south of Delancey), Lower East Side, New York City, NY 10002, USA
Tel: *withheld*

This legendary, small and exclusive venue serves absolutely amazing drinks: the classic cocktails of the Prohibition era. Should you be lucky enough to gain entry, be aware that you can only pay in cash and that old-school house rules are strictly enforced.

PEGU CLUB

●●●●◐

77 West Houston Street, New York City, NY 10012, USA
Tel: *+1 212 473 7348,*
www.*peguclub.com*

Inspired by a famous club in colonial Burma, Pegu Club is spearheaded by Audrey Saunders, a leading light in New York's cocktail culture. The well-made list changes with the seasons and majors on infused spirits: don't miss the eponymous, tart house cocktail.

Milk & Honey

Employees Only

Temple

East Side Company Bar

TEMPLE BAR

●●●●◐

332 Lafayette Street (btwn Bleecker & Houston Sts), Soho, New York City, NY 10012, USA
***Tel:** +1 212 925 4242,*
***www.**templebarnyc.com*

This classy little place with its cherry oak bar and thick curtains feels rather like a classic hotel bar. Attentive servers deliver well-made drinks, including quirky favourites like the Bicicleta and Sgroppino.

PARIS, FRANCE

BAR LE FORUM

●●●●◐

4 Boulevard Malesherbes (@ Pl de la Madeleine), Paris, 75008, France
***Tel:** +33 (0)1 4265 3786,*
***www.**bar-le-forum.com*

The original 1930 interior in the style of an English gentlemen's club gives Le Forum a wonderful old-school feel. However, the bar staff are young and keen, and the 16 page drinks list includes most of the classics.

HARRY'S NEW YORK BAR

●●●●◐

5 Rue Daunou (btwn Ave de l'Opéra & Rue de la Paix), Paris, 75002, France
***Tel:** +33 (0)1 4261 7114,*
***www.**harrys-bar.fr*

Harry MacElhone bought this bar in 1923, and the trip through the swinging, wooden, saloon-style doors is a step back in time. Knowledgeable, friendly bartenders make brilliant classic cocktails, including the Bloody Mary, which, like several others, was created here.

Bar Le Forum

BAR HEMINGWAY

●●●●◐

Ritz Hotel, 15 Place Vendôme, Paris, 75001, France
Tel: +33 (0)1 4316 3030,
www.ritzparis.com

This wonderful little bar is tucked away in a back corner of the huge Ritz hotel and was once a favourite haunt of El Papa. The small, circular tables are crowded with well-to-do international tourists, many of whom are regulars, drawn by the excellent cocktails made by Colin Field and his team.

SAN FRANCISCO, USA

ABSINTHE BRASSERIE & BAR

●●●●◐

398 Hayes Street (@ Gough), Hayes Valley District, San Francisco, California, CA 94102, USA. Tel: +1 415 551 1590,
www.absinthe.com

This fine dining restaurant and bar is styled as a French bistro. The bound wine, spirits and cocktail list impresses; classic drinks are wonderfully made; contemporary creations are fantastic; and the atmosphere drives one to revisit.

RANGE

●●●●◐

842 Valencia St (btwn 19th 20th), San Francisco, CA 94110
Tel: +1 415 282 8283,
www.rangesf.com

The bar section of this restaurant is small, and the cocktail selection is short, but don't let you put that off this fantastic little place. Quirky décor and fantastic service support daily special cocktails and 15 wines by the glass.

TOMMY'S MEXICAN RESTAURANT & BAR

●●●●◐

5929 Geary Boulevard (btwn 24th & 23rd Aves), Outer Richmond, San Francisco, California, CA 94121, USA
Tel: +1 415 387 4747,
www.tommystequila.com

Tommy's is an authentic Mexican restaurant owned and operated by the Bermejo family since 1965. It is also a Mecca for tequila lovers and widely acknowledged as serving the best Margaritas in the world.

SYDNEY, AUSTRALIA

JIMMY LIKS

●●●●◐

188 Victoria Street, Potts Point, Sydney, NSW 2011, Australia
Tel: +61 (0)2 8354 1400,
www.jimmyliks.com

Dark yet warmly lit, this sharp bar and restaurant imparts a touch of Tokyo style. The creative, Asian-influenced cocktails are superbly balanced: don't miss the Watermelon & Coriander Margarita.

LOTUS BAR

●●●●◐

22 Challis Avenue Potts Point, Sydney,
Tel: +612 9326 9000,
www.merivale.com

This retro-elegant cocktail bar serves some of the best drinks in Sydney in two secluded, atmospheric rooms behind an equally bijou restaurant and illuminated by tiny lotus flower spotlights.

ZETA BAR

●●●●○

Hilton Hotel, Level 4, 488 George Street, Sydney, NSW 2000, Australia. Tel: +61 (0)2 9265 6070,
www.zetabar.com.au

This contemporary hotel bar offers innovative cocktails, many of which use cooking techniques to caramelise or otherwise enhance ingredients. Try a Grilled Pineapple & Cracked Pepper Martini, or a Burnt Lemon & Vanilla Margarita.

VENICE, ITALY

TIEPOLO BAR

●●●●◐

The Westin Europa & Regina Hotel, San Marco 2159, Venice 30124, Italy. Tel: +39 041 240 0001, www.westin.com

Set in a five-star luxury hotel lavished with marbles of all colours, this bar combines splendour with warm lighting to produce an implausibly cosy feel. In the summer the Grand Canal terrace is a wonderful spot to enjoy the mostly classic cocktails.

WASHINGTON DC, USA

DEGREES

●●●◐○

The Ritz-Carlton Georgetown, 3100 South Street Northwest, Washington, DC 20007, USA
Tel: +1 202 912 4100,

Degrees lies behind the lobby of The Ritz-Carlton Georgetown and, like the hotel, has plenty of style. The long, shiny 25 seat granite bar is set against 1930s bare brick walls and black slate floors.